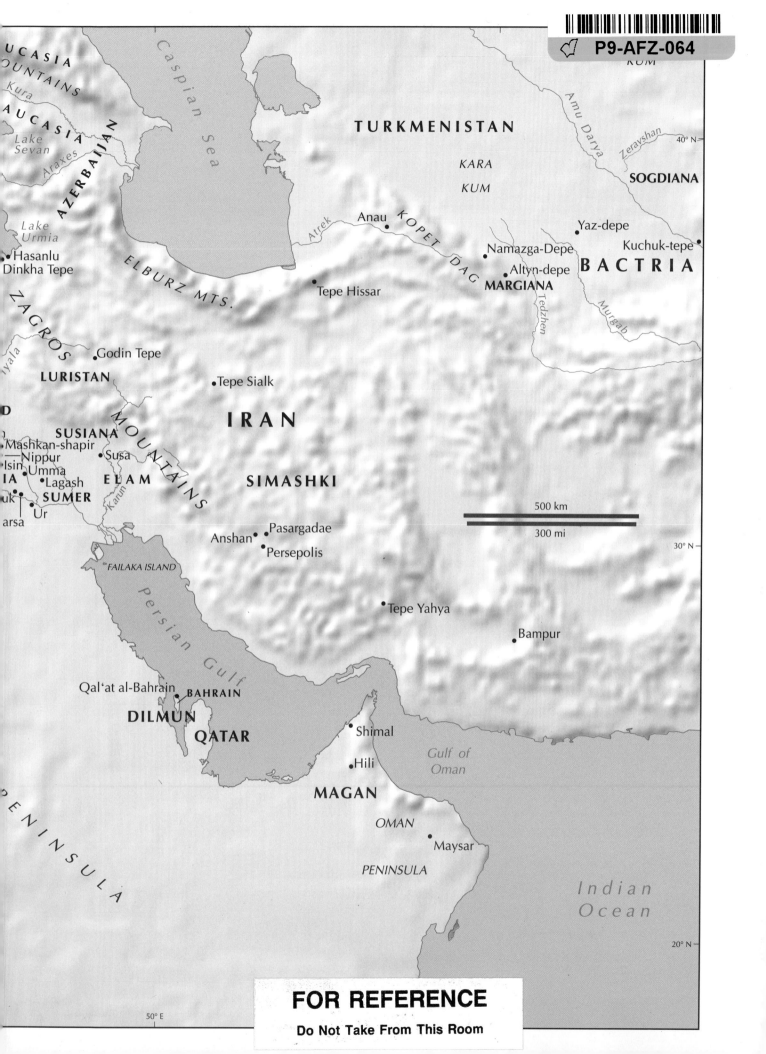

UCASIA
OUNTAINS

AUCASIA

Kura

Lake
Sevan

Araxes

AZERBAIJAN

Lake
Urmia

Hasanlu
Dinkha Tepe

ZAGROS

iyala

Godin Tepe

LURISTAN

D

SUSIANA

Mashkan-shapir
Nippur

Isin Umma

IA Lagash

uk SUMER

arsa Ur

ELAM

Susa

Karun

MOUNTAINS

Caspian Sea

ELBURZ MTS.

Atrek

Anau

Tepe Hissar

Tepe Sialk

IRAN

SIMASHKI

Anshan

Persepolis

FAILAKA ISLAND

Persian Gulf

Pasargadae

TURKMENISTAN

KARA
KUM

KOPET DAG

Amu Darya

Zeravshan

40° N

SOGDIANA

Yaz-depe

Namazga-Depe

Altyn-depe

MARGIANA

Tedzhen

Murgab

Kuchuk-tepe

BACTRIA

500 km

300 mi

Tepe Yahya

Bampur

30° N

Qal'at al-Bahrain

DILMUN

BAHRAIN

QATAR

Shimal

Hili

MAGAN

Gulf of
Oman

PENINSULA

OMAN

Maysar

PENINSULA

Indian
Ocean

20° N

50° E

Civilizations
of the
Ancient Near East

Civilizations
of the
Ancient Near East

JACK M. SASSON

EDITOR IN CHIEF

JOHN BAINES
GARY BECKMAN
KAREN S. RUBINSON

ASSOCIATE EDITORS

VOLUME IV

CHARLES SCRIBNER'S SONS
MACMILLAN LIBRARY REFERENCE USA
SIMON & SCHUSTER MACMILLAN
NEW YORK

SIMON & SCHUSTER AND PRENTICE HALL INTERNATIONAL
LONDON   MEXICO CITY   NEW DELHI   SINGAPORE   SYDNEY   TORONTO

Charles Scribner's Sons

An Imprint of Simon & Schuster Macmillan
866 Third Avenue
New York, NY 10022

LIBRARY OF CONGRESS CATALOGING-IN-PUBLICATION DATA

Civilizations of the ancient Near East / Jack M. Sasson, editor in
  chief.
        p. cm.
    Includes bibliographical references and index.
    ISBN 0-684-19279-9 (set)—ISBN 0-684-19720-0 (vol. 1)—ISBN 0-684-19721-9
    (vol. 2)—ISBN 0-684-19722-7 (vol. 3)—ISBN 0-684-19723-5 (vol. 4)
    1. Middle East—Civilization—To 622.   I. Sasson, Jack M.   95-1712
    DS57.C55 1995   CIP
    939'.4—dc20

1 3 5 7 9 11 13 15 17 19 V/C 20 18 16 14 12 10 8 4 2

PRINTED IN THE UNITED STATES OF AMERICA

The paper used in this publication meets the minimum requirements
of American National Standard for Information Sciences—Permanence
of Paper for Printed Library Materials. ANSI Z3948-1984.

Contents

VOLUME IV

Contents

PART 10   VISUAL AND PERFORMING ARTS

PART 11   RETROSPECTIVE ESSAYS

Contents

Contents

Contents

9

Language, Writing, and Literature

Record Keeping Before Writing

DENISE SCHMANDT-BESSERAT

A SYSTEM OF CLAY TOKENS used to store and manipulate economic data emerged in the Near East about 8000 BCE and constitutes the earliest code for communication before the invention of writing. This simple but brilliant prehistoric invention of encoding concepts in clay symbols opened new channels for transmitting information that deeply affected the human condition: first, the token system apparently evolved into the Sumerian script, the earliest known writing system; second, the tokens provided the immediate background for the invention of abstract numerals, upon which is founded mathematics; third, accounting with tokens forced the development of new socioeconomic patterns.

THE ARTIFACTS

Tokens are small artifacts about one to three centimeters (½ inch to one inch) across. They were made by simply pinching or rolling a lump of clay between the fingers or the palms of the hands and forming it into specific shapes. Tests such as differential thermal analysis (DTA) and electron microscopy have determined that from the beginning, tokens were consistently baked at a low temperature, which explains their varied colors ranging from buff-pink to greenish and black.

There are sixteen main types of shapes of tokens: (1) cones, (2) spheres, (3) disks, (4) cylinders, (5) tetrahedrons, (6) ovoids, (7) rectangles, (8) triangles, (9) biconoids, (10) paraboloids, (11) bent coils, (12) oval/rhomboids, (13) vessels, (14) tools, (15) animals, and (16) miscellaneous other shapes, including hyperboloids. These forms are interesting because, except for categories 13, 14, and 15, they are abstract. In fact, these diversely shaped tokens exploited systematically all the basic geometric figures known to us.

The counters can be further classified into subtypes according to intentional variations in size or by the addition of markings. Cones, spheres, disks, and tetrahedrons are consistently represented in two sizes, small and large (fig. 1). Spheres also occur as fractions, such as hemispheres and three-quarter spheres. The markings consist of incised lines, notches, punches, pinched appendices, or appliqué pellets. The lines were incised with a pointed tool, probably a stick or stylus. The punch marks take the form of either a fine pitting produced with a point as sharp as a needle, small circles done probably with a reed, or, more frequently, a deep circular impression made with the blunt end of a stick.

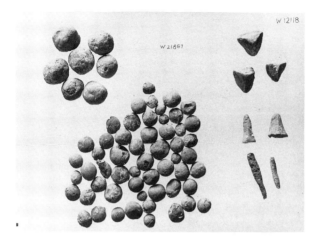

Fig. 1. Plain tokens (3200 BCE): large and small spheres, tetrahedrons, cones, and cylinders from Uruk, Iraq. GERMAN ARCHAEOLOGICAL INSTITUTE, BERLIN

THE EVOLUTION OF TOKENS

At the beginning of the token system, about 8000–7500, and until the fourth millennium, tokens were plain (fig. 1). The forms consisted mainly of geometric shapes, such as cones, spheres, flat and lenticular disks, cylinders, tetrahedrons, and only occasionally ovoids, rectangles, triangles, biconoids, and hyperboloids. The naturalistic shapes, such as vessels and animals, were also few. Although the earliest assemblages of the eighth millennium produced some tokens with an occasional incised line or a punctation, markings remained rare. It should be well understood that the plain counters continued to be part of all token collections from the beginning to the end of the system about 3000.

After four millennia, about 4000–3500, the system reached a second stage when new types and subtypes supplemented the plain tokens. These complex tokens (fig. 2) have a larger repertory of shapes. They feature additional geometric forms, including paraboloids, bent coils, and ovals-rhomboids. Triangles, ovoids, rectangles, and biconoids become more widely used and acquire multiple subtypes. New naturalistic forms also appear, such as miniature tools, furniture, fruit, and humans. A profusion of markings on all types of tokens is another distinctive feature of the complex counters. The markings are displayed on the most conspicuous part of the object; for example, in the case of flat tokens, such as disks, they appear on a single face. It is important to note that complex tokens of the same form and bearing identical markings are found at sites distant from each other. For instance, series of triangular tokens from Susa (biblical Shushan, modern Shush) in Iran (fig. 3) find exact parallels in Uruk (biblical Erech, modern Warka) in Iraq and Habuba al-Kabira in Syria.

GEOGRAPHIC DISTRIBUTION

Tokens pervaded most inhabitable regions of the Near East, from Israel to Syria, Turkey, Iraq, and Iran. Proceeding from west to east, tokens have been reported in eight Palestinian sites, including 'Ain Ghazal and Jericho, and sixteen Syrian sites, among them Tell Aswad, Tell Ramad, and Habuba al-Kabira. In Turkey, tokens

Fig. 2. Complex tokens, 3300 BCE: (*left to right*) bent coils, triangle, paraboloids, and rectangle, from Susa, Iran. LOUVRE MUSEUM, PARIS

Fig. 3. Triangle tokens (3300 BCE) with 2, 3, 4, 5, and 8 lines, from Susa, Iran. LOUVRE MUSEUM, PARIS

seem limited to sites located in the Taurus Mountains, such as Gritille and Çayönü (pronounced chayonu) Tepesi or along the Mediterranean coast, like Can (pronounced Jan) Hasan, Suberde, and Beldibi. There is no evidence, however, for the use of counters in Çatal Hüyük (pronounced Chatal Huyuk) or Hacilar (pronounced Hajilar), suggesting that perhaps the token system never reached central Anatolia. Iraq and Iran with forty-three and forty sites, respectively, have produced the greatest concentration of tokens. North and south Mesopotamian

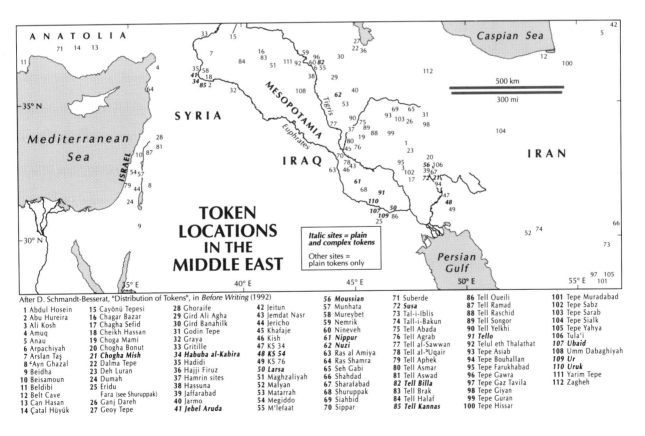

TOKEN LOCATIONS IN THE MIDDLE EAST

Italic sites = plain and complex tokens

Other sites = plain tokens only

After D. Schmandt-Besserat, "Distribution of Tokens", in *Before Writing* (1992)

1 Abdul Hosein	15 Cayönü Tepesi	28 Ghoraife	42 Jeitun	56 *Moussian*	71 Suberde	86 Tell Oueili	101 Tepe Muradabad
2 Abu Hureira	16 Chagar Bazar	29 Gird Ali Agha	43 Jemdat Nasr	57 Munhata	72 *Susa*	87 Tell Ramad	102 Tepe Sabz
3 Ali Kosh	17 Chagha Sefid	30 Gird Banahilk	44 Jericho	58 Mureybet	73 Tal-i-Iblis	88 Tell Raschid	103 Tepe Sarab
4 Amuq	18 Cheikh Hassan	31 Godin Tepe	45 Khafaje	59 Nemrik	74 Tall-i-Bakun	89 Tell Songor	104 Tepe Sialk
5 Anau	19 Choga Mami	32 Graya	46 Kish	60 Nineveh	75 Tell Abada	90 Tell Yelkhi	105 Tepe Yahya
6 Arpachiyah	20 Chogha Bonut	33 Gritille	47 KS 34	61 *Nippur*	76 Tell Agrab	91 *Tello*	106 Tula'i
7 Arslan Taş	21 *Chogha Mish*	34 *Habuba al-Kabira*	48 *KS 54*	62 *Nuzi*	77 Tell al-Sawwan	92 Telul eth Thalathat	107 *Ubaid*
8 ʿAyn Ghazal	22 Dalma Tepe	35 Hadidi	49 KS 76	63 Ras al Amiya	78 Tell al-ʾUqair	93 Tepe Asiab	108 Umm Dabaghiyah
9 Beidha	23 Deh Luran	36 Hajji Firuz	50 *Larsa*	64 Ras Shamra	79 Tell Aphek	94 Tepe Bouhallan	109 *Ur*
10 Beisamoun	24 Dumah	37 Hamrin sites	51 Maghzaliyah	65 Seh Gabi	80 Tell Asmar	95 Tepe Farukhabad	110 *Uruk*
11 Beldibi	25 Eridu	38 Hassuna	52 Malyan	66 Shahdad	81 Tell Aswad	96 Tepe Gawra	111 Yarim Tepe
12 Belt Cave	Fara (see Shuruppak)	39 Jaffarabad	53 Matarrah	67 Sharafabad	82 *Tell Billa*	97 Tepe Gaz Tavila	112 Zagheh
13 Can Hasan	26 Ganj Dareh	40 Jarmo	54 Megiddo	68 Shuruppak	83 Tell Brak	98 Tepe Giyan	
14 Çatal Hüyük	27 Geoy Tepe	41 *Jebel Aruda*	55 M'lefaat	69 Siahbid	84 Tell Halaf	99 Tepe Guran	
				70 Sippar	85 *Tell Kannas*	100 Tepe Hissar	

sites alike yielded tokens, as well as all settled parts of Iran, from Azerbaijan to Seistan. The largest collections of counters recorded in Iraq were 2,000 at Jarmo (circa 6000 BCE) and 850 at Uruk (circa 3300 BCE), and in Iran, 780 at the Proto-Elamite site of Susa (circa 3300 BCE).

ADVANTAGES OF THE TOKEN SYSTEM

Each token shape, with its own markings, had a specific meaning and stood for a particular commodity; the format may have inspired the development of a writing system by the Sumerians hundreds of years later. For example, the cone and sphere seemingly represented two separate measures of grain equivalent to our modern liter (quart) and bushel (36 liters), respectively; the ovoid stood for a jar of oil; and a disk with an incised cross meant a sheep. Other tokens, such as the lenticular disk, may have referred to a collection of animals, such as a flock (perhaps ten animals).

The three-dimensional clay symbols represented a new way of handling data and were a breakthrough in communication. The system made it feasible, for the first time, to manipulate simultaneously information concerning different categories of items, bringing a complexity of data processing never reached previously. Furthermore, the system was open—that is, new signs were added when necessary by creating new token shapes and the ever-increasing repertory constantly pushed the device to new frontiers of complexity. In fact, the tokens were the first code—the earliest system of signs used for transmitting information. This first code was based on the following features: Counters were modeled in striking, distinct, mostly geometric shapes that were easy to recognize and simple to duplicate. Each of these forms was endowed with a unique, discrete meaning. The tokens were systematically repeated, always carrying the same meaning; a sphere, for example, always signified a particular measure of grain. The many token shapes constituted a repertory of interrelated concept symbols concerning goods and commodities.

The counters abstracted data in three ways. First, the tokens translated concrete information, such as numbers of animals and units of goods, into abstract symbols. Second, they removed the data from its context; for example, sheep could be counted without handling the animals. Third, they separated the knowledge from the knower, presenting the data bare, devoid of any bias. This was a departure from verbal communication, which relies upon voice inflection and body language. In the vocabulary of Marshall McLuhan, the information communicated by tokens was in a "cold" and static form, unlike the "hot" and flexible spoken language.

The counters facilitated data manipulation in three main fashions. The counters were movable units easy to handle, and they encouraged the manipulation of information by making it easy to add, subtract, and rectify data at will. Next, the system was a mnemonic device by which to handle and store an unlimited quantity of data without risking the damages of memory failure. Last, the system enhanced logic and rational decision making by allowing the scrutiny of complex data.

DISADVANTAGES OF THE TOKEN SYSTEM

The tokens also had major drawbacks. They were in many ways a rudimentary device. First, the system worked according to the simplest or most basic principle of one-to-one correspondence, which consisted in matching each unit of a set to be counted with a token. Accordingly, one jar of oil was shown by one ovoid, six jars of oil by six ovoids, and so on. There were seemingly only a few tokens that stood for a collection of items, like the lenticular disk that probably means a "flock" or perhaps ten animals. More important, the token system did not allow expressing numbers discriminately. There was no token for "one," "two," or "three" independent of the commodity counted.

The counters also were limited in that they could communicate economic data only. Each token stood for a specific unit or a collection of goods with no possibility of conveying any other information. There were no tokens expressing the quality of the products, and no tokens to express whether, for instance, the merchandise was credited or withdrawn.

The format of the tokens was yet another major shortcoming. Although they are small, the counters are cumbersome when used in large quantities. Consequently, the tokens were restricted to handling small amounts of goods. The system was also inefficient because each commodity was expressed by a special token; it thus required an ever-growing repertory of signs. Finally, the counters were impractical to use for permanent records, since a group of small objects can easily become separated and can hardly be kept in a particular order for any length of time.

ENVELOPES TO HOLD TOKENS

The difficulty in storing the counters inspired the creation of clay envelopes so that they could be kept in discrete groups (fig. 4). These envelopes would remain of esoteric interest but for their importance in the invention of writing. Between 8000 and about 3350, tokens were probably held in a jar, as they are sometimes found in excavations. Starting in the second half of the fourth millennium, some tokens were enclosed in clay envelopes. There were spherical or oblong hollow clay balls, about 5–7 centimeters (2–3 inches) in diameter, made very easily by rolling a piece of clay in the hands and poking a cavity into it with the fingers. Tokens were deposited in the opening before closing the envelope with a patch of clay. About two hundred

Fig. 4. Envelope and six of the seven incised ovoids it contained, from Uruk, Iraq, 3500 BCE. GERMAN ARCHAEOLOGICAL INSTITUTE, BERLIN

such envelopes have been recovered in various states of preservation. Some eighty are still intact, keeping and hiding an unknown number of tokens. Others were found crushed with the token contents still fully or partly associated. The artifacts come from ten sites, including Uruk in Mesopotamia; Susa, Chogha Mish, and Tepe Yahya in Iran; Habuba al-Kabira in Syria; Dumah in Palestine; and Dharan in Saudi Arabia.

The envelopes were useful in keeping together two important kinds of information. First, the quantities of goods involved in a given transaction were represented by the tokens enclosed. Second, the individuals or officials who took part in the deal impressed their signets on the surface of the clay case when it was moist. These were seals, usually a small stone carved with a particular design, equivalent to a modern rubber stamp or signature. The major drawback of the envelopes was that they concealed the counters: once the tokens were enclosed, they were no longer visible. It was probably to overcome this difficulty that a system of markings developed. It consisted of impressing tokens, like the seals, on the face of the envelope when the clay was still soft. The resulting impressed markings were shown in one-to-one correspondence, with each token enclosed indicated by one marking on the surface of the case. For example, an envelope holding six tokens displayed six markings. In fact, the markings indicated not only the number of tokens included but also the shape of each counter. In other words, the markings translated into two-dimensional signs the information expressed by the three-dimensional tokens held inside. For example, an envelope from Susa yielded three lenticular disks and three cylinders, which were translated by three circular and three long markings. The meaning of these markings could be read as "thirty three animals (sheep?)." The accountants who initiated the new method of impressed markings to communicate information probably never realized the importance of the event: they had invented writing.

FROM TOKENS TO IMPRESSED TABLETS

The system of markings on envelopes ushered in a new phase of the token system. It became obvious to the accountants dealing with the envelopes that it was unnecessary to repeat the information, first with tokens inside the envelope and second with markings outside. Thus, solid clay tablets bearing impressed signs replaced the hollow envelopes holding tokens (fig. 5). These signs impressed on tablets were the same as those featured on the envelopes. They perpetuated the shapes of the tokens, but they assumed an entirely new function. Whereas the markings on envelopes repeated only the message encoded in the tokens held inside, the signs impressed on tablets were the message. The first tablets were a decisive new step in the development of the Sumerian writing system. About 240 impressed tablets are presently known from such sites as Uruk and Khafaje in Iraq; Susa, Chogha Mish, Tepe Sialk, and Godin Tepe in Iran; and Habuba al-Kabira and Jebel Aruda in Syria.

FROM TOKENS TO PICTOGRAPHIC WRITING

The impressed signs satisfactorily translated the shapes of the former plain tokens. The complex tokens with multiple markings, however, did not lend themselves to being impressed and gave rise to incised signs traced with a stylus (fig. 6). The resulting Sumerian script therefore had a repertory of impressed and incised signs, the

Fig. 5. Impressed tablet from Susa, Iran, 3100 BCE. LOUVRE MUSEUM, PARIS

Fig. 6. Pictographic tablet (circa 3100 BCE) from Godin Tepe, Iran. ROYAL ONTARIO MUSEUM, TORONTO

former perpetuating the shape of the plain tokens, and the latter, those of the complex counters. None of these techniques was new, since punched and incised markings had been placed on clay tokens from the beginning of the eighth millennium.

Pictography started by impressing or drawing signs in the form of the former tokens. But, when the principle of communicating by small pictures was established, it was applied to things other than tokens. The repertory of signs therefore increased to include sketches of items that were never handled in accounting and possibly never could have been with tokens. For example, "a man" was expressed by a small sketch. This was the true launching of Sumerian writing, since it enlarged its capacity to communicate information pertaining to all possible fields of human endeavor. In fact, some scholars regard pictography as the actual beginning of writing. Others equate the genesis of writing with yet another extraordinary development that took place in the Sumerian script in the late fourth millennium, when signs took a phonetic value. Indeed, this was an event of major importance, since this marked the first merging of visible and spoken language, which was to lead progressively to syllabaries and ultimately to the alphabet. The sign for "man," for example, which, in McLuhan's words, previously only "spoke to the eye," came to "speak to the ear" and took the phonetic value of LU, the sound for that word in Sumerian. I presume that, at first, phonetic writing was devised to allow transcription of an individual's name. Sumerian personal names were particularly appropriate for being rendered phonetically because they often consisted of a phrase or even a full sentence: "Servant of deity/king," "He belongs to his god," or the like. (See the next essay on "Sumerian Language.")

The following fundamental features of the token system were particularly significant in influencing the development of Sumerian writing: (1) semanticity—each token was meaningful and communicated information; (2) discreteness—the information was specific and each counter shape had a unique meaning; (3) systematization—each token shape was repeated over and over systematically with the same meaning; (4) codification—the system consisted of many interrelated elements, and so it was possible to deal simultaneously with data about different items; (5) openness—the repertory of counters could be increased to include new items; (6) discontinuity—tokens of related shapes could refer to completely unrelated concepts; (7) arbitrariness—many tokens were modeled in a shape totally unrelated to the form of the item expressed; for example, there is evidence that a cylinder stood for one animal; (8) independence of phonetics—the tokens were a nonverbal communication system, unrelated to spoken language. The tokens were symbols of particular goods that could be understood by individuals speaking different tongues or dialects; and (9) syntax—it is likely that the tokens were manipulated according to practical rules, and so, for example, there is evidence suggesting they were arranged in sets of counters of the same kind, with the larger units placed to the right.

THE MEANING OF TOKENS

The hypothesis that there was an evolution from tokens to Sumerian pictographic writing allows us to establish meaning for the early impressed and incised signs by retrospecting from cuneiform signs used in the third millennium. Eventually, Assyriologists will find it possible to trace the evolution of cuneiform characters backward through increasingly archaic forms to their prototypes of the late fourth millennium. This is the case, for example, for the signs for particular domesticated animals such as sheep, ewe, lamb, dog, and cow; staple foods or raw materials, including cereals, oil, and metal; and finished products such as types of textiles and garments. These cases are few, because writing evolved rapidly in the first centuries after its inception. The Sumerian script underwent, for example, a major phase of sign elimination. Around 3000 BCE the number of signs was reduced from an original repertory estimated at about a thousand signs to some five hundred. Apparently, the same was true when tokens were transposed into graphic signs. This is demonstrated, for example, by three triangular signs with three, five, and six lines, which seem to be the only surviving forms deriving from a large series of triangular tokens bearing numbers of lines ranging from one to twelve (fig. 3).

FROM CONCRETE TO ABSTRACT COUNTING

The token system paved the way not only for pictographic writing but also for the invention of the abstract numerals that are fundamental to mathematics. The accounts preserved in envelopes suggest that the prehistoric cultures of the Near East used a counting system different from ours. For example, the group of incised ovoid tokens enclosed in an envelope from Uruk (fig. 4) illustrate two major archaisms: the tokens were used in one-to-one correspondence (six jars of oil were indicated by six tokens) and each category of item counted required a special counter. (Jars of oil were counted with ovoids, and ovoids could only refer to numbers of jars of oil.)

Consequently, the token system suggests that the cultures that invented them used a rudimentary counting system. In particular, the tokens suggest that in the Near East before the fourth millennium there was no conception of numbers existing independent of the commodities counted. In other words, abstract numbers such as "one," "two," and "three," referring to any possible set of items, were not known. Instead, the prehistoric system of counting was concrete. That is to say, types of items were counted with different counters, probably corresponding to different numerations. It is difficult for us to conceptualize concrete counting. The closest to that mode of counting in our own culture would be numerical expressions such as "twin," "triplet," and "quadruplet," referring to different numbers of children of the same birth, and "duo," "trio," and "quartet," pertaining to groups of musicians.

Abstract numerals—signs to express 1, 2, 3,—unrelated to any particular commodity are first attested at the stage of pictographic writing. On the pictographic tablets, the incised signs encoding commodities like "jars of oil" were no longer repeated as many times as the number of units involved. Instead, the pictograph for "jar of oil" was preceded by abstract numerals showing that, at this stage, the concepts of quantity and of the commodity counted were finally abstracted from each other. For instance, a tablet from Godin Tepe, Iran, bearing the notation "33 jars of oil" displayed a single pictograph for "jar of oil" and expressed "33" with three impressed circles $(10 + 10 + 10)$ and three wedges $(1 + 1 + 1)$ (fig. 6). It is interesting to note that although abstract numbers made a breach in the age-old principle of one-to-one correspondence, they still did not put an end to it. "Three" was still represented by three wedges and "thirty" by three circles, and so on.

The first numerals were impressed wedges and circular markings. In fact, they were not symbols specifically created for representing abstract numbers. Instead, they were the impressed signs that formerly indicated measures of grain but were now endowed with a new numerical value. The wedge that derived from the cone (representing a small quantity of grain) now stood for 1, and the circle deriving from the sphere (representing a larger quantity of grain), for 10. In fact, the impressed signs that came to represent the first numerals never lost their primary meaning. Instead, according to the context, they had either an abstract value, 1 and 10, or a concrete value, a specific measure of grain.

The study of tokens therefore makes it increasingly clear that counting and writing are two closely interrelated processes. It is remarkable that the first writing system developed from a counting technology. It is no less remarkable that the invention of abstract numerals coincided with pictography and phonetic writing. This strongly suggests that numeracy and literacy are connected in ways that we do not yet comprehend. (For a different opinion, see "Memory and Literacy in Ancient Western Asia" later in Part 9, in this volume.)

THE SOCIAL IMPLICATIONS OF ACCOUNTING

The fact that the token system started in the late eighth millennium, when agriculture came about, and that the complex tokens first appeared in the fourth millennium, the period of urban formation, is of great significance because it shows that the evolution of communication coincided with major moments in human communal development. There can be no doubt that counting and keeping records of goods became necessary when survival depended on domestication of grains and on accumulating the products of harvests. The invention of the token system can therefore be considered as directly influenced by the "Neolithic Revolution." It is likely, however, that the beginning of accounting with tokens was not merely a response to farming but was sponsored by new social and political structures that arose because of agriculture. In particular, record keeping may be related to the creation of an elite overseeing a redistributive economy.

The fact that the token types and subtypes multiplied in the fourth millennium was also not accidental. The propagation of complex tokens corresponded to the creation of workshops and to the more diversified urban economy that followed. The need for more accurate and more comprehensive accounting techniques arose with the increase of bureaucracy typical of state formation. The direct implementation of the token system in the rise of an elite is suggested by three sets of data.

First, the creation of the token system coincided with a new settlement pattern characterized by larger communities. For example, at Mureybet in Syria, there is no evidence for the use of counters in the two earliest phases of the site, about 8500–8000, when it was a small compound of 0.5 hectare (1.25 acres). Tokens occur in the third phase, about 8000–7500, when the hamlet had grown to become a village covering 2 or 3 hectares (5–7.5 acres). It is difficult to evaluate the size of the population of Mureybet level III; it is estimated, however, that the community then exceeded the number of individuals managcable in an egalitarian system. Therefore, as probably happened elsewhere, the first token assemblage from Mureybet coincided with the advent of a society characterized by a new type of ranked leadership overseeing the community resources.

Second, in rare but significant instances, tokens have been recovered in a funerary context. Among the thousands of graves dating from 8000 to 3000 excavated in the Near East, only a dozen are known to have yielded tokens. These were located, for example, at Hajji Firuz (one), Arpachiyah (one), Tell es-Sawwan (four), and Tepe Gawra (six). The counters found in these sites were visibly restricted to the occasional richly furnished tombs of individuals of high status. The interments of Tell es-Sawwan held a variety of alabaster vessels and ornaments of dentalia shells and carnelian. Three of the burials of Tepe Gawra were among the richest at the site, holding gold rosettes and beads and precious vessels of obsidian, serpentine, and electrum. These particular tombs also included symbols of power, such as mace-heads and lapis lazuli seals. Other burials at Hajji Firuz and Tepe Gawra included special architectural features. A shrine, for instance, was erected above Tomb 107 of Tepe Gawra, and the burial of this prestigious individual was furnished with six stone spheres as the only offering. The rarity of funerary tokens and their association with comparatively luxurious burial deposits, artifacts symbolizing power, and special architecture indicate that the counters did not belong to the masses, but were the privilege of an elite. Apparently, they were used by individuals of high status and therefore came to be regarded as symbols of office, conferring the idea of authority. The fact that tokens were included among the trappings of power also suggests that during the Neolithic and Chalcolithic periods (8000–3500) the use of counters served an elite to command the control of real goods. In other words, numeracy played in prehistory the same role as literacy in historic times.

Third and last, the remarkable consistency and stability of the token system throughout the five thousand years of its existence makes it unlikely that it underwent a disjunction in use and function. Instead, it strongly supports the idea that the protohistoric tokens found in envelopes in the fourth millennium and those found as simple units in the fifth to eighth millennia had a similar use. In turn, the function of the fourth-millennium envelopes yielding tokens can be deduced from that of the pictographic tablets that replaced them. It is unchallenged that the pictographic tablets were temple records of entries and expenditures of goods. They listed small amounts of merchandise either brought to the temple as dues or worshipers' "gifts to the gods" or stipulated the disbursement of goods for rations or other purposes. The pictographic tablets provided the elite governing the first city-states with a device by which to establish an economic control.

It seems clear that the tokens held in envelopes assumed the same function of economic control as did the pictographic tablets. The fact that tokens and tablets dealt with identical data is indicated by the use of the same symbols in both media. For example, the symbols for grain, animals, oil, textiles, and garments, the most typical Mesopotamian commodities, exist as three-dimensional tokens, as well as impressed or incised signs. Envelopes and tablets also deal with similar quantities of merchandise. The small number of tokens enclosed in each case is comparable to the amounts of goods recorded on the tablets. In other words, because accounting was the key to the control of real goods, the evolution of the token system influenced socio-economic developments. The appearance of tokens in the earliest rank societies, their inclusion in rich burials, and the similarity of envelopes holding tokens to pictographic tablets suggest that from the beginning, counting and record keeping were the privilege of an elite and that the more the system became efficient and precise, the more power it wielded.

CONCLUSION

The system of nonverbal communication based on tokens played a major role in the ascent of civilization in the ancient Near East. The tokens were a record-keeping device that led to the invention of writing. They were counters, forerunners of abstract numbers. They were an instrument of power and favored the rise of an elite. Foremost, they were necessary for establishing the redistributive economy that was the basis of the first city-states.

BIBLIOGRAPHY

Sources

A comprehensive study of the near eastern token system is presented in DENISE SCHMANDT-BESSERAT, *Before Writing*, vol. 1, *From Counting to Cuneiform*, and vol. 2, *A Catalog of Near Eastern Tokens* (1992). See also H. J. NISSEN, P. DAMEROW, and R. K. ENGLUND, *Archaic Bookkeeping. Writing and Techniques of Economic Administration in the Ancient Near East* (1993).

Studies

Excavation reports or special studies including information on particular token collections include PIERRE AMIET, *Mémoires de la délégation archéologique en Iran* 43, *Glyptique Susienne*, pt. 1, *Texte* (1972); VIVIAN L. BROMAN, "Jarmo Figurines and Other Clay Objects," in *Prehistoric Archeology Along the Zagros Flanks*, edited by L. S. BRAIDWOOD, R. J. BRAIDWOOD ET AL., Oriental Institute Publications 105 (1983); JACQUES CAUVIN, *Les Premiers Villages de Syrie-Palestine du IXème au VIIème Millénaire avant J.C.*, Collection de la Maison de L'Orient Mediterranéen Ancien, no. 4, Série Archéologique 3 (1978); HENRI DE CONTENSON, "Recherches sur le Néolithique de Syrie (1967–1976)," *Comptes Rendus, Académie des Inscriptions et Belles-Lettres* (1978); M. W. GREEN and HANS J. NISSEN, *Zeichenliste der Archaischen Texte aus Uruk*, Ausgrabungen der Deutsche Forschungsgemeinschaft in Uruk-Warka 11, Archaische Texte aus Uruk 2 (1987); JULIUS JORDAN, *Zweiter vorläufiger Bericht über die von der Notgemeinschaft der deutschen Wissenschaft in Uruk unternommenen Ausgrabungen*, Abhandlungen der Preussischen Akademie der Wissenschaften, Phil.-hist. Klasse, 1930/4 (1931); ALAIN LE BRUN and FRANÇOIS VALLAT, "L'origine de l'écriture à Suse," *Cahiers de la Délégation Française en Iran* 8 (1978); HEINRICH J. LENZEN, *XXII. Vorläufiger Bericht über die von dem Deutschen Archäologischen Institut und der Deutschen Orient-Gesellschaft aus Mitteln der Deutschen Forschungsgemeinschaft unternommenen Ausgrabungen in Uruk-Warka* (1966); EVA STROMMENGER, *Habuba Kabira: Eine Stadt vor 5000 Jahren* (1980); ARTHUR J. TOBLER, *Excavations at Tepe Gawra*, vol. 2, *Levels IX–XX* (1950); MARY M. VOIGT, *Hajji Firuz Tepe, Iran: The Neolithic Settlement*, University Museum Monograph 50 (1983); HARVEY WEISS and T. CUYLER YOUNG, JR., "The Merchants of Susa: Godin V and Plateau–Lowland Relations in the Late Fourth Millennium B.C.," *Iran* 13 (1975).

For a critical response to the theory presented in this essay, see the following studies: P. MICHALOWSKI, "Early Mesopotamia Communicative Systems: Art, Literature, and Writing," in A. C. GUNTER, ed., *Investigating Artistic Environments in the Ancient Near East* (1990); and S. J. LIEBERMAN, "Of Clay Pebbles, Hollow Clay Balls, and Writing: A Sumerian View," *American Journal of Archaeology* 84 (1980).

SEE ALSO **Ancient Western Asia Before the Age of Empires** (Part 5, Vol. II); **Metrology and Mathematics in Ancient Mesopotamia** (Part 8, Vol. III); and **The Story of the Semitic Alphabet** (Part 9, Vol. IV).

The Sumerian Language

D. O. EDZARD

SUMERIAN IS, alongside the earliest written Egyptian, the world's oldest language attested in writing. The earliest documents date from the turn of the fourth to the third millennium BCE. Sumerian disappeared as a spoken language during the first centuries of the second millennium, but its written use and its cultural impact continued well into the first millennium. The Sumerians immigrated into southern Mesopotamia from the east or southeast at an unknown time. The linguistic affiliation of their language is unknown, and efforts to relate it to modern languages or language groups (Turkish, Hungarian, and Sino-Tibetan, among others) have remained unconvincing, because they are exclusively based on an often rather naive comparison of sound and meaning. Since the oldest reconstructable phonetic form of Sumerian dates only to about 2300 BCE, and there is a gap of at least two thousand to three thousand years between that date and the oldest comparable form of the languages under consideration, it is always possible that sound similarity is due to chance rather than to common ancestry.

Typologically speaking, Sumerian shares features with such diverse languages as Basque, Georgian, and the Paleo-Asiatic language Chukchee in Kamchatka, Siberia: agglutination, a series of prefixes and suffixes "glued" to a nominal or verbal base and serving to express both morphosyntactic and lexical functions; ergativity, a morphological distinction of "subject" markers depending on whether they head a transitive or intransitive verbal form; a class, instead of gender system (personal versus nonpersonal). This does not, however, help to elucidate parentage, since similar features occur independently all over the world and, moreover, individual languages may change their type in the course of history.

Close contact with the Semitic language Akkadian over several centuries caused Sumerian to acquire certain features of the neighboring language and vice versa, thus giving rise to a "linguistic area" (*Sprachbund*). In addition, Sumerian of course underwent its own internal evolution, as regards phonetics, morphology, syntax, and lexicon. A few dialect features can be detected as well. For all this, however, we are all but exclusively limited to the written form of Sumerian, and it is only through spelling variants that we sometimes may guess at phonetic peculiarities. This brief overview is based essentially on the literary language as attested at the end of the third millennium and during the first two centuries of the second millennium BCE. (In this chapter, Sumerian words are set in small capital letters, separated by a hyphen, but with a period when explained morphologically. Akkadian words are in italics.)

Our names Sumer and Sumerian go back to Akkadian *māt Šumerim*, "land of Sumer," or *lišānum šumerītum*, "Sumerian language." The origin and etymology of the stem *šumer-* are unknown. In Sumerian itself, the respective terms were KI.EN.GI(.R) and EME.(E)GI(.R).

Sumerian Writing

Different Sumerian words (mostly monosyllabic, but occasionally bisyllabic) were treated as homophones (words pronounced alike but differing in meaning) by the Akkadian scribes, who provided them with identical glosses in syllabic script in the vocabularies they created, e.g., DUG, "pot," DUG, "good," and DUG, "to say." These words, in many cases, were not truly homophones but were distinguished from each other by different vowel length or different shades of vowel quality ($u, \bar{u}; o, \bar{o};$ or the like) in spoken Sumerian. The Akkadian scribes, however, either were indifferent to such phonetic subtleties or were unable to denote differences of pronunciation in their syllabic glosses.

Modern Assyriologists have developed a system of identifying such alleged homophones by the addition of accents or numerical indices, as in DUG, "pot"; DÙG, "good"; DUG₄, "to say." (An acute accent [´] replaces the index ₂; the grave accent [`] replaces the index ₃. The indices were assigned on the basis of supposed relative frequency of the homophones in the texts.) It is to be stressed that this is a modern device completely irrelevant to the actual pronunciation of Sumerian. The term "transliteration" is used for the sign-by-sign transposing of cuneiform into Latin script (including the use of accents and numerical indices). The term "transcription" or "normalization" is used for spelling a Sumerian word in Latin script regardless of its original cuneiform spelling. Thus, the verbal form "he/she said to him/her" is transliterated as MU-NA-AN-DUG₄ but transcribed or normalized as MUNANDUG. In this article, hyphens join the transliterations of signs making up a word, while (somewhat unconventionally) periods join the normalizations or morphemes making up a word. Superscript letters represent the determinatives that mark words as referring to a member of a class, including d for "god" (ᵈNINGIRSU), KI for "city" (LAGAŠᴷᴵ), and GIŠ for "wood(en object)" (ᴳᴵˢKIRI₆).

WRITTEN SUMERIAN

Sumerian is written in cuneiform with a mixed system of word signs and syllabograms: *ba, da, bi, ab,* and so on (that is, CV or VC) and, less frequently, *bar, dam,* and so on (that is, CVC, where C is a consonant and V is a vowel). Nominal and verbal bases are primarily written with word signs. The two sign types are not, however, mutually exclusive. Thus, BA, as a word sign, means "to attribute," but as a syllabic sign, it may be used purely phonetically, as in the sequence *ba-ra-* (BARA), a bisyllabic prefix of the verb ("must not"). Since morphemes do not always coincide with syllables, the morpheme boundary may be within a syllabogram, as in *-ba* of GUB-BA (GUB.A), "standing," composed of the verbal base GUB, "stand," and a suffix *-a*. In this case, the *b* of *ba* is part of the verbal base GUB, whereas the *a* of that syllabogram is the suffix proper.

The way we transliterate Sumerian into Latin script—and consequently the way we read it—is dictated almost exclusively by the analogy of our reading of Akkadian. Our reconstruction of the phonetic system of Akkadian is itself strongly influenced by our knowledge of the sound sys-tems of the related Semitic languages Hebrew, Aramaic, and Arabic. Consequently—and this should always be kept in mind—at least two steps have distanced our reading and pronunciation of Sumerian from their actual form and acoustical identity, so that in all likelihood we would be totally unintelligible to native speakers of Sumerian who happened to hear our version of their language.

Our reading of most of the Sumerian word

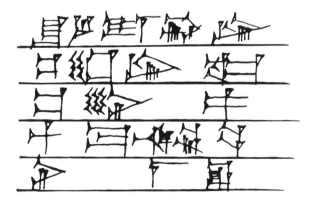

Paragraph of the *Code of Lipit-Ishtar of Isin,* twentieth century BCE. H. F. LUTZ, SELECTED SUMERIAN AND BABYLONIAN TEXTS (1919)

signs is guided, aided, and confirmed by glosses made by the ancient scribes in the lexical lists, but we are also guided by the numerous Sumerian loanwords that have passed into Akkadian, such as NAR > *nārum*, "singer, musician," or SAĜ.DILI > *sagdilû*, "bachelor."

SOUND SYSTEM

With these cautions in mind, we may present the (minimal) phoneme inventory of Sumerian as follows:

PA, "twig"	BA, "to attribute"	MA-, "to me" (verb prefix)
TAR, "to cut"	DAR, "to split"	NAR, "musician"
KAL, "dear"	GAL, "big"	ĜÁL, "to exist"

(ĝ was most probably a velar nasal, as in "si**ng**," perhaps with a labial component, ng^w, but its exact phonetic identity is unknown; therefore ĝ is primarily a symbol to differentiate it from G.)

ĜÁL, "to exist"	ĜAR, "to put"	
SU, "to sink"	ZU, "to know"	ŠU, "hand"
ḪI, "to mix"		

(š represents the *sh* sound; ḫ was probably some sort of guttural *kh* sound, reflected in loanwords in Akkadian by Semitic ḥ.)

Sumerian vowels are—again minimally—*a, e, i, u,* and, most probably, *o.* From the fact that Sumerian loanwords in Akkadian have short or long vowels (in a consistent pattern), we can deduce evidence for Sumerian vowels of differing quantity (length), so that oppositions of the type *a:ā* and so on are possible. Instead of quantity, however, different vowel qualities (open:closed) are as likely to have been relevant. The Sumerian spelling system does not reveal any such distinctions.

WORDS

The great majority of Sumerian words are mono- or bisyllabic (most words of more than three syllables are—or are suspected of being—originally compounds); they are given here in their best attested forms: E₄, "water"; RA, "to beat"; ÁB, "cow"; TUR, "small"; ERE, "city"; SAĜA, "main temple administrator"; ENIM, "word"; ANŠE, "donkey"; KISAL, "courtyard"; ABSIN, "furrow"; BANŠUR, "table." If initial or word-final consonant clusters existed (*KRA-, *-ARK, and the like, where the asterisk indicates a hypothetical form), the syllabic system convention would not have been able to denote them. Therefore, we cannot say whether such clusters actually occurred.

Parts of speech may be distinguished not by their form, but by their morphosyntactic behavior (before the parentheses is the spelling; within the parenthesis is the morphological analysis).

ŠAḪ-TUR, "piglet" ("pig" + "small"); ŠAḪ-A-NI, "his pig"; ŠAḪ-DA, "with the pig." ŠAḪ is defined as a substantive, because it can be combined with an adjective, with a possessive pronoun, and with a postposition (here, the comitative).

ĜIDRI-ZI(D), "rightful scepter" ("scepter" + "trustworthy"); ZI-DÈ-EŠ (ZID.EŠ), "in a trustworthy way." ZI(D) is defined as an adjective, because it can qualify a substantive or can be combined with the adverbiative ending .EŠ.

Use of Sumerian

It is impossible today to draw a language map exactly indicating the areas where, century by century, native speakers of Sumerian lived. It may be taken for granted that the greater part of southern Mesopotamia from the latitude of Nippur (modern Nuffar) southward was Sumerophone until about the twenty-fourth century BCE. Thereafter, the region was gradually taken over by the Akkadian-speaking population. Nothing is known yet about speakers of Sumerian living beyond the borders of southern Mesopotamia, either in (modern) Iran or along the southern coast of the Persian Gulf. Sumerian had probably died out as a living spoken language by the end of the nineteenth century. As a literary language, however, Sumerian continued well into the first millennium BCE, both as a vehicle of literary tradition and as the prestige language of royal inscriptions. At the very end of the tradition of cuneiform writing, during the first century BCE and the first century CE, Sumerian words were noted in Greek script on clay tablets, the so-called Greco-Babyloniaca.

MU-UN-DAḪ (MU.N.DAḪ) "he added"; DAḪ-ḪE-DAM (DAḪ.ED.AM), "it is to be added." DAḪ is defined as a verb, because it is combined with morphemes not occurring with nouns.

Certain adjectives may, however, be turned into verbs, in which case they become combinable with morphemes that are typical of verbs, such as DÙG, "good," and MU-UN-DÙG (MU.N.DUG), "he caused (it) to be good." In addition, we may distinguish pronouns, numerals, adverbs, conjunctions, and exclamations.

NOUNS

The Sumerian noun is characterized by the grammatical categories of class, case, and number. There is no gender, at least not morphologically marked; but a secondary gender distinction can be expressed, as in DUMU-NITA and DUMU-MUNUS, "male child" and "female child" (that is, "son" and "daughter").

Class

Every noun is, by class, either "personal" or "nonpersonal." The distinction is not "animate" versus "inanimate," since in Sumerian, animals are nonpersonal (unless, of course, they act like persons in a myth or fable). Class is not marked in the word itself but is shown by concord: LUGAL-A-NI (LUGAL.ANI), "his master, owner" (of a slave), as opposed to LUGAL-BI, "its owner" (of a house), with the referents "slave" and "house" being personal and nonpersonal, respectively. Class difference is also shown in plural marking and in case syntax.

Case

Case is unmarked or is expressed by postpositions. The unmarked absolute is the subject of an intransitive verbal form or the object of a transitive verb, as seen from the point of view of our subject language type. The absolute is also the quotation form in lexical entries.

The ergative (the case denoting the subject of a transitive verbal form) is marked by -E. This may coalesce with a preceding vowel.

The genitive is marked by -A(K). Here, complicated phonotactic rules apply: the K of -A(K) is not noted in final position; the A is elided when the noun ends in a vowel; the K is noted if another vowel follows: DIĜIR-RA (DIĜIR.A(K)), "the god's"; AMA (AMA.(A)(K)), "mother's"; AMA-KAM (AMA.(A)K.AM), "it is mother's."

The locative in -A is reserved mostly for nouns of the nonperson class: ERE-A, "in the city." It denotes situation "at," "in," "on"; note also U$_4$-DA (UD.A), "at the day" (that is, "today").

The dative is used exclusively with person-class nouns. It ends in -RA or -R; in the latter case, the sign containing the R includes the final vowel of the preceding noun or pronoun, LUGAL-A-NI-IR (LUGAL.ANI.R), "to his/her master." The dative denotes the goal of the action spoken of, giving and the like, and also of love and hate. Locative and dative are in practice used in complementary distribution with the nonperson and person classes, respectively.

The comitative in -DA denotes accompaniment, meeting, and mental participation as in AMA-DA, "with mother," and ÁB AMAR-BI-DA, "the cow with its calf."

The ablative-instrumental in -TA denotes point of departure, locally or temporally, or the object by means of which something is made or accomplished. Its use is restricted to nouns of the nonperson class: ERE-TA, "from the city"; U$_4$-BI-TA, "since that day"; TUKUL-TA, "by means of the weapon."

The terminative .ŠE denotes movement toward a goal and, in the abstract, reason: ERE-ŠÈ, "to the city"; MU-BI-ŠÈ, "toward its name" (that is, "therefore"). The stress is on motion proper, not on arrival at the goal; in the latter case, the locative-terminative would be preferred.

The locative-terminative ends in -E, like the ergative, with which it shares phonotactic rules. A common origin of the two cases is nearly certain, but since they behave differently in syntax, they must be clearly distinguished. The locative-terminative denotes either immediate surface contact or motion toward a goal with resulting contact: KAR-SIRARAN-NA-KE$_4$ (KAR.SIRANAN.AK.E), "(he landed the boat) at the quay of Siranan."

Standing apart as a postposition is -GIM, variant -GIN$_7$. It may follow a noun in the absolute, as in the proper name A-BA ᵈEN-LÍL-GIM (ABA EN-

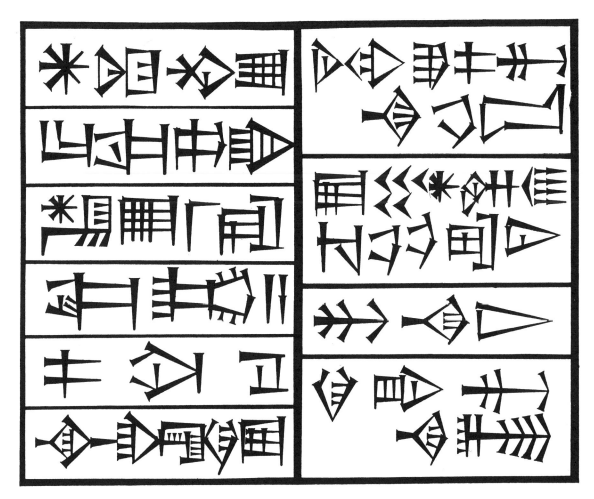

Stamped-brick inscription of Gudea from Lagash, twenty-first century BCE. D. D. LUCKENBILL, *INSCRIPTIONS FROM ADAB* (1930)

LIL.GIM), "Who-Is-Like-Enlil?" But it may also supersede another case postposition, such as -TA (ablative-instrumental), as in GU₄-AN-NA-GIM (GU.AN.A(K).GIM), "as (by means of) the Bull of Heaven."

Number

A plural in the strict sense (more than one) is available only for nouns of the person class: DIĜIR-RE(-E)-NE (DIĜIR.ENE), "gods"; AMA-NE (AMA.(E)NE), "mothers." This plural is attested only for ergative, genitive, dative, and comitative. Postpositions are added after the plural morpheme: LUGAL-E-NE-RA (LUGAL.ENE.R), "to the kings."

Nouns of the nonperson class are in principle indifferent to number; context alone indicates whether one or more than one are intended: ANŠE, "donkey(s)."

Apart from a numerical plural, there are means of specifying other kinds of plurality. Reduplication may indicate totality, as in KUR-KUR, "all the lands" and ĜIŠ-GI-ĜIŠ-GI, "all the canebrakes." Suffixed -DIDLI stands for an individuated plural, as in KIŠIB-DIDLI, "the single sealed documents." Heterogeneous plurality is denoted by suffixed -ḪI-A ("mixed"), as in UDU-ḪI-A, "diverse sheep and goats." Some adjectives must be reduplicated when joined to a substantive in the plural, as in GAL, "big, great," for example, DIĜIR-GAL-GAL-E-NE (DIĜIR.GALGAL.ENE), "the great gods."

PRONOUNS

The pronominal system essentially includes free personal and suffixed possessive pronouns: ĜÁ-E, "I"; ZA-E, "you" (singular); É-ZU, "your house." The inflectional pattern of personal pronouns is restricted in comparison to that of substantives. Possessive suffixes precede the plural marker and case postpositions: DUMU-ĜU₁₀-NE-DA (DUMU.ĜU.(E)NE.DA), "with my children." There are only singular and plural; a dual is unknown. For the first-person plural pronoun, a distinction between inclusive ("you and I") and exclusive ("they and I") forms has been suggested but not proven beyond doubt. In the third singular, the person and nonperson classes are kept apart.

Demonstrative pronouns are rare; in the expression U₄-UL-LÍ-A-TA (U.ULLIA.TA), "since that day" (that is, "since those days"), UL-LÍ-A is a loan from Akkadian *ullī'um*, "that one."

NUMERALS

The Sumerian number system is sexagesimal in the sense that in the sequence 1 to 10, 10 to 60, 60 to 600, 600 to 3600, and so on, ten and six steps alternate. Sumerian 100 would be 1,40 (that is, one unit of 60 plus 40), and 1995 would be expressed as 3 units of 600 plus 3 units of 60 plus 10 plus 5. Since numerals are almost exclusively written with number signs, information on their pronunciation is scarce. Among the digits, 7 (IMIN) and 9 (ILIMMU) are compounds of 5 plus 2 and 5 plus 4, respectively. ŠÁR, "3600," also serves to denote "myriad," or a very large number.

Cardinal numbers follow the thing counted, although for practical reasons (visual prominence) they usually precede in writing: 2 UDU, "two sheep," read UDU.MIN.

VERBS

As in many languages of the inflecting and agglutinating types, verbal morphology is by nature more complex than nominal morphology. The verbal base alone, as in DAḪ (Akkadian (*w*)*aṣābu*), "to add," is the form cited in lexical lists; but in a fuller context, the base rarely occurs without additional morphemes, prefixed and/or suffixed. The various morphemes follow each other in strict and unalterable rank order.

Finite Verbs

Finite verbal forms, where person is marked, and nonfinite forms can be clearly distinguished. Finite forms may be nominalized by means of a morpheme -A and thereafter be inflected as nouns. The finite verb has three conjugation patterns characterized by (1) the position (prefixed or suffixed) of the markers for the ergative and absolutive (or agent and patient) person elements and (2) the use of different forms of the base. The morpheme inventory of the finite verb includes markers of person and number, class, direction, mood, and connection, as well as markers not yet sufficiently understood.

The meaning of the verb is essentially conveyed by the base but may be modified by a directional morpheme. With a dative prefix, DUG₄ means "to say to someone," as in MU-NA-AN-DUG₄ (MU.NA.N.DUG), "he/she said to him/her" (with -NA- for third-person dative); with prefix BÍ-, DUG₄ has the meaning "to make a deposition." Moreover, a rather vague and general meaning may become precise when combined with a special subject or object; thus, DU₇, "to make a straight and direct movement toward a goal," becomes "to gore" when an ox is the subject, but combined with ŠU, "hand," the meaning is "to render perfect." A few verbs, like AG, "to make," and DUG₄, "to do, speak," often function as auxiliary verbs or verbalizers, such as KIN AG, "to do (AG) work (KIN)," meaning "to work," and ŠU DUG₄, "to . . . the hand (ŠU)," meaning "to create." There are as many as 210 so-called compound verbs just with the base DUG₄.

In reduplicated form, the verbal base may express different sorts of plurality (great number of objects, repetition of the action, intensity). Besides such lexicalized reduplication, there is full or partial reduplication, which, with certain verbs, predictably occurs in the "present" conjugation pattern (for example, ĜAR > ĜÁ-ĜÁ; ZI(G) > ZI-ZI; KU₄(-R) > KU₄-KU₄). A restricted number of verbs use different bases for singular and plural, such as ÚŠ, "to die" (one person), UG₆, "to die" (plural).

Transitive Verbs: Preterite In texts that are written in Sumerian but also give an Akkadian translation ("bilinguals"), the basic conjugation pattern of the transitive Sumerian verb corresponds to the Akkadian preterite (*iprus*), and it is labeled as such by the majority of Sumerologists, in spite of the inadequacy of the term (in both Akkadian and Sumerian the verb is primarily aspect-oriented, not tense-oriented). Here are considered only forms of the first-, second-, and third-person singular and the third-person plural as regards the ergative markers, since the first- and second-person plural are not attested frequently enough to allow them to be reliably incorporated into the paradigm.

The ergative marker comes immediately before the base: MU-UN-ḪUL (MU.N.ḪUL), "he destroyed (something)." An absolutive marker for first and second person may immediately follow the base: MU-UN-TU-DÈ-EN (MU.N.TUD.EN), "she (.N.) bore me (.EN)." The pattern is as follows:

1st sing.	-*V-B* (*V*=undefined vocalic element, *B*=base)
2nd sing.	-E-*B*
3rd sing.	-N-*B* (person class)
	-*B-B* (nonperson class)
3rd plur.	-N-*B*-EŠ (person class only)

The pattern of the absolutive marker is as follows:

1st sing.	-*B*-EN
2nd sing.	-*B*-EN
1st plur.	-*B*-ENDEN
2nd plur.	-*B*-ENZEN

Not all the ergative and absolutive markers can be combined; for instance, third plural plus first plural, "they bore us," cannot occur. In such cases, the speaker probably had to resort to a free form of the personal pronoun.

The preterite pattern utilizes the base referred to as *ḫamṭu* in the Akkadian lexicographers' terminology. The preterite pattern is used in the indicative mood, in the affirmative mood (positive or negative, "he certainly did [not] . . . ") of the past, and in the cohortative or optative mood ("let me . . . ," "let us . . . ").

Transitive Verbs: Present The second conjugation pattern of the transitive verb corresponds to the Akkadian present (*iparras*) in bilinguals. Here, the positions of ergative and absolutive markers are reversed, the former following, and the latter preceding, the base. The present pattern is as follows:

1st sing.	-*B*-EN
2nd sing.	-*B*-EN
3rd sing.	-*B*-E (both person and non-person class)
1st plur.	-*B*-ENDEN
2nd plur.	-*B*-ENZEN
3rd plur.	-*B*-ENE (person class only)

The pattern of the absolutive marker is as follows:

1st sing.	-(E)N-*B* (?)
2nd sing.	-(E)N-*B* (?)
3rd sing.	-N-*B* (person class)
	-*B-B* (nonperson class)

The present pattern has the base referred to as *marû* in the Akkadian lexicographers' terminology. The present pattern is used in the indicative mood, in the precative mood ("may you . . . ," "may he . . ."), and in the prohibitive mood ("you, he shall not . . .").

There are different verb classes defined according to the identity of the *ḫamṭu* and *marû* bases: (1) Both may be identical, as in SUM, "to give." This is the nonchanging class; it probably constitutes about two-thirds of Sumerian verbal bases. (2) In the reduplication class, *ḫamṭu* offers a simple form and *marû* a reduplicated form. In contrast to reduplication that is lexically relevant, the *marû* reduplication is characterized by phonetical reduction of the simple form; for example, ĜAR, "to put," loses its final consonant: ĜÁ-ĜÁ. The reduplication class comes next in frequency after the nonchanging class. (3) In the base-alternating class, some change other than reduplication occurs; for example, È, "to bring out" (*ḫamṭu*), has ÉD in the *marû* base. (4) Finally, there are cases of heteronymy, such as DE₆, "to carry away" (*ḫamṭu*), versus TÙMU (*marû*).

Both DE₆ and TÙMU are written with the same sign DU, and it is only from lexical glosses and from the phonetic behavior of some suffixed morphemes that the difference becomes clear. It is possible that more *ḫamṭu* and *marû* base differences than we are aware of are still hidden behind invariant spelling.

Intransitive Verbs The intransitive verb has but one conjugation pattern, with absolute markers immediately following the base:

1st sing.	-*B*-EN
2nd sing.	-*B*-EN
3rd sing.	-*B*-∅ (both person and nonperson class)
1st plur.	-*B*-ENDEN
2nd plur.	-*B*-ENZEN
3rd plur.	-*B*-EŠ (person class only)

In a few cases, as with the verb "to go," a *ḫamṭu* and a *marû* variant of the base are distinguished. Within the same conjugation pattern, ĜEN is used for preterite and DU for present. When no such distinction is available, present may be stressed by the addition of a morpheme .ED immediately after the base. BA-RA-BA-ZÀḪ-E-DÈ-EN (BARA.BA.ZAḪ.ED.EN) means "I (.EN) will (.ED.) certainly not (BARA.) run away (ZAḪ, with locative prefix BA. indicating point of departure)." (For passive constructions, a more-specialized Sumerological discussion must be consulted.)

Verb Prefixes While .ED and the ergative and absolutive markers are closest to the base in rank, a whole set of more distant morphemes occurs, mostly independent of the respective conjugation pattern. Both the general idea of whether there is movement toward or away from the speaker or person referred to and such adverbial expressions as "to me," "for you," "with him/her," "from it," and "next to you" are incorporated, or infixed, in the chain of preverbal morphemes: MU-E-DA-ĜAL (MU.EDA.ĜAL), "it is found with you (.EDA.)"; MA-AN-SUM (MA.N.SUM), "he/she gave (something) to me (MA.)"; BA-ĜEN, "he/she went away," IM-MA-ĜEN (I.MA.ĜEN), "he/she came here."

It is impossible to set out here the complex system of directional morphemes in more detail. The direction-mindedness of the Sumerian verb very probably had a strong impact on neighboring Akkadian, whose "ventive," permeating the whole verbal system, can only partly be explained as an outcome of its Semitic heritage.

The directional morphemes (two, more rarely three, of which may be combined and which follow each other in strict rank order) are preceded by MU. or I., whose function, in spite of the most intensive and varied efforts, has not yet been established beyond doubt and which,

unfortunately, are still disregarded in our translations.

Both MU. and I., in turn, are preceded by a set of opening morphemes that either denote mood or have a connective function. Among these belong GA., the cohortative (or optative) mood marker, as in GA-MU-RA-AB-SUM (GA.MU.(E)RA.B.SUM), "let me (GA.) give (.SUM) it (.B.) to you (.(E)RA.)"; ḪE., precative marker, as in ḪÉ-MU-NA-AB-SUM-MU (ḪE.MU.NA.B.SUM.E [assimilated to preceding *u*]), "may (ḪE.) he/she (.E, ergative) give (.SUM) it (.B.) to him (.NA.)"; connecting U., for example, Ù-MU-NA-AG (U.MU.NA.E.AG), "after (U.) you (.E., ergative, not expressed in spelling, since it coalesces with the preceding vowel) made (.AG) (something) for him (.NA.)."

The imperative occurs only in positive form; the negative imperative is expressed by the prohibitive mood. In the imperative, the base heads the verbal complex, and the normally prefixed morphemes of the nonimperative finite forms are suffixed, as in DUG₄-MU-NA-AB (DUG.MU.NA.B), "say (DUG) it (.B) to him (.NA.)." The plural form, "say it (all of you) to him," would be DUG₄-MU-NA-AB-ZÉ-EN (DUG.MU.NA.B.ZEN), with suffixation of the second-person plural marker .ZEN.

Nonfinite Verbs

The nonfinite verb has constructions with both the *ḫamṭu* and the *marû* base. During the centuries in which the Sumerian described in this survey was used, the *ḫamṭu* base plus .a usually denotes an intransitive, or passive, participle, such as DUG₄-GA (DUG.A), "said, spoken," and DÙ-A, "built." On the other hand, the *marû* base plus .ED (the D of which is not represented in the spelling when it is found in word-final position and the E of which may coalesce with a preceding vowel) denotes an active participle, as in EME ÉD-DÈ (EME ED.E(D)), "stretching out (one's) tongue."

The *marû* base plus .EDE or .EDA functions as an infinitive construction, "to . . ." or "in order to . . . ," as in KAR-RE-DÈ (KAR.ED.E), "in order to take away." The *marû* base plus .EDAM (that is, .ED plus copula .AM) serves for such expressions as "has to be . . . ," as in ZI-RE-DAM (ZIR.ED.AM), "must be destroyed."

In the frequent so-called compound verbs, where the verbal complex is preceded by a frozen nominal base, the noun normally functions as an object and stands in the absolute case, as in KI ÁĜ, "to love," literally "to . . . the ground," and ŠU ÙR, "to smooth, to erase (an inscription)," literally "to pass (one's) hand (over something)." Since the Sumerian verb cannot govern two different absolutives, the object of such a verb must appear in a dimensional case. With the verb KI ÁĜ, "to love," it is the dative: KI MU-RA-ÁĜ-EN (KI MU.(E)RA.AĜ.EN), "I (.EN, ergative) love (KI . . . AĜ) you (.(E)RA.)."

The verb "to be" (the copula) is ME. It follows the conjugation pattern of the intransitive verb, except for the third-person singular, where a special form, ÀM, is used. The copula has no prefixes; it is suffixed directly to a noun, as in AMA-ĜU₁₀-ME-EN (AMA.ĜU.ME.(E)N), "you are (.ME.(E)N) my mother," and UGULA-ME-EŠ (UGULA.ME.(E)Š), "they are overseers," versus LUGAL-ÀM (LUGAL.AM), "he is king."

WORD ORDER

The basic word order of the Sumerian sentence is ergative–absolutive (or absolutive–ergative)–verb. A topicalized noun may exceptionally be placed after the verb. Adverbial expressions often head the sentence; they must, in any case, precede the verb. Sumerian word order most probably influenced the subject–object–verb (SOV) order of Mesopotamian Akkadian (as opposed to twenty-fourth-century Eblaite of northern Syria, where VSO is quite frequent).

Instead of using subordinate clauses headed by a relative pronoun or a conjunction, Sumerian makes use of nominalized sentences. An independent sentence is turned into a noun by means of the suffixed nominalizer .A, and this newly created noun may then be provided with a postposition. Thus, a nominalized verbal complex with .TA (postposition of the ablative-instrumental) may render a temporal clause, beginning "after . . . ," or "since . . . ," such as SAĜ-KI-GÍD-DA ᵈEN-LÍL-LÁ-KE₄ KIŠᵏⁱ GU₄-AN-NA-GIM IM-UG₅-GA-TA (SAĜKI.GIDA ENLIL.AK.E KIŠ GU.AN.A(K).GIM I.M.UG.A.TA), "after (.TA) the wrath (literally, forehead-lengthened) of Enlil (wrath-Enlil-of, ergative) had killed (I.M.UG) Kish (absolutive) like (.GIM) (by means of) the Bull of Heaven (GU AN.A(K))." Here, the verb I.M.UG is

nominalized by means of .A and then provided with the postposition .TA.

Main clauses follow each other in juxtaposition and without any conjunction, but the word Ù, "and," has been borrowed from Akkadian (where U < *wa*). It is a latecomer in Sumerian, where it is used to connect nouns within a sentence but not separate clauses or sentences. If temporal precedence of verb A over verb B has to be emphasized, verb A may get a connective prefix Ù- (which is not related to the Akkadian loanword), as in Ù-UL-PÀ ZI-RE-DAM (U.(A)L.PA ZIR.ED.AM), "when it (that is, a document declared as lost and replaced by a duplicate) is found (again), it must be destroyed."

Verbal forms with prefix Ù- are sometimes used as polite imperatives: Ù-NA-A-DUG₄ (U.NA.E.DUG), "after (U.) you (.E., ergative, assimilated to preceding vowel) have said (DUG) to him (.NA.)," meaning "would you please say to him."

When two or more parallel parts of a clause or sentence occur in succession, certain morphemes (for example, postposition, plural marker) may be deleted, except from the last part, as in AMA A-A-(E)NE, "mothers (and) fathers (mother father-plural)," and AN KI-A, "in heaven (and) on earth (heaven earth-locative)."

STYLE

There is a clear distinction between colloquial, administrative, and elevated prose styles, literary style, and poetry, each marked by a partially different choice of vocabulary and phraseology and, in the case of literary and poetic style, by word parallelism and syllable count—that is, some kind of metric device. Internal rhyme also occurs.

EMESAL

In addition to ordinary Sumerian, there is a variant reserved mainly for the quotation of the speech of women. It is termed EMESAL (*ummi-sallu* as a loanword in Akkadian), literally "fine" or "thin (that is, high-pitched) tongue." Emesal words may differ phonetically (for example, DUG versus Emesal ZEB, "good") or by heteronymy (use of different words, such as NIN versus Eme-

Text Specimens (see figures; second text only partially analyzed)

(1)

TUKUMBI	LÚ	ᴳᴵˢKIRI₆	LÚ-KA	ĈIŠ	IN-SÀG
TUKUMBI	LU(.E)	KIRI	LU.(A)K.A	ĈIŠ	I.N.SAG
if	person (+ ergative)	date garden	person + genitive + locative	wood, absolutive	I + 3rd sing. ergative + cut, "preterite" conjugation pattern

MAŠ	MA-NA	KÙ-BABBAR	I-LÁ-E
MAŠ	MANA	KU.BABBAR	I.LA.E
half	mina, absolutive	bright (metal) white, absolutive, appositive to MANA	I + (cause to) hang + 3rd sing. ergative, present conjugation pattern

Translation: "If someone cuts a tree in someone's date garden, he will pay one-half mina of silver."

(2)

ᴰNIN-ĜÍR-SU	UR-SAĜ-KAL-GA	ᴰEN-LÍL-LÁ	LUGAL-A-NI	GÙ-DÉ-A	ÉNSI
NIN.GIRSU (.a)(k)	URSAĜ.KALGA	ENLIL.A(K)	LUGAL.ANI(.R)	GUDEA	ENSI
Ningirsu(k), dative deleted	warrior, mighty	Enlil + genitive (dative deleted)	master, his (+ dative not written)	Gudea	prince

LAGAŠᴷᴵ-ke₄	É-NINNU	MU-NA-DÙ
LAGAŠ.AK.E	ENINNU	MU.NA(.N).DU
Lagash + genitive + ergative	Eninnu, absolutive	MU + 3rd sing. dative (+3rd sing. ergative) + build, "preterite" conjugation pattern

Translation: "For (god) Ningirsu(k) (= lord of Girsu), the mighty warrior of (god) Enlil, his master, Gudea, prince of Lagash, has built the (temple) Eninnu (= House: The Fifty)."

sal GAŠAN, "lady"). The rules for when and why scribes note women's speech in Emesal are not yet clear.

BIBLIOGRAPHY

PASCAL ATTINGER, *Eléments de linguistique sumérienne, Orbis Biblicus et Orientalis. Sonder band* (1993); JEREMY A. BLACK, *Sumerian Grammar in Baby-lonian Theory,* Studia Pohl Series Major 12 (1984); DIETZ OTTO EDZARD, "ḫamṭu, marû und freie Reduplikation beim sumerischen Verbum," *Zeitschrift für Assyriologie* 61 (1971), 62 (1972), 66 (1976); ADAM FALKENSTEIN, "Das Sumerische," in *Handbuch der Orientalistik,* vol. 1, pt. 2 (1959); THORKILD JACOBSEN, "The Sumerian Verbal Core," *Zeitschrift für Assyriologie* 78 (1988); W. H. PH. RÖMER, *Einführung in die Sumerologie* (5th ed. 1984); ÅKE W. SJÖBERG, ed., *The Sumerian Dictionary,* vol. 2, *B* (1984), and vol. 1, part 1, *A* (1992); MARIE-LOUISE THOMSEN, *The Sumerian Language,* Mesopotamia 10 (1984).

SEE ALSO **The Decipherment of Ancient Near Eastern Scripts** (Part 1, Vol. I); **Scribes and Scholars of Ancient Mesopotamia** (Part 9, Vol. IV); **Sumerian Literature: An Overview** (Part 9, Vol. IV); and **Ancient Mesopotamian Lexicography** (Part 9, Vol. IV).

Semitic Languages

JOHN HUEHNERGARD

THE SEMITIC LANGUAGES are humanity's longest-attested language family and constitute the dominant linguistic group in much of the Near East throughout history, from the mid third millennium BCE, when Akkadian and Eblaite documents appear, down to the present. In most periods, moreover, one or another Semitic language has served as a lingua franca for the entire region: Akkadian during the second millennium BCE, Aramaic from the mid first millennium BCE to the mid first millennium CE, and Arabic since then. Besides Akkadian and Aramaic, other important Semitic languages of antiquity are Hebrew and Phoenician. Modern Semitic languages are Arabic, one of the world's most widely spoken tongues; Amharic, Tigrinya, and many other languages of Ethiopia; Israeli Hebrew; scattered dialects of Aramaic; and remnants of South Arabian languages in Yemen and Oman. The Semitic family is the easternmost member of the Afroasiatic language phylum.

SURVEY OF LANGUAGES

The Semitic languages fall into two principal branches, conventionally labeled East Semitic and West Semitic. Their genetic subgroupings and an overview of the attested ancient and modern Semitic languages, presented according to those subgroupings, appear as tables 1 and 2. The linguistic grounds for these subdivisions are cited below, under "Grammatical Sketch." The present section surveys the languages in detail, also by subgrouping.

East Semitic

This branch until recently consisted of only one known member, Akkadian, the preeminent Semitic language of the ancient civilization of Mesopotamia. It is written from left to right in the logosyllabic cuneiform script invented for the writing of Sumerian. Akkadian forms begin to appear in texts as early as the twenty-sixth century; during the dynasty of Sargon of Akkad (Agade), the language is used for royal inscriptions, letters, legal documents, and literary works. Akkadian dialects of the third millennium are referred to collectively as Old Akkadian. Thereafter, the dialects of Assyrian in northern Mesopotamia are distinguished from the Babylonian dialects in the south. Linguistic changes also lead scholars further to recognize chronological divisions in both Assyrian and Babylonian.

Old Assyrian is the language of some fifteen thousand texts, mostly from the site of Kültepe (ancient Kanesh, Nesha) in eastern Turkey (Cappadocia) but also from a few other sites in both Anatolia and Assyria; these letters and legal and economic texts document the trading enterprises of Assyrian merchant families and their Anatolian business outposts during the twentieth through eighteenth centuries. While fewer in number than Old Assyrian, Middle Assyrian texts exist in a variety of genres dating to about

TABLE 1
Schematic Tree of Semitic Subgroupings

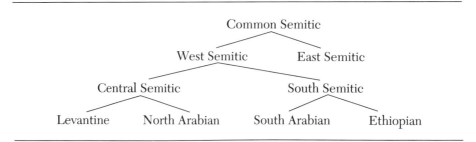

TABLE 2
Overview of Attested Semitic Languages, by Subgroup
(living languages in italics)

EAST SEMITIC
Akkadian
  Old Akkadian dialects:
    26th–20th c. BCE
  Assyrian
    Old Assyrian: 20th–18th c. BCE
    Middle Assyrian: 15th–11th c. BCE
    Neo-Assyrian: 10th–7th c. BCE
  Babylonian
    Old Babylonian: 20th–16th c. BCE
    Middle Babylonian: 16th–11th c. BCE
    (literary Standard Babylonian: from
      12th c. BCE)
    Neo-Babylonian: 10th–7th c. BCE
    Late Babylonian: 6th c. BCE–1st c. CE
Eblaite: 24th–23rd c. BCE

WEST SEMITIC
South Semitic
Ethiopian
  Northern
    Geʿez (Classical Ethiopic):
      4th–10th c. CE
    Tigre
    Tigrinya
  Southern
    Amharic
    Argobba
    Chaha and other *Gurage* languages
    Gafat: to 20th c. CE
    Harari
South Arabian
  Old (Epigraphic) South Arabian
    (Ṣayhadic)

Sabaean: 6th c. BCE–6th c. CE
Qatabanian: 5th/4th c. BCE–3rd c. CE
Minaean: 4th–2nd c. BCE
Ḥaḍramitic: 4th c. BCE–3rd c. CE
Modern South Arabian
  Mehri (and *Ḥarsūsi, Baṭhari*
    dialects)
  Hōbyōt
  Jibbāli (*Śheri*)
  Soqoṭri (and *ʿAbd el-Kūri* dialect)

Central Semitic
North Arabian
  Arabic
    Preclassical North Arabic Dialects
      Thamūdic: 6th c. BCE–4th c. CE
      Dedānite: 6th/5th c. BCE
      Liḥyānite: 5th–1st c. BCE
      Ḥasāʾitic: 5th–2nd c. BCE
      Ṣafāʾitic: 1st c. BCE–3rd c. CE
    Classical Arabic: from 4th c. CE
    Modern Arabic dialects
Levantine (Northwest Semitic)
  (Early cuneiform, Egyptian, and
    alphabetic evidence)
Ugaritic: 14th/13th c. BCE
Canaanite
  (Canaanitisms in Akkadian texts
    from Amarna: 14th c. BCE)
  Hebrew
    Archaic (older biblical poetry):
      12th–11th c. BCE
    Classical (biblical and
      epigraphic): 10th–6th c. BCE

Central Semitic continued
    Late Classical (biblical,
        epigraphic): 6th–2nd c. BCE
    Middle (Qumran, Samaritan,
        Mishnaic): 2nd c. BCE–5th c. CE
    Medieval
    Modern Israeli: from 19th c. CE
    Phoenician
      Byblian: 10th c. BCE–1st c. CE
      Standard
        Littoral (Phoenicia, Syria)
          9th–2nd c. BCE
        Mediterranean (colonies,
          outposts): 8th–2nd c. BCE
        Punic: 5th–2nd c. BCE
        Neo-Punic: 2nd c. BCE–5th c. CE
    Ammonite: 9th–6th c. BCE
    Moabite: 9th–6th c. BCE
    Edomite: 8th–6th c. BCE
    Aramaic
      Early
        Old Aramaic dialects:
          9th–6th c. BCE
        Official (Classical, Imperial):
          6th–4th c. BCE

      Middle: 3rd c. BCE–2nd c. CE
        Palestinian (Daniel, Qumran,
          early Targums, Bar Kosiba)
        Nabataean
        Palmyrene
        Hatran
      Late: 3rd–9th c. CE
        Western
          Galilean (Jewish: Palestinian
            Talmud, Midrashim, later
            Targums)
          Christian Palestinian
          Samaritan
        Syriac
        Eastern
          Babylonian (Talmud)
          Mandaic
      Modern
        Western: *Maʿlula, Jubbʿadin,*
          Bakhʿa (Syria)
        Central: *Ṭuroyo, Mlaḥso*
        Eastern: *Neo-Syriac* dialects
        Neo-Mandaic
    Deir ʿAlla plaster text: 8th c. BCE

1500–1000, including letters, legal and economic texts, royal inscriptions, and an important collection of laws. Neo-Assyrian, attested in a very large number of documents, is the spoken language of Assyria during the first millennium, the period of the Assyrian Empire until its destruction near the end of the seventh century BCE.

Old Babylonian is the term used for several closely related dialects from the twentieth century to the end of the First Dynasty of Babylon (1595), the best known of which is that of Hammurabi's chancery; there are vast numbers of Old Babylonian texts in the form of letters, laws (such as the *Code of Hammurabi*), legal contracts, economic dockets, omens, royal inscriptions, lexical lists, and literary works such as the *Epic of Gilgamesh*, the flood story of *Atrakhasis*, and the myth of Anzu. Much less common are texts in Middle Babylonian (sixteenth–eleventh centuries), which is known from letters, dockets, and a few royal inscriptions. Throughout much of the second millennium, Akkadian, especially

Old and Middle Babylonian, was used as a lingua franca in much of the Near East; for example, many Akkadian texts of the Late Bronze Age have been found at sites in Anatolia, Syria, Palestine, and Egypt. Neo-Babylonian is attested by a large number of nonliterary texts, especially letters and records, from the beginning of the first millennium until the fall of the Assyrian Empire. Thereafter, the term Late Babylonian is used for the final period of Akkadian textual material; the last texts date to the first century CE. During the first half of the first millennium BCE, and probably beginning earlier, both Babylonian and Assyrian scribes wrote literary works (such as *Enuma Elish*) and other learned texts (such as royal inscriptions) in an archaizing, nonspoken dialect called Standard Babylonian.

Excavations in the mid 1970s at the Syrian site of Tell Mardikh (ancient Ebla) produced a large number of cuneiform tablets dated to the twenty-fourth or twenty-third century. While the majority of these tablets were written in Sumerian, a substantial number revealed a new Semitic language, dubbed Eblaite (or Eblaic) after the ancient name of the site. Among the many Ebla tablets, the Semitic language is found especially in bilingual lexical texts, certain administrative documents, and some literary texts and incantations, some with parallels in texts found at the Mesopotamian sites of Fara (Shuruppak) and Abu Salabikh. Because of the presence of a number of words and other features not found in Akkadian, Eblaite was first considered by many scholars to be an early form of West Semitic; more recently, however, there has been a growing consensus among Semitists and Assyriologists (especially specialists in third-millennium cuneiform) that Eblaite is a form of East Semitic, either a separate subbranch closely related to Akkadian or even a dialect of Akkadian.

West Semitic

All Semitic languages other than Akkadian and Eblaite belong to the western branch of the family. West Semitic in turn comprises two main subbranches, South Semitic and Central Semitic, and each of these may be further subdivided into two groups (see table 1).

South Semitic: South Arabian Languages Old (or Epigraphic) South Arabian is a set of related languages attested in inscriptions that span just over a millennium, from about the sixth century BCE until the sixth century CE. By far the most common of these is Sabaean (also called Sabaic), the language of the kingdom of Sabaʾ (biblical Sheba) in the central and western part of northern Yemen. To the east are found Minaean (or Minaic) inscriptions; these are also attested at al-ʿUla (Alula, ancient Dedan), a Minaean trading settlement in the northern Hejaz. Farther south, the region of the Wadi Ḥarīb and the Wadi Bayḥān has produced inscriptions in Qatabanian (or Qatabanic). Ḥaḍramitic inscriptions are attested from a royal residence at Shabwa in the western Hadramawt (Hadhramaut); a few come from other sites, some as far away as Oman. While the majority of Old South Arabian inscriptions are mere graffiti, a good number are more substantial in their content: building inscriptions commemorating public works (construction of walls, waterworks); his-

torical texts commemorating victories, enthronements, and treaties; legal documents concerning boundaries, real estate, water regulation, and commerce; and religious texts, such as confessions, cultic decrees, and consecrations of firstfruits. Old South Arabian texts are written in an alphabetic script; the direction of writing is boustrophedon (alternate lines reading in opposite directions) in the earliest inscriptions, but later always right to left. The alphabet represents each of the twenty-nine Common Semitic consonants (see below) distinctly; vowels are not normally indicated, with the probable exception of $\bar{u}$ and $\bar{\imath}$ in some instances. The languages of Old South Arabian have sometimes been referred to collectively as Himyaritic; a leading student of these languages, A. F. L. Beeston, proposes the term Ṣayhadic for the group.

The Modern South Arabian languages are spoken by a small and diminishing number of people in the easternmost province of Yemen and the westernmost province of Oman. Some sixty thousand people speak several dialects of Mehri (including Ḥarsūsi and Baṭhari); the other languages are all on the verge of extinction: Hōbyōt; Jibbāli, also called Śheri (and, incorrectly, Shkhawri); and Soqoṭri, on the island of Suquṭra (Socotra). It is likely that there is a genetic relationship between the Modern and the Old South Arabian languages, especially Ḥaḍramitic; this is disputed, however, and it has been suggested that Old South Arabian is to be classified with the Central Semitic languages (see below).

South Semitic: Ethiopian Languages Speakers of the ancestors of the attested Ethiopian Semitic languages, which are closely related to the South Arabian languages, probably came to eastern Africa from the southwestern part of the Arabian Peninsula (today's Yemen) sometime during the first millennium BCE. Ethiopian Semitic may be subdivided linguistically into two groups, a northern and a southern.

The northern group has the only anciently attested member of Ethiopian Semitic, Geʿez, the classical language of the Ethiopian Christian church. Attested beginning in the fourth century CE, Geʿez was originally the language of Aksum (now in the northern province of Tigre). Early Geʿez inscriptions are written in Old South Arabian alphabetic characters; these were later modified with the addition of marks to indicate the vowels. Also an early development was the consistent left-to-right direction of the writing. Geʿez probably ceased to be a spoken language during the ninth or tenth century, with the end of the Aksumite Empire, but continued in use as a literary language until recently; the oral composition of *qəne* poetry (religious poetry) in Geʿez is still performed, and Geʿez is mined by the modern Ethiopian languages for technical vocabulary, just as Latin and Greek are mined by modern European languages. There are two modern varieties of northern Ethiopic: Tigrinya, spoken by more than three million people in the highlands of Tigre and Eritrea; and Tigre, the language of about one hundred thousand people of the lowlands and coastal areas of Eritrea.

Southern Ethiopic has no ancient representatives. Amharic, the national language of Ethiopia, is the Semitic language with the second-greatest number of native speakers, over seven million; it was first written, in the script used for Geʿez, as early as the sixteenth century CE. A dialect of Amharic is Argobba. Other southern Ethiopic languages are Harari, Soddo, Gogot, Mukher, Misqan, and three dialect clusters of Gurage (Eastern, Peripheral Western, Central Western); these have fewer than one million speakers altogether. Another language, Gafat, is probably now extinct; its last speakers were recorded by the Ethiopicist Wolf Leslau in the 1940s.

Central Semitic: North Arabian The North Arabian branch of Central Semitic consists of early inscriptional North Arabic dialects, Classical Arabic, and the modern Arabic dialects. Old (or Early) North Arabic refers to several pre-Islamic dialects attested in inscriptions written in scripts derived from the Old South Arabian alphabet. The roughly one thousand Thamūdic graffiti, which date from the sixth century BCE to the fourth century CE, are found over a widely scattered area, but are concentrated in central and western north Arabia; a subgroup of inscriptions from Tayma are the earliest North Arabic texts. The graffiti express a variety of sentiments, such as friendship, and activities, including herding and hunting; others invoke one or more of a number of deities. Dedānite and Liḥyānite inscriptions are found around Dedān, an ancient oasis in northwestern Arabia. The dating of both types is uncertain: the few Dedānite texts may date to the sixth or fifth century BCE, while the Liḥyānite inscriptions may date to the fifth through first centuries; it is possible that Liḥyānite is linguistically a continuation of Dedānite. Most Liḥyānite inscriptions are simple graffiti, but a few building, funerary, and votive inscriptions are attested. The few Ḥasaean (or Ḥasāʾitic) inscriptions found in northeastern Arabia near the Persian Gulf are mostly funerary in nature; their dating is uncertain, perhaps fifth to second centuries BCE. The largest and latest group of Old North Arabic inscriptions is the Ṣafāʾitic, with some fifteen thousand graffiti dating from the first century BCE to the third century CE. This is also the northernmost dialect, with inscriptions found east of Damascus and across to the Euphrates, and south to northern Saudi Arabia. The contents of the Ṣafāʾitic graffiti are generally similar to those in Thamūdic.

Classical Arabic is the literary language of Islam. Inscriptions from the fourth century CE reveal a dialect or dialects similar to the later classical language, but the latter, reflecting the spoken language of the Hejaz region of central western Arabia, truly began with the Koran in the seventh century. The language was standardized by grammarians during the eighth and ninth centuries, with features of the early poetic koine, and has remained essentially unchanged since. Modern standard literary Arabic differs from the old language only in its updated vocabulary. Arabic script is a modification of the Aramaic alphabet of the Nabataeans; it is written from right to left in an alphabet in which most long vowels are indicated, with optional diacritical marks to indicate short vowels and other features. Alongside the classical language, vernacular forms of Arabic have naturally evolved over the centuries, and some modern dialects are not mutually intelligible; today, with more than one hundred million speakers, Arabic is one of humanity's most widely used languages. The term Middle Arabic refers to compositions in the literary language that reflect features of the writers' spoken dialects; the latter have otherwise not normally been written down.

Central Semitic: Levantine (Northwest Semitic) Languages Evidence of early forms of

Central Semitic, particularly of Levantine or, as they are traditionally called, Northwest Semitic dialects, is found in the Middle and Late Bronze ages in cuneiform sources, in Egyptian, and in the first alphabetic inscriptions. Cuneiform texts from the late third and early second millennia attest a large number of personal names (some six thousand at last count) that are clearly Semitic but are not Akkadian. Some of the people with these non-Akkadian Semitic names are labeled in the texts with the Sumerian term MAR.TU, "westerner." In Akkadian this is *amurrû*, and in Hebrew *'ămōrî*, which is rendered in English as Amorite. Some of these Amorite names have features typical of Northwest Semitic, such as an initial *y* where other Semitic languages have *w*, as in the name *Yatarum*, "excellent," from the Semitic root **wtr* (an asterisk marks a hypothetical or reconstructed form), and the entire group of such names is thus often categorized as Northwest Semitic. Yet dialectal variation is discernible within the names themselves, and since the names span a wide geographical region and several centuries, it is unlikely that they constitute a single linguistic entity; rather, the so-called Amorite names probably reflect several languages (see "Amorite Tribes and Nations of Second-Millennium Western Asia" in Part 5, Vol. II).

It was noted above that Akkadian served as a lingua franca during much of the second millennium. Some texts from sites west of Mesopotamia exhibit evidence of local languages. Middle Bronze Age Akkadian texts from Mari (Tell Hariri), for example, occasionally use words attested in West Semitic languages but not found in other Akkadian texts, such as *qatālum*, "to kill"; in rare instances, the West Semitic active suffix-conjugation appears, as in *mi-ša-ta-an-ni*, "you despise me." Northwest Semitic words and constructions appear in Late Bronze Age Akkadian texts from Syro-Palestine, such as those found at Ras Shamra (ancient Ugarit; e.g., *bittu*, "daughter," in a text written at Carchemish [Karkamish]), Meskene (ancient Emar; e.g., *ðābiḫu*, "sacrificer"), and cities from which the letters found at Amarna (ancient Akhetaten) in Egypt were sent (some of which are discussed in more detail below, under "Canaanite"). Personal names appearing in texts written at these sites also frequently reflect Levantine Semitic dialects.

A few hieroglyphic Egyptian documents also furnish details about early Semitic in the Levant. Examples are the Execration Texts of the twentieth to nineteenth centuries BCE, in which the names of foreign, including Levantine, vassal rulers were inscribed on vases and statuettes to be smashed in symbolic gesture; slave lists from the eighteenth century; and lists of Syro-Palestinian toponyms (names of places) in various documents over a long period of time, the most important of which is a list from the reign of Thutmose III (mid fifteenth century).

History's earliest alphabetic inscriptions have been found at sites in Palestine and at Serabit al-Khadim in the Sinai; the dating of these inscriptions is controversial, but is usually given as seventeenth to thirteenth centuries. This aboriginal alphabetic script is pictographic in nature and indicates only consonants. Interpretation of the majority of inscriptions is quite uncertain, but they are considered by most scholars to represent one or more early dialects of Northwest Semitic. (See also "The Story of the Semitic Alphabet" later in this volume.)

From the last part of the Late Bronze Age onward, we may distinguish several distinct subbranches of Northwest Semitic, including Canaanite and Aramaic. The classification of Ugaritic (see below) is much debated, some placing it with the Canaanite languages, others viewing it as a separate strain of Northwest Semitic; the latter is the position taken here.

Excavation beginning in 1929 at Ras Shamra revealed documents in many languages, including hieroglyphic Egyptian, Cypro-Minoan, hieroglyphic Luwian, and several languages written in Mesopotamian syllabic cuneiform script: Sumerian, Hurrian, Hittite, and, of course, Akkadian. Many clay tablets, however, were in a different cuneiform script, which proved upon its rapid decipherment to be an indigenous alphabet used to write the local Northwest Semitic language, dubbed Ugaritic. The alphabet is consonantal; vowels are indicated only with the consonant ' (aleph), for which three signs exist, transliterated *'a*, *'i*, and *'u*. More than thirteen hundred Ugaritic texts and fragments have been published thus far. Well over half of these are administrative documents; there are also literary tablets (some of them quite large) relating myths and epics of local gods, heroes, and kings; ritual texts and lists of gods and of offerings; omens; letters; a few legal contracts; and school exercises. All the texts stem from the fourteenth and thirteenth centuries BCE.

Canaanite, one of the two large dialect clusters of Levantine Semitic, is first discernible in the language of some of the Akkadian texts discovered a century ago at Amarna. Some of these texts, all of which date to the first half of the fourteenth century, were sent to their Egyptian overlords by Syro-Palestinian vassal princes. The language of many of these documents is a curious mixture of Akkadian vocabulary (for the most part) and Northwest Semitic morphology and syntax (as in the morphology of the verb: instead of normative Akkadian *ašpur* for "I wrote" we find *šapar-tī*, which may be compared with Hebrew *kātab-tî*); such evidence has proved invaluable for tracing the early history of this branch of Semitic. (See also "The Amarna Letters from Canaan" later in this volume.)

The best-known and best-attested Canaanite language is Hebrew. Hebrew is extant in inscriptions from the tenth century BCE, but some biblical texts, such as the poems in Judges 5 and Exodus 15, show signs of having been composed one or two centuries earlier; such early texts, which may be termed Archaic Hebrew, show a few linguistic features that are not found in later forms of Hebrew. Biblical texts and extrabiblical inscriptions from the period of the monarchy (tenth to early sixth century) may be referred to as Classical Hebrew. Biblical and epigraphic Hebrew of the postexilic period, or Late Classical Hebrew, displays certain linguistic changes vis-à-vis that of the earlier period, especially in syntax. The extrabiblical documentation shows at least two geographical dialects, a southern (sometimes called Judean) and a northern (Israelian). The biblical text is relatively less varied linguistically, because of the harmonizing work of editors; as just noted, however, chronological differences may be discerned, and some linguistic variation is evident in a text like Ecclesiastes. It is likely that Hebrew died out as a spoken language in most areas in the second and first centuries BCE, when it was succeeded by Aramaic. From the second century BCE to the fifth century CE is the period of Middle Hebrew, which comprises the written dialects of Hebrew in texts from Qumran (the Dead Sea Scrolls) and in the Mishna, as well as Samaritan Hebrew.

Writers in the medieval Near East and Europe also used Hebrew as a written language for a large literature. Modern Hebrew is a national language of the state of Israel; the revival of Hebrew as a spoken tongue in the last century is a unique phenomenon among languages. The original forms of the Hebrew alphabet, which is written from right to left, were borrowed from the Phoenicians; the forms in use after the end of the monarchy to the present reflect the adoption of an Aramaic script.

Also Canaanite, and closely related to Hebrew, is Phoenician, the language of the coastal city-states of Byblos (biblical Gebal, modern Jubayl), Tyre, Sidon, and their surrounding areas and colonies. Dialectal differences may be discerned among the local forms of Phoenician and are particularly apparent in inscriptions from Byblos, which is therefore accorded special dialectal status. Phoenician inscriptions are attested at Byblos from the tenth century BCE and elsewhere from the ninth century. The dialect of Carthage (from Phoenician *qart ḥadašt, "new town"), a colony established by Tyre, is called Punic and is extant from the fifth century BCE; the term Neo-Punic refers to inscriptions written after the fall of Carthage in 146 BCE, until the last texts in the fifth century CE. The Phoenician alphabet, consisting of twenty-two consonants (vowels were rarely written until late in the history of Phoenician), was also used for the writing of other languages, including Aramaic, early Hebrew, and Greek.

Other Canaanite languages are very sparsely attested. Moabite is extant in one well-preserved, relatively long ninth-century inscription of Mesha, king of Moab; in two small fragments; and perhaps in a number of names on seals found in Moab. Students familiar with Biblical Hebrew have little difficulty reading the Mesha inscription, although there are a few features that distinguish it from Hebrew. Ammonite is attested, from the ninth to the sixth centuries BCE, in a small number of inscriptions and in names on a large number of seals. Finally, Edomite is extant in a few ostraca and possibly in names on a few seals, from the eighth to the sixth centuries.

The other main dialect cluster of Northwest Semitic is Aramaic, which has been extant in a large number of dialects from the ninth century BCE until the present. The earliest Aramaic, known as Old Aramaic, is attested by a small number of inscriptions, the first of which is the recently discovered ninth-century bilingual (Akkadian-Aramaic) inscription found at Tell al-Fakhariya (ancient Sikan) in northern Syria. Each of these Old Aramaic inscriptions differs somewhat from the others linguistically, so that no standard dialect is in evidence. During the Persian Empire, Aramaic was designated an official language. A large number of texts in closely related dialects of this period, collectively referred to as Official or Imperial Aramaic, have been found in Egypt (some written elsewhere, such as in Persia) and Palestine; the Biblical Aramaic of part of the book of Ezra is also an example of Official Aramaic.

From the third century BCE until the second century CE is the period of Middle Aramaic, which comprises many texts in several dialects, including Hatran, Nabataean, Palmyrene, and Old Syriac (the language of the city of Edessa [Urfa]). This period in Palestine also produced the Aramaic of about half of the biblical book of Daniel, the Aramaic texts from Qumran, and the early Aramaic Targums (translations of the Bible). Other Aramaic texts from this period have been found from Egypt to Afghanistan.

Late Aramaic, from the third century CE on, comprises three branches: Western, Eastern, and Syriac. Under Late Western Aramaic are subsumed Galilean (or Jewish) Aramaic, the dialect in which the Palestinian Talmud, Midrashim, and Targums are written; Judean Aramaic (also called Christian Palestinian Aramaic, Syro-Palestinian, or Palestinian Syriac); and Samaritan Aramaic. Late Eastern Aramaic consists of Babylonian Aramaic, which is the language of the Babylonian Talmud; Mandaic, the dialect of the gnostic Mandaeans of southern Babylonia; and the language of a large group of magical incantations written on clay bowls from the fourth to the seventh centuries CE. Syriac, a literary language based on the Old Syriac of Edessa, is the language of an extensive Christian literature from the fourth to the thirteenth centuries.

Several forms of Aramaic continue to be spoken in towns in Syria, Turkey, and Iraq; recent emigrations have brought some of these peoples to Armenia, Georgia, Germany, Israel, Russia, Sweden, and the United States. Modern Aramaic may be subdivided into four branches. Western Aramaic is spoken in three villages northeast of Damascus (Maʿlula, Jubbʿadin, and Bakhʿa); Central Aramaic, spoken in southeastern Turkey, comprises several dialects of Ṭuroyo and the recently reported dialect of Mlaḥso; Eastern Aramaic, or Neo-Syriac (although not directly descended from classical Syriac), consists of a large number of linguistically diverse dialects spoken by several hundred thousand people in and near Kurdistan; finally, Neo-Mandaic is spoken by a small group of Mandaeans in western Iran.

The last entry under Northwest Semitic is the language of a long inscription on plaster found at the site of Deir ʿAlla in Jordan. This eighth-century text has been called a form of Canaanite by some scholars and a form of Aramaic by others. Since it exhibits none of the innovative linguistic features that characterize either Canaanite or Aramaic, however, it seems preferable to conclude that the dialect of the Deir ʿAlla plaster text represents another, heretofore unknown branch of Northwest Semitic.

GRAMMATICAL SKETCH

The following paragraphs present a brief overview of the phonology and morphology of Common Semitic and of some of the individual languages.

Phonology

The vowel system of Common Semitic is relatively simple, consisting of three short vowels, *a*, *i*, *u*, and their corresponding long forms *ā*, *ī*, *ū*. This system is found essentially unchanged in classical Arabic.

The Semitic languages exhibit several unusual consonant phonemes, such as the pharyngeal fricatives ʿ and *ḥ* signified by [ʕ] and [ħ], respectively, in the International Phonetic Alphabet (IPA). For Proto-Semitic, twenty-nine consonants may be reconstructed, all of which remained distinct in some Old South Arabian dialects. In table 3 the traditional representations of the consonants appear in italics, followed by likely or possible pronunciations, as represented by the IPA symbols in square brackets.

TABLE 3
The Proto-Semitic Consonants

	Bilabial		Dental			Alveolar			Palatal	Velar			Pharyngeal		Glottal
	voiceless	voiced	voiceless	voiced	emph.	voiceless	voiced	emph.	voiced	voiceless	voiced	emph.	voiceless	voiced	voiceless
Plosive	p [p]	b [b]	t [t̪]	d [d̪]	ṭ [t̪']					k [k]	g [g]	q [k']			ʾ [ʔ]
Nasal		m [m]		n [n̪]											
Trill						r [r]									
Fricative			θ [θ]	ð [ð]	θ̣ [θ']	š [s]				ḫ [x]	ġ [γ]		ḥ [ħ]	ʿ [ʕ]	h [h]
Affricate						s [t͡s]	z [d͡z]	ṣ [t͡s']							
Lateral fricative						ś [ɬ]									
Lateral affricate								ṣ́ [t͡ɬ']							
Approximant		w [w]				l [l]			y [j]						

The pronunciations of some of the Proto-Semitic consonants are subject to considerable debate, and those given in table 3 reflect only one set of the suggestions that may be found in recent scholarly literature. The consonant given as *p* is [p] in Aramaic and Hebrew (where it also has an allophone, or variant, [f]) but [f] in Arabic, Ethiopic, and Modern South Arabian. The consonants usually represented as *s*, *z*, and *ṣ* are given here as affricates ([t͡s], [d͡z], and [t͡s'] on the basis of recent discussion, but many Semitists continue to believe that they were simple alveolar fricatives, respectively [s], [z], and [s'] or [sˤ]. The original nature of the consonant usually represented as *š* is also uncertain. While it appears as the postalveolar [ʃ] in some of the languages (as in Hebrew *šēm*, "name," as well as in Aramaic, the Babylonian form of Akkadian, and the Modern South Arabian language Jibbāli; it has generally become [h] in other Modern South Arabian languages), it is the alveolar [s] in others (as in Arabic *ism*, "name," as well as in Ethiopic

and the Assyrian form of Akkadian) and in cognate forms elsewhere in Afroasiatic. The so-called emphatic consonants are presented in table 3 as glottalic pressure sounds, or "ejectives," as they are pronounced in the Ethiopian Semitic and the Modern South Arabian languages—that is, [k'], [t'], and so on. It is possible that they were instead velarized or pharyngealized, as in Arabic, in which case, we would represent *ṣ* as [t͡sˤ] or [t͡s] (or [sˤ] or [s]), *ṭ* as [tˤ] or [t] and *θ* as [θˤ] or [θ]; further, *q* would probably have been the uvular [q], as in Arabic, rather than [k']. It is now generally accepted that the phonemes rendered *ś* and *ṣ́* (or *ð̣*) were in fact laterals, *ś* the voiceless fricative [ɬ] and *ṣ́* either an affricate or another fricative and, like other emphatics, either glottalic [t͡ɬ'] or [ɬ'] or pharyngealized [t͡ɬˤ] or [ɬˤ].

It was noted above that Old South Arabian preserves each of the Common Semitic consonants as a distinct phoneme (although their pronunciations in those languages are unknown).

Text Specimens

In order to illustrate the writing system, phonology, and morphology of some of the Semitic languages, a selection of text samples is given below. To facilitate comparison of the grammatical structures of as many languages as possible, a biblical passage, Genesis 11:7, is presented in the original Hebrew, followed by translations into Aramaic (Syriac, the Pšiṭṭå), classical Arabic, classical Ethiopic, and Amharic (southern Ethiopian). In each case, the passage is presented in the original script, then in the standard transliteration used by Semitists, then in transcription in the International Phonetic Alphabet, or IPA (with bound morphemes separated by =; stress on final syllable unless marked with ˈ); these are followed by a word-by-word English rendering of the passage. An idiomatic translation for the passage in each case approximates the

Hebrew, which reads, "Come, let us go down and confuse their language there, so that they may not understand each other's language."

Following the last of the translations (the Amharic), an Akkadian sentence is presented, from the Old Babylonian *Code of Hammurabi;* the lines with the copy of the original script give a sign-by-sign transliteration, a normalized Semitistic or Assyriological transcription, an IPA transcription, a word-by-word rendering, and an idiomatic translation.

Finally, a brief passage from a Modern South Arabian language, Ḥarsūsi, is cited. Since Ḥarsūsi is not a written language, the text is given only in Semitistic and IPA transcriptions, followed by a word-by-word rendering and an idiomatic translation.

Hebrew (Genesis 11:7)

הָבָה נֵרְדָה וְנָבְלָה שָׁם שְׂפָתָם אֲשֶׁר לֹא יִשְׁמְעוּ אִישׁ שְׂפַת רֵעֵהוּ:

hā́bā nērədâ wanāḇəlâ šām śəp̄āṯām ʾăšer lōʾ yišməʿû ʾîš śəp̄aṯ rēʿḗhû.

ˈhɔvɔ nerəɔ wə=nɔvəlɔ ʃɔm ɬəfɔθ=ɔm ʔᵃʃer loʔ jiʃməʕu ʔiʃ ɬəfaθ reʕe=hu

give(impv.m.sg.) let-us-descend and=let-us-confuse there language=their(m.) RELATIVE not they(m.)-hear man language-of associate=his

Aramaic (West Syriac; Genesis 11:7)

ܬܰܘ ܢܶܚܘܬ ܘܢܰܦܠܶܓ ܬܰܡܳܢ ܠܶܫܳܢܳܐ. ܕܠܳܐ ܢܶܫܡܥܘܢ ܓܒܰܪ ܠܶܫܳܢ ܚܰܒܪܶܗ.

taw neḥut wanp̄aleḡ tamān lešånå dlå nešmʿun gḇar lešån ḥaḇreh.

taw nɛħuθ wa=nfalɛɣ tamɔn lɛʃɔnɔ d=lɔ nɛʃmʕun gvar lɛʃɔn ħavr=ɛh

come(impv.pl.) we-will-descend and=we-will-divide there language RELATIVE=not they-will-hear man/one language-of associate=his

Classical Arabic (Genesis 11:7)

هَلُمَّ نَهْبِطْ وَنُبَلْبِلْ هُنَاكَ لُغَتَهُمْ حَتَّى لَا يَفْهَمَ بَعْضُهُمْ لُغَةَ بَعْضٍ.

halumma nahbiṭ wanubalbil hunāka luġatahum ḥattā lā yafhama baʿḍuhum luġata baʿḍin.

haˈlum:a ˈnahbɨt wa=nuˈbalbil huˈna:ka ˈluɣata=hum ˈħt:a: la: ˈjafhama ˈbaʕdu=hum ˈluɣata ˈbaʕdin

come!(INTERJ) let-us-descend and=let-us-confuse there language=their(m.) so-that not he-may-understand one=their language-of one

Classical Ethiopic (Geʿez; Genesis 11:7)

ንዑ ፡ ንረድ ፡ ወንክዐዎ ፡ ለነገሮሙ ፡ ከመ ፡ ኢይሳሳምዑ ፡ ነገሮሙ ፡ አሐዱ ፡ ምስለ ፡ ካልኡ ፡፡

nəʿu nərad wanəkʿawo la-nagaromu kama ʾiyəssāməʿu nagaromu ʾaḥadu məsla kāləʾu.

ˈniʕu niˈred wa=nikʕɛˈw=o lɛ=nɛgeˈr=omu ˈkɛmɛ ʔi=jis:aˈmiʕu nɛgeˈr=omu ʔɛħɛdu ˈmislɛkaliʔ=u

come(impv.m.pl.) let-us-descend and=let-us-disperse=it TOPIC=speech=their(m.) that not=
they(m.)-may-hear-reciprocally speech=their(m.) one with associate=his

Amharic (Genesis 11:7)

ኑ ፡ እንውረድ ፤ አንዱ ፡ የአንዱን ፡ ነገር ፡ እንዳይሰማው ፡ ቋንቋቸውን ፡ በዚያ ፡ እንደባልቀው ።

nu ǝnnǝwräd andu yä'andun nägär ǝndaysämaw qʷanqʷaččäwǝn bäziya ǝnnǝdäbalqäw.

nu in:iwrɛd and=u j(ɛ)=and=u=n nɛgɛr ind=a=jsɛma=w kʼʷankʼʷa=ˈtʃ:ɛw=ǝn bɛzija in:idɛbalkʼ=ɛw

come(impv.pl) let-us-descend one=the of=one=the=OBJECT speech that=not=he-hears=it
language=their=OBJECT there let-us-confuse=it

Akkadian (Old Babylonian; *Code of Hammurabi*, Law 1)

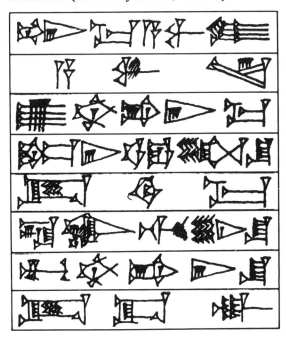

šum-ma a-wi-lum a-wi-lam ú-ub-bi-ir-ma ne-er-tam e-li-šu id-di-ma la uk-ti-in-šu mu-ub-bi-ir-šu id-da-ak

šumma awīlum awīlam ubbirma nērtam elīšu iddīma lā uktīnšu mubbiršu iddâk.

ˈʃumma aˈwi:lum aˈwi:lam uˈb:ir=ma ˈne:rtam eˈli:=ʃu iˈd:i:=ma la: ukˈti:n=ʃu muˈb:ir=ʃu id:a:k

if man(nom.) man(acc.) he-accused=and murder(acc.) upon=him he-threw=and not he-convicted=him accuser=his he-will-be-executed

If a man accused a(nother) man and charged him with murder, but has not convicted him, his accuser will be executed.

Ḥarsūsi (Modern South Arabian; T. Johnstone, *Bulletin of the School of Oriental and African Studies* 33, 1970, p. 512)

nǝḥa syōrǝn ḥǝyūmǝt aθθalāθa ǝmbuwmǝ ho wǝṣaḥbi ðǝnǝma ðǝyɣǝtūri ðǎlmǝn tǝh ḥarsiyyǝt wǝsyōrǝki . . . ǝm-buwmǝ u xaṭūfki.

nǝħa ˈsyo:rǝn ħǝ=ˈyu:mǝt aθ-θaˈla:θa ǝm=ˈbuwmǝ ho wǝ=ˈsaħb=i ˈðǝnǝma ðǝ=iˈɣǝˈtu:ri ð=ˈa:lmǝn t=ǝh ħarˈsiy:ǝt wǝ=ˈsyo:rǝki . . . ǝm=ˈbuwmǝ u xaˈtʼu:ʃki

we we-went the=day the=three(Arabic) from=here I and=friend=my(Arabic) this RELATIVE=he-speaks RELATIVE=I-teach OBJECT=him Ḥarsūsi and=we-two-went . . . from=here and=we-two-departed

We went on Tuesday from here, I and this friend of mine, who speaks—whom I am teaching Ḥarsūsi; we went . . . from here and departed.

In all other languages, some mergers and other phonemic losses have occurred, while in some cases new consonantal phonemes have arisen.

Classical Arabic exhibits one merger, of two sibilants (Common Semitic *š* [s] and *s* [t͡s] in table 3) to [s]. (Other mergers have occurred in most of the spoken dialects.)

In the Modern South Arabian languages, few changes have occurred, but ʾ and ʿ tend to merge, and in Mehri and Soqotri, the original *š* [s] has become [h] and merged with the original *h*.

Classical Ethiopic shows the merger of *ð* and *z* to *z*; ʿ and *ġ* to ʿ (which later also merged with ʾ); *š* ([s]), *s* ([t͡s]), and *θ* to *s* (later joined also by *ś* [ɬ]), *ṣ* and *θ̣* to *ṣ* (i.e., [s']). Original *ṣ́* remained distinct for a time (transcribed *ḍ*), but also became *ṣ* relatively early. Four labialized velar phonemes developed: *gʷ*, *ḫʷ*, *kʷ*, *qʷ*, as in *kʷaraba*, "to hew," versus *karaba*, "to collect."

Old Aramaic orthography compared with that of later dialects indicates that most of the Common Semitic consonants were still distinct in the early stages of Aramaic. Later, a number of mergers occurred: Interdentals merged with homorganic stops: *ð* and *d* to *d*; *θ* and *t* to *t*; *θ̣* and *ṭ* to *ṭ*. Further, *ḥ* merged with *h*, and *ś* with *s*; *ṣ́* is written with ⟨q⟩ in early Aramaic texts, but later merged with ʿ and *ġ* to ʿ. The stops *b, d, g, k, p, t* developed spirantized allophones when post-vocalic and not doubled ([v], [ð], [ɣ], [x], [f], [θ]); in some instances these achieved independent phonemic status.

In Hebrew, *ð* and *z* merged to *z*; *š* and *θ* to *š* [ʃ]; and *ṣ, ś, and θ* to *ṣ*. Further, ʿ and *ġ* merged to ʿ, and *ḥ* and *h* to *ḥ*; evidence from Greek transliterations of Hebrew names and words suggests that the last two mergers took place rather late in the history of Classical Hebrew. Original *ś* [ɬ] remained distinct during the classical period, but was written with the same sign as *š*; it later merged under Aramaic influence with *s* and was differentiated graphically from *š* by means of a diacritical dot. As in Aramaic, postvocalic, nondoubled *b, d, g, k, p, t* developed spirantized allophones.

In Akkadian the consonantal system underwent significant decay under the influence of Sumerian: the gutturals ʾ, *ḫ, ḥ,* ʿ, and *ġ* merged to a glottal stop [ʔ], which was lost in most environments in Old Babylonian; *w* and *y* were also lost in certain environments. Further, *ð* and *z* merged to *z*; *ṣ, ṣ́,* and *θ̣* to *ṣ*; *š, ś, š* and, after the Old Akkadian period, *θ* merged to one consonant, transcribed *š* (pronounced [ʃ] in later Babylonian and [s] in later Assyrian).

Morphology

Pronouns Personal pronouns in Semitic distinguish gender not only in the third-person forms but also in second-person forms; first-person forms are common gender. Besides the singular and plural forms listed in table 4, Common Semitic also possessed dual pronouns, apparently of common gender; second- and third-person dual pronouns are attested in Old Akkadian, Classical Arabic, Ugaritic, and the Modern South Arabian languages (the last two also have first-person dual forms).

Roots Semitic lexical bases may be classified according to whether they are associated with verbal description; nouns that are not derived from verbal bases are termed "primitive" or "unmotivated." Many Common Semitic primitive nouns exhibit fixed bases (in the singular) consisting of two consonants and an intervening vowel or three consonants with one or two intervening vowels; examples are **ʾil-*, "god"; **ʿiṣ́-*, "tree, wood"; **dam-*, "blood"; **mut-*, "man, warrior"; **yad-*, "hand, arm"; **ʾuðn-*, "ear"; **ʿayn-*, "eye"; **kalb-*, "dog"; **raʾš-*, "head"; **šinn-*, "tooth"; **ðirāʿ-*, "arm"; **paraš-*, "horse"; **raḥil-*, "ewe." Apart from such primitive nouns and from the pronominal system, however, lexical bases, especially of verbs, are discontinuous morphemes comprised of sequences of three consonants, called the root (sometimes marked √). (There is evidence of an earlier, pre-Semitic, system in which some verbal roots had two consonants, as in certain roots with first consonant *w* that "lose" the *w* in some forms: e.g., √*wrd*, "to descend," but **ya-rid*, "he descended," and **rid-(a)t-*, "descending.") Morphological information is carried by vowels and other affixes in and around these sequences. An example is the consonant sequence (root) *l-m-d*, which denotes the semantic field "learn" in Akkadian (and other languages); typical forms based on this root are *nilmad*, "we learned"; *talammadī*, "you (feminine singular)

TABLE 4
Personal Pronouns (Independent Nominative Forms)

	Proto-Semitic	Akkadian (Old Bab.)	Ethiopic (Geʿez)	Ḥarsūsi (MSA)	Arabic (Classical)	Hebrew (Biblical)	Aramaic (Syriac)
Singular:							
1st comm.	ʾană̆, ʾanākŭ	anāku	ʾana	ho(h)	ʾana	ʾănî, ʾānōkî	ʾenå
2nd masc.	ʾantă̄	atta	ʾanta	hēt	ʾanta	ʾattā	ʾatt
2nd fem.	ʾantĭ	atti	ʾanti	hēt	ʾanti	ʾatt	ʾatt
3rd masc.	šuʾa	šū	wəʾətu	ha(h)	huwa	hûʾ	hu
3rd fem.	šiʾa	šī	yəʾəti	sē	hiya	hîʾ	hi
Plural:							
1st comm.	niḥnŭ	nīnu	nəḥna	ənḥā	naḥnu	ʾănaḥnû	ḥnan
2nd masc.	ʾantum(±ū)	attunu	ʾantəmu	ʾətōm	ʾantum	ʾattem	ʾattun
2nd fem.	ʾantin(±ā/nă̆)	attina	ʾantən	ʾətēn	ʾantunna	ʾattēn(n)ā	ʾattēn
3rd masc.	šum(±ū)	šunu	ʾəmuntu	hōm	hum	hēm(mā)	hennun
3rd fem.	šin(±ā/nă̆)	šina	ʾəmāntu	sēn	hunna	hēnnā	hennēn

will learn"; *limdā*, "learn (plural)!"; *ulammid*, "I taught (= made learn)"; *lummudum*, "instructed"; *talmīdum*, "apprentice."

Nouns Semitic substantives and adjectives exhibit two genders, masculine and feminine. Some primitive noun pairs have different bases, as in *ʾab-*, "father," and *ʾimm-*, "mother"; *ḥimār-*, "male donkey," and *ʾatān-*, "female donkey"; in other noun pairs and in adjectives, gender is distinguished by means of a specific morpheme, usually of the form *-t* or *-at*, to mark the feminine, as in *śarr-*, "prince," *śarrat-*, "princess."

There are three numbers: singular, dual, and plural. The dual is marked by a set of endings. Some plurals are also denoted by a set of special endings, which probably appeared originally only on adjectives and on substantives derived from adjectives. Other plurals are indicated by pattern replacement (called "internal" or "broken" plurals). Such plurals are the norm in South Semitic languages and in Arabic (e.g., "dog" ~ "dogs" is Ethiopic *kalb* ~ *ʾakləbt*, Ḥarsūsi *kawb* [< *kalb] ~ *kəlōb*, Arabic *kalb-* ~ *kilāb-*); in Akkadian this means of pluralization has essentially disappeared in favor of the external endings; the same obtains in the Northwest Semitic languages, except for nouns of the type CVCC

(where C stands for any consonant and V for any vowel), which regularly form their plurals with the insertion of *a* between the last two consonants but also take the external plural endings (e.g., Hebrew *keleb* < *kalb-*, "dog," pl. *kəlābîm* < *kalab-īma*).

On the basis of Akkadian, Arabic, and Ugaritic, a simple case system may be reconstructed for the protolanguage, with each of three cases marked in the singular by one of the short vowels: *-u* in the nominative, for subjects of all clauses, for predicates of verbless clauses, and for topicalized forms; *-i* in the genitive, for the possessive and as the case governed by all prepositions; and *-a* in the accusative, for the object of the verb and for a range of adverbial nuances. In the dual and the external plural the genitive and accusative fall together in an oblique case; the dual endings are nominative *-ā* and oblique *-ay*, and the external plural markers are nominative *-ū* and oblique *-ī*. The short case-vowels of the singular were lost in many of the languages over time (in Modern South Arabian, Hebrew, Aramaic, late Akkadian dialects, and modern Arabic and Ethiopian dialects; in Classical Ethiopic the accusative *-a* remained); in most of these, the loss of case distinction in the singular was accompanied by the generalization of the oblique form in the external plural.

The other major morphosyntactic category for which substantives and adjectives are marked in the protolanguage is boundness: forms that are not bound to a following genitive element, which may be another noun or an enclitic pronoun, are closed by a specific morpheme, whereas bound (or "construct") forms lack that morpheme. On singular forms, the morpheme was probably *-m originally; thus, unbound (nominative) *kalbu-m, "dog," contrasts with bound (nominative) *kalbu śarri-m, "prince's dog," and *kalbu-kĭ, "your (feminine singular) dog." (*-m became -n in Arabic and was lost in Ethiopic, Modern South Arabian, and Northwest Semitic; in the last, differences in stress eventually came to mark at least some bound forms.) In forms with dual or external plural markers, the allomorph marking forms as unbound was originally *-na, as in (nominative) *yaśarū-na, "upright people," but *yaśarū ʾarṣi-m, "the upright of the land"; (nominative) *ʿaynā-na "(two) eyes," but *ʿaynā śarri-m, "the eyes of the prince," *ʿaynā-kă, "your (masculine singular) eyes." (*-na was lost in plural forms and became -n in the dual in Akkadian, became -ni in the dual in Arabic, and became -m(a) in some Northwest Semitic languages, such as Hebrew.) The foregoing elements of nominal inflection, and developments in some of the languages, are illustrated in table 5.

Verbs The Common Semitic verbal system may be reconstructed with two finite forms, two verbal adjectives (for active roots), and one or more verbal nouns. Both of the finite forms are inflected for person by means of a set of prefixes (and suffixes in some persons); the semantic distinction between these forms is primarily one of aspect: a form with the base $C_1C_2V_2C_3$ is marked as perfective and functions, inter alia, as a past tense, as in *yapqid, "he sought" (also as a jussive, frequently, but not obligatorily, with a proclitic particle *la-, as in *la-yapqid, "let him seek"); the other form, which has the middle consonant geminated, $C_1aC_2C_2V_2C_3$, is unmarked, as in *yipaqqad, "he seeks." Below is the complete paradigm of the perfective finite form:

	Singular	Plural
3rd masc.	*yapqid	*yapqidū
3rd fem.	*tapqid	*yapqidnă
2nd masc.	*tapqid	*tapqidū
2nd fem.	*tapqidī	*tapqidnă
1st comm.	*ʾapqid	*napqid

The verbal adjectives are the active participle *pāqid- ("seeking, seeker"; extant for active verbs only) and the perfective form *paqid-, the meaning of which depends on the semantics of the verbal root: passive for transitive roots (thus, *paqid-, "sought"), resultative for active intransitive roots (e.g., *waθib-, "seated," from the root wθb, "to sit"), and descriptive for adjectival or stative roots (e.g., *yaśar-, "upright, just," from the root yśr, "to be upright, just"). Both adjectives can be inflected attributively in the manner outlined above (see the paradigm of the participle *pāqid- in table 5). In addition, the perfective adjective can be inflected as a predicate with a set of enclitic subject pronouns (related in the first and second persons to the independent pronouns listed in Table 4), as in *paqid-a, "he is/was sought":

	Singular	Plural
3rd masc.	*paqid-a	*paqid-ū
3rd fem.	*paqid-at	*paqid-ā
2nd masc.	*paqid-tă	*paqid-tum(±ū)
2nd fem.	*paqid-tĭ	*paqid-tin(±ā/nă)
1st comm.	*paqid-(ā)kŭ	*paqid-nŭ

The forms of the verbal nouns among the various languages are diverse. Akkadian, Hebrew, and Ugaritic attest a form *paqād- that regularly functions as an infinitive, and Ugaritic and, sporadically, Hebrew also have an infinitive of the form *pidq-; in most dialects of Aramaic, the infinitive is of the form mipqad, while in Classical Ethiopic it is faqīd. In Arabic the shape of the verbal noun associated with any particular root is largely unpredictable. The situation in the protolanguage is therefore difficult to reconstruct with certainty.

TABLE 5
Nominal Declension: Active Participle of the Root √*pqd*, "to seek"*

		Proto-Semitic	Akkadian (Old Bab.)	Ethiopic (Geʿez)	Arabic (Classical)	Hebrew (Biblical)	Aramaic (Syriac)
Masculine:							
Sing.	nom.	pāqidu-m	pāqid-um	*fāqəd	fāqidu-n	pōqēd	påqed
	gen.	pāqidi-m	pāqid-im	(*fāqəda)	fāqidi-n		
	acc.	pāqida-m	pāqid-am	*fāqəda	fāqida-n		
Dual	nom.	pāqidā-na	pāqidā-n	—	fāqidā-ni	pōqədayim	—
	obl.	pāqiday-na	pāqidī-n	—	fāqiday-ni	(pōqədê)	
Plur.	nom.	pāqidū-na	pāqidū	*fāqədān	fāqidū-na	pōqədîm	påqdin
	obl.	pāqidī-na	pāqidī	(*fāqədāna)	fāqidī-na	(pōqədê)	(påqday)
Feminine:							
Sing.	nom.	pāqid(a)tu-m	*pāqidt-um	*fāqədt	fāqidatu-n	pōqedet	påqdå
	gen.	pāqid(a)ti-m	*pāqidt-im	(*fāqədta)	fāqidati-n		(påqdat)
	acc.	pāqid(a)ta-m	*pāqidt-am	*fāqədta	fāqidata-n		
Dual	nom.	pāqid(a)tā-na	*pāqidtā-n	—	fāqidatā-ni	pōqidtayim	—
	obl.	pāqid(a)tay-na	*pāqidtī-n	—	fāqidatay-ni	(pōqidtê)	
Plur.	nom.	pāqidātu-m	pāqidāt-um	*fāqədāt	fāqidātu-n	pōqədōt	påqdån
	obl.	pāqidāti-m	pāqidāt-im	(*fāqədāta)	fāqidāti-n		(påqdåt)

* The forms that include the elements after hyphens are free or unbound forms; elements after hyphens are lost in bound (construct) forms. (For Ethiopic, Hebrew, and Syriac, bound forms are given in parentheses when they differ from the free forms.) Ethiopic forms have an asterisk because the active participle is *faqādi*; the pattern *fāqəd* is an infrequent adjective pattern. In Akkadian the sequence -*dt*- in the feminine singular becomes -*tt*-; in Ethiopic it becomes -*dd*-. The Akkadian masculine plural forms given are those of nouns; participles may inflect like adjectives, which differ from nouns only in their masculine plural forms: nom. *pāqidūt-um*, obl. *pāqidūt-im*. Aramaic nouns also occur in a form called the emphatic or full form, which ends in -*å* (originally the definite article): masculine singular *påqdå*, feminine singular *påqedtå*, masculine plural *påqdē*, feminine plural *påqdåtå*.

The predicative construction of the perfective verbal adjective, illustrated by *paqid-a, paqid-at*, "he, she is sought," and so forth, above, is in full use only in Akkadian. (It is also attested with the same meaning in a morphologically related form in early Egyptian.) Elsewhere in Semitic it occurs as such only vestigially, with stative roots, in forms such as Hebrew *zāqantā* (< *ðaqin-tă*), "you (masculine singular) are old." Otherwise, in a development that defines the division between East and West Semitic, all languages other than Akkadian and Eblaite attest this form (usually with a vowel change, *paqada*) not as a predicate adjective but as an

active, perfective finite verb, "he has sought." The endings of the second and first person are also significant for classification: Akkadian has -*k*- in the first-person singular and -*t*- in second-person forms, while South Semitic languages have leveled -*k*- throughout and Central Semitic languages have leveled -*t*- throughout. Table 6 illustrates this form in several of the languages.

The innovative *paqada* replaced the earlier *yapqid* (as in the Akkadian preterite *ipqid* and precative *lipqid*) as the primary perfective form in West Semitic. The latter was retained in most languages in secondary uses. It continued to function as a jussive (often preceded by a pro-

TABLE 6
Forms of the Predicate Adjective (East Semitic)/Suffix-Conjugation (West Semitic)

	Akkadian	Ethiopic	Ḥarsūsi	Arabic	Hebrew	Aramaic
Singular:						
3rd masc.	paqid	fəqada	fəqōd	faqada	pāqad	pqad
3rd fem.	paqdat	fəqadat	fəqədōt	faqadat	pāqədâ	peqdat
2nd masc.	paqdāta	fəqadka	fəqōdək	faqadta	pāqadtā	pqadt
2nd fem.	paqdāti	fəqadki	fəqōdəš	faqadti	pāqadt	pqadt
1st comm.	paqdāku	fəqadku	fəqōdək	faqadtu	pāqadtî	peqdet
Plural:						
3rd masc.	padqū	fəqadu	fəqadəm	faqadū	pāqədû	pqad(un)
3rd fem.	paqdā	fəqadā	fəqōd	faqadna	pāqədû	pqad(ēn)
2nd masc.	paqdātunu	fəqadkəmu	fəqōdkəm	faqadtum	pəqadtem	pqadtun
2nd fem.	paqdātina	fəqadkən	fəqōdkən	faqadtunna	pəqadten	pqadtēn
1st comm.	paqdānu	fəqadna	fəqōdən	faqadnā	pāqadnû	pqadn

clitic particle), for example, in Ethiopian Semitic (as in Geʿez *(la-)yəfqəd*), Modern South Arabian (as in Ḥarsūsi *yəfqād*), Arabic *(li-yafqid)*, Hebrew *(yipqōd)*, and some dialects of Aramaic (early Aramaic **lipqud*). It also continued as a past tense in restricted environments in many of the West Semitic languages, as in Classical Ethiopic after the conjunctions *ʾəm-qədma* and *za-ʾənbala*, "before," in Arabic after the negative particle *lam*, and especially in Classical Hebrew in the extremely common consecutive preterite form *way-yipqōd*. Table 7 shows the reflexes of the original finite perfective form **yapqid* in several representative languages.

The Proto-Semitic aspectually unmarked form **yipaqqad* is attested in Akkadian (*ipaqqid*, the "present") and South Semitic (as in Classical Ethiopic *yəfaqqəd*, Harsusi *yəfōqəd*; the latter shows simplification of the originally doubled middle consonant). In Central Semitic, however, this form fell out of use completely; it was replaced by a new form based on the early perfective **yapqid*, marked with *-u* on forms ending in a consonant (as in third masculine singular **yapqid-u*) and *-na* on forms ending in *-ī* and *-ū* (as in second feminine singular **tapqidī-na* and third masculine plural **yapqidū-na*). The origin of this form is obscure, but it may be related to the Akkadian subordinative ("subjunc-

tive"; i.e., *ša ipqid-u*, "who inspected"). In Hebrew and Aramaic, a sound change caused the loss of the distinctive final *-u* that marked many of the forms of this paradigm, with the result that the **yapqid* and **yapqidu* forms fell together for most roots. In Hebrew, vestiges of the distinction between the two original forms are preserved in certain weak root types, as in *yāšûb < *yaθūbu*, "he returns," versus *yāšōb < *yaθub*, "let him return"; *yibke < *yabkiyu*, "he weeps," versus *yēbk < *yabki(y)*, "let him weep." Part of the **yapqidu* paradigm is also seen in Hebrew in an optional final *-n* that may appear on forms ending with *-î* and *-û*; forms with this *-n* are always imperfective. Paradigms of the nonperfective finite verb in some representative languages are shown in table 8.

All the verb forms cited thus far reflect what is termed the "basic stem" of the verbal root. Most verbal roots also occur in one or more of a set of derived stems that are characterized by internal changes, by prefixes (some of which became infixes in some of the languages), or by a combination of such modifications, and that effect more or less predictable alterations in meaning vis-à-vis the basic stem. Examples of the major derived stems, as represented by the **yapqid* form in Akkadian and Hebrew, follow:

TABLE 7
Verbal Conjugation: Perfective Forms

	Akkadian	Ethiopic	Ḥarsūsi	Arabic	Hebrew	Aramaic
Singular:						
3rd masc.	ipqid	yəfqəd	yəfqād	yafqid	yipqōd	nepqud
3rd fem.	tapqid	təfqəd	təfqād	tafqid	tipqōd	tepqud
2nd masc.	tapqid	təfqəd	təfqād	tafqid	tipqōd	tepqud
2nd fem.	taqidī	təfqədi	təfqād	tafqidī	tipqədî	tepqdin
1st comm.	apqid	ʾəfqəd	əfqād	ʾafqid	ʾepqōd	ʾepqud
Plural:						
3rd masc.	ipqidū	yəfqədu	yəfqədəm	yafqidū	yipqədû	nepqdun
3rd fem.	ipqidā	yəfqədā	təfqədən	yafqidna	tipqōdnā	nepqdån
2nd masc.	tapqidā	təfqədu	təfqədəm	tafqidū	tipqədû	tepqdun
2nd fem.	tapqidā	təfqədā	təfqədən	tafqidna	tipqōdnā	tepqdån
1st comm.	nipqid	nəfqəd	nəfqād	nafqid	nipqōd	nepqud

G: The basic stem (German *Grundstamm;* in Hebrew grammar called the *qal*): Akkadian *izkur,* Hebrew *way-yizkōr,* "(and) he remembered"; Akkadian *išlim,* Hebrew *way-yišlam,* "(and) he became whole."

N: Passive of the basic stem (the Hebrew *niphal*), marked with a prefixed *n* (which assimilates to the first consonant of the root in some forms in certain languages); this stem has been lost in South Semitic and in Aramaic: Akkadian *izzakir,* Hebrew *way-yizzākēr* (both < *yinðakir), "(and) he was remembered."

C: Causative (the Akkadian Š stem, Hebrew *hiphil*), marked with a prefixed *š, h,* or ʾ in the various languages: Akkadian *ušazkir,* Hebrew *way-yazkēr* (< *yuhaðkir), "(and) he caused to remember."

D: Factitive, pluralic, and other meanings (the Hebrew *piel*): Akkadian *ušallim,* Hebrew *wa-yšallēm,* "(and) he made whole."

TABLE 8
Verbal Conjugation: Finite Nonperfective Forms

	Akkadian	Ethiopic	Ḥarsūsi	Arabic	Hebrew	Aramaic
Singular:						
3rd masc.	ipaqqid	yəfaqqəd	yəfōqəd	yafqidu	yipqōd	nepqud
3rd fem.	tapaqqid	təfaqqəd	təfōqəd	tafqidu	tipqōd	tepqud
2nd masc.	tapaqqid	təfaqqəd	təfōqəd	tafqidu	tipqōd	tepqud
2nd fem.	tapaqqidī	təfaqqədi	təfēqəd	tafqidīna	tipqədî(n)	tepqdin
1st comm.	apaqqid	ʾəfaqqəd	əfōqəd	ʾafqidu	ʾepqōd	ʾepqud
Plural:						
3rd masc.	ipaqqidū	yəfaqqədu	yəfōqədəm	yafqidūna	yipqədû(n)	nepqdun
3rd fem.	ipaqqidā	yəfaqqədā	təfōqədən	yafqidna	tipqōdnā	nepqdån
2nd masc.	tapaqqidā	təfaqqədu	təfōqədəm	tafqidūna	tipqədû(n)	tepqdun
2nd fem.	tapaqqidā	təfaqqədā	təfōqədən	tafqidna	tipqōdnā	tepqdån
1st comm.	nipaqqid	nəfaqqəd	nəfōqəd	nafqidu	nipqōd	nepqud

The G, C, and D stems may be further modified by a prefixed or infixed -*t*-; these tG/Gt, Ct, and tD/Dt stems are semantically passive, reflexive, or reciprocal. (In Hebrew the tG and Ct have essentially been lost; the tD is called the *hithpael*.) Hebrew and other languages (Ugaritic, Arabic) also exhibit passive verbs that are forms of the G, C, and D stems modified by internal vowel changes (Hebrew *qal* passive, *hophal*, *pual*). Of these derived stems, the N, the C, and the *t*-forms have analogs in other Afroasiatic languages, while the D stem seems to be a Semitic innovation.

BIBLIOGRAPHY

See TH. NÖLDEKE, "Semitic Languages," in *Encyclopaedia Britannica* (11th ed. 1911). Though it is approaching its centennial, the most comprehensive work on the Semitic languages and their grammar remains the two-volume masterpiece of CARL BROCKELMANN, *Grundriss der vergleichenden Grammatik der semitischen Sprachen* (1908–1913). Also still very much worth reading, both because of its very reliable presentation of the grammar of individual languages and because of its extended text specimens, is GOTTHELF BERGSTRÄSSER, *Introduction to the Semitic Languages: Text Specimens and Grammatical Sketches* (original German ed. 1928), translated with notes, bibliography, and an appendix on the scripts by PETER T. DANIELS (1983). Because of their age, these works are naturally quite out-of-date in some respects. A somewhat superficial but still useful review of Semitic grammar is *An Introduction to the Comparative Grammar of the Semitic Languages: Phonology and Morphology*, written by a team of specialists in the various branches of Semitic and edited by SABATINO MOSCATI (1964). Overviews of scholarship in Afroasiatic, in comparative Semitic, and in individual languages (Akkadian, Classical Arabic, modern Arabic dialects, Aramaic, Hebrew, Ethiopic, and South Arabian), also by eminent scholars, may be found in volume 6 of *Current Trends in Linguistics*, edited by THOMAS A. SEBEOK (1970). A tour de force of linguistic reconstruction may be found in a volume by the great linguist JERZY KURYLOWICZ, *Studies in Semitic Grammar and Metrics* (1973). The classification of the Semitic languages is a much-disputed topic; the scheme presented here is based largely on a number of articles by ROBERT HETZRON, such as "Two Principles of Genetic Reconstruction," *Lingua* 38 (1976).

The following works on individual Semitic languages or branches may also be consulted: ERICA REINER, *A Linguistic Analysis of Akkadian* (1966); *Ebla 1975–1985: Dieci anni di studi linguistici e filologici*, edited by LUIGI CAGNI (1987); ROBERT HETZRON, *Ethiopian Semitic* (1974); A. F. L. BEESTON, *Sabaic Grammar* (1984); T. M. JOHNSTONE, "The Modern South Arabian Languages," *Afroasiatic Linguistics* 1 (1975); *Grundriss der arabischen Philologie*, vol. 1, edited by WOLFDIETRICH FISCHER (1982); STANISLAV SEGERT, *A Basic Grammar of the Ugaritic Language* (1984); E. Y. KUTSCHER, *History of the Hebrew Language* (1982); KLAUS BEYER, *The Aramaic Language*, translated by JOHN F. HEALEY (1986); and W. RANDALL GARR, *Dialect Geography of Syria-Palestine, 1000–586 BCE* (1985).

SEE ALSO **The Decipherment of Ancient Near Eastern Scripts** (Part 1, Vol. I); **Aramaean Tribes and Nations of First-Millennium Western Asia** (Part 5, Vol. II); **The Phoenicians** (Part 5, Vol. II); **The Story of the Semitic Alphabet** (Part 9, Vol. IV); and **Recovering Canaan and Ancient Israel** (Part 11, Vol. IV).

Ancient Egyptian and Other Afroasiatic Languages

ANTONIO LOPRIENO

THE AFROASIATIC LANGUAGES

Ancient Egyptian is a branch of the language family variously called Afroasiatic (in the United States and in modern linguistic terminology), Hamito-Semitic (in western Europe and in traditional comparative linguistics), or Semito-Hamitic (mainly in eastern Europe). Afroasiatic is one of the most widespread language families in the world, its geographic area comprising, from antiquity to the present time, the entire area of the eastern Mediterranean, northern Africa, and western Asia.

Most of the important languages of the ancient and modern Near East—major exceptions being Sumerian and Hurrian—belong to this language family, which is characterized by the following general linguistic features: the presence of bi- or triconsonantal lexical roots, capable of being inflected in various ways; a consonantal system displaying a series of "ejective," "emphatic," or "glottalized" phonemes alongside the voiced and the voiceless series; a vocalic system originally limited to the three vowels /a/ /i/ /u/; a nominal feminine suffix *-at (an asterisk indicates a reconstructed vocalization; see section on phonology below); a rather rudimentary case system, consisting of no more than two or three cases; a nominal prefix *m-*; an adjectival suffix *-ī* (called *nisba*); a basic opposition between prefix (fientive) and suffix (stative) conjugation in the verbal system; and a verbal conjugation pattern using these prefixes: first-person singular, *a-*; second-person singular, *t-*; third-person singular masculine, *y-*, and feminine, *t-*; and first-person plural, *n-*, with supplementary suffixes in the second- and third-person feminine plurals.

There are six branches of the Afroasiatic family. Besides ancient Egyptian, to which this essay is primarily devoted, and the Semitic languages (see the chapter on those tongues earlier in this volume), they are Berber, Cushitic, Chadic, and Omotic.

Berber

Berber comprises a group of related languages and dialects currently spoken (mostly in competition with Arabic) by at least five million people in northern Africa from the Atlantic coast in the west to the oasis of Siwa in the east and Mali and Niger in the south. Although written records exist only since the nineteenth century CE, some scholars take Berber to represent the historical outcome of the language of the more than one thousand "Libyan" inscriptions, written in a native script or in the Latin alphabet and documented from the second century BCE onward. The linguistic territory of Berber can be divided into seven major areas (the names following in parentheses refer to both the people and the locally spoken variety of Berber): the Moroccan Atlas (Tachelhit, Tamazight), central Algeria (Zenati), the Algerian coast (Kabyle), the Jebel Nefusa in Tripolitania (Nefusi), the oasis of Siwa in western Egypt (Siwi), the Atlantic coast of Mauretania (Zenaga), and the central Sahara in Algeria and Niger (Tuareg). Isolated communities are also found in Mali, Tunisia, and Libya. The Tuareg have preserved an old writing system called *tifinagh*, ultimately related to the alphabet of the old Libyan inscriptions.

Characteristic of Berber phonology is the presence of two varieties of a certain number of phonemes: a "tense" articulation, generally connected with consonantal length, and a "lax" one, often accompanied by spirantization. For example, the two variants of /k/ are [kk] (tense) and [χ] (lax). Masculine nouns normally begin with a vowel, whereas feminine nouns both begin and end with a *t*-morpheme. In the verb, oppositions of "aspect" (unmarked, intensive, perfect) are conveyed by prefixes, the subject being indicated by a prefix (first-person plural and third-person singular), a suffix (first-person singular and third-person plural), or a discontinuous affix consisting of a prefix and a suffix (second person). The usual order of the sentence, which can be modified by contextual emphasis, is verb–subject–object (VSO).

Cushitic

The Cushitic family of languages is spoken by at least fifteen million people in eastern Africa, from the Egyptian border in northeast Sudan to Ethiopia, Djibouti, Somalia, Kenya, and northern Tanzania. The existence of the Cushitic languages has been known to the West since the seventeenth century. While this language family does not seem to be documented in the ancient world—Meroitic, the still imperfectly understood language used and written in the kingdom of Napata and Meroë between the Third and Sixth cataracts of the Nile from the third century BCE to the fourth century CE, was a Nilo-Saharan language—one of the modern Cushitic languages, Beja, shows closer linguistic ties with

ancient Egyptian than any other Afroasiatic language. Cushitic languages are divided into four major groups: northern (Beja, in coastal Sudan); central (Agaw, in northern Ethiopia); eastern, further subdivided into Saho-Afar in southern Eritrea, Somali in Somalia, Oromo in central Ethiopia, Highland East Cushitic in central and southern Ethiopia, and various other languages in Ethiopia, such as Dullay and Western Omo-Tana, and in northern Kenya, such as Rendille; and southern (Alagwa, Burunge, Iraqw, and so on, spoken in southern Kenya and Tanzania).

Cushitic languages are characterized by the presence of a set of glottalized consonants (implosive, ejective, or retroflex) and, in some cases, such as Somali, by vowel harmony (whereby the vowels in any particular word come from a restricted set of the available vowels). Although they use distinctive tones, these are (unlike, for example, in Chinese) determined in the grammar rather than in the lexicon. In the area of morphology, Cushitic languages tend to use many inflectional endings; there are two genders (masculine, often covering the lexical areas of "greatness" or "importance," and feminine, often used for the semantic realm of "smallness"), a complex system of plural formations, and a varying number of cases. The Proto-Cushitic two-case system with nominative (-*u* or -*i*) and absolutive case (-*a*) has either been abandoned, as in southern Cushitic, or has evolved into a more complex system with numerous cases derived from the melding of function words into suffixes. The verbal system tends to replace the common Afroasiatic prefix conjugation (still present in Beja and Saho-Afar, with remnants in other languages as well) with a suffix conjugation based on the auxiliary verb "to be"; it is very rich in tenses, which are often derived from the grammaticalization of conjunctions and auxiliaries. Cushitic languages express pragmatic ("real-world," discourse-oriented) concepts, such as topic or focus, by grammatical means, while the verb normally comes at the end of the sentence.

Chadic

Chadic is a family of about 140 languages and dialects spoken by more than thirty million people in sub-Saharan Africa (Nigeria, Cameroon, Chad, and Niger) around Lake Chad.

They are currently subdivided into the following groups: western (Hausa, Bole, Ron, Bade/ Warji, Zaar, etc.); Biu-Mandara (Tera, Bura/ Higi, Mandara, Daba, Bata, etc.); eastern (Somrai, Nancere, Kera, Dangla, and so on); Masa. The most important language of this family, Hausa, enjoys the status of first language in northern Nigeria and Niger and of second language and regional lingua franca in the entire western Sahara. Chadic languages normally have a very rich consonantal inventory: like Cushitic, they display glottalized consonants, and they are often tonal. There is no gender distinction in the plural; verbal forms are normally not conjugated for person. The normal word order is SVO.

Omotic

Omotic is a family of languages spoken by approximately one million people along both shores of the Omo River and north of Lake Turkana in southwest Ethiopia, formerly thought to represent the western branch of Cushitic. It is still a matter of scholarly discussion whether Omotic really belongs to the Afroasiatic language family. Characteristic features of the Omotic languages are the absence of pharyngeal phonemes and the almost total loss of gender oppositions.

HISTORY OF THE EGYPTIAN LANGUAGE

Ancient Egyptian shows the closest relations to Semitic and Berber and more distant ones to Cushitic (except Beja, to which Egyptian shows closer ties than with any other Afroasiatic language) and Chadic. With its more than four millennia of productive history (3000 BCE–1300 CE), Egyptian proves an ideal field for both diachronic (historical) and typological investigation. The history of the Egyptian language can be divided into two main stages, characterized by a major typological change from synthetic (combining) to analytic (expressing each atom of meaning with a separate morpheme) patterns in the nominal syntax and the verbal system. Each of these two stages of the language can be further subdivided into three different phases, affecting primarily the writing systems.

Older Egyptian

Older Egyptian is the language of all written texts from 3000 to 1300 BCE, and it survived in formal religious texts until the second century CE. Its main phases are as follows: Old Egyptian, the language of the Early Dynastic period, Old Kingdom, and the First Intermediate Period (3000–2000), is mainly evidenced in the religious corpus of the Pyramid Texts and a number of so-called autobiographies of the administrative elite. Middle Egyptian, also termed Classical Egyptian, dating from the Middle Kingdom to the end of the Eighteenth Dynasty (2000–1300), is the classical language of Egyptian literature, differing from Old Egyptian mainly in its regularized orthography, which is the mirror of a centralized educational system. Late Middle Egyptian, the language of formal (mainly religious) texts from the late New Kingdom to the end of Egyptian civilization, maintains the linguistic structures of the classical language, but especially in the Greco-Roman period (Ptolemaic Egyptian, third century BCE–second century CE), it shows an enormous increase in its set of hieroglyphic signs (see below) and generally a change in the underlying "philosophy of writing."

Linguistically, Older Egyptian is characterized by its preference for synthetic grammatical structures: for example, it displays a full set of morphological suffixes indicating gender and number: masculine singular *nṯr.0*, "god"; feminine singular *nṯr.t*, "goddess"; masculine plural *nṯr.w*, "gods"; feminine plural *nṯr.wt*, "goddesses." It exhibits no definite article (*rmṯ*, "the man, a man"); it maintains the VSO order in verbal formations, as in *sḏm=k n=f*, "may you listen to him." (The *ṯ* represents English *ch; ḏ* represents English *j*, as in *judge;* and *0* represents the absence of any explicit ending.) In the transliterations, which follow common egyptological conventions, the dot separates the word stem from a morphological affix, such as a feminine or plural ending for nouns or a conjugational element for verbs, whereas the double hyphen is used to indicate the presence of a suffix pronoun.

Later Egyptian

Later Egyptian is documented from the end of the Eighteenth Dynasty down to the Middle Ages (1300 BCE–1300 CE). Late Egyptian (1300–

700 BCE) is the language of written records from the second part of the New Kingdom, following the Amarna Period. It primarily conveys the rich entertainment and wisdom literature of the Nineteenth Dynasty and of the Third Intermediate Period, and it was the vehicle of Ramesside bureaucracy. Demotic (seventh century BCE–fifth century CE) is the language of administration and literature during the Late and Greco-Roman periods. While grammatically it closely continues Late Egyptian, it differs radically from it in its writing system (see below). Coptic (fourth–fourteenth centuries CE) is the language of Christian Egypt, written in a variety of the Greek alphabet supplemented by six or seven demotic signs to indicate Egyptian phonemes absent in Greek. As a spoken and progressively also a written language, it was superseded by Arabic from the ninth century CE, but it survives to the present in the liturgy of the Christian church of Egypt, which is also called the Coptic church.

Later Egyptian tends to develop analytic features. For example, suffixal markers or morphological oppositions tend to be dropped and to be functionally replaced by prefixal indicators such as the article: *p-son*, "the brother"; *t-sōne*, "the sister"; *ne-snēw*, "the brothers." The demonstrative "this" and the numeral "one" progressively evolve into the definite and the indefinite articles: Coptic *p-rōme*, "the man" < Classical Egyptian *pꜣ rmṯ*, "this man," and *w-rōme*, "a man" < *wꜥj rmṯ*, "one man." Periphrastic patterns in the order SVO supersede older verbal formations: Coptic *mare-pek-ran wop*, literally, "let-do your-name being-pure" > "your name be hallowed," as opposed to the synthetic Older Egyptian construction *wꜥb(.w) rn=k*, literally, "shall-be-purified your-name."

Dialects of Egyptian

Because of the centralized nature of the political and cultural models underlying the evolution of ancient Egyptian society, there is hardly any evidence of dialect differences in pre-Coptic Egyptian. However, the origins of Older Egyptian are probably to be seen in Lower Egypt, around the city of Memphis (modern Mit Rahina), which was the capital of the country during the Old Kingdom, and those of Later Egyptian in Upper Egypt, in the region of Thebes, the cultural, religious, and, for a time,

political center of the New Kingdom. Coptic displays a variety of dialects that do not vary profoundly: they differ mainly in graphic conventions and sporadically in morphology and lexicon, but hardly at all in syntax and pragmatics.

Unless otherwise specified, the following grammatical sketch refers to Older Egyptian, specifically to the language of classical Middle Egyptian literature.

THE WRITING SYSTEM

The basic writing system of ancient Egyptian is hieroglyphs, a term that has been used since the Ptolemaic period as a Greek counterpart of the Egyptian expression *mdw.w-nṯr*, "god's words." This is a variable set of signs, ranging from about 1,000 in the Old Kingdom down to approximately 750 in the classical language but increasing dramatically to many thousands in Ptolemaic Egyptian. Hieroglyphic signs represent living beings and objects, such as gods or categories of people, animals, parts of the human or animal body, plants, astronomical entities, buildings, furniture, vessels, and so on (see fig. 1).

In this writing system, phonological and ideographic principles are combined. A word consists of a sequence of uniconsonantal, biconsonantal, or triconsonantal signs called "phonograms," which convey a substantial portion of its phonological structure: normally all the consonants and occasionally also the semivocalic phonemes, but with vowels remaining for the most part unexpressed. The sequence of phonograms is usually followed by a "semagram," normally called "determinative" by Egyptologists, which indicates iconically the semantic sphere of the word: for instance, a sitting man expresses the lexical sphere of "man, mankind," a scribe's kit indicates the semantic realm of "writing," and the stylized map of a settlement denotes the word as a place-name. While some words in common use (pronouns, prepositions, a few lexical items such as *ḏd*, "to say") are written only phonologically, many items of basic vocabulary are expressed only by semagrams that represent, evoke through rebuses, or symbolize their own semantic reference: these are called "logograms" (often termed "ideograms" by Egyptologists). For example, the hieroglyphic sign representing the enclosure of a house means "house" (**pār*). In order to distinguish the logographic (⌐⌐ = /pār/ = "house") from the purely phonological use of the same sign (⌐⌐ =/p-r/, independently of the lexical sphere of the word in which it appears), logographic uses are often marked by a vertical stroke following the sign. Egyptian writing displays a set of twenty-four "alphabetic," that is, uniconsonantal signs. Although these covered almost completely the inventory of consonantal and semiconsonantal phonemes of the Egyptian language (the only exception being /l/, for which a separate sign appears only in Demotic), this set of signs never developed into a genuine alphabetic system.

Within the hieroglyphic system, the increasing consciousness of the symbolic potential inherent in the relation between the signs used to write words and the meaning of the words themselves led to the development of new phonological associations and of cryptographic exercises in Ptolemaic Egyptian. On the one hand, this evolution progressively threatened the accessibility of the system and eventually favored its decay; on the other hand, it extended the meaning of the individual hieroglyphs and made

the system more perfect as a pictorial-linguistic form. This radical change in the nature of the writing system in the Greco-Roman period is at the origin of the view, which has been held in the Western world since late antiquity and until the emergence of modern Egyptology (but still surviving to the present day in some aspects of popular culture), of the "symbolic" rather than functional character of the hieroglyphic writing.

The hieroglyphic system was used mainly for monumental purposes and, more rarely (in a cursive form), for religious texts in the Middle and New kingdoms. During its history, it developed cursive varieties: hieratic (2600 BCE–third century CE), which represents a direct cursive rendering (with ligatures and diacritic signs) of a sequence of hieroglyphic signs; and Demotic (seventh century BCE–fifth century CE), which radically modified the writing conventions by introducing a shorthand-like simplification of hieratic sign groups. The basic orientation of the Egyptian writing system—and the only one used in the cursive varieties—is from right to left; in epigraphic, monumental texts, this order is often reversed for reasons of symmetry or artistic composition (but the people and animals

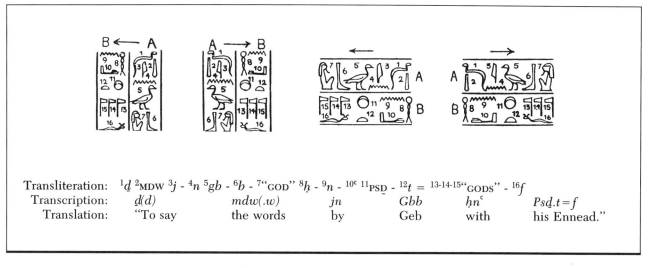

Transliteration:	¹*ḏ* ²MDW ³*j* - ⁴*n* ⁵*gb* - ⁶*b* - ⁷"GOD" ⁸*ḥ* - ⁹*n* - ¹⁰ᶜ ¹¹PSD - ¹²*t* = ¹³⁻¹⁴⁻¹⁵"GODS" - ¹⁶*f*						
Transcription:	*ḏ(d)*		*mdw(.w)*	*jn*	*Gbb*	*ḥnᶜ*	*Psḏ.t=f*
Translation:	"To say		the words	by	Geb	with	his Ennead."

Fig. 1. An example of how the hieroglyphic system worked. Numbers indicate the sequence of the individual signs; phonograms are indicated in italics, logograms in small capitals, semagrams in small capitals and quotation marks; supplements necessary to complete the grammatical structure of the corresponding words are added in parentheses. The four versions of the hieroglyphic text show the four basic directions of writing in use for the script. HIEROGLYPHIC TEXT FROM ALAN GARDINER, *EGYPTIAN GRAMMAR* (1957)

Ancient Egyptian Conceptions of Language and Writing in Context

For the Egyptians, as for many other cultures, language was not a passive medium for expressing thought. Language modeled the world, and the forms of words showed how the world was constituted. Speech could even create the world. Ritual exploited this power of language, and texts used wordplay to associate offerings with the deities to whom they were offered; such methods were also common in magic. Thus, humanity (*rmt-w*) was stated to originate in the tears (*rmjt*) of the creator. Numerous New Kingdom and later mythological narratives provide etiologies for the presence or meaning of features of the religious landscape in terms of linguistic associations, often turning on a sentence a divine actor is said to have pronounced on a mythical occasion.

As language and texts evolved, written tradition became more complex, as did the choice of language forms. Explanatory glosses were inserted into the body of some texts. From the later New Kingdom on, there were two distinct forms of written Egyptian. At first these were Classical or Middle Egyptian and Late Egyptian, while from the mid first millennium BCE, they were Classical Egyptian and Demotic. Little from the repertory of traditional texts moved into the new written idioms, and much disappeared. (Monumental inscriptions continued to be composed in Classical Egyptian.) A few texts were formally translated. Examples are the *Ritual for Repelling the Aggressive One*, a set of incantations against the god Seth preserved in a Ptolemaic manuscript in a version in Classical Egyptian together with a "translation" into Late Egyptian, and an astronomical treatise inscribed in the cenotaph of Sety I at Abydos (thirteenth century BCE) that is paralleled by a Demotic version on a papyrus from around 100 CE.

These texts demonstrate impressive continuity while reminding us that most Egyptian written culture involved learning a new language, because the written and the spoken diverged strongly no later than the standardization of Classical Egyptian in the Twelfth Dynasty. The translator of the astronomical treatise manipulated two alien idioms, Classical Egyptian and Demotic, which had been formalized many centuries before his time. This process continued. One of the latest major texts is an onomasticon, an encyclopedia-like compilation, preserved on a papyrus of the second–third centuries CE. This is written in hieratic in Classical Egyptian but has interlinear glosses in Greek letters (a pagan use of Greek writing known as Old Coptic). These glosses, which show that the writers were more familiar with the Greek

script than with Demotic, evince the decay of traditional Egyptian written culture, but they also show that, so long as its tradition continued, it could be transposed into another written form (which had itself been in the country for half a millennium). Another example of this use of Greek writing is Papyrus BM 10808, quoted in the main text of this essay. Despite the potential exemplified in these texts, native Egyptian culture soon succumbed to Christianity, and the knowledge of hieroglyphs, hieratic, and Demotic was gradually lost.

Writing was integral to the definition of Egyptian culture. Although the hieroglyphic script might in theory be separated from other aspects of Egyptian civilization, in practice such a split would have been almost unthinkable. Hieroglyphs, with their pictorial potential, conveyed essential meanings. From the Old Kingdom on, extended styles of writing known as cryptography (fig. 2) exploited pictorial implications of signs or unusual phonetic associations to create new

Fig. 2. Section of a hymn to Khnum in his temple at Esna, Roman period, first century CE. The text is an extreme example of cryptography, written almost entirely with hieroglyphs of rams. The ram was the manifestation and sacred animal of Khnum.
ADAPTED FROM SERGE SAUNERON, *LE TEMPLE D'ESNA II* (1963)

meanings. Until the Late Period, this practice was restricted to just a few contexts, but demotic created a vast potential by completing the separation of literacy in hieroglyphs from competence in everyday writing. From about 600 BCE, the range of hieroglyphs grew from a few hundred signs to some thousands, of which many had several different consonantal values. This elaborated script became its own domain of knowledge. It enhanced pictorial compositions and was integral to the vast proliferation of native Egyptian temple reliefs in the Greco-Roman period. The hieroglyphic writing in these reliefs varies from plain styles with a somewhat extended range of signs to extremes where the meaning is nearly as much pictorial as linguistic. Among examples of the latter is a hymn to the ram god Khnum in the Roman-period temple of Esna that is written almost exclusively with hieroglyphs of rams. Only those who knew the text beforehand could have deciphered this. (See fig. 2.)

The Greco-Roman temples, their hieroglyphs, and their furnishings and manuscripts formed the richest expression of traditional Egyptian culture that was perhaps ever achieved. At that time Egypt's rulers belonged to another civilization and could not comprehend the works they financed, although they evidently appreciated their importance for the native elite. Few people had access to these repositories of learning and values. Perhaps one in a thousand people could comprehend fully their inscriptions, which are more accessible to us than they were to most ancient Egyptians. In any case, many inscriptions could not be read once they had been inscribed because they were carved in dark places high up on walls. The gods were in a real sense the primary audience. These temples show great creativity and a sense of progress in which each structure seemingly strived to surpass its predecessors. It was necessary to maintain the reciprocity of gods and humanity and to celebrate the gods, without whom the world would not prosper, but the goal of this progress was not simply pragmatic.

The temples formed a self-sustaining world. They embodied a sacred science that the elite probably valued more highly than the knowledge of such domains as medicine, in which the Egyptians also excelled. This restricted knowledge of hieroglyphs and religious concepts impressed classical antiquity more than Egypt's practical achievements and contributed to the country's image as the source of ancient and secret wisdom. This classical and early medieval evaluation of Egyptian wisdom, which modern scholars have often dismissed, should be taken seriously as indicative of what was important to elites within and outside native Egyptian society.

JOHN BAINES

always face the beginning of the line). Figures 3 and 4 show samples of hieratic and Demotic writing, followed by the hieroglyphic transcription, but it should be noted that the conversion from Demotic into hieroglyphs is a purely artificial exercise whose sense would not have been comprehended in antiquity.

The hieroglyphic-based system was superseded in Coptic by an alphabet derived from that of Greek, with the addition of six or seven

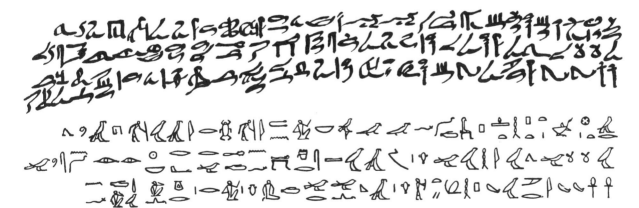

Fig. 3. Sample of literary hieratic writing, Twelfth Dynasty, followed by its hieroglyphic transcription. ALAN GARDINER, *EGYPTIAN GRAMMAR* (1957)

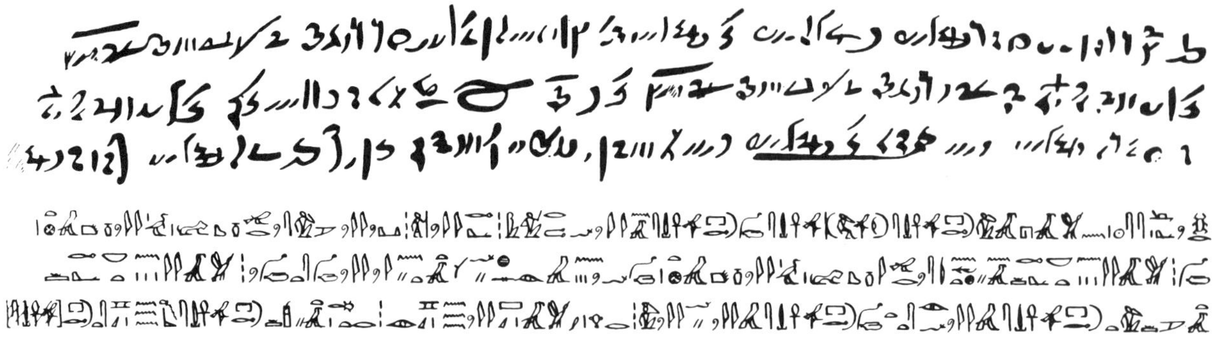

Fig. 4. Sample of literary Demotic writing, third century BCE, followed by its hieroglyphic transcription. ALAN GARDINER, *EGYPTIAN GRAMMAR* (1957)

Demotic signs for the indication of phonemes absent from Greek: ⲱ = /š/, ϥ = /f/, ϩ (in some dialects ⳉ) = /χ/, ϩ = /h/, ϫ = /c/, ϭ = /kʲ/, ϯ = /ti/. Coptic is written from left to right.

PHONOLOGY

The reconstruction of the phoneme inventory of Classical Egyptian is bound to remain very hypothetical. The exact phonological value of many consonants is obscured by difficulties in establishing reliable Afroasiatic correspondences; vowels and stress patterns can only be reconstructed by combining the contemporary, but not always unequivocal, Akkadian transcriptions of the second millennium BCE (which mirror spoken forms corresponding to late Middle Egyptian or Late Egyptian) with the later Greek transcriptions of the Late Period (corresponding roughly to spoken Demotic) and the Coptic evidence of the first millennium CE. In this article, reconstructed vocalizations (often referred to as "Paleocoptic" or *Urkoptisch* in Egyptological literature) are always accompanied by an asterisk, in order to distinguish them from actually documented consonantal sequences.

For Older Egyptian, we can posit the phonological inventory below, using conventional Egyptological transcriptions, including some alternatives.

Consonants

The Egyptian consonant system (table 1) does not display the "emphatic" phonemes common to many Afroasiatic languages. The most frequent Egyptian etymological counterpart to the Afroasiatic emphatic phonemes *ṣ and *ṭ seems to be the dental voiced *d*, the Egyptian voiced palatal *ḏ* often correlating with Semitic ʿ (ʿayin): Egyptian *sḏm* = Semitic *smʿ*, "to hear." Egyptian ʿ (ʿayin) corresponds to Afroasiatic *d, whereas the phoneme conventionally transcribed ʾ (aleph) probably corresponds to Afroasiatic *r or *l. The existence of the phoneme /l/ in Egyptian seems to be established by Afroasiatic correspondences (Egyptian *ns* = Semitic *lis-ān*, "tongue") as well as by its presence in Coptic (*las*, "tongue"); yet, unlike all other consonantal phonemes, /l/ shows no unequivocal graphic rendering, being expressed in different lexemes by <ʾ>, <n>, <r>, or <nr>.

Historically, the opposition between voiced and voiceless consonants tends to be progressively neutralized into the voiceless variant. During the second millennium, the following sound changes took place: the point of articulation was progressively moved to the front (velar to palatal, palatal to apical); oppositions between fricatives in the palatal region (/š/, /ç/, /χ/) tended to be neutralized into /š/; and final /r/ and /t/ tended to become /ʾ/ and then disappear. During the first millennium BCE, the opposition between ʿayin/ʿ/ and aleph/ʾ/ was also neutralized.

Vowels

The original set of vowels (table 2) underwent a certain number of historical changes. Already during the second millennium BCE, short stressed /i/ and /u/ merged into /e/, while long

TABLE 1
The Consonants of Older Egyptian

	Labial	Apical	Alveopalatal	Palatal	Velar	Uvular	Pharyngeal	Glottal
Stops								
Voiceless	p /p/	t /t/			k /k/	ḳ, q /q/		', 'ꞽ, j /ʔ/
Voiced	b /b/	d /d/			g /g/			
Affricates								
Voiceless				ṯ /tʲ/				
Voiced				ḏ /dʲ/				
Fricatives								
Voiceless	f /f/	s /s/	š /ʃ/	ḫ /ç/	ḫ /χ/		ḥ /ħ/	h /h/
Voiced		z /z/					ꜥ /ʕ/	
Nasals	m /m/	n /n/						
Lateral		', n, r /l/						
Vibrant		r /r/						
Glides	w /w/			y, jj /j/				

/u:/ turned into /e:/. Around 1000 BCE, long /a:/ became /o:/, a phonetic evolution similar to the contemporaneous "Canaanite shift" in Northwest Semitic. There was also a change in the short tonic from /a/ to /o/, but Coptic shows that this affected only a portion of the Egyptian linguistic domain. As a general rule, Egyptian unstressed vowels progressively lost phonological status and became realized as schwa.

TABLE 2
The Vowels of Older Egyptian

	Short	Long
Front	/i/	/i:/
Middle	/a/	/a:/
Back	/u/	/u:/

Syllabic Structures

In the classical language, the stress could lie only on the last or next-to-last syllable (table 3). While both closed and open syllables are found before a stressed syllable, the only possible structure in syllables following the stress is the closed syllable with short vowel. The stressed vowel of a penultimate open syllable is long; some scholars posit the existence of extralong sylla-

bles under final stress. In addition to final /j/ (i.e., y), /w/, /t/, and /r/, unstressed vowels were dropped between 2000 and 1600, leading to a global reorganization of syllabic structures in Later Egyptian.

MORPHOLOGY

Nouns

As is common in Afroasiatic, the basic Egyptian morphological unit is a biliteral or triliteral root, which is modified by suffixes (nṯr, "god," nṯr.w, "gods"; mꜣꜥ "true," mꜣꜥ.t "Truth") or, less frequently, by prefixes affecting meaning (ꜥḥꜥ, "to stand," m:ꜥḥꜥ.t, "tomb"). (See table 4.) There is no evidence that Egyptian ever possessed the paradigm of three cases (nominative in -u, accusa-

TABLE 3
The Syllabic Structures of Older Egyptian

Pretonic	Tonic	Posttonic
#CvC '___	'CvC (___)	'___ CvC#
#Cv '___	'Cv: (___)	
	'Cv:C#	
	'CvCC#	

TABLE 4
Nominal Morphology in Older Egyptian

	Masculine	Feminine
Singular	.∅, .w	.t
Dual	.wj	.tj
Plural	.∅, .w, .ww	.t, .jjt, .wt

tive in -*a*, genitive in -*i*) known from many other Afroasiatic languages. Although some scholars detect remnants of the Afroasiatic case system in the Egyptian verbal paradigm, the syntactic structure of Classical Egyptian (see below) was so rigid that cases could not have played a productive role in the language in historical times. Moreover, short unstressed vowels in final position are not posited for Classical Egyptian (see above).

As in other Afroasiatic languages, adjectives are morphologically and syntactically treated like substantives. Very common is the derivational pattern called "nisbation," in which a morpheme -*j* is added to a noun to form its corresponding adjective: *nṯr*, "god," *nṯr.j*, "divine"; *jmn*, "the right side," *jmn.t*, "the West," *jmn.tj*, "western."

Pronouns

There are three sets of personal pronouns in Egyptian (table 5). Independent pronouns are used for the topicalized subject of sentences with nominal or adjectival predicate in the first person (*jnk jtj=k*, "I am your father") and for the focalized subject of a nominal or verbal cleft sentence: *nft zꜣ wsjr*, "*he* is Osiris's son"; *jnk jnj=j sw*, "it is *I* who shall bring it." Dependent pronouns are used as the object of a transitive verb (*sḏm=f wj*, "he will hear me") and as the subject of a qualifying nominal sentence (*nfr tw ḥnꜥ=j*, "you are happy with me") and of an adverbial sentence (in the first and second persons only after an initial particle): *mk wj m-bꜣḥ=k*, "look, I am in front of you." Suffix pronouns are used as the subject of verbal forms, as the possessive pronoun, and as the object of prepositions: *ḏj=k r=k n=j ḥ.t=j*, "you shall truly (literally, to-you) give me (=to-me) my possessions."

Demonstratives are characterized by a deitic element ("this," "that") preceded by the indicator of gender and number, *pn, pf, pw* for the masculine and *tn, tf, tw* for the feminine: *rmṯ pf*, "that man"; *ḥjm.t tn*, "this woman." They normally follow the noun they refer to. The plurals *nn, nf, nn* are also used with a following genitive as pronouns in partitive constructions:

TABLE 5
Personal Pronouns in Older Egyptian

		Independent	Dependent	Suffix
Sing.	1 c.	*jnk*	*wj*	=*j*
	2 m.	*ntk, twt*[a]	*tw*	=*k*
	2 f.	*ntt, tmt*[a]	*tn*	=*t*
	3 m.	*ntf, swt*[a]	*sw*	=*f*
	3 f.	*nts, stt*[a]	*sj, st*	=*s*
Dual	1 c.		*nj*	=*nj*
	2 c.	*nttnj*	*tnj*	=*tnj*
	3 c.	*ntsnj*	*snj*	=*snj*
Plur.	1 c.	*jnn*	*n*	=*n*
	2 c.	*nttn*	*tn*	=*tn*
	3 c.	*ntsn*	*sn, st*	=*sn*

[a] *twt, tmt, swt,* and *stt* are archaic forms found mainly in Old Kingdom religious texts.

nn nj srjw.w, "these officials." Later Egyptian developed a set of definite articles from the prefixed demonstrative series masculine p', feminine t', plural n': p'-rm(t), "the man"; t'-ḥm(.t), "the woman"; n'-srj.w, "the officials." It also developed an indefinite article from the numeral wᶜj, "one": wᶜ-rmt, "a man."

The relative pronoun is masculine ntj, feminine nt.t, plural ntj.w, "who, which, that." It only refers to specific (that is, semantically determined) antecedents, since in Egyptian indefinite antecedents are not referred to by a relative but by a circumstantial clause: rmt ntj rḫ.n=j sw, "the man whom I know," literally, "man that I know him," as opposed to rmṯ rḫ.n=j sw, "a man that I know," literally, "man—I know him." Peculiar to Egyptian is the presence of a relative pronoun that semantically incorporates negation: masculine jwtj, feminine, jwt.t, plural jwtj.w, "who, which, that not."

Basic interrogative pronouns are m, "who? what?" (very common in Afroasiatic); jḫ "what?"; jšst, "what?" They can be combined with prepositions or particles to form complex pronouns: jn-m, "who?" literally, "FOCUS-OF-CLAUSE-who"; ḥr-m, "why?" literally, "on-what?"

Numerals

The most common numerals show many etymological connections with other Afrioasiatic languages. (In table 6, the numbers 1–10 are presented, followed by their tentative vocalization.) It is noteworthy that 5 is etymologically a *nisba* of Afroasiatic *yad, "hand" (*jadi:jaw), which is no longer a productive word in historical Egyptian; that 20 (dʲawa:taj) is an old dual of

10 (mu:dʲaw); and that 30 is an m-prefix formation from a root ᶜb', "command." Numbers are seldom written out: they are mostly rendered graphically, strokes indicating the units and special hieroglyphs being used for the powers of 10. Ordinals are derived from cardinals through the addition of the suffix .nw (from 2 to 9: ḥmt.nw, "third") or the prefixation of the participle mḥ, "filling," to the cardinal number (from 10 onward: mḥ-20, "twentieth").

Verb

Finite forms are built by annexing a suffix pronoun to the root, either directly (mrr=f, "that-he-loves"; mrj=k, "you love") or after the insertion of a morpheme indicating tense, aspect, or voice features (ḏd.n=j m mᵡ.t "I have spoken in truth"; sḥtp.w=ṯn nṯr.w−ṯn, "you shall satisfy your gods"). The most important verbal indicators are .n (past tense: sḏm.n=j, "I heard"), .t (perfective, sometimes prospective aspect: n sḏm.t=f, "he had not heard"; jw.t=f, "he shall come"), .w (prospective aspect and passive voice: jrj.w=f, "it has been/shall be done"), and .tw (passive voice: sḏm.tw=k, "you are heard"). Classes of "weak" verbal roots, whose third radical is a semiconsonant (j or w), show the reduplication of the second radical and the presence of a stressed vowel between the two resulting consonants (*ma|ra:rˣf) in a form that in Semitic languages indicates the imperfective aspect or the factitive stem, such as the imperfective in Akkadian (iparras) and the D-stem throughout Semitic (for example, uparras in Akkadian and yukattibu in Arabic); in Classical Egyptian this form, which is conventionally called

---

TABLE 6
Numerals in Older Egyptian

1	wᶜj [wuᶜj]	10	mḏw	100	šn.t
2	sn.wj [si'newwaj]	20	dw.tj	1,000	ḫ'
3	ḥmt.w ['ḥamtaw]	30	mᶜb'	10,000	ḏbᶜ
4	jfd.w [jaf'daw]	40	ḥm	100,000	ḥfn
5	dj.w ['di:jaw]	50	ty.w	1,000,000	ḥḥ
6	srs.w [sar'saw]	60	sjsy.w		
7	sfḥ.w ['safḥaw]	70	sfḥy.w		
8	ḥmn.w [ḥa'ma:naw]	80	ḥmny.w		
9	psḏ.w [pi'si:dʲaw]	90	psḏy.w		

"emphatic," fulfills the function of pragmatic "theme" of the sentence in which it appears: *mrr=s wj*, "(the-fact-that-)she loves me." In such sentences, the pragmatic stress normally lies on an adverbial modifier (see below). The nonreduplicated verbal form is further subdivided into temporally unspecified and future functions (*mrj=f*, "he loves, loved, will love," depending on the temporal setting of the context; *sdm=f*, "he will hear"); largely because of the defective nature of the hieroglyphic writing system, it cannot be fully determined to what extent these two forms—called in Egyptological literature "circumstantial" and "prospective," respectively—represent morphologically different structures.

The imperative has no suffix element in the singular: *dd*, "say!" But sometimes, especially with weak verbs, it has a suffix *.w* or *.y* in the plural: *rm.y*, "weep (plural)."

Egyptian also exhibits a verbal form—variously called "old perfective" or, more recently, "stative" in the English-speaking world and "pseudoparticiple" in continental Europe—that indicates the wide semantic range of verbal "perfectivity," from perfective aspect with intransitive verbs to passive voice with transitive verbs. This form displays a set of suffix pronouns that are etymologically linked to the forms of the Semitic suffix conjugation (table 7). Examples are *prj.kw*, "I have come forth"; *ḫpr.tj*, "you have become"; *rdj.w*, "it has been given."

Nonfinite forms of the Egyptian verb are the participle and the infinitive. The participle (*nomen agentis*) exhibits nominal morphology (masculine *.0*, *.w*, *.j*; feminine *.t*, etc.: see table 4) and is derived from the verbal stem: *sdm.j*, "listener" > "judge"; *mꜥ.t*, "the Straight One" (feminine) > "Truth, Order." It follows from what

was said above concerning the adjective that there appears to be no clear distinction between the categories of adjective and participle in Egyptian. The infinitive (*nomen actionis*) shows a suffix *.0* in the regular verbs (*sdm*, "to hear," "hearing") and a suffix *.t* in some classes of weak verbs (*mrj.t*, "to love," "love"). A special type of infinitive characterized by the suffix *.w* is used after verbs of negative predication: *tm*, "not to do," *tm=t ḫnj.w ḥr-m*, "why do you not row?" It is a matter of scholarly dispute whether the radical element in finite forms was originally a *nomen agentis* (*mrj=f*, "a-loving-one-is-he" > "he loves") or a *nomen actionis* (*mrj=f*, "loving-of-him" > "he loves"). Verbal predications could also be expressed analytically by prepositional constructions (*sw ḥr sdm*, "he is on hearing" > "he is hearing"; *jw=f r mrj.t*, "he is toward loving" > "he is going to love, he will love"), a construction that was to characterize the evolution of the verbal system in Later Egyptian.

Prepositions and Particles

The most frequent prepositions are *m*, "in, with"; *n*, "to, for"; *r*, "toward"; *mj*, "as, like"; *ḥr*, "on"; *ẖ.r*, "under"; *ḥnꜥ*, "with"; *ḫft*, "according to"; *ḫntj*, "before." Prepositional phrases follow the noun or the verb they modify. Particularly noteworthy is the presence of the preposition *ḥr*, "near," whose original semantic value (A *ḥr* B, "A is near B") was applied to any situation in which the two participants A and B find themselves at different hierarchical levels, A being socio-culturally higher than B (*sdd=f ḥr msj.w*, "he will speak to the children") or, vice versa, B higher than A (*jmꜢḥy ḥr ntr ꜥ*, "honored by the Great God").

The basic negative particle is *n* (cf. probably Semitic **laꜢ*): *n rḫ.n=f*, "he does not know." A variant of this, conventionally transcribed *nn*, is used as predicative negation: *nn mꜥ.tjw*, "there are no trustworthy people."

TABLE 7
The Stative in Older Egyptian

	Singular	Plural
1	*.k(j)* > *.kw*	*.wjn*
2	*.tj*	*.twnj*
3 m.	*.(j)* > *.w*	*.w*, *.y*
3 f.	*.tj*	*.tj*

SYNTAX

Egyptian exhibits three sentence types, which are classified on the basis of the syntactic nature of their predicate, the subject being always a nominal phrase. "Nominal sentences" are those in which the predicate is either a substantive or an adjective. In categorical statements or qualifying adjectival sentences, the normal order of constituents is predicate–subject: *Rꜥ w pw*, "this is Ra," *nfr mtn=j*, "my path is good." This sequence is modified into subject–predicate in identifying sentences, when both the subject and the predicate are semantically determined or specific (*sn.t=f spd.t*, "his sister is Sirius"), and in cleft sentences, when the subject is focalized (*jn sn.t=f sꜥnḫ rn=f*, "it is his sister who causes his name to live"). Nominal phrases can be topicalized by being placed at the beginning and referred to by a coreferential pronoun (*jr ḫꜣ.t NN nhnw pw*, "as for NN's body, it is a rejuvenated one," *tꜣ=n pḥ=n sw*, "our land—we are reaching it").

"Adverbial sentences" are those in which the predicate is an adverbial or prepositional phrase; the order is always subject–predicate: *jw NN jr p.t*, "NN is toward heaven," *ḥr.t=k m prw=k*, "your rations are in your house." "Verbal sentences" use a verbal phrase; the order is predicate–subject(–object): *ḫꜥ.y=k* "you shall appear," *ḫꜥm.n=f wj*, "he charged me."

In Egyptian sentences, verbal forms often appear embedded as pragmatic topic (theme) or, symmetrically, as emphasized comment (rheme) of the utterance. In the Egyptological literature, this phenomenon is known as "transposition," the theme-rheme sequence being labeled "complex adverbial sentence": *jrr=t pꜣ jb ḥr-m*, "that-you-do this mood is on-what" (emphatic form) > "Why are you in this mood?"; *wgg ꜣs.n=f wj*, "weakness is in-that-it-has-seized me" (circumstantial form) > "weakness has seized me." This terminology goes back to the particular linguistic paradigm adopted by Egyptologists from the 1960s to the 1980s, the "Polotskyan model," in

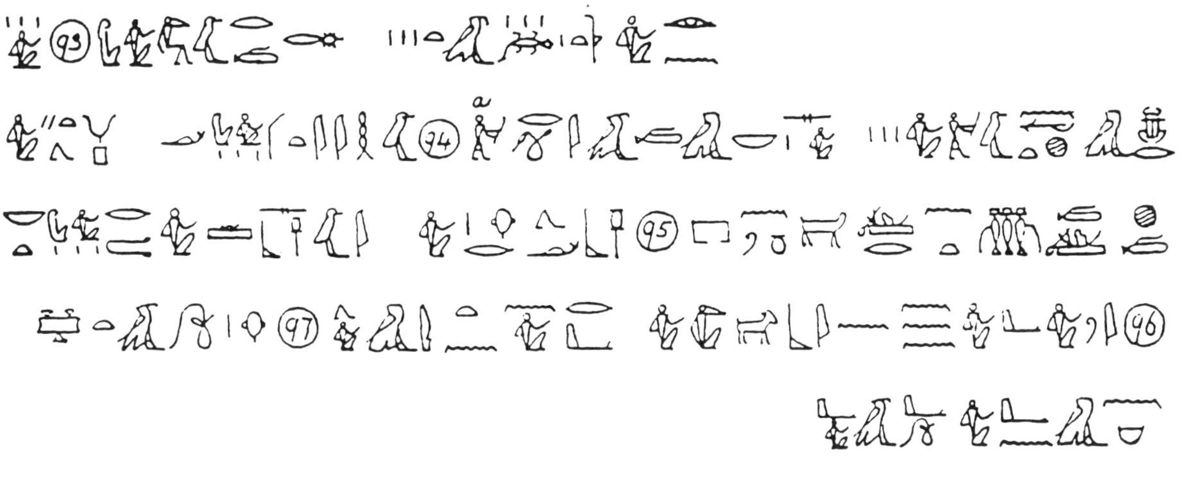

jr.n=j rnp.wt [ran'pawwi(t)] *ꜥšꜣ.wt ḥrd.w=j ḫpr(.w)* ['χapraw] *m nḫtj.w z(j) nb* ['zij-nib] *m ḏꜣr wḥy.t =f wpw.tj* [wap'wu:tij] *ḫdd ḫnt(j) r ẖnw* ['ça:naw] *ꜣb =f ḥr=j* [ḥi'raj] *jw sꜣb=j rmt.w nb.t* ['ni:ba(t)] *jw=j ḏj =j mw* [maw] *n jb(j)* ['ja:bij] *rḏj.n=j tnm ḥr wꜣ(j).t* ['wi'ja(t)] *nḥm.n=j ꜥwꜣ(j)* ['a'waꜣj(aw)]

I spent many years, and my children became strong men, each of them the chief of his own tribe. The messenger who came north or went south to the Residence would stop by me. I let everyone stay (i.e., I provided hospitality). I gave water to the thirsty, I showed the way to the one who had gone astray, I saved him who had been robbed.

Fig. 5. A passage from *The Story of Sinuhe*, circa 1900 BCE (text begins on top line and goes from right to left). HIEROGLYPHIC TEXT FROM A. M. BLACKMAN, *MIDDLE EGYPTIAN STORIES* (1932)

which "transposed" verbal forms of Older Egyptian are believed to convert themselves fully into syntactically nominal or adverbial phrases. This model, which has come to be termed the "Standard Theory," is being progressively abandoned in favor of a more verbalistic approach, in which transposed verbal forms are seen as keeping their predicative force, the opposition between "emphatic" and "circumstantial" forms being seen to operate at the level of their pragmatic salience—in the sense of their conveying conversationally more or less relevant information—within the utterance, rather than of their syntactic function as subject or predicate within the sentence. While in the Standard Theory the verbal form in the example above, *jrr=ṯ pꜣ jb*, "you do this mood," would be considered the subject of the sentence and the adverbial phrase *ḥr-m*, "why?" its predicate, a more conventional linguistic analysis, in which the verbal form presents the sequence predicate–subject and the interrogative pronoun is considered to be the pragmatic focus, has returned to favor in recent research: "Why (*ḥr-m* = adverbial focus) do you (= *ṯ* = nominal subject) do this mood (*jrj pꜣ jb* = verbal predicate + object)?"

TEXT SAMPLES

The first sample text (fig. 5) is a passage of the *Story of Sinuhe*, the most famous narrative of Classical Egyptian literature (about 1900 BCE). The hieroglyphic text, itself a transcription from the original hieratic, is followed by the conventional Egyptological transcription in Roman alphabet; semiconsonantal phonemes not conveyed by the hieroglyphic (originally hieratic) text appear in parentheses. Because of the many uncertainties in the reconstruction of the vocalic system of ancient Egyptian, Egyptian is traditionally "read" by inserting a short vowel [e] between consonants and by vocalizing both ꜣ and ꜥ as [a]. For words or phrases whose vocalization can be reconstructed with a certain degree of methodological reliability, a transcription in bracketed symbols of the International Phonetic Alphabet (IPA) is provided. Stress is indicated by a vertical stroke before the syllable it affects.

The second sample here (fig. 6), from the magical text of British Museum papyrus 10808, has been chosen because it represents an ideal combination of Older and Later Egyptian and displays the main historical tendencies in the devel-

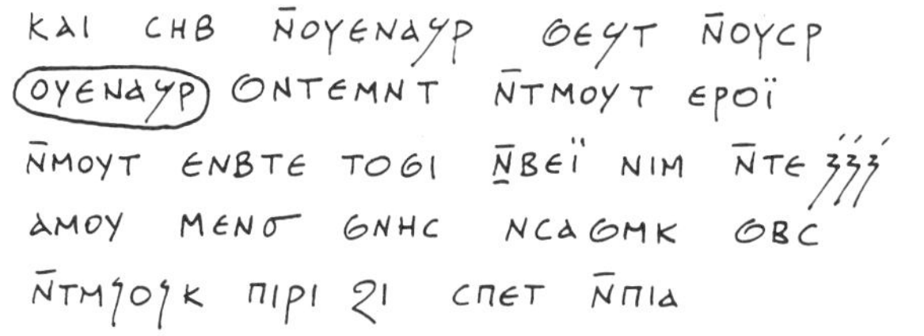

KAI CHB ⲚOYⲈNAⳍP ⲐⲈⳍT ⲚOYCP

ⲞⲨⲈNAⳍP ONTEMNT ⲚTMOYT ⲈⲢOÏ

ⲚMOYT ⲈNBTE TOⳠI ⲚBEÏ NIM ⲚTE 333

AMOY MENⲄ ⳠNHC NCAⳠMK ⳠBC

ⲚTM7OⳐK ΠIⲢI ⳌI CΠET ⲚΠIA

kai sēb n-ouenafr heft n-ousr ouenafr hnt-emnt nt-mout e-ro=i n-mout e-nbte-t-oḥi nbei nim nt-e MN *am=ou menc hnēs n-saḥm=k hbs nt-m-hoh=k piri hi spet n-pi-a*

[kaj se:b ᵉnwenʹnafᵉr χeft ᵉnu:sᵉr wenʹnafᵉr χenteʹmᵉnt ᵉntʹmu:t eʹroj ᵉnmu:t enᵉbteʹtꜣoχi ᵉnʹbej nim ᵉnte MN ꜣꜥamu menkʲ χne:s ᵉnʹsaχmᵉk χᵉbs ᵉntᵉmʹhohᵉk ʹpiri hi sᵉʹpet ᵉnpiʹꜥa]

Ky sbj nj Wnn-nfr.w ḫftj nj Wsjr (Wnn-nfr.w) ḫntj-jmn.tt ntj ḥr mḏ r rꜣ=j m mḏ r ntb ṯꜣ ʾḥ.t nby.t nb.t ntj-jw MN *ḥr ꜥm=w mnq ḥnzw nj sḫm=k ḥbsw ntj m ḫḫ=k prj hꜣj spd.tj m pꜥj wꜥ*

O Kai, enemy of Wennofre, opponent of Osiris Wennofre, the Foremost of the Westerners, you who go down deeply thanks to my spell, until the fire consumes all the flames which NN swallowed, stop the wandering of your power and the violence which is in your throat, going up and down, for you are sharp in great glare.

Fig. 6. A passage from the magical text of British Museum papyrus 10808, second century CE. HIEROGLYPHIC TEXT FROM J. OSING, *DER SPÄTÄGYPTISCHEN PAPYRUS BM 10808* (1976)

opment of the Egyptian language. The Old Coptic script of the text was in Greek letters, with the addition of a few Demotic signs, and it dates to the second century CE; while its grammar is essentially Late Middle Egyptian, it displays Later Egyptian phonology clearly. In the transcription, morpheme boundaries have been added; alphabetic signs are transcribed in italic, and Demotic groups (MN, that is, a sign indicating an unknown individual) in small capitals; the sign [-ᵉ-] indicates a short indistinct vowel (schwa). The text is transliterated into the Roman alphabet and followed by a tentative phonetic rendering in IPA based on current scholarly assumptions on the development of Later Egyptian phonology and then by a conversion into Classical Egyptian transliteration.

BIBLIOGRAPHY

This bibliography lists only some of the basic reference works on Afroasiatic languages in general and a selection from the vast contemporary literature on Egyptian grammar. The grammars and dictionaries are given in the order of the stage of the language treated.

Afroasiatic

CARLETON T. HODGE, ed., *Afroasiatic: A Survey* (1971); I. M. DIAKONOFF, *Afrasian Languages* (1988); JOSEPH H. GREENBERG, *The Languages of Africa* (3rd ed. 1970); and HANS-JÜRGEN SASSE, LOTHAR STÖRK, and EKKEHARD WOLFF, "Afroasiatisch," in *Die Sprachen Afrikas*, edited by BERNDT HEINE, THEO C. SCHADEBERG, and EKKEHARD WOLFF (1981).

Berber

ALFRED WILLMS, *Die dialektale Differenzierung des Berberischen*, Afrika und Übersee Beiheft 31 (1980).

Chadic

EKKEHARD WOLFF, "Grammatical Categories of Verb Stems and the Marking of Mood, *Aktionsart*, and Aspect in Chadic," *Afroasiatic Linguistics* 6, no. 5 (1979).

Cushitic

ROBERT HETZRON, "The Agaw Languages," *Afroasiatic Linguistics* 3, no. 3 (1976); M. LIONEL BENDER, ed., *The Non-Semitic Languages of Ethiopia* (1976); AN-

DRZEJ ZABORSKI, *Studies in Hamito-Semitic I: The Verb in Cushitic* (1975).

Egyptian

GRAMMARS

ELMAR EDEL, *Altägyptische Grammatik*, 2 vols. (1955–1964); ALAN H. GARDINER, *Egyptian Grammar: Being an Introduction to the Study of Hieroglyphs* (3rd ed. 1957); WOLFGANG SCHENKEL, *Einführung in die klassisch-ägyptische Sprache und Schrift* (1991); JAROSLAV ČERNÝ and SARAH ISRAELIT GROLL, *A Late Egyptian Grammar* (3rd ed. 1984); J. VERGOTE, *Grammaire copte*, 2 vols. (1973–1983).

DICTIONARIES

ADOLPH ERMAN and HERMANN GRAPOW, *Wörterbuch der ägyptischen Sprache*, 7 vols. (1926–1963); RAYMOND O. FAULKNER, *A Concise Dictionary of Middle Egyptian* (1962); W. E. CRUM, *A Coptic Dictionary* (1939); WOLJA ERICHSEN, *Demotisches Glossar* (1954); WERNER VYCICHL, *Dictionnaire étymologique de la langue copte* (1983).

SPECIALIZED STUDIES

JAMES P. ALLEN, *The Inflection of the Verb in the Pyramid Texts* (1984); A. M. BLACKMAN, *Middle Egyptian Stories*, Biblioteca Aegyptiaca 2 (1932); JOHN B. CALLENDER, "Afroasiatic Cases and the Formation of Ancient Egyptian Constructions with Possessive Suffixes," *Afroasiatic Linguistics* 2, no. 6 (1975); MARK COLLIER, "The Circumstantial $s\underline{d}m(.f)/s\underline{d}m.n(.f)$ as Verbal Verb-Forms in Middle Egyptian," *Journal of Egyptian Archaeology* 76 (1990); *Crossroad: Chaos or the Beginning of a New Paradigm, Papers from the Conference on Egyptian Grammar, Helsingør 28–30 May 1986*, edited by GERTIE ENGLUND and PAUL JOHN FRANDSEN (1986); "Proceedings of the Second International Conference on Egyptian Grammar (Crossroads II) Los Angeles, October 17–20, 1990," edited by ANTONIO LOPRIENO, in *Lingua Aegyptia* 1 (1991); ERIC DORET, *The Narrative Verbal System of Old and Middle Egyptian* (1986); PAUL JOHN FRANDSEN, *An Outline of the Late Egyptian Verbal System* (1974); JANET H. JOHNSON, *The Demotic Verbal System* (1976); FRIEDRICH JUNGE, *Syntax der mittelägyptischen Literatursprache: Grundlagen einer Strukturtheorie* (1978), and "Sprachstufen und Sprachgeschichte," *Zeitschrift der Deutschen Morgenländischen Gesellschaft*, Suppl. 6 (1985); ANTONIO LOPRIENO, *Das Verbalsystem im Ägyptischen und im Semitischen: Zur Grundlegung einer Aspekttheorie* (1986); JÜRGEN OSING, *Die Nominalbildung des Ägyptischen*, 2 vols. (1976); *Der spätägyptische Papyrus BM 10808*, Ägyptologische Abhandlungen 33 (1976); H. J. POLOTSKY, *Col-*

lected Papers (1971), "Les Transpositions du verbe en égyptien classique," *Israel Oriental Studies* 6 (1976); *Grundlagen des koptischen Satzbaus*, 2 vols. (1987–1990); WOLFGANG SCHENKEL, *Die altägyptischen Suffixkonjugation: Theorie der innerägyptischen Entstehung aus Nomina actionis* (1975); ARIEL SHISHA-HALEVY, *Coptic Grammatical Categories: Structural Studies in the Syntax of Shenoutean Sahidic* (1986); PASCAL VERNUS, *Future at Issue—Tense, Mood and Aspect in Middle Egyptian: Studies in Syntax and Semantics* (1990).

SEE ALSO **The Decipherment of Ancient Near Eastern Scripts** (Part 1, Vol. I); **Semitic Languages** (Part 9, Vol. IV), **The Scribes of Ancient Egypt** (Part 9, Vol. IV); **The Story of the Semitic Alphabet** (Part 9, Vol. IV); and **Rediscovering Egypt of the Pharaohs** (Part 11, Vol. IV).

Indo-European Languages of Anatolia

H. CRAIG MELCHERT

WE HAVE EVIDENCE FOR at least half a dozen Indo-European languages in Anatolia and northern Syria during the second and first millennia BCE. Except for Phrygian, all of these share a number of features pointing to a period of common prehistoric development that we may call Common Anatolian. One may therefore speak of an Anatolian subgroup of Indo-European languages comparable to Germanic, Slavic, or Celtic. To this group belong Hittite, Palaic, Luwian, Lycian, and Lydian. It is now virtually certain that we should add Carian, Pisidian, and Sidetic, but our evidence for and understanding of these languages remain very limited.

It is important to bear in mind that the Anatolian family as just defined is primarily a linguistic concept. The existence of such a subgroup of Indo-European languages is entirely independent of any theories about migration or diffusion of population groups. The speech community associated with the reconstructed prehistoric Common Anatolian stage may or may not have lived on the soil of Anatolia.

The Anatolian subgroup is attested in documents dating from the sixteenth century BCE to the first centuries CE and in three very different writing systems: cuneiform, hieroglyphic, and alphabetic. The first two systems use a mixture of logographic and syllabic spellings. Since the use of the different systems is roughly chronological, it is convenient to group the languages according to the writing system employed.

The Cuneiform Languages

Texts in Hittite, Palaic, and a form of Luwian (Cuneiform Luwian) appear in cuneiform documents. Most of these were discovered in the capital of the Hittite Empire, Khattusha (modern Boğazköy), in central Anatolia, but significant Hittite texts have also been found farther east at Maşat Hüyük (pronounced Mashat Huyuk) and at ancient Ugarit (modern Ras Shamra) on the Syrian coast, and there have been scattered finds elsewhere.

With the exception of one magnificent bronze specimen, the cuneiform is inscribed on clay tablets dating from the sixteenth to the thirteenth centuries. Recent advances in scholarship now permit us to give a relative chronology for most manuscripts and compositions, and we may distinguish Old Hittite (1570–1450), Middle Hittite (1450–1380), and Neo-Hittite (1380–1220). This division, details of which remain subject to revision, refers to periods of the language, which correspond only indirectly to political developments.

Phrygian

Our evidence for the Phrygian language is twofold. First, we have more than a hundred inscriptions of Old Phrygian, dating from roughly the eighth to the fourth century BCE, written in an alphabet related to that of Greek. These texts are on stone or various objects, chiefly pottery, discovered in Gordion and other sites in west-central Anatolia. Second, there are the "Neo-Phrygian" inscriptions, dating from the second and third centuries CE, written in the Greek alphabet. Virtually all of these are curse formulas appended to tomb inscriptions that are otherwise written in Greek.

There is general agreement that Phrygian is an Indo-European language totally distinct from Anatolian languages in the narrow sense. (For the appearance of a few Indo-Aryan words in the Hittite "horse-training" texts and Indic gods in Hittite-Hurrian documents, see the article on Mitanni in Part 5, Vol. II.) Phrygian shares a number of features with Greek, including notably the "augment," an *e*-prefix marking past tense in the verb. Nevertheless, the dialectal position of Phrygian within Indo-European is a matter of dispute and is likely to remain so, pending major new discoveries that would dramatically increase our understanding of the language.

The appearance of a few Hittite words (for example, *išḫyuli,* "obligation, contract") in Assyrian texts from Kanesh (modern Kültepe) dating from the nineteenth century shows that Indo-European languages were already in the central Anatolian area at the beginning of the second millennium, although actual texts in the languages appear only several centuries later.

The documentation for Hittite is extensive. Virtually all genres of texts are represented, but the bulk of the material deals with aspects of the state religion: cultic administration and practice, and associated mythology. The Cuneiform Luwian texts are limited to variations on fewer than a dozen compositions, chiefly rituals, while for Palaic we have merely a few fragments.

Hittite

Hittite was the chief administrative language of the Hittite Empire. To what extent it functioned as a spoken language at various places and times in the empire is impossible to determine. It is noteworthy that the Hittites themselves called the language *nešili*—that is, "of Nesha [Kanesh]."

Hittite is an unmistakably Indo-European language in all respects. All sure influence from other languages, such as Hattic, Hurrian, and Akkadian, is confined to loanwords. Earlier claims about heavy non-Indo-European "substrate" or "adstrate" effects on Hittite—features of other languages in the area before or alongside Hittite occupation—were grossly exaggerated.

Even in the case of vocabulary, the borrowing of words is largely limited to expected areas: terms relating to aspects of the cult, items of higher culture, and the names for some flora and fauna. The impression that Hittite replaced most of its inherited vocabulary is false, being based merely on the fact that most of our documentation relates to ritual practice. At least 75 percent of the core vocabulary is based on inherited Indo-European material.

Fig. 1. Hittite cuneiform inscription on clay from Boğazköy, circa 1500 BCE. Adapted from HEINRICH OTTEN AND CHRISTEL RÜSTER, *KEILSCHRIFTTEXTE AUS BOGHAZKÖY,* VOL. 22 (1974)

The Hittite sound inventory includes eighteen consonants. The sounds represented by the symbols *b, d, g, k, l, m, n, p, r, s, t, w,* and *y* are roughly equivalent to those of English (*g* equals the hard g of "gun"). The Hittites spelled their voiceless sibilant with the cuneiform signs of the "shin" (*š*) series. In Akkadian texts this sound represented a palatal similar to English *sh,* and by convention Hittite personal and place names are transliterated in these volumes with *sh.* The actual pronunciation in these cases is hard to determine. In ordinary Hittite words the sound was certainly a dental *s,* and it is given as such in this article. There is also a *ts* sound, as in "cats," plus *kʷ* and *gʷ,* similar to the initial sounds in "queen" and "Gwen." Finally, there are two harsh *h*-like sounds rendered imprecisely here as *ḫ* and *g̑.* Hittite has four vowels, each in contrasting short and long varieties: *a, e, i,* and *u.* The symbols have the values of western European languages, roughly English "ah," "say," "see," and "sue," respectively.

As an ancient Indo-European language, Hittite is of the expected "inflectional" type, marking the function of most words in a sentence by variations in their endings. The noun has two numbers, singular and plural. Alleged traces of a dual are highly dubious. Old Hittite does often distinguish a count plural from a collective plural ("leafy branch": count plural, "leafy branches"; collective, "foliage"). There are only two grammatical genders, animate and inanimate. Recent research has shown that the Anatolian languages did inherit a separate feminine gender from Proto-Indo-European but subsequently merged it with the masculine.

Old Hittite distinguishes a maximum of eight cases in the singular: vocative, nominative, accusative, genitive, dative-locative, allative, ablative, and instrumental. Vocative merges with nominative, and allative with dative-locative in the plural. Note also that the ablative and instrumental each have a single form for both singular and plural. As in other older Indo-European languages such as Greek or Latin the inanimate gender does not distinguish nominative and accusative.

In Neo-Hittite, the case system has been much reduced, with only five cases in the singular (nominative, accusative, genitive, dative-locative, and ablative-instrumental) and three in the plural (nominative-accusative, genitive-dative-locative, ablative-instrumental). Most case endings in the noun are either inherited from Proto-Indo-European or built on inherited Indo-European material.

Pronouns are predictably irregular in both stem formation and inflection. Most of the stems are recognizable as Indo-European: for example, *wēs,* "we"; * āntsas,* "us"; and *kwis/kwin,* "who/whom." The stem for "this" is inherited: *ka/i-* (compare Latin *ci-trā,* "on this side"). However, the stem *abā-,* "that," reflects an important Anatolian innovation. Unlike the noun endings, several of the pronominal inflectional endings are quite unusual, and there is not yet any totally convincing explanation for their origin.

The Hittite verb distinguishes the expected three persons and two numbers, singular and plural. There are only two moods: indicative and imperative (the latter for commands). Wishes and conditions are expressed not by a subjunctive or optative mood but by a conjunction-particle *mān/man.*

An active voice is opposed to a mediopassive. The latter marks the passive ("is hit") and many actions internal to the subject ("sit down"). As in Greek or Latin, there are also "deponent" verbs, which are mediopassive in form but active in meaning.

There are only two tenses: a present-future and a preterite. Hittite does have a phrasal construction with the verbs "have" and "be" plus the past participle, but the meaning is that of an attained state, not that of a true perfect tense as in modern European languages. There is also an interesting "serial" construction with the verbs "come" and "go" which is strikingly similar to that of modern English ("Why did you go and do that?"), but its precise function is not yet clear.

Hittite has a single participle, which has a past meaning with action verbs ("eaten," "gone") but usually a present meaning with stative verbs ("knowing," "standing"). There are an infinitive ("to go") and a gerund or verbal noun ("going"), both of restricted use. Finally, there is a "supine," which occurs only in combination with the verbs "to put" or "to step," meaning "to begin" or "to undertake" to do something.

There are no obvious traces in Hittite of the opposition between "imperfect" and "aorist" seen in Sanskrit or Ancient Greek. How and to what extent Hittite distinguishes "aspect" in the verb remains to be determined. While most of the inflectional endings of the Hittite verb are inherited from Proto-Indo-European, it contains many surprises in both formal and functional respects, and the relationship of the Hittite (Anatolian) verb to that of the other ancient Indo-European languages remains a matter of great controversy.

The following Hittite text sample (shown in fig. 1) is from an administrative text criticizing officials for improper behavior. Both composition and manuscript are of the Old Hittite period. The text reads left to right, top to bottom.

> *ta ḫapinántas īstẽni párna-sa páysi ẽtsi ẽkʷsi piyanãtsi-ya-ta*

> tah khahpeenAHntahs eestAYnee pAHrnah-sah pIEsee AYtsee AYk(u)see peeyahnAHtsee-yah-tah

> And (the bidding) of the rich (man) you do. To his house you go. You eat, you drink, and he gives you presents.

Every word in this passage reflects inherited Indo-European material. To name only the most obvious *ḫapinant-*, "rich," has the same source as Latin *ops*, "wealth"; *ed/t-* matches English "eat"; and the final suffixed *-ta*, "you," is related to "thee."

Palaic

Palaic was once the spoken language of Pala, a land that lay to the north of the Hittite heartland in central Anatolia, in all likelihood northwest of the Halys River in classical Paphlagonia. Pala is mentioned as a separate part of the empire in the Old Hittite Laws, but it does not appear in later texts and presumably no longer existed during the later empire. Palaic was surely extinct as a spoken language by the fourteenth century and may have already been so by the time of our first texts in the sixteenth.

We owe what little Palaic we have to its cultic use by the Hittites, particularly for rituals offered to the Hattic god Zaparfa. It is generally said that the non-Indo-European Hattic had more influence on Palaic vocabulary than it did on that of Hittite, but this impression may be based merely on the fact that most of our Palaic texts deal with the Zaparfa cult. When it borrows

Hattic words, Palaic does also borrow the foreign sound *f* from Hattic, unlike Hittite, which substitutes *p* or *w*.

Palaic is clearly an Indo-European language closely related to Hittite and Luwian, in some ways more conservative than either. The very fragmentary nature of our evidence limits our understanding considerably.

Cuneiform Luwian

The cuneiform texts from Khattusha include a number written in a form of Luwian. There are also many Luwian words scattered through the Hittite texts, both as foreign words and as genuine loanwords. We know that Luwian was spoken over a large area of southern and southwestern Anatolia and into Syria (see below). We do not yet have enough information to integrate the

Fig. 2. Language specimen of hieroglyphic Luwian from Kululu (Turkey), early first millennium. ADAPTED FROM PIERO MERIGGI, *MANUALE DI ETEO GEROGLIFICO*, PART 2, 1ST SER. (1967)

Luwian of the cuneiform documents into an overall geographic picture of Luwian dialects. (It is conceivable that one portion of the cuneiform texts, the "Istanuvian Songs," belongs to a different dialect of Luwian from the rest, but we understand these texts too poorly to assert this with confidence.)

In any case, there is no justification whatsoever for regarding the language of the Cuneiform Luwian texts as a dialect of Khattusha itself. At present, the only prudent course is to follow the majority of scholars in viewing Cuneiform Luwian as a coequal dialect with Hieroglyphic Luwian, whose chronological and geographic relationships remain to be determined. Minor differences between the two dialects are mentioned in the grammatical sketch below.

HIEROGLYPHIC LUWIAN

The Hittites obviously borrowed the cuneiform writing system from Mesopotamia, probably through a north Syrian intermediary. However, the so-called Hittite hieroglyphs are apparently a native creation of Anatolia.

The Hittite hieroglyphs first appear on personal seals, the oldest of which date from the fifteenth century. Monumental inscriptions on stone begin in the fourteenth century. The use of the hieroglyphs survives well beyond the end of the Hittite Empire in former vassal states of northern Syria, where we have large numbers of texts dating from the tenth to eighth centuries.

Most of the hieroglyphic inscriptions on stone are concentrated in southern Anatolia (classical Cilicia and Commagene) and in northern Syria, but there are also examples from central Anatolia, including Khattusha itself, and a few from as far west as modern İzmir.

Most of the inscriptions on seals contain only names and titles. The titles are almost always written logographically, and the names often are as well (see "The Decipherment of Ancient Near Eastern Scripts" in Part 1, Vol. I, for further discussion of logographs). The earliest inscriptions on stone are also heavily logographic. Under these circumstances, the question of what language is being written becomes moot. Indeed, it is likely that for these texts we should speak not of "logographs" but of "ideographs"; that

is, the signs stand not for words in a particular language but for concepts meant to be readable for anyone knowing the system, whatever the reader's language. This use of ideographs is comparable to our modern "Arabic" numerals, which are virtually universally understood.

If we leave aside the strictly logographic texts above, then, except for a few one-word glosses, all texts in the Hittite hieroglyphs discovered thus far are in a form of Luwian. Based on the distribution of the stone inscriptions cited above, we may be sure that this form of Luwian was spoken in southern Anatolia and northern Syria. To what extent and at what periods it may have been spoken in central Anatolia cannot yet be determined. It is likely that forms of Luwian were spoken across wide stretches of western Anatolia during the second millennium, and there remains the tantalizing suggestion by Calvert Watkins, not yet proven, that the language of the Trojans was a form of Luwian as well.

Most of the stone inscriptions are dedicatory in some sense, but many contain lengthy historical preambles. We also have a handful of personal letters and economic documents inscribed on soft lead strips. The Hieroglyphic Luwian texts are the most extensive and varied in content of any of the Anatolian languages, except Hittite.

Luwian resembles Hittite in many respects, but is generally more innovative in its grammar. It has the same consonants as Hittite, minus g^w. Luwian distinguishes only three vowels: *a*, *i*, and *u* (again both long and short). One difference between Cuneiform and Hieroglyphic Luwian is that the latter shows frequent "rhotacism"; that is, it replaces *d* (and often *l*) with *r*.

As in Hittite, the noun shows a singular and a plural, again sometimes with the distinction of count plural versus collective plural. There are likewise only two grammatical genders, animate and inanimate, although Norbert Oettinger in 1987, following a proposal by Frank Starke, has shown that some forms of the animate continue the Proto-Indo-European feminine in formal terms.

The Luwian noun distinguishes four cases in the singular: nominative, accusative, dative-locative, and ablative-instrumental. Cuneiform Luwian shows the same distinctions in the plural, but Hieroglyphic Luwian has merged animate nominative and accusative in the plural. The ablative-instrumental has a single form for singular and plural. There are a handful of vocative singulars distinct from the nominative. The case endings mostly match those of Hittite, but Luwian has built several new plural endings based on the original animate accusative plural.

Hieroglyphic Luwian has some examples of a genitive singular, but it for the most part and Cuneiform Luwian entirely have replaced the genitive of the noun with a "relational adjective" which agrees with the noun possessed: "father's house" is expressed by "paternal house." While this construction occurs in Hittite and indeed in other Indo-European languages, its functional replacement of the genitive case is a significant characterizing innovation of the western Anatolian languages: Luwian, Lycian, Lydian, Carian, Pisidian, and Sidetic. One disadvantage of the new procedure is that the adjective cannot indicate whether the possessor is singular or plural. Cuneiform Luwian has partially remedied this by creating new forms for the relational adjective in which the dative-locative plural ending is inserted between the stem and some case endings to mark plurality of the possessor.

The categories of the Luwian verb generally agree with those of Hittite: three persons, two numbers (singular and plural), two moods (indicative and imperative), two tenses (present-future and preterite), and two voices (active and mediopassive). Luwian also has a single participle, an infinitive, and a verbal noun. There are equivalents for some, but not all, of the phrasal constructions cited above for Hittite.

The following text sample (shown in fig. 2) is from a funerary stela. In this case, the text is divided into three panels, or "registers." Within each register the signs are read roughly vertically from top to bottom, starting at the left or right. This text begins at the upper left, and the first register reads left to right, the second right to left, and the third again left to right. The logographs for "couch" and "eat" are easily recognizable.

> *wa-ta amíyants ísanants adámmīs uwámmīs pádī sándadi árḫa waríḫa*

> wah-tah ahmEEyahnts EEsahnahnts ahdAHmees uewAHmees pAHdee sAHndahdee AHrkhah wahrEEkhah
> On my couch having eaten (and) drunk, there through (the grace of) Sanda I died.

Except for the divine name Sanda, all the words in this passage are ultimately derived from Proto-Indo-European. This is clearest in *ami-*, "my," and *ad-*, "eat." The verb *wari-*, "die," which may be related to the Old English verb *cwelan*, "die," shows the replacement of *l* by *r* mentioned above.

THE ALPHABETIC LANGUAGES

The remaining languages of the Anatolian subgroup are all attested in western Anatolia from the middle of the first millennium BCE to the third century CE in various alphabets either derived from or closely related to the Greek alphabet.

Lycian

We possess 170 to 180 inscriptions on stone written in the native language of Lycia, which lay on the southwest coast of Anatolia. There are also a number of very short inscriptions on coins. All the texts date from the fifth and fourth centuries.

All but a handful of the inscriptions on stone are funerary texts with highly stereotyped contents. One notable exception is the inscribed pillar of Xanthus, a lengthy dedicatory text with significant historical sections, unfortunately mostly unintelligible because of problems of vocabulary. Another is the "Létôon Trilingual," a stela inscribed with a Lycian text dealing with the establishment of a cult of Leto, accompanied by Greek and Aramaic translations.

Of all our Lycian texts, just two thus far are written in a distinct dialect called either "Milyan" or "Lycian B" (the latter opposed to "Lycian A," that is, ordinary Lycian). While Milyan is in some ways more conservative than Lycian, it would be inaccurate to consider it an older form of Lycian. We must treat Lycian and Milyan as two coequal dialects whose precise relationship remains unknown, just as in the case of the two forms of Luwian.

Lycian shares a large number of features with Luwian, and this has led some scholars to speak prematurely of a "Luwo-Lycian" or "Luwoid" subbranch of Anatolian. The close relationship between the two languages is undeniable, but there are also important differences, and some of the common features are shared with other western Anatolian languages such as Lydian. On the other hand, Luwian also shares certain innovations with Hittite and Palaic to the east. It therefore seems more useful at this point to view the Anatolian languages as a continuum of dialects rather than to try to divide them into clearly distinct "branches." (See also "The Lycian Kingdom of Southwest Anatolia" in Part 5, Vol. II.)

Lydian

Slightly more than a hundred texts in the native language of the western Anatolian kingdom of Lydia survive. Only a few dozen of these are of significant length and reasonably complete. All thus far have been found in the confines of Lydia, and all but a handful in the ancient capital of Sardis.

Except for a few short inscriptions on coins, some of which may be as old as the eighth century, our Lydian texts date from the fifth and fourth centuries and are thus roughly contemporaneous with our Lycian material.

So far as we can understand them, most of the longer Lydian texts are dedicatory in nature, and indeed mainly funerary. There are a few that appear to be decrees dealing with the granting of privileges or with property settlements. It is noteworthy that several of the texts are in verse, with a fairly rigid meter (based on word accent) and vowel assonance in the last word of each line.

There is one short bilingual text in Lydian and Aramaic that gave the first entry into the language, but we still lack a Lydian-Greek bilingual of any significant length. For this reason, our understanding of Lydian lags behind that of the other Anatolian languages mentioned above. We can for the most part analyze the grammatical structure with some assurance, but our grasp of the vocabulary remains vague.

Lydian clearly shares certain innovations with the rest of the Anatolian subgroup, and several specifically with the other western languages Lycian and Luwian. However, in many respects, it is unique among the Anatolian family. Given the relatively late date of its appearance and our limited comprehension of the language, we cannot yet determine whether the differences in its structure are due to archaisms preserved

only here or to a long series of prehistoric innovations. In either case, Lydian certainly did share in the prehistoric developments of Common Anatolian. The idea that Lydian appears in Asia Minor as the result of a separate development from that of the other Anatolian languages is erroneous. (See also "Croesus of Sardis and the Lydian Kingdom of Anatolia" in Part 5, Vol. II.)

Pisidian, Sidetic, and Carian

We must also make mention of three more languages of southwestern Anatolia that almost certainly belong to the Anatolian group of Indo-European languages. First, our evidence for Pisidian consists of some thirty-odd tomb inscriptions from northern Pisidia, located in southwestern Anatolia. These contain only names of the tomb occupants and patronymics, and date from roughly the second and third centuries CE.

For Sidetic, the language of Side, a city on the coast of Pamphylia, we have even less evidence: six inscriptions, all but one apparently dedicatory in nature, dating from the third century BCE, and a few older monograms on coins from the fifth and fourth centuries.

Texts in the native language of Caria, in the extreme southwest, are more extensive but widely scattered in space and time. We have a single fragmentary Greek-Carian funerary text from Athens from the end of the sixth century BCE. There are several inscriptions, also chiefly funerary, from Caria itself dating from the fourth and third centuries, as well as a few coins from the fifth century. The most extensive Carian texts come from Egypt, where there were several colonies of Carian immigrants. Dating from the seventh to the fourth century, most are funerary texts on stone, but there are a few dedicatory inscriptions on other objects and several graffiti.

Decipherment of the Carian script has been difficult and controversial. John Ray has at last established the values of some of the signs on an objective basis, using Egyptian renderings of Carian names. His work has confirmed some earlier proposals and refuted others. Much remains to be done. (See also "Soldiers to Pharaoh: The Carians of Southwest Anatolia" in Part 5, Vol. II.)

Despite the fragmentary and problematic evidence, we can already affirm that Pisidian, Sidetic, and Carian are Indo-European Anatolian languages, on the strength of one highly characteristic construction: the use of the relational adjective to mark possession cited above for Luwian. The Anatolian languages use two suffixes for this purpose. The more widespread of these had an original shape *-*āsso/ī*- (the asterisk marks a hypothetical, reconstructed form). We thus find in Hieroglyphic Luwian *Halparuntiyas Laramassis nimuwitsas*, "Khalparuntiya, of Larama son," where *Laramassis* shows the suffix in the animate nominative singular, agreeing with the possessed noun *nimuwitsas*, "son," and the son's name, *Halparuntiyas*.

In Lycian, where original *s* becomes *h* between vowels and disappears at the end of a word, the above pattern appears as *Kudali Tsuhriyah tideymi*, "Kudali, of Tsuhri son" (*-ah* < *-*āssos*). Similarly, in Pisidian we find as a tomb inscription *Musita Tas*, "Musita, (son) of Ta." Here, as in Lycian, the original final *-s* of the nominative singular has been lost in both noun and adjective, and the final unaccented vowel of the latter has also been deleted, but the new final *-s* of *Tas* clearly continues the original double *-ss-* of the Anatolian adjectival suffix. The same pattern is repeated in Sidetic, as in *poloniw pordors*, "Apollonius, (son) of Apollodoros," and in Carian, as in *uksmu lkorś*, "Uksmu, (son) of Lkor," where the symbol *ś* indicates that the result of original double *-ss-* is somehow different from ordinary single *s*.

The other suffix used for the relational adjective contained an *-l-*. This is seen in Lydian, as in *es wanas maneliš aluliš*, "This tomb (is) of Mane, (son) of Alu" (the final nominative *-s* becomes *-š* in the last two words because of the preceding *i*). Carian also uses this suffix beside the continuant of *-*āsso/ī*- given above.

DISTINGUISHING FEATURES OF ANATOLIAN

The Anatolian languages (omitting Phrygian) share a number of innovative features that distinguish them from other subgroups of Indo-European languages. Some of these, particularly those involving the system of sounds or the syntax, are too complex to be discussed here. I merely cite four brief examples.

First, the word for "me" has a *u*-vowel in the second syllable, apparently under the influence of the word for "thou/thee": Hittite *ammug*, Palaic suffixed *-mu*, Hieroglyphic Luwian *(a)mu*, Lycian, and Lydian *amu* after the model of Hittite *tug*, Palaíc *tū*, and Hieroglyphic Luwian *tu-u* "thee."

Second, the Common Anatolian word for the demonstrative "that" is *obó*-, appearing as Hittite, Palaic, and Cuneiform Luwian *aba*-, Hieroglyphic Luwian *(a)ba*- Lycian *ebe*-, Lydian *pi*-, and perhaps Carian *ubi*-. In the last three languages, the meaning has shifted to "this."

Third, in Proto-Indo-European, "giving" and "taking" were viewed as parts of a single reciprocal act, one word for which was a verb *ay*-. In Anatolian, as elsewhere, societal changes brought a breakdown in the notion of reciprocity, and "give" and "take" became opposing ideas. The new Anatolian word for "give" as opposed to "take" was formed by adding an adverb *pe*, "away," to *ay*-. This is reflected in Hittite *pe/pi*-, Hieroglyphic Luwian *piya*-, Lycian *piye*-, Lydian *pi(d)*-, and indirectly in the Carian name *par-pyém*-.

Note that the first two examples are pronouns, where borrowing is unlikely, while the third involves a very specific shift in meaning combined with a particular formal device. All these cases thus surely reflect innovations of the Common Anatolian period.

Finally, Andrew Garrett has shown that the Anatolian languages develop "split ergativity," a feature of syntax by which grammatically inanimate nouns enter into quite a different system of relations with verbs than animate nouns do: for example, they must be marked with a distinctive inflectional ending when they function as agents (as in "The water washes the roof").

Developments since the 1960s, including the discovery of crucial multilingual texts, have only recently brought our understanding of the Anatolian languages other than Hittite to the point where we can begin serious comparative study of this subgroup. Further investigation will surely reveal much more about their structure and relationship to each other as well as to the rest of Indo-European and to neighboring unrelated languages.

BIBLIOGRAPHY

Cuneiform and Hieroglyphic Languages

ONOFRIO CARRUBA, *Das Palaische* (1970); ANNALIES KAMMENHUBER, "Hethitisch, Palaisch, Luwisch und Hieroglyphenluwisch," in *Handbuch der Orientalistik*, vol. 1, pt. 2, edited by B. SPULER (1969); EMMANUEL LAROCHE, *Dictionnaire de la langue louvite* (1959); MASSIMILIANO MARAZZI, *Il geroglifico anatolico* (1990).

Alphabetic Languages

CLAUDE BRIXHE, "La Langue des inscriptions épichoriques de Pisidie," in *A Linguistic Happening in Memory of Ben Schwarz*, edited by YOËL ARBEITMAN (1988); ROBERTO GUSMANI, *Lydisches Wörterbuch* (1964); ALFRED HEUBECK, "Lydisch," and GÜNTER NEUMANN, "Lykisch," both in *Handbuch der Orientalistik*, vol. 1, pt. 2, edited by B. SPULER (1969); GÜNTER NEUMANN, *Phrygisch und Griechisch*, Sitzungsberichte der Österreichische Akademie der Wissenschaften, phil. hist. Klasse 499 (1988), and "Die sidetische Schrift," *Annali della Scuola Normale Superiore di Pisa*, ser. 3, vol. 8, no. 3 (1978); JOHN RAY, "An Approach to the Carian Script," *Kadmos* 20 (1981):150–162; and "An Outline of Carian Grammar," *Kadmos* 29 (1990): 54–88.

Anatolian in General

ANDREW GARRETT, "The Origin of NP Split Ergativity," *Language* 66 (1990); NORBERT OETTINGER, "Bemerkungen zur anatolischen *i*-Motion und Genusfrage," *Zeitschrift für vergleichende Sprachforschung* 100 (1987); CALVERT WATKINS, "The Language of the Trojans," in *Troy and the Trojan War*, edited by MACHTELD MELLINK (1986).

SEE ALSO **The Decipherment of Ancient Near Eastern Scripts** (Part 1, Vol. I); **Less-Understood Languages of Ancient Western Asia** (Part 9, Vol. IV); and **Resurrecting the Hittites** (Part 11, Vol. IV).

Less-Understood Languages of Ancient Western Asia

GENE B. GRAGG

FROM THE EARLIEST recorded periods, the Mesopotamians were aware of the ethnic and linguistic diversity that existed to the east. A bilingual inscription of Hammurabi talks of "the man of Elam, Gutium, Subar, and Tukrish, whose land is far and whose tongue is confused." Mesopotamians contacted, invaded, and were invaded by peoples living east of the Tigris River and up into the Zagros. Moreover they seem to have had a realization, if somewhat less precise, of a world that stretched down the Persian Gulf and over the Iranian Plateau to the limits of Afghanistan and the Indus Valley. Later, during the second and first millennia BCE, Assyrian and Hittite contact with the northern Zagros Mountains, the Taurus Mountains, eastern Anatolia, and the edges of Transcaucasia revealed a plethora of new peoples. (This territory is plotted in the maps in the chapters on King Khattushili III and on the Lycian Kingdom in Part 5, Vol. II.)

Although many dozens of geographic, ethnic, and possibly linguistic designations can be identified, there are immense differences in how much we know about these groups and in the certainty with which we can associate them into wider linguistic subgroups. Roughly speaking, the groups can be divided into three categories: written languages, nearer neighbors, and distant lands.

Written Languages

Written languages include four special cases in which "other" speech communities not only contributed to the ongoing elaboration of some aspect of ancient Near East civilization but, initiating or adopting a writing tradition, left direct traces of their language with their written records. These are Elamite in Khuzestan, from the third to the first millennium; Hurrian east of the Tigris from the Diyala north and through the Tur-Abdin–Khabur area to Cilicia, from the late third to the late second millennium; Urartian on the upper Euphrates and around Lakes Van, Urmia, and Sevan, in the first half of the first millennium; and Hattic, whose speakers once occupied what became the core of the Hittite Empire, attested, after they were replaced by Hittites, in texts from the second half of the second millennium. These are the only cases where texts give us the possibility of making any detailed statement about the language, and the bulk of this chapter will deal with them.

Nearer Neighbors

Known only by rulers' names or a limited number of glosses, but apparently representing distinct groups, are several ethnic groups in Luristan: the Kassites, the Guti, and the Lullubi. The

Kassites, who occupied Babylonia in the middle of the second millennium, are known from a long series of royal names and a few glosses. The language of the Guti, who occupied parts of southern Mesopotamia between the Old Akkadian period and the Third Dynasty of Ur period (about 2100) is attested only in a much smaller inventory of royal and personal names. The Lullubi, more southeast of Lake Urmia, are known for all practical purposes by name only; the only inscription by a self-identified ruler of the Lullubi is in Akkadian, and the ruler bears an Akkadian name. The *bi* element of the name may be related to the normal plural suffix of Elamite (see below), and *lul(l)u* may simply mean "foreigner," as it does in fact in Urartian.

Subar (Subir, Subartu) is definitely a generic term for foreign peoples living to the east of the Tigris, north of the Lullubi. It is clearly used to designate Hurrians in the second millennium and describes glosses and texts that seem to represent Hurrian or some dialect of Hurrian. Later, it is used to describe Assyrians and groups whose language was probably Aramaic. It is of course possible that the name Subar was used also to designate the predecessors or non-Semitic competitors of the Hurrians in the area, for the term is attached to certain uninterpretable texts that cannot be clearly identified as Hurrian or any other known language. Note that onomastic studies in the Subarian area (principally around the city of Nuzi) seem to reveal a group of non-Semitic names that do not seem to be Hurrian either. This possibly pre-Hurrian population has sometimes been referred to as the "Banana people" from the characteristic identical second and third syllables in many of the names.

A final group to be mentioned here is the Kashka—a designation that may have been used for more than one ethnolinguistic entity. The Kashka, whose depredations and invasions are chronicled in the Hittite texts, lived to the north of the Hittites on the Black Sea, at the mouth of the Halys River (Kızıl Irmak), and in territories to the east. Their personal names reveal next to nothing about their wider linguistic classification, although circumstantial evidence would suggest a possible connection with Hattic.

Distant Lands

Known through largely indirect trade relations and preserved in texts of a literary character, as well as in a limited number of economic texts, names like Magan (Oman), Melukkha (Makran, Indus?), Aratta (Afghanistan?), Markhashi (eastern Iran?), and Tukrish (northern Iran?) afford some idea of the Mesopotamian conception of the world to the east and south, but provide no real evidence for linguistic identities.

ELAMITE

As far as we can judge from the available evidence, by the beginning of the third millennium at the latest, an Elamite-speaking population was occupying the river-irrigated lowlands of Khuzestan and, to an undetermined extent, adjacent highlands to the north and east. Elamite cultural influence (attested for the earliest period by a writing system and a system of accounting of Elamite origin and for the latest period by accounting documents drawn up in the Elamite language itself) extended far over the Iranian Plateau, reaching Afghanistan and the thresholds of the Indus. But we have no way of knowing whether the affected populations spoke Elamite or languages in any way related to Elamite. (See also "Susa and Susiana in Second-Millennium Iran" in Part 5, Vol. II.)

Language Divisions

Although it is embodied in a much smaller, less diversified, and less well-understood corpus, the Elamite language is known over a span of time that nearly rivals that of Akkadian—from shortly after the middle of the third millennium until the Achaemenid period (fourth century). This Elamite language corpus can be conveniently divided chronologically and typologically into five fairly distinct groups, with greater or lesser gaps between them, and relatively few attested intermediate or transitional texts.

Proto-Elamite   The Proto-Elamite subcorpus stretches from as early as the middle of the fourth millennium down to around 2200. The designation "Proto" is unfortunate from a linguistic point of view, because it is not meant to convey any reference to an early or reconstructed stage of the Elamite language. Indeed, no direct definitive evidence whatsoever has as yet been discovered in the texts as to the identity of the language(s) underlying the script, and it is only a plausible assumption that the creators of the writing system were speakers of Elamite. The earliest Proto-Elamite texts—attested at Susa (biblical Sushan, modern Shush), at other Khuzestan and Zagros sites, and on the western plateau—contain only numerals and seal impressions and apparently served language-independent administrative and accounting functions. Before the end of the fourth millennium nonnumerical signs, some of which are pictographic, were added, and the use of the system became widespread over the whole Iranian area. In a final stage, around 2200, attested principally at Susa, a more linear version of the script was developed with a greatly reduced sign inventory. This version of the script was used in a relatively small number of what appear to be monumental or votive inscriptions, perhaps associated with contemporary Elamite rulers, although no generally accepted interpretation of these texts has yet been made. Typologically the Proto-Elamite script may be compared to the roughly contemporary archaic (presumably Sumerian) cuneiform, although the two writing systems originated and developed independently of each other. In any case, the Elamite script developed no further than its late-third-millennium linear stage, for at this point, which corresponds to the Old Akkadian period in Mesopotamia, Mesopotamian cuneiform was introduced into Elam; thereafter, Mesopotamian cuneiform became the sole medium of written communication, used principally to write Sumerian or Akkadian, but also on occasion adapted to Elamite.

Old Elamite The earliest Elamite written in cuneiform is Old Elamite. At present, this stage is principally represented by a long (six-column) poorly preserved, and very poorly understood text, the Treaty of Naram-Sin, so designated because of repeated mention of the Old Akkadian ruler's name and a phrase that might allow the interpretation "The enemy of Naram-Sin is my

enemy, the friend of Naram-Sin is my friend." By paleography, as well as by content, the text can be placed in the Old Akkadian period, when cuneiform writing was first introduced to Elam. Out of the mainstream of Elamite is the small group of apparently Elamite incantations that occur on Old Babylonian tablets from Mesopotamia. These tablets (about two dozen of them) constitute a small corpus of extracanonical incantations and contain texts in various combinations of Akkadian, Sumerian, Elamite, Hurrian, and possibly one or more other languages or pseudo-languages.

Middle Elamite The next sure attestation of written Elamite comes only after a hiatus of many centuries. In the thirteenth and twelfth centuries, in a period of national revival, the king Khumban-numena and his successors commemorate an intense building activity with a series of votive inscriptions on various objects—in particular, on hundreds of bricks (see example below). Although there are many individual inscriptions, the form and content of these highly stereotyped texts yield only a tantalizingly limited amount of data on Elamite grammar and vocabulary. Although in some centers (such as Haft Tepe, near Susa), economic and administrative texts from this period continue to be written in Akkadian, the existence of an archive of Elamite administrative texts from the Elamite highland center at Anshan (Tepe Malyan) shows that Elamite had been (re)adopted for this function also. This period of Elamite renaissance apparently came to an end with the anti-Elam campaign of Nebuchadnezzar (Nebuchadrezzar) I around 1100.

Late Elamite Several centuries were to follow before the final blossoming of an independent Elam—a spurt of Late Elamite writing between about 717 and 640, preceding Elam's political eclipse before, successively, the Assyrians, the Medes, and the Persians. This period witnesses the greatest variety of Elamite text genres. In addition to the usual votive inscriptions, there are rock inscriptions, a stela, a large number of economic texts, a small corpus of letters, some contracts, and even two literary texts—one collection of astrological (and perhaps other) omens and the other a fragment of a text, discovered far to the north, in Urartian territory.

Achaemenid Elamite The language of Elam as a satrapy of the Persian Empire enjoyed something of an afterlife in the trilingual and bilingual monumental inscriptions of the Persian rulers. These inscriptions, in which the Elamite is accompanied by an Old Persian and sometimes an Akkadian translation and which are much longer and more varied than the monolingual Middle and Late Elamite votive inscriptions, were what made possible the decipherment of Elamite in the first place. Even today they provide the surest basis of our knowledge of Elamite. There is little in the vocabulary and, to a lesser extent, the grammar of Elamite that we are sure of that does not occur in the royal Achaemenid inscriptions. Finally, important both for the language and for the light they throw on Achaemenid administrative practices are several thousand Elamite economic texts discovered at Persepolis.

The Elamite Language

The Elamite scribes who adopted the cuneiform system for writing their language streamlined the inventory of signs considerably. Only a few logograms were retained, and most of the texts are written with a relatively small number of CV, VC, and V signs (sixty-six for Achaemenid Elamite), plus a few dozen less-frequent CVC signs (C = consonant, V = vowel). Since this writing system was not created to represent Elamite, we have little exact idea how it was pronounced.

The inflectional system of Elamite is based on a relatively small number of verbal and nominal suffixes and clitics. As can be seen in the text sample below, the most salient characteristic of Elamite grammar is the way it builds up (marks out) complex nominal phrases (noun plus modifier, noun plus genitive, noun plus relative clause) by attaching to the modifiers (and optionally to the head noun) pronounlike affixes that agree with the head noun along various dimensions of person and animateness. Table 1 gives these agreement affixes, together with the (active/transitive) verbal subject suffixes for contrast.

As can be seen from Table 1, the agreement suffixes distinguish at least three (and perhaps more) classes of inanimate nouns. The basis for this classification is not clear to us. The agreement suffixes can also be used to derive nouns of a given class from other words; thus, from *sunki(-r)*, "king" (third-person animate), comes *sunki-me*, "kingship" (inanimate), and from *li-*, "give" (verb), comes *li-n*, "gift" (inanimate).

The verb in Elamite has the following simple structure:

$$\text{Base} + \begin{Bmatrix} \text{Subject (=finite)} \\ \begin{Bmatrix} \text{-k- (passive)} \\ \text{-n- (active)} \end{Bmatrix} \quad (=\text{Participle}) \end{Bmatrix} + \text{Modal/Clitic}$$

The base can be simple (*kut-*, "carry") or reduplicated according to the formula $C_1VC_2 > C_1VC_1C_2$ (*kukt-*, "carry much/frequently"). The finite form uses the subject suffixes of Table 1 and is used in past-tense clauses (as *kuši-*, "build"; *kuši-ḫ*, "I built," below); the participial forms correspond to nonpast clauses (as *tela-k-ni*, below) and can also be used as nouns and modifiers (compare *ḫutta-*, "do"; *ḫutta-k*, "work" [noun]; "thing done"). The most frequent of the four or so clitics is the *-ni* marker of the optative (again, *tela-k-ni*).

The Elamite sentence always has the verb at the end. Often after the noun phrases in preverbal position will occur one or more pronouns recapitulating the roles of the noun phrases (and usually in this order: indirect object, subject, direct object). Independent pronouns as direct object may be marked with a suffix *-n;* relations of place, instrumentality, and the like are given by a restricted set of postpositions.

As Elamite developed into the first millennium, perhaps under the influence of Old Persian, it tended to lose its characteristic nominal-agreement and word order–based syntax. New connectives, case markers, and postpositions were developed (for example, a *-na* genitive suffix) as it shifted to a more Indo-European–like verb-oriented syntax.

HURRIAN

The Hurrian language is responsible for the largest, most diversified, and most unevenly understood corpus of texts treated in this chapter. The time range is relatively short, compared

TABLE 1
Elamite Suffixes and Prefixes

		(1) Agreement		(2) Verb Subject	
		Sing.	Plur.	Sing.	Plur.
Animate	1st pers.	=k	=k	-ḫ	-ḫu
	2nd pers.	=t	=t	-t	-ḫt
	3rd pers.	=r	=p	-š	-ḫš
Inanimate		=me			
		=t			
		=n			

[ḫ = kh; š = sh]; plural is not marked for inanimate.

with Elamite—from the late Ur III period to the last centuries of the second millennium (end of the Hittite Empire). The texts come from all over the ancient Near East (Mesopotamia, Syria, Anatolia, Egypt), from everywhere, in fact, but with perhaps a single exception, the core region where Hurrian must have been spoken as an indigenous language. This central area consisted of the Tur-Abdin range, with the upper Tigris to the north and the upper Khabur basin to the south, the region where, in their brief period of political hegemony, the Hurrians must have had their capital, the still-undiscovered Wasshukkani.

Our main evidence for the geographical waxing and waning of the Hurrian-speaking area is not the Hurrian-language texts as such but the presence in texts written in Akkadian, Ugaritic, and Hittite of large numbers of Hurrian proper names and, to a lesser extent, of Hurrian loanwords, phraseology, and references to Hurrian beliefs and institutions. Their presence evidences the existence of a Hurrian political entity in the upper Khabur basin already in the earliest cuneiform documentation concerning that area, the Old Akkadian. Subsequent Ur III and early Old Babylonian evidence shows a spreading of Hurrian down the east of the Tigris and the corresponding flanks of the Zagros, as far as the Diyala, and shortly thereafter a push down the Khabur in the direction of Mari (Tell Hariri) and to the west toward Ugarit (modern Ras Shamra) and Cilicia (Kizzuwatna). Farther north and west, in a vast arc reaching into eastern Anatolia, dozens of terms in later Assyrian and Hittite texts reveal a jigsaw puzzle of small ethnic groups and ephemeral kingdoms. Onomastic and cir-

cumstantial evidence (for example, the fact that most of them exist on territory that from 1500 to 1300 was controlled by the Hurrian-ruled Mitanni Empire) combine to suggest that many, if not most, of these groups were Hurrian. But a definitive collection and assessment of the evidence has yet to be made. After a period of political dominance in the mid second millennium, with a startling rapidity all evidence for a Hurrian presence evaporates in the southern parts of this area (where Aramaean-speaking populations seem to be their successors). First-millennium sources, Assyrian and Urartian, refer to political-geographic-ethnic entities that may be Hurrian in areas of Tur-Abdin and to the north and west, at the sources of the Euphrates (Diawhi?), Tigris (Shupria), Bohtan-Su (Khubushkia), and Zab (the Kardouchoi?). It is possible that an ethnic group in this area known to Herodotus and other classical sources as the Matieni may bear some last onomastic reminiscence (compare Mitanni) of the period of Hurrian power.

Divisions of the Hurrian Corpus

The Hurrian corpus itself can be conveniently divided into six bodies of evidence.

Old Hurrian   A single, short (twenty-five lines) monumental inscription (a foundation deposit) of Tish-atal, the Hurrian ruler of Urkish (upper Khabur), dates perhaps toward, or shortly after, the end of the Third Dynasty of Ur.

Old Babylonian Period   The evidence from the Old Babylonian period is a poorly under-

Elamite Text Sample

Many points about the Elamite language can be exemplified by a simple text. The following inscription of Untash-Naprisha (circa 1275–1240), on a baked brick, from M.-J. Stève, *Tchoga-Zanbil (Dur-Untash)*, vol. 3, *Mémoires de la délégation archéologique en Iran*, text 41 (1967), is typical of the Middle Elamite royal inscriptions. The meaning is fairly clear, although experts might differ in details of grammatical analysis. To show how the extensive concord system works, in the interlinear analysis a line is drawn from the agreement suffixes (-*k*- first person; -*r*- third-person inanimate singular; -*p*- third-person plural; -*me*-/-*n*- third-person inanimate singular) to the underlined governing noun (the subscript "agr" highlights this agreement). The problematic vocalic suffixes, some of which may function as connectives and complementizers, while others may be merely graphic, are left glossed simply as "+V." Parts of compound words are separated by "=" (as in *mur=ta*, "place," from *mur*, "earth," and *ta*, "set").

Transliteration

1. *ú* ᵐ*Un-taš*-DINGIR.GAL *ša-ak* ᵐᵈ*Ḫu-ban-nu-me-na-ki su-un-ki-ik*

2. *An-za-an Šu-šu-un-ka si-ia-an* ᵈ*Na-bu-me ú-pa-at ḫu-us-*

3. *si-ip-me ku-ši-iḫ* ᵈ*Na-bu-ú la-an-si-ti-ra ir a-ḫa-ar*

4. *mu-ur-taḫ ḫu-ut-tak ḫa-li-ik ú-me* ᵈ*Na-bu-ú*

5. *si-ia-an ku-uk-ra ul-li-na te-la-ak-ni*

Transcription and Interlinear Analysis

<u>u</u> *Untaš-Napriša šak Ḫumban* = *numena* + *k*(+ *i*) *sunki* + *k Ancan Šušun* + *k* + *a*

I Untash-Naprisha son Khumban = numena + 1$_{agr}$ (+V) king + 1$_{agr}$ Anshan Susa + 1$_{agr}$ +V

<u>siyan</u> *Nabu* + *me* <u>upat</u> *ḫussi* + *p* + *me kuši* + *ḫ*

temple Nabu + 3in$_{agr}$ brick baked + 3pl$_{agr}$ + 3in$_{agr}$ build + 1$_{subj}$

<u>Nabu</u> *lan-siti* + *r* + *a* <u>ir</u> *aḫa* + *r mur* = *ta* + *ḫ*

Nabu golden + 3an$_{agr}$ +V him there + 3an$_{agr}$ place + I$_{subj}$

ḫutta+k ḫali+k u+me

make+Pass labor+Pass I+3in$_{agr}$

Nabu siyan=kuk+r+a u+li+n+a tela+k+ni

Nabu acropolis+3an$_{agr}$+V I+give+3in$_{agr}$("for")+V set+Pass+Optative

Translation

I, Untash-Naprisha, son of Khumban-numena, king of Anshan and Susa,
built a temple of Nabu of baked brick.
I placed there a golden Nabu(-statue).
What I made and elaborated ("my made and elaborated [thing]")
for Nabu of the Acropolis by me for him ("as a gift") may it be dedicated.

---

stood mix of incantations in the Babylonian collection cited above for Old Elamite, plus seven texts from Mari—six magical religious texts similar to the Babylonian and one fragment of a royal letter.

Mitanni   A single long letter (more than 490 lines), written in Hurrian from the Mitanni ruler Tushratta to the Egyptian pharaoh Amenhotep (Amenophis) III, was discovered in an archive of cuneiform diplomatic correspondence in Amarna (ancient Akhetaten) in Egypt. (The rest of the correspondence—about a dozen letters—between Tushratta and the rulers of Egypt, preserved in the same archive, was carried on in Akkadian.) This impressive tablet (physically the largest single cuneiform tablet in existence), with its carefully worked-out and consistently applied orthography, leads us to suppose the existence in Wasshukkani of a highly professional chancellery accustomed to writing in Hurrian—but no other sure instances of Hurrian texts produced by it have survived. Apart from the Old Hurrian monumental inscription, this is the best-understood (one might even say the only relatively well understood) text in the corpus. Since the Akkadian letters in the archive provide "virtual bilinguals," great progress had been made in interpreting the text by the early years of the twentieth century. The first complete grammar of Hurrian (that of E. A. Speiser) is almost entirely based on the tablet, and even today our understanding of Hurrian is largely limited to forms, phrases, and constructions with close parallels in the Mitanni letter. (For a discussion of "bilinguals," see the chapter "The Decipherment of Ancient Near Eastern Scripts" in Part 1, Vol. I.)

Ugarit   Hurrian dominance in Syria is confirmed by the highly varied corpus of Hurrian texts discovered in the various campaigns in Ras Shamra. The corpus includes, in cuneiform, several bilingual and quadrilingual (Akkadian, Sumerian, Hurrian, Ugaritic) vocabularies, a bilingual collection of sayings in Akkadian and Hurrian, a fragment of a letter, and a small corpus of texts with musical annotation, unique in the ancient Near East. Ras Shamra also yielded a number of Hurrian texts (perhaps offering lists) written in the alphabetic script developed for Ugaritic.

Boğazköy   Because of their predominance in northern Syria, the Hurrians exercised a great religious and intellectual influence on the Hittites. It is even possible that they played a role in spreading the cuneiform writing system into Anatolia, where it was adapted to the writing of Hittite. Many Hittite rituals and ceremonies (especially those originating in Kizzuwatna/Cilicia) seem to have been modeled on Hurrian prototypes, and the Hittite archives at Khattusha (modern Boğazköy) contain many tablets and passages in Hurrian (frequently noted *ḫurlili*, "in the Hurrian language," in the texts where they appear in a Hittite context; compare below for Hattic). The Hurrian texts cover virtually all genres represented in Hittite religious literature: myths (including the *Epic of Gilgamesh*), legends, divination, rituals, and incantations. In spite of the fact that Hittite parallels, and more-or-less helpful translations, exist for many of the Hurrian passages, these texts remain very difficult to interpret and are much less understandable than the Mitanni letter.

Excavations in 1983–1985 added to the Boğazköy corpus some genuine Hurrian-Hittite bilingual texts, some of which, moreover, seem to represent a stage of Hurrian somewhat anterior to that of the Mitanni letter (see the box in "The Kingdom of Mitanni in Second-Millennium Upper Mesopotamia" in Part 5, Vol. II). It may be hoped that these texts will provide the entry point we have been missing into this hitherto intractable part of the Hurrian corpus. In order to make the Boğazköy Hurrian texts (by far the largest single constituent of the total Hurrian corpus) more accessible, a major project, the *Corpus Hurritischer Schriftdenkmäler* (Corpus of Hurrian Inscriptions) in Berlin is currently preparing reliable editions of this material; ultimately the Corpus will be extended to all Hurrian texts.

Emar   Excavations carried on at Emar (modern Meskene, on the Euphrates at about the latitude of Ugarit) since 1972 have yielded a small corpus, as yet unpublished, of Hurrian texts of varied content—reportedly lexical, medical, and omen texts.

The Hurrian Language

From all available evidence, the Hurrian sound system differed considerably from the systems of Sumerian, for which the cuneiform syllabary had been developed, and Akkadian, to which the syllabary had been adapted already at some point before scribes undertook to write Hurrian in cuneiform. We can still make only a tentative reconstruction of the Hurrian phoneme inventory (I point out here only the presence of a /f/ and a /ž/, the latter as voiced correspondent to /š/). In its most consistent orthographic representation, that of the Mitanni chancellery, a system of single and double writing of consonants seems to replace the use of the voiced (/b d g/) versus the unvoiced (/p t k/) consonants of Akkad-

ian—a system that is also used, with some variation, in Elamite and Hittite (and perhaps also Hattic).

The morphology of Hurrian involves complex chains of suffixes and enclitics, as can be appreciated by a simple inspection of the sample analyzed text given below. Any word, noun or verb, can be followed by an agreement constituent, an enclitic pronoun, and/or an enclitic conjunction. The enclitic pronoun is usually the absolutive noun that goes with the verb, namely, the subject of an intransitive verb or the object of a transitive verb; compare in the text below the many examples of -*lla*-, the third-person plural absolutive, glossed 3pl$_{enc}$, and -*(n)n(a)*, the third person singular absolutive, glossed 3sg$_{enc}$. The commonest enclitic conjunctions exemplified below are -*man*, -*nin*, -*an*, -*n*.

The nominal and verbal words themselves are too complex to be discussed in detail. But a general formula with numbered positions—o for the root, 1 for the first suffix, 2 for the second, and so on—can give an idea of what kind of morphological categories are involved. The formula for the noun is as follows:

o: *ROOT* + 1: *derivational suffix* + 2: *possessive* + 3: *article* + 4: *plural* + 5: *case* + 6: *agreement*.

Among the nominal categories exemplified below are derivational suffix (-*ithi*-), possessive (-*iff*, "my"), article (-*ne* singular, -*na* plural). For case we can establish the following partial paradigm:

Absolutive	-∅
Ergative	-*(u)š*
Genitive	-*we*
Dative	-*wa*
Directive	-*t/da*
Directive/Ablative	-*t/da-n*
Locative	-*(y)a*

The even more complex formula for the verb is this:

o: *Root* + 1: *derivational*$_1$ + 2: *tense* + 3: *derivational*$_2$ + 4: *plural* + 5: *transitivity* + 6: *negative*$_1$ + 7: *modal* / 8: *ergative* / 9: *impersonal* + 10: *negative*$_2$ + 11: *relative (plural)*.

Of these, notice below the tense markers (-*oz* past, -*ed*- future), the negative$_1$ (-*wa*-), the ergative (-*af* first person, -(*y*)*a* third person), the impersonal (-*a*), and the relative (-*šše*).

Word order is fairly fluid in Hurrian. However, enclitic pronouns and conjunctions tend to occur most frequently after the first word in the sentence. The relational structure of Hurrian is clearly ergative. In fact, with its clear marking of the ergative case (for the subject of transitive verbs) versus the absolutive case (for the subject of intransitive verbs and the object of transitive verbs) on both the noun and the verb, and clear marking distinctions for transitivity versus intransitivity on the verb, it could almost be taken as the type language for the category "ergative."

Hurrian Text Sample

The following is the text of a typical paragraph of the Mitanni letter, marked off as such in the letter itself (*Vorderasiatische Schriftdenkmäler*, vol. 12, text 200, col. 4, lines 30–39 [1915]). The letter is generally concerned with the marriage of Tushratta's daughter Tadu-Khepa to the pharaoh Amenhotep III and with what Tushratta can expect in re-

turn, both in strengthened diplomatic relations and in gifts. In the section given here, Tushratta is reminding Amenhotep, once more, of all that Tushratta has done for him, and he names the Egyptian and Mitannian envoys accompanying the letter (and perhaps Tadu-Khepa herself). The interpretation follows that of Gernot Wilhelm.

Transliteration

30. *un-du-ma-a-an i-i-al-li-e-ni-i-in ti-we-e-na*^MEŠ *šu-ú-al-la-ma-an*

31. *še-e-ni-iw-wu-uš ka-du-u-ša-a-aš-še-na ú-ú-ri-a-a-aš-še-na an-til-la-a-an*

32. *e-e-ma-na-a-am-ḫa ta-a-nu-ša-a-ú ti-ša-a-ma-a-an še-e-ni-iw-wu-ú-e šuk-kán-ni-en*

33. *pa-ti ti-we-e-ni-en ḫi-su-ú-ḫu-ši-uw-wi aš-ti-i-in še-e-ni-iw-wu-ú-e*

34. *a-ru-u-ša-ú še-e-ni-iw-wu-ú-e-ni-e-en ti-ša-a-an-na ši-ra-aš-še*

35. *un-du-u-un* ᴵ*Ma-ni-e-na-an še-e-ni-iw-wu-ú-e pa-aš-ši-i-it-ḫi un-du-u-un*

36. ᴵ*Gi-li-ya-na-an* ᴵ*Ar-te-eš-šu-pa-na-an* ᴵ*A-sa-a-li-in-na-a-an pa-aš-ši-i-it-ḫi-iw-wi*

37. ᴵ*Gi-li-ya-na-an ta-la-mi* ᴵ*A-sa-a-li-in-na-a-an tup-šar-ri-iw-wu-ú-un-ni*

38. *ki-i-pu-šu-ú-uš-ši še-e-ni-iw-wi-ta-al-la-a-an ni-i-ru-ša-e tiš-ša-an*

39. *pa-aš-šu-ša-a-ú še-e-ni-iw-wu-ú-ul-la-a-an wu-ri-e-e-ta*

Continued on the next page.

Continued from the previous page.

Transcription and Interlinear Analysis

30. *undu+màn ya+lle+ nin*   *tiwe+na*   *šua+lla+man*
thus+but whatever+3pl$_{enc}$+indeed   thing/word+pl   all+3pl$_{enc}$+but

31. *šen+iff+uš*   *kad+ož+a+šše+na*   *wur+ia+šše+na*   *andi+lla+àn*
brother+my+erg   ask+past+3sg$_{erg}$+rel+p   desire+3sg$_{erg}$+rel+pl   this+3pl$_{enc}$+and

32. *eman+am+ḫa*   *tan+ož+af*   *tiža+màn*   *šen+iff+we*   *šukk+ane+n*
ten+cause+adj   do+past+1sg$_{erg}$ heart+but   brother+my+of   far+deriv+by

33. *padi*   *tiwe+ne+n*   *ḫisuḫ+ož+iuwwi (<ewa+af)*   *ašti+n*   *šen+iff+we*
up-to(?)   word+art+by   annoy+past+not+1sg$_{erg}$ wife+3sg$_{enc}$ brother+my+of

34. *ar+ož+af*   *šen+iff+we+ne+n*   *tiza+n(n)+a*   *šir+a+šše*
give+past+1sg$_{erg}$ brother+my+of+art+3sg$_{enc}$ heart+n+obl   pleasing+impersonal+rel

35. *undu+n*   *Mane+n+an*   *šen+iff+we*   *pašš+ithi*   *undu + n*
now+3sg$_{enc}$ Mane+3sg$_{enc}$+and   brother+my+of   send+nom   now+3sg$_{enc}$

36. *Kelia+n+an*   *Ar-Teššuba+n+an*   *Asali+n(n)+an*   *pašš+ithi+iff*
Kelia+3sg$_{enc}$+and   Ar-Tesshub+3sg$_{enc}$+and   Asali+3sg$_{enc}$+and   send+nom+my

37. *Kelia+n+an*   *talami*   *Asali+n(n)+an*   *tupšarri+iff+n(n)i*
Kelia+3sg$_{enc}$+and   great   Asali+3sg$_{enc}$+and   scribe+my+N

38. *kib+ož+ušši*   *šen+iff+da+lla+àn*   *nir+ož+ae*   *tiššan*
set+past+???   brother+my+direct+3pl$_{enc}$+and   great+derv+adv   very

39. *pašš+ož+af*   *šen+iff+uš+lla+àn*   *wer+ed+a*
send+past+1sg$_{enc}$ brother+my+erg+3pl$_{enc}$+and   see+fut+3sg$_{erg}$

Translation

And now anything whatsoever
that my brother has asked for and desired
this I have done tenfold.
Furthermore my brother's heart even by a (single) word
I have not annoyed.
I have given my brother's wife,
pleasing to my brother's heart.
Now Mane, my brother's envoy,
and also Keliya, Ar-Tesshub, and Asali, my envoys
(Keliya as Great [-chief?], Asal as my scribe . . .),
I have sent to my brother in a grand manner.
And my brother will see them.

URARTIAN

Almost as soon as Hurrian and Urartian were identified, such lexical equations as Hurrian *šala* = Urartian *sila*, "daughter"; Hur. *pab-* = Ur. *bab-*, "mountain"; and Hur. = Ur. *ar-*, "give"; Hur. = Ur. *tan-*, "do," made it abundantly evident that the two languages were related. (Note also the morphological resemblances adduced below.) Moreover, the more we discover or deduce about the earliest stages of Hurrian, the more it looks like Urartian. To this extent, it has been estimated that Hurrian and Urartian could have been slightly divergent dialects as recently as the third millennium, only a few centuries before the first indirect attestations of the presence of Hurrian speakers to the north and east of the Old Akkadians.

The Urartians (as they are known to the Assyrians and the outside world; compare "Ararat," a related form of the word mentioned in Genesis 8:4 as a country with a mountain upon which landed Noah's ark) appear in the historical record in a region and a historical epoch quite different from that of the Hurrians. (See "The Kingdom of Urartu in Eastern Anatolia" in Part 5, Vol. II.) They begin to be noticed in inscriptions of the Assyrian kings from around the thirteenth century and then produce monumental inscriptions of their own shortly after the middle of the ninth century; by the end of the seventh century, they are no longer heard from. They are located in the region of Lake Van (a word derived from their own name for their country, Biayne-le) and in adjacent regions of the upper Euphrates and its sources to the west and Lake Urmia to the south and southeast. From the northwest to the south of them are located the putative remnants of the post-Mitanni Hurrians. It had once even been proposed that the Urartians themselves represented a Hurrian remnant that had been pushed back into the Taurus-Zagros hinterlands. The identification of a pattern of early linguistic resemblance and subsequent differentiation, however, has made this scenario extremely unlikely. In fact, the Van–Urmia–upper Euphrates area occupied by Urartians and Hurrian remnants in the early first millennium may well represent the homeland of Proto-Hurrian-Urartian, from which the early Hurrians may have begun to expand toward the Mesopotamian and Syrian plain in the third millennium.

Toward the end of their recorded history, before falling under the domination of the Medes and then the Persians, the Urartians were probably being encroached on by Armenian-speaking peoples. By the time documentation resumes under the Achaemenids, what used to be Urartu had become the Persian satrapy of Armina. It is possible that the tribe of the Alarodioi, reported in the area by Herodotus, continued the name of the Urartians.

The corpus of Urartian shows by the distribution of its texts that it is clearly different from a typical second-millennium "cuneiform culture" that we have seen exemplified, however unevenly, by Elamite, Hurrian, Hittite, and the various peripheral Akkadian "literatures." The cuneiform writing system seems to have been imported into Urartu for one principal purpose—to make monumental inscriptions on stone and, to a lesser extent, dedicatory inscriptions on various other kinds of objects. It was used extensively for this purpose, and nine rulers left more than five hundred monumental and dedicatory inscriptions. The earliest inscriptions, three identical inscriptions of Sarduri I, were in Akkadian, but all the rest are in Urartian, including two bilingual Urartian-Akkadian of Ishpuini and Rusa I set up on the border of Urartu and Assyria. It was not rare for inscriptions to commemorate military campaigns, and two rulers (Argishti I and Sarduri II) combined successive campaigns into lengthy annalistic inscriptions carved into the face of the cliff that dominates Lake Van at the site of the Urartian capital.

Other uses of writing were quite limited. Cuneiform signs are found on a large number of storage vessels, where they are used to indicate capacity. Mysteriously, storage areas in excavated sites have yielded hundreds of sealed clay bullae, almost without exception uninscribed; the bullae might have been used to attach to storage facilities accounts of contents, purpose, and provenance written on perishable materials. Apart from this, there are only a couple dozen clay tablets inscribed with cuneiform; almost all of them seem to be letters, plus a few ad hoc administrative documents. Still something of an enigma is the use of a system of hieroglyphic signs, both the familiar Neo-Hittite and a still-undeciphered Urartian system apparently inspired by, but distinct from, the Neo-Hittite. The inscriptions are all very short and, in many cases, seem to be capacity markings.

The Urartian Language

Like Hurrian, Urartian almost certainly had a rich inventory of consonant and vowel phonemes that could not be expressed directly in the cuneiform writing system. Unlike Hurrian and Elamite, Urartian made systematic use not only of the voiced (/b d g/) and voiceless (/p t k/) but also of the "emphatic" consonant signs (/ṣ ṭ q/) current in cuneiform. Like the other adaptations of cuneiform, it pared down the inventory of signs and eliminated most of the "homophony" and "polyphony" in the Akkadian syllabary, but still kept an active inventory of eighty-four CV and VC signs, nineteen CVC signs, fifteen determinatives, and a relatively large number of logograms. It seems most likely that it borrowed the cuneiform system directly from the Assyrians, and not by way of the Hurrians. By comparing Urartian writing with cognates in Hurrian and loanwords in Assyrian, Armenian, and other languages, Igor Diakonoff has been able to bring to light a number of details of Urartian phonology. In what follows, however, we will stick to a rather literal rendering of the Assyrian values of the signs.

The structural outline of the Urartian noun and verb is very close to that of Hurrian. One of the main differences between the two is the way formatives that are kept distinct in Hurrian tend to reduce and coalesce in Urartian. The general outline for the noun is sketched:

$$\text{Root} + \begin{Bmatrix} \text{Definite } (\text{-}ni\text{-}) \\ \text{Possessive} \end{Bmatrix} + \text{Plural} + \text{Case}$$

The distinction between "definite" and "nondefinite" (with and without -*ni*-) is very important in Urartian. We do not possess complete paradigms for many combinations of possessive, plural, and case. But the basic singular paradigm for the most important cases in the singular is as follows:

Absolute	-∅
Ergative	-*še*
Genitive	-*(e)y*
Dative	-*(y)e*
Directive	-*di*
Ablative	-*ni*
Locative	-*a*

The resemblance with Hurrian can be readily seen. There are in addition a number of derivational suffixes in the nominal system. Those that occur in the text below are -*ae*, -*ḫi* (adjectival); -*ši* (abstract); and -*usi*, -*ari* (function uncertain).

The general formula for the verb is basically that of Hurrian for the first eight positions, making allowance for some reductions. An innovation in Urartian for ergative/absolute marking, however, comes in the fact that it has one set of endings for absolute subject marking (that is, when the absolute is subject of the verb and there is no object, first column in Table 2) and

TABLE 2
Hurrian Suffixes

Subject	Object		
	zero	3rd sing.	3rd plur.
1st sing.	-*di*	-*bi*(=*ve*?)	-*ú-li*(=*ve-le*?)
3rd sing.	-*bi*	-*ni*	-*a-li*
3rd plur.	-*li*	-*itu-ni*	-*itu-li*

a slightly different one for combined marking of ergative-subject plus absolutive-object (second and third columns). Table 2 shows the combinations of first-person singular, third-person singular, and third-person plural subject with zero-object (that is, intransitive) and third-singular and third-person plural objects. Here it can be seen that -*li* is used consistently for the third-person plural absolutive and -*itu* for the third-person plural ergative. The first-person ergative seems to be -*ve* (recall Hurrian -*af*). However, the third-person singular ergative seems to change between -∅ and -*a*, while the third-person singular absolutive can be -*ni* (twice), -∅, or -*bi*. The fact that *manu*, "(it) was," does not conform to this generally valid paradigm is some indication of the complexity of the system. Finally, there is a participle in -*uri* that apparently occurs in both transitive and intransitive senses.

Syntactically, as we have seen, Urartian seems to be almost as markedly ergative in character as Hurrian, even if this works itself out in a slightly different fashion. A major difference from Hurrian is the absence of the long chains of enclitics so characteristic of Hurrian. (There is one particle, however, -*me*, "to me," not illustrated below, that behaves like the Hurrian enclitics.) Finally, in word order, Urartian is somewhat less free than Hurrian, tending toward a subject-object-verb order for transitives and a verb subject order for intransitives.

HATTIC

When Hittite was first identified, it was given a name based on the Hebrew and Egyptian designations for the inhabitants of northern Syria and

Urartian Text Sample

The following text (from *Handbuch der chaldischen Inschriften*, vol. 8, pl. 70, no. 90 [1967]) is typical of the short inscriptions commemorating canal construction. It comes from Kara Kalʿah, about twenty-one kilometers (about thirteen miles) west of Armavir in Armenia, at the head of a canal leading from the Araks River (ancient Araxes) to Armavir.

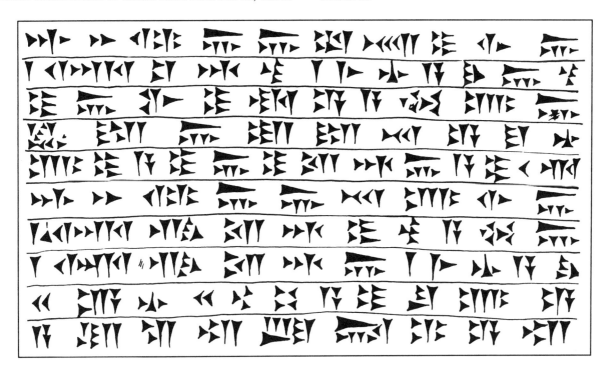

Transliteration

^{d}ḫal-di-ni-ni al-su-i-ši-ni

^{I}ar-giš-ti-še ^{I}me-nu-a-ḫi-ni-še

i-ni pi-i-li-e a-gu-ú-ni

qi-ra-ni și-ra-ba-e ma-nu

ú-i a-i-ni-i iš-ti-ni a-i-u-ri

^{d}ḫal-di-ni-ni ba-ú-ši-ni

^{I}ar-gi-iš-ti-i-še a-gu-ni

^{I}ar-gi-iš-ti-ni ^{I}me-nu-a-ḫi

LUGAL$_2$ *dan-nu* LUGAL$_2$ ^{kur}bi-a-i-na-ú-e

a-lu-si ^{uru}tu-uš-pa-e URU

Transcription and Interlinear Analysis

Ḫaldi+ni+ni   alsui+še+ni
Khaldi+definite+ablative   great+abstract+ablative

Argišti+še   Menua+ḫi+ni+še
Argishti+ergative   Menua+adj+definite+ergative

Continued on the next page.

Continued from the previous page.

ini   pili   ag+u+ni
this canal lead+transitive+3sg$_{sub}$3sg$_{obj}$

qira+ni   şira+b+ae   man+u
land+definite unused(?)+?+adj be+intransitive

ui   aini   ištini ag(>y)+uri
not anything there   lead+participle
Ḫaldi+ni+ni   bau(+?)še+ni
Khaldi+definite+ablative word(+abstract?)+ablative

Argišti+še   ag+u+ni
Argishti+ergative lead+transitive+3sg$_{sub}$3sg$_{obj}$

Argišti+ni   Menua+ḫi
Argishti+definite Menua+adj

erili tar+ae   erili Biaini+awe
king strong+adj king Biaini+genitive$_{pl}$

al+usi   Tušpa+ie   pat+ari
ruler+deriv Tushpa+genitive$_{sg}$ city+deriv

Translation

By the might of (the god) Khaldi
Argishti, son of Menua ("the one Menua's"),
built this canal.
The land was uninhabited.
No one was building ("leading") anything there (or "nothing was built").
By the word of Khaldi
Argishti built it.
Argishti, son of Menua, (is)
the mighty king, king of the Biaini country,
ruler of the city Tushpa.

eastern Anatolia. The Hittites themselves referred to their language with the term *nešili/našili,* "(in) the language of Nesha [Kanesh]." It was soon discovered that among the Hittite archives were texts and passages in a completely unrelated language that the Hittites themselves referred to with the term *ḫattili.* These passages frequently occurred in Hittite rituals, where they were often introduced by formulas such as "And the (singer/priest/etc.) says these words in the *ḫatti*-language," obviously referring to the language spoken by the inhabitants of the city Khattusha who lived there before the "Hittites" took it over and made it their capital. As with Hurrian, the Hittites evidently felt that certain

gods and religious practices were most effectively dealt with in a language already sanctioned by tradition.

The exact boundaries of Hattic have still to be fixed, but a Hattic-speaking population was clearly the principal pre-Hittite ethnic group in the area bounded by the bend of the Halys River (modern Kızıl Irmak) and dominated by the city Khattusha. In addition to ritual and mythological texts, and presumably the rites and beliefs underlying the texts, the Hattic peoples contributed a number of loanwords to Hittite. Farther to the east, personal names in the Old Assyrian texts from Kanesh (modern Kültepe) show an important Hattic population there in the period just before the rise of the Hittites; the Palaic language, an Anatolian Indo-European language closely related to Hittite and probably to be located to the north or northwest of the Hittites, reveals there also, by a set of Hattic loanwords independent of those in Hittite, the existence of an indigenous substrate Hattic population. By contrast, precisely the absence of such a set of loanwords in Luwian, another Indo-European cousin of Hittite to the south of the Halys, seems to limit the primitive distribution of Hattic to north-central and northeastern Anatolia.

Of the four isolated ancient near eastern languages represented by a corpus of texts, Hattic is by far the least well understood. This is in spite of the fact that the corpus is fairly extensive (more than one hundred and fifty published tablets and tablet fragments), and that a large proportion of the texts are accompanied by Hittite translations. But the corpus consists entirely of prayers, incantations, rituals, and myths—precisely the kinds of poetic, elliptic, idiosyncratic material that is so difficult to interpret when it occurs even in the better-understood language corpora of Elamite, Hurrian, and Urartian. Moreover, the translations themselves pose many problems, and there are indications that later generations of Hittite scribes had difficulties with these texts (some colophons comment on the poor state of the text) and with their translation into a language as different from Hattic as Hittite was.

The Hattic Language

In spite of the general obscurity of these texts, it is possible to distill from them a general idea of what the language was like. The following sketch is largely based on the work of C. Girbal, although a more complete presentation would have to take into account important differences in the view of Hattic presented by other authors cited in the bibliography.

Some suffixation occurs in the noun: feminine nouns can be marked by -*ḫ*, -*i*/*at* (*katte*, "king"; *kattaḫ*, "queen"; *uril katte*, "mighty king"; *uriet kattaḫ*, "mighty queen"). There are also three caselike suffixes on the noun: -*n* (genitive, general oblique marker—used after prepositions), -*tu* (another oblique marker), and -*šu* (perhaps

direct or indirect object, not obligatory). But unlike the other three languages considered here, the lion's share of nominal morphology is handled by prefixes. Table 3 gives a list of the prefixes that have been isolated to date (the underlined prefixes are illustrated in the sample text on the following page).

The verb is also predominantly prefixing, as can be seen from the following formula:

1: *negative*   2: *modal*   3: *directive*
4: *subject*   5: *preverb*   0: *ROOT*
6: *suffix*

A large variety of prefix chains can occur in principle in Hattic, although not all theoretically possible combinations are attested (in practice, verbs occur with anything from zero to four prefixes). The general structure of the verb is fairly clear, even if the interpretation of the individual formatives is quite tentative. In particular, the non-third-person subjects are very uncertain; this holds true also for independent pronouns. (We have almost no information about first-person pronouns; there may be a pronoun *weutta*, "you" [sing.]). The third-person singular *an-* seems to occur only with transitive verbs (third-person singular being unmarked with intransitives). But as far as we can tell, this is the only ergative-like feature of Hattic; there is no ergative/agentive case marking on the noun, and the third-person plural subject marker *es-*

TABLE 3
Hattic Prefixes

Possessive	Demonstrative
le- (his, their)	*ip-* (this?)
se- (her)	*at-* (that?)
te- (its)	

Location	Plural
ta- (in)	*es-*/-*as* (inanimate?)
ḫa-	*fa-* (inanimate and animate?)
zi-	
ka-	

Hattic Text Sample

The following passage (*Keilschrifturkunden aus Boghazköi*, vol 2, text 2, col. 2, lines 40–42 [1922]) is the first section of a well-known Hattic-Hittite bilingual "Building Ritual." The text has been treated repeatedly since the first attempts to decipher Hattic in the 1920s. The interpretation given here relies principally on the edition of H.-S. Schuster. The cuneiform signs containing *š* seem to correspond to a simple *s* in Hattic.

Transliteration

wa$_a$-aš-ha-ab-ma eš-wu$_u$-ur aš-ka-ah-hi-ir šu-ú-wa$_a$
^{uru}ha-at-tu-uš ti-it-ta-ah zi-la-at šu-ú-wa$_a$
ta-ba-ar-na ka-a-at-ti ta-ni-wa$_a$-aš

Transcription and Interlinear Analysis

fa+ashap+ma   es+fur   as+kahhir
pl+god+and/but pl$_{in}$+land 3pl$_{sub}$+determine
sufa   Hattus titta+h   zilat
but-they-set(? so Hittite) Khattus great+fem seat

sufa   Tabarna katte ta+nifas
but-they-set(?) Tabarna king location+sit

Translation

The gods determined (the fate of) the lands.
And they set up in Khattusha the great seat (throne).
And they set (it) up (so that) Tabarna the king might sit there.

seems to occur with both transitives and intransitives. The "preverbs" seem to be largely locative in character, and the first four seem to be identical with the "location" noun prefixes registered in the noun chart.

There is a fair amount of freedom in the word order of Hattic sentences, although in general the verb tends to occur in the initial position (except in the case of discourse-initial position, where the verb often occurs last). Nominal modifiers generally occur before the modified noun. An extensive set of enclitics (frequently attached to the first word in a clause) governs the relations between clauses and sentences.

FURTHER CONNECTIONS: LINGUISTIC PREHISTORY

A question that naturally occurs in the light of all this is, What connections are there among these languages, and between these languages and any other known languages? The question can be taken in either a typological sense (are these the same kinds of languages?) or a genetic sense (are these languages related to one another, or to other known language families? or to what extent does the linguistic prehistory of the ancient Near East link up with the linguistic prehistory of other regions of the Old World?). These questions have been asked by scholars since the first discovery of these languages and, indeed, were probably asked more often at the beginning of the twentieth century than later on. And from the beginning, the Caucasus, that "museum of peoples and languages," has been a prime candidate for both types of relationship.

The typological question has principally revolved around the feature of ergativity, prominent in many, if not most, of the languages of the Caucasus to such an extent that it certainly qualifies for an areal, if not necessarily genetic, feature of the languages of the region. In this respect, Hurrian and Urartian, as we have seen above, fit right in (as does Sumerian to only a slightly lesser degree). Elamite lacks the prominent case system of these other languages, but seems to give an important syntactic role to the distinction between active and stative predicates. In the opinion of some investigators (for example, Diakonoff), this is sufficient to qualify it also as essentially ergative in character; others would tend to see Elamite rather as a representative of a distinct linguistic type sometimes labeled "active." To date, Hattic does not seem to have revealed any obviously ergative features, but the material is still too obscure for any definitive judgment.

For the genetic question, at least for the more northern of the peripheral languages, the Caucasus likewise remains a principal focus. The most serious attempt at discovering pre-ancient near eastern relations in this area has been that of Diakonoff and Starostin to relate Hurro-Urartian to the Eastern Caucasian group of languages (whose own status as a unified family has not yet been established to everyone's satisfaction). There remain two other large groupings of languages in the Caucasus, Kartvelian (Southern Caucasian, with Georgian) and Western Caucasian. Arguments have been made for linking Hattic to both; of course, the same reservations have to be made as in the typology case. Note that if these hypotheses should turn out to be tenable, this would point to a prehistoric situation in which the north down to the sources of the Tigris and Euphrates and Lake Urmia was divided among the same groups that occupy the Caucasus today, and would lend plausibility to a working hypothesis that unassignable languages in this northern area would also belong most probably to one of these groups.

Quite a different situation obtains in Khuzestan, where, after some initial attempts to link Elamite with the Caucasus, more attention has been paid to a possible connection with Dravidian (the non-Indo-European family of languages presently occupying the southern part of India, but with isolated representatives west of the Indus River). This hypothesis might gain in geographical and historical plausibility if it could be established that the language of the Indus Valley inscriptions were also Dravidian.

The apparently limited distribution of indigenous Sumerians to southern Babylonia (as opposed to the much wider area of their cultural influence), along with the apparently secondary nature of Semitic Akkadian occupation of the rest of Mesopotamia, has invited considerable speculation as to the area of origin of the Sumerians and the identity of the "original" population(s) of Mesopotamia. At present, it can only be said that there is nothing in the linguistic or archaeological record to suggest anything more than a relatively local displacement of Sumerians within the northern Persian Gulf region. There are sets of possible loanwords in Sumerian, mostly dealing with cultural institutions, such as the cultivation of the date palm. Words of this sort are typically borrowed along with the objects and practices they represent, and could have had many sources, if in fact they are loanwords. Indeed, one possible source could be the hypothesized non-Semitic, non-Sumerian (and probably non-Hurrian) populations in Mesopotamia outside southern Babylonia.

BIBLIOGRAPHY

Overview

IGOR M. DIAKONOFF, "Media," in *The Cambridge History of Iran*, vol. 2, edited by ILYA GERSHEVITCH (1985), and *The Pre-history of the Armenian People*, translated by LORI JENNINGS (1984), give useful information about the peoples in the Taurus-Zagros area and their localization. The "Subarian" incantations are discussed in JAN VAN DIJK, "Fremdsprachige Beschwörungstexte in der südmesopotamischen literarischen Überlieferung," in *Mesopotamien und seine Nachbarn*, edited by HANS-JÖRG NISSEN and JOHANNES RENGER (1982). IGNACE J. GELB, *Hurrians and Subarians* (1944), is the classic synthesis of the subject. See PIOTR MICHALOWSKI, "Mental Maps and Ideology: Reflections on Subartu," in *The Origin of Cities in Dry-Farming Syria and Mesopotamia in the Third Millennium B.C.*, edited by HARVEY WEISS (1986), on the notion of Subar and the literature connected with it. PIOTR STEINKELLER, "The Question of Marḫaši: A Contribution to the Historical Geography of Iran in the Third Millennium B.C.," *Zeitschrift für Assyriologie* 72 (1982), gives an idea of the early Mesopotamian view of the world to the east. Information on the peripheral ethnic groups is also available in the *Reallexikon der Assyriologie*: "Gutium," by W. W. HALLO, in vol. 3 (1957–1971); "Kaškäer," by E. VON SCHULER, and "Kassiten," by J. A. BRINKMAN, in vol. 5 (1976–1980); and "Lullu(bum)," by H. KLENGEL, and "Magan," by W. HEIMPEL, in vol. 7 (1987–1990).

Elamite

PETER DAMEROW and ROBERT K. ENGLUND, *The Proto-Elamite Texts from Tepe Yahya* (1989), with a general introduction by C. C. LAMBERG-KARLOVSKY (pp. v–xiv), gives a survey of the Proto-Elamite corpus. A unique text was published by I. M. DIAKONOFF and N. B. JANKOWSKA, "An Elamite Gilgameš Text from Argištihenele, Urartu (Armavir-blur, 8th Century B.C.)," *Zeitschrift für Assyriologie* 80 (1990). The Elamite incantations from the Old Babylonian period are discussed in the article by JAN VAN DIJK mentioned above. FRANÇOISE GRILLOT-SUSINI, *Éléments de grammaire élamite* (1987), is a survey of the grammar. WALTHER HINZ and HEIDEMARIE KOCH, *Elamisches Wörterbuch*, 2 vols. (1987), lists all Elamite words attested in published texts, plus the major discussions of each word in the literature. HERBERT H. PAPER, *The Phonology and Morphology of Royal Achaemenid Elamite* (1955), is an exhaustive grammatical analysis of the largest Elamite corpus. ERICA REINER, "The Elamite Language," in *Keilschriftforschung und alte Geschichte Vorderasiens*, edited by B. SPULER, Handbuch der Oriental-

istik, vol. 1, pt. 2 (1969), is the starting point of all contemporary attempts to understand Elamite grammar. Middle Elamite economic texts have been published by MATTHEW W. STOLPER, *Texts from Tall-i Malyan I: Elamite Administrative Texts (1972–1974)* (1984).

Hurrian

FREDERIC W. BUSH, *A Grammar of the Hurrian Language* (1964), is the most exhaustive grammatical treatment of the language of the Mitanni letter. IGOR M. DIAKONOFF, *Hurrisch und Urartäisch* (1971), provides a new linguistic and comparative framework for the study of both Hurrian and Urartian and of their relation to one another. VOLKERT HAAS, ed., *Hurriter und Hurritisch* (1988), is a collection of articles giving modern orientations on Hurrian and the Hurrian Corpus project, including GERNOT WILHELM, "Gedanken zur Frühgeschichte der Hurriter und zum hurritisch-urartäischen Sprachvergleich," on Hurrian grammar, and ERICH NEU, "Zur Grammatik des Hurritischen auf der Grundlage der hurritisch-hethitischen Bilingue aus der Boğazköy Grabungskâmpagne 1983," on the Hurrian-Hittite bilinguals. EMMANUEL LAROCHE, *Glossaire de la langue hourrite* (1980), is a list, with glosses where possible, of all Hurrian words known by the mid 1970s. E. A. SPEISER, *Introduction to Hurrian* (1941), laid the foundation for our present understanding of Hurrian and is still an excellent introduction. GERNOT WILHELM, "EA 24," in *The Amarna Letters*, edited by WILLIAM MORAN (1992), gives a complete translation of the Mitanni letter.

Urartian

RICHARD D. BARNETT, "The Hieroglyphic Writing of Urartu," in *Anatolian Studies Presented to Hans Gustav Güterbock*, edited by KURT BITTEL, PHILO H. J. HOUWINK TEN CATE, and ERICA REINER (1974), summarizes what is known about Urartian hieroglyphs. WARREN C. BENEDICT, *Urartian Phonology and Morphology* (1958), is an earlier grammatical study of Urartian. IGOR M. DIAKONOFF, *Urartskie pis'ma i dokumenty* (1963), contains an edition, with photographs, of sixteen of the twenty-two known Urartian tablets. In addition to the works by Diakonoff cited under "Hurrian," the most basic tool in Urartian is G. A. MELIKISHVILI, *Urartskie klinoobraznye nadpisi* [Urartian cuneiform inscriptions] (1960), an annotated transcription and translation, with glossary, of all the Urartian inscriptions known up to the end of the 1950s; Melikishvili's grammatical introduction to that work, translated, revised, and expanded in *Die urartäische Sprache* (1971), is the best introductory grammar. GERNOT WILHELM, "Urartu als region der Keilschrift-Kultur," in *Das Reich Urartu: Ein altorientalischer*

Staat im 1. Jahrtausend v. Chr., edited by VOLKERT HAAS (1986), develops the idea of "cuneiform culture" and points out the nature of the relation between Hurrian and Urartian.

Hattic

CHRISTIAN GIRBAL, *Beiträge zur Grammatik des Hattischen* (1986), gives an overview of Hattic grammar. ANNELIES KAMMENHUBER, "Hattisch," in *Keilschriftforschung und alte Geschichte Vorderasiens*, edited by B. SPULER, Handbuch der Orientalistik, vol. 1, pt. 2 (1969), is basic and gives much lexical information. HANS-SIEGFRIED SCHUSTER, *Die hattischhethitischen Bilinguen*, vol. 1 (1974), besides giving much lexical and grammatical background information, is the most complete edition of a Hattic text (the text whose beginning lines are cited above).

Wider Connections

IGOR M. DIAKONOFF and SERGEI A. STAROSTIN, *Hurro-Urartian as an Eastern Caucasian Language* (1986), lines up the evidence for a possible wider relationship, to which RIEKS SMEETS, "On Hurro-Urartian as an Eastern Caucasian Language," *Bibliotheca Orientalis* 44 (1989), gives a reaction from the point of view of a specialist in the languages of the Caucasus. V. V. IVANOV, "Relations Between the Ancient Languages of Asia Minor," in *Šulmu: Papers on the Ancient Near East Presented at International Conference of Socialist Countries*, edited by PETR VAVROUŠEK and VLADIMIR SOUČEK (1988), is one statement of the thesis that Hattic is related to Western Caucasian (Christian Girbal, above, suggests a Kartvelian connection). BENNO LANDSBERGER, "The Beginnings of Civilization in Mesopotamia," in *Three Essays on the Sumerians* (1974), is a classic statement, first published in German in 1944, of the possibility of a pre-Sumerian substrate population in Mesopotamia. DAVID W. MCALPIN, *Proto-Elamo-Dravidian: The Evidence and Its Implications* (1981), is the most thorough presentation to date of the evidence for a possible relation of Elamite to Dravidian; KAMIL ZVELEBIL, "Dravidian and Elamite—A Real Breakthrough?" *Journal of the American Oriental Society* 94 (1974), represents the point of view of a prominent Dravidianist.

SEE ALSO **The Decipherment of Ancient Near Eastern Scripts** (Part 1, Vol. I).

Memory and Literacy in Ancient Western Asia

H. VANSTIPHOUT

TO SAY THAT WRITING is the ancient Near East's single most important cultural contribution is a truism that cannot be weakened by repetition. The consequences of that contribution are immense and can be appreciated only after a thorough and multidisciplinary study. I shall here raise issues only about literacy and its impact on the cultural systems involved. That I will draw illustrations mostly from cuneiform civilizations is not because of personal predilection: cuneiform is not only the earliest but also the most important writing system to come to us from the ancient Near East. Furthermore, our documentation for cuneiform writing is far richer than that for any other writing system of antiquity.

A writing system is the graphic representation of features of language—lexical, grammatical, and syntactic. This implies that there must be phonetization of some kind and that this phonetization must be at the same time systematic and abstracted from the contents, context, and intention of an actual individual message. Essential to any human language is that its basic element, the word, not be merely a label for an idea or an object but function in combination and within a phrase or sentence, obeying a system of rules we call "grammar." It is also important to note that the level and the method of so-called phonemic notation are not identical concepts, so that a writing scheme that uses an alphabet must not automatically be judged more advanced or developed than one that uses a syllabary or logographs. The efficiency by which the grammatical structure of a language is expressed is a much more important consideration than the language's number of signs.

Somewhat independently of this close link, or conceptual isomorphy, with language, writing as a cultural action may be said to show three interrelated specific aspects. First, the operational aspect consists of the execution of signs by means of an instrument on a carrier, signs meant to represent the linguistic features known as words, morphemes, or phonemes, or all three. Second, the functional aspect is closely related: the operation is intended to convey a "message"—or, perhaps better, a piece of language—by proxy and therefore consists of the fixation in time and space of an otherwise ephemeral linguistic communication. In terms of the general scheme underlying every communication, this means that the operation itself establishes contact and presumes the code, while the intention is precisely to get the message through in the absence of the addressee and sometimes the context. Therefore, the functional aspect may be said to cover also the conditions under which, and the reasons for which, the message is twice encoded. Third is the material aspect: the operation, originating under specific conditions and with specific intentions, results in a concrete

2181

object that is not identical to, or even coextensive with, the message.

ORIGIN AND DEVELOPMENT
OF WRITING

Sources and Critical Issues

True writing originated for the first and, according to some, for the only time in the ancient Near East. To be precise, it was in southern Iraq in the last centuries of the fourth millennium BCE that *homo literatus sumericus Urukeus* invented writing for his Sumerian language. The felicitous term is Marvin Powell's, and it implies that the invention of writing is related to the emergence of the city of Uruk (modern Warka, biblical Erech) as southern Mesopotamia's major urban center. The first written documents, which are economic and administrative in nature, are dated archaeologically to the period 3300–2900 and were located at or near the site of Uruk. The thorough and painstaking studies by M. W. Green have removed most of the doubts that the language of the documents is Sumerian. It is therefore not without interest that Sumerian literary tradition ascribes the invention of writing to a prince of Uruk. Not long afterward, the Nile Valley also shows evidence of a writing system that seems full-fledged. From the first two dynasties (circa 2900–2650), we have a relatively important number of written documents, such as private stelae, name tags, jar sealings, and inscriptions on pottery. Although at this stage the Egyptian writing system was in principle capable of recording all of language, the uses to which it was put were much more limited, and continuous language was not written down. For the sake of completeness, it should be noted that the Iranian Plateau offers early documents written in the Proto-Elamite script. Yet, these economic texts and early inscriptions hardly differ from their Mesopotamian counterparts, and this script is merely an early and short-lived variant application of Mesopotamian cuneiform.

Two questions may be posed: Was writing invented just once or several times? And how exactly did cuneiform writing, which is undoubtedly the first in any case, originate? Partisans of monogenesis point to the structural near identity between the oldest (Sumerian) system and its near contemporary, Egyptian. Ignace J. Gelb claims that he can follow the period of development into phonetization in much detail for Sumerian, in contrast to Egyptian or even Chinese. He also disallows the evidence of the great civilizations of the New World, the Maya and the Aztec; these would not, for him, constitute true writing, since they have not progressed from the vague and uncertain and partial principle of phonetization to systematic phonetic, or rather phonemic, writing. Yet, since recent progress in deciphering Maya has proven beyond a reasonable doubt that Maya is indeed a true writing system, it follows that writing can be discovered twice, just as metallurgy or agricultural techniques can. By the same token, the dependence of the Chinese system on Sumer is no longer the most probable hypothesis. Further, research after Gelb has observed that even the Egyptian system may have developed gradually and independently—by coincidence only slightly later than the invention in Sumer. In fact, polygenesis (multiple origins) now seems to be accepted as the more probable hypothesis.

A vexingly unexplained problem is the absence of evolutionary stages in some material. However, the argument seems to involve a *petitio principii:* we only call a system "true writing" precisely because of its relative completeness. Half a writing system is no writing system. One may have some sympathy with the view that the evolutionary approach to the origin of writing is irrelevant or plainly wrong. Furthermore, it is very much a matter of degree and appreciation; as noted, the earlier stages of Egyptian writing do show a gradual refining, adaptation, and, indeed, growth of phonetization. Still, the fact remains that we have much more material for the several steps the system went through in Mesopotamia. The reason might be twofold: the material lends itself much better to preservation, and it is probable that the incidence of writing was much higher since, from very early on, the distribution or functional spread is much wider. This last observation implies that an answer to the second question—how exactly true writing originated—can be attempted most fruitfully on the basis of the Mesopotamian evidence and example.

The Moment and the Conditions of the Invention of Writing

It should be remembered that writing, as such, was something completely new at its invention; indeed, just like human language, it may be said to have constituted a Lamarckian leap instead of a Darwinian evolution. But this does not mean that it was the first or the only sign system available to the Sumerians of the fourth millennium. To the contrary, there is plenty of evidence that these early Sumerians, just like every other community, used a number of slightly interrelated sign systems that may be roughly broken down in three groups.

First of all, there are drawings or other manufactured representations of objects, animals, and men on cylinder and stamp seals or on pottery or other artifacts. These are often highly stylized, so that a degree of abstraction, leading to a certain uniformity, may be said to have reached a systemic level. But the systematization seems dictated by representational or aesthetic considerations and traditions.

Second, and very probably arising out of the first group, there are representations that are loaded with symbolic value; we know, because some of them, such as the emblems belonging to a number of deities, survived until the very end of cuneiform civilization and maybe even beyond that, implying that their referent reaches much further than the single and individual object or animal. Such a system of symbols can only be effective if it reflects a common ideology or body of beliefs and convictions. This phenomenon is found all over the world, and in some cases, it results in the construction of "messages" by means of an assemblage of different symbols. Every history of writing contains illustrations of this, and there are some very fine examples on late Predynastic Egyptian objects. Strangely enough, these assemblages are rare in Mesopotamia: at most, a number of scenes depicted on seals might be interpreted in this way, but the impression remains that even in these cases the combined scene, as such, is generalized and becomes a new and composite symbol. In any case, such assemblages can hardly qualify as protowriting, since the linguistic link is absent. As a matter of fact, sign systems that are based on a combination of these first two groups and represent a coherent corpus of meanings while independent of any single language have been found everywhere and are certainly not restricted to societies without writing. Heraldry is one such system, and the modern world abounds with insignia: traffic signs, icons in airports and railway stations, signs on car dashboards, and icons in computer programs.

A third group consists of identifying or mnemonic devices: arbitrary simple linear designs used as marks on all kinds of objects in everyday use. These are frequent from early on in Egypt (potters' marks), but relatively rare in Mesopotamia.

Mesopotamia, with its northern and eastern border regions, abounds in another class of objects, the relevance of which has been noticed only since the 1960s. Excavations have yielded large numbers of very small clay objects of sun-dried simple shapes: spheres, cones, dice, discs, and the like, some of them incised with lines or crosses. These "tokens" are especially abundant from 3500 onward; the number of different shapes increases, and there are apparently no significant regional variations between findspots, such as northeastern Syria (Habuba al-Kabira), Sumer (Uruk), north-central Mesopotamia (Khafaje), central Iran (Tepe Sialk), and southern Iran (Choga Mish). Archaeologists used to give them scant attention—indeed, they often just threw them away—until Pierre Amiet built a theory on them, which was later worked out extensively by Denise Schmandt-Besserat. The theory (developed in the chapter "Record Keeping Before Writing," above) in broad outline runs like this: The tokens were used in a system of accounting, standing for (units of) goods. This economic system is of great age; tokens go back as far as the ninth millennium—when farming began. Starting as a simple bookkeeping device, they really come into their own with the advent of large-scale trading at about 3500. They then served also as bills of lading and the like; in order to restrain fraud, the tokens were enclosed in a ball of clay called a "bulla." Bullae often have marks on the outside corresponding with the tokens inside—sometimes made by actually pressing the tokens into the soft clay before closing up the ball. The next step was obvious: since the "contents" are marked by making a sign on the clay of the bulla, they may just as well be dispensed with, and so, the clay tablet was invented before writing itself.

Is this how writing was invented? From the technical point of view, there seems little doubt that this evolution in practice and function of a generalized token system indeed led to the use of clay tablets as carriers of economic messages in the broadest possible sense. But something is lacking: the token system does not imply a notation of phonemic or grammatical features. Indeed, if the spread of the system was as wide as has been claimed (almost the complete Fertile Crescent, including Egypt), such a notation would surely be impossible. Furthermore, the more specific the meaning of a token in such a system becomes, the more different tokens are needed, which would tend to make the system far too unwieldy. Two discoveries by M. W. Green are very important in this respect. First, she demonstrated that the repertoire of signs in the very early period was far greater than later, while obviously the content of the "texts" is highly conventional and extremely simple. Second, she also demonstrated that in the very early tablets the signs are arranged in boxes that do two things: they make visible the format of the "text," thus making it "readable," and within the boxes the arrangement and sequence of the signs becomes gradually more regulated. While the first aspect illustrates that the proliferation of signs was felt to become a problem from early on—indeed, the growth of the number of signs tapers off and is very much reduced once "full" writing appears—the second suggests that an important step had been made: not just the signs themselves but also, and perhaps more so, their sequence and arrangement carry meaning. In this way a combination of signs can be used for a meaning that is more than, and different from, the disconnected series of the separate signs. This happens in hieroglyphic as well as in cuneiform. But even more important is the implication that in this way an important (albeit rather abstract) linguistic feature can be expressed: syntax, being a rule-governed series or chain of distinct semantic units. The next step is obvious in hindsight: the system is used to express other linguistic features as well, and though we will probably never have certainty on this point, I would suggest that the conceptual route led from syntax notation over morpheme notation to pho-

neme notation, and not the other way around; in this respect also, true writing works like true language. The very probable hypothesis that this was done—in both hieroglyphic and cuneiform—by means of partial or complete homophony, of which general technique the hieroglyphic predilection for rebus writing is only a specialized instance, does not change this. And so we are back to Powell's *homo literatus sumericus Urukeus*, for however plausible and well founded the token theory is, it does not explain by itself the step to true writing. I would venture that the great invention was indeed just that—a conscious invention with perhaps a definite purpose, although partly based on an existing technique for limited and specific communication. As with all great inventions, novelty is but one, not very important, aspect. The main fact about the invention is that its applicability is raised to an incredible degree both as to domain and to substance.

Evolution and Implications

In both cuneiform and hieroglyphic, the invention relatively quickly led to more-general application and specific refinements or adaptations. This evolution, which is partly mixed with the invention itself, has four aspects. First, there is the emancipation from the system of tokens and symbols. This emancipation is of course implied in the transition from purely administrative to linguistic notation. This motif is splendidly illustrated in an episode from the Sumerian narrative poem *Enmerkar and the Lord of Aratta*: the Lord of Aratta is vexed and despondent when, looking at the tablet written—allegedly for the first time—by Enmerkar, he does not see the iconic or symbolic signs he may have expected, but "words" in the form of "nails."

Second, giving a linguistic content to the newly invented system has serious implications. Whereas the head of a donkey, a cow, or a sheep is just that in any language, now the drawing of a foot can be used for a range of different linguistic units: foot, to stand, to go, to walk, to run, and so on. This weakening of the significance of direct pictorial denotation—or, for that matter, of restricted conventionalism—leads in both systems to subsidiary systems that are remarkably alike. To the original set of logographs is added a set

---

Enmerkar Invents Writing

500 This speech was [too difficult?]; its contents were too long;
The Messenger's mouth was too slow; he could not repeat it.
Since the Messenger's mouth was too slow, and he could not repeat it,
The Lord of Kulab patted some clay and set down the words as on a tablet.
Before that day, there was no putting of words on clay;
505 But now, when the Sun rose, it verily was so:
The Lord of Kulab had verily put words on clay!

. . .

524 "Enmerkar, son of the Sun, gave me this tablet;
"O Lord of Aratta, look upon this clay; if you are able to grasp its meaning,
If you can tell me whatever you may find to reply,
[I will bring back that reply to Enmerkar].

. . .

536 After he had spoken thus
The Lord of Aratta took his
Brazier to the messenger.
The Lord of Aratta kept looking at the clay;
But the spoken word was but a nail; his brow darkened
While he kept looking at the brazier.

---

of classifiers and a set of purely phonographic additions, thus making it possible to identify correctly the intended word or phrase. In hieroglyphic, this generally works out as a conventional group of signs used on the level of the individual word or phrase, or almost on a lexical level, and such a group consists of one or a few basic logographs, some classifiers, and some so-called phonetic complements. These last are a relatively small set of single-consonant or biconsonant signs, of which the former might easily have been used as a more or less full-fledged consonantal alphabet, but which was never so used. In cuneiform, the phonemic notation gradually becomes more important, in that grammatical forms are spelled out more and more explicitly in Sumerian. When Akkadian starts using cuneiform, the phonetization is vastly extended. By translating from the one language into the other, the original set of logographic applications is doubled, as are the derived phonemic usages. On the whole, one might say that Sumerian remains a mixed system, while Akkadian is basically phonemic. The late and learned return to a plethora of logographs is to be understood as inkhorn preciosity or as a shorthand system, or both.

Third, the method of phonetization in the subsidiary system is a different one. Egyptian consists of a mixed system of a consonantal alphabet with a number of bi- and triconsonantals. (See the chapter "Ancient Egyptian and Other Afro-asiatic Languages," earlier in this volume.) The Sumero-Akkadian system is a complete syllabic set consisting basically of signs for the values V, VC, CV, and CVC (where V = vowel and C = consonant). Both facts are of great importance for the further spread of writing in the ancient world.

Lastly, the signs themselves undergo modification to various degrees. In Egyptian the early pictorial design of most signs is kept for monumental purposes and in some later periods is even more detailed than in the earlier periods. Writing in ink on such surfaces as papyrus, writing boards, and ostraca was in a cursive form that developed by the Old Kingdom into the distinct script known as hieratic that was partly replaced from the seventh century by a further development known as demotic. The hieroglyphic form remained in use not only for stone carving but also for other monumental uses (wall painting, sarcophagi, amulets, holy or magic objects, ritual texts, and the like); therefore, hieroglyphs are integrated into works of art, even when they record very long texts. It is no surprise to have monuments or objects whose adornment mixes to a degree written language with nonverbal, symbolic representation. The image remains very important.

In cuneiform, quite the reverse is true. From very early on, the material—wet clay and a sharpened reed stylus—almost obliterates the recognizable shape of the original "object," which in many cases was already highly stylized. Cuneiform, therefore, does not put any value at all on the image in writing. The image and meaning of writing, on the other hand, is all-important. Cuneiform writing, as such, acquires almost a mystical value, as does the carrier of the writing, the cuneiform tablet.

Spread and Transformation

From the early second millennium onward, writing spread all over the ancient world. Egyptian writing remained almost completely restricted to the pharaonic culture and, therefore, to the valley and delta of the Nile and to the Egyptian language. Almost, that is, since in the second century hieroglyphic provided the basis for the Meroitic alphabetic script, and demotic was the model for its cursive variant; the Meroitic language is still only partly understood. Nevertheless, Egyptian writing may very well have influenced some of the early Aegean scripts, as it certainly laid the foundation of the Proto-Sinaitic "alphabet."

Cuneiform knew its greatest expansion in this period. Babylonian cuneiform was used, sometimes in a simplified form and with slight adaptations, for such different languages as Hittite and its Anatolian relatives, Hurrian, Urartian, Elamite, and to a less certain extent, early forms of northwest Semitic. The Babylonian language itself was used internationally: when Egypt ruled the east it used Babylonian even for correspondence with its own Syrian possessions. On the purely technical level, cuneiform has also stood godfather to the Ugaritic and related early forms of the Semitic alphabet, and to the Persian syllabary. Furthermore, the idea of strict "syllabography," which is found at different places in the eastern Aegean in the second and first millennia, may also have been influenced by the simplified forms of Babylonian cuneiform.

There are also other monumental systems comparable with Egyptian hieroglyphic, such as the "Hittite" and Urartian hieroglyphs, although it is not known under which influence they originated (Egyptian, Aegean, or indigenous). And there are a number of undeciphered groups of texts or even single documents. But the greatest

renewal or transformation was, of course, the development of the Semitic alphabet, which begins to be used toward the end of the second millennium (a chapter on the Semitic alphabet appears below).

A major point resulting from this overview is that apart from a few exceptions (such as Ugarit), we possess no, or not nearly enough, evidence of the effect of literacy beyond the two high cultures and their immediate neighbors, who took over the writing systems.

PURPOSE AND IMPACT

What, if any, the original purpose of writing, beyond basic bookkeeping, may have been can no longer be traced with certainty, and I am not sure this is a meaningful question. What one can do, however, is to interrogate the earliest documentation and the subsequent developments.

The hieroglyphic and the cuneiform systems in their earliest stages show different uses of writing. In Egypt during the first two dynasties, monumental writing was used for various marks of ownership, such as seals and tags, and elaborate titularies for kings and high officials were recorded; purely administrative writing has been almost entirely lost. A bit later comes the most important group, funeral inscriptions, which contain important juridical, administrative, and economic information, in addition to the religious data. The earliest longer texts date to the Fifth and Sixth dynasties and include autobiographies of high officials (see "Ancient Egyptian Autobiographies," below). The extensive corpus of Pyramid Texts, inscribed in royal burial apartments and intended to further the king's destiny in the next life, points to the existence of large bodies of religious texts for use in the cult. In Mesopotamia the first documents are overwhelmingly economic or administrative in nature; inscriptional material comes later, followed closely by religious, literary, and, from very early on, "learned" material in the form of word lists. These developments are only approximations for two reasons. First, the invention itself quickly becomes autonomous, in that it tends to impose its own, new purposes; but the early stages still reflect in some way the pre-writing communication technology and its traditions. Second, the differences between the two systems in their early stages are to a degree dependent on the different material and societal circumstances and, to a lesser degree, on the accidents of preservation and excavation.

But in any case, the evidence allows us to question the dogmatic view that writing was invented solely for the purpose of economics and administration. Three things indicate that this is too restricted a view. First, the evidence shows that almost right from the beginning (in Egypt) or very soon after it (in Mesopotamia), writing was fully used for noneconomic or nonadministrative purposes. Second, an overview of the development of cuneiform economic documents shows a double and somewhat contradictory evolution. In the earliest phase, we see a falling of the number of object-specific signs, caused no doubt by the gradual spreading of true writing over nonlinguistic notation; in later times, the massive and all-pervading administrations of the Akkadian and Ur III periods show that, in fact, the vast majority of documents no longer contain language in a meaningful sense. They have become tabulated forms, and the bits and pieces of what once was language are now mere formulaic symbols, the one important exception being the nomenclature of persons, functions, places, periods, and activities. Third, the study of the archaic economic documents from Mesopotamia reveals that the most important linguistic information to be culled from them consists in the grouping of signs into boxes and the makeup of the document—in other words, in syntax, which, after all, is independent from, or unnecessary for, the substantial or referential information. Therefore, it seems much more correct to say that writing was invented at a time when society was in need of a sophisticated administrative and economic bureaucracy and that the new invention, partly based on the older system(s) of identification and accounting, was immediately put to use in order to achieve this organizational level. But it seems clear that the prime purpose of writing was the notation and recording of language, as such. The prime impact is, of course, that language, once recorded, can be stored and retrieved at will.

While nonliterate societies abundantly illustrate that the recording of language does not by itself enhance the importance of language, it nevertheless gives language a quite different and more permanent function. It depersonalizes language and its use, and thus plays a normative role as well, differentiating between nonwritten and written language; this split may create almost unbridgeable chasms. It emancipates language from the shackles of place, occasion, and, most of all, time. Since retrieval is always possible, it actually makes the language user more conscious of the qualities and properties of language itself. It formalizes, generalizes, and perpetuates the features and intentions of language by cutting it loose from a momentary utterance. Writing's virtually infinite possibilities for storage and retrieval undoubtedly tended to favor the systematization and structuring of knowledge, its immediate products, and even other cultural phenomena dependent on, or at least cognate with, language, such as ordered lists, publication, and thus confirmation of social and administrative principles, structuring of large-scale reflective and poetical discourse, and so forth. Thus, from the beginning, there seems a high degree of congruence between the purpose and the impact of writing. But, of course, writing can do all these things and more only if there is someone to record (and in many cases, preserve) and someone to retrieve the information. (See "Archives and Libraries" below.) Some of the native North American–derived scripts remained on the (nonexistent) level of literacy shown by Claude Lévi-Strauss's Nambikwara chief, since their inventor kept them to himself. In other words, literacy must spread to some degree, or writing will die.

THE STRUCTURES OF LITERACY

Apart from the hundreds of thousands of documents written in a disconcerting variety of scripts, we have no clear indications of the spread of literacy in the ancient world. What we do have are indications of the range of activities for which writing—and thus literacy—was important or even necessary. And these were manifold.

A first structural aspect of literacy can be said to consist in the social function fulfilled by literati. We know from the mass of documents that almost every aspect of life was subject to a detailed administration, much of which was, of course, kept in writing and, therefore, by literates. The different format, formulary, and intention of the classes of documents imply a degree of differentiation and specialization. There is in Mesopotamia a very broad common system of economic administration—or simply bookkeeping—underlying the whole system of government and society; although there are changes over the years, within any given period this remains essentially the same, whether the books are kept for temple, palace, or even private households or commercial firms. But temple, palace, and local government also require specialized services. In the case of the temple, these literati will be closely connected and even partially identical with cult personnel and the priesthood. The palace will supervise and control the civil, military, and big commercial services. Local government will be responsible for state policy on the local level, and an important task will be the administration of justice. All these functions will have to be executed under the supervision of literates. And so, the schools, where literacy in the broad sense is the main preoccupation, but where also the rudiments of specialized vocations are first set forth, are in a way the most important locations of the literacy system. They are responsible for the training of a class of literates, or "scribes"; they are also the places where "purely scientific" training is undertaken; these "scientists"—diviners, astrologers, physicians, and such—then have the opportunity to enter civil or temple service because of their specialized knowledge. (See "The Scribes and Scholars of Ancient Mesopotamia," later in this volume.) Specialists in literary texts also belong to this group, in that they may remain attached to the school but go into service in temple or at court. In any case, the school system results in a literate class, which normally has a rather important function in society.

This class of literates has its own internal structure. While the mass of alumni will probably have remained in the broad middle range of their specialized profession for the whole of their career—be it the law court, the temple, or one of the great branches of civil administration—there seems to be a top layer of very high officials. We know from biographies (mainly from Egypt) and a number of prosopographic studies (both in Egypt and Mesopotamia) that these top officials may well be put in charge of totally different branches of government during their active life (such as mayor of an important city, provincial tax collector, governor, or high courtier). We have no indication, and some doubt, that this system of promotion is based on academic or administrative excellence, rather than upon family relations. At least in the early phases in Mesopotamia (third and early second millennia), the academic profession seems to have its own organization, apart from temple and palace. And even in the first millennium, specialists such as physicians, diviners, and astrologers seem to have had their own department with local branches, albeit under the direct orders of the king, as witnessed by many reports to the palace coming from all parts of the country. There seems also to have been opportunities for free employment, perhaps not unlike public scriveners: economic documents, incantation texts, and the like drawn up for private persons are easily recognizable, being far less well written than temple or palace documents of the same kind. Also, as early as the beginning of the second millennium, the big commercial families of Asshur, being private persons, personally kept up the correspondence with their trading colonies in faraway Anatolia. (See the chapter "Kanesh" in Part 5, Vol. II.)

Now apart from the twin indications of the sheer mass of documents, and the diversity and all-pervading nature of writing on all levels of society, the spread and rate of literacy in Mesopotamia and Egypt—and, for that matter, elsewhere in the ancient world—is very uncertain. But the overwhelming importance of written documents in all walks of life suggests that literacy was more extensive than primary sources report. In fact, one may well surmise that in the early second millennium, which was a period of great literary flowering in Mesopotamia (as it was in Egypt), literacy was more widespread than at the end of that millennium and the beginning of the next, when, according to our documentation, all or most writing was closely linked to temple and palace. In any case, the relative complexity of the writing system will have had little or nothing to do with the spread of literacy. Japan has the highest degree of literacy by very far in comparison to some other industrial giants, which goes to prove that literacy is far more dependent on a nation's political and social priorities and prejudices than on the intricacies of the script. Also, the rate of functional illiteracy is growing alarmingly precisely in alphabet-using countries. And last, the introduction of the "simple" alphabet in the ancient Near East (well before 1000) made no perceptible change in the degree of literacy before the Hellenistic period, and certainly not an immediate one; even in the West, Greece remained for centuries a much more fundamentally oral society than Mesopotamia had been for the last two millennia.

The structure of ancient literacy can also be seen from the contents and perhaps even the method of education, which was always literate. Both Egypt and Mesopotamia possessed a standard system of formal education by 2000. In regard to Egypt, we are well informed about the general outlines, since we have numerous references in literary and other texts and, most of all, the priceless schoolboys' exercises from Dayr al-Madina (Deir el-Medina, 1300–1100). As regards Mesopotamia, our knowledge is much more detailed and, since it deals with two languages (Sumerian and Akkadian), perhaps also intrinsically more relevant. The Old Babylonian school, or Eduba (Sumerian É.DUB.BA, literally "tablet house"), provided its students with a fairly comprehensive education based on the two "major" subjects: cuneiform writing and the Sumerian language. By 1800, but perhaps even as early as 2000, Sumerian was no longer a spoken language, although the kings of the Third Dynasty of Ur had probably reintroduced it as the official language at the end of the third millennium. (See "Sumerian Literature," below.) Since the foundation of the two major academies at Ur and Nippur is ascribed to the most famous king of that dynasty, Shulgi (circa 2094–2047), there is probably a relationship between these facts. As soon as the basic drawing techniques had been mastered by simply repeating the different strokes, the signs and their readings were taught. These signs were learned from sign lists arranged in several ways: phonologically (such as the list *tu-ta-ti*, which arranged the signs ac-

cording to their vowel); graphically (such as the list *a-a*, *a-a-a*, arranged according to groupings of simple signs); or lists that gave the meaning and the Akkadian reading together with the Sumerian sign (such as *Ea = nâqu*). As the student progressed, he had to copy, and probably learn, the more complex lists, culminating in the study of the great encyclopedic lexical list UR₅.RA-*ḫubullu*, or kindred works (see the chapter "Ancient Mesopotamian Lexicography"). By that time, Sumerian grammar had to be learned as well. For this purpose, there were lists of grammatical paradigms comparing systematically the Sumerian nominal and verbal grammatical system to its Akkadian counterpart. Syntax and style were probably taught in this phase by two means: by studying simple texts culled from the collections of proverbs and the like and from a few texts apparently composed with this didactic purpose in mind, since they most systematically progress from simple to more-complicated verbal and syntactical constructions, of which only a very few are repeated; and by copying and probably analyzing literary works.

The classics to be studied consisted of the great narratives about the deeds of the gods, the hymn collections, the historical lamentations, and the epics about the heroic house of Uruk (Enmerkar, Lugalbanda, and Gilgamesh) from which the dynasty of Ur pretended to descend. Copies of real or invented royal inscriptions were recopied and studied. There are indications that composition in Sumerian was a subject as well, and it is probably in this light that one must interpret the numerous and always delightful compositions known as "School Essays," "Dialogues," and certainly the "Disputations." Two practical subjects connected with writing were instruction in legal formulas and letter writing. Probably connected to hymnology, music was also taught, and on the so-called practical side, mathematics and surveying. The overall picture is that the main vehicle and the central point of the whole educational system was the mastery of Sumerian cuneiform. The scribal character of education remains preponderant throughout: the Mesopotamians summarized scribal education, including linguistic, literary, and scientific training and competence as NAM.DUB.SAR (Akkadian *ṭupšarrūtu*), "the scribe's competence," and GU.SUM (Akkadian *miḫiltum*) "orthocalligraphy."

THE ORDERING AND SHAPING OF MEMORY

Since writing in any form or shape intends at the very least to perpetuate an otherwise ephemeral utterance, it may also be said to replace memory. This implies that there must be a reason why a specific utterance was deemed worthy of being recalled. Then, too, the technology and nature of writing will influence the external organization and the immanent structure of language in its memorable aspects.

Organizing the Message

Recent analyses have done much to elucidate the major role writing played in achieving organization. Since the invention of writing was so closely linked to the concept of economic and administrative notation, it should not be surprising that an administrative document clearly shows the advantage of a written format. Apart from mere preservation, these advantages include the following: (1) listing, which unburdens human memory; (2) classification, difficult in speech or memory when the unclassified mass of factual information is great and complex; (3) clear reciprocal tabulation, which would be cumbersome when not visible or easily retrievable; (4) high definition by unequivocal sign differentiation of terms that might otherwise be either easily confused with one another or whose difference would otherwise demand extensive explanation; and (5) permanence and therefore ease of control. These features have led to more or less fixed models for administrative documents, which after the advent of true writing can become even more explicit. It is remarkable that in both the hieroglyphic and the cuneiform systems, these latter linguistic explicitations in later times revert to language-based tabulating formulas. A last and very important effect of writing technology is that only in this way can the mass of organized documents themselves be grouped, summarized, and classified. The process can be repeated virtually endlessly on a geometrically progressing scale of magni-

tude, with the documents engendering meta-documents. The point is that the mental effort needed for drawing up and using this documentation is no longer simple memory—except, of course, that the format of the document must be remembered—but is instead the use of a conceptual structure suggested by a certain technological layout that writing makes visible and thereby possible.

The link between administrative listing and classification of information and "other" writing can be perceived clearly in some of the oldest written documents. In the archaic Mesopotamian documents, one sees the growing impact of phonetization and syntax notation, illustrated by the grouping of signs in boxes whose disposition defines and explains the document. But also some very old "literary" pieces have passages that almost qualify as economic or administrative lists. Examples are a number of the official inscriptions from Lagash (modern Tell al-Hiba) in southeastern Mesopotamia, and the opening of the Egyptian *Story of the Eloquent Peasant*, which includes a list of products in the middle of the narrative flow.

In Mesopotamia the format of administrative documents generated a special kind of literary (in its broadest possible meaning) document, the royal inscription. A simple type of administrative document would note that (1) a commodity has been (2) forwarded to (3) a destination by (4) an official on (5) a certain occasion. Very early we find a kind of ideological or narrative counterpart somewhat like this: (1) for the god X, (2) the ruler Y (3) has built (4) temple Z. These texts grow by natural but ordered accretion, not unlike the systematics of an administrative document. The names of the "officials" as well as of the "destinations" are expanded with titles, descriptions, and so on, which grow into a fixed system of titles. Also the activities are expanded from a single building activity to a multitude of disparate actions undertaken for a series of divinities and at different locations. Out of these very simple origins, elaborate "biographies" or "annals" grew, and they represented a kind of royal account rendered to the divine patron.

Both in Mesopotamia and in Egypt, the organized-list format had an effect on the organization of language itself. However, the documentation in cuneiform is far richer, far more significant, and, because of the bilingual nature of much of the material, far more relevant. From the very beginning of true writing, and no doubt primarily for educational reasons, so-called lexical lists were drawn up. They listed either words arranged thematically (such as professions, fish, geographical names, vessels, or artifacts) or signs with their pronunciation. Soon afterward, an Akkadian column was added to both types, so that via the Akkadian the "meaning" was noted as well. Still later came comparative lists of contrasted grammatical forms in Sumerian and Akkadian, which in turn led to lists noting Sumerian particles with their grammatical function. The important point is that the principle underlying all this effort of collection, classification, organization, and analysis is the principle of writing. To the Mesopotamians themselves, therefore, the term approximating what we would call "science" or "knowledge" was simply *ṭupšarrūtu*, "the art, knowledge, and technique of the scribe." Ancient reflection upon reality and the world was based on language in its written, not its spoken form, as was the case with, for instance, much of Greek philosophy. Therefore, even our thematic lists are not treatises on botany, medicine, government, or law. They are, instead, scribal collections of appropriate terms that do have their own graphic structure and articulation but also their graphic dynamics. They tend to expand by accumulation or accretion. But this accretion is governed by the organization of the sign list, in that subseries (such as geographical provenance, color, or size) can be entered at different points of the base list and so applied to different lemmata. Nor is the accretion exclusively caused by the need for actual completeness: reality is transcended, in that also obviously impossible entries, which are never found in actual texts outside the lexical material, are listed as well, since the system seems to predict them. The sign is all-pervading and more important than its contents. Somewhat paradoxically, this overriding preoccupation with writing also implies that for the first time in intellectual history, the student is thrown back onto language itself, not its referential aspect. This explains why the analysis of their linguistic material led ancient scribes to the discovery of the principles of language structure and typology, of morphemics and even phonemics, millennia

before the formulation of structuralism and centuries before the Greek views on and discourse about language, or rather about the "meaning" of (spoken) words, which were essentially philosophical and rhetorical, and not linguistic. All this tends to show that writing very soon became emancipated from its utilitarian application and was used and studied for its own sake, since it was the basic method of dealing with language, reality, and thought.

Ordering the Discourse and the Text

Mainly but not exclusively in literary or in official compositions (a distinction that is not meaningful for the ancient world), we find even more-penetrating influences of writing on the text. The impact of writing is felt even on the textural and decorative level. On Egyptian monuments the hieroglyphs are very often integrated into the design to form essential elements in artistic and architectural compositions. Some hieroglyphs acquire human limbs to become active emblems. Also both in Egypt and in Mesopotamia there are plenty of fancy writings, aberrant spellings, and sign plays, not necessarily with corresponding phonic properties or even with attempts at conscious and meaningful ambiguity, which are to be regarded as having the same function as mere sound- or wordplays. The authors and their public doubtless regarded them as such, and they are as much a part of elegant discourse as other poetic tactics. In both Egypt and Mesopotamia there were specialized uses of the signs in the script to enhance the meaning of texts or to create new forms. In Egypt these practices led to forms of cryptography and to elaborate developments of the hieroglyphic script, especially in the Greco-Roman period, when lists of signs and their readings and meanings were also compiled (see the sidebar in the chapter "Ancient Egyptian and Other Afroasiatic Languages"). In Mesopotamia this specialized style engendered a type of literary text and was ultimately derived from literacy-based "philology" consisting of the different possible intervention(s) of signs or sign groups, which, after all, is the system underlying some of the most developed Mesopotamian "lexical" lists and is the major method in their native commentaries. This style consists of breaking down a sign group or a statement into its constituent parts, elaborating upon these parts by alternative readings, other interpretations, other meanings, and the like and repeating the proceedings even with alternate spellings of the same original "base" signs. A splendid and well-known example is the last tablet of *Enuma Elish*, the Babylonian didactic theological poem about the creation, the organization of the universe, and praise for Marduk's ominpotence. This tablet lists and comments on the fifty names of Marduk, using this technique with as much gusto, albeit in a poetic vein, as is spent on the more abstruse passages in some of the major lexical lists. The interpretations are all based on the written-list format and can come only from works like these. Nor is the usage restricted to this somewhat late composition. Far earlier, it is found in a number of hymns, which by their format might as well be called litanies. Famous examples are the great *Hymn to the City of Nippur* and the didactic *Hymn to the Hoe*, but there are many more examples. This style is common to all of them in an almost exclusive way, so that stylistics, based on literacy-based "learned" philology, has created a genre or type belonging to itself.

On the level of composition or structure, literacy works in a more subtle way. As our literary competence in reading ancient Egyptian and Mesopotamian grows, it is becoming gradually clearer that these texts usually show a closely knit structure, far greater and stricter than that of many other literatures that seem less emancipated from a possible previous oral stage or a particular oral performance. A prime example is the Sumerian tale *Gilgamesh and Agga*, a short piece of 114 lines that uses only about 160 different words. The story is admittedly simple and straightforward, but well and cleverly articulated. An analysis, however, shows how sophisticated the arrangement of the text really is. By the use of repetitions, antitheses, reciprocal passages, dialogic structures, and other kinds of parallelism, the simple linear structure is buttressed by at least three other structural lines: serial congruence, where passages "answer" earlier passages; pivotal congruence, where the format of a passage is repeated in a similar structural context; and the dialogue structure. Furthermore, even in the repeated passages, there is a tendency to give them in reverse order, a

lovely trick that was featured in many compositions. Indeed, even in much longer narratives, the clever and meaningful structural use of repetition and parallelism becomes a major compositional technique. Now the point is that repetition in written literature by itself is sometimes regarded as a hallmark of oral composition, although verbatim repetition is not accomplished all that easily in a purely oral environment. But the highly sophisticated use of diverse kinds of structural parallelism is surely dependent on fixation of the text as part of the composer's work. It is true that fixation can also happen by means of learning by heart. But this is in a way immaterial: the fixation of the text is the cause of all these structural techniques, whether this is done by remembering or by writing. And it seems somewhat perverse to posit a complicated and difficult training to learn long compositions by heart—a phenomenon for which we have no evidence whatsoever—when we possess thousands of written texts, originating in an academic environment dedicated to writing. Even when a Renaissance sonnet or a Japanese haiku are learned by heart, they are products of the learned and the literate. A high degree of structural organization does seem to be an outcome of literacy, the reason being again the easy retrievability implied by writing.

Specific to Mesopotamia is one more interesting aspect of literacy shaping the text. The Mesopotamians had a great admiration, verging on veneration, for the cuneiform tablet. Indeed, the fate of the universe was written down on a "Tablet of Destinies" (*tup šimātim*), worn around the neck or on the garment of the supreme deity. The decisions of the gods could be read from the liver of sacrificed sheep, because the gods had written it down on that liver as on a tablet. Native tradition had it that the tablet was so venerable that it even antedated writing itself. In the narrative poem *Enmerkar and the Lord of Aratta*, it is said that Enmerkar initiated writing when he "patted some clay and set words on it as if on a tablet." In the Old Babylonian period, which saw the greatest flowering of classical Sumerian literature, the most common and most handy tablet format was an oblong of about 13 by 9 centimeters (5 by 3 inches), which would carry about 30 to 35 lines of writing on each of its two sides. Analysis of some thirty Standard

Sumerian compositions reveals that they range between 60 and 640 lines each, but that there is a marked tendency toward multiples of 60/70. Indeed, the most popular lengths seem to have been 120 to 140 and about 280 lines. Furthermore, some compositions show clear structural pivots regularly at around 60 and 70 lines. Thus, it seems safe to say that at least in Mesopotamia, even the format of the medium has controlled the length and articulation of the text. Certainly in the later Babylonian tradition, larger works were divided into tablets functioning like our chapters or perhaps volumes, in most cases with their specific structure or special topic. As the term itself implies, there is an almost complete ideological homology of *ṭupšarrūtu* and the tablet, since the former literally means something like "tabletology."

Shaping the Memory by Creating the System

There is one last, important way in which literacy has influenced or even shaped the cultural and poetic memory. The principle of intertextuality is fully at work in the literatures of both Egypt and Mesopotamia. This intertextuality takes different forms, starting with somewhat straightforward copying and adaptation, such as the way in which huge chunks of older material rightly belonging to compositions about the gods Enlil, Enki, and Ninurta are incorporated into the new creed expressed in *Enuma Elish*. Many compositions contain allusions to others, and in a few cases, a composition can only be fully understood when we become familiar with other members of a group or cycle of texts. Thus, the Akkadian poem about Sargon of Akkad known as *Šar tamḫāri* makes little sense unless other parts of this wonderful cycle are also known. At the same time, it alludes clearly and in some detail to the Sumerian cycle about Gilgamesh. But as Goodnick Westenholz has shown, this cycle also illustrates how at least some of the cycle is based on much earlier written material in the form of official inscriptions from the times of Sargon and Naram-Sin themselves. In other compositions, one often sees intrusions from text types of an altogether different nature. Some of the learned or semilearned compositions called "Disputations" contain much lore and learning

culled from the lexical lists, and even a heroic narrative like *Enmerkar and the Lord of Aratta* includes a listing of dogs of different colors, which parallels what is found in an encyclopedic list. Furthermore, works reflecting historical ideology or theory, such as the historical laments and in a way the *Curse of Agade*, are based on the system presented in the Sumerian kinglist—a literary work if ever there was one. Examples like these could easily be multiplied. The important point is that even barring the influence of one literary composition on another, all these intertextualities ultimately derive from the actual environment in which every important document was drawn up, studied, copied, or handed down—the school, which was not only devoted to writing but whose whole existence and intention was meant to elaborate, foster, and perpetuate literacy.

Now the articulate system of literature in its broadest sense is also manifestly based on intertextuality in the sense of organized literacy. Unequivocally, oral literary systems—and there are remarkably few of those—teach us that oral literature uses at best only about half a dozen clearly discriminate types of discourse and that to a large extent originality or creativity is a factor of the recreative performance of existing pieces, and much less of the conception and construction of "original" work. With literacy the constraints of immediate performance fall away; the text is divorced from its occasion; it becomes truly autonomous precisely because it is fixed as such. This also makes it possible to bring out, or to grasp better, all or at least more aspects of its immanent poetical structure, its virtual ambiguities that enrich rather than weaken its "meaning." The greater distance created by its existence as an objective, material thing—a tablet or a papyrus—also allows for the detection and intellectual use of the way in which it means what it means. The possibilities for refining and discriminating among different kinds of discourse and for reserving well-defined types for sundry intentions become virtually infinite, since, although some kind of public performance remains important and must be presumed for most of our material, the moment and the circumstances of such a performance are deferred and can thereby no longer wholly or for the most part dictate the construction of the piece. Literacy allows for clear and fine distinctions between discourse types, be it on the level of texture, structure, or both. Also, and somewhat parallel to what happened with administrative documents, it allows for grouping and classification based on the distinctions carried by those features that are foregrounded as being more meaningful than others, which in turn allows for metatextuality alongside of intertextuality. Going by G. K. Chesterton's famous dictum that once you have seen an elephant you may call it "tiny," the finely distinguished and at least synchronically stable system of literature also allows one to play around with it. It takes a high degree of literacy, even of literary competence, to create an effective satire or parody. Although parody is a basic mode of metaphorical social behavior, a literary form has to create a constant concinnity between an underlying "serious" model and the mock-

ingly applied or totally inverted system of anti-values, with the resulting text and the masked intentions hovering somewhere in between.

That these effects of literacy were present then as now is splendidly illustrated by the pitiful remains of what once was the Babylonian *Tale of the Fox*. Fragmentary though it is, the material makes it clear beyond doubt that it heralds the creation of a "new" genre, namely, the satirical animal epic. Furthermore, this genre is manifestly constructed out of at least five different preexisting genres, which by themselves are unconnected. These are (1) animal fables and stories, responsible for the actors and the tonality of the piece; (2) disputations, responsible for the dialogic structure and also for the animals being presented as standing for different attitudes or values; (3) court tales, responsible for the actual argument presented as a series of

---

From *The Tale of the Fox*

1. The Contestants as Animals.

> They were chased away, and entered their holes;
> The Fox crept away deep inside his hole;
> The Wolf crouched in the midst of his lair;
> The Dog kept guard at the entrances, and kept looking out. . . .

2. Dog's Boast in Mock-Heroic Terms.

> The Dog opened its mouth and bayed;
> Fearful to them was his barking;
> Their hearts were so overcome that they vomited.
> "My strength is overpowering; I am the talon of the Thunderbird, the ferocity of the Lion.
> "My legs run faster than birds in flight;
> "At my call mountains and rivers dry up;
> "I take up my heavy duty before the sheep;
> "Their very life is entrusted to me instead of to shepherd or herdsman!
> "I am sent on the rounds in the open and near the watering places; I encircle the fold.
> "With the din of my terrible weapons I chase away . . .
> "At my baying panther, tiger, lion, wildcat flee;
> "Birds cannot fly away or set their course;
> "No rustler can steal from my pens!"

3. Fox, Being Accused by Dog, in Turn Accuses Wolf: A Self-Righteous Defense Against Treason and Slander, Based upon Common Wisdom in the Form of Proverbs.

> Fox replied, weeping bitterly;
> His heart grew heavy; his tears were profuse.
> He spoke to them:
> "Wolf, you are verily a slanderer;
> "You are the evil one who cuts even his friend's throat.
> "Why do you keep adding flames to the already burning reed?
> "Why do you stoke up the smouldering thicket?"

4. A Mock Declaration of Innocence, on the Grounds of Moral Impossibility.

> "[I did not] bite flesh, nor did I drink blood;
> "I did not tear skin, nor did I make wounds.
> "[And still, as an] enemy, I am bound.
> "[Should I] have done injury, I would gladly bear the punishment.
> "[But] Dog has spoken slanderous words.
> "[While] our very children, those of the house of truth . . .
> "And I myself am the [trustee] of Enlil!"

5. Fox Tricks the Gods into Forgiveness by Promising to Go on Pilgrimage: A Mock *Votum*.

> "[. . .] I shall bring torch and pitcher into the temple;
> "[. . .] let [all my sins?] be expelled in your presence;
> "[I] will sacrifice with my whole family to my lord Enlil!"
> Thus did Fox pray to Enlil.

pleas before a court; (4) serious heroic narrative, responsible for the tongue-in-cheek high-flown speeches and the epic conventions; and (5) serious tales about the works of the gods and their responsibility for the universe, effecting the pervasive and heavily satirical tone of mock seriousness. It is highly relevant that in Egyptian literature an identical or at least very comparable natural evolution can be observed. Among the compositions, *The Story of Sinuhe* is a new creation in generic terms, consciously using existing modes and types in order to compose a new kind of literature, which goes beyond the confines and articulations of the system out of which it was put together. Here we perceive clearly intertextuality and metatextuality at their best even as a totally new artifact was being created. And this could only happen in a literate environment. The perception of the world, of language, and of self has here been fundamentally altered through literacy.

BIBLIOGRAPHY

Origin and Development of Writing

SOURCES AND CRITICAL ISSUES

JERROLD S. COOPER, "Writing," in *International Encyclopedia of Communications*, vol. 4, edited by ERIK BARNOUW ET AL. (1989); IGNACE J. GELB, *A Study of Writing* (1952; 2nd rev. ed. 1963); M. W. GREEN, "The Construction and Implementation of the Cuneiform Writing System," *Visible Language* 15 (1981); ROY HARRIS, *The Origin of Writing* (1986); JOHN SÖREN PETTERSSON, *Critique of Evolutionary Accounts of Writing* (1991); MARVIN A. POWELL, "Three Problems in the History of Cuneiform Writing: Origins, Direction of Script, Literacy," *Visible Language* 15 (1981); GEOFFREY SAMPSON, *Writing Systems: A Linguistic Introduction* (1985); H. L. J. VANSTIPHOUT, "Enmerkar's Invention of Writing Revisited," in *DUMU-E₂-DUB-BA-A: Studies in Honor of Åke W. Sjöberg*, edited by H. BEHRENS ET AL. (1989).

THE MOMENT AND THE CONDITIONS OF THE INVENTION OF WRITING

PIERRE AMIET, "Il y a 5000 ans les Élamites inventaient l'écriture," *Archéologia* 12 (1966), and "La Naissance de l'écriture ou la vraie 'révolution,'" *Revue biblique* 97 (1990); JOHN BAINES, "Literacy and Ancient Egyptian Society," *Man*, n.s. 18 (1983), and "Literacy, Social Organization, and the Archaeological Record: The Case of Early Egypt," in *State and Society*, edited by JOHN GLEDHILL, BARBARA BENDER, and MOGENS TROLLE LARSEN (1988); J. S. JUSTESON, "The Origin of Writing Systems: Preclassic Mesoamerica," *World Archaeology* 17 (1985–1986); R. LEBRUN AND F. VALLAT, "L'Origine de l'écriture à Suse," *Cahiers de la délégation archéologique française en Iran* 8 (1978); E. S. MELTZER, "Remarks on Ancient Egyptian Writing with Emphasis on Its Mnemonic Aspects," in *Processing of Visible Language*, edited by P. A. KOLERS ET AL. (1979); DENISE SCHMANDT-BESSERAT, *Before Writing* (1992); WOLFGANG SCHENKEL, "Schrift," in *Lexikon der Ägyptologie*, vol. 5, edited by WOLFGANG HELCK and WOLFHART WESTENDORF (1984); HERMAN TE VELDE, "Scribes and Literacy in Ancient Egypt," in *Scripta Signa Vocis*, edited by H. L. J. VANSTIPHOUT ET AL. (1986).

EVOLUTION AND IMPLICATIONS

JOHN BAINES, "Communication and Display: The Integration of Early Egyptian Art and Writing," *Antiquity* 63 (1989); D. O. EDZARD, "Keilschrift," in *Reallexikon der Assyriologie und vorderasiatischen Archäologie*, vol. 5 (1976–1980); H. L. J. VANSTIPHOUT, "Miḫiltum, or the Image of Cuneiform Writing," *Visible Religion, Annual for Religious Iconography* 6 (1988); HERMAN TE VELDE, "Egyptian Hieroglyphs as Linguistic Signs and Metalinguistic Informants," *Visible Religion, Annual for Religious Iconography* 6 (1988).

SPREAD AND TRANSFORMATION

M. DIETRICH and O. LORETZ, *Die Keilalphabete, Die Phönizisch-kanaanäischen, und altarabischen Alphabete in Ugarit* (1988); and G. R. DRIVER, *Semitic Writing: From Pictograph to Alphabet* (1944; 2nd ed., revised and edited by S. A. HOPKINS, 1976).

Purpose and Impact

JEAN BOTTÉRO, "Symptômes, signes, écritures," in *Divination et rationalité*, edited by J.-P. VERNANT ET AL. (1974), *Mésopotamie: L'Écriture, la raison, et les dieux* (1987), and "L'Écriture et la formation de l'intelligence en Mésopotamie ancienne," *Le Débat* 62 (1990); JACK GOODY, *The Domestication of the Savage Mind* (1977), *The Logic of Writing and the Organization of Society* (1986), and *The Interface Between the Written and the Oral* (1987); JACK GOODY, ED., *Literacy in Traditional Societies* (1968); JOHN HALVERSON, "Goody and the Implosion of the Literacy Thesis," *Man* 27 (1992); ERIK A. HAVELOCK, *The Literate Revolution in Greece and Its Cultural Consequences* (1982); ROBERT K. LOGAN, *The Alphabet Effect: The Impact of the Phonetic Alphabet on the Development of*

Western Civilization (1986); JOSEF VACHEK, *Written Language Revisited* (1989).

The Structures of Literacy

BENDT ALSTER, "Interaction of Oral and Written Poetry in Early Mesopotamian Literature," in *Mesopotamian Epic Literature: Oral or Aural?*, edited by M. VOGELZANG and H. L. J. VANSTIPHOUT (1992); JAN ASSMANN, "Schrift, Tod, und Identität: Das Grab als Vorschule der Literatur in Ägypten," in *Schrift und Gedächtnis*, edited by ALEIDA ASSMANN ET AL. (1983), and *Das kulturelle Gedächtnis: Schrift, Erinnerung, und politische Identität in frühen Hochkulturen* (1992); HELMUT BRUNNER, *Altägyptische Erziehung* (1957); CHRISTOPHER EYRE and JOHN BAINES, "Interactions Between Orality and Literacy in Ancient Egypt," in *Literacy and Society*, edited by KAREN SCHOUSBOE and MOGENS TROLLE LARSEN (1989); MOGENS TROLLE LARSEN, "What They Wrote on Clay," in *Literacy and Society*, edited by K. SCHOUSBOE and M. T. LARSEN (1989); PIOTR MICHALOWSKI, "Orality and Literacy and Early Mesopotamian Literature," in *Mesopotamian Epic Literature: Oral or Aural?*, edited by M. VOGELZANG and H. L. J. VANSTIPHOUT (1992); Å. W. SJÖBERG, "The Old Babylonian Eduba," in *Sumerological Studies in Honor of Thorkild Jacobsen*, edited by S. J. LIEBERMAN, Assyriological Studies 20 (1975); ROSALIND THOMAS, *Literacy and Orality in Ancient Greece* (1992); H. L. J. VANSTIPHOUT, "How Did They Learn Sumerian?" *Journal of Cuneiform Studies* 31 (1979).

The Ordering and Shaping of Memory

ORGANIZING THE MESSAGE

JEREMY A. BLACK, *Sumerian Grammar in Babylonian Theory* (1984); MIGUEL CIVIL, "The Sumerian Writing System," *Orientalia* 42 (1973), and "Lexicography," in *Sumerological Studies in Honor of Thorkild Jacobsen*, edited by S. J. LIEBERMAN, Assyriological Studies 20 (1975).

ORDERING THE DISCOURSE AND THE TEXT

H. L. J. VANSTIPHOUT, "Some Remarks on Cuneiform *Écritures*," in *Scripta Signa Vocis*, edited by H. L. J. VANSTIPHOUT ET AL. (1986), "Towards a Reading of 'Gilgamesh and Agga.' Part II: Construction," *Orientalia Lovaniensia Periodica* 17 (1986), and "Repetition and Structure in the Aratta Cycle: Their Relevance for the Orality Debate," in *Mesopotamian Epic Literature: Oral or Aural?*, edited by M. VOGELZANG and H. L. J. VANSTIPHOUT (1992).

SHAPING THE MEMORY BY CREATING THE SYSTEM

JOAN GOODNICK WESTENHOLZ, "Heroes of Akkad," *Journal of the American Oriental Society* 103 (1983), and "Oral Traditions and Written Texts in the Cycle of Akkade," in *Mesopotamian Epic Literature: Oral or Aural?*, edited by M. VOGELZANG and H. L. J. VANSTIPHOUT (1992); JOHN BAINES, "Interpreting *Sinuhe*," *Journal of Egyptian Archaeology* 68 (1982); CHRISTOPHER J. EYRE, "Why Was Egyptian Literature?" in *Sesto Congresso Internazionale di Egittologia: Atti*, vol. 2 (1993); H. L. J. VANSTIPHOUT, "Lore, Learning, and Levity in the Sumerian Disputations: A Matter of Form, or Substance?" in *Dispute Poems and Dialogues in the Ancient and Mediaeval Near East*, edited by G. REININK and H. L. J. VANSTIPHOUT (1991).

SEE ALSO **The Scribes of Ancient Egypt** (Part 9, Vol. IV) and **The Scribes and Scholars of Ancient Mesopotamia** (Part 9, Vol. IV).

Archives and Libraries in the Ancient Near East

J. A. BLACK and W. J. TAIT

ARCHIVES AND LIBRARIES WERE a vital element both of the cuneiform scribal traditions of the ancient Near East and of the almost completely independent hieroglyphic and hieratic scribal tradition of Egypt. They played a key role both in administrative practice and in the handing on and development of the literatures. Unfortunately, intact archives and libraries rarely survive, and their original locations have not often been the object of competent archaeological work; the evidence from Egypt is particularly disappointing in this respect.

NATURE AND LOCATIONS

Cuneiform World

Almost any group of documents excavated together can be called an "archive," on a broad definition of the word. Within Mesopotamia and the rest of the regions using cuneiform writing, "library" tends to be reserved for a collection including literary, historical, and perhaps scientific texts, in an institutional building such as a palace or temple or in a private house—where it might be the property of a scholar-scribe or priest, such as the library of Qurdi-Nergal at Sultantepe, or that in the house of Rap'anu at Ugarit. In practice the distinction between archive and library is often impossible to make, since administrative, legal, and business records may be stored in the same room as traditional or scientific texts used for scribal training, and priests or scholars kept their family records at home with their private libraries. Occasionally archival records (state letters and legal documents) were incorporated into the educational repertoire and repeatedly copied.

Temples may have had a limited involvement in legal procedures, but they do not appear to have served as storage places for official records (except those of their own commercial activities, such as the "bank" operated from the temple of Nabu at Nimrud [Kalkhu] in Neo-Assyrian times). However, scholarly libraries of literary, scientific, and pedagogical texts and copies of historical documents existed at the temples of Nabu in the Assyrian capitals—Nineveh (modern Tell Kuyunjik, Nebi Yunus), Nimrud, and Dur-Sharrukin (modern Khorsabad)—and at the temple of Shamash at Sippar (modern Abu Habba) in Babylonia.

The time span covered by documents from individual private archives seems to range up to as much as two hundred years, (for example, the Egibi family archives, or Ur-Utu's archive from Tell al-Der), while the archives from Nuzi (Nuzu, modern Yorghun Tepe) span some five generations. But most documents will belong to the last couple of generations. Within the literary tradition, the Sippar library contained one tablet more than five hundred years old, but this was probably exceptional.

Egypt

A distinction seems to have been recognized in Egypt, at least in principle, between official archives and libraries, in that different terms are used for them. For example, for archives, the "Office of Writings of the Vizier" is mentioned in the Twentieth Dynasty Papyrus Abbott (edited by T. E. Peet) as the place in which a document has been lodged, rather than where it was written, while libraries were termed "House of Books (or Book-rolls)." Royal and temple libraries are known, and it is normally assumed that in practice they contained a far wider range of material than just literary or religious texts. Temples certainly kept elaborate accounts. Although it is generally inferred that every branch of the Egyptian bureaucracy maintained extensive archives, the surviving documentation is heavily weighted in favor of temple records. The extensive and elaborate Papyrus Wilbour of the reign of Ramesses (Ramses) V (circa 1150–1145 BCE) surveys different kinds of land within a limited district: it is a matter of debate whether the text was a product of state or temple administration. Military records—by which is meant not just accounts of royal campaigns, but regular reports on routine and trivial tours of duty—were evidently generated in great quantities. Although it remains disputed just what kind of legal documentation was, for example, available to the New Kingdom vizier when dispensing justice, it is clear that official and private archive material played a part in the work of Egyptian courts at all periods.

A few private libraries have survived. For ex-

Retrieving Tablets from an Archive

Letters on cuneiform tablets from the court of King Zimri-Lim of Mari (early eighteenth century) allow us to form some impression of the procedures involved in retrieving documents from a storeroom to which access was classified. Evidently at Mari a rather cumbersome system was in use, necessitating the participation of several specifically authorized persons. Interestingly, not all of these needed to be literate. Queen Shiptu writes to the king:

> Tell my lord, thus speaks Shiptu, your handmaid. The palace is in good order. My lord wrote to me, "Herewith I am sending Yassur-Addu to you. Send inspectors with him to retrieve tablets from a location he will indicate. These documents should be kept with you until my arrival."
>
> So now, in accordance with what my lord wrote to me, I have had Mukannishum, Shubnalu, and (a third person) accompany this man Yassur-Addu. He showed the inspectors whom I sent along a storeroom in a workshop supervised by Etel-pi-sharrim. They opened the door of the storeroom he identified, breaking the seal of Igmillum of the Central Office in doing so. They retrieved two baskets stamped with the seal of Etel-pi-sharrim. With their seal impressions still intact, these baskets are now with me, awaiting my lord's arrival. Meanwhile I have used my own seal to reseal the door of the storeroom they opened.

In another letter, Mukannishum writes to the king about a similar occurrence:

> When Igmillum . . . showed us the containers with the tablets of the district which were stamped with Sammetar's seal, Tabat-sharussu and I retrieved them into our own custody. As my lord had instructed me, I did not open any container, but I merely brought out two baskets and had them sent to my lord.

The high priestess Inibshina, sister of the king, writes to her brother to confirm these details:

> According to the written request you sent me, I have opened the archive room bearing your own sealing, and, while Mukannishum and Tabat-sharussu were standing by, Igmillum showed them the containers *according to his knowledge* (translation uncertain) and they took into their own custody the containers with the census records; but I have sent you the sealed documents needed for the inventory.

However, not all palace chancelleries were so carefully administered. Half a millennium later, in the mid-thirteenth century, the Hittite king Khattushili (Hattusili) III, writing from Anatolia to Kadashman-Enlil II, king of Babylonia, laments the fact that

> At that early date you, my brother, were a youngster and they did not read the tablets to you. Currently the scribes of those days are no longer alive, and the tablets were not even archived such that they would have been able to read the old tablets to you now.

ample the Ramesseum papyri were found in a wooden box within a modest late Middle Kingdom tomb later hidden beneath one of the storehouses of the New Kingdom Ramesseum in western Thebes. The owner's name is unknown, but Sir Alan Gardiner suggested that his interests were those of "a magician and medical practitioner." The texts comprise religious, magical, medical, and literary material; documents seem to have been present only as scrap paper. From the New Kingdom, a family library from Dayr al-Madina was discovered early in the twentieth century, but became scattered between several collections (some are known as the Chester Beatty papyri). The precise contents and size of the library are uncertain, but it comprised at least forty papyri, including literary and magical-medical texts, as well as letters and private and official documents. It was added to for a period of more than one hundred years, although its later owners (in contrast to the preferences of the presumed owner of the Ramesseum papyri) seem to have regarded the literary material as expendable. The author of the *Petition of Petiese* (P. Rylands IX) was able to compile a detailed chronicle of his family's misfortunes for a century and a half, from the reign of Psamtik (Psammetichus) I (664–610) down to the time of writing (the reign of Darius I [521–486]).

PHYSICAL CHARACTERISTICS

Cuneiform World

Sun-dried clay tablets (the principal medium for cuneiform writing) can be damaged by water, salts, or crushing; but, when baked in a kiln, or accidentally in a conflagration (as happened relatively often), they are much more likely to survive for thousands of years. Their preservation may be deliberate, or accidental (if reused as packing and fill in building or simply discarded as rubbish). It is clear from colophons (paragraphs written at the end of the last column of text on a tablet) that waxed wooden boards were also extensively used, especially for library texts, but these have universally perished. Two sets of ivory boards are known: one from the fourteenth-century BCE Uluburun shipwreck and one from the Northwest Palace at Nimrud.

Papyrus too was widely used in the first millennium, but labels or summaries on clay, attached to the papyrus documents, are all that has survived.

Tablets could be stored in various containers—in a jar, basket, bag, or box, possibly wrapped in a reed mat or piece of cloth. Thousands of tablets might be kept in a special room, which might have been sealed. Such a room might have low storage-benches around the walls or (as at Nimrud) a narrow well in the corner. The tablets might be stacked on the floor leaning against the walls, or stacked in rows facing inward on several levels of wooden shelving, as in the archive room of the palace of Ebla (modern Tell Mardikh). Tablets were also stored in groups in pigeonholes, as at Sippar, Dur-Sharrukin, and Nineveh. The shaded sunlight of a doorway or portico outside the storage room offers ideal light conditions for reading cuneiform texts; the interiors of rooms would probably have been too dark for writing.

The desirability of retrieving tablets from storage without reading through the whole of each document necessitated some organization. Sometimes the physical shape and size of a tablet, or the layout of a text, was enough to identify the nature of a document or the genre of a composition. Colophons are of crucial importance for the study of literary and scientific texts. They may give the identity of and position within the series of the tablet, a catchline to the next tablet, information on the textual ancestry (source of the original exemplars from which the tablet was copied), name and family of the scribe, occasionally that of the person for whom the tablet was written, restrictions on access to the text, and library to which the tablet belonged, as well as a curse on anyone who damaged or destroyed the tablet.

At Mari (modern Tell Hariri) a red stripe, painted lengthwise over an account tablet, indicated that its contents were consulted when establishing an inventory. Occasionally it was also used to delete names of deceased individuals from lists. Some account tablets from Ebla had the most recent month written on the upper edge of the tablet, making selection from a stack easy. Similarly, some Old Babylonian administrative texts had a short summary note on their left (upper) edge. From the seventh century, notes in (alphabetic) Aramaic were written in ink on tablets for the benefit of those too busy to read the Akkadian cuneiform; there is limited evidence for Aramaic annotations on the Elamite cuneiform documents from Persepolis. Jars containing personal archives sometimes had the person's name written on the outside of the jar. Label-tablets survive, summarizing briefly the contents of individual containers to which they were attached: "tablet-box (or basket) containing . . ." (usually giving a date and names of officials involved). It is clear, for example, from the Ebla "system," that some labeling registered not the final storage place of the documents but the *movement* of people and products through the system, and so some records are in transit, intended to be only temporarily in the archive, but trapped there for posterity by whatever disaster sealed the archaeological deposit.

Egypt

Papyrus was the basic writing material in Egypt, and hieratic, written with rush pen and ink, the basic script for most literature and for all documents (the hieroglyphic script was used principally for monumental and other similar purposes). Papyrus was always manufactured in the form of a roll, and Egyptian scribes generally worked with the complete roll, not separate sheets. The commonest Egyptian term for "book (in the form of a roll)" is also the commonest word for a literary book.

Papyrus is a relatively tough material. It normally cannot survive fire, although a few carbonized rolls, some of importance, are known from Egypt to set alongside the famous Herculaneum papyri and a large find was made at Tanis in the Delta in 1993. Papyrus rolls suffer grievously from rough handling (the number of rolls that survive with beginning and end intact is extremely small) and above all from damp. Thus the bulk of surviving papyri come from tombs or special contexts such as the New Kingdom necropolis workmen's village of Dayr al-Madina, or the administrative headquarters of the necropolis, based (at one period) in the Madinat Habu mortuary temple of Ramesses III, both situated on the dry desert edge, outside the area of cultivation. Wooden writing boards with a gesso surface, which were written on with pen

and ink, were commonly employed, especially for accounts and in school. Material was probably not stored in this form. Ostraca (potsherds or limestone flakes) were widely used for ephemeral purposes. Leather rolls rarely survive and were probably employed for special purposes, which certainly included ritual books. The inscribed version of the annals of Thutmosis III (circa 1479–1425) at Karnak, however, specifies that an account of his siege of Megiddo was recorded on a leather roll deposited in the temple.

Papyrus rolls, when tightly rolled up, were regularly secured by a thong of loosened papyrus fibers, and this was sealed with a small quantity of mud, which might bear a seal impression. A little evidence suggests that rolls could also be tied together to protect one another, and were often stored in groups in boxes, baskets, pots, or bags—and no doubt other containers were also used. Specific rooms in, for example, temples or administrative offices seem to have been set aside for the storage of papyri, but there is no sign that they had any special kind of arrangement or permanent furniture (an image of the god of writing, Thoth, may have been a common feature), and reading and writing of papyri clearly was done elsewhere. Remarkably little is known about the labeling of collections of books or documents, although the systematic labeling of containers of many kinds is well attested, and was no doubt applied to papyrus storage. Papyrus rolls of different heights were preferred for various types of text and document (and the preferences changed from one period to another). Only the occasional imposing document or religious text had a roll height in excess of sixteen inches (forty centimeters), and New Kingdom literary rolls were often eight inches (twenty centimeters) or less in height. These differences, however, can hardly have provided much help in retrieving material from storage. Rolls, when closed and sealed, could be annotated on their outside surface, although this is commonly found only in the case of letters, which regularly bear an external address. Two small faience "book labels" of King Amenhotep (Amenophis) III (circa 1390–1353) are perhaps isolated evidence for the labeling of single rolls.

Egyptian "daybooks" and records and accounts of many kinds give prominence to the dates that head the entry for each day (they are

Papyrus Manufacture

In Egypt, the papyrus roll was, throughout dynastic history, the standard surface used to bear writing. The papyrus plant is not self-evidently a promising source of writing material. Papyrus, however, had been used for such purposes as basket- and boat-making for much of Egyptian prehistory, and the properties of its white inner pith would have been well understood. The plant grows in swamps, and at the start of dynastic history was extremely widespread in Egypt. By the end of the Middle Ages the exploitation of the plant and the reclamation of swampland for agriculture had eradicated papyrus from the Nile Valley within Egypt, although it still thrives in the Sudan. The plant grows by sending up from a substantial root-formation a succession of tall triangular stems, up to two inches (five centimeters) in thickness, each one bearing a feathery flower head. It is likely that in the Old Kingdom papyrus was gathered from the wild; in the Ptolemaic period it is clear that the plant was farmed.

The methods of manufacture of a papyrus roll must be deduced from surviving ancient papyri and from modern experiments, as the Egyptians did not describe or depict the process, and information from classical writers is suspect or barely intelligible. After the removal of the tough outer rind from the stems, the soft pith was cut or torn into long strips, anything from half an inch to a little more than an inch (one to three centimeters) wide, and very thin. A papyrus sheet is made up of two layers of these strips. A dozen or more strips were laid down flat, side by side, just touching each other, to form the first layer. A second set of strips was immediately laid down over the first. The strips of the two layers were arranged to run at right angles to each other; thus the length of one set of strips would correspond to the height of the finished sheet, that of the other to the width. The sheet was consolidated by hammering or by pressure and was left to dry.

The finished sheets might sometimes have been polished, for example, by a smooth pebble. A papyrus roll consisted of several sheets (twenty was a standard number) fastened together. Each sheet was made to overlap the next by about half an inch (one to two centimeters) and a starch paste was used to join them securely. The manufacturer seems always to have made the sheets up into rolls, and, if an individual

Drawing of a papyrus plant. F. WOENIG, *DIE PFLANZEN IM ALTEN AEGYPTEN* (1886)

sheet was required, the scribe would himself cut it from the roll. Clearly, much experience and skill were needed in harvesting the papyrus stalks and in making the sheets. The most successful modern attempts at manufacture fall short of the whiteness, evenness, and thinness of the best ancient papyrus, some surviving examples of which retain the suppleness that makes papyrus a particularly pleasant writing material.

The papyrus roll was already employed in the First Dynasty, as is indicated by the discovery of a blank roll in a tomb of the period. The hieroglyph that depicts a sealed papyrus roll was also in use then. It is plausible that the development of the hieratic script went hand in hand with the introduction of the Egyptian scribe's standard equipment—papyrus roll, rush pen (a flexible, almost brushlike writing implement), and carbon ink—and led to developments in the use of writing.

often picked out in red ink). Literary works regularly each occupy one roll and begin with a statement of their title. School texts and unpretentious private copies may include several works upon one roll. The division of a single work between rolls was unnecessary, as rolls could be pasted together to accommodate virtually any length of text. Documentary material might be treated in the same way. For example, the Great Harris Papyrus records the temple donations of King Ramesses III (circa 1187–1156) in a single roll some forty-seven yards (forty-two meters) long. When records occupied a series of rolls, it seems likely that no more elaborate system of cross-reference was employed than uniform headings and the prominent use of dates. In particular, documents both public and private regularly began with a conspicuous date, which would have assisted in arranging them chronologically. Colophons at the end of texts were common. They would have been difficult to consult, if it is correct to assume that books were regularly rolled back to their beginning after consultation. Most commonly, colophons record the scribe who copied a text and assert the accuracy of the copy.

ARCHIVES

Cuneiform World

Tens of thousands of cuneiform documents can be described as originating from archives, but not generally in the sense of "repositories of records no longer in use but preserved for their historical value" (as described by K. R. Veenhof). Instead they were, typically, working archives, continually in use (sometimes terminated by catastrophe). It was relatively rare for records that were no longer needed for consultation to be kept, and they were usually thrown away or used as fillers for mud benches or the like (which does not preclude their being found by modern excavators). Although many of these documents are the products of officials exercising their functions within some organizational system (temple, palace, or governmental institutions), it is necessary to include here private archives, the records of individuals. The distinction between official and private is not always

easy to make: officials might keep personal or family documents or correspondence in their workplaces, and some government business, for example during the later Old Babylonian period, was carried on by privatized contracting out to independent agents, whose archives illustrate their government work as well as their private activities. The Middle Babylonian landowners of the Nuzi area have left private archives that demonstrate their almost feudal control of local administration. The archives of large family firms in the Neo-Babylonian and Achaemenid periods, such as Egibi and Murashu, cover several generations and a wide range of business activities. (See "Private Commerce and Banking in Achaemenid Babylon" in Part 6, Vol. III.)

Bureaucratic bookkeeping procedures were a fundamental stimulus to the development of writing itself and can be observed in the earliest surviving written documents from Uruk (modern Warka, biblical Erech), found among later rubbish but dating to perhaps as early as 3400. At Ebla detailed monthly allotment and expenditure accounts were stored temporarily pending the transfer of the information in summary form to smaller tablets for longer-term storage. Perhaps the most complex bureaucracy of the ancient Near East was that of the empire of the Third Dynasty of Ur, whose traditions were to some extent bequeathed to its immediate successors, the kingdoms of Isin (modern Ishan Bahriyat), Larsa (modern Tell Senkereh), and Babylon. A highly involved recording system was devised for use at Puzrish-Dagan (modern Drehem) to render enormous numbers of workers accountable for the entry into, passage through, and exit from the administration of all human personnel, every single animal (dead or alive), and all material goods. Such systems require great care if they are to function satisfactorily. Interesting evidence from the royal kitchen accounts from the Old Babylonian palace at Mari has demonstrated considerable discrepancies in record keeping, confirming that scribes were (like their modern counterparts) frequently careless and inaccurate in their computations. Sometimes multiple "bureaux" existed at different locations within one institution, as with the eight partially interrelated archives from the royal palace at Ebla, the several discrete archives from Mari—such as the diplomatic, royal kitchen, and customs archives—or the western and eastern archives of the palace of Ugarit, each positioned near an entrance to the palace.

Assyriologists try to reconstruct the administrative infrastructures by a systematic analysis of the documents from these archives. Some scribal offices may have been not only centers where incoming documents were read and filed but also chancelleries responsible for drafting state letters, royal inscriptions, year names, and annals. The existence in such archives of some apparently private records raises questions of the role of the palace and the extent of state control, through centralized administration, over the lives of ordinary citizens. The evidence for centralized cadastral surveys, as a basis for census, taxation, or land sales or allocations, is limited, and such as there is may be more closely connected with military conscription. Similarly, there is no very clear evidence for systematic registration of legal records, a notable exception being the apparent attempt at Girsu (modern Tello) under the Third Dynasty of Ur to compile a centralized archive of *ditilas* (completed legal verdicts), possibly with a view to establishing some sort of case law. Normally legal records were retained privately by those personally concerned in the suits. Temples may have been responsible for administering the oaths sworn by witnesses or parties in lawsuits or have been the place where courts met, but they seem to have had little legal authority as such.

Some archives as excavated are clearly not complete but form the core of a larger archive, from which the most important documents have been selected and preserved (perhaps hidden against disaster), such as the archive from Kutalla (modern Tell Sifr) of Ṣilli-Ishtar, who wrapped certain documents in a reed mat and hid them beneath the bricks of the floor of his house. The importance of letters in archives must be stressed. Among the Old Assyrian merchants operating at Kanesh (modern Kültepe) in Anatolia, it was frequently the custom to keep copies of letters sent. Numerous letters, however, were found in uncontrolled excavations out of any archival context. This raises the possibility of modern reconstruction of archives from tablets scattered in different museums and collections, on the basis of prosopographical data (for example, letters all addressed to the same

person or to related persons, or records of the activities of an interconnected group of officials). While this can be a useful procedure, it is severely limiting in that it draws together only such documents as can be plausibly linked. The importance of an archive excavated in a detailed archaeological context—say a jar full of tablets, or a kiln full of tablets that were baked (as in one example of the thirteenth century at Ugarit in Syria)—is that it offers an authentic assemblage of documents that would not otherwise have been reunited, and whose presence together may indeed be perplexing to explain.

Egypt

In Egypt also, "archives" were essentially working archives, and there is no indication that material of a strictly documentary kind was retained for its historical value or out of any sense of reverence. Officials and others plainly reused discarded rolls for private purposes, including the copying of literary works, and papyrus was also recycled within official archives. Archive material, then, more commonly survives by chance, as incoherent groups of fragments—in fact, as rubbish. The prime Egyptian example of an archive simply abandoned *in situ* was the royal archive at Akhenaten's short-lived capital of Akhetaten (Amarna), from which came the *Amarna Letters,* cuneiform tablets preserving royal correspondence between Egypt and other kingdoms of the ancient Near East. Virtually none of the material was found in regular excavations, and the opportunity to study its organization was lost. The texts cover only a couple of decades, but, as Akhetaten was built up from nothing as an administrative center, this cannot tell us what other royal archives might have been like.

Curiously, the most explicit statement as to the documentation that a ruler might expect to call upon is contained in the literary *Report of Wenamun.* This story recounts the journey, during the final years of the collapse of the New Kingdom, of an official of the Karnak temple of the god Amun-Re to Byblos, whose independent ruler imitated the pharaonic style, to acquire timber for the rebuilding of the sacred boat of the god. A dispute as to whether or not Egypt had on previous occasions actually paid for timber is settled when the ruler of Byblos "had fetched

The Abusir Papyri

The Abusir papyri are our earliest substantial group of Egyptian documentary material. As with so many other Egyptian archives, the papyri—all fragmentary—first came to light in illicit excavations, apparently in 1893, and were soon in the possession of several museums and private purchasers. Subsequent excavation found further fragments in the funerary temple of the Fifth Dynasty king Neferirkare Kakai (circa 2400) on the desert edge near Abusir. The archive had evidently been housed in a room of this temple. The material now known is divided between at least six museums.

The archive covers a period of about eighty years, commencing some fifty years after the death of Neferirkare. The papyri evidently represent only a small fraction of the documentation that must have been produced during that period, and it is probably chance that has denied us of earlier or later material from the same source. Not all the types of document originally stored in the archive are necessarily represented by those that survive. These include inventories of temple furniture and other objects, compiled regularly as one group of priests handed over responsibility for the running of the temple to another, with notations of any damage; inspections of the fabric of the temple; accounts of various types, notably daily and monthly accounts of temple income and accounts of issues of food and the like; and rosters of the daily duties of temple staff.

The papyrus upon which the documents are written is of very fine quality—apparently a general feature of Old Kingdom material. The papyri have often,

however, had a previous text erased, presumably for economy and because such regular routine documentation soon lost its relevance. No kind of register intended to be valid over a considerable period of time seems to be present. Many documents are laid out as elaborate tables, evidently following well-established principles, with horizontal and vertical lines ruled to aid the eye of the reader. Sometimes every tenth horizontal line is ruled in red ink (the Egyptian week comprised ten days), and red is used in other ways to make aspects of the tables clearer. The tabular form does not seem to have been employed in order that information might be entered piecemeal, but simply as a matter of presentation. Monthly accounts appear to have been compiled from more frequent ones, and it has been suggested that even the daily accounts are fair copies.

The Abusir archive has been comprehensively studied. In 1979 a few fragments from another royal temple archive were discovered at Abusir, and in 1982 numerous small fragments came to light from the Abusir temple of Reneferef. The indications are that the Neferirkare archive was typical of temple administration of the period, and the evidence of some slightly earlier papyri from Gebelein (Pathyris, Aphroditopolis) in the south suggests that this was not merely a local phenomenon. The presence in the Neferirkare archive, apart from the types of document already mentioned, of many letters (perhaps copies of letters) and of much miscellaneous material might hint that the temple stored, at least for a while, virtually all its paperwork.

the daybooks of his ancestors. He had them read before me, and a thousand *deben* of silver came to light, and all kinds of things, according to his books." Although the text sometimes makes a point of introducing local color from the Levant, the terminology here suggests Egyptian practice, and the context indicates that such documentation was to be expected.

The Abusir papyri (see box) suggest that in Egypt a comprehensive recording of the movement of personnel, animals, and goods was attempted, similar to that mentioned above for Puzrish-Dagan. Accounting errors may similarly be found. The relationship between different branches of the bureaucracy is more difficult to chart and may reflect an actual weakness in the

Egyptian system as a whole. The notion of registering documents with the central authority, however (an obsession of the Greco-Roman period, in the case of both demotic and Greek documents), seems clearly evidenced for the office of the vizier in the New Kingdom. From several periods, we know of documents drawn up with the expectation that they would be binding upon future generations. Evidence also exists that courts would take into consideration archives of documents dating over hundreds of years, and that documentation would be scrutinized for falsification. Indeed, there is considerable evidence for mistrust of written documents, such as wills, unsupported by the testimony of witnesses to their contents.

SPREAD

Cuneiform World

The cuneiform scribal tradition is an unbroken one, lasting at least thirty-four centuries. In particular the tradition of the so-called lexical texts, designed for scribal training, can be followed for the whole of that period. The literary tradition of individual works is long-lived also: the proverb collection *The Instructions of Shuruppak* can be traced from an Old Sumerian version (about 2400 from the literary archive found at Abu Sala-bikh) to a Middle Assyrian translation (about 1100), while Sumerian cultic lyric poems of about 1800 were still being copied—almost un-changed, but accompanied by an interlinear Akkadian translation—at Babylon in the first century BCE. The extent to which a tradition of bureaucratic procedures can be traced down the centuries deserves further study; it is known that chancellery practices reached Ebla in Syria from Sumer through Kish (modern Tell al-Uhaimir, Tell Ingharra) and Mari in the third millennium, and that Babylonian scribal procedures (especially the format of letters and treaties—inescapably bound to the international language, Akkadian) reached the Hittite Empire and also Syria again, this time through the Hurrian state Mitanni, in the second millennium. From Syria they were transmitted to Egypt and are known from the tablets found at Akhetaten (Amarna).

Egypt

Although the initial development in Egypt of the hieroglyphic script probably took place because of an awareness of the development of writing in Mesopotamia, the Egyptian scripts thereafter had a virtually independent evolution, and the rapid establishment of hieratic as the script of everyday life ensured that Egyptian scribal practices were very different from those of cuneiform. Egyptian language and script had remarkably little influence or imitations abroad (the chief exceptions being the Meroitic script, invented around 200, and the practice at Byblos). The Egyptian scribal tradition remained unbroken until the gradual infiltration of some Greek practices began in the Ptolemaic period, and it did not perish until the final demise of the native scripts relatively late in the Roman period.

Within Egypt, even in the earlier New Kingdom the existence of Thebes as the nominal capital city of the Eighteenth Dynasty alongside Memphis (modern Mit Rahina) as the favored administrative center allowed minor variations in scribal practice to develop. Under the Twenty-sixth (Saite) Dynasty (664–525) which gradually reunified a country that had been increasingly fragmented ever since the final collapse of the New Kingdom, a new cursive script, demotic, was developed in the north and gradually supplanted the abnormal hieratic script, which had been the natural development from

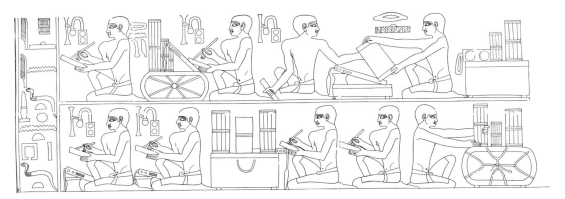

Relief of scribes at work, from the Tomb of Ti at Saqqara, mid Fifth Dynasty, circa 2400 BCE. Six write, one unrolls a papyrus to show to another, and one arranges rolls on a traylike base. Also shown are boxes for papyri, more papyrus rolls, scribes' palettes, and water pots. HENRI WILD, *LE TOMBEAU DE TI*, VOL. 3, *LA CHAPELLE* (1966).

the late New Kingdom hieratic of Thebes in the south. Demotic in due course became the regular script for both literary and documentary material. In the Persian period, various new concepts relevant to archival and library practice may have been introduced. For example, a section of the papyrus known as the *Demotic Chronicle* (because of another text preserved upon it) records that Darius I ordered that previous Egyptian law of all kinds "down to year 44 of king Amasis" (that is, down to 526, the eve of Persian control of Egypt) should be "written." The point of this order cannot have been that hitherto unrecorded law should be committed to writing. Later evidence indicates that laws might be cited by the regnal year of their enactment, and the comprehensive listing of laws by date was probably the essential feature of the innovation.

LIBRARIES

Cuneiform World

The very existence of a cuneiform literary tradition implies the transmission from one library to another, as well as from one private collection to another, of the same, similar, or related texts. Colophons give explicit information about this. Old Sumerian archives, predominantly of literary tablets, were found both at Shuruppak (Fara) and at Tell Abu Salabikh, in each case dispersed through several rooms of a building. Although there was apparently a scribal academy under royal patronage at Nippur (Nuffar) during the Third Dynasty of Ur, which was a crucially important center for the collation and copying as well as the composition of many Sumerian literary works, libraries as such are more a feature of the first millennium (and, to a limited extent, the second). A royal library at Khattusha (modern Boğazköy) combining political documents and religious and literary texts survived until the fall of the Hittite Empire about 1200: some of its catalogs may date from the fifteenth or fourteenth century. A library collection at Asshur (modern Qalat Sharqat) was probably begun by Tiglath-pileser I (1114–1076) and continued by Tukulti-Ninurta II (890–884), although precise excavational data about this are limited.

At each of the other three Assyrian capitals (Dur-Sharrukin, Nimrud, and Nineveh), the temples of the scribal god Nabu (and similarly the temple of Nergal at Tarbisu [modern Tell Sherif Khan], residence of the crown prince) housed libraries of literary, scientific, religious, and historical texts. These have been recovered with varying degrees of completeness. At Nineveh royal libraries were housed in both the Northwest and the Southwest palaces at Kuyunjik, collections probably begun by Sennacherib and continued by his grandson Assurbanipal. A letter from Assurbanipal addressed to one of his officials gives detailed instructions for the (enforced) collection from the temple of Nabu at Borsippa (Birs Nimrud) in Babylonia, and from private scholarly collections in that city, of certain rare magical and religious texts that are "needed in the palace" but not available in Assyria. "No one is to withhold tablets from you; search for and acquire any other tablets which are good for my palace as well." Just such a Babylonian temple library was found *in situ* at Sippar.

Literary texts were sometimes copied exactly, with the same format maintained. Sometimes the format was altered, with one or more whole compositions copied onto one large library tablet, or, alternatively, one composition divided up into sections on smaller tablets (perhaps what might be called performance editions). It has been argued that the typical size of a Sumerian literary tablet influenced the typical length of literary works. (See the preceding article, "Memory and Literacy in Ancient Western Asia.") Later, on the other hand, compendious scholarly works of reference might be spread in a series over fifty or more tablets. Indices exist that list the incipits (first words or lines) of these tablets in sequence; library catalogs list a variety of works, sometimes of the same genre, sometimes apparently descriptive handlists of actual libraries. Other catalogs seem to be more normative in intent. When a scribe writes, "checked; all that were available; many could not be traced and were therefore not included," it is clear that he is already aware of some standardized sequence. Mesopotamian scribes were themselves conscious of some process of standardization of the literary repertoire, as the occasional use of the term *ahû*, or "extraneous (version)," indicates.

The Sippar Library

In January 1986 Iraqi archaeologists from the University of Baghdad, excavating in the E-babbara (temple of the sun-god Shamash) at Sippar in northern Babylonia, made the exciting discovery of a small Neo-Babylonian library in a room leading off a long room which itself led off a larger room. To their amazement they found the tablets still ranged in the pigeonholes. The walls of the library were preserved up to a height of 1.6 yards (1.5 meters) or more. The modest-sized room, about 1.6 yards (1.5 meters) wide and 1.1 yards (1 meter) from front to back, was in a part of the temple probably built by Nabonidus (555–539), the last king of Babylon before the Persian conquest. In the left, right, and back walls were a series of pigeonholes built out from the mud-brick walls, each about 7 inches (17 centimeters) high and about 1 foot (30 centimeters) wide, with four ranks in the side walls and six in the back wall. There were probably originally four levels of niches, and thus fifty-six pigeonholes altogether. Each pigeonhole was about 28 inches (70 centimeters) deep, made of clay but with plastered reeds forming an inside lining for the sides and roof, so that each had a slightly tunnel-shaped or arched interior. Up to sixty tablets were stacked in each niche, on their long sides, two or three rows deep. There would have been room for about two thousand tablets, although it appears that not all the niches were filled.

Of the tablets recovered so far (many badly encrusted with salt), almost all were literary, some described in their colophons as "copied from originals" from Babylon, Nippur, Agade, and elsewhere. They indicate that overall the content of this library conformed to the range of compositions known from other libraries; such finds are gradually filling the gaps in the reconstructed texts of these works. The latest dated tablet was an administrative document of 529. There were some copies on clay of inscriptions on stone stelae or metal tablets. One or two royal inscriptions, Neo-Babylonian copies of documents up to fifteen hundred years older and previously unknown, have been identified. Among the other texts were hymns, prayers, divination texts, astrological omens, mathematical texts, and lexical texts. Several sets of well-known literary works of the standard Babylonian corpus, including *Atrakhasis* and the *Creation Epic* (*Enuma Elish*), have also been found. Among the novelties was a unique circular "astrolabe" text giving interstellar distances and indicating by sketches the arrangement of stars in the constellations. Several of the tablets were written by the same scribe, one Nabium-etir-napshati of the family Pakkharu, and other scribes are named in colophons. Work on this collection will continue for some time to come.

Egypt

A single, evolving literary tradition endured throughout Egypt's independent history, and libraries must have played a key role in this. Although our best information about actual libraries comes from the Ptolemaic and Roman periods, the earliest mentions of libraries in documentary texts date to the Old Kingdom. In several temples of the Ptolemaic period, the actual rooms in which books were stored are securely identified by wall inscriptions. A few substantial hauls of papyri of the Late Period and Ptolemaic and Roman periods come from a temple context, and may, in whole or in part, be the remnants of temple libraries. Notable examples are the Elephantine hieratic papyri and the papyri from Dimai (Soknopaiou Nesos) and Tebtunis (Tell Umm al-Breigat) in the Faiyum. Little of this material stems from official or well-recorded excavations, and in every case it is difficult to determine whether a particular text came from an institutional library, private collection, or rubbish dump.

Literary texts of the Middle Kingdom and later allude to personal royal interest in religious texts and literature and in libraries. For example, a king is said to have discovered a text in a library or is portrayed as writing down a text with his own hand; these are undoubtedly fictions but presumably represent credible or at least intelligible behavior. The royal court and the major temples are assumed to have been the centers of literary endeavor in the widest sense.

There is no difficulty in seeing a continuous tradition of religious texts in Egypt. Thus, passages from the Pyramid Texts, first committed to writing in the Old Kingdom, still appear, in demotic script, in the Roman period. Literary material, such as fictional narratives and wisdom, or instruction, texts, is more problematic. A significant number of texts survive in only a single copy. Only a proportion of Middle Kingdom texts certainly or probably remained in circulation in the New Kingdom, and there is another, apparently more marked, break between the New Kingdom and the Late Period. Texts copied in school provide the bulk of our physical evidence, especially for the New Kingdom, both for the dissemination of texts and for their longer-term survival. Nevertheless, there are clear indications that some Middle Kingdom literature was still known in the Late Period. Our surviving literary material is neither sufficiently copious nor sufficiently evenly distributed to enable us to argue confidently that texts did not survive, merely on the basis of lack of evidence.

Papyri frequently claim, sometimes with scant justification, to contain a complete and accurate copy of an exemplar, and lacunae in the original are sometimes noted. We have no indication of any practice of rejecting books—or individual passages in books—that failed for any reason to meet expected standards. The general tendency is illustrated by the collections of funerary texts, known to us through three millennia as the Pyramid Texts, subsequently as the Coffin Texts, and finally as the *Book of the Dead*. These collections in turn incorporated a wide range of new material, and they discarded spells on grounds that had nothing to do with any narrow form of textual criticism. There are only occasional and exceptional instances where the original physical format of a text seems deliberately to have been reproduced. The general nature of scribal practice in the hieratic script would not have encouraged this, as hieratic texts were not normally arranged in fixed line, or paragraph, or page lengths. However, the fact that a hieroglyphic inscription would normally be drafted in hieratic is relevant here, since inscriptions often had to fit into a predetermined space and shape, for example, on a tomb wall or on a stela. Examples are known of the copying of hieroglyphic inscriptions in hieratic. The only concrete indication from Egypt of any canon of texts is of the Greco-Roman period, when the walls of the libraries of temples such as that of Horus at Edfu bore a permanent list of the religious and magical books they were supposed to contain. It seems probable that an inventory of contents must always have been a standard feature of Egyptian libraries.

CONCLUSIONS

Both in the cuneiform world and in Egypt, the preservation of documents and, therefore, the maintenance of archives were essential both in public administration and for the operation of private business and the management of private property. Libraries were crucial for the transmission of literate culture, and their mere existence led to the emergence of scholarly—or even scholastic—approaches to written texts.

BIBLIOGRAPHY

Mesopotamia

KLAAS R. VEENHOF, ed., *Cuneiform Archives and Libraries: Papers Read at the 30ᵉ Rencontre Assyriologique Internationale, Leiden, 4–8 July 1983.* Uitgaven van het Nederlands Historisch-archaeologisch Instituut te Istanbul 57 (1986), see especially KLAAS R. VEENHOF, "Cuneiform Archives: An Introduction," with an extensive bibliography in the footnotes, covering most aspects of the subject. ERNST POSNER, *Archives in the Ancient World* (1972) is a useful overview that includes the classical world; not fully adequate for the ancient Near East. OLOF PEDERSÉN, *Archives and Libraries in the City of Assur: A Survey of the Material from the German Excavations*, Studia Semitica Upsaliensis, vols. 6, 8 (1985, 1986), is an exemplary attempt to reconstruct individual archives on the basis of archaeological information. DOMINIQUE CHARPIN, "Une pratique administrative méconnue," *MARI* 3 (1984), discusses the red ocher marks on tablets from Mari. E. FIANDRA, "The Connection Between Clay Sealings and Tablets in Administration," in *South Asian Archaeology 1979*, edited by H. HÄRTEL (1982). C. B. F. WALKER, "Some Mesopotamian Inscribed Jars," *Iraq* 42 (1980). WARWICK BALL and JEREMY A. BLACK, "Excavations in Iraq, 1985–1986," *Iraq* 49 (1987), under "Sippar." H. CURTIS WRIGHT, *Ancient Burials of Metallic Foundation Documents in Stone Boxes*, Occasional Papers of the University of Illinois Graduate School of Library and Information Science, no. 157 (1982), is a pamphlet that collects evidence on the topic of the title.

The Mari documents discussed in the box, "Retrieving Tablets from an Archive," are treated in J. M. SASSON, "Some Comments on Archive Keeping at Mari," *Iraq* 34 (1972). The Hittite letter is given in A. LEO OPPENHEIM, *Letters from Mesopotamia* (1967), no. 83.

Egypt

G. P. F. VAN DEN BOORN, *The Duties of the Vizier: Civil Administration in the Early New Kingdom* (1988). MORRIS L. BIERBRIER, ed., *Papyrus: Structure and Usage,* British Museum Occasional Paper no. 60 (1986). HELLMUT BRUNNER, *Altägyptische Erziehung* (1957). GÜNTER BURKARD, "Bibliotheken im alten Ägypten," *Bibliothek: Forschung und Praxis* 4 (1980). JAROSLAV ČERNÝ, *Paper and Books in Ancient Egypt* (1952). SIR ALAN H. GARDINER, *The Ramesseum Papyri: Plates* (1955); his *The Wilbour Papyrus,* 4 vols. (1941–1952). NICOLAS-CHRISTOPHE GRIMAL, "Bibliothèques et propagande royale à l'époque éthiopienne," in *Livre du centenaire 1880–1980, Mémoires de l'Institut Français d'Archéologie Orientale du Caire* 104, edited by JEAN VERCOUTTER (1980). WOLFGANG HELCK, "Archive," in *Lexikon der Ägyptologie,* vol. 1, edited by WOLFGANG HELCK and EBERHARD OTTO (1972); his *Zur Verwaltung des Mittleren und Neuen Reichs* (1958), and *Register* (1975). THOMAS ERIC PEET, *The Great Tomb-Robberies of the Twentieth Egyptian Dynasty,* 2 vols. (1930). PIETER WILLEM PESTMAN, "Who Were the Owners, in the 'Community of Workmen,' of the Chester Beatty Papyri," in *Gleanings from Deir el-Medîna,* edited by R. J. DEMARÉE and JAC. J. JANSSEN (1982). PAULE POSENER-KRIÉGER, *Les Archives du temple funéraire de Néferirkarê-Kakaï (Les Papyrus d'Abousir): Traduction et commentaire,* 2 vols. (1976). PAULE POSENER-KRIÉGER and JEAN LOUIS DE CENIVAL, *Hieratic Papyri in the British Museum, Fifth Series: The Abusir Papyri* (1968). DONALD B. REDFORD, *Pharaonic King-Lists, Annals, and Day-books: A Contribution to the Study of the Egyptian Sense of History* (1986); his "Tagebuch," in *Lexikon der Ägyptologie,* vol. 6, edited by WOLFGANG HELCK and WOLFHART WEITENDORF (1986). ADELHEID SCHLOTT, *Schrift und Schreiber im Alten Ägypten* (1989). SIEGFRIED SCHOTT, *Bücher und Bibliotheken im alten Ägypten: Verzeichnis der Buch- und Spruchtitel under der Termini technici* (1990). WILHELM SPIEGELBERG, *Die sogenannte demotische Chronik des Pap. 215 der Bibliothèque nationale zu Paris, nebst den auf der Rückseite des Papyrus stehenden Texten,* Demotische Studien 7 (1914). EDWARD F. WENTE, *Letters from Ancient Egypt* (1990). VILMOS WESSETZKY, "Bibliothek," in *Lexikon der Ägyptologie,* vol. 1, edited by WOLFGANG HELCK and EBERHARD OTTO (1972).

SEE ALSO **Ebla: A Third-Millennium City-State in Ancient Syria** (Part 5, Vol. II); **The Scribes of Ancient Egypt** (Part 9, Vol. IV); and **The Scribes and Scholars of Ancient Mesopotamia** (Part 9, Vol. IV).

The Scribes of Ancient Egypt

EDWARD F. WENTE

IN TREATING THE SUBJECT of Egyptian scribes, this essay draws primarily upon the abundant evidence from the New Kingdom. Earlier periods are also considered insofar as they contribute to the overall picture or illustrate significant developments.

An appreciation of the semantic range of the Egyptian word for scribe, *zakhau* (Coptic *sakh*), is attained if it is realized that the primary meaning of the word was "one who uses the brush," not only to write but also to draw and paint. Thus, for example, a "scribe of contours" was a draftsman, who drew in outline the pictorial decoration of a tomb or temple wall, and a "column scribe" was a painter of pillars. Modern scholarship, however, generally understands scribe as a writer of texts, even equating "scribe" with "official," for the ability to read and write was a prerequisite to a career in the administration, and high officials proudly retained the title of scribe that they had acquired by virtue of their education.

The title of scribe did not, however, necessarily indicate rank. Indeed, from the point of view of the bureaucratic elite, writing was something that subordinates should do. In older letters an inferior writing to a superior might obliquely refer to the addressee as "your scribe," implying that the recipient was of such exalted status that he would not have to read the letter himself but would have it read out to him by a subordinate scribe. Like a modern executive, a ranking official had one or more secretaries to take care of correspondence and accounts. Sometimes the word "scribe" placed before an individual's name meant simply that he was literate.

Reflecting the primary meaning of the term, this discussion begins by considering the concrete, material aspects of the scribal occupation.

TOOLS OF THE TRADE

The scribe's basic writing implement was the rush brush, of which one end was cut diagonally and then chewed to produce a suitable writing tip. Not until Roman times did Egyptian scribes adopt the reed pen, which Greeks in Egypt had already been using for several centuries. The two inks the scribe employed were black, produced from powdered carbon (commonly soot taken from cooking vessels), and red from red ocher. Both substances were mixed with gum and water and allowed to dry in the form of cakes. The scribe gripped the brush between the thumb and forefinger of his right hand, and, using water as a lubricant, handled the pigments in much the same manner as modern watercolors. While black ink served for inscribing most of a text, the scribe frequently highlighted portions as "rubrics" in red ink. To avoid having to wash the brush clean as he changed inks, he had several brushes at hand, often tucked above the ear like a modern stenographer. Erasures were made by washing away the mistake with a damp rag, and a smooth pebble or a special implement of hardwood or ivory served to burnish the writing surface.

The original form of the scribal kit comprised a reed tube holding several brushes, a small sack containing the pigments, and a rectangular palette with two depressions for working them up. For convenience these three components were linked together by a cord. In the Fifth Dynasty a different form of scribal kit became standard: a thin rectangular box, usually of wood, provided with a slot to contain the brushes and two receptacles on top for the black and red inks. Nonetheless, throughout pharaonic history the older form of scribal kit remained the standard hieroglyph for the words "write" and "scribe," and was also retained as an occupational insignia of the scribe, who was sometimes depicted with the kit draped over his shoulder. (See the preceding essay "Archives and Libraries in the Ancient Near East" for an illustration of scribes shown with their tools.)

Preeminent as a writing surface was papyrus, manufactured seasonally in rolls from freshly cropped papyrus plants, which flourished particularly in the Delta. (See the preceding essay "Archives and Libraries in the Ancient Near East" for an account of the manufacture of papyrus and for an illustration of a papyrus plant.) In Ptolemaic Egypt, papyrus was a royal monopoly, and a commonly accepted etymology of the word "papyrus" as meaning "that of pharaoh" has been taken to indicate that papyrus was also a royal monopoly in earlier times. Another possible etymology, "that of the administration," points simply to the importance of papyrus in government affairs without implying a royal monopoly. The production of papyrus paper required specialized craftsmen, who were primarily state employees.

In manufacturing papyrus paper, stalks of the plant three to six meters (three to six yards) long were used. Horizontally and vertically positioned fibers were superimposed and pounded together, the binding agent deriving from the pith itself. Sheets were produced in heights of forty-two to forty-seven centimeters (seventeen

to nineteen inches) while the length varied from sixteen to forty-two centimeters (six to seventeen inches). These sheets were then glued together with a starch paste to create a normal roll of twenty sheets. Usually the height of the roll was reduced to half the manufactured height to facilitate handling, and still smaller heights are attested.

Papyrus was an ideal material for documents. Substantially more durable than our paper, it has survived quite well in desert conditions, though few papyri have been recovered from town sites located on the damp alluvium. Papyri could be rolled up, tied with a string, and sealed. Being light in weight, papyrus documents were easily transported and could be conveniently stored in containers for future reference.

Papyrus was moderately expensive, the cost of a roll being equivalent to a fifth of a skilled workman's monthly salary. Because of cost and seasonal shortages, it was common for a scribe to recycle an old papyrus by washing away the outdated text and re-inscribing it with a new text, producing a palimpsest. In letter writing it was even the preferred practice to reuse sheets cut off from an old roll. Having inscribed a letter on such a sheet, the scribe folded the document to form a small packet that was then tied with string and provided with a seal after he had written the address on the exterior. In this way the integrity of the communication within was assured. For more valuable documents and frequently consulted texts, such as the lector-priest's ritual, the scribe might use parchment. Very few leather scrolls, however, are extant.

The scribe obtained potsherds at no cost from the town's kitchens, where there was constant breakage of pottery, or flakes of limestone that were readily available in desert areas where new tombs were being excavated. These materials, known as ostraca, were inscribed with a wide variety of texts, including accounts, drafts of documents, and letters, and were much used by student scribes during their education. Because of their weight and irregular shape, ostraca were not as easily stored as papyri, and letters on ostraca could not be sealed to ensure confidentiality. Discarded ostraca have been of immense value in reconstructing daily life in the Ramesside village of Deir el-Medina (Dayr al-Madina), where lived the artisans who constructed and decorated royal tombs in western Thebes. In fact, this is the only dynastic site yielding large numbers of ostraca.

For student scribes there were writing boards, coated on both sides with gesso for easy erasure of exercises. Learning a text written on one side of the board, the student could then turn the tablet over and try his hand at reproducing the passage from memory. Writing boards were also used for short notes, accounts, and name lists by scribes working in the countryside. ("Material, Technology, and Techniques in Artistic Production" in Part 7, Vol. III shows a wooden drawing board.) Occasionally a scribe even wrote on his palette, making notations of deliveries or using it as a reckoning board.

INSCRIBING DOCUMENTS

When represented in sculpture in the round, the scribe is shown seated cross-legged on the ground, inscribing a papyrus roll that extends from his left hand across the lap (see fig.). Normally the scribe used the hieratic script, except when preparing certain religious texts like the *Book of the Dead*, for which cursive hieroglyphs were generally employed. In the Old and early Middle kingdoms, the scribe wrote in vertical columns proceeding from right to left. During the Twelfth Dynasty it became customary to inscribe horizontal lines of fairly uniform length, a sequence from seven to as many as twenty-six lines constituting a "page." This alteration may have been instituted to avoid smudging previously penned lines, but more important perhaps was the desire to make consultation of the document easier by organizing it into pages. The transition to horizontal lines also had the effect of permitting more ligaturing of the hieratic signs, thereby increasing writing speed.

Characteristic of scribe statues is the accompanying papyrus roll, indicating that a significant document was being prepared. The gaze of the scribe is normally aimed straight ahead, as though seeking inspiration, although in New Kingdom examples he may look downward as he writes. While it may be said that such statues expressed the scribe's subserviency to the pharaoh, more important, the statues conveyed the

Fifth Dynasty painted limestone statue of a seated scribe, found at Giza, circa 2400 BCE. WILLIAM STEVENSON SMITH, *ART AND ARCHITECTURE OF ANCIENT EGYPT* (1958)

individual's status as an elite official in the act of composing a text, not simply taking dictation as a subordinate secretary. Significantly, the earliest scribe statues are of Fourth Dynasty princes.

By contrast, it was the exception when an official was portrayed on the walls of his tomb chapel in the act of writing. Here, decorum was such that writing was an activity delegated to subordinate scribes, who did not assume the pose of the elite scribe of the statuary. These clerks were conventionally depicted squatting with the left leg bent upright to support the lower left arm holding a papyrus roll or sheet, or they might even be standing to write accounts and reports on behalf of a superior official overseeing their work.

In the mid Eighteenth Dynasty, a different method was devised for inscribing business documents. Instead of writing lines running horizontally across the papyrus, the writer, who might at this date sit on a stool, held the papyrus perpendicularly to his body rather than horizontally across his lap. Thus, in inscribing a document, the scribe began at the top short edge of the papyrus and penned horizontal lines until he completed the text; or, he estimated when he had written half of what he had to record, cut the sheet off the roll, and then inscribed the reverse side with the remainder. (See "The Amarna Letters from Canaan" later in this section.)

LITERACY

Literacy Among Kings

Although decorum prevented the king from being depicted in the act of writing, there is sufficient textual information to suggest that kings were normally literate. Moreover, the fact that kingly gods, even when in the company of the divine scribes Thoth and Seshat, might occasionally be shown in the act of writing on the leaves of a sacred tree supports the notion that their earthly counterparts were literate. The Fifth Dynasty king Djedkare Isesi, who wrote letters "with his own two fingers," may even have fostered the development of the epistolary genre, for kings were patrons of literature. In general, however, the pharaoh had personal secretaries who handled most of his correspondence, so that to receive a personal letter inscribed by the king himself was a special honor. The proud recipient of a royal letter might have it copied in stone on a wall of his tomb chapel or on a stela.

The Spread of Literacy

It appears that in the Old Kingdom only the sons of officials received a scribal education, so that there was little opportunity for the nonelite population to become literate. This situation changed dramatically after the collapse of the Old Kingdom administration. In the Middle Kingdom a concerted effort was made to reconstitute a bureaucracy loyal to the king, and to this end children of people of diverse origins were encouraged to become scribes. Particularly in the New Kingdom one finds instances of boys of modest background being educated at schools

and later attaining high rank in the officialdom. It was the desire of parents that their child should take up the scribal profession, although at this time the military also offered an attractive alternative for advancement. Compositions designed to encourage the pupil to persevere in his studies understandably cast the profession of soldier in a most unfavorable light.

The Literacy Rate

It has been estimated, primarily on the basis of Old Kingdom evidence, that the literacy rate was about 1 percent overall. Naturally the rate was higher in major administrative centers than in the provinces. In the case of Deir el-Medina, where the draftsmen decorating the royal tombs with hieroglyphic inscriptions had been taught writing as well as drawing, literacy probably reached 5 percent or more.

Female Literacy

As early as the Fifth Dynasty, Seshat, the goddess of writing and accounting, was depicted in the act of writing, but there is no positive evidence for female literacy during the Old Kingdom. One official, however, mentioned that for two successive reigns of the late Fourth Dynasty he was educated at the palace among the royal children, male and female. The fact that no distinction was made regarding the nature of the education of the two sexes over the span of time involved suggests that writing may have been taught to princesses as well as princes.

The title of female scribe does rarely appear in the Middle Kingdom in contexts where it cannot be an abbreviation of the obscure title "female scribe of her mouth," designating an illiterate woman who was possibly a cosmetician. Although there are no instances of the title of female scribe from the New Kingdom, women are occasionally depicted seated with scribal equipment under their chairs. Several indirect references to female literacy exist, and some of the letters composed by women may actually have been inscribed by them. While a scribal education for women may have been largely for the purpose of making them cultivated members of New Kingdom society, one cannot exclude the possibility that they on occasion used their scribal talent in affairs of daily life.

EDUCATION

In the Old Kingdom the education of a scribe was on an apprenticeship basis: either a father educated his own son to follow in his footsteps or an official in loco parentis took on a student as a sort of spiritual son. Such a one-to-one relationship is implied in the earliest wisdom literature, where the term "son" also connoted "pupil." The official serving as instructor taught in his own office and had a close pedagogical relationship with a single student or at most several, who learned the techniques of writing and the duties of a scribe. In the Old Kingdom, there was no independent calling of teacher, as it was the duty of experienced officials themselves to train future bureaucrats. Nor did schools exist during the Old Kingdom, except perhaps at the palace, where the sons of high-ranking officials, particularly sons of provincial governors, were educated in the company of princes. The practice of educating children of certain commoners at court continued throughout most of pharaonic history and established a close bond between a future king and his officials.

With the breakdown of the government of the Old Kingdom and its tightly knit bureaucracy, there was increased provincialism, with local officials having little or no tie with the central residence. It was in this sort of decentralized situation that schools developed, responding to the need for local scribes. The earliest mention of a school, literally "chamber, or department, of instruction," is in a tomb inscription of the First Intermediate Period, where there is reference to "every scribe and every wise man, who is skilled in his calling, perfect in writing and perfect in learning, who has acquired the designation of a man of rank, and who has taken up a position, after he has gone to school." By attending school, a person gained wisdom and a station in life. The establishment of schools not only permitted more students to be gathered together for instruction in classes but also allowed for greater uniformity in education than had previously existed in the master-apprentice form of tutelage, which, however, was retained for the instruction of advanced students.

In the Middle Kingdom the premier school, staffed with teachers who were also officials of the civil administration, was located at the royal residence at Itjtawy (modern al-Lisht) near Memphis. Although this was the school to which sons of the elite were sent, a boy of humbler background could attend this school.

The system of education in the New Kingdom continued the pattern established in the Twelfth Dynasty. When a boy approached the age of ten, his parents made the decision to send him to elementary schools. Such schools, generally open to the air, were attached to a temple or to a department of the government. At school the boy was first introduced to the oldest known pedagogical text, the *Book of Kemit*, meaning "summation" or "completion." Compiled in the early Middle Kingdom in epistolary form, this composition employed simple forms of hieratic signs, inscribed in vertical columns, and introduced the beginner to the phraseology of letters and biographies. Since papyrus was somewhat costly, the beginning student wrote his exercises on ostraca or writing boards. The fact that vast numbers of ostraca contain portions of *Kemit* suggests that many beginners never progressed beyond this primer.

Subsequently, the student learned how to write hieratic in horizontal lines, the set texts used being well-known literary compositions of the Twelfth Dynasty, starting with the *Satire on the Trades* (or *Instruction of Khety*), which had as its theme the exaltation of the scribal calling to the denigration of other occupations. In teaching hieratic, the instructor first provided a sample of the text to be copied by the students, but as they gradually learned to write, he read passages out loud for them to record from dictation. The pupils then memorized the text and wrote out copies from memory, perhaps as homework. Although there is evidence that students in school recited or chanted texts in unison, the writing of texts was to be done silently.

During their elementary education, pupils concentrated on learning the classics composed in the language of the Middle Kingdom. From the numerous errors and textual reinterpretations found in Ramesside copies of these texts on ostraca, it is clear that students experienced difficulty in understanding many of the passages, for by this time the language had evolved considerably into Late Egyptian. The primary aim was to master the principles of the difficult hieratic script rather than the content of the classical texts, though after four years of elementary education the student must have absorbed at least some of the ideals expressed in Middle Kingdom literature. Contrary to what one might expect, the young student did not learn hieroglyphs before mastering the hieratic script. Since hieratic writing, unlike hieroglyphs, involved ligatures of signs, the student learned to write whole words and phrases, even sentences, rather than spell out words sign by sign. Thus, the method of education was holistic rather than analytical.

Although the child's parents had made the initial decision to send him to elementary school, the choice of a more advanced education lay with the student, who was now a partly trained scribe in his teens. At this point he selected the type of school appropriate for a career in the administration, the priesthood, or in the military as an officer. This second phase of the student's education could last as long as twelve years, during which time he learned to write texts in colloquial Late Egyptian and was exposed to such disciplines as mathematics, accounting, geometry, surveying, and simple engineering.

As the student progressed, his instruction became more personalized, and he was designated an apprentice scribe. Again the master provided model compositions, usually in epistolary form, for the student to learn. Some texts were copies of genuine letters, pulled from the teacher's files, while others were specially concocted so that the student might become familiar with rare words, often of Semitic origin. Through such diverse texts, modernly called *Miscellanies*, the student learned the names of deities and cult places, foreign localities, and exotic products, and how to formulate an extended royal titulary. Following the model of the *Satire on the Trades*, the theme of the superiority of the scribal profession over other callings, including soldiering and even priesthood, was expounded at length. A fair number of *Miscellanies* papyri have survived from this phase of the student's education. Since students were told to bring their papyrus rolls to school, and the quality of the copies is often imperfect, it seems that these *Miscellanies* were inscribed by apprentice scribes rather than by their teachers.

In his secondary education the student mastered three types of hieratic: the uncial or book hand, the more cursive business hand, and, if he was attached to the palace school, the elegant chancellery hand for royal documents. At this stage he might also be instructed in hieroglyphs, to prepare him for drawing up inscriptions on monuments. Because of the nature of hieroglyphic writing, which was not ligatured, the apprentice scribe learned to spell out words sign by sign, and thus to think analytically about the writing system. Perhaps the most dreary part of his education was memorizing word lists, where designations of occupations, localities, parts of the body, and the like were organized topically as a sort of embryonic encyclopedia. These apprentice scribes were mature young men, often subject to carnal temptations and running off. The unruly pupil could receive a severe thrashing, as it was believed that "a youth's ears are on his back."

For those entering the priesthood, the place of instruction was the House of Life, a temple scriptorium, where old religious and magical texts were copied and new theological treatises composed. Since New Kingdom temples possessed vast estates, young men training for the priesthood also learned how to manage temple holdings and personnel, for priests were administrators as well as ritualists. The Houses of Life were Egypt's intellectual centers, where future physicians, astronomers, magicians, and interpreters of dreams were also educated.

Whereas most students studied to become civil administrators, education as an army scribe opened the way to a career as a military officer. One schoolboy composition, the long satirical letter of Papyrus Anastasi I, is noteworthy in that it does not denigrate the military profession in its polemic against the rote memorization that characterized much of the traditional education. It was not a matter of merely regurgitating Asiatic place-names, but the student also had to explain the topography of Syro-Palestine and routes connecting various places. Although this satire, written early in Ramesses (Ramses) II's reign, was intended for the education of military scribes, portions of it were often copied on ostraca by students not contemplating a military career. The satirical letter posed challenges to improve the quality of the student's mind, and educators must have considered it a valuable adjunct to the pedantic *Miscellanies*.

The intensity of foreign relations during the New Kingdom necessitated the training of officials in such languages as Akkadian, Canaanite, Hittite, and Minoan or Mycenaean. Although student scribes were familiar with those foreign loanwords that had entered the Egyptian language, proper instruction in writing a foreign language was accorded only to those select scribes who were educated at the foreign office and then possibly sent abroad to improve their language proficiency.

EMPLOYMENT

Upon completing his education, the student became a full-fledged scribe, normally employed in the department of government where he had served his apprenticeship. There is some indication that the names of superior graduates were listed as qualified candidates to be selected by appropriate governmental agencies. All young scribes became employees of either state (civil or army) or temple administrations.

Although it has been surmised that there were self-employed village scribes in pharaonic Egypt as there were in the Greco-Roman Period, there is no firm evidence that this was so. If, for example, an illiterate desired to have a legal instrument written, he or she went to a local government scribe, who, for a fee, drew up the document using the appropriate protocol. Before the Late Period, the mere fact that a legal document was penned by a scribe was a sufficient warranty of its official cachet, there being no need for the signatures of witnesses, whose names were simply listed by the scribe; signatures of witnesses appear first on demotic documents.

Although in the New Kingdom there were private traders who were unattached to any institution, no evidence exists that they were literate or had scribes in their employ. Such traders were not highly esteemed in Egyptian society. No scribe would boast of being a trader, though as an official or army officer, the scribe might employ one. On the other hand, traders connected with temples could have been literate, as may be suggested by a Twentieth Dynasty letter addressed to the merchant Amenkhau of the temple of Amun.

Since agriculture was the most important economic activity in ancient Egypt, many scribes found employment in those departments like the treasury that had to do with assessing the annual harvest of grain and collecting the revenues. For this work the scribe had to be more than a "penman"—he also required the skills of practical geometry and arithmetic. Each year there were plots to be surveyed, estimates of crop yields to be made, and assessments to be imposed. Scores of lower-echelon scribes throughout the land recorded the necessary measurements and estimated the yields, a percentage of which went to the state in the form of taxes or to the temples as their due. The scribe was a tax assessor, backed by bailiffs armed with cudgels to make the delinquent peasant cough up.

The records of local scribes surveying the fields were incorporated into a coherent unified report by a more senior scribe or scribes. For the student scribe to be told in the *Miscellanies* that he would assess both Upper and Lower Egypt meant that he and his colleagues would be involved in this massive project. In theory it was the king who assessed all Egypt, but in practice the office of the overseer of the Treasury was responsible for the final compilation. It was possible for the intelligent young graduate to advance quickly and make the assessment of the entire land. This we know of Ramesses II's viceroy of Kush, Setau, who boasted that soon after completing his education he, as the vizier's chief scribe, assessed the entire land with his "mighty reed brush." Other accountant scribes were involved in such matters as taking the annual census of the herds for purposes of taxation.

In addition to his role in the productive economy, the scribe was involved in building projects, such as the construction of temples and royal tombs. As with the cadastral surveys, these enterprises required precise measurements and calculations. The Egyptians had devised methods for calculating such requirements as the number of man-days of work to cut a given amount of stone, or the amount of rations for the work force to get a particular job accomplished.

One of the duties of an army scribe was to take the census for purposes of recruitment. One such scribe of the Eighteenth Dynasty, the Scribe of Recruits Tjanuny, was credited with taking the census of the entire land, and was depicted on the walls of his tomb chapel as a scribe, enlisting soldiers and informing them of their duties. This kind of registration was a far more exalted activity than enregistering grain. Scribes recruited organized companies of men to send off to war, and they also had disposition over the labor force to advance building projects, as was the case of Amenhotep (Amenophis), son of Hapu, of the reign of Amenhotep III. He was so highly honored for his organizational talent and familiarity with the population that his statues at the temple of Karnak functioned as intermediaries, interceding with the god on behalf of passersby. He was a sort of hero, who subsequently became deified.

STATUS IN SOCIETY

Texts designed for the scribal education in the Middle Kingdom stress the advantages of being a scribe. The early Middle Kingdom *Book of Kemit* concludes with the words, "As for the scribe in whatever position he has at the Residence, he can never become miserable in it." This passage is cited in the Twelfth Dynasty *Satire on the Trades*, which states further of the scribal profession, "It is greater than all occupations. There is none equal to it in the land. . . . There is no occupation without a boss, apart from the scribe; he is boss." The theme of the scribe's superiority is developed further in the New Kingdom *Miscellanies*, accentuating the positive benefits of scribedom. Above all, the individual is absolved from hard manual labor and the performance of unpleasant tasks that might sully his composure and sense of well-being. The stress is on the scribe's privileged status and access to the circle of the elite. Only the occupation of scribe, so it was argued, afforded the opportunity to advance and become an official controlling others.

Since the *Miscellanies* were the product of the official class, interested in perpetuating itself, the arguments presented are tendentious in their exaggeration of the scribe's exalted lifestyle. There is an unctuous self-serving aspect to these descriptions. The successful scribe is sleek-bodied, fine-limbed, with soft refined hands untarnished by manual labor—by no means the epitome of physical prowess. Dressed in white, he is saluted by courtiers as he has gained entrée to the well-to-do and influential. As an official he acquires a mansion, landscaped with a garden and trees, and provided with well-stocked granaries, barns with cattle, and aviaries with fowl. He has male and female slaves and fields for the growing of vegetables and grain and may even possess ships, importing exotic luxuries.

One of the advantages of being a scribe was that he was not subject to taxation. This was true insofar as there does not seem to have been a tax on his scribal output or the wages he received as a scribe. But some scribes in due time would have accumulated enough wealth to purchase fields for cultivation. In that case the scribe, as a gentleman farmer, was probably taxed on his agricultural income, but in general the scribe was viewed as a tax collector rather than taxpayer.

The Ramesside community of Deir el-Medina, from which there is both abundant archaeological and philological information, can provide something of a corrective to the inflated picture of the scribe in the *Miscellanies*. This exceptional village, located at the base of the Theban desert escarpment, was inhabited by a community of artisans engaged in preparing the royal tombs of the New Kingdom. Numbering roughly four hundred inhabitants, including men, women, and children, the town was financed by the state. There were comfortable dwellings for the families, but the houses of the several administrative scribes did not differ significantly from those of ordinary workmen. Although an administrative scribe received a salary in grain that was 35 percent higher than a workman's, his wages were identical to those of the two foremen, who were superior in rank to the scribe. Both the foremen and administrative scribes were appointees of the vizier. The former organized work on the royal tomb and supervised its decoration, while the latter compiled the journal of work, recorded the workers' attendance and the project's progress, and kept detailed accounts of the materials used and the payments made in kind to the workers. Occasionally when there were arrears in the grain deliveries from the royal granary, the administrative scribe went into the countryside to collect grain directly from the farmers.

These scribes were very much a part of the community and dealt personally with the complaints of the villagers. They served as members of the village tribunal, where they were frequently witnesses to oaths they administered. If the civil court failed to reach a verdict, it was the scribe who wrote out questions to be presented to the local oracle for a divine decision. For the illiterate the scribes would write and read out letters and draw up sale records and legal documents for a fee. An administrative scribe who had been educated in drawing and painting at the local school could make substantial extra income decorating such items as coffins or stelae for village clients. Such a scribe was a "brush man," not simply a "penman." These administrative scribes did not, however, participate in the work of tomb decoration, as this was carried out by draftsmen, who also possessed some knowledge of reading and writing.

Some scribes became wealthy members of the community and owned fields, cultivated for grain and vegetables by a slave or two, and some scribes might even have several tombs prepared for themselves and relatives. Like most Egyptians they had numerous children. A scribe who had no children might adopt a son to succeed him, for the tendency was for the office to be inherited. Generally the scribes were well liked by the villagers, but there were a few who were tyrannical and not above taking bribes.

Although there was no formal teaching of history in the schools, scribes acquired some sense of the past by copying literary works of earlier periods. In their work, scribes were more concerned with the present and immediate past, so the phenomenon of antiquarianism was a rarity among them. One exceptional individual was the Deir el-Medina administrative scribe Qenhikhopeshef, who, in the Nineteenth Dynasty, had catholic interests that included lexicography, the interpretation of dreams, and history. In his jottings he made lists of kings and princes and recorded a portion of the poem on the Battle of Qadesh.

THE SCRIBES' LEGACY

Scribes were the intellectual elite of the land, the principal artisans of high culture. It is signifi-
cant that the nonroyal heroes of Egyptian culture were not men of war but were scribal officials noted for outstanding organizational ability. Although their function was primarily administrative, ensuring them a privileged and envied place in society, scribes were also the preservers of the literary tradition, which in ancient Egypt was largely written rather than oral. Throughout pharaonic history scribes, particularly during the period of their education, were continually copying past works of literature; and in the Houses of Life scholarly priests, immersed in past traditions, copied and sometimes revised and updated ancient theological, liturgical, medical, and magical texts.

But scribes were also encouraged to write in the broad sense of the word, that is, to compose new works that would enlighten and edify. In the Old Kingdom the authors of the predominant literary form at that time, the instructions, were men of the highest rank: princes and viziers. It should be noted, however, that some scholars believe that such instructions as Ptahhotep's were pseudepigraphical works of later date. With altered political conditions after the fall of the Old Kingdom, the writing of literature expanded in the Middle Kingdom to include stories and other forms of belles lettres, and at the same time the circle of authors broadened to include scribes of lower status. The increased role of education and its organization by schools supported this expansion of literary creativity that was to continue to the end of the New Kingdom.

Some scribes achieved fame for their literary output. In one Ramesside work, Papyrus Chester Beatty IV, the argument is made that only learned scribes attain immortality, because tombs and funerary monuments perish, whereas authors' memories survive in their books. Of the eight sages named in this text, six are known to us from copies of their writings, and four were depicted as mummified beings on the walls of a Ramesside tomb chapel at Saqqara. These eight were obviously considered to be the great writers of the past, but there are other less renowned authors, some anonymous, whose works have survived.

Following the advice of Papyrus Chester Beatty IV that the scribe should concern himself more with being an author than with traditional modes of ensuring a blessed afterlife, some scribes of Deir el-Medina even tried their hand at writing literature. It is perhaps significant that Papyrus Chester Beatty IV, with its disparagement of, indeed blatant attack on, traditional burial practices, was found among the writings of a scribe at Deir el-Medina, whose raison d'être was the construction and decoration of royal tombs! The suggestion can be made that during the Ramesside period there was a movement among scribes toward secularism that touched even those involved in providing tombs with orthodox religious compositions.

Unlike the scribe who wrote secular literature and received credit for its authorship, the priestly scribe of the House of Life was not named as the author of religious texts. Rather, such writings, known as "the words of the god," were ascribed to such deities as Thoth, Atum, and Horus, with an occasional archaic king or Old Kingdom sage being credited with the authorship of a magical spell, medical recipe, or *Book of the Dead* spell. The major religious texts, however, such as those that the Deir el-Medina crew inscribed in the royal tombs, were too sacrosanct to be ascribed to a human author.

Indeed, as writers of hymns and other works of theological nature, anonymous priestly scribes of the House of Life achieved more quantitatively than the larger circle of secular scribes. Since we do possess works of six of the eight great authors, and often numerous copies of portions of other literary works, it is unlikely that the literary production over nearly two millennia vastly exceeded what has actually survived, if those works in fragmentary form are included in an estimate. There seems to have been a limited demand for belles lettres, whereas the need for religious and funerary literature was considerable.

There are some rare examples of Egyptian literary criticism. In searching for a new subject, the Twelfth Dynasty author Khakheperresonb bemoaned the hackneyed rehashings of old themes in the literature of his day. The author of the satirical letter in Papyrus Anastasi I berates his literary opponent for having quoted a maxim of the renowned Old Kingdom sage, Prince Hardjedef, without knowing whether it was good or bad.

While skeptically minded scribes of the Ramesside age were moving in the direction of secularism, in the end they too were buried in the very sort of tombs whose value some of their composition decried. Butehamon, one of the last of the administrative scribes of the Deir el-Medina milieu, captured in writing the final mood of a scribe when he wrote these egalitarian lines in a letter to his dead wife, "The sun-god Pre has departed and his ennead following him, the kings as well, and all humanity in a single body following their fellow beings. No one shall stay alive, for we shall all follow you."

BIBLIOGRAPHY

General

T. G. H. JAMES, *Pharaoh's People: Scenes from Life in Imperial Egypt* (1984), chaps. 5 and 6, primarily for the New Kingdom scribe, amply provided with relevant translations; ADELHEID SCHLOTT, *Schrift und Schreiber im Alten Ägypten* (1989), the best work on the subject with many new observations; H. TE VELDE, "Scribes and Literacy in Ancient Egypt," in *Scripta Signa Vocis: Studies about Scripts, Scriptures, Scribes, and Languages in the Near East, Presented to J. H. Hospers*, edited by H. L. J. VANSTIPHOUT, K. JONGELING, F. LEEMHUIS, and G. J. REININK (1986), a succinct and accurate account.

Sources in Translation

RICARDO A. CAMINOS, *Late-Egyptian Miscellanies* (1954), for the New Kingdom *Miscellanies;* MIRIAM LICHTHEIM, *Ancient Egyptian Literature*, vol. 1 (1973) for the *Satire on the Trades* and *The Lament of Khakheperresonb*, vol. 2 (1976) for the *Miscellanies* of Papyrus Lansing and Papyrus Chester Beatty IV; EDWARD F. WENTE, *Letters from Ancient Egypt* (1990), for the *Book of Kemit*, Papyrus Anastasi I, the letter to the merchant Amenkhau, and Butehamon's letter to his dead wife.

Tools of the Trade

JAROSLAV ČERNÝ, *Paper and Books in Ancient Egypt* (1952; repr. 1977); A. LUCAS, *Ancient Egyptian Materials and Industries* (1926; 4th ed., rev. by J. R. HARRIS, 1962); NAPHTALI LEWIS, *Papyrus in Classical Antiquity* (1974), for technical aspects.

Inscribing Documents

GERRY DEE SCOTT III, "The History and Development of the Ancient Egyptian Scribe Statue," 4 vols. (Ph.D. diss, Yale, 1990) and JAC. J. JANSSEN, "Literacy and Letters at Deirel-Medîna," in *Village Voices*, edited by R. J. DEMARÉE and ARNO EGBERTS (1992).

Literacy

JOHN BAINES, "Literacy and Ancient Egyptian Society," *Man*, n.s. 18 (1983); JOHN BAINES and C. J. EYRE, "Four Notes on Literacy," *Göttinger Miszellen*, vol. 61 (1983); BETSY M. BRYAN, "Evidence for Female Literacy from Theban Tombs of the New Kingdom," *Bulletin of the Egyptological Seminar* 6 (1984); HENRY GEORGE FISCHER, "Administrative Titles of Women in the Old and Middle Kingdom," in his *Varia*, Egyptian Studies I (1976).

Education

HELLMUT BRUNNER, *Altägyptische Erziehung* (1957), the basic study, well documented; ELMAR EDEL, *Die Inschriften der Grabfronten der Siut-Gräber in Mittelägypten aus der Herakleopolitenzeit* (1984), pp. 109–111, for the earliest mention of school; GEORGES POSENER, *Littérature et politique dans l'Égypte de la XIIᵉ Dynastie*, Bibliothèque de l'école des hautes études, vol. 307 (1956), for the use of literature in education; and ANDREA MCDOWELL, "Awareness of the Past in Deir el-Medîna," in *Village Voices*, edited by R. J. DEMARÉE and ARNO EGBERTS (1992), for the effects of education in a local community.

Employment and Status in Society

JAROSLAV ČERNÝ, *A Community of Workmen at Thebes in the Ramesside Period*, Bibliothèque d'étude 50 (1973), for the Dayr al-Madina scribes; JOHN ROMER, *Ancient Lives: Daily Life in Egypt of the Pharaohs* (1984), a well-researched, popular account with chapters on various scribes; SUSANNE BICKEL and BERNARD MATHIEU, "L'ecrivain Amennakht et son Enseignement," *Bulletin de l'Institut Français d'Archéologie Orientale* 93 (1993), for a local scribe as literary author; EDWARD F. WENTE, "A New Look at the Viceroy Setau's Autobiographical Inscription," in *Mélanges Gamal Eddin Mokhtar*, vol. 2, edited by PAULE POSENER-KRIÉGER, Bibliothèque d'étude, vol. 97 (1985), for a young scribe who assessed the entire land.

Legacy

LEONARD H. LESKO, "Some Comments on Ancient Egyptian Literacy and Literati," in *Studies in Egyptology Presented to Miriam Lichtheim*, vol. 2, edited by SARAH ISRAELIT-GROLL (1990), for a critique of Egyptian literature; GEORGES POSENER, "Literature," in *The Legacy of Egypt*, edited by J. R. HARRIS (2nd ed. 1971), a good overview of the scribes' literary output; R. B. PARKINSON, "Teachings, Discourses and Tales from the Middle Kingdom," in *Middle Kingdom Studies*, edited by STEPHEN QUIRKE (1991), a comprehensive survey of literary production in the classical period.

SEE ALSO **Legal and Social Institutions of Pharaonic Egypt** (Part 4, Vol. I); **Archives and Libraries in the Ancient Near East** (Part 9, Vol. IV); and **The Scribes and Scholars of Ancient Mesopotamia** (Part 9, Vol. IV).

Ancient Egyptian Literature: An Overview

DONALD B. REDFORD

WITHIN A FEW GENERATIONS of its invention, the hieroglyphic script had developed into a system which could visibly encode any speech. That it was not initially used to commit literary works to legible form is more a comment on societal custom and the nature of oral composition and transmission than on any inherent limitation of this mode of writing.

ORAL COMPOSITION AND TRANSMISSION

The common grouping of Egyptian narrative and poetry under the rubric "literature" should not deceive us as to the mode of composition and transmission: the vast majority of the population in ancient Egypt remained illiterate, and pieces were composed and delivered orally. Writing down an oratorical creation never had anything to do with making it available for the diversion of a wider public; many of the surviving manuscripts come from scribes' private collections and were exercises in penmanship as much as composition. The first lengthy inscriptions are at pains to put testaments and decrees on permanent display, so that the law would be "published" in an immutable form: "Make copies of this decree and have them sent to every nomarch of Upper Egypt and set it on a sandstone stela at the gate of (every temple) where your monu-

ments are, so that the sons of the sons of the people may seek it." Even the "address to the living," carved in a prominent place in the tomb, had an essentially practical purpose: to cajole the scribe or literate priest who chanced to pass by to make an offering to the deceased. In the realm of belletristic creations, the written copies that have survived served as little more than an aide-mémoire to reciter or scribe.

Skill in speech was one of the most coveted accomplishments in social intercourse for Egyptians. As the *Instruction of Ptahhotep* records, "Fine speech is more hidden than the emerald, (yet) it is found with servant girls at the grindstone . . . it is a craftsman who (knows how to) speak in council: oratory is more difficult than any occupation." According to the *Harper's Song of Antef* the ideal was "one who knows the (appropriate) word for the frustrating situation . . . one who silences weeping with a happy saying . . . one who knows how to speak in any office . . . who speaks honestly in any office, incisive speaker in situations of meanness."

The orator (literally, one who is adept at speaking) and raconteur (storyteller) are both well known in Egyptian texts. Their basic function as entertainers is nicely conveyed in the *Prophecy of Neferti* by the characterization of their delivery as "a few fine words and choice phrases at the hearing of which (one) may be diverted." "For you," says the writer of a satirical letter, "I have made by way of diversion a document which will be amusing to listen to" (P. Anastasi I). The fact that there were many practitioners of the art inevitably produced pedestrian and hackneyed compositions shot through with time-honored locutions and repetitive vocabulary. The purist could only crave "unknown locutions, recherché phrases with new words not used (before), free of repetition," as explained in the *Lament of Khakheperresonb.* So effective was skill in speaking and so potentially influential the orator that, in revolutionary times, the able speaker fell under suspicion and provoked resentment. "The orator is scum! Suppress him! Slay [him]!" says King Merykare's father, King Akhtoy, in the *Instructions for King Merykare.* " 'Informer' is what they call a wise-man, 'chatterer' is what they call an orator," wails one member of the intelligentsia of the lack of culture and education during the revolutionary times of the First Intermediate Period.

The structure and vocabulary of many of the pieces of Egyptian literature betray their origin and transmission within a living, word-of-mouth tradition. In hymns, poems, and narrative alike one senses a great enjoyment of wordplay and alliteration; mnemonic devices can frequently be detected. Some supposed literary works, indeed, like the Middle Kingdom model letter and the *Admonitions of Ipuwer,* hang together in the arbitrary sequence of pericopes largely on the basis of wordplays and homonymous passages that could be appreciated only orally and that provide mnemonic links in what otherwise would be a meaningless ordering of material. In hymnic material, especially in the so-called penitential psalms and the royal encomia, the compositions are clearly of the oral formulaic kind, in which phrase accommodates rhythm. The speaker has, as it were, a store of stock locutions that can be used as building units in the creation of a piece. Even the formal temple inscriptions that gloss relief scenes of the king addressing his court come from "live" speeches: "Pay attention to my words!" says Ramesses (Ramses) III, "and listen to them; for I am speaking to you that I might instruct you . . . !" In examples that are drawn in sufficient detail, a group of scribes is shown to one side busily recording the king's words.

Types of writing that we moderns might ex-

pect to have taken precedence over the spoken word are found to be coupled with a reading of the contents. The Egypto-Hittite treaty of Ramesses II, for example, was composed of "these words upon the tablet of silver"; but the king had to read them in the hearing of the people. Letter writing was an art demanding that the scribe be conversant with complicated epistolary terms; yet the common letter formula "I have *heard* all the matters you sent me about" shows that the messenger had to read the contents. Formal written reports were often based on oral communication, and school texts were often read to the pupils. Even the hymns on the formal stelae, set up in the precincts of the temple, were intended for public reading: Ramesses III speaks to Amun-Re with reference to "the many beatifications and hymns that I made in your name at the hearing of which your heart might be content." Private mortuary texts reflect a context in which people were regaled with the content of a tomb biography read out to them: "O every scribe who will read, and all you people who will listen. . . ."

At the level of popular folklore a lively oral tradition operated. Some of its products may be reflected in the Late Egyptian stories or even in the snippets of myth vouchsafed in secondary contexts. Two phrases colorfully signal the presence of this type of oral tradition: "the converse of the people" and "from mouth to mouth." The content of such oral transmission is made plain by frequent allusion to it: the mighty acts and fame of the king, the power of the god, one's reputation after death, wisdom, father's advice, prescriptions for the cult, tales of faraway places, or events that occurred long ago. In this last connection the "converse of the people" acquired a reputation for wild exaggeration, and many a scribe made a contemptuous remark about the lack of veracity inherent in anything passed "from mouth to mouth." A common statement declares that some fantastic occurrence "has not been seen in the writings of the ancestors nor has it been [recounted] verbally, mouth to mouth."

Side by side with the popular oral transmission of the masses, and overshadowing it completely at an official level, was the strong scribal tradition of court and temple. A marked archival tendency informed the scribal mind from the very founding of the state and imparted to the "House of Books" and "the Chamber of Writings" a reputation as the sole repositories of reliable information. When the king wished to discover the "truth" about the gods and their cults and images, he repaired, not to his wise men, but to the library. Ramesses IV, having found in the temple library an old book describing Re and primeval times, assures us that "this is recounted in writing, not in oral tradition." Even in those genres, such as "teaching" (*sbōyet*), where the form itself demands oral composition and lends itself to oral transmission, a strong written tradition existed down through the ages side by side with the oral. The wording of the Old Kingdom *Instruction of Ptahhotep*, for example, and even the internal order of the pericopes had achieved almost a "canonical" written form by Ramesside times. The *Instruction for Kagemni* concludes with the following significant scene:

> Then the vizier summoned his children after he had completed "The Condition of Man"(—possibly) . . . and finally he said to them: "As for anything that is in writing on this scroll, hearken to it as I said it. Do not embellish what is authorized." Then they took it into their hearts, and recited it in accordance with that which was in writing.

LITERARY CATEGORIES

In the realm of narrative discourse a number of genre terms betray the origin of a piece and its subsequent transmission as oral. As pointed out above, the burden of the raconteur might be categorized under the heading of "the converse of the people" if it constituted a narrative. A formal declamation or a monologue, often in a juridical setting, might be called *mdt* ("word" or "speech") while *tpt-r* ("utterance," literally, "that which is upon the mouth") was used in a slightly wider context for any proclamation (of god or king), incantation, songs, addresses to the living, and other similar texts. Aphoristic or pithy speech, sometimes in meter and delivered in a declamatory style, could be termed *ḥn* ("speech," "utterance," or "song").

Hymns and poetry together make up a large proportion of ancient Egyptian literary produc- tions. The most common term for hymn was *dw'w* (literally, "praising"), under which one might subsume formal "supplication" (*snmḥw*) and "adoration" (*snsw*), often in the mouth of a king, and the popular forms identified by their incipits "hail to you . . ." (*jnḏ ḥr.k*) and "praise to you . . ." (*j'w n.kj*) or "giving praise" (*rdjt j'w*). When carved on a wall or stela all these subtypes might be shown next to a figure of the hymnist (king or commoner) with hands raised in adoration. Long dirge-like declamations deploring the social and economic conditions of the land, a favorite theme in the First Intermediate Period and Middle Kingdom, seem to have gone under the rubric of "lament" (*nḥwt*); if an element of prophecy informed the piece, the verb *sr* ("predict," "prophesy") might be used, although this never developed into a genre term. Polite society during all periods of Egyptian history favored dancing and singing as entertainment. The latter was usually provided by choristers and (especially) a harpist who extemporized songs. The harpist soon became a stereotype in Egyptian literature and was pictured and described as a corpulent wit, a wine-bibbing "good old boy." In a courtly setting he acquired more dignity and authored hymns of praise in honor of the king, his acts, and his regalia. By the Ramesside age such encomia had become stilted and somewhat brittle, being organized into stanzas full of the most hackneyed imagery, each ending in the formal titulary and cartouches of the monarch. One stela, for example, labels such a piece as a "song" to be sung to the accompaniment of the harp. Another type of eulogy, which might be dubbed "longing for city X," consists of a poetic description, metrically arranged, of a particular settlement, in the course of which a description of its layout and decoration is given. One such poem is introduced by the title "narrative (*sḏd*) of the triumphs of the Lord of Egypt." Secular love poetry goes under the rubric "song of entertainment," or "sweet phrases" or the like, none of which approximates a true genre term.

From an early period in Egypt's history there appears an amorphous body of texts compiled with pedagogic intent for the training of scribes. While much of this material is the routine, prosaic categories a government scribe would require knowledge of in his job (letters, memo-

Highlights of Egyptian Literature

Middle Kingdom Instructions (*Sbōyet*)

The Dialogue of a Man with His Ba

Number of manuscripts: One papyrus (P. Berlin 3024) of Middle Kingdom date.

Date of composition: Early (?) Middle Kingdom (twentieth century BCE).

Content: A dialogue between a man contemplating death and his *ba* (manifestation of personality) over the efficacy of funerary preparations and the true nature of the afterlife. The ba's view appears heterodox, if not downright agnostic. Appended to the dialogue are several hymns extolling the peace of death.

Translations: James B. Pritchard, *Ancient Near Eastern Texts: Relating to the Old Testament* (2nd ed. 1955); R. O. Faulkner, "The Man Who Was Tired of Life," *Journal of Egyptian Archaeology* 42 (1956); Miriam Lichtheim, *Ancient Egyptian Literature*, vol. 1 (1973).

Harper's Song of Antef

Number of copies: One papyrus (P. Harris 500 vi, 2–vii, 3) and a relief in the tomb of Pa-Aten-em-heb (Saqqara, now in Leiden).

Date of composition: Possibly 2100 (although a date in the seventeenth century has been championed).

Content: A song, said to have been copied from a standard scene of a harper before a tomb owner from the tomb of a King Antef. The singer adopts an agnostic tone and denies that knowledge of the afterlife is possible. He insists that one should seize the pleasures of the moment and ignore preparation for death.

Translations and commentary: Pritchard; Lichtheim, vol. 1; Jan Assmann (1977).

Instruction of Ptahhotep

Number of copies: Four papyri (P. Prisse, Paris; P. British Museum 10371, 10435, 10509), one writing board, and five octraca (Carnarvon Tablet I).

Date of composition: Middle Kingdom; copies date from the Twelfth to Nineteenth dynasties (twentieth to seventeenth century)

Content: Practical advice couched in a series of thirty-seven maxims, with the intent to inculcate the sort of behavior that will make a man successful in his life and profession.

Translations: Zbyněk Žába, *Les Maximes de Ptahhotep* (1956); Pritchard; Lichtheim, vol. 1.

Instructions for King Merykare

Number of copies: Three papyri (P. Hermitage, St. Petersburg, 1116A; P. Moscow 4658; P. Carlsberg 6), and one ostracon (ODM 1476).

Date of composition: Probably twenty-first century (First Intermediate period); papyri date from the Eighteenth and early Nineteenth dynasties (fifteenth and fourteenth centuries).

Content: A statement by a king on the point of death for the benefit of his son and successor. As such it constitutes a sort of treatise on statecraft by a pharaonic mind and provides an intimate view of Egyptian kingship.

Translations: Pritchard; Lichtheim, vol. 1; Wolfgang Helck, *Die Lehre für König Merikare* (1977); Joachim Friedrich Quack, *Studien Zur Lehre für Merikare* (1992).

Instruction of King Amenemhet

Number of copies: Two major papyri (P. Berlin 3019; P. Sallier II = British Museum 10182), numerous fragments, one leather roll, three tablets, and more than one hundred ostraca.

Date of composition: Early Twelfth Dynasty; all manuscripts and ostraca are of New Kingdom date (from the fifteenth to twelfth centuries).

Author: Apparently a scribe, Akhtoy, perhaps writing at the behest of Senwosret (Sesostris) I.

Content: The deceased King Amenemhet I is represented as speaking from the grave to his son Senwosret I. The main burden of his testament (born of bitterness at how, for all the good he did, he had suffered an assassination attempt) is his advice that his son should be circumspect and watchful toward all around him. His tone and single-minded message mark the piece as part of the so-called propaganda literature of the early Twelfth Dynasty.

Translations: Pritchard; Lichtheim, vol. 1; Wolfgang Helck, *Der Text der "Lehre Amenemhets I. für seinen Sohn"* (1969).

The Prophecy of Neferti

Number of copies: One papyrus (P. Hermitage, St. Petersburg, 1116 B), two writing tablets (Cairo 25224, British Museum 5647), and about twenty ostraca.

Date of composition: Early Twelfth Dynasty; copies range from the fifteenth to thirteenth centuries.

Content: Neferti, a legendary wise man of the Delta, is described as prophesying for the predilection of King Sneferu (Fourth Dynasty, circa 2650) the time of troubles that would follow the collapse of the Old Kingdom and the coming of Amenemhet I, the deliverer of Egypt (founder of the Twelfth Dynasty, circa 1940). The composition is therefore part of the propaganda literature extolling the accomplishments and promoting the interests of the Twelfth Dynasty.

Translations: Pritchard; Lichtheim, vol. 1; Wolfgang Helck, *Die Prophezeiung des Nfr.tj* (2nd ed. 1992).

The Eloquent Peasant

Number of copies: Four papyri (P. Berlin 3023, 3025, 10499; P. Butler = British Museum 10274), all of the Middle Kingdom.

Date of composition: Late Twelfth Dynasty.

Content: A peasant en route to the capital to trade is waylaid and robbed by a tenant of a high steward. The peasant appeals to the latter but shows such oratorical skill that the steward delays judgment, so that the peasant will have to return day after day and unwittingly provide further examples of his spoken art. The framework of the story provides occasion for a profound discourse on *ma'at* and sheds light on contemporary social conditions.

Translations and commentary: Pritchard; Lichtheim, vol. 1; further literature in William Kelly Simpson, "The Political Background of the Eloquent Peasant," *Göttingen Miszellen* 120 (1991); R. B. Parkinson, "Literary Form and the *Tale of the Eloquent Peasant*," *Journal of Egyptian Archaeology* 78 (1992).

Satire on the Trades

Number of copies: Four New Kingdom papyri (three in the British Museum, one in the Pierpont Morgan Library), two drawing boards (the Louvre), and about one hundred ostraca of Ramesside date.

Date of composition: Middle Kingdom.

Content: A man from the northernmost (and provincial) part of Egypt conducts his son by boat to the scribal school located in the capital. During the journey he describes a wide variety of occupations, all in highly derogatory terms, except for that of the scribe, which is praised unstintingly. The text ends with advice on how to behave in office.

Translations: Pritchard; Lichtheim, vol. 1; Wolfgang Helck, *Die Lehre des Dw'-ḥtjj*, 2 vols. (1970).

Middle Kingdom Narrative

The Story of Sinuhe

Number of copies: Six papyrus manuscripts, more than two dozen ostraca.

Date of composition: Early Twelfth Dynasty.

Content: Couched in format suggesting the self-presentation of an individual in a biographical statement, the story rapidly transforms itself into a narrative of adventure. Sinuhe, an employee of the queen, flees Egypt at the death of Amenemhet I, fearing implication in plots he never specifies, and spends many years in the Levant. At length persuaded to come home by the magnanimous Senwosret I, Sinuhe returns to Egypt, where he is forgiven and reinstalled at court. Though intended at one level as propaganda for the Twelfth Dynasty, the *Story of Sinuhe* develops into a well-told narrative of a romantic nature, and while the hero is perhaps fictional, the writer presents a vivid and accurate picture of contemporary Egypt and Western Asia.

Translations: Pritchard; Lichtheim, vol. 1; full bibliography in William Kelly Simpson, "Sinuhe," in *Lexikon der Ägyptologie*, edited by Wolfgang Helck and Wolfhart Westendorf, vol. 5 (1984).

Papyrus Westcar

Number of copies: A single papyrus (P. Berlin 3033).

Date of composition: Middle Kingdom; the papyrus is of the seventeenth to sixteenth century.

Content: The sons of Khufu (Cheops) vie with each other in telling their father tales of miracles, performed by legendary magicians, to relieve his boredom. The last tale devolves into a current event, that is, the miraculous birth of the three sons of the sun god who were eventually to supplant the house of Khufu and found the Fifth Dynasty.

Translation: Lichtheim, vol. 1.

Neferkare and the General Sisene

Number of copies: A papyrus (P. Chassinat I) in Paris and an ostracon (Oriental Institute 13539) in Chicago.

Date of composition: Middle Kingdom.

Content: The very fragmentary text (lacking beginning and ending) deals with Pepy II and his nocturnal visits to the house of his general. What the point of the story was, or whether a homosexual theme was in question, is not at all clear.

Translations and Commentary: Georges Posener, "Le Conte de Néferkarè et du général Siséné (Recherches littéraires, VI)," *Revue d'Egyptologie* 11 (1957); R. B. Parkinson, "'Homosexual' Desire in Middle Kingdom Literature," *Journal of Egyptian Archaeology* 81 (1995).

The Shipwrecked Sailor

Number of copies: One papyrus (P. Hermitage, St. Petersburg, 1115); now in Moscow.

Date of composition: Middle Kingdom.

Content: A retainer, to encourage his commander, recounts a tale of ill fortune in which he was shipwrecked on a deserted island, inhabited only by a gigantic snake. The latter rescues him and predicts, correctly, his safe return to Egypt. Interpretations vary.

Translations: Lichtheim, vol. 1; Antonio Loprieno, "The Sign of Literature in the Shipwrecked Sailor," in *Religion und Philosophie im alten Ägypten: Festgabe für Philippe Derchain*, edited by Ursula Verhoeven and Erhart Graefe (1991).

Continued on the next page.

Continued from the previous page.
New Kingdom Narrative
Tale of Apopis and Seqenenre

Number of copies: One papyrus with two partial copies of the text, on recto and verso (P. Sallier I; British Museum).
Date of composition: Early Nineteenth Dynasty.
Content: The tale is loosely based on the circumstances attending the expulsion of the Hyksos and ascribes the opening of hostilities to Apopis's absurd complaint that the noise of the hippopotamuses at Thebes is disturbing his sleep five hundred miles (eight hundred kilometers) away.
Translations and commentary: Pritchard; Edward F. Wente, "The Quarrel of Apophis and Seknenre," in *The Literature of Ancient Egypt*, edited by William Kelly Simpson (1973); Hans Goedicke, *The Quarrel of Apophis and Seqenenreʿ* (1986).

The Taking of Joppa
Number of copies: One papyrus (P. Harris 500; British Museum).
Date of composition: Early Nineteenth Dynasty.
Content: The tale describes the capture of the Canaanite city of Joppa under Thutmose III by General Djehuty. Interest centers upon the "Ali Baba" ruse of hiding soldiers in the panniers of donkeys and secreting them into the city under the guise of a merchant caravan.
Translation: Edward F. Wente, in *The Literature of Ancient Egypt*, edited by William Kelly Simpson (1973).

The Report of Wenamun
Number of copies: One papyrus (P. Moscow 120).
Date of composition: Early Twenty-first Dynasty (eleventh century).
Content: A commercial agent of the temple of Amun reports on a trip to Byblos to buy lumber for the divine bark of the god, an expedition shot through with misadventures and bad luck. The account, which shows a marked literary treatment, has elicited different interpretations from scholars as to its historicity.
Translations: Pritchard; Lichtheim, vol. 2; interpretation and bibliography, Wolfgang Helck, "Wenamun," in *Lexikon der Ägyptologie*, vol. 6, edited by Wolfgang Helck and Wolfhart Westendorf (1986).

New Kingdom Folktales

The Prince and His Fate (or *The Doomed Prince*)
Number of copies: One papyrus (P. Harris 500; British Museum).
Date of composition: Early Nineteenth Dynasty.
Content: A prince, an only child, is fated at birth to die by a snake, a dog, or a crocodile. Seeking his fortune in western Asia, he marries a Mitannian princess and has dompted one of his fates at the point

where the papyrus breaks off. Scholars are divided as to the outcome and implications of the plot.
Translations: Lichtheim, vol. 2; Wolfgang Helck, "Die Erzählung vom verwünschenen Prinzen," in *Form und Mass: Beiträge zur Literatur, Sprache und Kunst des alten Ägypten: Festschrift für Gerhard Fecht*, edited by Jürgen Osing and Günter Dreyer (1987).

The Tale of Two Brothers
Number of copies: One papyrus (P. d'Orbiney, British Museum 10183).
Date of composition: Nineteenth Dynasty.
Content: A wife, avid of the sexual services of her husband's younger brother, wrongfully accuses him (upon rejection) of improper advances toward herself. The younger brother castrates himself to prove his sincerity, and the story degenerates into an aetiological tale of the bull-god Bata with significant influence of Canaanite motifs.
Translations and commentary: Pritchard; Lichtheim, vol. 2; Jan Assmann, "Das ägyptische Zweibrüder-märchen (Papyrus d'Orbiney)," *Zeitschrift für ägyptische Sprache und Altertumskunde* 104 (1977).

Allegory

Truth and Falsehood
Number of copies: One papyrus (P. Chester Beatty II, British Museum).
Date of composition: Nineteenth Dynasty.
Content: Falsehood wrongly accuses his brother Truth of having stolen his knife, which, to enhance his argument before the court, is described as a gargantuan artifact. Truth is condemned and blinded, but his son (by an evil woman whose doorkeeper he has become) avenges him by accusing Falsehood of having killed and eaten the son's prize bull, which is also described in terms reminiscent of Paul Bunyan's beast.
Translation: Lichtheim, vol. 2.

Mythological Tales

The Book of the Cow of Heaven or *The Destruction of Humanity*
Number of copies: Six hieroglyphic versions in royal tombs at Thebes, from Tutankhamun to the Twentieth Dynasty (fourteenth to eleventh centuries).
Date of composition: Possibly Eighteenth Dynasty.
Content: The first pericope of a much longer aetiology describes how the sun-god Re, faced with a rebellion of mankind, sends his "Eye" down to earth in the form of a lioness that proceeds to devour men. When called back she refuses to come and has to be deceived into sedating herself by imbibing a potent brand of beer colored red to look like blood. The theme of the

Destruction of Humanity is alluded to in both earlier and late literature.

Translations and commentary: Lichtheim, vol. 2; Erik Hornung, *Der ägyptische Mythos von der Himmelskuh: Eine Ätiologie des Unvollkommen* (1972; 2nd ed. 1991).

Astarte and the Sea

Number of copies: One tattered papyrus in the J. Pierpoint Morgan Library, New York.

Date of composition: Probably Eighteenth Dynasty.

Content: A paraphrase of the Canaanite myth about how ʿAleyan Baal, with the help of Astarte, defeated the monster Yamm (the wild Sea). In this version "Seth" plays the hero role of Baal, and the Ennead is used for the Canaanite assembly of the gods. There is some evidence to suggest that the immediate model for the Egyptian version was Hurrian.

Translations and commentary: Pritchard; Rainer Stadelmann, *Syrisch-Palästinensische Göttheiten in Ägypten* (1967); Wolfgang Helck, "Zur Herkunft der Erzählung des sog. 'Astartepapyrus,'" in *Fontes atque pontes: Eine Festgabe für Hellmut Brunner,* edited by Manfred Görg (1983); Donald B. Redford, "The Sea and the Goddess," in *Studies in Egyptology Presented to Miriam Lichtheim,* edited by Sarah Israelit-Groll (1990).

The Contendings of Horus and Seth

Number of copies: One papyrus (P. Chester Beatty I, Dublin).

Date of composition: Nineteenth Dynasty.

Content: The trial of Horus versus Seth in court before the Ennead for the office of Osiris and the rule of Egypt is treated in eighteen episodes in somewhat picaresque fashion. The court setting is suspended in the middle of the sequence by four acts of trial by combat, which draw on very old mythological material. The final episodes are cast in satirical form and play upon the antipathy between the sun-god and Osiris.

Translations: Lichtheim, vol. 2; Pritchard; A. Kirk Grayson and Donald B. Redford, *Papyrus and Tablet* (1973).

---

randa, accounts), a certain amount turns out to be poetical or prose compositions that aimed both to entertain and to instruct. Temple libraries contained stories and mythological treatises, and even a scribe's private collection might include stories, love poetry, and hymns. Broadly speaking, much of this material falls under the heading "teaching," a term that whether or not it can be construed as a genre, relates more to intent and purpose than form. While "teaching" can encompass many life situations, in general it applies to a type of composition in which a wise man (father, king, or simply a superior) addresses a discourse on worldly wisdom to a subordinate. It therefore assumes the form of a monologue with suitable introduction and ending.

The format of Egyptian belletristic works varies somewhat, but remains basically rudimentary. Not always is a piece introduced by title and genre term; but in complete examples one might encounter "Here begins the . . ." "Sections" or "columns" are occasionally mentioned, and the headings thereof (often employing obsolete verb forms) are in red. Hymns and poetry are often divided into formal "stanzas" ($ḥwt$), sometimes numbered, the beginning of each stanza again being in red ink. A formal and carefully written text on papyrus was normally provided with a colophon incorporating the rubric "it has come to a successful end . . ." followed by the name of the one to whom the work was dedicated and the name of the scribe who wrote the text. Sometimes an imprecation was added: "as for him who shall criticize this writing, Thoth shall be an opponent to him!"

Genre terms frequently arose from the specific forms of compositions. The letter format, for example, was commonly used to convey instruction, and the contents could range from father-to-son chat to satire. It could also be used for a satirical exchange of insults between people at loggerheads with each other; occasionally for a lament. Similarly the text carved on a wall or a freestanding stone, the "stela" ($wḏ$), could be used with adjective or attributive phrase to qualify a genre of text, thus "stela of the king" (royal decree), "stela of victories" (rhetorical account of a military triumph), "stela to regulate" (published rules), "stela of summons" (written answer to an oracle), and so on. The terms for papyrus could be combined with qualifiers to produce titles, if not in some cases formal designations of genres: "document (ʿ) of . . . ," "scroll ($šfdw$) of . . . ," "book ($mḏ\!t$) of . . . ," and the like.

NARRATIVE

Several examples of Egyptian narrative survive from the Twelfth, the Nineteenth, and especially the Twentieth dynasties, and from the Persian-Roman periods. On the basis of internal criteria at least three types of narrative may be separated out (see also "Tales of Magic and Wonder from Ancient Egypt" later in this volume).

Adventure tales are represented from the Middle and New kingdoms by about a half-dozen examples, although the epitome of Manetho's *Aegyptiaca* suggests that many more once existed. These tales are set in the real world, often dated by reference to "the time (that is, the reign) of king so-and-so," and deal, it would seem, with real figures of history and real places. Often, though by no means always, the interest resides in, and the plot in fact turns on, some trick performed by the lead character, or on a surprise ending. Papyrus Westcar (Middle Kingdom, circa 1980–1630 BCE) is a collection of short tales told by the sons of Khufu (Cheops) to amuse their father that focus on wonders performed by magicians: the animation of a wax crocodile and its transformation into the real animal, the folding back of water to reveal dry ground, the restoration of decapitated animals to life, and so forth. (In the preserved version, the last of the these stories is expanded into an aetiology and a prophecy on the coming of the Fifth Dynasty.) New Kingdom (circa 1539–1075) tales reveled in the exploits of the warrior-kings of the Eighteenth Dynasty. The *Tale of Apopis and Seqenenre* told how Seqenenre accused Apopis of disturbing his sleep by maintaining a pool of noisy hippopotamuses at Thebes, a fantastic charge since Apopis lived in Avaris (Pi-Ramsese), five hundred miles (eight hundred kilometers) from Seqenenre. Presumably, the lost ending of the story recounts how Seqenenre won in what turned out to be a battle of wits. The great conqueror Thutmose III became the subject of a cycle of tales, but only one has survived in more than a small fragment, *The Taking of Joppa*. This tells of the capture of the city by means of the Ali Baba ruse of hiding soldiers in donkey panniers.

Egyptian narrative also throws up examples of what one might call fairy tales or folktales. These differ from adventure stories in that personal names and toponyms are consciously avoided, and terms of relationship are favored for the main characters (for example, "brother," "sister," "king's son," and "lad"). Thus a sort of timelessness is lent to the narrative and interest perforce centers on the well-crafted plot. In the Middle Kingdom *Shipwrecked Sailor*, a sailor, after the manner of the later Sindbad, is shipwrecked on a mysterious island. He is rescued and cared for by a giant talking snake. When the sailor finally leaves, the island disappears into the sea and is never found again. In the New Kingdom *The Prince and His Fates* (or *The Doomed Prince*), a prince, fated at birth to die by a dog, snake, or crocodile attack, seeks his fortune in Naharin and wins the local princess's hand. One major focus, the supposed inevitability of succumbing to one's fate, cannot now be appreciated because the final pages of the papyrus are lost. In another New Kingdom piece, *The Tale of Two Brothers*, a wife, whose sexual advances toward her young brother-in-law have been rebuffed, accuses him of sexual importuning. Her husband becomes enraged with his younger brother, who castrates himself to prove his innocence.

The largest preserved group of narratives are those set in the realm of the gods; these might be dubbed "mythological stories." The characters are the gods themselves. Several are based on popular myths that are well known and resemble variations on a theme. Some develop a myth or are spin-offs of one particular plot. But far from maintaining a reverent tone, all are bawdy and freewheeling and recall the tenor of an Atellan farce or medieval miracle play. Arguable though it may be that the mythological stories reflect the folk culture of the masses as the social stratum of their origin, nonetheless our exemplars give evidence of a secondary use in cultic aetiology, mortuary literature, and prophylactic magic.

The Book of the Cow of Heaven contains numerous aetiological explanations of "facts" of the cult, mostly based on wordplays, and incidentally preserves the myth of the destruction of mankind, in which the feline "Eye of Re" is dispatched to earth by the sun-god to decimate the human race. The extant copies of *The Book of the Cow of Heaven* are carved on the walls of several New Kingdom royal tombs. Equally inappropriately placed are the stories of Shu and

Geb, the gods who ruled after Re, the creator god. These stories are placed on a granite shrine originally intended for the temple of Sopd at Saft al-Hinna, yet they deal, among other things, with the incest of Geb and how he was bitten on the rump by a serpent. Other stories of this genre tell of the never-ending battle in the skies between Seth and the monster Apopis, of the journey of Anhur to bring back the straying lioness goddess, and of King Osiris and his vizier Khentyamentiu. A good number center on episodes in the Osiris myth: Isis deceives Re into revealing his hidden name to her, thus becoming the most powerful goddess; the baby Horus in the arms of his mother, in flight from his uncle Seth, is stung by a scorpion or a snake, or bitten by dogs. All stories on this theme were secondarily pressed into service as magical charms against the bite of noxious insects or animals. (See also "Witchcraft, Magic, and Divination in Ancient Egypt" in Part 8, Vol. III.)

The longest connected tale on an Osirian theme has been preserved in a papyrus in the Chester Beatty collection, and is now called *The Contendings of Horus and Seth*. The papyrus dates from the Twentieth Dynasty, but it is clearly composite and employs some material of very early origin. The conflict between the adolescent Horus and the villainous Seth becomes the backdrop for the piece, which comprises eighteen more or less unconnected episodes. These are strung out within the loose framework of a court trial held in the presence of the Ennead, or council of the gods, with the purpose of deciding which of the two shall be awarded the office of the deceased Osiris. Into this is inserted a block of seven episodes derived ultimately from the age-old myth of the physical combat between the two gods. These episodes are followed by a treatment of the conflict theme in the form of a satirical exchange of letters between Re and Osiris. The storyteller achieves considerable success in his characterization of the principals: Seth appears as a macho buffoon, Horus as a clever Puck-like stripling, Isis an insufferable nag, Neith a crotchety old woman, Re-Harakhty a sulky fellow, and so on. The tone and the development are picaresque throughout.

Narrative of the classical period of Middle Egyptian (Twelfth to Fifteenth dynasties) for the most part springs from a native milieu and owes little to external influence. For the New Kingdom period of the empire the picture changes dramatically. Egypt, victorious on the battlefields of Canaan and Nubia, succumbed to the belletristic influences of the conquered, who boasted communities of congeners ensconced beside the Nile. While we know next to nothing of the Nubian contribution, the literary influence of Canaan and Syria proved great.

The Canaanites brought a rich literary heritage into the Nile Valley, and it made an impact on the Egyptian narrative repertoire through the influence exerted by the cult. We find the Canaanite myth of Baal versus the Monster Sea (Yamm), well known from Ugarit (modern Ras Shamra), rendered into Egyptian apparently through the intermediary of a Hurrian version: Yamm, who has reduced the council of gods to tributaries to himself, now lusts after the beautiful Astarte, until the hero-god Baal (here transmogrified into Seth) comes to the rescue and defeats him. This example is a conscious adaptation from a West Asiatic original, but Canaanite motifs also crept into Egyptian literature imperceptibly. The lascivious Yamm pawing the voluptuous goddess on the Levantine coast turns up in *The Tale of Two Brothers*, as does the emasculated god (of the Adonis type). Baal, set upon by wild beasts at a water hole, informs the pericope dealing with the fate of the prince in *The Prince and His Fates*, and the same tale gives up a euhemerized "Astarte at the Window" in the person of the princess in the Tower. The satire of the two brothers, Truth and Falsehood, in the tale of the same name, seems to mirror the Hurrian tale *Good and Bad*.

Narratives of the Late Period (664–332) took on a more somber ambience, as the country suffered repeated invasion. A type of story arose and underwent permutations associated with an oral tradition; it plays on the paranoia of the Egyptian underclass and offers hope for the future. Set both in the past and future, the stories begin with a prophecy that, for its sin, Egypt will be invaded from the north by vile foreigners who will devastate the land. This comes to pass in due course, but then the gods relent. A deliverer appears from the south, drives out the invaders, and restores the country. Another plot type ascribes Egypt's woes to the presence within the country of a dissident group, whether diseased or merely socially unacceptable. When these are rounded up and disposed of or expelled, the gods are pleased and happy days return. (This motif is best known within the context of the Judeo-pagan polemic of Hellenistic times, when the plot was used to explain the origin of the Jews.)

These later narratives—of which some are preserved in Egyptian Demotic and some in Greek versions—are often more didactic and seriously aetiological. Many are intent on pointing up a moral and display a crass patriotism. As in Middle Kingdom literature, lector-priests, or "magicians" as the term had come to denote, appear as leading protagonists, but their role has little to do with something as innocent and trivial as a pharaoh's amusement: now they are called upon to save the nation. In these tales, northerners invade, a Nubian warlock vaunts himself against the nation, a pharaoh finds he has but days to live, a seven-year famine afflicts the land—calamities that provide the foil for the wisdom and sorcery of the magician. Sometimes the authors weave a rags-to-riches theme into the narrative: the wise man/magician languishes unknown or forgotten, occasionally in prison, as the country goes to ruin, and once he is summoned and solves the problem he vaults to wealth and celebrity.

Xenophobic as Egyptians of the first millennium might well have been, they owed a literary debt to the outside world. Well-known themes, motifs, and characters in Greek literature turn up more frequently than one might expect. The scribe of the myth of Horus at Edfu and the author of the demotic story *Armor of Inaros* apparently both knew of the *Iliad*, and in the tale *Egyptians and Amazons* Djoser fights the Amazons and the Assyrians. The consequences of hubris, upon reflection an unlikely preoccupation of traditional Egyptian authors, are explored in the case of a lector-priest whose fabulous magical skill and whose greed lead to disaster. Elsewhere we encounter the Didymus-Lazarus and Tantalos themes, and wise men visit Hades.

The magician-protagonists of these late pieces are drawn from figures of the illustrious past: Imhotep under Pharaoh Djoser; Amenhotep, son of Hapu, under Amenhotep (Amenophis) III; and especially Setna Khaemwaset, modeled on Khaemwaset, fourth son of Ramesses II. Others may or may not be historical: Meryre under a king Si-Sobek (of the Thirteenth Dynasty?), Phritiphantes under an Amenhotep, Onkhsheshonqy, Hi-Hor, to name a few.

THE BIOGRAPHICAL STATEMENT

Autobiography is the oldest genre in Egyptian literature, and many exemplars achieve a high literary quality. The Egyptian genre term for this type of piece is not altogether clear; since its origin is ostensibly oral it can be termed "my statements" or "words," but since it is a catalogue of honors, "my offices," is also found. Although influenced, if not at times informed, by the sophisticated speech of pharaoh's court, the biographical statement takes its rise in the practice, discernible already in the Early Dynastic period, of identifying the deceased by name, title, and representation (in relief, painting, or statue) in his tomb or on a stela associated with the tomb. As mortuary installations grew in size and adornment, they became an attraction for the general populace as a place to visit and sightsee, and the chance to communicate with posterity was not lost on the tomb owner. Appended to his name and titles by the close of the Third Dynasty is often a statement introduced by the words "he says," in which the dead person addresses "all you who pass by." Initially the purpose is practical: the owner enjoins future generations to give him offerings or at least to pronounce the offering formula, while forbidding them to damage the tomb for any reason. Well before the close of the Old Kingdom, however, the deceased speaker feels the need, in the interests of presenting a case to posterity, to deliver a well-crafted monologue on his doings in life. Not all his deeds are passed in review—the criterion of his selection appears often to be beyond recovery—but all is recounted with a verve and brazenness that only the exigency of self-promotion could justify. Since the opportunity of advancing the reputation and desires of the speaker suggests a didactic intent, the biographical statement might spill over into the category of instruction texts, with the constellations of form and content contained therein: "Ho, all you living upon the earth and you who shall be young men some day! I will tell you the way of life. . . ."

The biographical statement underwent the complex evolution over the centuries that one expects from a "living" genre. In the chaotic world of the First Intermediate Period (circa 2130–1980), when a kind of rugged individualism informed provincial society, the crudely written and prosaic but lively summary of military successes was the norm. The Middle Kingdom witnessed a polishing of the form, which carried over into the New Kingdom, when a biographical statement occasionally took on a poetic cast. Lauding one's own exploits in life gave way during the Ramesside age to the piety of intoning hymns of adoration to the deity. When in the Late Period in the Twenty-fifth and Twenty-sixth dynasties a general return to recording deeds done on earth took place, the content centered in the main on benefactions done for the temples and the gods by the individual on the king's behalf.

The form of the biographical statement, in light of its purpose and intended audience, is often pressed into service as a vehicle for loyalist instruction. Although the blatancy of the approach might be expected to detract from the aesthetic quality of the result, this extended use of biography gives up some exciting compositions. Chief among these, and the one in which loyalist propaganda is least marked, is the Middle Kingdom *Story of Sinuhe*. After the formal list of titles and name, and the rubric "he says," the author launches into a breathtaking adventure story in which the usual biographical framework and the "hidden persuaders" indicative of the propagandistic intent are infrequent and seldom in evidence. The hero is driven to flight in Asia in the aftermath of Amenemhet (Ammenemes) I's death, and after many adventures, reappears timorously at pharaoh's court, only to be welcomed back and reinstated by the magnanimous Senwosret (Sesostris) I. The high literary standard achieved far outweighs for us (and probably for the ancients too) the ephemeral purpose of contemporary politics, and the result is that it became one of the most popular creations of the entire corpus of ancient Egyptian belles lettres. (For more information on this genre, see the chapter "Ancient Egyptian Autobiographies" below.)

THE LITERATURE OF PROTEST AND DESPAIR

The catastrophe at the close of the Old Kingdom gave rise to a good deal of soul-searching and reappraisal. For the first time in Egypt's history there came to be written down a number of heterodox oratorical creations that were outside the mainstream of government and society, and whose gifted authors stood in opposition to existing ways. It is not the ruling class that we hear speaking in these works; often the words are put in the mouths of those who are at odds with it. All are highly critical about the way things have been done up to the present, and have no qualms about saying so. The times were ripe for such individualists. Their ability to express themselves and hence their threat to the establishment called forth pejorative terms used to describe them. New literary forms appeared, suited specifically to convey the peculiar messages that were being promulgated: the lament (possibly also called the statement, literally the "word" of so-and-so), the dialogue, the prophetic message (back-dated or contemporary), and the cynical song.

The lament was fairly popular. That it enjoyed a considerable vogue in the Twelfth Dynasty, by which time it had become a hackneyed and overused vehicle, militates strongly in favor of the traditional view that it was a product of the earlier First Intermediate Period. The description is organized into sections that are usually the length of a single couplet, each beginning with the same deictic expression. Section is related to section either by similarity of content or by punning on homonyms. The framework may vary—the speaker may address one of the authorities or he may soliloquize—but the content usually centers on the calamitous condition of human society, as expressed in *The Admonitions of Ipuwer*:

> Really, the poor have become owners of
>   luxuries:
>   he who never made sandals for himself is now
>   possessor of riches. . . .
>
> Really, the heart is aggressive; plague is
>   throughout the land,
>   blood is everywhere, death gives no offence;

. . . Really many dead are buried in the river,
    the stream is a tomb—indeed the embalming
    place has become the stream!

Really the rich are in mourning while the poor
    rejoice;
    every city says "Let us drive the influential
    out from among us!"

The speaker of these words, the otherwise unknown Ipuwer, goes on to castigate the individual to whom he is speaking, in this case the sun-god himself, with having allowed his creation and society at large to go to ruin.

Dialogue is employed to stunning effect in a curious piece preserved in a single Twelfth Dynasty manuscript. *The Dispute Between a Man Tired of Life and His Ba*, as it is now called (the original title is lost), is a work in which a man converses with his *ba* (his personality or alter ego) regarding the imponderables of death and the beyond (see "Death and the Afterlife in Ancient Egyptian Thought" in Part 8, Vol. III): The man appears to be weary of life and is contemplating death (although scholarly opinion differs on the translation of key passages), but first he must make preparation for death by building a tomb, establishing a mortuary endowment, and awaiting the birth of an heir. This preparation corresponds to traditional funerary practice. His *ba*, on the other hand, denies that customary preparation for death and all the mortuary ritual this entails are of any use whatsoever: if the man is going to die, better to do it immediately and have done with it; for we know nothing of the beyond in any case.

"If you goad me on to death in this manner," says the man to his *ba*, "you will not find where to alight in the West! Have patience, my *ba*, my brother, until my heir shall appear who shall make offering and attend to the tomb(?), on the day of burial that he might spread the funerary couch of the necropolis!" My *ba* opened his mouth to me and answered what I had said: "If you think on burial it's a heartache, it brings on tears by making a man miserable. It means dragging a man out of his house and casting (him) upon the high ground. You won't be able to go heavenward to see Re! As for those who built with new stone and constructed halls in fine pyramids as excellent work, when their builders became gods (that is, died), their offering tables went to ruin, just as if (they had been) weary ones

who died on the river with no survivor (that is, the poor), they to whom, when the inundation has taken its toll and the sun likewise, the fishes of the shallows talk! Listen to me, for listening is good for people: follow the happy day and forget care!"

Thus the man and his *ba* espouse views diametrically opposed, struggling for supremacy in the same soul: the traditional belief in the efficacy of the mortuary cult and the afterlife, and an agnostic view that these practices are useless, that the rich who die fare no better for all their funerary preparation than the poor, and that the afterlife cannot be known. While at the close of the piece, after the inclusion of a lengthy poem in the vein of the lament (above), the man seems to win the argument, this outcome was perhaps but a perfunctory nod in the direction of orthodoxy. Certainly the *ba* seems to have the better of the argument.

The *ba*'s advice to his owner—that he should cease to contemplate things he can never know and enjoy the pleasures of the moment—is taken up by the harper's songs which unabashedly preach hedonism. Harpers, singers, and dancers were standard entertainment at the banquets of the wealthy, and they are frequently depicted in Old Kingdom art. After the close of the Old Kingdom harpers' songs became a literary vehicle of sorts; in a mortuary context recalling the parties enjoyed in life, the solitary harper was depicted directing an extemporized song to his master. It is this form of the song that became a vehicle for a much more serious, and, for the ancients, jarring message.

The song which is in the tomb of (king) Antef, deceased, which is in front of the singer with the harp: "Prosperous is this good prince though a happy fate has failed. One generation passes away and another settles in since the time of those of long ago; and the gods who lived long ago now rest in their pyramids. . . . Mansions were built, but their seats exist not—see! what has been made of them! I have heard the words of Imhotep and Hardjedef (Djedfehor) whose talk is talked about so much. Look at their (cult) seats! Their walls are denuded, as though they had never existed; and nobody comes (back) from over there that he might tell us their condition or tell us their state to allay our concern until we journey where they have gone. . . . (So) make holiday and be not concerned with it! Lo! No man is allowed to take his things with him! Lo! No one who goes comes back again!

The harpers' songs enjoyed an increasing popularity throughout the New Kingdom. The agnostic and hedonistic tone that informs them could not fail to call forth a rebuttal. "Extolling the earthly and belittling the land of the dead" was, from the standpoint of the righteous Egyptian, unseemly if not immoral; but a somber note had been struck. The blessed afterlife in the Elysian Fields or the heavenly realm of the sun was not only unattainable: it was not even verifiable. The exact opposite was feared: an eternity of darkness and misery. A spirit appears at the offering stone of his tomb and reveals the truth about the afterlife in terms of a pointed rebuttal of the tenets of traditional belief: "My desire is not to flow(?) like the Nile. . . . (In the Afterlife?) there is no eating, no drinking, no o[ld, no yo]ung, no seeing the rays of the sun, no breathing the [north wind]. Darkness engulfs the face constantly, no one rises early to go forth." A deceased wife describes the next life to her living husband: "As for the West, it is a land of sleep and thick darkness, a resting place for those that are there. Slumber is their (only) occupation—they waken not to see their brothers, they do not behold their fathers and mothers, their hearts long for their wives and children!"

COURTLY LITERATURE

Apart from the setting up of decrees in public places, the kings of the Old Kingdom did not adopt the practice of broadcasting their exploits on stelae for all to see, an omission curiously explained in late tradition by the assumption that these early kings had accomplished nothing worth recording. The biographical statement, coupled with an individual's name and titles, was the preserve of the private individual, to be placed prominently in the tomb for future generations to read (or have read to them). The kings of the Eleventh Dynasty were themselves once commoners, provincial squires with no royal blood in their ancestry at all; and not surprisingly it is with them that royal biographical statements begin to be found. Before the close of the Eleventh Dynasty these biographical state-

ments, occurring initially as tradition demanded in a mortuary context, were supplemented by true narrative discourse—speeches from the throne, as it were—inscribed on stelae in public places. In the Twelfth and Thirteenth dynasties, when kings were not exactly the untouchable gods-on-earth that their Old Kingdom predecessors had been, the propaganda value of such public texts (especially if accompanied by relief scenes) could not be overestimated.

By the beginning of the New Kingdom a full-fledged literature of the court was in the process of taking final shape. Central to it was what the Egyptians called the "royal sitting," or sometimes the "king's appearance," a formal seance of the court at which the king delivered a speech that either detailed policy or announced the results of some action. Scribes were on hand to take down the proceedings, and soon the whole evolved into a self-conscious rhetorical exercise. That the royal speeches which derive from such sittings and presently survive on stelae are most often verbatim transcriptions can be argued on the basis of style and vocabulary. The king's addresses in the New Kingdom stelae can often be allocated, without recourse to the obvious labels of name and titulary, to a particular reign on the basis of individual style. This is especially true of texts coming from the reigns of Thutmose I, Thutmose III, Amenhotep II, probably Amenhotep III, Akhenaten (first known as Amenhotep IV), probably Horemheb (though doubtful), Ramesses II, Ramesses III, and Ramesses IV. It is not true of texts that can be otherwise dated to the reigns of Ahmose, Amenhotep I, Thutmose IV (probably), Sety I, or the later Ramessides. Such texts from "sittings" can be highly stilted, and some have a prosodic form. Sometimes a speech is interlarded at irregular intervals with sections of editorial comment that refer to the king in the third person, and probably come from the hand of the redacting scribe. In many examples a stela recording the king's speech terminates with a pericope recording the response of the assembled court.

But the job of the scribe at pharaoh's court involved something more than merely taking dictation. From the Old Kingdom a lively tradition of adulation of the king had sprung up in court circles, consisting of hymns (placed in the mouths of courtiers) extolling the virtues and might of pharaoh, and even his crowns and accoutrements. The sort of panegyric that extolled the bucolic pleasures of fishing and fowling also produced exemplars in which the king and his court enjoyed an outing in the marsh and became the subject of a poet's (rather tedious) encomium. The military victories that accompanied the creation of the empire in the Eighteenth Dynasty evoked an atmosphere ripe for extolling the supposedly mighty acts of pharaoh in the sophisticated though brittle creations of a sort of poet laureate. The reign of Thutmose III witnessed the appearance of a type of prose that went under the title "Collection of Deeds" of a given king. Although the precise context that produced it eludes us, its origin in an exercise of oratory for the edification of the commons cannot be denied. In a chatty manner the author selects specific campaigns, hunting parties, and feats of strength from the manifold acts of the pharaoh and expatiates upon them in shameless and exaggerated language. The evolutionary link between the two cannot be demonstrated, but at the Ramesside court the same adulation is realized by a song in set strophes, to be sung to the accompaniment of the harp. Each strophe ends with the cartouches of the king, and the content amounts to little more than a series of high-flown epithets. Sometimes a specific military success would trigger the production of what the Egyptians called a victory stela, in which the date and brief allusion to the event provided the occasion for a panegyric on the king's superhuman strength and intelligence.

The context of this encomiastic literature is not difficult to discern. The pharaoh kept singers and dancers to perform at court, as did the temples, and a festive atmosphere centering upon Hathor, goddess of love and music, is frequently alluded to. Two other situations were used to good effect in the composition of victory stelae: the arrival of the messenger and the king-in-council. The former adopts as point of departure the moment (replete with regnal year, month, and day, clearly derived from an entry in the royal daybook) when a messenger arrived bearing bad news: foreigners have invaded, a rebellion has occurred, a disaster threatens. The king, then, is usually said to react by "raging like a southern panther," and he immediately determines to come to grips with the situation. He leads or sends forth his army, and the enterprise issues in victory and glory for the king. In the motif of the king-in-council a crisis similarly looms, but this time, rather than act alone, the king summons his advisers and questions them: Where can I find information on the gods? Shall we go to war or not? Which route shall we take against the enemy? Shall we lay siege to or assault the city? In most cases the council advises caution and the king interprets this as cowardice. He disregards their counsel and proposes to act immediately and with force. The pattern is used to play up pharaoh's foresight, energy, and courage, by contrasting his actions with the timidity of his entourage.

> I come that you might trample the western
> lands,
>   Crete and Cyprus are in awe of [you];
> I let them view your majesty as a young bull,
>   confident and sharp-horned, who cannot be
>   attacked!

Thankful for the construction work done on his behalf, Amun-Re speaks to Queen Hatshepsut:

> Welcome, my sweet daughter, my favourite, king
>   of Upper and Lower Egypt . . . who makes
>   my beautiful monuments . . .
>
> You are the king . . . you satisfied my heart at
>   all times.
> I have given you all life and satisfaction from
>   me,
>
> I have given you all countries wherein your
>   heart is glad.
> I have long intended them for you . . .

Sometimes the deity's message is couched in the form of a dream. A prince (the future Thutmose IV) is promised the throne if he will clear the sphinx of sand. The army is rusty, the threat serious, and the king requires the encouragement of the god; by means of symbols a Nubian pharaoh is promised the rule of Egypt if he attacks. Oracles, too, were widely used, from the mid Eighteenth Dynasty on, to convey a god's will to the king, but neither oracle nor dream became a favored device in literature.

Pharaoh's conversation with the gods took the form of the same kind of hymns and prayers that his subjects used, but they are grandly characterized as "the mighty and effective beatifications, supplications, hymns, and prayers." Often their content is purely liturgical, and the king adopts the role of the priest, but sometimes the tone is more personal, as the king makes report and beseeches the god.

HYMNS AND POETRY

Egyptian poetry was intended to be sung (*ḥsj*), chanted (*g'*), or intoned (?—*dd m 'nn*) to the accompaniment of such instruments as reed pipe, lyre, flute, and percussion. It was performed against a strong rhythmic backdrop provided by hand-clapping, castanets, or toe-tapping, and was itself strongly accentuated. To such an extent did prosodic patterns inform Egyptian poetry that the singing of the priests in the temple was likened to the rhythmic chatter of baboons at the rising of the sun. We cannot speak of the uniformity of musical meter, however. Scanning is impossible on classical terms, the forms approximating modern "rap" poetry to a far greater extent. Basic to Egyptian poetry is the stich of two cola, each colon receiving usually two or three stresses. Stichs can be grouped into couplets or quatrains, and these again into stanzas, although the subtleties of specific rules (if such there were) are lost to us.

While little more can be said about Egyptian poetic structure despite what has been written on it, a large body of written material exists that, beyond doubt, belongs under the heading of poetry. Hymns abound, finding their context in the cult. Temples employed choirs of male and female singers to intone morning and evening hymns. Some hymns achieve a sublimity of concept that raises them to a prominent place in the ranks of world hymnology: one may cite the hymns to and lamentations over Osiris, the prayers of Isis for her baby, the hymns to Amun-Re and Re, the sun hymn of Akhenaten, and the great didactic paean to Ptah.

Love poetry, apart from individual examples scattered over the centuries, has survived in four collections: Papyrus Harris 500 (circa 1300), a Turin Museum papyrus (circa 1200), Papyrus Chester Beatty I (circa 1150), and a large ostracon in the Cairo Museum (see "Love Lyrics from the Ancient Near East" later in this volume).

Usually narrated in the first person, the stanzas are placed alternately in the mouth of the boy (the "brother") or the girl (the "sister"), rarely a third party. Couplets are frequent, lines of six beats (3:3 or 4:2) being common. Themes include the catalogue of the lover's charms, the sickness of the lovers, the separation of the lovers, the coming of dawn, the locked door, and the like. The charms of the beloved are thus passed in review:

> . . . With flashing eyes of beauty,
> Her lips sweet of speech—
> Yet she lacks a word too much—
> With lofty neck and radiant breasts,
> Real lapis lazuli her hair;
> Her arms outdo gold,
> Her fingers are like lotus flowers;
> With declining rump and trim waist,
> Whose thighs show forth her beauty,
> Of graceful step when she treads the earth,
> She has seized my heart in her embrace!
> She causes the neck of every male
> To turn about at the sight of her;
> Happy the one whom she embraces!
> He thinks himself the foremost of lusty males!

SATIRE, ALLEGORY, AND FABLE

The Egyptians loved the give and take of a lively dispute. We sense this in courtroom settings where the exchange was oral; but the format of an exchange by letters also enjoyed a vogue. In *The Contendings of Horus and Seth*, Osiris excoriates Re-Harakhty for blocking his son Horus's assumption of Osiris's office, especially since Osiris has the important task of ensuring that the crops grow. Re writes back that crops would grow even if Osiris did not exist, to which Osiris responds that Re has been so concerned with heavenly matters that he has neglected justice.

A king's scribe blasts a colleague for pretending to competence in the various disciplines in which a king's scribe ought to be proficient, and in the course of his long letter (Papyrus Anastasi I) he seeks by every means to hold the addressee up to derision. One scribe writes to another accusing him of giving himself up to pleasure and neglecting his scribal duties. In the *Instruction of Any* a wise man and his son enter into a lively debate over wisdom and the education of children of differing capacities. In all examples the form fosters a search for obscure vocabulary and convoluted ways of couching the requisite insults.

Arguably to be classed between the extended parameters of satire is the report, informed by an explicit or implicit complaint. The piece is written in the first person and has been infelicitously dubbed pseudo-autobiographical; but like Papyrus Anastasi I or the pericope in *Horus and Seth,* the favored format is the letter. In one instance a former civil servant is driven from office, cruelly persecuted by unnamed personal enemies, and driven to exile; he suffers robbery, the murder of relatives, and vilification (P. Pushkin 127). In the *Report of Wenamun* a commercial agent, on a mission to Lebanon for the temple of Amun, experiences robbery, loss of credentials, the hostility of the local administration, and piracy. A minor official complains earnestly in the *Letter of Complaint* about his inability to fulfill assigned tasks because of the implacable opposition and machinations of a rival in office (P. Anastasi VI). Throughout the didactic corpus used in training scribes, many model letters exhibit similar characteristics. This subgenre arises out of a real-life situation, that is, the need rhetorically to make a strong case of an apologetic kind. The cuneiform diplomatic correspondence in the Amarna letters abounds in real exemplars of the genre, many of which rival *Wenamun* in skillful composition and persuasive rhetoric (see the chapter on the Amarna letters later in this volume).

Neither allegory nor fables are well represented in the surviving literary corpus. *Truth and Falsehood,* an example of these forms of late New Kingdom date, recounts the dispute between two brothers, named in the title. The former, though maligned and punished by his brother, was eventually vindicated through the agency of his son. A fable of the dispute between the body and the head over bodily supremacy is known from a badly preserved schoolboy's exercise tablet.

CONCLUSION

Ancient Egypt bequeathed a rich literary heritage to the ancient world. Its principal contributions, perhaps, were the short story and the wisdom text, although Egyptian love poetry and the hymn exerted a certain influence in Levantine culture. Influenced during the New Kingdom by Canaanite and Hurrian literature, Egyptian literature nonetheless had developed a number of themes and plot motifs that are distinctively Nilotic and can be traced into Europe and the Middle East in medieval times. Egyptian literature was also one of the first bodies of writing to wrestle with moral problems inherent in theodicy, to question accepted dogma in an agnostic manner, and to explore such imponderables as first cause, substance, and life itself.

Though grounded in oral composition, Egyptian literature was always tied to the scribe, that gifted, literate wise man who exemplified all the traits of a polymath. Greece and Rome revered this wise man in concept, but the literature he produced no Roman or Greek could read. It was largely through Egyptian literature's influence on nascent Christianity that any impact was made on the (late) classical world.

BIBLIOGRAPHY

General

JAN ASSMANN, ERIKA FEUCHT, and REINHARD GRIESHAMMER, eds., *Fragen an die altägyptische Literatur: Studien zum Gedenken an Eberhard Otto* (1977); HELLMUT BRUNNER, *Grundzüge einer Geschichte der altägyptischen Literatur* (4th ed. 1986), and "Literatur," in *Lexikon der Ägyptologie,* vol. 3, edited by WOLFGANG HELCK and EBERHARD OTTO (1980), and *Altägyptische Weisheit: Lehren für das Leben* (1988); MIRIAM LICHTHEIM, *Ancient Egyptian Literature: A Book of Readings,* 3 vols. (1973–1980); GEORGES POSENER, "Les Richesses inconnues de la littérature égyptienne," *Revue d'Égyptologie* 6 (1951), 9 (1952), and "Literature," in *The Legacy of Egypt,* edited by J. R. HARRIS (1971); and JAMES B. PRITCHARD, *Ancient Near Eastern Texts Relating to the Old Testament* (3rd ed. 1969); and *Ancient Egyptian Literature: History and Forms,* edited by ANTONIO LOPRIENO.

Oral Composition and Transmission

DONALD B. REDFORD, *Oral and Written Tradition in Ancient Egypt* (forthcoming, 1996).

Literary Categories

ANTONIO LOPRIENO, *Topos und Mimesis: Zum Ausländer in der ägyptischen Literatur* (1988); and ADEL-

HEID SCHLOTT, *Schrift und Schreiber im Alten Ägypten* (1989).

Narrative

FRANCIS LLEWELLYN GRIFFITH, *Stories of the High Priests of Memphis: The Dethon of Herodotus and the Demotic Tales of Khamuas* (1900); WOLFGANG HELCK, "Zur Herkunft der Erzählung des sog. 'Astartepapyrus,'" in *Fontes atque pontes: Eine Festgabe für Hellmut Brunner*, edited by MANFRED GÖRG, Ägypten und Altes Testament 5 (1983); GEORGES POSENER, *Littérature et politique dans l'Égypte de la XIIᵉ dynastie* (1956), and *Le Papyrus Vandier* (1985); and H. S. SMITH and W. J. TAIT, *Saqqâra Demotic Papyri 1* (1983).

The Biographical Statement

JAN ASSMANN, "Schrift, Tod, und Identität: Das Grab als Vorschule der Literatur im alten Ägypten," in *Schrift und Gedächtnis*, edited by ALEIDA ASSMANN, JAN ASSMANN, and CHRISTOF HARDMEIER (1983); JOHN BAINES, "Society, Morality, and Religious Practice," in *Religion in Ancient Egypt: Gods, Myth, and Personal Practice*, edited by BYRON E. SHAFER (1991); GEORGES POSENER, *L'Enseignement loyaliste: Sagesse égyptienne du Moyen Empire* (1976); and WILLIAM KELLY SIMPSON, "Sinuhe," in *Lexikon der Ägyptologie* vol. 5, edited by WOLFGANG HELCK and WOLFHART WESTENDORF (1984).

The Literature of Protest and Despair

GERHARD FECHT, *Der Vorwurf am Gott in den "Mahnworten des Ipu-wer"* (1972); FRIEDRICH JUNGE, *Die Welt der Klagen*," and JAN ASSMANN, "Fest des Augenblicks—Verheissung der Dauer: Die Kontroverse der ägyptischen Harfnerlieder," in *Fragen an die altägyptische Literatur: Studien zum Gedenken an Eberhard*

Otto, edited by JAN ASSMANN, ERIKA FEUCHT, and REINHARD GRIESHAMMER (1977); and R. B. PARKINSON, "Teachings, Discourses, and Tales from the Middle Kingdom," in *Middle Kingdom Studies*, edited by STEPHEN QUIRKE (1991).

Courtly Literature

ALFRED HERMANN, *Die ägyptische Königsnovelle*, Leipziger Ägyptologische Studien 10 (1938); and RICARDO A. CAMINOS, *Literary Fragments in the Hieratic Script* (1956).

Hymns and Poetry

JAN ASSMANN, *Liturgische Lieder an den Sonnengott: Untersuchungen zur altägyptischen Hymnik, I*, Münchner ägyptologische Studien 19 (1969), and *Ägyptische Hymnen und Gebete* (1975); GERHARD FECHT, "Prosodie," in *Lexikon der Ägyptologie* 4, edited by WOLFGANG HELCK and WOLFHART WESTENDORF (1982); JOHN L. FOSTER, *The Love Songs of the New Kingdom* (1974); MICHAEL V. FOX, *The Song of Songs and the Ancient Egyptian Love Songs* (1985); and HEIKE GUKSCH, "'Sehnsucht nach der Heimatstadt'": Ein ramessidisches Thema?" *Mitteilungen des Deutschen Archäologischen Instituts, Abteilung Kairo* 50 (1994).

Satire, Allegory, and Fable

RICARDO A. CAMINOS, *A Tale of Woe: From a Hieratic Papyrus in the A. S. Pushkin Museum of Fine Arts in Moscow* (1977); HANS-WERNER FISCHER-ELFERT, *Die satirische Streitschrift des Papyrus Anastasi I*, Ägyptologische Abhandlungen 44 (1986); and RONALD J. WILLIAMS, "The Sages of Ancient Egypt in the Light of Recent Scholarship," *Journal of the American Oriental Society* 101 (1981).

Demotic Literature

— W. J. TAIT

The demotic script (a highly cursive adaptation of hieratic) was first developed in the seventh century BCE for the writing of legal contracts and other documentary material. At some point before the late fourth century (exactly when is not yet clear), it came to be employed for the recording of literature.

By the Early Roman period, from which the greatest quantity of demotic literary papyri survives, the literature was made up of a wide variety of texts. The two most strongly represented genres are stories (fictional narratives) and wisdom literature. However, the range of texts also includes prophecy and satire as well as religious, astrological, medical, and magical texts. New kinds of material undoubtedly still await discovery, since museum collections of papyri have only partly been explored.

Narratives are attested in our earliest substantial group of demotic literary material, which was found

Continued on the next page.

Continued from the previous page.

in excavations at North Saqqara. Many of these papyri probably date from the fourth century. From the middle of the Ptolemaic period, just the beginning of a narrative survives in which King Amasis seeks distraction from a hangover by demanding to be told a story. The surviving copies of most texts, however, belong to the first century BCE and the first two centuries CE.

Demotic stories are always expressed in prose. They sometimes form cycles of stories that deal with the exploits of the same character or group of characters. One such cycle concerns Setna Khaemwaset, a son of the New Kingdom king Ramesses II. These Setna stories all seem closely similar in content. Setna is fascinated by magical texts and by the funerary monuments of the past, and so encounters the "ghost" of a long-dead magician—within his tomb, in at least one case. In a "story-within-a-story," he learns of an episode in the magician's life; it seems that usually the "ghost" and Setna also both play a role in an episode set in Setna's own time. The texts occupy a world halfway between the traditional Egyptian view of the magician as learned priest and that of the magician as sorcerer that we meet in the Greek and demotic Magical Papyri of the third century CE.

The Inaros (or Petubastis) Texts describe the adventures of warriors, principally numerous members of the "family" of Inaros. The stories seem to be set in the seventh century BCE but include confused reminiscences of other late dynastic periods; Inaros himself has no obvious historical counterpart. Egypt is depicted as divided into numerous princedoms, over which a Pharaoh Petubastis is, in a few texts, shown to hold a precarious control. The plots are highly varied. Some deal with contests within Egypt and seem deliberately to emphasize the fragmentation of the country; in one, for example, warriors rally to either side of a dispute over the possession of a priesthood. Others recount exotic adventures abroad, such as an expedition to the "Land of the Women," while another text includes a description of a battle against a gigantic griffin.

Demotic wisdom literature also survives mainly from the first century BCE and the first two centuries CE and includes two substantial, well-preserved examples. The text of Papyrus Insinger, the longer of these, is also attested in several other fragmentary copies. Only one copy is known of *The Wisdom of ʿOnkhsheshonqy*. There are a few other short texts or fragments. All the texts are built up of independent, single-sentence maxims or commands, each of which is normally laid out on a single line in the manuscript. Two or more of these may be closely connected in their subject matter, and sometimes an extended sequence of sentences may be parallel in structure and related

in sense. Papyrus Insinger is the most highly organized, being divided into twenty-five chapters, each dealing with a different topic and each introduced by a heading, which either describes its subject matter or provides a typical maxim. For example, chapter 8 is headed, "The eighth teaching: do not be greedy, in case you meet with poverty," and deals with gluttony and greed in general. Chapter 18 is entitled, "The eighteenth teaching: the wisdom of being patient until you have (properly) reflected, in case you cause offense." Much of the text concerns the distinction between the wise and foolish man, and it pays particular attention (more than do the other texts) to the role of fate and the fickleness of fortune—but also to the inescapable vengeance of god upon the wicked. *The Wisdom of ʿOnkhsheshonqy* begins with a lengthy narrative introduction that tells how ʿOnkhsheshonqy came to compose his text while languishing in prison. The maxims themselves, many of which have the character of proverbs, concentrate upon practical wisdom and self-interest rather than morality or a sense of divine justice.

The relationship between demotic literature and that of pharaonic Egypt is problematic. Hardly any hieratic wisdom material survives from after the New Kingdom, and the only hieratic narrative later than 1000 BCE is Papyrus Vandier, which perhaps dates to the middle of the first millennium BCE; it tells the story of a visit to the underworld by a magician, and has close links both in language and in subject matter with demotic tales. It is conceivable that Egyptian fictional traditions continued solely in oral form after the New Kingdom. There is only a little evidence for the actual survival of any literary (as opposed to religious) texts of the Middle or New kingdoms into the period of demotic.

Significant differences may be seen between the demotic and the earlier literatures. Demotic shows little sign of the elaborate metrical structures that are an essential part of pharaonic material. Narratives do not seem to have continued to be used in school education. Although the royal court figures at some point in most demotic narratives, "court literature" —such as hymns to the king—does not appear to occur. This is hardly surprising if, as seems plausible, demotic literature was chiefly current in temple communities. The authors of demotic texts are evidently aware of a wide range of foreign literatures—at the least of Babylonian, Hebrew, Aramaic, and Greek, although not necessarily at firsthand—and adopted and adapted themes, stories, and structures from them. Very rarely were texts simply translated. The vitality of demotic literature needs no defense.

Demotic Literature

PAUL J. FRANDSEN, ed., *The Carlsberg Papyri I: Demotic Texts from the Collection* (1991); MIRIAM LICHTHEIM, *Late Egyptian Wisdom Literature in the International Context: A Study of Demotic Instruction* (1983); GEORGES POSENER, *Le Papyrus Vandier* (1978); H. S. SMITH and W. J. TAIT, *Saqqâra Demotic Papyri 1* (1983); W. J. TAIT, "Demotic Literature and Egyptian Society," *Life in a Multi-cultural Society: Egypt from Cambyses to Constantine and Beyond*, edited by JANET H. JOHNSON (1992); and HEINZ-JOSEF THISSEN, "Graeco-ägyptische Literatur," in vol. 2 of *Lexikon der Ägyptologie*, edited by WOLFGANG HELCK and WOLFHART WESTENDORF (1977).

SEE ALSO **The History of Ancient Egypt: An Overview** (Part 5, Vol. II); **Ancient Egyptian Autobiographies** (Part 9, Vol. IV); **Tales of Magic and Wonder from Ancient Egypt** (Part 9, Vol. IV); **Akkadian Literature: An Overview** (Part 9, Vol. IV); **Hittite and Hurrian Literature: An Overview** (Part 9, Vol. IV); and **The Literatures of Canaan, Ancient Israel, and Phoenicia: An Overview** (Part 9, Vol. IV).

Ancient Egyptian Autobiographies

OLIVIER PERDU

THE GENRE OF BIOGRAPHY was not known in pharaonic Egypt. Autobiographies, however, are well attested, although the texts that Egyptologists term autobiographies may not correspond to the Western expectation of literary works in which people give accounts of their lives, principally in order to present their personal experiences as food for thought for their peers. There are a number of Egyptian fictional narratives in which a narrator tells his story, such as the *Story of Sinuhe,* but in these the protagonist restricts himself to reporting a part of his life, an adventure of which he is the hero. Moreover, what is important for these texts is less the man himself than the events in which he participates.

Egyptologists apply the term "autobiography" to inscriptions, carved or painted on a variety of nonroyal monuments, in which the owners evoke their own personalities. Almost all belonged to men, but a few women were commemorated in this way in the first millennium BCE, including at least one who had died when still a child. All are in the form of narrative in the first-person singular, introduced by the traditional formula "he says," which is preceded by an indication of the owner's titles and name. A single example from about 2000 BCE is partly composed in the second person, as if it were taken from a funerary address to the deceased. Their length, which varies considerably, depends, in part, on both the available space and the subject's importance in society. The text addresses itself to a limited number of individuals—to those who happen to pass by—and its goal is less to inform them than to serve the autobiographer's goals for the afterlife.

There are two kinds of material in the autobiographies. One type is simply descriptive and focuses on the self-portrait that the subject wishes to present. Often long and tedious, it is a sequence of epithets of varying length and of more or less elaborate expressions that evoke his personality through his character traits, his tastes, and his attitudes. These expressions were also used in the titularies of nonroyal individuals as soon as it became possible, in the Fifth Dynasty (circa 2450 BCE), to extend these beyond simple enumerations. The second type of material consists of narrative passages in the form of continuous text that relates in chronological order the owner's career, or at least its principal stages.

These two categories of material, which differ in both form and content, can occur independently or may be linked in a single inscription. In such cases the description generally precedes the narration. It is difficult to summarize patterns of usage here, because the treatment of the material is very flexible.

TRADITIONAL AUTOBIOGRAPHIES

Monuments preserving autobiographies whose frequency renders their type deserving of the designation "classical" are found in necropolises (burial grounds) and in temples. In tombs the autobiographies are inscribed at the entrance or in the chapel, directly on a wall or on a stela, but always in a position where they would be noticed by the passersby to whom they were addressed, whether these individuals were servants of the deceased or common visitors. These inscriptions had to persuade the readers to do what was required in the appeal addressed to them, by showing how much the tomb owner was worthy of their attention. These two messages—the praise of the owner and the request—are very closely related, even when they are not combined in a single inscription. The deceased needed to obtain a contribution to his funerary cult, the principal requirement of which was the presentation of food offerings. The practice of the earliest texts to ask for gifts in kind, in the form of food and libations, quickly gave way to requests that the formula which accompanied such offerings be recited.

The autobiographies in temples are on objects set up in open courtyards in front of the roofed areas where the deities dwelt. They are carved on stelae or on statues of their beneficiaries. Here, too, the inscriptions were intended to elicit actions on behalf of their owners by portraying them as deserving people. The difference lies in the identity of those addressed and what was asked of them. Because the setting was a temple, the inscriptions were directed at the priests (rather than the deity), who were beseeched to take care of the monument—and thus to sustain the deity's memory of its owner—and, above all, to reserve for the owner portions of the daily offerings after they had been presented to the statue of the deity.

There was, however, no fundamental difference between the aims of autobiographies set up in tombs and those in temples. It was always necessary to persuade the person who one hoped would perform an action that the recipient was in all respects worthy. People were better disposed toward a person of rank and considered it more satisfying to perform a service for a great personage. Such an action was believed to be highly advantageous, if the recipient promised in return to intercede with the gods, for the more highly placed the intercessor, the greater the chances that his intercession would be successful.

Thus, to make an impression through one's qualities and actions; to elicit sympathy, respect, and admiration; in short, to present oneself as the perfect man: these were the aims that preoccupied those who commissioned the carving of their autobiographies. The texts, however, also needed to arouse interest, to surprise, and to stimulate the reader's curiosity, because the content was just as capable of attracting attention as the quality of carving or the beauty of the objects on which they were inscribed. In temples, where many monuments accumulated, it became vital to catch the priests' eyes, if one was to benefit from their generosity.

It goes without saying that these considerations affected greatly the veracity of what was said in autobiographies. Each of the aims just mentioned above is a constraint that stands in the way of a realistic presentation. Even when a large amount of space is allotted to a text, so that it will strike the reader, there is no question of going into detail. Everything negative is forgotten, despite constant affirmations that the owner wishes to tell the whole truth. The texts include only what redounds to the subject's credit; even that information tends to be inflated, although there are frequent denials of any tendency to exaggerate. It is understandable, therefore, that autobiographies had no space for objectivity. Egyptologists have to be extremely careful when evaluating what the texts say. The statements must be placed in context, and it must be borne constantly in mind that they contain only a small proportion of the truth—the part that is most flattering and spectacular.

Portraits

Every portrait attempts to show its subject to best advantage. It would be quite impossible to list the expressions that texts exploit to this end:

they are far too numerous, and their variants still more so. The most that can be done is to delimit the general themes employed that were deemed essential throughout pharaonic history. People of any period assessed themselves according to the same criteria and hence invariably claimed the same merits. Such innovations as are found are minor and have the character more of adjustments than of profound changes. For the sake of clarity, I shall present a classification, but it should not be imagined that the ancient Egyptians shared this need. On the contrary, disorder seems to reign over the sequences of epithets, even though logical groupings can be discerned here and there. This lack of order complicates interpretation still further.

To begin with, the subject presents himself to everyone as just and virtuous, loving justice, detesting lies, and doing only what is good. His conduct is irreproachable, and he is incapable of performing an evil act, such as seizing someone else's property. His happy disposition and agreeable temperament are at once generous and charming. Vivacious and never gloomy, he knows how to please and to win the approval of others. He is discreet, calm, and reserved; he knows his status and never loses his self-control.

At work, he is intelligent and competent, clever and farsighted. His words are so well considered and weighed that his colleagues welcome his timely interventions. He is vigilant and indefatigable, playing an important part in what is done. If he commands, he does so with authority, and his orders are exactly what is needed. He is able to display the aptitudes appropriate to whatever office he may take on: if he is a vizier, he is an impartial judge who settles matters to general satisfaction by listening carefully to petitioners, while nevertheless adhering rigorously to principle. If a military leader, he proves to be a warrior who arouses fear as he travels through foreign lands, and he is full of strength on the day of battle.

Toward his god, he wishes naturally to be a faithful servant, who sticks to the right path without going astray, who does not consort with those who ignore the deity's power. He is pious and unceasingly attentive to the wishes of the deity, which he is therefore able instantly to turn into realities. (Texts that focus on religious concerns date mainly to the New Kingdom and later.)

Among his fellow citizens, he is helpful and useful, always alert to their problems. He is like a rampart around a town: defending the widow, aiding the wretched, or protecting the weak against the powerful. He is generous, always ready to extend a helping hand. He gives bread to the hungry, water to the thirsty, and clothing to the naked, even going so far as to ensure burial for those who cannot afford it.

In his family, he is a son honored by his father, praised by his mother, and cherished by his brothers and sisters. To his friends, he is a companion with whom they can celebrate, who likes to drink himself into a state of drunkenness.

With the pharaoh—if his duties bring him into such contact—he is a loyal subject who aspires to gain the king's affection and to become his confidant. He is careful to obey orders and is conscientious in his duties, serving with unflinching loyalty. Once he has been singled out because of his excellence, he merits praise, gifts, privileges, and promotions; he has become someone eminently suited to conversing alone with the king. Finally, when he is among the courtiers, he proves himself to be the greatest among them, enjoying their respect because of his wise views.

In short, the possessor of an autobiography is someone unique, whose perfection has no equal. In this perspective, the portrait reveals more of what an individual wished to be than of what he was in reality. These texts therefore manifest the Egyptian conception of an ideal man.

Realism

In view of this idealizing tendency, we may wonder whether descriptions that contradict the traditional canon, which can be found in a few texts, were composed from a desire to present as lifelike an image as possible of their subjects. But even in these cases, the evocation of someone's life conserves the memory only of the episodes that contributed to his glorious reputation, naturally leaving aside anything for which he might be criticized. In one or two texts, episodes that were not to the subject's credit are indeed evoked, but these are presented very indirectly and in such a way as to count after all in his favor. Otherwise, events in which the individual distinguished himself are recalled, notably the successes of his professional life and the rewards he received for them, which give a measure of his merit. These less-stereotyped narratives start with the promotions that the protagonist received and continue with each similar achievement, without shrinking from tedious repetition. Such texts allow us to follow the stages through which some high officials rose in their careers.

Although these texts share a common orientation, officials pursued careers that were sufficiently diverse for their autobiographical narratives to exhibit far more originality than do portraits. This tendency emerges most strongly if one compares the autobiographies of people whose occupations were quite different from one another. Thus, an architect may speak at length of the works he directed, commenting on the magnitude and quality of his projects and not hesitating to offer a wealth of technical details. A soldier may narrate his campaigns abroad and the battles in which he participated, in order to boast of his prowess in the face of the enemy. Nonetheless, the same is true even when individuals share their specialties. However much their careers may have resembled each other, there are always original allusions to the situations, periods, and places in which the protagonists were active. These texts are rich in details of every sort about the administration, the economy, and history, as well as matters of daily life. In consequence, their importance exceeds greatly the narrow compass of their subject.

Whether an inscription was set up in a tomb or in a temple, nothing prevented the speaker from listing all his successes, wherever he might have achieved them. But if the text was to be placed in a sanctuary for which the owner had worked a good deal, it tended to emphasize his actions at that site, even to the point of passing over his other achievements. Since it was important to influence the local priests—and their divine master was well—it was natural to dwell on the arguments that meant the most to them. Like their god, the priests were undoubtedly better disposed toward an individual whose largesse they had previously enjoyed. For this reason some stelae or statues destined for a specific temple reflect the fact that their owners provided things for that temple, such as food for offerings, cult equipment, the construction of a new building, the restoration of decayed structures, the reorganization of the clergy, or the performance of a ritual.

In Transit

On the margin of the autobiographical genre are inscriptions that were left in stone quarries or on the desert routes of commercial or military expeditions. These are less numerous than those in temples and tombs, and most are much shorter, often being reduced to just a few sentences. Relatively poorly executed, they generally take the form of graffiti carved in the living rock. The inscriptions' main distinctive characteristic is that, rather than being concerned with the whole life of the protagonist, it recalls only the occasion when he passed by. The texts focus on the extraction of stone and on what methods and suffering were involved in the process, or they bring out the owner's role in a military campaign by describing it and its goals. In this respect, these inscriptions are comparable with the texts in temples that mention only temple concerns. The difference between the two is that, with a few rare exceptions, the desert inscriptions do not include any appeal to the traveler for some sort of service. Indeed, their principal aim was to record, for all time, the fact that a person had passed by. The protagonist's action is presented as spectacular; if differences in status are taken into consideration, they were to nonroyal individuals what triumphal stelae were for kings who commemorated their victories. Far better than a simple inscribed signature, they could present the significance of the undertaking in which the owner was proud to have played his part. It is for this reason that they include details of the scale of an expedition's accomplishments.

Sarcophagi

In just a few cases, an autobiographical inscription was carved, surprisingly, on a sarcophagus. The real purpose of these texts, which give a summary of the deceased's sojourn on earth, was to plead on his behalf for the next world. Like the praise of the subject in other autobiographies, this testimony was meant to act as advocate for the deceased before the god of the dead, who was to rule on that individual's entry into the paradise of the blessed. Autobiographies on sarcophagi all date to the Twenty-sixth Dynasty and later. A particularly interesting one belonged to the dancing dwarf Djeho (fourth century BCE), who pleaded to the gods of the next world on behalf of his patron—who probably commissioned the sarcophagus.

HISTORICAL SURVEY

Autobiographies appeared early in Egypt and were employed almost throughout the three millennia of pharaonic history. Despite the common features autobiographies retained, which render them coherent as a genre, developments over this vast span of time were sufficiently distinctive that they can be charted. The range of places in which the texts were set up increased very gradually, parallel with the expansion of their functions; the same applies to the categories of objects on which they were inscribed. The frequency of autobiographies increased progressively, as did the range of people they commemorated. In parallel, their content evolved in several ways, becoming richer and more prolix, varying the topics treated, and sometimes sacrificing its elements to fashion.

Old Kingdom

From the first major period of united Egypt, during which writing was used to record continuous language (circa 2625–2130 BCE), come the earliest autobiographies. Most are from tombs, and several are of exceptional length. From as early as the Fourth Dynasty, a few texts are preserved in which the tomb owner narrates briefly its construction, at the same time giving some incidental details about himself.

Only later, however, especially in the Sixth Dynasty, did autobiographies begin to develop further. The majority are concentrated in the necropolises around the capital Memphis (modern Mit Rahina), such as Saqqara, where an appreciable number have been found. There are others in the provincial cemeteries; among them are Elephantine, Edfu, Abydos (modern Araba al-Madfuna), and Dayr al-Gabrawi. Depending on the topography of the particular site, they may be in mastabas (rectangular freestanding tombs)

or in rock-cut tombs. Only the finest funerary monuments were considered worthy of an inscription in this genre. Because the funerary cult required a large amount of space, these buildings contained sufficient wall areas for the carving of long autobiographies.

Since such inscriptions were only within the means of the elite, it is hardly surprising that, in an age which celebrated the triumph of the centralized monarchy, the subjects of the texts are invariably those close to the center of power, who make constant allusions to their connections with the king. The subjects include viziers, courtiers, provincial governors and high priests, all of whom explain how they served the king and record how he expressed his gratitude for their services. In doing so, they give much original information, breaking the monotony of narrative schemas that involve much repetition, especially in long inscriptions.

To give some idea of the tone of Old Kingdom autobiographies, it is sufficient to present the following extract from the Sixth Dynasty autobiography of the architect Nekhebu, from his tomb in Giza.

> I was a servant of the king of Upper and Lower Egypt, Meryre (Pepy I), my lord. His Majesty sent me to direct works on his monument at Heliopolis. I did so in a manner which His Majesty appreciated. I spent six years supervising the work, and His Majesty congratulated me about this each time I came to the Residence on business. Everything was done thanks to me, because of the vigilance I displayed to accomplish all that His Majesty had commanded, [doing] all that I could. His Majesty found me, one among many masons, and appointed me (successively) Inspector of Masons, Director of Masons, and Chief of the Team. His Majesty appointed me Master of Royal Masons, and Subordinate of the King and Master of Royal Masons. His Majesty proclaimed me Sole Companion and Master of Royal Masons in the Two Houses. His Majesty did all this inasmuch as he favored me exceedingly. (Kurt Sethe, *Urkunden des alten Reiches*, fascicle 3 [1933]: 215–216)

Among Old Kingdom autobiographies, that of Weni is celebrated for the quality of its composition and its rich content. It consists of some fifty columns of text inscribed on a wall of Weni's mastaba at Abydos, now displayed in the Cairo

Museum. As he recounts one reign after another, Weni recapitulates the various successful missions that won him rapid promotion under the first three pharaohs of the Sixth Dynasty. He

tells of his first appointments, his role as judge in a trial of a matter involving the royal harem, and his expeditions to the east against the "Sand Dwellers." He explains how he took on the ad-

Exemplary Egyptians

The following excerpts from three major autobiographies, drawn from different periods, typify the tone of these texts. The stela of Taimhotep is one of the rare autobiographies of a woman. The autobiography of Weni, a high official of the late Old Kingdom, is one of the longest of its period, describing the excellence of its narrator, his many offices, and his expeditions.

> When I was chamberlain of the palace and sandal-bearer, King Mernere, my lord who lives forever, made me Count and Governor of Upper Egypt, from Yebu (Elephantine) in the south to Medenyt (a district a little south of Memphis) in the north, because I was worthy in his majesty's heart, because I was rooted in his majesty's heart, because his majesty's heart was filled with me. When I was chamberlain and sandal-bearer, his majesty praised me for the watch and guard duty which I did at court, more than any servant of his. Never before had this office been held by any servant.
>
> I governed Upper Egypt for him in peace, so that no one attacked his fellow. I did every task. I counted everything that is countable for the residence in this Upper Egypt two times, and every service that is countable for the residence in this Upper Egypt two times. I did a perfect job in this Upper Egypt. Never before had the like been done in this Upper Egypt. I acted throughout so that his majesty praised me for it.
>
> His majesty sent me to Ibhat (near Aswan) to bring the sarcophagus "chest of the living" together with its lid, and the costly august pyramidion for the pyramid "Mernere-appears-in-splendor," my mistress. His majesty sent me to Yebu to bring a granite false-door and its libation stone and granite lintels, and to bring granite portals and libation stones for the upper chamber of the pyramid "Mernere-appears-in-splendor," my mistress. I traveled north with (them) to the pyramid "Mernere-appears-in-splendor" in six barges and three tow-boats of eight ribs in a single expedition. Never had Yebu and Ibhat been done in a single expedition under any king. Thus everything his majesty commanded was done entirely as his majesty commanded. (Lichtheim, vol. 1, p. 21)

Carved on a stela from Abydos, the late Twelfth Dynasty autobiography of Sehetepibre is a good example of the kind of text found near temples, in which the narrator's exemplary acts at the site are stressed. The continuation of the text, not reproduced here, is an

excerpt from the *Loyalist Instruction*, one of the major literary texts of the period.

> The Prince, Count, Royal Seal-bearer, Temple-overseer, Deputy Chief Seal-bearer, Sehetepibre, the justified, says:
> I have had this monument consecrated. Its place has been established. I have made contracts for payments to the priests of Abydos. I have officiated as "his beloved son" in the service of the gold-house, in the mystery of the lord of Abydos.
> I have directed the work on the sacred bark; I fashioned its cordage. I conducted the *ḥ'kr*-ceremony for its lord, and the Procession of Wepwawet. All the offerings were done for him, recited by the priests. I clothed the god in his regalia in my rank of master of secrets, my function of stolist (priest in charge of clothing). I was openhanded in decking the god, a priest whose fingers are clean, so that I may be a follower of the god, so as to be a mighty spirit (*akh*) at the shrine of the lord of Abydos. (Lichtheim, vol. 1, p. 127)

The Ptolemaic inscription of Taimhotep, the wife of the high priest of Ptah at Memphis, is one of the latest surviving Egyptian autobiographies. Taimhotep died on February 15, 42 BCE, at the age of thirty.

> The heart of the high priest rejoiced over it greatly. I was pregnant by him three times but did not bear a male child, only three daughters. I prayed together with the high priest to the majesty of the god great in wonders, effective in deeds, who gives a son to him who has none: Imhotep Son of Ptah.
> He heard our pleas, he hearkened to his prayers. The majesty of this god came to the head of the high priest in a revelation. He said: "Let a great work be done in the holy of holies of Ankhtawi (a part of Memphis), the place where my body is hidden. As reward for it I shall give you a male child."
> When he awakened from this he kissed the ground to the august god. He gave the orders to the prophets, the initiates, the priests, and to the sculptors of the gold-house also. He ordered them to carry out an excellent work in the holy of holies. They did as he had said. He performed the opening of the mouth for the august god. He made a great sacrifice of all things. He rewarded the sculptors on behalf of the god. He gladdened their heart with all good things. In return he (the god) made me conceive a male child. (Lichtheim, vol. 3, p. 62)

ministration of Upper Egypt and details his travels to quarries to bring back pieces of equipment for the king's pyramid. All these achievements permit Weni to offer himself as an example of an exemplary Egyptian: "I am indeed loved by my father, praised by my mother, and cherished by my brothers, the Prince, True Overseer of Upper Egypt."

Dating slightly later are some autobiographies in the rock-cut tombs of the governors of Elephantine at Qubbet al-Hawa. Their authors, who were primarily explorers, speak of their long expeditions to discover unknown regions and new riches, notably in Nubia. The most famous of these texts is that of Harkhuf, who undertook three journeys to "reconnoiter the route" to the country of Yam, possibly in the region of Dongola in Sudan. These are unique narratives, in which travel alternates with adventure and exoticism, and they are equally important as evidence for commercial relations with areas outside Egypt.

At the end of the Old Kingdom, autobiographies appear in stone quarries, for example at Hatnub and in the Wadi Hammamat, which were sources of calcite (Egyptian alabaster) and schist, respectively. These texts are few and brief, with information that tends to be restricted to such facts as the personnel sent on the mission and the number of blocks removed from the site, so that their character is similar to that of a report on a task that had been commissioned.

First Intermediate Period

Despite the political turmoil and social upheaval of the First Intermediate period (circa 2130–1980), autobiographies continued to be written. Among them are remarkable examples, such as that of Ankhtifi in his tomb at Moʻalla, which recounts the troubles in the south of Egypt, or that of Tjetji, whose funerary stela in the British Museum documents the restoration of order under the Theban rulers of the Eleventh Dynasty. A common preoccupation in the literature of this period is the anarchy that engenders both insecurity and famine, which the authors of inscriptions evoke in order to narrate the steps they took in their regions to make up for the absence of a central authority. Whether they be soldiers or governors, royal butlers or majordomos, all present themselves as helpful men who protected the weak and provided for the subsistence of their fellows.

Middle Kingdom

With the resurgence of a united Egypt in the Middle Kingdom (circa 1980–1630), autobiographies multiplied in number and diversified in type during the Twelfth Dynasty. They appeared in temples, and the range of social groups who formed their subjects expanded to include lower ranking people than heretofore. The subject matter of the texts became significantly richer. During this period in particular, the repertory of laudatory epithets was elaborated. Autobiographies of later times borrow copiously from this material, especially those of the first millennium, when there was a fashion that is termed "archaizing."

Middle Kingdom tombs that contain autobiographies continued to be those of members of the wealthy elite. It is, however, a sign of the times that more are known in the provinces than at the capital. From Elephantine to Beni Hasan, passing by Asyut (ancient Lykopolis) and Dayr al-Barsha, the necropolises contain numerous inscriptions evoking the characters of local potentates whose influence waxed in the face of a state that was still relatively weak. As in the case of Hapydjefai at Asyut, the texts may consist of little more than a string of eulogistic epithets and phrases following on the deceased's appeal to the goodwill of passersby. More often, however, there is a true narrative, and some of these develop into veritable family chronicles of considerable length. This is the case at Beni Hasan in the tombs of Amenemhet and of Khnumhotep II, whose text extends to 222 columns that cover the base of the four walls of the chapel. The owner proudly reports the favors he won, relates the great honor conferred on him by the king in appointing his eldest son to administer a neighboring province, and continues with a digression on the son's activities in his new role. Taken together, the inscriptions of these two dignitaries allow us to follow through the first four reigns of the Twelfth Dynasty the fortunes of a line of governors who extended their control over a whole region of Middle Egypt, until the capital succeeded in imposing a tighter control.

In the quarries, the number of autobiographies becomes greater with the frequency of expeditions and the increased size of the area exploited. Not only are there many more inscriptions at Hatnub and in the Wadi Hammamat, but they are also found in regions where there had hitherto been none: in the desert outside Aswan near the amethyst mines of Wadi al-Hudi, and in Sinai, not far from the turquoise mines of Serabit al-Khadim. Except at the latter site, where the texts were inscribed on dressed stelae in a temple near the quarries, the inscriptions were always carved like graffiti on the surrounding rocks. Whereas many of the inscriptions at Hatnub are very similar to the portraits encountered in tombs, elsewhere they still have much of the character of reports on tasks commissioned. Their terseness, however, is tempered by a new eagerness to tell of the conditions of the journey, even to the extent of adopting an anecdotal tone.

In addition to these autobiographies, great numbers are preserved from Abydos, where the context was again unusual, although in certain respects it resembled that at Serabit al-Khadim. Abydos had been promoted to be the domain of Osiris in Upper Egypt, and the city became a magnet for the faithful, especially when the procession took the god to his tomb in Poqer, the

Painted limestone stela of Montuwosre with autobiographical inscription, Twelfth Dynasty, Abydos. METROPOLITAN MUSEUM OF ART, NEW YORK.

sacred district near the escarpment behind the low desert. High-ranking officials who had been sent to supervise the event, pilgrims from far away, and local devotees of Osiris all wished to bring memory of themselves to the attention of the deity and of his priests. According to their means, they constructed chapels or set up simple stelae on the elevation near the temple. Large or small, many of these monuments had space for autobiographies, even brief ones, which pleaded their owners' cause. Thus, such texts begin to spread beyond the restricted circle of high functionaries into a segment of the population that included artisans, scribes, and numerous other people of similar status. Now subordinate officials had their say, as with Sihathor, the assistant chancellor, who proclaims on his stela (now in the British Museum):

> I have traveled through the mine districts in my youth; I astonished the Great Officials by washing gold; I brought back turquoise. I reached Nubia, and the Nubians came, prostrating themselves because of their fear of the Lord of the Two Lands. I went to the land of Ha (to the south of Egypt), traveling throughout its territory and bringing back *sesh*-plants. (British Museum, *Hieroglyphic Texts* 2 [1912], pl. 19)

Alongside traditional narratives of this type are those with more unusual content, relating to the offices their owners held. Such texts were set up by people at the site where they worked on the maintenance of a temple or in the celebration of its rituals. They preferred to dwell upon this particular aspect of their careers rather than to evoke matters that had no direct connection with the place where they had left their memorial. The best example of this type is narrated by Ikhernofret, "overseer of seal-bearers," whose stela in Berlin enumerates his responsibilities in organizing the festival of Osiris, from the preparation of equipment to the performance of the ceremony itself, during which he "performed the great procession," "sailed the bark of the deity," "opened the way toward his tomb in Poqer," "protected His Person on the day of the great combat," and "routed all his enemies on the banks of Nedit (the mythical place where Osiris was killed)."

The Middle Kingdom ended with the installation of the Hyksos rulers in the north of the country, which marks the beginning of the Second Intermediate Period (circa 1630–1539/23). This period is synonymous with decline, but in temples and tombs at Edfu, Hierakonpolis, Abydos, and even Buhen in Nubia, there are, nevertheless, modest stelae inscribed with autobiographies, the conciseness of which does not rule out the literary qualities inherited from the previous period.

New Kingdom

The war of liberation waged by Thebes against the occupying Hyksos inaugurated the New Kingdom (1539–1075), a highly auspicious period for Egypt, when the country expanded greatly as the center of a vast empire. This epoch, which is characterized by its architectural and artistic achievements, is also the one that has left the most numerous and original autobiographies. The majority are longer than those of earlier times, and many of them devote much space to narratives in which the subject expounds not just what he did but also how he behaved, in terms comparable to those of a portrait. As illustrated by the Theban stela of the herald Inyotef (now in the Louvre in Paris), the series of laudatory phrases are normally integrated into the introductory titularies, where they are interspersed among the honorific titles and designations of office that precede the owner's name.

With the exception of a few sites such as Elkab or Amarna, tombs containing autobiographies are concentrated on the West Bank at Thebes, where they number in the dozens. There, as a result of the prosperity and importance the city acquired by becoming the capital of the empire, the proportion of fine tombs rose in proportion with the numbers of high officials or of people who could henceforth aspire to own a funerary monument. The owners, men who exercised a wide range of responsibilities in various sectors of the administration, generally inscribed the texts in which they presented themselves to visitors in their tomb chapels, often on a round-topped stela.

The proliferation of private monuments in temples, however, led to the greatest increase in the number of autobiographies. This development, which had begun in the Middle Kingdom, can be seen primarily at the temple of Karnak in the capital, but it is also found throughout the

province, especially in the capitals of nomes (provinces), even if the numbers of texts from these places are much smaller. Some people whose offices conferred on them sufficient wealth are known from several monuments with different and complementary autobiographical inscriptions. Almost all earlier autobiographies set up in temples were on stelae. In the New Kingdom they were mostly on statues—a new setting. Autobiographies are found on most statue types, but the block statue was the preferred vehicle for them. In addition to their strength, these statues had the advantage of providing large flat surfaces for inscription. On whatever surface these texts were inscribed, they could, like earlier ones, either recount the whole range of the subject's activities or focus on his achievements in the place where the inscription was located.

Outside tombs and temples, the number of autobiographies tends to stay constant or diminish. There are a few groups of them along expedition routes, as on the island of Sehel in the First Cataract, at the beginning of the way to the south. They are equally rare in the quarries, whether in the Wadi Hammamat or in Sinai, although regular expeditions continued to be sent there.

The wide range of people attested and the originality of the narratives combine to produce compositions that cast a far more vivid light on numerous aspects of the period than do official accounts.

At the beginning of the Eighteenth Dynasty, the ship's captain Ahmose, son of Ebana, is the earliest to tell us, in his tomb in Elkab, of his successes in the first campaigns of the New Kingdom, notably in the battles to expel the Hyksos from their capital, Avaris:

> The town of Avaris was besieged, and I displayed valor on foot in the presence of His Majesty. I was assigned to the ship "Emergence in Memphis," and we fought on the water at Padjedku, near Avaris. I took prisoners and I brought back a hand (as proof of killing an enemy). This was reported to the Royal Herald, and I was given the gold of valor.

Later, with the policy of conquest pursued by such kings as Thutmose III and Amenhotep (Amenophis) II, this style was emulated by other autobiographers, such as Amenemheb and Tja-nuny, who reminisce with equal pride about the part they played in other, ever more distant victories. As the country harvested the benefits of its expansion and launched a vast program of construction, architects too began to recount the works they had directed, in temples at Karnak and in the provinces. At Karnak their inscriptions enrich our documentation for buildings that still stand today, while for the provinces they allude to monuments that archaeology has not been able to reveal. From the reign of Amenhotep III there is the example of the famous Amenhotep, son of Hapu, who refers to the installation of the renowned "Colossi of Memnon," which represents the king at the entrance of the royal funerary temple:

> The king appointed me Overseer of Works in the quartzite quarries to direct the making of monuments for his father (the god) Amun in Karnak. I brought very great monuments, statues of His Majesty in fine craftsmanship which were transported from Northern Heliopolis (near the quarries) to Southern Heliopolis (Thebes) so that they might be set up in Western [Thebes]. (Wolfgang Helck, *Urkunden der 18. Dynastie*, Section 21 [1958], p. 1833)

During the interlude when Amenhotep IV (later Akhenaten) attempted to impose a new doctrine, we find one of the king's adherents proclaiming in his tomb at Amarna his devotion to the cause of this self-styled mystic and his diligence in following the royal teachings.

Third Intermediate and Late Periods

The end of the New Kingdom heralded the political decline of Egypt and the beginning of the Third Intermediate Period (circa 1075–656). Seven centuries later, pharaonic Egypt was no longer an independent kingdom, as the country fell to Greek and then Roman control. In the Late Period (664–332) there were two principal attempts to check the collapse: under the Twenty-sixth Dynasty, after the Libyan anarchy and the Ethiopian occupation; and under the Thirtieth Dynasty, between the two periods of Persian rule. These intervals of renewed vigor coincided with an increase in the incidence of autobiographies that is linked to the production of greater numbers of private monuments than in the immediately preceding periods. But throughout these many centuries, and even later during the Ptolemaic period (332–30), such inscriptions were always produced. The continuation of the tradition was never threatened, but the quality of the objects bearing the texts suffered occasionally from the disorders of the times.

The effects of the crisis can be seen especially in the necropolises. Only in the Ptolemaic period, in the tombs of Abydos, Akhmim, and Saqqara, does one find numerous stelae of increasing size that bear autobiographies. Earlier in the first millennium, the texts were inscribed on the walls of funerary chapels. Tombs that possessed such chapels are very rare, because they were too expensive, and the same applies to autobiographies. Examples are confined to a few exceptional cases, such as the Twenty-sixth Dynasty portrait of Ibi in his tomb in western Thebes, or the fourth-century narratives of Petosiris and Wennofer at Tuna al-Gebel and North Saqqara, respectively.

Political events did not hinder individuals from depositing their monuments in temples, so that the genre of autobiography continued to develop. Karnak, with its great cache of statues buried in the Ptolemaic period; other major temples such as those in Memphis and Sais (modern Sa el-Hagar); the Serapeum at Saqqara; and a host of secondary sanctuaries spread throughout the country have together yielded significant numbers of examples. Except at the Serapeum, where they were inscribed on stelae, the texts were almost always carved on statues. The proportion of block statues drops off in favor of increasing numbers of kneeling or standing statues, some of which are covered with inscriptions from head to foot.

The most notable changes are in the content of the texts. People no longer address themselves solely to the local priests but also speak directly to their god. They no longer request only that the gods stand guard over their monument, but also that they guarantee them a long and joyful life and a fine burial. Later in the period, a majority of the texts are concerned exclusively with the owners' actions on behalf of those gods whose favor they are requesting, while the recompense they expect is presented more and more as their just reward for their efforts.

From these epochs, which were as turbulent as they were various, several autobiographies deserve note both for their intrinsic qualities and for their historical interest. The biography of the chief physician Udjahorresne, whose statue from Sais is now in the Vatican in Rome, speaks of his conduct before the Persian conqueror Cambyses and places the Persian occupation of Egypt in a less negative light than is found in other sources.

Here we should mention the autobiography of Somtutefnakht, the chief of *wab* priests of Sakhmet, whose stela from Herakleopolis (Ihnasya al-Madina) reached Naples by way of the Roman temple of Isis at Pompeii. Somtutefnakht recalled the last native dynasty (the Thirtieth), the Second Persian period, and the conquest of Alexander. In these events, which he experienced personally, he sees signs of the benevolence of his god Herishef of Herakleopolis. He considered this attention to be the consequence of his own piety, the demonstration of which was the chief purpose of the inscription:

> You eased my path to the palace, and the heart of the Perfect God (pharaoh) was pleased with what I said. You distinguished me before the multitude, when you turned away from Egypt. You inspired affection for me in the heart of the Ruler of Asia (Persian king), so that his courtiers thanked god for me, when he appointed me to the office of Overseer of *wab* priests of Sakhmet, replacing my uterine brother, the Overseer of *wab* priests of Sakhmet for Upper and Lower Egypt Nakhtheneb. You protected me through the offensive of the Greeks as soon as you repelled Asia (Persia); they killed a multitude around me; but there was none who raised a hand against me.

The final autobiography to be mentioned here is one of the longest from this period: that of Petosiris, the high priest of Thoth of Hermopolis (al-Ashmunein) and another contemporary of Alexander the Great. In his tomb at Tuna al-Gebel, Petosiris described, in a text that mixes narrative with religious and moral sentiments, his reorganization of the temple of Hermopolis after the disasters caused by the return of the Persians.

Despite the variety of forms of the autobiographies and their development over the course of ancient Egyptian history, these texts are remarkably consistent. Their accuracy as portraits of individuals can be questioned, because of the selective inclusion of facts, but they are definitely a portrait of Egyptian society: its ideals, aspirations, organization, and history.

Translated from the French by Peter Daniels

BIBLIOGRAPHY

Anthologies

Unless a bibliographic citation is specifically attached to a translated autobiography, readers can find a full rendering of that particular text in the three-volume work of MIRIAM LICHTHEIM, *Ancient Egyptian Literature* (1973–1980), or in her *Ancient Egyptian Autobiographies*, cited below. These volumes also contain translations of many autobiographies that are not mentioned in this contribution. She gives a useful introductory paragraph and bibliography for each of the autobiographies she translates. ALESSANDRO ROCCATI, *La Littérature historique sous l'Ancien Empire égyptian* (1982), gives translations of diverse documents of the Old Kingdom.

Major Works on Autobiographies

HEIKE GUKSCH, *Königsdienst: Zur Selbstdarstellung der Beamten in der 18. Dynastie*, Studien zur Archäologie und Geschichte Altägyptens 11 (1994); KARL JANSEN-WINKELN, *Ägyptische Biographien der 22. und 23. Dynastie*, 2 vols., Ägypten und Altes Testament 8/1–2 (1985). JOZEF JANSSEN, *De traditioneele egyptische Autobiografie vóór het Nieuwe Rijk*, 2 vols. (1946). MIRIAM LICHTHEIM, *Ancient Egyptian Autobiographies Chiefly of the Middle Kingdom: A Study and an Anthology*, Orbis Biblicus et Orientalis 84 (1988), and *Maat in Egyptian Autobiographies and Related Studies*, Orbis Biblicus et Orientalis 120 (1992); and EBERHARD OTTO, *Die biographischen Inschriften der Ägyptischen Spätzeit: Ihre geistesgeschichtliche und literarische Bedeutung*, Probleme der Ägyptologie, 2 (1954).

Background

GEORG MISCH, *Geschichte der Autobiographie* (1949–1950) is a review of autobiographies throughout the ages. BAUDOUIN VAN DE WALLE, "Biographie," in *Lexikon der Ägyptologie*, vol. 1, edited by WOLFGANG HELCK and EBERHARD OTTO (1975), is a handy overview of the subject.

The following two articles describe the development of autobiography and its relation with literature: JAN ASSMANN, "Schrift, Tod und Identität: Das Grab als

Vorschule der Literatur im alten Ägypten," in *Schrift und Gedächtnis: Beiträge zur Archäologie der literarischen Kommunikation,* edited by ALEIDA ASSMANN, JAN ASSMANN, and CHRISTOF HARDMEIER (1983); WOLFGANG HELCK, "Zur Frage der Entstehung der ägyptischen Literatur," *Wiener Zeitschrift für die Kunde des Morgenlandes* 63/64 (1972). HERMAN TE VELDE, "Commemoration in Ancient Egypt," *Visible Religion: Annual for Religious Iconography,* vol. 1, *Commemorative Figures,* edited by H. G. KIPPENBERG (1982), has a broad discussion on the connection between afterlife and memory.

SEE ALSO **The Middle Kingdom in Egypt** (Part 5, Vol. II) and **Ancient Egyptian Literature: An Overview** (Part 9, Vol. IV).

Tales of Magic and Wonder from Ancient Egypt

SUSAN TOWER HOLLIS

TALES OF MAGIC AND wonder, often called fairy tales or folktales, have enchanted young and old for millennia, but it was not until 1852 that the modern world learned the ancient Egyptians also enjoyed this form of narrative. In that year, Emmanuel de Rougé published *The Tale of Two Brothers* from Papyrus d'Orbiney, a tale rife with magic and wonders that provides many parallels to tales known to the modern world. With time many other tales emerged from papyri and ostraca unearthed in Egypt, leading to T. E. Peet's assertion in the Schweich Lectures of 1929 that Egypt was "the home of the short story." Interestingly, however, we know of no specific term used by the ancient Egyptians to designate or refer to these tales, although such a tale might have been called *sdd*, "narrative," a term which usually refers to narratives about kings or gods, or maybe *tsi ndm*, "diversion," or *shmh-ib*, "distraction of the heart," "enjoyment." The absence of a clear designation could suggest that their appearance in writing is anomalous and that such stories existed primarily in oral form. In fact the term *sdd*, narrative, from the causative of *dd*, "to speak," implies orality.

CRITERIA FOR CLASSIFICATION

The classification of a written piece as a "short story" can mean many different things, for example, biography and autobiography, legend, myth, anecdote, fable, and of course a tale of magic and wonder. Characteristics for each include brevity, simplicity, minimal details, and drama. Additional characteristics that usually define tales of magic and wonder include the intersection of the otherworld with this world, a clear delineation between good and bad, a lack of depth, a lack of character development, the presence of magical figures and objects, emotions, expressed in acts rather than words, a lack of physical reaction to injury, abnormal time, unidentifiable space, primary colors, sharp contrasts, triads, abstraction, and anonymous characters. This list of characteristics derives, however, from the study of modern folktales, most especially those from the European continent, including Russia, and it needs qualification for use with ancient Egyptian narratives.

For the present purpose, ancient Egyptian tales of magic and wonder, like the European tales, are defined as short, dramatic narratives. They exhibit an intersection between this world and the otherworld, a clear delineation between good and bad, a lack of depth, a lack of character development, timelessness, repeated actions, and the presence of magical objects, figures, and actions. In addition, like the modern folktales, though perhaps to a greater degree, the ancient Egyptian tales clearly reflect their cultural context, detailing specifically Egyptian ideas, beliefs, and practices. The significance of this fact can be appreciated through the insight of modern folktale scholarship that the audience participates actively in the narration. To identify and study the individual acts and ideas of one of these ancient tales is to allow oneself to participate as closely as possible, seeking to understand what beliefs and concepts would have been part of the common thinking of the ancient Egyptian audience. For example, in *The Tale of Two Brothers*, the episode in which the hero severs his sexual organ contains very clear reflections of the story of Osiris that would have no meaning for a similar act in another culture. In a number of the tales, otherworld references designate either lands to the northeast or to the far south of Egypt proper, reflecting the Egyptians' sense of exile and virtual death when outside the bounds of the Nile Valley. In modern narratives, the otherworld lacks any such specificity—it is just not the everyday world one commonly encounters.

Despite the initial analogy of Egyptian tales of magic and wonder with modern fairy tales and folktales, only two Egyptian examples truly come close to the European form in their entirety: *The Tale of Two Brothers* and *The Prince and His Fates*. A number of other tales from ancient Egypt incorporate aspects of what we term magic and wonder, that is, the extraordinary, a fact which suggests the limitations inherent in using modern terms for ancient forms.

SOURCES

The copies of the tales we have date from the Middle Kingdom through the Greco-Roman period, though one set of tales purports to come from the Old Kingdom. None of them occurs on more than one papyrus, and several of these papyri are damaged. Those narratives discussed here as tales of magic and wonder include *The Shipwrecked Sailor* (P. Hermitage, Saint Petersburg 1115), the tales in Papyrus Westcar (P. Berlin 3033), *The Prince and His Fates* (P. Harris 500, verso in the British Museum), *The Tale of Two Brothers* (P. d'Orbiney, in the British Museum), stories about Setna

Khaemwaset (or Khaemwas): *Setna I* (P. Cairo 30646) and *Setna II* (P. British Museum 604 verso), as well as several other fragmentary Setna stories in Cairo and Copenhagen, *Hi-Hor, the Magician* (Berlin Jar 12845), and *The Shoe of Rhodopis* (Strabo, *Geography* 17.1.33). This last story is written in Greek, *Hi-Hor* and the Setna tales in Demotic, while the others are Middle and Late Egyptian tales written in hieratic.

ORAL TRADITION

Because many collections of modern folktales derive from oral sources, the question of an oral-traditional origin for ancient Egyptian tales commonly arises in discussion. Although often mentioned, the subject has been minimally studied, in part because scholarship addressing oral-traditional narrative refers largely to epic poetry and its performance in classical and modern cultures or documents actual tale tellers, none of which is relevant for ancient tales known only from single papyrus copies.

Nevertheless, since the level of literacy was no better than one percent in ancient Egypt, presumably a great number of narratives circulated orally, but how close any of the tales we have is to the oral tradition is hard to say. The presence of certain formulas, such as "Now many days after this" and "Now after the land was light and a second day began" in *The Tale of Two Brothers* and *The Prince and His Fates*, suggests orality. Examples of paronomasia, such as *i'wt* (cattle) and *i't* (office) in *The Contendings of Horus and Seth*, are a play on words that would be most delightful in aural experience. In addition, the presence of parallel clauses like those at the beginning of *The Shipwrecked Sailor* and proverbial sayings like the one at the end of the same tale could imply an oral origin. We might also see orality in the single-copy existence of the narratives, particularly of those most similar to our modern day concept of the folktale. But with all these examples, only the suggestion is there, not the proof. In the end we must deal with the tales as they have been transmitted to us: written and thus from the more elite strata of society.

STRUCTURE

In overall structure and presentation, these tales come to us in two guises: cycles of tales and integral tales. Tales from cycles are set within a frame story similar to the well-known *Tales of a Thousand and One Nights*. Examples date from the Middle Kingdom, the earliest period from which we have fictional narratives, and also from the Greco-Roman period. The absence of any examples from the New Kingdom reflects both the accident of preservation and the likely orality of such materials. Chance, however, has preserved for us a few individual tales of magic and wonder from every period.

In composition, each of the tales classified as a tale of magic and wonder contains a number of "motifs," Stith Thompson's designation for "the smallest element in a tale having a power to persist in tradition," and "types," his term for "a traditional tale that has an independent existence." A narrator's combination of different motifs and tale types results in a complex narrative that we recognize as a folktale, or more specifically as a tale of magic and wonder. In fact, certain patterns of combinations exist, and a person who is really familiar with such narratives finds it fairly easy to predict the direction any given set of motifs might take. The lack of large numbers of ancient Egyptian tales makes similar predictions less sure.

NEW KINGDOM TALES

A close look at the two New Kingdom tales of magic and wonder, *The Tale of Two Brothers* and *The Prince and His Fates* (often called *The Doomed Prince*), will help illustrate why scholars perceive them as similar to the modern folktale and yet different from the modern form. *The Prince and His Fates* is found on the reverse of Papyrus Harris 500, dating to around 1300 BCE, and lacks an ending because of damage to the papyrus. It begins as follows:

> There was once a king to whom no son was born. [When His Majesty begged] for himself a child from the gods of his domain, they commanded that one be born to him. And he lay down with his wife in the night, and then [she became] pregnant. When she completed the months of childbearing, a son was born. The Hathors came to determine his fate for him, and they said, "He will die of the crocodile or the snake or the dog." When the people who were beside the child heard, they reported (it) to His Majesty, (and) His Majesty's heart became very very sad. His Majesty had one build [for him a house] of stone in the hill country, equipped with people (and) with every good thing of the royal house. The young prince did not go outside.

The beginning, "There was once. . . ," recalls clearly the "Once upon a time. . . ." so familiar to every child as the opening of a fairy story, an opening that actually occurs in *The Tale of Two Brothers*. For us—and quite likely for the ancient Egyptians—these key words signal that we are entering the realm of wonder and fantasy, one in which the audience can expect the unusual to occur. As the opening of the *Prince* continues, one finds several motifs common in modern tales: (1) child born in answer to prayer; (2) three fates prophesied at child's birth (threefold death, death from dog or snakebite, death by crocodile); and (3) confinement in a tower to avoid fulfillment of prophecy. This last particularly reminds the reader of modern tales such as *Rapunzel*, where the heroine lives in a tower, even though in the Egyptian story it is a male who is confined there. The prophecy of the fates at the infant's birth, while recalling tales like *Sleeping Beauty*, differs significantly from the modern form in that the Hathors simply announce the child's fate rather than grant gifts. Nevertheless, in parallel with traditional folktales, we expect these fates to play a central part in the narrative—and they do.

As the tale progresses, the prince sees a hound puppy and requests one like it. His father obliges him despite the decree. Then, when grown, the boy decides to confront his fates straight on, and equipped by his father and supplied with a servant, he goes on his way to "act as he wishes until the god does what is in his heart to do." The prince's travels lead him to Mitanni (Naharin), where its ruler had placed his daughter in a tower. She is to become the wife of the man who can jump up to her window. The Egyptian prince, who hides his true identity, leaps successfully. The Mitanni ruler, not wishing an upstart for a son-in-law, only agrees to it when his daughter twice threatens to kill herself unless she is allowed to marry the Egyptian.

Eventually the Egyptian prince tells his bride about his three fates. She immediately wants to have the dog killed, but he does not allow it. She does, however, kill the snake which threatens him, getting the snake drunk first. The audience learns that the crocodile has followed the hero from Egypt, and when the dog chases the prince to the water, the crocodile seizes the young man. It turns out, however, the crocodile itself is being besieged by a demon, and as the papyrus breaks off, the crocodile seems to be on the verge of setting up a bargain with the prince to help kill the demon. There are two possible endings for the tale, each of which has been supported by scholarly discussion. In the first, the young man falls victim to his fates; in the other he overcomes them successfully.

The kinds of motifs and tale types present in this story lead us to identify it with modern folktales, as does its general pattern: the hero rescues the heroine, who in turn looks out for him, and once he overcomes his fates, we can suppose the two of them "live happily ever after," presumably returning to Egypt in accordance with the Egyptian view that the Nile Valley is the central place in the world and the only place where an Egyptian can live and die properly. As in the traditional European tale, the characters are nameless, the hero seeks his "fortune" elsewhere, he overcomes his predicted fate, he wins a bride with his superhuman action, animals talk, his birth is miraculous, and his wife, originally confined to a tower, helps him. Finally the tale's content suggests an apparent purpose of pure entertainment: boy leaves home, has adventure, earns wife, and returns home. The perception, however, that folktales, or indeed any folk narrative, ever exist only to entertain is spurious. In the case of this story, the specificity of the locale—the northern Euphrates territory—suggests that one or more of the different marriages of the Mitanni ruling family with Egyptian pharaohs underlies the tale and accounts for one reason why it appears in writing.

The Tale of Two Brothers, roughly contemporaneous with the *Prince*, begins with an episode in which an older, powerful woman, one who has served as a mother figure, attempts unsuccessfully to seduce a young, virile male, an incident which recalls the well-known attempted seduction of Joseph by Potiphar's wife in Genesis 39. Like Joseph, Bata, the hero of *Two Brothers*, must leave his home and position as a result, but he eventually returns to a ruling position and a successful life. Like the *Prince*, *Two Brothers* contains many well-known folktale motifs and several tale types, all of them combined into a unified story detailing the rise of a young herdsman to become king, the oldest known shepherd-becomes-king narrative.

Following the failed seduction of her brother-in-law, the woman falsely accuses him, with the result that his older brother seeks to kill him. Bata, having been warned of the danger by his lead cow, flees, eventually gaining help from the sun god who separates the two antagonists by creating a river. The following day, after explaining the truth to his brother, the hero cuts off his sexual organ, throwing it into the river where it is eaten by a catfish, an act recalling Osiris's similar loss in Plutarch's *De Iside et Osiride*. Bata than announces that he is going to the "Valley of the Pine" in Syria, where he will place his heart on a tree. His brother will know Bata is in trouble when his beer foams, at which point he should come to rescue him.

Once in the valley, the hero sets up house. Worried that he is lonely, the gods create a wife for whom the Hathors decree death by the knife. Nevertheless Bata desires her greatly; however, he also warns her, "Do not go out lest the sea seize you because I will not be able to save you from it because I am a woman like you. Further, my heart is placed on top of the flower of the pine." With these words he reveals to her all his vulnerabilities. As in all traditional tales, the warning is ignored and the sea chases the woman, but it gets only a lock of her hair. This it takes to Egypt where, because of its odor, the king falls in love with her, sight unseen. Eventually the king has her brought to him and has Bata killed. The older brother, learning of the death, rescues his younger sibling and journeys with him back to Egypt. There the hero twice reveals his continued existence to his former wife, being killed and resurrected in new forms each time, finally being reborn to her as crown prince. Following the death of the king, Bata accedes to the throne, at which time his wife-mother is judged and presumably punished. He then rules for thirty years, being succeeded by his older brother.

Among the numerous traditional motifs here, we should note that the odor of the woman's hair relates to her divine origin and the special odor of divinity, a concept common in the ancient Egyptian and Greek worlds. In addition, the motif of the fulfillment of the decreed fate should not be seen to contradict the presumed abrogation of the decreed fate in the *Prince*, since here the decree is made against the antagonist and there against the protagonist.

Although its motifs link *Two Brothers* to modern tales, its strongly mythic overtone, generally common to Egyptian tales, sets it apart. Furthermore, not only does each of the main male characters have an individualized name—in contrast to tales in the modern world—but their names, Anubis and Bata, relate them to the mortuary realm and the myth of Osiris. Anubis was the age-old mortuary deity whose ministrations were essential to the deceased's successful entrance to the underworld, and Bata was an old or alternative form of Osiris, king of the underworld, possibly serving as the underworld deity for the nonroyal individual, since in the Old Kingdom period Osirian benefits were limited to royalty. Among the other mythic imagery present is that of Kamutef, "bull of his mother," a designation for each pharaoh of the New Kingdom related to the begetting of his heir.

Given the specificity of the male names, the lack of names for the women in this tale stands out. Both female antagonists are divine, the one as wife of the god Anubis and the other expressly created as such. It is probable, however, that each is a manifestation of Hathor in her more negative forms, although the women's respective deaths in no way reflect on the goddess. The extreme misogyny present in the tale can be interpreted as an aversion to the historical strength of numerous Seventeenth and Eighteenth Dynasty queens. From another viewpoint, the negative roles of the women parallel those of wicked stepmothers and witches in more modern tales. Although often described as misogyny, there actions to such women in both the ancient and modern tales—all of which re-

flect androcentric cultures—embody the ambiguous attitude of men toward women: the mother/ wife cares and nurtures but also demands growth and change, death to the old ways. She thus is simultaneously loved and hated, even as are the women in *Two Brothers*.

While *Two Brothers*, like the *Prince*, functions primarily to entertain, it also carries a certain didactic tone. For example, the fates of the two women bespeak expected conjugal behavior and penalties for violation, and the sequence about the conception and birth of Bata points to the major birth narratives known from the earlier Twelfth and Eighteenth dynasties. It may even contain a hint of royal legitimation, reflecting a specific historical situation in the birth of the recognized royal heir by a foreign wife. In this tale, as in other Egyptian tales, a land outside Egypt serves as the otherworld in which the hero undergoes transformation from one status in his community to another: from single to married and from herdsman to king. All these concepts are the stuff of traditional but more modern tales of magic and wonder.

MIDDLE KINGDOM TALES

Middle Kingdom tales of magic and wonder differ from the New Kingdom tales discussed and the usual modern folktale in that their heroes do not undergo any real change of status. Nevertheless, they entertain extremely well with their magical and wondrous episodes, some of which occur as stories within stories. The so-called frame story consists of a narrator and his audience, the former telling a tale for the benefit of the latter. In *The Shipwrecked Sailor* (P. Hermitage, Saint Petersburg, 1115) an attendant relates his adventures to his lord, in order to reassure the latter on his return from an apparently less-than-successful trip. As we have it, the story opens with the attendant saying,

> Renew your heart, my nomarch. Behold we have reached home. The mallet has been seized, the mooring post driven in, (and) the bow-line placed upon land. Praise is given; God is thanked; each man embraces his companions. Our crew has come safely; there were no lost soldiers. We reached the land of Nubia; we passed Sehmet (Biga Island).

Behold we have come safely. We have reached our land. Listen to me, my prince. I am empty of exaggeration. Wash yourself; place water over your fingers. Then you answer when you are addressed. May you speak to the king courageously; may you answer and not stammer. A man's word can save him. His speech causes one to indulge him.

The narrator then proceeds to tell of his own experiences as a sailor wrecked on a fantastic island, ostensibly for the purpose of reassuring his lord. After three days alone on this island, the sailor hears a thundering noise and experiences trembling ground. On uncovering his face, he sees

a snake coming. He was of thirty cubits. His beard was greater than two cubits, his body was overlaid in gold, (and) his eyebrows were real lapis lazuli. He was bent up in front.

After interrogating the sailor, this fantastic creature recounts his own story of devastation (a story within a story within a story), identifying himself as the lord of Punt, the possessor of much exotic material such as myrrh, special oils, spices, cosmetics, perfumes, various animals and animal parts, and "all good riches." After assuring the sailor that he will return home to be among his family and will "die in (his) town," the lord of the exotic land of Punt laughs at the sailor's promise to send gifts and make sacrifices to him, both because he has innumerable riches of his own and also because when the sailor leaves the island, he will not see it again, for it will have become water. The island is a fantasyland, an otherworld. When the sailor is finally rescued, the lord of Punt gives him some of his riches which the sailor presents to the king on his return. The sailor is then made a royal attendant.

Despite the happy ending for the sailor-attendant, the high official in the frame story apparently fails to be reassured by the tale, for the text ends with the latter's rhetorical question, "Who will give water to a duck when day will break to its early slaughter?" Thus one senses that, contrary to the attendant's suggestion at the tale's opening, the nomarch has just given up, and is not even listening.

Nevertheless, for us the tale is a short, entertaining narrative of a journey that begins in the real world, progresses to the world of the fantastic with a splendid talking serpent, and ends in a return to the everyday world, recalling numerous similar tales from other cultures. Like the tales previously discussed, this one includes other possible levels of interpretation, both political and philosophical. Stylistically the opening phrases, the prince's final words, and much in between reflect traditional ways of speaking. Many sentences contain clauses with a formulaic flavor, while the final question suggests the economical wisdom of a proverb. Both modes of speaking appear in known written and oral materials from more recent sources.

Papyrus Westcar, a Second Intermediate Period document, contains a series of tales told by the sons of King Khufu (Cheops) of the Fourth Dynasty to entertain him. Although the first of the five tales is virtually lost and the second contains large lacunae, what is known of these first two and the contents of the other three make up a clear and chronological cycle of entertaining tales about magician-priests from the Third and Fourth Dynasty royal courts. The extant fragments of the second tale tell of a priest whose wife cuckolds him with a townsman. Upon discovering the adultery, the priest constructs a crocodile of wax, which is magically commanded to seize whoever bathes in the priest's pool—and of course the townsman is seized and dies. And when the priest takes up the crocodile, it becomes a figure of wax again. So as not to think the adulterous wife goes free, the narrator relates that she is set afire and her ashes scattered into the river. Thus the entertaining vignette, while showcasing the magical powers of the priest, also details the results of adultery and, by implication, contains an injunction against it.

The third tale tells of a group of beautiful young women from the king's palace who row on the palace lake for the king's pleasure. One of them loses her pendant in the lake and then refuses to continue until it is retrieved. When she rejects a substitute, demanding instead the original, the chief lector-priest says magical words over the lake with the result that one half of the water is laid on top of the other, the pendant is found and restored to its owner, and the lake's waters are returned to their normal place.

The tale ends with appropriate celebration and reward, having demonstrated the power of the magician. This episode recalls the emptying out of lakes in order to find rings and other such items in more modern European tales such as *The Drummer-Boy* from the Grimm Brothers collection and *Jack and King Marock* from Appalachia, and it perhaps presages the control of the Sea of Reeds when the Israelites fled Egypt, as related in Exodus 14:10–29.

In the fourth tale, the king is enchanted to learn of a magician from Upper Egypt who not only can join a severed head to its body and control wild animals but more importantly is reputed to know the number of secret chambers of the sanctuary of the god Thoth. This man Djedi, who eats a prodigious amount of food daily—five hundred loaves of bread, half an ox, and one hundred jugs of beer—indeed demonstrates that he can join the head and body of a goose, but he refuses to allow a man's head to be severed for the same purpose, stating that humans are "noble cattle." His description of humankind suggests not only an abiding respect for humanity but also humanity's place as part of the created world, a concept which pervades ancient Egyptian instructional and wisdom literature from all periods.

When this remarkable magician is asked about the number of Thoth's secret chambers, he denies personal knowledge but assures the king that the number may be found in a special chest in Heliopolis, telling him that the information will be brought to him by the eldest of the three children in the womb of Reddjedet, the wife of a priest of Re, lord of Sakhbu. With this information the fifth story begins. It continues by describing the births of these three children who are actually to be the first three kings of the Fifth Dynasty. Their births are attended by the same deities who also appear in the pictorial cycles told about the births of kings in the Eighteenth and Nineteenth dynasties, suggesting a similar divine concern and involvement and reflecting the royal ideology of the day in which the king was the son of the sun god but not the sun god himself. A mildly comic note appears when these deities, Isis, Nephthys, Heket, Meskhenet, and Khnum, feel the need to leave evidence for the infants' father, Re, of their involvement. This they do by placing three crowns in a sack of barley which is then stored in a sealed room. Later the sounds of singing, music, dancing, and shouting come from this room, thus revealing a divine presence. Like the story of the waters, the crowns in the sack recall the episode from Genesis in which first money and later a royal cup are placed in the sacks of Joseph's brothers (42:25–28 and 44:1–2).

The last narrative is important for describing the transition from the Fourth to the Fifth Dynasty and for presenting the theme of the divine birth of the king. It is also one of the oldest stories dealing with real-life prophecy, written, of course, after the fact from the reader's viewpoint though not from that of the narrator. It demonstrates an approach to actual occurrences that one finds in Egyptian pseudepigrapha, such as the *Prophecy of Neferti*.

GRECO-ROMAN TALES: DEMOTIC

The Greco-Roman period produced at least two known cycles of stories, that is, stories which focus on a specific person but which may or may not form a series of sequential episodes. Both were written in Demotic. One features a magician named Hi-Hor, but only one tale of the cycle remains and it is incomplete. The other, a story-cycle focusing on Setna Khaemwaset (a name with many variant spellings) consists of two nearly complete manuscripts and numerous fragments. The hero was a real prince, the fourth son of Ramesses (Ramses) II and high priest of Ptah at Memphis. The older, usually called *Setna I*, dates from the third century BCE, and the other, generally referred to as *Setna II*, dates to the first or second century CE. These tales provide an excellent example of how a man who became famous during his lifetime as a wise man later had attributed to him great powers as a magician. On one hand, the tales reflect Hellenistic influence, as seen in their underworld trips. On the other, they present traditional Egyptian ideas, such as the concern with the secrets of Thoth, and recall Egyptian materials relating to other legendary personalities, for example, Imhotep, the patron of writing and the architect of Djoser's pyramid complex, and the sage Hardjedef, famous for his wisdom teaching.

Besides being linked together as a cycle through the character of Setna, each tale contains several stories. In the case of *Setna I*, or the story of *Setna Khaemwaset and Naneferkaptah*, the lost beginning of the tale, reconstructed from another papyrus fragment, relates how the spirit of the wife of the priest Naneferkaptah tells Setna Khaemwaset of the fateful search for and acquisition of the magic book of Thoth by her husband at the eventual cost of his, her, and their son's lives. Not to be deterred from his own search, Setna, a priest himself, seizes the book after a magical battle with the spirit of Naneferkaptah. When Setna tells this adventure to his father the king, the pharaoh warns him to return the book, a warning the prince does not heed, as he had not heeded the earlier one.

In an apparently separate episode, the prince sees and becomes thoroughly enchanted with the beautiful Tabubu. Through an intermediary, he offers her gold in order to effect a tryst. Seemingly willing, she orders him to come to her and then makes increasing demands on him, including signing over to her all his possessions and killing his children, in order that she fulfill his desire. When the climax comes, he awakes in terror, naked, and learns this was a dream sent to punish him for his misdeeds toward Naneferkaptah. On the advice of his father, he then returns the book he had taken, while simultaneously bringing the bodies of the priest's wife and child from Koptos (Coptos) to the priest's tomb in Memphis. In the end the narrator has restored the hero to heroic stature by making the entire episode a dream—after the fact. The narrator also portrays a most vicious and cold-hearted prostitute, rivaling any known, thus reminding the audience in a most graphic fashion that one must stay away from "other" women, as is counseled as far back as the Old Kingdom.

The many magical and wondrous details of *Setna I* include wax figures enlivened to become real, ghosts, magical boxes, visions, and the ability to understand animals, along with an episode of fighting a serpent three times before victory and assuring victory only by separating the parts of the cut-up serpent with sand. Although providing a showcase for these entertaining magical acts, this tale clearly means to emphasize that the boundary between the human and divine worlds is not to be transgressed at will, even by royalty. Perhaps in a world where the Ptolemaic rulers had arrogated to themselves Egyptian divine kingship, this tale reminded the Egyptians that even under the Ramessides, there had been a separation between gods and humanity.

Setna II actually focuses on Si-Osire, a child divinely/magically conceived by Setna and his wife. The narrative consists of two parts. In the first, Si-Osire, a rapidly growing and precocious child, quickly outpaces the skills of his teacher and shows his father Setna the virtues of a life in which the good deeds outweigh the bad. The child accomplishes this latter feat by taking his father to the underworld, so that he can see how the man who was rich in his burial is tortured in his next life, while the man with the poor burial is elevated to the entourage of Osiris himself, as a result of their deeds in this world. At the end, the twelve-year-old boy is unsurpassed in magic and the use of spells by any scribe or learned man in Egypt, recalling the wondrous childhoods of epic figures from numerous other cultures.

The second part of *Setna II* gives the background of the child's birth by explaining how he is able to read the writings in a document bound to a Nubian messenger's body without opening it. The writings that he reads tell of an earlier magical battle between two magicians—a Nubian and an Egyptian—in which each transported the other's ruler to his own homeland by means of an enlivened wax litter and entourage. As it turns out, Si-Osire's miraculous birth and precocious childhood represent the preparation for a renewal of this earlier battle, for the Nubian messenger is the released Nubian magician from fifteen hundred years earlier and Si-Osire himself is the original Egyptian magician.

Obviously a tale full of magic and wonder, *Setna II* may reflect tensions between Egypt and its southern neighbors as well as carrying overtones of conflict over the kingship, since Si-Osire means "son of Osiris," an epithet of the king as the embodiment of Horus.

TALES FROM GREEK SOURCES

A number of Egyptian tales come to us via Greek writers. Particularly pertinent to the topic of magic and wonder is the tale of Rhodopis, a woman first mentioned by Herodotus (2.134–135) in the fifth century BCE and then by Strabo (*Geography* 17.1.33), writing at the turn of the era. The tale Strabo narrates recalls the more modern narrative of Cinderella and tells of a courtesan brought to Egypt and freed. One day, as she was bathing, an eagle seized her shoe and flew off with it to Memphis. There the bird flung it into the lap of the king, who subsequently searched the land for its owner with whom he had fallen in love, sight unseen, reminding the modern reader of Bata's spouse. Ultimately, the woman was reunited with her shoe and became the wife of the king.

FUNCTIONS OF THE TALES

In general, as the brief summaries given here suggest, the Egyptian tales function like their modern counterparts. Most obviously, the tales entertain, while some also provide a sense of release from ordinary strictures of behavior and belief, as seen in the tongue-in-cheek mockery of ordinarily venerated figures like the king driven by his appetites in *The Tale of Two Brothers*. On a more serious level, they serve as vehicles of education, exemplified in the warnings—shown by means of punishment—against adultery. Less obviously, they transmit cultural values of all kinds, ranging from respect for human life—demonstrated by Djedi the magician—to the view of foreign lands as places of exile—as in the New Kingdom tales. Expression and validation of particular practices or beliefs, the "why" of a practice or belief, normally present in what we commonly designate as "myth" (for example, the inviolability of humanity exemplified by Djedi), also appears in the tales, reemphasizing the problems inherent in using modern terminology to define ancient forms. Finally, individual tales address and reflect specific historical, political, and philosophical realities and beliefs. For example, the birth story from Papyrus Westcar expresses, if not legitimizes, the

transition from the Fourth to Fifth Dynasty, and *Setna I* relays the message that even kings cannot violate the preserves of the deities.

As a whole, Egyptian tales contain features specific to Egypt that identify the narratives as explicitly Egyptian. Even those tales which are "the most fabulous"—the two New Kingdom narratives—share this trait. In a few of them, one also finds the transition from one social status to another (shepherd to king, boy to man) that is so typical of modern tales. Finally, there is no question that each of the stories contains tale types and motifs that are ubiquitous in later stories from every part of the world. This is not to suggest that Egypt served as the origin of such tales, which were then borrowed or otherwise diffused elsewhere, but rather that in these ancient writings are some of the earliest examples of motifs and tale types that appear in other times and places.

BIBLIOGRAPHY

Sources

Most of the tales discussed here appear in English translation in MIRIAM LICHTHEIM, *Ancient Egyptian Literature*, 3 vols. (1973–1980). All of them can be read in German in EMMA BRUNNER-TRAUT, trans. and ed., *Altägyptische Märchen*, 8th edition, (1989). Other sources include WILLIAM KELLY SIMPSON, ed., with translations by R. O. FAULKNER, E. F. WENTE, JR., and W. K. SIMPSON, *The Literature of Ancient Egypt: An Anthology of Stories, Instructions, and Poetry* (new ed. 1973); JAMES B. PRITCHARD, ed., *Ancient Near Eastern Texts Relating to the Old Testament* (3rd ed. 1969); and the English translation of Adolf Erman's German rendering of the tales, published as *The Ancient Egyptians: A Sourcebook of Their Writings* (1966).

Translations of the stories and references from Greek sources can be found in *Plutarch's De Iside et Osiride*, translated and edited by JOHN GWYN GRIFFITHS (1970).

STRABO

The "Geography" of Strabo, 8 vols., translated by HORACE LEONARD JONES (1949).

HERODOTUS

Histories, vol. I, books translated by A. D. GODLEY, (1920; reprinted 1975), see especially vol. 2.134–135.

Studies of Egyptian Tales

EMMA BRUNNER-TRAUT discusses folk motifs in "Märchenmotive," *Lexikon der Ägyptologie,* vol. 3 (1980), and folktales in "Volkserzählungen," vol. 6 (1986). Commentaries on specific tales include WOLFGANG HELCK, "Die Erzählung vom verwünschenen Prinzen," in *Form und Mass: Beiträge zur Literatur, Sprache und Kunst des alten Ägypten, Festschrift für Gerhard Fecht,* edited by JÜRGEN OSING and GÜNTER DREYER (Ägypten und Altes Testament, 12; 1987); SUSAN TOWER HOLLIS, *The Ancient Egyptian "Tale of Two Brothers": The Oldest Fairy Tale in the World* (1990); and JOHN BAINES, "Interpreting the Story of the Shipwrecked Sailor," *Journal of Egyptian Archaeology* 76 (1990).

General discussions of Egyptian literature in English can be found in GEORGES POSENER, "Literature," and RONALD J. WILLIAMS, "Egypt and Israel," in *The Legacy of Egypt,* edited by J. R. HARRIS (2nd ed. 1971). POSENER surveys Egyptian literary texts known as of 1960 in "Recherches littéraires I–VII," *Revue d'Égyptologie,* 6–12 (1951–1960). For a more recent listing of Middle Kingdom tales, see R. B. PARKINSON, "Teachings, Discourses and Tales from the Middle Kingdom," in *Middle Kingdom Studies,* edited by STEPHEN QUIRKE (1991).

Studies in Folklore and Folktales

STITH THOMPSON provides the major sources of tale and motif analysis as well as a major study of the folktale: *The Folktale* (1946; repr. 1972); *Motif-Index of Folk-Literature,* 6 vols. (rev. and enlarged; 1955–1958); and *The Types of the Folktale: A Classification and Bibliography,* by ANTTI AAINE, trans. and enlarged (1964). MAX LÜTHI, *The European Folktale: Form and Nature,* translated by JOHN D. NILES (1982) and *The Fairytale as Art Form and Portrait of Man,* translated by JON ERICKSON (1984); and VLADIMIR PROPP, *Morphology of the Folktale,* 2nd ed., translated by LAURENCE SCOTT, revised and edited by LOUIS A. WAGNER (1968), each provide studies of modern folktales which help in the analysis of the ancient tales. The classic work on oral traditional narrative is ALBERT BATES LORD, *The Singer of Tales,* Harvard Studies in Comparative Literature 24 (1960), complemented by his *Epic Singers and Oral Tradition* (1991), while RICHARD BAUMAN, *Verbal Art as Performance* (1977; 2nd ed. 1984), is one of numerous works addressing actual performance.

WILLIAM R. BASCOM, "Four Functions of Folklore," in *The Study of Folklore,* edited by ALAN DUNDES (1965), reprinted from *Journal of American Folklore* 67 (1954), is the classic article on this subject.

SEE ALSO **The Middle Kingdom in Egypt** (Part 5, Vol. II); **The Kingdom of Mitanni in Second-Millennium Upper Mesopotamia** (Part 5, Vol. II); **Witchcraft, Magic, and Divination in Ancient Egypt** (Part 8, Vol. III); and **Ancient Egyptian Literature: An Overview** (Part 9, Vol. IV).

The Scribes and Scholars of Ancient Mesopotamia

LAURIE E. PEARCE

The scribal art is the mother of speakers, the father of scholars.

THIS SUMERIAN PROVERB demonstrates the high regard generally accorded scribes and scholars in ancient Mesopotamia. Although the scribes themselves remain largely in the background—anonymous recorders of civilization—the training, responsibilities, and activities of Mesopotamian scribes and scholars can be deduced from the texts they produced. Documentation unevenly reflects details related to the training of the scribes, the existence of a scribal academy, and the nature of cuneiform in scholarship. In order to present the broadest possible picture of cuneiform scribes and scholars, evidence from all periods is included here.

Scribes functioned in a society in which the vast majority of people were illiterate. The basic responsibility of scribes was to write documents for themselves and others. They acquired literacy and numeracy in schools dedicated to that purpose. Having mastered those fundamental steps, the scribe was equipped to serve the business communities, both private and public. Scribes with exceptional interest or talent engaged in additional study, mastering advanced bodies of knowledge: science, literature, religion. These scholars were responsible for preserving the cultural heritage of Mesopotamia.

SOCIAL STANDING OF THE SCRIBES

Scribes and scholars belonged to the social elite. A bilingual Sumero-Akkadian proverb notes: "The scribal art, receiving a handsome fee, is a bright-eyed guardian, the need of the palace." Students in the scribal school were male children of members of the upper strata of society. Their fathers were well-to-do merchants, priests, governors, ambassadors, kings, and occasionally scribes. (As in most areas of Mesopotamian society, women were denied access to the scribal academy. See the accompanying sidebar for a discussion of women scribes, scholars, and authors.)

One text tells of a failed scribal career. Yasitna-abum, the scribe of a very flowery letter from Tell al-Rimah (around 1750 BCE), had been told to "Learn the art of scribes! I shall make you into a household of gentlemen." Although Yasitna-abum gave up food and water in order to master the scribal arts, he met with little success and never achieved prominent employment: "Because I have nothing, I cannot serve in the palace."

Among the Hittites, the scribe could be counted with the dignitaries of the court and might be called upon as the king's substitute to deliver prayers before a god. Payment to an archive administrator of a salary equal to one-half of that of the high priest's substitute during the reign of Bur-Sin in the Third Dynasty of Ur (Ur III) period attested to the prominent social standing of the scribes.

MATERIALS OF THE SCRIBAL PROFESSION

The cuneiform scribe most frequently executed his tasks with clay tablet and reed stylus, ready materials in the riverine environment of Mesopotamia. However, a variety of materials were used for cuneiform inscriptions. The entire range of tools and materials is considered here.

Tools Used for Writing

The stylus used to impress clay tablets was most frequently fashioned out of reed and was known by the Sumerian or Akkadian words for that material, GI and *qanû*, respectively. At first, the rounded end of the reed was impressed into the tablet. Soon, scribes began to shape the reed's end into a triangular cross-section that gave cuneiform signs their characteristic wedge shape.

Wall reliefs in palaces of several Neo-Assyrian kings, including those of Adad-nirari III, Tiglath-pileser III, and Sennacherib, portray scribes at their tasks. Reliefs from Nineveh (Kuyunjik) variously depict two scribes recording the spoils of war and the numbers of enemies slain in military campaigns (see fig. 1). The Aramaic scribe holds pen and papyrus; the other scribe holds either a hinged writing board coated with wax or a cuneiform tablet and a stylus.

When writing on wax, scribes employed a metal (bronze) stylus because of its strength and durability. Writing on wood was done with ink and brush. With a pointed tool, scribes outlined inscriptions to be chiseled in stone by expert stoneworkers.

Women Scribes

While the vast majority of scribes were men, there were notable exceptions. The first was Enkheduanna, the earliest named woman scribe and author. She was a daughter of Sargon of Akkad and author of a lengthy Sumerian poem praising Inanna. Nin-shata-pada was priestess of the underworld deities, Meslamtaea and Lugal-girra, and daughter of Sin-kashid of Uruk (Warka). In her literary letter to Rim-Sin of Larsa, she appealed to the conquering king for mercy. Her elegant prayer became the object of study in subsequent generations of apprentice scribes. The wife of Ur-Nammu (circa 2100) may have composed a lament following his death in battle. The wife of Shulgi may have created the lullaby to her son.

Women scribes are attested in Old Babylonian Mari and Sippar (Abu Habba). Some were daughters of scribes. At Sippar, the women scribes were members of the cloister that functioned as an important social and economic entity in that city. These scribes served to record the transactions of the members of the cloister. Their position as scribes further indicates the social and economic achievement of these women.

At Mari, the names of at least ten women scribes are known. Nine of these received rations small enough to suggest that, although they were literate, they were held in low regard and were slaves of the harem. Slave-girls trained as scribes were occasionally given to princesses as part of their dowries. Just as at Sippar, these women scribes served the documentational needs of other women in their society.

Evidence of women scribes as scholars is limited to one fragment of a vocabulary text written by one Belti-remenni in the Old Babylonian period. Female counterparts to diviners, physicians, performers, and artists are all attested. But their activities, too, are overshadowed by those of their male counterparts.

Fig. 1. Assyrian relief from the Southwest Palace of Nineveh showing military scribes listing booty and soldiers slain during the war in southern Babylon (note the heads at the scribes' feet). BRITISH MUSEUM, LONDON

Clay Tablets: Preparation and Layout

Surviving tablets reflect the quality of the materials available to the scribes, as well as the attention paid by the scribe to the preparation of the tablets themselves. Some tablets were prepared from clay filled with inclusions, impurities in the clay such as small pebbles, grit, straw, and other organic material. Other tablets were formed from a fine clay body.

The quality of the clay body and the layout of the text were related to the type of text to be written on the tablet. Literary and historical texts are the most aesthetically pleasing to the modern eye, because the scribes took great care to proportion the size of the tablet to the amount of material to be inscribed. The standardized and formulaic language of some text genres, such as contracts, encouraged scribes to adhere to a prescribed layout of text on tablet.

Some late-first-millennium cuneiform tablets also contained scribal notations inscribed or painted in the Greek or Aramaic alphabetic scripts. The scribe of an incantation text found on a tablet from Uruk engaged in the unusual practice of employing the cuneiform script to graphically represent the Aramaic in which the incantation was composed.

A variety of other markings appeared on some tablets. Vertical or horizontal lines, found on literary, historical, lexical, religious, and scientific texts, divided texts into various sections comparable to poetic stanzas or book chapters. The rulings also provided reference points to sections of the text and aided the scribe in allocating the text on the tablet.

From the Middle Babylonian and Middle Assyrian periods on, some literary tablets were impressed front to back or side-to-side with holes. The suggestion that the purpose of these holes was to prevent the rupture of the tablet during firing is dubious, as many large tablets were successfully fired in antiquity without such precautions. Although their purpose remains unclear, it became traditional to impress such holes on many literary tablets. Tablets of the *Erra Epic* could be hung on votive statues once a cord was passed through holes bored in the clay. Holes in the corners of the bronze tablet found at Boğazköy, recording a treaty between the Hittite king, Tudkhaliya IV, and Kurunta of Tarkhuntassha, may have served a similar function.

Other marks included impressions of a fingernail or the hem of a garment, evidence of an individual's participation in the recorded transaction. Some economic tablets that were reviewed when taking inventory of stocks bore a thick red marking painted on its face. Scribes drew maps and representations of astrological material on tablets. Impressions of a stamp or cylinder seal sometimes accompanied cuneiform inscriptions. When a scribe noticed mistakes in the text, he might correct them by rubbing the surface of the clay with his fingers. The clarity of corrections depended on the elasticity of the clay when the scribe made the correction. Variation among scribes' handwritings occasionally makes it possible to identify groups of tablets as the product of a specific, albeit anonymous, scribe.

Scribes inscribed tablets from the left edge to the right and from top to bottom. Tablets were generally turned on the horizontal rather than vertical axis: top to bottom, as it were. Multicolumned tablets read from left to right on the obverse, and continued from right to left on the reverse. For want of space, scribes also filled the edges of a clay tablet and occasionally squeezed words between lines. The layout of text on clay objects other than tablets conformed to the constraints imposed by their unique shapes.

Clay Tablets: Shapes and Sizes

The majority of clay tablets were rectangular in shape; the vertical axis was generally the longest. Some Ur III land surveyors used circular tablets to record their results. Students of the Ur III and Old Babylonian period schools wrote elementary exercises in sign composition and beginning vocabulary development on round tablets.

Royal inscriptions, commissioned by kings to commemorate their great deeds, appear on variously shaped writing surfaces, including clay barrels, and six- and eight-sided prisms. Each face of a prism contained a column of text. Barrels were inscribed along their long axes, so that when they were stored or displayed vertically (on a spindle that fit through the hole running the length of the barrel), the inscription appeared perpendicular to the direction in which it was intended to be read.

Clay cones with broad flat nail-heads and bronze nails, decorated with a figure carrying a work basket on his head, contain inscriptions attesting to the piety of the ruler responsible for the buildings into whose sides these cones were inserted. Inscriptions on clay cones began at the flat-head side of the nail; sometimes the nail was ruled into registers and the text divided into two columns. The shape of these foundation deposits developed from the practice at Early Dynastic Uruk of facing walls and columns with cones, the heads of which were set in mosaic-like patterns. Foundation-deposit inscriptions are also attested on rectangular tablets of precious metals.

Surfaces on which cuneiform inscriptions appear vary greatly in size. The smallest clay tablets, just a few centimeters in length and width, could contain tens of lines of writing on each side. The ability to write so much in limited space is a tribute to the dexterity and skill of the scribe. Large texts recording literary, historical, and political records may measure as much as 45 by 30 centimeters (18 by 12 inches). While the bronze treaty tablet mentioned above was somewhat smaller, measuring 35 by 23.5 by 1 centimeters, its weight of 5 kilograms (11 pounds) is remarkable! Scribes in the service of the Neo-Assyrian king Esarhaddon executed copies of treaties concluded with his vassals on tablets of such dimensions. Among the largest surfaces containing inscriptions were walls in the palaces of Assyrian kings, such as those of Assurnasirpal II, and the escarpment of the mountain pass at Behistun (Bisitun), Iran, on which the Persian king Darius I had a trilingual inscription carved. (See the chapter on Darius in Part 5, Vol. II.)

Other Uses of Clay

Scribes fashioned clay into other objects related to writing. Clay tokens, in a variety of shapes and sizes, may have been the original source and inspiration for the shapes of some cuneiform signs. Bullae were of two types: hollow spheres of clay contained clay tokens; flattened rings of clay surrounded some papyrus and parchment documents and served as the medium onto which witnesses impressed their seals in attestation to the transaction recorded therein. (See "Record Keeping Before Writing" earlier in this volume.)

Clay casings, termed envelopes, enclosed some administrative documents (fig. 2). The text of the transaction was recopied, in part or whole, onto the envelope. The envelope inscription served either to provide a duplicate copy against which the original text could be compared if questions about the validity of the transaction arose or to offer a ready indication of the contents within, facilitating storage and retrieval of the tablet in an archive. Although attested from the Ur III to Neo-Assyrian periods, the practice was largely abandoned after the Old Babylonian period.

Inscriptions on Stone and Metal

Stone and metal were generally reserved for inscriptions commissioned by members of royalty, although not all royal inscriptions were written on these materials. Since Mesopotamia was poor in mineral resources, gold, silver, and basalt were imported. Metals were attested only infrequently as a writing material and were reserved for texts of importance to the crown, such as several found at Persepolis.

Inscriptions on Ivory and Wood

Another medium for cuneiform inscriptions was writing boards, flat pieces of ivory or wood

Fig. 2. An example of a tablet encased in a clay envelope, Middle Babylonian period. BRITISH MUSEUM, LONDON

bound together with hinges. Writing boards of silver and gold are rarely mentioned. Writing boards, in use from the Ur III to Late Babylonian periods, were coated with a layer of wax to which orpiment was added. This allowed the wax to flow easily to coat the surface of the boards and to retain its malleability for the inscription. This malleability also made it possible for the scribes to erase and reuse the wax, rendering it ideal for the preliminary composition of texts. Once the preliminary copy was completed, the scribe copied all of the data onto a durable clay tablet. The wax was then erased and reused and this process was repeated. The texts composed on wax writing boards recorded a variety of data compiled over a period of time, including religious and ritual matters, royal reports and orders, registers of people, and astronomical observations. The Mesopotamians depicted the "tablet of life" as a wax-covered board on which the god Nabu recorded the names and deeds of kings and their sons. Some wax boards were attached together by means of hinges to form a "book." Recent excavation of a shipwreck near Uluburun, on the southwestern coast of Turkey, delivered a rare example of such a "book." (See "Sea and River Craft in the Ancient Near East" in Part 6, Vol. III.)

Scribes also wrote on papyrus and leather. Because these materials were not easily impressed with cuneiform signs, their use did not become widespread until the development and spread of alphabetic scripts in the first millennium. Inscriptions employing these scripts used pen or brush and ink. Scribes who wrote on these materials were designated leather or papyrus scribes, respectively.

THE SCRIBAL SCHOOL AND CURRICULUM

Archaeological evidence for the existence and activities of the scribal school comes from sites such as Ur (Muqayyar), Sippar, and Nippur (Nuffar), where rooms replete with cuneiform tablets have been identified as schools.

All education related to the scribal arts occurred in a school or under the tutelage of experienced scribes. The scribal school, known as "the tablet house" (Sumerian É.DUB.BA.A; Akkadian *bīt ṭuppi*), achieved its greatest prominence in the Old Babylonian period. There, all aspects of the scribal profession were taught, from the preparation of tablet and stylus to the mastery of a curriculum covering four major areas of instruction: language (including vocabulary and grammar), literature, mathematics (including surveying), and music.

By the Old Babylonian period, Akkadian had replaced Sumerian as the appropriate language of commerce and diplomacy throughout Mesopotamia. Although the students' native language was generally Assyrian or Amorite, Sumerian retained its exalted position as the literary and religious language of school and cult and was

probably the language of instruction in the Old Babylonian school. Thus, students would had to have learned Sumerian upon entrance into the school. Scribes preserved Sumerian compositions, either unilingual or bilingual (with Akkadian translations), until the end of cuneiform usage.

The difficulties inherent in mastering the cuneiform system, in particular the complexity of sign-forms and multiple phonetic readings of individual signs, ensured a lengthy period and process of scribal education. These difficulties guaranteed the limited spread of literacy throughout Mesopotamian society. With the exception of one possible example discussed below, modern scholars lack the biographical data that, when correlated to scribes' activities, would make it possible to determine the ages at which scribes entered or graduated from the academy, or began and ended their careers. Although the length of many scribes' careers can be determined, this is relative, not absolute, data.

The early stages of language study were combined with instruction in tablet preparation and sign production. The teacher or his assistant wrote the day's lesson on the obverse of round tablets; the student copied the lesson on the reverse. At first, this consisted of learning how to impress the horizontal, vertical, and diagonal wedges that, combined in differing arrangements, produced cuneiform signs. The students progressed to form individual signs and words. Inscriptions on these lenticular tablets reflect the rudimentary stages of scribal education: crudely fashioned signs and only the briefest of connected textual passages, usually short proverbs and maxims. Once students mastered the fundamentals of sign composition, they advanced to the study of the components of language and literature.

Language study was acomplished through the copying and studying of lists. Scribes and scholars generated four kinds of philological lists: sign lists, vocabularies, syllabaries, and grammatical lists. Sign lists were either single- or multi-columned; in the latter case the right-hand column gave the names of signs listed on the left. Vocabularies or lexical lists of two or three parallel columns offered translations into Akkadian for designated Sumerian terms. Syllabaries

Fig. 3. Round school tablet inscribed with a Sumerian proverb by a student, Old Babylonian period. BRITISH MUSEUM, LONDON

presented cuneiform signs in standardized orders governed by orthographic or phonetic conventions. Some word lists provided Akkadian equivalents to Sumerian grammatical (verbal or nominal) forms. Once the student mastered the fundamentals of language and a basic vocabulary, he proceeded to advanced and specialized study in a variety of disciplines. (See "Ancient Mesopotamian Lexicography" below.)

Pedagogic practices in the Old Babylonian school were responsible for the preservation of Sumerian literature. Copying literary texts provided instruction in Sumerian composition and syntax for more advanced students. Among the literary texts thus preserved were royal hymns, proverb collections, mythological texts, and dialogues between hypothetical rival parties (such as the pickax and the plow) in which each presented evidence to support its claim to superiority or greater worth (see fig. 3).

The student achieved competence in epistolary and contractual style and structure by copying practice letters and model contracts. He mastered the terminology of a discipline by copying lists of technical vocabulary. The practice of grouping words according to subject matter facilitated this endeavor. The complex composition and syntax of the majority of cuneiform lists show they were intended for the use of advanced students in the scribal school or as reference works to be consulted by scholars. Other areas of advanced training and study included the vocabulary of priestly and administrative offices, the preparation of stelae, and the copying of law codes and trial proceedings.

Mathematics constituted the third area of instruction in the scribal curriculum. Mathematical exercise texts, preserved from the Old Akkadian, Old Babylonian, and Seleucid periods, belong to one of three types: table texts dealing with multiplication, reciprocals, squares, and square roots; coefficient lists presenting fixed values for various items; and problem texts covering matters such as algebra, geometry, and surveying. Texts containing practical problems prepared scribes for a variety of administrative positions. (See "Metrology and Mathematics in Ancient Mesopotamia" in Part 8, Vol. III.)

Individuals who would enter temple service received training in music, the fourth curricular area. Music instruction included mastery of Sumerian technical terms, such as GIŠ.GI₄.GAL (Akkadian *miḫru*), ŠID (Akkadian *manû*), and KI.ŠU₂ (Akkadian *kīlu*), roughly equivalent to our terms antiphon, recital, and finale. Students in the scribal school mastered performance of several instruments. They also learned the different names of various songs and the versification of lyrics. This training was essential preparation for the chief singer of lamentations and dirges in the temple. Ordinary performers in the cult, however, probably did not read or write. (See "Music and Dance in Ancient Western Asia" later in this volume.)

Sequence of Instruction

Several Sumerian texts deal with students' experiences in school. Known by their modern titles, "Examination Text A" and "Schooldays" provide a comprehensive picture of the composition and pedagogic practices of the faculty. While the surviving texts themselves date from the Late Babylonian period, they are believed to reflect conditions during Old Babylonian times, the heyday of the scribal academy. The teacher, designated as *ummānu*, "expert, professor," presided over the school, the students, and the curriculum. The advanced student, called "big brother," served as his assistant. The "son of the tablet house" occupied the lowest rung in the student hierarchy.

The primary task of the school day was the preparation, writing, and reading of tablets. Students partook of a midday meal brought from home. The teacher meted out corporal punishment for tardiness and lack of decorum. The teacher held power over the student's career, for he could ensure, or at least influence, the student's placement in a desirable position.

After the Old Babylonian period, the academy as an institution died out. The heretofore uniform school curriculum became less clearly defined and less widespread in its application. Although texts describing the educational process ceased to be produced, students continued to receive formal education from masters of the scribal arts. Scholars instructed pupils in their homes or in smaller schools. Some of these were located in proximity to the place in which scribes fulfilled their professional duties, for example, the private study of a master scribe associated with the temple complex at Hellenistic Uruk.

Evidence of pedagogic activity is available in the continued production of copying exercises and lists, and indirectly from notices of scribal activities contained in the texts and in colophons appended to texts. It was customary for scribes to append to the ends of tablets colophons that included some or all of the following notations: catch-line, which gave the opening line of the next tablet in the series; name and number of a tablet in a series; number of lines on the tablet; source of the copy; names of the owner or scribe who produced the copy; reason for writing the tablet; curse or blessing; date; and disposition of the copy. The colophon might also contain the name of the owner of the tablet, that of the tablet scribe, or both names. Prosopographic notices in colophons from texts, particularly of the Hellenistic period, afford a unique glimpse at the transmission of knowledge and the development of personal libraries and study collections. The statements of purpose in the colophon contain phrases related to the pedagogic process. The phrases "for reading," "for instruction," "for dictation," or "for his own study" indicate

some of the activities in which scholars were engaged.

SCRIBAL TITLES

The Akkadian and Sumerian terms for scribe, *ṭupšarru* and DUB.SAR, meant "tablet writer." Other scribal titles reflected either the material on which a scribe wrote or some aspect of his duties, for example, wood-tablet scribes known from the Hittite Empire and, as mentioned above, leather or papyrus scribes.

A sample of translated Sumerian and Akkadian scribal titles offers some indication of the broad range of responsibilities borne by cuneiform scribes. Not all titles were in use throughout the entire period of cuneiform writing, and the specific duties associated with each title varied through time.

deaf writer (probably a copyist)
female scribe
field scribe, land-registrar, geometer
inscriber of stone
judge's scribe
mathematician
military scribe
scribe for laborer groups
scribe of the property of the temple of Anu
scribe of the *nadītu* (cloistered) women
scribe of (the omen series) *Enūma Anu Enlil* (an astrologer)

Scribes could hold titles indicating additional nonscribal responsibilities. For example, at Hellenistic Uruk some scribes held as many as three titles, including that of *kalû*, "lamentation priest." Furthermore, scribal titles indicate that a scribe could hold several scribal positions, either concurrently or consecutively.

DUTIES AND RESPONSIBILITIES OF SCRIBES

Cuneiform scribes were involved in every facet of life where the script was employed. Distribution of scribes across various specialties is estimated as follows: 70 percent administrative; 20 percent private; and 10 percent scientific and quasi-scientific activities.

Scribes Engaged in Private Enterprise

As private individuals, scribes recorded business transactions, prepared contracts, served as notaries, and functioned as witnesses both to transactions they recorded and to those in which they had an interest. While scribes received compensation for their work, the great fortunes some scribes amassed derived from a variety of activities, including the sale and rental of real estate, accumulation and trading of shares held in temple offerings, and loans of silver. As private individuals, scribes engaged in activities appropriate to any member of their social strata.

Tablets from the Old Assyrian trading colony at Kanesh (modern Kültepe) demonstrate that some merchants were literate, having received training sufficient to enable them to send letters and maintain business records. However, most merchants hired scribes to do this work for them.

Scribes were particularly in evidence as businessmen in entrepreneurial firms of the late first millennium. Records from the House of Egibi, a Neo-Babylonian business firm, provide information about the activities of individual scribes as businessmen. Of these, the most renowned was Itti-Marduk-balatu, son of a man who was a scribe and businessman. Although Itti-Marduk-balatu wrote many legal documents, mercantile activity was his primary concern. In his lifetime he amassed a fortune that included more than one hundred slaves and sixteen houses in Babylon and Borsippa. His resources enabled him to provide his sister and daughters with substantial dowries. (See "Private Commerce and Banking in Achaemenid Babylon" in Part 6, Vol. III.)

Scribes were among the members of the community who served as agents for business activities of the Achaemenid firm of Murashu. Like other landholders with whom the Murashu firm did business, scribes were grouped into special associations in which a foreman allocated shares in the fiefdom to the association members. One such association was of the "scribes of the army/people." The foremen of this group were, among other things, responsible for ensuring payment of rent from their own association's lands to the Murashu firm and for issuing written authoriza-

tion for collection of rents due on lands of other associations. Individuals titled *sepīru,* an Aramaic loanword often rendered "translator-scribe," made and received payments on behalf of their principals. Additionally, these individuals, competent in both Akkadian cuneiform and Aramaic, worked outside the firm as low-level administrators in private real-estate firms.

In contracts, the scribe served either as a notary or a witness. Scribes of Hellenistic contracts typically recorded transactions to which they were not witnesses. But individuals known and designated by title as scribes appear in witness lists of other contracts, indicating that a scribe, just as any member of the social elite, could witness contractual agreements. However, seal impressions on Old Babylonian tablets indicate that scribes in that period could serve simultaneously as notaries and witnesses.

Scribes in the Palace

Palace scribes recorded the activities of kings and the affairs of kingdoms in ancient Mesopotamia. Scribes served a variety of administrative functions, including arrangement and storage of texts for future retrieval from palace archives and libraries, collection of taxes and supervision of workers, and supervision of public buildings such as granaries. As secretaries to kings, scribes exercised control over communications intended for royalty. Some seal inscriptions of Old Babylonian scribes designated an individual scribe as servant of a particular king.

Particularly in the first millennium, scribes in their capacities as scholars achieved the greatest proximity to and influence over matters at court. Among the areas of scholarly specialization were haruspicy, astrology, exorcism, medicine, and performance of hymns to appease angered gods.

The tablets of Nabu-zuqup-kenu, a scribe in the palace of the Neo-Assyrian kings Sargon and Sennacherib, inform us of the activities of a scholar in the palace employ. The colophons appended to many of the tablets he copied indicate that he traveled to other cities to consult original texts in order to prepare copies for the library at Nimrud (Kalkhu). The colophons to six texts written by Nabu-zuqup-kenu note that the texts were copied "for his reading." This attests to his continuing personal study in addition to the execution of professional obligations.

Besides being a copyist, Nabu-zuqup-kenu authored an mathematical text, known as I.NAM.GIŠ.ḪUR.AN.KI.A. A tablet preserving an extract of this series contains a chart, the three columns of which established equivalences among divine attributes, numerals, and the deities' names. The colophons to these tablets were a vehicle by which the scribes could assert, in a self-perpetuating way, that learning was only for those initiated into its secrets. Warnings to this effect might read: "A secret of the scholar. The uninitiated shall not see." However, the ease with which many of the putative scribal secrets can be deciphered mitigates the force of this claim.

Scribes as Translators

As Mesopotamian kings turned their political ambitions to empires, the need for translators arose. Scribes, already trained in the spoken and written forms of two languages, were the natural choice to assume this task. However, there is little indication of how scribes achieved proficiency in additional languages.

At the time of the Akkadian Empire, references to translators of the languages of Melukkha and Kutha appear. The Ur III king Shulgi boasted that in his palace he alone knew how to speak Elamite and Amorite. The Mari tablets of 1780 BCE mention the presence of translators in trading caravans. In the Middle Babylonian period translators were needed to deal with the Mitannian army. International activity between Egypt, Mesopotamia, and the Hittite empires in the middle and late second millennium necessitated translators from cuneiform into Egyptian. Texts from the Egyptian city of Amarna (Akhetaten) refer to cuneiform scribes learning Egyptian, as well. The appearance of the title "head of the translators" indicates that there was an organized cadre of these professionals.

Translators, in great demand throughout the first millennium, achieved special prominence during the Achaemenid period. When the kings of the Achaemenid Empire adopted Aramaic as their official language, it became necessary to prepare copies of royal promulgations in the native languages of the subject populations. Following the Neo-Assyrian period, the Akkadian term *targamannu,* "translator," is replaced by *sepīru,* "parchment scribe." *Sepīru* in fifth-century Nippur served as translators for various laborers employed in that city.

Temple Scribes

Scribes associated with the temple were not officiants in the temple cult. They functioned largely in administrative and bureaucratic roles. They received incoming staples for the temple, including commodities such as grain, fish, wool, and silver. They traveled to various cities to fulfill official duties, such as the purchase of grain for the temple complex.

Temple scribes aided temple archivists by classifying records, indicating categories under which tablets were to be stored. They also helped to prepare tablets as votive offerings to the gods. The nature and organization of archives, both private and public, is discussed under the title of "Archives and Libraries" earlier in this volume.

One area of scribal activity that reflects the interconnection between temple and palace activities is the composition of ephemerides, late first millennium texts on which scribes kept track of and recorded astronomical data. In order to determine the propitiousness of an action at any given time, the king ordered the observation of a variety of natural and celestial phenomena. Priests interpreted the signs as beneficent or malevolent. Archive staff members prepared reports and disseminated them to interested parties. Records of these observations and the ensuing actions taken provided comprehensive catalogs of everything that transpired in the court and empire. Preparation of these reports called upon the expertise of many specialists, including priests, astronomers, archivists, and scribes.

CUNEIFORM SCHOLARS

Most scribes wrote mundane business documents and left little indication of their personalities, backgrounds, or intellectual interests. A few scribes, however, stand out for achievements that earn them the title of scholar. Cuneiform scholars were individuals who, having mastered the basics of the scribal curriculum, received advanced training in one or more specialized fields. Scholars amassed collections of tablets for personal, family, or royal libraries. Facility in a particular genre or discipline led some to author or edit unique compositions which may then have been copied by generations of scribes.

In general, anonymity characterized cuneiform literature. However, the few named authors of literary texts left remarkably rich insights into the nature of their involvement with their work. Kabti-ilani-Marduk, author of the *Erra Epic*, claimed to have completely and accurately copied the poem that had been divinely transmitted to him through a dream.

Saggil-kinam-ubbib, author of *The Babylonian Theodicy*, allowed his sense of whimsy and innovation to creep into his famous composition. When the syllabic signs beginning each line of each successive stanza of this acrostic poem are arranged sequentially, they read: "I, Saggil-kinam-ubbib, the incantation priest, am adorant of the god and the king." Sin-leqe-unninni, the legendary editor of a recension of the *Epic of Gilgamesh*, was said to have lived around 1300. Hundreds of years later, a few scholars regarded him as a putative ancestor.

Many families of scholars associated themselves, through patronymics recorded in colophons, with a prestigious ancestor. At Hellenistic Uruk, most scribes claimed descent from either Sin-leqe-unninni, Ekur-zakir, Akhu'tu, or Kuri. Scribes claiming descent from Sin-leqe-unninni concentrated their efforts on the copying of scholarly and scientific texts. Scribes in both the Sin-leqe-unninni and Ekur-zakir "clans" developed personal tablet collections once they retired from actively writing tablets.

Sumero-Akkadian bilingual hymns from Babylon were largely composed by scribes claiming descent from the ancestor Nana-Utu. The family tree reconstructed for the scribes of this genre of texts includes four generations. In almost all cases the writer of a particular tablet was the son of the individual who owned it. The fathers of the scribes had themselves frequently been scribes of this genre of texts. From the dates of these texts, it is possible to determine that these scribes assumed scribal duties only after their fathers were no longer writing tablets.

The term *ummānu*, defined as teacher, carried the basic meaning of master, one proficient in a particular area of knowledge. In this sense the term was applied to practitioners of various disciplines, including diviners and exorcists, who consulted gods about important events; astronomers, who observed celestial phenomena; astrologers, who interpreted omens portended in the heavens and on earth; and physicians, who ministered to the mental and physical health of the court. The king regularly availed himself of the talents of these specialists and counted them among his most trusted advisors. The technical literature mastered by these professionals constitutes the body of Mesopotamian science.

By the end of the Neo-Assyrian period, the association of the scientific literature with the temples as well as the palace was strong, leading some modern scholars to consider their ancient counterparts priests. However, this conclusion conflicts with the evidence from most periods, as the duties and responsibilities of scholars and priests were clearly differentiated. This specialization is reflected in part by the distinctive titles held by members of particular professions. Only in the Hellenistic period, when the use of cuneiform was limited to a few traditionalists in the major cities of Mesopotamia, did an individual hold multiple titles once reserved for separate offices.

Astronomers and astrologers constituted the largest group of scholars. By 700 BCE, astronomers could predict eclipses and planetary phases and had discovered the periodicity of various astronomical phenomena. Records show that some physicians diagnosed conditions based on the appearance of a variety of symptoms. An extensive corpus of letters written by scholars to the king during the Neo-Assyrian period documents communication between these two parties.

Scholars were not merely copyists of earlier traditions. They perused earlier tablets of particular omen series and took the information they deemed necessary or appropriate for the particular occasion and edited it into a new composition. Increasingly, scholars found ways to leave their personal imprint on texts.

In the first millennium, scholars began to engage in whimsical and erudite orthographies. Numerals sometimes substituted for syllabic or logographic signs in normal orthographies of some omen texts and commentaries. We encounter a comparable practice in modern times when, for example, the homophony of the numeral "four" and the preposition "for" allows us to write "4 sale." This curious practice was also tested on some scribal names preserved in colophons. As the numbers in these curious cuneiform orthographies have no intrinsic relationship to the cuneiform signs for which they substitute, we must conclude that the scribes manipulated the system for their enjoyment and intellectual diversion.

ROYALTY AND THE SCRIBAL ARTS

While scribes and scholars may have served the needs of temple and palace, several royal figures claimed to have mastered or at least achieved proficiency in the scribal arts. Enmerkar, putative builder of Uruk, makes a literary claim to having invented writing itself. Otherwise, the first, already mentioned above, was Enheduanna. (See an illustration of Enheduanna in "Art and Ideology in Ancient Western Asia" later in this volume.) In self-laudatory hymns, Shulgi claimed to have mastered various aspects of the scribal curriculum, including music and divination. He asserted that none of the young students could write tablets as well as he, and that Nisaba, patron deity of writing, provided him with intelligence and wisdom. In the hymns he also credited the scribal school with preserving tradition. (For further discussion on Shulgi, see the chapter on him in Part 5, Vol. II.)

Other kings responsible for the development of libraries were Tiglath-pileser I, who brought together tablets at his palace at Kalkhu, and As-

An Individual Scribe's Career

Evidence from the scribal curriculum demonstrates how and what the scribes learned. An understanding of the breadth of scribal and scholarly activity is deduced from the documents they produced. While the career of an individual scribe is generally difficult to trace, it is possible to determine that some scribes served that profession for their entire adulthoods. Scribal careers of thirty or more years, while not typical, are attested. Evidence from the careers of two scribes at Hellenistic Uruk affords a rare opportunity to examine aspects of an individual scribe's career at a particular place and time. It would be unfair, however, to generalize the conclusions based on this evidence to all periods of scribal craft.

This brief glimpse into a scribe's career focuses on Anu-belshunu and his grandson, who, in accordance with the practice of papponymy common at Uruk, bore the same name. Both were involved, either as owner or scribe, with some two dozen texts. Between the years 230 and 193 BCE, the grandfather wrote a variety of texts, including a contract recording a real-estate purchase, omen tablets, lamentations, and a ritual to be followed by the *kalû* priest. A horoscope indicates that he was born in 248. Therefore, this man began his scribal career no later than his seventeenth year and practiced his profession until he was fifty-five years old. When his name appeared in other colo-

phons, he was the owner of astronomical texts that date from 192–176. Thus, Anu-belshunu served as a scribe and began to collect scientific documents, probably for a personal reference library, once he no longer was an active scribe.

His grandson adheres to this pattern of scribal and scholarly activity. He wrote texts from 178–172. These texts were records of real-estate transfers and a letter describing the training of scribes. Evidence from the remainder of his career, spanning 186–164, shows him as a tablet owner of some of the most unusual texts of the time, including a unique list of the names of antediluvian sages. Either this Anubelshunu had access to some of the more esoteric material in the Hellenistic cuneiform corpus, other exemplars of which have not survived, or he was uniquely creative and talented. In either case, the evidence from the careers of this grandfather and grandson, combined with that from other scribes of this clan at Uruk, overwhelmingly suggests that the careers of scribes adhered to this pattern: they began by writing routine formulaic texts, such as legal contracts, and as their interest or talent increased, progressed to copy scholarly treatises. Some became collectors of tablets, in much the same way that modern scholars build personal reference libraries in their areas of interest or expertise.

surbanipal. Like Shulgi, Assurbanipal was not modest about his erudition:

> I am versed in the craft of the sage Adapa [an antediluvian hero]; I studied the secret lore of the entire scribal craft, I know the celestial and terrestrial portents. I discuss with competence in the circle of the masters; I argue about the text "If the liver is a correspondence of the sky" with expert diviners. I can solve the most complicated divisions and multiplications which do not have a solution. I have read intricate tablets inscribed with obscure Sumerian or Akkadian difficult to unravel, and examined sealed, obscure, and confused inscriptions on stone from before the Deluge.

More significant evidence of Assurbanipal's interest in scholarly activities is the library he created at Nineveh. One letter from a scribe to Assurbanipal indicated that the king was personally involved in deciding which tablets were to be included in the collection. The scribe noted that all texts he suggested for the king's consideration were worth preserving for eternity. In a letter to a second scribe, Assurbanipal directed the scribe to find designated tablets in various houses and in the temple of Nabu at Babylon. The king instructed the temple overseer and magistrates to place at this scribe's disposal any tablets he deemed suitable for the palace library.

Nabonidus, the last Neo-Babylonian king (see the chapter on him in Part 5, Vol. II), has long been known for his antiquarian interests. In attempting to reestablish aspects of the cult of the moon god Sin, Nabonidus consulted older stelae and tablets for the proper procedures. He claimed to have taken out old tablets and writing boards and to have restored the works according to ancient customs. The Royal Chronicle recorded that while Nabonidus claims to have consulted the earlier documents, he handled the texts ignorantly.

The cuneiform scribes are responsible for producing the written evidence from which modern scholars are able to learn about Mesopotamia. The enormity of the cuneiform record, both in sheer numbers and in breadth and depth of content, attests not only to the complexity of its civilization but to the prodigious efforts of its recorders.

BIBLIOGRAPHY

The Sumerian proverb opening this chapter is cited from J. LAESSØE, "Literacy and Oral Tradition," in *Studia Ioanni Pedersen . . . dicata* (1953).

Scribal Training

STEPHANIE DALLEY, C. B. F. WALKER, and J. D. HAWKINS, *The Old Babylonian Tablets from Tell al-Rimah* (1976), contains the text of Yasitna-abum, the unsuccessful scribe described above. ADAM FALKENSTEIN, "Die babylonische Schule," *Saeculum* 4 (1953), is an early study of the general characteristics of the Babylonian school. C. J. GADD, *Teachers and Students in the Oldest Schools* (1956), is a general introduction to the topic. S. N. KRAMER, "Schooldays: A Sumerian Composition Relating to the Education of a Scribe," *Journal of the American Oriental Society* 69 (1949), has an English translation of the Sumerian text on which much of our knowledge of the scribal school is based; it contains commentary suitable for the general reader. See also his "The First Schools" and "The First Case of 'Apple Polishing,'" in *History Begins at Sumer* (1959; 3rd rev. ed. 1981), which present a thumbnail sketch of the Mesopotamian scribal academy. BENNO LANDSBERGER, "Babylonian Scribal Craft and Its Terminology," *International Congress of Orientalists* 23 (1954), presents a list and basic discussion of terms relating to the scribal school, the pedagogic process, and scribal titles; see also his "Scribal Concepts of Education," in *City Invincible*, edited by C. H. KRAELING and R. M. ADAMS (1960). KAREN RHEA NEMET-NEJAT, "Cuneiform Mathematical Tests as Training for Scribal Professions," in *A Scientific Humanist: Studies in Memory of Abraham Sachs*, edited by E. LEICHTY AND M. DEJ. ELLIS (1988), details all types of cuneiform mathematical texts and explores their relationship to the scribal curriculum. A. L. OPPENHEIM, *Ancient Mesopotamia* (1964; 2nd ed. rev. by ERICA REINER, 1977), discusses the scribes, their training, and responsibilities. A. W. SJÖBERG, "The Old Babylonian Eduba," in *Sumerological Studies in Honor of Thorkild Jacobsen*, edited by S. LIEBERMAN (1975), describes the scribal curriculum as recovered from a variety of sources, including the royal hymns. In "How Did They Learn Sumerian?" *Journal of Cuneiform Studies* 31 (1979), H. L. J. VANTISPHOUT considers the place of lexical lists in the process of learning Sumerian. He suggests that some royal hymns may have provided students with instruction in progressively more difficult stages of Sumerian.

Women Scribes

See W. W. HALLO, "Women of Sumer," in *The Legacy of Sumer*, edited by D. SCHMANDT-BESSERAT (1976). In addition to female scribes and scholars Enkheduanna and Nin-shata-pada, Hallo discusses women and their presence in the religious, economic, and political life of Mesopotamia. See also RIVKAH HARRIS, "The Female 'Sage' in Mesopotamian Literature (with an Appendix on Egypt)," in *The Sage in Israel and the Ancient Near East*, edited by J. G. GAMMIE AND L. G. PERDUE (1990).

Scribal Materials

In GEORGE F. BASS, "Oldest Known Shipwreck Reveals Splendors of the Bronze Age," *National Geographic* 172 (December 1987), both the text and superb photographs record a significant archaeological find. See HEINRICH OTTEN, *Die Bronzetafel aus Boğazköy: Ein Staatsvertrag Tuthalijas IV* (1988), for the publication of the bronze treaty tablet mentioned above. C. B. F. WALKER, *Cuneiform* (1987), is a small volume that covers the origin, development, and geographical distribution of cuneiform, the process of its decipherment, scribes and libraries, and the variety of texts produced in cuneiform. D. J. WISEMAN, "Assyrian Writing Boards," *Iraq* 17 (1955), presents evidence of the production, use, and organization of this inscriptional medium.

The Scribal Process

W. G. LAMBERT, "Ancestors, Authors, and Canonicity," *Journal of Cuneiform Studies* 11 (1957), is a consideration of the contributions of ancient cuneiform scholars to the literary "canon"; see also ALASDAIR LIVINGSTONE, *Mystical and Mythological Explanatory Works of Assyrian and Babylonian Scholars* (1986). A. L. OPPENHEIM, "The Intellectual in Mesopotamian Society," *Daedalus* 104, no. 2 (1975), discusses the contributions of the scribe to the intellectual history of Mesopotamia and considers the scribe in his roles as bureaucrat, scholar, and poet. In SIMO PARPOLA, *Letters from Assyrian Scholars to the Kings Esarhaddon and Assurbanipal* (1971), the introductory material of vol. 1 discusses the nature of Mesopotamian science, the responsibilities of the cuneiform scholars, and the relationship of the scholars to the crown. FRANCESCA ROCHBERG-HALTON, "Canonicity in Cuneiform Texts," *Journal of Cuneiform Studies* 36 (1984), examines evidence for the existence of a native Mesopotamian concept of canon as applied to its literary and scientific texts. Three streams of tradition are defined. The problems are considered in detail with regard to the celestial omen series *Enūma Anu Enlil*. MAXIMILLIAN STRECK, *Assurbanipal und die letzten assyrischen Könige bis zum Untergang Ninivehs* (1916), discusses the inscriptions of Assurbanipal from which the excerpt above was quoted.

SEE ALSO **Legal and Social Institutions of Ancient Mesopotamia** (Part 4, Vol. I) and **The Scribes of Ancient Egypt** (Part 9, Vol. III).

Sumerian Literature: An Overview

PIOTR MICHALOWSKI

THE OLDEST PRESERVED LITERATURE in the world was written in the Sumerian language. Nine or so generations after the invention of writing early in the third millennium BCE, the inhabitants of Mesopotamia began writing texts that were not administrative in nature but were the product of imagination. Where that literature came from we do not know. It could be maintained that writing preserved a rich oral literature that no doubt existed in Sumer. One could also argue that writing provided a completely different medium of expression, and that from the very beginning the literature of the clay tablets was fundamentally different from the oral compositions that circulated in society. Literacy was always highly restricted in the ancient Near East, and only an elite, scribes as well as government and temple officials—could read and write.

A MULTICULTURAL ENVIRONMENT

Sumerian literature is defined here as literature in the Sumerian language. Most of the texts that we have come from periods when the language was no longer spoken by the population at large but was maintained in the schools and temples. After the Sumerian language died out, most people in Mesopotamia spoke various Semitic lan-guages and dialects, and literature was com-posed in literary versions of some of these languages, primarily in Akkadian. Already at the time when writing was invented Sumer was a multicultural and multilingual place, and so it is fair to say that Sumerian was always written in a multilingual environment, and that the politics and aesthetics of written language choice are not linked in a simple way with the spoken language of a people or peoples. For this reason, and be-cause for most of its history this literature coex-isted with Akkadian, it is difficult to speak of a separate Sumerian literature although for the sake of this introductory essay we do precisely that.

Authors

Most ancient literary works cannot be easily dated. An examination of the script and the writ-ing, or the investigation of the archaeological context, can tell us when a given work was in-scribed; but it rarely determines when a text was composed. We know almost nothing about the poets who wrote the literary compositions; autho-rial anonymity was the rule. The rare exceptions to this are of significance. The earliest poet known by name was Enkheduanna, daughter of King Sargon of Akkad and high priestess of Nanna, the moon-god, in the city of Ur (modern Tell al-Muqayyar). Ancient tradition, probably baseless, ascribed to her three separate poems:

the collection of "Temple Hymns," a hymn to the goddess Inanna, and the autobiographical hymn known as the *Exaltation of Inanna*. It is interesting to note that in a profession dominated by men, the world's first identified poet was a woman. (See "Kings of Akkad: Sargon and Naram-Sin" in Part 5, Vol. II.)

The creative process involved only a small number of people, and their labors were read only by a privileged few. The average man or woman probably knew nothing of the poems and stories that we have recovered from the ground of Mesopotamia, and therefore we should not identify the sentiments and values of the literature with the ideals of all members of those ancient societies.

Form and Style

Tablets.   Sumerian literature was written on clay tablets and cylinders of various forms. The early texts were inscribed on large square tablets, with rounded edges, in multiple columns. Shorter exercises and incantations were written on round tablets. Beginning with the Ur III period, round and multiple-sided prisms, only sporadically attested before, came into general use. Although one can observe a certain local standardization of formats, a variety of forms persisted, often differing according to the level of instruction. Many of the Old Babylonian school exercises were written on rectangular IMGIDAS, "long tablets," which contained between fifteen to forty lines of text in single columns on each side. There were also multicolumn tablets that contained two hundred or more lines, but these are less common, and often have inferior versions.

Style.   Almost all of Sumerian literature is poetry. There are prose texts—law codes, literary letters, copies of royal inscriptions—but they constitute a small portion of the literature. As far as we know, Sumerian did not use meter and rhyme as its primary poetic devices. The formal study of Sumerian poetics is seriously hampered by our rudimentary knowledge of the phonology of the language, but we can recognize some of the underlying principles.

The dominant form of poetic organization was syntactic parallelism. Short lines were organized into larger units of two, three, four, or more lines by parallelism of all levels of language. Repetition of units of various sizes was an important element. One of the most well-known Shulgi hymns begins thus:

> LUGAL MEN SHATA URSANG MEN
> SHULGI MEN BATUDENATA NITA KALGA MEN
> PIRING IGI KHUSH USHUMGALE TUDA MEN
> LUGAL AN UBDA LIMMUBA MEN
>
> King am I, warrior from the womb am I,
> Shulgi am I, mighty male from birth am I,
> Lion fierce of eye, born to be a dragon am I,
> King of the four corners of the universe am I.

Here the repeated use of the verb MEN, "I am," which goes on for another fifteen lines, frames a section of four lines in which synonyms are used to establish a poetic pattern. The repetition of that most important word, LUGAL, Sumerian for "king," frames the section. The fourth line is a standard epithet commonly found in royal inscriptions, as is NITA KALGA, "mighty male," in line two. Here they are introduced as the natural consequences of proper royal birth, which is established in the first line. The parallelism of the word for "king" and the name of Shulgi, with the epithet preceding the proper name, is another typical device found in the opening lines of hymns. Sometimes poets went against the grain in order to make it new, as in the first line of the longest of all Old Babylonian hymns, which began not with an epithet but with the name of Sumer's most important god: "Enlil—his utterance is mighty and his instructions are holy for ever!"

Many of these devices are difficult to render in English. For example, in Sumerian the normal possessive construction works on the pattern LUGAL KALAM.AK, "king-land.of," that is, "king of the land." In order to stress the second part, a different construction was used: KALAM.AK LUGAL.BI, "land.of—king.its," or "of the land—its king." This semantic shift is common in poetic texts and often accounts for the artificial and awkward tone of many modern translations.

The heightened attention to all levels of language provided various motivations for poetic composition. On the lexical level the word lists were drawn on for a complex vocabulary. Word-plays and the use of synonyms and antonyms were characteristic devices. The phonological level is the most difficult to appreciate since that is the part of the language we know the least about at present, but certain poetic devices are quite obvious even to the modern reader. One extreme example is the *Song of the Hoe*. Since the Sumerian word for a hoe was AL, the text is built around words that contain the syllable "al."

EARLY SUMERIAN TEXTS

Lexical Texts

The earliest writing in the world first appears in the city of Uruk (modern Warka) and dates to approximately 3100. It is assumed, but cannot be proven, that these tablets were written in Sumerian. The earliest texts are economic and administrative in nature. They record the collection and redistribution of various items such as animals, grain, oil, and cloth and the management of personnel by economic institutions such as temples and large households. Very soon a new type of text makes its appearance: the lexical lists. These are lists of words arranged either by theme, such as professions or geographical names, or by the shape of the cuneiform signs. The didactic purpose of these lists is clear: they were the first textbooks of cuneiform, and although it may seem strange to the modern reader, one should perhaps refer to this production as the first written literature. These lexical texts have the longest history of any written genre because they continued to be copied, changed, and composed anew for more than three thousand years. (See the essay "Ancient Mesopotamian Lexicography" later in this section.)

Imaginative Writing

The earliest narrative and poetic texts date to the end of the Early Dynastic period (around 2500), and have been excavated primarily in two ancient cities: Fara (ancient Shuruppak) and Abu Salabikh (ancient name unknown). Smaller finds of literary tablets from this period have been made in such other cities in southern Mesopotamia as Nippur (modern Nuffar), Adab, Uruk,

Girsu (modern Tello), and Ur. They have also been found in Syria: at Mari (Tell Hariri) on the Euphrates and, farther west, at Ebla (modern Tell Mardikh).

The scribes of Early Dynastic compositions wrote elements basic to every sentence and the reader was expected to supply the remaining parts from memorized texts. Needless to say, this causes great difficulties for modern scholars, and the only texts that can be well understood are those that survived into later times, in copies made hundreds of years later. Another obstacle to the understanding of the earliest literature was a separate writing convention that was used alongside the standard form. In this type of writing, known as UD.GAL.NUN (the writing for the name of the god Enlil), the same signs as used in the standard system were read differently, and as a majority of these different readings are still unknown to us, we remain in the dark about the meaning of such texts.

Whatever the writing convention, not a single one of these early pieces of literature can be fully translated, although we do understand parts of them to various degrees. A small number of tablets contain magical charms against diseases. One text tells of the adventures of a legendary king, Lugalbanda of Uruk, who, in later times, becomes the subject of two long heroic poems. In another piece, a king gives proverbial advice to his son.

Most texts from the early period, however, treat mythological subjects. Some of these begin with cosmological introductions: "After the heavens were separated from the earth, after the earth was separated from the heavens"; or, "In those ancient days it was, in those ancient nights it was, in those ancient years, in those ancient years it was." One litany of short hymns to the major deities of Sumer begins with a longer invocation to the main god of the land, Enlil.

> O city that grows to the heavens, O (city) Nippur,
> Bond of the Heavens and the Earth, O Enlil,
> lord Nunamnir, lord whose command is unalterable . . . ! Enlil established his seed on the earth,
> and uttered the praises of the great gods.

The world slowly comes into being and is reshaped by divinities, as when Enlil takes matters into his own hands and personally separates earth from the sky. The gods of Sumer build temples, make love, and have children. Generations follow each other, grow up, and have their own adventures.

Although there is much that we do not understand, we can ascertain that, but for one very important text, the earliest Mesopotamian literary works were written in the Sumerian language. The one exception is a hymn to the sun-god, found in two versions: one from Shuruppak and one from the Syrian city of Ebla. This hymn was written in a Semitic language, perhaps in an early dialect of Akkadian, and is but a signal of another literature that still awaits discovery.

At Ebla there is a handful of other literary compositions in at least two Semitic languages or dialects; there can be no doubt that there were other such writings throughout the ancient Near East. One of the important discoveries of the last few decades has been the unearthing of third-millennium writing and the discovery of the wide spread of literature at that time. Although this vast area was politically fragmented and power resided in locally centered city-states, strong economic and cultural contacts resulted in many common features, and the use of a common writing system, with a shared school curriculum, was an important aspect of the culture of the time. No matter what dialect was spoken locally, the bureaucrats learned Sumerian and other written languages throughout Mesopotamia and Syria, and perhaps in other places. The common literary tradition was one element of this shared bureaucratic culture.

The Agade and Ur III Periods

Around the year 2300, Mesopotamia was united under the rule of one city and one dynasty, centered around the as-yet-undiscovered capital of Agade (Akkade, Akkad). Sargon, the founder of the Akkadian dynasty, and his successors ruled the land for slightly more than a century (2334–2154). This unprecedented centralization of power in Mesopotamia required a whole new propaganda apparatus: scribes were centrally trained and sent out to the provinces to run the local bureaucracies. Although one suspects that a whole new literature was created at this time, much of it in the Akkadian language, very little of it has survived.

After the fall of Sargon's empire and the ensuing disorder, a new government was able to dominate Mesopotamia from the city of Ur. The Third Dynasty of Ur (Ur III) ruled the land for 109 years (2112–2004). Its five kings—Ur-Namma (Ur-Nammu), Shulgi, Amar-Sin, Shu-Sin, and Ibbi-Sin—were celebrated in Sumerian poetry. Although we have found only a small number of literary texts from the period, the songs and poems from the court and temples of Ur were adapted and recopied by later generations of scribes, and therefore we have access to some of these compositions.

One should also mention the *Gudea Cylinders*, the combined texts of which provide the longest and most complex surviving early Sumerian literary work. Gudea was a ruler of the state of Lagash, who was contemporary with the first years of the Ur III Empire. The poem, inscribed on two large clay cylinders, describes how Ningirsu, the titular deity of Lagash, appeared to the king in a dream and commanded him to build the Eninnu, his temple, in the capital city of Girsu (modern Tello). The main portion of the text describes in great detail the fulfillment of that task, and is a source of much information on building techniques and on ritual practices of the time. The *Cylinders* are unique, and as far as we know, the poem never entered the school curriculum nor was it read again by future generations.

THE OLD BABYLONIAN CURRICULUM

The widest variety of Sumerian literary compositions is found in the Old Babylonian period, from the eighteenth century, when Sumerian was certainly no longer a living language. (See the next essay in this volume "Akkadian Literature: An Overview.") The best-known texts from this period were retrieved from the private houses of the cities of Nippur and Ur, although smaller finds have been made in other southern Mesopotamian cities, in Isin, Uruk, Larsa (modern Tell Senkereh), and elsewhere. As far as we know, there were no temple or private libraries in the south during this time. A different mixture of texts comes from the north of Babylonia, from cities such as Sippar (modern Abu Habba), Babylon, and Kish (modern Tell al-Uhaimir). Many literary pieces that are preserved in museums are of unknown origin.

Southern Babylonia

By far the largest number and the best-known of the texts are those from Nippur. As is the case with most southern literary texts of this period, the surviving tablets represent the curriculum of the scribal schools. All evidence seems to indicate that we have recovered the major part of the Old Babylonian school curriculum from the time of King Samsu-iluna of Babylon (1749–1712 BCE), when Nippur was abandoned for a few hundred years, and the exercises of the last two or three generations of pupils were preserved. We can retrace the steps that a schoolboy took on the road to literacy, and literature was a vital component of these studies. Schooling prepared the aspiring clerks and bureaucrats for membership in, and service to, the elite ranks of the state. The literature that they learned and recopied on clay was part of the indoctrination process.

Although there seems to have been a fairly uniform curriculum of instruction in Old Babylonian times, in the south at least, education was not controlled by the state. Most probably instruction took place in the houses of scribes and priests, who taught their own sons together with other neighborhood children. Literary texts such as *Schooldays* describe the learning environment of an institution called the EDUBA'A (EDUBBA) or "school," but it is quite possible that these are idealized representations and not realistic descriptions of Old Babylonian scribal education.

Classification: Ancient and Modern. Since the southern literature of the Old Babylonian period has been recovered to a large degree, a brief survey of its contents may best illustrate its range. We assign names such as hymn or epic to categories of text, but the reader should keep in mind that these designations are modern. The same is true of the titles of texts; the Mesopotamians usually referred to texts only by quoting all or part of a composition's first line. Indeed, the modern generic classification of Sumerian texts is a matter of intense debate that has yet to be resolved. As there are no native classifica-

tions to help us, we are forced to rely on Western schemes for the organization of texts, although one is always aware that these categories may be totally inappropriate for an ancient literature. Without descriptive labels it would be impossible to discuss the texts, and therefore the labels that we use are necessary, even if they are only heuristic devices that should not be taken too seriously. The ancient scribes left no system of their own, although some texts have subscripts that may indicate some of their thinking on the matter, even if we sometimes fail to recover a full consistency of usage.

There is an Early Dynastic collection of short hymns to deities from Abu Salabikh in which each section ends with "To divine so-and-so, let praise be!" Such endings are quite common in a variety of texts from later times, including hymns, epic tales, and other compositions. The expression "let praise be" (Sumerian ZÀ.Mĺ) was even borrowed by Akkadian as *sammû;* it clearly was thought to characterize certain texts. Yet, we would never group together the wide variety of compositions that end in this manner, and it is not at all certain that the ancients considered them to belong to one class.

Other endings are easier to understand, and seem to refer to an accompanying instrument, as in ÉR.ŠÈM.MA, "lament of the *shem* instrument," or BALAG, "(song of) the *balag* drum." There are also other descriptive phrases, such as ŠÌR.GIDA, "long song," or ÉR.ŠÀ.HUN.GÁ, "lament to pacify the heart (of an angry god)." Some subscripts such as KA.IMIM.MA used at the end of incantations, or ADAB and TIGI, types of hymns named after musical instruments, have predictable structural organization and are used in ways that conform to our expectations. Others, such as ŠÌR.NAM.ŠUB, are used for a variety of texts that we would not have gathered under a single label. The law codes provide a characteristic example.

There are three such Sumerian "codes," all of which antedate the famous Hammurabi (1792–1750) stela. All three are preserved in school copies. They were structured as royal inscriptions and were designed to be written on stone stela for public display. None is completely preserved. All three probably began with a historical introduction, followed by a long section of legal provisions, and then by an epilogue that included standard curses found in other monumental inscriptions. To the modern reader the term "legal code" invokes the concepts of prescriptive law and sanction, and of statutory law that has practical application in the courts. There is absolutely no evidence that these "codes" had any practical judicial function. They must be treated as abstract demonstrations of royal wisdom and justice, together with the hymns and other examples of the literature of the court.

Court Literature

Most of the texts that were adapted to school use in Old Babylonian times had been written much earlier. The process of sifting through and selecting materials for preservation was as important as the composition of new texts, and therefore a good portion of the literature concerned the earlier rulers of Mesopotamia. The roots of the central Sumerian Old Babylonian school tradition go back to the Ur III period. Shulgi, the second king and great consolidator of the dynasty, initiated a number of political, bureaucratic, and military reforms. In connection with these structural changes, he also probably restructured much of the school curriculum. He was one of the few Mesopotamian kings who claimed to be able to read and write. In one royal hymn he asserts: "Since I was a child I (studied in) the school, I learned the scribal art from the tablets of Sumer and Akkad, (and) among the children no one could write a tablet like I could!" (See the essay "Shulgi of Ur: King of a Neo-Sumerian Empire" in Part 5, Vol. II.)

It is impossible to evaluate the veracity of such statements, but it does seem that Shulgi and his successors paid particular attention to the use of Sumerian literature as cultural and political propaganda. We only have a handful of original literary pieces from the period, but one can see the effects of this royal patronage in the later tradition, which is built around works connected with the Ur III kings. The numerous royal hymns are the most obvious survival, but one can also point to the "debates," some of which include references to performance at the court of Ur; the love songs of King Shu-Sin; the *Curse of Agade*, which describes the fall of the earlier major state in Mesopotamia and was written in Ur III times; the "law code" of Ur-Namma; and

even a fragmentary text that may be a lullaby written for a son of Shulgi.

There are reasons to believe that the heroic tales of the legendary kings of Early Dynastic Uruk—Enmerkar, Lugalbanda, and Gilgamesh—may have been composed at this time. The Ur III kings came from Uruk and the queen mother maintained her palace there throughout much of the reign of the dynasty. The commemoration of these illustrious ancestors constituted part of the foundation myth of the royal family, and Shulgi repeatedly mentions his connections with his divine "brother," Gilgamesh. This legendary ruler of Uruk was the son of King Lugalbanda and the goddess Ninsun; after his death he became a judge in the Netherworld. During the middle of his reign, Shulgi resurrected a tradition first introduced by the Akkadian king Naram-Sin, and proclaimed himself divine. The descent from Gilgamesh thus provided an important element of the ideology of divine kingship; therefore, it is not surprising to find allusions to the court of Ur in some of the Gilgamesh compositions.

Other historical or historiographic texts were also studied and recopied by aspiring Old Babylonian scribes, including the Sumerian Kinglist, a tendentious and partially fictive list of dynasties from successive cities that supposedly ruled Mesopotamia since before the Flood, and the *Curse of Agade*, mentioned above.

The literary biographies of ancient kings, if one might call them that, were molded into specific patterns that contrasted certain views of kingship and human destiny. A short poem, *The Ballad of Heroes of Old*, which is known from Old Babylonian and later sources, summarized the ambivalent Mesopotamian attitude toward fame and historical achievement. Asking where were the heroic kings of legend, such as Gilgamesh, the poet seeks but one happy day of life and proposes to find solace in the domain of the beer goddess. A small number of short compositions on similar themes, one of which begins "nothing is (better) than the sweet life," were copied alongside the *Ballad*.

Hymnic Literature

The life of kings was filled with ritual and ceremony. Hymnic texts were composed for these occasions, and many of them were preserved by later generations. Ur-Namma, the first king of the Ur III dynasty, was one of the few Mesopotamian kings who was killed in battle. This was such an unusual occurrence that a long poem was composed to commemorate this sad and ominous event. His son Shulgi, one of the most famous rulers of early Mesopotamia, was celebrated in more than twenty-four royal hymns; a selection of his letters was excerpted for school use. The last king of Ur, Ibbi-Sin, was the subject of hymns, but as the kingdom deteriorated and fell during his reign, he was primarily remembered through a selection of possibly fictive letters that detailed the process of disintegration of the state, and in a long poetic lament that described the fall of Sumer and the capture of the king by enemies from Iran (*The Lamentation over the Destruction of Sumer and Ur*).

In the centuries that followed, kings of the succeeding dynasties of Isin, Larsa, Uruk, and Babylon commissioned similar royal hymns, right up to the last years of the Old Babylonian period, as more than 130 of them are known. None of them was more fervent than Ishme-Dagan, who reigned at Isin more than a century after Shulgi and who patterned his numerous royal hymns after the achievements of his predecessor. Poetic laments similar to the one described above were written during his reign.

The royal hymns are closely related to hymns to deities. Since many of the former are actually hymns to gods or goddesses addressed by or on behalf of kings, it is often difficult to make a distinction between the two categories. There are more than 120 divine hymns known at present. Most of the major gods and goddesses of the pantheon were so honored; in each case the author treated the deity as if he or she were one of the most important in the universe. There is also a smaller category of hymns extolling temples and the deities worshiped within them. Best known are a series of short hymns to the temples of Sumer and Akkad (the *Temple Hymns*); the *Hymn to the Ekur*, the temple of Enlil in Nippur, which was the major cult center of Sumer; and the *Kesh Temple Hymn*, which is already attested among the Early Dynastic texts from Abu Salabikh.

Personal lyrical poetry is absent in Sumerian literature. This is partly a function of the public nature of the texts we have at our disposal. Intimacy and public spectacle were often combined, as in the hymns that celebrated union between King Shu-Sin and his wife Kubatum. There are a number of short poems concerning the doomed love affair of the goddess Inanna and the divine shepherd Dumuzi that could be considered lyrical poems. They are often couched in dialogue form, with the two lovers exchanging highly erotic speeches. In these texts, date syrup, lettuce, and beer all serve as metaphors that are charged with sexual meaning. These erotic, sometimes playful, often humorous poems have a darker side, as they cannot be separated from other compositions such as *Dumuzi's Dream*, *Inanna's Descent*, and *Damu in the Netherworld*, which describe the betrayal and death of Dumuzi, Inanna's lover.

All of these poems concern kings and queens, gods and goddesses. Private individuals rarely make their appearance in Sumerian literature, and when they do, we do not know if they celebrated real individuals or idealized figures. Such is the case with two elegies that commemorate the death of Nannamu and Nawirtum, the parents of one Ludingira, who had ventured to a foreign land and had been summoned back to his ailing father's side. Quite different in tone is a highly metaphorical poem, in which another Ludingira—the name ("Man of a god") may be the Sumerian equivalent of "Everyman," albeit of high status—sends a messenger to his mother, Shat-Eshtar, in Nippur, and provides him with a series of descriptions by which he may recognize the woman. The son spares nothing in his praise and tells the envoy that "my mother is like a bright star of the horizon, a doe in the mountains, a morning star (shining even) at noon, a precious (jewel of) carnelian, a topaz from (the land of) Markhashi."

Mythmaking

There was a smaller group of narrative poems concerning deities that might be called myths. Although they differ from each other in story line and in cast of characters, many of them share a common theme: the problem of order and disorder in the universe. Typically, they begin with an anomalous situation in which the order of the world is either disturbed, as when the mythical

Anzu (or Zu) bird stole the Tablets of Destinies, or is not fully established, as in *Enki and the World Order,* which describes the creation of the cosmos and its allotment to individual gods. The action of the text leads to the reinstatement of order, or in the establishment of proper control under the rule of the hierarchy of deities. The mythological tales differ in detail and often present contradictory narratives. There are, to provide one salient example, two contemporaneous narratives that describe completely different stories of the courtship and marriage of Enlil, god of Nippur and of all Sumer, and the goddess Ninlil (*Enlil and Ninlil, I* and *II*). The two versions were undoubtedly read by the same eyes, at least in the Old Babylonian period, but it is characteristic of the culture that the contradictory narratives were not harmonized. Other texts seem to provide etiological explanations of the origin of culturally important elements such as fire (*Inanna and the Numun-Plant*) and grain (*How Grain Came to Sumer*).

Although there were hundreds of deities in the Sumerian pantheon, each city was presided over by a specific god or goddess, who dwelt in the central shrine of the town. On certain sacred occasions they would visit each other, and their statues were ceremoniously transported by boat to neighboring cities. There are mythological accounts of such visits, narrated in poetic form (for example, *Enki's Journey to Nippur* or *Nanna's Journey to Nippur*).

A myth that has attracted much contemporary attention is *Inanna's Descent to the Netherworld;* it serves as a good example of the kind of narrative one encounters in these myths. Inanna, who dwells in the heavens as goddess of war and carnal love, impetuously sets out for the Netherworld, the domain of her sister Ereshkigal. As she passes each of the Netherworld's seven gates, she is made to give up one item of her clothing or jewelry, each representing one aspect of her power. She reaches the Netherworld's core bereft of clothing, hence powerless, a sack of skin hung out to dry. Her return to the land of the living depends on finding a god to take her place in the Netherworld. Inanna searches among the gods but can locate only Dumuzi, her lover. After vainly trying to escape his fate, Dumuzi is captured by demons and

dragged to the Netherworld. There are variant recensions to the end of the tale as well as separate tales about Dumuzi's capture (*Dumuzi's Dream* and *Damu in the Netherworld*).

The sense of order is central to all Sumerian literature, and even if it is most explicitly set out in the myths, it is to be found in almost every kind of composition. Most characteristically, it is expressed by the notion of ME, a Sumerian word that is notoriously difficult to pin down. It denotes the proper way of being in the world. It can apply to things and to actions, particularly to rites, as they must be done in the exact proper fashion. The MES are, in turn, closely connected to a Tablet of Destinies, which could not be altered even by the gods. The MES and the Tablet of Destinies (that is, the physical embodiments of destiny) had their proper place, and myths were written about the effects of their displacement. In one such text (*Inanna and Enki*) it is Inanna who steals the MES from Enki; in another, the lion-headed eagle Anzu flies off with the Tablet. The return of the MES and the Tablet is the stuff of the ensuing narratives and of the new reality that is created as order is restored to the universe.

This same sense of proper balance is found in other parts of Sumerian literature. While most royal texts extol the might and wisdom of the king and celebrate the institution of kingship, others appear to do quite the opposite. The poem of the death of Ur-Namma, the literary letters concerning the last days of the house of Ur, and the *Curse of Agade* and the *Lamentation over the Destruction of Sumer and Ur,* which describe in vivid language the fall of the empires of Sargon and Shulgi, all seem to go against the tendency to praise kings and their states. Seen in context, however, these sad tales of the deaths of kings serve to delimit the boundaries of royal power and to establish the proper semantic definition of kingship. Since even the gods themselves were beholden to an abstract notion of destiny and order, nothing less could be expected of kings, even if some of them were considered divine.

Other Literary Forms

Among the other texts that were studied in the Old Babylonian schools were more than twenty collections of short proverbial stories and sayings, and a much smaller group of riddles. The young scribes also studied collections of older letters. Although normal correspondence by this time was carried on in Akkadian, around forty Sumerian letters were preserved among the literary texts. The largest group originated, if we are to take them at face value, in the chancellery of the Ur III kings; a smaller group was ascribed to kings of the succeeding dynasty of Isin. In addition, there were miscellaneous letters and a few odd items such as a public announcement of the loss of an inscribed cylinder seal and a copy of an old votive inscription. We have no way of establishing which, if any, of these older royal letters were authentic; their language and written style were certainly modernized in Old Babylonian times, but it is also possible that some, if not all, of them were written as school exercises.

These elaborate Sumerian letters gave way to a new genre—the poetic letter of petition, sometimes referred to as letter-prayers. These prayers and petitions to gods and kings, addressed as if they were letters, were deposited before statues with the hope that they would be answered. We have three Akkadian letters from the period, addressed from a goddess to the chief administrator of her temple. It is possible that this represents one of the ways in which the deities answered letters of petition. One of the most elaborate of these was addressed by Ninshatapada, high priestess in the city of Durum and daughter of King Sin-kashid of Uruk, to Rim-Sin (1822–1763), the king of Larsa who had conquered her city.

Among the major textual types, one must refer to the debate poems in which idealized characters such as Summer and Winter, Silver and Copper, or Cattle and Grain, exchange self-praise, insults, and taunts. These compositions are an invaluable source of information on the formal attitudes of the Mesopotamian poets toward their culture and the world that surrounded them.

Another important category of texts was the incantation, or magical charm. These were recited to help heal sick persons; to purify cultic objects; to ward off evil demons, pests, and dangerous animals; or to undo the effects of bad omens. Because of their complex poetic tone and rich metaphorical imagery, these compositions led a double life: they were used in rituals and also copied in the schools as literary examples. Such incantations are already found among the Early Dynastic texts from Abu Salabikh and Ebla and were copied or created down to the very end of Mesopotamian culture. From there, they came into the literature of Diaspora Jews living in Babylonia.

LITERATURE IN NORTHERN BABYLONIA

In contrast with the southern Mesopotamian cities, the northern ones such as Babylon, Sippar, and Kish were not abandoned during the eighteenth century, but continued to be parts of the Old Babylonian kingdom until its end in 1595. There is some evidence that their populations expanded with the influx of people from the south. Many Sumerian literary tablets from the north have survived, albeit few are from modern controlled excavations, and therefore we know little about their origin. From the published materials it would appear that texts from north and south differed substantially. In contrast to the wide variety of texts known from the Nippur schools, in the north we have primarily Sumerian compositions that were used in cultic settings. Texts such as laments, hymns, and prayers dominate, and although there are also examples of compositions known also from the south, we often find substantial differences when comparing these versions.

Two characteristics stand out from among the northern materials: syllabic spellings and the use of a literary dialect of Sumerian known as EME.SAL. Of necessity, EME.SAL texts often used the syllabic orthography, so the two phenomena are related. Syllabic spellings were used to indicate more exactly the pronunciation of words. Thus, the word GAL (big) would normally be written with one cuneiform character, but in this orthography it could be expressed by a sequence of two signs: "ga" + "al." The EME.SAL dialect differed in pronunciation from the main Sumerian literary tongue. For example, in this dialect, the god Enki was Amanki. The term EME.SAL means literally "thin tongue" and it may have referred to the way in which these texts were pronounced aloud. It was reserved for texts used in the liturgy by a special caste of priests who were called in Sumerian GALA (Akkadian *kalû*), and for the direct speech of women or goddesses in other literary compositions. In the past, this was sometimes translated as "women's tongue," but there is no basis for this rendering. (See also "Ancient Mesopotamian Lexicography" later in this section.)

These features are also found in certain southern texts, but they are not as common as in those from the north. The differences in the literatures of the two regions may be explained in a variety of ways. One may posit that the predominance of liturgical texts in the north was a result of the abandonment of the south; as priests migrated upstream, they may have been forced to commit to clay the liturgy that had hitherto been transmitted from generation to generation mainly by oral means. The disruption of the normal workings of apprenticeship and of the passing down of tradition from generation to generation may have pressured them to write texts down and to assure proper pronunciation by more extensive use of syllabic writings.

SUMERIAN LITERATURE AFTER THE OLD BABYLONIAN PERIOD

After the end of the Old Babylonian period, we have hardly any Mesopotamian literary texts for close to three hundred years. This may be due to accident of discovery, to unknown social and historical forces, or to both. By this time the cuneiform script and written forms of the Akkadian language were in use throughout western Asia, and therefore we can study Mesopotamian literature from texts that were used in the Hittite capital of Khattusha (modern Boğazköy) in Anatolia, in Ugarit (modern Ras Shamra) on the Syrian coast, in Emar farther inland in Syria, and even in Egypt. The creative effort was now clearly centered around literature in the Akkadian language, but selected Sumerian texts remained in circulation. Lexical texts, crucial for teaching the cuneiform script, were retained, as

were many incantations, prayers, and liturgical compositions. A small number of myths and other kinds of texts continued to be studied and copied. Most conspicuously, however, the core legacy of the Ur III tradition—the royal hymns, epics, and other historiographic compositions—were no longer part of the written tradition.

The end of the second and the whole of the first millennium were times of ordering and restructuring of the literature of Mesopotamia. The temple and palace scribes of Assyria and Babylonia collected and edited the rich literary legacy of the land. By then there were hardly any monolingual Sumerian texts; bilingual versions were the norm, and standardization was the rule. In the restructuring of the literary corpus, many older Sumerian compositions were discarded, and those that were preserved were supplied with Akkadian translations. The most common format of bilingual texts was interlinear; that is, each Sumerian line was followed by a rather literal translation, sometimes indented and written in a smaller hand. There were also other ways of doing this: a line could be divided in half and the Akkadian translation was inserted in the middle, often bounded by small double cuneiform wedges that resemble our own quotation marks. Very few monolingual Sumerian texts are found from the later periods, and these are primarily incantations. It was also not standard practice to circulate the Akkadian translations without the Sumerian originals, and only a handful of such one-language examples are known.

There remained regional differences, and we often find that redactions differed in details between scribal centers. The owners and directors of private, temple, and palace libraries went to great pains to create authoritative redactions of individual compositions, often collating manuscripts from different cities in order to establish a complete text. The best-known efforts at such standardization were undoubtedly those carried out by the scribes who compiled the Nineveh libraries of Assurbanipal (668–627), one of the last kings of Assyria. Since the libraries were destroyed soon after his reign, when Nineveh was sacked, the tablets that were collected there had a larger impact on modern scholarship than they had on knowledge in antiquity.

MESOPOTAMIA UNDER FOREIGN RULE

The political end of Assyria around 614 and of Babylonia a century later did not put an end to Mesopotamian literature; the complex cultures of the land outlasted the state structures. Scholars continued their redactional activities under the Persian, Seleucid, and Parthian kings, primarily in the cities of Uruk and Babylon. Many of the Sumerian and bilingual texts from Babylon, some of which were copied into the first century BCE, were liturgical songs that were the domain of the lamentation priests and were found in the private collections of priestly families. Priests and rich individuals copied or commissioned the copying of literary texts for deposition as devotional objects in temples. Certain texts were explicitly copied "for singing" during various festivals, ceremonies, and rituals, and some bore additional notations to guide musical performance. There can be no doubt that only the Sumerian was pronounced aloud, and that the Akkadian translations, probably equally foreign by this time, were transmitted only by the requirements of tradition.

Mesopotamian literature survived into later times. The last known dated cuneiform tablet is an astronomical text from 75 CE Babylon. There may be later texts however. There is a handful of literary exercises, including Sumerian magical charms, that have cuneiform on one side and phonetic Greek transcriptions on the other. It has been suggested recently that these may date as late as the second century, and are but a small indication of the survival of Mesopotamian traditions into late antiquity.

This most ancient of all literatures was read and recopied by scribes throughout the Near East for almost three thousand years. The recovery of this intellectual achievement is one of the great scholarly adventures of our time, and we are only now beginning to appreciate the richness of the universal legacy that the Mesopotamian scribes unknowingly left us. By chance, they wrote on clay, a material that has proved more durable than bronze, paper, or papyrus. Because texts were recopied for generations, many literary compositions have been preserved in more than one copy, and therefore we can restore broken tablets with the preserved portions of duplicate copies. The unexcavated mounds of the Near East and the neglected storerooms of modern museums provide, and will continue to provide, new cuneiform tablets containing works of literature, and therefore the history of Sumerian literature is constantly being revised as new materials become available.

BIBLIOGRAPHY

There are very few up-to-date English translations of Sumerian literary texts. The difficulties that we still have with the lexical and grammatical aspects of the language and the radical differences between Sumerian and English poetic diction have made it difficult for scholars to offer popular translations without learned commentary. One recent exception to this is THORKILD JACOBSEN, *The Harps That Once . . . : Sumerian Poetry in Translation* (1987).

There is no convenient listing of translations of Sumerian literature, but one can consult the bibliography in *The Sumerian Dictionary of the University Museum of the University of Pennsylvania*, vol. 2 (1984), and in MARIE-LOUISE THOMSEN, *The Sumerian Language: An Introduction to Its History and Grammatical Structure* (1984).

Sumerian Texts in Translation

The most reliable translations are to be found in scholarly editions of the cuneiform texts. We are only beginning to reconstruct the full range of Sumerian literature and such editions are a necessary, if sometimes tedious, foundation for any serious research. They may be difficult to read for the uninitiated, but they are an invaluable source of information for scholars and nonscholars alike. Following is a selected bibliography of modern renderings of Sumerian texts into English:

The works of Enkheduanna are discussed in WILLIAM W. HALLO and J. VAN DIJK, *The Exaltation of Inanna* (1968); her other compositions are edited by ÅKE W. SJÖBERG and EUGEN BERGMANN, *The Collection of the Sumerian Temple Hymns and the Keš Temple Hymn* (1969), and by ÅKE W. SJÖBERG, "In-nin šàgur₄-ra: A Hymn to the Goddess Inanna by the en-Priestess Enheduanna," *Zeitschrift für Assyriologie* 65 (1975).

Old Babylonian texts dealing with earlier kings are to be found in SAMUEL NOAH KRAMER, "The Death of Ur-Nammu and His Descent to the Netherworld," *Journal of Cuneiform Studies* 21 (1967), and "Uₛ-a a-ù-a: A Sumerian Lullaby," in *Studi in onore di Eduardo Volterra*, vol. 6 (1969), a lullaby for a son of Shulgi; and THORKILD JACOBSEN, *The Sumerian King List* (1939).

Hymns

The best discussion of the royal hymns of the Ur III kings, with editions of three such texts, is in JACOB KLEIN, *Three Šulgi Hymns: Sumerian Royal Hymns Glorifying King Šulgi of Ur* (1981). Royal and divine hymns, with examples of the latter, are analyzed by DANIEL D. REISMAN, "Two Neo-Sumerian Royal Hymns" (Ph.D. diss., University of Pennsylvania, 1969). For two very different examples of divine hymns, consult WOLFGANG HEIMPEL, "The Nanshe Hymn," *Journal of Cuneiform Studies* 33 (1981) and MIGUEL CIVIL, "A Hymn to the Beer Goddess and a Drinking Song," in *Studies Presented to A. Leo Oppenheim* (1964).

Myths

Editions of Sumerian myths are found in CARLOS BENITO, " 'Enki and Ninmah' and 'Enki and the World Order' " (Ph.D. diss., University of Pennsylvania, 1969); BENDT ALSTER, *Dumuzi's Dream: Aspects of Oral Poetry in a Sumerian Myth* (1972) and " 'Ninurta and the Turtle': UET 6/1, 2," *Journal of Cuneiform Studies* 24 (1972). MIGUEL CIVIL, "The Sumerian Flood Story," in *Atra-hasīs: The Babylonian Story of the Flood*, edited by W. G. LAMBERT and A. R. MILLARD (1969); JERROLD S. COOPER, *The Return of Ninurta to Nippur* (1978); THORKILD JACOBSEN and SAMUEL NOAH KRAMER, "The Myth of Inanna and Bilulu," *Journal of Near Eastern Studies* 12 (1953); SAMUEL NOAH KRAMER, *Enki and Ninhursag: A Sumerian "Paradise" Myth* (1945), "Inanna and the Numun-Plant: A New Sumerian Myth," in *The Biblical World: Essays in Honor of Cyrus H. Gordon* (1980), and "The Marriage of Martu," in *Bar-Ilan Studies in Assyriology* (1990); and GENE G. GRAGG, "The Fable of the Heron and the Turtle," *Archiv für Orientforschung* 24 (1973).

Other Literary Forms

The two versions of the courtship and marriage of the deities Enlil and Ninlil can be found in MIGUEL CIVIL, "Enlil and Ninlil: The Marriage of Sud," *Journal of the American Oriental Society* 103 (1983), and JERROLD S. COOPER, review of *Enlil und Ninlil: Ein sumerischer Mythos aus Nippur*, by HERMANN BEHRENS, *Journal of Cuneiform Studies* 32 (1980).

The myth of Inanna's descent has been treated by WILLIAM R. SLADEK, "Inanna's Descent to the Netherworld" (Ph.D. diss., Johns Hopkins University, 1974). For editions of two examples of divine journeys and

a discussion of other texts see ABDUL-HADI AL-FOUADI, "Enki's Journey to Nippur: The Journeys of the Gods" (Ph.D. diss., University of Pennsylvania, 1969), and A. J. FERRARA, *Nanna-Suen's Journey to Nippur* (1973).

For translations and discussions of literary letters, see FADHIL ABDULWAHID ALI, "Sumerian Letters: Two Collections from the Old Babylonian Schools" (Ph.D. diss., University of Pennsylvania, 1964), and PIOTR MICHALOWSKI, "The Royal Correspondence of Ur" (Ph.D. diss., Yale University, 1976).

The letter-prayer of Ninshatapada is translated by WILLIAM W. HALLO, "Royal Correspondence of Larsa: III. The Princess and the Plea," in *Marchands, diplomates, et empereurs: Études sur la civilisation mésopotamienne offertes à Paul Garelli* (1991). City laments are found in JERROLD S. COOPER, *The Curse of Agade* (1983); PIOTR MICHALOWSKI, *The Lamentation over the Destruction of Sumer and Ur* (1989); and STEVE TINNEY, *The Nippur Lament* (1993).

The three extant law "codes" are dealt with by J. J. FINKELSTEIN, "The Laws of Ur-Nammu," *Journal of Cuneiform Studies* 22 (1969); FRANCIS R. STEELE, *The Code of Lipit-Ishtar* (1948); and PIOTR MICHALOWSKI and C. B. F. WALKER, "A New Sumerian Law Code," in *DUMU-E₂-DUB-BA-A: Studies in Honor of Åke W. Sjöberg* (1989).

Most of the proverb collections remain unedited. For a discussion and translations of a group of such texts see EDMUND GORDON, *Sumerian Proverbs: Glimpses of Everyday Life in Ancient Mesopotamia* (1959).

For riddles see MIGUEL CIVIL, "Sumerian Riddles: A Corpus," *Aula Orientalis* 5 (1987).

Examples of dialogs, debates, and taunts are BENDT ALSTER and HERMAN VANSTIPHOUT, "Lahar and Ashnan—Presentation and Analysis of a Sumerian Disputation," in *Acta Sumerologica* 9 (1987); and ÅKE SJÖBERG, " 'He Is a Good Seed of a Dog' and 'Engardu, the Fool,' " *Journal of Cuneiform Studies* 24 (1972).

For descriptions and celebrations of scribal education, see SAMUEL NOAH KRAMER, *Schooldays: A Sumerian Composition Relating to the Education of Scribe* (1949), and ÅKE SJÖBERG, "In Praise of the Scribal Art," *Journal of Cuneiform Studies* 24 (1972).

The "Message of Lu-dingira" has been studied by MIGUEL CIVIL, "The 'Message of Lú-Dingira to his Mother' and a Group of Akkado-Hittite 'Proverbs,' " *Journal of Near Eastern Studies* 23 (1964), and, more recently, by M. CIĞ and S. N. KRAMER, "The Ideal Mother: A Sumerian Portrait," *Belleten Türk Tarih Kurumu* 40 (1976).

The elegies for the parents of another Ludingira were translated by SAMUEL NOAH KRAMER, *Two Elegies on a Pushkin Museum Tablet: A New Sumerian Literary Genre* (1960).

Many liturgical texts, including late bilingual versions, are to be found in: MARK E. COHEN, *Sumerian Hymnology, The Eršemma* (1981), and in his *The Canonical Lamentations of Ancient Mesopotamia* (1988).

For a modern rendition of a representative group of incantations see MARKHAM J. GELLER, *Forerunners to Udug-hul: Sumerian Exorcistic Incantations* (1985).

SEE ALSO **The History of Ancient Mesopotamia: An Overview** (Part 5, Vol. II); **Myth and Mythmaking in Sumer and Akkad** (Part 8, Vol. III); **Akkadian Literature: An Overview** (Part 9, Vol. IV); and **Epic Tales from Ancient Sumer: Enmerkar, Lugalbanda, and Other Cunning Heroes** (Part 9, Vol. IV).

Akkadian Literature: An Overview

JEAN BOTTÉRO

WHEN WE SPEAK OF Mesopotamian literature, we should remember that it was not, as in our own time, a domain easily accessible to all. Both reading and writing were confined, in principle, just to the guild of the literate and of the scribe. The contents of this literature might have filtered down gradually to the public by word of mouth. However, it is safe to say that most of the population, including individuals of high rank, conveyed literature by word of mouth. This oral tradition paralleled the written one, but about it we are almost totally in the dark.

GROWTH AND DECLINE OF AKKADIAN LITERATURE

Whatever may be said of the scattered examples of writing composed before the middle of the third millennium—votive inscriptions, compositions for exorcists, fragments of myths, not to speak of a large sampling of "lists," plausibly the oldest form—as a collective enterprise, Mesopotamian literature written in Akkadian, a Semitic language, was likely born during the Akkad (Akkade, Agade) Dynasty at the latest (around 2330–2200 BCE). Even though the Akkad Empire quickly proved fragile and ephemeral, it is hardly conceivable that so mighty a political entity, with Semites at its helm, could have been established without advancing the cause of the language spoken by the new rulers. What we call Akkadian literature originated in the activity of a court or temple "academy" that entertained themes and topics somewhat removed from daily life, recording them for diffusion within its own circles in its own time.

Of this most ancient literature written in the Akkadian language, practically nothing has survived, and today we can scarcely reconstruct its early manifestation. After the fall of the Akkad Empire and especially during the Third Dynasty of Ur (around 2100–2000), Sumerian literature not only enjoyed a veritable renaissance but apparently also attained its peak of invention and perfection. Only after the integration into the population of a new wave of Semitic Amorites, and after the creation of a solid and durable political structure by an Amorite, Hammurabi of Babylon (circa 1792–1750), were Semitic speakers given a second opportunity to create literature. By then Sumerian was more than likely extinct as a living language and speakers of diverse dialects of Semitic had become the sole occupiers of Mesopotamia. From then on it was possible for Mesopotamians to compose diverse types of literary works in Akkadian. Fairly quickly they wrote exclusively in that language, turning Sumerian into an erudite jargon accessible to a progressively shrinking class of lettered scholars who, even when they learned or understood it, reduced it to the level of our "schoolboy Latin" or used it to draft pieces of very little merit.

These were the early years of a revitalized creative effort, and even if time has so far been stingy in delivering to us examples of these renewed beginnings, we may nevertheless say that literature of Akkadian character truly began during the Old Babylonian period, around the eighteenth century BCE. After that it continued to develop without interruption, even broadening, like a river swollen by successive tributaries, during Mesopotamia's long history. After 1500 it developed in accord with the partition of the land into two rival realms: Babylonia in the south and Assyria in the north. Around the middle of the first millennium, Akkadian in its turn was supplanted in current usage by Aramaic. From that moment, as with ancient Sumerian, Akkadian became no more than a language for the erudite, the scholarly, and lettered individuals, none of whom could manipulate it with the resilience needed to compose truly original literature. Rather, these academics hardly did more than tirelessly recopy and reread those texts inherited from the past, gaining much satisfaction from merely commenting on the portions of their legacy that had become obsolete or obscure.

The fundamental fact of Mesopotamia's literary history is that after an initial millennium of preponderant, if not almost exclusive, use of Sumerian, there followed, timidly during the third millennium, then boldly and without reserve from the eighteenth century on, a literary production in the Akkadian language which, over fifteen centuries, became increasingly vast and progressively exclusive. We must confront this truth if we wish to recapture as much as possible this literature in its proper context. We must also confront a double issue it forces on us: Following upon a rich and diverse Sumerian-based literature, in what ways was literature in Akkadian influenced or affected by a vision and rhetoric that is distinctive to speakers of Sumerian? On the other hand, at what point was it liberated from its predecessor, thereby developing traits and characteristics that were unique to Akkadian culture, by its choice of genres or models as much as by its stylistic and ideological treatment?

For lack of sufficient or complete documentation, it is hardly possible in our day to offer a true history of Mesopotamian literature. To answer the twofold question we have just posed, it may be useful first to compile a brief inventory, by category, of Akkadian works that fit the definition of literature offered above. We can then describe how they differed from each other and define the vision specific to their authors. (See the preceding chapter, "Sumerian Literature: An Overview.")

A CATALOG OF GENRES

Akkadian Literature with Sumerian Prototypes

Translation of Akkadian literary texts into the Sumerian language seems to have occurred rarely and relatively late in Mesopotamian history. As examples we cite the *Poem on the Return of Marduk to Babylon*, written under Nebuchadnezzar (Nebuchadrezzar) I (1126–1105), and doubtless stemming from an even later period, the short "Prologue" to the large *Treatise on Astrology*. Beginning in the first half of the second millennium, Sumerian documents were rendered into Semitic Akkadian, most often on the same tablet interlinearly, giving us what are wrongly labeled "bilinguals." Sometimes a translation was prepared separately, on a tablet of its own, as with the second part of the Sumerian *Gilgamesh, Enkidu, and the Netherworld.* This particular translation was attached to the Nineveh version of the *Epic of Gilgamesh*, appearing as its twelfth and last tablet. A quantity of literary pieces in all genres was thus translated, including myths and legends, even "archaic" examples (such as *Enlil and Ninlil*, LUGAL.E, *Lugalbanda*, and the *Sumerian Legend of Sargon*), and cultic songs and poems (such as diverse *Hymns to the Great Sanctuaries*, the *Hymn to the Goddess Nanshe*, and *The Exaltation of Inanna*). Also translated were orations and formulas attributed to exorcists (for example, the Sumerian UDUG.ḤUL.A.KAM) (Akkadian *utukkū lemnūtu*) and a number of other pieces, often of lesser caliber, that exorcists would recite over many generations). Finally, we may include in a broad category of learned texts such "academic" fragments as the famous *Examinations* (to cite just one), and didactic pieces as *Advice of a Father to His Son*, Proverbs, and Fables.

What controlled the choice of literature to be translated from Sumerian was a phenomenon no doubt akin to the process by which we label selected inherited literature as classics. There was the feeling that what should be translated from the Sumerian were the most notable, or the most important, works of the ancestors; by taste or usage, such documents had also become indispensable to a program of training future generations of learned scholars. (Later on, in fact, the same process of "canonization" would be applied to the literary production originally created in Akkadian.) A large part of Sumerian literature in this way become accessible to users of the Akkadian language, and its preservation could and did offer Akkadian speakers models for ideas, vehicles for composition, and a repertoire for literary expression.

Despite this reliance on Sumerian prototypes, Akkadian literature nevertheless proved itself no less original, above all in the choice of genres that it exploited. That Akkadian writers retained an interest in a certain number of readily available literary categories was, given the level of the culture and the mentality of the country, without doubt because eliminating them would have risked losing the means of expression and reflection fundamental to the vision they had of their world.

We tackle first the religious dimension, which continued to dominate practically all of existence. How could anyone turn away from the "calculating imagination" we call myths? As constructs they alone were disposed to answer the great questions about the universe and how it functions, about human beings and why they exist, about the supernatural and its constant internal disturbances and interference with the course of earthly events. From such speculation, we get the mythological works in Akkadian, sometimes rather freely transposed from parallel works in Sumerian. Thus the Akkadian *Descent of Ishtar into the Netherworld* is adapted from the Sumerian *Inanna in the Netherworld*, and the Akkadian *Ishtar and Ishullanu* is a rendering from the Sumerian *Inanna and Shukaletuda*. But often we have compositions that are more or less original to Akkadian. In addition to myths regarding the creation of gods, the cosmos, or human beings, they include *The Flood, The Great Dragon, Labbu, Agushaya, Anzu, Nergal and Ereshkigal,* and the *Poem of Erra*.

In all religions that are based on diverse anthropomorphic manifestations of the gods,

people communicated with the deity either officially, through solemn addresses and with songs that exalt their glory or beseech their assistance; or individually, by direct appeal for relief, for deliverance from the ills and the misfortunes that plague existence. Accordingly, the ancient euchological tradition—labeled "hymnic" or "incantatory" but also more accurately "exorcistic"—was kept up and developed naturally in the Akkadian language. For now we cite only the exquisite Old Babylonian *Hymn to Ishtar,* stemming from the reign of King Ammiditana of Babylon (about 1683–1647). With time, this particular mode of communicating with the gods took on diverse manifestations and acquired a more fundamental inflection, as we will explain. For unknown reasons another channel to the divine, itself launched by the Sumerians, retained its popularity. It consisted of letters written by individuals, often rulers, to a specific god. Additionally, Akkadian writers continued to exploit a vein of narratives and legends that had as subjects mortals whose destiny the gods surreptitiously guided. *Etana* is one such narrative, and *Adapa* is another. The *Epic of Gilgamesh,* more grandiose and magnificent than either, stands out among them all. On a less imaginative level, the Akkadians remained somewhat faithful, at least initially, to the general format of the Sumerian votive, dedicatory, and commemorative inscriptions.

Several other Sumerian literary models likewise persisted in Akkadian, in particular the polemical "disputations": two "beings" belonging to opposite sides in the same animal, plant, or object category clash in a contest in which each praises its own virtue and quality but also occasionally belittles those of its adversary, using exclusively utilitarian and economic arguments. *The Tamarisk Against the Palm* is one such disputation.

Sumerian Literature with Limited Akkadian Continuity

In the aforesaid categories of literature, there was an undisputed continuity between the Sumerian and Akkadian traditions. However, from the outset to some degree, and more definitely with time, Akkadian authors ignored or eliminated a number of themes and models familiar to the Sumerians, probably because such topics dealt with subjects no longer corresponding to the way Akkadians viewed their universe. For this reason we no longer find voyages and mutual visits of the gods as the subject of myths; for Sumerians such narratives provided explanations for holy places or for rituals, but they must have lost their meaning in an Akkadian theology that was becoming increasingly universalistic and in a cult that was vastly redesigned. (See the chapter on "Theologies, Priests, and Worship in Ancient Mesopotamia" in Part 8, Vol. III.) Thus the *Hymns to the Sanctuaries* lost their significance as soon as religious evolution began to depersonalize sacred places and sacred objects so that only the gods were considered holders of supernatural power and therefore worthy of supplication. Similarly, the supernatural and divine character of ruling kings, which seems to have crystallized in Mesopotamia around the end of the third millennium, rather quickly receded before the conviction (perhaps more congenial to Semitic religiosity) that transcendence appertains solely to divinities. If we still find examples of royal hymns dedicated to Hammurabi and to his immediate successor, Samsuiluna (circa 1749–1712), these are the last echoes of a genre that had a peculiar success in Sumerian literature.

With the new political regime in which the older city-states no longer had autonomy or true political importance, power was centralized once and for all. The famous Sumerian *Lamentations*, composed to deplore as well as justify the defeat and loss of predominance of one city-state or another, inevitably went out of fashion. (See "Lamentations and Prayers in Sumer and Akkad" in Part 8, Vol. III.) A similar change in political conditions accounts for the disappearance of the largely fictional and apologetic historical works, such as the famous *Sumerian Kinglist*, which was actually intended to recall the successive transfer of power from one city-state to another, always to the benefit of the most recent center of power. It may be arguable that such lists were replaced by the epic narratives that glorified the conquest of power now not by cities but by kingdoms and empires, through the warlike deeds of kings who felled enemies as well as rivals. They include the epics of *Zimri-Lim of Mari* during the Old Babylonian period and, a few centuries later, of *Adad-nirari* and

Tukulti-Ninurta in late second millennium Assyria. Although such epics, heroic in inspiration and elevated in style, may have been amplifications of an old Sumerian legacy, of which *Gilgamesh and Akka* is a good example, it is equally possible that these creations may have emerged from inner explorations within the Akkadian literary traditions that are not yet fully displayed in the extant documentation. (See also "The Deeds of Ancient Mesopotamian Kings" later in this volume.)

The movement away from Sumerian literary traditions may also be charged to the diminishing prestige and shrinking privileges of the Akkadian scribal profession. Over time this development led Akkadian writers away from speculations that were self-absorbed or that gave them opportunity to brilliantly display their erudition and imagination, culture and spirit: essays, puzzles and riddles, word plays, portraits, and proverbs.

Literature Particular to Akkadian

To counterbalance this desertion of and lack of interest in some types of Sumerian compositions, in the course of time a number of recast or entirely new literary models began to appear that were written solely in Akkadian. They included topics and material that the writers of Sumerian never entertained, indeed could not have imagined in their time, given their level of culture and capacity for reflection.

The most unexpected, surprising, and opulent works, divergent in compass from Sumerian antecedents, with their narrower sense of time and more limited goals, are the Akkadian works of broad cultural synthesis. They include the myths *Atrakhasis*, or *The Ultra-Wise; Enūma Elish* or *The Creation Myth;* and the *Poem of Erra.* In a category entirely its own is the *Epic of Gilgamesh.* Because they are so vital to our topic, we will return to them soon.

Compositions about Gods and Their Worship In the category of works celebrating the gods, aside from songs, canticles, and numerous humns that more often than not cultivate inherited Sumerian prototypes (see above), there appeared, for the first time, long pieces in a liturgical style. Such pieces give the impression of being reworked compositions, scholarly in character, with a lyricism that seems borrowed rather than fresh, as is only too often the case in Mesopotamian poetry. However, such works—dedicated to deities who became objects of intense devotion, often late in Mesopotamian history—could be strongly lyrical and very personal in idiom, vocabulary, or imagery. Among these are works dedicated to Ishtar, Marduk, Nabu, and Shamash.

On the subject of the gods and, more specifically, how they were worshiped, rituals are examples of a literature in Akkadian that was totally unknown previously, presumably because the topics they considered had been left to the oral tradition. These ritual texts record with precision the diverse operations that occurred during liturgical ceremonies, whether ordinary or singular, daily or festival. They also cite prayers and hymns by name and occasionally include complete texts of the relevant prayers. The Akkadian rituals preserved in writing were not only of official cults in honor of the gods but also of sacramental cults that were carried out for the benefit of the worshipers. (See below.) In a distinct subdivision of this category, we should include the menologies and hemerologies, respectively monthly and daily calendars of activities that regulated the spiritual and ritual observances of the faithful.

Literature on "Wisdom" Themes   Also new in Akkadian literature were a number of works couched as essays, reflections, or theological discussions. Commonly presented as dialogues but occasionally also as monologues, they were the product of a sustained religious maturation that generated issues beyond the capacity of the inherited mythology to describe or solve. Among the more famous examples of this literature are the *Dialogue of a Man with His God* from the Old Babylonian period and, from a later date, *In Praise of the Lord of Wisdom* (often cited by its first Akkadian words, *Ludlul bēl nēmeqi*) and the *Babylonian Theodicy*. Belonging to this category, but displaying its own unique character, if not also ambiguity, is the *Dialogue of Pessimism*. (See "The Contemplative Life in the Ancient Near East" later in this volume.)

Literature about Rulers   Novelties abound also in official literature that treats earthly

power, the communal good, and the life of the country as subjects but uses the king as emblem of power over civilization. The inherited "royal inscription" style, which was used to commemorate briefly the main accomplishments of a ruler, in the course of time developed into long and sometimes detailed narratives of military campaigns and battlefield successes as well as of nonmilitary achievements including the building of temples, palaces, and major monuments. In Assyria, late in the second millennium, this literary type evolved into what we call the *Annals*, in which the expeditions and conquests of the king are recounted, year by year.

Based loosely on the above-mentioned *Sumerian Kinglist*, but with a completely different spirit and purpose, are the *Chronicles*. These compositions gather and place in chronological order the events of successive reigns that were deemed important. Because the breadth and contents of compilations depended on the perspectives of the writers, these chronicles vary in content, sometimes going far back into the past in search of material and sometimes restricting themselves to a well-defined period. Around this literature with historical concerns emerged a whole range of ancillary writings. We thus have lists of kings and of reigns as well as compilations of "year-names" and eponyms that, in the absence of a dating system based on an absolute chronology (such as our own), placed the years of a succession of kings in a consecutive order. In such lists a year would be named after a notable event that had happened earlier; thus Hammurabi of Babylon's thirty-fifth year of rule was called "Year: Upon the command of Anu and Enlil, he [Hammurabi] destroyed the walls of Mari and Malgium." In Assyria each year was assigned an eponym honoring a high official of the realm; thus one year in the reign of Tiglath-pileser III was called "Beldan, governor of Kalkha (Kalkhu)."

It is fitting to mention here the self-praises that leaders bestowed on themselves, one such example being the lyrical segment Hammurabi created as an introduction to his *Law Code*. Belonging in this category, too, are briefer works with political overtones and propagandistic objectives, such as the Neo-Assyrian *Vision of the Netherworld*. This narrative aimed to dictate a political act by having a message reach a crown prince to whom the Realm of the Dead is revealed through a dream. We must locate also in this category a certain number of fictive biographies, normally with famous kings as protagonists. (See also "Autobiographies in Ancient Western Asia" later in this volume.) Written in the third person, these narratives simulate with varying success the historicizing style of inscriptions carved on stone monuments (*narû*). *Sargon, King of Battle* and *The Conquests of Sargon* are two such narratives. Other pieces are couched as first-person narratives and are therefore meant to be taken as true autobiographies. Among these are *The Birth of Sargon*, famous for contents that allegedly parallel the story of the birth of Moses, and *The King of Kutha*. Somewhat similar are the literary letters, which read as if dictated by famous kings or leaders but are fictional, having been created for didactic, apologetic, or even entertainment purposes. (See "Kings of Akkad: Sargon and Naram-Sin" in Part 5, Vol. II.)

Literature about Conduct and Experience
There are a good number of works, some of them brief, in which religion, politics, government, and history are not obvious concerns. Rather these pieces seem to aim at educating individuals and addressing their personal needs for amusement and diversion. In addition to material already discussed—the anthologies of counsels and proverbs, of fables and disputations—we are left with at least one satirical tale (*The Poor Man of Nippur*) and smaller pieces in a similar vein, such as *The Fuller and His Client* and *Discourse of a Clown* (*aluzinnu*). (See "Humor and Wit in the Ancient Near East" later in this volume.) Love was not beyond Akkadian literary interest; from the Old Babylonian period we have the very beautiful but curiously chaste *Dialogue of Lovers*. From later times we have a compendium that contains the first lines of more than fifty songs or love songs. We know the full text of at least one of these—*To a Gallant Shepherd*, a charming ballad apparently composed toward the end of the second millennium. (See "Love Lyrics from the Ancient Near East" later in this volume.)

Although we have broached it already under the rubric of sacramental cult, we must return for a moment to a whole literature that, while it had Sumerian prototypes well-known if only for their appreciable number, also had an Akkadian development that was internally invigorated by a new vision of reality. We are speaking of the literature of exorcism, of which we possess a prodigious number of Akkadian examples. A very ancient practice, inasmuch as the oldest illustrations come from the Fara period (around 2600 BCE), exorcism aimed to eliminate the various afflictions that troubled the lives of sufferers. The tormented individual imagined being plagued, for no good cause, by various supernatural beings—we might call them demons—and by other evil forces. Such attacks were effectively rebuffed through a cluster of conjurations, often accompanied by gestures and bodily movements. Eventually this type of magic became integrated into a religious system that ascribed evil to gods who used demons to punish those contravening their will, therefore sinning against them. Nevertheless the divine sentences were not believed so fatal as to preclude using the ancient gesticulations and magic utterances in two ways: as prayer to the gods to reverse their initial censure and as the gods' instrument for obtaining grace in stopping their demonic executors and distancing them from their victims.

On such a theological system was developed a broad variety of literary genres that must be discussed briefly, not only because they loom large in Akkadian records, but also because they seem to be of great importance to the ancient users. They include concise rituals for exorcists, often an interweaving of words that must be spoken and instructions for gestures that must be made. These rituals developed into compact ceremonies meant to prevent all possible afflictions: sickness; evil portents; sorcery; acts by "evil bringers"; and misfortunes of all other sorts. Now and then these manifestations of a sacramental cult were classified by their goal and turned into anthologies of various sizes. Of these we have only fragments, but occasionally they are significant. In exceptionally serious cases or for highly influential people, some of these ceremonies became long and solemn liturgies, the copying of which took up ten tablets. The most famous examples of such compilations are *Shurpu* and *Maqlû*.

Literature Based on Casuistic Principles
Completely unknown to Sumerian writing, and therefore a category singular to the Akkadian language, is a literature of divination based on deductive logic. Building on speculations first developed during the Akkad Dynasty, observation of a series of events allowed the Akkadians to establish a correlation among such events. An event that initially seemed unexpected, unusual, strange, extraordinary, or singular was seen as a divine message heralding the coming of the second event. In the United States, an equivalent logic claims that "on February 2, if a groundhog comes out of its hole and sees its shadow, there will be six more weeks of winter."

No later than the early second millennium, scribes used this type of reasoning to collect as many occurrences as possible and to link conditional events with their predicted consequences. The linked observations were then classified and entered into long lists that eventually became vast treatises, extending over dozens of tablets and embracing a rich variety of ancillary writing: reports on inspection of ominous phenomena; divinatory questions asked of gods before reading the omens; rituals for these examinations of phenomena; and prayers of diviners, as required by the circumstance. Proceeding from the favorable or threatening prognostications that were retrieved through this system of observation, Akkadian scribes eventually compiled anthologies of predictions that occasionally come close to matching the apocalyptic style that is best known from some chapters in the biblical book of Daniel.

Together with the material on exorcism, divination and its allied literature makes up the bulk of the available Akkadian documentation. In their divination treatises, Mesopotamians did no more than apply casuistic logic (if something occurs, something happens) to the domain of fortuitous occurrences. Much as today's addition and multiplication tables instill in us arithmetic principles without explaining them, Mesopotamians, who lacked the ability to smoothly manipulate ideas, abstractions, theories, and principles, relied on time-precise and context-specific analyses to arrive at their formulations. These analyses were varied enough to suggest that the Mesopotamians might have possessed a deeper and broader awareness of how things worked than we have normally allowed them.

While hardly noticeable in Sumerian documents, this type of logic was common to other areas of knowledge that excited the curiosity of Akkadians and gave rise to a whole range of literary documents. Based too on casuistic logic are those manuals of jurisprudence that we tend to label law codes. Examples are, in Sumerian, those from the Third Dynasty of Ur and Isin (King Lipit-Ishtar) and in Semitic Akkadian, those from Eshnunna (Tell Asmar), Babylon (King Hammurabi), and second-millennium Assyria. We have at least one great medical treatise, the *Treatise of Medical Diagnostics and Prognostics*, accompanied by numerous collections of therapeutic and pharmacological diagnoses and remedies, most often classified by illnesses to be treated. We also have mathematical exercises and primers for arithmetic, field survey, geometry, and algebra (from early in the second millennium!), with lists and tables giving users essential tools with which to calculate. (See also "Metrology and Mathematics in Ancient Mesopotamia" in Part 8, Vol. III.)

Babylonian natural sciences, which concerned themselves with heaven and earth, minerals, plants, animals, and human beings, were exemplified, partly by extensive analysis of divinatory exercises, partly by a rationally argued nomenclature (see below)—more precisely by descriptive catalogs.

Knowledge about Knowledge Working on a very old paradigm that Sumerians had already exploited nicely but rather narrowly (since they treated nouns only), Akkadian scholars doubled the lists of words, first by giving Akkadian equivalents to Sumerian terms already compiled. These listings of words inspired a number of developments. Semantically and lexicographically, words were paired with their synonyms and antonyms and gathered with those similar in phonetic composition, related by perceived origin (etymology), or associated by alleged equivalence in usage. Sumerian phrases and idioms (especially those still circulating in scholarship or commerce) were reproduced grammatically or rhetorically in the Akkadian language. The masterpiece of this genre, which betrays a drive to explore and classify objects by moving beyond the meaning of words, is a veritable encyclopedia of terms in three loosely connected parts. Using an organizational logic that remains foreign to us, this immense work sought to classify, and hence to give order to, the entire content of the universe as known to the Mesopotamians: on the one hand, there was all that was known about the numerous gods, about nature, and about civilization; and on the other, there was everything that concerned the state, the professions, and the human condition. (See "Ancient Mesopotamian Lexicography" immediately following this chapter.)

Dealing with know-how rather than knowledge was the technological treatise, a practically new branch of literature that hardly existed in Sumerian but that came to inspire a whole class of writing. Set down in writing were traditional but efficacious and practical methods for raising, training, and curing horses; making colored glass (as a substitute for precious stones); preparing perfume; mixing dyes; and brewing beer. We even have cooking recipes, which reveal the odd tastes of Babylonians during the first half of the second millennium. Among types of treatises, we may once more make mention of pharmaceutical texts and medical treatments. (See above.) In Akkadian literature technological treatises are represented by tens of thousands of cuneiform tablets, a proud record of achievement.

THE FORMS

A portion of Akkadian literature, including the historical narratives, the scientific works, and technical treatises, was written in prose. It would be overly fastidious to dwell here on the characteristics of Akkadian prose style; it often reflected the idiom current at the time of composition. Poetry was reserved primarily for myths, epics, hymns, and songs, religious or profane. Some pieces belonging to the scholarly or academic literature were also written as poetry. During the early periods, poets wrote their works, particularly those of elevated style and lyrical inspiration, in a distinct dialect of Akkadian. The dialect was ostensibly archaic and relatively artificial, of unconventional grammar and exclusive vocabulary, the whole not likely ever

experienced as a spoken form. Subsequently the language of poetry remained distinctive and separate from the common language.

Two thousand years after its extinction, the written idiom of Akkadian literature cannot be compared to any living phonetic tradition. Without the necessary evidence, therefore, it would be foolhardy to expound authoritatively on the formal composition of poetic works or on how they differed from each other. We can only say that, as it concerned Akkadian, poetry depended above all on rhythmic alternations of stressed measures (strongly accented syllables) separated by unstressed syllables of unfixed number. The oldest verses, ordinarily of two hemistich (half-lines separated by a caesura), are shorter and better coined, and this gives them, in our judgment, more vigor. In time verses tended to become longer and occasionally overloaded, slack, and ponderous. However, it is possible that this deterioration of style is partly due to the written tradition, for copyists did not always respect poetic unity. Rhymes did not follow a systematic pattern, but alliterations and diverse phonetic, actually semantic, "games" became a major mechanism by which to create poetry. During the first millennium mostly, poets used acrostics to forge a poetic format.

The rules for the general layout of a poetic composition and for arranging the verses within it escape us for the most part, as does the typology of poetic genres. They seem to us, however, less elaborate than those for Sumerian poetry. In the early stages, Akkadians stuck close to the rules of Sumerian poetics. The great *Poem of Agushaya,* for example, is explicitly constructed on a fairly complicated Sumerian model. More so than in Sumerian, however, parallelism in all of its manifestations seems to have played a major role here. Compositional techniques dependent on Sumerian prototypes include the following:

- Progression from the vague to the precise:

  Sing of the Goddess, most dominant of goddesses
  Sing of Ishtar, most dominant of goddesses

- Repetition, occurring quickly, of a complete passage, restated ad nauseam two, three, even four times, for example to predict a sudden change of fortune or to rehearse it afterward; and

• Use of epithets that are formulaic and repeated, such as "Ea-the-Prince," "Shamash-
the-Valiant," and "Ramparted Uruk."

In contrast, we hardly ever find in Akkadian
poetry the profusion of images, common to Sumerian poets, drawn from raising livestock and
other aspects of a bucolic life. Conversely, we
meet with a variety of features that are unique
to the elevated narrative style; they consist of
stereotypical idioms such as the following one
used to introduce direct discourse: "[He/She]
opened the mouth, took up speech//and spoke
to. . . ."

If one must hazard an aesthetic judgment of
the whole, we might say that because Akkadian
poetry is distant from us and from our taste, it
does not often succeed in reaching us. Linguistic
discontinuity has blocked us from appreciating
its sonorous qualities; its idioms often seem to
us tedious; its imagery is stock, alien to our own,
cold and narrow. Rarely do we resonate to it,
and when we do, the harmony is minimal and
quite unlike what we feel when reading other
poetry from antiquity, such as Hebrew, Greek,
Latin, or even Chinese. Yet occasionally we
chance upon verses that strike responsive chords
in us by their powerful lyricism and their imagery, grandiose or tender. The previously mentioned great *Hymn to Shamash* is indisputably
one such success.

INTELLECT

Where Akkadian authors unquestionably scintil-
late with originality and virtuosity is in their
discourse, in the way they think about a subject,
broach it, and actualize it in writing. We can say
that their most successful and exceptional works
easily surpass the best efforts of their Sumerian
predecessors.

In Mesopotamia, the richest literary works are
without doubt the myths, since they fruitfully
engage vital issues of human concern through
prose narratives. Sumerians produced brief
myths that normally attacked a single subject,
often of local interest: How was Enki's sanctuary at Eridu (Abu Shahrain) promised endless
glory? Why were Enlil's descendents dispersed
among Heaven, Earth, and the Netherworld?

Even as polished a work as *LUGAL.E*, albeit more
than seven hundred verses long, moves unswerv-
ingly toward its goal of explaining how successive wars and heroics brought Ninurta an
extraordinary promotion among the gods.

With its first major works, Akkadian literature
suddenly and precociously generated a completely new narrative. Broad and organic, but
never simply linear, it is a compact synthesis in
which a large number of complementary problems are rehearsed and solved.

We first take up *Atrakhasis*, the earliest of
these works, commonly dated to the beginning
of the seventeenth century. It is larger than
LUGAL.E, not just in its twelve hundred lines—itself a trivial matter—but in its goal. *Atrakhasis*—the title means "ultra-wise" and is the
name of the tale's hero—seeks to explain a host
of issues, both individually and mutually: why
mortals came to be; their link to the gods; the
meaning and value of their lives; and their role
in the management of the universe. These are
questions more fundamental than those aired in
Sumerian myths. In accomplishing their aim, the
authors of *Atrakhasis* filled a vast scene, stretching from before humankind's existence to the
point at which an eventful process of evolution
brought it to its present condition, so that it has
endured since time immemorial.

With great coherence the authors integrated
a series of originally independent myths so that
the issues developed in each found answers in
the others, issues such as: How did the gods
behave when people did not yet exist? Why did
they create people? How did people come to
face cruel choices (some of which we still face)
when in conflict with their creators, and how
did they learn to fend off evil consequences?
How did they survive the worst among these
god-ordained ordeals, the universal Flood? (See
"Flood Narratives of Ancient Western Asia"
later in this volume.) How was the span of years
allotted humankind modified to its present duration, and how did this preclude future conflicts
with the gods? All the answers that myths give
to these questions were attached or clustered
into a flowing narrative, natural and spontaneous, an intricate story that maintains its integrity
and, from one episode to another, strives vigorously to shed light on the meaning of life, on
our role within the universe, and on what binds

us to the gods. In *Atrakhasis* we find a breadth of vision, a controlling intelligence, a power of synthesis, a capacity for comprehension, a logic for coherence, and a desire for clarity—virtues and characteristics for which nothing in Sumerian literature prepares us.

Atrakhasis was no aberration, no shining but isolated success. The inspiration that made it a considerable improvement on inherited literature is also at work in a contemporaneous masterpiece, the first version of the *Epic of Gilgamesh.* Despite its fragmentary condition, this Old Babylonian version of the great epic undoubtedly served as model for the more complete standard or Ninevite account produced a half millennium later. Working with brief Sumerian episodes, each of which contains a discrete tale about Gilgamesh—an ancient king of Uruk (modern Warka, biblical Erech)—a truly inspired Akkadian forged them into a broad, dynamically structured narrative that was driven by a central theme: the quest for endless life. In situating and integrating the Sumerian originals within his work, the author strove for an imposing yet touching portrait of a superman haunted by a will to live and to survive. Gilgamesh seeks earthly fame and human glory through heroic deeds, for he initially has a petty and, in truth, giddy notion of immortality that equates extraordinary human achievement with perpetuity or even divinity. Gilgamesh later looks for it as nondeath, as life without end, and to find it makes an incredible effort that takes him to the end of the earth. Ultimately Gilgamesh realizes the vanity of reaching for the impossible and accepts his mortal lot. (See "The Gilgamesh Epic: A Masterpiece from Ancient Mesopotamia" later in this volume.)

In this portrait, so solid in itself, nothing is lacking, not even what affects the heart: love, sorrow, longing, hope. Is it not a mark of genius to have transformed into a true friend the Enkidu who, in the Sumerian accounts, was merely a servant of Gilgamesh? For when Gilgamesh sees Enkidu—in fact his other self—dying before his time, in his very arms, our hero grasps what horror death is; at that moment he decides to do everything to avoid it. No less than in *Atrakhasis*, we have here a monumental and luminous fresco, a demonstration at once convincing and moving of an art that is strangely distant from the shortsighted, bland, and commonplace perspective of the Sumerian traditions of the epic.

One more illustration is warranted. Where else among mythologies could we find a better example, or one better suited to its culture and time, than in the *Enūma Elish?* This myth, too, was created by gathering together myths that originally existed in well-known Sumerian and Akkadian prototypes with narrowly defined purposes. Where could we find a more lucid justification, at once rational and religious, for the promotion of Marduk to kingship over the community of gods, for saving them from extreme peril, and over humankind, for inventing and creating them?

If we maintain that cultures should be judged by their most perfect successes, these three examples of the Akkadian literary art—*Atrakhasis, The Epic of Gilgamesh,* and *Enūma Elish* should suffice for an evaluation. With this literature a new era dawned on Mesopotamia as it embraced a tougher logic and a more mature viewpoint, thus taking a giant stride toward the convictions of modern Western culture. It came closer still during the Hellenistic period, when a creative and independent Akkadian literature reached its final destination.

*Translated from the French by Ulla Kasten
and J. M. Sasson*

BIBLIOGRAPHY

Overviews

For an excellent overview of works cited in the above essay along with additional references, see WOLFGANG RÖLLIG, "Überblick über die akkadische Literatur," in *Reallexikon der Assyriologie* 7 (1987). ERICA REINER provides a fuller sketch of our topic in "Die Altorientalische Literaturen," in *Neues Handbuch der Literaturwissenschaft,* edited by WOLFGANG RÖLLIG (1978).

Translations

A great number of Akkadian literary texts are translated and presented in JAMES B. PRITCHARD, ed., *Ancient Near Eastern Texts Relating to the Old Testament,* with *Supplement* (3rd ed. 1969). More up-to-date renderings of mythological and ritual texts can be found in JEAN BOTTÉRO and SAMUEL N.

KRAMER, *Lorsque les dieux faisaient l'homme: Mythologie mésopotamienne* (1989), and BENJAMIN R. FOSTER, *Before the Muses*, 2 vols. (1993).

Literary Studies and Appreciation

Three volumes that are worth consulting for their diverse literary studies are: JACK M. SASSON, ed., *Studies in Literature from the Ancient Near East, Dedicated to Samuel Noah Kramer* (1984); FRANCESCA ROCHBERG-HALTON, ed., *Language, Literature, and History: Philological and Historical Studies Presented to Erica Reiner* (1987); and I. TZVI ABUSCH ET AL., eds., *Lingering over Words. Studies in Ancient Near Eastern Literature in Honor of William L. Moran* (1990). Aside from those concerned with the *Epic of Gilgamesh*, works of appreciation of Akkadian literature are still few. I mention here only ERICA REINER, *Your Thwarts in Pieces, Your Mooring Rope Cut: Poetry from Babylonia and Assyria* (1985).

Culture and Mentality

Issues relevant to the culture and mentality of the Mesopotamian world are discussed in JEAN BOTTÉRO, *Mésopotamie: l'écriture, la raison, et les dieux* (1987), available in English as *Mesopotamia, Writing, Reasoning, and the Gods*, translated by ZAINAB BAHRANI and MARC VAN DE MIEROOP (1992).

SEE ALSO **The History of Ancient Mesopotamia: An Overview** (Part 5, Vol. II); **Myth and Mythmaking in Sumer and Akkad** (Part 8, Vol. III); **Theologies, Priests, and Worship in Ancient Mesopotamia** (Part 8, Vol. III); **Prophecy and Apocalyptics in the Ancient Near East** (Part 8, Vol. III); **Sumerian Literature: An Overview** (Part 9, Vol. IV); and **The Gilgamesh Epic: A Masterpiece from Ancient Mesopotamia** (Part 9, Vol. IV).

Ancient Mesopotamian Lexicography

MIGUEL CIVIL

LISTS OF WORDS are a characteristic feature of ancient Mesopotamian culture. In fact, the whole of its "science" consists in the enumeration and classification of all natural and cultural entities. These are then compiled in lists. Some of the lists focus on the elements of the writing system or represent an inventory of the lexicon of the languages (mainly Sumerian and Akkadian) used in the area. These are the lists that are considered "lexical."

Many hundreds of clay tablets of word lists of a lexical nature written in cuneiform script have been recovered in excavations of ancient cities. They have been unearthed not only in Mesopotamia proper but also in all peripheral areas where cuneiform writing was used at one time or another: Elam, Anatolia, Syria, Palestine, and Egypt.

HISTORY OF LEXICAL TEXTS

Lexical lists appear among the earliest cuneiform tablets, at the beginning of the third millennium BCE, and they continue to be written as long as cuneiform writing was in use, until Hellenistic and Roman times. The history of Mesopotamian lexical texts can be divided into four periods. The Archaic period extends from the invention of cuneiform writing until the end of the third millennium and is subdivided into the following phases: Uruk; Fara (Fara, Abu Salabikh, Nippur); Sargonic (including the texts from Ebla); and Ur III. The Old Babylonian period runs from the end of the Ur III Empire to the end of the first Babylonian dynasty and is subdivided into the following phases: Isin-Larsa; Early Old Babylonian (Kings Hammurabi and Samsu-iluna of Babylon); and Late Old Babylonian (after Babylon's loss of the southern provinces). The Middle Babylonian period lasts until the twelfth century. Finally, the Canonical period extends from the twelfth century to the disappearance of cuneiform. (See "The History of Ancient Mesopotamia: An Overview" in Part 5, Vol. II.)

Development and Elaboration

The lexical texts and the educational system of scribes associated with them are the backbone of Mesopotamian culture. Despite local, political, and cultural differences, and their changes through time, the body of lexical compilations tends to be extremely uniform. The very same compilations that are first attested in the earliest Uruk tablets were copied, with very minor changes, for more than one millennium. They are found not only in southern Mesopotamia, their place of origin (besides Uruk, the bulk of recovered material comes from Fara and Abu Salabikh), but also in a vast area that stretches from Elam in the east to Syria in the northwest. The body of lexical texts excavated at Ebla (modern Tell Mardikh) is particularly significant because it offers data on the earliest known Semitic language and because it includes the earliest known instances of bilingual lists and phonological definitions of logographic cuneiform signs. Strangely enough, the Ur III Empire, which represents a period of intense scribal activity, has left us practically nothing of a lexical nature. Word lists must certainly have been used in the training of the hundreds of scribes known by name from this time. Archaeologists have not been able to excavate any place of scribal training of Ur III times. Lexical fragments found in Nippur (modern Nuffar) seem to indicate that the oldest traditional lists were still in use.

When lexical tablets again appeared, with most of the material dating from the eighteenth century, the word lists differed from the ones used until then. In contrast with the textual stability of the oldest lists, schools of this time, while keeping the same general system, tended to freely adapt the new lists to local needs. Some recensions were more successful than others either because of the prestige of the school in which they were created or because of their in-

trinsic quality. When the south—where Nippur and Ur were the centers of scribal culture—was lost, shortly after the end of Hammurabi's reign, the scribal schools emigrated north to the Babylon area. There the lists received their final Old Babylonian form.

After the destruction of Babylon, the history of lexical lists in southern Mesopotamia is obscure for several centuries. Scribes seem to have emigrated north and northwest, and the Babylonian lists traveled with them to peripheral areas such as Boğazköy, Alalakh (modern Tell Atchana), Ugarit (modern Ras Shamra), and Emar (modern Meskene). It is likely that there was a local, ancient, lexical tradition in the northwest and in the Asshur area, possibly related to the type of texts found at Ebla, but nothing certain can be said at present about it. The texts recovered from these areas are of Babylonian origin, as shown by the names of cities mentioned in them and by their zoological and botanical terminology. The lexical tradition continued in Kassite Babylonia, under conditions unknown to us.

Around the twelfth century, the text of the lexical lists becomes standardized, in the so-

Modern Scholarship on Cuneiform Lexicography

When in the nineteenth century modern scholars deciphered the cuneiform writing system used in the tablets and inscriptions that were being discovered in great numbers at the time, they found many lexical lists among them and used them to better understand how the ancient languages of the region worked. These scholars were faced by two tasks: the textual reconstruction of the native lists that were recorded on clay tablets and the compilation of dictionaries to be used by modern students of these languages. For several decades, the list reconstruction advanced by leaps and bounds, but no full series was restored except for the simplest syllabaries. From the 1930s on, Benno Landsberger, a European scholar who also worked in Turkey and in the United States, provided a comprehensive overview of the lexical lists and began their systematic publication.

Today all the major lexical texts are published in the monumental *Materials for the Sumerian Lexicon*, started by Landsberger. Additionally, there are now two modern dictionaries of the Akkadian language.

W. Von Soden's *Akkadisches Handwörterbuch* (1965–1981) is a three-volume work that was completed in 1981. What is commonly cited as the *Chicago Assyrian Dictionary*, or simply as the CAD, is nearing completion. Von Soden's work is a compact dictionary with minimal information: a suggested meaning for a word, a basic citation of where it occurs in cuneiform texts, and brief phonological and etymological proposals. The CAD additionally excerpts from the documents all significant passages where a word occurs.

For the Sumerian language, except for incomplete glossaries such as Friedrich Delitzsch's *Sumerisches Glossar* (1914), there is not yet a modern dictionary available. The first volume of the *Sumerian Dictionary of the University Museum of the University of Pennsylvania* was published in 1984 and the second in 1992. Because of its problematic nature as a language with no known linguistic relatives and with a mainly logographic writing system, Sumerian makes the task of compiling a dictionary a daunting enterprise.

called canonical versions. Until then, the lists show the influence of oral tradition and a good deal of local variability; frequently we find two or three different but parallel recensions of the same list in Ugarit and Emar. In the "canonical" period, the lists are meticulously copied from tablet to tablet, with variations among models and damaged passages carefully noted. The pedigree of a tablet is often given in a colophon. These standardized texts are copied and recopied everywhere, virtually unchanged, until the demise of the cuneiform script in Roman times. Among the latest recovered school exercises with copies of lexical lists, a few exist with the entries transcribed into the Greek alphabet.

LEXICAL LISTS AND SCRIBAL TRAINING

Although some carefully edited "library" copies of the lists have been preserved—especially from the "canonical" period—the great majority of sources used to reconstruct lists consists of school exercises. Scribal education essentially involved repeated copying and memorization of traditional word lists. It is possible to reconstruct a curriculum of such lists since a "catch line" at the end of one list often gives the name of the list that follows it.

Scribal training must have produced a staggering number of clay tablets that were filled with student exercises. Such by-product tablets were "melted" and reused, a practice that accounts for the scarce remains of school activities in certain places and at certain times. Only when a war or a natural calamity brought such activities to a sudden halt have significant numbers of such school exercises been preserved.

We may assume that there was a certain level of competence among the teachers of southern Mesopotamia. The situation is not the same in peripheral areas. Even tablets that belonged to the large "library" collections at Ebla, Ugarit, and Emar in Syria or at Boğazköy in Anatolia, show severe errors of comprehension and a poor understanding of the Sumerian and Akkadian languages. In some cases, unfavorable conditions can justify poor results, as when a jailed Emar scribe wrote a tablet, full of mistakes. But the real reason for problems is that most word lists were originally drawn up in southern Mesopotamia and were full of references that were alien to the scribes beyond its borders. Such scribes not only spoke different languages, but they must have found very limited use for items they inherited with these lists, for example, names of canals in the Babylon region or terms for fish found only in south Mesopotamian marshes.

The modern textual reconstruction of ancient lexical lists is based to a large extent on school exercises. The Assyriologist must therefore account for such frequent errors of the apprentice scribes as malformed, omitted, or confused signs and incorrect spellings of words. On the positive side, these errors can have, linguistically speaking, a diagnostic value; a misspelling, for instance, may be a clue to the pronunciation of a word.

DESCRIPTION OF WORD LISTS

We refer to the lexical lists by following the practice of ancient scribes who labeled them by their opening lines (incipits). Major lists, especially when they span several tablets, are called lexical "series." In the examples given below, we observe the following conventions:

Sumerian words are given in lowercase roman transliteration, syllable by syllable separated by hyphens (as in ga-ša-an) or continously (gašan). (Editor's Note: Small capital letters are used for Sumerian in all other essays in the four volumes.)

Akkadian words are given in italic transliteration separated by hyphens (as in *e-ze-bu*) or continuously (*ezēbu*).

Transliteration in capital letters (as in DU) designates a given cuneiform sign, regardless of its actual pronunciation. In the case of two or more syllables, periods are used to separate them (as in U.AD). The accents and subscripts on individual signs are used by Assyriologists to distinguish signs that share both the same consonant and vowels but which may have been pronounced differently. Diacritics, such as a macron or circumflex, indicate length when placed over vowels in Akkadian words.

Types of Lists

External Classification The lexical lists are written on clay tablets, prisms, or cylinders of various sizes, shapes, and formats. Only the most important are mentioned here:

Type I refers to generally large tablets, found in all periods, with a full lexical list or a substantial part thereof and nothing else.

Type II is limited to the period of the Old Babylonian schools. Such tablets contain divergent material on each of its two sides. To the left of the flat side (II/1) there is a carefully written lexical passage extracted from a fuller list, apparently the work of an instructor, while to the right the passage is copied by a student. On the convex side (II/2) of a Type II tablet, there is a multicolumn excerpt from a longer list.

Type III tablets are found in all periods and contain just one column with material extracted from a longer list.

Type IV are plano-convex (flat on one side and convex on the other) round (lenticular) tablets that come from the Old Babylonian and, less frequently, the Middle Babylonian periods. On the flat side, they have two to four lines of text written by the instructor and copied underneath by the student. On some of them, the convex side gives the reading of the signs in syllabograms and/or their Akkadian translation.

Type V are small, oblong tablets, from the Middle Babylonian or early New Babylonian times, with a literary citation written parallel to the longer axis on one side, and a lexical excerpt, written at a ninety-degree orientation, on the other side.

Type VI are small, one-column tablets, first encountered in the Neo-Babylonian era, with several lines with a literary quotation, followed by several sections, from four to six lines long, with excerpts from successive tablets of a lexical series.

Type VII, also Neo Babylonian and later, is a large tablet with several columns. On the obverse, it contains part of a lexical list; on the reverse, there are multiple columns with varied matter that includes model contracts, brief and repeated literary quotations, verbal forms, personal names, and short lexical excerpts, often repeated several times.

Lexical lists can be unilingual or multilingual. The first type contains words that in most cases were Sumerian. The majority of bilingual lists give words in Sumerian and in Akkadian, but there are also unique examples of Kassite-Akkadian and Egyptian-Akkadian bilinguals. In multilingual lists, this core can be expanded to include one or more additional languages, such as Hittite, Ugaritic, or Hurrian.

The lexical tablets can also be classified according to the number of subcolumns for each entry. In the tablet descriptions it has been found to be useful to designate the subcolumns as follows:

0: A cuneiform vertical wedge that opens the entry (at the left margin) in some types of lists; it may have made the line-count easier.

1: The phonological description of the word represented by the logogram in subcolumn 2 given by a set of simple "basic" syllabograms. It can be present as a formal subcolumn through the entire tablet, or it can be added only to selected entries as a gloss (frequently in smaller-size signs).

2: The Sumerian logogram, the essential part of the entry.

3: The names used by the scribes to refer to the logogram in subcolumn 2. This procedure is first attested in the Middle Babylonian period.

4: The Akkadian translation.

5: Translation(s) into additional languages, for example, Hittite.

When materials are transliterated into the Roman alphabet, items in gloss size are given as superscripts; optional items are enclosed in parentheses.

All these elements appear in the fullest form of an entry. The majority of lists lack one or more of the subcolumns. For example,

0	1	2	3	4	5
(a)					
I	du-u	KAK	gakku	*banû*	—
(b)					
—	tak-tak	TAK₄.TAK₄	tak minnabi	*ezēbu arḫa dalumar*	

These entries are to be interpreted in the following manner:

Example (a): when pronounced du, the Sumerian logogram called gakku (but transliterated KAK by today's Assyriologists) means in Akkadian *banû*, "to build." The "I" at the left edge represents a vertical wedge, without any linguistic significance.

Example (b): when read tak-tak, the Sumerian logogram TAK$_4$.TAK$_4$ called "double (minnabi) tak" means in Akkadian *ezēbu*, "to abandon," and in Hittite *arḫa dalumar*, "forsaking."

Lists that have only subcolumns 1 and 2 are called "syllabaries," since their function is to give the pronunciation of the logogram in subcolumn 2 with the help of simple syllabic signs in subcolumn 1. The other lists are usually called "vocabularies."

Internal Classification According to the contents, the lexical lists can be sorted into: lists organized according to shape, or some other characteristic, of the cuneiform signs (or logograms); lists organized thematically, according to the meaning of the logograms; lists organized phonologically, following the reading of the logograms; etymological lists; synonym lists; and miscellaneous lists.

In bilingual and multilingual lists, the entries are ordered according to one of the languages. Although the physical arrangement of the subcolumns in bilingual lists is always the same—Sumerian to the left, Akkadian to the right—the contents of the lists can be ordered according to either one of these languages. There are thus Sumero-Akkadian lists (the great majority) and Akkado-Sumerian ones. In the multilingual glossaries derived from traditional Sumero-Akkadian ones, the more exotic languages are located in the right subcolumn. Akkadian is found at the right in the exceptional cases of the Kassite-Akkadian and Egyptian-Akkadian bilingual glossaries.

Sign Lists or Syllabaries The earliest sign lists appear in the Fara period. The ordering criterion is not apparent; it includes compound signs alongside simple ones. A sign may be repeated several times to account for its different readings, but those are not given on the tablet. One Ebla sign list gives for the first time the pronunciation in the form of semiticizing sign

names (the Sumerian pronunciation + the Semitic ending -*um*). This list is unique in that the signs are selected from existing lists (an archaic list of dignitaries and a list of domestic animals), with no regard to shape or sound. The explanatory nature of the list is shown by the presence (side-by-side) of easily confused signs corresponding to a single sign in the primary list. Thus, the very similar signs EDIN and BAḪAR in the sign list correspond only to BAḪAR in the list of dignitaries. Examples of entries follow (note the unusual format 2-1):

BAḪÁR	*ba-ḫa-ru₁₂-um*	(= *baḫar* + *um*)
TIR	*ti-i-ru₁₂-um*	(= *tir* + *um*)

The major sign list (with the opening entry: "Ea = *nâqu*") appears, in the Early Old Babylonian period, in the form of a 918-line list (known as "Proto-Ea"), which is preserved in school exercise tablets with only the logograms (format 0-2) or with their pronunciation added (format 0-1-2). Only rarely is the Akkadian translation included (format 0-1-2-4). Examples:

su-un	BÚR
bu-ur	BÚR
du-un	BÚR
ù-šu-um	BÚR

And with the Akkadian translation:

mu-ul	MUL	= *kakkabu*	"star"
		= *šiṭirtu*	"written document"
		= *napāḫu*	"to shine"
		= *nabāṭu*	"to be bright"
sú-ḫub	MUL	= *šuḫuppu*	"shoe"

The signs are arranged according to the stylus strokes needed to write them. The Nippur recension of this list is quite uniform, but there are local variations in other schools, especially in Late Old Babylonian times. One of these recensions, which was much shorter, was standardized in the Syllabary A (format 1-2-[3]), and it was used as a didactic tool until the end of cuneiform writing. A variant recension of this syllabary with Akkadian translations added (Vocabulary of Syllabary A, format 1-2-4) was the main "textbook" during Middle Babylonian times in Assyria and in Syria and Anatolia in the northwest. Proto-Ea was expanded during the Late Old Babylonian and Middle Babylonian periods until it became a series of forty-two tablets (Aa = *nâqu*) with about 14,400 entries; its companion is a condensed recension of eight tablets (Ea = *nâqu*) of about twenty-four hundred entries (70 percent preserved). The format is 0-1-2-(3)-4. The main difference between the two series is that while Aa = *nâqu* lists all known translations of a Sumerian word, Ea = *nâqu* gives, as a rule, only a single translation, rarely more. For instance,

| Ea II 152–53: | bu-ru | U | *šup-lu* | "depth" |
| | [same] | U | *pil-šu* | "hole" |

is compared with,

Aa II/4 86–137:	bu-ru	U	*pa-la-šu*	"to pierce"
			pi-il-šu	"hole"
			šu-up-lum	"depth"
			šu-pa-lum	"beneath"
			ša-pa-lum	"to be(come) low"
			hu-ub-tum	"cavity"
			bu-rum	"well"
			ka-lak-ku	"pit"

In this instance there are fifty-two translations. The compilers added—next to genuine, independent meanings—derivations from the same root, synonyms, and divine names and placenames, often at great length. Thus, one reading of the sign TAR receives no fewer than 73 translations in Aa = *nâqu*, and the sign BAR receives 195 in Aa = *nâqu*.

Like all the major lexical series, the Ea/Aa = *nâqu* list took its "canonical" form around the twelfth century. In its final form it was the main reference work of the Mesopotamian scribes; it was the object of school commentaries and was provided with an index according to the Sumerian readings of the entries. In later times, Syllabary A was partially replaced by Syllabary B, a list 743 lines long in two tablets, as a way of learning the writing system without the complexities of the full Aa = *nâqu* series.

The lists of the Ea-family include only single cuneiform signs. Many Sumerian words are represented by a combination of several cuneiform signs. The constituents of these compound logograms may keep their original pronunciation, or the whole may have a pronunciation different from that of its constituents. In the first case,

they are called "Izi-compounds"; in the second, "Diri-compounds," from the titles of the major series in which they are collected. For instance, the compound EN + NU + UN, read en-nu-un, "watch, guard," is an Izi-compound; KI + KAL, read ḫirin, "a plant," is a Diri-compound. The Izi-compounds are collected in the series Izi = *išātu* and in the so-called acrographic (or less precisely "acrophonic") lists, ordered according to the initial sign of the (compound) logogram.

Acrographic lists are found for the first time in Ebla in rather large compilations (the major one has about twelve hundred lines) and are frequently provided with Semitic (Proto–Old Akkadian or local dialects) translations. Thus, the first 132 lines are entries, of which the first sign is GAR; the next 35 lines have GAR (or its derivations PAD and SUR) in noninitial positions. The next sixty-three entries start with the sign KA and are followed by some with KA in the secondary position. These mid-third-millennium texts are the ancestors of the Old Babylonian acrographic compilations, although there is no direct textual dependency between them.

"Proto-Izi" is an Early Old Babylonian series, 1,072 lines long, that is organized in a sequence which is basically graphic but with many thematic and phonological associations. For instance, one section lists eight terms for "road," with no common initial sign. It is followed by a twenty-line section with ŠID, purely acrographic, and then, by phonological association with the reading sid, comes sig₄, "brick," and its various types. This in turn attracts a section about walls, which is followed by terms for "shadow" by conceptual association. More rigorously acrographic are the series "Ká-gal = *abullu*" (542 lines), "Nig-ga = *makkūru*" (579 lines), and "Sag = *awīlu*" (312 lines) of the same period. These series only partially survived the Old Babylonian period.

The series "Diri = *watru*" of the Diri-compounds appears for the first time in Early Old Babylonian as a list of about seven hundred entries. In its final, canonical form, it becomes a series of seven tablets with at least eighteen hundred entries, not counting the seventh tablet, which is a list of divine names that has not been satisfactorily reconstructed.

Thematic Lists Collections of logograms grouped solely according to their meaning are found among the oldest cuneiform tablets in the Uruk period. There are lists of animals, trees, and metal objects. Alongside exhaustive monographic lists there appear, already in the Fara period, "practical vocabularies" with the more frequently used terms of material culture: stones, metal objects, garments, wooden implements, containers, and perfumes, collected on a single large tablet. The tendency to write encyclopedic compilations culminates in the series "ḪAR-ra = ḫubullu."

Known in Early Old Babylonian times, the canonical recension of "ḪAR-ra = ḫubullu"—now restored in almost its entirety—has twenty-four tablets with close to ten thousand entries. Tablets 1 and 2 contain terms needed for writing legal and administrative documents. They are followed by a list of trees (tablet 3); wooden objects (4–7); reeds and objects made of reeds, an important construction material in southern Mesopotamia (8–9); clays and pottery (10); skins and leather objects (11); metals (12); domestic animals (13); wild animals (14); meat cuts (15); stones (16); plants and vegetables (17); birds and fish (18); textiles (19); geographic terms (20–22); and food and drink (23–24). Considering that each tablet in this series is 300 to 400 lines long, the value of this series for reconstructing the natural resources, technology, and geography of Mesopotamia, on the one hand, and for understanding of technical terms in Sumerian and Akkadian texts, on the other, is enormous.

The "ḪAR-ra = ḫubullu" series is completed by a compilation of kinship terms, social classes, and human conditions (series "Lú = ša"). An archaic list of dignitaries is already found in Uruk. Lists of professions are known from the Fara period. There are two such lists in Early Old Babylonian times. One, "Proto-Lú" or "Lú = šu," has 846 lines, the other, "Azlag = ašlakku," has more than 500. The first is the ancestor of the canonical series "Lú = ša," which has at least four tablets that have yet to be fully recovered. The second, with a wider anthropological outlook than the first, contains mostly terms and phrases describing psychological qualities, bodily characteristics, morbid states, and human activities that are usually of a nonprofessional nature. This series did not survive after Middle Babylonian times.

More restricted in scope is an Early Old Babylonian thematic list of parts of the human body (more than 270 entries) that includes:

nundum-mu	"my lips"
nundum-an-ta-mu	"my upper lip"
nundum-ki-ta-mu	"my lower lip"
ka-mu	"my mouth"
eme-mu	"my tongue"
zú-mu	"my teeth"
zú-ga-mu	"my milk tooth"
zú-kinkin-mu	"my molar"

Worth noticing is the presence of the first-person possessive suffix (mu); the Sumerian names of the parts of the body belong to the linguistic category of "obligatorily possessed," that is, to a class of words that should normally be provided with a possessive.

Lists of divine names appear in the Fara period and are very frequent after Early Old Babylonian times. The final, standard compilation with about eighteen hundred divine names is the series "An = *Anum*." Its first line means "AN represents the name of the god Anu." Complicated syncretistic processes—many local deities were assimilated to the ones of politically dominant towns—and the personification of divine epithets resulted in an extended synonymy of divine names. This series arranges the names in families and households. The left column is the main entry; the right gives a synonymous name, the kinship relation with other deities, or the role of a given deity in another deity's court or household.

Long lists of place-names are part of the thematic series "ḪAR-ra = ḫubullu." Extensive onomastic listings—both Sumerian and Akkadian—with many hundreds of personal names were often copied as an exercise in the schools.

Phonological Lists An elementary teaching exercise in the Early Old Babylonian schools was a list of triplets of the most basic syllabograms of the form: consonant + vowel, vowel + consonant, or consonant$_1$ + vowel + consonant$_2$. One finds there series of syllables such as tu-ta-ti, ub-ab-ib, and pur-par-pir. The only other list ordered by sounds is an index to

Ea = *nâqu* (format 0-1-2-(3)-4), infrequently attested and only partially preserved, that is the ancient equivalent of a modern list of homophones. Following are examples that are somewhat modified by placing in parentheses the Assyriologists' transliteration and by omitting the Akkadian translation that is found on the tablet:

gi-ir	LAGAB	(gir_8)	"to roll over"
	U.AD	(gir_4)	"oven"
	DU	(gir_7)	"to run"
	KAS_4	(gir_5)	"to run"
	GÌR	(gir)	"foot"
	IN	(gir_{12})	"a rodent"
	GÍR	($gír$)	"knife"
	NE	(gir_{10})	"angry"
	ÁBxŠÀ	(gir_{16})	"a pot"
	GIR	(gir)	"pig"
	KÉS	(gir_{11})	"to tie"

Etymological Lists The series "SIG_7.ALAN = *nabnītu*" is divided into paragraphs that deal with an Akkadian root and its Sumerian equivalents. It is an Akkado-Sumerian vocabulary and was presumably used in translating Akkadian texts into Sumerian. The Akkadian roots themselves are organized within a general semantic theme of names of body parts from head to feet, and activities associated with them. The Mesopotamian scribes had a much more elastic concept of "root" than that of the modern linguist, and often only a vague phonological similarity connects the entries within a paragraph. For instance, we find the following entries mixed in the same paragraph: *kamāmu* "to nod," *kamû* "to roast," *kummu* "inner room," *kumû* "a bird," *kamû* "to capture," *kamû* "outside," *kimtu* "clan," *kamūnu* "truffle," and *kamānu* "a type of cake." The series can be reconstructed, with considerable gaps, up to tablet 32. Starting with tablet 31 there seems to be a shift to a thematic organization. An ancient catalog compiled by a Sippar scribe indicates that the series had as many as fifty-four tablets. Rather surprisingly, though apparently nothing is preserved from tablets 33 to 54, it is possible that tablets usually assigned to other series were considered part of *nabnītu* in Sippar. In any case, considering that the better-preserved tablets have well in excess of three

hundred lines, the original must have had more than fifteen thousand lines: an impressive amount of lexical material.

Synonym Lists Late post–Old Babylonian lists have been found that have normal Akkadian words in the right subcolumn, while in the left column are unusual, poetic, obsolete, or foreign synonyms. The main compilation of this type is "Malku = *šarru*," a collection of at least eight tablets. It seems to be continued by two or three tablets with the title "An = *Anum*." This happens to be the title of the main god-list series, mentioned above, and perhaps these tablets were considered its continuation. "Malku = *šarru*" must have held at least two thousand entries in total. The entries are organized along themes, such as kinship terms and names of weapons. Following is an excerpt from the list:

iššu	= *sinništu* "woman"
ašbutu	= [same meaning]
umāmatu	= *umāmtu* "female animal"
muḫterkun	= [same meaning] in Elamite
aštu	= [same meaning] in Hurrian

The first synonym of *sinništu* is northwest Semitic or Canaanite (compare *iššu* to Hebrew *'iššâ*). The second is a word of unknown filiation, reported only here. This list is purely philological and is reminiscent of the lexicographic work of Hesychius of Alexandria many centuries later (fifth century CE). But there are also Mesopotamian "dictionaries of ideas," more in the style of our own modern thesaurus. The series "Erimḫuš = *anantu*" (meaning "battle") consists of six tablets with 1,450 lines divided in paragraphs of mostly three (sometimes two, rarely four or more) lines containing one group of synonyms or otherwise closely related words, sometimes with an antonym added at the end. "Antagal = *šaqû*" is a similar, though longer, series that is not too well preserved; apparently it was used only in Assyria. Here is a brief extract from Erimḫuš:

kuš-è	= *kâṣu*	"to skin"
zil	= *qalāpu*	"to peel"
gar-ra	= *šaḫāṭu*	"to remove clothing"

Slightly more complicated is the following sequence:

a-tar-lá-lá	= *šuteṣû*	"to quarrel"
lú-kúr-dug₄-dug₄	= *qābi šanīti*	"one who says hostile things"
zú-bir	= *ṣuḫḫu*	"to deride"
pe-el-lá	= *qullulu*	"to ridicule"
dugud	= *kubbutu*	"to respect"

Miscellaneous Lists A dialect known as "emesal" in Sumerian and *lurû* in Akkadian (the exact meaning of these terms is unknown) is characterized by a different articulation of certain sounds and by some variations in the vocabulary. In literary texts, this dialect is used in women's speech, regardless of the gender of the addressee (see "Sumerian Literature" earlier in this volume). A class of temple cantors also used this dialect, at least in liturgical songs. Written forms of this dialect found in literary tales and liturgical songs were collected in a three-tablet series with the title "dimmer = dingir = *ilu*." It has three subcolumns, the left has the "emesal" form, the central the standard Sumerian form, and the right the Akkadian translation. This series, with close to five hundred entries, is a late one; it seems to be the creation of Neo-Assyrian scribes. Here are some examples of entries:

ga-ša-an	= nin	= *bēltu*	"lady"
u₅-mu	= ì-giš	= *ellu*	"vegetable oil"
zé-èg	= šúm	= *nadānu*	"to give"

In addition to the large, well-established lexical compilations that are preserved in several copies, one finds many tablets that were created for some specific purpose, never gained much popularity, and were hardly ever copied. Among the more remarkable examples are the two brief bilingual lists of words in Kassite-Akkadian and Egyptian-Akkadian. The latter was found at al-Amarna in Egypt, where it may have been created to train the scribes of the Egyptian chancellery.

Some practical manuals for teaching how to give orders related to the performance of some craft or activity are known from the Early Old Babylonian period. There was a time when the supervisors or instructors were expected to conduct their duties in Sumerian. Whether this was still true in Early Old Babylonian times or whether it was an old tradition, by then a memory, we cannot say. In any case, there are tablets with instructions on how to prepare malt for brewing and another that teaches how to examine the intestines of a lamb sacrificed for divination. There are fragments with instructions on such matters as how to prepare a tablet on which to write and how to harvest grain.

INTERPRETATION OF THE LISTS

Although the majority of entries in the Mesopotamian lexical lists are simple and direct, there are limitations inherent in the system as well as scribal conventions that must be taken into account if we are profitably to use the lists.

Owing to the nature of the writing system or to scribal conventions, there are restrictions in how to represent the sound of words. Thus, the syllabic nature of the script makes it impossible to represent clusters of consonants in an initial or final position; for instance, a word starting with two consonants and followed by a vowel (C_1C_2V) can only be represented by creating two separate syllables, either by adding a superfluous vowel before the first consonant $([V]C_1\text{-}C_2V\text{-})$ or after the first consonant $(C_1[V]\text{-}C_2V\text{-})$.

When the words or grammatical elements represented by the cuneiform signs come in contact with other elements of the language, their phonological shape may be altered. For instance, the Sumerian verbal modal prefix of the optative mood—used in the verbal forms expressing a wish or a polite order—changes its vowel to harmonize with the vowel in the syllable right after it. For example, it becomes ḫu- before a syllable with u and ḫa- before a syllable with a. This type of phonological modification is often not overtly indicated in the lists.

The lists may also give alternative forms of the phenomenon just described in such a way that they seem to be dealing with entirely different words. For example, the Sumerian word "dug" means "good"; but it has a short form that is found only when it is in combination with other elements, such as in du(g)-ga. The lists, however, can give this word as du-u *and* as du-ug, and we must realize that these are two forms of the same word.

The cuneiform writing system evolved over a long period. As a result, the value of some signs changed and occasionally it is difficult to determine how to read them. Thus, in Old Babylonian texts, the sign MU is used to represent not only the syllable "mu," but also the syllable "gu." Later on, however, the sign GU is used for "gu." The ambiguity now shifts because GU can now also be read as "qu." In a related phenomenon, some Sumerian sounds were not used in Akkadian and so are represented by two or more approximations. Thus, "to gore" was pronounced something like "dʳu"; but the vocabularies split it into two, probably spurious, forms giving it as du-u "to gore, said of a bull" *and* as ru-u "to gore, said of a ram."

We must also take into account scribal conventions that might affect our understanding of the entries. Scribes did not always indicate whether a form belonged to the women's dialect (emesal) mentioned above. A potential problem arises from the fact that Sumerian has a very high number of compound words but scribes sometimes assign to a single, isolated component of a compound the meaning that is correct only for the compound form. Thus, the compound ki-ág means "to love," but in some lists this meaning is given to the element "ág" alone, even if ág by itself does not have this meaning. This particularly insidious feature has often caused problems for Assyriologists.

Somewhat related are two other pitfalls. Scribes often fail in Sumerian to indicate that different verbal roots could have the same meaning, one form for the singular and another for the plural. Thus, tuš means "to sit down," said of one person, but durun is used when referring to several subjects. The meaning scribes assign to a given word may be correct only for certain grammatical constructions with particular subjects or objects. In the following examples, all Sumerian entries are translated by Akkadian *nakāpu* "to gore, to knock down," but qualifica-

tions (the subject, object, or synonym) are entered to establish distinctions:

sag-ta-dug$_4$-ga	= *nakāpu*,	"(said) of the head"
sag-sìg-ga	= [same meaning]	
du$_7$	= *nakāpu*,	"(said) of oxen"
ru$_5$	= *nakāpu*,	"(said) of rams"
si-tu$_{10}$	= *nakāpu*,	"(said) of oxen/bulls"
kur-ku	= *nakāpu*,	"(said) of a flood"
ru-gú	= *nakāpu*,	"(said) of a finger"
si-ga	= *nakāpu*,	"(said) of a garment"
si-ga	= *nakāpu*,	"(said) of a woman's sex organ"

Note that the last entry properly belongs not to *nakāpu* but to *naqābu*, "to deflower." The two Akkadian verbs themselves were at times confused by the scribes. In any case, the scribes did not use definitions proper.

As the world's oldest body of lexical material, the Mesopotamian lexical lists are of enormous linguistic and historical interest. In addition, they help us reconstruct the Mesopotamian view of the world and are indicators of cultural, and even political, change in the ancient Near East.

BIBLIOGRAPHY

Sources

ANTON DEIMEL, *Sumerisches Lexikon* (1928–1933), a collection of largely uninterpreted source material, is mostly outdated, but not yet replaced. *Materials for the Sumerian Lexicon* (1937–) is a series of individual volumes that includes the complete corpus of all lexical series. It was begun by BENNO LANDSBERGER and has been continued by other editors.

General

MIGUEL CIVIL, "Lexicography," in *Sumerological Studies in Honor of Thorkild Jacobsen on His Seventieth Birthday, June 7, 1974,* Assyriological Studies, vol. 20 (1975), gives a general overview of the issues; ANTOINE CAVIGNEAUX, *Die sumerisch-akkadischen Zeichenlisten: Überlieferungsprobleme* (1976), deals with the internal structure of the lists; RYKLE BORGER, *Altorientalische Lexikographie, Geschichte und Probleme* (1984), is a history of modern Sumero-Akkadian lexicography.

SEE ALSO **The Use of Knowledge in Ancient Mesopotamia** (Part 8, Vol. III); **The Sumerian Language** (Part 9, Vol. IV); **The Scribes and Scholars of Ancient Mesopotamia** (Part 9, Vol. IV); and **Sumerian Literature: An Overview** (Part 9, Vol. IV).

Epic Tales from Ancient Sumer: Enmerkar, Lugalbanda, and Other Cunning Heroes

BENDT ALSTER

THE ORIGIN OF EPIC POETRY IN SUMER

With the progress made over the last fifty years in understanding Sumerian literary texts, it is now possible to trace not only sacred literature, such as hymns, myths, and lamentations, but also epics, literary debates, love songs, proverbs and proverb collections, didactic poems, folktales, and animal tales, back to the beginning of the second millennium BCE, and in some cases even back to the Early Dynastic period (approximately 2600–2500). The question has naturally been raised whether some of these types of literature, including epics, actually originated with the Sumerians and spread from them to other geographical areas. However, such an avenue would probably be much too simple.

What we can learn from the Sumerian sources is really what common sense might already have told us, namely, that proverbs, folktales, and storytelling are much older than the oldest written sources known to us, and, in fact, may already have existed thousands of years prior to the world's oldest written sources. Yet, in the case of heroic epic poetry it is true that we may be able to fix the approximate date when this phenomenon first appeared, and, although we may not accept the idea that the genre as such spread from Sumer to the rest of the world, then at least there are good reasons to debate whether the appearance of such poetry in different countries was conditioned by similar cultural developments.

Students of Mesopotamian epics are in a favorable position compared to classical scholars, because their sources cover a long span of time and represent various stages of a tradition. We are able to see, at least in glimpses, how the Akkadian *Epic of Gilgamesh* came into being. We have fragments of an Old Babylonian version preceding the Neo-Assyrian one, and still earlier epic tales in the Sumerian language. We know that parts of these were incorporated in the Akkadian Gilgamesh epic, but other parts disappeared from the literary tradition of the second and first millennia. (See the chapter on the Gilgamesh epic below.)

Most of the Sumerian sources come from the scribal schools of Nippur (modern Nuffar) and

Ur (modern Tell al-Muqayyar) and date to the Isin-Larsa period, (approximately 1900–1800), but they were probably composed somewhat earlier. A single fragment of the *Epic of Lugalbanda in Khurrumkurra* may be earlier than 2000. A tablet inscribed with a much older short poem of Lugalbanda found at Abu Salabikh dates to approximately 2600. Although it has a very different character, it does contain one of the fundamental components of the later epic tradition in that it deals with the ruler Lugalbanda and his relations to the goddess Inanna.

THE TEXTS

The following Sumerian compositions can with some right be regarded as epics. They are all short poems, ranging from about one hundred to not much more than six hundred lines in length, in other words, not much longer than one song of the Homeric epics. What entitles us to use the designation "epic" regarding the Sumerian poems of Enmerkar, Lugalbanda, and Gilgamesh is that they evidently share their subject matter with other poems widely acknowledged as epics: the rulers of the early city-states, their leadership and cunning, conquests, war and peace, international and national threats, and in addition, the relations between the rulers and their gods.

Enmerkar and the Lord of Aratta

The two Enmerkar epics deal with the Sumerian ruler Enmerkar of Uruk (modern Warka, biblical Erech) and his antagonist, the ruler of Aratta, a foreign city in Iran.

In *Enmerkar and the Lord of Aratta*, it is Enmerkar who challenges the Lord of Aratta. He requests that he recognize him as his overlord and provide Sumer with precious stones and metal with which to build and embellish the sanctuaries of Sumer. In order to threaten the Lord of Aratta, an incantation of the god Enki is recited to the effect that all languages will become harmonized, in other words, that the citizens of Aratta will have to speak Sumerian. The Lord of Aratta agrees to comply, provided that Enmerkar can solve a series of seemingly impossible tasks, and Enmerkar then outwits him three times. His invention of cuneiform writing is an exquisite proof of Enmerkar's superior cunning. The peaceful outcome finds trade relations established between the two cities.

Enmerkar and Ensukhkeshdanna

In *Enmerkar and Ensukhkeshdanna*, it is Ensukhkeshdanna, the lord of Aratta, who requests that Enmerkar acknowledge him as his superior and the favorite of the goddess Inanna. Enmerkar absolutely refuses to do this. Humiliated, Ensukhkeshdanna consults his council. A traitor from the city of Khamazu (a sarcastic perversion of Sumerian HAMAZI, meaning "may he learn") suggests a plan to make Enmerkar surrender and is offered a miserable payment of five minas of gold and silver. A sorcerer from Aratta then persuades the cows and goats of the city of Eresh to withhold their milk. Two shepherds, who are twins, ask the sun-god Utu for help. This results in a fishing competition in which a sequence of five animals caught in the river by the sorcerer of Aratta are devoured by a matching sequence of larger animals caught by a clever old woman acting on behalf of Uruk. The outwitted magician is then thrown into the Euphrates. In both Enmerkar poems the lord of Aratta finally acknowledges Enmerkar as his superior.

The Lugalbanda Epics

The two Lugalbanda epics belong together in a cycle, similar to the *Iliad* and the *Odyssey*. In *Lugalbanda in Khurrumkurra*, Enmerkar summons an army to conquer Aratta. Seven brothers are chosen as leaders, and Lugalbanda, the youngest brother, is "their eighth." He becomes sick on the way to Aratta. They leave him asleep in a cave, providing him with food so that he can survive if he wakes up. So he does, and with great skill in praying and bringing offerings to the gods, he makes them favor him. He survives by baking primitive bread and overcomes all sorts of dangers.

In *Lugalbanda and Enmerkar*, Lugalbanda continues to demonstrate his cunning by flattering the mythical Anzu bird, with the result that it offers him various gifts. He is clever enough to choose what he really needs, namely, the ability to run fast. As in any good folktale, he receives this as a gift on the condition that he will not reveal to anybody how he attained possession of it. When he reaches the army that is besieging Aratta, his brothers welcome him with joy and serve him a meal. However, after a year of unsuccessful siege, Enmerkar needs a courier to deliver a message from the goddess Inanna in Uruk that provides the means by which Aratta can finally be conquered. Now the brothers reveal themselves as true cowards. Only Lugalbanda, trusting in his secret ability to run fast, is brave enough to volunteer. Envious, they change their attitude toward him and bark at him like dogs; but he leaves them without listening to their words. This time they do not even give him any travel provisions. He quickly completes his mission, and Aratta is conquered. Uruk is provided with precious stones and handicrafts from Aratta.

Gilgamesh and Khuwawa

In *Gilgamesh and Khuwawa*, Gilgamesh decides to establish a great name for himself that will last after his death. He summons his men to set out to defeat Khuwawa (or Khumbaba), the guardian of the cedar forests. The fearless and undaunted Gilgamesh is balanced by his more cautious friend Enkidu. On having seen Khuwawa, Enkidu is stricken with panic. He arouses Gilgamesh, who has fallen asleep at the most critical moment, and begs him to abandon the project. Unimpressed, Gilgamesh approaches Khuwawa's abode. Received like a visitor by a sheikh, he tricks Khuwawa into giving up his seven coats of protective splendor. When he begs for his life, Gilgamesh, like a gentleman, is ready to show him compassion; yet Enkidu interferes, warning that Khuwawa may block the road and prevent them from returning home. When Khuwawa calls Enkidu a mercenary, Enkidu, acting accordingly, kills Khuwawa. On returning home with Khuwawa's head, they are unexpectedly reproached by the god Enlil for what they have done. The seven coats of Khuwawa's divine splendor are conferred on dangerous places and animals (like the mountains, lions, etc.). Finally, it is laconically said that Gilgamesh "entered the sea," that is, died in a supernatural way.

Gilgamesh, Enkidu, and the Netherworld

In this poem the goddess Inanna wants a mortal man to cut a bed from a *khuluppu* tree that has survived a huge cosmic storm. Gilgamesh does so, but also crafts two tools, the *pukku* and *mekku*. Playing with them, he drops them through a hole into the netherworld. Enkidu offers to descend and fetch them, but failing to listen to Gilgamesh's advice not to associate with the dead, he cannot return from their world. Gilgamesh then conjures up Enkidu's spirit through a hole, and Enkidu gives him a description of life in the netherworld. It appears from the cases he mentions that the best thing the living can hope for is to have children who can provide their parents' graves with food offerings. Those who showed disrespect toward their parents or committed perjury are punished. The text ends in a humorous statement that the spirit of the man whose body was burned ascended with the smoke to heaven. This total annihilation would be the only escape from the eternal dependence between the living and the dead. The whole point of the story becomes clear from some related fragments, namely that Gilgamesh, in spite of his aspirations to become immortal, cannot escape death. He has to take care of his parents' grave, and we tacitly understand that someone will have to take care of his.

Gilgamesh and Agga

Gilgamesh and Agga deals with a war between Gilgamesh of Uruk and Agga (Aka), the ruler of the neighboring city of Kish (modern Tell al-Uhaimir, Tell Ingharra). Agga sends a message to Gilgamesh, requesting that he surrender. Uruk's council of elders is afraid of resisting, but the young men are ready to fight. Agga besieges Uruk, but the impression of Gilgamesh's personal aura is so strong that it is enough to defeat Agga's army and take Agga captive. Instead of killing him, Gilgamesh generously releases Agga, referring to a previous act of kindness that Agga has performed.

Other Gilgamesh Tales

The tales of *Gilgamesh's Dream* and *Gilgamesh's Death* are perhaps fragments of a single poem. They deal with Gilgamesh's concern that he shall die and with his burial. *Gilgamesh and the Bull of Heaven* is a fragment that apparently anticipates the episode of the Akkadian Gilgamesh epic in which Gilgamesh resists Inanna's love.

The Sargon Legend

The *Sargon Legend* is a brief story that tells how Sargon, founder of the first Akkadian dynasty (circa 2334–2279), originally was an official at Ur-Zababa's court at Kish. He had a dream that predicted that Ur-Zababa would drown and, implicitly, that Sargon would become his successor. When Ur-Zababa learned about the dream, he tried to misinterpret it as if it were Sargon who was to drown, but he also made plans to have Sargon burned in a smith's furnace. Yet, nobody can do harm to the favorite one of the gods, and Sargon escaped the danger. Ur-Zababa then hatched a new plan. He sent Sargon to Lugalzagesi's court in Uruk with a letter ingeniously concealed in the world's first envelope, instructing Lugalzagesi to kill Sargon (see box below). The end of the tale is missing, but we may safely assume that Sargon was clever enough to break the envelope and take the necessary precautions, acting like Bellerophon in the *Iliad* and Prince Hamlet in Shakespeare's tragedy but—unlike the biblical Uriah (2 Samuel 11:14–15)—he avoided being killed.

LITERARY CHARACTERISTICS

Oral or Written Composition and Transmission?

In contrast to the Homeric epics, the Sumerian tales came into being in a society where writing had already been used to record literary compositions. Does this mean that they are "pen" compositions, created by poets who used stylus and clay instead of pen and paper? The immediate impression of their style is suggestive of oral poetry, but the answer may not be so straightforward. (See "Sumerian Literature" above.)

In twentieth-century scholarship the theory of oral improvised composition, initiated by Milman Parry, has become very influential. Parry compared the poetic technique of the Homeric epics—their poetic expressions and the way in which they are told—to that of Serbo-Croatian heroic poetry, and he saw them as creations of the oral art of singers who were able to produce and transmit poems by means of a stock of traditional poetic expressions (formulas) and sets of themes common to many poets. According to this theory each performance of a poem was a unique recreation, in which the singer adjusted length and details to the response of his audience, rather than a complete verbal repetition of a fixed text memorized by heart. Therefore "oral" literature tends to be in a constant "flow," because no two performances are exactly alike, and it is fundamentally different from "written" literature, which, according to the theory, is transmitted in a basically "fixed" form. The theory has provided insight into how such poems could have come into being long before writing was applied to literary purposes. However, when seen from the perspective of Mesopotamian literature, the distinction between oral and written literature may not be so sharp. (See "Memory and Literacy in Ancient Western Asia" above.)

What we can see, in particular from the Sumerian schools of the Isin-Larsa period, is that the transmission had both an oral and a written aspect. The pupils undoubtedly learned the texts by heart and wrote excerpts of them by dictation, but in addition to scribal art the pupils also learned rhetorical technique. This explains why we find variants in copies of the same texts that are characteristic of oral transmission or composition—such as the addition of expressions traditionally associated with specific situations and elaborate expanded versions of exciting episodes—along with variants that are features typical of written transmission, including minor dictation errors and omissions. In Sumerian texts we have evidence for blind singers, like Homer, and indirectly for literate singers, like the goddess Geshtinanna, who was said to be an expert in clay tablets as well as in songs. The art of the singer was probably the highest step of scribal education and considered even more difficult. In the middle of the third millennium when writing was first used for recording literary compositions, these were written in an incomplete way, indicating that they could have been read only by someone who was familiar with their wording in advance. This shows very clearly that in early Mesopotamian culture poetry existed before writing. The scribes undoubtedly played an important role in creating standardized texts, but the audible and the visible aspects in literature continued to be two aspects of the same process.

Some Sumerian poems may have been conceived in a fixed form in the mind of a single poet before the first performance. They then may have been transmitted orally in the same form before they were written down. On the other hand, once written down, the transmission to some extent may have been continually influenced by living oral poetry. It is also conceivable that orally transmitted poems or tales could have been repeated so many times that they finally received an almost standardized form, in an interplay between the performers and an audience who played an active role in checking and refining the tradition. In fact, many features suggest that Sumerian compositions were fundamentally meant to be recited before an audience. Therefore, instead of distinguishing between "oral" and "written" literature, it might be more appropriate to distinguish what can be called "performance poetry" from other kinds of literature.

Sumerian "Performance Poetry"

Sumerian poetry in general can be characterized by the following features:

1. The *syntax is straightforward* with no complex digressions, and if recited, the texts will be easy for a listener to follow. Rigid metrical patterns, such as the Greek hexameter, were not used in Sumerian poetry, but rhythmical and syntactic patterns were frequently repeated in a way that made it easy for a listener to recognize clusters of related phrases and transitions from one situation to the next. The plots were almost pedagogically built up in blocks, within which the story might move leisurely along with lengthy repetitions of entire passages. However, such repetitions were not used mechanically. *Enmerkar and the Lord of Aratta* starts with a sequence of messages conveyed by envoys and repeated at great length, but later the action is effectively speeded up when unnecessary repetitions are omitted. Toward the end of the text,

the transitions from one episode to the next become so abrupt that the plot is very difficult for a modern reader to follow. This creates the impression of a performance in which the tension between predictability and surprise was exploited. It is highly likely that the recital was accompanied by gestures and mime to indicate that different characters were speaking.

2. A *special poetic language* is used with many traditional expressions. Contrary to what is often asserted, the Sumerian language may have been a living and spoken language when the Sumerian epics were composed. Although little is known about the language of daily life, there can be no doubt that the Sumerian poetic language was a different formulation. A characteristic of this poetic language is that simple notions may be expressed through figures of speech or similes that present an idea in a nonstraightforward way. For example, to suggest the idea that something "covers (a large area)," the following traditional phrase could be used: "it covered like a garment, was spread out like linen." This might refer to clothes or to the splendor of a city, but, strangely enough, also to audible phenomena, such as the sound of a screaming voice or of heroic words. The texts shared a recognizable set of traditional similes and descriptions of typical situations, as well as patterns of parallelism and repetition, a characteristic way of beginning a story and introducing speakers, and so on. The poets did not normally strive to vary their descriptions. Linguistic originality was restricted to coining poetic expressions that alluded in a recognizable manner to familiar phrases. Examples are "Utu (the sun-god) went with his head raised to the lap of his mother" (that is, the sun set), and "the year returned to its mother" (that is, a year passed). Recurring expressions are fundamentally anonymous and not meant as deliberate quotations, but they can be meant as allusions to commonly known motifs.

3. A high level of "intertextuality" is characteristic of all texts. This means that each text shares with others a complex *set of allusions* to whole poems, stories, themes, characters, events, expressions, or proverbs, which a listener is supposed to know in advance in order to enjoy the point. An example is the allusion made in the Sargon legend to *Enmerkar and the*

Lord of Aratta. It is necessary for the listener to know the story of Enmerkar inventing writing to appreciate the point that now Ur-Zababa invents the envelope. Decisive events may be told in so few words that the narrative presupposes knowledge and understanding on the part of a listener or reader. An example is the phrase "he is wise and equally effective," used of Lugalbanda, in which the whole point of the Lugalbanda epics is embedded. One version of *Gilgamesh and Khuwawa* has expanded some points of the story to bring the trade relations between Sumer and the land of the cedar forests into focus, but simultaneously other parts of the story have been abbreviated to such an extent that to understand the plot the audience must have been familiar with the information that was left out.

Sometimes the outcome of a sequence of events is anticipated from the very beginning, so suspense and surprise in the sense of a modern novel was obviously not the point. In fact, the very plot structure of the poems generally depends on a high degree of predictability. Occasionally two poems, or versions of the same poem, appear to be variations on a common theme. This is the case with the two Enmerkar epics, whose plots correspond to each other like a mirror. What the audience expects is not so much an entirely new story but rather an old story in new clothes. Even a modern reader can

enjoy the effect, recognizing behind the story of Lugalbanda a folktale about a younger brother prevailing over his seven older brothers, similar to the biblical story of Joseph and Benjamin. Despite its abrupt ending, the story's true outcome, that Lugalbanda qualified to become Enmerkar's successor to the throne of Uruk, is another point that is supposed to have been evident to the listener. In the case of Sargon's dream, even today we can enjoy the effect of recognizing the similarity with the biblical stories of Joseph's dream and of Uriah's letter. This recognizability makes us feel familiar with the story, and even permits us to enter it, because we know approximately what to expect.

4. The use of preexisting *blocks of traditional descriptions* affects the appearance of the texts, so that one can sometimes literally see how they were glued together, like patchwork. Scenes are often described with this traditional material, and not always adjusted to specific circumstances. Occasionally, the attentive reader can discover minor slips of logic. When Enmerkar is besieging the foreign city of Aratta, his abode is called a "palace," although what we expect in this specific situation is a tent.

The Selection of Poetry for Academic Purposes

Like the works of classical literature that have survived to our time, the standard Sumerian liter-

---

Samples of Sumerian Epic Poetry

Enmerkar Invents Cuneiform Writing

The section to be quoted here of the poem *Enmerkar and the Lord of Aratta* (lines 500ff.) tells the story of the invention of cuneiform writing: an envoy had to deliver a message from Enmerkar to the Lord of Aratta; it was so difficult to remember that Enmerkar wrote it down on a clay tablet.

In the following translation of the passage, the symbols [] indicate that some cuneiform signs have been restored. "The lord of Kulaba (Kulab)" is another name for Enmerkar.

> His speech was [elaborate], its meaning was intricate,
> it was too heavy for the envoy's mouth, he could not repeat it.

> Because it was too heavy for the envoy's mouth, so that he could not repeat it,
> the lord of Kulaba formed a clay tablet in his hand, he wrote the words down as you do on a tablet.
> In those days there was no writing down words on clay,
> but now, under the sun of that day, thus it came about indeed!
> The lord of Kulaba wrote the words [down on the clay tablet], and thus it came about indeed!

On arriving at Aratta, the envoy speaks to the Lord of Aratta. He presents the tablet and promises to bring the answer back to Enmerkar. The description of Enmerkar as an impressive ruler, favored by the mother goddess ("the mother cow") and called the son of the sun-god Utu, aims at convincing his antagonist that he has little chance against Enmerkar (lines 524ff.):

> "Enmerkar, the son of Utu, gave me the clay tablet.
> O Lord of Aratta, when you have examined the clay tablet and learnt the meaning of the words,
> whatever you speak to me, when you have said it,
> I will tell it to the scion whose beard is blue like lapis lazuli,
> whose mother was the mighty mother cow in the land of pure rites,
> who was reared in Uruk's soil,
> who was nursed with milk at the breast of the good mother cow,
> who is fit to be the lord of Kulaba, the land of the pure rites,
> to Enmerkar, the son of Utu,
> I will deliver this message as good tidings in the shrine of Eanna.
> In his courtyard, abounding in fruits like the fresh *celtis*-tree,
> I will repeat it for my lord, the lord of Kulaba."
> Thus, he spoke to him,
> and the Lord of Aratta received
> from the envoy the baked tablet(?).
> The Lord of Aratta examined the clay.
> The spoken words were nails, his face was frowning,
> while the Lord of Aratta was examining his baked tablet(?)!

The word translated "baked tablet(?)" normally means oven or brazier, but since this would hardly make sense here, it is assumed that in this case it refers to the baked tablet produced from the oven. The implication may actually be that the Lord of Aratta watched the tablet being baked before his eyes, but if this is the case, the account of the sequence of events is abbreviated beyond recognition. Since, in antiquity, only extraordinarily important documents were baked, the point may be that the beautifully baked tablet made the Lord of Aratta realize his inferiority in cunning. The cuneiform script representing the spoken message is very accurately likened to nails.

Although obviously the Lord of Aratta could not read the world's first letter—and this is what caused his wrath—he unquestionably got the point of the message indirectly. Yet this did not cause him to give in right away. The plot continues with an episode that gives the Lord of Aratta new hope. After heavy rainfalls, piles of grain are heaped up in his courtyard, and he proudly answers that the grain harvested in Aratta is never to become the property of Enmerkar. Two warriors are then selected to fight on behalf of each ruler. The letter episode thus appears to be a story within the story, in which the poet showed his skill in producing an exciting variant of the theme of the envoy delivering a message.

That Enmerkar was traditionally associated with the invention of writing also appears from the poem *Enmerkar and Ensukhkeshdanna*. There it is said that, in response to Ensukhkeshdanna's claim of superiority, Enmerkar "formed (some clay) like a tablet in his hand, and examined it like a clay tablet" (line 77). In this case it is not explicitly stated that Enmerkar's message was inscribed on the clay tablet and delivered by an envoy to Aratta, but the comparison of the two texts actually suggests that this is how the text is to be understood. However, the story is told in so few words that we merely get the impression of a hint at a motif that must once have been commonly known but is not told in detail in the present case.

King Ur-Zababa Invents the Envelope

The *Sargon Legend* (lines 53–56) contains an episode in which the poet formed a story of King Ur-Zababa inventing the envelope on allusions to the story of how Enmerkar invented the letter.

Ur-Zababa of Kish wanted to get rid of his official Sargon, so he sent him on a mission to his colleague Lugalzagesi in Uruk, with a letter instructing Lugalzagesi to kill Sargon. To keep the matter secret he concealed the letter in the world's first envelope. Cuneiform documents of legal contents were normally contained in clay envelopes inscribed with the same texts as those of the documents themselves. We may surmise that Ur-Zababa concealed his intention by writing a document that was not a precise duplicate of the text of the envelope. The story reads as follows:

> In those days writing on clay tablets existed, but putting the clay tablets in envelopes did not exist.
> King Ur-Zababa dispatched Sargon, the creature of the gods,
> with a document written down on a clay tablet, a thing that would cause his own death,
> to Uruk, to Lugalzagesi.

Also in this case the extremely brief formulation of the story is remarkable. We have to compare the text with the Enmerkar episode to understand that after the first line the following logical continuation might be added "and now, thus it came about that envelopes came into being." The text does not even explicitly mention the fact that the letter was put in the envelope.

These examples illustrate how the poems play on allusions to traditional themes and notions, whose implications must have been evident to the contemporary audience but which can be very difficult for a modern reader to grasp. This poetry was at home in a circle of connoisseurs familiar with the basic themes. Appreciating recognized themes and presenting them in new combinations and variations were essential aspects of the art of the poet.

ary works of the Isin-Larsa period were transmitted, or channeled, as it were, through the academic circles of the schools. They were selected as literary models to be used for scribal exercises and education. Consequently, the works that have survived may be only one-sided fragments of the total tradition that once existed. The schoolmasters not only compiled previously existing literature, but they also created new poems in which the academic life in the schools was described, often satirically. However, we have no direct information about the original use and social context of most of the poems transmitted through the schools.

Entertainment and Glorification

Although we have no explicit evidence for this, we may guess that the Sumerian epic poems were first created and performed at the royal courts to entertain and glorify the king. It has been suggested that one purpose was to postulate a connection between the Third Dynasty of Ur (circa 2112–2004), and in particular its mighty King Shulgi (circa 2094–2047), with the Early Dynastic rulers Enmerkar, Lugalbanda, and Gilgamesh of the First Dynasty of Uruk (circa 2800–2700). Yet this suggestion explains only one aspect of their function.

The Story Behind the Story: The Aspirations of the Little Man

If the primary aim of the Lugalbanda epics or the *Epic of Gilgamesh and Khuwawa*, for example, had been to legitimize a ruler, then one might wonder why this was not done is a much more direct way. The stories of Lugalbanda, the youngest brother falling sick and being left alone in a cave in the mountains, and Gilgamesh falling asleep when his attention was most needed or inciting the wrath of the gods, could not have been the most obvious paradigms for King Shulgi. These are examples of stories that had their own values and follow their own principles. Nothing should prevent us from assuming that the primary function of the poems known to us was simply that of good and entertaining storytelling.

Yet, if we try to read the stories behind the stories, we see that in the case of the Lugalbanda epics, and the *Sargon Legend* as well, we find expressions of the ideology characteristic of all folktales, namely that the little man will prevail over his superiors, because he is cleverer than they are, and he is born to be a lucky man. This brings us to the true point of such storytelling, which is that wisdom prevails over strength. The little man used such tales to express his aspirations to become mighty. Such stories belong to the international cultural heritage of mankind, and storytelling may well have flourished in particular among illiterate people who had few material possessions.

Historicity

It is often more or less tacitly assumed that the stories told in the Sumerian epics are based on actual historical events, or even that they reflect a so-called heroic age of the first half of the third millennium. None of the three rulers, Enmerkar, Lugalbanda, or Gilgamesh, is attested in contemporaneous written documents; however, we do have an inscription of Enmebargesi, who is reported to have been the father of Gilgamesh's opponent, Agga of Kish, so the idea that these rulers lived in history is realistic.

Nevertheless, one must take into account that at the time when the poems were composed, there was no detailed knowledge—whether preserved in oral tradition or in written sources—about the early history of Mesopotamia. One has to accept the fundamental fictional character of literary art, and the poems can at most be used as historical sources for earlier periods in a very general sense. Neither can true historical facts of the Early Dynastic period be used directly to explain features of later literary sources. They do contain allusions to the lapis lazuli trade routes, governmental institutions, such as the council of elders, and other information that may be approximately correct. However, it serves little purpose to discuss whether the stories contain anachronistic details, because, as is generally the case with legends and folktales, they telescope everything into exemplary behavior where the realistic is imagined, and they do not aim at correctness in any historical sense.

A few examples deserve mention. The *Epic of Lugalbanda and Enmerkar* refers to the so-called Martu-wall surrounding Uruk, to describe the fortification of the city. That this wall did not exist at the time when the poem pretends to take place was not an issue for the poet. "Martu" was a designation of the nomads who threatened to invade Sumer from the west in the late second millennium, and the Martu-wall was constructed during the Third Dynasty of Ur. The epic tradition also ascribed the wall of Uruk to Gilgamesh, and although this may rest on very old and correct tradition, it is equally possible that it does not. In *Enmerkar and the Lord of Aratta*, the invention of writing is attributed to Enmerkar, and there is also a brief allusion to this in the other Enmerkar epic, but it is in fact anachronistic, and the poets knew less about the origin of writing than we do today.

Much more interesting in terms of literary understanding are many sophisticated allusions to realistic activities, which presuppose that the plots were plausible. The ancient oriental custom of political marriage is satirically ridiculed in the story of how Gilgamesh tricked Khuwawa by offering him his sister in marriage. It is possible that the story hints at a particular ruler of Elam, Sumer's northern neighbor, but all details escape us.

Social and Literary Background

It was the growing political influence of the institution of kingship and state formation that created the mental environment in which epic poetry could grow. But even if we posit that the first epics were created by court poets, presumably in the late third millennium, a number of specific factors may have been decisive in the start of the epic tradition.

One was the development of a new type of lengthy autobiographical royal inscriptions and temple hymns in which the deeds of the rulers carrying out the orders of their gods are minutely described in realistic terms. The best examples are the two long cylinder inscriptions in which Gudea of Lagash (circa 2144–2124) reported how he built the temple Eninnu, and an inscription of Utukhegal of Uruk (circa 2116–2110) which describes how he defeated the Gutians, a foreign tribe that had invaded Sumer. These texts reveal a growing interest in realistic accounts of the deeds of great rulers.

A second factor was the existence of a poetic language with many traditional phrases, whose history can in some cases be traced back to the earliest written literary sources, around 2600. We thus know that the phrase "wise and equally effective," used of Lugalbanda, originally had a shorter form, "also wise," but later the longer form became generally accepted. It is mostly assumed that this poetic language belonged exclusively to the educated classes, but this is far from certain. There is plenty of evidence that popular poems, such as love songs, workers' songs, and shepherds' songs, lie just beneath the surface of the poems transmitted to us.

A third decisive factor was undoubtedly the presence of a rich tradition of folklore and mythology, most of which is now lost to us. In other words, the art of storytelling existed and just had to be modified to suit the new purposes. This explains why the poems themselves combine features of mythology and folktales with realistic scenes belonging to the royal court.

Narrative Technique

The art of storytelling in the Sumerian epics fundamentally conforms to the list of "epic laws," as formulated in the early twentieth century by the Danish scholar Axel Olrik to characterize the narrative technique of storytelling transmitted orally.

1. Most of the Sumerian tales have a leisurely beginning, which often starts with a retrospective look into the past. Normally a tale also has a leisurely ending, but there are exceptional examples of abrupt endings (*Gilgamesh and Khuwawa* and *Lugalbanda and Enmerkar*).
2. Repetition, mostly threefold, is present everywhere.
3. Normally no more than two persons are active at one time.
4. Contrasting characters, good and bad, encounter each other. (Khuwawa is a rare example of a more complex type of personality. He may have been a frightening obstacle to traveling merchants, but we feel sorry for him.)
5. If two persons appear in the same role, they may become antagonists, like Lugalbanda and his brothers, or the two rulers Enmerkar and the Lord of Aratta, both of whom are favorites of Inanna.
6. The weakest in a group (Lugalbanda) turns out to be the best.

7. The characterization is simple and only refers to such qualities as affect the story. The characters have no life outside the story.
8. The plot is simple. Only one story is told at a time, and there are no subplots.
9. No attempt is made to secure variety in descriptions (there are exceptions to this, such as the varied descriptions of messengers in the Enmerkar epics).

One may add that different Sumerian tales may well tell contradictory stories about the same persons, but they do not violate the principle that one character stands for one particular quality. This point is particularly relevant when we try to understand why the story of Enkidu's journey to the netherworld was added to the Akkadian Gilgamesh epic as its twelfth tablet, at a point where Enkidu was supposed to be dead.

Unlike the Homeric epics, those from Sumer did not develop methods to deal with interwoven subplots, which are undoubtedly a sign of more sophisticated literature handled by literate men. There is no room for any development of the personal character of the hero: a good man is good, and a bad man is bad. The Lugalbanda epics simply serve to bring the true character of Lugalbanda and his brothers to light with as much consequence as possible. The brothers do not learn from their mistakes, and they are not given a chance to repent. The Akkadian Gilgamesh epic is the first epic that successfully deals with the development of the character of the hero, and both the Homeric epics (Achilles) and the Hebrew Bible (King David) master this to an eminent degree.

SOME OF THE THEMES

The Sumerian epics contain a number of themes and motifs attested there for the first time in world literature, such as the visit to the netherworld (Enkidu), and the hero (Gilgamesh) falling asleep at the most unfortunate moment. Some of these definitely belong to the tradition of court epic and are clearly distinct from the themes found in folktales.

The Half-Divine Hero

In heroic literature there is usually a special connection between the hero and a goddess. Enmerkar was the favorite, or even consort, of Inanna, and Gilgamesh was the son of Lugalbanda and the goddess Ninsun. The main theme of the Akkadian Gilgamesh epic, that is, his unsuccessful quest for immortality, is anticipated in the Sumerian tales and reflected later in the myths about Achilles, son of Thetis and Peleus, who was nearly made immortal by Thetis.

Chivalrous Contests and Impossible Tasks

In the *Epic of Enmerkar and Ensukhkeshdanna*, a particular expression meaning a "contest" is used of the combat of the two rulers. This word also refers to a ceremonially performed verbal contest, and this may explain the background of the Enmerkar poems: there is good evidence that entertaining verbal contests were performed when rulers or chieftains visited each other. When the winner is said to eat the geese fed by the loser, this may be a hint at a banquet served at the conclusion of such entertainments.

Some love songs give the impression that contests could also be performed in order to select a husband for a young woman, and there is evidence of a running competition with the same purpose. This may throw additional light on the contest between Enmerkar and Ensukhkeshdanna, because there can be no doubt that the winner was to become Inanna's consort.

Some details in the Enmerkar epics make us think of other types of contests. Enmerkar is asked to find a solution to three impossible tasks. The first of these was to transport barley in sacks with huge meshes. Enmerkar solved this by making the barley germinate before it was loaded in the sacks to be transported by donkeys. When the malt was sown on the fields, it could not grow, and the result was severe starvation in Aratta. The second task was to provide a scepter not made of wood, metal, or stone. Enmerkar solved this by sending a scepter made of a particular type of reed. The third problem was to provide a dog without any natural colors to fight with the Lord of Aratta's dog. Enmerkar solved this by covering the dog with a garment (perhaps a kind of harness?) that fulfilled the condition.

At this point the modern translations have "warrior," instead of "dog," but the word does in fact mean "dog," and there are clear allusions to the whole sequence in lexical series and in incantations, where the meaning clearly is "dog." This makes one think of an animal contest, in which two dogs fight on behalf of each party. Yet, the text is not easy to understand here, because in the continuation of the story the contestants actually seem to be warriors wearing helmets.

These are the earliest attestations of the solving of impossible tasks. Other early examples can be found in the Syriac legend of Ahiqar, where the wise Ahiqar is asked to provide a rope made of sand, and in the Nordic saga of Ragnar Lodbrog, where Kraka is asked to appear not dressed, but not naked, and not accompanied by someone, but not alone. Ahiqar's solution was to bore five holes in a wall and to fill them with sand to be dried in the sun. Kraka appeared dressed only in her long hair and was accompanied by a dog.

The Cunning Hero

In *Gilgamesh and Khuwawa*, Gilgamesh appears as the prototype for the Eastern and Greek tradition of the cunning hero capable of tricking his antagonist. He is received at Khuwawa's abode as an official visitor in audience. He is asked to bow down politely and then stand up and speak. Like any polite visitor he then presents his gifts. Since he knows that loneliness and the lack of noble ancestry are Khuwawa's weak points, he offers him his sister in marriage. Khuwawa greedily accepts this, but is invited to reciprocate by handing over his seven coats of splendor. This leaves him unprotected, like Samson having lost his hair. The sly, cool, and almost technical way in which Gilgamesh deceives Khuwawa makes one think of Odysseus tricking Polyphemos.

The Generous Hero

In *Gilgamesh and Agga*, Gilgamesh much rather represents the timeless ideal of the magnanimous, chivalrous ruler, who is generous enough to set his enemy free at the moment when he has a unique chance to get rid of him. We easily recognize the motif in the story of David sparing Saul's life in the cave at En-Gedi and later in

Saul's own camp (1 Samuel 24:11, 26:9). Many such themes have disappeared from modern literature but have been revived in operas, in this case in Mozart's *Die Entführung aus dem Serail*.

Wisdom Is Better than Force

The antiquity and persistence of the themes that appear for the first time in the Sumerian epics are amazing. The only thing a modern reader might miss is a true love story. The reason is that human love stories could only be told indirectly, with the girl disguised as the goddess Inanna and her lover as Dumuzi. What we can learn from the Sumerian epics is the timeless lesson that wisdom or cunning is better than force. The *Iliad* ultimately stayed true to this tradition, because, like Aratta, Troy was finally conquered by guile rather than by arms.

BIBLIOGRAPHY

Sources

ADELE BERLIN, *Enmerkar and Ensuḫkešdanna* (1979); JERROLD S. COOPER and WOLFGANG HEIMPEL, "The Sumerian Sargon Legend," *Journal of the American Oriental Society* 103 (1983); D. O. EDZARD, "Gilgameš und Ḫuwawa," *Zeitschrift für Assyriologie* 80 (1990), 81 (1991); D. KATZ, *Gilgamesh and Akka* (1993); MARIA DEJONG ELLIS, "Gilgamesh's Approach to Ḫuwawa: A New Text," *Archiv für Orientforschung* 28 (1982); SAMUEL NOAH KRAMER, *Gilgamesh and the Ḫuluppu-Tree* (1938); "The Death of Gilgameš," *Bulletin of the American Schools of Oriental Research* 94 (1944); "Gilgameš and Agga," *American Journal of Archaeology* 53 (1949); *Enmerkar and the Lord of Aratta: A Sumerian Tale of Iraq and Iran* (1952); WILLEM H. PH. RÖMER, *Das sumerische Kurzepos "Bilgameš und Akka"* (1980); CLAUS WILCKE, *Das Lugalbandaepos* (1969).

Translations

THORKILD JACOBSEN, *The Harps that Once . . . : Sumerian Poetry in Translation* (1987), includes translations of *Enmerkar and the Lord of Aratta, Lugalbanda and Enmerkar,* and *Gilgamesh and Agga*.

Studies

BENDT ALSTER, "A Note on the Uriah Letter in the Sumerian Sargon Legend," *Zeitschrift für Assyriolo-*

gie 77 (1987), and "Court Ceremonial and Marriage in the Sumerian Epic 'Gilgameš and Ḫuwawa,'" *Bulletin of the School of Oriental and African Studies* 55 (1992); WILLIAM W. HALLO, "Lugalbanda Excavated," *Journal of the American Oriental Society* 103 (1983); AARON SHAFFER, "Gilgamesh, the Cedar Forest, and Mesopotamian History," *Journal of the American Ori-*

ental Society 103 (1983); HERMAN L. J. VANSTIPHOUT, "Enmerkar's Invention of Writing Revisited," in *DUMU-E₂-DUB-BA-A: Studies in Honor of Å. W. Sjöberg*, edited by H. BEHRENS, D. LODING, and M. T. ROTH (1989); CLAUS WILCKE, "Lugalbanda," *Reallexikon der Assyriologie und Vorderasiatische Archäologie* 7 (1987).

SEE ALSO **Sumerian Literature: An Overview** (Part 9, Vol. IV).

The Gilgamesh Epic: A Masterpiece from Ancient Mesopotamia

WILLIAM MORAN

THE SUMERIAN BACKGROUND

According to Sumerian tradition, Gilgamesh (originally Bilgamesh) was an early ruler in the city-state of Uruk (Warka, biblical Erech). The evidence, admittedly meager and indirect, puts him there around 2700 BCE, a period of intense intercity rivalries. Nothing is known of his actual achievements in this setting except perhaps what is reflected in the later tradition of Gilgamesh as heroic warrior and the builder of his city's walls. Not very long after his death, Gilgamesh appears in a god-list.

The memory of Gilgamesh lived on in the oral tradition of the Sumerians, especially at the court of Uruk, where he became the subject of heroic tales. How early these tales, and how many of them, may have been committed to writing is not known. The earliest compositions we have probably do not go back beyond the late third millennium. By that time, Gilgamesh had become a very popular figure, especially among the rulers of the Third Dynasty of Ur. As befits a hero, he has a distinguished parentage. His father, Lugalbanda, was another divinized ruler of Uruk, and his mother was the goddess Ninsun.

Gilgamesh is celebrated in a number of works, which in view of their length (115–450 lines) are perhaps better called lays rather than epics. These lays contain themes and tales that would later reappear in the Babylonian epic. In one lay, Gilgamesh, accompanied by Enkidu and other retainers, in order to achieve the immortality that comes with heroic deeds, sets out to confront the monster Khuwawa in the Cedar Forest. In another, Gilgamesh is the oppressor of Uruk, and Enkidu is trapped in, and must remain in, the underworld. In another, for reasons that are not clear, the goddess Inanna (Akkadian Ishtar) sends the Bull of Heaven against Gilgamesh. In yet another version, Gilgamesh protests against his mortality. While these are all independent compositions, they do manifest a certain unity. Death—the fear of death, everlasting fame as victory over death, life after death—is a common

2327

theme and distinctive of the late Sumerian Gilgamesh tradition. (See also "Epic Tales from Ancient Sumer" earlier in this volume.)

THE OLD BABYLONIAN VERSION

Sometime early in the second millennium the various Gilgamesh traditions, Sumerian and perhaps Akkadian, oral or written, were sorted out, adapted, and profoundly transformed into either a single composition, which seems more probable, or a two-part cycle. This earlier version of the *Epic of Gilgamesh* has come to be known as the Old Babylonian Version. Though preserved only in fragments, it is clearly a work of great originality. Written in the Babylonian dialect of Akkadian and not a mere translation from the Sumerian, it is poetry of remarkable freshness and simplicity. Its thousand or more lines, like Homer's *Odyssey,* are unified around a central character and a single pervasive theme—the hero's quest for immortality.

With occasional reliance on the later Standard Version, we can reconstruct the narrative line. After a brief hymn in praise of the hero, we are introduced to a Gilgamesh who, driven by his superhuman energies and powerful ambitions, has by his excessive and relentless demands on his people become their oppressor. In answer to the people's prayers, the gods create a match for Gilgamesh, someone of comparable strength, to refocus his energies and ambitions. This is Enkidu. They become friends, and soon Gilgamesh conceives a project that will bring him the immortality of undying fame, a battle with Khuwawa. Thus begins the journey to the Cedar Forest, the confrontation, and the victory.

The characterization of Enkidu here is new, but the Khuwawa adventure, with Enkidu a participant, is based on an earlier, Sumerian tradition. The Old Babylonian Version then goes its own, original way. Enkidu dies, undoubtedly as divine punishment for his part in the slaying of Khuwawa. This is one innovation, and another follows. Gilgamesh, confronted now with death in the person of a beloved friend, becomes consumed with grief and is suddenly riven with fear. Faced with the reality of death, he will now be content only with true immortality, the immortality reserved to the gods. Thus begins another journey, this one to the end of the world to find the lone exception to human mortality—Ut-napishtim (Old Babylonian Uta-napishtim, Sumerian Ziusudra), the Babylonian Noah, the one survivor, along with his family, of the Flood.

After a long journey full of harrowing experiences, Gilgamesh finally reaches Ut-napishtim, at which point the reconstruction of the narrative becomes only partial at best. We still do not know exactly how the Old Babylonian Version ended. Certainly Gilgamesh failed in his quest for divine immortality and learned that his death was inevitable. But how did he react to this discovery? Did he return to Uruk, frustrated and embittered, a broken and tragic figure? Or did he, as in the later Standard Version (see below), recover some sense of purpose, of human goals, and of the satisfaction of human achievements? At present, these are questions for which there are no sure answers.

This long narrative seems to pivot on three seven-day periods, each of which is associated with a profound transformation, first of the nonhuman into the human, then of the human into the nonhuman, and finally of the nonhuman back into the human. These transformations are associated with corresponding rites of passage, especially those of cleansing and clothing. The underlying theme of evolution is evidently germane to a work that studies someone trying to come to terms with his humanity.

The first transformation is that of Enkidu. The Old Babylonian Enkidu is utterly different from the Sumerian Enkidu. As created by the gods, he is a savage, hairy wild man who lives on the steppe with the animals and acts as their friend. As described, he may ultimately reflect the myth and representations, dating as far back as the early third millennium, of the Bull-Man who fights the Naked Hero. More immediately, however, Enkidu is modeled on a concept of antiprimitivism found elsewhere in Sumerian, Babylonian, and classical sources. According to this notion, the beginning of human existence was neither a golden age nor a period of pristine simplicity. On the contrary, life was savage, and man differed little, if at all, from other animals. Primal man was a beast, and the Babylonian Enkidu was primal man *redivivus,* a figure who introduced into the epic a sharp nature-culture contrast that became a recurrent theme.

The humanization of Enkidu begins with seven days of uninterrupted lovemaking with a harlot sent into the steppe to seduce him. In one of the most amusing and lighthearted passages in Babylonian literature, the humanization proceeds as Enkidu is bathed, anointed, clothed, and then introduced to human fare—bread and beer. He drinks seven kegs of beer and breaks into song. At this point, he is introduced to shepherds, transitional figures who are, by definition, at the outer edge of human society and urban life. Enkidu's humanization is complete when, having entered Uruk, he finally kneels in submission before Gilgamesh and acknowledges his kingship, the institution that in the Mesopotamian worldview was the sole guarantee of the guided, the ordered, the fully human life. Now fully human, Enkidu can become the friend of Gilgamesh, and the story can move into what we may call its heroic phase.

The second transformation occurs when, for seven days and seven nights, Gilgamesh grieves over the body of his dead friend, "until a maggot dropped from his nose." His friend gone, Gilgamesh refuses to end his grief or to put away the signs of grief. He does not wash; he puts on no fresh clothes. He will not be reintegrated into human society. Instead, his body covered with grime and wrapped in animal skins, he departs into the steppe. The transformation is radical. He who once voiced so eloquently the heroic ideal—declaring his contempt for death and chiding Enkidu for fearing it as long as there was the prospect of dying gloriously and unforgettably—now utterly rejects that ideal and all the values associated with it. Gilgamesh the hero is dead. Gilgamesh, the anti-man, the would-be god, appears.

The last seven-day period and last transformation, is reconstructed from the Standard Version. In view of the evidence for other, smaller periods of transformation in the Old Babylonian Version, however, it seems virtually certain that the Standard Version reflects the earlier tradition. To prove to Gilgamesh that he does not have the stuff of immortality, Ut-napishtim challenges him to stay awake for seven days. Gilgamesh accepts the challenge and immediately falls asleep—for seven days. Awakened and confronted with the facts, he finally yields, and in evidence of his inner transformation and of his at least grudging acceptance of his mortality, he allows himself to be bathed. His animal skins are cast off and carried away by the sea, and with

---

"The Tears of Things"

My friend, whom I still love so very much,
Who journeyed through all hardships with me,
Enkidu, whom I still love so very much,
Who journeyed through all hardships with me,
Did journey to the fate of all mankind.

For days and nights did I weep over him,
And would not let them bury him,
As if my friend might rise at my cries
—for seven days and seven nights—
Until a maggot dropped from his nose.

And since he's gone, I have not found life,
Though roaming, trapper-like, about the steppe.
And now, dear Alewife, I behold your face.
The death I ever dread may I not behold!

The Alewife addresses Gilgamesh:
"Where can you reach in your wanderings?

The life you seek you shall never find.
For when the gods created human kind,
Death did they establish for human kind,
Life did they keep just for themselves.

You, Gilgamesh, with belly full,
For days and nights do celebrate,
And of each day a feasting make,
For days and nights do dance and play.

And let your garments be clean and fresh,
Your head be washed, your body bathed,
Your eyes upon the child that holds your hand.
Your wife should rejoice, rejoice in your
    embrace.
Such work is meant for human kind."

(From the Old Babylonian Version, "Meissner Fragment"—Standard Version, Tablet 10)

a new cloak to cover him, Gilgamesh accepts his humanity.

DIFFUSION, EXPANSION, AND ESTABLISHMENT OF THE TEXT

In the centuries that followed, knowledge of the epic spread into Anatolia, Syria, and Palestine. Fragments of the *Epic of Gilgamesh* both in the Babylonian language and in Hittite and Hurrian adaptations have been found, and they date to the fourteenth and thirteenth centuries BCE. They establish the existence of a text that followed the Old Babylonian story at least in broad outline, but they also include what was probably material unknown to the earlier version, most notably Ishtar's sexual advances to Gilgamesh and the slaying of the Bull of Heaven. In other words, almost the entire narrative of the later Standard Version seems to be in place. At times, the language of the text is quite close to that of the older version; at others, it is closer to the language of the Standard Version; at still others, it goes its own way. A stable story and a fluid text exist well into the late second millennium.

THE STANDARD VERSION

Late in the second millennium Babylonian literature took on more or less stable forms. The text of the *Epic of Gilgamesh* seems to have been established around this time. Tradition credits this edition to a poet-editor by the name of Sin-leqe-unninni. (See "The Scribes and Scholars of Ancient Mesopotamia" earlier in this volume.) The text is known mainly from copies of the seventh century in the Nineveh library of the Assyrian king Assurbanipal, but substantial parts have also been found at other sites—Sultantepe, Nimrud (modern Kalkhu), Asshur (modern Qalat Sharqat), Babylon, Uruk—and in copies as late as the first century BCE. Known as the Standard Version—the existence of competing versions is doubtful—it was originally a work of about three thousand lines, traditionally distributed over eleven tablets; a twelfth tablet, a kind of appendix, was a later addition. At present, we possess about three-fifths of the original.

Prologue

The Standard Version begins by repeating and expanding the prologue of the Old Babylonian Version. Line 27 (in the Kovacs translation quoted herein) has been identified as the first line of the latter; thus, lines 1–26 are a later addition, probably from the hand of Sin-leqe-unninni, and are meant to guide our understanding of the narrative that follows.

The earlier prologue, which perhaps contains later additions but certainly nothing dissonant, is a hymn to the unique strength, dignity, and kingship of Gilgamesh. He is first presented as a giant: "He was bigger than (all other) kings, in stature most renowned." (In the Hittite version, he was eleven cubits tall.) The text then goes on, for twenty lines, presenting origins that make him partly divine, his leadership, and his distant journeys. He is mighty, and his deeds are mighty.

How different the Gilgamesh of lines 1–26. In sharp contrast with the earlier hymn, this Gilgamesh suffers and is worn out: "He came back from a long journey and was weary." The feats celebrated in the hymn all become simply "wearying toil," and lest we forget this, just as we are about to begin the celebratory hymn, we are reminded that "Gilgamesh every hardship bore." This is another Gilgamesh, a more human Gilgamesh, a Gilgamesh who, however great his strength and however splendid his achievements, had to pay the price. Behind this expression of admiration are values different from those inspiring the ancient hymn.

Even more than the hero's sufferings, these opening lines stress his vast experience, knowledge, and wisdom. The very first words introduce Gilgamesh as "The one who saw all." Moreover, he was "possessed (?) of wisdom" and

> Secret things he saw, hidden ones revealed,
> Knowledge brought of days before the Flood.
>
> (1.5–6)

Here again the later poet-editor complements and refocuses the hymn that follows. The earlier hero's long journeys are seen simply as feats of strength. Here they become sources of knowledge. Here, too, the hero is not only strong but wise, possessed of a quality of mind in the experiential and practical order that is a guide to action in all its manifold forms. This Gilgamesh not only has *emūqān*, physical strength, but *nēmēqu*, wisdom. In short, he is a complete king, something the earlier text did not make clear.

To prove his point and to illustrate this *nēmēqu*, the poet-editor addresses his reader. (It is important to note that the prologue addresses a second participant. The author is not a singer or a reciter but a writer, and his audience is not a group listening to him, but individuals, readers with tablet in hand.) The reader's attention is directed to one of Gilgamesh's most famous achievements, the great walls of Uruk and its renowned temple of the goddess Ishtar, "the like of which no king, no man, will ever build":

> Go up on the walls and walk about.
> Examine the terrace and study the brickwork,
> If its brickwork be not all of baked bricks,
> Its foundations not laid by the Seven Sages.
> One *sar* city, one *sar* orchards, one *sar* pasture and pond—and the fallow fields of Ishtar's house—
> Three *sar* and fallow fields—Uruk you will see [?].
>
> (1.17–22)

Here is a work of Gilgamesh's *nēmēqu*, conspicuous and resplendent, begun indeed with the assistance of the great and most ancient Seven Sages.

Before turning to the walls of Uruk, the poet-editor tells us two more important things about Gilgamesh. The first is that he is not just weary; he is "weary but at peace." This is a Gilgamesh who contrasts vividly with the Gilgamesh of the older narrative following. The earlier figure is totally unfamiliar with peace. His energies consume him, and he drives everyone around him to exhaustion. His heart is ascribed the wildness of a storm-demon, and even his mother complains of her son's "restless heart." All his projects, whether in Uruk or on his long campaigns and journeys, bespeak anything but peace. Whence, then, this peaceful if weary man?

We are also told that Gilgamesh left a record of his labors: "From a far journey he returned, was weary but at peace. On stone chiseled each wearying toil." The walls having been celebrated, we—still readers, still alone—are told

this (some uncertainty attaches to the translation of the beginning of some of these lines):

> Find the copper chest.
> Remove the locks of bronze.
> Open the cover to the treasure there.
> Take up and read diligently the tablet of lapis lazuli,
> How he, Gilgamesh, every hardship bore.
>
> (1.22–26)

There can be little doubt that the inscription chiseled on stone must be identified with the lapis lazuli tablet we are now instructed to read so diligently. In context, it does not seem likely that the two are distinct. Moreover, there is other evidence that kings were supposed to leave records of their labors and deposit them in chests (see below). Note, too, how strongly *kalû mānaḫti*, "each wearying toil," is echoed in sound and sense by what we are now told to read about on the tablet, *kalû marṣāti*, "every hardship" borne by Gilgamesh.

The object on which Gilgamesh writes is called a *narû*, often a "stela," freestanding and on public display, like the Code of Hammurabi stela (pictured in "King Hammurabi of Babylon" in Part 5, Vol. II). But if the *narû* here is identical with the tablet, it is not a stela. Moreover, it lies in a chest, probably in the room of some temple (see below). By implying that the source for the following narrative—and certainly this is implied—was the text inscribed by Gilgamesh himself and by inviting the reader to a comparision with the original, the poet-editor undoubtedly wishes to authenticate his tale. But the text implies more. It implies a particular approach to, and understanding of, the epic.

Babylonian literature possessed a genre known as "pseudo-autobiography," which is characterized by its didacticism. The best-preserved example is very instructive for the interpretation of the prologue. It is called *The Legend of Naram-Sin*, and it is attested in both an Old Babylonian and a later form. (See the chapter on Sargon and Naram-Sin in Part 5, Vol. II.) In the latter, we find Naram-Sin, the famous king of Akkad, in the broken first line advising the reader to "read diligently the *narû*." It is, moreover, now virtually certain that the break should be restored to read "open the chest." The text that follows is badly broken. Speaking in the first person, Naram-Sin tells about some fabulous bird-men, and the narrative concludes with his reporting an oracle he says he received from Ishtar. The king then addresses the reader:

> Whosoever you may be, whether governor or
>   prince or anyone else,
> Whom the gods shall call to rule over a kingdom,
> I have made for you a chest and inscribed for
>   you a *narû*,
> And in the city of Cuthah, in the temple
>   Emeslam,
> In the chamber of the god Nergal, deposited it
>   for you.
> Find this *narû* and listen to what this *narû* says,
>   and then . . .
>
> (1.147–152)

There follows a long exhortation that reflects the oracle of Ishtar just reported.

The parallels to the prologue are obvious: the address to the reader, the chest, the *narû* within, the command to read it diligently. The parallels from a kind of didactic literature fit perfectly with the Gilgamesh we are first introduced to, the man of *nēmēqu*. Moreover, as most modern interpreters of the epic have stressed, the epic is a kind of bildungsroman, the story of Gilgamesh's education and progress to maturity. It is, in its way, a lesson. In alluding to Gilgamesh's autobiography as his source, the author has thus given us final and formal guidance on how we are to read what follows. We are to read, tablet in hand, quietly, reflectively, intent on learning what the life of Gilgamesh has to teach us. What follows is *narû*-epic, epic in a new key, epic in "the key of wisdom."

Tablets 1.52–2:
Gilgamesh and Enkidu

Where preserved, the text follows the Old Babylonian narrative rather closely, but with considerable amplification: Gilgamesh the oppressor; the creation and humanization of Enkidu; his confrontation with Gilgamesh in Uruk; their friendship; Gilgamesh's proposal to fight Khuwawa, now called Khumbaba.

Tablets 3–4:
The Khumbaba Adventure

In broad outline, but again with expansions, some now of folkloristic origin, the text follows the old story. The role assigned to Shamash is an innovation, but probably not of the late edition. Counselor and protector in the Old Babylonian Version, he is presented in the Standard Version as the instigator of the whole enterprise. Ninsun charges him with having "touched" her son and set him on his way to Khumbaba, and Khumbaba himself holds Shamash as ultimately responsible for his plight. Later, too, at least according to the Hittite version, when it is decided by the gods that the slaying of Khuwawa and the Bull of Heaven may not go unpunished, Shamash protests, though in vain, that Gilgamesh and Enkidu have only acted on his orders. What may lie behind this apparent conflict between Shamash and the other gods is not clear; a mythic dimension of the text eludes us here.

The Standard Version also enlarges and elevates the purpose of the journey: "Until he [Gilgamesh] slays the fierce Khumbaba, / And makes perish from the land every evil that you [Shamash] hate." No longer is the sole consideration that lasting glory of Gilgamesh. Shamash has his own motive, be it to destroy all moral evil or everything baneful. It seems a loftier view of the whole enterprise and one quite consonant with the didacticism of the late edition. The alleged Old Babylonian parallel is quite uncertain.

Also new and shocking is the manifest hubris of the two companions. As they face Khumbaba, Enkidu speaks of having to contend with the anger of the gods for what they are about to do, but he does not hesitate to urge Gilgamesh to kill. They seem to think that making a great cedar door and bringing it back to Nippur (Nuffar) will placate the gods. As the two heroes head back in apparent triumph, the fifth tablet finishes with a very strong sense of foreboding that the Khumbaba story is not over. The foreboding is only reinforced by the next series of events.

Tablet 6:
Ishtar and the Bull of Heaven

Back in Uruk, bathed and decked out in all his finery, Gilgamesh catches the eye of Ishtar, who, smitten by his charms, offers to take him in marriage. Gilgamesh not only rejects her offer but pours out on her a stream of insults. Scorned and enraged, the goddess persuades her father, Anu, to unleash against Gilgamesh the Bull of Heaven only to have Gilgamesh and Enkidu slaughter the Bull, empty its innards, and lay them before Shamash. Ascending the city wall to look down on the scene below, Ishtar "took a stance of mourning, uttered a loud wail, / 'Woe to Gilgamesh, who has insulted me, killed the Bull of Heaven.' " On hearing her, Enkidu tears off the Bull's haunch and hurls it at her as he screams, "Oh that I could reach you and make you just like him."

Whether Tablet 6 serves as a polemic against the ancient institution of the sacred marriage, king and priestess uniting symbolically as god and goddess, remains uncertain, but the context of the Gilgamesh narrative certainly establishes hubris as a quality that makes divine retribution inevitable. There is something undeniably terrifying about the figure of the great goddess standing high on the wall over her city and crying "Woe to Gilgamesh." The gods are not mocked.

Tablets 7–8: The Death of Enkidu

That very night, after a great banquet in celebration of the heroes' return, Enkidu has a dream wherein he learns (here we are briefly dependent on the Hittite version) that the gods have decided he must die while Gilgamesh is to be spared. His resentment is deep and bitter, and he is full of curses for the great door, for the trapper who brought the harlot to him, and for the harlot herself, all of them responsible in some way for his imminent death. Reproached by Shamash for forgetting the blessings of civilized life and the friendship of Gilgamesh that the harlot had led him to, Enkidu relents and blesses her. Thus does the epic celebrate once more culture over nature. Enkidu also has a terrifying dream about life in the underworld. Finally, he falls sick, lingers on for twelve days, and dies. Stricken with grief, Gilgamesh recalls at length their many adventures together, buries his friend after a week of mourning, erects a statue in his honor—and is transformed.

Tablets 9–10: The Great Journey

The journey to Ut-napishtim leads Gilgamesh through a strange and awesome world. He meets the Scorpion-Man and his wife, who try to dissuade him from going on, but on he goes, on and on under the earth, surrounded by darkness, emerging into a garden of trees loaded with jew-els. He has left all that is human, all that is of this world. He reaches a tavern keeper named Siduri, who tries to dissuade him, but eventually she directs him to Urshanabi, Ut-napishtim's boatman, who can bring him across the Waters of Death to his master.

The Ut-napishtim whom he reaches is for Gilgamesh a bitter disappointment. Unlike the superman he had imagined, Ut-napishtim is quite ordinary. But he is also a sage and he chides Gilgamesh with the question "What have you gained?" He is full of brief sayings on the frailty of man "snapped off like a reed," on the transitory nature of whatever man does, and, above all, on death—invisible, faceless, silent, certain. And finally he explains that, after the Flood,

After Ellil had pronounced my blessing [of immortality],
The Anunnaki gods being assembled,
Mammetum, creatress of destiny, with them decreed the destinies.
They established death and life.
The days of death they did not define.
(10.305–309)

In this meeting, for the first time, the gods made death part of the established order of things. Later—originally, probably in the next line—Ut-napishtim asks rhetorically, "Now who is going to assemble the gods for you?" Obviously, no one. Gilgamesh has journeyed in vain.

Tablet 11: The Flood Story: Conversion and Journey Home

It is generally conceded that the Flood was not part of the original epic, which may have referred to it, but only briefly. The long account in Tablet 11 seems to be told for its own sake. It seriously interrupts not only the flow of dialogue between Ut-napishtim and Gilgamesh but the otherwise smooth and natural transition from the end of Tablet 10, where Ut-napishtim tells Gilgamesh about the assembly of the gods after the Flood, to Ut-napishtim's rhetorical question. Finally, the story as told here is not an independent account; it draws on an identifiable source, the myth of Atrakhasis.

It is also generally conceded that the one who added the story was the poet-editor of the prologue. He has a manifest interest in, and esteem for, "the knowledge of days before the Flood" that Gilgamesh brought back. He also speaks in

Babylonian Flood Stories

There were two Babylonian versions of the Flood Story, one long and one short. In the former, the myth of Atrakhasis (Ut-napishtim), the Flood comes as the culmination of a long series of events reaching back into mythic time when humans did not exist. It is a story that begins with some gods forced to labor for the others. Eventually the subdued deities refuse to work any longer. The solution to the crisis, proposed by the crafty god Ea, is the creation of humans to form a new labor force, which only leads to another crisis: the ever-increasing numbers of humans produce such a din that the god in charge of the earth, Ellil (or Enlil), can get no sleep. What follows is a tale of growing anger and frustration, as Ellil's attempts to reduce the number of humans is thwarted by Ea. Finally, Ellil decides not merely to reduce but to annihilate humanity. He sends the Flood—and Ea saves Ut-napishtim.

In this amusing, rather naïve tale, Ellil may appear as a somewhat pathetic figure. His anger may be excessive and the indiscriminate destruction of humanity both reprehensible and even stupid. After all, the gods need humans. Nevertheless, his decision is also understandable, and it does make some sense.

The short version is quite different. Two examples of it are known, one the account in the Gilgamesh epic, the other on a tablet of the thirteenth century BCE discovered at Ras Shamra (ancient Ugarit) in Syria. The latter is extremely fragmentary, but enough is preserved—the very beginning and the very end—to show its basic similarity to the Gilgamesh version. It begins, "When the gods took counsel about the lands / They sent a flood upon the world" ("Récit du Déluge," lines 1–3). Then Ut-napishtim introduces himself as Atrakhasis and begins to tell of Ea's communication to him. At the very end, Ut-napishtim and his wife are being granted immortality.

In the Gilgamesh version, the story begins:

> Shuruppak—a city you yourself know,
> Lying on Euphrates' bank—

This city was old, the gods within it,
And their heart moved the gods to send a flood.

(11.11–4)

It continues, as does the Ugarit tablet, with Ea's revelation to Ut-napishtim and ends with Ellil touching the foreheads of Ut-napishtim and his wife as they kneel at his feet and declaring that they shall no longer be like men but immortal like gods. The absence of any clear motivation for sending the Flood is distinctive of the short version. The decision to destroy mankind has no prior history, no background; it simply happens. It may not be an act of sheer caprice, but we shall never know why. The waters wash over humanity, and it disappears, swallowed up in mystery.

The part of the long version in which Ut-napishtim is given immortality is lost, and so comparison of the two versions is not possible. It may be noted, however, that, in the short version as preserved in the epic, the gift of immortality strikes one as no less capricious or mysterious than the sending of the Flood. The god Ellil, who had been mainly responsible for the destruction of humanity and who only moments before, on arriving and finding a few survivors, had become quite enraged, now not only spares these survivors but makes them immortal. Why such extraordinary largesse? The conclusion of the story makes no more sense than the beginning. We start with an apparently arbitrary destruction of life and end with an equally arbitrary extension of life into eternity.

The inscrutability of the gods was ancient and common in Mesopotamian religious thought, and it became an essential part of the wisdom of the sage. Reflective individuals of this period concluded from their life experience that the gods were not only inscrutable but held humanity to norms of behavior that they would not reveal and that humans could not discover. It even seemed that good was evil and evil good. The Flood Story contained in the epic, the primeval paradigm of the human situation, belongs within this tragic view of humanity. (See also "Flood Narratives of Ancient Western Asia" below.)

the prologue of the secret things revealed by Gilgamesh but with only two formally identified, one of them the Flood Story. If the poet-editor was not the one who added the story, he certainly directs his reader to it and implies its importance.

In the learned world of Sin-leqe-unninni, the Flood Story is certainly important in that it is knowledge that, were it not for Gilgamesh, would have been lost. And it is not just any knowledge. It is knowledge about the most terrible event in human history. It is knowledge about a terrible truth: the gods can destroy and one may never know why. A wise man, Gilgamesh, should know this.

Another essential truth is revealed in the episode of the Plant of Rejuvenation. Convinced finally by his week-long sleep that he must die, Gilgamesh, as already noted, yields, accepts his mortality, and allows himself to be bathed and clothed in fresh garments. He is ready to return to Uruk. Before he is gone for good, Ut-napishtim and his wife, wishing to give him some reward for his labors, tell him of the Plant of Rejuvenation. It can make him young again, and its existence is identified as the second matter of secret knowledge. Gilgamesh secures the plant, but, returning to Uruk accompanied by Urshanabi, he sets it down as he plunges into the cool waters of a pool, only to watch helplessly as a serpent makes off with it, sloughing off its skin as it goes.

Here Gilgamesh is betrayed simply by his humanity, its frailty and its limitations. Weeping, he delivers his final judgment on his journey across the Waters of Death to the end of the world. He says quite simply, "I should have turned back." He sees now the radical impropriety of the whole enterprise: one should attempt neither to escape death nor even to cheat it. A wise man, Gilgamesh, should know this too.

The story does not end here. Gilgamesh and the boatman push on to Uruk, and the language echoes the earlier journey to the Cedar Forest. We are being drawn back to the memory of earlier events. And, finally, on their arrival Gilgamesh addresses the boatman:

> Go up on the walls and walk about.
> Examine the terrace and study the brickwork,
> If its brickwork be not all of baked bricks,
> Its foundations not laid by the Seven Sages.
> One *sar* city, one *sar* orchards, one *sar* pasture
>   and pond—
>   and fallow fields of Ishtar's house—
> Three *sar* and fallow fields . . .
>
> (11.314–319)

These are the last words of the epic, and we have come full circle. We hear again the words of the prologue that were addressed to the reader, and we have a sense of finality and completeness. We began in Uruk, and we end there. In this new context, however, after all that has

gone before, the solid, material nature of it all—walls and measurements and topography—tells us, and tells us forcibly, that Gilgamesh is back from a world of jeweled trees and monsters and regions not meant for man. He returns to a definable, measurable, human world, a world indeed made by man. And Gilgamesh, pointing to this man-made world of Uruk, suggests an intuitive if inarticulate perception that the work proper to man and his destiny is to build, to create a world of his own, as well as to die. This perception gives meaning to life and makes whole the wisdom of Gilgamesh: "From a far journey he returned, was weary but at peace."

Tablet 12: Appendix

Tablet 12 is a literal translation of part of the Sumerian composition *Gilgamesh, Enkidu, and the Netherworld*, and it is certainly a later but not an altogether happy addition, destroying the narrative symmetry of the earlier eleven-tablet work. Nor are the motives for the addition clear. Since Enkidu instructs Gilgamesh on the life of various classes of people in the netherworld, it has been suggested that merely by questioning Enkidu, Gilgamesh implies his readiness to accept his role in the next life as god and king of the netherworld. And there have been other proposals, none convincing.

With the end of cuneiform civilization, Gilgamesh was not completely forgotten. At Qumran, site of the discovery of the famous Dead Sea Scrolls, in the apocryphal literature associated with the biblical patriarch Enoch, he appears as one of the giants along with the monster Khumbaba, who is also found in the Manichaean *Book of the Giants*. Later, in his *On the Characteristics of Animals*, Aelian (circa 175–230 CE) recounts a curious tale about a Gilgamos who became king of Babylon. In the seventh century CE, the scholiast Theodore bar Konai, writing in Syriac, mentions among ancient kings a certain Gmigmos (Gmengos, Glimgos) as a contemporary of Abraham.

Whether (and if so, to what extent) the epic itself may have survived in various transformations remains a matter of discussion. The arguments for influence on works such as the *Alexander Romance*, originally a Greek composition of the fourth century CE, and on the journeys of Buluqiya in the *Arabian Nights* seem the most plausible.

BIBLIOGRAPHY

Primary Sources

Cuneiform copies and critical editions are listed in JEFFREY H. TIGAY, *The Evolution of the Gilgamesh Epic* (1982); To Tigay's Boğazköy fragment (p. 305), add GERNOT WILHELM, "Neue akkadische Gilgameš-Fragmente aus Ḫattuša," *Zeitschrift für Assyriologie* 78 (1988); to Tigay's Uruk (GEUW) fragment (p. 306), add E. VON WEIHER, *Spätbabylonische Texte aus Uruk*, Teil II, Ausgrabungen der deutschen Forschungsgemeinschaft in Uruk-Warka, Band 10, no. 30 (1983); and "Ein Fragment der 5. Tafel des Gilgameš-Epos aus Uruk," *Baghdader Mitteilungen* 11 (1980). For Gilgamesh in Elamite, see I. M. DIAKONOFF and N. B. JANKOWSKA, "An Elamite Gilgamesh Text from Argištihenele, Urartu (Armavi-blur, 8th Century B.C.)," *Zeitschrift für Assyriologie* 80 (1990). For the translation and more on *The Legend of Naram-Sin*, see O. R. GURNEY, "The Sultantepe Tablets: IV. The Cuthean Legend of Naram-Sin," *Anatolian Studies* 5 (1955). For a discussion of "Récit du Déluge," see JEAN NOUGAYROL, *Ugaritica V*, Mission de Ras-Shamra, Tome XVI, no. 166 (1968).

Translations

In English translation, see MAUREEN GALLERY KOVACS, *The Epic of Gilgamesh* (1985); and STEPHANIE DALLEY, *Myths from Mesopotamia: Creation, the Flood, Gilgamesh, and Others* (1989). DAVID FERRY, *Gilgamesh: A New Rendering in English Verse* (1992), is quite free, but real English verse and very moving.

Interpretation

Three important sources are THORKILD JACOBSEN, *The Treasures of Darkness: A History of Mesopotamian Religion* (1976), pp. 195–219, and, with a somewhat different interpretation, "The Gilgamesh Epic: Romantic and Tragic Vision," in *Lingering over Words: Studies in Ancient Near Eastern Literature in Honor of William L. Moran*, Harvard Semitic Studies 37, edited by T. ABUSCH, J. HUEHNERGARD, and P. STEINKELLER (1990), pp. 231–249; and G. S. KIRK, *Myth: Its Meaning and Functions in Ancient and Other Cultures*, Sather Classical Lectures 40 (1973). For Rilke's appreciation, see *Rainer Maria Rilke, Katharina Kippenberg, Briefwechsel*, edited by BETTINA VON BOMHARD (1954); for the post-cuneiform Gilgamesh, see JEFFREY H. TIGAY, *The Evolution of the Gilgamesh Epic*, pp. 241–255; and STEPHANIE DALLEY, "Gilgamesh in the Arabian Nights," *Journal of the Royal Asiatic Society*, 3rd ser., no. 1 (1991).

SEE ALSO **Near Eastern Myths in Greek Religious Thought** (Part 1, Vol. I); **Death and the Afterlife in Ancient Mesopotamian Thought** (Part 8, Vol. III); **Sumerian Literature: An Overview** (Part 9, Vol. IV); **Akkadian Literature: An Overview** (Part 9, Vol. IV); and **Epic Tales from Ancient Sumer: Enmerkar, Lugalbanda, and Other Cunning Heroes** (Part 9, Vol. IV).

Flood Narratives of Ancient Western Asia

BRIAN B. SCHMIDT

INTRODUCTION

The world's great catastrophic traditions testify to humanity's persistent quest to derive meaning from calamity. Occupying principal place within that legacy are oral and written accounts of life-threatening floods caused by torrential rains, raging rivers, glacial melts, seismic waves, or the rising surge of subterranean seas. So ominous was the encounter with the flood's destructive power, so evocative humanity's response, that in widely divergent cultures, there arose the belief in, even the characterization of, the flood as an act of the gods.

Anthropology and Folklore

Although not every society preserves traditions about destructive waters in its myth and legend, peoples of every continent do perpetuate such lore. In fact, recent estimates of the total number of such accounts worldwide surpass three hundred. Their antiquity, diversity, and geographic distribution negate the view that all such narratives reflect a common source such as the flood account in the book of Genesis. The preservation of older Mesopotamian traditions in Genesis 6–9, and the presence of elements from Mesopotamian traditions alongside Israelite ones in later classical sources, likewise render such an idea unlikely.

In much of the world's myth and folklore, inundation signifies something other than a consummate destructive force, more than the divine dictum for primordial genocide. In sundry traditions, the flood manifests a re-creative act, a new beginning for humanity, Where the gods seek to exterminate the existing generation by means of a flood, a minuscule remnant survive to become the founders of a new world order.

Not surprisingly, numerous symbolic meanings and interpretations flow from the flood as cosmic re-creative act. Illustrative of this fact is the proposal by Alan Dundes that in a wide range of ethnographic data, including the biblical flood account and other ancient near eastern traditions, the flood functions as a *male* narrative of re-creation. The major protagonists are male deities and heroes, and when female companions of flood heroes are mentioned, they are merely *anonymous* actors on the narrative stage. For those who suggest that male pregnancy envy provides the impetus for the production of these myths, the flood is interpreted as expressive of the masculine desire to imitate the creative power of the feminine, a strategy detectable in some creation narratives as well. The narrator has transformed life's emergence from the rush of amniotic fluid into humanity's appearance from the primordial deluge.

Alongside such psychological drives as the male assertion of creative power and the sober reality of life-threatening floods, the inclination to offer etiological explanations for mountain lakes and seashell deposits has no doubt contributed to the transformation of the flood into an ancient near eastern mythological motif, a mythologem. But is the presence of reservoirs and ancient aquatic life at high altitudes evidence for a universal flood as some have proposed? Near eastern archaeology suggests otherwise.

Near Eastern Archaeology

At a number of sites in Mesopotamia, such as the ancient cities of Ur, Kish, Shuruppak, Nineveh, Uruk, and Lagash, archaeologists have exposed sediment layers initially interpreted as floodwater deposits. However, these data are open to various explanations. In some cases, winds, not water, probably deposited the sediment. In others, the fluctuating channel courses and water tables of the Tigris and Euphrates rivers or intruding ocean waters might have resulted in accumulation. Flooded areas uncovered thus far are restricted to a relatively small region as indicated by the fact that some cities, while located near others with sediment, show no signs of flooding. Although the city of Eridu (modern Abu Shahrain) is located near Ur (Tell al-Muqayyar), Eridu preserves no evidence for flooding. In a number of the cities with deposits, the flooding is only partial, and in still others torrential rains probably caused the flooding and so no deposits accumulated. Moreover, the dates of flood levels from city to city vary by as many as nine hundred years and a few sites have multiple flood levels. Finally, most excavated sites in Syro-Palestine lack any evidence for flooding. In other words, while cataclysmic waters were frequent and violent enough to inspire ancient Mesopotamian poets, ancient near eastern archaeology does not confirm the historical occurrence of a universal flood.

Likewise, scientists have not been able to confirm claims that Noah's ark or parts thereof have been recovered from any of the locations identified as Noah's landing site. Under laboratory testing, wood samples retrieved from one of the more widely acclaimed sites, Ağrı Dağı in Turkey, were found to date only to the seventh century CE. Moreover, eyewitness citings have been shown to be contrived or contradictory, and pinpointing the supposed whereabouts of Noah's ark on the basis of Christian, Jewish, and Muslim accounts poses numerous problems. These sources list various sites in Arabia, Armenia, Kur-distan, Iran, and Turkey as the landing site of Noah's ark. Moreover, before the geographical details contained in such reports can be properly assessed, the historical value of the biblical flood story upon which the later accounts are based must be carefully evaluated.

FLOOD NARRATIVES OF ANCIENT WESTERN ASIA

In Mesopotamia, the common term for "flood" or "storm" (Sumerian A.MA.RU, Akkadian *abūbu*) appears in a wide variety of cuneiform texts (hymns, lists, and royal inscriptions) as a metaphor for inescapable destruction. It is variously applied to warrior-kings on campaign, to invading armies and, by extension, to their weapons, and even to malevolent demons. The flood as primordial re-creative event is attested as a narrative motif in the Mesopotamian literary traditions from the Old Babylonian period onward.

Ancient Egypt preserves no narratives of a primeval deluge designed by the gods to exterminate mankind or to start civilization anew. To be sure, the annual inundation of the Nile was personified in the form of the god Hapy, and the infinite watery expanse that surrounded the formless world at creation was termed the "great flood." However, a destructive or regenerative primeval deluge is nowhere documented in Egyptian literature. The same can be said of literatures representative of the Levantine cultures. Fragments of flood stories recovered thus far from Anatolia, Syria, and Palestine are but versions or copies of the Mesopotamian traditions. As widely recognized, the biblical flood story qualifies as a variation on those same traditions. Indeed, narratives about a primordial flood were perpetuated by the Persians, Greeks, and Romans. Still later Jewish, Christian, and Muslim writers preserved elements from both the ancient near eastern and classical flood traditions (see bibliography).

In the selection of texts surveyed below, the reference to a primordial flood that is at once destructive and regenerative is common to all. This warrants our treatment of otherwise generically unrelated texts under the common rubric, "flood narrative." Where multiple versions of a particular flood narrative exist, our analysis relies on modern reconstructed composites without any implication that the composite texts are intended as definitive reconstructions of a hypothetical prototype. As a final qualification, the reader should note that the dates posited for most of the relevant texts can only be approximated.

Mesopotamia

The Epic of Atrakhasis (First Half of the Second Millennium BCE*)* Despite the impression conveyed by the closing lines of the Atrakhasis epic, namely, that the flood is its main theme—"I have sung of the flood to all the peoples, hear it!"—the deluge comprises only a subplot, albeit an important one, within the larger story. The *Atrakhasis* tradition as a whole is concerned with the primeval history of mankind.

The epic opens with several junior gods who, wearying of both their perpetual maintenance of and care for the world, rebel against their taskmasters, the senior gods. The confrontation is resolved by creating mortals to do the labor of the junior gods and to serve all the gods. Humans are created by mixing clay with the blood and flesh of the slain leader of the rebellion. From an initial seven pairs, humanity quickly multiplies on the earth and its noise ultimately disturbs the sleep of Enlil (or Ellil). Exasperated, Enlil devises a series of schemes to curtail this noise (elsewhere in the Mesopotamian literary traditions, humanity's noise embodies mankind's attempt to gain its independence from the menial task of serving the gods). Enlil first unleashes plagues, then drought, and lastly, famine, but each measure is frustrated by his rival, the god Enki, who instructs his pious devotee, the mortal Atrakhasis (*atra* + *ḥasīs*, "Exceedingly Wise"), on how to appease the gods most responsible for each calamity.

Enlil and the other gods eventually devise another form of devastation, the flood, designed to limit humanity's increase and independence. Once more Atrakhasis is warned by Enki, who circumvents a vow of silence in order to instruct Atrakhasis to build a boat. Claiming that Enlil and Enki are at odds and that he must leave, Atrakhasis gathers the local craftsmen who help him build a boat. Kith, kin, and diverse animals enter just as the fierce flood begins. Following the flood, which lasts for seven days and nights and terrifies even the gods, Atrakhasis disembarks and makes offerings to the gods, who swarm like flies over the sacrifices (a simile perhaps intended to lampoon the gods for their dependence upon human servants).

Having learned their lesson, the gods lament their involvement in the catastrophe and fully blame Enlil. Although faced with insurrection, Enlil nevertheless is angered at the sight of survivors. Enki openly reproaches Enlil for his planned extermination of humanity and claims credit for preserving human life. Thereafter, the gods consider less-drastic means of reducing humanity's noise while maintaining its servitude. They decree that women must often suffer sterility, stillbirth, and socially imposed chastity, and so the account closes with an explication of the harsh realities of life especially for women, "since the flood."

The Eridu Genesis *(Circa 1600)* Although written in the Sumerian language, the *Eridu Genesis* or *Sumerian Flood Story*, is probably derivative of Semitic tradition. It is concerned with the creation of the human race, the foundation of kingship and the first cities, and the reestablishment of the world after the flood. The text is severely damaged, with the beginning and end missing. The hero of this flood story is Ziusudra (ZI.U₄.SUD.RÁ, ("Life of Long Days"), a king of the city of Shuruppak (Fara).

Following what appears to be an initial dispersion of mankind over the earth that threatens their continued existence, the god Enki proposes to gather the people and to build cities endowed with life-giving waters. This is followed by reports on the (new?) creation of the "black-headed people" (or Mesopotamians) and the multiplication of various animal forms. An unnamed god inspects the newly constructed cities, institutes kingship, names the five royal municipalities (Eridu, Bad-tibira, Larak, Sippar, and Shuruppak), dedicates each to a particular deity, and designs a system of irrigation.

At the end of a lengthy break in the narrative, we learn that the gods decide to bring about a great flood. One of the gods (probably Enki) shirks his oath of secrecy and warns Ziusudra, his pious devotee, of the impending disaster, so the hero finds(?) a boat. The flood subsides after seven days and nights and the sun reappears. Ziusudra makes an opening in his boat, steps onto dry land, and, as an expression of his piety, offers an ox and a sheep to the god Utu (or Shamash), the god of justice. Although initially outraged to discover that a mortal had survived, Enlil finally relents at the rebuke of Enki and the other gods. As the story draws to a close, Ziusudra is rewarded with "life like a god," and is taken to "the land of Dilmun, the place where the sun rises." (See also the overview of Sumerian literature, later in this volume.)

The Epic of Gilgamesh (Second and First Millennia; Diverse Versions) The central theme of the Gilgamesh epic is humanity's struggle to come to terms with its mortality. As in *Atrakhasis*, the flood account in tablet eleven of the Gilgamesh epic comprises only one episode within a larger narrative. Gilgamesh, son of Lugalbanda, king of Uruk, seeks out Ut(a)-napishtim (Akkadian *ūta + napištim*, "He/I found life"), the survivor of the great flood and recipient of eternal life. However, upon meeting him, Gilgamesh is unimpressed by his less than heroic stature, and so his hope for immortality soars. In order to explain how he received the gift of immortality, Ut-napishtim recounts the flood story.

He begins by retelling how Ea (Sumerian Enki), although having sworn an oath of secrecy, warned him of the impending catastrophe while addressing him from the other side of a reed hut and a brick wall (he offers no reason why the gods decree the flood). He builds a boat as directed by Ea, but deceives his neighbors by claiming that Enlil had rejected him, and that he must leave the city in order that the people might continue to receive Enlil's blessing. He then constructs a multileveled, multichambered craft which he launches before the coming of the flood. It is laden with precious metals, "the seed of life of all kinds," animals of every kind, his kith and kin, and artisans. The flood lasts for six days and seven nights until "all of man had returned to clay." Afterward, Ut-napishtim sends out a dove, then a swallow, but both come back. When a released raven does not return, Ut-napishtim disembarks and sacrifices to the gods, who then swarm like flies at the smell of the offering. In spite of having been rebuked for instituting the flood, Enlil rages with anger at the sight of the mortal survivors. Thereafter, Ea chastises him for failing to consider more modest means of population control such as unleashing the warrior-god Erra. Ea also urges the gods to distinguish between sinner and innocent in future dispensations.

As Ut-napishtim's review of the flood episode comes to a close, he recounts how Enlil responds to Ea's reprimand by awarding Ut-napishtim and his wife life "like the gods," and placing them "far off at the mouth of the rivers." He then sets before Gilgamesh the type of rhetorical question that anticipates a negative response: "So now (O Gilgamesh), who can gather the gods on your behalf, that you may find eternal life which you seek?" The expected answer is, "No one." This underscores the singularity of the calamitous event, the uniqueness of the gift bestowed on the survivors of the great deluge, and the grievous fate of the hero Gilgamesh that he must die. (See also the chapter on the Gilgamesh epic earlier in this volume.)

The Sumerian Kinglist *(2000–1700)* There are significant differences evident among the fifteen known copies of the *Sumerian Kinglist*. The various copies display differences in the names of the kings, their lengths of reign, order, and number. These variations suggest that it was an adaptable reconstruction of dynastic succession in which political power is transferred from one city-state to another by the gods. The fact that the *Sumerian Kinglist* stops with a particular dynastic line, the Isin kings, confirms its function as a propagandistic tool for legitimating not only that dynasty, but the others mentioned as well.

Whether the flood or storm in the *Sumerian Kinglist* functions as the great temporal divide between primordial and historical time or as a symbol or emblem of political, military, or economic catastrophe of early history is debated by scholars. Most likely it is that the flood functions as a great temporal divide, for the historical-catastrophe interpretation does not readily explain why the lengths of rule that follow the flood are progressively shortened. The flood or storm of the *Sumerian Kinglist* separates a series of kings of "history past" from an earlier series of primordial rulers. Kingship as created by the gods "comes down from heaven," and lodges first at Eridu. From there it passes from city to city. This repeated trope is only temporarily suspended by the great flood, for kingship begins anew at the city of Kish, "after the flood had swept over (the earth?)." In sum, the flood of the *Sumerian Kinglist* looks very much like the primordial flood of *Atrakhasis, Eridu Genesis,* and *Gilgamesh.*

The Lagash Kinglist *(Early Second Millennium)* The *Lagash Kinglist* offers an imaginative register of the ancient rulers of the city of Lagash (modern Tell al-Hiba). The list is generally understood to presuppose, but also to burlesque, the claims of the *Sumerian Kinglist,* in response to the latter's omission of the Lagash kings. The flood is first mentioned in the beginning of the narrative, and reference to its survivors is concise. The *Lagash Kinglist* emphasizes the central role of that city and its rulers in the founding period of Mesopotamian kingship.

Unlike the *Sumerian Kinglist,* the *Lagash Kinglist* lacks an antediluvian list of kings. It begins instead with a report on the world's condition "after the flood had swept over (the land?)," a period which, in contradistinction to the entire *Sumerian Kinglist* tradition, includes the initial absence of kingship and only the belated beginnings of agriculture. Moreover, with the statement, "the name of man having been called," the *Lagash Kinglist* depicts the postdiluvian age as a second creation, for this is the language used for what has been created.

Other elements worthy of note include the flood's total destruction of civilization (though the question remains whether this is the primordial flood or the metaphorical language of cataclysm), the portrayal of the postdiluvian period as a wholly new beginning, the characterization of that new beginning as a time when humanity soon began to wane rather than increase owing to insufficient food sources, and the artificial nature of the royal genealogies.

The Poem of Erra and Ishum *(First Millennium)* Erra and Ishum reports the god Marduk's remorse over the senselessness of the flood's devastation, omits the high god's second bout of raging anger at the sight of survivors (as in *Atrakhasis* and *Gilgamesh*), and records Marduk's unsolicited sparing of the remnant. The narrator of *Erra and Ishum* thereby portrays the perpetrator of the deluge as a contrite, compassionate god who, for enacting such tragedy, has suffered immensely the loss of his former glory. Marduk's lost grandeur stands as a portent of consequences for acting on unchecked anger. Erra, warrior god of destruction, rouses himself from his chamber to destroy Babylon and to do battle with Marduk. Initially beset by languor, he is eventually urged on by the Sebitti, a group of seven hostile gods, to take up his cause once again and to enter the temple of Marduk in Babylon. Upon entering Marduk's shrine, Erra mocks Marduk by criticizing his drab attire. In response, Marduk recounts how his image and adornment were tarnished upon rousing the flood. The broader context suggests that the flood was caused by the forces of chaos in the absence of divine order. In response to humanity's neglect of his cult, Marduk had angrily departed and remained absent from his sanctuary shrine, the center of the universe, resulting in a cosmic disruption in which, "heaven and earth dissolved," and devastation reigned.

Erra counsels Marduk to have his image refurbished and offers to sit in his place in the meantime, thereby enticing Marduk to abandon his rule again so that Erra might freely destroy Babylonia's inhabitants. Marduk descends to the lower regions to have his attire restored by the only craftsmen sufficiently skilled to complete the task, the seven prediluvian sages whom he had banished below following the flood. With Marduk out of the way, Erra inaugurates his reign of terror on Babylon and its environs. His vizier, Ishum, god of fire, fails to dissuade Erra from slaughtering the innocent along with the wicked; he then concedes Erra's authority, even goes to battle on Erra's behalf, and in the end ironically placates Erra by completing the destructions.

Comparing the details of this account with the other Mesopotamian traditions suggests that this poem preserves a distinct flood tradition. To be sure, elements attested in the other flood stories are missing (a divine assembly, the rival Enki/Ea, a warning, a flood hero, a boat, an offering, and accusing gods), and there are new elements (the relegation of the prediluvian sages to the sweet-water abyss, called the Apsu; the cosmic disturbance; and the sparing of the city of Sippar, the sun-god's cult center—an element contradicted by the *Babyloniaca* of Berossus, which is discussed below).

Be that as it may, *Erra and Ishum* uses as background the mythic flood recalled by *Atrakhasis*. The writer refers to the flood as an event of hoary antiquity ("long ago") and expresses ambivalence about whether the survivors of the flood should be destroyed or spared. As in the *Lagash Kinglist*, the remnant's numbers initially wane for lack of food, but Marduk introduces agriculture and rescues them from total extermination. Moreover, the parallel roles accorded Marduk and Erra in *Erra and Ishum* and Enlil in *Atrakhasis*, as well as the resonance of human noise in both, could suggest that *Erra and Ishum* conveys a theological critique of divine action in cases where the alleged crime is minor compared to the punishment that the gods mete out.

The writer of *Erra and Ishum* disparages the senseless desolation wrought by the gods as typified in the primordial flood and by the divine zest for war. He exposes the flood for what it really is when stripped of its re-creative attachments, the epitome of meaningless destruction. Nevertheless, he partially exonerates the gods for their past failings, distant and immediate, by recounting their remorse, goodwill, and retributive suffering.

Berossus's Babyloniaca *(the Hellenistic Period)*   In writing the *Babyloniaca*, a history of Mesopotamia in Greek, Berossus, a Babylonian priest of the third century BCE, sought to inform the new masters of Mesopotamia, the Greeks, about the Babylonian priestly legacy. This heritage was founded upon traditions whose origin goes back to the time before the flood, to the origin of the cosmos when gods and men experienced more immediate relations. Berossus recounts how the gods preserved the priestly legacy from the devastation of the flood, and in so doing he attempts to establish the holy status of that priestly tradition.

The story begins with the flood hero, Xisouthros (the Greek rendering of Sumerian Ziusudra), being alerted in a dream by Kronos to prepare for an impending catastrophic flood. Although it is designed to destroy mankind, no

reason for the flood is offered. Kronos directs Xisouthros to bury all extant writings in the city of Sippar, to build a boat, and to take on board his family, close friends, food, drink, and winged and four-footed creatures. In the event that another asks whither he is sailing, Berossus is to mislead his interrogator by claiming that he is going out, "to the gods to pray for good things for men." After the flood has ceased its advance on either the second or third day (variant traditions are present here), Xisouthros sends out birds (perhaps doves) to find dry land, but to no avail: the birds return. The available traditions report that either the second or third (and last) wave of birds returns to the boat muddied. The boat then lands on a mountain located in Armenia in the mountainous range of the Korduaians (classical Gordyene or Gordion). Berossus relates that portions of the boat survived the flood to his day, and the variant traditions record that either pitch or the wood from the boat was used later for amulets. With the boat having landed, Xisouthros then departs with his wife, daughter, and boatman. After making offerings to the gods, they disappear from sight and take up residence with the gods. Those left behind are commanded by a voice from the heavens to return to Babylon in order to reestablish it. They are to recover the buried writings from Sippar and dispense the priestly traditions to mankind.

Review   A dream tradition is reported in *Gilgamesh*, *Babyloniaca*, and perhaps in *Atrakhasis*, but in the last Enki also admits to warning the flood hero directly, whereas in *Gilgamesh*, Ea denies having disclosed the plan of the gods to the flood hero. In *Eridu Genesis*, a dream is categorically denied. In *Atrakhasis*, *Gilgamesh*, and *Babyloniaca*, the flood hero misleads others as to the purpose of building the boat. In *Babyloniaca*, Berossus stands in the tradition of *Gilgamesh* and *Eridu Genesis* by rewarding the flood hero with some form of beatific afterlife. Reference to such a reward has been seen in the damaged lines of the concluding section of *Atrakhasis*, but it is equally plausible that Atrakhasis's mentioned longevity is his full reward.

In *Atrakhasis*, *Eridu Genesis*, the *Sumerian Kinglist*, the *Lagash Kinglist*, and *Babyloniaca*, the flood marks the beginning of "history" after which follows, or beyond which is projected, civilization's beginnings with its arts, inventions, or institutions. Their antiquity serves to establish their legitimacy. In *Gilgamesh,* the flood similarly functions to distinguish between mythic and "historical" time, but in so doing, it underscores the singularity of the gods' gift of immortality to a human. Unique to *Erra and Ishum* is the flood's embodiment of unjustified divine violence.

When the cause of the flood is mentioned, it is invariably humanity's noise. Noise as the flood's cause is explicitly reported in *Atrakhasis,* inferred in Ea's listing of less drastic alternatives to limit the excesses/numbers in *Gilgamesh,* and perhaps assumed in *Erra and Ishum* where it underlies the patterning of the account: humanity's din, divine arousal, anger, and destruction of humanity. However, in *Erra and Ishum,* Marduk's abandonment of the universal shrine also plays a role in bringing about the flood. In any case, noise probably suggests more than simply humanity's overpopulation and something other than its depravity. As in the Mesopotamian literary traditions more generally, noise symbolizes mankind's active, creative quest for autonomy, while silence reflects its inactivity or passivity. In other words, humanity's numerical increase or excessive technological productivity serves as a synecdoche for mankind's varied attempts at trespassing divinely established limits.

Syro-Palestine

Excerpts from the *Gilgamesh* flood tradition have been recovered at Megiddo (modern Tell al-Mutasallim) in Canaan (fourteenth century) and at Emar (modern Meskene) in Syria (thirteenth century). These, along with fragments from *Atrakhasis* found at Ugarit (modern Ras Shamra; fourteenth century), illustrate the early diffusion of the Mesopotamian traditions into Syro-Palestine and corroborate the theory that the biblical flood story is closely related to the Mesopotamian (see the summary below). Estimated dates for the composition of the Israelite flood narrative range from the tenth to sixth centuries.

The Israelite Flood Story The flood story as preserved in chapters 6–9 of the book of Genesis

serves as a transition from the primordial era to an age of "history as we know it." An earlier age in which violence reigned, and gods and mortals engaged in carnal improprieties, is followed by a succeeding age wherein humanity is offered renewed hope for its survival. In spite of this, humankind soon after the flood fails to regain paradise lost. The recurring pattern of crime and punishment throughout primeval history prepares the reader to anticipate humanity's certain postdiluvian dereliction. But what causes humanity's repeated failure and justifies its punishment?

Two accounts dealing with the violation of sexual prohibitions bracket the flood narrative. The first, Genesis 6:1–4, reports the intermingling of gods and humans resulting in a hero or giant race. Nevertheless, this quintessential act of hubris justifies Yahweh's decision to bring about the flood only in part, for elsewhere in the flood account the writer underscores humanity's violence as the reason for divine punishment (6:13). Following the flood, a second account, Genesis 9:20–27, reports that one of Noah's sons, Ham, "looked upon his father's nakedness" while Noah was inebriated. The statement may be read euphemistically, for the violation of sexual prohibitions is a motif repeated elsewhere in the book of Genesis (e.g., the story of Lot's two daughters in 19:30–38; see also Leviticus 18:7–8 and 20:11 for the possible incestuous overtones attached to this idiom). Ham's act results in a severe curse upon his descendants, the Canaanites, who are to be perpetually enslaved to Shem's descendants, the Israelites. This account is soon followed by man's collective act of hubris against Yahweh reported in the Tower of Babel incident (11:1–9) and the consequent confusion of languages and dispersion of peoples.

As for the flood account proper, the *observable discrepancies* contained therein—in particular the differences in chronology, the number of animals taken on the ark, and the diverse sources of the floodwaters (rains and subterranean waters)—have convinced a number of scholars that what we now have in the Bible is a composite tradition, a weaving of two originally separate versions of the flood, one being supplemented by the other. This theory also finds support in a number of the repetitions present throughout the composite story. Of the two versions, one is attributed to a tradition that typically uses Yahweh as the name for the Israelite god ("Lord" in English translations). Thus, this version is commonly referred to as the Yahwistic version. The second version uses Elohim (English "God") as the deity's name and displays a keen interest in ritual purity and cultic observance and has been labeled the Priestly version. It is the Priestly version that has been preserved more fully, and the Yahwistic version supplements it.

In the plot summary that follows, what comprises the Yahwistic version is set in regular type (Genesis 6:5–8, 7:1–5, 7:7, 7:10, 7:12, 7:16b–17, 7:22–23, 8:2b–3a, 8:6–12, 8:13b, 8:20–22, 9:18–19), while those elements identified as Priestly are italicized (Genesis 6:9–12, 6:17–22, 7:6, 7:8–9, 7:11, 7:13–16a, 7:18–21, 7:24–8:2a, 8:3b–5, 8:13a, 8:14–19, 9:1–17). The long-recognized discrepancies between the two versions are enclosed by asterisks, and those few lines the authorship of which is disputed are set in brackets (e.g., Genesis 6:13–16).

The flood story in Genesis 6–9 begins with Yahweh's decision to destroy both man and beast by means of a great flood. The reasons given are man's sexual improprieties [*and the rampant violence on the earth*]. Yahweh spares a pious man, the six-hundred-year-old Noah, his wife, and family from the impending destruction. He directs Noah to build a boat [*made of wood and covered with pitch with multiple levels and compartments and having precise height, width, and length specifications*], to gather every kind of creature in *pairs/ seven pairs of every clean creature*, to put provisions on board, and to enter the boat with his family. Noah does as he is commanded. After seven days *the rains begin/the underground seas burst forth*, and *the rains last for forty days and forty nights/one hundred and fifty days*. As the waters rise, the boat is launched, *the mountains are covered*, and all life forms are ended. Yahweh sends a wind, the waters recede, *and the boat comes to rest on the mountains of Ararat*. In order to discern favorable conditions for leaving the boat, Noah opens a window and dispatches a raven. He then sends out a dove that returns, another that returns with an olive branch seven days later, and finally, after another seven-day wait, a third dove that does not return. *God instructs Noah to disembark. He and his family do so*, and immediately construct an altar and make sacrifices to Yahweh. Yahweh smells the pleasing odor and promises never to destroy the earth and its inhabitants with a flood again. *This is symbolized by placing his rainbow in the sky (his "weapon laid to rest"?)*. Yahweh then directs Noah to repopulate and cultivate the earth, but prohibits the eating of animal blood and the murder of fellow humans. Noah dies at the ripe old age of nine hundred and fifty (9:28).

Outside Genesis, only two biblical writers make mention of the flood. Their oracles are contemporary with Judah's exile in Babylonia. In Ezekiel 14:14, 20, the writer lays emphasis on the heroic and exemplary life of Noah. Isaiah 54:9 parallels Yahweh's promise of no destruction after the flood with his assurance that he will cease being angry with the generation of the exile. As in Genesis 5:1–32, Noah is listed in the tenth generation after Adam in the post-exilic genealogical record of 1 Chronicles 1:4.

Ancient Flood Traditions and Lucian's De Syria Dea   More than one hundred and sixty mythical flood accounts are preserved in the ancient Greek and Latin literature that has survived down to modern times. One of the earliest references to the flood is found in Pindar's *Olympian Odes* (9:42–46; early fifth century BCE). In the opening of the epic known as the *Cypria* (attributed by Pindar to Homer, by other ancients to Stasinus), there is a fragment that contains a prose narrative listing the flood as one of the more radical means to rid the earth of humanity. That at least the main contents of the *Cypria* might have been known as early as 650 BCE is suggested by the depiction of the Judgment of Paris on a vase from Chigi. Unlike the flood in *Atrakhasis* and *Gilgamesh* XI, however, the flood mentioned in the surviving scholia of the *Cypria* is rejected in favor of the decreed marriage of a god and a mortal eventually leading to the Trojan War.

The longest surviving flood narrative is preserved in the *Bibliotheca*, a work that has been mistakenly attributed to the second-century BCE writer Apollodorus of Athens. The *Bibliotheca* is more likely the work of Pseudo-Apollodorus of the second century CE. The author of the *Bibliotheca* reports that the high god Zeus creates the flood in order to destroy ancient man. The hero Prometheus instructs his son Deucalion to build a boat to survive the flood. Deucalion stocks it with provisions and embarks on it with his wife Pyrrha, the daughter of Epimetheus and Pandora. The rains last for nine days and nights, flooding first the greater part of Greece and then, after the mountains of Thessaly divide, the lands beyond.

After safely landing on Parnassus, the couple sacrifices to Zeus, and so Zeus sends Hermes to grant Deucalion's wish. Deucalion requests the company of more people. Deucalion and Pyrrha (are instructed to?) create other human beings by casting stones over their heads. Those stones cast by Deucalion become men, while those cast by Pyrrha become women. Other mortals had escaped by ascending high mountains and survived the first stage of the flood, but whether or not they survived the second stage is not clear. While the fate of the animals is not explicitly mentioned, that some were sacrificed points to their survival after the flood, that is, unless they were spontaneously created after the flood as in Ovid's *Metamorphoses* dating to the early first century CE. In sum, the *Bibliotheca* of Pseudo-Apollodorus mentions a surviving couple, children born to them after the flood abated, survivors who had escaped to the high mountains, and other postdiluvian life-forms that were created by stone throwing.

Lucian of Samosata (120–180 CE), a Greek satirist and contemporary of Pseudo-Apollodorus, reports in his *De Syria Dea* that Deucalion "the Scythian," or Deucalion Sisitheus, built a temple at Hierapolis in Syria over the spot where the flood receded. The element Sisitheus in the name Deucalion Sisitheus might be a late recasting of Sumerian Ziusudra (like Berossus's Xisouthros). As in Ovid's *Metamorphoses*, Lucian identifies the cause of the flood as humanity's sinfulness, a motivation for divine judgment also attested in other Greek and Latin traditions. Because of his prudence and piety, Deucalion, his wife, and children were spared the flood brought about by torrential rains and the earth's bellowing forth of subterranean waters. According to Lucian, the hero's sizeable boat took on board all kinds of animal life, all in pairs, all of which Zeus rendered harmless to Deucalion. Having survived the flood, Deucalion and his family became founders of a new people.

In another of his works, *Timon*, Lucian parodies old Zeus who, as a young god, would have stood up to all forms of crime and violence as proven by his commencement of the flood in the days of Deucalion. Nevertheless, Lucian qualifies his endorsement of the young Zeus's decision to bring about the flood. For Lucian, it was a clear case of overkill—everyone, save a few, died. Lucian accentuated this squandering of human life by noting that although a handful survived in a small boat that landed on top of Lycoreus, the following generation of the human race was one consumed by even greater wickedness.

A configuration of themes unattested in earlier classical traditions first appears in the flood accounts of Lucian and Pseudo-Apollodorus. It is the threefold element of (1) a flood that is (2) survived by a hero who (3) boarded a boat. Moreover, unlike Ovid, Lucian's *De Syria Dea* explicitly mentions children and animals on board the boat. In Ovid, all other life-forms were destroyed, and following the flood, new animal life was spontaneously formed from the earth. While Ovid shares with the *Bibliotheca* of Pseudo-Apollodorus the theme of postdiluvian forms of life created by the casting of stones, such is absent in the works of Lucian.

In addition to those themes attested in both *De Syria Dea* and the classical flood traditions, Lucian's indebtedness to ancient near eastern flood traditions is widely recognized. To begin with, he preserves a name of the flood hero at home to Mesopotamian traditions. Moreover, the large boat, the paired animals taken on board (Genesis 6:19), their having been rendered harmless by the deity, and the absence of a mountain are all elements that Lucian's account shares with the ancient near eastern flood traditions over the classical tradition. As in near eastern flood traditions, Lucian reports that more than the flood hero and his wife survived and the character of the flood hero is similarly contrasted with that of the antediluvian generation. Lastly, Lucian's cause of the flood has its parallel in near eastern texts. The swelling up of the earth's underground waters is attested in the Israelite flood account (Genesis 7:11), the *Babyloniaca*, and perhaps *Gilgamesh*. Lastly, *De Syria Dea* uniquely shares with near eastern flood accounts the reference to a sign commemorating the event. In Genesis, the sign is a rainbow (9:12), in Lucian, the sign is the construction of the Hierapolitan temple. (For further comparison of flood-story elements, see the table.)

A Comparative View of Flood Narratives of Ancient Western Asia

	Atrakhasis	Eridu	Gilgamesh	Sumerian Kinglist	Lagash Kinglist	Erra and Ishum	Babyloniaca	Genesis
Cause of Flood	Hubris [Noise]	[missing text]	[Hubris/Noise]	—	—	[Hubris/Noise]	—	Hubris (Yahwistic) Violence (Priestly)
Revelation	(?)	Denied	Dream	—	—	—	Dream	[Divine Speech]
Hero	Atrakhasis	Ziusudra [king]	Ut-napishtim	—	—	—	Xisouthros	Noah
Family Survivors	Yes	—	Yes	—	—	—	Yes	Yes
Deception by Hero	Yes	—	Yes	—	—	—	Yes	—
Form of Flood	Rains	Rains	Rains/Springs(?)	Rains	Rains	Rains/Springs	—	Rains/Springs
Flood Duration	7 days/nights	7 days/nights	7 days	—	—	—	3 days	40 days/nights or 150 days

2346

Boat	Yes [reed hut]	Yes	Yes [reed hut]	—	—	—	Yes	Yes [gopher wood]
Birds	[missing text]	—	Dove, Swallow, Raven	—	—	—	3 bird groups [unnamed]	Raven, Dove, Dove
Landing Spot	[missing text]	—	Mt. Nimush (= Nineveh)	—	—	—	Armenia	Mountains of Ararat
Sacrifice to God(s)	Yes	Yes	Yes	—	—	—	Yes	Yes
Reward for Hero	Longevity [+ missing text]	Afterlife	Afterlife	—	—	—	Afterlife	Renewal of Humanity
Other Survivors	Animals [+ missing text]	[Kingship Renewed]	Animals, Craftsmen	[Kingship Renewed]	[Kingship and Farming Begin]	City of Sippar [general population]	Animals, Friends [Kingship Renewed]	Animals [Farming Renewed]

OVERVIEW

Scholars who compare Mesopotamian, Israelite, and Hellenistic flood narratives typically interpret the elements held in common by these traditions as indicative of one literary tradition's dependency upon another: the Israelite flood narrative is judged to be a derivative of the Mesopotamian, particularly the *Gilgamesh*, tradition, and the Hellenistic flood traditions are likewise regarded as the descendants of both the Israelite and Mesopotamian flood narratives.

To be sure, the themes and motifs held in common by the respective narratives from East and West illustrate a common repertoire of elements pertaining to a mythic flood, albeit more consistently in the former than in the latter. For example, that Israelite writers were familiar with Mesopotamian flood traditions in addition to *Gilgamesh* is corroborated by the adoption of features peculiar to *Erra and Ishum* in the biblical book of Ezekiel; however, the question remains whether or not this indicates derivation. Moreover, the themes of humanity's quest for autonomy, the resultant dispensation of the gods to prevent it, and the divine assurance of a future for humanity are shared by all. The same can be said for such motifs as the inauguration of the universal flood, a surviving remnant, the escape by boat, and sacrifice as an act of obeisance. But these parallels might simply reflect a shared tradition, rather than the borrowing by one tradition from another (see the table).

However one imagines the interdependence among the flood stories, it would be fallacious to conclude that their dissimilarities are the result of qualitatively distinct religious "mentalities." This is an assessment that is unfortunately prevalent in past comparative treatments. For example, scholars often have attempted a contrast between the "morally superior" Israelite flood story and the stories from Mesopotamia. The Israelite tradition seems to justify Yahweh's initiation of the flood as a response to a breach of sexual propriety and rampant violence. While neither of these specific factors is explicitly mentioned as a cause for the flood in Mesopotamian traditions, and while both do comprise unique Israelite contributions to the constellation of themes found in the ancient near eastern flood traditions, it would be erroneous to conclude that such moral dimensions of the human condition were exclusively Israelite concerns.

Humanity's moral culpability, or more specifically as in the case at hand, sexual impropriety and senseless violence, do provoke divine retribution elsewhere in Mesopotamian and Greek literatures. Moreover, within the Israelite context, these violations might hint at a more acute motive for the flood. Humanity's first violation comprises more than mere carnal debauchery, for the cohabitation of "the daughters of men" with "the sons of God/gods" (Genesis 6:1–4) epitomizes humanity's attempt to transgress its mortal confines, to attain divine status, and ultimately to secure its autonomy vis-à-vis the divine realm. In this respect, the Israelite and Mesopotamian traditions share a common concern. The deity's decision to bring about the flood in the Mesopotamian tradition is not simply a capricious response to humanity's din or overpopulation, for "noise" might epitomize humanity's quest for technological advancement and numerical growth, that is to say god-like power. Both are believed necessary to achieve autonomy from the gods. It is this breach of the status quo that provokes the gods to send the flood.

Divine compassion and concern for human perpetuity as expressed in the aftermath of the flood are likewise not unique to the Israelite religious milieu. In the Mesopotamian tradition, the god responsible for the punishment has a change of heart and the divine council institutes moderating sanctions on him following the flood. Furthermore, in *Erra and Ishum,* the god's violent and genocidal bent is disparaged. The divine concern to preserve humanity is also embodied in the offer of eternal life or longevity to the Mesopotamian flood survivors.

Does the absence of such a motif in the Noah flood tradition reflect ancient Israel's peculiar religious emphasis on the finality of death? Not only is such stark realism evident elsewhere in early Greek and Mesopotamian literature more generally, but Gilgamesh's encounter with Utnapishtim highlights the singular uniqueness of such a reward and underscores the finality of death as every Mesopotamian's certain fate. Furthermore, while Noah is not so rewarded, he is granted longevity of life. Years are added to Atrakhasis's life as well. In any case, the unfounded notion that Atrakhasis attains a blessed afterlife as well is controvertible since the relevant lines of the text are fragmentary and claims to this effect are entirely dependent upon the theme's occasional presence in other Mesopotamian flood traditions. Israelite writers did, in special cases, offer their heroes eternal life as a reward for piety. Both post- and prediluvian heroes were so blessed, as is illustrated in the heavenly ascensions of Enoch, the forefather of Noah (Genesis 5:24), and of the prophet Elijah (2 Kings 2:1, 11).

Distinctiveness in the case of the respective flood narratives is best explained as the consequence of unique configurations of otherwise common motifs and themes rather than as the expression of unique religious mentalities. Illustrative of these respective thematic configurations is the peculiar role that the theme of violence plays in the Israelite and Mesopotamian flood traditions. In Genesis, human violence is condemned and brings about the flood. The genocide wrought by the deity's enactment of the flood, however, is nowhere condemned; only divine regret and the promise never again to destroy humanity with floodwaters are mentioned. However, in *Erra and Ishum* the violence of the god responsible for the flood is singled out, and he is severely censured for it. Although human violence is not explicitly identified as an immediate cause for Mesopotamian floods, tumultuous growth in population and advances in technology would not only create the increased demand for those resources needed to gain autonomy, but they would also provide the violent means to obtain them. In other words, such conditions are the catalyst for war, the real plague of human existence.

Conclusion

The similarities and differences evident among Mesopotamian, Israelite, and classical flood traditions on balance indicate that, despite their divergences, they share a common tradition and function as a mode of discourse for exploring the prospects of divine justice and human existence in the face of those calamities brought on by rampant human violence and the inevitability of death.

BIBLIOGRAPHY

Anthropology and Folklore

JAMES G. FRAZER, *Folk-Lore in the Old Testament: Studies in Comparative Religion, Legend, and Law*, 3 vols. (1919), see especially volume 1, pp. 104–361; B. LANG, "Non-Semitic Deluge Stories and the Book of Genesis: A Bibliographical and Critical Survey," *Anthropos* 80 (1985); ALAN DUNDES, "The Flood as Male Myth of Creation," in *The Flood Myth*, edited by A. DUNDES (1988).

Near Eastern Archaeology

M. E. L. MALLOWAN, "Noah's Flood Reconsidered," *Iraq* 26 (1964); E CARTER, "The Babylonian Story of the Flood: An Archaeological Interpretation," in *Mountains and Lowlands: Essays in the Archaeology of Greater Mesopotamia*, edited by L. D. LEVINE and T. C. YOUNG (1977); L. R. BAILEY, "Wood from 'Mount Ararat': Noah's Ark?" *Biblical Archaeologist* 40 (1977), also *Noah: The Person and the Story in History and Tradition* (1989).

The Atrakhasis *Epic*

W. G. LAMBERT and A. R. MILLARD, *Atra-Hasīs: The Babylonian Story of the Flood* (1969); E. A. SPEISER, "Atrahasis," in *Ancient Near Eastern Texts Relating to the Old Testament*, edited by J. B. PRITCHARD (3rd ed. 1969), with additional texts by A. K. GRAYSON; W. L. MORAN, "The Creation of Man in Atrahasis I 192–248," *Bulletin of the American Schools of Oriental Research* 200 (1970); also "Atrahasis: The Babylonian Story of the Flood," *Biblica* 52 (1971) and "Some Considerations of Form and Interpretation in Atrahasis," in *Language, Literature, and History: Philological and Historical Studies Presented to Erica Reiner*, edited by F. ROCHBERG-HALTON (1987); R. A. ODEN, JR., "Divine Aspirations in Atrahasis and in Genesis 1–11," *Zeitschrift für die Alttestamentliche Wissenschaft* 93 (1981); S. DALLEY, "Atrahasis," in *Myths from Mesopotamia* (1989).

The Eridu Genesis

M. CIVIL, "The Sumerian Flood Story," in *Atra-hasīs: The Babylonian Story of the Flood*, edited by W. G. LAMBERT and A. R. MILLARD (1969); S. N. KRAMER, "The Deluge," in *Ancient Near Eastern Texts Relating to the Old Testament*, edited by J. B. PRITCHARD (3rd ed. 1969); T. JACOBSEN, "The Eridu Genesis," *Journal of Biblical Literature* 100 (1981); also *The Harps That Once . . . : Sumerian Poetry in Translation* (1987); S. N. KRAMER, "The Sumerian Deluge Myth: Reviewed and Revised," *Anatolian Studies* 33 (1983).

The Gilgamesh Epic

A. HEIDEL, *The Gilgamesh Epic and Old Testament Parallels* (1946); N. K. SANDARS, *The Epic of Gilgamesh* (1960); E. A. SPEISER, "The Epic of Gilgamesh," in *Ancient Near Eastern Texts Relating to the Old Testament*, edited by J. B. PRITCHARD (3rd ed. 1969), with notes and additions by A. K. GRAYSON; J. H. TIGAY, *The Evolution of the Gilgamesh Epic* (1982); also "The Evolution of the Pentateuchal Narratives in the Light of the Evolution of the *Gilgamesh Epic*," and "The Stylistic Criterion of Source Criticism in the Light of Ancient Near Eastern and Postbiblical Literature," in *Empirical Models for Biblical Criticism*, edited by J. H. TIGAY (1985); M. KOVACS, *The Epic of Gilgamesh* (1989); S. DALLEY, "The Epic of Gilgamesh," in *Myths from Mesopotamia* (1989); P. MICHALOWSKI, "Presence at the Creation," in *Lingering over Words: Studies in Ancient Near Eastern Literature in Honor of William L. Moran*, edited by T. ABUSCH, J. HUEHNERGARD, and P. STEINKELLER (1990).

The Sumerian Kinglist

T. JACOBSEN, *The Sumerian King List* Assyriological Studies, vol. 11 (1939); J. J. FINKELSTEIN, "The Antediluvian Kings," *Journal of Cuneiform Studies* 17 (1963); W. W. HALLO, "Beginning and End of the Sumerian King List in the Nippur Recension," *Journal of Cuneiform Studies* 17 (1963); also "Antediluvian Cities," *Journal of Cuneiform Studies* 23 (1971); A. L. OPPENHEIM, "The Sumerian King List," in *Ancient Near Eastern Texts Relating to the Old Testament*, edited by J. B. PRITCHARD (3rd ed. 1969); R. R. WILSON, *Genealogy and History in the Biblical World* (1977); P. MICHALOWSKI, "History as Charter: Some Observations on the Sumerian King List," *Journal of the American Oriental Society* 103 (1983).

The Lagash Kinglist

E. SOLLBERGER, "The Rulers of Lagaš," *Journal of Cuneiform Studies* 21 (1967); R. R. WILSON, *Genealogy and History in the Biblical World* (1977).

The Poem of Erra and Ishum

W. G. LAMBERT, "Review of F. Gössman, *Das Erra-Epos*," *Archiv für Orientforschung* 18 (1957–1958); L. CAGNI, *L'Epopea di Erra*, Studi Semitici, vol. 34 (1969), text edition with Italian translation and commentary; also *The Poem of Erra*, Sources from the Ancient Near East, vol. 1/3 (1977), English translation and commentary; P. MACHINIST, "Rest and Violence in the Poem of Erra," *Journal of the American Oriental Society* 103 (1983); S. DALLEY, "Erra and Ishum," in *Myths from Mesopotamia* (1989); D. BODI, *The Book of Ezekiel and the Poem of Erra* (1991).

Berossus's Babyloniaca

A. HEIDEL, *The Gilgamesh Epic and Old Testament Parallels* (1946); W. G. LAMBERT and A. R. MILLARD, "Berossus," in *Atra-hasis: The Babylonian Story of the Flood* (1969); G. KOMORÓCZY, "Berossos and the Mesopotamian Literature," *Acta Antiqua Academiae Scientiarum Hungaricae* 21 (1973); S. M. BURSTEIN, *The Babyloniaca of Berossus*, Sources from the Ancient Near East, vol. 1/5 (1978).

Syro-Palestine

C. WILSON, *The Ebla Texts: Secrets of a Forgotten City* (3rd ed. 1979), see pp. 58–59 for a possible flood narrative at Ebla; W. G. LAMBERT and A. R. MILLARD, *Atra-hasis: The Babylonian Story of the Flood* (1969), see pp. 131–133 for Ugarit; J. H. TIGAY, *The Evolution of the Gilgamesh Epic* (1982), see pp. 123–129 for Megiddo, p. 130, n. 1, for Emar; R. A. ODEN, JR., *Studies in Lucian's "De Syria Dea,"* Harvard Semitic Monographs, vol. 15 (1977), esp. pp. 24–36.

The Israelite Flood Story

W. M. CLARK, "The Flood and the Structure of the Pre-patriarchal History," *Zeitschrift für die Alttestamentliche Wissenschaft* 83 (1971); D. L. PETERSEN, "The Yahwist on the Flood," *Vetus Testamentum* 26 (1976); B. W. ANDERSON, "From Analysis to Synthesis: The Interpretation of Genesis 1–11," *Journal of Biblical Literature* 97 (1978); G. W. COATS, *Genesis with an Introduction to Narrative Literature*, The Forms of the Old Testament Literature, vol. 1 (1983); C. WESTERMANN, *Genesis 1–11*, translated by J. J. SCULLION (1984); J. A. EMERTON, "An Examination of Some Attempts to Defend the Unity of the Flood Narrative in Genesis (Parts 1 and 2)," *Vetus Testamentum* 37 (1987) and 38 (1988); J. VAN SETERS, "The Primeval Histories of Greece and Israel Compared," *Zeitschrift für die Alttestamentliche Wissenschaft* 100 (1988); also *Prologue to History: The Yahwist as Historian in Genesis* (1992); L. R. BAILEY, *Noah: The Person and the Story in History and Tradition* (1989); JOSEPH BLENKINSOPP, *The Pentateuch* (1992).

The Genesis Flood Story in Judaism, Christianity, and Islam

J. P. LEWIS, "Noah and the Flood in Jewish, Christian, and Muslim Tradition," *Biblical Archaeologist* 47 (1984); also "Flood," in vol. 2 of *Anchor Bible Dictionary*, edited by D. N. FREEDMAN (1992).

Greece

G. A. CADUFF, *Antike Sintflutsagen*, Hypomnemata, vol. 82 (1986), contains one hundred and sixty Greek and Latin references to mythic floods; J. G. FRAZER, *Folk-Lore in the Old Testament: Studies in Comparative Religion, Legend, and Law*, 3 vols. (1919), see especially volume 1, pp. 146–174; E. G. KRAELING, "Xisouthros, Deucalion, and the Flood Traditions," *Journal of the American Oriental Society* 67 (1947).

Persia

J. DARMESTETER, "(Fargard 2): Yima," in *The Zend-Avesta. Part 1: The Vendidād*, The Sacred Books of the East, vol. 4 (1880; repr. 1965); J. G. FRAZER, *Folk-Lore in the Old Testament: Studies in Comparative Religion, Legend, and Law*, 3 vols. (1919), see especially volume 1, pp. 179–182; M. BOYCE, *Textual Sources for the Study of Zoroastrianism* (1984), see pp. 94–96.

SEE ALSO **Ancient Mesopotamia in Classical Greek and Hellenistic Thought** (Part 1, Vol. I); **Near Eastern Myths in Greek Religious Thought** (Part 1, Vol. I); and **The Gilgamesh Epic: A Masterpiece from Ancient Mesopotamia** (Part 9, Vol. IV).

The Deeds of Ancient Mesopotamian Kings

MARIO LIVERANI

TWO PROCEDURES ARE AVAILABLE to the modern historian of ancient Mesopotamia: either to painstakingly collect the administrative, epistolary, and archaeological primary documentation in order to reconstruct anew the development of socioeconomic, political, and cultural relationships; or else to be satisfied with easy recourse to the historical summaries provided by the royal inscriptions—from the shortest dedications to the lengthy "annals," where military and civil enterprises are chronologically arranged.

The first procedure would provide quite a banal image of ancient Mesopotamia, of anthropological and mundane character: the image of a society and a life-style endowed with their own peculiar features, differentiated by socioeconomic level and political environment, gaining mastery of space and following the rhythms of time as dictated by the available technological equipment. This procedure has only recently become available to scholarship.

The second, more widespread procedure has yielded a supercharged and quite memorable image of ancient Mesopotamia as a country inhabited by great kings devoted to building temples and palaces, to digging canals, to fighting enemies and repulsing invaders, to dispensing justice and providing for the prosperity of their people, according to directions coming directly from the gods.

We all know that this second image is grossly exaggerated, one-sided, and unreliable. A single example among hundreds of similar cases—an inscription by Sin-kashid of Uruk (circa 1850 BCE)—will suffice:

> During his reign, according to the market rate of his land, one shekel of silver was the price of 3 *gur* of barley, of 12 minas of wool, 10 minas of copper, 3 *ban* of oil. His years were years of abundance!
> (After Frayne, *Old Babylonian Period*, 1990)

The information coming from the contemporary administrative texts demonstrates that the real prices were three times higher. Why did the king issue such a deceitful "summary" of the economic life of his reign? Obviously, prices are low in times of abundant commodities, and high in times of want. The utopian picture thus effectively provided, in apparently technical (although patently forged) terms, the evidence for the final statement "His years were years of abundance," thereby celebrating the king's capability.

Historians' use of the celebrative texts issued by the ancient kings requires an understanding of their background and their purposes, and of the communicative conventions in use, in order to reach a deeper level of reading, to recover truth behind propaganda, and to identify the real problems behind their verbal resolution. Ideology is not seldom a virtual inversion of reality.

WHY DID THE ANCIENT KINGS PUBLISH THEIR ACHIEVEMENTS?

The first question to be asked in seeking deeper historical insight is about the audience: Who was expected to read the messages of the ancient kings? The official answer, provided by the texts themselves, is that the royal inscriptions address a purely ideological audience: the gods and future kings. The former have to be told how properly and successfully the man behaved whom they had selected to fulfill the difficult task of government. The latter have to learn how to behave in difficult circumstances and have to restore and care for the old inscriptions (instead of appropriating or destroying them), in order to ensure their predecessors of survival after death, which is only entrusted to the "name" (*šumu*), that is, to fame. The properly ideological character of such an audience is confirmed by the fact that in most cases the celebrative inscriptions were inaccessible to a real public—buried under the foundations of buildings, or located in secluded rooms—in any case written in a very complicated writing system that 99 percent of the population was unable to understand.

If we read the ancient inscriptions, however, and if we try to analyze them using a normal semiological grid, we get a different answer: they were written for a human audience, and for the purposes of present, not future, times. They were written to become known—in some way—to subjects and enemies; they were written for self-justification, or to obtain or increase sociopolitical control, or to mobilize, or to impress, or even to frighten.

The "imaginary" and the "semiological" answers are distant, even opposed, yet not necessarily contradictory. They are simply located at different levels of interpretation and elaboration of reality. Consider, for example, the letter written by Sargon II to the god Assur (Ashur) in 714 to announce the triumphal result of the campaign he led against Urartu (Armenian plateau).

The letter must, in fact, have been read to the god in the course of a ceremony, presumably in the presence of representative groups of the populace, and perhaps accompanied by the exhibition of the plundered goods and the prisoners. In the frame of the Assyrian ideological system, such a report is dutiful, since the king is but a regent of the state in the name of Assur. Assur and the other gods gave the order (*qibītu*) to start a campaign against the enemies and to enlarge the borders of Assyria; from the gods came the oracular guarantee (*tukultu*) that the campaign would be a success. There could hardly be a clearer example that the gods are the hypostasis of the sociopolitical community, and that when addressing Assur the king is in fact addressing Assyria. And the message is that the war had been necessary and victorious, that the treachery of the enemies and the obstacles of an alien landscape have been overcome by the king's courage and decision, that the political order of the area has been changed to the advantage of Assyria, that the plundered goods pay for the expenses of war, that the human casualties have been insignificant. Not too different, after all, from modern bulletins after a victorious war.

SPHERES OF AUDIENCE AND LEVELS OF MOBILIZATION

The message certainly serves to strengthen the king's position within the political community and to further his activity. But how could such a message reach its audience? In the form we have it—a tablet inscribed in cuneiform characters (inaccessible without long, specific training) and kept in an archive—it was available to very few people, no others but the scribes. This limited audience, the very same people who issued the text, is able not only to read the document, but also to understand all the political implications, and to appreciate all its allusions and nuances. This "inner" audience comprises palace officials, priests, courtiers, and administrative personnel and is the only one that really needs to understand the text in all its details.

A second, wider audience comprises the Assyrians (of course free, male, adult Assyrians) who live in the capital city or in other towns: although they have no access to writing, nonetheless they gain some access to the content of the message through the channels of oral transmission, ceremonial staging, and iconic representation. In this way the message loses part of its political meaning and narrative elaboration but remains perfectly adapted to the purpose of mobilization. The populace has no part in formulating the political decisions and could not appreciate its theoretical (or theological) frame, but it provides the (military, working, fiscal) base for the king's action and must be convinced and satisfied.

A third audience is even more peripheral, in the social sense (above all, women) or in the topographical (the villages): it will be reached only via a pale echo of the celebration, deformed by the intermediate passages and kept to the essential facts. This outer audience needs only to know that in the remote capital city, inside an impressive palace, a king is living and acting, beloved by gods and people alike, able to ensure well-being and justice, victorious over enemies, and protecting the borders.

The enemies themselves (be they actual or just potential enemies) are the addressees of the message, or parts of the message, or of some communicative features of the message. The ambassadors admitted into the Assyrian palace have to wait in a hall decorated with scenes of victory and cruel destruction and of exemplary punishment of those who "rebelled" against Assur. At the opposite (lower) end of the communicative range, the only Assyrian "message" received by the mountain tribes is the cloud of dust raised by the approaching army—a message expressive enough to make them fly to the remotest recesses of their mountains, to be "swallowed by caves and gullies." In any case, the enemies have to realize the truth of the Assyrian statement that the transgressors of the loyalty oath (*adû*) will sooner or later be reached by divine punishment, through the action of the Assyrian king and his army.

AUTHORS AND SPONSORS, FORM AND CONTEXT

As the audience is diverse and the communicative level is more or less elaborated accordingly, so also are the promulgators of the texts. The scribes who actually composed the inscriptions are certainly important, and they were the best in their profession. (Only some of the scribes were able and allowed to compose royal celebrative inscriptions.) They sometimes produced elegant and well-organized texts. Yet they are almost completely overwhelmed by two elements: the burden of tradition and the personal interest of the sponsoring king. There is an evolution in the composition, phraseology, and style of the royal inscriptions, but it is a slow process, affecting generations rather than individuals. The literary model of a royal inscription is very rigid and based on previous inscriptions; all a scribe can normally do to show his literary talent is to devise a new combination of the usual time-honored, ideologically dictated set of verbs and nouns. If any individualistic features emerge, they always belong to the king: to his idiosyncracies and personal background, to his political problems and projects.

Sumerian and Old Babylonian

The most evident developmental trend is dictated by material (even technological) conditioning; but the most meaningful is dictated by the ideological development of kingship. The earliest royal inscriptions are very short votive epigraphs on objects dedicated to the gods, sometimes mentioning the origin of the object itself: "from the booty of land X" or "when he vanquished/destroyed country Y." Just as short are the earliest, simplest forms of building inscription, on bricks or foundation tablets. Yet as early as the middle of the third millennium we find more elaborate and extensive "historical texts," in which the narration of past events proves that the present king operated according to right and justice, following divine advice, and against treacherous enemies. The "origin of historiography" in the legalistic attitude of proving oneself to be right can be found in the narration of both internal political competition and external military encounters. As an example of the former, the "reform" text of Urukagina (or Uru-inimgina) is paramount:

> Formerly, from days of yore, from (the day) the seed (of man) came forth, the man in charge of the boatmen seized the boats. The head shepherd seized the donkeys. The head shepherd seized the sheep. The man in charge of the fisheries seized the fisheries. . . .The *sanga* (in charge) of the food

(supplies) felled the trees in the garden of the indigent mother and bundled off the fruit. . . .

The houses of the *ensi* (and) the fields of the *ensi*, the houses of the (palace) harem (and) the fields of the (palace) harem, the houses of the (palace) nursery (and) the fields of the (palace) nursery crowded each other side by side. From the borders of (the god) Ningirsu to the sea, there was the tax collector.

(But) when Ningirsu, the foremost warrior of Enlil, gave the kingship of Lagash to Urukagina, (and) his (Ningirsu's) hand had grasped him out of the multitude (literally, "36,000 men"); then he (Ningirsu) enjoined upon him the (divine) decrees of former days.

He (Urukagina) held close to the word which his king (Ningirsu) spoke to him. He banned the man in charge of the boatmen from (seizing) the boats. He banned the head shepherds from (seizing) the donkeys and sheep. He banned the man in charge of the fisheries from (seizing) the fisheries.

(After S. N. Kramer, *The Sumerians*, 1963, pp. 317–319)

As an example of the latter case, the narration by Entemena of the Gu-edinna war against Umma (Tell Jokha) is just as famous and typical:

Enlil, king of all lands, father of all the gods, by his authoritative command, demarcated the border between Ningirsu (i.e., Lagash) and Shara (i.e., Umma). Mesalim, king of Kish, at the command of Ishtaran, measured it off and erected a monument there.

Ush, ruler of Umma, acted arrogantly: he smashed that monument and marched on the plain of Lagash. Ningirsu, warrior of Enlil, at his (Enlil's) just command, did battle with Umma. At Enlil's command, he cast the great battle-net upon it, and set up burial mounds for it on the plain.

(After Jerrold S. Cooper, *Sumerian and Akkadian Royal Inscriptions*, 1986, p. 54)

And the text goes on to narrate the full sequence of events, with treacherous Umma always transgressing the gods' decision and righteous Lagash always winning thanks to the gods' support.

But it is only with the Akkadian Dynasty that a real propagandistic apparatus is set up, and the monuments of Sargon and Naram-Sin are located in the major temples of the country, especially the Ekur, the Enlil temple in Nippur (modern Nuffar). The Akkadian monuments are equally significant in their iconic and textual features: the heroic and individualistic personages engraved on the Naram-Sin stela of victory, freely acting in an open landscape where the gods are reduced to mere symbols, make a sharp contrast with the Sumerian city phalanx and city ruler acting as mere instruments of the preeminent and overpowering city god in the Stela of Vultures. (See "Aesthetics in Ancient Mesopotamian Art" below for an illustration of the Naram-Sin stela.) The textual counterpart of such a new attitude is easily found in inscriptions celebrating the bold enterprises of the Akkadian kings, who were effective not in restoring the time-honored order of things, but in changing it and in opening new horizons:

Sargon, king of Kish, won 34 battles, destroyed the city walls up to the sea shore. He made ships of Meluhha [Melukkha], ships of Magan, ships of Dilmun dock at the harbor of Akkad. Sargon, the king, bowed down in prayer to Dagan in Tuttul, and (the god) gave him the Upper Country: Mari, Yarmuti, Ebla, up to the Cedar Forest and the Silver Mountains. Sargon, the king to whom Enlil gave no rival: 5400 people daily had their meal in his presence.

Since the establishment of humankind, no king among kings had ever ravaged Armanum and Ebla. Nergal opened the road of Naram-Sin, the strong one, and gave him Armanum and Ebla, and offered him also the Amanus, the Cedar Mountain, and the Upper Sea. Thanks to the weapon of Dagan, exalting his kingship, Naram-Sin, the strong one, vanquished Armanum and Ebla.

(For these documents, see "Kings of Akkad" in Part 5, Vol. II)

The monuments of the Akkadian kings, kept for centuries in the main temples of Sumer and Akkad, visible to future generations, were an effective channel for perpetuating the fame of their enterprises and giving rise to a whole series of popular narratives and poems.

The "heroic" kingship of Akkad remained a model to be imitated, or at least to be taken into account, even though the following Ur III and Isin-Larsa periods in southern Mesopotamia saw the revival of a "cultic" kingship, more interested (at least in the official propaganda) in the welfare of the country than in its military power and expansion. Celebrative inscriptions were still being composed (some of them clearly in the tradition of the Akkadian ones), but the most typical kind of texts in which the king expresses his program and narrates his achievements are the royal hymns. These are addressed to an inter-

Detail of the Stela of the Vultures found at Girsu, circa 2450 BCE. The stela records the victory of Eannatum of Lagash over the city of Umma. In the stela, the soldiers of Eannatum I are shown trampling over corpses of enemies as they follow the king. In the lower register, Eannatum holds a long spear from his vantage point in a battle wagon. LOUVRE MUSEUM, PARIS

nal audience of temple and palace officials, and wider diffusion of their content (parallel to that of the royal monuments) is unlikely. Internal cultic and civic activities are the principal topics, while war activities are minimized, sometimes even denied (Shulgi goes so far as to imagine setting up an antiheroic stela of "no-victory," with the boast, "Cities, I did not destroy; walls, I did not pull down").

While the Neo-Sumerian and Old Babylonian kings in the south (the land of Sumer) based their royal image and their prestige among the populace on cultic activities, culminating in self-divinization, and on administrative skill and public works, ensuring the welfare of the country,

the contemporary kings in the north (the land of Akkad and upper Mesopotamia) preserved and revived the Akkadian tradition, underscoring military achievements and heroic behavior. The royal inscriptions of Yakhdun-Lim of Mari or Shamshi-Adad of "Assyria" contain lengthy and elaborate "historical" passages, taking up far more space than was required by the traditional formulaic "historical" sections of the genre (see "Shamshi-Adad and Sons" in Part 5, Vol. II). Not by chance, shortly afterward northern Syria and the Old Hittite kingdom were prompt in following the example of northern Mesopotamia by developing their own historical narrative. Again and not by chance, at the same time the model of kingship provided by the kings of Akkad finds other ways of expression, in spurious royal inscriptions (the so-called *narû* stelae) and in short poems (usually called "epics" by Assyriologists) that do not emanate directly (or officially) from the kings' will and are not explicitly intended to ensure the kings' success and fame. They derive, though, from the very scribal circles that produced the royal inscriptions and provide additional details on the political ideologies and debates of their time.

Kassite and Middle Assyrian

After the "classical" achievements of the Old Babylonian period, the royal inscriptions of the Kassite Dynasty are almost insignificant as media for celebrating the king's image and his "historical" achievements. Yet the Late Bronze period is not at all devoid of examples of the use of history and politics as arguments for celebration and propaganda. In the highly international world of the time, the most significant topos is provided by the declarations of war, already well attested in the Old Babylonian period but now spread all over the Near East, in the wars between Egyptians and Hurrians and Hittites, Kassites and Assyrians and Elamites. The declarations of war are significant because the issuing king has to condense into a few words all the reasons for his being right and the enemies' being guilty, for the gods to support him and abandon the other country. This is demonstrated by tracing back the course of past relations between the two countries, in a style of argument quite similar to that of legal contests. Just as the royal inscription is the best record of all the arguments a king can produce to build support inside his kingdom, so functions the war declaration in the field of external relations.

At the same time, the Middle Assyrian kingdom becomes a privileged center for the elaboration and the improvement of old and new literary tools in the service of the palace. On the one hand, the narrative sections of the royal inscriptions become ever longer and more complex, culminating with Tiglath-pileser I (circa 1100) in a clearly annalistic arrangement of the military campaigns, and consolidating a stock of sentences and stylistic features that will last for almost a millennium. On the other hand, the deeds of the kings are also recorded and celebrated in different kinds of compositions: chronicles (a genre to be further developed in the first millennium), which originate by joining the political aim of celebration with the practical task of chronological recording; poems (the poem of Tukulti-Ninurta I is paramount in this genre), which now have as protagonists the present kings instead of the model heroes of the past; and even letters to foreign kings, or prayers to the Assyrian gods that beyond the peculiarities of their genre contain political messages as well.

Neo-Assyrian

The further developments of the "annalistic" royal inscriptions under the Assyrian kings in the ninth to seventh centuries are well known. They provide by far the most important corpus of political addresses from Mesopotamia, in which the problems of political communication in the ancient Near East can be most conveniently studied and exemplified. Among the arguments of interest, we must at least mention: (a) the literary and stylistic development through which the original patterns of the building and votive inscriptions become but a pretext for independently conceived and developed historical narratives; (b) the connection between the texts, their architectural context, and the iconic representation of the same events (the "historical" reliefs)—three media using quite different codes yet physically superimposed and mutually interdependent; (c) the connection between royal titulary and historical narrative, the latter being to some extent a justification (or a detailed demonstration) for the use of the former; and (d) the periodic rewriting of the annals (for some kings many successive "editions" have been preserved), in order not only to add new campaigns and bring the record up to date, but also to correct previous statements under the influence of subsequent developments.

Scholarly attention has obviously focused on the royal inscriptions, but other political compositions are also known from the Neo-Assyrian period (as from the Old Babylonian and Middle Assyrian periods). Epic poems are still composed to celebrate the Assyrian kings (e.g., Shalmaneser III); the prayer to the god Assur becomes a real historical narrative (best exemplified by Sargon II and Esarhaddon); and the chronicles become a tool for ideological and political debate between Assyrian and Babylonian scribes (and their respective royal palaces).

Neo-Babylonian

In the Neo-Babylonian period, the royal inscriptions are—in a sense—a compromise between the local tradition of the sober and mostly cultic- and building-oriented content of the Kassite and Middle Babylonian inscriptions, and the unavoidable model of the Neo-Assyrian historical narratives. The chronicles become instead the paramount literary expression of the kings' right to impose their own reconstruction of history. It has repeatedly been noted that as much as the Assyrian royal inscriptions are biased, exaggerated, bombastic, and self-celebrative, so the Babylonian Chronicles are sober, accurate, even prompt to record failures besides successes. This is certainly true and partly to be credited to the different cultural backgrounds of Assyrian and Babylonian political ideologies. But we have to remember that the Assyrian inscriptions were real political addresses (to be received in one way or another by a large audience), while the chronicles were "scholarly" documents circulating inside the closed world of the scribal schools. Their bias is somewhat subtler and goes back to a theology of history rather than to an immediate search for support. But the borders between historiography and politics, between theology and practice, are uncertain in the Neo-Babylonian period—as always in world history. Babylonian independence, it is well known, ends in a military struggle between the local dynasty and the Persian invaders, but when reading the inscriptions of the last Babylonian king, Nabonidus, or the polemical texts that the victors addressed against him, or even the (apparently neutral) chronicles, we get the impression that the basic problems at such a juncture were theological in character: whether Babylonian kingship was granted by Sin or by Marduk; whether the New Year celebrations had been omitted due to the king's neglect or to his concern to avoid risks; whether the king had correctly understood the divine signs or not; and so on. The political elite of priests and scribes, officials and administrative personnel, was certainly involved in such debates, wherein the basic problem of legitimacy was discussed according to the specific code of the time. We can hardly be sure

that a similar concern and a similar competence were widespread among the common people.

SUCCESS AND LEGITIMACY

Not all kings equally needed, and not all were in the position, to issue celebrative messages. First, most Mesopotamian kings did not live and reign long enough to have anything to celebrate, be it a new building or a military success. Also, many of them met with such internal political or economic (even meteorological!) difficulties as to be unable to mobilize the necessary resources and human consent for any kind of celebration. These are the kings who have no place in the history books, who are just the silent majority against which the successful rulers stand out. In terms of ancient ideology they prove—by the way of contrast—the exceptionality and legitimacy of those few who really had something to celebrate.

Success and legitimacy are related: while in practice success generates legitimacy and acceptance, in ideological terms (in the characteristic inversion of reality) success proves the existence of a previous true (though hidden) legitimacy. Legitimacy is an important matter. It means a correct chain of relationships from god to king and from king to people. In case a king lacks (or loses) legitimacy, he will be unable to ensure order and prosperity for his country: it will be a disaster for the people, and to wait for "proofs" of legitimacy could make it too late. The population of any kingdom is therefore very concerned (and understandably so) with the legitimate origin of a new king; and the critical points in any reign are the beginning and the end, his enthronement and the designation of his heir. Between these two points, the rest of the reign is almost routine—provided the gods assist.

Now, if a new king is the son of the previous ruler, if he was designated by his father as heir to the throne (an inheritance hardly to be shared among brothers!), no special "proof" of legitimacy is necessary, and the populace will remain confident unless or until some specific problem arises. But if the king achieves his position through some irregular procedure, he has to justify himself, in various ways. If he is a member of the royal house but not the legitimate heir to the throne, he can try to turn his position around, from usurper to legitimate heir threatened by aggressive and treacherous brothers. If his access to power is related to opposed socioeconomic interests, the usurper will assume the role of the restorer of order and justice—as we have already seen in the case of Urukagina. If no excuse at all can be found to justify the usurpation, the final possibility will be to underscore the very lack of previous and apparent justifications, implying that the decision of the gods was based on hidden qualities that will later become evident to everybody: remember again Urukagina singled out from among thirty-six thousand people!

In fact, the most important and decisive legitimation comes from good government and therefore becomes known after, rather than before, the exercise of power. This is true at the level of actual political relations, since an effective and successful government increases consent and leaves no room for opposition, while a negative government produces disaffection, hostility, and rebellion. This is also true at the ideological level, since success is only possible with divine help, and divine help is only granted to legitimate kings—while the unsuccessful ruler is clearly one who has been abandoned by the gods. A military defeat or a series of unfavorable growing seasons are equally indicative of a lack of the proper connection between gods and people that should be ensured by the presence of a proper king on the throne.

In royal inscriptions, the properly ideological "code" is generally used: the king claims to have divine support in order to receive (automatically) the people's support. Very seldom is popular support directly celebrated—as if the attitude of the populace were not the result of different possible options but the necessary issue of the quality of rule. The crude mechanism is: Peace and availability of goods make people happy. But the ideological code is: The gods put on the throne the right king.

BUILDING AND FIGHTING FOR THE GODS

Provided that the problem of legitimation has been solved, the celebration of the normal, day-to-day activity of government mainly concerns two sectors: buildings and wars. The successful Mesopotamian king is portrayed as a relentless builder and a victorious warrior. This characterization requires some comment, since it is not directly connected with real advantages to the population: in this sense we would rather expect a celebration of economic prosperity and of the correct administration of justice. These are indeed sometimes celebrated, especially in periods of "paternalistic" attitudes, like the Old Babylonian period. Yet the celebration of economic prosperity is rather the frame than the real subject of celebration; only the digging of canals (the most important agricultural infrastructure in ancient Mesopotamia) is the object of direct celebration. As for the quality of the king as a righteous judge, it finds expression in specific kinds of texts, namely the law codes, whose aim is to demonstrate, through a lengthy list of practical examples, how correctly the kingdom was run under the king who authored the code.

By and large, the most common celebration is that related to temple-building or restoration and to dedication of cultic objects inside the temples. This means—again—that Mesopotamian society is deeply embedded in ideology, an ideology shared by the ruling elite and the common people, so that the religious code is preferred to the realistic one. The very same activity of building temples and concentrating wealth in their furnishings is a metapolitical activity: it is devoted not to the direct care of the country and people, but to the care of the gods who are ideologically considered to be responsible for the care of country and people. Consequently, the celebration of temple-building instead of more direct economic intervention has a precise meaning, in the sense of a "fatalistic" society whose problems and expectations receive an answer which is more symbolic than technical, more formal than real.

The other royal feature to be celebrated, namely success in war, is also not directly concerned with the prosperity of the country (since war generally means death of people and destruction of material goods) and seems not even to be a part of the most ancient repertory. Clearly enough, it is the result of competition for control of the limited resources within the landscape (land, water, and work force), and to a lesser extent for access to remote sources of raw materials. Yet it must be noted that in a condition of balanced coexistence of different states, the celebration of victory is quite moderate in tone and extent. The topic becomes pivotal, and almost obsessive, only in the case of states especially engaged in an expansionistic and "imperialistic" policy, from the Akkadian Dynasty down to the Neo-Assyrian Empire. In differing formats (the few lines of the Akkadian monuments versus the many columns of the Assyrian "annals"), the purpose is the same: to accredit the image of a king "who has no rival" (*lā šanān, ša māhira lā išu* or the like) throughout the world and who exerts his power not only in avoiding the threat of a barbarian invasion, but in extending by force of arms the control of the inner country over the periphery (*murappiš miṣri* and the like) in every direction.

In this context, the obvious topoi of the enemy as treacherous and vile have a secondary relevance, in comparison to the pure and simple exaltation of the king's valor, success, and cruelty. Here is Assurnasirpal II (circa 875):

> I approached the city Tela. The city was well fortified; it was surrounded by three walls. The people put their trust in their strong walls and their large number of troops and did not come down to me. They did not seize my feet. In strife and conflict I besieged (and) conquered the city. I felled 3,000 of their fighting men with the sword. I carried off prisoners, possessions, oxen (and) sheep from them. I burnt many captives from them. I captured many troops alive: I cut off of some their arms (and) hands; I cut off of others their noses, ears, (and) extremities. I gouged out the eyes of many troops. I made one pile of the living (and) one of heads. I hung their heads on trees around the city. I burnt their adolescent boys (and) girls. I razed, destroyed, burnt, (and) consumed the city.
> (A. Kirk Grayson, *Royal Inscriptions*, 1991)

The modern (secondary, and unforeseen) audience of such a passage is disgusted at the brutal display of cruelty and sadism. As a matter of fact, this text and the related images (not to speak of the "operative" message on the spot) contain an exemplary warning to other possible "rebels." But in terms of Assyrian ideology, such a crude attitude is somewhat sublimated and justified: in refusing Assyrian suzerainty, the enemies refused to acknowledge the world order established by the gods; in their impious hubris, they put their trust in purely human features, while the Assyrians put their trust in God their sponsor. The enemies were wicked—this is the recurrent message of every victor, in order to overcome the guilt complex of murder—and it was *their* fault if we had to kill them.

THE CONTRASTIVE UNDERSCORING

The purposes of celebration and mobilization, which are the very kernel of the royal inscriptions, are best realized through the use of very simple formal devices—commonly used in propagandistic texts of all times—mostly centered on the pattern of counterposition. Counterposition is effective at a very basic psychological level: it produces self-identification and mobilization against the alien; it makes easier and obvious the choice, and the moral reasons for the choice.

Most common is counterposition with respect to time. Of course the present time, under the happy government of the ruler who issues the texts, is quite positive. Its positiveness is enhanced by contrast with a past time (under the ineffective predecessors) when the gods withdrew their support, the enemies prevailed, the country was threatened or even invaded, and so on. And the positive present time is even more highlighted by linking it to the remote past of origins, to the happy "golden age" when things (just created by the gods) functioned perfectly. So the present reign is a restoration of the original positive time, after an interval of dysfunction and disorder. The present king is to some extent repeating the divine work of creation by restoring the primeval state of affairs as established by the gods and therefore endowed with inherent superiority.

A variant form of the motif of the "restorer of order" is the motif of the "first discoverer." Here the celebration of some positive achievement by the king is underscored by counterposition to a past when such an achievement did not yet exist. The achievement can be of any kind: the opening of a new road or the reaching of a remote land, the possession of an exotic product or the introduction of a technological improvement, even the building of a new temple or the establishment of a new festival. Here is Sennacherib, circa 690:

> In times past, when the kings, my fathers, fashioned a bronze image in the likeness of their members, to set up in their temples, the labor on them exhausted every workman; in their ignorance and lack of knowledge, they drank oil, and wore sheepskins to carry on the work they wanted to do in the midst of their mountains. But I, Sennacherib, first among the princes, wise in all craftsmanship, great pillars of bronze, colossal lions, open at the knees, which no king before my time had fashioned —through the clever understanding which the noble Nishiku (= Ea) had given to me, (and) in my own wisdom, I pondered deeply the matter of carrying out the task, following the advice of my head and the prompting of my heart I fashioned the work of bronze and cunningly wrought it.
> (After D. D. Luckenbill, *Ancient Records of Assyria and Babylonia*, 1927)

In this way the king is claiming a role in the process of organization of the world. Of course, the basic arrangement had been provided by the gods—from the organization of the cosmos in its physical features to the creation of man. But the elements of human culture were subsequently provided by old "heroes" (kings and "sages") who introduced all the features of human culture as it is now. Finally, the present king can also become a member of such an honorable congregation by discovering something new and unprecedented, by leading human possibilities a step further than his predecessors.

Counterposition in space is more strictly concerned with the problem of mobilization. The "inner" country is well ordered, prosperous, and civilized, thanks to the positive action of the king. The foreign lands, mostly with "no king" (or not the right one) and "no god" (or just minor ones), are still in a state similar to the chaos before creation, without the advantages of order and civilization, often without the basic requirements of physical life. The counterposition is effective in two ways: first, as proof of the positive role played by the king, and therefore as an element favoring social and political cohesion; second, as justification for the king's intervention against foreign lands, intervention that will prove advantageous to the conquered lands themselves, which for the first time are put in a condition to become part of the cosmos.

In a sense, the distinction between center and periphery is eliminated thanks to the conquering and civilizing action of the king of the central country. But in another sense, this is a structural and permanent distinction. Landscape itself is significantly different: not by chance is the central country a fertile plain, while the periphery is built up of impassable mountains and arid steppes. Only the central country produces all the elements (first of all food) that are necessary for life, while the peripheral lands are entrusted with the production of just one commodity each: one land (or mountain) produces cedar, another lapis lazuli, still another copper, and so on. Clearly, the gods have arranged such a "topography of commodities" with the advantage of the central country in mind, where all the products converge and find their use. The central country is the only land of life; the outer lands exist for its sake, and not for their own—how could a land (and a people) survive on lapis lazuli alone?

Yet the empty periphery, inconvenient for human life, seems from time to time to host numberless peoples, all of them pressing to get hold of the treasures of life and culture contained in the towns of the central country:

> The (foreign) countries surround the city Asshur from everywhere with a circle of evil, and their assemblage hates the shepherd you appointed to keep your people in order. . . . For your city Asshur the work of the battlefield is standingly prepared, and all the onslaughts of the flood are raised against it. Your adversaries and enemies keep looking at the site of your residence, and they made a wicked agreement in order to plunder your country, Assyria. Night and day the (foreign) countries are longing for the destruction of your marvels, and apply themselves to destroy your towns from above and below.
> (Prayer of Tukulti-Ninurta I to Assur, circa 1225; after M.-J. Seux, *Hymnes et Prières aux Dieux de Babylonie et d'Assyrie*, 1976)

These peripheral peoples, pressing at the borders, are aggressive and wicked, uncivilized and unfearful of the gods; it could even be suspected that they do not properly belong to humankind (compare the Gutians "with human instinct but canine intelligence and monkeys' features" or the Martu "with instincts like dogs or like wolves"). Happily, the central country will prevail owing to its superior civilization, but especially owing to the presence of the right king on the throne and to his positive relations with the gods. The motifs (at the same time literary and ideological) of "conspiracy," "confederation," "encirclement," "treachery," and "agreement-breaking" are the typical constitutive features of a real syndrome (the "siege" complex) of a civilized people surrounded by a multitude of barbarians. The use of such a syndrome (and of such literary motifs) has a sure mobilizing effect and provides the psychological—even the moral—justification for what is in reality the aggression of the central country against the peripheral lands and its hold on and exploitation of their economic and human resources. Once again, ideology is the inversion of reality.

MODELS FOR KINGSHIP: FROM HISTORY TO WISDOM

While mobilization of the population is the basic and original reason for writing royal inscriptions, some products of this literary genre follow a development of their own, partly unrelated to the functional use of the texts, and limited to restricted scribal circles. The celebrative monuments of the early kings, kept in the main temples of the country for centuries and centuries, gave rise to a "historical" interest in the visitors, at various cultural levels. The common people were interested in the memory of the famous heroes of the past, whose adventures (partly stimulated by etiological explanations of the monuments themselves) became the subject of popular stories and anecdotes. The learned scribes copied (as a paleographic exercise) the early inscriptions, made calculations of their chronology, tried to translate into contemporary terms the archaic (and mostly obsolete) toponyms, used the early monuments as reservoirs of stylistic features and of stereotyped boasts, and above all suggested to their kings the most appropriate models of behavior. Since the most effective celebrative apparatus had been set up by Sargon and Naram-Sin, these kings became the standard heroes to be imitated by later kings.

The most obvious case is the direct imitation of old inscriptions by later rulers. To mention just a couple of examples, when Shamshi-Adad restored a temple in Nineveh (Kuyunjik, Nebi Yunis) that had been built by the Akkadian king Manishtushu, he recovered the original building inscriptions and assumed a titulary that he found there. Or when a minor king of Kish (modern Tell al-Uhaimir, Tell Ingharra), Ashduni-yarim by name (circa 1880), had to fight against his neighbors, he decided to imitate the inscriptions in which Naram-Sin had celebrated the general rebellion of the entire world against him. The boast sounds rather pathetic and awkward:

> When all the four quarters of the world rebelled against me, during eight years I made war, and in the eighth year my worth was reduced to nothing and my army was reduced to 300 people. But when my lord Zababa decided in my favor, and my lady Ishtar came to my rescue, although I had taken just a little bread as my food, and I had left for an expedition of one day only, I held the country in awe for 40 days.
> (After E. Sollberger and J.-R. Kupper, *Inscriptions royales Sumériennes et Akkadiennes*, 1971)

But the most elaborate texts in this vein were not intended for publication as new building or celebrative inscriptions. They circulated instead among the learned people (scribes, priests, and palace officials) as false inscriptions, "stelae" (*narû*) in the spirit of the early heroes. The purposes of such fabrications cover a range of possibilities, from the most "candid" one of pure erudition or story-telling, to the most purposefully "functional" falsification providing a new decision with the juridical and religious sanction of time past. The so-called Cruciform Monument of Manishtushu is this kind of fraud from Late Babylonian times but was composed on the basis of authentic early texts. Most of the texts are to be located between these two extreme points: they belong to the political debates of their times and were composed in order to provide one or the other of the contending parties with the authoritative support of the model kings of the past.

While traditional (Assyriological) interest has been focused on the search for the "historical kernel"—always presumed to be found under the anachronisms and literary embellishments of the historical poems—the most important information we can extract therefrom is certainly related to the political problems for whose solution they had been written. The "King of Battle" (*šar tamḫāri*) probably has to do with the resuming of Old Assyrian trade activities in Cappadocia at the time of Shamshi-Adad. The "Curse of Akkad (Agade)" probably has to do with the restoration work in the Ekur by Ur-Nammu of Ur (or perhaps by Ishme-Dagan of Isin). The "General Rebellion" was reworked in the frame of the wars between Kish and Babylon. And so on. In all these cases, the discovery of the historical context is only a reasonable hypothesis, since the extant literary compositions are the only evidence for the debates from which they originated.

In their actual political activities, the kings and their advisers had to decide on the basis of their practical knowledge of the affair, but they had to use the cultural codes of their times. There are basically two codes. The main code of Mesopotamian politics was that provided by divination, a set of techniques putting the king in direct contact with the divine world, the only source for correct instruction. Spontaneous omens (especially dreams) and solicited omens (especially extispicy, inspecting entrails) assured the ruler about the feasibility of his projects. The two opposed attitudes are "to be afraid" (*palāḫu*) and "to be confident" (*takālu*) about the issue of the enterprise. Even though the difficulties might seem excessive, the king has nothing to fear, provided he is confident in the gods' assent. By the way, the behavior of enemies is opposite to the correct one: instead of being confident in the gods and not fearful of natural or human elements, they are confident in natural or human elements (the mountains, the city walls, the numbers of their troops, their allies) but are not afraid of the Assyrians and of the gods' verdict. This behavior is clearly impious and foolish and cannot but end in disaster.

Besides this basic code of decision making, the literary and historical models provide an additional code, or perhaps just some additional elements. The achievements of the early heroes can suggest the correct choice, can demonstrate that the enterprise is not beyond human capabilities, and can stimulate the competition for fame. The two model Akkadian kings are endowed with opposite characters. Sargon is the model for correct behavior, the one who followed divine advice even when human judgment would have suggested caution or renunciation. On the con-

trary, Naram-Sin is the one who did not care for gods or for omens and made his decisions according to purely human evaluations, on the basis of human information (see "Kings of Akkad" in Part 5, Vol. II). In the *Legend of Naram-Sin*, the king sends a scout to test the possibility of defeating the enemies and does this before asking the gods' advice:

> I summoned an officer and instructed him: 'Take a lance, take a spear, touch them (= the enemies) with the lance, prick them with the spear. If blood comes out, they are men like us; if blood does not come out, they are evil spirits, spectres, ghosts and fiends, creatures of Enlil.'
> (After Oliver R. Gurney, "Sultantepe Tablets," 1955)

No wonder that eventually the omens will turn out to be negative. And at this point, Naram-Sin's second mistake (or "sin") is to imagine that he is able to do without the consent of the gods:

> What lion ever observed oracles? What wolf ever consulted a dream-priestess? I will go like a robber according to my own inclination, taking with me a spear of iron. (After Gurney)

A similar concern for the omens is to be found throughout the epic literature of historical content, where the success or failure of kings is explained by their pious or impious behavior, by their capability of listening to the advice coming from the gods. Such literature is therefore deeply embedded in the political and theological theories of ancient Mesopotamia. Only secondarily is it a poetic celebration of the heroic qualities of the king and his soldiers.

The final development of the genre is wisdom, a development already implicit beforehand, since the political and theological principles pointed out above are the very basis for wise behavior, and the example of the model kings of the past has a didactic value for later kings. While the "true" royal inscriptions put their emphasis on celebration (underscoring the valor and the success of the king), the "false" ones—the literary fabrications originated by, and giving origin to, the scribal learned debates—put their emphasis on teaching. Here is the close of the "Legend of Naram-Sin":

> Whoever you are, whether governor or prince or any one else, whom the god shall call to rule over

a kingdom . . . read this document and listen to the words thereof. . . . Let wise scribes read aloud your stele. You who have read my stele and kept out of trouble, you who have blessed me, may a future one bless you.

(After Gurney)

And here is the close of the "Synchronistic History":

Let a later prince, who wishes to achieve fame in Akkad, write about the prowess of his victories. Let him continually turn to this very stele (and) look at it that it may not be forgotten. . . . May the praises of Assyria be lauded forever. May the crimes of Sumer and Akkad (= Babylonia) be bruited abroad through every quarter.

(After A. Kirk Grayson)

The kings' desire for eternal fame (the only possible survival after death) generated the "historical" narratives in the royal inscriptions. But the scribes' pride added the further qualification that the most heroic enterprises of the most powerful king would not have survived, and would not have functioned as models for kingship, were it not for the scribes who put them into writing. We can add a further consideration that is not present in the ancient inscriptions—since it belongs to the "materialistic" level of understanding that the royal inscriptions tried to sublimate and conceal: namely that even the most powerful kings would not have been able to keep their kingdoms in subjection by pure force, were it not for the words of propaganda causing people to believe that the social and political imbalances were necessary for the benefit of the exploited and the exploiters alike, and that the efforts of the whole community had to be addressed to the care of the gods—and of the king, their delegate on earth.

BIBLIOGRAPHY

Mesopotamian Historiography

BERTIL ALBREKTSON, *History and the Gods: An Essay on the Idea of Historical Events as Divine Manifestations in the Ancient Near East and in Israel* (1967); J. J. FINKELSTEIN, "Mesopotamian Historiography," *Proceedings of the American Philosophical Society* 107 (1963); JEAN-JACQUES GLASSNER, *Chroniques mésopotamiennes* (1993); A. KIRK GRAYSON, "Histories and Historians of the Ancient Near East: Assyria and Babylonia," *Orientalia* 49 (1980); MARIO LIVERANI, "Memorandum on the Approach to Historiographic Texts," *Orientalia* 42 (1973); JOHN VAN SETERS, *In Search of History: Historiography in the Ancient World and the Origins of Biblical History* (1983).

Historical Traditions Concerning the Akkadian Kings

HANS G. GÜTERBOCK, "Die historische Tradition und ihre literarische Gestaltung bei Babyloniern und Hethitern," *Zeitschrift für Assyriologie* 42 (1934) and 44 (1938); MARIO LIVERANI, "Model and Actualization: The Kings of Akkad in the Historical Tradition," in *Akkad, the First World Empire*, edited by MARIO LIVERANI (1993).

Assyrian Royal Inscriptions

RYKLE BORGER and WOLFGANG SCHRAMM, *Einleitung in die assyrischen Königsinschriften*, I–II (1961–1972); *Assyrian Royal Inscriptions: New Horizons in Literary, Ideological, and Historical Analysis*, edited by F. MARIO FALES (1981); A. T. OLMSTEAD, *Assyrian Historiography: A Source Study* (1916); *History, Historiography and Interpretation*, edited by HAYIM TADMOR and MOSHE WEINFELD (1983).

Ideology and Propaganda in the Royal Inscriptions

J. J. FINKELSTEIN, "Early Mesopotamia, 2500–1000 B.C.," in *Propaganda and Communication in World History, I, The Symbolic Instrument in Early Times*, edited by HAROLD D. LASSWELL, DANIEL LERNER, and HANS SPEIER (1979); A. LEO OPPENHEIM, "Neo-Assyrian and Neo-Babylonian Empires," ibidem; MARIO LIVERANI, "Ideology of the Assyrian Empire," in *Power and Propaganda*, edited by MOGENS TROLLE LARSEN (1979); PETER MACHINIST, "Assyrians on Assyria in the First Millennium B.C.," in *Anfänge politischen Denkens in der Antike*, edited by KURT RAAFLAUB (1993); TREMPER LONGMAN III, *Fictional Akkadian Autobiography: A Generic and Comparative Study* (1991).

War and Building Accounts

JERROLD S. COOPER, *Reconstructing History from Ancient Inscriptions: the Lagash-Umma Border Conflict* (1983); SYLVIE LACKENBACHER, *Le palais sans rival. Le récit de construction en Assyrie* (1990); MARIO LIVERANI, *Prestige and Interest: International Relations in the Near East ca. 1600–1100 B.C.* (1990); MANFRED WEIPPERT, "'Heiliger Krieg' in Israel und Assyrien," *Zeitschrift für die alttestamentliche Wissenschaft* 84

(1972); K. LAWSON YOUNGER, *Ancient Conquest Accounts: A Study in Ancient Near Eastern and Biblical History Writing* (1990); BUSTENAY ODED, *War, Peace and Empire: Justification for War in Assyrian Royal Inscriptions* (1992).

Translations

JERROLD S. COOPER, *Sumerian and Akkadian Royal Inscriptions, I: Presargonic Inscriptions* (1986); BENJAMIN R. FOSTER, *Before the Muses*, I–II (1993); DOUGLAS FRAYNE, *The Royal Inscriptions of Mesopotamia, Early Periods, IV: Old Babylonian Period* (1990), and *The Royal Inscriptions of Mesopotamia, Early Periods, II: Sargonic and Gutian Periods* (1993); A. KIRK GRAYSON, *Assyrian and Babylonian Chronicles* (1975), and *The Royal Inscriptions of Mesopotamia, Assyrian Periods, II: Assyrian Rulers of the Early First Millennium BC* (1991); OLIVER R. GURNEY, "The Sultantepe Tablets. IV: The Cuthaean Legend of Naram-Sin," *Anatolian Studies* 5 (1955); DANIEL DAVID LUCKENBILL, *Ancient Records of Assyria and Babylonia*, vols. 1–2 (1927); SAMUEL NOAH KRAMER, *The Sumerians: Their History, Culture, and Character* (1963).

SEE ALSO **The Historiography of the Ancient Near East** (Part 9, Vol. IV) and various chapters in PART 5: HISTORY AND CULTURE.

Hittite and Hurrian Literatures: An Overview

ALFONSO ARCHI

FOR THE HITTITES the acquisition of cuneiform script meant undergoing a profound process of acculturation. In addition to Sumerian-Akkadian word lists (necessary for a correct use of cuneiform), which had to be provided with Hittite equivalences, the scribal school absorbed literary models that were curricular because of the prestige of Mesopotamian culture and because Akkadian was the written language in the entire Syrian region. And so it follows that discoveries in the archives of Khattusha (Boğazköy), the Hittite capital, turned up rituals, auguries, hymns, wisdom texts, and some parts of the Gilgamesh and Atrakhasis poems, all in Babylonian, in addition to the legends about Sargon and Naram-Sin, the two great kings of the Akkad dynasty, in Hittite translation. Even if some of the hymns—to the sun-god, to the storm-god, to the goddess Ishtar—and the wisdom texts were imported during the period of the Empire and translated into Hittite, they did not influence Hittite styles of expression. But there are two hymns in Hittite that date to the Hittite Middle Kingdom (the last decade of the fifteenth century BCE), one to the storm-god and the other to the sun-god, of which there are no known Mesopotamian parallel texts. Both are clearly Babylonian in form and motif; while the first case is surely a translation into Hittite from an original now lost to us, the second could be the work of a Hittite poet who had a direct and thorough knowledge

of Babylonian hymnody. The distribution of this hymn to the sun (there exist separate versions to be recited by the king, by "a man," and by "a son of mankind") was so widespread that some of its sections served as introductions to prayers for various other divinities such as Telipinu and the sun-goddess of Arinna. However, other prayers, in particular those devoted to a specific circumstance, lack hymns and represent an entirely independent style. In such prayers, the rulers themselves unfold the events that brought about a particular situation and are forced through an introspective examination to admit their own guilt, and perhaps to give historical explanations that differ from the versions consecrated in the official documents (see "Hittite Prayers" in Part 8). In spite of the impact of Babylonian culture, Hittite forms of expression maintained a particular identity. The numerous incantations and festivals (texts of an eminently practical nature) that describe magical and cult actions step by step were not influenced in form by the Assyro-Babylonian incantations, which were composed in large part of elaborate invocations. There is only one genre that the Hittites owe totally to outside influence: the poems of myth and legend (called "songs," like the Babylonian examples) that were absorbed from the Anatolian and Syrian centers of Hurrian culture.

The Hittites did not feel it necessary to define the forms in which they articulated their written work, excluding terms like "incantation," "prayer," "festival," and "(political) treaty." But the documents may be classified according to their functions, and within some categories there are texts that present such expressive elaboration that they become recognizable as literary works.

THE FORMATION OF GENRES IN THE OLD HITTITE KINGDOM

Edicts

There is evidence from the period of Khattushili I (Hattusili; 1650–1620 BCE), the second king of the dynasty, of genres such as edicts, heroic narratives, and annals in very mature stylistic forms that would be taken as models for later work. It was in these practical normative and historical documents that the Hittite scribal school found its strongest expression. The extraordinary personality of Khattushili, who made the Hittite state one of the great powers of its time, comes out vividly in an edict in which he presented his own successor, Murshili I, to the dignitaries of the realm. It is a true political last will and testament, dictated when the king was sick. It is infused therefore with the pathos of a man who, feeling the nearness of death, is obliged to trust to a young and unseasoned descendant the fortunes of a kingdom that is torn by internal strife. Because of the drama of the situation and the simplicity of the language, his message reaches us even today with an immediacy that perhaps has no equal in any other historical document of the ancient Near East. Although the colophon specifically states that the *Edict of Khattushili* was sent out "when the great king . . . named the young Murshili to ascend to the throne," there is no discourse on the office of royalty that might serve ideological purposes by invoking divine rights of kings. Everything is resolved in the scope of a personal association with the king, and only those who observe the king's word can be just and authoritative: "(Labarna) did not shed tears, and did not show mercy; he is cold and heartless. . . . Until now no one in my family obeyed my will . . . keep your father's word!" There is frequent recourse to images taken from the animal world, with a

realism that will not occur again in later Hittite compositions: "Then his mother bellowed like an ox, 'They have torn asunder the womb in the living body of me, a mighty ox!' . . . His mother is a serpent! . . . The god will appoint only another lion to the place of a lion!" The text reflects the concerns of a period of state formation, and in the press of events the king is obliged to present himself directly rather than through a screen of an elaborate ideology of royalty.

Khattushili insists upon obedience in another (fragmentary) edict as well, with the same expressive force: "As long as you keep my words . . . and blow on the fire of the hearth [symbol of the unity of the clan], you will not transgress my words; . . . or else it will happen that the serpent will entwine itself around Khattusha!" And this message is taken up by his successor, Murshili I (1620–1598), who left a large collection of anecdotes concerning officials of the realm that intentionally represents the "father of the king" (that is, Khattushili) as a paradigmatic figure, guardian of good government. From the anecdotes emerges a picture of a small-scale society that revolves around a sovereign ruler who controls everything and who punishes dishonesty wherever it can be found. Other documents of the same period reinforce the charge imposed on officers to act on behalf of the disinherited, with precepts similar to those of royal Egyptian and Mesopotamian propaganda. These texts insist on true "works of charity": "Give bread to the hungry, give oil to whoever is chapped, clothes to the naked; whoever is tormented by heat lead into the coolness, and whoever is tormented by cold lead into the warmth!" And again it is "the father (of the king who) seeks to expose your scandals before the entire assembly!" This pressing preoccupation with justice that the ruler imposes on his officers is a motif that appears only in this stage of the formation of the state, and then disappears together with the patriarchal characteristics of the early Hittite royalty.

The *Edict of Telipinu* (1525–1500) also expresses a moment of profound crisis, but it speaks to a broader purpose than the *Edict of Khattushili*. The *Edict of Telipinu* sought to establish the fundamental principles of the organization of the state. The introductory section narrates the course of past events to seek the causes of weakness in the present, which is attributed to a failure of unity. The kings in older times (Labarna, Khattushili, Murshili) were victorious because their "sons, brothers, all their relatives and soldiers were united." This theme goes back to Khattushili: "Let your clan be united like that of a wolf!" Khattushili, too, had appealed to past events in order to lend force to his arguments. Now, with Telipinu, the historical precedent was given in a preamble, a form that would be repeated in later decrees and political treaties. These were versions of history codified in political documents and certainly not inquiries into the sense of historical truth. The reconstruction of events given by Telipinu, who presents himself as the author, is particularly far reaching. As the narrative approaches more recent events, the tone becomes more dramatic. Khantili I, who was the first to make his way to the throne by regicide—Murshili, conqueror of Aleppo (ancient Halab) and Babylon, was his victim—is represented as a man tortured by remorse: "Khantili was afraid: 'Who will protect me?'. . . Wherever he moved, the lands (rebelled against him). . . . 'What did I do to deserve this?' And then the gods took their (revenge for) the blood of Murshili."

As was the case in the *Edict of Khattushili* (but not in those texts of the Empire period) there is no reference to the influence of particular divinities. Man is the master of his own destiny, but the gods guarantee moral order. Khantili had violated that order, and consequently he is presented as a completely negative figure. His queen is murdered, and while Khantili is on his deathbed, Zidanta, who had participated in the conspiracy against Murshili, murders his son and all of his descendants. And the narrative gets gloomier as it proceeds from crime to crime through the reigns of Zidanta, Ammuna, and Khuzziya, until it reaches the point when Telipinu takes control. *The Edict of Telipinu*, a text surely dictated by the king and one that makes frequent use of direct discourse (a technique initiated by Khattushili), has an energy that would be lost in later works, when the edicts of a stiff and pompous chancery sought to glorify the ideology of royalty. The energetic style of the older edicts was due in part to the fact that they were read aloud before the assembly in Khattusha.

The second part of the document prescribes rules and standards, including the rules for succession to the throne and the methods for dealing with criminals guilty of high crimes. In order to break recurrent patterns of revenge, the edict abolishes the responsibility of families for the actions of individual family members. The entire administrative system is reorganized. Historical precedence is sought in references to the ideals of good government fixed by Khattushili, and pregnant expressions like "drinking the blood of the country" were borrowed from him to describe the actions of officers who sought advantage to the detriment of the population. In this document, broad reformist commitments find their appropriate literary form.

Annals and Chronicles

The historical inscription of Anitta dates back to a pre-Hittite phase, when the ruler Anitta moved from Kusshar, where the dynasty of Khattushili also had its origin, to become the king of Nesha (Kanesh, modern Kültepe). The text is in Old Hittite, but it is not clear whether or not it was originally written in Assyrian. At the beginning, Anitta refers briefly to the deeds of his father and to some of his own conquests. Then there is a sharp break in the narrative, and a formula, used to close Assyrian-Babylonian inscriptions but foreign to the Hittite tradition, appears: "[I wrote] these words on a tablet, on my gate. In the future no one may break this tablet! Whoever breaks it, let that person be an enemy of Nesha!" The narration of further deeds follows, along with a description of the building works undertaken at Nesha. After another campaign, Anitta receives from the king of Purushkhanda a throne and an iron scepter, symbols of his supremacy. The composition is not unified, but it is rather a compilation of several inscriptions, with insufficient transitions between events. The condemnation of a rival city that will never be repopulated (Khattusha), ritually expressed by sowing weeds, is found also in the history/story of the town of Zalpa, where the acting king probably is Khattushili I; but various other elements belong only to the Mesopotamian tradition, like the vanquished king carried as prisoner to the city of the victor, the fortification of the capital, the construction of temples for the major gods, and the ritual hunt.

Less rich in its range of subjects is the *Deeds of Khattushili*. This text exhibits the characteristics of annals, such as the first-person narrative of the deeds of the ruler. This text follows five years of Khattushili I's reign, from western Anatolia to beyond the Euphrates. The division of time is given by the formula "and in the following year . . ." without progressive numbers, a system that Murshili II uses about 300 years later in his *Ten Year Annals*. The narrative scheme of the *Deeds of Khattushili* is very simple in its vocabulary and syntax: "I went to the city. . . . I destroyed it, I carried off from it [such and such]." The few variations and clarifications are mostly of a military nature. In contrast, lists of booty dedicated to the gods are given in great detail. The aid of the sun-goddess is often acknowledged, but the primary picture is of a heroic king who battles and defeats the enemy cities, and piously honors the gods. The king is compared to the lion that "holds at bay" and "prevails with his claws" against his enemy. There is an Akkadian version of the *Deeds of Khattushili*, as well as of the *Edict of Khattushili* and the *Edict of Telipinu* (addressed to a Hittite-speaking audience); in the Akkadian version, the narrative is in the third person. The existence of these Akkadian versions is powerful evidence of the importance of the original documents. During the Old Hittite period, Akkadian was considered the written language par excellence, much in the way that Latin and Arabic were considered prestigious in later historical epochs. The only literary echo of Mesopotamian origin appears at the conclusion of the part narrating the expedition against the cities of Khakkhum and Khasshum in the area of the Euphrates, an achievement discussed at greater length at the end of the document. In a sort of crescendo, Khattushili compares himself to Sargon the Great of Akkad: "No one had crossed the Euphrates; But I, the great king Tabarna crossed it on foot, and my army crossed it after me. Only Sargon had crossed it, and had beaten the troops of Khakkhum, but had left Khakkhum itself intact. But I . . ."

Ample summations of the deeds of Khattushili and, above all, of Murshili in eastern Anatolia against the Hurrians and the coalitions united under Aleppo (ancient Halab) are preserved in texts that are so fragmentary that it is not possible to analyze them.

A tablet with an edict of Ammuna (a predecessor of Telipinu) is also too fragmentary to analyze. The back of the tablet contains some sections of a chronicle relating the activities of an unknown king and his officers, who are named, narrated in yearly sequential order ("in the second year," "[in the third ye]ar," and so forth). The style is richer in data than that of Shamshi-Adad, the king of Asshur (eighteenth century BCE).

Sagas and Epics

Some archaic texts introduce elements of legend into the course of historical narratives. A very fragmentary composition describes Anumkhirpi, the eighteenth-century king of Mamma, as a foundling who grew up at the court of Zimri-Lim of Mari. Notable characters reflect the relationships that bound eastern Anatolia and Mari during this period. Remote countries often inspire tales of bizarre customs, like the cannibalism attributed to a people of the Syrian steppe, and give the impression that the campaigns of Khattushili and Murshili had reached the very ends of the earth: "Any man who comes there, they eat him. If they see a fat person, they kill him and they eat him." The explorers devise a way to test the nature of these strange beings: "If he realizes it (that flesh of pigs—not of humans—is offered to him), he is a god; but if he does not realize it, he is a man, and we should fight him!"

Elements of legend open the history of the relationship between Zalpa, a city on the Black Sea, and the Hittite dynasty. It seems that by showing how Zalpa was colonized by the people of Nesha, who spoke Hittite, the narrative attempts to justify the right of the Hittites to hold that city under their control. It employs the well-known motif of rejected children who succeed in finding their parents. The queen of Nesha gives birth to thirty sons "in a single year," and, horrified, she shuts them up in a basket and throws it into the river. The currents take them downriver to Zalpa, near the sea. When they grow up, they learn about the queen of Nesha and the fate of her thirty sons, and also that she later bore thirty daughters. Understanding that they have found their mother, they go back to her. Not recognizing her sons, she offers her thirty daughters for them to take as wives. But the youngest son, realizing that these women are his sisters, avoids committing incest. At this point, with a benediction of the sun-god to allow Zalpa to prosper, the narration of historical events begins. After various struggles, the elders of the city ask the Hittite king for one of his sons to be their lord. But when even his own son contends with him, the Hittite king (probably Khattushili) conquers Zalpa. The vows/benediction of the sun-god come to pass in an unintentionally ironic way: the prosperity of Zalpa is in its annexation into the Hittite kingdom. Of a notable literary quality is the story of crossing the Taurus Mountains, which describes in mythological-poetic language the Hittite expansion toward northern Syria. Dramatic situations follow one upon the other in rapid succession, and there is ample use of symbolic images. This story begins after a break in the text, with the king having decided not to succumb to the difficulties that surround him.

> He (the king) is dressed in a multicolored shirt, and on his head he wears a basket (as a quiver) and he carries a bow in his hand. He called for help, "What have I done? What? I never took anything from anybody. . . . Why are you doing this to me? Why do you lash me to this yoke? I will bring the chill of death upon you with this quiver. I will fight and I will destroy this land, using this arrow that I will shoot into their hearts!"

A usurper rises up against him and installs himself as king in the sacred city of Arinna. But the true king exalts his own role, which is to maintain the cosmic order as the representative of the gods on earth:

> Who did you lead to Arinna? Him, my foe! Is he not my donkey? I will set myself against him. Take me there! Who rules all the lands (with his hand)? Is it not I who hold fixed (in their places) the rivers, the mountains and the sea? I set the mountain in such a way that it does not move; I set the sea in such a way that it does not overflow!

At this point it is probably the king who takes on the semblance of a bull and opens with his horns a passage across the mountain (Taurus Mountains) so that the army can move against Aleppo. The king "became a bull; his horns are slightly curved. I ask, 'Why are your horns curved?' He answers, 'When I went into battle, the mountain was in my way.' Behold, it was the bull. . . . (There) stands the sun-god, who orders the messengers: 'Go to Aleppo!'" The historical situation—Hittite expansion to the south—and the lively phraseology make it possible to identify Khattushili I as the hero whose deeds are mythologized in this text. The following sections, badly preserved, narrate the struggle against Aleppo and the tension of the soldiers who sing as they wait for the Hurrian enemy: "The Hurrians have not come yet, and four years have passed. There are two warriors who sing, 'Garments of Nesha, garments of Nesha. Come to me, come! Bring me to my mother. Come to me, come! . . . What is that crowd of people?'"

The *Siege of Urshu* recounts another episode in the life of Khattushili (there is corollary mention of it in his *Annals*). The text is known to us only in an Akkadian version, probably from a lost Hittite original. Here the dialogues are particularly dramatic, at times even explosive. The character of the king, who is dedicated to righting the errors of his officers, acquires an epic dimension:

> The king said, "If the city is destroyed, it would be an offense, it would be a crime." They replied, "We will give battle eight times, and the city will be destroyed, but we will wipe out the crime." The king gave his assent. But they broke the battering ram. The king became furious; his face grew dark (and he said), "They always bring me bad news!"

The intention is to glorify the king's skill as a commander, which stands in contrast to the ineptitude of the Hittite generals, for whom he spares no sarcasm: "Why did you not fight? Are you standing on a chariot made of water? Or have you yourself turned to water?"

THE EMPIRE PERIOD

Already by Khattushili's time the Hittites had a memory of the glorious kings of Akkad, but it is not certain what they knew of the epic narratives that told of their exploits. These compositions were widely disseminated beyond Mesopotamia during the Amarna period (fourteenth century). More than a few fragments in Akkadian come from Khattusha in loose translations, such as the *King of Battle*, whose hero is Sargon, and the story of Naram-Sin in Asia Minor. These texts are interesting because they recount the ancient history of Anatolia in the form of fables and legends. Sargon, answering the pleas of merchants, comes to Anatolia and establishes a friendship with the king of Purushkhanda, the city that according to Anitta maintained hegemony in Anatolia before Nesha. Naram-Sin battled against a coalition that included, among others, the kings of Khatti, Nesha, and Purushkhanda. These Anatolian countries are presented as being far away from the known world, whose inhabitants could be not humans but gods, a motif that we have already encountered in the epic concerning the Hittite expansion in eastern Anatolia: "I shall stab them with a spit, and I shall slice them with a razor. If blood spurts out of them, they are mortal and I will march against them; if no blood spurts out, they are gods and I will not march against them." These compositions had no influence on the historical narrative style of the Empire, but if they were previously known to the Hittites, they could have inspired Old Hittite narratives like the *Conquest of Urshu* and the story of the struggle against Aleppo and its allies. (See "Kings of Akkad: Sargon and Naram-Sin" in Vol. II.)

In the Empire period the Hittite kings forged alliances with various rulers of Anatolia and Syria, and they established relations at various levels with the courts of Babylonia and Egypt. These political accomplishments and greater political stability are reflected in narratives of a broader historical scope. The rulers' confidence in their power is apparent in the style of the Empire period narratives. Murshili II (1339–1306) wanted to leave a memorial record of his own deeds and those of his father, Shuppiluliuma I, who had decisively beaten Mitanni, effectively resisted the Egyptians, and had married a princess of Babylon, a recognition of his status as great king. Murshili produced the *Deeds of Shuppululiuma*, the *Ten Year Annals* (covering his own first ten years of rule), and the *Detailed Annals* that cover nearly the entire period of his

own rule. It is not possible to determine the chronological sequence with which these histories were composed. Taken together the result is a narrative that covers about seventy years.

Before Murshili II, other kings of the Hittite Middle Kingdom, like Tudkhaliya and Arnuwanda, had already taken up the ancient rulers' tradition of dictating their own exploits. However, a remarkable development in talent and skill was necessary to broaden the traditional scope of such narratives and to detail events occurring over a long span of time: the *Deeds of Shuppiluliuma* (composed by Murshili II) covers the events in the life of that king, who during a long reign fought repeatedly in the regions south of the Caucasus and in western Anatolia and who boasted of having the Euphrates and Lebanon as borders for his empire. Perhaps the fact that these narratives are given in the third person allows them to assume more of a historical perspective. Not only are the actions of the generals reported (as they are in the *Annals*), but episodes of simultaneous action sometimes occur. A strict sequential order of material by year is observed only in the *Ten Year Annals* and the *Detailed Annals*. The symmetrical structure of the *Ten Year Annals* (the only ones preserved almost in their entirety) is formed by a descriptive pattern that alternates between battles and exchanges of letters or messages. There are also passages of reflection on preceding events and persuasive argumentation turned against adversaries, as in the historical prologues of the political treaties. The articulation of the text into sections that present a certain symmetry could be the result of an intelligent selection and arrangement of material. The rhetorical instruments, and the excellent syntactical control (the use of hypothetical phrases, concessive and causal), make the *Annals of Murshili* the apex of Hittite historiography.

Of a completely different character is the so-called *Autobiography* or *Apology of Khattushili III* (1275–1250). Formally this work is an edict that institutes a religious foundation in honor of Ishtar, the tutelary goddess of the king, using the assets of defeated enemies. But the disposition section occupies only about twenty lines of the more than three hundred lines that make up the whole text. The document is cleverly constructed to justify the coup d'état with which

Khattushili installed himself in place of his nephew Urkhi-Teshub (Murshili III), who had ascended to the throne by legitimate succession. Khattushili presents himself as having been an instrument in the hands of Ishtar since childhood. His loyalty was tested in more than one trial presided over by Muwattalli, his brother and predecessor, who placed such faith in him as to trust the government of the entire northern region to him, and then even the city of Khattusha. In turn, upon the death of Muwattalli, Khattushili enthroned his son Urkhi-Teshub, whom he later deposed because Urkhi-Teshub returned evil for Khattushili's good deed. There is practically no phrase that does not echo one of the main themes—fidelity, divine favor—that run through the entire text, which is an absolute masterpiece of the art of persuasion. (See "Khattushili III, King of the Hittites" in Vol. II.)

MYTHS

Between the fifteenth and the fourteenth centuries, the scribal school of Khattusha opened itself up to various outside literary influences. Its contacts with Canaanite culture probably go back to the military undertakings of Shuppiluliuma I (1380–1340). In Hittite there are sections of a myth involving Elkunirsha (the West Semitic El, Creator of the Earth), his wife Ashertu (Asherah), and Baal. Another fragment of a text dedicated to the activities of a personified mountain Pishaisha (somewhere in Syria), mentions the victory of the storm-god over the sea, which recalls the Ugaritic myth of Baal and Yamm.

The epic story of Gurparanzakh is native to the Hurrian world, as shown by the name of the hero, Aranzakh being the Hurrian name of the Tigris River. The story takes place, however, in Akkad. Gurparanzakh helps Impakru, certainly the king of Akkad, to kill a bear. Upon returning to Akkad, he proves his valor again by defeating the best heroes of the city ("sixty kings, seventy heroes") in an archery contest. Perfumed with oil, Gurparanzakh prepares himself for a night of love, but instead he has a talk with his wife Tatizuli, who is perhaps the cause of the despair to which he falls victim in a second fragment. The river Aranzakh, fast as an eagle, flies to him in Akkad, and asks him the reason for his sorrow.

The story that the hero tells, in tears, is poorly preserved; but at its conclusion, Aranzakh flies to the goddess of destiny for advice.

The great Hurrian cycle of Kumarbi, known to us only in the Hittite language, was acquired by the Hittites probably toward the end of the fifteenth century. This work is formed by a number of assorted "songs" (Sumerian sìr), such as "Kingship in Heaven," "Ullikummi," "Khedammu," and "Silver," that exhibit an expansive capacity to build narrative. Each song extends over an as yet unknown number of tablets, and each tablet contains about 250 lines. The songs clearly present formal literary elements. There are formalistic repetitions, parallel clauses, fixed epithets, and formulas for opening and closing direct discourse. Considering a syntactical clause as a unit, segments vary from twelve to seventeen syllables, perhaps in free verse. The origin of the text is obscure, and it is not certain that the Hittite version depends directly upon a written recension in Hurrian (only a fragment about Ullikummi remains in the Hurrian language). The Hittite text, where it is documented by many manuscripts, presents only minimal variants and therefore constitutes a unique recension. (See "The Kumarbi Cycle" in Part 8, Vol. III, for further details.)

There is a mythological narrative from the Hurrian tradition, whose title is *Song of Remission* (of debts) and whose function is to establish ground rules for human behavior. In the introduction, the sun-goddess of the earth, Allani, invites the storm god Teshub to a sumptuous feast, to which the "ancient" gods who inhabit the netherworld are also invited. The harmony thus established between the two divinities that rule the world above and the world below constitutes the theological condition for procuring the repayment of debts and a general harmony among men.

How men ought to conduct themselves is shown from certain negative examples, which belong to the heritage of wisdom of the ancient Orient and which are always introduced by the formula: "Harken to this message, I wish to tell you wise things."

A smith forged a cup of copper, for his own glory. He chiselled it and adorned it with marvellous decorations. He made it sparkle in every detail.

Then the foolish copper began to curse him who had forged it: "May your hand be smashed, you who have forged me, may the tendons of your arms be cut!" When the smith heard this, he grieved in his heart and said: "How can the copper which I have forged curse me?" (After V. Haas and I. Wegner, *Orientalische Literaturzeitung* 86 [1991]: 387)

And then the smith cursed the copper. The following example is of a son who does not love his father and abandons him in his old age. The gods, however, curse the son.

A situation is then presented in which the adduced examples ought to serve as ammunition. Megi, lord of the city of Ebla, entertains six kings, and three other kings are entertained in a neighboring city. To them is presented a tenth king, who seeks the liberation of the nine kings; otherwise he will destroy Ebla: "I will shatter the wall of the mean city of Ebla like a glass; I will reduce the wall of the citadel like a heap of rubble. I will annihilate like a glass the foundations of Ebla in the market square." Thus ends, abruptly and inappropriately, the sixth tablet of this composition.

In the Empire period the Hittites created new literary genres with documents of high quality. The *Annals of Murshili II*, and those drawn up by him through his father Shuppiluliuma I, constitute stylistically the most notable historical narratives of the second millennium. The *Apology of Khattushili III* is a model for the subtle use of rhetoric.

Through epic compositions and literary elaborations of myths, the Hittites were entirely indebted to Hurrian culture, but they can be credited with having transmitted these texts. Their works are translations, whose excellent stylistic quality owes much to the originals. In these literary genres, narratives of Hittite origin do not flow together. The expressive forms in which the Hittites excelled are all connected to their political history.

These literary texts, of foreign origin, all come from the temple libraries. They were vehicles for religious concepts that the Hittites collected in part between the fifteenth and fourteenth centuries, and they include various Hurrian divinities. These literary texts were of interest to the temple scribal school but not to the chancellery.

Apparently no one in the palace sought entertainment in literature.

Hattic-Hittite mythological narratives, in contrast to Hurrian ones, are often known through various recensions, even in abbreviated form. These narratives are embedded in ritual contexts because they were recited as part of magical rites. These texts were found in the royal palace as often as in the temple libraries.

The Hittites acquired Anatolian myths in large part from the Hattic people who had settled central Anatolia and whose culture had a profound influence on them. Some of these texts survive in Hattic versions, a language that has only been partially deciphered; others, in Hittite, are set in the Hattic region or include Hattic divinities. Sometimes the same mythic motifs are transferred to Hittite divinities. The redactions that have come down to us do not go back before the fifteenth century. The themes are few and repetitive; the expressive form does not show any literary intent.

The Hittite mythological heritage, which had been codified in a written tradition, was indubitably the poorest in variety of all those that have been transmitted by peoples of the ancient Near East who had knowledge of script. This does not mean, however, that the Hittites did not have other myths. Functioning as sections of rituals that use magic to remedy a crisis are those myths that present two fundamental stages: an event that disturbs a given balance and a divine intercession that restores order. Only myths that follow this pattern were recorded by the Hittites. The celebrant would recite myths together with magic formulas. These myths provide a kind of setting for a mimetic dramatization of the story. In order to function as rituals, they offer a very simple structure, with brief phrases and repetitions designed to hold one's attention. The fascination of these documents lies in their very simplicity, which makes them seem to flow directly out of an archaic world.

Myth is the root of ritual. A Hattic ritual tells that once upon a time the gods had built a palace and had authorized the kingship of the Labarna (the dynastic title of the king) by establishing the throne and instituting the regal vestments. In order to placate the storm-god "when he thunders terribly," another Hattic ritual (in Hittite translation) envelops a myth that projects a similar situation upon the world of the gods. Men are able to counter adverse events by means of a process analogous to the one the gods themselves use. The moon-god, fallen from the sky (a motif prompted by lunar phases), is seized by anguish because no one seems to care what has happened to him. Only the goddess Katakhzipuri (Kamrushepa in Hittite), looking down from the sky, takes notice of his predicament and administers a ritual conducted with the assistance of the god Khapantali in order to eliminate his "fear and anguish." The myth occupies only about twenty lines, but repetition of each phrase provides the narrative with rhythm: "The moon-god fell from the sky and fell upon the gate, but no one saw him. The storm-god sent rain after him; he sent rains after him. Fear seized him; anxiety seized him."

The image of Katakhzipuri looking down from the sky, seeing an unfortunate condition, and then correcting it is a common one in Hattic rituals, where the mythological section of the ritual can be extremely abbreviated. Kamrushepa, together with Khapantali, assumes a decisive role in the myth of the vanishing god, the most productive myth of all, adapted to many divinities. Telipinu, a god of Hattic origin who presides primarily over agriculture (his symbol is the ear of grain), has the part of the vanishing god in the most elaborate known version of this myth. Telipinu is angry (his motives are never given), and in his state of agitation the god puts his shoes on the wrong feet. (In the version adapted to the goddesses Anzili and Zukki, they reverse the lacing of pectorals and veils—a sign of the popular origin of the story.) Going away, Telipinu carries off all "grain, fertility, luxuriance, growth, and abundance" with him. As a consequence,

> Mist seized the windows. Smoke seized the house. In the fireplace the logs were stifled. At the altars the gods were stifled. In the sheep pen the sheep were stifled. In the cattle barn the cattle were stifled. The mother sheep rejected her lamb. The cow rejected her calf.

The rhythm, suggested by the repetition, is similar to that of the myth of the moon. Humankind and animals are no longer able to reproduce. The gods themselves, gathered at a banquet, "ate but could not get enough; drank but could not quench their thirst." Then the storm-god, realizing that Telipinu is absent, sends the eagle to seek him out. When the eagle fails to find him, the storm-god himself goes, but he searches in vain. On the suggestion of the mother goddess Khannakhanna, a little bee is sent to find the absent god and succeeds where the "great and the small gods" had failed. The bee stings Telipinu and wakes him from sleep. The angry god nearly gets away, but Kamrushepa exorcizes Telipinu's anger with a ritual in which Kamrushepa sacrifices twelve rams of the sun-god that Khapantali had shepherded. Here the divine plane blends with the human, since it is the priestess performing the ritual who acts in place of Kamrushepa and sacrifices twelve rams. The anger of Telipinu is purged by reconciling him, through the telling of the story and the sacrifice, with the offerant of the ritual. With Telipinu's anger eliminated, health returns, and as a symbol of perennial prosperity, a hunting bag is hung from an evergreen tree. Like a cornucopia, the bag contains "sheep fat, fecundity, wine, cattle and sheep, longevity, and progeny." The images are all taken from the world of nature, and perhaps in its origin the myth was tied to seasonal rites. But in the historical period the ritual was celebrated in order to placate the offended divinity. There are different versions that were written for specific cases, like those of the queens Ashmunikal and Kharapshili, or of the scribe Pirwa.

The ritual might also have been performed as a prophylactic action, to ingratiate oneself before a divinity, such as was the case of the ritual for the storm-god in Kuliwishna that was celebrated "annually, whenever it pleases the head of the house." There are three versions of the myth about Telipinu that vary in detail. There are several other incomplete ones in which it is the storm-god or even a goddess such as Anzili, Zukki, or Khannakhanna, who disappears. The version where the vanishing god is the sun should be considered distinct from all others. Without the sun, the personified ice, a sort of Jack Frost, is free to act. He paralyzes the land and freezes the water. The storm-god sends assorted gods to find the missing sun-god, but the

Jack Frost–like character captures them. The text of this myth is particularly long; the narrative structure is complex and makes use of direct discourse. We do not know the final strategy by which ice is defeated because the conclusion of the story is missing.

The myth of the killing of the serpent Illuyanka, of Hattic origin, was recited on the occasion of a seasonal feast (*purulli*), when "the land prospers and thrives." Two versions are preserved, both of them dictated by a priest, Kella, and collected on the same tablet. The style is restrained, and the narrative passages are rapid. The two versions differ sharply, but they present the same essential structure: (1) the storm-god is defeated by the serpent; (2) in order to regain his power, the storm-god seeks an ally who, by means of a trick, could help him defeat his adversary; and (3) the victory of the storm-god and the death of the serpent occur. In both versions the storm-god's ally is sought among men. The alliance between gods and men is necessary, but it is limited by man's mortality. The myth is tied to the seasonal cycle—the forces above (represented by the storm-god) must have the advantage over the forces below (represented by the serpent) in order for nature to be reborn in the Spring. In the first version it is the goddess Inara who devises the strategy to defeat the serpent, but she seeks the help of Khupashiya, a man who asks for her love in exchange. Inara consents to this. Then the goddess serves a feast to the serpent and his children at which they eat and drink so much that they cannot return to their lair. Khupashiya ties them up, and the storm-god kills them. Inara proposes that Khupashiya live with her on condition that he renounce the world from which he came: "If you look out of the window," she tells him, "you will see your wife and children!" Khupashiya does not pass this test, and it may be that he forfeits his life (the text is badly preserved).

In the second version, the serpent neutralizes the storm-god by removing his heart and eyes. The storm-god then "takes as his wife the daughter of a poor man," with whom he has a son. This son marries the daughter of the serpent. Then, instructed by his father, the son has his wife return the heart and the eyes to his father. The storm-god, thus restored, "went again to the sea to battle." He is about to deliver the coup de grace to the serpent when he sees his own son with the serpent. The son calls up to his father in the sky for his father not to spare him, and thus the son is killed together with the serpent. The second version has some elements in common with a Greek myth that narrates the struggle between Zeus and Typhoeus in Cilicia. But the first version and the ritual associated with both versions certainly take place in northern Anatolia.

There are a few narrative texts that belong to a cultural koine of the western region of the Near East. Concerning the "Song of Kesshi," of Hurrian origin, there are a few fragments in Hurrian which come from Khattusha, and others are in Hittite. Another fragment in Akkadian was found at Amarna (Akhetaten) in Egypt. In the Hittite version, regulations governing hunting are spelled out. These regulations are sacred because not everyone is allowed to hunt and kill animals. Kesshi, who is a hunter, marries a beautiful woman and, lost in fascination with her, neglects the hunt and the offerings due the gods. When, at his mother's urging, he finally goes out hunting, he has no success, and he returns after three months with nothing to show for it. At home, he falls asleep and has seven dreams, all of them inauspicious. This is the only part of this story that the Hittite fragments reveal to us.

In the story of Appu, many folkloric motifs acquire literary form. The stylistic technique (parallelism, repetition, narrative formulas) come to this text through the songs of Kesshi and the cycle of Kumarbi. Appu is the wealthiest man of his city, but he is unhappy because he has no children. At last the gods grant him his desire and his wife bears two children, who take on the programmatic names of Wrong and Right. The two brothers, upon their father's death, decide to separate, and in dividing their inheritance Wrong tries to cheat Right by ceding to him a sterile cow, while he takes for himself an ox and a plow. But the gods, who make the cow fertile again, favor Right. Other differences probably divided the two brothers in the missing text, but the story probably concludes with the triumph of Right, according to what was first stated in the prologue: "[the sun-god] who always exalts just men, but chops down evil men like trees." The sorrow over having no children, the sterility corrected by the beneficence of a god, the contrast between brothers, and the division of goods are all motifs found in several settings, including the Bible and some Egyptian works. The Egyptian story that has for its subject the two brothers Truth and Falsehood constitutes the most fitting point of comparison.

Perhaps the Hittite story of the sun-god, the cow, and the fisherman belongs to the same cycle. The sun, smitten with lust for a cow, appears to her as a youth and provokes her by denying her the right to graze in a pasture. He then impregnates her. When the cow later realizes that she has given birth to a child, she is horrified: "[My calf] should have four legs. Why have I borne this two-legged thing?" She wants to eat it, but the sun-god saves the child. A fisherman finds it and carries it to his wife, telling her to feign having given birth to it so as to fool the villagers into believing that it was their child.

The compositions of a heroic character and the edicts of the Old Kingdom are characterized by an expressive form and the immediacy of their message, as though, in the period that corresponds to the formation of the Hittite state and to its appearance on the international scene, things of themselves were pressed into speech. Except for certain letters, the archives of the ancient Near East have not preserved other documents of equal freshness.

Translated from the Italian by Rodger Friedman

BIBLIOGRAPHY

Collections of Texts in Translation

OTTO KEISER, *Texte aus der Umwelt des Alten Testaments* (1982–), a good selection from every genre of Hittite texts.

General Overview

HANS GUSTAV GÜTERBOCK, "Hethitische Literatur," in *Altorientalische Literaturen (Neues Handbuch der Literaturwissenschaft)*, edited by WOLFGANG RÖLLIG (1978), important for its citations of various editions and bibliography.

Historical Texts

HUBERT CANCIK, *Grundzüge der hethitischen und alttestamentlichen Geschichtsschreibung* (1976); HANS GUSTAV GÜTERBOCK, "Die historische Tradition und ihre literarische Gestaltung bei Babyloniern und Hethitern bis 1200, zweiter Teil: Hethiter," *Zeitschrift für Assyriologie* 44 (1938): 45–145, a study of Old Hittite documents; HARRY A. HOFFNER, JR., "Histories and Historians of the Ancient Near East: The Hittites," *Orientalia* 49 (1980): 283–332; ANNELIES KAMMENHUBER, "Die hethitische Geschichtsschreibung," *Saeculum* 9 (1958):136–155.

Myths

BERT DE VRIES, "The Style of Hittite Epic and Mythology" (Ph.D. diss., Brandeis University, 1967); HANS GUSTAV GÜTERBOCK, "Hittite Mythology," in SAMUEL NOAH KRAMER, *Mythologies of the Ancient World* (1961), pp. 139–179; HARRY A. HOFFNER, JR., *Hittite Myths* (1990), the latest English translation; FRANCA PECCHIOLI DADDI and ANNA MARIA POLVANI, *La mitologia ittita* (1990), a collection of translations, also valuable for its introductions to texts.

SEE ALSO **From Hittite Mythology: The Kumarbi Cycle** (Part 8, Vol. III); **Hittite Prayers** (Part 8, Vol. III); **Akkadian Literature: An Overview** (Part 9, Vol. IV); and **The Literatures of Canaan, Israel, and Phoenicia: An Overview** (Part 9, Vol. IV).

The Story of the Semitic Alphabet

WILLIAM D. WHITT

THE INVENTION OF THE alphabet is often claimed as one of the major achievements of antiquity. What are the reasons for such a claim? Some have argued that because the alphabet is based on the principle of "one letter per sound," it hastened the development of logical thought; others have supposed that the simplicity of the alphabet led to a democratization of knowledge. These arguments, however, are not borne out by the evidence from either China and Japan or the ancient Near East. Chinese thought is not less logical even though the Chinese use an ideographic system. And the alphabet does not necessarily lead to a democratization of knowledge; Japan, with its ideographic and syllabic systems, has for centuries had a higher rate of literacy than European societies with their wholly alphabetic system. The same points can be made for the ancient Near East. Few would claim that the inhabitants of Syria or Palestine were more rational than the inhabitants of Mesopotamia simply because the former used an alphabet and the latter did not. In fact the furthest advances in astronomy and mathematics were made in Babylonia, where a syllabic system of writing predominated. Nor did the alphabet lead to a democratization of knowledge in the Near East; with few exceptions, only wealthy landowners, merchants, the governing elite, and the religious elite used or had genuine need of writing (see "Memory and Literacy in Ancient Western Asia" earlier in this volume).

The place of alphabetic writing in ancient society will be taken up at the end of this essay; for now, it suffices to note that the alphabet did not have a revolutionary impact and that its role in society was not significantly different from that of other writing systems. Regardless of what writing system or language was used, writing in the ancient Near East was almost always done by a professional class of scribes, and the literacy rate among the population as a whole remained extremely low. The main advantages that the alphabet had over a syllabic or ideographic system of writing were that it was potentially easier (and less expensive) to train a scribe to write fluently in an alphabetic script and that an alphabetic script can be written more economically.

ORIGINS OF ALPHABETIC WRITING

It is not easy to say when alphabetic writing was first used. This is not solely a problem of archaeology; it is also a problem of definition. By emphasizing or deemphasizing the role of certain types of signs, scholars have made very different claims. Most think that alphabetic writing was first used in Syria-Palestine during the first or second half of the second millennium BCE, but some have proposed that it began in Egypt early in the third millennium and others that it began in Greece in the early eighth century. In the position taken here, writing that uses signs to represent a single sound-unit of speech (a phoneme) is alphabetic. If it contains nonalphabetic signs as well as alphabetic ones, it is semi-alphabetic; if it contains only alphabetic signs, it is fully alphabetic. This definition accords no importance to the presence or absence of vowel signs.

The origins of the earliest writing systems known to us—in Sumer and Egypt—are obscure, but at a very early stage, both seem to have combined three different types of signs: *logographic, ideographic,* and *phonetic.* Logographic signs in their most primitive form are word signs that represent objects, actions, or numerals. Ideographic and phonetic writing seem to have been developed because of the inability of logographic writing to express abstract concepts and personal names. Ideographic writing, in which individual signs express ideas, came about through what is called secondary association; for example the logographic sign for "sun" was used secondarily to represent the concepts of "bright" or "white" or "day." In phonetic writing individual signs represent the sounds of speech rather than words or ideas. This kind of writing has its origin in the rebus principle, where the picture-sign of an object is used to express the sound of the object's name rather than the object itself.

In Mesopotamia, phonetic writing was syllabic—that is, each sign represented the sound of a syllable—and the writing system there came to use a mixture of ideographic and syllabic signs. In Egypt, however, the application of the rebus principle took a slightly different course. Here logographic signs were reinterpreted to represent the consonantal sounds contained in the object's name. These signs cannot be said to be syllabic, for no vowel is indicated. For example the word for "house" in Egyptian was *pāru;* thus the sign for "house" came to express the consonantal sequence *p-r.* Because Egyptian word roots could have one, two, or three consonants, signs that were originally logographic developed into uniconsonantal, biconsonantal, and triconsonantal signs. The system used in Egypt thus came to be largely a mixture of ideograms and these three different types of consonantal signs. Of most interest are the uniconsonantal

signs; these are true alphabetic signs, for each represents a single phoneme. At best the Egyptian writing system can be described as partially alphabetic; a few common words were written solely with alphabetic signs, and many other words were spelled alphabetically, but almost always in combination with multiconsonantal signs or determinatives. Yet the potential for fuller alphabetic writing was there, and it was the Egyptian use of these alphabetic or uniconsonantal signs that may have provided the eventual impetus for the invention of the Semitic alphabet, which was the first fully alphabetic writing system.

THE INSCRIPTIONS FROM SERABIT AL-KHADIM

The inscriptions from the vicinity of Serabit al-Khadim in the Sinai Peninsula are generally thought to provide the earliest evidence for the Semitic alphabet. The first inscriptions were found there in the Hathor temple by the noted archaeologist W. M. F. Petrie in 1905 (one is shown in fig. 1). To date, more than thirty inscriptions have been discovered, most of them very short, crudely drawn, and poorly preserved. There is some dispute about the date of these inscriptions; for a long time, there was a consensus for a date in the Eighteenth Dynasty (1540–

Fig. 1. Underside of an inscribed statuette found in the Hathor Temple at Serabit al-Khadim (Sinai 346). BENJAMIN SASS, *THE GENESIS OF THE ALPHABET AND ITS DEVELOPMENT IN THE SECOND MILLENNIUM B.C.* (1988)

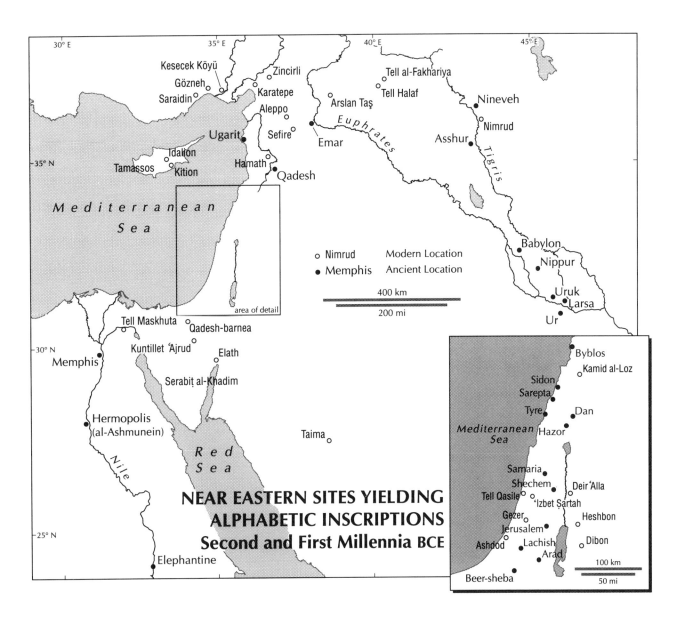

NEAR EASTERN SITES YIELDING ALPHABETIC INSCRIPTIONS Second and First Millennia BCE

1290), but a recent study suggests that a Twelfth Dynasty date (1940–1760) is more probable.

The signs in these inscriptions are pictographic and bear a close resemblance to Egyptian hieroglyphs; it is generally held that most of the signs were in fact based on the Egyptian signs. Fewer than thirty signs are used in the inscriptions, but because of the poor state of preservation, the exact number is not clear. The script does not have a standard direction; most inscriptions are written vertically, but some mix vertical and horizontal writing, and a few are written horizontally. One inscription is written in *boustrophedon;* this term refers to "back and

forth" writing, in which a line written to the right is followed by one written to the left so that each line takes the reverse direction of the preceding one. Nor do the letters point in any standard direction. The fish sign, for example, is sometimes written facing to the right, sometimes facing to the left, and sometimes facing up.

The earliest success at deciphering these inscriptions was achieved by the Egyptologist Alan H. Gardiner in 1916. He showed that the letter forms of the earliest Semitic alphabet must have been pictographic, with their values based on the principle of *acrophony.* (Acrophony is the use of a picture of an object to represent the initial sound of the object's name; for example, the picture of a house, which in early Semitic had the name *baytu,* represents the sound /b/.) Because the form of several of the signs in the Serabit al-Khadim inscriptions correlated with the names of the letters in the Phoenician alphabet, Gardiner suggested that these inscriptions were an early form of the Semitic alphabet. He noted that one sequence of four signs appeared several times: house—eye—ox goad—cross. By applying the principle of acrophony, he came up with the reading *lbʿlt,* "for the Lady," which he identified as a Semitic epithet of the Egyptian goddess Hathor. Despite this initial success and the continuing work by several scholars, the inscriptions remain undeciphered, though it seems certain that their language is a Semitic dialect.

OTHER EARLY EVIDENCE FOR THE ALPHABET

Apart from the Serabit al-Khadim inscriptions, there are more than twenty probable alphabetic inscriptions that predate the stabilization of the direction of the letters and the script in the eleventh century. Moreover there are a number of items (mainly potsherds, jars, and arrowheads) that have incised marks which probably are not alphabetic. These early alphabetic inscriptions are very problematic and their relationship to the Serabit al-Khadim inscriptions is unclear; the most the evidence allows us to say is that the Semitic alphabet was invented somewhere in the southern Levant in the first half of the second millennium.

The earliest alphabetic inscription is often thought to be a group of four signs on a dagger found in a tomb at Lachish from the second half of Middle Bronze Age IIB (1700–1650). However, only two of the four signs can be identified as belonging to the early alphabetic script, so it is quite possible that this inscription is actually a nonsense inscription or an inscription in an unknown pictographic script.

Six inscriptions should possibly be dated before 1300: sherds from the Palestinian sites of Gezer, Hazor, Lachish (Tell al-Duwayr), Tell al-Najila, and Tel Reḥov and a fragment of a limestone relief found at Shechem (modern Nablus; see fig. 2). However, like the Lachish dagger, these inscriptions are quite problematic. None can be firmly dated by archaeology, and the signs are so few, so poorly preserved, and so inconsistently formed that meaningful decipherment is not possible. It is true that several of the signs bear a close resemblance to those of the Serabit al-Khadim inscriptions, but it is by no means clear that any of these six are intelligible alphabetic inscriptions in a Semitic language, as there is evidence for non-Semitic speakers living in Palestine at this time. The only inscription with enough signs for meaningful palaeographic analysis is the relief from Shechem. Although some signs of this inscription are every bit as pictographic as those from Serabit al-Khadim, other letter forms are drawn in a more linear and simplified manner.

Benjamin Sass dates eight alphabetic inscriptions to the thirteenth or twelfth centuries: one ostracon each from Beth-Shemesh and ʿIzbet Sartah; a ewer and two bowls from Lachish; a bowl from Qubur al-Walaida; the handle of a storage jar from Khirbet Raddana; and a sherd from Sarepta. Some of these inscriptions are fairly long (the ʿIzbet Sartah inscription has eighty-four letters), and many of the letters are clearly

Fig. 2. Shechem plaque, obverse. BENJAMIN SASS, *THE GENESIS OF THE ALPHABET AND ITS DEVELOPMENT IN THE SECOND MILLENNIUM B.C.* (1988)

formed, but with the possible exception of the Lachish ewer, none has yielded an intelligible meaning. The 'Izbet Sartah ostracon (see fig. 3) is of particular interest because a twenty-two-letter abecedary is written on its last line in an order very close to the standard order of the Phoenician alphabet. This is the earliest unambiguous example of the "short" form of the linear alphabet. (There are earlier examples of the cuneiform alphabet in the short form.) The short form has twenty-two letters and differs from the twenty-seven-letter "long" form in that five pairs of consonants have merged with each other: z and d̲; ḥ and ḫ; ʿ and ġ; ṣ and ḍ (and ẓ?); and š and t̲ (and ś?). There is much variation in the letter forms of these inscriptions, but none of the letter forms is obviously pictographic, and on the whole, the letters are drawn in a more simplified and linear manner than they are in earlier alphabetic inscriptions.

The latest inscriptions in a pre-Phoenician alphabetic script are on nine arrowheads (five found near Jerusalem at al-Khadr; see fig. 4) and a fragment of a pottery cone found at Byblos (modern Jubayl). These inscriptions are usually dated by palaeography to the twelfth or eleventh centuries, and all ten have an intelligible meaning; each records the name of the object's owner. The purpose of the arrowheads is unknown; vari-

ous scholars have proposed that they are votive, that they were used in divination, or that they were simply for military use. Although the stance of the letters in these inscriptions is still not completely consistent, the letter forms appear more "developed." For example the dot for the pupil in the ʿayin is rarely drawn, and the *beth* looks very similar to its form in the Phoenician alphabet.

Most of our knowledge about the early alphabetic inscriptions is uncertain. These inscriptions are very short and fragmentary, and only a few have an intelligible meaning. They were written before a standardized alphabet had been developed and thus show a wide variation in the direction of writing and the forms and stances of the letters. Especially when the archaeological context is not certain, dating these early inscriptions is highly conjectural and not subject to any real controls. Although it is clear that the later letter forms are a simplification of a pictographic script, it does not follow that inscriptions with more pictographic letters are necessarily earlier than those that used simplified letter forms. There is no reason that a more pictographic script could not have continued on in some locations even after the script had been simplified elsewhere. This makes dating by palaeography more hazardous than is usually admitted, mean-

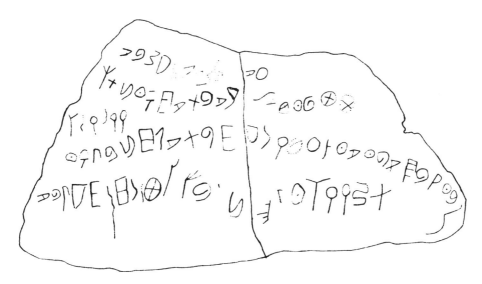

Fig. 3. Ostracon found at 'Izbet Sartah. From left to right, the abecedary on the last line reads ʾ *b g d h w* ḥ z* ṭ y k l n s p ʿ ṣ q q š t*. Uncertain readings are marked by an asterisk. TEL AVIV 4 (1977).

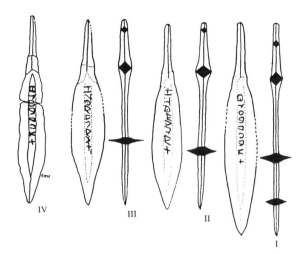

Fig. 4. El-Khadr arrowheads I-IV. Reading down, I and III are inscribed *ḥṣ ʿbdlbʾt* ("arrow of ʿAbd-labiʾat"). The same inscription is found on II and IV, but II omits the *aleph* and IV omits the second *beth;* both omissions are probably accidental. BENJAMIN SASS, *THE GENESIS OF THE ALPHABET AND ITS DEVELOPMENT IN THE SECOND MILLENNIUM B.C.* (1988)

ing that the consensus opinion on the topic— that there is a range of error of a century or so at the end of the second millennium—is probably too optimistic.

THE CUNEIFORM ALPHABET

The term "cuneiform" refers to the wedge-shaped writing that is impressed into clay tablets with a stylus. Cuneiform is closely associated with the mixed syllabic and ideographic system of Mesopotamia. However, in Syria in the middle of the second millennium, cuneiform was used to record a new alphabetic script. Almost all the evidence for the cuneiform alphabet comes from Ugarit—more than thirteen hundred tablets from Ras Shamra and one hundred from nearby Ras ibn Ḥani. Only ten examples have been found elsewhere: a tablet from Beth-Shemesh (see fig. 5); a cup from Hala Sultan Teke on Cyprus; a knife from Naḥal Tabor; two jar handles from Sarepta; a jar from Tell Nebi Mend (Qadesh), Syria; a tablet from Tell Soukas; a tablet from Tell Taʿanak; and a jar handle and

a pithos from Kamid al-Loz (Kumidi). The spread of the evidence makes it clear that the cuneiform alphabet was used throughout the Levant. While it is impossible to determine where in the Levant it was invented, the impetus for its development seems to have been knowledge of the early Semitic alphabet discussed above. The most distinctive characteristic of the cuneiform alphabet is that it uses three signs for *ʾaleph;* these have the syllabic values /ʾa/, ʾi/, and ʾu/. The syllabic values mean that, strictly speaking, this is a semi-alphabetic writing system.

The origin of the forms of the letters in the cuneiform alphabet is not entirely clear. Some of the signs correspond closely to early forms of the linear alphabet—in particular, b, g, h, ḫ, w, z, ʿ, and š. On the other hand, several of the cuneiform letters closely resemble Akkadian signs. It is impossible to say what the origin is of the cuneiform letter forms, but the similarities to the early linear alphabet seem too many to be coincidental; at least some of the letter forms of the cuneiform alphabet must have been influenced by the linear alphabet.

The cuneiform alphabet was used at Ugarit almost exclusively to record the local language, which is a dialect of northwestern Semitic and is closely related to Phoenician and Hebrew. But on some thirty tablets, it was used to record the Hurrian language, and on four tablets it was used to record Akkadian. Any genre of document, from economic accounts to myths, might be written in the cuneiform alphabet, although judicial and diplomatic documents occur only rarely.

Fig. 5. Beth-Shemesh abecedary in the short alphabet. Beginning in the upper right, the writing goes counterclockwise around the edge of the tablet. DRAWING AFTER *UGARIT-FORSCHUNGEN* 23 (1991)

The earliest alphabetic tablets are no later than the mid thirteenth century (in the reign of Ammishtamru II of Ugarit), but it may well be that the cuneiform alphabet was in use a full century earlier (in the reign of Niqmaddu II). The earliest possible alphabetic tablet is a copy of a treaty between Niqmaddu II and Shuppiluli-uma, the great king of Khatti. However, there is no way to know when this copy was made; it could easily have been made many years after Niqmaddu II died. Two mythological tablets are dated to *Nqmd,* or Niqmaddu, king of Ugarit, but this is just as likely Niqmaddu III as it is Niqmaddu II. Nevertheless a date between Niqmaddu II and Ammishtamru II seems to be confirmed by their personal seals; the seal of Niqmaddu is written in syllabic Akkadian, and the seal of Ammishtamru is written in the cuneiform alphabet.

Almost all of the tablets from Ugarit use the long form of the alphabet and are written from left to right. This is our earliest evidence of the long form of the alphabet. Two tablets from Ugarit and one inscribed jar handle from nearby Minet al-Beida use the short alphabet and are written from right to left. An inscription on the head of a large clay votive nail found near the Baal temple at Ugarit possibly should be included with these as well. Most interestingly, of the ten inscriptions in alphabetic cuneiform found elsewhere, all but the one from Tell Sou-kas (which was on Ugarit's southern border) were in the short alphabet; five of these were also written right to left. Though we have little evidence, this suggests that the long alphabet was used only within Ugarit's borders and that the short cuneiform alphabet was standard throughout the rest of the Levant. The tablets in the short alphabet all seem to date to the thirteenth and twelfth centuries. The tablet from Beth-Shemesh is of extreme interest because it is an abecedary, with the order of the letters following the order of the south Semitic alphabet in the Arabian Peninsula. (Could this have been the usual letter order of the short cuneiform alphabet?) It is quite different from the abecedaries from Ugarit, which, when the extra consonants are removed, have the same letter order as the Phoenician alphabet (see "Ugarit" in Part 5, Vol. II).

THE PHOENICIAN ALPHABET AND ITS SPREAD

Following the political and social upheavals of the early twelfth century, the Levant suffered a period of severe decline, and cuneiform writing there (both alphabetic and syllabic) quickly died out. But the linear alphabet, perhaps because it was simpler and thus did not require state-supported training to learn, remained in use. The linear alphabet first appears in a standard form in Phoenician inscriptions of the eleventh and tenth centuries: the stance of the letters is fixed, the direction of writing is right to left, and the short (twenty-two letter) form is used. It was in this general form that the alphabet spread throughout the Levant, west to Mesopotamia, south to Arabia, and northwest to Greece. But the event that had the greatest long-term effect on how the alphabet spread through the Near East was the gradual adoption of the Aramaic language and script in the Assyrian Empire during the ninth and eighth centuries, where it was used alongside the Akkadian language and the traditional syllabic cuneiform script. Because Assyria was the world power of the day, the Aramaic language came to be used with, and then replaced, Akkadian as the language of international diplomacy and commerce.

As with the earliest alphabetic inscriptions, using palaeography to date inscriptions written in the standard Phoenician script is highly problematic; this is especially true for those inscriptions thought to be from the ninth century and earlier. The main problems are that most of these inscriptions do not come from clearly stratified archaeological contexts; that the inscriptions are too few, too short, and too fragmentary to give trustworthy typological sequences; and that there is no way to determine whether the peculiar features of a certain inscription are due to local variation in script or to its date. The unreliability of dating by palaeography is supported by the inscription on the Tell al-Fakhariya (ancient Sikan) statue. This was dated to the eleventh century by Joseph Naveh, but the historical evidence demands a ninth-century date. The claim that the inscription was deliberately written in an "archaizing script" begs too many questions.

Letters, Numbers, and Letters as Numbers

The word "alphabet" has its etymology in the names of the first two letters of the Greek alphabet, *alpha* and *beta*. Just as we sometimes today refer to "our ABCs," so too in antiquity did the Greeks refer to their "alpha-beta." The Greeks borrowed both the names and the forms of the letters from the Phoenicians. Not all the Phoenician letter names are known, but there is evidence that they are closely related to the Hebrew names. Note the close resemblance between the Greek and Hebrew letter names (the Greeks merely added a final /a/ to each name): *alpha* comes from *'aleph; beta* from *beth; gamma* from *gimel; delta* from *daleth; iota* from *yod;* and so on. In the Semitic alphabet, the names of the letters are based on their original pictographic forms. For example, originally a picture of a hand was used to represent the sound /y/. The Phoenician word for "hand" was *yod* (or *yad*), and, thus, the name of this letter was *yod* as well. The meanings of thirteen of the twenty-two letter names are known: *'aleph* is "ox"; *beth* is "house"; *daleth* is "door"; *waw* is "hook, nail"; *yod* is "hand"; *kaph* is "palm of hand"; *lamed* is "ox goad"; *mem* is "water"; *'ayin* is "eye"; *pe* is "mouth"; *reš* is "head"; *šin* is "bow"; and *taw* is "mark, cross."

Letters were not always used to represent speech; a system known as alphabetic numeration was developed in which letters were given the values of numerals. In Hebrew *aleph* (the first letter) has a value of 1, *beth* (the second letter) has a value of 2, and so on. The earliest examples of alphabetic numeration are in Greek and date to the end of the fourth and early third centuries BCE. The oldest indisputable examples in Semitic are coins struck under Alexander Jannaeus (king of Judea) early in the first century BCE, although an unpublished, fourth-century Phoenician text has recently been cited as using alphabetic numeration. Alphabetic numeration was especially common on coins, where it was used to mark the date of minting, and in economic accounts.

At some point, alphabetic numeration led to the development of a hermeneutic device called *gema-*

tria. One or two examples of gematria possibly occur in the Bible, meaning that it may be as old as the fourth or third century BCE, but it became common only with the rabbis, who used it to find the "hidden meaning" of biblical texts. Rabbinic gematria may have been influenced by a similar hermeneutic device from Babylonia, although the Babylonian evidence comes from earlier centuries. There are several types of gematria, but in the most common cases, the rabbis find a veiled reference to a person in a number or they equate two words that had the same numerical value. For example it was supposed that the 318 men who accompanied Abram (Abraham) in Genesis, chapter 14, are in fact a reference to his servant Eliezer, since the numerical value of his name is 318.

The origin of the names and forms of the numerals used today is completely unrelated to the origin of the letter names and forms. The names of the numerals in English can be traced back to the names of the numerals in early Indo-European. For example, our words "one" and "three" are clearly related to the reconstructed Indo-European roots for these words, *oi-no-* and *tri-*. Although the forms of our numbers are known as "Arabic numerals," they actually originated in a system developed in southern India no later than the sixth century CE. The written form increased the number of angles from one (1) to nine (9). The zero, lacking angles, was also an Indian innovation and was added to this system sometime during the following two or three centuries. The Indian system became known to Arabs in the eighth and ninth centuries through astronomical texts, and it seems to have been gradually adopted throughout the Muslim world over the course of the ninth and tenth centuries. This system came into Europe through Spain, where it was used by the Umayyads after the Muslim conquest of the Iberian Peninsula. During the tenth century, European scholars visiting Spain learned of the Arabic numerals and developed a new counting board based on them. As use of this counting board spread throughout Europe in the eleventh and twelfth centuries, the Hindu-Arabic numerals gradually took hold.

It is more probable that this is an example of a local script that retained older features. Because the societies of the ancient Near East had, at best, very rudimentary educational systems, local variation in script is exactly what we would expect as the alphabet spread from one region

to another. In fact this is what we see in the Greek evidence: numerous variations in script sprang up as the alphabet spread across the Aegean, Ionia, the Peloponnese, and central and northwestern Greece.

Reservations about accuracy in dating aside,

almost all of the earliest inscriptions written in the "standardized" alphabet come from Phoenicia, which suggests that the alphabet probably spread from there to the rest of the Near East. However, even here caution is needed. One would like to use the archaeological record to trace the spread of the alphabet and the increase in its use. Unfortunately hazards of preservation and excavation affect each region differently, so that comparing the archaeological record of one region with another gives a skewed picture. For example, Palestine and Israel have been much more intensively excavated and surveyed than either Syria or the Transjordan. Consequently the number of inscriptions found in Palestine relative to, for example, Syria is in no way indicative of the relative amount of writing that went on in both places. Moreover, objects are preserved much better in dry than wet climates. That we have many more inscriptions from ancient Judah (in southern Palestine) than from ancient Israel (in northern Palestine) is a reflection of differences in climate rather than of differences in the use of writing.

Very few inscriptions are commonly dated to the tenth century. There are ten inscriptions from Byblos, five inscribed arrowheads from the Lebanon, a bowl from Crete, and a "calendar" inscribed on a small block of limestone from Gezer. There is some question as to whether the Gezer calendar should be considered Phoenician or Hebrew, but all the other tenth-century inscriptions are clearly Phoenician. The most important of these inscriptions are the five royal inscriptions from Byblos, the earliest of which is the Aḥiram sarcophagus (table 1, line 1).

Beginning in the ninth century, inscriptions appear in Aramaic and Hebrew as well as Phoenician. The tenth-century inscriptions all come from a small area along the eastern coast of the Mediterranean. But by the ninth century, the alphabet had spread throughout western Asia. Alphabetic inscriptions from this century are attested from the Anatolian peninsula, Cyprus, all of Syria and Palestine, the Transjordan, the Arabian Peninsula, and Mesopotamia. The earliest inscriptional evidence of Phoenicians in the western Mediterranean—two inscriptions found

TABLE 1
West Semitic Scripts, 1000–400 BCE (Written from Right to Left)

| t | š | r | q | ṣ | p | ʿ | s | n | m | l | k | y | ṭ | ḥ | z | w | h | d | g | b | ʾ | |

Key: 1. Sarcophagus of Aḥiram, Byblos, circa 1000 BCE. From H. Donner and W. Röllig, *Kanaänische und aramäische Inschriften* (1962–1964).
    2. Kilamuwa inscription, Zincirli, circa 825 BCE. From Joseph Naveh, *The Development of the Aramaic Script* (1970), fig. 1.
    3. Lion weights from Nineveh, late eighth century BCE. From Naveh (1970), fig. 2.
    4. Siloam tunnel inscription, late eighth century BCE. From Joseph Naveh, *The Early History of the Alphabet: An Introduction to West Semitic Epigraphy and Paleography* (2nd ed. 1987), fig. 70.
    5. Saqqara papyrus, circa 600 BCE. From Naveh (1970), fig. 3.
    6. Letter of Arsham (Cowley, no. 26), 412 BCE. From Naveh (1970), fig. 6.

on Sardinia—also dates to the ninth century. The most important development of that century was the use of certain consonants as vowel letters by Aramaic scribes to mark final (and occasionally medial) long vowels, *waw* being used to mark /ō/, *he* to mark /ā/ or /ē/, and *yod* to mark /ī/.

There are only three lengthy inscriptions from the ninth century: the Mesha stela; the Tell al-Fakhariya statue (a bilingual inscription in Aramaic and Akkadian cuneiform); and the Kilamuwa inscription from Zincirli (pronounced Zinjirli; see table 1, line 2). Three important short inscriptions of the ninth century are the Bar-Hadad stela, an inscribed block of sandstone found on Cyprus (the "Honeyman inscription"), and the *Mlktn* stela from Sardinia. The only ninth-century inscriptions from Palestine are a few inscribed bowls and potsherds from Hazor. The paucity of inscriptions is surprising given how intensively the region has been excavated and surveyed. Possibly we should conclude from this that the alphabet was not in widespread use in either Judah or Israel at this time.

There are not enough ninth-century inscriptions to trace regional variations in script. With the exception of the Tell al-Fakhariya statue, the ninth-century scripts exhibit only slight differences from the tenth-century script. The main differences are that in the ninth-century script, the crossbar on the *'aleph* is shifted slightly to the right, the *kaph* gains a tail, and the stance of *mem* is rotated slightly and a tail is added. In the Bar-Hadad and Kilamuwa inscriptions, the *dalet* gets a small tail, the leg of the *waw* is shifted to the right, and the leg of the *ṣade* is lengthened. With the exception of the *aleph*, all these changes can be explained as a move to a more cursive style.

ALPHABETIC INSCRIPTIONS OF THE EIGHTH–SIXTH CENTURIES

There are noticeably more inscriptions dating to the eighth century than to the ninth. The earliest major find of inscribed ostraca (the Samaria ostraca) dates to this century; inscribed seals, barely attested in the ninth century, become quite popular, and inscribed pottery becomes more common. The increase in the number of inscriptions is due primarily to the abundant evidence from Palestine. Graham Davies has cataloged over three hundred pieces of writing from eighth-century Palestine alone—more than 100 inscriptions from Samaria (mostly ostraca and ivories), almost 150 seals and seal impressions, and 50 or so ostraca and inscribed jars and bowls. As dramatic as the increase in the Palestinian evidence is the dearth of Phoenician evidence from the mainland. Except for the Karatepe inscriptions, the Phoenician inscriptions are all from Phoenician outposts or colonies in the Mediterranean. This dearth is most likely attributable to the lack of controlled excavations at sites in the Lebanon. (Sarepta is the only major site that has yielded evidence from the Iron Age.)

There are a number of important inscriptions dating to the eighth century. Besides the ninety or so legible Samaria ostraca, important Hebrew inscriptions include the Siloam tunnel inscription in Jerusalem, the large corpus of *lmlk* (belonging to the king) seal impressions on storage jars from Judah, and a number of inscriptions from Kuntillet ʿAjrud (interesting principally for their religious implications; see "Myth and Mythmaking in Canaan and Ancient Israel" in Part 8, Vol. III). The only important Phoenician inscriptions are the three copies of the Karatepe inscription from south-central Anatolia (long bilingual inscriptions in Phoenician and hieroglyphic Luwian). For Aramaic the most important ones are the eight inscriptions of Pannamuwa and his son Bar-rakkub from Zincirli in Anatolia, the Zakkur stela from Hamath, three copies of the Sefire treaty (near Aleppo [Halab]), and the Deir ʿAlla plaster text (see "Aramaean Tribes and Nations of First-Millennium Western Asia" in Part 5, Vol. II).

In the eighth-century inscriptions, differences begin to appear in the Phoenician, Aramaic, and Hebrew scripts. The lapidary inscriptions in Phoenician and Aramaic are largely indistinguishable; the main development in both is in the *kaph*, where two of the "fingers" have partially merged. However, cursive examples of Aramaic show more development (see table 1, line 3), especially in the head of the *qoph*, the presence of only a single crossbar in the *ḥeth*, and the leftward shift of the cross in the *taw*. The Siloam tunnel inscription in Jerusalem and numerous seals make up our evidence for the Hebrew lapidary script (table 1, line 4). This script has developed in several places toward a more cursive style; this is apparent particularly in the *'aleph, waw, zayin, mem, ṣade,* and *qoph*.

When seals and seal impressions are included, there is even more inscriptional evidence from the seventh and early sixth centuries than from the eighth. Both Hebrew and Aramaic are well attested, but the Phoenician evidence is particularly sparse. In the seventh- and early sixth-century inscriptions, we see a rise in the popularity of inscribed seals and inscribed pottery, and finds of ostraca are more numerous than in earlier centuries. In Hebrew the most important inscriptional finds are the Lachish ostraca, the Arad ostraca, a group of more than two hundred bullae known as the "Burnt Archive," two silver plaques from Ketef Hinnom, and the tomb of the royal steward at Silwan (near Jerusalem). In Aramaic the most important inscriptions are the two Narab stelae, the Necho letter from Saqqara (written on papyrus), some epigraphs on a group of clay tablets from Nineveh (Kuyunjik, Nebi Yunus), and the Asshur ostracon.

The Silwan inscription and various inscribed seals comprise the evidence for the Hebrew lapidary script in the seventh and early sixth centuries. In this period the lapidary script developed further toward a cursive style. *'Aleph* began to lose its triangular shape, the tops of *dalet* and *he* were extended to the right, the tail on *nun* was extended to left, the bars of the *samek* are sometimes connected, and the leg on *pe* was also extended to the left. The cursive Hebrew script became even more simplified, as is especially apparent in the *mem* and *nun*. The Aramaic script underwent a great deal more development than the Hebrew. Several letters in the Aramaic cursive (which is far better attested than the lapidary) were much simplified (see table 1, line 5); the tops of letters that were previously closed—the *beth, daleth, ṭet, 'ayin,* and *resh*—opened up, and crossbars were lost on the *he* and *ṣade*. Although evidence for the Phoenician script in the seventh century is sparse, here, too, several letters seem to have been simplified and drawn in a more cursive manner.

THE ALPHABET IN THE PERSIAN PERIOD

The inscriptional evidence for the Persian period (about 540–330), especially in Egypt, is abundant; writing was undoubtedly more common in this period than in preceding centuries. Because Persia had adopted the Aramaic language and script for administrative purposes, both came to be used throughout the Near East (from Afghanistan in the east to Anatolia and Egypt in the west). Consequently the evidence for the Hebrew and Phoenician scripts in the Persian period is quite sparse. In the Persian provinces of Yehud and Samaria (which corresponded more or less with the heartland of the former kingdoms of Judah and Israel), Aramaic-language documents soon outnumbered those in the Hebrew language, and most of the Hebrew documents that we do have are written in the Aramaic script. The Judeans retained the old Hebrew script mainly for their holy books; the only evidence we have of the Hebrew script in the Persian period is coins and seals. The Phoenician script of the Persian period is attested mostly in a few lapidary inscriptions from Cyprus, Byblos, Tyre and Sidon, and Carthage.

The most important Persian period inscriptions in Aramaic include the large corpus of Elephantine papyri and ostraca from Upper Egypt, letters of the Persian satrap Arsham, a number of very fragmentary papyri and inscribed objects from Saqqara, a huge number of inscribed ritual vessels and unpublished tablets from Persepolis, dockets of the Murashu family from Nippur, administrative ostraca from Arad and Beersheba, papyrus conveyance deeds found at the Wadi ad-Daliyah (near Samaria [modern Sabastiyah, Roman Sebaste]), and a group of stelae from Teima (biblical Tema) in the Arabian Peninsula. The most important Phoenician inscriptions are royal inscriptions: the Shipṭibaal and Yeḥawmilk inscriptions from Byblos and the Eshmunazar inscription from Sidon.

Our evidence for the cursive Aramaic script is much fuller than that for the lapidary script. The letter forms in the Persian period are further simplified, usually by reducing the number of strokes used. This can be seen in the formal cursive hand of the Arsham letters (late fifth century), which are good examples of the cursive script in the Persian period (table 1, line 6). For example, the fingers of the *kaph* are simplified into a bar with a hook, the wavy squiggles of the *mem* are replaced with a downward stroke drawn through the top bar, and the *šin* is drawn with only three strokes instead of four as previously. Most of the Phoenician inscriptions of this period are lapidary inscriptions, so the letter forms remain somewhat closer to the script of the previous centuries. For example the *he* and the *ḥeth* retain all three bars in Phoenician, whereas in Aramaic, both letters are simplified, being written with only one bar.

THE ADOPTION OF THE ALPHABET IN THE GREEK WORLD

The earliest Greek inscriptions come from Ionia and date to the first half of the eighth century. In these earliest inscriptions, neither the stance nor the form of the letters is standardized. The direction of the script is not standardized either; inscriptions may be written either right to left, left to right, or boustrophedon. There are no Greek inscriptions that can be dated by archaeology to the ninth century. Given this evidence and the greatly increased contact between Phoenicians and Greeks in the eighth century, classicists prefer to date the coming of the alphabet to the latter century. On the other hand, on palaeographical grounds semiticists have proposed dates ranging from the eleventh to the eighth centuries. Some semiticists think that the variation in direction of writing and stance and form of the letters is best explained by an early date of adoption, before the Semitic alphabet itself had been standardized. But such a conjecture ignores the important point that it would be impossible for a society with no previous experience of writing to achieve immediate uniformity in how the script is written. It takes time for such a society to learn in what ways it is useful, and it takes time for writing to become common enough and widespread enough for standards to be adopted. This implies that the argument for borrowing can only be based on letter forms; it cannot be based on the direction of script or the stance of the letters, for these

will vary indiscriminately while a society is still learning how to use writing. If only the forms of the letters are considered, then the borrowing is best dated to the late ninth or, more probably, the early eighth century. This is quite close to the date suggested by classicists, who base their arguments more on historical considerations and the archaeological evidence.

One of the most interesting aspects of the adoption of the Phoenician alphabet by the Greeks is that the signs for the gutteral consonants and the glide consonants were adopted as vowels in the Greek alphabet. Some scholars have described the adoption of signs to indicate vowels as a "brilliant" or "crucial" or "revolutionary" invention that shows the superiority of the Greeks over the Phoenicians. (Such claims overlook the fact that vowel signs were already in use in the Semitic alphabet.) In fact, the Greek-speaking peoples would not have distinguished the guttural or the glide consonants very clearly if at all when they heard Semitic speech. *Waw* /w/ and *yod* /y/, the two glide consonants, were heard as *upsilon* /u/ and *iota* /i/ respectively. Because the guttural consonants could not be heard, it was assumed that each of these letters signified the vowel that followed the guttural: thus *ʾaleph* /ʾ/ was heard as *alpha* /a/; *he* /h/ was heard as *epsilon* /e/; *ḥet* /ḥ/ was heard as *eta* /ē/; and *ʿen* /ʿ/ was heard as *omicron* /o/. (The seventh vowel letter, *omega*, was a Greek invention.) The invention of six of the seven vowel letters was thus a natural consequence of the inability of the Greeks to hear all the phonemes in Semitic speech; this can hardly be called a brilliant or revolutionary invention. And in any case, as any reader of Arabic or Hebrew will attest, an alphabet that indicates all vowels is wholly unnecessary. As long as there are letters to indicate final and medial long vowels, diphthongs and triphthongs, and the presence of initial vowels (as in the Semitic writing system), any language so written—even classical Greek—can be read easily by its native speakers.

THE SOUTH SEMITIC ALPHABET

Early in the first millennium, a new alphabetic script begins to appear in the Arabian Peninsula. This script is known as the "south Semitic" or "(south) Arabian" alphabet. About thirty inscriptions in this alphabet predate the Persian period. The earliest inscriptions that can be firmly dated are two seals; their designs are suggestive of the ninth-eighth centuries and the eighth century. More than half of the thirty inscriptions are seals of unknown provenance (twelve in the Mesopotamian style and six in the Syro-Palestinian style); most of the seals date on stylistic grounds to the eighth-seventh centuries. The remaining inscriptions consist of an incised jar, a stela (fig. 6), and two rock graffiti from the Arabian Peninsula; two pottery fragments, a label, a brick, and two tablets from Mesopotamia; and some sherds found in Jerusalem.

From the seventh century down through the first centuries CE, the evidence for south Semitic writing increases enormously; a few thousand inscriptions, mostly graffiti on rocks, have been found in northern Arabia, Jordan, and the Syrian Desert. Safaitic inscriptions (those written by

Fig. 6. Stela from Marib, circa eighth century BCE(?). From left to right, the inscription reads *yšrḥ'l* | *'yln* | . BENJAMIN SASS, *STUDIA ALPHABETICA: ON THE ORIGIN AND EARLY HISTORY OF THE NORTHWEST SEMITIC, SOUTH SEMITIC, AND GREEK ALPHABETS* (1991)

Acrostics, Mnemonics, and the Order of the Letters

There has been a great deal of speculation about how the letters of the Semitic alphabet came to be ordered: Why does *beth* follow *aleph* or *nun* follow *mem*? Why not *ṣade* after *qoph*? Many of the proposals are far-fetched; among the more fantastic are that the order of the letters is based on the Sumerian musical scale, that every pair of letters spells out the Egyptian names of various body organs, that the scribes applied ancient phonological theory to fit the letters into a matrix, and that the order is based on lunar and astral theories. Other conjectures seek a connection between the order of the letters and didactic poems and mnemonic devices. All of these proposals lack even a shred of hard evidence, and it is hard to imagine that any evidence relating to this problem will ever turn up. Perhaps the best position is the one that refuses to look for a logical system behind the order of the letters, stating instead that the order was determined by custom and is of no significance at all.

Poets sometimes composed verse that used the order of the letters as a literary device. These poems, which are known as alphabetic acrostics, are normally twenty-two lines or stanzas; the first line or stanza begins with *'aleph*, and each line or stanza thereafter begins with a successive letter of the alphabet. Although it is commonly thought that alphabetic acrostics belong to "wisdom literature," there is no evidence that these ever had a didactic purpose; in fact,

the most common type of alphabetic acrostics are hymns and prayers, which have a setting in the cult.

The appeal of the alphabetic acrostic lay in the "enumerative aesthetic" of Semitic poetry, where items were piled up one after the other. How much this produced a feeling of completeness in the reader or audience is hard to say, but it is clear that anyone who knew the alphabet would know what to expect next and would know exactly when the poem should end. Yet alphabetic acrostics do not always have a rigid structure and are not always complete, which is odd if completeness really was as important as is claimed. For example an acrostic in Lamentations reverses the letters *pe* and *'ayin*, Psalm 25 lacks lines beginning with *waw* and *qoph* and has two lines that begin with *resh*, the poem in Nahum stops after *kaph*, and the acrostic in Psalms 9–10 lacks *daleth* and *he* and skips from *lamed* to *qoph*.

Another interesting use of the alphabet is in simple arrangements of letters that serve as mnemonic devices (that is, tricks to spur the memory). This use of the alphabet is first known from the Talmudic literature of the earliest centuries CE. A well-known example is the mnemonic for the ten plagues—*deṣak 'adas be'aḥab*—where the first consonant stands for the first letter of the first plague, the second consonant the first letter of the second plague, and so on.

the Safa tribe) come mainly from the Syrian Desert; Lihyanic and Thamudic inscriptions (written by the Lihyan and Thamud tribes) are most common in Jordan and northern Arabia. Because so little is known of the history of these areas, these inscriptions are impossible to date with any real precision.

The form of the letters in the earliest south Semitic inscriptions is very distinctive, as practically all the units of composition are simple geometric shapes—straight lines meeting at forty-five- or ninety-degree angles, full circles, and half circles. The alphabet has twenty-nine letters and is usually written from right to left, although inscriptions written from left to right do occur, and some Thamudic inscriptions were written vertically. And in large monumental inscriptions of a later date, boustrophedon is common.

Similarities in letter forms suggest that the south Semitic script is an offshoot of the Phoenician alphabet. However, there is some disagreement as to when the south Semitic alphabet split off. One scholar thinks that the split must have occurred in the fourteenth–thirteenth centuries BCE, when the long form of the alphabet was still in use (though this is not proven) and when the direction of writing had not yet been standardized. On the basis of the forms of the *nun* and the *lam*, another scholar has suggested that a split in the eleventh–tenth centuries is more likely. The same point made above for the Greek alphabet applies here: the argument based on the direction of the script has no merit, for a society must gain experience in writing and its uses over a long period of time before it can settle on a standardized script. Thus the later date is preferable. However, it may be doubted that these eighteen seals and twelve short and fragmentary inscriptions are sufficient for a trustworthy palaeographical dating, especially as the (admittedly incomplete) archaeological evidence points more toward the ninth–eighth centuries.

THE TECHNOLOGY OF ALPHABETIC WRITING

Alphabetic writing from the ancient Near East has been found on an enormous variety of objects; these objects were composed of a wide range of materials and had many different uses (not always related to the writing on the object). An array of relatively simple skills was needed to produce these objects and the writing on them: preparing inks; manufacturing writing implements and inkwells; producing papyrus paper and preparing animal skins; constructing wooden writing boards; collecting beeswax and mixing plaster; dressing and chiseling stone; and engraving gems and cast metal. All this warrants speaking of writing as a technology. Because the technology of writing influences how writing is used, it is important to understand something of this technology if we are to appreciate the role of writing in ancient societies and avoid the anachronism of applying modern criteria of literacy to the ancient past.

A scribe wrote with ink on papyrus or potsherds, probably using a reed pen or a slender wood brush. The writing bristles seem to have been formed by cutting the reed or wood at an angle and then bruising the tip in order to make the fibers separate. The inks used were either carbon-based or a carbon and iron mixture, the former producing a black ink and the latter a brown or red ink. The carbon for making ink was probably soot, which could easily be obtained by scraping cooking vessels. Ink could be erased with spittle or a wet rag or a small stick of sandstone. Several "inkwells" have been found in Palestine and Israel; these are small stone mortars in which the dried carbonaceous or ferrous material could be finely ground and mixed with gum and water.

The most common type of writing material to survive was sherds of broken pottery; a sherd that has been used for writing is known as an ostracon. Generally ostraca were fairly small, about the size of the scribe's hand or a little larger. Because potsherds cost nothing and were in practically unlimited supply, they served much as scrap paper or notepaper function today. Owing to size limitations, the sorts of writing most commonly found on potsherds are short letters and administrative or economic memoranda. Wooden writing boards covered with wax or gypsum plaster were another very common writing material; these could be reused merely by smoothing out the wax or plaster or by removing it and applying a new coat. Writing boards would have been only marginally more expensive to use than potsherds, for beeswax and gypsum were abundant and available year-round. Writing boards were often used for writing memoranda and drafts of documents (the fair copy being written on papyrus). And because writing boards were easily reused, they were ideal for writing exercises in scribal training. (Writing boards are used this way even today: students in Koranic school in parts of the Muslim world write their lessons on wooden writing boards covered with lime.)

In the southern Levant, papyrus was the most common type of writing material for any document of more than ephemeral significance. The proximity to Egypt made papyrus fairly easy to obtain. Documents typically written on papyrus include long or important letters, literary texts, all types of legal documents, important administrative documents, and all manner of ritual and religious documents. Papyrus offered several advantages. Sheets could be pasted together to make long rolls (usually not more than 30 feet [10 meters], but the two longest rolls known are over 120 feet), so that very long texts could be written on a single roll. Because adding sheets was a simple process, papyrus rolls could be tailored to fit the size of the text being recorded. Papyrus was also very easy to trim; if a text did not fill a whole sheet, the excess could be cut off and used at a future time (see the box "Papyrus Manufacture" in "Archives and Libraries in the Ancient Near East" earlier in this volume). In Judah, writing on leather seems to have been quite exceptional before the Persian period; leather apparently was used mainly for special display books in the temple. During the Persian period, when a canon of holy writings was first adopted by the Jews of Yehud, the use of skins seems to have been extended from the book of Deuteronomy to all the canonical books.

The situation in the Assyrian Empire was a good deal more complex. Early in the first millennium, almost all documents were written in the Akkadian language in the syllabic cuneiform script; the two main types of materials were clay tablets and wooden writing boards. From Nimrud (Kalkhu) we know of writing boards being joined in folding leaves to form primitive "books." In the ninth century, as the Aramaic-speaking peoples were subsumed into the Assyrian Empire (by deportation, migration, and military conquest), their language spread, and with it use of the linear alphabet. In Assyria and the rest of Mesopotamia from the ninth century onward, documents were increasingly recorded in the Aramaic language and written in the linear alphabetic script. The material most commonly used for alphabetic documents was undoubtedly animal skins, for importing papyrus all the way from Egypt would have been fairly expensive. This was also the case in Persia, as is shown by leather letters of Arsham, which were sent from Persia to Egypt. For several centuries documents were commonly written in both Akkadian (on clay tablets and writing boards) and in Aramaic (on skins). But by the Hellenistic period, the alphabetic script had all but supplanted syllabic cuneiform in Mesopotamia. The use of both languages in official administrative documents is quite clear from the iconographical evidence. In Assyrian art there are a number of stock depictions of a pair of scribes working together: one scribe is always depicted with a beard and writes with a stylus on a clay tablet or writing board, while the other is always shown as clean shaven and writes on a skin with a brush. It is commonly assumed that the scribe using the stylus is writing Akkadian and that the scribe using the brush is writing Aramaic; presumably both men are recording the same information. (See "The Scribes and Scholars of Ancient Mesopotamia" earlier in this volume.)

Throughout western Asia from the eighth century onward, personal stamp seals inscribed with one's name were quite popular. The material used undoubtedly reflected in some way one's social status and wealth. The most common material that seals are made of is limestone; these must have been used mainly by people of low and middle social status. Other materials for "low-status" seals include bone, granite, bronze, rock crystal, and marble. Stones that are hard and have interesting coloration are typical in "high-status" seals: jasper, agate, carnelian, serpentine, chalcedony, opal, amethyst, and so on. Personal seals were used in a variety of personal, judicial, and business circumstances. Legal documents and letters were rolled up, tied, and then sealed with a daub of clay, thus identifying the owner (or sender) of the document and providing evidence to a future reader that the document had not been tampered with. The handles of commodity jars were often sealed, probably to identify the owner or the sender. Anything to which one wished to limit access—a room, a box, a jar, or a document—could be sealed so as to provide evidence of tampering. Seals were almost always worn as jewelry, either placed on a string and worn as a necklace or set in metal and worn as an arm band or finger ring.

Inscribed vessels of pottery are found frequently in the archaeological record. The inscriptions could be made either before or after firing and could either be scratched in or painted on. The purpose of these inscriptions varied widely, being used to mark ownership, to specify contents and capacity, to give over as an offering, to identify the sender of the jar, or to identify the receiver of the jar.

Other materials on which writing is commonly found include stone, brick, plaster, metal, and ivory. We should assume that writing on wood was also common, although no examples have been preserved. Monumental inscriptions (commemorating a deed or act, usually of the king) were typically written on buildings, rock faces, stone stelae, or statues. On occasion a dead person might be commemorated with an inscription on a stone stela or a coffin; if the person was buried in a rock-cut tomb, as was common in Judah, the inscription might be carved on the outside face near the entrance or on one of the inside walls (though the grave inscriptions from Khirbet al-Qom are written in ink). Commemorating the dead with inscriptions became increasingly popular over the course of the first millennium. At Deir 'Alla, a fairly long religious text (the Balaam inscription) was found written on plaster; it is unclear how common long texts written on plaster were. (See "Witchcraft, Magic, and Divination in Ancient Israel" in Part 8, Vol. III, and "The Literatures of Canaan, Ancient Israel, and Phoenicia" below.) Objects made of metal and ivory were often inscribed. These were usually valuable personal items and family heirlooms, such as amulets, incantation bowls, or boxes for jewelry and toiletries. Presumably the writing in some way served to increase the efficacy of the amulet or bowl. In the case of luxury items, the writing served to mark ownership and give added prestige to the item. Votive inscriptions might be written in any of these materials—on a stone stela, on a jar identifying the contents of what is offered, or on a luxury item such as a metal bowl or an ivory box.

SCRIBAL COMPOSITION

It is worth giving some thought to how a scribe went about composing a document. First, a scribe chose the writing material appropriate to the kind of document he or she (female scribes are known, but they were quite rare) was preparing to compose. In turn each material called for its own particular writing implement—a brush for a potsherd, a pen for papyrus, or a stylus for a waxed writing board. Writing could be either at the dictation of another or by self-composition. There is no way to know how often documents were dictated or how often they were the scribe's own composition. Certainly, though, most administrative documents, such as work rosters or inventories of goods shipped or received by the palace, were composed by scribes, while most letters were dictated. For important texts a scribe probably took dictation on a waxed writing board and then made a fair copy on papyrus. The script used by a scribe depended on the kind of document being composed. For an administrative document, the scribe used a cursive hand that could be written quickly. In making monumental inscriptions, a scribe traced a more formal script on the surface of the stone, which a mason then chiseled into the face of the monument.

Ancient notions of layout and format were quite different from modern ones. This is often easy to forget, as most contemporary readers' contact with these inscriptions is limited to the transcriptions found in collections of inscriptions, where the texts are laid out in a modern format. The only mark of punctuation was a dot (or dots) or a short vertical line used to indicate word division. Its use was very inconsistent, being largely a matter of each scribe's personal preference. In some monumental inscriptions, such as the Mesha inscription, the punctuation appears between almost all words. In other monumental inscriptions, such as the Karatepe inscriptions, it never appears, and the words in each line are strung together as a continuous sequence of letters. It was quite common for a line to end in the middle of a word. This can be disconcerting at first to a modern reader, for there was no punctuation mark indicating that the word is continued on the next line. In some texts the scribe drew a rule so that the line of writing would be straight; the letters were commonly written below, not above, the line.

THE EXPERIENCE OF WRITING

Writing played an important role in ancient society, and practically all adults must have had some experience with writing. But is it possible to say what this experience of writing was? When considering this question, it is necessary to distinguish between the different social classes and the situations in which each would have had some need of writing. Practically all of the writing in the ancient Near East was done by scribes, craftsmen, merchants, and landowners, for these are the only groups who would have had an incentive to learn to write. Needless to say, the literacy of scribes was very different from the literacy of craftsmen, merchants, and landowners. Scribes played important roles in government, where writing was used for carrying out administration and conducting diplomacy, and in the cult, where writing was used to preserve and transmit knowledge of the gods (myth) and of how to communicate with them (ritual). Composing and copying such texts required a very high level of literacy that could be achieved only through extensive education. In many cases scribal ability to read and write must have been equal to that of a modern university-educated person (although examples of barely literate scribes are known). This was a very small segment of the population, less than 1 percent of all adult males.

The most we can suppose of craftsmen, merchants, and landowners is that they possessed the skills to compose and read simple texts, such as accounts or inventories; there is no reason to believe that very many of them could read difficult literary or religious texts. Most men in this group would be considered semiliterate by today's standards. The size of this segment of the population is difficult to estimate and must have varied from region to region, but in the Levant it was probably less than 10 percent of all adult males.

The rest of the men and almost all of the women would be considered illiterate in the modern sense of the word. The only literate skill that the remaining adult males might have had an incentive to learn would be the ability to sign one's own name, for in some places it was customary for witnesses to judicial procedures to do this. The contracts from Elephantine (Upper Egypt) are enlightening. Although the scribes often wrote the names of the witnesses, there are many instances in which witnesses signed for themselves. In almost every case, the hand is unpracticed, showing that the signature was made with difficulty. By modern standards most of these people would be considered functionally illiterate.

One important point that is sometimes forgotten is the nondocumentary or visual function that writing could have in the ancient world. Time after time we find writing on objects that could be understood entirely on their own apart from what was written on them. Looking at such objects must have been one of the most common ways that people had contact with writing. For example memorial stelae and tombs sometimes had inscriptions and sometimes did not; it was not necessary for a passerby to be able to read the inscription to know what its purpose was. Amulets often had magic spells inscribed on them, but one did not have to read the inscription to know what the amulet's function was. Jars containing offerings to gods sometimes had inscriptions naming the giver, the gift, or the recipient; however, a worshiper in a temple would immediately have known a jar's purpose without having to read its inscription. In many cases the object that the inscription appeared on was just as or more important than the inscription. To the ancient worshiper who saw the Tell al-Fakhariya statue in the temple of Hadad, for example, the inscription was much less important and, in a way, communicated less of the intended message than the statue itself. Although few royal monuments from the Levant survive, these too would have often been inscribed; the main purpose of monumental writing was as a "display" of the king's authority and power, a message that could easily be grasped by the illiterate.

It is often hard for us to understand that the ability to read and write was not a necessary skill in the ancient world. Illiteracy was rarely a disadvantage, either socially or economically.

Reading and writing were highly specialized skills. In situations that called for reading or writing, there was almost always an intermediary present (usually a scribe) who could perform the necessary tasks for a fee. An interesting example is the case of the anonymous scribe who hired out his services on the wharf at Syene (on the east bank of the Nile opposite the island of Elephantine). This scribe's work is known from some thirty ostraca found at Elephantine that were all written in the same hand. These ostraca consist mostly of short letters and memoranda written for persons who needed something done back at Elephantine. The subjects of these were always mundane: requests for a family member to send some barley or a small drinking cup from home; an invitation to help shear a lamb; and instructions from husbands sent to their wives. Through examples such as this, we begin to see that the important thing was how writing was used, not the ability to use it. We also begin to see how extraordinarily adaptable ancient society was to its limitations. Lack of state resources for education, an economic structure that had little need for literate workers, and the absence of an ideology that promoted reading and writing meant that literacy rates would always remain very low, yet society adapted in such a way that writing could become an extraordinarily powerful tool in almost all areas of life.

BIBLIOGRAPHY

The Significance of the Alphabet

On the scholarly prejudice in favor of the (Greek) alphabet, see MAURICE BLOCH, "Literacy and Enlightenment," in *Literacy in Society*, edited K. SCHOUSBOE and M. T. LARSEN (1989), and ROSALIND THOMAS, *Literacy and Orality in Ancient Greece* (1992). (The latter work is also useful for gaining an appreciation of the role of writing and literacy in premodern societies; see below.)

Origins of Writing

On the origins of writing and the development of different types of writing systems, see IGNACE J. GELB, *A Study of Writing* (1952; rev. ed. 1963).

Early Alphabetic Inscriptions

For the first (and only) success at deciphering the Serabit al-Khadim inscriptions, see ALAN H. GARDINER, "The Egyptian Origin of the Semitic Alphabet," *Journal of Egyptian Archaeology* 3, part 1 (1916). The most recent comprehensive treatment of these inscriptions and all other pre-Phoenician alphabetic inscriptions is BENJAMIN SASS, *The Genesis of the Alphabet and Its Development in the Second Millennium B.C.* (1988). Less comprehensive but otherwise excellent is the study of ÉMILE PUECH, "Origine de l'alphabet: documents en alphabet linéaire et cunéiforme du IIᵉ millénaire," *Revue Biblique* 93, no 2 (1986). (This work also has a good discussion of the cuneiform alphabet; see below.) For an important caveat on dating early alphabetic inscriptions, see STEPHEN A. KAUFMAN, "The Pitfalls of Typology: On the Early History of the Alphabet," *Hebrew Union College Annual* 57 (1986).

The Cuneiform Alphabet

On the cuneiform alphabet, see ALAN R. MILLARD, "The Ugaritic and Canaanite Alphabets—Some Notes," *Ugarit-Forschungen* 11 (1979); A. LOUNDINE, "L'Abécédaire de Beth Shemesh," *Le Muséon* 100 (1987); and MANFRIED DIETRICH and OSWALD LORETZ, *Die Keilalphabete* (1988).

Scripts and Inscriptions of the First Millennium

The most useful compilation of northwest Semitic alphabetic inscriptions is H. DONNER and W. RÖLLIG, *Kanaänische und aramäische Inschriften*, 3 vols. (1962–1964); these volumes contain full bibliography, philological commentary, glossary, and a number of hand copies and photographs. A complete collection of Hebrew inscriptions in transcription (but without bibliography, commentary, or hand copies) is GRAHAM I. DAVIES, *Ancient Hebrew Inscriptions: Corpus and Concordance* (1991). Essential for any study of Aramaic inscriptions is JOSEPH A. FITZMYER and STEPHEN A. KAUFMAN, *An Aramaic Bibliography, Part I: Old, Official, and Biblical Aramaic* (1992), a complete bibliography of all known Aramaic inscriptions down to 200 BCE.

The standard work on the development of the Aramaic script is JOSEPH NAVEH, *The Development of the Aramaic Script* (1970). The best and most thorough study of the Phoenician script is JOHN BRIAN PECKHAM, *The Development of the Late Phoenician Scripts* (1968).

The Origins of the Greek Alphabet

For semiticists' opinions on the adoption of the alphabet in the Greek world, see PETER KYLE MCCARTER,

The Antiquity of the Greek Alphabet and the Early Phoenician Scripts (1975) and JOSEPH NAVEH, *The Early History of the Alphabet: An Introduction to West Semitic Epigraphy and Paleography* (1982; 2nd ed. 1987). (This work also contains a useful discussion of the south Semitic alphabet; see below.) The arguments of classicists (with a critique of the semiticists) can be found in LILIAN H. JEFFERY, *The Local Scripts of Archaic Greece* (1961; rev. ed. 1990).

The South Semitic Alphabet

On the origin and early history of the south Semitic alphabet, see JACQUES RYCKMANS, "Aux origines de l'alphabet," *Bulletin des Séances de l'Académie Royale des Sciences d'Outremer* 36 (1986); "Le rôle de la paléographie dans la datation des inscriptions," in *L'Arabie antique de Karib'il à Mahomet: Nouvelles données sur l'histoire des Arabes grâce aux inscriptions*, edited by CHRISTIAN ROBIN (1992); and BENJAMIN SASS, *Studia Alphabetica: On the Origin and Early History of the Northwest Semitic, South Semitic and Greek Alphabets* (1991). The Sass work also contains the most recent discussion of the date of the Serabit al-Khadim inscriptions; see above.

The Scribes and Their Materials

An excellent discussion of ancient scribes and their materials is ANDRÉ LEMAIRE, "Writing and Writing Materials," in *The Anchor Bible Dictionary*, edited by DAVID NOEL FREEDMAN, vol. 6 (1992). On the use of papyrus and leather, see MENAHEM HARAN, "Book-Scrolls in Israel in Pre-Exilic Times," *Journal of Jewish Studies* 33, nos. 1–2 (1982), and "Book-Scrolls at the Beginning of the Second Temple Period: The Transition from Papyrus to Skins," *Hebrew Union College Annual* 54 (1983). Technical discussions of writing materials in Egypt (which provides the fullest evidence) can be found in ALFRED LUCAS, *Ancient Egyptian Materials and Industries*, edited by J. R. HARRIS (1926; 4th ed. 1962).

Writing in Premodern Societies

On literacy and the experience of writing in premodern societies, see MICHAEL T. CLANCHY, *From Memory to Written Record: England 1066–1307* (1979; 2nd ed. 1993); WILLIAM V. HARRIS, *Ancient Literacy* (1989); and SEAN WARNER, "The Alphabet: An Innovation and Its Diffusion," *Vetus Testamentum* 30 (1980). On writing and literacy in Egypt, see JOHN BAINES, "Literacy and Ancient Egyptian Society," *Man*, n.s. 18 (1983); for Mesopotamia, see H. L. J. VANSTIPHOUT, "Some Remarks on Cuneiform *Écritures*," in *Scripta Signa Vocis: Studies About Scripts, Scriptures, Scribes, and Languages Presented to J. H. Hospers*, edited by H. L. J. VANSTIPHOUT et al. (1986).

Letters, Numerals, and Acrostics

On the numerical value of letters and on the Hindu-Arabic numerals, see GEORGES IFRAH, *From One to Zero: A Universal History of Numbers*, translated by LOWELL BLAIR (1985). On gematria, see STEPHEN J. LIEBERMAN, "A Mesopotamian Background for the So-called *Aggadic* 'Measures' of Biblical Hermeneutics?" *Hebrew Union College Annual* 58 (1987). For acrostics in the ancient Near East, see WILLIAM M. SOLL, "Babylonian and Biblical Acrostics," *Biblica* 69, no. 3 (1988).

SEE ALSO **The Phoenicians** (Part 5, Vol. II); **Record Keeping Before Writing** (Part 9, Vol. IV); and **Memory and Literacy in Ancient Western Asia** (Part 9, Vol. IV).

The Literatures of Canaan, Ancient Israel, and Phoenicia: An Overview

SIMON B. PARKER

THE PRODUCTION AND APPRECIATION of written literature in the ancient Near East was a luxury limited almost exclusively to scribes of palace and temple. While the invention of the alphabet in Syro-Palestine made the mastery of writing and reading vastly simpler than in the neighboring civilizations of Mesopotamia and Egypt, it did not precipitate a great increase in literacy. Governments had no interest in promoting literacy beyond their own agents, and the vast majority of people had no motivation to learn to read or write. Oral performance remained normal, and writing, prestigious, as is reflected in the line "My tongue is the pen of an expert scribe" (Psalm 45:1). (See the essays "Memory and Literacy in Ancient Western Asia" and "The Story of the Semitic Alphabet" earlier in this volume.)

The bulk of the "literature" of Syro-Palestine was oral. Working with more or less established genres, poets, storytellers, priests, and sages created and transmitted individual works orally, adjusting their performances to particular audiences and to particular situations. Since there is no evidence of a long scribal tradition outside the Bible, it is likely that the occasional literary deposits that have been recovered are fairly direct reflections or adaptations of oral traditions.

In short, Syro-Palestinian literature, being predominantly oral, is largely inaccessible to us. Moreover, when scribes did commit to writing versions of these "standardized oral forms" (to use Jack Goody's term for the oxymoron "oral literature"), they would generally have used perishable materials. As a result, only in special cases have Syro-Palestinian literary works been preserved. This limited evidence may be supplemented by reference to the occasional literary features of nonliterary texts—letters, graffiti, monumental inscriptions—which are much more common.

HISTORICAL OVERVIEW

Early expectations of Canaanite literature from third-millennium Ebla (modern Tell Mardikh) have not yet been fulfilled. In the rich, cosmopolitan city of Ugarit (modern Ras Shamra), where the Mesopotamian technique of writing on clay (which was then baked and so preserved) was adapted to write the local language in a new alphabet, some scribes undertook—or were commissioned—to record some of their traditions in this form (fourteenth to thirteenth centuries BCE). A few major narrative poems have been recovered, none completely, but to an extent sufficient to allow a fair judgment of their scope and character. There are also several shorter myths and related pieces, mostly too damaged or obscure to permit a persuasive interpretation. Though only a fraction of the size of the Hebrew Bible and of a limited range of genres, these texts constitute the only other body of Syro-Palestinian literature from pre-Hellenistic times. (On the Amarna letters and Idrimi inscription, see "The Amarna Letters" and "Autobiographies in Ancient Western Asia" below.)

From the first millennium there are numerous alphabetic inscriptions of different genres written in the various northwest Semitic dialects. Despite occasional claims to the contrary, these are all in prose, though sometimes a very formal prose. A comprehensive study of the various genres has yet to be undertaken, but dedicatory, votive, memorial, diplomatic, and funerary inscriptions may be provisionally distinguished. Although generally mundane and repetitive, a few of these inscriptions stand out as more fully developed and original, disclosing the rhetorical and compositional resources and abilities of their authors. Even some which are no more than graffiti reveal traces of their culture's rhetoric. These sources assume a certain importance, not only because of the paucity of properly literary material but also because of their rhetorical connections with Ugaritic and Israelite literature.

The Deir 'Alla inscription on plaster (from eighth-century Transjordan), damaged and incomplete as it is, is quite atypical of these inscriptions and seems to be a copy of a literary text made for public display. In better condition is the Aramaic proverb collection and accompanying narrative of Ahiqar. This text is preserved because it was in the possession of speakers of Aramaic who had migrated to Upper Egypt, where they wrote it down on papyrus, which if untouched by the Nile can survive in the dry climate. This is the earliest version of a later widely known and well-attested work. Although the papyrus dates to the late fifth century, the proverbs and story themselves doubtless date back to the first half of the millennium.

Finally, a number of Hebrew literary works survived the destruction of the state of Judah in 586 BCE and were transmitted and elaborated through the following centuries, to be incorporated into what finally became the Hebrew Bible. Although most of the Hebrew Bible was probably written down, and certainly put into its present form, after 586, much of it originated during the preceding centuries. It is by far the most extensive body of literature from Syro-Palestine prior to the Hellenistic period. Despite, and partly because of, its long, complicated history of transmission and compilation, it remains a literature of unparalleled richness and complexity.

BASIC FORMS

Poetic forms are best exemplified in the literatures of Ugarit and Israel. In the major narrative poems from Ugarit, poetic verses usually consist of two, less frequently, three cola—phrases or clauses—sharing some semantic and syntactic parallelism (occasionally repeated words). In bicola, the first colon gives all the essential syntactic information, and the second often omits one or more constituents of the first including, most significantly, the verb:

> He took a sacrificial lamb in his hands
>   A kid in both.

Tricola are often formed by the prefixing of a colon to a bicolon attested elsewhere. This first colon is often incomplete, full syntactic information being given only in the second:

> May Horon break, my son—
> May Horon break your head,
> Athtart-name-of-Baal your skull.

Occasionally the parallelism will extend beyond a bicolon or tricolon to produce larger verses (quadricola, etc.) or larger formal units of two or more bicola. The succession of parallel cola consisting of single clauses or phrases maintained through long poems tended to produce cola or bicola of approximately the same length. This consistency of length may have reflected a

The Deir ʿAlla Text

In 1967 a team of Dutch archaeologists discovered a number of fragments of inscribed plaster in a complex building at Deir ʿAlla, a settlement east of the Jordan and just north of the river Zerqa which appears to have been a religious and trading center. The fragments were found in a destruction layer, having apparently fallen from a plastered wall during an earthquake. Many of them were reassembled into various "combinations," the first two of which yield some continuous text and sense. They were all published by J. Hoftijzer and G. van der Kooij in *Aramaic Texts from Deir ʿAlla* (1976).

The texts are written in a local version of the Transjordanian script and dialect and are probably to be dated to the later eighth century. The following is a translation of the clearest opening lines:

> [   ] account [of Balaam, son of Be]or, who was a seer of gods. Gods came to him at night, and he saw a vision like a divine oracle. They said to Balaam, son of Beor: "Thus . . ." Balaam arose the next day . . . and wept helplessly. Then his people came up to him [and said to h]im: "Balaam, son of Beor, why are you fasting and weeping?" He said to them: "Sit down. I will tell you what the mighty [ones (*shaddayin*) have done]. Come, see the deeds of the gods." The gods assembled and the mighty ones took their positions in the assembly and said to Sh[   ]: "Sew up, lock up the heavens with cloud for there will be darkness and not light there . . ."

Balaam, son of Beor, appears as a character in a biblical narrative in Numbers 22–24. (See also "Witchcraft, Magic, and Divination in Canaan and Ancient Israel" in Part 8, Vol. III.) Here too he is a seer, to whom God comes in the night (22:20), who sees a vision of a Mighty One (Shadday—24:4, 16), and who pronounces oracles on the basis of what has been revealed to him (23:8, 20; 24:4, 16). The biblical narrative treats of a quite different subject—Balaam is hired to curse the Israelites, but God intervenes to make him bless them—and itself reflects the amalgamation of different traditions. The biblical and Deir ʿAlla texts together tantalizingly suggest the diverse narrative traditions that legendary figures such as Balaam could generate.

---

consistency of rhythm in terms of major stresses—most frequently three, sometimes two, to the colon. While this was not strong enough to produce the more precise consistency of line length familiar from the classical languages and their heirs, it was strong enough to allow the occasional deviation for effect.

Also characteristic of Ugaritic narrative poetry is the use of formulas. Invariable formulas usually consist of a name and epithet, which may form part of a colon, a whole colon, or be extended over a bicolon or tricolon:

> Danil, man of Rapiu . . .
> the hero, man of the Harnemite

Variable formulas (varying in person, number, gender, etc.) usually consist of a single colon and refer to standard acts, such as arrival and departure, and to standard narrative moves, such as the introduction of direct speech. Longer or shorter clusters of formulaic cola, with and without parallelism, appear in certain standard narrative situations—for example, to describe a journey or someone's reaction to good or bad news.

A repertoire of such formulas is obviously useful to poets developing their stories orally.

Several smaller Ugaritic texts suggest that the preceding description may not hold for all poetic genres. Unfortunately, many of these texts are too short, obscure, or damaged to permit a general description of their conventions.

While the literature recovered from Ugarit consists primarily of narrative poetry, Israelite literature is almost completely lacking this genre. However, Israel had a rich tradition of cultic, devotional, prophetic, proverbial, discursive, and love poetry. Despite the differences in genre, many Ugaritic poetic expressions recur in Israelite poetry (and sometimes prose), indicating a degree of continuity in poetic tradition.

The forms of Israelite poetry are far more diverse than the Ugaritic. Parallelism and formulas are less ubiquitous, and the forms and length of individual cola are more varied. Moreover, the boundaries between poetry and prose are sometimes less clearly discernible, since one of the features of more-formal prose (as in the prose of many literatures) is a high degree of parallelism.

West Semitic prose is best represented in the Hebrew Bible, where it is used to great expressive effect in such diverse narrative passages as Genesis 1:1–2:4, Genesis 22, and 2 Samuel 9–20 with 1 Kings 1–2. Biblical prose ranges in style from the economy of the laws in Exodus 21–23 to the prolixity of the homilies of Deuteronomy 1–12. A few small-scale examples of West Semitic prose are found among the Phoenician and Aramaic royal inscriptions, the Moabite inscription of King Mesha, the Aramaic treaty from Sefire, and the story of Ahiqar from Elephantine. Among these, the Phoenician inscription of King Kilamuwa of Sam'al (modern Zincirli, pronounced Zinjirli) stands out for both its structure and its rhetoric.

The remainder of this article surveys three broad genres: narrative, cultic, and wisdom literature. These include most of the significant extrabiblical literature. Biblical literature will be invoked chiefly as it relates to this material. There are two reasons for this: at least parts of the Bible are more familiar to most people, and there are many easily accessible introductions to biblical literature. (See "Myth and Mythmaking in Canaan and Ancient Israel" in Part 8, Vol. III.)

NARRATIVE

The peoples of Syro-Palestine must have told stories from time immemorial. Basic story types appear in various versions not only here but also in neighboring Egypt and Khatti. Their presence in literary works from such different regions indicates the ubiquity of such stories in the oral culture.

The earliest surviving large-scale narratives are those from Ugarit. The tales of *Aqhat* and *Keret* focus on human actors. In *Aqhat*, Danil (Danel) is an elder; but beyond formulaic references to his giving justice to widow and orphan at the town gate, the story gives no indication of his social context outside his family. One may compare the biblical patriarchs (in many of the Genesis stories) or Job. Keret (Kirta) is a king, whose family is at the center of the action, but whose larger public world also figures in the story. Similarly, the stories about David in 2 Samuel, while focusing on the royal family, refer also to the larger public world. In neither Ugaritic story is there any attempt to relate the action to a particular historical context. This is also true of Job and was probably true of many early Israelite stories, but the biblical writers have conferred on most a specific historical setting. Thus, the stories about David are fitted into a larger historical context. Even the patriarchal stories have a quasi-historical locus.

In the Ugaritic stories, human actors are from time to time assisted or harmed by a deity. Such divine intervention may be portrayed by a deity appearing as an actor in the human realm or by a shift of scene and action from the world of men and women to the world of the gods. Both devices were used in Israelite narration, though they appear only in limited contexts in the Bible: Genesis 18–19, 32:24–30; Judges 6:11–22, 13:3–23; and Job 1–2.

The Ugaritic tales, but especially *Aqhat*, have fantastic elements other than divine visitations. 'Anat places her henchman in her girdle and then, while flying above Aqhat, releases him onto the boy, whom he kills. The high god, El, makes a creature to cure Keret's sickness, and sends her flying over towns and settlements to accomplish her mission, which she does. Such features are virtually absent from Israelite stories as they appear in the Bible.

The action in the Ugaritic stories is linear, moving forward without flashbacks or anticipations. The narrative world is never interrupted by authorial explanations, summaries, or judgments such as are common in biblical narrative. However, the pace may vary considerably. The Ugaritic authors sometimes make extensive use of epic repetition and clusters of formulas that slow the action down and, at other times, by minimal use of such devices, move it rapidly onward. The biblical authors are sparing in their use of epic repetition, but may use an accumulation of detail to retard the action.

Both Ugaritic tales—*Aqhat* and *Keret*—are clearly composed of shorter, simpler stories of standard types that must have been widely told in oral form: the story of a childless person appealing to the gods and being granted a son (compare 1 Samuel 1); the story of a divine visitor leaving a reward with those who have shown him generous hospitality (compare Genesis 18); the tale of a difficult expedition for a wife, proceeding through delicate negotiations to a successful conclusion (compare Genesis 24). Such traditional stories are handled differently in the two larger narratives. In *Aqhat* they form a concatenation of episodes each of which builds on the preceding one and leads into the next. In *Keret* the poets have simply juxtaposed each new tale to the preceding, with only slight superficial adjustments to suggest an ongoing plot.

Keret

Keret opens with a prologue that shows Keret bereft of family. The action begins with Keret's retiring to bed, weeping, where he dreams that El appears to him and asks what is the matter. This motif of a divine offer to grant a monarch's wish reappears in 1 Kings 3 and in the royal psalms: Psalms 2:8, 20:4–5, 21:2 and 4. Wealth, long life, and dominion are the three common requests (compare 'Anat's offer to Aqhat, below). When told of Keret's plight, El gives lengthy, detailed instructions for what he is to do. Keret carefully follows these: he performs a sacrifice, gathers provisions, musters an army, and marches to the town of Udum. There is one intrusive element: during the journey he makes a vow to the goddess Asherah, promising her a rich gift if she will give his expedition success. He then continues to follow El's instructions, besieging the town of Udum and negotiating with its king for the hand of his daughter. After a gap in the text, El and the gods gather, and El blesses the couple, promising them many children, which are then born.

The sudden loss and rapid restoration of a family at the beginning and end of this story are echoed in the books of Job and Ruth. In *Keret* the action between these limits is shaped by the structure of the dream theophany, in which an expression of need elicits a divine response with instructions, the execution of which results in the meeting of the need. This same structure appears on a small scale in, for example, 1 Kings 19, Genesis 16:6–15 and 21:14–19. The particular subject here, however, is the expedition for a wife. This, too, has a typical narrative structure—need of family, journey to land of potential spouse, and negotiations leading to marriage and childbirth—which is also found in Genesis 24, Ruth (with reversal of gender roles), and, more loosely, the story of Jacob.

Next, we see Keret seriously ill, thus precipitating the action of the second story. This is linked with the preceding by a reference to Keret's failure to keep his vow to Asherah; the sickness is thus her punishment of him. There is severe damage to the next several columns of text, but it is at least clear that Keret's wife invites his lords and nobles and other guests to a banquet and that some of his children begin to mourn and are given directions by him. Whether this has to do with attempts to heal him or to assure the succession, or both, is not clear. Next, we seem to be in the divine court, where note is taken of a famine that has begun, the natural consequence of Keret's sickness. Various gods are called for and sent (again there are large gaps in the text). Finally, after challenging the other gods to heal Keret, El himself makes a creature to cure him. Thus, the second crisis in Keret's life is over. The outline of this story reappears in the tale of Job, where a member of the heavenly council strikes Job with sickness, and responses by different parties in his social world are finally succeeded by God's response and Job's restoration (Job 2:7–13, 42:7–10).

Keret's son, Yassub, now proposes to take over the throne because of his father's failure to exercise justice. The text links this new story with the preceding one by citing Keret's sickness (now past!) as another reason for this bid. Keret curses his son—and there the preserved text ends. The bid to displace the present ruler(s) on the grounds of his/their injustice or misrule is a motif found also in 2 Samuel 15 and Psalm 82.

Keret treats of three crises that kings may face: lack of progeny, sickness, threat of deposition. The theme of the poem, so far as we have it, seems to be the power, wisdom, and benevolence of the god El and Keret's total dependence on him in these crises. The larger work, which would have included at least the remainder of the third story, may have laid more emphasis on the theme of royal succession. In any case, there seems to be a balance between a lack of succession in the first story and an overzealous succession in the third.

Aqhat

In *Aqhat*, Danil is also introduced as childless. He appeals to the gods, who respond with a blessing. Informed that he will have a son like his peers, he entertains the Katharat, goddesses of marital fertility, and his wife conceives and gives birth to Aqhat (compare also 1 Samuel 1, and, in outline, Genesis 25:21, 25:25–26, and 30:1, 22–23). After a gap, the craftsman god, Kothar, visits Danil and his wife, enjoys their hospitality, and delivers a composite bow to Danil, who hands it over to Aqhat (note also Genesis 18:1–15, 19:1–16; 1 Kings 17:10–16; 2 Kings 4:8–17).

The goddess ʿAnat now tries to get Aqhat to give her the bow, promising him silver and gold and then immortality. Aqhat rejects her offers, pointing out how she can get the materials for a bow for herself and that death is the universal human fate (the latter is a cliché; e.g., Psalm 89:48; Joshua 23:14; Job 30:23). Offended, ʿAnat goes off to El and bullies him into letting her have her way with Aqhat. (This material also bears comparison with the sixth tablet of the *Epic of Gilgamesh.*) Soon, ʿAnat is engaged in negotiations with a new character, Yutpan, which result in a plan for her to carry him like a bird of prey, fly among a flock of such birds, and release him to fly down and strike Aqhat. This she does, and Aqhat is killed. But ʿAnat does not get the bow, and the vegetation withers because of the crime (for this motif, see also 2 Samuel 21:1–2; Jeremiah 12:4; Hosea 4:2–3).

Danil, accompanied by his daughter, undertakes ritual pronouncements and acts to revive the vegetation, but then two messengers arrive and tell them the real cause of the drought. Danil calls on Baal to bring down the birds of prey so that he can see if Aqhat's remains are in their viscera. After finally recovering the remains in this manner and burying them, Danil curses three towns near the site of the crime (compare the law in Deuteronomy 21:1–9) and returns home, where mourners bewail his dead son for seven years. He then offers up a sacrifice, and his daughter asks him to bless her on an errand of vengeance. He does so, and she puts on male weapons under her woman's dress and sets out. The preserved part of the tale ends with her arriving at Yutpan's camp and joining him in a drinking party.

Several features of this errand of vengeance anticipate the mission of Judith in Judith 8–13, which in turn suggests the conclusion of this episode. The motif of the warrior killed (shame-fully) by a woman reappears in Judges 4:9, 4:21, 5:26–27, and 9:53–54, and the motif of the hidden weapon recurs in Judges 3:16.

Again, the lack of an ending (as well as the various gaps in the story) hampers any attempt to give a definitive interpretation. The central act of the poem—to which everything preceding leads up and from which everything that follows devolves—is the murder of Aqhat by ʿAnat. Reversals of traditional gender roles lead up to the crime and to the revenge. The goddess ʿAnat wants the male weapon, the bow, and kills when she cannot get it. The daughter, Pughat, dons male clothes and weapons to avenge the murder. In contrast, detailed and repeated attention is given to traditional family roles, duties, and rituals: a litany of the duties of a son is repeated four times in the opening section, and each of the duties undertaken by Danil after Aqhat's death is repeated two or three times.

Danil is also mentioned in what may have been a lengthy mythological tale, of which we have only parts of five columns from three tablets. The remains include repeated invitations to the Rephaim (deified ancestors) and an elaborate banquet scene. But the larger subject or theme, as well as the purpose of this work, remains obscure. That different stories about Danil—or versions of the same story—were in any case popular over a wide area and long period is indicated by later evidence of a Judean version (Ezekiel 14:14, 14:20, and 28:3).

Baal

The other major subject of Ugaritic narrative poetry is the struggles of the god Baal. Various mythological topics and motifs are developed into a major literary work that uses narrative and poetic forms similar to those of the two preceding narratives, but exceeds them as an expressive and imaginative achievement. Since the damaged state of the tablets does not permit a secure judgment on the unity of the work, it is usually referred to as a "cycle"—suggesting a loosely connected series of myths about the same deity. It is preserved on six large tablets that treat of three successive subjects: the conflict between Baal and Yamm ("Sea"), the building of a palace for Baal, and the conflict between Baal and Mot ("Death").

The first tablet is very damaged, so that the beginnings of the story are uncertain, but they clearly involve El's establishment of Yamm as ruler by giving him a new name, "beloved of El," and commissioning Kothar to build a palace for him. In the second tablet Yamm seeks to establish his rule by demanding that Baal be delivered to him. El agrees to this, but, nevertheless, Baal defeats Yamm with the aid of two magic maces produced by Kothar. With the death of Yamm, Baal becomes king.

Variant versions of a sea monster's defeat are found in other fragmentary tablets, and allusions to the same motif are found elsewhere in the main cycle and in Israelite literature where Yahweh replaces Baal as victor. The original myth may have had cosmogonic import, as well as reflecting meteorological phenomena (such as appear in a storm at sea) but in the *Baal Cycle* it is developed into a narrative concerned with a struggle for power. Israel's literature preserves the theme's cosmogonic associations (Psalms 74:12–17, 89:9–13); historicizes it, relating it especially to the crossing of the Sea during the Exodus (Psalm 77:16–20; Isaiah 51:9–10); and eschatalogizes it, using it to depict God's final conquest of the powers of evil (Isaiah 27:1).

The next tablet opens with a banquet scene at which Baal is regaled with food, drink, and song, presumably in celebration of his recent victory. After a brief gap in the tablet, ʿAnat is slaughtering warriors, wading up to her knees in blood, and hanging heads and hands on her person. Finally, she washes herself off. (Another Ugaritic text concludes with lines similar to these, but begins with a unique description of Baal, comparing him to a mountain, and referring to various parts of his body.) Baal now sends messengers to ʿAnat. She is to pour peace into the earth and come to him, and he will tell her his secret. On her arrival, Baal complains of his continuing dependent status and lack of a palace of his own. This precipitates the second major development. ʿAnat volunteers to bully El into letting Baal have a palace. She threatens El, as in *Aqhat*, but apparently in vain. Next, Baal commissions from Kothar gifts that he and ʿAnat take to Asherah. With these, Asherah goes and presents Baal's petition to El, who now grants the request. Baal summons Kothar and commissions

him to build a palace, rejecting Kothar's proposal to put a window in it. The palace is built, and Baal sacrifices large numbers of animals, inviting all the gods to a great feast. He makes a show of strength by campaigning through town after town, claiming them as his. Returning home, he finally asks Kothar to put a window in his palace and then gives voice to his thunder through the window.

This lengthy narrative may once have been related to the building of an actual temple for Baal. Temple building was of momentous significance in the societies of the ancient Near East, as attested in description of the building of the Temple in Jerusalem in 1 Kings 6–8 and of the tabernacle in Exodus 25–30 and 35–40. But the account here, rather than identifying the palace of the story with any historical building, as in the Babylonian *Enuma Elish*, mystifies its construction and shows more interest in the relations among the various gods and the literary development of mythological details than in the practice of the earthly cult.

Baal now takes on the last enemy. He sends his messengers down to Mot ("Death"). At the beginning of the next tablet, they return with a message extolling Mot's appetite and inviting Baal to go down Mot's throat. Baal expresses his fear of Mot, who has "one lip to the earth/ underworld, one lip to the heavens . . . tongue to the stars." (The first two phrases are used of Shahar and Shalim, see below, and the whole is recast in Psalm 73:9, where it refers to the wicked. The ravening Mot, sometimes under the name Sheol, becomes a powerful image in other biblical texts, notably Habakkuk 2:5 and Isaiah 5:14.) Baal now declares himself Mot's perpetual servant. After two badly damaged columns, someone is telling Baal to go down into the underworld with his retinue like mortals.

When the text resumes, two messengers are reporting to El that they have found Baal dead on the ground. El immediately goes into mourning. ʿAnat goes out, finds the body, and also goes into mourning. With the assistance of Shapsh, the sun-goddess, ʿAnat takes the corpse to Baal's mountain, where she buries it and slaughters numerous sacrificial animals. El calls on Asherah to nominate (at least) two of her offspring for him to make king in Baal's place, but neither can fill Baal's role as warrior or ruler. ʿAnat longs for Baal: "As the heart of a cow for its calf, as the heart of a ewe for its mother, so is the heart of ʿAnat for Baal." She grabs hold of Mot, who tells her how he chewed Baal up like a lamb. Finally, she destroys Mot with sword, sieve, fire, and millstones, scattering him over land and sea, and announces to El that Mot is dead. El now dreams that the heavens rain (olive) oil and the wadis run with honey, a sign that Baal is alive. He tells ʿAnat to appeal to Shapsh to find Baal. When Baal reappears, he strikes down his enemies and resumes his rule. After seven years Mot also returns, complaining to Baal of his treatment at ʿAnat's hands. Threatening to consume humankind, he demands one of Baal's fellows. Baal refuses, and they fight like wild animals, both equally strong, until they collapse on the ground. Shapsh rebukes Mot, warning him that El will overthrow his dominion if he contends with Baal. Mot finally acknowledges Baal's rule. The cycle ends with a hymn to Shapsh, who is given authority over the denizens of the underworld.

Mot ("Death") is the ultimate and enduring enemy. While he cannot defeat Baal, neither can Baal defeat him. Thus, the cycle concludes with the establishment of Baal's rule, but also the limitation of his rule and so of his beneficence to humanity. Humanity is assured of his fertilizing rain and his more general support of life, but also knows that occasionally ("seven years") death breaks in and indeed can never finally be escaped. In the cycle as a whole, the political struggles of an aristocracy—the alliances and rebellions, the messages and visits with their appeals and threats, the occasional hand-to-hand fights, all set against a background of lavish hospitality and celebratory banquets—are transferred to the divine realm and invested with cosmic significance.

Shorter Narratives

Beyond these major works there are several shorter stories, many of which are too damaged to be susceptible of interpretation. It is clear that some were borrowed or created for practical (ritual) purposes and that births, fights, banquets, and marriage negotiations recur as basic material. Several tablets preserve different versions of passages in the *Baal Cycle* or other epi-

sodes about similar topics. The remains of one three-column tablet, sometimes called "The Loves of Baal and ʿAnat," depict ʿAnat seeking out Baal, who, she learns, has gone hunting in a region well populated with wild bulls and cows. The real concern of the story, it transpires, is the birth of a worthy offspring for Baal. The text ends with Baal rejoicing at the good news brought him by ʿAnat: a bull has been born to him. (This recalls a brief episode in the main cycle: immediately before he is overcome by Mot, Baal copulates with a heifer that gives birth to a child.) This myth transfers the motif of childlessness to the divine world. Baal and ʿAnat themselves solve the problem.

In the remains of a myth on another partially preserved tablet, El supports the birth of "devourers" resembling bulls. Baal comes across them while hunting at the edge of the steppe. He is apparently defeated by them, falling like a bull, and nature is desiccated in consequence. Here, as in the *Baal Cycle*, El seems to authorize and support opposition to Baal, whose demise traumatizes nature.

El's efforts to produce offspring are the subject of a myth recorded on an almost complete text that opens with an invocation of "the lovely gods" and references to several cultic acts. The myth begins with El's efforts at coition with two women. They eventually conceive and give birth to Shahar and Shalim ("Dawn" and "Dusk"), who are placed in the heavens. Then, after a rubric indicating a fivefold repetition of conception and birth, they give birth to the lovely gods, whose voracious appetites consume the birds in the heavens and the fish in the sea and still are not sated. They are put in the steppe. After seven years they approach the guard of the cultivated land and ask him to let them in, which he apparently does, offering them food and wine.

A distinctive banquet scene appears in another short narrative in which Yarkh (Yarikh), the moon-god, roams about under the table like a dog, and El, the host, has to be helped home, finally falling in his own feces as if dead. ʿAnat and Athtart go off and bring back something that revives him. The epilogue is evidently a prescription for drunken stupor.

Marriage negotiations figure in two short myths. A text that focuses on the disposal of snake venom concludes with a myth describing how Horon disposes of the venom for the Mare, the daughter of Shapsh, and then seeks admission to her house. But having locked herself in, she first demands that he produce the snakes as her bride-wealth, which he does. In the other myth ("The Marriage of Nikkal"), Yarkh sends a message to Khirikhbi, "King of Summer," requesting in marriage his daughter Nikkal (a moon-goddess imported from Mesopotamia) and offering generous bride-wealth. Khirikhbi tries to get Yarkh to marry one of Baal's daughters. But Yarkh insists on Nikkal, and the story ends with Nikkal's family preparing the scales to weigh out the gifts. The context, including a hymn to the Katharat and a reference to a young woman bearing a child, suggests that this text was used to enhance the fertility of a marriage.

Two extrabiblical narratives are preserved from the first millennium. Like Danil the patriarch, Balaam the seer was evidently a popular subject of story. Known especially from the biblical narratives in Numbers 22–24, he has now reappeared in what seems to be a copy of a literary text inscribed on plaster fragments from Deir 'Alla. The work is headed "Inscription of [Balaam son of Be]or, seer of gods." Gods came to Baalam at night with a message. He arose the next day in great grief. When his people asked why he was fasting and weeping, he gave them a detailed account of a vision, starting with a divine assembly. What is preserved of the vision is reminiscent of the more poetic and symbolic biblical oracles and visions.

The Aramaic tale of Ahiqar begins traditionally by introducing a childless man, but uses this feature quite differently from the Ugaritic tales. Ahiqar, counselor and confidant of the Assyrian king, is growing old, so he resolves to adopt his nephew, impart his wisdom to him, and prepare him as his successor in the king's service. Eventually, the nephew, Nadin, is installed, only to accuse Ahiqar of treachery. The king orders that Ahiqar be put to death. Fortunately, the officer sent to dispose of Ahiqar had himself once been condemned to death. On that occasion, Ahiqar hid him and then told the king he had killed him. Later, when the time seemed auspicious, Ahiqar had produced and vindicated the officer. Ahiqar now successfully appeals to the officer to do the same for him. Although the sequel is lost, in the later versions the king eventually wishes Ahiqar were back and the officer produces him. Ahiqar is reinstated, and Nadin is punished. Thus, *Ahiqar* shares with the story of Mordecai in the book of Esther a basic bipartite structure: (1) A saved B, who was in danger from X; (2) B, being reminded of (1); now saves A, who is in danger from Y.

More generally, *Ahiqar* bears comparison with the biblical stories of Esther and Joseph and some of the stories in the early chapters of Daniel. All of these reflect court life in the great near eastern empires: the rise and fall of officials, intrigues, the risk of treachery. The hero is the truly wise and virtuous person who is victimized but finally prevails. *Ahiqar* (so far as we have it) is devoid of miracle and magic, of divine intervention, and indeed of specifically religious acts such as prayer. The biblical stories differ from this to varying degrees. Esther's virtue and courage are emphasized, and she initiates one religious act, a three-day fast. In Joseph and especially Daniel, mantic wisdom is prominent. Joseph acknowledges God's general guidance of human affairs and specific aid in giving the interpretation of dreams. The stories of Daniel repeatedly refer to, and hymn, the God who reveals hidden knowledge, solves mysteries, and intervenes to save his servants.

CULTIC LITERATURE

While the Psalms constitute an unparalleled collection of (largely) cultic literature, there is sufficient evidence from Ugarit and the inscriptions to indicate the existence of a more widely spread tradition. Much of this derives from the existential situation of desperation in which an individual (or community) appeals to the deity (who may reply through prophets). After the deity has intervened, the individual responds with a public acknowledgment of what the deity has done. So far as the appeal takes the form of a vow, there is a specific correspondence between what was promised and what is now said and done.

A ritual text from Ugarit anticipates in poetic form the first stages in this sequence of events:

When another power attacks your gates,
  a warrior your walls

Lift up your eyes to Baal:
"O Baal,
If you will drive the power from our gates,
the warrior from our walls . . ."

This vow continues with the promise of various sacrifices and of a procession to Baal's sanctuary and is followed by the assurance:

Then Baal will hear your prayer:
He will drive the power from your gates,
the warrior from your walls.

The Aramaic king Zakkur (Zakir) recorded in an inscription his retrospective view of a similar sequence of events. He recounts how an alliance of kings laid seige to his city, Hadrak: "They raised a wall higher than the wall of Hadrak, and plowed a ditch deeper than its ditch. And I lifted my hands to Baalshamein and Baalshamein answered me, and Baalshamein spoke to me through seers and prophets." A prophetic oracle promising deliverance is then quoted. The following broken lines presumably told of Zakkur's actual deliverance.

Both texts describe a similar situation of desperation and the oral forms that are used in that situation. In the first case, the wording of the prayer is given; it is an explicit vow, a promise conditional on the deity's granting a request. In the second case, there is an immediate verbal answer through prophets, who give the king an oracle of reassurance, promising deliverance.

The same situations and types of utterance are referred to in biblical texts. In the account of the dedication of the Temple, King Solomon prays that when in various kinds of crisis the community appeals to Yahweh, Yahweh will hear and take appropriate action (1 Kings 8:33–52). Second Chronicles 20:1–30 recounts such a crisis in a community's life, quoting both the prayer appealing for divine aid and the divine response through a prophet.

The biblical laments (or complaints or supplications) are examples of prayer in a desperate situation. Although they do not contain formal vows, there is often an implied vow in the simple juxtaposition of appeal and promise (e.g., Psalm 80:18). In any case, there are many references after the fact to vows and their subsequent fulfillment, and formal vows uttered in situations of desperation are quoted in biblical narratives

(1 Samuel 1:11; Numbers 21:2; Judges 11:30–31; 2 Samuel 15:8; Genesis 28:20–22; compare Keret's vow, mentioned above).

The divine "answer"—an oracle giving reassurance and promise of deliverance—is rare in the psalms (but see Psalms 85:8, 35:3; Lamentations 3:57), though some think it is presupposed by the shift from supplication to expressions of confidence or thanksgiving in some psalms. The oracle that King Zakkur records in his Aramaic inscription uses phrases that appear in Hebrew oracles of salvation: "Fear not, for I made [you k]ing, [and I will b]e with you, and I will deliver you from all [these kings who] have laid siege to you." Oracles of this type appear in more-developed literary forms in Israel: in royal psalms, such as Psalm 21:8–12, and addressed to the community, especially in Isaiah of Babylon (Isaiah 40–55). Thus, at least some forms of biblical prophecy (and the prophecy of the Deir 'Alla Balaam) are a literary development of oral (and inscribed) oracles that were more widely spread among the West Semites.

The last stage in this sequence of events and corresponding expressions is the public acknowledgment of divine aid. Votive inscriptions are the simplest such testimonies, as in "Stela which Barhadad . . . king of Aram, erected for his lord, Melqart, who heard his voice when he made a vow." Zakkur's inscription is itself such a testimony. The biblical psalms of thanksgiving are the most developed form of this genre. They, too, are offered in recognition of God's having "heard" the speaker (see Psalms 6:8–9, 28:6; Jonah 2:2). Such psalms often recall the initial plight, the appeal to God, and God's intervention—just as in Zakkur's inscription—thus giving the specific reason for the present thanksgiving and praise.

We surmise that the Canaanites, Aramaeans, and Phoenicians may have had more literary laments and thanksgiving psalms than the lapidary inscriptions reveal. The Ugaritic ritual text certainly suggests this. If so, the different genres of psalms may have been more clearly distinguished and related to the appropriate situation than many of the biblical psalms. These were compiled, edited, and put to different uses over centuries, and so in many cases are now complex fusions of different genres.

After laments, hymns are the next most frequent genre among the Israelite psalms. Brief hymnic passages open and conclude the Ugaritic song of Nikkal: "I shall sing of Nikkal-and-Ib" and "I shall sing of the Katharat." The same formal proclamation opens several Israelite songs (e.g., Psalms 89:1, 101:1, 108:1), and such songs are promised at the end of some laments (e.g., Psalms 13:6, 59:17). The ritual text "The Lovely Gods" opens with another formal cry: "I call on the lovely gods." This, too, appears in Israelite cultic literature (Psalm 18:3, 6 [= 2 Samuel 22:4, 7]; Deuteronomy 32:3).

Two Ugaritic texts concerned with the cult of deceased monarchs end with a blessing on Ugarit, to last, in the words of one, "as long as the days of the sun and moon." Israel's royal psalms, while focusing on the living (and reinterpreted after the monarchy to refer to the future) are in the same broad tradition of royal ideology, already seen in the royal oracles. Similar blessings are wished on the current monarch in Psalms 72:5, 17 and 89:36–37 (and in the inscription of King Azatiwada of Karatepe, discussed in "Autobiographies in Ancient Western Asia" later in this volume.)

WISDOM LITERATURE

The occasional quotation of a proverb in narrative literature or correspondence hints at the existence of a "wisdom" tradition. (See also "The Contemplative Life in the Ancient Near East" for more discussion of wisdom literature.) This is well represented in Israel by the collections of proverbs preserved in the book of that name. This tradition is challenged from within and its scope expanded in different ways in the books of Job and Ecclesiastes.

Outside the Bible, the wisdom tradition is best represented by the *Proverbs of Ahiqar,* of which about one hundred are more or less preserved and understood. These are obviously part of the same international tradition as the biblical proverbs, and sometimes they echo individual biblical sayings; for example, "Do not withhold your son from the rod; otherwise you will be unable to save him [from death?]" (number 3; compare Proverbs 23:13–14), or "Hunger sweetens what is bitter, and thirst [sourness?]" (number 90; compare Proverbs 27:7). Other common themes include the divine origin of wisdom (number 13; compare Proverbs 8:22–31), the virtue of cautious speech (numbers 14–16; Proverbs 12:23), the danger of a monarch's anger (number 19; Proverbs 16:14), the godlikeness of a monarch (numbers 25–26; Proverbs 25:2–3), respect for parents (number 49; Proverbs 20:20), and the destruction of the wicked (number 75; Proverbs 14:11). Characteristic forms include numerical sayings (number 12; Proverbs 30:15–31), rhetorical questions (number 21; Proverbs 17:16), and the juxtaposition of metaphors with the topic to which they refer (number 21; Proverbs 26:3). There is even a brief fable (number 73) not unlike that quoted in 2 Kings 14:9 (see also Judges 9:8–15).

While there are significant differences among the literary remains from Ugarit, Israel, Phoenicia, and Aram (differences that may be exaggerated by the accidents of preservation and recovery), there are also striking similarities that indicate a common broad stream of tradition. An awareness of this tradition helps both to compensate for the poor condition of many of the nonbiblical texts and to enhance our appreciation of the oral and literary roots of what finally became the Bible.

BIBLIOGRAPHY

Sources

UGARITIC

G. DEL OLMO LETE, *Mitos y Leyendas de Canaan* (1981), the best and most comprehensive introduction with texts and translations. MICHAEL D. COOGAN, *Stories from Ancient Canaan* (1978) and JOHANNES C. DE MOOR, *An Anthology of Religious Texts from Ugarit* (1987), English translations.

OTHER

JOHN C. L. GIBSON, *Textbook of Syrian Semitic Inscriptions,* 3 vols. (1971–1982), a wide selection with commentary. J. M. LINDENBERGER, "Ahiqar," in *The Old Testament Pseudepigrapha*, vol. 2, edited by JAMES H. CHARLESWORTH (1985), good translation and useful introduction. FRANZ ROSENTHAL, "Canaanite and Aramaic Inscriptions," in *Ancient Near Eastern Texts*, edited by J. B. PRITCHARD (1969), translation of several of the most important inscriptions.

Analytic and Comparative Studies

NARRATIVE AND MYTH

SIMON B. PARKER. *The Pre-Biblical Narrative Tradition* (1989), the poetic and narrative composition of *Keret* and *Aqhat* and their relations with biblical and other narratives. KENNETH T. AITKEN, *The Aqhat Narrative* (1990), a structuralist analysis. MARK S. SMITH, "Interpreting the Baal Cycle," *Ugarit-Forschungen* 18 (1986), good overview of the issues raised by this work. JOHN DAY, *God's Conflict with the Dragon and the Sea* (1985), lucid treatment of the biblical echoes of the divine battle with the sea (monster). J. HOFTIJZER and G. VAN DER KOOIJ, eds., *The Balaam Text from Deir ʿAlla Re-evaluated* (1991), review of various aspects of this difficult text.

CULTIC LITERATURE

PATRICK D. MILLER, "Psalms and Inscriptions," in *Congress Volume: Vienna, 1980,* Supplements to *Vetus Testamentum,* vol. 32 (1981) and "Prayer and Sacrifice in Ugarit and Israel," in *Text and Context: Old Testament and Semitic Studies for F. C. Fensham,* edited by W. CLAASSEN (1988); JULIA M. O'BRIEN, "Because God Heard My Voice: The Individual Thanksgiving Psalm and Vow-Fulfillment," in *The Listening Heart,* edited by KENNETH G. HOGLUND ET AL. (1987); JAMES F. ROSS, "Prophecy in Hamath, Israel, and Mari," *Harvard Theological Review* 63 (1970); H. J. ZOBEL, "Das Gebet um Abwendung der Not und seine Erhörung in den Klageliedern des Alten Testaments und in der Inschrift des Königs Zakir von Hamath," *Vetus Testamentum* 21 (1971), all good discussions of specific texts and topics.

Rhetoric

JONAS C. GREENFIELD, "The Hebrew Bible and Canaanite Literature," in *The Literary Guide to the Bible,* edited by ROBERT ALTER and FRANK KERMODE (1987), and "Scripture and Inscription: the Literary and Rhetorical Element in Some Early Phoenician Inscriptions," in *Near Eastern Studies in Honor of William Foxwell Albright,* edited by H. GOEDICKE (1971), trace mythological/rhetorical/idiomatic continuities in Ugaritic/Phoenician and biblical literature. M. O'CONNOR, "The Rhetoric of the Kilamuwa Inscription," *Bulletin of the American Schools of Oriental Research* 226 (1977), a good study of the rhetorically most ambitious Phoenician inscription.

SEE ALSO **The History of Ancient Syria and Palestine: An Overview** (Part 5, Vol. II); **Myth and Mythmaking in Canaan and Ancient Israel** (Part 8, Vol. III); and **The Amarna Letters from Canaan** (Part 9, Vol. IV).

The Amarna Letters from Canaan

SHLOMO IZRE'EL

HISTORICAL SETTING

The Amarna letters are named after the site in Middle Egypt where they were discovered. Tell al-Amarna, or ancient Akhetaten, was the city chosen by Akhenaten (Amenhotep IV) to be his capital when he left Thebes.

By the fourteenth century BCE, the Egyptian Empire was dominating the Levant up to the borders of the Hurrian kingdom of Mitanni. This was an age of turbulence and disorder in the Levant. Both the Mitannian kingdom and the more remote political powers, like Assyria and Babylonia, maintained good relations with the Egyptians. But another dominant power was rising to threaten the northern borders of the Egyptian Empire. These were the Hittites, who, in the course of the Amarna period, had gained enough power to attract to their side the important strategic area of the Amurrite (Amorite) state. Peace and political tranquillity did not prevail within the Asiatic territories of the empire. Power struggles erupted among the local city chieftains and between leading personalities of individual cities. Moreover, a class of outsiders known by their West Semitic label 'apiru (or ḥabiru) further complicated the political situation by encouraging diverse populations to rebel against their own leaders.

Resident commissioners, who could be either Egyptian or Canaanite, supervised the country on behalf of the pharaoh from a number of principal cities in Canaan. These commissioners did not have complete authority over the leaders of the Canaanite city-states; for these city-state leaders tried to plead their cases directly to the pharaoh in exchanges of letters with him. This correspondence forms the bulk of the tablets that now constitute the Amarna corpus.

The tablets themselves became known to the scholarly world thanks to an accidental discovery, probably in 1887. According to the reported history of the find, we owe their initial discovery to a peasant woman who was digging among the ruins of the ancient site for compost to cultivate her field. After this woman sold some tablets she had found to an interested client, the local inhabitants started digging the place, and managed to find many more tablets. These tablets eventually found their way to antique dealers and to museums. Following the original discovery, systematic excavations yielded some further tablets. There are now about 380 texts and fragments preserved in diverse museums, mainly in Europe and in Egypt.

An important part of the Amarna corpus is letters sent into the Egyptian court by Egypt's vassals in the Levant. Other letters were sent on behalf of the kings of Babylonia, Assyria, Khatti, Mitanni and Alashiya (Cyprus), and from minor princes and rulers of the Near East. In addition, some copies or drafts of letters sent from Egypt on behalf of the Egyptian king have been preserved. The find includes not only letters but also some material of use to Egyptian students learning Akkadian.

THE CULTURAL-LINGUISTIC BACKGROUND

Although Egypt had a written and an epistolary tradition as ancient as that of Mesopotamia, the correspondence of the Egyptian court, both for its international affairs and with its vassals in southwest Asia, was conducted not in the language of the Egyptian Empire, but in the Akkadian language and in the Akkadian cuneiform script (two of the Amarna letters were written in Hittite; one in Hurrian). Perhaps the internal correspondence of the Egyptian Empire with its vassals was not written in Egyptian script or language because of the esoteric character of the Egyptian linguistic, scriptural, and cultural lore. Another probable reason is that there was an old and widespread non-Egyptian tradition of letter-writing and of writing in general in Syria and Palestine.

Cuneiform writing in the regions of Syria and Palestine is documented from the third millennium BCE. At Ebla (modern Tell Mardikh in Syria), cuneiform documents in Sumerian and Semitic languages were written in the third millennium for internal administration. Byblos (modern Jubayl), a coastal city well represented in the Amarna archive, has yielded a cuneiform document of the third millennium. Second-millennium sites outside Mesopotamia are even more bountiful in this respect. The Old Babylonian dialect of the Akkadian language became the norm for written communication throughout the entire Near East. Akkadian, or rather one of its branches called Peripheral Akkadian, served during the second millennium as the *lingua franca*, the diplomatic and trading language, of the ancient Near East.

Peripheral Akkadian was, in effect, much more than a language used for intercultural communication. Until relatively late in the second millennium, in many of the societies of western Asia, it was the main language used to preserve knowledge and information; for some of these cultures, in fact, it may have been the only language they wrote. Thus, administrative documents in cities like Emar (modern Meskene) and Alalakh (modern Tell Atchana) were written mainly in Akkadian, and no written document in the local languages has so far been recovered. The "autobiography" of King Idrimi of Alalakh is written in this peculiar form of Akkadian. (See "Autobiographies in Ancient Western Asia" below.) In the Syrian coastal city of Ugarit (modern Ras Shamra), the local language began to be written (alongside Akkadian) only after an alphabetic writing system using wedges impressed on clay tablets had been developed. Even after written forms were developed for local languages of Anatolia, Syria, and Canaan, Akkadian still served as a common administrative language. From Hazor in northern Canaan, a legal suit formulated in Akkadian has been recovered. In Hebron of southern Canaan, a list of sheep, also written in cuneiform, has been unearthed. Spreading outward from Mesopotamia, Akkadian served not only as a vehicle for diplomatic relations but also as a transmitter of Mesopotamia's ancient cultural heritage. All over western Asia, scribes were trained using literary texts in Akkadian and sometimes also in Sumerian. To varying extents, the Sumero-Akkadian culture was assimilated throughout the entire Near East.

By the time of the Amarna period, people of the eastern Mediterranean regions had been bilingual—in some regions multilingual—for centuries; they wrote Mesopotamian languages, but conversed in their local languages. It is not surprising, therefore, that Sumero-Akkadian culture penetrated the West Semitic dialects in both language and style. Beside words such as "chair" (Akkadian *kussī-*, Sumerian GU.ZA, Aramaic and Arabic *kursi*, Hebrew *kissē*), "sailor" (Sumerian MÁ.LAH₄, Akkadian *malāḫ-*, Hebrew *mallāḫ*), "palace" (Sumerian É.GAL, literally: "big house," Akkadian *ekall-*, Hebrew *hēkāl*), or "price" (Akkadian *maḫīr-*, Hebrew *meḫîr*), a significant number of technical terms were taken directly from Akkadian, and occasionally also from Sumerian: "scribe" (Sumerian DUB.SAR, Akkadian *ṭupšarr-*, Aramaic, and via Aramaic also Hebrew, *ṭipsār*); "written document, letter," later "book" in Hebrew (*sēper*, which recalls Akkadian *šipr-*, denoting "sending" of persons, messengers, and messages). From the latter root,

Hebrew also possesses the more regular and ancient term for "scribe," namely *sōpēr*.

STYLE, PHRASEOLOGY, IDIOM

As is common for correspondence in most cultures, Amarna letter-writing was formulaic. The Amarna scribes inherited, and occasionally adapted, conventions of correspondence derived from Mesopotamia. The conventions of written correspondence were rooted in oral exchanges of information.

Formulaic structure and conventions reflected the social status and stratification of the respective correspondents. For example, in these letters, a man with a lower status would always address his superior by the title "my lord." Kinship terminology was used metaphorically to indicate the relative social status of the respective correspondents. Terms of address like "father," "son," "brother," and "family" are common in the letters. Aziru of Amurru addresses Tutu, an Egyptian official to whom he is not related, as follows: "To Tutu, my lord, my father: Message of Aziru, your son, your servant: I fall at the feet of my father. May all be well with my father" (EA 158).

Later in the same letter, Aziru finds it suitable to emphasize the familial, respectful relationship that, in his view, should exist between the two correspondents: "Look, you are my father and my lord, and I am your son. The lands of Amurru are your lands, and my house is your house. Whatever your request may be, write here, and I shall indeed give your entire request."

A Letter of Ammunira of Beirut to the Pharaoh (EA 141)

Say to the king, my lord, my sun,
my divinity, the breath of my life:
Message of Ammunira,
Man of Beirut, your servant, the dust (gloss:
  'aparu) of your feet:

I fall at the feet of the king, my lord, my sun,
  my divinity,
the breath of my life, 7 and 7 times.
Furthermore, I have heard
the words of the tablet of the king, my lord,
my sun, my divinity, the breath of my life,
and the heart of your servant,
the dust of the feet of the king, my lord,
my sun and my divinity, the breath of my life,
  rejoices
very much, since the breath of the king, my
  lord,
my sun, my divinity, went out
toward his servant, the dust of his feet.

Furthermore, that the king,
my lord, my sun, wrote to his servant,
the dust of his feet:
"be prepared for
the troops of the king, your lord"—

I have heard very well,
and now I am prepared
with my horses and
with my chariots and with
everything
that there is with
the servant of the king, my lord, for
the (arrival of) the troops of the king, the lord.
May the troops of the king, my lord, my sun,
  my divinity,
smash the head of his enemies,
and may the two eyes of your servant watch
the life (= victory) of the king, my lord.

Furthermore, behold: The ⟨troops⟩ of the king,
  the lord,
my sun, my divinity, the breath of my life,
will treat his servant favorably.
Now, I am the servant of the king, the lord,
and the stool of his feet.
Here I guard
the city of the king, my lord, my sun,
the breath of my life,
and its wall (gloss: ḫōmītu)
until I see with (my own) two eyes
the troops of the king, my lord
  . . .

This obsequiousness is conventional for people making requests. Thus, Abdikheba of Jerusalem addresses even the scribe of the Egyptian king as his "lord" when, in a postscript to a letter to the pharaoh, he asks the scribe in Egypt to "bring good words to the king," that is, to present his case favorably before the pharaoh.

Formulaic phrases and sentences, whether in opening addresses or in the body of a letter, harmonize with the transmitted message, the correspondents tending to use suitable formulas that advance their immediate purposes. The correspondence mostly rehearses either of two recurring general themes. The first includes a variety of requests of the pharaoh, for example, to send goods and slaves or to prepare for a forthcoming Egyptian military campaign. The second includes the complaints or requests of Egyptian vassals for help against the rulers of neighboring cities, marauders, or the pharaoh's own commissioners. In the correspondence from the north, the threat of the rising Hittite Empire and of its allies from within the immediate vicinity is commonly bemoaned.

According to the Amarna letters from Palestine, the authority of some of the loyal and sincere vassals of the Egyptians in Canaan was progressively weakening. The most loyal, Ribhaddi (Rib-Haddu), ruler of Byblos in northern Canaan, fled to Beirut when his own people joined Aziru, the king of the rising state of Amurru. (Ironically, toward the end of his career, Ribhaddi was put back on the throne by none other than his—and the pharaoh's—bitterest enemy, Aziru of Amurru.) Ribhaddi's large correspondence with the Egyptian court is full of detailed complaints regarding his depressing situation, such as: "Why are you (the pharaoh) silent (and do not speak)?"; "all my cities have been captured"; "all the countries have joined the Apiru"; "there is war against me." Likewise, Abdikheba of Jerusalem states: "May the king take counsel concerning his land! All the land of the king is lost!" (EA 188).

Such sentences are so common to many of the Amarna letters and are couched in so similar a style that we can label them formulaic. Perhaps they were even taught as traditional epistolary material at Canaanite cuneiform scribal schools. It seems, then, that Canaanite scribes during the Amarna period were constrained in their linguistic usage by reliance on learned phraseology and epistolary patterning.

An illustration of this condition is available in a letter from the Egyptian king to the rebel Aziru. Full of accusation and threats, this letter was probably the last the pharaoh sent to a king who had transferred his allegiance to the Hittites. While the letter conveys to Aziru the pharaoh's anger, it also desperately seeks to bring Aziru back, to use a commonplace of the time, "under his feet." As is usual in letters from the pharaoh, a terminal formula ends this letter too, using the third person with reference to the pharaoh by his own scribes: "You should know that the king is wholesome like the sun in heaven. His numerous troops and chariots, from the upper land to the lower land, from the east (literally: rising of the sun) to the west (literally: setting of the sun), are very well" (EA 162).

Earlier in this letter, the pharaoh reminds Aziru of his former promise of loyalty to Egypt: "Have you not written to the king, your lord, thus: 'I am your servant like all the loyal (or: former) mayors who were in this city?'" Indeed, Aziru did once write such an admission. However, even then, Aziru never really intended to stand behind his words.

Once learned and absorbed, the tradition of cuneiform letter-writing permanently affected the compositional styles of Syria and Palestine. The scribes of Ugarit wrote letters in their own language that drew heavily on Akkadian phraseology. Letters written in first-millennium northwest Semitic languages such as Aramaic and Hebrew, although not entirely devoid of native formulas, generally exhibit contemporary epistolary conventions absorbed from Mesopotamian or Egyptian letter writing. In contrast to the majority of the Hebrew and Aramaic letters of the first millennium, the only Phoenician letter known to us (found at Saqqara in Egypt; sixth century), and possibly one of the Hebrew letter-fragments from Wadi Murabba'at near the Dead Sea (possibly early seventh century), still retain much of the older, basically Mesopotamian, epistolary style of the second millennium. This formulaic convention has further been adapted for dedications in some Hebrew (Kuntillet Ajrud) and Phoenician (Sarepta) traditions.

The Akkadian *lingua franca* that was used in Egypt and in Canaan is permeated with ele-

A Letter of the Pharaoh to Milkilu of Gezer (EA 369)

Amarna letter 369 is a copy of a letter that was to be sent from the pharaoh to Milkilu, ruler of the city-state of Gezer in southern Palestine. In this letter, Milkilu is asked to send the pharaoh forty "very beautiful women-cupbearers." These women served drinks at banquets, and—as we learn from other documents as well—Canaanites were sent to the Egyptian court to serve in this capacity.

> To Milkilu, Man of Gezer:
> Message of the king: I herewith send you this tablet
> to say
> to you: I herewith
> send you Khanya,
> the (inspector of) the stables of the troops,
> with everything (needed) to take
> beautiful woman-cupbearers (gloss: *šāqītu*):
> silver, gold, clothing (gloss: *malbaši*),
> carnelian, all (kinds of precious) stones, ebony chairs,
> likewise, everything beautiful.
> Total of 160 *diban* (an Egyptian measure of weight).
> Total: 40 women-cupbearers,
> 40 (shekels of) silver (being) the price of (each) woman-cupbearer.
> So send women-cupbearers
> very beautiful,
> that there will not be any one deficient among them,
> so that the king, your lord
> will say to you:
> "This is good,
> conforming to the order
> that he had sent you."
> You should know that
> the king is wholesome like the sun.
> His army, his chariots,
> his horses, are very well.
> Now, Amon (Amun) has placed
> the upper land
> (and) the lower land, the east (literally: rising of the sun)
> (and) the west (literally: setting of the sun), under
> the two feet of the king.

In this letter, some linguistic features suggest that it was not written by an Egyptian scribe, but by a Canaanite one. Additionally, it is exceptional among the Amarna letters from Egypt in that it includes glosses in two languages: Akkadian and Canaanite.

How would a scribe whose mother tongue is Canaanite write a letter to Canaan in a foreign language (Akkadian) and still make sure that the pharaoh's specific requests were understood if he lacked a term conveying their exact meanings? He would either borrow a word from his mother tongue or coin a neologism in Akkadian. In many cases, he would offer them as glosses translating Sumerian logograms. In this letter, the scribe seems to vacillate between the choices, finally resorting to one of each. In one case he took an Akkadian word, *šāqû* "cupbearer," and coined its feminine counterpart, namely *šāqītu*, a term otherwise unattested in Akkadian literature. In the second case, he turned to his own Canaanite dialect when he wrote: *malbašu* "clothing."

ments borrowed from native linguistic systems. It can be shown that in the Akkadian documents, written as well as received by the pharaoh or by his officials, there are several idioms or phrases that are conventional to Egyptian letter-writing. For example, Aziru of Amurru assures the Egyptians that he intends to arrive in Egypt promptly by using the following wording: "I shall arrive in peace, so that I may see the face of my lord, the beautiful (one)." Many centuries later, Aramaic letters found at Hermopolis in Egypt exhibit similar phraseology in their complimentary addresses: "I bless you before Ptah, that he may let me see your face in peace."

Among the Egyptian idiomatic conventions is the reference to the pharaoh's orders or message that uses the word "breath" (Akkadian *šāru* or *šēḫu*, Egyptian *ṯ'w*) in the often-repeated phrase, "the breath of the king." The following is an example taken from a letter sent by Aziru of Amurru: "My country and my brothers, the servants of the king, my lord, and the servants of Tutu, my lord, are very very glad, since the breath of the king, my lord, has come to me" (EA 164).

Another phrase is "the strong arm of the king," used by the scribes of Jerusalem and Tyre. The following is a well-known citation from a letter

Abdikheba of Jerusalem sent to the pharaoh: "The land of Jerusalem—neither my father, nor my mother gave (it) to me; the strong hand of the king gave (it) to me." The word for "arm" is written with a Sumerian logogram (šu, for Akkadian *qātu*), which, in its broader sense, means "hand." The scribe, demonstrating his awareness of the expanded meaning, specified its meaning by glossing this logogram with the Canaanite word for "arm," namely, *zorōʿ* (spelled *zu-ru-uḫ*; compare Hebrew *zĕrōaʿ*).

Although Akkadian, like other Semitic languages, uses "hand" in the sense of "authority," in the letters written in Tyre it is employed in a way that betrays Egyptian usage. Here are examples (EA 147, 149):

> —Here I guard Tyre, the principal city, for the king, my lord, until the strong hand of the king comes out toward me, to give water for me to drink and wood for my heating.
> —If the strong hand of the king comes, it will kill them.
> —My lord is the sun(-god)
> Who sets out upon the lands day after day,
> . . .
> Who sets the whole land in tranquillity by the strength of his hand (gloss: *ḥapši*),
> . . .

The Egyptian word *ḥapši* or "strong hand" (in Egyptian writing: *ḫpš*) explains the Sumerian logogram ZAG, denoting "right (hand)." The third example, in fact, is a plan that strings a series of Egyptian stereotypical sentiments. Indeed, the Tyre letters attest so many egyptianisms as to suggest that the scribe who wrote them was a speaker of the Egyptian language who seems also to have had intimate knowledge of Egyptian literature.

ECHOES OF AMARNA: CULTURAL SYNCRETISM IN THE BIBLE

The Mesopotamian metaphor "right hand," itself molded by the Egyptian notion of "strong hand," is recalled in the Hebrew Bible (Exodus 15:6): "Your right hand, O Lord, is majestic in strength; your right hand, O Lord, shatters the enemy."

Perhaps the most conspicuous comparison between Amarna speech-forms and Biblical Hebrew verses may be found in the following statements, cited from a letter from Aziru: "What else should I seek? I seek the beautiful face of the king, my lord," and from the Hebrew Bible (Psalms 27:8): "'Come,' my heart has said, 'seek my face.' I will seek your face, O Lord."

Another example may be extracted from a letter of a son of Aziru to the pharaoh, while Aziru was detained in Egypt (EA 169):

> You can give me life,
> and you can put me to death.
> I look at your face:
> it is you who are my lord.

The rhythmic nature of this passage suggests that it depends on a common saying, which could definitely have been taken from indigenous colloquial sources. A similar idea, no doubt deriving from the same cultural stock, is available in biblical poetry (Deuteronomy 32:39):

> See then that I, I am He.
> There is no god beside me.
> I put to death and I keep alive,
> If I wound, I will heal:
> No one can rescue from my grasp.

While both the divine pharaoh and the god of Israel are perceived as having the capability of healing, that would not be the case with the king of Israel. Nevertheless, Jehoram, king of Israel, falls back on this concept when he is quoted as saying (2 Kings 5:7): "Am I god to kill and to make alive?"

Another example is the following, cited from a letter from Tagi, ruler of Gath-Carmel in central Palestine, to the Egyptian king (EA 264):

> Whether we ascend to heaven (gloss:
>   *šamêma*),
> whether we descend to earth—
> our head (gloss: *rōšunu*) is in your hands.

Because of its rhythmical nature and metaphoric idioms, this statement too seems to rely on a popular saying. It may be noteworthy in this respect that two key words of this saying, namely "heaven" and "our head," were glossed with Canaanite words. Two biblical verses are comparable to this passage:

> If I climb up to heaven, you are there:
> If I make my bed in Sheol, again I find you.
>
> (Psalm 139:8)

> If they dig down to Sheol,
> From there shall my hand take them;
> If they climb up to heaven,
> From there will I bring them.
>
> (Amos 9:2)

CUNEIFORM LEARNING AND THE SPREAD OF MESOPOTAMIAN CULTURE TO THE WEST

Phrases and metaphors, proverbs and similes, are capable of straightforward transfer between societies in contact. Linguistic structures, and especially the internal units of the individual words, that is, the syntax and the morphology of a language, are less easily transferred. Yet, even in the domain of the most intricate linguistic structural strata, namely its sentence structure

---

A Letter of Baʿlushiptu of Gezer to the Pharaoh (EA 292)

This letter is a typical example of Canaanite letters to the pharaoh, where a local ruler informs the Egyptian king of the fulfillment of his demands, and also applies for help against mischiefs he has been suffering from both local bandits and the pharaoh's own officers. In his endeavor to submit obediently to the pharaoh, his master, the scribe uses especially elaborate prostration formulas which draw their phraseology from local practice.

Say to the king, my lord,
my divinity, my sun:
Message of Baʿlushiptu, your servant,
the dust of your two feet:
I fall at the feet of the king, my lord,
my divinity, my sun, seven times
(and) seven times.
I looked here
and I looked there,
and there was no light; yet
I looked at
the king, my lord, and there was light.
A brick may move off
from beneath its companion;
but I shall not move off
from beneath the two feet of
the king, my lord. I have heard
the words that the king,
my lord, wrote to his servant:
"Guard your commissioner
and guard the towns of
the king, your lord." Here

I guard and
listen day
and night to the words of
the king, my lord. May the king,
my lord, be informed regarding his servant:
There is war against me
from the mountain, so I built (gloss: *banīti*)
one place—its name is Mankhate—
to prepare for
the troops of the king, my lord,
and, behold, Maya took it
from my hands, and installed
his commissioner therein.
So order Reʿanap,
my commissioner, that he return
the town to me, so that
it be prepared for
the troops of the king, my lord.
Furthermore, note the deeds of
Piʾiya, son of Gulate,
against Gezer, the maidservant
of the king, my lord: How many
days does he rob her!
Hence she has become like
a damaged pot
because of him. From
the mountain
people are redeemed for 30 (shekels of) silver, but from
Piʾiya for a hundred (shekels of) silver. Be attentive to these words of your servant!

and word formation, the language used for the Canaano-Egyptian correspondence has undergone numerous mutations. Peeling away, one by one, the cultural, literary, and linguistic layers in the Amarna material allows us to draw the following conclusions:

1. There is a correlation between the provenance of a letter and its linguistic structure. In general, the farther south in Canaan an Amarna letter originated, the more remote is its language from Akkadian, and the closer it is to the Canaanite vernacular of that region. Thus, a scribe of Amurru, who was located just north or northeast of the Canaanite city Gubla (Byblos)—although making much usage of local phraseology and idioms—would use a language which is very much like other Akkadian dialects, of both the western periphery and the core of Mesopotamia. By contrast, a scribe working for the ruler of Gath in southern Palestine uses cuneiform script to write a language which, in its grammar (rather than its lexicon), is almost wholly Canaanite.

2. Toward the second half of the second millennium, schools of Akkadian of various traditions were widespread all over the ancient Near East. There is ample evidence that such schools existed throughout the western Mesopotamian periphery from Khatti in the north, through Ugarit and Emar, to Egypt in the south. In all these schools, direct contact with contemporary Mesopotamian and other major centers of cuneiform learning resulted in a relatively continuous renewing of the linguistic resources. This is suggested by the very nature of the Peripheral Akkadian dialects attested in cuneiform tablets from that period, as well as by the nature of the educational cuneiform material found in the respective sites.

In contrast, the linguistic data drawn from the Canaanite Amarna letters show stagnation and reliance on older Akkadian layers. One may therefore wonder whether the cuneiform schools which are known to have existed in Palestine at about the same period were indeed used to educate local scribes in contemporary Akkadian. The bulk of evidence allows us to suppose that the Canaanite scribes were taught not (or not only) contemporary Akkadian, but mainly the mixed language they were using. Indeed, Canaano-Akkadian, or to coin a suggestive label,

"Amarnaic," seems to have been an institutionalized diplomatic language. Indeed, a letter in Amarnaic written on a clay cylinder from Tagi of Gath-Carmel to Lab'aya of Shechem, discovered at Beth-Shan, proves than Amarna Akkadian was the vehicle also for internal communication.

3. The emergence of such a language, and especially its institutionalization, suggests restricted contemporaneous contacts with the Mesopotamian core. This observation is supported by historical data. The area of Syria and Palestine represented by letters written in Amarnaic, that is, the land of Canaan, was part of the Egyptian Empire of the Eighteenth Dynasty, and, especially from the time of Thutmose III, was—at least with regard to independence in terms of cultural politics—virtually isolated from the northern political and cultural powers with which it had been in contact before. This detachment from Mesopotamia proper and from the less remote centers where Akkadian was used allowed the surfacing of local linguistic and cultural affinities. In turn, these cultural traits resulted in the emergence of a unique corpus of cultural-linguistic artifacts such as the Amarna letters, thus allowing us a glance not only into the history of Syro-Palestine during the Amarna period, but also into its linguistic, its sociolinguistic, and its cultural life.

BIBLIOGRAPHY

Background and General

W. F. ALBRIGHT, "The Amarna Letters from Palestine," in chapter 20 of *The Cambridge Ancient History*, vol. 2, pt. 2: *History of the Middle East and the Aegean Region c. 1380–1000 B.C.*, edited by I. E. S. EDWARDS, C. J. GADD, N. G. L. HAMMOND, and E. SOLLBERGER, (3rd ed. 1975); DONALD REDFORD, *Akhenaten the Heretic King* (1984); DIETZ OTTO EDZARD, "Amarna und die Archive seiner Korrespondenten zwischen Ugarit und Gaza," in *Biblical Archaeology Today* (1985); and CYRIL ALDRED, *Akhenaten, King of Egypt* (1988).

Text Editions and Translations

J. A. KNUDTZON, *Die El-Amarna-Tafeln* (1915); ANSON F. RAINEY, *El-Amarna Tablets 359–379* (1970; 2nd rev. ed., 1978); and WILLIAM L. MORAN, *The Amarna Letters* (1992).

Epistolography

ERKKI SALONEN, *Die Gruss- und Höflichkeitsformeln in babylonisch-assyrischen Briefen* (1967); and F. BRENT KNUTSON, "Cuneiform Letter Writing," *Semeia* 22, *Studies in Ancient Letter Writing* (1982).

Style, Phraseology, Idiom, and the Lexicon

ANTON JIRKU, "Kanaʿanäische Psalmenfragmente in der vorisraelitischen Zeit Palästinas und Syriens," *Journal of Biblical Literature* 52 (1933); W. F. ALBRIGHT, "The Egyptian Correspondence of Abimilki, Prince of Tyre," *Journal of Egyptian Archaeology* 23 (1937); FRANZ M. TH. DE LIAGRE BÖHL, "Hymnisches und Rhythmisches in den Amarnabriefen aus Kanaan," in *Opera Minora* (1953); STANLEY GEVIRTZ, "On Canaanite Rhetoric: The Evidence of the Amarna Letters from Tyre," *Orientalia* 42 (1973); MARIO LIVERANI, "Political Lexicon and Political Ideologies in the Amarna Letters," *Berytus* 3 (1983); DANIEL SIVAN, *Grammatical Analysis and Glossary of the Northwest Semitic Vocables in Akkadian Texts of the 15th–13th c. B.C. from Canaan and Syria* (1984); RICHARD S. HESS, "Hebrew Psalms and Amarna Correspondence from Jerusalem: Comparisons and Implications," *Zeitschrift für die Alttestamentliche Wissenschaft* 101 (1989); and MARIO LIVERANI, "A Seasonal Pattern for the Amarna Letters," in *Lingering over Words: Studies in Ancient Near Eastern Literature in Honor of* William L. Moran, edited by TZVI ABUSCH, JOHN HUEHNERGARD, and PIOTR STEINKELLER (1990).

Grammatical Studies

FRANZ M. TH. BÖHL, *Die Sprache der Amarnabriefe mit besonderer Berücksichtigung der Kanaanismen* (1909); WILLIAM L. MORAN, "A Syntactical Study of the Dialect of Byblos as Reflected in the Amarna Tablets" (Ph.D. diss., Johns Hopkins, 1950); ANSON F. RAINEY, "Reflections on the Suffix Conjugation in West-Semitized Amarna Tablets," *Ugarit-Forschungen* 5 (1973), also "Morphology and the Prefix Tenses of West-Semitized el-ʿAmarna Tablets," *Ugarit-Forschungen* 7 (1975); and SHLOMO IZREʾEL, "The Gezer Letters of the el-Amarna Archive—Linguistic Analysis," *Israel Oriental Studies* 8 (1978), and *Amurru Akkadian: A Linguistic Study* (1991).

Scribal Education

A. LEO OPPENHEIM, "A Note on the Scribes in Mesopotamia," in *Studies in Honor of Benno Landsberger on His Seventy-fifth Birthday, April 21, 1965* (1965); PINḤAS ARTZI, "Studies in the Library of the Amarna Archive," in *Bar-Ilan Studies in Assyriology Dedicated to Pinḥas Artzi*, edited by JACOB KLEIN and AARON SKAIST (1990); and AARON DEMSKI, "The Education of Canaanite Scribes in the Mesopotamian Cuneiform Tradition," in *Bar-Ilan Studies in Assyriology Dedicated to Pinḥas Artzi*, edited by JACOB KLEIN and AARON SKAIST (1990).

SEE ALSO **The History of Ancient Egypt: An Overview** (Part 5, Vol. II) and **The History of Ancient Syria and Palestine: An Overview** (Part 5, Vol. II).

Autobiographies in Ancient Western Asia

EDWARD L. GREENSTEIN

THERE IS NO AUTOBIOGRAPHY as such in the ancient world, if we describe "autobiography" as the retrospective interpretation of the author's own life—a contemplative self-scrutiny of the past. Modern critics suggest a variety of theories by which to understand and classify autobiography, but there is a general consensus that it is not a specifically definable literary genre. Autobiographical styles vary, and some authors even choose discourse in the third person rather than the first person. There are, however, ancient texts that seem autobiographical, in which first-person narrators recount what they represent as parts of their own lives.

We may therefore speak of "autobiographical" texts in the ancient world, and in the ancient Near East in particular, without implying that such texts tell the actual history of a life. (See "Ancient Egyptian Autobiographies and Biographies" earlier in this volume.) Ancient Mesopotamian royal inscriptions, which typically commemorate a king's achievements or chronicle a campaign, and ancient Egyptian tomb inscriptions, which typically trace a career and highlight scenes from a life, might then be viewed as autobiographical. An important qualification is that these ancient texts were nearly all the direct product of scribes, not of the autobiographical subjects themselves.

The term "autobiography" and its German equivalent, *Selbstbiographie*, were introduced around the turn of the nineteenth century to describe full-scale personal accounts such as Benvenuto Cellini's *Vita* (Life), which is usually referred to as his *Autobiography* (1558–1563) and is often held to be the first true instance of a quintessentially modern genre. On the other hand, many critics consider the first autobiography to be the *Confessions* of Augustine (early fifth century CE). The introspective nature of Augustine's work is often taken as a sine qua non of genuine autobiography. If that criterion were strictly applied, few ancient near eastern autobiographical texts would meet it. The Hellenistic novels that began appearing in the first century BCE—largely romances about star-crossed lovers—do feature monologues, but these shed no light on a character's inner thought; rather, they display the speaker's rhetorical virtuosity.

Confessional and contemplative modes of expression characterize such Hebrew Bible literature as some of the (anonymous) Psalms and passages in the prophets (especially Jeremiah 14–15), the book of Job (especially chapters 29–31), and Ecclesiastes (Qoheleth). Of these, only the prophetic passages are at all autobiographical, and the few prophetic passages that externalize inner feeling capture moments, not a life story.

Inner thought is, nevertheless, not altogether absent from autobiographical texts in the ancient Near East. The first-person speaker in the biblical book of Nehemiah (early fourth century) recounts how a report of the ruined state of the walls of Jerusalem moved him to tears and then action, as he obtained royal permission to return to Judea and supervise the necessary repairs (Nehemiah 1–2). His pleasure at finding acceptance among his people and his efforts to overcome waves of local opposition (chapters 2, 4–6) resemble the story pattern of Idrimi. In the two texts we shall survey here, the story of Idrimi, a royal inscription from fifteenth-century Syria, and the inscription of Azatiwada, a royal-style inscription from eighth-century-BCE Asia Minor, the first-person speaker discloses some of his motives and intentions. This is particularly so of the extraordinarily personal account of Idrimi.

Subcategories and Features of Autobiography

It is useful, at this point, to differentiate between autobiography and memoir and to delineate the various, often mixed purposes that are attributed to the former. Autobiography seeks to render an account of a life that has reached a certain peak of development (e.g., old age) or achievement. As we have seen, autobiographies in the modern sense may serve as vehicles for self-scrutiny and meditation or for self-discovery. However, they may also construct and project a certain self-image; and it is this feature of the genre which comes closer to the functions that typify autobiographical texts in the ancient Near East, especially in inscriptions of the royal type. There, as elsewhere, they tend to publicize, commemorate, or justify what their subjects have done for the sake of gaining acceptance or legitimacy, appreciation or sympathy.

A famous example is the great stela inscription of King Hammurabi of Babylon (eighteenth century), which includes his so-called code of laws. In this text—one of the lengthiest near eastern royal inscriptions—Hammurabi recounts how the various leading deities entrusted him with "shepherding" the people of Mesopotamia and with promulgating justice among them. In the prologue to the laws, the king dwells on the shrines he refurbished, and in the epilogue as well as the prologue he represents his 282 laws as evidence that he has performed his duty to promote justice and well-being. The self-legitimizing character of the inscription is reflected in such lines as these:

With the mighty weapon with which (the gods) Zababa and Inanna have endowed me, with the wisdom that Ea has allotted me, with the ability that Marduk has given me, I have rooted out enemies above and below; I have ended warfare; I have made the land prosper; I have made the people of the country lie down in towns—I did not allow any to terrorize them. (col. 24, ll. 22–39)

The whole would seem calculated to impress the gods with what the king has done on their behalf and, vicariously, for Mesopotamia. Typically, the inscription ends with a series of divinely dispensed curses on anyone who would tamper with the text. (See also "Legal and Social Institutions of Ancient Mesopotamia" in Part 4, Vol. I, and "King Hammurabi of Babylon" in Part 5, Vol. II.)

In contrast to such "autobiographical" characterizations, memoirs present a recollection and understanding of significant events that one has observed. While the memoir genre is little attested in the ancient Near East, to consider it highlights a perpetual problem in handling the ancient autobiographical texts. The issue raised concerns the extent to which such texts can be considered recollected memories of events. After all, they are for the most part patently self-serving and were composed by scribes who were commissioned to write them. In general, on the basis of comparative documentary and archaeological evidence, historians tend to trust the "who," "where," and "when" of the autobiographical materials, while remaining cautious concerning the "what" and "how" and skeptical of the "why." Each document must be individually assessed.

In the end it may not be clear whether texts like the inscription of Idrimi are even truly autobiographical, that is, composed or commissioned by the subjects themselves. The autobiographical text of Adad-guppi (mid sixth century), mother of the Babylonian king Nabonidus, for example, opens in the first person and relates at length how her faithful service to the moon-god Sin and other deities was rewarded by a long and healthy life. The next part of the text, however, describes her death and burial in the third person, leading one to suspect that she may not have written the first part either.

The Egyptian *Story of Sinuhe* (circa 1900), the first-person tale of a runaway statesman who prospers in Syria and is invited back to the Egyptian royal court, like the story of Idrimi, includes several folkloristic elements and resembles in part the story of Moses in Midian (Exodus 2–4). The Sinuhe narrative evinces authentic ethnographic detail. Yet, the folktale qualities of the text, together with the fact that the story is told posthumously, strengthen the impression that this unique autobiographical narrative is essentially fiction. Similarly, scholars differ on whether the *Report of Wenamun* (circa 1100), the first-person tale of an Egyptian emissary's mishaps in Lebanon, is an actual diplomatic brief or a historical romance.

Typology

Analysis of the form and content of "autobiographical" materials can reveal consistent typological features of the genre. Indeed, for various purposes some ancient near eastern authors adopted such a style for clearly pseudepigraphical works. Tremper Longman has investigated fifteen Akkadian (Mesopotamian Semitic) autobiographical prose texts that he regards as fictional, including Idrimi's (some were written much later than their subjects and one is of the god Marduk). Longman divides each narrative into three parts: a "first-person introduction," a "first-person narrative history," and a variable third section that may indicate something of the document's purpose. For each of these texts, there are four possible endings: the invocation of a blessing on the subject or a curse against someone else; the mention of cultic donations the subject has made (which would benefit the priests of the recipient shrines); a didactic lesson drawn from the subject's experiences; and a prediction or "prophecy" delivered by the speaker. The last two types of fictional autobiography would ostensibly enhance the conviction of their messages by ascribing them to authoritative figures. For example, Longman compares the biblical book of Ecclesiastes, whose somewhat cynical advice for living, presented in first-person discourse, claims authority on the basis of experience and on the apparent identification of the speaker with the legendarily wise King Solomon.

Longman classifies fictional Akkadian autobiography according to these four types of endings.

Alternatively, there are other possible ways to group ancient near eastern autobiographical texts: the nature of their narratives (chronological or selective, private or public, etc.), the degree of their confessional tone, their apparent motivation, or the kind of self-image that they project. From a formal aspect, the Idrimi and Azatiwada inscriptions both conclude with invocations of blessings (though there is a significant twist in that of Idrimi). With respect to their narratives, however, while Idrimi relates a tale of personal setback and comeuppance before recounting his civic accomplishments, Azatiwada begins at a point of triumph and almost immediately memorializes the diverse and substantial achievements of his regime. Indeed, the apparent purpose of the Azatiwada inscription is memorialization, while the purpose of Idrimi's autobiography would appear to be something else.

THE INSCRIPTION OF IDRIMI

The text of the inscription is incised on 104 lines across the front of a statue of its subject, Idrimi, king of Alalakh, an ancient city in northwest Syria, modern Tell Atchana. The statue is 41 inches (103 centimeters) tall, sculpted in white stone, which was polished, inscribed, and (originally) colorfully painted. Idrimi sits face forward, looking solemn, his right hand over his heart, his left hand in his lap. He is wearing a headdress and robe. The statue was set into a stone throne, which was flanked by lions in royal fashion and placed on a stone pedestal. When the statue was excavated by the British archaeologist Leonard Woolley in 1939, it appeared deliberately buried, albeit in pieces, next door to its chamber in a temple when that temple was destroyed about 1200 BCE. Woolley observed that the statue was treated like that of a god. There are reasons to think that the statue was made as a cult object and the inscription was composed to justify that function.

The inscription is written in cuneiform characters in Akkadian, the language of diplomacy and culture during the second millennium. Its language and writing indicate the influence of Hurrian, spoken in the then-regnant Mitanni

Upper part of the statue of Idrimi found at Alalakh. The long inscription covering the body details events in this ruler's life. BRITISH MUSEUM, LONDON

Empire, but there are also several indications of West Semitic (Canaanite) language and literary style. It would seem that the scribe, whose name is given as Sharruwa, was Hurrian and that he made use of West Semitic literary conventions. The local language was probably West Semitic, and so is Idrimi's name, which may mean "(The God) is my help" (the suffix -mi stands instead of a divine name). Unfortunately, the inscription was written inconsistently and copied onto the stone with less than complete professionalism. For those reasons and because of some linguistic problems, certain passages are difficult to interpret.

History and Purpose

There was an Idrimi, king of Alalakh, and we have a contemporary treaty between him and Pilliya, king probably of Kizzuwatna (Cilicia), a territory in south-central Anatolia, north of Alalakh. The treaty mentions Parrattarna, the Mitanni king who was overlord to Idrimi and Pilliya. This Parrattarna figures prominently in the statue inscription. A royal seal bearing Idrimi's name was used by his son Niqmepa. Since Niqmepa apparently built the palace in Alalakh that is datable to the second half of the fifteenth century, we can place Idrimi at about 1475. For independent reasons, we can date Parrattarna to the same time. (See "The Kingdom of Mitanni in Second-Millennium Upper Mesopotamia" in Part 5, Vol. II.)

The statue inscription concludes, "Thirty years I was king. My achievements I have inscribed on my statue" (ll. 102–103). The inscription is autobiographical in character but not strictly autobiography; it may have been commissioned by Idrimi, but it was composed after his death. The scribe, Sharruwa, is known to have worked in the employ of Idrimi's son and royal successor Niqmepa. Sharruwa, who says that he wrote the text of the statue (ll. 98–99), in an extraordinarily peculiar manner invokes the gods' blessing of life on himself at the point where it is customary to invoke a blessing for the king (ll. 99–101). This oddity may be explained by the hypothesis that Idrimi was dead and Sharruwa had provided the statue and composed the inscription as an object of veneration, perhaps in an ancestral cult. Idrimi would no longer need divine blessing, and Sharruwa would merit divine favor for his piety. Indeed, Sharruwa describes himself as "the servant of the storm-god, the sun-god, the moon-god, and (the god) AN.ŠUR."

It would be no accident, then, that the last of Idrimi's achievements that the inscription commemorates is his restoration of the cultic rites of Alalakh "just as . . . our fathers performed them" (ll. 87–90). Idrimi says that he himself "continually performed" these rites and that he entrusted them to his son, Adad/Teshub-nirari (ll. 90–91). Throughout the inscription Idrimi seeks to restore the institutions of his fathers, which his brothers would not endeavor to do. The theme of respect for the "fathers" sits well with the notion that Idrimi should be enshrined for ancestor worship. The inscription's conclusion supports this interpretation. In it, he bids that people "look upon" his record of achievement and requests, "And let them continually bless me" (ll. 103–104).

Content and Form

The inscription may be divided broadly into six parts: (1) an introduction of "Idrimi, son of Ilim-ilimma" in the first person, which oddly does not identify him at the outset as king but as "the servant of the storm-god (probably the Hurrian deity Teshub), (the goddess) Khepat, and (the goddess) Shaushga, the lady of the city of Alalakh, my lady" (ll. 1–2); (2) a lengthy narrative (ll. 3–91); (3) an invocation of curses on anyone who would alter or efface the inscription (ll. 92–94); (4) an invocation of blessing on Sharruwa the scribe (ll. 98–101); (5) a first-person summary (ll. 102–103); and (6) an appeal for veneration (ll. 103–104).

Overall the structure of the text conforms to that of a Mesopotamian royal inscription. Two features, however, set this inscription apart, besides those items mentioned above. The lengthy narrative of Idrimi's adventures in obtaining and securing his throne is unlike any Mesopotamian text and has its closest parallels in the Egyptian *Story of Sinuhe* and the biblical stories of Jacob, Joseph, Moses, Jephthah, David, and Nehemiah. Second, the many parts of the inscription display a remarkable thematic coherence, reinforced by the recurrence of motifs and key terms. What Idrimi does for the people of Alalakh may be interpreted as a direct response to his own experience.

Analysis and Interpretation

The Flight Idrimi's story begins with what folklorists informed by the work of Vladimir Propp would call an "initial situation" (which prompts an ensuring action): "In the city of Aleppo, the house of my father, there was an evil" (ll. 3–4). Idrimi does not specify the nature and cause of this "evil" here, but a plausible explanation emerges at a later point in the inscription: "Now for seven years Parrattarna . . . was hostile toward me" (ll. 42–44). The Mitanni king may have conquered Aleppo (ancient Halab), which lies east of Alalakh and closer to Mitanni, and deposed—and perhaps even executed—Idrimi's father. Since Idrimi will govern Alalakh only at the pleasure of Parrattarna, it would be politic of Idrimi to omit from his tale the sorry circumstances of the evil in Aleppo. In

reaction to the evil, he and his brothers fled to Emar (modern Meskene), located directly southeast of Aleppo, where Idrimi's family, he says, had relatives.

The Theme of Home Emar is the first of five places where Idrimi bides his time and builds a power base. He and his brothers "stay" in Emar for an undefined period (ll. 6–8). The verb "to stay," which is repeated here, also means "to dwell." This verb, as well as cognate nouns, functions as a *Leitwort* ("guiding word"), or term whose recurrence conveys a central theme: the importance of having a place to stay or dwell—a home. The verb is also employed (in a West Semitic usage) to describe the location of Ammiya: "In the land of Canaan the city of Ammiya is *situated*" (ll. 19–20). That is where Idrimi's compatriots from Aleppo and elsewhere "dwell" (ll. 20–23). That is also where Idrimi "stayed" among the ʿApiru "for seven years" (a round number). The verb is used no fewer than six times in a passage in which Idrimi boasts that he made the "dwelling" of those who had dwellings "secure" (ll. 84–85) and provided dwellings for those who had none (ll. 85–86). Idrimi's concern to provide safe habitations for his subjects is similar to concerns expressed in conventional royal inscriptions, including those of Hammurabi and Azatiwada. However, this civic achievement of Idrimi is made particularly poignant because it is preceded by a narrative in which the hero has been dislocated from his home and must travel from place to place to prepare and launch his comeback. The inhabitants of Idrimi's realm will not be homeless, as he was for so long.

Homelessness and alienation (as in the Egyptian *Story of Sinuhe*), as well as humiliation, are the personal ills Idrimi explicitly seeks to remedy. He says, "My brothers who were older than I stayed with me, and the things that I was thinking no one was thinking" (ll. 7–9). Idrimi formulates his plan in a quasi-proverbial style: "One who [seeks? possesses?] the house of his father is the foremost, great son; and one who [stays?] among the sons of the city of Emar is a servant" (ll. 10–12). Reflecting a literary motif well known from such Hebrew Bible stories as

From the Story of Idrimi (ll. 1–63)

(1–2) I, Idrimi, son of Ilim-ilimma, servant of [the storm-god] Teshub, Khepat, and Shaushga, the lady of the city of Alalakh, my lady—

(3–6) in the city of Aleppo, the house of my father, there was an evil, and we fled to the people of the city of Emar, relatives of my mother, and we stayed in the city of Emar.

(7–9) My brothers who were older than I stayed with me, and the things that I was thinking no one was thinking. (10–12)—said I: "One who . . . the house of his father is the foremost, great son, and one who [stays] among the sons of the city of Emar is a servant."

(13–17) My horse, my chariot, and my groom—I took them, and I crossed the land of the desert, and I entered the midst of the troops of Sutu. With them I spent the night in the midst of my covered chariot. (17–20) On the next day I set out and went to the land of Canaan. In the land of Canaan the city of Ammiya is situated. (20–23) In the city of Ammiya sons of the city of Aleppo, sons of the land of Mukishkhe (Mukish), sons of the land of Ni'i (Niya), and sons of the land of Ama'e dwell. (24–27) When they saw that I was the son of their lord, they gathered to me. Thus did I say: "I have been made great, I have been appointed."

(27–28) And in the midst of the troops of the ʿApiru (Khabiru) I stayed for seven years. (28–30) I released birds and I inspected sheep (entrails), and in the seventh year (the storm-god) Teshub turned back to me.

(30–31) And I built ships. The auxiliary (?) troops—I boarded them on the ships. (32–34) And I proceeded by sea to the land of Mukishkhe, and I reached dry land at Mount Cassius (Khazzi), and I went up. (35–36) When my land heard about me, they brought oxen and sheep to me; (36–39) and in one day, like one man, the land of Ni'i, the land of Ama'e, the land of Mukishkhe, and the city of Alalakh, my city, turned back to me. (39–42) When my brothers (i.e., allies) heard, they came before me. When my brothers allied with me, I confirmed them as my brothers.

(42–44) Now for seven years Parrattarna, the mighty king, king of the troops of Hurri, was hostile toward me. (45–48) In the seventh year to Parrattarna the king, king of the troops of Hurri, I sent Anwanda, and I related the treaty terms of my fathers, when my fathers were allied with him. (49–51) And our words were pleasing to the kings of the troops of Hurri, and they established between them a binding oath. (51–54) When the mighty king heard the treaty terms of our predecessors and the oath between them, he respected the oath because of the words of the oath and because of our treaty terms. (54–56) He accepted my tribute, and I conveyed (?) (gestures of) loyalty, which were substantial, I made many oblations, and I restored a lost house to him. (57–58) As a vassal, in loyalty, I swore a binding (oath) to him, and I became king over the city of Alalakh.

(59) Kings to my right and to my left went up against me, (60–63) and just as they had piled up on the ground corpse (?) upon corpse (?) of my fathers, I made piles on the ground, and their warfare I brought to an end.

those of Jacob, Joseph, and David, Idrimi is a younger brother whose ambition drives him to surpass his elders.

Idrimi's reference here to "the house of his father" is significant in the context of this inscription. Idrimi first speaks of Aleppo as "the house of my father" (l. 3). When Idrimi ends his exile and gains local power as a vassal of Parrattarna, he says that by taking control of Alalakh and submitting to the Hurrian's domination, he "restored a lost house to him" (l. 56). The return of an estate, a "house," is obviously of paramount importance to Idrimi. After fighting off his enemies and collecting booty, the first thing he does

in Alalakh is to build a palace, a "house" (l. 80). This edifice forms a neat contrast to the "covered chariot" in which he spent the night among the seminomadic Sutu (ll. 16–17). The verb used for "spending the night" is cognate with the word for "house." Idrimi replaces his makeshift housing with a permanent home.

Idrimi probably could not return to his native Aleppo, because it was closer to the Hurrian power center and was ruled directly by Mitanni. But Idrimi would seem to regard Alalakh as an adopted home. He anticipates its centrality for him by naming the goddess of Alalakh in the introduction and refers to it redundantly and possessively as "the city of Alalakh, my city" (ll. 38, 78) and to his domain as "my land" (ll. 35, 84, 86) and "my cities" (l. 87).

The Return　From Emar, Idrimi embarks on a series of adventures whose potential drama is hardly exploited and whose fantastic character is rendered matter-of-factly. The narrative interest is subordinated to the steps by which Idrimi goes home and establishes himself as king. The end, more than the means, controls the narrative pace. Leaving Emar, "my horse, my chariot, and my groom—I took them, and I crossed the land of the desert"—a long and dangerous journey—"and I entered the midst of the troops of Sutu" (ll.13–16). The fact that Idrimi made such a trip virtually alone is pure bravado. One suspects that the entire episode is contrived to impress the reader with Idrimi's heroism. Since nothing eventful occurs, the stay among the relatively wild Sutu would seem gratuitous, a rite of passage demonstrating Idrimi's courage and stamina.

"On the next day" he sets out for the land of Canaan. It is here, in the city of Ammiya, near the Mediterranean coast about a hundred miles south of Alalakh, that Idrimi is joined by other displaced compatriots, who recognize him as the son of their former king. He boasts, "Thus did I say: 'I have been made great, I have been appointed' " (ll. 26–27). The verb "I have been made great" echoes the sentiment he felt when he was in Emar that the one who reclaims his heritage is "great" (l. 11).

Recognition　Idrimi sees in this initial recognition by his fellow exiles confirmation of his quest. Similarly, when Idrimi makes an amphibious landing up the Syrian coast, near Alalakh, his people unanimously offer both material and political support (ll. 35–39). That the entire population came out for him "in one day" is improbable as history but is an attested literary convention. To be recognized and accepted in stages is a pattern that is reminiscent of biblical narratives in which Moses returns from Midian to Egypt and David amasses support as he rises to power. Idrimi's triumph reaches its climax when Parrattarna agrees to reaffirm the historical treaty terms between Idrimi's dynasty and the

Hurrians (ll. 51–58). Idrimi does not—perhaps cannot—suppress his vassal status, but it is this that enables him to go home and reign as king.

A Favorable Turn　In Canaan, Idrimi dwells among the 'Apiru, a class of landless people who are known to have worked as mercenaries. (See "Administration of the State in Canaan and Ancient Israel" in Part 4, Vol. I.) Jephthah and David, too, are said to draw support from the dislocated (Judges 11:3; 1 Samuel 22:2). Idrimi, reminding us of his piety, seeks a divine omen that the time is ripe for his return: "I released birds and I inspected sheep (entrails), and in the seventh year the storm-god turned back to me" (ll. 28–30). The turning-back of the god follows the turning-back of his people; together they pave the way for his own turning-back to the land of Mukishkhe (l. 77).

Idrimi accomplishes his initial return by building ships, boarding troops, and sailing to the land of Mukishkhe (ll. 32–34). Idrimi enjoys the support not only of his people but of other local rulers, too, significantly called his "brothers": "When my brothers heard, they came before me. When my brothers allied with me, I confirmed them as my brothers" (ll. 39–42).

It is then that Idrimi relates the background of the treaty with his Hurrian overlord. He claims, "For seven years Parrattarna . . . was hostile to me" (ll. 42–44). It is unclear whether these seven years are the same as those in which, and perhaps because of which, Idrimi remained in exile among the 'Apiru. The passage, in any event, provides a transition to the next part of the narrative.

Another Setback　As soon as Idrimi is enthroned in Alalakh and truly returns home, kings from areas surrounding him attack (l. 59). Hostilities doubling those that caused Idrimi's initial flight threaten to dislodge the hero again. This time, however, Idrimi avenges in kind the treatment his predecessors received: "And just as they had piled up on the ground corpse (?) upon corpse (?) of my fathers, I made piles on the ground, and their warfare I brought to an end" (ll. 60–63).

Enjoying the Spoils　His military prowess proved, Idrimi attacks "seven cities" under the protection of the Hittites, the dominant power in Anatolia and rival of the Hurrians (ll. 65–68). It is not stated whether Idrimi initiated the campaign preemptively, under orders from Parrattarna, or for the spoil he would remove. What Idrimi does assert is that no one dared oppose him: "The land of Khatti did not muster and did not come against me. I did according to my heart" (ll. 70–72). The fugitive who braved the hinterland alone nobly leads his army; he shares the loot with one and all: "I captured captives, and I took their goods, their possessions, and their property; and I divided (it) among my auxiliary troops, my brothers, and my friends" (ll. 72–76). His own share he will use to reconstruct Alalakh. Idrimi, however, is hardly selfless. He does not omit to say, "I made my throne like the throne of kings" (l. 81), and his statue has him indeed ensconced on a royal throne.

The Curse The curse against anyone who would efface the statue resembles Assyrian maledictions. But it conveys an unusual poignancy, given the background of the narrative, with its near obsession of restoring continuity with the "fathers" and with Idrimi's appointment of his son to attend to the cult—including presumably the veneration of Idrimi: "Whoever alters or erases(?) it (i.e., this statue of mine), may the storm-god, lord of heaven and earth, and the great gods annihilate his name and his seed from his land" (ll. 96–98).

Summing Up Idrimi's successes confirm the divine favor he received through the omens. Like such biblical protagonists as Joseph and David, personal triumph signifies divine election.

Many ancient near eastern royal inscriptions employ first-person discourse; but virtually no other text quotes the speaker's inner thoughts and personalizes the significance of his accomplishments as does the narrative on Idrimi's statue. A letter from eighteenth-century Mari (Tell Hariri), a city on the middle Euphrates, relates that when a prophet dreamed of entering a shrine to pay homage to its god, the god's statue opened its mouth and spoke. The text inscribed across the statue of Idrimi would seem to be the words that the scribe Sharruwa had his king,

now perhaps one of the gods, open his mouth and speak. Indeed, the final three lines, which sum up his achievements and request a blessing, are inscribed alongside the statue's face and might be taken as the very words of his mouth: "Thirty years I was king. My achievements I have inscribed on my statue. Let them look upon them, and let them continually bless me" (ll. 102–104).

THE INSCRIPTION OF AZATIWADA

The hilltop site of Karatepe (ancient Azatiwadiya) was excavated by the University of Istanbul beginning in 1945. In the next two years among the ruins of the ancient city, in the area of the city gate, five inscriptions bearing versions of the same text, two in Luwian hieroglyphic and three in West Semitic alphabetic characters, were found. The only fully preserved inscription was engraved near the base of the lower gate in Phoenician (a northern Canaanite dialect). It is written across adjoining orthostats in four columns and ends on one of the two stone lions that flanked the gate. This version of sixty-two lines is by far the longest Phoenician document we have. A hieroglyphic version in the local language, Luwian, accompanies it. In the upper gate area, too, are the remains of parallel Phoenician and Luwian versions of the inscription. A third Phoenician version appears on the four sides of a statue of the storm-god, Tarkhunza in Luwian, Baal in Phoenician.

History and Purpose

In contrast to the inscription of Idrimi, which purports to summarize a career and in this respect resembles a true autobiography, the inscription of Azatiwada memorializes the founding and construction of a city, named for him, Azatiwadiya. There is no reason to doubt that it was Azatiwada, builder of the city, who commissioned the text.

Azatiwada's detailed description of his activities gives a well-rounded picture of the responsibilities and accomplishments of an ideal local governor in Cilicia, southeast Anatolia, in the mid eighth century. If Awariku, king of the Danunians, who is mentioned in this inscription, is identified as the Cilician king called Urik(ki) in Assyrian royal documents of the late eighth century, Azatiwada's inscription may be dated to about 730–710. If, on the other hand, Azatiwada was the regent of Awariku until the latter came of age, the inscription may be dated a generation earlier. The dating is inconclusive, and some scholars place it a century earlier. (See "Karkamish and Karatepe: Neo-Hittite City-States in North Syria" in Part 5, Vol. II.)

Form and Style

The native culture of the site, like the style of the statuary, would seem to be Luwian, the dominant, ethnically mixed culture in Asia Minor in the early first millennium. The inscription of Azatiwada, however, reflects the structure and formularies of Mesopotamian prototypes, such as the stela inscription of Hammurabi discussed above; it also resembles other Phoenician and Aramaic commemorative texts of the early first millennium, such as the Phoenician inscription of Kilamuwa, king of nearby Sam'al (Zincirli, pronounced Zinjirli) from about 825. (See "Aramaean Tribes and Nations of First-Millennium Western Asia" in Part 5, Vol. II.)

The fullest Phoenician version of the inscription may be divided for convenience into five sections: (1) a first-person introduction of the subject (col. 1, ll. 1–3); (2) a lengthy first-person recounting of achievements (col. 1, l. 3, to col. 3, l. 2); (3) an invocation of blessing for the subject and his dominion that switches according to convention, but unlike Idrimi's, from first- to third-person discourse (col. 3, ll. 4–11); (4) a curse on anyone who would efface the inscription or destroy the gate (col. 3, l. 12, to col. 4, l. 1); and (5) a brief reprise of blessing for the subject (col. 4, ll. 1–3).

Only the first two sections of the text employ the first person and are accordingly autobiographical, but the themes and motifs of the "autobiography," as with Idrimi's, cohere with the sections containing the blessings and curses. The narrative of the autobiographical sections, unlike the story of Idrimi, has barely any drama; indeed, the only challenge Azatiwada acknowledges is his need to compete with and outstrip the past. The inscription is, however, a masterful exercise in rhetoric.

Analysis and Interpretation

Azatiwada the Kingmaker Azatiwada introduces himself as the "steward of Baal, servant of Baal, whom Awariku, king of the Danunians, made powerful, whom Baal made father and mother to the Danunians" (col. 1, ll. 1–3). The Danunians are the people of the territory that the inscription describes as "the Plain of Adana." Significantly, Azatiwada is careful never to identify himself as king. It would seem, therefore, that he was a regional governor under, or very possibly the regent of, Awariku of the "House of Mupsh(os)." As a powerful arm of the king of the Adana Plain, "I set up the house of my lord in good [prosperity], and I made good for the scion of my lord. I seated him on the throne of his father" (ll. 9–11). Azatiwada presents himself as the kingmaker, a role consistent with that of the regent of a boy king. Though not the monarch himself, Azatiwada takes credit for foreign relations: "I made peace with every king, and every king treated me like a father on account of my justice, my wisdom, and my good-heartedness" (ll. 11–13). Azatiwada's repeated characterization of himself as "father" would also seem to reflect his role as regent.

"By the Grace of the Gods" The cultic tenor of Azatiwada's self-identification as the "servant of Baal" conforms to themes and purposes of the inscription. Azatiwada represents his activities as the fulfillment of a divine mandate. Three of his major achievements he says he accomplished "by the grace of Baal and by the grace of the gods," a phrase that is almost a refrain structuring the narrative. As the first of these accomplishments, he amassed economic and military power: "I filled the storehouses of Pa'ar, and I acquired horse upon horse, shield upon shield, and army upon army" (ll. 6–8). As the second, he established security in his realm (col. 2, ll. 1–6). The third is his building, or rebuilding, of his city, which he claims to have done "because Baal and Resheph of the Stags (?) commissioned me to build it" (ll. 10–12); there he appropriately replaces "and by the grace of the gods" with "and by the grace of Resheph of the Stags (?)." A fourth instance of the phrase occurs in the blessing formula, in which Azatiwada bids the gods bless him and his city and see that its

inhabitants "serve Azatiwada and the House of Mupsh by the grace of Baal and the gods" (col. 3, ll. 10–11).

Azatiwada makes certain to mention that he installed the local storm-god, Baal Krntryš (Tarkhunza in Luwian), in his newly (re)built city and that "an (animal) offering was established for every molten image: the annual offering—an ox; and at plou[ghing season]—a sheep; and at harvest season—a sheep" (col. 2, l. 19, to col. 3, l. 2). It is Baal Krntryš whom the inscription invokes above all to "bless Azatiwada with life, well-being, and powerful strength over every king" (col. 3, ll. 3–4). He is apparently the god depicted on the aforementioned statue.

Achievements   On behalf of his people, to whom Azatiwada was "father and mother," he claims to have performed two major boons. He made the land prosper, filling it with "satiety (plenty) and good things (delectables)," a phrase he employs no fewer than four times. And he made the land secure, an accomplishment he elaborates at unusual length: "I built strong walls (i.e., fortresses) on all the borders of the territories, in places where there were evil men, leaders of gangs, no one of whom was a servant of the House of Mupsh. But I, Azatiwada, put them under my feet" (col. 1, ll. 13–17). He goes on to say that he deported the unsubmissive population to the west and replaced them with Danunians. The Adana Plain became so safe that "in places where before people were fearful, so that a man would fear to walk on the road, during my days, mine, a woman could walk alone with her spindles (i.e., obliviously spinning wool)" (col. 2, ll. 3–6). It is these two achievements that Azatiwada summarizes: "There was during all my days satiety and good things, and good (i.e., safe) dwelling and peace of mind for the Danunians and for the entire Adana Plain" (col. 2, ll. 7–9).

Immortalization   The crowning achievement of Azatiwada, and the manifest occasion for this inscription, is the (re)construction of this fortress, which he names for himself: "I built this city, and I named it Azatiwadiya . . . that it be protection for the Adana Plain and for the House of Mupsh" (col. 2, ll. 9–10, 14–15). He

repeats these facts a few lines further on: "I built this city; I named it Azatiwadiya" (ll. 17–18). Although Azatiwada maintains that the purpose of the city is to defend the region, the rhetoric of the inscription suggests that its purpose, like that of the inscription itself, is to immortalize Azatiwada.

No fewer than eight times does the inscription mention the name of its subject, Azatiwada. The conventional section of curses threatens "any king among kings, or governor among governors, or any man whose name is 'man' (a commoner without a title), who erases the name of Azatiwada from this gate and puts his own name (there) . . . or (who would) make for (the city) a strange gate and put his name on it" (col. 3, ll. 12–16). Preservation of the name is paramount. The curse that is invoked on any would-be effacer of Azatiwada's name does not involve losses in battle, plague, or even extirpation of lineage. The gods are bidden to "wipe out" the perpetrator (l. 19)—the same verb that was used for the "erasure" of Azatiwada's name. Following this curse of oblivion, the blessing invoked on Azatiwada is briefly but tellingly reprised. Whereas above, the blessings chiefly invoked are power and longevity, here it is immortal fame: "Only may the name of Azatiwada be eternal like the name of the sun and the moon!" (col. 4, ll. 1–3). Indeed, the curse formula invokes the solar deity as "Eternal Sun" (col. 3, l. 19).

Solar Symbolism   The simile using the sun and moon is conventional; compare, for example, Psalm 72:5 and 17, the latter of which reads, "May his [the king's] name be eternal like the sun." In the context of this inscription, however, the simile gains in significance. East and west are repeatedly and typically referred to as "where the sun rises" and "where the sun sets." Azatiwada claims to have "widened the land of the Adana Plain from where the sun rises to where it sets" (col. 1, ll. 4–5). Here the sun's compass is the measure of space. In the curse and concluding blessing, it is the measure of eternity. By implication, it is also the symbol of good. Azatiwada says that in his time "the Danunians never had any night" (col. 2, ll. 16–17). If "night," darkness, represents the bad, then light, and by metonymy the sun, signifies the good. In this document, the comparison with the sun connotes Azatiwada's sunlike virtues as well as his desire for immortal fame.

Contrasts   The opposition of day and night is one of several contrasts on which the rhetoric of the inscription revolves. The "good" that Azatiwada repeatedly reminds us he has provided for the Danunians contrasts with the "evil men" and the general "evil" he has "removed" from his domain (col. 1, l. 9). In the passage impressing us with how he established law and order, Azatiwada explains that a woman could walk alone where formerly a man would fear to tread.

In fact, the most striking and recurrent opposition would seem to be the contrast Azatiwada draws between what he was able to accomplish and what his predecessors could not — a theme that also figures prominently in the Phoenician inscription of Kilamuwa of Sam'al. Only once does Azatiwada explicitly compare himself to former rulers: "I subjugated mighty lands where the sun sets, which all the kings who were before me did not subjugate" (col. 1, ll. 18–19). But instead of reiterating the failures of his predecessors, as Kilamuwa does by mentioning each of them by name, Azatiwada accentuates what he achieves "during (his) days." He relegates his anonymous predecessors to the past and highlights his own performance; he uses the pronoun "I," often redundantly like his name, a full twenty-four times.

Blessing   In recognition of the good days Azatiwada gives the Plain of Adana, he asks the gods for "length of days and many years" (col. 3, ll. 5–6) for himself and eternal commemoration for his name. We do not know whether Azatiwada ruled many years, but his name has been assured academic perpetuation.

CONCLUSION

In the modern era autobiography flourishes, a result of, among other factors, a fashionable interest in individual lives, a long-evolving tendency toward introspection, and the general accessibility of publication to people both "great" and "small." In the ancient Near East, on the other hand, autobiographical works nearly all concern the lives and accomplishments of public figures, mainly kings, who, in a world where the few dominated the many, led lives that could make an extraordinary impact. Such ancient authors writing in the first person understandably sought to justify and promote themselves or, in the case of scribal authors, their patrons. When that is all they do, their literary products have little more than historical interest.

When, however, the writing involves personal conflicts and aspirations with which we may all identify, even the self-serving story of an ancient life may affect readers across time and space. Idrimi's struggle to transcend the vicissitudes of history and restore his home and Azatiwada's need to surpass his predecessors and leave a permanent mark reflect themes that have characterized Western literature beginning with such Greek and Roman classics as Homer's *Odyssey* and Virgil's *Aeneid*. Biblical parallels to Joseph, Moses, David, and other personalities have also been cited above. And beyond the rhetoric, Idrimi and Azatiwada may also elicit our sympathy because they are both rulers who can never be better than second best; their individual talents and efforts remain constrained by their dependency on more powerful persons.

BIBLIOGRAPHY

General Studies

GEORG MISCH, *A History of Autobiography in Antiquity*, 2 vols., translated by E. W. DICKES (1950); JAMES OLNEY, ed., *Autobiography: Essays Theoretical and Critical* (1980). On the history of narrative in general, see ROBERT SCHOLES and ROBERT KELLOGG, *The Nature of Narrative* (1966).

Ancient Near Eastern Studies

EMMA BRUNNER-TRAUT, "Altägyptische Literatur," and ERICA REINER, "Die akkadische Literatur," in *Altorientalische Literaturen*, edited by WOLFGANG RÖLLIG (1978); MIRIAM LICHTHEIM, *Ancient Egyptian Autobiographies Chiefly of the Middle Kingdom: A Study and an Anthology* (1988); TREMPER LONGMAN III, *Fictional Akkadian Autobiography: A Generic and Comparative Study* (1991).

Texts in Translation

JAMES B. PRITCHARD, ed., *Ancient Near Eastern Texts Relating to the Old Testament* (3rd ed. 1969); many of the texts discussed in this essay can be found in translation in this volume, for example, Idrimi on pp. 557–558, Azatiwada on pp. 653–654, Hammurabi on pp. 163–180, Adad-guppi on pp. 560–562, Sinuhe on pp. 18–22, Wenamun on pp. 25–29, the Mari prophecy on p. 623, and Kilamuwa on pp. 654–655. MIRIAM LICHTHEIM, *Ancient Egyptian Literature*, 3 vols. (1973–1980), includes translations of many Egyptian "autobiographical" texts from a wide range of periods.

Idrimi Inscription

M. DIETRICH and O. LORETZ, "Die Inschrift der Statue des Königs Idrimi von Alalaḫ," *Ugarit-Forschungen* 13 (1981); EDWARD L. GREENSTEIN and DAVID MARCUS, "The Akkadian Inscription of Idrimi," *Journal of the Ancient Near Eastern Society of Columbia University* 8 (1976); GARY H. OLLER, "The Autobiography of Idrimi" (Ph.D. diss., University of Pennsylvania, 1977); SIDNEY SMITH, *The Statue of Idri-mi* (1949). For a different dating, see JACK M. SASSON, "On Idrimi and Šarruwa, the Scribe," in *Studies in the Civilization and Culture of Nuzi and the Hurrians in Honor of Ernest R. Lacheman*, edited by MARTHA A. MORRISON and DAVID I. OWEN (1981).

Azatiwada Inscription

FRANÇOIS BRON, *Recherches sur les inscriptions phéniciennes de Karatepe* (1979); JOEL F. DRINKARD, "The Literary Genre of the Mesha Inscription," in *Studies in the Mesha Inscription and Moab*, edited by ANDREW DEARMAN (1989); JOHN C. L. GIBSON, *Textbook of Syrian Semitic Inscriptions*, vol. 3, *Phoenician Inscriptions* (1982). For the archaeological context and dating, see J. D. HAWKINS and W. ORTHMANN, "Karatepe," in *Reallexikon der Assyriologie* 5 (1976–1980), pp. 409–411 and pp. 411–414, respectively.

SEE ALSO **Ancient Egyptian Autobiographies** (Part 9, Vol. IV); **The Deeds of Ancient Mesopotamian Kings** (Part 9, Vol. IV); and **The Historiography of the Ancient Near East** (Part 9, Vol. IV).

The Historiography of the Ancient Near East

JOHN VAN SETERS

My subject is not the methodology of modern historians but rather the way the ancient scribes themselves wrote "history." The topics are not unrelated, because modern historians must depend heavily upon ancient texts for their own reconstructions of the past. Consequently, an understanding of the nature and limits of ancient historiography is a prerequisite for modern historiography as well.

Yet it is fair to ask what constitutes historiography in the world of near eastern antiquity, because before the Hellenistic period, there are no examples of literary works from the ancient civilizations of Babylonia, Egypt, and the Hittites that would easily be recognized as a national history. There was no circumscribed group of literati known as historians. Yet there are many different kinds of literary works from antiquity that treat historical subjects or reflect historical concerns in all of the great civilizations of the Near East over a very long period of time. Just to classify and enumerate them would take more space than is available for this essay and would do little more than suggest the diversity of interest in the historical past.

Consequently, this essay will focus on two contrasting types of historiography and the ways in which a variety of different genres of "historical" texts in the Near East reflect them. The first presents *recent events* from immediately accessible sources to offer accountability and me-morialize the events for future generations. For the Near East the primary actor of such accounts is the king, so that this first type of historiography often has a strongly biographical bent and includes not merely specific public events but the life of the king, his character, and achievements. The second type of historiography involves the re-presentation of the *remote past* for the purpose of explaining and understanding the present in terms of origins and primary causes. While origins and primary causes may be viewed by the ancients as belonging to a mythological beginning and are explained in theological terms, they are "historical" when they stand in chronological continuity with the present and when they are explained in terms of historical realities.

These two aspects of historiography are most distinct at their extremes, the distant past and the recent past, but there is often no clear line of demarcation between them. Yet even in antiquity, the chronicling of recent events was viewed as quite distinct from antiquarian interests in remote history, both in terms of the kind of sources available and with respect to the motivation for writing. The various genres of historiography in antiquity tend to differentiate more easily along these two lines than they do in modern historiography, where "in-depth" explanation of causes seems quite necessary even for journalistic history concerning the most recent events.

The question of the audience to which ancient historical works were directed is also more complex than our modern notions of publishing histories for the inspection of any interested member of the general public. Some works dealing with recent events glorifying the king were intended for public presentation. Others dealing with the remote past were learned antiquarian documents of interest to only a limited circle of scribes. In addition, some historical texts were directed at the deity as the primary or exclusive audience. These were often deposited in places inaccessible to the general public. It should also be kept in mind that literacy in antiquity was very limited; only texts that could be read aloud or performed had a large audience.

THE TREATMENT OF RECENT EVENTS

Mesopotamia

In ancient Assyria and Babylonia, the writing of recent history dealt almost entirely with the activity of the king. From the earliest simple dedicatory inscription naming the benefactor of a temple or cult object, royal inscriptions developed in time into lengthy commemorative texts whose subject was the construction of temples and palaces and the conquest of the king's enemies in battle. While some of these inscriptions may appear on display along with pictorial representation on the walls of palaces or on stelae to memorialize the greatness of the king, many of the most detailed accounts were concealed from view as foundation deposits or in other inaccessible places. The reason for this is that the king was accountable first to the gods, to whom he frequently gave credit for his successes. The detailed record of his activity was, therefore, an expression of his piety, offered with the hope that the deity would acknowledge it and continue to support and bless him. Also, because of frequent renovation of public buildings, rulers knew that their texts might be discovered by future kings, from whom they expected continued recognition and credit for their deeds. By the same token, they acknowledged the building record of past kings and often included a summary history of a temple being restored.

While Babylonian inscriptions dealt almost entirely with royal building activity, the Assyrian kings gave great emphasis to their military campaigns. These may be in the form of "annals" that narrate, in autobiographical style, the royal campaigns in chronological order as yearly endeavors. The most recent campaign would be derived from the field records themselves and the booty list, but after an "official" version had been composed, it would become the source for future texts. Thus, the earlier campaigns would be extracted and summarized from previous inscriptions, while only the current year's campaign would be treated in more detail. Royal building activity was not treated within the chronological framework but loosely joined to the military recital by a vague connective, "at that time," leading to the false impression that only after the cessation of all military activity did the king engage in building temples. In addition to the annals, there were also display inscriptions that commemorated the king's deeds, but not in chronological order.

The term "annals," as applied to Assyrian royal inscriptions, is a misnomer, for the concern was not to maintain a strict chronological record of major public events for posterity. The royal inscriptions are highly ideological documents in which the annalistic form for the military campaigns is used to convey the continuous and overwhelming power of the king over all his enemies. The ideology is expressed directly through the rather verbose recitation of the honorific epithets ascribed to the king and of his special relationship to the deity. The inscriptions, though autobiographical, were not, of course, the work of the king himself but of the court scribes and poets whose task it was to present the contemporary events in the king's own image as hero and pious servant of the gods. Royal inscriptions served as paeans of praise to the king, and he was their most important audience.

The historical epic, though more polished in form, was similar in purpose to the commemorative inscription. It resembles the heroic epic but its subject is the exploits of a contemporary monarch. To judge from the epic of Tukulti-Ninurta I (late thirteenth century BCE), celebrating his victory over Babylon, the historical epic incorporated the basic components of the royal inscription but skillfully included other literary and religious genres and themes, such as the royal hymn to the king, the account of a god's abandonment of the doomed city, and the penitential prayer as a confession of guilt by the defeated Babylonian king. A broad range of literary features are employed to reconstruct the "historic" event. The blatant ideology and propagandistic tone, the elevated style and the manipulation of literary presentation for dramatic effect, all make the epic suspect by the canons of modern historiography. But this was Assyria's form of commemorating a major event for future generations.

Similar in purpose but quite different in style is the genre known as the "letter to the god." In the mid first millennium the Assyrian king might commission a special text for presentation in a public "triumph" celebrating an important military victory. An example of this genre is the report of Sargon II's eighth campaign against the land of Urartu (714 BCE), in the form of an address to the god Assur and to the gods and citizens of the city of Asshur (modern Qalat Sharqat). It renders praise to the king for his great victory and eulogizes as "heroes" those fallen in battle. While it has some similarities to the annals, it is much superior as a work of artistic composition. It devotes attention to interesting detail regarding the topography, fauna and flora, and customs of the foreign regions traversed in a manner that anticipates the style of Herodotus. But the text is also ideological in that it is conscious of the need to justify Sargon's actions, particularly the destruction of the most holy city in Urartu with its gods and temple. This it does by reporting three divine signs the king received before the attack on the city. The accountability of the report is to both the gods and citizens of Asshur, while at the same time it memorializes the great victory in a rather sober and realistic account.

Egypt

In ancient Egypt the development of a historiography that centered on the king faced two conflicting realities. At a very early stage, the Egyptian bureaucracy inaugurated a remarkable system of official record keeping and a chronological scheme for recording important events. These records or "annals" begin as year names,

of which examples are preserved on wooden and ivory labels; these names were probably recorded serially for individual reigns and then eventually compiled on scrolls of papyrus. From at least the Middle Kingdom (circa 1980–1630) onward, these rudimentary records are supplemented by daybooks covering a wide range of administrative affairs of the temple and the court.

At the same time, during the earliest period of Egyptian history an ideology of kingship emerges in which the king is regarded as manifesting the gods on earth and the defender of the cosmic order. Change threatened disorder, so the ideal was political and social stability in which the king would rule "for ever and ever." Pictorial portrayal of royal activity, therefore, symbolized the meaning of the institution rather than any specific event or achievement.

In contrast with this presentation of absolutism are the tomb inscriptions of high officials. These took the form of autobiography, spelling out the accomplishments of the deceased in the service of pharaoh, giving the official's titles and honors and how he achieved them. These texts were put on public display in funerary chapels in the hope of receiving continued offerings and benefactions for the dead. Officials also set up stelae detailing the faithful execution of royal commissions. Both types of texts are major sources of historical information, especially for the period prior to the New Kingdom (circa 1539–1075). Their "history" is directly related to their sense of accountability to the king as a god. With the breakdown of centralized authority at the end of the Old Kingdom (circa 2675–2125), the administrative districts or nomes gained a certain independence that they retained, to a large measure, even after reunification in the Middle Kingdom. The nomarchs or local magnates continued to inscribe the walls of their tomb chapels with records of their own achievements. In one such tomb of the Twelfth Dynasty, the deceased nomarch carefully outlines the history of his family's control over the region to establish the boundaries by historical precedent and to confirm his own hereditary rights.

Few royal inscriptions are preserved from the Middle Kingdom, but those that are suggest some important innovations in this period. In a few cases involving the dedication of a temple or the introduction of cult reform, discursive narration is employed to tell of the circumstances under which these projects were undertaken. This becomes an important feature in royal inscriptions of a later period.

Not until the rise of the New Kingdom, however, did the pharaohs set up royal inscriptions to commemorate their military exploits in detailed narration. Kamose, the last Theban king of the Seventeenth Dynasty, left a long account of his military victory over the Hyksos of Avaris (circa 1550). The inscription was prominently displayed on three stelae, two of which are preserved, in the temple of Amun-Re in Thebes to celebrate his claim to the rule of all Egypt.

During the New Kingdom, the question of who was the legitimate heir to the throne arose repeatedly. One way for the king to attest his right to the throne was victory over foreign armies as a proof of divine favor. This is reflected in the "Annals of Thutmose III," which retell the pharaoh's conquest of the Levant in seventeen campaigns over twenty-one years. The work is written in an unadorned, precisely dated style. Some sections were told with great narrative skill. The first campaign, being the most significant, is presented in the greatest detail, while the remaining portions are abbreviated. The author also makes reference to his sources as the "daybooks" of the temple and palace. The spoils of war are listed in detail and offered to the god Amun-Re. In a quite separate poetic composition, a "Hymn of Victory," the god Amun-Re acknowledges the pharaoh as his true son to whom he has given all the nations and peoples of the earth. This became a favorite genre with later pharaohs, who borrowed parts of it for their own use.

Thutmose III was the first New Kingdom pharaoh to use this annalistic style, and not all of his commemorative inscriptions made use of it. Only in the case of his son, Amenhotep (Amenophis) II, were annals used again (for campaigns in his seventh and ninth years). Except as a brief experiment in literary style, therefore, annalistic historiography never became established in Egypt and the term "annals" is misleading even in the cases of Thutmose and Amenhotep.

Early in his reign, Ramesses (Ramses) II undertook a major campaign against the Hittites with the decisive battle taking place at Qadesh (Tell Nebi Mend) in Syria. A record of the event was produced by three authors in the form of two written versions and a set of captioned reliefs. While all three treat the same event, they complement and supplement each other in information, indicating that they derive from common, detailed field records. The account gives a full description of the battle, with deployment of forces, strategies of ambush and attack, the decisive turning point, and the consequences. Alongside the realistic details, one version gives an idealized, poetic rendition of the battle that presents Ramesses's military prowess as godlike. Nowhere else in Egyptian historiography is the contrast between the dogma of royal ideology and the skill of reporting an historical event as it happened more apparent than here. (For more on Ramesses II, see the chapter on him in Part 5, Vol. II.)

The great stela of Piye, an egyptianized ruler of Kush (modern Sudan), is another example of historical reporting of recent events. It is that ruler's account of a victorious march from the south over a coalition of princes of Middle and Lower Egypt that allowed Piye to become the principal ruler of both Kush and Egypt. James Breasted described it as the "clearest and most rational account of a campaign which has survived from Egypt." In the introduction the king compares his deeds with those of his ancestors and declares his divinity. There follows a finely crafted narrative of the conduct of the campaign. The portrayal of the king seems particularly realistic, revealing his piety, his love of horses, and his generosity toward his enemies. By contrast, there is no great concern for exact dates or lists of booty, and the work seems based on recollections by participants in the action.

The Hittites

Most Hittite historical texts deal with recent events, presented in royal inscriptions dating from the oldest historical period to the end of this civilization in Anatolia. The earliest historiographical text is that of King Anitta, who may or may not have been a Hittite, describing events in the first half of the eighteenth century. Anitta begins by reviewing some of his father's deeds before recounting his own achievements. His deeds, intended to reflect on the greatness of the king, include not only military activity but the building of temples and a royal hunt. The text seems to be a rough compilation of several individual inscriptions that were originally set up for public display. These inscriptions were then copied as one text at some later time on the model of the later annals, but without any chronology.

Hittite royal inscriptions take the form of public pronouncements of the king and are of two kinds. One is in the style of annals that report the king's military activity year by year. The earliest, from the Old Kingdom, is by Khattushili (Hattusili) I and is clearly meant to impress the reader or hearer by a comparison drawn between the king's deeds and those of Sargon of Akkad, who had become legendary even among the Hittites. The reporting of the king's "manly deeds" (the Hittites' term for this literary genre) reaches its high point during the reign of Murshili II. His scribes not only compiled two versions of his own deeds but also composed an edition of the deeds of his father, Shuppiluliuma I. The "Ten-Year Annals" were written for the specific purpose of dealing with the king's own "manly deeds," as if to justify his accession to the throne by his personal accomplishments. The "Detailed Annals" cover not only a greater time frame in greater detail but also recount the activity of other Hittite princes and generals. The Assyrian and Egyptian annals, by comparison, always leave the impression that no successful military venture ever took place without direct royal involvement. There is also greater uniformity in the treatment of all the campaigns and a greater explanation of strategy and of the reasons for taking, or delaying, action against an enemy than in Assyrian and Egyptian annals. However, a precise chronology of events beyond vague references to seasons or year sequences is lacking.

The style of the annals is autobiographical, except in the case of the "Manly Deeds of Shuppiluliuma," where these activities are reported by Murshili as the deeds of "my father." Divine intervention is recognized in a variety of ways similar to that of the Assyrian inscriptions. Defeat or mistakes are never mentioned, because these would reflect impiety and divine punishment. They could, however, be recognized and mentioned in a different context, that of peni-

tential prayer, such as the "Plague Prayers" of Murshili, where Murshili admits to his father's disregard of an old treaty that resulted in plagues as divine punishment.

A second type of Hittite text that deals with recent history reflects the attempt to give legitimacy or justification for past action. The emphasis on accountability is one of the most distinctive aspects of Hittite historiography. The earliest example of this type is the "Political Testament" of Khattushili I, in which the king addresses the assembly (*panku*-), the nobles, and the members of the royal family. The text excuses the king's unorthodox selection of a grandson as an adopted son and heir to the throne on the grounds of the evil behavior of certain members of the royal family. The king cites events from the past in support of his royal edict, but not in chronological order. The use of historical precedent becomes a feature of Hittite historiography and gives to it a certain legal quality.

The "Apology" of Khattushili III is a text written in autobiographical style to justify dethroning a nephew in order to occupy the throne and to relate subsequent actions taken against an important nobleman's family. In the "Apology" Khattushili honors the goddess Ishtar of Shamukha for guiding and protecting him throughout his career. In concluding his "Apology," the king bestows certain cultic rights and properties in perpetuity to Ishtar's temple. The text is difficult to classify because it combines the autobiographical style of annals with the argument of historical precedent from royal edicts and treaties and with the apology for justifying actions that do not conform to custom or the law of succession. It is a highly literary work that renders an account of the king's career and memorializes his life in the service of the goddess. (See the chapter on Khattushili III in Part 5, Vol. II.)

Syro-Palestine

The treatment of contemporaneous history in Syro-Palestine is represented primarily by "memorial inscriptions," a designation that covers royal inscriptions in autobiographical style. These were written in a form of Luwian, in Aramaic, and in Phoenician and were found in sites from southern Anatolia, Syria, and Phoenicia to

Moab in the south, dating from the thirteenth to the eighth centuries. These memorial inscriptions include the king's relationship to the deity to whom the inscription is dedicated, an account of royal deeds, and a request to be remembered in perpetuity with a blessing on those who preserve this record and a curse on those who do not. The royal deeds are not given any clear chronology and can scarcely be said to reflect an annalistic tradition. They may include remarks about the career of the king's father or a reference to setting up a memorial to him. The texts are clearly meant to memorialize the accomplishments of the king; most were composed late in his reign or, more usually, after his death.

These texts often refer to a troubled period of civil strife or foreign domination that was ended by the present ruler and to the ensuing return to order and prosperity. Some may highlight a specific event or accomplishment. The inscription of King Zakkur (Zakir) from Hamath commemorates a divine deliverance of the king when he was under siege by a coalition of enemy forces. The stela of Mesha, king of Moab, tells how he liberated his land from Israelite domination and describes his building activity in Dibon. The deeds recorded in the inscriptions are meant to attest to the righteousness of the king and the divine favor bestowed on his reign. As such they are deserving of perpetual remembrance.

No memorial inscriptions are extant from Israel or Judah, although it is reasonable to assume that some may have existed in antiquity. Some information about military activity and building ventures during the monarchy may have been used by the writer(s) of Kings. The "memoirs of Nehemiah" in the book of Nehemiah has a certain resemblance to memorial inscriptions with its autobiographical style, its treatment of a time of crisis when things were set right by Nehemiah, and his plea to be remembered for his deeds of righteousness. But the resemblance is not so close that it preserves the text of an inscribed monument. It might be that an inscription of a governor inspired this literary rendering of events regarding Jerusalem's restoration.

Some scholars have also seen in the narratives about David, particularly in the "Succession Story" (2 Samuel, chapters 9–20; 1 Kings, chapters 1–2), a contemporary eyewitness reporting of events. The work is interpeted as providing for the legitimacy of Solomon's succession. To support this view, comparisons have been made with the Hittite historiographic tradition. The "Succession Story" is regarded by many as the foremost example of Israelite historiography because of its realistic presentation of the monarchy. However, the view that the "Succession Story" represents an early source for David's reign has become increasingly difficult to maintain. Thus, the "Succession Story" is no longer to be regarded as a source used by the historian of Samuel and Kings, but a late postexilic addition to the history that calls into question the use of the divine promise of an "enduring house" of David (2 Samuel, chapter 7) as justification for reviving the Judean monarchy. Consequently, within the Hebrew Bible we have no treatment of recent history.

HISTORIOGRAPHY OF THE REMOTE PAST

Mesopotamia

Turning to the second aspect of historiography, namely, treatment of the remote past, we are confronted in Mesopotamia with a variety of literary genres that reflect antiquarian concerns. Indispensable to the presentation of past history is a chronological framework. This developed in Mesopotamia, in the first place, as a response to the practical necessity of dating administrative documents. The system in Babylonia was to give a name to each year corresponding to an important event of the preceeding year. Such year-names were compiled into datelists to enable ancient scribes to ascertain the proper order of a particular year-name. It was then possible to tally the datelists to arrive at a chronology of Babylonian kings. Such chronologies eventually spanned most of the second and first millennia. In Assyria a similar system was devised by naming each year after an important official (*limmu*) and then compiling lists of such eponymous years. Unfortunately this system was not regularly linked to the chronology of the Assyrian kings until the late tenth century.

A kinglist, however, could be used not only for chronology but to express an understanding of the remote past, including the origins of kingship and, therefore, of the state. This can be seen in the case of the "Sumerian Kinglist," a literary work of the early second millennium preserved in several versions. In its oldest form it tells how kingship descended from heaven and was established at Kish (modern Tell al-Uhaimir, Tell Ingharra). It then enumerates the dynasties of the various cities, each of which in turn ruled over the whole of Babylonia, over a very long period of time. The author, by collecting the dynastic traditions of various cities, wished to demonstrate that there could be only one true kingship in Mesopotamia at any one time. The "Sumerian Kinglist" was later extended back in time to include the period "before the Flood" when kingship came down to Eridu (Abu Shahrain); it gave the names of semidivine kings with very long reigns who ruled in five cities. In this way Babylonian "history" reached back to the time of human origins. This "Sumerian Kinglist" became a classic of Babylonian historiography and was continued for several centuries.

The classical tradition of the Assyrian Kinglist developed somewhat differently. An erudite scribe of the thirteenth century brought together several different documents based upon his research of library texts and monuments to produce a list of Assyrian kings that would reach back into hoary antiquity and thus rival the tradition of kingship in Babylonia. It was a purely nationalistic document which suggested that Assyria had been an independent state from its origins (which is historically untrue). Once this Assyrian historiographical tradition was established, the Assyrian Kinglist became classic and was continued faithfully by the addition of new rulers' names for at least another five hundred years. This is another case of reconstructing the past based on traditional sources in order to explain the state's origins and distinct identity primarily in terms of the origin and continuity of kingship.

The "Babylonian Chronicle" is another historiographic genre aimed at reconstructing the national tradition of the Chaldean Dynasty in Babylonia from its beginning in the mid eighth century. It represents a true annalistic tradition with precise chronology by dated regnal years and covers a range of military and public affairs of the Babylonian kings and their Assyrian over-

lords. A single chronicle may cover the reign of several kings, both native and foreign, and a series of such texts, with variant versions, extends down to the Hellenistic period. The sources for such texts are disputed, but they seem to reflect an extensive system of record keeping. Although somewhat rudimentary for the early period, by the early seventh century the chronicle becomes quite precise and detailed in its account. The chronicles give an impression of objectivity and factual reporting free from the propagandistic and ideological bombast of the Assyrian annals. While kings are still the central figures in such chronicles, the texts are not written for their aggrandizement or the justification of their actions. The virtue of the chronicle seems to be that of recording the activity of the successive rulers with little interpretive commentary.

The genre of chronicle, once created and perpetuated, seems to have given rise to the creation of a chronicle series comparable to the "Babylon Chronicle" that extended back to the time of Sargon of Akkad in the third millennium and continued down to the point where the "Babylonian Chronicle" begins, thus filling the gap of previous history. Babylonian scholars did not have access to annalistic records from this period because they did not yet exist, so they extracted historical material from a variety of traditional texts: kinglists, omen collections, and special literary works in the scribal libraries. Whatever reservations one may have about the results achieved by such an enterprise, it nevertheless gives evidence of research into the remote past for the purpose of constructing a continuous account of the Babylonian historical tradition from its beginning down to contemporary history. It expresses a concern to trace the nation's origin and an understanding of the many vicissitudes in Babylon's long history. This tradition of historiographical research and reconstruction of the remote past was inherited by Berossus (third century), who wrote a Babylonian history using the "Sumerian Kinglist," the "Babylonian Chronicle," and other literary works as a corrective to the Greeks' history of Babylonia.

Egypt

When it comes to considering the way in which Egyptian historiography dealt with the remote past, we must turn again to the "annals" and year-names of the Old Kingdom. In the late Fifth Dynasty (about 2350), a complete compilation of the annals and datelists was made, covering about seven centuries, which was preserved in stone on a monument known as the Palermo Stone. It contains the names of all the kings and the years each ruled Egypt from Predynastic times with one or more principal events for each year of the Dynastic period. For the Old Kingdom, these include building activity and military enterprises, but the latest entries are confined to the subject of donations to the cult. The annals tradition did not develop as a form of narrative history in the subsequent period. Yet the Palermo Stone itself, as a compilation of all the kings of Egypt, created a most important historiographic genre, the kinglist. Its eventual successor is the "Turin Canon of Kings."

The "Turin Canon of Kings" is a fragmentary papyrus from the Ramesside period (thirteenth century) that originally contained a list of all the kings of Egypt with the lengths of their reign and the capital city with which they were associated (preserved sections go down to the Seventeenth Dynasty). While this is the only exemplar of a kinglist from the pre-Hellenistic period, it is clear that the tradition continued to Hellenistic times, where it reappears in the work of the Greco-Egyptian historian Manetho. Alongside the "Turin Canon," there are many monuments that contain groupings of ancestral royal names or images reflecting a strong cult of royal ancestors. These begin as early as the Old Kingdom but become especially numerous in the late New Kingdom. Such texts attest a strong interest in the remote past and in a sense of continuity and stability that the succession of kings represents.

Furthermore, the "Turin Canon" is not just an administrative record of succession but the product of research that brought together sources from different centers. This was especially important for the Second Intermediate Period and the time of rule by the Hyksos when the country was divided. For this period it lists some kings as ruling successively when it is known that they were contemporaneous. Thus, the kings of Thebes of the Seventeenth Dynasty were contemporary with the rulers of the Fifteenth and Sixteenth dynasties of Avaris and the Delta.

One feature of the "Turin Canon" calls for special attention. During the course of the Old and Middle Kingdoms, the notion had developed that the king was divine not only by virtue of his birth as a god but by the fact that kingship was a divine institution in that the gods themselves had ruled over Egypt in the distant past and had brought about the unification of Upper and Lower Egypt. This meant that in place of the "historical" kings of the Predynastic period (around 3000), who are recorded on the Palermo Stone, the "Turin Canon" substitutes the rule of gods, demigods, and spirits. This is also the form in which the kinglist tradition survives in Manetho. Clearly, some of the historical record has been sacrificed for the sake of royal ideology and cosmology. The kings of Egypt are the heirs to the rule of the gods, and whenever the principal deity's authority is expressed in universal terms, as it was during the empire in the New Kingdom, then the king of Egypt is also considered to be the universal ruler. The kinglist tradition, as reflected in the "Turin Canon," is not itself a national history, but it was the indispensable framework for the development of such a history in the work of Manetho.

The Hittites

The Hittites did not develop a way of treating the remote past comparable to that of Mesopotamia and Egypt. Their civilization was much shorter in duration and they do not seem to have had any interest in long-range chronology or kinglists. In those texts that deal with the past beyond one or two generations, history often served as prologue to other concerns, such as treaties or legal agreements, where the establishment of precedent was important. One text that did treat past history extensively is the "Proclamation of Telipinu (Telepinu)." Its purpose was to regulate dynastic succession and to establish future jurisdiction over the royal family. It does this by setting forth the past history of the monarchy to show that unity and harmony in the royal family led to great success abroad, whereas civil strife led only to disaster. The history extends from the first king, Labarna, to Telipinu's own time, in which case it offers an apology for his own actions as a usurper.

The "Proclamation" lays down a series of regulations for the succession to be administered by the king. The form owes something in style and character to that of the earlier "Political Testament" of Khattushili I and is imitated later by the "Apology" of Khattushili III. The major difference between the "Proclamation" and both of these is that beyond the treatment of Telipinu's own actions, the "Proclamation" reflects an effort to research past history through several generations, to set forth the material in chronological order, and to lay down some fundamental principles for the understanding of the state in a historical preamble to its constitution. It is also "objective" in presentation without appeal to the deity, and the whole of their history is rendered accountable to the Hittite people. (See "Royal Ideology and State Administration in Hittite Anatolia" in Part 4, Vol. I, for further discussion of the "Proclamation.")

Syro-Palestine

Texts that deal with the remote past of Syro-Palestine, apart from the Hebrew Bible, are very limited. From ancient Ugarit (modern Ras Shamra) comes a list of the names of about thirty deceased kings. There is no indication of filiation and no chronology, so it is not a regular kinglist. The kings are all deified, suggesting a cult of royal ancestors similar to what was very popular in Egypt at this time, which was the period of the Egyptian Empire. In the works of the historian Josephus, there are references to the "Annals of Tyre" which give information about Tyre's monarchy contemporary with the Israelite and Judean monarchies. These "Annals" contain data that strongly suggest the existence of a kinglist with chronology and some other rudimentary details about the succession. Apart from this, however, the information is not clearly dated and does not resemble an annalistic or chronicle tradition. The "Annals of Tyre" may very well be a work of Hellenistic historiography, using some old sources and popular traditions.

The historiography of Israel in the Hebrew Bible is a problem because it is not like anything in the rest of the Near East and resembles most the histories of ancient Greece. Nevertheless, some sources used by biblical historians, especially for the monarchy, belong to the genres of

historical texts treated above. A second problem is the great diversity of scholarly opinion regarding literary analysis of the biblical histories. It is scarcely possible to do justice to the debate over these issues. What follows is a simplified sketch of one possible view of biblical historiography.

Genesis to 2 Kings, in its present form, is a history that extends from the beginning of the cosmos down to the end of the Judean monarchy (586). This history is not a unified literary work but represents the writings of at least three major historians. The first of these writings extends from Deuteronomy to 2 Kings and is a single historical corpus stretching from the time of Moses through the periods of the conquest under Joshua, the Judges, and the Monarchy, to the end of the national state. Deuteronomy, with its law code, serves as an ideological prologue to which the historian makes frequent reference throughout his work. For this reason the corpus is dubbed by scholars the "Deuteronomistic History." It understood Israel's existence in the promised land as conditioned upon loyalty to the national god, Yahweh, and obedience to his laws as revealed through Moses. While the monarchy is a form of the state instituted by the deity, with David as the ideal, few kings live up to this standard and the wickedness of the kings ultimately dooms both kingdoms.

As sources for the monarchy, the historian had access to the kinglists of Judah and Israel, a "book of the deeds of Solomon," and "chronicles" covering some of the important military and building activities of the kings of Israel and Judah. Apart from the kinglists, there is little precise dating, and the historian did not feel obliged to use much of his official sources. Most of his history covering the Judges, the stories of Saul and David, and much of the Monarchy seems based upon popular, orally communicated tradition. For the early period some source "documents" have been proposed: (1) a collection of stories about local heroes in Judges 3–16; (2) a narrative about the ark (1 Sam. 4–6; 2 Sam. 6); (3) an early Saul tradition (1 Sam. 9–11, 13–14); (4) an account of David's rise to power (1 Sam. 16—2 Sam. 5); (5) the story of the throne succession (2 Sam. 9–20; 1 Kings 1–2). About these documents, however, there is still much disagreement. Behind the conquest of Joshua, on the other hand, there is only the historian's "reconstruction" of how Israel gained possession of the land, based upon the experience of the military invasions by the Assyrians and Babylonians. To the original history many additions were made, but these do not constitute a separate edition, only unsystematic expansions of the national tradition.

That part of the history covered by Genesis to Numbers did not belong to the original "Deuteronomistic History" but was the work of later authors. Since these four books, along with Deuteronomy, constitute the Torah or Pentateuch, the first division of the Hebrew Bible, its literary development has always been viewed quite independently from the "historical" books. There is good reason to believe, however, that Genesis to Numbers was composed as a supplement to extend the national history back to the time of creation and the ancestors of the nation. The first stage of this expansion was carried out by a historian, known in the scholarly discussion as the Yahwist ("J" for German "Jahwe"). Using antiquarian traditions from both Mesopotamia and the eastern Mediterranean region, "J" constructed the history of a primeval age from the first humans to the tower of Babel story (Gen. 2–11). He then took up traditions about the patriarchs—Abraham, Isaac, Jacob, and the sons of Jacob—and, by using a framework of genealogy and itinerary, combined the different popular traditions into a single work. The divine promises of land and nationhood to the patriarchs, which run as a common theme throughout these stories, were the means by which the patriarchal traditions served as prologue to the tradition of national origins in the exodus from Egypt. This tradition of the deliverance from slavery and the wilderness trek to the promised land was filled out by "J" with vivid detail.

Mesopotamian and Egyptian historiography began their national kinglists with traditions of a reconstructed primeval age. But it was especially in the west, as reflected in Greek historiography, that one finds strong antiquarian interest in national origins. Such histories contained genealogies and stories of eponymous ancestors who migrated from old civilizations to establish new peoples and nations. The Yahwist also was an antiquarian who preserved many old traditions about the ancestors and skillfully recon-

structed them into a prologue for the older national history.

A later author, known as the Priestly Writer ("P" for Priestly) expanded this prologue considerably at a number of points. He began the work with a more complete cosmology (Gen. 1), a common feature of such histories in antiquity, and added a more precise chronology to the whole of Genesis–Numbers. He also introduced a periodization of history by means of customs, laws and covenants, and the progressive revelation of the divine name. Beginning with creation, "P" establishes the ideal cosmos with humanity as vegetarian, the animals as herbivorous, and the sabbath rest as an institution reflective of the created order. After the flood, laws against homicide are inaugurated along with regulations concerning the slaughter of animals for food and an "eternal covenant" that promises no future deluge (Gen. 9).

With Abraham and Sarah, God makes an "eternal covenant" establishing their offspring as the deity's distinctive people who practice the rite of circumcision as a covenantal sign (Gen. 17). The deity reveals himself to the patriarchs using the name El Shaddai ("God Almighty"). The nation itself begins with the deliverance through Moses and the revelation of the divine name, Yahweh (Exod. 6). Through Moses the laws for the regulation of the religious life of the people are laid down at Sinai and on the wilderness journey. Preparations are made for the division of the land by tribal allotment (Num. 26, 27, 34–36) which is carried out by Joshua (Josh. 13–21).

While the interests of "P" lie primarily with priestly law and lore, his work is historiographical in that he locates such laws and customs in the remote past as the time of divine revelation. He attempts to do this with great chronological precision. The Priestly Code is a theocratic program associated with the constitutional age of Moses but intended for the time of the author in the postexilic period. In the ancient world, antiquarian historiography was a major preoccupation of priestly circles, who used the authority of the remote past as support for their religious programs, and the national histories of Greece also included extensive treatments of the state's "constitution," often reshaped to express the politics or ideology of the historian. The three historians—the author of the "Deuteronomistic

History," "J," and "P"—represent three different conceptions of national identity in their reconstructions of the time of Israel's origins.

Another major historical corpus in the Hebrew Bible is 1 and 2 Chronicles with closely related "supplements" in Ezra–Nehemia. There is much scholarly debate about whether these all represent the work of one author or of several within a complex redactional development. These issues need not concern us here. The historian of Chronicles was primarily interested in presenting a revised history of the monarchy of Judah while ignoring the kingdom of Israel. For this he drew heavily upon the history of Samuel–Kings, omitting what he did not wish to use and adding material of his own. He was not averse to making chronological or other factual changes for his own ideological purposes. He appeals to a large number of sources by name as authorities for his version, but these are clearly fictional. This is a practice common to Hellenistic historiography. As a prologue to the Judean monarchy, the Chronicler constructs an elaborate genealogy from creation to King Saul, derived largely from genealogical information in Genesis–Kings in its final form.

For the Chronicler, David and Solomon were completely idealized, and he places his "constitutional age" in this period. He seems to regard a dyarchy of political and religious authorities as the ideal system of governance. His history is highly moralistic, with both good and bad kings receiving the divine rewards or punishments they merited. His work reflects the historical method and perspective of Jerusalem in the Hellenistic period.

The book of Ezra is a continuation of Chronicles, beginning with the edict of Cyrus in 538 that allowed for the return from exile and the restoration of the temple and the community in Jerusalem. It attempts to fill in the historical picture down to the time of Ezra's mission, which is the main concern of the work. The author makes reference to official documents that he quotes as sources, but whether any are authentic is debatable. The book of Nehemiah is written in the autobiographical style of memoir, as discussed above, by a governor about his efforts to rebuild the walls of Jerusalem and about some religious reforms. The work was edited by the Chronicler's school to make his activity contemporaneous with that of Ezra, but the historical relationship between the two is much debated.

CONCLUSION

The above survey has attempted to show that the "uses of the past" as reflected in ancient near eastern historiography are very diverse and presented in many different forms. Generalizations spanning different civilizations over so long a period are always hazardous. Most of near eastern historiography in the form of annals, chronicles, kinglists, and commemorative inscriptions is related to concerns of the monarchy, its glorification and legitimation in the eyes of the people and its accountability before the gods. Disinterested research into the past or objective reporting of current events was virtually nonexistent in antiquity. The "Babylonian Chronicle" may be an exception, but even that is disputed.

While Israelite historiography made use of various near eastern genres, such as kinglists for chronology and perhaps royal inscriptions and chronicles for the deeds of the king, it went beyond anything yet known in the scope of its presentation of national history. Its focus is the origins, election, and "manifest destiny" of the people as a whole. The remote past and the recent past form the same continuum of divine activity in national and human affairs. Kings may be important actors and agents in this history, but so are other divinely appointed leaders, such as prophets and judges. It is the whole nation in its entire history that is accountable to the deity. In its concern to articulate national origins and identity and in its search for the causes of recent events in the remote past, Israelite historiography shares much with the early Greek historians and anticipates the rise of national histories in the modern world.

BIBLIOGRAPHY

Sources in Translation

MESOPOTAMIA

THORKILD JACOBSEN, *The Sumerian King List* (1939); A. K. GRAYSON, *Assyrian and Babylonian Chronicles*

(1975); and DANIEL D. LUCKENBILL, *Ancient Records of Assyria and Babylonia*, 2 vols. (1926–1927).

EGYPT

JAMES HENRY BREASTED, *Ancient Records of Egypt*, 5 vols. (1906–1907); and MIRIAM LICHTHEIM, *Ancient Egyptian Literature: A Book of Readings*, 3 vols. (1973–1980).

THE HITTITES

A collection of historiographic texts in translation is not easily accessible. A selection of literary texts from the ancient Near East including some Hittite and Syro-Palestinian historical texts may be found in JAMES B. PRITCHARD, ed., *Ancient Near Eastern Texts Relating to the Old Testament* (1950; 3rd ed. 1969).

ANCIENT ISRAEL

See the Hebrew Bible in various translations.

Studies

JOHN VAN SETERS, *In Search of History: Historiography in the Ancient World and the Origins of Biblical History* (1983), gives a more complete survey of the subject. See also ROBERT C. DENTAN, ed., *The Idea of History in the Ancient Near East* (1955), a collection of essays by various scholars on near eastern historiography.

MESOPOTAMIA

A. K. GRAYSON, "Histories and Historians of the Ancient Near East: Assyria and Babylonia," *Orientalia* 49 (1980); HANS GUSTAV GÜTERBOCK, "Die historische Tradition und ihre literarische Gestaltung bei Babyloniern und Hethitern bis 1200," *Zeitschrift für Assyriologie* 42 (1934) and 44 (1938); A. LEO OPPENHEIM, *Ancient Mesopotamia: Portrait of a Dead Civilization* (1964), especially pp. 144–153; PETER B. MACHINIST, "Literature as Politics: The Tukulti-Ninurta Epic and the Bible," *Catholic Biblical Quarterly* 38 (1976); and W. W. HALLO, "Sumerian Historiography," in *History, Historiography and Interpretation: Studies in Bibli-*

cal and Cuneiform Literatures, edited by H. TADMOR and M. WEINFELD (1983).

EGYPT

ALAN H. GARDINER, *Egypt of the Pharaohs: An Introduction* (1961), in which chapter 4 contains a useful introduction to some important Egyptian historical texts; E. OTTO, "Geschichtsbild und Geschichtsschreibung in Ägypten," *Die Welt des Orients* 3 (1966); ANTHONY J. SPALINGER, *Aspects of the Military Documents of the Ancient Egyptians* (1983); DONALD B. REDFORD, *Pharaonic King-Lists, Annals, and Day-Books* (1986); JOHN BAINES, "Ancient Egyptian Concepts and Uses of the Past: 3rd to 2nd Millennium BC Evidence," in *Who Needs the Past? Indigenous Values and Archaeology*, edited by ROBERT LAYTON (1989); and DAVID O'CONNOR and DAVID P. SILVERMAN, eds., *Ancient Egyptian Kingship: New Investigations* (1994), which contains several essays relevant to this chapter.

THE HITTITES

HUBERT CANCIK, *Grundzüge der hethitischen und alttestamentlichen Geschichtsschreibung* (1976); HANS GUSTAV GÜTERBOCK, "Hittite Historiography," in *History, Historiography, and Interpretation*, edited by H. TADMOR and M. WEINFELD (1983); HARRY A. HOFFNER, "Histories and Historians of the Ancient Near East: The Hittites," *Orientalia* 49 (1980).

ANCIENT ISRAEL

Basic to modern discussion of biblical historiography is the work of MARTIN NOTH, *Überlieferungsgeschichtliche Studien* (1943), translated into English as *The Deuteronomistic History* (1981) and *The Chronicler's History* (1987). See also GERHARD VON RAD, "The Beginnings of Historical Writing in Ancient Israel," in his *The Problem of the Hexateuch and Other Essays* (1966). On the Deuteronomistic history, see BURKE O. LONG, *First Kings with an Introduction to Historical Literature* (1984), and ANDREW D. H. MAYES, *The Story of Israel Between Settlement and Exile* (1983). On the historiography of the Pentateuch, see JOHN VAN SETERS, *Prologue to History: The Yahwist as Historian in Genesis* (1992).

SEE ALSO **Chronology: Issues and Problems** (Part 5, Vol. II); **The Deeds of Ancient Mesopotamian Kings** (Part 9, Vol. IV); and **Autobiographies in Ancient Western Asia** (Part 9, Vol. IV).

The Contemplative Life in the Ancient Near East

JAMES L. CRENSHAW

WHEN THE SAGES of ancient Egypt, Mesopotamia, and Israel contemplated reality, they assessed matters in two distinct ways; one firmly grounded in experience, the other abstract and philosophical. Central to both modes of understanding reality, the principle of analogy facilitated a moving from the better known to the less well known. From the beginning, philosophical ponderings of life's enigmas took the form of extensive dialogue in which opposing viewpoints found expression and vied for acceptance. In contrast to this dialogic way of addressing the world around them, others observed what was accessible to the naked eye and crystallized insights about human beings or nature in brief aphorisms, riddles, and popular sayings.

In time the gnomic apperception of reality receded as teachers expanded earlier insights in an effort to communicate with students. Modern scholars therefore distinguish between sayings and instructions. Stimulated by the natural tendency to view the universe in terms of binary opposition—for example, light and darkness, good and evil—this approach encouraged an exploration of deeper reasons for the presence of troublesome aspects of reality along with the good. The two ways of viewing reality therefore reinforced one another.

THE LITERATURE

Instructions

In Egypt a technical term, seba'it, designates instructions, although the expression also refers to other forms of literature (these forms are discussed in "Ancient Egyptian Literature: An Overview" in this section). Among the earliest instructions are some that purport to offer advice from pharaohs to their young sons, the heir apparents. Hence, the subject matter was essentially directed toward preparing princes and their high officials for later responsibilities in government: for example, appropriate etiquette, table manners, conduct in the presence of officials, eloquence, restraint, behavior with respect to women, control of passions, knowing when to speak and when to be silent. Not all instructions were restricted to royalty, for the majority of texts are attributed to courtiers wishing to prepare their sons to succeed them at the royal court. The demotic instructions known from the Greco-Roman Period were probably written by ordinary, literate citizens—as a sort of manual for self-improvement.

Over the two millennia from the earliest instructions to these products of popularizing reflection, a decisive change is discernible. At first those who formulated these teachings looked confidently on the order of the universe and took the deity's control for granted. In their view, persons deserving favor received it and those whose conduct merited punishment did not prosper. With the coming of the Middle Kingdom, optimism such as Ptahhotep's "Baseness may seize riches, yet crime never lands its wares" waned and an altogether different mood apparently set in, with serious consequences.

Accompanying the anxiety generated by notable social changes was a piety in which individuals sought to incur divine favor by prayer and virtue. During the period of demotic literature the power of fate began to dominate the surviving instructions, chiefly *Ankhsheshonqy* (*'Onkhsheshonqy*) and Papyrus Insinger. Both instructions stressed the necessity of pleasing the gods, never reconciling the contradiction between fate and the power of the gods but allowing the two notions to function in a complementary manner.

Another decisive change occurred in these late instructions, the adoption of a form that adhered to a single line for each saying. Earlier teachings had begun with a conditional statement, followed by an observation and an explanation or justification for the comment. Because all instructions seek to shape character and to stimulate action, they regularly employ imperatives, a feature biblical scholars have exaggerated in formal analysis. Papyrus Insinger and *Ankhsheshonqy* link the imperatives together in chain fashion, with verbal links connecting anaphoric chains. Whereas older Egyptian instructions influenced biblical Proverbs, the demotic ones have left their impact on Qoheleth (Ecclesiastes) and Sirach (also known as Ecclesiasticus or Ben Sira, whose text is replete with paragraph-length instructions).

The oldest Mesopotamian proverbs, the *Instructions of Shuruppak*, use the technical expression "my son" in the sense of student, a characteristic of Egyptian and biblical instructions also. The latter comprise the initial collection of Proverbs, chapters 1–9, as well as a section betraying the influence of the Egyptian *Instruction of Amenemope*, 22:17–23:22, and a brief unit attributed to King Lemuel's mother in chapter 31:1–10. The Neo-Assyrian text, *Counsels to a Prince*, also belongs to this instruction genre, as do *Counsels of Wisdom* and *Counsels of a Pessimist*.

Sayings

No Egyptian collection of sayings has survived, but numerous traditional sayings and aphorisms are scattered throughout the instructions and are embedded in other literary forms, especially narrative. Collections of proverbs exist in Sumerian and Old Babylonian, just as they do in the Bible, chiefly in Proverbs but also in Qoheleth and Sirach. An Aramaic collection of riddles and proverbs, *The Sayings of Ahiqar*, resembles Mesopotamian texts and thus renders plausible its narrative framework about a Mesopotamian setting.

Dialogue

The other way of assessing reality—philosophical reflection—deals with weighty matters, especially the problem of life's inequities. Only one text from Egypt, *The Admonitions of Ipuwer*, addresses the issue of theodicy (divine justice) as such, and this particular section may be a later addition. Other works take up many issues typically found in theodicies, especially *The Harper's Songs, The Dialogue of a Man with His Ba*, and to some extent *The Tale of the Eloquent Peasant* and *The Book of the Dead*. Two biblical exemplars of this genre, Job and Qoheleth, have greatly influenced Western thinkers. Both Sirach and Wisdom of Solomon contain mini-discussions of the anxiety generated by evil in a universe supposedly created and ruled by a benevolent deity. A few psalms also broach the issue, either to deny that any problem exists, as in Psalm 37, or to forge new insights, as in Psalms 49 and 73.

Several examples of theodicy derive from Mesopotamia. *The Sumerian Man and His God* is the oldest known expression of the Job problem, but the later *I Will Praise the Lord of Wisdom* and *The Babylonian Theodicy* develop the form in the direction that the biblical Job adopts. *A Pessimistic Dialogue Between a Master and His Slave* struggles with the problematic nature of reality that causes such consternation in Qoheleth. These Mesopotamian texts set precedent for: blaming the gods; recommending repentance and correct ritual; arguing with a friend about God's justice; introducing and concluding poetry with a mythological framing narrative; and considering both sides of opposing intellectual positions.

COMPOSITION

Myths

What prompted the authors of these sapiential insights to adopt forms of expression intended to convey their meaning to a wider public? A didactic impulse seems to have accompanied dialogue and instruction—perhaps, even sayings—from their inception. This inherent didacticism does not exclude a conscious attempt at a later time to turn simple statements into *literary* products. The functional aspect of knowledge prevailed, its capacity to enrich life in quite tangible ways. According to a royal myth echoed in Proverbs 25:2, deity and king enacted a reciprocal drama by hiding and seeking valuable facts about the universe and its inhabitants. Presumably, the creator concealed such data in observable reality and thereby presented a challenge for humankind, especially its representative leader, to search for insights that would facilitate steering life's course into safe harbor. The operative phrase "What is good for men and women?" survived the very questioning of the intellectual quest's validity. Qoheleth retained the myth of the deity's concealing essential data (3:11) but pronounced a negative judgment on human ability to profit from this dubious gift. Similarly, the author of Job 28 restricted something called wisdom to the deity, announcing that no one else came any closer to it than secondary reporting. Sirach goes a step farther, attributing secrecy to wisdom itself.

Underlying this myth was a significant theological issue—the freedom of God. That prerogative of deity to act without restraint from external sources seems threatened by the sapiential notion of an order governing the universe. In Egypt the principle of *ma'at* represented this divine order that assured governmental, societal, and individual well-being. A corresponding principle in Mesopotamia seems to be implied by the Tablets of Destiny, called in the Sumerian language ME. The Israelite concepts of justice, *mišpat*, and right dealing, *ṣᵉdāqāh*, functioned in the way *ma'at* and ME did elsewhere.

At first glance this objective order appears to compromise the deity's freedom, but even this principle remained subject to God's free will. At the same time, sages spoke openly of deeds that carried within them the capacity to set into motion events commensurate with the originating act, whether for punishment or for reward. Occasional canonical sayings within the book of Proverbs accentuate the fundamental limits imposed on the human intellect; these reminders that "humans propose but God disposes" resemble sayings in Egyptian instructions. The latest surviving Egyptian instruction, Papyrus Insinger, develops this notion of fate into a refrain while also acknowledging the deity's active involvement in shaping human destiny. Resolving apparently contradictory statements was not essential in the ancient world; rigorous thinkers have always managed to flourish without pressing for closure on disputed matters.

Forms

This open-ended worldview of sages achieved expression in specific forms, chiefly saying and instruction, but also in related ones. Interpreters generally assume that the elemental form, the saying, existed initially as a product of popular insights. Brief maxims and aphorisms simply registered the way things were without pronouncing judgment or advocating corrective action. Several traditional sayings have survived in the narrative and prophetic literature of the Bible; others, in expanded form, may be embedded in the wisdom corpus. Occupying a transitional stage between popular saying and didactic poem, riddles captured the surprise of discovery and directed it toward the teaching task. Only Mesopotamian wisdom has preserved riddles intact, but once again Israelite narrative, more particularly the story of Samson in Judges 14, fills the gap left tantalizingly open by explicit references to riddles as a sapiential concern (Proverbs 1:6; Sirach 39:1–3). Several proverbs structured by ascending numbers betray affinities with riddles, and in one instance the specific allusion to numbers has vanished but the normal interrogative form of riddles takes its place (Sirach 1:2–3).

The popular saying, often only a half line, commanded assent by its content alone. Instructions relied on motivation clauses and warnings to persuade others that their teachings were valid. This extended discourse developed into didactic poems which treated single themes at greater length than occurred in sayings and instructions. At this point erotic overtones color the expression of paternal will, either in the form of positive seduction to the intellectual enterprise or in the guise of negative warnings about strange women who lured young men to the grave.

Other didactic poems tackle the vexing problem of aging and its final victory, they acknowledge the tyranny of time over all flesh, or they celebrate the worth of a good woman. An impressive group of poems explores the means through which deity communicates with mortals, at first envisioning nothing more than poetic metaphor but afterwards contemplating an actual expression of the divine will in legal form, and eventually opting for a virtual hypostasis in which the deity becomes manifest on earth. Echoes of a polytheistic environment persist in this mythologos, with features deriving from Egyptian *ma῾at* traditions and eulogies of Isis cast in the form of speeches or aretologies. Didactic poems delve into the wonder and majesty surrounding the creative process, both the divine act by which everything came into existence and the human intellectual adventure that endeavors to make sense of reality as it presents itself to inquiring minds.

Pedagogic interests generated yet another form of communication, the exemplary tale. The autobiographical character of these stories bestows credibility and authority on them. A concerned teacher reports on the fatal attraction of two people who come together for illicit sexual pleasure, an older person recalls near-disastrous personal decisions during his youth, an astute observer calls attention to the undesirable results of laziness, a fictional monarch sums up his life's work and assesses its worth, a sober social analyst registers dismay over society's lack of appreciation for the contribution of scholars, and so on.

Of course, such communicative devices gave birth to related ones, for example, exemplary tale to parable, parable to allegory, and dialogue to dispute. One parable uses the ant's furious pace in preparing for winter's scarcity as incentive to action. Such appeal to lessons from nonhuman creatures played a significant role in ancient wisdom. Mesopotamian disputes between animals or trees over the merits of different species reflect a similar epistemological assumption that nature itself functions as a bearer of knowledge. That polytheistic environment also encouraged informed evaluation of rival deities through disputes. In Israel the dispute form developed into internal debate, a conversation with the self in which Qoheleth considers what he has seen and draws rational conclusions from the available evidence. The Egyptian *Dispute Between a Man and His Ba* differs dramatically in its view of an entity, the *ba*, that survives death. The arrangement of aphorisms into a statement, then a contradiction, an objection, or a confirmation demonstrates the sages' fondness for dialogue.

Not all stylistic devices employed by the sages

Foreign Woman

Beware of a woman who is a stranger,
One not known in her town;
Don't stare at her when she goes by,
Do not know her carnally.
A deep water whose course is unknown,
Such is a woman away from her husband.
"I am pretty," she tells you daily,
When she has no witnesses;
She is ready to ensnare you,
A great deadly crime when it is heard.

Instruction of Ani

You will be saved from the loose (strange)
   woman,
from the adventuress with her smooth words,
who forsakes the companion of her youth
and forgets the covenant of her God;
for her house sinks down to death,
and her paths to the shades;
all who go to her cannot come back
nor do they regain the paths of life.

Proverbs 2:16–19 (*cf.* 5:20; 6:24; 7:5)

On Old Age

O king, my Lord!
Age is here, old age arrived,
Feebleness came, weakness grows,
Childlike one sleeps all day.
Eyes are dim, ears deaf,
Strength is waning through weariness,
The mouth, silenced, speaks not,
The heart, void, recalls not the past,
The bones ache throughout.
Good has become evil, all taste is gone,
What age does to people is evil in everything.
The nose, clogged, breathes not,
Painful are standing and sitting.

Ptahhotep

Remember also your Creator in the days of your youth, before the evil days come, and the years draw nigh, when you will say, "I have no pleasure in them"; before the sun and the light and the moon and the stars are darkened and the clouds return after the rain; in the day when the keepers of the house tremble, and the strong men are bent, and the grinders cease because they are few . . . the almond tree blossoms, the grasshopper drags itself along and desire fails. . . .

Ecclesiastes 12:1–7

(I was) a youth, (but now) my luck, my strength, my personal god and my youthful vigour have left my loins like an exhausted ass. My black mountain has produced white gypsum . . . my mongoose which used to eat strong smelling things does not stretch its neck towards beer and butter. My teeth which used to chew strong things can no more chew strong things. . . .

The Old Man and the Young Girl

are unique to their literature. The book of Job makes copious use of the lament form, common to Psalms and to comparable texts from Mesopotamia. Later wisdom, especially Sirach, introduced prayer and hymn into the sapiential vocabulary. Prior to this embracing of religious language, the only prayer occurs in the late excerpt attributed to Agur and the nearest semblance to a hymn heightens the tension between Job and his friends by pointing to the mystery of the universe and its maker. The hymnic praise of the creator comes into its own in Sirach; in addition, Ben Sira adapts a Hellenistic form, the encomium, to heap accolades on heroes of the past.

Social Settings

Do these rhetorical devices indicate the social setting for their use? Unfortunately, one cannot move from literary genre to precise locations in society. This issue must be addressed from country to country, and even within a given environment distinctions readily surface. Egyptian instructions presuppose a royal context, but this intimate connection with the court is not absolute. Scribal schools existed primarily as a function of area temples, instructing religious personnel in the necessary ritual and in theological texts. The language and themes of individual instructions do not provide easy access to the social location of the authors. Villagers can readily discuss royalty and their doings, just as courtiers can talk about agrarian tasks. The fact that only about one-tenth of *Ankhsheshonqy's* sayings deal with agricultural topics hardly settles the question of origins. The Sumerian school, EDUBBA, may have served as a locus for learned discourse, as well as for education at all levels of instruction. Here, as also in Egypt, noun lists, or onomastica, assisted in the study of language and grammar, perhaps also in providing data for a broader education itself.

Ancient Israelite literature derives from several different social contexts. The authors of Proverbs, Job, Ecclesiastes, and Sirach occupied distinct social worlds, and a single book like Proverbs reflects several settings. To be sure, most of the sayings revolve around life in small villages and restrict themselves to the nuclear family. The latter point detracts from the hypothesis of clan wisdom, for members of an extended family are never mentioned. The instructions are directed to yet another group, young urban men, possibly potential officials at the royal court. Given the court's minor role in these sayings and instructions, perhaps one should assume that both forms eventually played a significant role in the scribal school, for which the earliest firm evidence is the second-century BCE remark by Ben Sira. Inscriptional evidence has generated a hypothesis of widespread schools in Palestine from early monarchic times, but these data—particularly abecedaries, exercise tablets, crude drawings, and foreign-language texts—can be readily explained without resort to the claim of a vast educational network. Literacy in the ancient world rarely exceeded 10 percent, and in most instances it ran considerably lower. The modern advance in literacy is a direct result of several factors: the invention of the printing press; the industrial revolution's need for trained workers; state sponsorship of education, assisted by exceptional philanthropists; Protestantism's emphasis on knowing the Bible; the availability of eyeglasses; population density sufficient to support public education; and affordable writing materials. Ancient literacy was ordinarily restricted to males with administrative legal functions; exceptions occurred only with respect to the daughters of a few rulers and high officials. (For a further discussion, see the chapters on "Memory and Literacy in Ancient Western Asia" and "The Story of the Semitic Alphabet" in this section.)

At least three social groups factor into the discussion of the book of Job, according to a recent plausible theory. Two wealthy groups, one of which objects to taking advantage of the poor, contend for supremacy. The cruel upper class against which Job rails has no compassion for the underprivileged who in their view exist only to be used. Qoheleth belonged to an acquisitive society, one in which financial success counted heavily. He has been accused, with dubious justification, of membership in a cruel, calculating upper crust within society that held the poor in contempt. Such a harsh reading of the book ignores the pathos of Qoheleth's observation about defenseless victims of oppression. Strictly speaking, one can only conclude that Qoheleth's *audience* possessed the means to enjoy life that he enjoins as a way of dealing with absurdity everywhere.

Although Egyptian and Mesopotamian wisdom had a positive relationship with the royal court, Israelite attitudes toward kingship and a discernible enthusiasm for simpler societal structures produced conflicting texts. Despite a royal myth that includes attributing collections of sayings and even two entire books, Ecclesiastes and Wisdom of Solomon, to a king, the nature of the proverbial sayings and the celebration of Edomite sagacity imply that in some circles marginal existence apart from society's corrupting influence was viewed as more pristine. Presumably, in that purer state knowledge came much more naturally.

THEMES

Creation

The fundamental themes of wisdom literature are religion and knowledge. Beginning with an assumption that truth applies universally and thus was not confined to private experience or limited to any geographical area, sages concentrated on the initiating event that made life possible in its manifold localities and variants. In Israelite wisdom the creative act was placed under the umbrella of divine justice, for it was believed that appropriate reward or punishment could only be dispensed by one who controlled the universe. Even social distinctions on the basis of access to property failed to efface the unique feature uniting all humanity in a single community—their mortality—or to compromise the fact that rich and poor had the same maker. Radical dissenters like Qoheleth did not challenge the common conception that the created world was a thing of beauty, despite occasional examples of twistedness. According to the wisdom myth, the original act of creation culminated in rejoicing on the part of the morning stars and, in one bold text, the creator's youthful female companion, unless one accepts the alternative reading, master craftsman.

One type of creation myth included a battle between the power representing order and an opposing force characterized by instability. This "struggle against chaos" has left its imprint on numerous hymnic texts within the Bible, especially those incorporated in Deutero-Isaiah and

Psalms. This version of creation in which the Israelite deity prevails over chaos has close parallels in ancient Babylon, best known from the conflict between Marduk and Tiamat recorded in *Enuma Elish* (this myth is examined in "Myth and Mythmaking in Sumer and Akkad.") The belief that a violent event fashioned the arena for life's drama evoked similar myths throughout the ancient world, competing with the explanation of origins in natural, or sexual, imagery. Some interpreters think the struggle between Baal and Yamm (Yam) in Ugaritic myth actually disguises the creative act under the story about constructing a palace for Baal.

Isrealite sages transformed the chaos myth into a story about domesticating the forces of evil, or more accurately, restricting their scope. Thus the deity who spoke to Job in the whirlwind boasts about setting limits for the chaos monster, circumscribing its movement and wrapping it in swaddling bands. In this version of the myth the real problem of chaos shifts to the human arena, and the faintest hint of divine weakness over this evil probably achieves expression. In its social dimension evil poses a constant problem requiring perpetual vigilance on the part of the deity and virtuous mortals.

Fear of God

The sages' emphasis on creation acknowledged major indebtedness on the part of human beings toward the deity, for life itself derived from the creator. Occasionally this knowledge led to the rejection of any claim with respect to the deity based on virtuous conduct, for no gift to or from God could ever rival the one already freely bestowed on mortals. Given this situation, it is a little surprising that a concept of reward and retribution became common belief, virtually hardening into dogma. At the same time, the sages also recognized their complete dependence on the creator's good will, hence the necessity for proper fear. This notion of fear before the deity included the sense of dread in the presence of a potential threat as well as genuine submission in obedient love. In its fullest sense the expression "fear of God" is the closest the sages ever came to the modern idea connoted by the word "religion."

Although the evidence lacks clarity, some in-terpreters think the sentiment expressing fear of God was originally missing from the sayings. In modern categories, they would have been thoroughly secular. This understanding of the sayings underscores the fact that several aphorisms whose form bears the marks of great antiquity are remarkably silent about any deity, relying solely on human action without regard to transcendent motivation. Such silence does not necessarily mean that the authors of these texts were irreligious. Egyptian wisdom literature also betrays a growing overt pietism as a direct consequence of the collapse of traditional values during the era immediately preceding the composition of *The Instruction of Any* (Eighteenth Dynasty). In this work and in subsequent ones personal piety replaced a strong sense of self-reliance characterizing earlier wisdom. One seems drawn to the conclusion that the world was viewed as less penetrable than had been the case during the early days of Egyptian and Israelite wisdom.

The failure of traditional belief may have affected only a small segment of the population, whereas secular sayings may derive from well-placed individuals at the palace. Perhaps the authors of these precepts saw no need to articulate self-evident views that temple functionaries explicitly mentioned in their literature. A conviction that a person could cope with every eventuality may easily have existed alongside the belief that divine assistance was essential to successful endeavor. Hence modern attempts to discern an increase in piety reflecting a crisis of confidence may be correct for only a select group of ancient thinkers.

Esoteric Knowledge

Although the formula "Let the initiate instruct the initiate; the uninitiated may not see" does not always imply esoteric knowledge, certain texts in Egypt and Mesopotamia, intentionally secret, suggest an elitist—perhaps even a mystical—tradition as early as the second millennium, one that goes far beyond the elitism accompanying literacy and possession of information concerning magical ritual. Egyptian initiation texts, such as the *Book of Amduat*, the *Book of Gates*, the *Book of the Heavenly Cow*, and the *Book of the Dead* (chap. 148), restrict gnosis to a select group or claim extraordinary knowledge of ritual for a chosen person such as the vizier User (see "Death and the Afterlife in Ancient Egyptian Thought" in Part 8, Vol. III, for further discussion). Mesopotamian mystical and mythological explanatory works employ the numerical device, gematria; they also comment on mystical numbers and names of deities, identify gods with various parts of the world through analogy or specification, offer mystical descriptions of gods, explain state rituals in terms of the myths by which people lived, and interpret the god's (Marduk's) ordeal existentially. Some of these texts state that the contents are "a secret of the scholar," adding that "the uninitiated shall not see." Occasionally, a scribe expects readers to know another text by heart; for instance, one ancient scholar cites only the first line of *Enuma Elish*. An aim of a few texts was identification with a deity, sharing mythic conflicts and victories.

Within seventh-century Israel a quasi-mystical surge in the thinking of two prophets, Jeremiah and Ezekiel, may have taken place. Claiming to have been given access to the divine council, Jeremiah insists that his opponents were not similarly gifted. He even uses language that accords with a mystical understanding of the word, which he characterizes as a fire and a hammer (23:29). His contemporary Ezekiel describes the divine departure from the temple of Jerusalem in mystical categories, leading to later restrictions on just who could read these visions. Prophetic books, such as Joel, cite earlier prophecies and interpret them in new ways; thus, an exegetical tradition emerges to prominence in postexilic and Hellenistic Judaism. Apocalyptists soon boasted of esoteric knowledge, comparable to Jeremiah's claim to special disclosure. An elitist tradition flourishes at Qumran and in pseudepigraphic literature, partly because some contemporaries believed that revealed writings necessarily derived from ancient worthies. (For a further discussion, see "Prophecy and Apocalyptics in the Ancient Near East" in Part 8, Vol. III.)

Personified Wisdom

The tension between self-reliance and resort to the deity in special circumstances, or indeed in all circumstances, was eventually eased through a remarkable myth. Israel's poets frequently spoke of abstract divine qualities in a personified manner, for example when picturing righteousness and truth as kissing one another. The wisdom of God naturally lent itself to such personification, as did divine power and speech, which were personified by the Aramaic terms *gebûrâ* and *memra*. Wisdom, *ḥokmâ* in Hebrew, represented the divine logic by which the universe took shape, the structuring of things into a coherent order.

The erotic dimension inherent to all knowledge found suitable expression in this personification of the thought processes, the inexplicable seduction of the human mind by the unknown. Curiously, Israel's stout resistance in official circles to fertility religion did not prevent enthusiastic development of an erotic relationship between students and wisdom. The sages spoke freely about wisdom as a seductress who lures young men to her banquet, but they also conceded that she had a rival in this game of love, one who capitalized on her exceptional physical attributes inflaming youthful passions by smooth limbs and speech. The personified wisdom thus was forced to adopt extreme measures, hence the emphasis on her turning to human beings in love, a notion that does not appear in Egyptian description of a comparable figure, *maʿat*, the goddess of "right order." In Israelite wisdom, seekers of knowledge are invited to pitch their tent near wisdom's and to pursue her relentlessly, ignoring her initial rebuff in assurance that perseverance will reap rich reward. A partial defusing of this myth occurs in the Hellenistic Wisdom of Solomon, where the intellectual quest has achieved its goal and gained wisdom, now the familiar Sophia from Greek philosophy, as wife. Here love's ardor burns under the protective canopy of piety.

Quite a different redirection of erotic ardor takes place in Sirach, where daughters in particular do not receive adequate appreciation—despite Ben Sira's enthusiasm for some women and an appendix to the book that is arguably rich in eroticisms. The development by certain psalmists of something called Torah piety led Ben Sira to a bold move, the identification of Torah with God's wisdom. In this way a divine attribute has taken up residence in Jerusalem, assuming

Human Plans and Divine Action

God is ever in his perfection,
   Man is ever in his failure.
The words men say are one thing,
   The deeds of the god are another.

Amenemope 19:14–17

The plans of the god are one thing, the
   thoughts of [men] are another.

Ankhsheshonqy 26:24

The plans of the mind belong to man,
   but the answer of the tongue is from the
   Lord.

Proverbs 16:1

Many are the plans of the mind of a man,
   but it is the purpose of the Lord that will
   be established.

Proverbs 19:21

Formation of Character

How did wisdom express itself in the lives of sages? In both Egypt and Israel, four character traits distinguish wise from foolish, good from evil: silence, eloquence, timeliness, and modesty. The first requires control over passions; the silent person does not permit anger, lust, greed, or envy to dominate thought or action. The opposite, the heated individual, gives passion a free rein. The second quality, eloquence, enables sages to persuade others and to communicate effectively, while timeliness, the third quality, implies an awareness about the appropriate moment for speaking, valuing non-speaking as a powerful form of communication. The fourth, modesty, indicates humility arising from knowledge that life's mysteries will never be fully divulged to those who search for truth.

The premise underlying the sages' elevation of these characteristics is clearly opportunistic. Some interpreters prefer the term eudaemonistic (hedonistic). The fundamental question, "What is good for men and women?" reveals

visible form in the Mosaic covenant, the law. Furthermore, this wisdom evokes comparison with knowledge in the story of the fall, for the paradisaic myth of the rivers recurs here in Ben Sira's musings about the composition of his book.

Why this striving to mediate transcendence in a tangible manner? The sages' concept of God is remarkably silent with regard to the saving deeds extolled within official Yahwism. This theological position is a corollary of an ethical view emphasizing self-worth, a coping with life on one's own. As confidence in one's ability dwindled, particularly after the collapse of the concept of the extended family and later the state, sages began to recognize their own reliance on divine compassion. Wisdom mediated God's concern for mortals. The transcendent creator draws near and makes known the secrets to success and happiness. Most revealing of all, for those who think of the divine law as oppressive, the person who equates wisdom and Torah also introduces the attribute of divine mercy into the discourse of the sages to a degree unprecedented in his time.

Good Deeds

Do a good deed and throw it in the water;
   when it dries you will find it.

Ankhsheshonqy 19:10

Cast your bread upon the waters,
   for you will find it after many days.

Ecclesiastes 11:1

The Shame of Begging

Better is the short time of him who is old
   than the long life of him who begs (or has
   begged).

Papyrus Insinger 17:19

My son, do not lead the life of a beggar;
   it is better to die than to beg.

Sirach 40:28

their anthropocentric orientation. Nevertheless, the sages believed that their virtuous conduct did more than guarantee good rewards in the form of wealth, health, progeny, and honor. They also thought their actions sustained the order of the world, preventing a return to chaos. Hence eudaemonism was rooted in ethical philosophy, transforming an apparent selfish act into a moral and religious deed. In their view, the world was always at risk. This fear explains their incessant struggle against those who posed the most formidable threat—fools—and the fervent pleading with vulnerable students—called sons—that they adopt their teacher's worldview.

Sporadic victories by representatives of evil called into question the comfortable eudaemonism and forced sages to reckon with suffering and mortality. The lyrical "I" soon led to a heightened ego, an almost inevitable consequence of the hurting self, and eventuated in uncommon pride of authorship, at least for Ben Sira. With Qoheleth, egoism affects the form of expression, the teacher daring to assess everything as absurd on the basis on his own personal experience. The union of epistemology and theology persists in Qoheleth, who drew the painful conclusion that human beings cannot discern whether or not the deity turns to them in love or hate, all the while speaking effusively about divine gifts. The problem lay in the changed status from one who earned life's rewards to a person depending on divine handouts over which the recipient had no control. More specifically, the apparent arbitrary conduct of the deity generated increased anxiety.

FUNCTION

Education

The literature produced by ancient near eastern sages served several purposes, all of which belong to the general category of education. Egyptian and Sumerian school texts assisted in the task of instructing students for the many demands of professional life, potentially at the court, but also as scribes responsible for all sorts of economic transactions. Training in requisite languages, contract forms, epistolary style, and regulations pertaining to international commerce probably occurred in the schools, and such instruction required paradigms and exemplars of diverse kinds. Sample examination questions have been identified among surviving Egyptian scribal texts, particularly in Papyrus Anastasi I, indicating that students learned considerable general knowlege of local geography, perhaps while practicing grammar and calligraphy. The complex hieroglyphs and cuneiform signs necessitated close attention to detail beyond the aesthetics of nicely shaped letters. The abecedaries recovered from Palestine probably indicate scribal practice in forming the vastly simpler Hebrew alphabet, but the silence in Hebrew literature concerning schools has elicited opposite explanations: no schools existed, or schools were so prevalent that no one ever thought about mentioning them.

Debate

Possibly the most useful texts in implementing pedagogical strategies for advanced students, the philosophical debates covered a wide range

---

On Disciplining One's Son

Withhold not your son from the rod, else you
    will not be able to save [him from
    wickedness]. If I smite you, my son, you
    will not die, but if I leave you to your
    own heart [you will not live].

Sayings of Ahiqar 4

He who loves his son will whip him often,
    in order that he may rejoice at the way he
    turns out.

Sirach 30:1

He who spares the rod hates his son,
    but he who loves him is diligent to
    discipline him.

Proverbs 13:24

You beat my back; your teachings entered my
    ear.

Papyrus Lansing

of responses to difficult intellectual problems. Such literature offered alternative solutions to the vexing issues the populace encountered every day, although the stellar example of this genre in Israel, the book of Job, portrays its disputants as pastoralists rather than as scribes or sages. This unusual feature highlights the simple fact that ancient learning, however academic, did not occur within the confines of an ivory tower but took place at the center of daily activity and addressed pressing questions that directly affected human lives. The same point underlies the description of woman wisdom in Proverbs as a rhetor practicing her trade in busy streets where she had to compete with vendors of all types. In this respect the similarity with Hellenistic peripatetic philosophers comes to mind.

Entertainment

Debate did not always focus on serious existential issues, for the sages found time to enjoy the art of storytelling and the clever defense of an intellectual position. An example of the former is the remarkable contest of Darius's guards recorded in 1 Esdras 3:1–4:41, which examines the relative merits of wine, king, woman, and truth under the rubric "What is greatest?" An intriguing remark by the servant in the *Babylonian Dialogue Between a Master and Slave* suggests that intellectual exchange occurred at banquets, hence that symposia played a significant role in early education. That incidental remark has parallels in Egyptian wisdom literature also, and the pseudepigraphic Epistle of Aristeas develops the notion of scintillating, greatly detailed conversation during meals. Mesopotamian fables served a dual purpose of entertainment and practice in defending a particular viewpoint. These fables sometimes required students to make discerning judgments about the relative merits of various aspects of society—for example, tools, animals, vocations, deities. The combined sayings and instructions reflect societal values about numerous topics, but they do not constitute a complete moral code, for some important dimensions of life are strangely missing.

Taxonomies

A few texts from Egypt and many more from Mesopotamia comprise zoological and botanical taxonomies, an exhaustive list of various species. A curious legend in 1 Kings 4:29–34 (Hebrew 5:9–14) attributes this sort of learning to Solomon, who is said to have compiled proverbs about trees, beasts, birds, reptiles, and fish. Those interpreters who consider this text historically credible understand Solomon's contribution to the genre to be the actual formulation of poetic sayings incorporating such taxonomies. Encyclopedic lists in Egypt and Mesopotamia probably served a dual function, facilitating the practice of language and writing.

Ritual

Mesopotamian scribal texts served an important role in ritual, especially magic. Incantations dealing with all kinds of circumstances enabled society to reckon with multiple threats to existence. Liturgical paradigms such as *I Will Praise the Lord of Wisdom* enjoined proper religious response to calamity. Egyptian ritual incantations also claimed the attention of learned scribes, and the biblical Job's protestations of innocence in chapter 31 resemble oaths of innocence in Egypt and Mesopotamia. Otherwise biblical wisdom practiced restraint with respect to religious ritual prior to Ben Sira, whose priestly leanings led to unchecked exuberance at witnessing the high priest in procession on a holy day. This late biblical sage also compiled an expansive eulogy honoring great men of the past; in doing so, he incorporated Yahwistic tradition into wisdom thought.

Polemic

Some sapiential texts functioned polemically to defend the scribal profession, perhaps necessitated by harsh measures employed in the classroom, for which several scribal texts in Egypt and at least one school text from Sumer provide vivid documentation. Ben Sira's defense of the scribe's vocation has some affinity with the much earlier Egyptian *Instruction of Khety*, although the phenomenon of polygenesis may be at work here rather than direct literary dependence. Naturally, opposing views among the sages resulted in literature rich with polemic. Sometimes polemical attacks on outsiders intrude into sapiential texts, as when Ben Sira explodes against traditional enemies of Israel and Wisdom of Solomon launches a verbal assault against Egyptian idolaters.

Counsel

Just as Egyptians had officials at the royal court who needed instruction, Mesopotamians also employed scribes for whom appropriate guidance was necessary, as the story of Ahiqar implies. Whether or not an actual royal counselor advised biblical kings remains unclear, although the story about David mentions two counselors, Ahithophel and Hushai. The obscure title "men of Hezekiah" alluded to in Proverbs 25:1 indirectly links these sayings with royalty.

CONCLUSION

A significant literature from ancient Egypt, Mesopotamia, and Israel possesses sufficient thematic and formal unity to suggest a common context of origin and purpose, allowing for distinctions in the several areas. Those texts comprise the ancient effort to acquire knowledge and to embody wisdom in personal character. To achieve that worthy goal, the sages collected traditional insights of the populace and added their own learned conclusions about reality. In doing so, they bequeathed an important legacy to posterity.

BIBLIOGRAPHY

Israelite Wisdom

JAMES L. CRENSHAW, *Old Testament Wisdom* (1981), is a general introduction to Israelite wisdom in its ancient near eastern context; and his *Studies in Ancient Israelite Wisdom* (1976), provides an extensive collection of essays by various scholars; JOHANNES FICHTNER, *Die altorientalische Weisheit in ihrer israelitisch-jüdischen Ausprägung* (1933), is a valuable synthesis of the scholarly interpretation of an earlier time; JOHN G. GAMMIE and LEO G. PERDUE, eds., *The Sage in Israel and the Ancient Near East* (1990), is an important collection of articles covering a wide range of topics; and JOHN GAMMIE ET AL., eds., *Israelite Wisdom: Theological and Literary Essays in Honor of Samuel Terrien* (1978), offers articles on many facets of biblical wisdom; ROLAND E. MURPHY, *The Tree of Life: An Exploration of Biblical Wisdom Literature* (1990), provides nontechnical treatment of biblical wisdom literature intended for educated lay readers; GERHARD VON RAD, *Wisdom in Israel*, translated by JAMES D. MARTON (1972), explores the limits of knowledge and provides good analyses of biblical wisdom books; and HORST DIETRICH PREUSS, *Einführung in die alttestamentliche Weisheitsliteratur* (1987), is a useful introduction, often expressing views at variance with much scholarship.

Social Context

CLAUS WESTERMANN, *Wurzeln der Weisheit: Die ältesten Sprüche Israels und anderer Völker* (1990), studies the social context within which Israelite wisdom flourished; and R. N. WHYBRAY, *The Intellectual Tradition in the Old Testament* (1974), views wisdom as a product of upper-class intellectuals rather than of a professional class.

Babylonian Wisdom

W. G. LAMBERT, *Babylonian Wisdom Literature* (1960), includes texts and translations of major works; M. LIVINGSTONE, *Mystical and Mythological Explanatory Works of Assyrian and Babylonian Scholars* (1986).

Egyptian Wisdom

ALEIDA ASSMANN, JAN ASSMANN, and C. HARDMEIR, eds., *Schrift und Gedächtnis* (1983), collects essays on ancient thought; JOHN BAINES, "Restricted Knowledge, Hierarchy, and Decorum: Modern Perceptions and American Institutions," *Journal of the American Research Center in Egypt* 27 (1990), discusses the social position of ancient elite knowledge; HELLMUT BRUNNER, *Altägyptische Weisheit: Lehren für das Leben* (1988), is a translation of ancient Egyptian wisdom literature; and MIRIAM LICHTHEIM, *Ancient Egyptian Literature*, 3 vols. (1973–1980), contains translations of the relevant texts, with notes.

Colloquia on Ancient Near Eastern Wisdom

Les Sagesses du Proche Orient ancien (1963), reproduces essays from a colloquium in Strasbourg in 1962; and MAURICE GILBERT, ed., *La Sagesse de l'Ancien Testament* (1979; 2nd ed. 1990), gathers essays delivered at a colloquium on Old Testament wisdom in 1978 at Louvain, Belgium.

Worldwide Wisdom

Jack M. Sasson, ed., "Oriental Wisdom," *Journal of the American Oriental Society* 101, no. 1 (Spring 1981), essays on Egyptian, Israelite, Mesopotamian, Arabic, Asian, and Indian wisdom, also published as a monograph; and "Wisdom, Revelation, and Doubt: Perspectives on the First Millennium B.C.," *Daedalus* 104, no. 2 (Spring 1975), offers perceptive articles by specialists in different ancient cultures.

SEE ALSO various chapters in PART 8 VOL. III: RELIGION AND SCIENCE; **Ancient Egyptian Literature: An Overview** (Part 9, Vol. IV); and **Akkadian Literature: An Overview** (Part 9, Vol. IV).

Humor and Wit in the Ancient Near East

BENJAMIN R. FOSTER

HUMOR IS THE perception and expression of the ludicrous or amusing. It often ridicules people by pointing to truths they prefer to ignore. It seeks to provoke laughter, to entertain, to embarrass, to create a mood of relaxed inhibitions. The point lies in breaking a taboo, undermining or reversing expectations, or making fun of discrepancies between convention and actuality.

No society, ancient or modern, is without humor, and numerous examples of humorous discourse survive from the ancient Near East. While the humor of some themes and subjects transcends the millennia, one cannot always be certain of the original intent of a passage now perceived as humorous. Likewise, what was intended as humorous in antiquity may not be taken that way today.

The examples that follow include short jokes, humorous passages or episodes in otherwise non-humorous compositions, and extended narratives that were intended to be amusing and entertaining. They are drawn from such documents of everyday life as letters, from such formal compositions as historical or commemorative narrative, and from such didactic or instructional materials as might have been used by youngsters seeking to acquire the literate arts. The examples are arranged typologically in ascending order of sophistication, beginning with remarks the humor of which depends on inappropriate or crude references to bodily functions or sex, then proceed-

ing to satire based on appearance, behavior, profession, or social position, and next turning to caricature, irony, epigrams, and political and ethnic jokes. Finally, attention is given to extended humorous narratives and to humor as a defensive strategy to mask emotional pain or anger. In a number of examples, the crude outweighs the subtle, but this need not be considered fully representative of the humor of ancient near eastern peoples. The examples show only what modern readers with an imperfect knowledge of the languages and cultures concerned can readily apprehend.

BREAKING TABOOS

At its most basic level, humor lies in reference to matters not normally referred to in social discourse, with the intent to provoking laughter. Examples include allusion to bodily functions such as excretion, flatulence, and urination. Here the point can lie in unappetizing imagery, as in this Babylonian parody on the practice of prescribing monthly dietary restrictions intended to promote health and well-being: "In the ninth month what is your diet? Thou shalt eat donkey dung in bitter garlic, and emmer chaff in sour milk. In the eleventh month what is your diet? Thou shalt eat whole a jackass's anus

2459

stuffed with dog turds and fly dirt." Or the point may lie in inappropriateness: a Babylonian scholar inflects the verb to "break wind" in a grammatical treatise on the Sumerian verb. A scurrilous Babylonian poem berates a prospective lover: "Why did you break wind and feel mortified? Why did you stink up your boyfriend's wagon like a wild ox?" A ribald Sumerian expression for our "tempest in a teapot" alludes jocosely to a girl's breaking wind in her nuptial bed. Prolixity is derided in another Sumerian saying: "While the backside was breaking wind, the mouth brought forth babble." Delusions of grandeur are pilloried in the Sumerian vignette of a boastful fox who opines that his urine gave rise to the ocean. Flatulence may be discussed soberly, as in Babylonian and Egyptian medical texts, but in connection with marriage ditties, verb paradigms, or portrayals of intimacy, reference to it must be considered humorous or malicious, perhaps both. Scatological references do not occur, for example, in letters and so were not part of normal polite discourse. They are rare outside of overtly humorous texts, though once the Assyrian king Sennacherib makes a grim joke of the incontinence of his discomfited foes, and the same embarrassment has been proposed for Belshazzar (Daniel 5:6). Likewise the prophet Elijah, in his challenge to the priests of Baal, demands to know if Baal has not responded to their appeals because he has "gone aside," that is, to relieve himself (1 Kings 18:27). Allusion to menstruation is the element of humor in Genesis 31:35, where Rachel sits on the stolen household gods and tells her father that she cannot move because "the way of women" is upon her.

DISCOMFITURE OR LOSS OF DIGNITY

Literatures of the ancient Near East are rich in stories wherein someone is outwitted or put to shame by a person ostensibly less clever or in a disadvantageous position. The duel of wits between Jacob and Laban is a prime instance from the Bible (Genesis 30:32–36), and another is the manipulations of Abigail (1 Samuel 25). Another

instance, a Mesopotamian example wherein a poor man outwits a mayor, is discussed below.

Loss of dignity through drunkenness is a familiar theme, amusing to those who enjoy the abasement of someone else. An Egyptian tomb painting shows an elegant lady vomiting after a drinking bout, the humor lying in the contrast between her fine appearance and the indignity of her situation. In another drawing, a lady remarks, "My throat's parched; I'm going to drink twenty jars!" An Egyptian vignette shows workmen grumbling that their foreman has passed out from drink; he protests indignantly. In a light moment in the Mesopotamian *Epic of Gilgamesh*, the wilderness man Enkidu is introduced to the pleasures of civilization in the form of seven jugs of liquor: "His mood became relaxed and cheerful, he was light-hearted, his features glowed." He has never drunk liquor before, so he begins with a heroic quantity. The mock-serious invocation of inebriation is found in Babylonian lullabies. Parents troubled by a fretful baby sometimes croon that they wish their baby were a tavern keeper's child, in a stupor from the presumably alcoholic content of the mother's milk. Another frustrated parent may use a magic spell climaxing with the words "burp like a drunkard!"

Gluttonous appetites are alluded to humorously in a Babylonian buffoon's routine: "I've waxed large from starvation and enormous from eating, ten quarts for breakfast and thirty for dinner, I don't rest until I've filled the 'bushel' to the brim."

SEX

Sexual behavior or lack of it was a favorite subject of humorous observation in the ancient Near East. As always, the humor takes on meaning only in the context of usual prudery, discretion, or reserve about such matters (see "Love Lyrics from the Ancient Near East" and "Erotic Art in the Ancient Near East," both in this volume). The attitudes of Egyptians, Babylonians, Hebrews, and Canaanites toward sex no doubt varied as widely by culture, class, and individual as attitudes vary today, but a universal sense of privacy provides the background for most jokes about sex. In some instances, humor and pleasure intermingle in laughing surrender of inhibition. Before Sumerian weddings, for example, the bride's girlfriends might sing her chaffing songs of encouragement, with abundant allusions to plowing, irrigation, harvesting of fruit, and the like. A more seasoned Sumerian barmaid mockingly asks a customer ardent for her favors to swear to her that he is not a foreign spy: "Your right hand shall be placed on my private parts, your left shall hold up my head. When you have brought your mouth close to my mouth, when you nibble my lips with your teeth, then you must swear the oath." At this point, as intended, the beery customer becomes a "pillar of alabaster"; there is no indication that he bothers with the oath. Laying hands on the male genitalia in connection with solemn oaths is well attested in the Hebrew Bible (Genesis 24:2, 9; 47:29); if the same practice was known in Sumer, part of the joke may lie in role reversal of male and female roles.

A Babylonian "love lyric" abounds with uninhibited material, much of it mocking and ribald: "By night there's no prudish housewife, by night no man's wife makes objection!" An *odi et amo* passage celebrates the beloved's ugliness: "I saw my girlfriend and was stunned. You are chalky like a gecko, your hide is swart like a cooking pot!" Continuing in a mock-passionate vein, the singer finds his beloved's person none too clean nor exclusive:

> Babylon-town is looking for a rag to swab your vulva, to swab your vagina. So let him say to the women of Babylon, "Won't they give her a rag, to swab her vulva, to swab her vagina?" Into your vulva, where you put your confidence, I'll bring a dog and fasten the door, I'll bring a watchbird so it can roost. Whenever I go out or come in, I'll instruct my little watchbirds, "Please, my little watchbirds, don't go near the fungus! Please, my little watchbird, don't go near the stench of her armpits!"
> (After Benjamin R. Foster, *Before the Muses*, p. 828)

Impotence and frustration could also be the butt of humor. An Ugaritic poem builds a humorous episode around the temporary impotence of the chief god, El; a biblical story reflects on King David's loss of authority by focusing on his sexual impotence (1 Kings 1); a Babylonian narrative poem dealing with the sexual frustration of the queen of the dead is discussed below.

SOCIAL SATIRE

Jokes about professions or social ineptitude in the ancient Near East were usually told from the point of view of scribes or literate folk who felt that their training made them superior to those whose work did not require writing. In the Egyptian satire on professions, a scribe surveys a variety of tradesmen with distaste. The copper worker, for example, has fingers like crocodile claws, and he stinks "worse than fish dirt." As for the potter, he is covered with earth, though still among the living, and he burrows in fields like a pig. The brickmaker has little to wear but "a thread for his buttocks" and is exhausted from kneading dung the livelong day. As for the launderer, "There is no part of him that is clean, he cleans the clothes of women in menstruation." A Sumerian joke about a cleaner goes, "Men say, 'I'm dirty!' 'By god, I'm dirty too!' says the launderer."

In an unusual reversal of this motif, a gruff cleaner has the better of a confrontation with a Babylonian fop who discourses in detail about the intricacies of cleaning his coat:

> You should lay flat the fringe and the border, you should stitch the front to the inside, you should pick out the thread of the border, you should soak the fringed part in a brew, you should strain that with a strainer. . . you should [tap it] with a cornel branch, you should dry it in the cool of the evening. Lest the weaving get too stiff from the sunlight, you should put it in a trunk or chest, make sure it's cool!

The cleaner crushes the client with a diatribe:

> Lay off! Nobody but a creditor or [tax collector] would have the gall to talk the way you do. . . . The big job on your hands you can tend to yourself. Don't miss your chance, seize the day! Do ease if you please the countless [burdens] of a cleaner. If you can't give yourself more breathing room, the cleaner's not yet born who will pay you any mind, they'll think you're a ninny.

An Egyptian artist satirizes the stonemason in a lively drawing of a brutish lout, with unshaven chin and mouth hanging open, who has given himself a cauliflower ear by repeated blows with his own mallet.

Learned men were not exempt from satire, as demonstrated in a Babylonian tale of a physician who goes to Nippur (modern Nuffar), a center of Sumerian learning, to collect a fee. His client gives him abstruse directions to his house. As the physician makes his way there, he asks the way in Babylonian of a woman in the street, who answers him in Sumerian, the language of learning and scholarship, which, as a learned man, he is supposed to have mastered. The physician fails to recognize Sumerian and remonstrates with the woman for cursing at him. Then she translates her reply into Babylonian, indignant that he would think she was cursing. After

several reprises of this, he learns that his client is not at home anyway, and the author suggests that the students get together and run such an ignoramus out of town.

A Babylonian buffoon, parodying an exorcist, brags that he can rid any house of a ghost: the procedure consists of burning the house down! Other fragments of the buffoon's routine depend for effect on internal contradictions such as, "Stealing is an abomination to me, whatever I see doesn't stay where it was." Dressing (we surmise) as a woman, the buffoon lauds his allure as a lover: "My limbs are elephantine, my face a hyena's, in stature tall as a tortoise, I have no equal. I'm vigorous, I'm a lively one, so much would my lover fondle me that he keeps scuttling around, backwards and forwards from me, like a snared crab."

Kings and their grandiose claims could be sati-

Comical image of a stone mason at work, circa 1305–1080 BCE. He has given himself a cauliflower ear by repeated blows with his own mallet. Ostracon found at Dayr al-Madina. FITZWILLIAM MUSEUM, CAMBRIDGE, ENGLAND

rized; for example, the same Babylonian buffoon claims a heroic journey to distant lands in the style of kings of old. A Babylonian pseudonymous letter in the name of Gilgamesh, the legendary Sumerian king, makes gargantuan demands on the recipient: "Send me 70,000 black horses with white stripes, 100,000 mares whose hides have markings like wild tree roots, 40,000 continually gambolling miniature calves, 50,000 teams of dappled mules, 50,000 fine calves with well-turned hooves and horns intact. . . ." In an Egyptian story, Apophis, a king in northern Egypt, writes to his rival Seqenenre Tao II at Thebes, far to the south, claiming that the roaring of hippopotamuses in a Theban canal deprives him of sleep, and he demands that the Theban king get rid of them. A stupefied Seqenenre promises to look into the matter and summons his officials for a consultation. (At this point, the text breaks off.)

Limitation of royal power in the face of a woman's will is shown by a lighthearted Egyptian story. Here, as the pharaoh watches harem girls row, one of them drops a jewel into the lake. She is inconsolable at her loss and ignores all royal blandishments, saying she wants "the whole pot" (an unclear expression that may mean that she will not settle for anything but the actual piece). A magician folds one side of the lake water over the other, and the jewel is found miraculously on top of a potsherd. Another Egyptian anecdote, well known in its day, involved a Canaanite king treed by a bear.

In an Egyptian satire on a bungled military expedition, the would-be warrior gets too far ahead of his troops and stumbles along, lost and terrified, over rocks and brambles. Eventually abandoning his chariot in a fit of temper, he scrambles up a hill, imagining the enemy on all sides. Finally, he camps for the night unmolested. No doubt he went on to grander exploits the following day.

Priests could also bear the brunt of humor. A singer of Sumerian cultic laments is pilloried for his absurd piety: if his boat sinks, he wishes the river-god enjoyment of his cargo; if he slips and falls, he is doubtful of the propriety of rising, since his mishap was a visitation from heaven.

One of the most appealing of Babylonian parodies was sketched by some earthy scholar weary of magical lore who devised a spoof magi-

cal spell to be used by someone kept awake by a bleating goat. Here the god of wisdom, Enki, sends off his son, Marduk, the Babylonian national god, to deal with the problem. While in serious incantations the two gods consult courteously as to the correct procedure to follow, here the angry Enki sends off Marduk without preamble. After what might be called "ear for an ear" reprisal, the goat falls dead, and the speaker imagines heaven and earth erupting in praise and thanksgiving at the great god's mighty deed:

> The goat is sick, it cannot [shut?] its mouth! The shepherd is disturbed and cannot sleep. It disturbs its herdboy, who must go about, day and night, forever herding. Enki saw it, he called the Wise One (Marduk), sent him off with weighty charge, "A goat in pen or fold is disturbing me. Go, it must not disturb me! Take its dung, stuff it into its left ear. That goat, instead of falling asleep, let it drop dead!" May Shamkan, lord of the beasts, hold nothing against me, nor serve me summons for this case. Folk and land will sing your praises, even the great gods will praise what you can do.
>
> (Benjamin R. Foster, *Before the Muses*, p. 138)

Jokes on social institutions include a Babylonian quip on marriage and family: "The man with a wife and child is one-third robust and two-thirds a weakling." A Babylonian bit of homespun wisdom offers what may be mock-serious advice on choosing a wife: "Do not buy an ox in the springtime, do not choose a girl on a holiday. Even a bad ox will look good in that season, a bad girl just wears good clothes for the occasion." An Egyptian drawing of a harvest scene shows a supercilious foreman reproving indignant field hands while, unknown to him, others lie asleep under a tree.

FABLES AND CARICATURE

From Mesopotamia and Egypt numerous animal caricatures survive, lighthearted, satiric representations of animals carrying out human activities. A Sumerian inlay shows a goat, despite his hoofs, playing a lyre, while an officious cat butler does honors with a roast. In an Egyptian caricature, a monkey plays the flute and a crocodile the lute, accompanied by a donkey at the harp.

Animal stories and debates often seem humor-

Animals in human occupations as shown on a humorous Egyptian papyrus, circa 1305–1080 BCE. A lion and antelope are playing a board game, while a cat herds poultry. BRITISH MUSEUM, LONDON

ous in intent. In a Babylonian debate between a dog and a fox, the dog lavishes praise on himself and his importance to the human race:

> I am mighty in strength, the talon of a storm-bird, the fury of a lion, my legs run faster than birds on the wing. At my loud outcry mountains and rivers come to naught. I take my onerous place before the sheep, their lives are entrusted to me, instead of shepherds or herdsmen. . . . At my baying panther, tiger, lion, wildcat take to flight.

On a different note, a homesick Sumerian monkey sends a plaintive screed to his mother: "I am being fed on offal(?) alone! Don't let me die of hunger for fresh bread and fresh beer! Send me some by courier. This is urgent."

Eternal conflicts (fox and fowl, cat and mouse), familiar in our own times from cartoon films and comics, amused the Egyptians as well. A notable Egyptian group of drawings suggests the existence of popular stories about a war between cats and mice. Scenes include a delegation of mice asking a cat pharaoh for peace, and an army of mice laying siege to a cat fortress, which is about to fall. Here the general of the mice rides in a chariot pulled by two rearing bitches. In other scenes, a mouse and a cat fight a duel, and a cat submits to a mouse officer. Another series of vignettes shows cats in the domestic service of mice, serving food, fanning them, assisting a mouse grande dame at her toilette, and undertaking mouse child-care.

RIPOSTE, IRONY, SARCASM

The arts of verbal offense and defense often use humor to parody or ridicule another. In Sumer-

ian school debates, for example, the interlocutors plied each other with elaborately artificed insults about each other's genealogy, appearance, and level of education, presumably with an eye to raising a laugh in the gallery. An example begins, "He is spawn of a dog, seed of a wolf, stench of a mongoose, a helpless hyena's whelp, a carapaced fox, an addlepated mountain monkey whose reasoning is nonsensical." The parents of a Sumerian scholar who is failing in school invite his teacher for dinner. After a fine repast and a handsome present, the teacher discourses warmly on the youngster's talents and prospects.

As an instrument of criticism, humor is closely related to irony. Like irony, humor draws attention to incongruity between what is and what ought to be. But unlike humor, which often relies on overstatement for effect, irony normally relies on understatement or suggestion, presuming the reader's perception of the truth of the matter and the narrator's intent at the same time. Although irony uses some of the same rhetorical strategies as humor, it need not be humorous in intent.

Overstated irony can become sarcasm. This shares with humor and irony allusion to a discrepancy between a situation and what is right or proper, but leaves little to the imagination, as this example from a letter by a Babylonian to his sister illustrates:

> Do go on being such a good sister to me! Even though we grew up together, you didn't pay me two cents' worth (text: a quarter of a shekel) of attention when you got your big break . . . if that big chief you're married to needs timbers, he can write me. I'll send him five timbers . . . you send

me in return a hundred locusts and a cent-and-a-half's worth (text: one-sixth of a shekel) of food, so I can see what sort of sister you are.

An Assyrian king acidly compares the Babylonians to an ungrateful potter's dog, who, once warm at the potter's oven, sets to barking at him; the Babylonians are to see themselves as the dog, of course, and the king as the potter affording them comfort and protection.

WIT

The artful turn of phrase, the flash of cleverness, the ingenious paradox that might have delighted a fine-tuned sensibility millennia ago must often now, if perceived at all, be labored to death with an elaborate commentary. For example, an elegant Babylonian note invokes a magic spell to request a prompt visit: "So long as you have not seen my eyes, may you swallow neither bread nor beer! Also, so long as you do not come to me, do not sit on a chair!" An Egyptian king enjoys a pun on his correspondent's name, Senedjemib ("Who Makes the Heart Joyful"): "Indeed, it is true that my heart was made joyful by this, and I am not just saying this." Nabal's name and that of the Calebite clan are vehicles for a series of clever puns in 1 Samuel 25.

PROVERBS AND EPIGRAMS

Proverbs, like jokes, often make use of inappropriate juxtaposition for effect, as in the Sumerian saying "Would you pay cash for a pig's squeal?" Some have an earthy quality that may seem humorous to some readers, like other Sumerian sayings, such as "Eat no fat, void no blood" or "Is she pregnant without intercourse? Fat without eating?" or, returning to the scatological level, "When the ox has diarrhea, the trail of dung is a long one!" Some involve sex, such as a Sumerian saying about a woman's eye for opportunity: "Who is wealthy? Who is rich? For whom shall I reserve my intimacy?" or "She looked at you, how far will she go with you?" "Gallows" humor is found at the end of the Egyptian Story of the Shipwrecked Sailor, wherein a pessimistic lieutenant, dreading his reception by the pharaoh, is unsuccessfully distracted by the tale of his more optimistic companion's shipwreck. "Who would give water at dawn," asks the lieutenant, "to a goose that will be slaughtered in the morning?" The audience may have understood that "the executioner" was meant, for at least in modern Egypt a bird is often watered before slaughter.

Laughter in ancient near eastern texts is generally at the expense of someone or in the context of lasciviousness. When Adapa, a Mesopotamian sage, is shown up as a bumpkin in heaven, the chief god bursts out laughing and sends the mortal home, cheated of immortality. In one Babylonian narrative poem, when the god Nergal returns to the netherworld and sees the lustful queen of the dead, he laughs aloud and they embrace. Malicious laughter is foretold for the Babylonian rash enough to marry a prostitute, for "she will snigger at you when you are embroiled in controversy."

HUMOROUS STORIES

Stories of a light and entertaining character occasionally survive from the ancient Near East. A unique manuscript from the seventeenth century BCE preserves a Sumerian tale of this type, which opens as follows:

> Once there were three friends, citizens of Adab, who fell into a dispute one with the other, so went to seek justice. Many were the words they had on the matter, so they went before the king. "Our liege, we are cattle drivers. One man has an ox, one man a cow, and one man a wagon. We became thirsty and we had no water. 'If the ox driver would get water, then we will all drink.' A lion might devour my ox, then I would be out my ox.' 'If the cowherd would get water, then we will all drink.' 'My cow might wander off in the steppe, then I would be out my cow.' 'If the wagon driver would get water, then we will all drink.' 'The load might make my wagon coast off(?), then I would be out my wagon.' 'Well, let's all go off together, then let's all come back together.' The ox mounts and mates with her, the cow conceives and drops her calf, which eats the load on the wagon. Whose is the calf? Who shall take the calf?"

The king cannot solve the dilemma, so goes to a woman in the palace. Although the manuscript is damaged thereafter, it appears that she refutes the claim of each man, but the outcome is uncertain.

In an Egyptian story, King Neferkare Pepy II is attracted by his bachelor general, Sisene. Rumor that the king is sneaking out of his palace at night reaches a certain Theti (Tjeti), who plays detective by shadowing the king. He watches the king toss a brick at the general's window shutter. A ladder is lowered, whereupon the king climbs into the house and spends four hours there. The patient Theti then follows the king back to the palace, at which point the rest of the story is lost.

A well-preserved Babylonian story tells of a poor man's vengeance against the mayor of Nippur. The poor man, Gimil-Ninurta, sells his last garment for something to eat. Intending to buy a sheep, he ends up with a three-year-old goat, but is then loath to slaughter it at his house: "My friends in my neighborhood will hear of it and be angry, my kith and kin will be furious with me" (for not having been invited to partake). He takes his goat to the mayor, expecting him to prepare a feast for him to share, but the mayor gives him a bone, a piece of gristle, and a quaff of third-rate beer. As he leaves, the poor man vows, "For the one insult you laid upon me, I will requite you three." The poor man's revenge takes up the rest of the story, of which one episode is given in the accompanying box.

Gimil-Ninurta ultimately tricks the mayor into giving him a fine meal, a suit of new clothes, and a pound of gold: he has the further satisfaction of giving the mayor three severe thrashings. Aside from its exploitation of the "clever fool" motif, well known, for example, from the Arabic Juha stories or Armenian folklore, the story has numerous individual humorous touches that make it a fine example of its kind.

POLITICAL AND ETHNIC JOKES

Political and ethnic jokes were familiar fare in ancient times. The Hebrews enjoyed satirical jokes on the ancestry of their neighbors. For example, Esau, ancestor of the Edomites, was born

---

Gimil-Ninurta's Revenge

Gimil-Ninurta came before the king. He fell down and did homage before him. "O noble one, prince of the people, king whom a guardian spirit makes glorious, let them give me at your command one chariot, so that, for one day, I can do whatever I want. For my one day my payment shall be a pound of finest gold." The king did not ask him, "What is it that you want, parading about all day in a chariot?" They gave him a new chariot, fit for a nobleman, they wrapped him in a sash. . . .

He mounted the new chariot, fit for a nobleman, he set out for Nippur. Gimil-Ninurta caught two birds, stuffed them in a box and sealed it up. He went off to the gate of the mayor of Nippur. The mayor came outside to meet him. "Who are you, my lord, who have traveled so late in the day?" "The king, your lord, sent me. . . . I have brought gold for the Ekur, temple of the god Enlil." The mayor slaughtered a choice sheep to make a lavish repast for him. After they had sat together over it, the mayor said, "Ho-hum, I'm tired!" But Gimil-Ninurta sat up late with the mayor one whole watch of the night. The mayor finally fell asleep from exhaustion.

Gimil-Ninurta got up stealthily in the night, opened the lid of the box, and the birds flew up in the sky. "Wake up, mayor! The gold has been taken and the box opened! The boxlid is open, the gold has been taken!" Gimil-Ninurta tore his clothes in a passion, he set upon the mayor, making him beg for mercy. He thrashed him from head to toe, causing him much pain. The mayor howled at his feet, begging for mercy, "My lord, do not destroy a citizen of Nippur! The blood of a protected person, sacred to the god Enlil, must not stain your hands!" They gave him for his present two pounds of finest gold, for the clothes he had torn, he gave him others.

As Gimil-Ninurta went out the gate, he said these words to Tukulti-Enlil, who minded the gate, "Joy of the gods to your master! Say this to him, 'For the one insult you laid upon me, I've requited you one; two remain.'" When the mayor heard that, he cried(?) all day.

(Benjamin R. Foster, *Before the Muses*, pp. 831–832)

---

with a "hairy coat" (*śēʿār*), and was a hairy man (*śāʿîr*), puns no doubt on the Hebrew word for goat (*śāʿîr*) and the mountains of Edom (*śēʿîr*) (Genesis 25:25, 27:11). In like manner, the ancestry of the Ammonites and Moabites is tied to acts of drunken incest initiated by Lot's daughters (Genesis 19:31–38). The Egyptians were amused by contemptuous references to the "wretched Asiatics" who lived in the mud like crocodiles. The Sumerians made jokes about the barbarous Amorites.

An Amorite nobleman allows himself a political joke in writing to the queen of Qatara, a city in northern Syria. Acknowledging her dispatch of a shipment of small fish, such as her own husband, the king of Qatara, esteems, he writes, "Just as your husband Aqba-khammu has learned to appreciate 'little fish' when in Qatara and Karana [two small kingdoms], I myself have always had a liking for the 'big fish' in Shubat-Enlil, Ekallatum, Mari, and Babylon [capitals of major kingdoms]. Since there are no big fish around (where you are), you send me little ones, but who would eat them?"

THE HUMAN CONDITION

Humorous discourse is sometimes the defense of the sensitive spirit unable to deal otherwise with painful reality. Penetrating social and personal satire suggests to some readers withdrawal and alienation, and to others healthy insouciance, but in any case, intense personal involvement, along with superior perception and dissatisfaction.

A Babylonian satire on the bondage of love portrays a woman besotted with a selfish man. He rejects her declarations: "He who sprawls next to a woman treasures up empty air! If he doesn't look out for himself, he is no man worthy of the name. . . . I remember better than you your old tricks, give up! Be off with you, tell your divine counsellor how we've sobered out of it." She replies, "I'll hang on to you, and this very day I shall make your love harmonize with mine. . . . I shall have your eternal good will, darling, freely given." His reaction continues brutal: "I despise a woman who can't seduce me, I have no desire for her charms." In a soliloquy, the woman muses, "I shall hug him! I shall kiss him! . . . So very tired my eyes are, I am weary for looking out for him, I keep thinking he will pass through my neighborhood. The day has gone by, where is [my darling]?" After a final bluster ("Your love is nothing more to me than anxiety and bother"), he gives in: "My one and only, your face wasn't bad-looking before, when I used to stand next to you and you leaned your shoulder against me. Call you 'sweetie,' dub you 'smart lady,' say the other woman is our ill omen, Ishtar be my witness!" Perhaps this is

---

A Capricious Master and His Servant

"Servant, listen to me." "Yes, master, yes." "Quickly, get me the chariot and hitch it up for me so I can drive to the palace." "Drive, master, drive, it will bring you where you want to go, the others will be outclassed, the prince will pay attention to you." "No, servant, I will certainly not drive to the palace." "Do not drive, master, do not drive. The prince will send you off on a mission, he will send you on a journey that you do not know. He will expose you to discomfort day and night."

"Servant, listen to me." "Yes, master, yes." "I will fall in love with a woman." "So, fall in love, master, fall in love. The man who falls in love with a woman forgets sorrow and care." "No, servant, I will certainly not fall in love with a woman." "Do not fall in love, master, do not fall in love. A woman is a pitfall, a pitfall, a hole, a ditch, a woman is a sharp iron dagger that slashes a man's throat."

"Servant, listen to me." "Yes, master, yes." "Quickly bring me water (to wash) my hands, give it to me so I can sacrifice to my god." "Sacrifice, master, sacrifice. The man who sacrifices to his god makes a satisfying transaction, he makes loan upon loan." "No, servant, I will certainly not sacrifice to my god." "Do not sacrifice master, do not sacrifice. You will train your god to follow you around like a dog. He will require of you rites or a magic figurine or what have you."

(Benjamin R. Foster, *Before the Muses,*
pp. 815–817)

to be read as it stands, like the second elegy of Theocritus on the same theme, or perhaps the whole is a marriage ditty with mock dialogue between bride and groom; the unique manuscript provides no clue. The opposite situation is found in the Samson and Delilah story (Judges 16) and the Egyptian story of Setne Khamwas and Tabubu.

An effective Babylonian social satire reflects on such matters as public service, fame, the pleasures of sport, the table, love, and marriage through a dialogue between a capricious master and a glib servant. (Excerpts are given in the accompanying box.) Eventually the master asks the servant what he suggests, and the servant proposes suicide. When the master answers that he will kill the servant first, the servant ripostes, "Then my master will certainly not outlive me even three days!" Whatever this piece lacks in subtlety, it makes up in brilliance and originality.

Sophisticated humor is worked into multilayered discourse, an overtone, a connotation. In such instances, modern readers lack the cultural competence to be sure of the intent. A passing reference in a Babylonian prayer, for instance, wherein an old man notes with nostalgia the marking-off of the years, remarks on his assiduity in prayer: "I am breathless from prostration, before mankind I am like a whirlwind!" One may detect a note of wry self-depreciation at the futility of his exertions ("I have seen no favor, I have had no mercy").

A more complex case is provided by a subplot in the *Epic of Gilgamesh*, which might be subtitled "What Every Woman Knows." Here each turn in Gilgamesh's progress is made possible by the intervention of a woman, not by the hero's valor or intelligence. A harlot brings him his friend, his mother ensures by prayer the outcome of his vainglorious expedition, the wife of a guardian monster lets him through an impasse, a female tavern keeper tells him how to cross the river of death, the wife of the flood hero arranges for him to take home a reward for his expedition to the frontiers of existence. A parody of male vainglorious heroism? A celebration of the importance of female roles in success? No matter how read, it is a treatment of remarkable subtlety, like the best of humor.

The Babylonian mythic story of Nergal and Ereshkigal provides an instance of a narrative being reworked with the addition of a subplot that is not without elements of humor. In an earlier version of this story, the god Nergal takes over the netherworld by a heroic feat: he stations various demons at the gates of the netherworld, then rushes in, seizes Ereshkigal, queen of the netherworld, but refrains from killing her in return for marriage. In a later version, he comes as a guest to the netherworld, becomes aroused at Ereshkigal's stripping to take a bath, and has intercourse with her for seven days and nights. Then he slips away and leaves her at dawn. When she arises in a leisurely fashion and calls for the rooms to be freshened and breakfast to be served, she learns that her lover has absconded. In a bitter lament, with tears dripping off the end of her nose, she sets forth her isolation and sexual frustration as queen of the dead and demands her lover back at any price. This part of the story is told with both humor and pathos, and adds considerable emotional interest to an otherwise simile tale.

Statements sometimes encountered in modern books that the Mesopotamians, Egyptians, or Israelites were devoid of humor, were heavily imbued with religious awe, and were fatalistic or preoccupied with their afterlife may safely be dismissed as ridiculous. Among ancient near eastern peoples, as among any other populations, there were no doubt those unblessed with a sense of humor, to whom laughter was license, amusement frivolity, and inhibition a way of life. Yet, the serious student of the past cannot form a balanced picture of a society without considering its jokes, insults, and entertainments, for these often point to truths accessible in no other way. Although in many literate cultures one can find references to humor as being low, common, vulgar, or, at best, not to be taken seriously as artful discourse, humor had its arts and letters, and it can be judged like any other cultural phenomenon. Humorists have consoled themselves for their lack of cultural prestige by recalling, with a Greek sage, that the best of humor is produced by the few for the enjoyment of the many.

BIBLIOGRAPHY

Egypt

EMMA BRUNNER-TRAUT, *Altägyptische Tiergeschichte und Fabel* (1968), collects evidence for animal stories in ancient Egypt; SILVIO CURTO, *La satira nell'antico egitto*, Quaderno del Museo Egizio di Torino 1 (n.d.), has excellent illustrations of Egyptian caricatures, with reconstructed drawings; ADOLF ERMAN, *Reden, Rufe und Lieder auf Gräberbildern des alten Reiches* (1919), includes discussion of humorous passages; WALTRAUD GUGLIELMI, *Reden, Rufe und Lieder auf altägyptischen Darstellungen* (1973); GERALD E. KADISH, "The Scatophagus Egyptian," *Journal of the Society for the Study of Egyptian Antiquities* 9 (1979), discusses Egyptian attitudes toward filth and is useful for underlying attitudes toward scatological insults; MIRIAM LICHTHEIM, *Ancient Egyptian Literature*, 3 vols. (1973–1980), has many Egyptian texts referred to in this essay in translation and commentary, with citation of bibliography; B. VAN DE WALLE, *L'Humour dans la littérature et dans l'art de l'ancienne Égypte* (1969), gives citation and discussion of examples; see also his "Humor," in *Lexikon der Ägyptologie*, vol. 3 (1980); and R. J. WILLIAMS, "The Fable in the Ancient Near East," in *A Stubborn Faith*, edited by E. C. HOBBS (1956), although it is dated in many respects—it is still a useful survey of near eastern animal stories for the nonspecialist.

Israel–Syro-Palestine

EDWIN M. GOOD, *Irony in the Old Testament* (1965); FLEMMING F. HVIDBERG, *Weeping and Laughter in the Old Testament: A Study of Canaanite-Israelite Religion* (1962), is a survey of weeping and laughter in alleged cultic or religious contexts, with some discussion of humor; MARVIN H. POPE, "Ups and Downs in El's Amours," *Ugarit-Forschungen* 11 (1979), studies erotic episodes in Ugaritic poetry, with reference to willing spirit and weak flesh; YEHUDA T. RADDAY and ATHALYA BRENNER, *On Humour and the Comic in the Hebrew Bible* (1990), contains fourteen essays, with numerous examples, analyses, and additional bibliography; and EDWARD ULLENDORF, "The Bawdy Bible," *Bulletin of the School of Oriental and African Studies* 42 (1979), surveys the language of lewdness, prurience, scatology, sex, and euphemism in the Hebrew Bible, with citation and discussion of examples.

Mesopotamia

SALLY DUNHAM, "The Monkey in the Middle," *Zeitschrift für Assyriologie und vorderasiatische Archäologie* 75 (1985), is a survey of the portrayal of monkeys in ancient near eastern art and literature, sometimes for humorous effect, BENJAMIN R. FOSTER, *Before the Muses: An Anthology of Akkadian Literature* (1991), includes Babylonian literary texts in translation and with commentary, with citation of bibliography; and see his "Humor and Cuneiform Literature," *Journal of the Ancient Near Eastern Society of Columbia University* 6 (1974), which gives citations and discussions of examples from Sumerian and Akkadian; W. G. LAMBERT, *Babylonian Wisdom Literature* (1960), provides translation and commentary on Assyro-Babylonian fables and debates among animals, most of which are preserved only in fragments; see also A. LIVINGSTONE, "'At the Cleaners' and Notes on Humorous Literature," in G. MAUER and U. MAGEN, *Ad Bene et Fideliter Seminandum* (1988); and MAGGIE RUTTEN, "Les Animaux à attitudes humaines dans l'art de l'ancienne Mésopotamie," *Revue des Études Sémitiques* (1938), a study of Mesopotamian animal caricatures.

SEE ALSO **Ancient Egyptian Literature: An Overview** (Part 9, Vol. IV); **Sumerian Literature: An Overview** (Part 9, Vol. IV); and **Akkadian Literature: An Overview** (Part 9, Vol. IV).

Love Lyrics from the Ancient Near East

JOAN GOODNICK WESTENHOLZ

IN THE ANCIENT NEAR EAST, love was more than a passing emotion individuals felt for each other; it was not divided between the sacred and the profane, human and divine, emotional and physical. Love engulfed men and women, gods and worshipers, rulers and ruled, parents and children.

Further, love, the emotion, and sexuality, the physical attraction, that occur between two individuals (gender distinction not being particularly important) were not perceived as separate forces. In our rhetoric we tend to value emotional love as nobler than physical sex. In antiquity, these two aspects of human attachment were deemed reflexes of the same relationship. For the ancients the love metaphor remained physical, whether it reflected a love that was not sexual (parents and children) or sex that was not loving (rape). Thus, the mystical union between humans and deities could be depicted symbolically as a "sacred marriage" or evoked lyrically in the Song of Songs. Accordingly, the love poetry of the ancient Near East encompasses explicit references of an erotic character both in texts used for divine liturgy and as worldly entertainment. Rich imagery with its joyous portrayal of sexuality permeated poetry and myth and found expression in statuary and reliefs.

The ancient Near East includes various distinct cultures. Each culture has its unique perception of love and its own response to the trials and triumphs of lovers; each understands differently the feelings and emotions of love, the manner in which lovers relate to themselves and to their society, and love's role in the structure of the universe.

Not only the perception but also what is implied in the word "love" differs in the various cultures of the Near East. The Sumerian word for "love," KI.ÁG, may have developed from a quantifying outlook on the universe, if the etymology "to measure (ÁG) the place (KI)" is at all correct. The object of such a love can either be someone (construed in the dative) or something (construed in the locative or locative-terminative). Both persons and abstractions can be the recipients of KI.ÁG: "When she loved her city, she hated me, . . . when she loved me, she hated her city"; "I love justice, I do not love injustice."

In Akkadian, the verb for love is *râmu*, and it is construed directly with its object. Gods can love a variety of objects: other gods, people, animals (Ishtar is said to have had an affair with her horse and Sin was in love with his cow), heaven, kingship, reigns, life, justice, prayer, and sacrifice. People can love gods, other people (including sexual love), places, temples, and abstract nouns. Even animals can love—their offspring and their owners. In Akkadian, the essence of love is personified as *irʾemum* (Old Akkadian), *irimum* (Old Babylonian):

"Ir'emum, the son of Ishtar, sitting on her lap, in the fragrance of incense"; "Erimu, Erimu, his horns are (like) gold, his beard(!) like lapis lazuli; he is in the heart of Ishtar." When the love force is visualized as a mythological figure, it can be invoked in spells and charms, such as that for arousing love in a maiden's coldly cruel heart. It is a concept akin to the Greek Eros, that is, partly a personification of love and sexual desire, partly the impersonal force itself. As the latter, it is the quality of attraction that makes its possessor irresistibly attractive to the opposite sex.

Hebrew speakers also love God and other people, objects and abstracts, using the same term *'āhab*, with the same love. However, human "love" is limited to children, spouses, and God, while parents are to be "honored" rather than loved. On the other hand, the slave "loves" his master, the inferior his superior. A characteristic biblical injunction urges people to "love their brethren," though it is debated whether this applies universally or communally. Another injunction to "love the stranger" definitely refers to a person outside and foreign to the group.

The Egyptian root meaning "love," *mry*, applies to an emotion that is generally expressed from the higher to the lower, god's love for people rather than the other way around. The king loves the commoner. The husband loves the wife. From the bottom up, one tends to speak of awe, prayer, and honor, in particular during the Old and Middle Kingdoms. This dichotomy is similar to that seen in biblical language, where the child "honors" rather than "loves" his parents. The vocable is used to express both the emotional and physical aspects of love ("his love entered into her limbs"). The range of meaning of *mry* extends beyond the sense "to love," one of the most frequent uses being "to wish, to desire, to prefer."

When we turn from the emotion "love" to the vehicle in which it is expressed—"lyrics"—we find a lack of agreement on this term. Critical attempts to define lyrical poetry by reference to its brevity, metrical coherence, subjectivity, passion, sensuality, or imagery are particular to the specific literature on which the definitions were based. Originally, lyric poetry earned its name in Greece, where it was sung to the accompaniment of the lyre by either a single voice or a chorus. The Greek lyrics gave expression to the poets' mood, hopes, fears, and longings and

to their love, patriotism, and rejoicing. Lyrical poetry came in a variety of forms: the simple lyric, an unrestrained, immediate expression of the poet's overflowing emotion; the lyric that presents not the emotion but the scene or incident from which the emotion springs; and the reflective lyric, the result of emotion recollected in tranquility. In all cases, there was one voice in a monologue.

Unfortunately, this division of literature is not easily applicable to the ancient Near East. In particular, ancient near eastern love lyrics partake of both the dramatic and the lyric. There are usually two or more voices, so these poems depart from the conception of lyrical forms. Further, love lyrics are embedded in epics and hymns of praise—narrative and nonnarrative, liturgical and nonliturgical.

MESOPOTAMIA

For over two thousand years, the land between the Euphrates and Tigris yielded poetic texts, in Sumerian and in Akkadian, whose subject was love. The theme is found in the mythic tales of Inanna, the goddess of love, and her shepherd husband, Dumuzi; divine and royal hymns; and love songs and love charms. The distribution of these documents is skewed over the centuries: abundant for some periods and nonexistent for others.

Sumerian

Sumerian love poetry can be arranged into three categories: (1) deities assume the role of lovers; (2) individual Sumerian kings are praised as they unite with their consorts or with the goddess Inanna; and (3) lovers are not gods or kings.

Most Sumerian love poetry is in the first category, telling of the love between Dumuzi and Inanna, although we know from the cylinders of Gudea of a marriage ceremony for Ningirsu and Bau, the gods of the city of Lagash (modern al-Hiba). The cycle of texts includes various stories of Dumuzi's courtship of Inanna, preparations for the wedding, and the wedding itself. Although there exist Early Dynastic texts (circa 2500 BCE) whose laconic vocabulary might indicate their belonging to this literary category, their difficulty for decipherment and deficiency

Stone sculpture of a seated couple from the Temple of Inanna, the goddess of love, Nippur.
ORIENTAL INSTITUTE, UNIVERSITY OF CHICAGO

in expressing essential elements of the sentence render them inadequate for literary analysis. The tablets on which we must base our analysis are those that stem from a period after Sumerian was no longer a living language. Love lyrics appear in both narrative myths and nonnarrative songs.

The passion for love as well as the joy its consummation achieved were deemed attributes of Inanna (or of her Akkadian counterpart, Ishtar).

Accordingly, any manifestation of love betrayed her presence and activity. Dumuzi, her lover and spouse, was a shepherd who, according to the Sumerian Kinglist, was the king of Bad-tibira before the gods sent a flood to wipe out humanity. As in all metaphorical poetry, the literal identity of the protagonists is not what is immediately relevant; rather, they epitomize a union that is paradigmatic or archetypal because it is divine.

The second category, hymns in praise of god and king, forms another large percentage of Sumerian literature. The love songs, in which the love object is a king, are common, but they are most plentiful when addressing the fourth king of the Third Dynasty of Ur, the deified Shu-Sin. In this case, these songs were written by the wife of his body and the votary of his divinity, Kubatum. They were composed in two modes of discourse—as monologues and dialogues. The motifs are the king's beauty and his virile prowess.

The love lyrics extolling the king and Inanna are embedded in "sacred marriage" texts such as the Iddin-Dagan Hymn which describes the mystical union of king and goddess as a festive occasion during the New Year's holiday: to renew the harmony of the world, to determine the fates of the king, the people, and the land for the coming year.

The third category, much rarer than the literature described above, consists of those poems where love does not refer to gods or kings but to passions between ordinary human beings. Further, the vocabulary and phrases of love lyrics are also incorporated into other pieces of literature. An example of the latter is the "Message of Ludingira to His Mother," in which the beloved mother's anatomy is described in highly erotic language.

The native classification for all three categories of texts is BAL.BAL.E, apparently denoting a dialogue or duet. Other designations, such as "composition for a TIGI (harp)" or "for a KUN.GAR instrument," also exist. On occasion, the narrator provides the transition between the sections with different labels and indicates a change of speaker, but this is not a common occurrence. The structure of the majority of the poems is narrative, having a beginning, a climax, and a denouement.

Passionate love and sexual yearnings for the beloved characterize almost all the songs. Moreover, the marriage theme permeates the poetry; the bridal sheets, laid out on a marriage bed, are where the consummation of love is to take place. Jerold S. Cooper has claimed that Sumerian love poetry expressed female sexuality, that it "privileges the female organ over the male," whereas Sumerian narrative poetry praised male sexuality in telling the exploits of the god Enki, god of sweet waters and organizer of the universe, "where penises and sexual intercourse are mentioned by name, and where lovemaking leads to ejaculation, conception and birth." Although he regards Sumerian love poetry as having little relationship with fecundity, Cooper does recognize that it is this poetry which "is associated with agricultural fertility and abundance, that, in the sacred marriage ritual, are generalized to other areas of successful rulership."

The temporal setting of the poetry is at sunset or later, when day has passed and night has come, the time of lovers. The place is in the city of Uruk (modern Warka, biblical Erech)—its streets, squares, and houses.

The characters in these dramatic poems are several; Inanna and Dumuzi are not alone but are joined by his sister, her brother, girlfriends of the bride acting in chorus, and narrator(s). The marriage theme is evoked by the invocations of "bridegroom" and "bride." Other terms of endearment, "brother" and "sister," were used among lovers without implying actual kinship: "With arousing glances, I shall induce the brother to enter, I shall make Shu-Sin—all ready—reveal himself a lusty man"; "My sister, why have you shut yourself in the house? . . . My brother coming from the palace, . . . let him bring the fine butter and cream."

One noteworthy feature of the discourse is that female lovers commonly employed the first person plural instead of the first person singular, especially when referring to bodily features, perhaps in the sense that they are sharing them with their lovers.

Love imagery reaches for diverse effects: it conjures up an enchanting atmosphere and portrays specific objects as well. Physical imagery is taken from the natural world. Metaphors such as the apple tree and the pillar of alabaster symbolize the male member. The apple tree may rise in a garden or the pillar of alabaster may

Cylinder-seal impression of a garden scene (cylinder at left). BRITISH MUSEUM, LONDON

stand in dark blue lapis lazuli stone. "Garden" and "stone" are the pubic hair, and whether it belongs to a swain or to his beloved, it could also be described by its texture as "wool" or "lettuce."

All the senses are actively stimulated by the poetry: *smell*—"O that someone would tell my mother Ningal, and she would sprinkle cedar perfume on the floor! Her dwelling, its fragrance is sweet"; *sight*—"The young lady stood waiting—Dumuzi pushed [open] the door, and like a moonbeam she came forth to him out of the house. He looked at her, rejoiced in her, took her in his arms [and kissed her]"; *touch*—"When you touch [our] hair with your hand. . . ."; *taste*—"Like her beer her vulva is sweet"; and *hearing*—"Cow of the good voice, . . . The faithful shepherd, he of the sweet chant, will verily recite a song of jubilation for you, goddess who sweetens everything (in) song."

Above and beyond the physical imagery and the sensual stimulation, there is an obsession with jewelry. Although the many descriptions of jewels and gems could refer to bridal gifts and ornaments and allusions to the "plowing of ŠUBA-stones" could be a euphemistic expression for sexual intercourse, there is more to the mention of jewels than meets the reader. First, on the most mundane level, a bride's quality or worth parallels the wealth in the jewelry offered by a groom. On the second level, the beauty of the bride, according to Sumerian tenets, rested on the perfection of her adornments and not just on

natural attributes. In one text, Dumuzi brings precious stones and jewelry and portrays how Inanna covers her body completely from head to toe in jewelry. Jewelry is used metaphorically: "My brother of fairest face, press it toward our bosom, My (beloved) with a lapis-lazuli beard, . . . You are my pin, my gold, Piece (of art) shaped by the skilled carpenter, My (be-

Female statue wearing a pendant showing a couple embracing, third millennium BCE. *FESTSCHRIFT HUNDERT JAHRE BERLINER GESELLSCHAFT FÜR ANTHROPOLOGIE, ETHNOLOGIE UND URGESCHICHTE 1869–1969 II* (1970)

loved) manufactured by the skilled copper smith!"

The context in which the songs of the first category were sung has been long debated. Clearly, they were chanted as part of the Inanna-Dumuzi cult, but whether they were sung by priests and priestesses before the statues of the deities or in a dramatic reenactment of the roles of divinities cannot be determined on the internal evidence of the texts. Furthermore, the specific rite during which the performance took place may have been either the New Year's festival, which included the bringing of a variety of edible gifts by the worshiper, or the "sacred marriage" ceremony performed as a cyclical festival of the royal calendar (as were certain songs of the second category). Poetic allusions to an impending marriage are frequent, such as in an address by the bride's parents to their future son-in-law and in the advice of a ladylove to her suitor on the best method of getting her parents' consent to the marriage. Other texts describe the actual ceremony in which the opening of the door by the bride to the bridegroom functioned as the formal act that concluded a Sumerian marriage.

Akkadian

Akkadian love poetry may be divided into two periods: from its beginnings in the third millennium to the fall of the Old Babylonian hegemony in southern Mesopotamia (circa 1720 BCE) and from then until the demise of the Babylonian culture. The great divide between the two is due to the destruction of the Sumerian school system and the end of its cultural and religious dominance. The sexual metaphor in myth and ritual changed with time and place. With the passage of the millennia, the symbolization of the union of divine and human in ritual intercourse, and the immanence of the divine in the world, were replaced by the image of gods first as parents, and then as transcendent remote deities.

From the first half of the second millennium, the extant Akkadian love poems express three subjects. First, there is one dialogue relating to the love between deities, a dialogue between Nanaya and Muati from Babylon. Second, there is also a solitary example of a "sacred marriage" text from Larsa (modern Tell Senkere) in the

time of Rim-Sin. A descriptive ritual from Mari (Tell Hariri) also seems to refer to some such ceremony between the king and Ishtar, but no lyrics are preserved and the incipits that are quoted are in Sumerian. Third, there is a unique nonreligious dialogue between a lovesick woman and her less than loving beloved. Other fragments containing the theme of love and sexual union come from the city of Kish (modern Tell al-Uhaimir; Tell Ingharra), but as yet it is uncertain if they belong to the first or third category. Further, love lyrics are embedded in the love charms, the earliest of which dates to circa 2250. After a collapse of the southern centers, there appears for the first time a type of literary composition that combines aspects of the first and second types above. It is a prayer or hymn addressed to a female goddess to intercede with either her lover or husband for blessings on the king. The example in the first category, the dialogue of Nanaya and Muati, is really an example of this mixed genre. The sensual and amatory vocabulary is used both of the relationship between goddess and husband as well as between goddess and king.

From the late second millennium comes an ancient library catalog from the northern city of Asshur (modern Qalat Sharqat), capital of Assyria. It was found in the Assur temple complex in the courtyard of Nunnamnir in a later, first millennium context. It lists literary works by the first lines of the compositions and demonstrates clearly the degree to which Mesopotamian amatory literature has been lost. Of the original eight-column tablet, only six columns are preserved from the upper two-thirds of the tablet. Thus, only half the tablet is attested, in which occur the incipits of 275 out of 400 songs and hymns. Of these, at least two-fifths are in Sumerian and the remainder in Akkadian. Of all these songs, two or perhaps three of the Sumerian songs are known to us and one of the Akkadian songs. The character of this collection is not clear, since the conclusion is missing. The varied nature of the library texts with which it was found precludes any definite statements as to the possible liturgical character of the original songs. Some seem to be hymns, since they directly address the gods by name; some amatory, pastoral ballads, probably concerned with the love between Ishtar and Dumuzi but not explicitly religious. Most were labeled *zamāru*, "song," sung to musical accompaniment. A broken section also contained an unknown number of Sumerian BAL.BAL.E-dialogues, such as discussed above.

Another fragment of a catalog from southern Mesopotamia from a few hundred years earlier preserves six titles, also of amatory content. One of these preserves the name of the Old Babylonian king Ammisaduqa. Since Ishtar is addressed in one, it is possible that these are titles of liturgical hymns from her temple. Further, the complete song that is preserved from this period, written in a Middle Babylonian hand on a tablet of unknown provenance, contains a song whose title is preserved in the Assyrian catalog and speaks of the love between the shepherd Dumuzi and Ishtar. Its colophon states that it is a library tablet of an officer in the temple of Ishtar.

First-millennium Akkadian love poetry can be described under two categories. There are liturgical texts, including the dramatic mystery play, and nonliturgical texts. Liturgical texts range from those whose main concern is the love between two divine beings to those which feature complete rituals. There is far more evidence of marriage rituals (*ḫašādu, ḫadaššūtu*) than texts concerning them. Rituals associate the god Nabu with both Tashmetu and Nanaya, consorts in the Assyrian center of Kalkhu (modern Nimrud), Nabu with Nanaya in Babylon; Shamash with Aya in the Babylonian center of Sippar (modern Abu Habba); Marduk with Sarpanitu in Babylon; Anu with Antu in Uruk (modern Warka, biblical Erech); and perhaps the goddess Banitu with her spouse Ninurta in an unknown Assyrian center. From the several remarks in letters, administrative texts, royal inscriptions, and ritual calendars, we know that there was more love poetry that has been lost to us.

Of the ritual texts, the most complete are those dealing with the ritual of Ishtar of Babylon, which have been termed "Divine Love Lyrics." The rites of Ishtar of Babylon contain a dramatic mystery play in which the main actors are Marduk, the main god of Babylon, his consort Sarpanitu, and Ishtar of Babylon, his "girlfriend." Not one word of love appears, with the exception of the stereotypical erotic phrase "to the garden of your (feminine) love." As Dietz Otto Edzard

states, "the Love Lyrics are neither very loving nor very lyrical." He believes the text to be "measures against rivals," an elaborate incantation drama. Thus, it would link up with other incantations of jealous men and women, such as an Old Babylonian collection of love incantations from Isin (Ishan Bahriyat). Other actors include the gardener whose poisonous brew is sought, the comic *kurgarrû*, and the dance of the *assinnu*.

True love lyrics are found in the Neo-Assyrian dialogue between Nabu and Tashmetu.

Under the heading of nonliturgical texts are the love chants used in sympathetic magical rites to enthrall the desired and unwary object of one's affections. The love charms and spells contain the same phraseology as the love lyrics such as the themes of the garden of love and the erotic jewels.

Dialogue is the preferred form of the Akkadian love lyrics. Most often names of the speakers are not given; changes in person and gender of grammatical elements give hints, but not explicit information. Some transitions are marked by narration. The content of these poems plays on the theme of love. The message is identical, whether in liturgical or non-liturgical contexts, since all are encoded in the same amatory and erotic vocabulary.

The archetypal characters, Inanna and Dumuzi, again appear in varied contexts. In an Old Babylonian love charm from Isin, the simile is explicit: "I shall hold you as tight as Ishtar held Dumuzi." In addition to the main personae, the chorus again appears as a group of women or a group of worshipers. The terms of endearment have changed. The brother-sister forms of address have given way to the son and king in reference to the male beloved and queen in reference to the female beloved. The royal metaphor is the leitmotif. The use of the grammatical first person plural by the female speaker again appears frequently.

The imagery is similar to the Sumerian. Horticulture, once more, provides similes for the expression and depiction of love: "She seeks the beautiful garden of your (male) delights." The synonyms for love are various words for fruits, in particular the word "fruits" (*inbū*) itself, and love is always "sweet." Orchards play a role as the setting for sacred marriage rituals, both as a backdrop to the meetings of lovers in the poetry and as metaphors for the physical attributes of the lovers. Eroticism of the most explicit nature often appears.

The adornment of the female beloved again plays a part in the love poetry. She comes bedecked with jewels to her meeting with her lover: "O by the diadem of our head, the rings of our ears, the mountains of our shoulders, and the charms of our chest, the bracelet with date spadix charms of our wrists, the belt hung with frog charms of our waist." No love encounter is complete without finery: "My lord, put an earring on me, let me give you pleasure in the garden! . . . My [Tashmetu], I will put on you bracelets of carnelian!"

SYRO-PALESTINE

The most famous love lyrics from this geographic area in ancient times are to be found in the biblical book entitled Canticles, Song of Songs, or Song of Solomon. Comparative material from Ugarit is embedded in narrative texts such as the short depiction of Lady Ḥry in the "Keret Epic" and the description of the marriage proposal in "Nikkal and the Moon." Other pieces of Ugaritic literature, such as the cycle of Baal and Anat do not provide any lyrics with a love theme, although there is a graphic account of sexual intercourse related to the birth of an heir.

The body of love lyrics contained in the Song of Songs is limited: eight chapters with a total of 117 verses. Despite various theories, there is no reason to attribute the origin of these love lyrics to Sumerian literary sources or to any direct importation of Egyptian love songs, given the appreciable distance in space or time.

In addition, love lyrics are incorporated into other books of the Bible. For example, there is Isaiah's "Song of the Vineyard": "Now, will I sing to my well-beloved a song of my beloved touching his vineyard" (5:1). Likewise, in Psalm 45, entitled a song of endearment, the author proclaims the grandeur and charms of the loving couple, the king and his royal bride, and their nuptials.

In form and structure, the Song of Songs has been analyzed both as a single song and as an anthology of love lyrics. Unity or diversity are the themes of the commentaries on this biblical book. In either case, the formal structure is based on the dialogue. While monologues are embedded in the discourse, there is always a listener within the fictional framework of the poem who is being addressed and who often responds. The dialogue emphasizes the interaction of the lovers and the mutuality of their communication by making the words of one lover echo the words of the other. The audiences are both implicit and explicit—the love monologue may sometimes have a double audience: an apparent (explicit) audience such as a group of outsiders, and the real (implicit) hearer, who is always the beloved.

The surface structure of the discourse is loose; the poem achieves unity through coherence of thematic and verbal texture. It has a cyclical structure of seeking and finding the beloved, with pauses for descriptive sections depicting the beloved and lyrical sections on the power and character of love itself. The superscript title of the book plainly presents it as a song par excellence. The literary language of the Song of Songs contains many obscure terms and words of multifaceted meaning. Word plays are abundant and often obscure to the modern reader. The sensation of sounds reverbrates throughout the composition.

The essential nature of the Song as love lyrics is not in controversy. Nevertheless, few agree on its theme. There are numerous modes of interpretation—allegorical, mystical, messianic, liturgical, historical, and secular. However, the earliest information that we possess on its evaluation indicates that it was considered national religious literature, a holy book in the canon of sacred scripture. The evidence for the canonicity of the Song is discussed in Mishna *Yadayim* 3:5, where the issue is whether the status of the Song had been in dispute at a council session at Jamnia that took place sometime between 75 and 117 CE. The sacredness of the book may be indicated by the existence of four fragments of the Song at Qumran, of which the only published one is dated to 50 CE. Furthermore, snippets from it were featured at diverse festivities. (For the 15th of Ab and the Day of Atonement celebrations, see Mishna *Taʿanit* 4:8; and for "at banqueting houses," see Tosefta *Sanhedrin* 12:10.) In the second century, Rabbi Akiva denounced the people who were singing its verses in improper places and manner as a secular song.

Whatever the message, it was encoded in the language of love. Even if the Song was originally oral literature and its stock of images came from formulaic diction, the poetic craft of the unknown author or authors reached extraordinary heights in the metaphorical comparisons based on the physical attributes of the lovers. Common motifs are: the praise of love itself; the courting of the beloved; the separation of the lovers; and the search for the beloved. The number of characters in the Song of Songs is in dispute. The minimum cast includes two lovers with the girls of Jerusalem and unnamed brothers. The maximum cast includes as many as ten characters in the libretto. There does not seem to be any narrator.

The relationship between the Song and King Solomon, who is mentioned by name in the first verse and in six other places in the text, is disputed. Apparently, the size of Solomon's harem was proverbial and must have given rise to an evaluation of Solomon as a voluptuary. Nevertheless, as Dumuzi is the Mesopotamian archetypical lover, King Solomon seems to play the same role in Song of Songs. In a similar vein, we should view the wider use of "king," "prince," and "noblewoman" to designate the lovers. Another appelative is "sister." The designation "bride" provides the only reference to marriage in the book.

The sensual imagery of the world and all that is in it permeates the biblical love lyrics. In particular, olfactory sensations arise from the perfumes and aromatics, and stimulating to the tastebuds are the ambrosial delicacies of the honey and wine:

> Awake, north wind,
> Come, wind of the south!
> Breathe over my garden
> To spread its sweet smell around
> Let my beloved come into his garden
> Let him taste its rarest fruits.
> I come into my garden
> My sister, my promised bride
> I gather my myrrh and balsam
> I eat my honey and my honeycomb
> I drink my wine and my milk.
>
> (4:16–5:1)

The images drawing on flora come from twenty-five varieties of trees, shrubs, flowers, herbs, fruits, nuts, spices, and nectars; among the fauna, the mare, dove, gazelle, deer, nightingale, turtledove, fox, lion, leopard, and raven appear. Even objects of human artifice, such as sculptural and architectural forms, serve as complementary sources of inspiration. These images simultaneously embody several layers of meaning: the literal, metaphorical, and euphemistic. Among the metaphors and symbols, the garden, the orchard and the vineyard have a special place. The garden, as a specific place and as an extended metaphor, has been equated with female sexuality, while pasturing has been identified with male sexual activity. Eating and drinking have been understood as erotic metaphors. The frequent use of military imagery and androcentric language in the depiction of the female and its virtual absence for the male has been noted by Carol Meyers.

The setting of the Song ranges over the lush cultivated countryside, the wild remote landscape, and the well-defended walled city with its houses and streets. Further, it expresses interior emotional space.

Although the rubrics of the Mesopotamian poetic texts attribute them to goddesses (which may or may not indicate their religious nature), and the superscriptions of many of the Egyptian love songs characterize them as entertainment, the Song of Songs is designated only as a song composed by or for Solomon. There is no internal evidence of a specific context for the Song of Songs, although over the millennia there has been much speculation on possible historical, religious, and social backgrounds. There is no evidence from the Song of a liturgy for an orgiastic fertility cult or a sacred marriage. External evidence adduced by Michael V. Fox for a context of pure entertainment is from the book of Ezekiel 33:31–32: "For they have a taste for erotica. . . . As far as they're concerned you're just a (singer of) erotic songs." There are certain surface similarities between the Song and the Arabic song of description, termed *waṣf*, which depicts through a series of images the parts of the male and female body. Although the *waṣf* songs are sung during wedding ceremonies, this social context is not necessarily that of the Song. Early references to the Song in no way point to an original use at weddings. The most cogent argument as to its origin and development seems to be that its early use at religious festivities (see above) led to the sacralization of the Song.

EGYPT

The ancient Egyptian love songs survive from a very limited period—there are about fifty love poems from the New Kingdom, from the thirteenth to the eleventh centuries BCE, in four groups: Papyrus Harris 500, vase fragments with the Cairo Love Songs, Papyrus Chester Beatty I, and Papyrus Turin 1966 plus other fragments. An estimate of the number of poems depends on the definition of the pause marks between poems, whether they separate distinct poems or just stanzas. The love poems often have an elite setting, but two groups (vase fragments with the Cairo Love Songs and Papyrus Chester Beatty I) were found at Dayr al-Madina, a craftsmen's village, which would indicate a wide appeal. Papyrus Harris 500 contains not only three groups of love songs but also a mortuary song ("Antef") and two popular stories ("The Doomed Prince" and "The Capture of Joppa"). However, these texts are written in literary Late Egyptian, which was not a vernacular dialect.

Some Egyptian love songs have headings giving the purpose or title of the composition(s) in red ink to differentiate them from the body of the texts, such as, *ḥʾt-ʿ m ḥs sḥmḥ-jb*, "Beginning of the song of entertainment." The singular *ḥs*, "song," is used in several of the headings, while *ts*, "saying," and *rʾw*, "utterances," also occur. Egyptian love songs are basically monologues. The speaker may address no one in particular, revealing innermost thoughts and feelings, or the monologue could be directed to an implicit or explicit audience. Nonhuman objects can be addressed. While the girls in the Egyptian love songs frequently address their lovers in the second person whether or not they are present, the boys never address the girls in that way, even when their presence is implied. Two poems consist of speeches of a boy and a girl in juxtaposition, but neither of these is a true dialogue; both of them are speaking their inner thoughts. The speakers do not exchange words or affect each other by speech.

Formal patterning creates a tight literary structure. Many songs are built up from repetition of a single motif. Each stanza is introduced in the same manner. In several poems, a set of wishes forms the structure. In one song, the puns on flower names, loosely related to the rest of a girl's words, realize and maintain a scene where she strolls in a garden with her lover.

The content of these love songs is limited to premarital courting and the sensual world of young lovers. The love poems present amatory fantasies in delicate tones in their description of the beloved's body and the dalliance on the bed, with few of the euphemisms known from the Mesopotamian or biblical material and none of the Mesopotamian anatomical details. These erotic fantasies of both sexes portray love as a state of pleasant harmony brought about mainly by the presence of a beloved and by mutually shared sensual contact. The Egyptian love songs are exceptional in that they are mainly introspective songs, describing emotions.

Not only the two lovers but also representatives from the animal and plant kingdoms crowd an Egyptian love poem. In three of them, trees speak, each showing a higher degree of generosity toward the lovers. Although the lovers are human, they can transform into gods, thus sharpening the perfection of their emotions and feelings: the "brother" is Re, the "sister" Hathor, or in the Cairo Love Songs, the boy is Nefertem and the girl is Sothis. The "brother" and "sister" are the most common epithets of the lovers, although royal and noble epithets for the lovers do appear. Infrequently, we hear the voice of the narrator.

The imagery reflects the Egyptian landscape—the Nile and the marshes figure prominently. Although literal rather than figurative expressions give voice to a lover's admiration, floral motifs are common in the comparison of physical attributes to flowers and woods, and the *rrmt*-fruit motif also appears recurrently. The senses are continually intoxicated—the intoxicant being love: "Your liquor is (your) lovemaking." The sweet fragrances come from Punt and permeate the "Flower Song." The sound of the turtledove is heard in the land of Egypt, as it is in Israel. The lovers stroll hand in hand. Jewelry is limited to the signet ring on the beloved's finger. The poems can be set any time of the day or night. Two songs take place at dawn, with the parting of the lovers occurring at daybreak, with love fulfilled.

Internal evidence of the actual context of the Egyptian love poetry can be adduced from the heading: "the beginning of the entertainment (*shmh-j'b*) song." Some external evidence is provided by tomb paintings. Those depicting singing and dancing at banquets are labeled *shmh-j'b*, although no love songs are recorded in this context.

Whereas Mesopotamian art from its inception portrayed sexual encounters, it was only in the graphic art of the Amarna period that the open display of intimacy and sensual pleasures came to be prominent motifs. In Ramesside art and literature, different views of sexuality are shown. Overt sexual activity on the part of men and women is not shown in the tombs but on ostraca, clay models, papyri, and probably in the decoration of private houses. For example, ostraca depict undressed women on beds as well as men and women coupling quite explicitly. An extreme example of blatant sexuality in Ramesside art is Papyrus Turin 55001, which depicts the adventures of a man with a prostitute. In narrative literature stemming from this same period, sexuality is a major theme: it is the moving force of the story in "Truth and Falsehood," it is repudiated in "Two Brothers," and it occurs as homosexual encounters in "Horus and Seth." While not depicted openly, visual intimations of sexuality are presented in tomb paintings, such as the motif of the pleasure trip in a papyrus boat with its erotic implications. On the other hand, the tender love story of "The Doomed Prince" offers us a romantic, although asexual, narrative. The love poetry with its direct and indirect references to sex was written down in this environment.

The annual cycle of daily life had its high points during religious occasions that brought opportunities for lovers' meetings. Participation in cultic activities forms the backdrop to a number of songs; for example, two songs describe a lover's journey to the cult centers of Memphis (modern Mit Rahina) and Heliopolis. Beyond the literary conventions of divine equations with the lovers, there does not seem to be any possible ritual aspect to this poetry, such as seen in the Mesopotamian sources. None of the love songs is a prayer or a hymn to Hathor, although marshes were particularly connected with her (a frequent setting of the songs).

One of the songs expresses a woman's hope of being able to marry her lover. However, generally the context does not mention marriage.

SUMMARY AND CONCLUSIONS

The love lyrics of the ancient Near East vary in form, structure, characters, setting, imagery, content, and context. An evaluation of the form of the poetic texts should answer the question posed at the outset of this article regarding the propriety of the label "lyrics." The form of the Egyptian poems, apparently, is that of free verse in a composition which is itself often free. It is a poetry of feeling and thus falls under the "lyric" designation with static descriptions, introspective monologues, and little narrative plot. Whereas Egyptian poetry depends on the short lyrical verse, the Mesopotamian cannot be so easily described. However, the presence of tight plot structure, fixed personae, unified portrayal of character for the voices, dialogue, and choruses are a sufficient basis on which to posit "drama" for the Mesopotamian love literature. The Song of Songs has the loosest poetic structure while it makes extensive use of dialogue, which indicates that it, too, could have been "drama." Note that the prosody of ancient Egyptian, Akkadian, Sumerian, and Hebrew are not fully known to us and seem to be based on a succession of fairly free rhythmic accents rather on a system of quantities.

The central characters of the love poetry are the lovers. In all the areas surveyed, these are portrayed as equal partners in a mutual giving relationship. In both Mesopotamia and in the Bible, the greatest lovers are kings, enhancing the notion later proposed by the Greeks that nobler individuals embody deeper feelings.

The setting and backdrop for the action of the poetry is seen in glimpses. The indications of place are exact and graphic, but fleeting, the ebb and flow of impressions counting infinitely more than external facts.

The Garden, The Orchard, and the Apple

Of the motifs and figurative expressions that are the common property of ancient near eastern love lyrics, one that is, so to speak, the hallmark of love poetry is the theme of "going down to the garden, the garden of love." Note the following:

> Sumerian: "My(?) sister, I would go with you to my garden."

> Akkadian: "Let my Tashmetu come with me to the garden"; "As I [went down] into the garden of your (feminine) love."

> Hebrew: "My beloved went down to his garden, to the beds of spices, to pasture his flock in the gardens and gather lilies."

> Ugaritic: "I'll make her field into a vineyard, the field of her love into an orchard."

> Egyptian: "When I am headed to the 'Love Garden' my bosom full of persea (blossoms), my hair laden with balm."

While the imagery may be the same, the meaning may not be. As Michael V. Fox has stated, "While a girl may be compared to a garden, the garden never seems to be an independent symbol for a girl or for feminine sexuality in the Egyptian love songs." Apparently, most cases of the garden imagery in Egyptian love poetry are to be taken on the literal level as the preferred venue for lovers' meetings, with few metaphorical overtones.

Related to this motif are the frequent comparisons of the beloved to fruits or fruit trees, in particular to that of the apple tree (whatever its exact botanical identity):

> Sumerian: "My blossom bearer in the apple garden, your appeal is sweet, My fruit bearer in the apple garden, your appeal is sweet"; "My budding garden of the apple tree, sweet are your charms! My fruiting garden of the apple tree, sweet are your charms!"

> Akkadian: "Praise of Mami is sweeter than . . . an apple"; "To my spouse I cleave as an apple to the bough."

> Hebrew: "As an apple tree among the trees of the wood so is my beloved among the boys, under its shadow I delighted to sit, and its fruit was sweet to my taste."

> Egyptian: "It (love) is like *rrmt*-fruit in a man's hand; it is like dates he mixes in beer."

The apple is not only used in figurative language but also in symbolic actions. For example, apples are mentioned in an incantation. The ritual specifies that the incantation is to be recited over an apple, which is then given to the desired woman to suck.

Of the three cultural areas surveyed, all employ imagery taken from the world of nature as multifaceted symbols of lovers' emotions and physical attributes. Beyond this generalization, there are differences and similarities. It has been claimed that the gentle eroticism of the Song of Songs is far removed from the detailed and explicit sexuality of the Mesopotamian liturgies. In Syro-Palestine and Egypt, there is an extended use of simile ("like a") rather than the metaphorical language found in Mesopotamia.

The most suggestive imagery is taken from the natural world. Often the scene is the garden and the charm of the flowers, fruits, and birds envelops the charm of the maidens. From the world of handicraft are brought comparisons to precious metals, gems, and jewelry. In the Song of Songs, the head, hands, and ankles of the beau are compared to gold, and the golden hands are further inlaid with beryl. The association between the garden imagery and the metaphor of the jewelry is often made: "'For what, for what, are you adorned, my Tashmetu?' 'So that I may [go] to the garden with you, my Nabû!'" The following combination provides the key to obsession with jewelry in the metaphors of the Mesopotamian world: "Lo, your love is obsidian, lo, your rapture is gold." They also appear in biblical descriptions of the ladylove: "Thy cheeks are comely with circlets, thy neck with beads. We will make thee circlets of gold with studs of silver." Apparently, sexual allure and attraction were projected by these adornments, but the erotic overtones of these enticing gems escape us with our own cultural perspective. However, it is more than just the brightness of the metal and the mesmerism of the sparkling ornaments. In Mesopotamia, beauty is found in the bodily adornments, and they eloquently demonstrate the worth of the prospective bride.

Literary phrases such as these clearly have various levels of significance. Some are little more than fixed formulae characteristic of oral poetry, which, however, could be used in widely different contexts with only minor adaptations. Others may be derived from the symbolic imagery of the deeper psychological levels. In between these extremes are the ordinary literary metaphors, recognized as such by the literary traditions of the culture. Unlike the fixed formulae, they were not limited to one language only, but could be freely shared by all.

Another noteworthy feature of these symbols and metaphors is their extreme plasticity and their capacity to refer to several levels of perception at the same time. Not only can the same metaphor be used in different contexts with quite different meaning, but it may even have several meanings at the same time in the same text. It is also difficult to read the Song of Songs without sensing that the distinction between the metaphorical and the literal meanings of the words vanishes like smoke—the scents and colors of the land and its trees and fruits blend with the descriptions of the beloved's charms into an indissoluble whole. Finally, the symbols and images were evidently capable of being understood differently by different individuals, without any single understanding being more "correct" than the others.

We thus arrive at a concept of a common near eastern pool of literary "building blocks" that the individual author could manipulate to promote imagery and realize moods. It follows from this that a work like the Song of Songs, which seems to be a collection of such "building blocks," cannot be dated at all—its elements are as timeless and as old as near eastern literature itself, oral or written. It also seems pointless to ask whether such love lyrics originated in Mesopotamia or not. As it happens, we have the oldest surviving witnesses to such literary compositions on cuneiform tablets, but that, of course, proves nothing except that the Mesopotamians wrote on clay, which is durable, and the others, if at all, on perishable papyrus or parchment. We should not doubt, therefore, that love

was sung even among those who have left us no written records of their passion.

Although the basic content of this poetry is the passion of lovers, the interpretations of the imagery built on this foundation have been numerous. The most influential and the oldest of them has been built on the substructure of the sacred love poetry of Mesopotamia—the divine allegory, an extended analogy between divine and human affairs, sought and found in the Song of Songs by the Tannaitic rabbis and early church fathers, and in the love poetry of Egypt by a few Egyptologists.

The most difficult aspect of love poetry is to determine a specific context for its transfer into writing and its authorship. The written compositions in our possession are remnants of a larger oral tradition. In particular, the love poetry of Israel does not lend itself easily to contextualization on internal evidence, and therefore the theories propounded are myriad. According to their captions, Egyptian texts are merely entertainment, which makes it more puzzling why they were written down. On the other hand, the Mesopotamian liturgical texts were written down by scribes and taught to the priestly singers. As to the authorship, a theory was once propounded that all love lyrics were written by men, betraying a male's fantasy of women aggressively seeking out lovers, thus reversing the role recognized as typical of females. This is now challenged by the clear evidence that the only credited authors ascribed to specific Sumerian and Egyptian compositions were women.

In conclusion, the love that eternally sprung from the hearts of the people of the ancient Near East was expressed through various types of love poetry of which only a few remnants have been preserved for our appreciation. Let us hope that more such poems are found in new excavations of either ancient tells or modern storerooms.

BIBLIOGRAPHY

Mesopotamia

General discussions can be found in the following: V. AFANASJEVA, "Zu den Metaphern in einem Lied der "Heiligen Hochzeit," in *Societies and Languages of the Ancient Near East*, edited by M. A. DANDAMAYEV

(1982); BENDT ALSTER, "Marriage and Love in the Sumerian Love Songs," *The Tablet and the Scroll: Near Eastern Studies in Honor of William W. Hallo*, edited by M. COHEN, D. C. SNELL, and D. B. WEISBERG (1993); JERROLD S. COOPER, "New Cuneiform Parallels to the Song of Songs," *Journal of Biblical Literature* 90 (1971), and "Enki's Member: Eros and Irrigation in Sumerian Literature," in DUMU-E₂-DUB-BA-A: *Studies in Honor of Åke W. Sjöberg*, edited by H. BEHRENS, D. LODING, and M. T. ROTH (1989); PHILIP M. HIBBERT, "Liebeslyrik in der arsakidischen Zeit," *Die Welt des Orients* 15 (1984); S. N. KRAMER, "The Biblical 'Song of Songs' and the Sumerian Love Songs," *Expedition* 5 (1962), and *The Sacred Marriage Rite* (1969); W. G. LAMBERT, "Devotion: The Languages of Religion and Love," in *Figurative Language in the Ancient Near East*, edited by M. MINDLIN, M. J. GELLER, and J. E. WANSBROUGH (1987); GWENDOLYN LEICK, *Sex and Eroticism in Mesopotamian Literature* (1994); and J. G. WESTENHOLZ, "Metaphorical Language in the Poetry of Love in the Ancient Near East," *La circulation des biens, des personnes et des idées dans le Proche-Orient ancien*, XXXVIIIᵉ RAI (1992).

TEXT EDITIONS OF SUMERIAN LITERATURE

BENDT ALSTER, "Sumerian Love Songs," *Revue d'Assyriologie* 70 (1985), and "The Manchester Tammuz," *Acta Sumerologica* 14 (1992); and S. N. KRAMER, "Cuneiform Studies and the History of Literature: The Sumerian Sacred Marriage Texts," *Proceedings of the American Philosophical Society* 107, no. 6, and "Inanna and Šulgi—A Sumerian Fertility Song," *Iraq* 31 (1969).

TEXT EDITIONS OF AKKADIAN LITERATURE

J. A. BLACK, "Babylonian Ballads: A New Genre," *Journal of the American Oriental Society* 103 (1983); ERICH EBELING, *Ein Hymnen-Katalog aus Assur* (1929); DIETZ OTTO EDZARD, "Zur Ritualtafel der sog. 'Love Lyrics,'" in *Language, Literature, and History*, edited by F. ROCHBERG-HALTON (1987); IRVING FINKEL, "A Fragmentary Catalogue of Lovesongs," *Acta Sumerologica* 10 (1988); MOSHE HELD, "A Faithful Lover in an Old Babylonian Dialogue," *Journal of Cuneiform Studies* 15 (1961) and 16 (1962); W. G. LAMBERT, "Divine

Love Lyrics from the Reign of Abi-ešuḥ," *Mitteilungen des Instituts für Orientforschung* 12 (1966), and "The Problem of Love Lyrics," in *Unity and Diversity*, edited by H. GOEDICKE and J. J. M. ROBERTS (1975); E. MATSUSHIMA, "Le rituel hiérogamique de Nabû," *Acta Sumerologica* 9 (1987), and "Les rituels du mariage divin," *Acta Sumerologica* 10 (1988); J. G. WESTENHOLZ and A. WESTENHOLZ, "Help for Rejected Suitors: The Old Akkadian Love Incantation MAD V 8," *Orientalia* 46 (1977); and J. G. WESTENHOLZ, "A Forgotten Love Song," in *Language, Literature, and History*, edited by F. ROCHBERG-HALTON (1987).

Syro-Palestine

For a bibliography on the Song of Songs, see MARVIN POPE, *Song of Songs* (1977). Beyond that resource, see: HAROLD BLOOM, ed., *The Song of Songs* (1988); MARCIA FALK, *The Song of Songs: A New Translation and Interpretation* (1990); OTHMAR KEEL, *Deine Blicke sind Tauben: Zur Metaphoren des Hohen Liedes* (1984); FRANCIS LANDY, *Paradoxes of Paradise: Identity and Difference in the Song of Songs* (1983); CAROL MEYERS, "Gender Imagery in the Song of Songs," *Hebrew Annual Review* 10 (1986); HANS-PETER MÜLLER, *Vergleich und Metapher im Hohenlied* (1984); J. M. SASSON, "Unlocking the Poetry of Love in the Song of Songs," *Bible Review* 1 (1985); and R. J. TOURNAY, *Word of God, Song of Love: A Commentary on the Song of Songs* (1988).

Egypt

For general discussions, see MICHAEL V. FOX, *The Song of Songs and the Ancient Egyptian Love Songs* (1985). See also: PIERRE DERCHAIN, "Le lotus, la mandragore, et le persea," *Chronique d'Égypt* 50 (1975); MICHAEL V. FOX, "Love, Passion, and Perception in Israelite and Egyptian Love Poetry," *Journal of Biblical Literature* 102 (1983); and J. M. SASSON, "A Major Contribution to Song of Songs Scholarship," *Journal of the American Oriental Society* 107 (1987).

TEXT EDITIONS

MICHAEL V. FOX, *The Song of Songs and the Ancient Egyptian Love Songs* (1988), and ALFRED HERMANN, *Altägyptische Liebesdichtung* (1959).

SEE ALSO **Sumerian Literature: An Overview** (Part 9, Vol. IV); **Akkadian Literature: An Overview** (Part 9, Vol. IV); and **Erotic Art in the Ancient Near East** (Part 10, Vol. IV).

10

Visual and Performing Arts

Art and Ideology
in Ancient Western Asia

MICHELLE I. MARCUS

IDEOLOGY IS DEFINED HERE broadly as any intersection between belief systems and political power. It refers to the way in which signs, meanings, and values help to reproduce a dominant social power. More specifically, ideologies can make use of cultural symbols to enhance or mask relationships of inequality and domination, serving to legitimate the special interests of hegemonic groups. The concept of hegemony—meaning the ways in which a governing power wins acceptance to its rule from those it subjugates—extends and enriches the notion of ideology, especially for some of the ancient near eastern ideologies discussed below. An important device by which ideologies achieve legitimacy is by universalizing and eternalizing themselves; values and interests that are in fact specific to a certain time and place are projected as the values and interests of all humanity and for all times.

Despite the application of metaphors derived from the interplay of art and language (or texts) in recent art historical and linguistic theory, it should be pointed out that visual materials have a unique role in expressions of ideology. Material culture can take on the responsibility of carrying certain messages that a culture cannot entrust to language. The ability of art and other material goods to carry messages nonverbally makes them an especially subtle and stealthy means for communicating certain potentially controversial political messages, without danger of protest, refusal, or controversy. In this way they can become powerful tools of persuasion by which one group of people wins the obedience of another.

The above understanding of the use of ideology ascribes an active intelligence to artisans and patrons of antiquity, granting them the same abilities and intentions that we would credit to ourselves as sentient social beings. It is such a perspective that allows and impels scholars to think about ideology in the archaeological record—something that anthropologists have been doing for some time, but which is still not a part of mainstream near eastern art history.

We will examine three kinds of ideology in the art of the ancient Near East: state, class, and gender. While other issues could be investigated, such as religious ideologies, they are at once more static (figures and symbols of deities) and somewhat less accessible in the visual record. Previous research on art and ideology in the ancient Near East has concentrated on the relief-sculpture of the Neo-Assyrian Empire, particularly royal architectural decoration from the imperial centers in northern Iraq. Such a concentration may be attributed in part to theories in sociology (dependent on S. N. Eisenstadt) that ideological politics originated in the Axial Age civilizations of the first millennium BCE, and that pre-Axial Age cultures did not have the same degree of principled ideologies.

Although it could be demonstrated that earlier

materials in the Near East and in preliterate cultures elsewhere clearly participated in ideological signification, I will feature selected examples from the Neo-Assyrian period, but will draw, as well, on the contemporary luxury goods and personal ornaments from Hasanlu in northwestern Iran. Adding Hasanlu to the picture allows me to compare cultural ideologies at the center of power and at its periphery, to find illustration in large-scale and small-scale art, and to constrast an imperial state that had recently begun to expand territorially with a settlement that was about to be overrun by a new population group. The Neo-Assyrian material, in which written documents complement artistic creations, can be used to clarify how ideology was meant to work for those who crafted it in ancient times. The Hasanlu material, however, lends itself to an evaluation of modern preconceptions and ideological agendas applied to the examination of artistic remains that do not include written texts.

STATE IDEOLOGY

The art of Shalmaneser III (858–824 BCE) continues traditions of historical narrative first established by his father, Assurnasirpal II (883–859). The focus here is on some of the differences between the ideology that is expressed in the art of father and son. In both cases, the use of historical narrative—scenes of battle and of tribute, with the king as both author and subject—serves to couch an imperialist ideology in what seems to be historical reality (figs. 1, 2). Typological features and signature elements of dress, headgear, landscape, or associated goods accentuate the realism of the place and of the moment. These elements therefore serve as verifiers of the supposed truth of the scene. By thus communicating to their subjects a visual version of social reality that is real and recognizable, the imperial ideology becomes more truly effective.

At the same time, the use of certain standard images that have a long history of representation in near eastern art also serves to eternalize and naturalize the legitimacy of the king and the state, by way of suggesting unity with the past. For instance, representations of the king receiving officials or tributaries, or holding a cup before attendants, are most reminiscent of so-called presentation scenes (often featuring worshipers before a deity) in earlier Sumerian and Babylonian artwork (compare fig. 3). Significantly the references are to Babylonian

Fig. 1. Limestone relief from the Northwest Palace at Nimrud showing the Assyrian king Assurnasirpal II (at center) shooting his bow in combat, with women and animals being led away as booty (at left), circa 865 BCE. BRITISH MUSEUM, LONDON

Although the reign of Shalmaneser III is not known for any of the large-scale carved orthostats (revetment slabs) characteristic of the palace decoration of Assurnasirpal II, it is associated nevertheless with three major monuments carved with scenes of historical narrative: the so-called Bronze Gates from Balawat (ancient Imgur-Enlil) (fig. 4); the Throne Base from Fort Shalmaneser at Nimrud (Kalkhu) (figs. 5, 6); and the Black Obelisk also from Nimrud (fig. 7). In each case, there are battle or tribute scenes carved in narrow horizontal registers, identified by short labels or epigraphs usually at the top of each register, as well as a longer inscription recording the military activities of the king.

Fig. 2. Limestone relief showing foreigners bearing gifts, Northwest Palace of Assurnasirpal II at Nimrud, circa 865 BCE. BRITISH MUSEUM, LONDON

imagery. It provides visual support for a particularly Assyrian ideology that consciously plays upon its Babylonian foundation, especially in religious matters, but with Assyria now as the new center of Mesopotamian culture.

The Bronze Gates from Balawat

The decoration on the Bronze Gates represents the earliest of the three artworks of Shalmaneser featuring scenes of historical narrative. It is distinguished from the other two works by its closer ties to the relief sculpture of Assurnasirpal II, specifically in the repeated narrative sequence of Assyrian victory in battle and subsequent collection of booty. The later monuments feature only the culmination of imperial might: the king's reception of foreign tribute (figs. 5–7).

Fig. 3. Drawing of a limestone relief showing the Assyrian king Assurnasirpal II seated with attendants; detail from the Northwest Palace at Nimrud, circa 865 BCE. The composition is reminiscent of so-called presentation scenes in early Sumerian and Babylonian artwork. BRITISH MUSEUM, LONDON

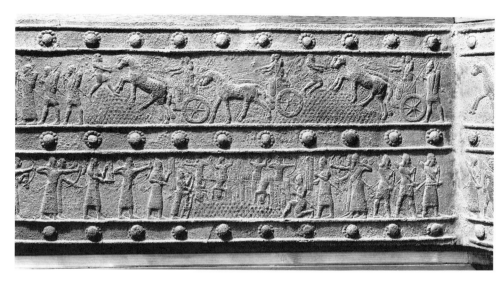

Fig. 4. Bands from the Bronze Gates of Shalmaneser III, at Balawat showing a campaign in the mountainous regions of Urartu in eastern Turkey, circa 848 BCE. BRITISH MUSEUM, LONDON

While military force might have been implied in these later images, the visual display of force is omitted. In fact, Shalmaneser seems to have deliberately edited out from these later representations his more aggressive campaigns and to depict instead campaigns in which tribute was collected without any prior battle (for instance, tribute from Gilzanu and Israel in the first two registers on the Black Obelisk [fig. 7]). That this selection process was a matter of ideology and not a function of the limited space available on these small-scale works is supported by the fact that battle scenes are featured even on small-scale objects attributed to Assurnasirpal II.

Fig. 5. Limestone throne base of the Assyrian king Shalmaneser III, circa 846 BCE, found at Fort Shalmaneser, Nimrud. The carving on the front of the dais shows a meeting between Shalmaneser and the Babylonian king Marduk-zakir-shumi; the side view shown (the southern side) depicts the Assyrian king receiving tribute from Babylonia. The base is now in the Iraq Museum in Baghdad. ANTON MOORTGAT, *ART OF ANCIENT MESOPOTAMIA* (1967)

Fig. 6. Detail of the relief-carving on the north side of the Throne Base of Shalmaneser III, showing tribute from Unqi in North Syria, circa 846 BCE. BRITISH SCHOOL OF ARCHAEOLOGY IN IRAQ

In other words, the display of military domination was less a part of the imperial ideology of Shalmaneser III than was the actual collection of raw materials and goods. The texts of Shalmaneser similarly pay greatest attention to economic and commercial gains: the number of cities conquered, the quantities of metals and other commodities received as booty and tribute. This commercial focus contrasts with the accounts of military exploits of Assurnasirpal II, which enumerate those massacred, impaled, burnt, and taken captive. Even the chosen titulary of Assurnasirpal describes his role as "ferocious predator, conqueror of cities," as opposed to the epithets employed by his son, which more often stress his role as extender of the empire. Shalmaneser is described, for instance, as the one "who finds his way among the most difficult paths, who treads the summits of mountains and highlands far and near, . . . who opens up trails, north and south"—literary metaphors that find their visual counterpart in early representations of his troops crossing mountains, dragging their horses behind them (fig. 4).

It is tempting to explain this adjustment in imperial ideology by reference to political theory suggesting that emerging nations had more of a need for the arrogant display of power than those already established. In other words, when Assyria was just beginning to expand territorially under Assurnasirpal II there was a greater need to display in art and texts signifiers of military might: to promote an image of king as predator. As the state developed, however, and as Assyrian force became more established by the middle of Shalmaneser's reign, the imperial ideology became centered around other issues, particularly prestige based on the collection of goods from the periphery and the geographical spread of Assyrian hegemony. The later artworks of Shalmaneser suggest that goods came into the center naturally, without any coercion; that the king's power and legitimacy went undisputed. The special attention to battle scenes in the decoration on the Bronze Gates may be explained perhaps by their early date and the subsequent need for Shalmaneser to re-establish Assyrian legitimacy following the death of his father, or by their location at Balawat, situated outside the capital, and hence the desire or need to impress a less urban audience.

This discussion raises the issue of the intended audience for the imperial imagery. While foreign subjects may have had access to some of

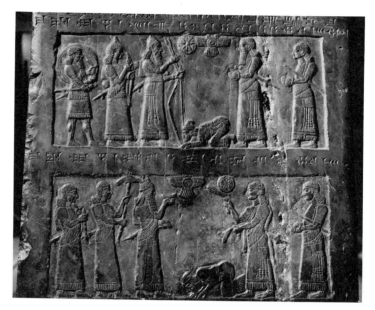

Fig. 7. Detail of the relief-carving of Side C of the Black Obelisk of Shalmaneser III from Nimrud, circa 827 BCE, showing the Gilzanite Sua (above) and the Israelite Jehu, son of Omri (below), paying homage to King Shalmaneser, who is accompanied by courtiers. Other scenes on the monument show tributaries bearing gifts including camels, elephants, and monkeys. BRITISH MUSEUM, LONDON

the more public monuments, one could argue that we are dealing with what social psychologists call self-symbolizing. This term refers to the representation of oneself the way one would like to be seen—a wished-for status that is a natural part of the process of self-completion. In this view, king and officials would be the intended target, the art serving to boost the national self-image, while at the same time ensuring loyalty and unity of the court by example.

The representation of foreign goods coming into the center further promotes an ideology that pits city against hinterland, insider against outsider. Part of the Assyrian ideology was the notion that the city was especially important, being the center of culture and civilization; it was an ideology that served to co-opt the outsider for the urban insider. By representing in art the large-scale collection of goods by the ruling elite as a natural order, a policy of territorial expansion and annual tribute giving is ratified. The capacity to collect goods legitimated the power of the court—in Assyria just as in Elizabethan England and seventeenth-century France.

It is important to point out that Shalmaneser's monuments do not depict the king receiving tribute and booty from just anywhere, but that the representations seem to have been governed by an underlying program based on the geographical ordering of events. All three cases seem to represent the collection of goods from states at the farthest borders of Assyrian hegemony. Such visual cues support an imperial ideology based on the geographical distance from which goods were reaching the center.

The Throne Base and Black Obelisk from Nimrud

Athough the throne-room reliefs of Assurnasirpal II may have been similarly organized around a geographical program, this agenda is more certain in the art of Shalmaneser, where epigraphs regularly identify the campaigns represented. The situation is perhaps most clear for the Throne Base and the Black Obelisk. The former places in opposition tributaries from the western border of the empire (Unqi [formerly Pattina, Patinu] in North Syria) on the northern side of the dais and those from the southern border (Babylon) on the southern side of the base (figs. 5, 6). This opposition of territorial extremities allows one to read the Throne Base as a statement of the extent of imperial power. The visual message would have been reinforced by the physical presence of the king enthroned at the center of the dais, above and between the reliefs of tributaries literally advancing toward him from the ends of his empire. With the king (or throne) thus marking the symbolic center of Assyria, the whole package (base and throne together) truly becomes a microcosm of the state, as I. Winter has previously suggested for the throne base of Sargon II (721–705).

The carvings on the Black Obelisk similarly oppose tributaries from the geographical limits of Shalmaneser's hegemony. Most clear is the opposition in the first two registers between tributaries from Gilzanu, in northwestern Iran, and from Jehu of Israel, who submitted to Shalmaneser in 841 BCE. The visual polarity between east and west correlates nicely with the chosen metaphor in Shalmaneser's inscriptions for the extent of the empire, in which Assyrian power is proclaimed from the "Lower Sea of the land of Nairi" (Lake Urmia in northwestern Iran) to the "Great Sea of the Setting Sun" (the Mediterranean Sea). Even the form of the obelisk can

be tied to the imperial ideology—specifically the use of a stepped top resembling a ziggurat or platform on which Mesopotamian temples were built. Like the Throne Base, the structure of the monument allows it to be read as a symbol of the city, and the tributaries as outsiders symbolically marching into the urban cultural center.

So far any references to parallelism between text and image have been with various annalistic accounts of Shalmaneser's military campaigns and not with the actual inscriptions on the monuments themselves. In fact, text and imagery on single monuments are not parallel, as they seem to be for Assurnasirpal II. More specifically, art and text often refer to different sets of campaigns, with the texts presenting a chronological ordering of military events characteristic of Assyrian annals, and the art presenting a geographical ordering of events more characteristic of so-called display or summary texts. Far from paralleling each other, text and image seem to complement each other, each nevertheless serving its own rhetorical ends.

CLASS IDEOLOGY

One of the characteristics of many of the luxury goods from the major ninth-century BCE settle-

Fig. 8. Fragment of an ivory pyxis in North Syrian style from Hasanlu, circa ninth century BCE. THE UNIVERSITY MUSEUM OF ARCHAEOLOGY AND ANTHROPOLOGY, UNIVERSITY OF PENNSYLVANIA

ment of Hasanlu in northwestern Iran is their connection with the art of the more powerful states of Assyria and northern Syria to the west. These goods include actual foreign imports, such as Neo-Assyrian–style cylinder seals and carved ivory plaques and northern Syrian–style pyxides and lion bowls (fig. 8); and locally made goods (ivories, metalwork, and cylinder seals) that incorporate subjects best known from royal Assyrian monuments, particularly scenes of warfare and the hunt (fig. 9) and more courtly designs of seated figures with attendants.

In terms of the relationship between the local Hasanlu art style and Assyrian art, it is possible to argue that there existed an ideology of prestige based on the collection and emulation of Assyrian artwork, specifically emblems of authority and power associated with royal imperial monuments. Hence, just as Assyrian ideology was based on the collection of raw materials and booty from the periphery, part of the ideology of prestige at Hasanlu seems based on the importation of goods and certain symbolic systems from the center.

It is easy to explain the transmission of themes in Assyrian art to Hasanlu, since there were ample opportunities for interaction. We know from the royal annals, for instance, that the Assyrians were campaigning in northwestern Iran in the mid ninth century BCE, and that dignitaries from the Hasanlu region were among the guests at the dedication ceremonies of Assurnasirpal's new capital at Nimrud around 865. The residents at Hasanlu could have heard descriptions of the Assyrian reliefs or even seen them firsthand. At the same time, small-scale objects bearing designs similar to the palace reliefs could have been brought to Hasanlu as diplomatic gifts or items of a mutual exchange: for example, ivories, textiles, metal objects, and cylinder seals.

Fig. 9. Detail of the silver beaker from Hasanlu, circa ninth century BCE. The detail shows a chariot scene reminiscent of scenes on Neo-Assyrian reliefs. The beaker is now in the Musée Iran Bastan in Tehran. THE UNIVERSITY MUSEUM OF ARCHAEOLOGY AND ANTHROPOLOGY, UNIVERSITY OF PENNSYLVANIA, PHILADELPHIA

Fig. 10. Skeleton number 263 with lion pins and beads *in situ* in the central court of Burned Building II, Hasanlu. The individual was trapped inside the structure when the citadel was destroyed by a military incursion and fire about 800 BCE. THE UNIVERSITY MUSEUM OF ARCHAEOLOGY AND ANTHROPOLOGY, UNIVERSITY OF PENNSYLVANIA, PHILADELPHIA

Despite the importance of Assyrian goods and imagery in expressions of cultural ideology at Hasanlu, it seems to be only a part of the picture. Any discussion of ideology at the site must also take into account the vast number of prestige goods found that have little relationship with Assyria, especially personal ornaments discovered actually on skeletons of individuals either buried in graves in a cemetery area at the base of the citadel mound or of those accidentally trapped inside major elite burned buildings on top of the mound when the citadel was destroyed by a military incursion and fire at the end of Hasanlu period IVB (roughly 800 BCE) (fig. 10).

Some personal ornaments from Hasanlu do have Assyrian parallels, judging from comparisons with representations on the Assyrian reliefs. These finds, which included single-pendant earrings, pectorals with Assyrian designs, and bracelets with lion- and calf-head terminals, were discovered primarily in debris from second-floor storage facilities at the site. In contrast, nearly all of the ornaments found *in situ* on skeletons (both in the cemetery and on the mound) are most at home in western Iran, to judge from excavated parallels at other sites in the region: for example, cast-bronze pins with geometric heads, and incised and knobbed bronze and iron bracelets (fig. 11). Also found on individuals were large iron pins with heavy cast-bronze finials in the form of lions or lion demons with wide-opened mouths, exposed teeth, and protruding tongues; so far these types of pins are unique to Hasanlu (fig. 12).

Fig. 11. Incised bronze bracelet from Hasanlu, circa ninth century
BCE. METROPOLITAN MUSEUM OF ART, NEW YORK

Many of the skeletons on the citadel mound were found in so-called Burned Building II, now tentatively identified as a temple on the basis of the architecture and the nature of the small finds. Although the body ornaments and the possible identity of the individuals in Burned Building II will be discussed in greater detail below, the evidence suggests that there were certain situations in which Assyrian imagery was appropriate at Hasanlu and situations in which it was not. It may be suggested even at this initial stage of research that for body decoration in mortuary

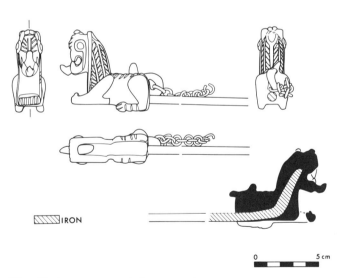

IRON

Fig. 12. Reconstructed drawing of cast-bronze lion pin from Hasanlu, circa ninth century BCE. The lion was originally cast onto an iron shaft, now broken off. The pin is now in the Metropolitan Museum of Art. UNIVERSITY MUSEUM OF ARCHAEOLOGY AND ANTHROPOLOGY, UNIVERSITY OF PENNSYLVANIA, PHILADELPHIA

contexts and in daily and perhaps temple life, traditional local customs were most appropriate; whereas for promoting the political and administrative power of the ruling elite, Assyrian and other western objects and images were ideologically more useful. In other words, while Assyrian emblems filled a gap in available displays of power at Hasanlu, there already existed well-established local symbolic systems in other spheres, including dress and adornment. Assyrian emblems of authority may be seen then as simply a superficial overlay, adopted by a culture that maintained its own cultural and ethnic identity through personal appearance cues.

Another dimension of the Hasanlu situation is the abundance of ornaments found on many of the skeletons in Burned Building II. Certain individuals (including perhaps female palace personnel) wore as many as thirty bronze bracelets, fifteen finger rings, and five or more garment pins, often including three or more huge, heavy lion pins. While this ostentatious display might be explained in terms of ritual clothing alone, it is tempting to draw on the political and social theory of display and power. Since, as argued above, emerging states often seem to have more need for display than those at their zenith of power, the same could be said for states on the verge of collapse. That the Hasanlu elite may have felt threatened for some time—not only by their Urartian neighbors but presumably also by the expanding Assyrian Empire and by new population groups, such as the Persians, evidently moving into the region in this pe-

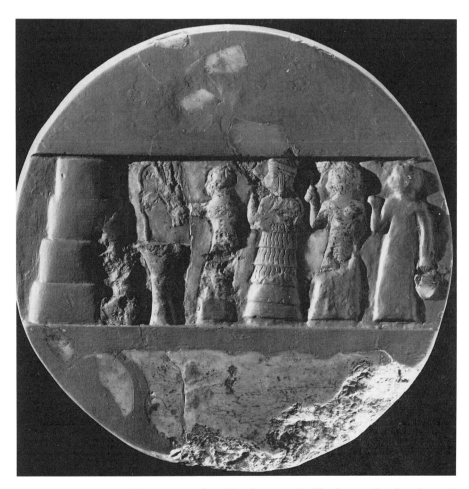

Fig. 13. Limestone disk, excavated at Ur, showing Enkheduana, the daughter of the Akkadian king Sargon, officiating in her role as high priestess to the moon-god at Ur, circa 2300 BCE. THE UNIVERSITY MUSEUM OF ARCHAEOLOGY AND ANTHROPOLOGY, UNIVERSITY OF PENNSYLVANIA

riod—is suggested by the major buildings on the citadel mound becoming more enclosed and self-contained around 1100 BCE. Did the weapon-like, bulky lion pins possibly serve then to over-compensate for feelings of vulnerability by the Hasanlu elite vis-à-vis the more powerful states around them? Was size and weight of body ornaments tied somehow to political ideology at Hasanlu, serving to legitimate the power of the ruling and temple elite at a time when their cultural and political integrity was being threatened?

GENDER IDEOLOGY

The explosion of feminist scholarship over the past twenty years has only recently affected archaeology. But by engaging the archaeological study of gender with feminist theory, we are immediately confronted by such questions as: What is the place of ideology in collective representation? Are analytical categories such as "domestic" and "political" useful? Feminist theory urges us to pay more attention to gender, to those ideologies that have attributed certain characteristics to men and others to women. Ideally it would be preferable not to segregate gender issues from matters of state ideology on the whole, since they are both related to issues of power and are both inherent parts of a culture's total ideological complex.

Studies in self-decoration, likewise well underway in ethnography, social psychology, and costume history, have also been slow to reach archaeology. This neglect can be attributed to strong gender biases, rooted in nineteenth-century presuppositions, that view adornment exclusively as a female issue. But it can be said that just as dress and ornament in modern societies help to define and communicate personal and social identity, being literally extensions of the body and hence signals of the self, they should likewise serve to clarify social identities in the past. More important, personal-appearance cues are intimately related to gender ideologies, for they bring to the surface the cultural categories assigned to men and women.

Women are rarely represented in the art (and texts) of the ancient Near East—clearly a func-

tion of ideology, since we need not prove that women existed. Their absence in representation serves to support the legitimacy of the patriarchal power structure: if only men are represented, especially in formal political positions, then we are led to believe that this is the way things have always been and will always be, and that women's roles are naturally marginal. Although there are many representations of female deities in Mesopotamian art, earthly women are generally depicted as barefoot political prisoners (fig. 1), as frenzied individuals clasping their heads in war scenes, in nurturing roles with children, in groups with other women and, in exceptional cases, as elite women in religious roles (fig. 13). Just as ideology did not encourage the depiction of daily activity in near

Fig. 14. Detail of a carved ivory pedestal showing a male figure wearing a large pectoral and armbands, which was found at Hasanlu, circa ninth century BCE. The ivory pedestal is now in the Musée Iran Bastan in Tehran. THE UNIVERSITY MUSEUM OF ARCHAEOLOGY AND ANTHROPOLOGY, UNIVERSITY OF PENNSYLVANIA

eastern art, it likewise did not encourage the representation of women.

There is still a tendency in contemporary scholarship to rely uncritically on early theoretical binaries that contrasted active men to inactive or passive women, and the public world of men to the private, secluded world of women. Such contrasts stem from early feminist discussions of "being" versus "doing" but ultimately are derived from the tendency to establish separate spheres (private versus public) for women and men. While such polarities can certainly be useful and remain a salient feature of many types of analysis within the social sciences, there is now a consensus that they are not universal: gender roles can be negotiated between partners, are subject to internal variation, and are historically and culturally specific. The Hasanlu material tests the validity of such rigid binaries for one part of the ancient Near East and poses the question of gender ideology in terms of social practice.

Excavations in the Iron II levels at the site (circa 1100–800) uncovered approximately fif-

teen hundred personal ornaments. About one thousand of these were discovered directly on or near skeletons: individuals either deliberately buried in graves in the cemetery (about ninety) or accidentally trapped inside the burned buildings on the citadel mound (about one hundred). The greatest concentration of adorned skeletons (over sixty) were found in Burned Building II; most of the individuals were found near the entranceway, where they scrambled to escape the burning building. The site provides a unique opportunity, therefore, to compare how individuals decorated themselves in aspects of daily or perhaps temple life, and how they were ornamented for burial. The well-preserved context of the personal ornaments should allow us to distinguish between gender ideology (both past and present) and actual gender roles in the past.

A comparative analysis of the anthropologically sexed skeletons in the cemetery area and the poorly preserved skeletons in the collapsed structures on the citadel mound suggests that men, women, and children shared the same basic ornament categories. These include stone

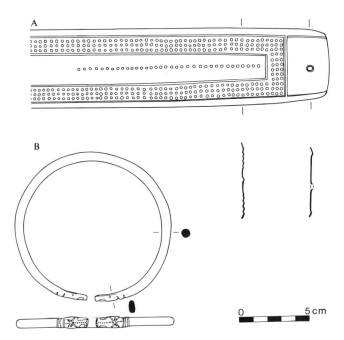

Fig. 15. Types of personal ornaments associated with males at Hasanlu. (A) bronze belt decorated with repoussé dots; (B) bronze armband. Both objects are now in the Metropolitan Museum of Art in New York. THE UNIVERSITY MUSEUM OF ARCHAEOLOGY AND ANTHROPOLOGY, UNIVERSITY OF PENNSYLVANIA, PHILADELPHIA

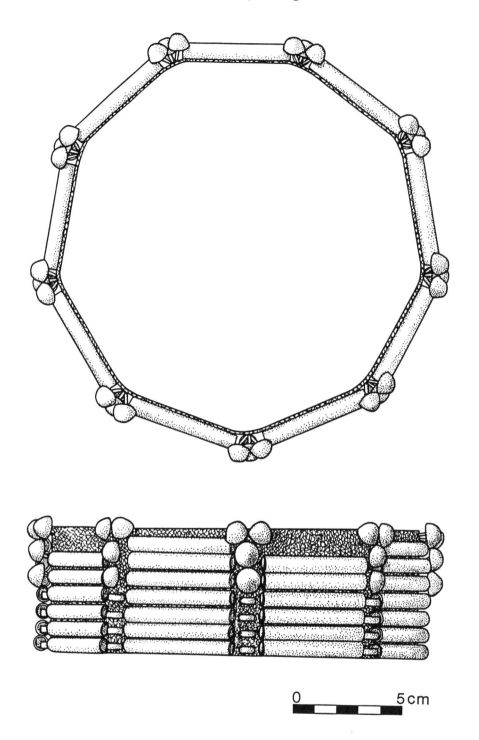

beads, seals, and other neck ornaments, and bronze and iron finger rings, anklets, and brace-lets. Only a few types of ornament can be tied exclusively to one gender or the other. Although women seem consistently to wear a greater quan-tity of jewelry than men, most men wear some

ornaments as well. Even small-scale images from the site sometimes emphasize male adorn-ment with oversized neckpieces and multiple bracelets (fig. 14).

The distinction between "being" and "do-ing"—previously based on the assumption that

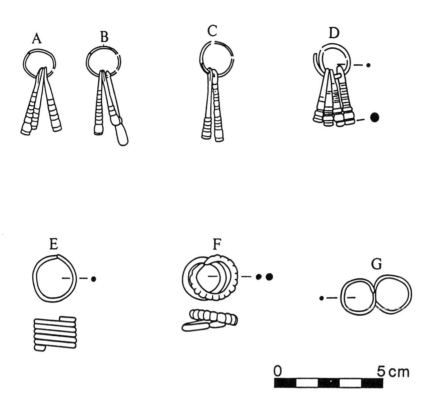

Fig. 16. Types of personal ornaments associated with females at Hasanlu: (opposite) copper/bronze head ornament (dark area represents original leather or cloth backing); (above) copper/bronze dangle earrings (A–D); copper/bronze hair ornaments (E–G). The head ornament is now in the Metropolitan Museum of Art in New York. The other objects are in the University Museum of the University of Pennsylvania in Philadelphia. THE UNIVERSITY MUSEUM OF ARCHAEOLOGY AND ANTHROPOLOGY, UNIVERSITY OF PENNSYLVANIA, PHILADELPHIA

personal adornment reflects passivity, hence female sensibility—is proving clearly artificial and oversimplified in practice. Nevertheless, some aspects of the old binary formulation seem to hold true as cultural ideology, that is, as one cultural mechanism for organizing gender. For instance, among the few gender-specific ornaments at Hasanlu seem to be metal belts and armbands for men, and head and hair ornaments and dangle earrings for women (figs. 15, 16). Since metal belts were often used to support weapons (to judge from evidence in burials and visual representations), they imply potential action—the case still for middle eastern tribesmen today and for earlier Persian dignitaries. By drawing attention to the biceps, armbands also imply strength and action. I would even suggest a possible relationship between men wearing arm-

bands and a royal ideology in the Near East of the strong-armed king. This association persists from the full-muscled representations of the Neo-Sumerian ruler Gudea through the use of enlarged casts of Saddam Hussein's forearms for his so-called Victory Arch in Baghdad.

In contrast, the head and hair ornaments and dangle earrings of women in Hasanlu, also common in the Middle East today, suggest something other than physical strength and action. They suggest an opposition between the emphasis on the head or face for women and the body for men—a notion that can be tied as well, perhaps, to Assyrian representations of women holding mirrors or looking out of windows (figs. 17, 18). It is unclear as yet just how to interpret this difference in terms of cultural ideology or social practice. At Hasanlu, for instance, could we be dealing with a woman's dowry and a desire to display in a highly visible place what represented independent wealth, or with different conceptions about male and female sexuality?

Especially compelling about the Hasanlu material is the identity of the highly decorated individuals in Burned Building II. If we are dealing with a temple, as some of the evidence mentioned above suggests, then we have to ask whether or not we are also dealing with temple personnel, a situation in keeping with texts from Mesopotamia that refer to male and female temple staff. The body ornaments and associated goods on some of the individuals in Burned Building II suggest different possible identities such as male and female temple elite or palace elite seeking shelter from the enemy attack. Most telling are the unique lion pins found on at least twenty-four of the roughly sixty adorned skeletons trapped in the structure.

The lion pins were evidently worn, usually in groups of three, on the upper chest and shoulders of individuals, somehow held in place by metal chains that were attached to a loop in the

Fig. 18. Carved ivory plaque from Nimrud showing a woman looking out of a window, circa eighth century BCE. BRITISH MUSEUM, LONDON

Fig. 17. Carved bronze fragment showing an Assyrian king and queen, circa 700 BCE provenance unknown. The queen, identified in an epigraph as Queen Naqya, holds a mirror. The king, who is unidentified, may be her husband, Sennacherib, or her son, Esarhaddon. LOUVRE MUSEUM, PARIS

lion's tail. The sophisticated technology involved in producing these elaborate cast bronze and iron pins, their material, size (about 7 to 8 inches long [some 17 to 20 centimeters]), weight (up to 10 ounces [280 grams]), and powerful imagery all suggest that they were signs of special status, as does the bulk of associated jewelry found with most of them on skeletons.

Unfortunately, the sexing of the individuals with lion pins is problematic, since, along with the other skeletons in the building, they were severely crushed by the fallen debris from a second story. Nevertheless, a re-examination of the skeletal material together with the types and sizes of the associated body ornaments tends to support the excavator's initial impression that they included young women and girls. In particular, a number of the skeletons have since been tentatively sexed as female from field photographs, while others wore dangle earrings, hair and head ornaments, and other items that can now be tied exclusively to females in the cemetery burials. Although we must allow for differ-

Fig. 19. Drawing of a shell plaque found in a temple at Mari showing a woman carrying an offering stand and wearing large garment pins, circa 2500 BCE. DIRECTORATE GENERAL OF ANTIQUITIES AND MUSEUMS, DAMASCUS

ent rules governing dress in mortuary, temple, or palace ritual, and especially for cross-dressing by palace eunuchs or temple berdache, for now the personal ornaments together with the skeletal data suggest that at least some of the lion pins were worn by elite females, including girls as young as six or seven.

In this interpretation, the lion pins take on new meaning as an extraordinary burden in terms of size, weight, and mobility on relatively small individuals. It suggests that, if one pin can be associated with women and girls, these individuals held formal, ceremonial roles in the temple, as opposed to associative roles as weavers or entertainers, for instance, or active roles

elsewhere at the site. Alternatively, they may have been palace elite seeking shelter in the temple, perhaps taking their dowry jewelry with them. In this context, the immobilizing quality of many of the alleged female ornaments may be better explained by the nature of ritual or royal dress than by any real dichotomy between active men and passive women. Context and class therefore remain critical for understanding gender roles and ideologies.

Women wearing large pins in religious contexts are not uncommon in representations from the Near East (fig. 19). They occur on shell plaques from a mid third-millennium BCE temple at Mari (Tell Hariri) on the middle Euphrates, as well as in the company of men on the Hasanlu gold bowl (fig. 20). We might even suppose that the unusual leonine form of the Hasanlu pins is related to the service of a divinity whose attribute is a lion or lion-demon, such as the goddess on the gold bowl or other figures from Mesopotamia and North Syria who sit on leonine thrones.

Whatever the original function of Burned Building II, the evidence from the destruction level suggests that its occupants were women, girls, and perhaps men from the temple and palace elite. Texts and art from Mesopotamia highlight the role of royal women in important religious positions (for example, fig. 13). Evidence that daughters and sisters of rulers were regularly dedicated to temples provides one possible explanation for the range in age of the individuals with lion pins at Hasanlu. Did the massive lion pins serve a cultural need to bolster the status and stature of females in public, religious positions, where an image of authority is required?

The issue of public and private also pertains to the relationship between Hasanlu and Assyria. The role of western imports at Hasanlu and the adaptation of royal Assyrian themes in the local art style are discussed in scholarly literature in connection with the way the Hasanlu elite incorporated some of the prestige associated with the imperial center. It would seem that only men had access to such foreign symbols of status, to judge from the exclusively male pursuits incorporated from Assyria into the local style: for instance, scenes of hunting and warfare that can be matched on contemporary Assyrian

Fig. 20. Drawing of the design on the gold bowl from Hasanlu, circa tenth to ninth centuries BCE. The three individuals wearing patterned tunics (two men and one woman) wear garment pins at the shoulder. A photograph of the bowl appears in "Art and Archaeology of Western Iran in Prehistory" in Part 5, Vol. II. The bowl is in the Musée Iran Bastan, Tehran. DRAWING BY MAUDE DE SCHAUENSEE; THE UNIVERSITY MUSEUM OF ARCHAEOLOGY AND ANTHROPOLOGY, UNIVERSITY OF PENNSYLVANIA, PHILADELPHIA

palace reliefs (cf. fig. 9). But if my speculations about the sex of some of the skeletons in Burned Building II are correct, some elite women wore Assyrian-style cylinder seals, and thus elite women also had access to symbols identified with the prestigious, foreign centers to the west.

CONCLUSIONS

No less than words, visual images and objects can be the most effective tools to legitimate the authority of a dominant social group. In Assyria, relief sculpture of battle and tribute scenes served to represent the power of the king and state as a natural order and to legitimate policies of political domination, territorial expansion,

and mass consumption of foreign tribute and booty. Outside the Assyrian heartland, at Hasanlu, a nationalist ideology incorporated Assyrian symbols of power and prestige, while at the same time maintaining local traditions in dress and ritual. Such a system would have served to legitimate the power of the ruling elite without compromising their own cultural and ethnic identity.

The personal ornaments from Hasanlu highlight the complexities of social roles and relationships in daily life. It is impossible to say, as yet, whether we can generalize from a single site in northwestern Iran to patterns in the whole Near East, or whether we are dealing with traditions of a specific ethnic or linguistic group distinct from the Sumerian and Semitic populations of

Mesopotamia. Nevertheless, it seems inappropriate, at least in the case of Hasanlu, to freeze gender roles and presumed spheres of activities. Rather, we must consider issues of class and context and must allow for gender ambiguities in actual practice. Although expensive adornment does not always correlate with real power, a preliminary contextual analysis of the Hasanlu materials suggest that under certain conditions, whether by dint of ability, marriage, or birth, women were able to occupy high status positions in Iran in the Iron Age.

BIBLIOGRAPHY

General

For some of the theoretical literature on ideology see MARGARET W. CONKEY, "Does It Make a Difference? Feminist Thinking and Archaeologies of Gender," in *The Archaeology of Gender*, edited by DALE WALDE and NOREEN D. WILLOWS (1991); TERRY EAGLETON, *Ideology: An Introduction* (1991); KRISTIAN KRISTIANSEN, "Ideology and Material Culture: An Archaeological Perspective," in *Marxist Perspectives in Archaeology*, edited by MATTHEW SPRIGGS (1984); GRANT MCCRACKEN, *Culture and Consumption: New Approaches to the Symbolic Character of Consumer Goods and Activities* (1988); DANIEL MILLER and CHRISTOPHER TILLEY, eds., *Ideology, Power, and Prehistory* (1984); and ARAM A. YENGOYAN, "Review Article, Digging for Symbols: The Archaeology of Everyday Material Life," *Proceedings of the Prehistoric Society* 51 (1985).

State Ideology

On art and ideology in the Neo-Assyrian period, see especially IRENE J. WINTER, "Royal Rhetoric and the Development of Historical Narrative in Neo-Assyrian Reliefs," *Studies in Visual Communication* 7 (1981). See also MICHELLE I. MARCUS, "Geography as an Organizing Principle in the Imperial Art of Shalmaneser III," *Iraq* 49 (1987); JULIAN READE, "Ideology and Propaganda in Assyrian Art," in *Power and Propaganda: A Symposium on Ancient Empires*, Mesopotamia, Copenhagen Studies in Assyriology, vol. 7, edited by MOGENS TROLLE LARSEN (1979); and JOHN MALCOLM RUSSELL, *Sennacherib's Palace Without Rival at Nineveh*

(1991). For some of the related historical issues see SHMUEL N. EISENSTADT, "The Axial Age: The Emergence of Transcendental Visions and the Rise of Clerics," *European Journal of Sociology* 23, no. 2 (1982); MARIO LIVERANI, "The Ideology of the Assyrian Empire," in *Power and Propaganda: A Symposium on Empires*, edited by MOGENS TROLLE LARSEN (1979); PETER MACHINIST, "The Assyrians and Their Babylonian Problem: Some Reflections," *Wissenschaftskolleg zu Berlin Jahrbuch* (1984/85), and "On Self-Consciousness in Mesopotamia," in *The Origins and Diversity of Axial Age Civilizations*, edited by S. N. EISENSTADT (1986).

Class Ideology

On art and ideology at Hasanlu see MICHELLE I. MARCUS, "Center, *Province*, and Periphery: A New Paradigm from Iron-Age Iran," *Art History* 13, no. 2 (1990); EDITH PORADA, *The Art of Ancient Iran: Pre-Islamic Cultures* (1965); and IRENE J. WINTER, "Perspective on the 'Local Style' of Hasanlu IVB: A Study in Receptivity," in *Mountains and Lowlands: Essays in the Archaeology of Greater Mesopotamia*, edited by LOUIS D. LEVINE and T. CUYLER YOUNG, JR. (1977). In general, see also ROBERT H. DYSON, JR., and MARY M. VOIGT, eds., *East of Assyria: The Highland Settlement of Hasanlu*, Expedition 31, nos. 2–3 (1989). For Hasanlu objects held at the Metropolitan Museum, see OSCAR WHITE MUSCARELLA, *Bronze and Iron: Ancient Near Eastern Artifacts in The Metropolitan Museum of Art* (1988).

Gender Ideology

On art and gender in the ancient Near East see MICHELLE I. MARCUS, "Incorporating the Body: Adornment, Gender, and Social Identity in Ancient Iran," *Cambridge Archaeological Journal* (1994); SUSAN POLLOCK, "Women in a Men's World: Images of Sumerian Women," in *Engendering Archaeology: Women and Prehistory*, edited by JOAN M. GERO and MARGARET W. CONKEY (1991); IRENE J. WINTER, "Women in Public: The Disk of Enheduanna, the Beginning of the Office of EN-Priestess, and the Weight of Visual Evidence," in *La Femme dans le proche-orient antique, Compte rendu de la XXXIIIᵉ Rencontre Assyriologique Internationale*, edited by JEAN-MARIE DURAND (1987); JOAN GOODNICK WESTENHOLZ, "Towards a New Conceptualization of the Female Role in Mesopotamian Society," *Journal of the American Oriental Society* 110, no. 3 (1990). See also BARBARA S. LESKO, ed., *Women's Earliest Records from Ancient Egypt and Western Asia* (1989).

SEE ALSO **Ancient Mesopotamian Religious Iconography** (Part 8, Vol. III); **Aesthetics in Ancient Mesopotamian Art** (Part 10, Vol. IV); **Art and Archaeology of the Achaemenid Empire** (Part 10, Vol. IV); and **Understanding Ancient Near Eastern Art: A Personal Account** (Part 11, Vol. IV).

Proportions in Ancient Near Eastern Art

GUITTY AZARPAY

A SURVEY OF THE HISTORY OF proportions in art reveals basic agreement between formulas used for the definition of proportions of the human form in Western art and those used in the ancient Near East and Egypt. These formulas are recalled in the ideal proportions of the human body devised by the first-century Roman architect and writer Vitruvius.

The Vitruvian model, a six-foot figure of ten face lengths inscribed in a circle and square, was the inspiration for Leonardo da Vinci's celebrated study depicting the body spread-eagled within a circle and, with arms extended and legs placed together, fitted into a square. In a treatise on sculpture, the fifteenth-century Italian architect and humanist Leon Battista Alberti prescribes the use of a ruler, protractor, and plumb line to achieve the ideal six-foot image of ten face lengths. Detailed measurements of the component parts of the ideal body, indicated by a system of coordinates, or expressed in numbers provided in scales, accompany the human form in Renaissance and later drawings in handbooks such as the *Four Books of Human Proportion* (1528) by the German artist and theorist Albrecht Dürer.

Although artists and architects of the age of humanism, such as da Vinci, Alberti, and Dürer, revived the Vitruvian model in their definitions of ideal proportions, they nevertheless were engaged primarily in the formulation and refine-ment of issues relevant to their own times and intellectual discourse.

The ancient Near East and Egypt have yielded no written treatises on proportions in art. Only the Egyptian grid system offers direct evidence for the invention and use of proportional guidelines in art. However, indirect evidence, based on written sources and comparative data, is used in recent studies to reconstruct and interpret the prevailing proportional systems in several periods in the history of the art of the ancient Near East: late-third-millennium BCE Sumer, Neo-Assyrian Mesopotamia, and Achaemenid Iran. That function and meaning were determining factors in the definition of the proportions of the human image in the art of the ancient Near East is suggested in studies by Irene Winter, Gay Robins, and Jeannine Davis-Kimball. These studies seek to explain the proportions of the image through comparison of ancient near eastern visual expressions with verbal representations from textual sources, by reference to Egyptian models, and by quantification of hierarchical proportions.

That artists of the ancient Near East, when depicting the human form, applied formal standards which included observance of proportional ratios is an assumption advanced in this article. Although other theories have been proposed to explain the formal particulars of the ancient near eastern artistic tradition, the case argued here for reliance of ancient near eastern artists on systems of proportion in figural representation may be kept in mind.

In the following treatment of the subject of proportions under regional and temporal headings, the continuity in application of a proportional system in Egyptian art, based on the grid system, is conspicuous by comparison with the seemingly irregular occurrence of artistic standards in ancient near eastern art. If the continuity of the cultural tradition of pharaonic Egypt is seen as an explanation for the perpetuation of the Egyptian grid system, then the apparent irregularity of the use of artistic standards in the art of the ancient Near East might be attributed to the latter's political discontinuity and cultural heterogeneity.

Among factors that may have controlled the tempo of artistic standardization in the ancient Near East, apart from the actual or supposed influence of the Egyptian model, are the role of patronage in promulgation of religious and political programs at various periods. That royal patronage was a driving force behind the development, refinement, and implementation of artistic standards in the ancient Near East is asserted in a number of studies. That view, treated sequentially here, is exemplified by studies on the age of Gudea of Lagash and the Neo-Assyrian period in Mesopotamia, datable to the late third and early first millennia BCE, respectively, and on the Achaemenid Persian dynasty of the sixth to the fourth century BCE.

A comprehensive treatment of proportions in ancient near eastern art requires information on proportional systems in as yet unstudied but important periods, such as the Early Dynastic and the Neo-Babylonian periods of Mesopotamian history.

EGYPT

Fundamental to the system of proportions in Egyptian art is the approximate determination of length and breadth ratios among different components of the human body. Canonic proportions of the human body in Egyptian painting, relief, and freestanding sculpture are based on a balance between empirical observation and calculation of simple regular ratios that describe a universal and standardized model rather than the proportions of particular individuals.

The earliest evidence for such a system of proportions in Egyptian art is found in guidelines used for the correct placement of the different parts of the body and is preserved in unfinished works of art from the Old Kingdom. From at least the Middle Kingdom, these guidelines were replaced by the use of a grid on which the standing human form was plotted on eighteen squares from the soles of the feet to the hairline, and seated figures on fourteen squares (fig. 1). In the later grid, used from the Twenty-fifth Dynasty to Roman times, standing and seated figures were plotted on twenty-one and seventeen squares, respectively, between the soles of the feet and the upper eyelid.

In the standing male image in the earlier eighteen-square grid, certain points of the body relate to particular grid horizontals. Thus the knee line corresponds with grid horizontal 6, the lower border of the buttocks with horizontal 9,

Fig. 1. Standardized proportions of male and female forms in the eighteen-square grid of Twelfth Dynasty Egyptian art from the tomb of Ukh-Hotep, Meir. A. M. BLACKMAN, *THE ROCK TOMBS OF MEIR II* (1915)

the small of the back with horizontal 11, the elbow with horizontal 12, the nipple approximately with horizontal 14, and the junction of the neck and shoulders with horizontal 16. Although the proportions of the human form remained largely unchanged in the transition from the eighteen-square to the twenty-one-square grid, the reduced size of the later grid produces different correspondences between grid lines and various points of the body. In the Twenty-sixth Dynasty grid system, horizontal 20 passes just below the nose, 17 through or near the nipple, the foot is roughly four squares long, and the length of the forearm, from elbow to fingertips, measured along the axis of the arm, is usually about six squares.

In depictions of the female form the body is slender, and the small of the back is placed higher than in male figures. Whereas women are of roughly the same height as men, the human figure, when depicted in mummified form, is one square shorter. In compositions that include several figures, same-scale images may be drawn on the same grid, whereas figures of dissimilar scale are drawn free hand or plotted on different grids within the composition. Figures of animals and hieroglyphs appear to be subordinated to the principal figure and systematically aligned within its grid lines.

Although the same basic principles governed the rendering of the proportions of the human form throughout the history of the art of pharaonic Egypt, stylistic differences may be associated with different periods. During the New Kingdom, the levels of the knee top, buttocks, and small of the back were progressively raised, thereby shortening the upper torso and lengthening the lower leg. In the late Third Intermediate Period and the Twenty-fifth Dynasty, on the other hand, there was a return to proportions of the classic art of the Old and Middle kingdoms. In the art of the Amarna period the royal image, represented by figures of Akhenaten (Amenhotep IV) and his family, which Gay Robins plots on a partly hypothetical twenty-square grid, departs from classic proportions by virtue of its larger head, longer neck, protruding stomach, heavy buttocks and thighs, thin limbs, and short legs. Except for the large head and short lower legs, the changes observed in proportions of images of Akhenaten have been described as

feminizing features. It is noteworthy, however, that in the art of the Amarna period female figures are shown with an even higher small of the back and are made more slender than their male counterparts. (See "Akhetaten: A Portrait in Art of an Ancient Egyptian Capital" in Part 5, Vol. II.)

Changes in proportions of the male form in periods other than the Amarna age are attributed by Robins to a quest for elegance rather than to a deliberate feminization of the male form. She attributes differences in proportions between male and female figures to actual physical differences between the sexes and finds that the proportions of the human form in Egyptian art reflect the actual height and natural proportions of ancient Egyptians as evidenced in their skeletal remains. Robins thus seeks a rough equation between the proportions of the human form in life and those of figures plotted on the eighteen- and twenty-one-square grids.

A different equation is proposed by Erik Iversen, who sees the interpretation of natural proportions of the human form as approximation of proportional ratios in Egyptian metrology. He identifies the grid square with a metrological unit and with the basic module used for determination of proportions in the Egyptian grid system. The Egyptian units of linear measure are the small and royal cubits preserved on surviving measuring rods. The small cubit (about 45 centimeters/18 inches in length) is divided into six palms, with each palm subdivided into four fingers; the royal cubit (about 52.5 centimeters/21 inches) is divided into seven palms. Both cubits are written with a hieroglyph depicting the forearm from elbow to fingertips.

Controversy has been generated by Iversen's interpretation of the length of the small cubit and its subdivision, represented by the fist. Robins questions Iversen's identification of the fist as a metrological unit and its correspondence with the side of the grid square. She also rejects the equation of the length of the small cubit with the distance from elbow to thumb tip, as proposed by Iversen, in favor of elbow to fingertips. The correspondence of the small cubit of forty-five centimeters to the length of the forearm from elbow to fingertips in effect allows the height of the image to approximate the 1665–1710 millimeters/5 feet, 5.5 inches to 5 feet, 7.5 inches assumed by Robins to represent the actual height of ancient Egyptians.

Iversen thinks the reason for the change from the eighteen- to the twenty-one-square grid was a metrological change in which the royal, or "reformed," cubit subdivided into six great palms (instead of the earlier seven palms), and replaced the small cubit as the standard unit of measure. For Robins, the change was due to a desire for a smaller grid square with correspondence to the palm of four fingers. The twenty-one-square grid prevailed in Egyptian art through Greco-Roman times when, under the influence of Greek art, fuller modeling of the body produced plumper figures.

MESOPOTAMIA

Third Millennium

From its inception in Late Uruk times, the art of ancient Mesopotamia displays stylistic conventions in the representation of the human form that suggest varying degrees of compliance with artistic principles governing its form and meaning. Unlike the art of ancient Egypt with its seeming formal continuity, throughout its history Mesopotamian art was marked by temporal and regional variations that obscure the continuity of its formal and iconographical conventions. Any study of the systems of proportions for the depiction of the human body that we may ascribe to the art of the ancient Near East is complicated by the lack of native tradition regarding their application, such as the proportional grid preserved on Egyptian works of art.

Hence, to reconstruct its rules and to appreciate its significance, we must adopt different means than obtain in the study of Egyptian art. The approaches adopted in recent studies include measurement of proportional ratios in works of art by means of photogrammetry, construction of hypothetical grids on the Egyptian model, and comparison with proportional ratios that are known to have prevailed in architecture in the contemporaneous cultures of the ancient Near East. We have occasions in the ancient Near East when there were standards applied in architectural proportions, based on measurements of the modular brick. It is the information in Mesopotamian textual sources on architectural proportions that has offered a key to the metrological study of figural representation on brick grids in architectural decoration.

That proportional ratios in the art of ancient Mesopotamia were governed by metrological considerations is proposed in a photogrammetric study of Neo-Sumerian sculpture from the reign of Gudea of Lagash (around 2100 BCE). The use of analytical photogrammetry is especially appropriate for the study of Gudea statues because proportional ratios thus obtained may be tested against, and supplemented by, a relatively rich body of information on the Neo-Sumerian systems of measure available in textual sources. The quantification of the Sumerian system of linear measures is graphically illustrated on two well-known statues of Gudea, from Tello, in the Louvre, Paris. Statues F and B, which are commonly called Architect with Measuring Rule and Architect with Building Plan, respectively, show Gudea seated with a stylus for use with the right hand and a graduated rule placed on the upper edge of the tablet.

Whereas the blank tablet on Gudea's lap in statue F may reflect his expectant readiness for divine instruction on how to build the temple of the goddess Gatumdug, the completed plan displayed on the table in statue B may attest to the fulfillment of this expectation. The measuring rule, shown on the tablets in statues F and B, records Gudea's cubit as equivalent to twenty-four fingers. The scale of the rule shows sixteen nominally equal divisions, or fingers, with a total length of 269 millimeters/10.76 inches and an average length of 16.6 millimeters/0.66 inch for each division. Five of the divisions on Gudea's rule are further subdivided into fifths, fourths, thirds, and halves. The Sumerian two-thirds of a cubit measure is represented by the rule of sixteen fingers. Proportional ratios obtained by measurement of actual statues and determined through photogrammetry are known for three standing statues of Gudea, represented by inscribed statues A and E in the Louvre (fig. 2) and by one uninscribed statue, BM 122910, in the British Museum. The use of these three statues as examples for determination of proportional ratios is complicated by the fact that the excavated statues A and E are headless. As to the British Museum example, consisting of a

Fig. 2. Neo-Sumerian statue of Gudea of Lagash, Statue E, from Tello. Because the level of craftsmanship flourishing during his reign was so high, Gudea was the subject of a number of statues. See "Reliefs, Statuary, and Monumental Paintings in Ancient Mesopotamia" later in this volume for other illustrations of Gudea. LOUVRE MUSEUM, PARIS

torso and head, fractured in antiquity and reassembled in modern times, it was obtained on the art market and its authenticity has been questioned by Flemming Johansen. To my mind, however, the assembled head and torso in the British Museum is sufficiently similar in both style and scale to the more fragmentary statues from the later period of Gudea's reign to justify its use as an example of that class of statues for purposes of measurement of the large divisions of the body.

These statues of Gudea may be regarded as embodiments of ideal standards of their age. They are of imported and precious diorite and dolomite stones, and are sculpted in monumental, life-size dimensions and standing postures. Statues A and E are also linked by their dedicatory formulas and Sumerian phraseology with important temples and with the last and most technically accomplished group of statues from Gudea's reign. Winter compares the formal properties of style and rendering in the statues of Gudea with verbal expressions of the qualities and attributes of the ideal ruler articulated in the inscriptions of Gudea. Thus images of Gudea that present him as a man of large stature and powerful build, broad-chested, strong-armed, wide-eared, and large-eyed, visually portray Gudea's verbally expressed attributes. The latter describe him as an ideal ruler who is strong, wise, pious, and attentive to divine command (wide-eared, large-eyed, clasped hands), authoritative, and protective of his people. The statue is thus seen as a literal embodiment of the qualities of the ideal, able, and righteous ruler.

Using Gudea's cubit of twenty-four fingers, a composite of the three standing statues of Gudea measured by means of metric photography (fig. 3) shows the overall height of the figure to be expressed in six multiples of the length of the forearm, measured from the inside of the elbow to the wrist (right elbow to wrist, at the juncture of the overlapped left hand). The breakdown of the six divisions of the body, as suggested by the major subdivisions of Gudea's cubit, is as follows: (1) head, (2) upper torso, (3) upper legs, (4) lower legs, and (5) hemline to (6) baseline. The six divisions of the body correspond to the bends of the body, roughly at the neck, waist, hips, knees, and ankles. Determination of the large divisions of the body in the Gudea figure is based on measurements taken from frontal, profile, and back views of the figure.

Since the figure is draped in a long robe that conceals the waistline, hips, and knees in front view, photogrammetric measurements of the large divisions of the torso are based on points of maximum concavity and convexity obtained for the waistline and buttocks, respectively, in profile and back views of the statue. The division between upper and lower torso is represented

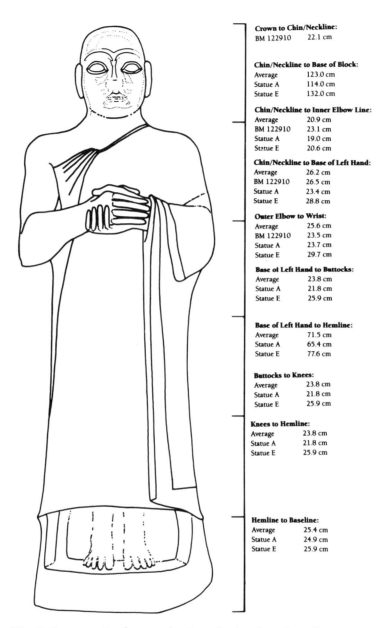

Crown to Chin/Neckline:
BM 122910	22.1 cm

Chin/Neckline to Base of Block:
Average	123.0 cm
Statue A	114.0 cm
Statue E	132.0 cm

Chin/Neckline to Inner Elbow Line:
Average	20.9 cm
BM 122910	23.1 cm
Statue A	19.0 cm
Statue E	20.6 cm

Chin/Neckline to Base of Left Hand:
Average	26.2 cm
BM 122910	26.5 cm
Statue A	23.4 cm
Statue E	28.8 cm

Outer Elbow to Wrist:
Average	25.6 cm
BM 122910	23.5 cm
Statue A	23.7 cm
Statue E	29.7 cm

Base of Left Hand to Buttocks:
Average	23.8 cm
Statue A	21.8 cm
Statue E	25.9 cm

Base of Left Hand to Hemline:
Average	71.5 cm
Statue A	65.4 cm
Statue E	77.6 cm

Buttocks to Knees:
Average	23.8 cm
Statue A	21.8 cm
Statue E	25.9 cm

Knees to Hemline:
Average	23.8 cm
Statue A	21.8 cm
Statue E	25.9 cm

Hemline to Baseline:
Average	25.4 cm
Statue A	24.9 cm
Statue E	25.9 cm

Fig. 3. A composite drawing by Jane Becker based on three incomplete standing statues of Gudea of Lagash, with reconstructed head, shown with proposed proportional scale.
COURTESY OF GUITTY AZARPAY

by the point of maximum concavity at the waistline in profile views of the statue. The juncture of the knees, clearly defined in seated statues, is placed at a point midway between buttocks and hemline. Unlike the Egyptian system of proportional measurement, in which the soles of the feet are used as the lowest point for measurement of the body, in the statues of Gudea the statue base serves as a baseline and is an integral part of the carved stone block that embodies the image.

Photogrammetric measurements, obtained for the same six key divisions of the body on the three measured statues yield similar vertical lengths for each of the six divisions of the body. The distorted view of the proportions of the statues suggested by the camera angle in figures 2 and 3 is corrected in the full frontal drawing of the composite figure.

In the absence of textual sources on artistic practices and of material evidence for the use of artistic guidelines in the ancient Near East, the results of the photogrammetric study cited here must remain unproven. The conclusions to be drawn from this study, albeit speculative, suggest that the human form in stone sculpture from the latest phase of Gudea statuary may have been conceived as tiers of six superimposed units or building blocks clearly divided at the bends of neck, waist, hips, knees, and ankles, with a ratio of head to body height of 1:6. In small-scale statues from the early and intermediate groups of Gudea statuary the proportional ratio was 1:4 and 1:5. The reduced height of the possibly intentionally squat statues may be attributed to limitations imposed by the dimensions of the imported and costly stone block, the rare and admired diorite that was absent among stones used in the earliest group of Gudea statues.

The intentional elimination, in the small-scale Gudeas, of one or more units from the standard six-tiered format may be interpreted by reference to Winter's observations on the significance of physical augmentation in representations of large-scale images of Gudea as ideal ruler. One may surmise that faced with limitations imposed by the proportions of the stone block, the sculptors of squat Gudea images may have opted to sacrifice nonsignificant anatomical parts (lower torso or upper legs) in favor of symbolically loaded anatomical features: head, shoulders, small of the back.

Second and First Millennia

Knowledge about proportional ratios in the architecture of the ancient Near East has been advanced in studies on metrology and on the identification of the dimensions of standard bricks used in the ancient Near East through Achaemenid times. Because works of art often functioned as architectural decoration and were adapted to, and coordinated with, the proportions of walls, stairways, and gates, they may be expected to be subject to the same, or similar, proportional considerations that obtained in their architectural contexts.

In Mesopotamian architecture, where brick was the traditional medium of construction, the architectural module was based on standard brick dimensions reflecting proportional ratios in the prevailing system of linear measure. The dependence of form on function, of art on its architectural context, is visibly evident in the proportions of figures of divinities represented on the molded-brick panels from the Kassite temple of Innin, built at Uruk (modern Warka) by Karaindash about 1415 BCE (fig. 4). The size of the head, measured from the brow (or hairline, above the eyes) to chin, is here dictated by the dimensions of the standard brick which is used to articulate also other anatomical components of the figures. The subordination of proportional considerations to architectural priorities is further notable in the elongation of bodies to accommodate and echo the vertical rhythm of the temple's niched facade. A similar proportional articulation by means of standard brick grids, and elongation of bodies in conformity with architectural requirements, is found in subse-

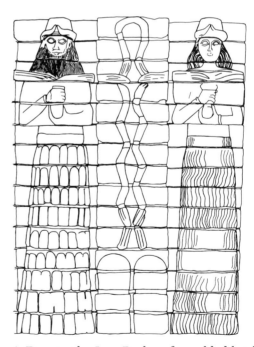

Fig. 4. Drawing by Jane Becker of a molded brick panel, circa 1425 BCE, from the facade of the Kassite temple of Innin, Uruk. STATE MUSEUM, BERLIN

2513

quent Middle Elamite constructions that adopted Middle Babylonian artistic conventions and the use of decorated molded brick panels on wall facades.

The use of a consistent system of proportions of the human form in Mesopotamian art of the Middle Babylonian period in media other than brick panels is suggested by the revised drawings of murals from the Kassite palace at Dur-Kurigalzu (modern ʿAqar Quf) (level II of unit H, doorway IV), dated to the thirteenth or twelfth century BCE. It is, nevertheless, the brick medium in mold-made brick images that suggests correspondence between proportional ratios in representations of the human form in Mesopotamian art and the dimensions of the Mesopotamian standard brick from at least the second millennium BCE. The standard brick, made to conform to specific dimensions expressed in ratios of the near eastern sexagesimal system of numeration, was used simultaneously as an architectural and an artistic module.

Robins has suggested a flexible system, based on the Egyptian model, for determining the proportions of the human form in Neo-Assyrian art. Figures of human- and eagle-headed genii, depicted in stone reliefs from the northwest palace of Assurnasirpal II at Nimrud (Kalkhu), when plotted on a hypothetical fifteen-square grid with the eye and the soles of the feet as fixed upper and lower reference points, display only a limited range of variation in the key dimensions of the body. However, since no single image here possesses dimensions that conform to all modes, the original model for the images of the genii is considered to be a distortion of natural proportions in favor of enhanced masculinity, represented by massive shoulders, bulging muscles, thick waists, and bulky torsos.

The practice of gender augmentation in royal imagery, for which Winter suggests continuity from the late third to the first millennium BCE, was evidently adopted in Mesopotamian non-royal imagery. It is noteworthy that the prevailing standards used for male proportions in Mesopotamian art may have differed from those used for female figures. In some Mesopotamian monuments, such as the Ur III stela of Ur-Nammu, gender differences are observed in the relatively more slender frame and higher small of the back in female representations.

IRAN

The Achaemenid Brick Grid

The definition of human proportions in Achaemenid art from Susa (modern Shush), exemplified by images on molded, glazed brick panels, is associated with guidelines created by the grid-like joints of bricks of standard dimensions. This conjectural use of a brick module for the rendition of human proportions implies correspondence between the system of proportions in Achaemenid brick art and Old Persian mathematical ratios that determined the dimensions of the Achaemenid standard brick. Achaemenid glazed bricks, recovered from Persepolis, Susa, and Babylon, have flat or relief decoration applied to the exposed sides. These bricks are either square, slightly wedge-shaped, or rectangular half-bricks, with the decoration usually applied to brick thickness or height in wall bricks and to the brick face in floor or ceiling tiles. The slightly wedge-shaped format served to produce a tight joint on the exposed side of the brick. Square wall-bricks generally measure 33 to 35 centimeters (about 13.5 inches) on each side and 8 to 9 centimeters (about 3.5 inches) thick, or four Persepolitan palms on each side and one Persepolitan palm in thickness.

Panels that depict the Archer frieze from Susa (reconstructed at the Louvre) are of the best preserved glazed bricks of Achaemenid date. These panels depict a procession of standardized figures of armed guards (fig. 5). First identified by Joseph Marie Dieulafoy with members of the Ten Thousand Immortals, the body of picked Persian troops known from Herodotus's account of Achaemenid royal guards, the archers are now more specifically identified with Susian guards and recognized by their twisted headbands, a feature distinctive of Elamites on labeled Achaemenid reliefs. Like the Susian guards on stone reliefs from the Apadana stairway at Persepolis, each archer in the version from Susa carries a spear with the circular butt on the toe, an uncased bow over the left arm, and a quiver over the shoulder, and is dressed in an ankle-length, flowing garment. The Susian guards in all versions of the Archer frieze display identical gestures and postures, shown facing right and left, framed by ornamental borders and sometimes by inscriptions.

Fig. 5. Frieze of archers at Susa, showing a Susian guard, Achaemenid period. LOUVRE
MUSEUM, PARIS

In the reconstructed version in the Louvre, the standard figure is four-fifths natural size, or about 1.46 meters (about 4.8 feet) tall, and is represented by seventeen brick thicknesses, each about 8.5 centimeters (3.4 inches), that define the figure from the soles of the feet to crown. In these panels it is the face length, from the hairline to the base of the nose, that fits exactly the space provided by the height of the standard brick (fig. 6). This modular unit, about 8.5 centimeters (3.4 inches) high, is equivalent to one Persepolitan palm of four fingers. The modular brick face is also equal to the width of the fist of five fingers, described as a brickfist, in the Susian brick grid.

A comparison of the ratios of anatomical units

Fig. 6. Detail from frieze of archers in molded brick, Susa, Achaemenid period. LOUVRE MUSEUM, PARIS

in the Archer frieze and the prevailing metrological ratios reveals a systematic effort on the part of the artist to fit discrete units of the human body into the format of the standard brick. The correspondence of anatomical units to brick dimensions is notable in the loose equation of graphic equivalents of the Persepolitan fist and forearm with their metrological equivalents represented by the height and length of the standard brick. Thus the image of a fist of five fingers may be fitted into the brick height with a metrological value of one palm (of four fingers). The graphic depiction of the cubital forearm is confined to the brick length, with a metrological value of two-thirds of a Persepolitan cubit of sixteen fingers (about 33 centimeters/13.2 inches).

Davis-Kimball's photogrammetric study of the Archer frieze provides computer-generated measurements that correct and refine an earlier schematic reconstruction of the proportional ratios of the human form in the Susian brick grid. Measurements taken from photographs and compiled with a computer spreadsheet program now offer mathematical relationships between anatomical units that could not be obtained through visual observation and brick count. Davis-Kimball compares proportions and attributes of the human image in the media of brick and stone relief by reference to points of the body that both coincide with brick joints and occur as measurable areas on Achaemenid stone reliefs.

The anatomical and costume divisions measured in this study are subdivided into primary and secondary measurements. Primary measures are those units into which others are sequentially ratioed so as to yield proportional relationships: represented by height, brick face, brickfist, and two forearm measures. Height is measured from soles of the feet to hairline (exclusive of hairstyle and headdress); brick face is the face length, from hairline to the base of the nose (exclusive of the variable beard); brickfist is the width of the clenched fist, and the two forearm measures are represented by elbow to fingertips and elbow to middle finger of the clenched fist. Secondary measures represent reference points that are not found on all figures, such as width, measured across the chest, which may be depicted in profile or frontally, and length of robe, which varies according to dress type.

Davis-Kimball's study reveals correspondences between proportional ratios of the human form in some Persepolitan reliefs and in the Susian Archer frieze, and Achaemenid architectural ratios. These correspond to the relative values of the Persepolitan cubit: four palms: one palm that have the relationship 6:4:1. The Persepolitan reliefs that display these ratios are four groups represented by the Apadana north and east Stairs, the Council Hall north stairs, and the Apadana Replacement Panels. Differences between the proportional ratios of these figures and ratios obtained for other figures in Achaemenid art may be attributed to several factors, not least the fact that the accuracy of the computer-generated measurements of the images in photographs clearly exceeds the technical abilities of the creators of the brick and stone reliefs. Variations in proportions of the human form in Achaemenid art are also associated with differences in ranks of individuals depicted, with differences in artistic hands, and with the chronological order of the reliefs.

Achaemenid Proportional Systems

The development of a system of proportions in Achaemenid art has been attributed to both external and internal conditions. Robins's study implies the appearance of the more technically accomplished and taller royal image, in the latter part of the reign of Darius I, with an impact on Achaemenid sculpture of the canonic conventions of Egyptian art. Davis-Kimball, on the other hand, attributes the change in the proportions of the royal image during Darius's reign to an internal development that led to a unique expression of hieratic proportions in Achaemenid art.

The colossal statue of Darius I (521–486), uncovered in 1972 at Susa by the French Archaeological Delegation in Iran, provides evidence of the influence of Egyptian conventions of stone sculpture on Achaemenid art. Carved in Egypt from local Egyptian gray granite, perhaps for the Atum Temple at Heliopolis, the statue is presumed to have been one of a pair of identical portal figures that were erected against the west facade of the main gate that gave access to the royal complex at Susa (illustrated in "The History of Elam and Achaemenid Persia" in Part 5, Vol. II). The quadrilingual inscription on the statue indicates that the monument was commissioned around 490 BCE by Darius I and erected according to his specifications. Darius's inscription states that the statue was created so that "he who saw it in the future would know that the Persian man had conquered Egypt." Indeed, Darius's view of himself as world ruler and master of Egypt is portrayed in the statue through a subtle blend of Egyptian and Achaemenid Persian artistic conventions.

The monolithic statue, which is estimated to have measured 2.70 meters (8.91 feet) in height (without the base) prior to the loss of its head and shoulders, rests on a rectangular base measuring 51 centimeters (20.4 inches) in height. The height of the base corresponds exactly to the absolute dimensions of the cubit-size standard brick, laid in six rows of nine upon the passage along the west facade of the gate in which the statue was placed. Robins, who notes the correspondence in the dimensions of the Egyptian reformed cubit and the Neo-Babylonian and Achaemenid cubits, finds a similarity in the proportions of the Darius statue to Egyptian sculpture from the Twenty-sixth Dynasty, or Saite Period (662–525). Robins observes that if the Darius statue is provided with a reconstructed head and plotted on a hypothetical Egyptian twenty-one square grid, as in Egyptian sculpture of the Late Period, horizontal 20 would pass between the reconstructed mouth and nose, horizontal 19 through the junction of the reconstructed neck and shoulder, 13 through the small of the back, and 9 beneath the fist of the hanging arm.

Although the loss of the head and shoulders of the Darius statue does not permit conclusive determination of the statue's face, width, and height ratios, its visual comparison with Achaemenid sculpture from the latter part of Darius's reign suggests the adherence of the whole group to a similar set of stylistic criteria. The Darius statue is linked especially closely in terms of style to the enthroned king from the Treasury Reliefs. The royal figure and its mirror image in the two Treasury Reliefs, originally intended as central panels on the north and east stairs of the Apadana, are perhaps the most carefully and skillfully executed among all the reliefs at Persepolis.

These masterpieces of Achaemenid sculpture, destined for public view at the two most promi-nently visible locations on the Apadana stairways, were ideally sited for graphic expression of the Achaemenid concept of ideal kingship. The image of the enthroned ruler from the Treasury Reliefs conveys the notion of the ideal king not only through its iconography, as persuasively argued by Margaret Root, but also through a complex set of formal and expressive devices that include reference to a system of proportions used for the depiction of the human form.

The proportions of the enthroned ruler from the Treasury Reliefs were computed by Davis-Kimball after theoretical height conversion that served to determine the standing height of the royal figure. The resulting proportional ratios of 6:4:1 (height: forearm [elbow to tip of thumb]: face) obtained for this figure are similar to those found for images of the guards in the Susian Archer frieze and to ratios obtained for Achaemenid architecture from the reign of Darius I at Persepolis.

Of special interest and significance in Davis-Kimball's study is her observation on the use of hierarchical proportions as a means of conveying information on social stratification in Achaemenid art. Although guards, nobles, and attendants have a superficial resemblance to the figure of the king, the latter is distinguished from them by virtue of his greater height and larger head. The king, important personages, the king's attendants, and nobles are portrayed in a descending order of body height and facial dimensions. The magnification of the royal countenance is seen as a pictorial statement about the Achaemenid concept of kingship and as reference to the king's temporal, and perhaps infinite, power. As an expression of the Achaemenid artistic koine and as a major monument displayed at the main gate in Achaemenid Susa, the colossal statue of Darius may be expected to have been provided with a head and countenance that expressed the hierarchical proportions that now appear to have been a pervasive hallmark of Achaemenid royal imagery throughout the course of its development.

Variations in proportions of the human figure in Achaemenid art are also associated in Davis-Kimball's study with the chronological sequence of the reliefs. The royal image, which is relatively attenuated and proportionately taller and more slender than other figures during the reigns of Darius I and his son Xerxes, becomes proportionately shorter and stockier in later Achaemenid reliefs. The exponential falloff observed in the height and width ratios of figures in Achaemenid sculpture over time may be attributed to the sculptors' increasing laxity in reproduction of stock figures. It may also conceivably suggest tacit approval of the resultant gender augmentation in these figures.

That the proposed Achaemenid system of proportions in art was modified to accommodate its architectural context is indicated at Persepolis by the differing heights of servant figures from the Xerxes palace stairway and by the variable proportions of nobles of equal rank from the northeast stairway of the Central Building. The blatant disregard of standardized proportions for like figures in these reliefs may be explained by spatial limitations imposed by the architectural setting of the reliefs. The disproportion between gigantic and diminutive figures, necessitated by the variable height of the wall, clearly demonstrates that artists could subordinate guidelines to aesthetic and architectural considerations.

Abrupt changes in the format and scale of figures within a single procession are also found in the medium of glazed-brick wall decoration of Achaemenid structures from Susa. Thus the scale and direction of figures in the Susian Archer frieze are determined by projections and angles along wall surfaces; figures in a single procession may suddenly shift direction to face a doorway, or the scale of one or more figures within a frieze may be reduced to accommodate a wall recess. Moreover, the Achaemenid brick mason readily trimmed and cut the decorated bricks for use as building blocks. Such tailoring of glazed bricks to architectural requirements distinguishes Achaemenid brick panels from the carefully fitted glazed bricks of Neo-Babylonian date.

The reduction in the scale of human figures in later versions of the Archer frieze may be explained by a parallel development in Achaemenid glazed bricks from Susa that depict processions of lions. The Susian Lion frieze is known in two versions represented by an earlier series, datable to the reign of Darius I, and a later one from the reign of Artaxerxes II (early fourth century BCE). Although the height and length of the lion in both versions are identical (about 1.5 by 2 meters/1.65 by 2.2 yards), in the older version the lion's height is defined by almost fourteen brick thicknesses, whereas only half that number define it in the later version, where bricks of double thickness are used. The use of bricks of double thickness in the later version was evidently intended to facilitate construction of the relief by reducing the number of horizontal joints. The joints of the brick grid used for the definition of proportions in the earlier version of the Lion frieze from Susa were thus gradually deprived of their importance as markers. It may be speculated that once anatomical proportions were fixed, standardized images might be rendered without direct reference to the original brick grid.

Despite a paucity of studies on animal imagery in the art of the ancient Near East, visible evidence for anatomical augmentation and the use of standardized proportions in depictions of lions in the glazed panels from Susa justify expectation of the observance of artistic standards for depiction of some, if not all, animals at various periods in the history of the art of the ancient Near East. It may be conjectured that the animals that were subjected to anatomical augmentation and standardization were surely those that, like the lion and the bull, were invested with special symbolism.

Like the two versions of the Lion frieze, the various versions of the Archer frieze from Susa and Babylon may be assigned to an earlier and a later type. Whereas the earlier type is represented by panels that manifest a correspondence between anatomical proportions and brick dimensions, the later type may be identified with versions that lack such correspondence. The reduced scale and formulaic figures that appear without reference to the brick grid are thus later versions, based on nearly life-size originals characterized by a correspondence between face length, or brick face, and the height of the brick itself. Although the Archer frieze panels from the Apadana at Susa appear to date from a period when repairs and additions were made to earlier Achaemenid structures at that site, they evidently reproduce the scale and format of the earliest panels datable to the reign of Darius I.

Origins of the Achaemenid Brick Grid

A search for the origins of the Achaemenid system of proportions in art must take into account information offered in Achaemenid texts about the nationalities of the work force engaged in the construction of the palace of Darius I at Susa. The foundation charter of Darius's palace credits Babylonian workmen with the tasks of laying the foundations and the preparation of molded and baked bricks used in the palace's construction. Babylonians evidently continued to perform the same tasks in Darius's later constructions at Susa, as indicated in foundation tablets uncovered there in 1970. This more recently uncovered textual source also serves to clarify an earlier incomplete and ambiguous reference to the role played by Ionians in the decoration of Darius's palace. Darius's earlier foundation charter states that the elements of decoration that ornamented the terrace were imported from Ionia. The elements of decoration of the palace mentioned here and understood earlier as a reference to brick panels, however, could refer to fixtures such as stone slabs or reliefs. Moreover, there is little in the form and content of the decoration of Achaemenid glazed bricks to argue for Greek workmanship.

If the leading role attributed to Babylonians in the manufacture of bricks for Achaemenid palaces at Susa accounts for similarities in the decorative schemes of Neo-Babylonian and Achaemenid glazed brick panels, the technology of Achaemenid brick production suggests the involvement in brick production also of native workmen who were presumably ignored in the lists given in the foundation charters because of the propagandistic nature of these texts. Apart from some glazed terra-cotta bricks of Neo-Babylonian type, the bulk of the bricks utilized in Achaemenid glazed-brick panels were of a glazed siliceous faience, frequently described as frit. This lighter, more porous and durable brick, not found in Neo-Babylonian structures, has a composition that is identical to that of Elamite bricks utilized in both Late and Middle Elamite structures. Despite considerable innovation in the range of colors of the glaze and in the method of its application to the decoration, Achaemenid frit bricks evidently continued the methods and materials of manufacture found in the older Elamite glazed-brick industry. That both Elamite and Mesopotamian artistic conventions contributed to Achaemenid glazed-brick production may thus be observed in technological conventions and, as argued in this study, in the artistic use of the brick module as a proportional guideline. Finally, the use of the standard brick as a metrological guideline in the art of the ancient Near East indicates a far earlier date than previously supposed for the use of a relatively large, abstract module in the rendition of proportions in art. The Byzantine module, identified with the face-length, for which Erwin Panofsky had in fact sought an eastern origin, now finds an early forerunner in the brick length used in a similar fashion in Achaemenid art. That Achaemenid art in turn relied on older, Mesopotamian systems of proportions and metrologies is an assumption that finds support in proportional ratios noted for Neo-Sumerian sculpture from the last quarter of the third millennium BCE.

These findings suggest that systems of proportions in art were remarkably conservative and that a long tradition links the canons of our own age with those of early historic periods in the ancient Near East and Egypt. That art is modeled on art, and not on life, is elegantly phrased by E. H. Gombrich (*Art and Illusion, A Study in the Psychology of Pictorial Representation* [1960], p. 315): "Even after the development of naturalistic art, the vocabulary of representation shows a tenacity, a resistance to change, as if a picture seen could account for a picture painted."

BIBLIOGRAPHY

Egypt

ERIK IVERSEN, *Canon and Proportions in Egyptian Art* (1955; 2nd ed., with Y. SHIBATA, 1975); GAY ROBINS, "Natural and Canonical Proportions in Ancient Egyptians," *Göttinger Miszellen* 61 (1983), "Standing Figures in the Late Grid System of the 26th Dynasty," *Studien zur Altägyptischen Kultur* 12 (1985), "Amarna Grids," *Göttinger Miszellen* 84 and 88 (1985), *Egyptian Painting and Relief* (1986), "Composition and the Artist's Squared Grid," *Journal of the American Re-*

search *Center in Egypt* 28 (1991), and *Proportions and Style in Ancient Egyptian Art* (1994); and HEINRICH SCHÄFER, *Principles of Egyptian Art*, translated and edited by JOHN BAINES (1974; revised repr. 1986).

Mesopotamia

GUITTY AZARPAY, "A Canon of Proportions in the Art of the Ancient Near East," in *Investigating the Artistic Environment in the Ancient Near East*, edited by ANN C. GUNTER (1990), and "A Photogrammetric Study of Three Gudea Statues," *Journal of the American Oriental Society* 110, no. 4 (1990); GUDRUN COLBOW, *Zur Rundplastik des Gudea von Lagaš* (1987); FLEMMING JOHANSEN, *Statues of Gudea: Ancient and Modern* (1978); M. A. POWELL, "Metrological Notes on the Esagila Tablet and Related Matters," *Zeitschrift für Assyriologie* 72 (1982); GAY ROBINS, "Proportions of Standing Figures in the North-West Palace of Assurnasirpal II at Nimrud," *Iraq* 62 (1990); HORST STEIBLE, "The Chronological Order of the Statues of Gudea of Lagash from the Point of View of a Sumerologist," *Journal of Cuneiform Studies* (1991); YOKO TOMABECHI, "Wall Paintings from Dur Kurigalzu," *Journal of Near Eastern Studies* 42 (1983); and IRENE J. WINTER, "The Body of the Able Ruler: Toward an Understanding of the Statues of Gudea," *DUMU-E₂-DUB-BA-A: Studies in Honor of Åke W. Sjöberg*, edited by HERMANN BEHRENS et al. (1989).

Iran

GUITTY AZARPAY, "Proportional Guidelines in Ancient Near Eastern Art," *Journal of Near Eastern Studies* 46 (1987); JEANNINE DAVIS-KIMBALL, "Proportions in Achaemenid Art" (Ph.D. diss., University of California, Berkeley, 1989); JOSEPH MARIE DIEULAFOY, *L'Acropole de Suse d'après les fouilles exécutées en 1884, 1885, 1886, sous les auspices du Musée du Louvre*, vol. 2 (1893); R. DE MECQUENEM, L. BRETON, and M. RUTTEN, *Mission de Susiane, Mémoires de la mission archéologique en Iran*, vol. 30 (1947); MICHAEL ROAF, "Persepolitan Metrology," *Iran* 16 (1978), and "Sculpture and Sculptors at Persepolis," *Iran* 21 (1983); GAY ROBINS, "Proportions in Persian and Egyptian Art," *Bulletin of the Egyptological Seminar* 19 (1987/1988); and MARGARET C. ROOT, *The King and Kingship in Achaemenid Art* (1979).

SEE ALSO **Artisans and Artists in Pharaonic Egypt** (Part 4, Vol. I); **Artisans and Artists in Ancient Western Asia** (Part 4, Vol. I); **Metrology and Mathematics in Ancient Mesopotamia** (Part 8, Vol. III); **Aesthetics in Ancient Mesopotamian Art** (Part 10, Vol. IV); and **Understanding Ancient Near Eastern Art: A Personal Account** (Part 11, Vol. IV).

Erotic Art in the Ancient Near East

FRANCES PINNOCK

EROTICISM, FROM ITS MOST spiritual to its crudest aspects, has always been present in human intellectual history. Because of its close connection with the sexual sphere of people's lives, eros, probably more than other feelings, is subject to the widest range of ideological and other nuances and to variations in the so-called communal sense of decency. Eroticism, in fact, may be considered the intellectual and aesthetic sublimation of love feelings, but the term frequently also means the most vulgar expressions of the sexual act, not to mention perversions.

In visual representations the borders between the different nuances become even more feeble, and today heated and often hectic discussions about the permissibility of artistic or pseudo-artistic productions with erotic subjects are not infrequent. On the basis of moral beliefs or moralistic conceptions, people attempt to distinguish eroticism (that is, acceptable artistic or "poetic" representation intended to arouse sexual desire within the sphere of love) from pornography (unacceptable vulgar exhibition of a mere physical sex act that lacks investment of affection). Eroticism, therefore, may be something that slightly trespasses the bounds of the communal sense of decency but still remains within the limits defined by the fulfillment of a feeling of love.

Pornography, on the other hand, is strictly related to obscenity. Particular stress is placed on aspects of the mere physical sphere, rather than the spiritual or emotional one. The material is therefore believed to be corrupting, offensive, and morally repugnant.

The ancient world produced several examples of works of art or handicraft with erotic subjects and written documents exalting both heterosexual and homosexual love. In this sphere, as well as in many other and perhaps more relevant ones, humans have not changed much from the time they became *Homo sapiens*. It is perhaps easier, when one studies cultures closer to contemporary western ones, to understand the aims of representations of erotic subjects or the feelings that inspired them. Written evidence is invaluable for such an understanding. From the classical Greek world, for example, come exaltations of the pleasures of homosexual love in connection with symposia. Kraters and drinking bowls depict male figures drinking and feasting, often in an evident state of excitement, accompanied by short inscriptions praising the beauty and vigor of the beloved boy. As concerns the culture of ancient Rome, the famous erotic paintings in Pompeian houses are only one part of a large and well-known body of evidence that spanned various areas from visual art to writing.

Did a similar body of work exist in the ancient Near East? Or rather, are we able to interpret correctly the surviving evidence? The answer to the first question is positive, but that to the second is rather problematic. First, we must limit the geographic sphere within which our search will take place.

EGYPT

Egypt had no art definable as erotic. Love poetry survives, although not of the very explicit type found in Mesopotamia. (See "Love Lyrics from the Ancient Near East" in Part 9, earlier in this volume.) There are some graffiti or ostraca, particularly from private houses, and sketches on the walls of tombs. These drawings belong to the sphere of unofficial, popular expressions and are uncommon. Rather than being considered artistic creations, they must be interpreted as a casual manifestation of a people's esprit. Moreover, the representations of the ithyphallic god Min cannot be considered erotic art, for they must have had a magical or ritual meaning. In Egyptian the phallus is also a hieroglyphic sign with different meanings, and it was employed in writing without sexual connotations.

The figures of ducklings or geese and the representations of stick fowling found in tombs are believed to be metaphoric or symbolic representations of the respective sexual roles of woman and man. One important piece of evidence for eroticism is Papyrus 55001 in Turin, clearly a satiric work, whose full meaning, however, escapes us. In this papyrus a row of animals is depicted in humanlike positions, below which humans are shown performing various kinds of sexual acts.

As concerns Egypt of the Late Period, Herodotus observed that, although in the Near East he had seen occurrences of prostitution and especially sacred prostitution, he was not sure that this phenomenon was known in Egypt. Moreover, according to Egyptian lore, prostitution was overtly condemned, and a married woman found guilty of adultery might be put to death.

ANATOLIA

In Anatolia, as well, eros is more hinted at than clearly represented. For instance, one box shows a man and a woman side by side in bed, covered by a blanket. Another interesting example is a large pithos, recently found at İnandık, richly decorated with four registers of painted relief. The top register depicts a banquet with music and the preparation of food, and the next one, cult scenes with music and libations for a sacred bull. The third register down likely represents cult scenes with music, in which gifts, presumably bull horns, are brought to a kind of altar, behind which two figures are shown crouching on a large stool or bed; one is probably a veiled woman. The last register has scenes of a feast with music and dancing or gymnastic exercises, and two personnages, most probably a man and a woman, are represented in a *coitus a tergo* (penetration from behind); both figures are dressed. The overall subject of the vase seems to be the celebration of a feast during which the characters, most likely priests and priestesses, joined for banquets or brought gifts to the deity, represented by the statue of a sacred bull. As the bull is a well-known symbol of fertility, it is not surprising that in the last register a sexual act is depicted among other scenes (which probably represent the feast and games that took place during the celebration).

MESOPOTAMIA AND SYRIA

Two regions only, Mesopotamia and Syria, show a definite interest in erotic representations. These can be divided into three main categories: handmade or molded clay figurines of naked women, cylinder seals, and molded clay or pierced metal plaques representing naked women or sexual acts. All three kinds of objects are attested in Mesopotamia, while in Syria the plaques are not present.

Figurines

The clay figurines, pervasive in the archaeological record, represent naked female figures and are attested from the Neolithic period until the

Persian period, although they vary over time. In the Neolithic period and until the Uruk period, the female figure, usually identified as the mother goddess, has strongly accentuated physical characteristics that might be related with the procreative function: big and heavy breasts, outsize buttocks, a large belly, a strongly stylized head. The figure is frequently in a sitting position, one of the traditional postures for childbirth. Sometimes the so-called mother goddess holds or feeds a baby in her arms.

With the Jamdat Nasr period, on the other hand, a new representation appears that endured, with slight variants, until the Persian period: a young, slender woman with small, well-modeled breasts (sometimes held firm by her hands, as in a provocative offering), her genitalia depicted by a big triangle filled with dots to render her pubic hair. The hair on her head is usually loose or plaited; it surrounds her face, falling to her shoulders. In the painted figures the woman has heavy makeup. In all the figurines the woman wears jewels, either earrings, necklaces, bracelets, anklets, or all of them. In Syria during the Early and Middle Bronze ages, these figurines are quite numerous, but they do not have human features: their faces and coiffures are distorted in peculiar ways until they lose any human characteristic.

The clay female figurine appears totally different from the representation of women in statues or seals with the exception of the squatting women: she is naked, while the others are dressed. With the later type of figurine, the differences increase: her hair is loose, while the others' is usually tied up in a kind of chignon on the nape of the neck; she wears jewels, while the others wear no ornaments (at least until the Isin-Larsa period), with the exception of single or multiple torque-like necklaces. Later on musicians, usually playing a tambourine, are represented in the same attire.

There are, however, objects related to the clay figurines. Particularly in the Late Bronze Age in Palestine and coastal Syria, the so-called Astarte plaques are common. These small clay or metal plaques represent a naked woman, sometimes only symbolized by her sex rendered once again as a dotted triangle. She is identified as the goddess Astarte or with some other female member of the local pantheons related to fertility. Quite famous are the silver and gold plaques used as pendants from Ugarit (modern Ras Shamra). In Syria such objects are also attested in the Iron and Persian ages but are more frequently made of clay. Another kind of representation belongs in this section: the well-known type called the "woman at the window" (although only her head is shown). This figure, represented on Phoenician ivories of the ninth to eighth centuries BCE, is usually explained as a harlot, attracting the passerby from the window of the brothel or of her house (see fig. 18 in "Art and Ideology in Ancient Western Asia," earlier in this volume).

The female figurines are ubiquitous; they are found in temples, houses, and tombs. It is therefore impossible to ascertain their purpose on the basis of their findspots. The Astarte plaques had a more definite votive nature, and they were more frequently found in temples, even outside Syro-Palestine proper. Hazael, king of Damascus, sent two big bronze triangular plaques with several figures in rows, forming a kind of pyramid, to the Heraion in Samos, as if identifying his own great goddess with that foreign one. The ivory pieces with the "woman at the window" were probably parts of pieces of furniture, like the other famous ivories of Phoenician or Syrian origin, although it is difficult to place this kind of representation in a definite ideological context.

Cylinder Seals

In glyptics two main representations can be singled out. The first depicts the very stylized figure of a naked woman in a frontal position with her legs spread apart, the so-called squatting woman, attested in Mesopotamia and Syria from the Uruk to the Early Dynastic I period (fig. 1). Usually, the figure appears in seals of cursory style, together with other figures or scenes related mostly to country or everyday life: domestic animals, vegetable motifs, the production of pots, and the preparation of food. The second type portrays an actual erotic scene with two characters who perform the sexual act facing each other in a horizontal position. Sometimes they are accompanied by attendants. One seal from the earlier levels at Ur (modern Tell al-Muqayyar) presents a couple over a kind of

Fig. 1. Cylinder-seal impression from Ur showing a squatting female. L. LEGRAIN, *UR EXCAVATIONS, VOL. 3, ARCHAIC SEAL IMPRESSIONS* (1936)

shrine, where a woman is probably performing a cultic rite. A variant is attested in which the two figures are standing, and one, most probably a female, turns her shoulders to the other. In seals, particularly those made in simpler style, it is sometimes difficult to identify the gender of the characters, but frequently the passive personage in the erotic scenes (that is, the one below in the canonical scene, or the one who is penetrated in the scenes of *coitus a tergo*) has a long ponytail and can therefore be identified as a woman.

This second type of scene was present in Mesopotamia, apparently from the Uruk to the Neo-Sumerian period, although very few specimens survive. Some occurrences of stamp or cylinder seals with erotic representations were also found, more or less in the same periods, from Syria to Iran to the Indus Valley. Apparently, the representations of the two standing characters, one behind the other, are more numerous than the rest. The next most frequent are those

of the couple standing face-to-face, followed by those of the couple in a horizontal position face to face (fig. 2). Until the Early Dynastic III period, the erotic scene is the main theme on the seals on which it appears (fig. 3). From the Akkadian period, it becomes a secondary motif on seals that may even have presentation scenes, in addition to eagles and lions. Seals with erotic scenes are not very common, generally speaking, and erotic scenes are not attested in seals of the refined style.

Plaques

The so-called votive plaques with erotic images, attested only in Mesopotamia, have the most lively representations, rich in variants of the subject, and are closer to the modern conception of erotic art. There are two main types. The first are molded clay plaques, mainly dating from the Old Babylonian period, that were found in several Mesopotamian sites, such as Nippur (modern Nuffar) or Kish (modern Tell al-Uhaimir, modern Tell Ingharra), and in the Diyala region, especially at Eshnunna (Eshnunnak, modern Tell Asmar) and Tutub (Dur-Samsu-iluna, Tupliash, modern Khafaje). The second type are the even livelier plaques of the Middle Assyrian period, which mainly date from Tukulti-Ninurta I's age (late thirteenth century). They are made of lead and were found in Ishtar's temple at Asshur (modern Qalat Sharqat) and at Kar-Tukulti-Ninurta (modern Telul al-Aqar).

Fig. 2. Cylinder-seal impression of couple in bed, Early Dynastic period, from Tell Asmar.
ORIENTAL INSTITUTE, UNIVERSITY OF CHICAGO

Fig. 3. Cylinder-seal impressions from Ur. L. LEGRAIN, *UR EXCAVATIONS*, VOL. 3, *ARCHAIC SEAL IMPRESSIONS* (1936)

The Old Babylonian clay plaques carry two scenes most frequently. In the first a man and a woman, both naked, stand facing each other and perform the sexual act; the woman usually raises one leg bent at the knee to form a right angle. In the second a naked woman bends down from the waist, with her body parallel to the ground, and sometimes she drinks through a tube from a jar. She is penetrated from behind by a naked standing man, who occasionally holds a vase in his hand. No attendants are present (fig. 4).

The material from Asshur consists of pierced lead plaques with a variety of subjects: squatting women spreading their legs apart with their hands; couples standing face-to-face, with the woman guiding the man by holding his member with her hand; and couples performing *coitus a tergo* (fig. 5). In a very peculiar variation, the woman reclines with her back on a rectangular support marked by lines inside, which seems to represent mud-brick, and the man stands in front of her. Sometimes an attendant, whose gender is difficult to ascertain, holds the woman from behind by her arms, in a pose sometimes adopted in cylinder seals.

In the clay plaques the two personages are usually naked, but the woman may wear jewels. In the lead plaques, however, the two characters are dressed and wear long skirts open in the front, when they are represented standing. The woman reclining on the support is naked, as is

probably the attendant, and the male wears the long skirt; he may also be naked. The squatting woman is always naked, but it is not clear, because of the metal's bad state of preservation, if she wears jewels.

Finally, there is another type of object seemingly related to the pierced plaques. Quite a number of representations in vitreous paste of male and female sexual organs were found in Ishtar's temple at Asshur. The male organs were pierced by a hole at one extremity, and the female organs had two holes at both ends of the upper part of the pubic triangle. These holes allowed these pieces to be suspended from a support, or be attached to some other object.

INTERPRETING THE EVIDENCE

On the basis of the examples from Mesopotamia and Syria, we can pose some questions. Who are the personalities represented in these scenes? Are they human beings, deities, or semidivine

Fig. 4. Clay plaque showing a couple. BRITISH MUSEUM, LONDON

Fig. 5. Lead plaques from Asshur. STATE MUSEUM, BERLIN

beings? To what purpose and for whom were these objects made? And, last, can all these manifestations be labeled erotic art in the sense already defined?

Persons Represented

In the existing evidence, the personages represented performing sexual acts or shown in positions hinting at the sexual act (the squatting women, for example), do not have patently divine characteristics. They do not wear, for instance, the horned crowns that distinguished the gods from the Akkadian age on. The glyptics or plaques contain no peculiar symbols that might be connected with a divine figure. These figures are not larger than the other characters in the scene; on the contrary, when other characters are shown, they are usually bigger. From this we should infer that these personages, male and female, are human beings and not divine or semidivine creatures. An exception to this might be the Syrian clay figurines of the Early and Middle Bronze ages, which, with their distorted features, might be the representations of nonhuman beings, although probably not of deities. The other clay figurines apparently represent human beings, including the late figurines that hold musical instruments, usually tambourines.

Henri Frankfort, in discussing an Old Syrian seal impression, proposed to identify the squatting woman as a temple prostitute. A further hint for the identification of the specific milieu of these scenes is offered by the Asshur plaques in which the woman is shown leaning on a support. This support looks like a kind of mud-brick pilaster or tower; it might be the representation of the town walls, near which harlots usually lived and probably practiced their profession. To this specific milieu might point also the scenes in which one personage or both drink from vases or cups; these images might be evocative of the tavern where men could enjoy themselves—drinking, listening to music, and having intercourse with the opposite sex. The characters acting in erotic scenes are human beings, and we are perhaps not too far from the truth in proposing that the females are prostitutes, at least in the plaques and probably also among a number of the clay figurines.

Purposes of the Objects

In order to evaluate the purpose served by the objects depicting erotic scenes, the use of the objects themselves must be considered. Cylinder seals, votive plaques, and clay figurines apparently do not belong to one and the same range of possible uses. The seals are related to administration, that is, to official milieus. (See also "Cylinder Seals and Scarabs in the Ancient Near East" in Part 7, Vol. III.) The plaques may be decorations but, as they are frequently found in temples, may also have a votive meaning; in either case they are also related to official settings, either palaces or temples. Clay figurines are ubiquitous, and their purpose has not yet been definitely ascertained, although it has been frequently debated. Apparently they belong to the popular sphere rather than the official one. (See fig. 7, a terra-cotta bed with figures, in "Furniture in Ancient Western Asia" in Part 7, Vol. III.)

In Egypt, because the objects depicting erotic scenes are only a cursory expression of popular feelings, they do not belong to a true genre of art. In Mesopotamia and Syria, on the other hand, erotic art may be considered a genre, albeit a minor one, and it stays midway between official art and popular expression. Human beings are represented naked, in seductive positions or performing sexual acts, on objects whose uses were diverse, but which can also be related, somehow, to the milieu of the administration of the state. It seems, therefore, that the best way to reach some conclusion is to analyze the different sets of evidence separately.

Cylinder Seals Used mainly in administration to seal goods or documents, cylinder seals may have had some amuletic value when they were worn as pendants hanging from the neck, but this must have been a secondary use. The seals that represent squatting women or mating couples, together with scenes of everyday life, do not belong to the production of the palatial milieus, first for the simplicity of their style and second for the subjects represented. They might therefore express an ideology linked with the everyday life of simple people. And yet, they still belong to an official—albeit not central—milieu; for it is likely, because of their specific function, that seals would belong only to persons somehow connected with the central administration.

It seems probable that these seals were products meant for a lower level of state officials (the owners of the country estates, for instance) instead of those living in town in close contact with the center of administration. In glyptics, the order of the world was represented in palatial style by themes related to kingship and the official cult, and in the rural style by simpler themes related to humankind and popular cult. These two kinds of seals might present a general concept of the world order as perceived by the upper and lower classes, each with its own aims

and justifications for occupying its place in society.

In interpreting these erotic seals, Frankfort and others have spoken of fertility cults, sacred marriage (in the case of the mating couples), and the New Year's festival. The themes of the squatting woman and of the mating couple may, as has often been proposed, refer in a general sense to fertility and to the benevolent forces of nature. Yet the relation between these subjects and the New Year's festival, which has been debated, probably should not be fully accepted. In fact, these scenes are not connected with clear images of fertility, like flocks or herds, but only with individual animals or branches. The personages do not possess attributes that might point to a sacral function. Even if the sacred marriage was enacted by humans, namely the king and a priestess, in that moment they *were* gods. Apart from their symbolic roles, they were still the king and the high priestess engaged in one of the most important cult ceremonies in the life of the community.

P. R. S. Moorey, in discussing the identity of the owners of the tombs in the Royal Cemetery at Ur, proposed that these tombs belonged to kings and queens who had taken part in the New Year's festival. One of the elements of evidence supporting his theory is the large number of cylinder seals with banquet scenes. The banquet scene, which is sometimes accompanied by the representation of flocks or herds, is believed to depict the New Year's festival. This may be true, especially in the case of banquets with two participants, a male and a female. In the banquet seals, the main scene never includes an erotic component; on the other hand, an erotic scene may be accompanied by the representation of a jar with a tube, which might hint at a banquet that has taken or will take place. No seal with an erotic content has been found in the Royal Cemetery, however.

If these representations—banquets with two characters of different sex and erotic scenes—hint at the same event, namely the New Year's festival and the sacred marriage, the officials in the palace and in the countryside stressed two different moments of the feast. In the palace they preferred to highlight the moment of the banquet, which might have been public and thus a moment of participation by the community. Palace and temple had to be the centers of community life and the main link between the populace and the deities; these officials stressed their social position rather than a realistic representation of what had to be performed. In their seals the peripheral officials may have wished to represent a more private moment, the sexual conjunction between the two main characters. This moment was so private that the personages were represented deprived of all signs of their official positions.

While this hypothesis may be true, the estate lords, whose environment was probably more conservative, may have wished instead to express their beliefs about their position in society through a simple representation of traditional symbols. In the Old Babylonian version of the *Epic of Gilgamesh,* Enkidu's passage from wildlife to civilization is accomplished with the help of a prostitute, who teaches him to eat bread, drink beer, dress, and become convivial. On the seals the representation of a naked female offering herself or of sexual intercourse could refer to that free love, and the symbols or plain scenes of everyday life (such as the preparation of food or the making of pots) to the bread and beer. The animals and branches on these seals might be symbols of the past wildlife. Together these images might be a kind of synthesis of the idea of civilization, of being human in opposition to being animal. The peripheral officials expressed their belonging to the same social order as their counterparts in the palace, but they used traditional subjects linked to popular beliefs that were different but not necessarily opposed to the official ones.

Figurines The clay figurines are probably another expression of the same kind of popular set of beliefs illustrated in the cylinder seals. While the cylinder seals in cursory style were connected almost exclusively with nonpalatial milieus, the clay figurines had a wider circulation and were frequently found in private houses and tombs. The material in which they were realized and their style indicate that the figurines are certainly part of a popular level of handicraft production. While figurines of so-called mother goddesses exist in stone (a "nobler" material, in a certain sense), these figurines of naked women

were never made of stone, even though they were sometimes painted. Although their craftsmanship is quite simple, the rendering of the details of features, jewels, and hairstyles, and even hands and feet, is sometimes accurate. Moreover, in the Syrian region, these figurines assume an odd aspect, with their strange, distorted faces.

Naked figurines and the provocative offering of the breasts, while not so patently provocative as the squatting women and not directly involved in sexual acts, seem to represent a sublimated and detached expression of the concept illustrated by the cylinder seals, and found in the more explicit and plain representations of erotic scenes. The clay figurines have two usual interpretations. On the one hand, they are considered a representation of the female reproductive function and are believed to have been placed in women's tombs for that reason. The connection in funerary contexts between these figurines and women, however, is not certain. On the other hand, the figurines are seen as a stylization of the goddess Ishtar, because of their richly painted or molded jewelry. Ishtar's connection with jewels and beads is attested in written evidence—for instance, in the poem *Inanna's Descent to the Netherworld.* This last hypothesis seems more probable, if we take into consideration the late development of the Astarte plaques.

Plaques The clay or lead plaques with erotic scenes represent a third aspect of the question. The production of the clay plaques is limited to the Old Babylonian period, and that of the lead ones to the Middle Assyrian period. The erotic scene is usually represented by itself, without secondary motifs or other scenes that might give a hint about its context. Clay and lead cannot be considered precious materials, and yet the workmanship of the plaques requires a certain degree of specialization. The clay plaques were molded and therefore presumably made in a workshop. The same applies to lead plaques, because of the requirements for handling the metal and their workmanship, which is by no means cursory. In fact, the metal is not simply molded; it is also pierced with great care. The choice of lead for the Asshur plaques is quite interesting, for the material is not frequently used in Mesopotamian art. It is not a precious material like gold or silver, and yet it is not a common material like clay. Once again the plaques are a handicraft in between official and popular art, but in this instance the aim of the representation seems to be the erotic scene itself; here, certainly, no deity is illustrated or hinted at.

Yet who ordered the production of these plaques and why? Because the plaques were found in a temple, they were not made solely for visual enjoyment. They might have been requested by men, who presented them as a kind of ex-voto for a particularly successful performance. Alternatively, they might have been commissioned by women. In that instance, because the plaques exclusively represent sexual acts or women in erotic positions, and because there is nothing in the representations suggestive of fertility or procreation, these women could have been temple prostitutes, who might have celebrated in the plaques their profession or the moment of their consecration to the goddess and to their profession. If the first hypothesis cannot be dismissed, the connection of the plaques to prostitution seems more probable.

In fact, the physical characteristics of the women on the plaques are totally different from those of other female representations in Mesopotamian and Syrian art. As with the clay figurines, they are frequently naked and their hair is loose—none of these traits is to be found in statues or seals that represent women. The other elements that appear in the plaques can also find an explanation through this interpretation: the scenes of drinking or the playing of music may be related either to some cult ceremony, in which the sexual act was also performed, or to the taverns, where prostitutes could be found. The mud-brick pillar or tower on some of the plaques has already been mentioned in relation to prostitutes.

The temple prostitutes were not exclusively in temples. These women, in fact, gathered in associations, distinguished by special names and under the protection of a deity, most frequently Ishtar. They were to be found at the borders of the physical space of the community, near the city walls, midway between the inside and the outside, or between the civilized and the savage world. Prostitutes were considered a part of the society, and yet they were women who had lost their proper destiny—that is, marriage and childbearing to ensure the continuity of the community. These groups were defined by a generic name, *harimtu* (literally, the separate ones), while their specific names of individual associations hinted at their garments, which were particularly luxurious or odd, their coiffure, or to their general appearance, which distinguished them from other women.

If prostitutes were women excluded from the normal destiny for women and if, from what can be inferred from the textual evidence, the Mesopotamian man protected the morality of his family, he was still allowed to practice free love to some extent, for free love was considered a part of humanity. The duplicity of Mesopotamian attitudes toward sex not linked to marriage and procreation is expressed in the story of Enkidu. As already mentioned, a prostitute was sent to Enkidu in order to bring him from savagery to civilization. In another passage of the poem, in a moment of bitterness for the suffering he has met, Enkidu curses the woman who has taken him out of the steppe, promising her a life of solitude and contempt from those same men she once made happy. Near eastern society in general was a man's society, or at least only the male point of view has survived. Free love was accepted, but women who practiced prostitution were women who "had lost their way."

Art with Erotic Subjects

The Mesopotamian and Syrian artifacts with erotic subjects do not belong to the domain of erotic art, in that they were not conceived and produced as a means to arouse sexual desire. Yet they are nevertheless erotic art, in the sense that they were the expression of the feelings those people had about eros. And while the production of seals and figurines is, generally speaking, quite monotonous in the repetition of standard themes or figures, the plaques reveal a liveliness and amusement, as if the craftsman at least took pleasure in making them. They can be compared to the Egyptian graffiti on tomb walls and sherds, which, in the domain of popular culture, certainly represent a lively, albeit vulgar, joke. Moreover, these objects were visible in the temples and could provoke reactions in the visitors, even if they were not specifically designed to do so. They might have been a kind of preparation for a forthcoming act or a pleasant souvenir of something that had already taken place.

From conjecture based on this artistic evidence, together with information from written sources, we might maintain that, generally speaking, Mesopotamians did not have problems with eroticism. They liked it, and they were not ashamed to represent erotic subjects on objects of everyday use, like cylinder seals, or those in public buildings, like the figurines and plaques (although possibly these were in not-too-prominent positions). In fact, lovemaking was considered a basic element of civilization, as if the possibility of having free sexual intercourse with the opposite sex, not strictly for the sake of reproduction and therefore not related to the cycle of nature, was a way of stepping out of the animal part of the human being. The application of these concepts was intense enough that when Herodotus visited Babylon he saw so many prostitutes walking in the streets that he believed that all Babylonian women dedicated themselves to that profession, which, of course, was by no means true.

But the relation between the Mesopotamian man and his sexuality was not completely free from contradictions and problems. Apparently, free heterosexual love was considered acceptable outside the legal bond of marriage. Homosexuality did exist, as is known from written sources. There were even male equivalents of the *harimtu*, but they were somewhat despised or considered a little ridiculous. Homosexual acts were never clearly represented in visual art. The only possible exception might be found in seals, where it is sometimes difficult to determine the gender of the protagonists. As already stated, the characters with the ponytail hairstyle are considered to be women, but homosexuals may have appropriated feminine garments and coiffures. No doubt can be possible, however, as to the sex of the figures represented on the plaques.

The twofold attitude of Mesopotamians to sex—on the one hand an accepted part of human life, and on the other a possible source of social disorder—is inherent in erotic art, or, to say it better, in the artistic expressions that represent erotic subjects. In fact, the themes deal with only a few facets of eroticism: mainly intercourse between a man and a woman, usually represented as youths, or naked, attractive young women offering themselves. The utilization of objects with erotic scenes was apparently not private but somehow entered the public sphere and, therefore, was subject to a kind of censorship.

The problem of the relation of at least a part of these compositions to fertility cults, New Year's festivals, and sacred marriage rites still remains unsolved. As already stated, it does not seem possible to identify the personages of erotic scenes directly, especially those on cylinder seals, as the main characters of these religious events. However, we cannot dismiss the hypothesis that erotic scenes incorporating animals or vegetables are related to fertility in a general way.

Perhaps there was a deep contradiction in the relation between the Mesopotamians and their sexuality, leading to the elimination from visual art of certain more reproachable, offensive, and disorderly subjects and to a double standard for prostitutes. But the erotic scenes we have are quite uniform in conveying an overall impression of gaiety and liveliness. The personages, men and women, are attractive and graceful; even the squatting women are so natural that their posture does not look like a vulgar accentuation of an offering but rather a mischievous exhibition.

Erotic art, or rather objects with erotic scenes, with the exception of clay figurines and their derivatives (the Astarte plaques, for example), have a temporally limited presence. The plaques are also geographically limited. No explanation has been found for these limitations. Moreover, the discussion of prostitutes and their position in society applies to Mesopotamia and not to Syria, where only the seals and figurines are attested, and where no written evidence exists for prostitution. Only in the late epochs did Herodotus observe the presence of sacred prostitution in Syria and its absence in Egypt.

Midway between sacred and profane, the representations of sexual acts and of squatting women belong to a period in which humans were perhaps closer to nature and its demands. The figure of the young and attractive naked woman may have become, for a time, a symbol of the goddess of love, but probably not the goddess herself. The clay and lead plaques, on the other hand, apparently originated in a specific milieu at a particular time for reasons that are so far difficult to ascertain.

It becomes clear that a subject, apparently so simple and easy to single out when it influences human feelings strictly linked with morals and social order, becomes quite difficult to interpret when one observes, as in this instance, the material evidence of distant cultures. With some dismay, we must conclude that the ancient Near East certainly had an art with erotic subjects, but whether it really was erotic art remains debatable.

BIBLIOGRAPHY

General

HARRY A. HOFFNER, JR., "Incest, Sodomy, and Bestiality in the Ancient Near East," in *Orient and Occident: Essays Presented to Cyrus H. Gordon on the Occasion of His Sixty-fifth Birthday*, edited by HARRY A. HOFFNER, JR. (1973); W. G. LAMBERT, "The Problem of the Love Lyrics," in *Unity and Diversity: Essays in the History, Literature, and Religion of the Ancient Near East*, edited by HANS GOEDICKE and J. J. M. ROBERTS (1975); and GWENDOLYN LEICK, *Sex and Eroticism in Mesopotamian Literature* (1994).

Egypt

LISE MANNICHE, *Sexual Life in Ancient Egypt* (1987); JOSEPH A. OMLIN, *Der Papyrus 55001 und seine satirisch-erotischen Zeichnungen und Inschriften*, Catalogo del Museo Egizio di Torino (1973); and LOTHAR STÖRK, "Erotik," in *Lexikon der Ägyptologie*, vol. 2, edited by WOLFGANG HELCK and WOLFHART WESTERNDORF (1977).

Mesopotamia and Syria

JEAN BOTTÉRO, "L'Amour libre et ses désavantages," in his *Mésopotamie: l'écriture, la raison, et les dieux* (1987); GEORGES CONTENEAU and ROMAN GHIRSHMAN, *Fouilles du Tépé Giyan près de Néhavend, 1931 et 1932* (1935); JERROLD S. COOPER, "Heilige Hochzeit. B. Archäologisch," in *Reallexikon der Assyriologie und voderasiatischen Archäologie*, vol. 4, edited by DIETZ OTTO EDZARD (1975); HENRI DE GENOUILLAC, *Fouilles françaises d'el-ʾAkhymer: premières recherches archéologiques à Kich, mission d'Henri de Genouillac, 1911–1912* (1924–1925); and THORKILD JACOBSEN, "Religious Drama in Ancient Mesopotamia," in *Unity and Diversity: Essays in the History, Literature, and Religion of the Ancient Near East*, edited by HANS GOEDICKE and J. J. M. ROBERTS (1975).

SAMUEL NOAH KRAMER, *The Sacred Marriage Rite: Aspects of Faith, Myth, and Ritual in Ancient Sumer* (1969); DONALD E. MC COWN and RICHARD HAINES, with DONALD P. HANSEN, *Nippur*, vol. 1, *Temple of Enlil, Scribal Quarter, and Soundings* (1967); J. TOBLER, *Excavations at Tepe Gawra*, vol. 2 (1950); and EDWIN M. YAMAUCHI, "Cultic Prostitution: A Case Study in Cultic Diffusion," in *Orient and Occident: Essays Presented to Cyrus H. Gordon on the Occasion of His Sixty-fifth Birthday*, edited by HARRY A. HOFFNER, JR. (1973).

FIGURINES

W. F. ALBRIGHT, "Astarte Plaques and Figurines from Tell Beit Mirsim," in *Mélanges syriens offerts à Monsieur René Dussaud* (1939); JAMES B. PRITCHARD, *Palestinian Figurines in Relation to Certain Goddesses Known through Literature* (1943); AGNÈS SPYCKET, *La Statuaire du Proche-Orient ancien* (1981); and E. DOUGLAS VAN BUREN, *Clay Figurines of Babylonia and Assyria* (1930).

CYLINDER SEALS

HENRI FRANKFORT, *Cylinder Seals: A Documentary Essay on the Art and Religion of the Ancient Near East* (1939); L. LEGRAIN, *Ur Excavations*, vol. 3, *Archaic Seal Impressions* (1936); and P. R. S. MOOREY, "What Do We Know about the People Buried in the Royal Cemetery," *Expedition* 20 (1977).

PLAQUES

WALTER ANDRAE, *Die jüngeren Ischtar-Tempel in Assur* (1935); RUTH OPIFICIUS, *Das altbabylonische Terrakottarelief* (1961); and AGNÈS SPYCKET, "Ex-voto mésopotamiens du IIᵉ millénaire av. J.-C.," in *De la Babylonie à la Syrie en passant par Mari: Mélanges offerts à M. J.-R. Kupper à l'occasion de son 70ᵉ anniversaire*, edited by Ö. TUNCA (1990).

SEE ALSO **Private Life in Ancient Mesopotamia** (Part 4, Vol. I); **Jewelry and Personal Arts in Ancient Egypt** (Part 7, Vol. III); **The Gilgamesh Epic: A Masterpiece from Ancient Mesopotamia** (Part 9, Vol. IV); **Love Lyrics from the Ancient Near East** (Part 9, Vol. IV); and **Reliefs, Statuary, and Monumental Paintings in Ancient Mesopotamia** (Part 10, Vol. IV); and VARIOUS CHAPTERS IN PART 5: HISTORY AND CULTURE.

Ancient Egyptian Reliefs, Statuary, and Monumental Paintings

ROBERT STEVEN BIANCHI

THIS ESSAY IS BASED UPON three principles: (1) Egyptian art is the visual manifestation of societal values formulated by an elite representing less than 5 percent of the total population of the country; (2) the art created for this elite was a canonical enterprise, conforming to established criteria that remained relatively invariable over time and that did not allow craftsmen the degree of freedom of expression that one associates with Western artists; and (3) as a visual means of expressing these societal values, Egyptian art may be regarded as an extension of the system of hieroglyphs, because the rules regulating the design of any given hieroglyph are precisely those governing the composition of any given visual image. Accordingly, ancient Egyptian painting and relief will be considered together, because both media reflect the concerns of two-dimensional representation.

INTRODUCTION:
THE PREDYNASTIC PERIOD

The earliest examples of representations are dated to the seventh millennium BCE and take the form of images cut into the living rock in the region of the Second Cataract. The interpreta-tion and chronology of these images, the earliest of which seem to be geomorphic or polymor-phous designs, deserve more intensive study than they have received to date. That study can now be more profitably undertaken because many of these images, having been removed from their original locations, are on view in a sort of open air museum at the site of New Kalab-sha near the Aswan High Dam. The relation-ships between these Epipalaeolithic images and those of the next three chronologically sequen-tial cultural phases—Badarian, Naqada I (Amra-tian), and Naqada II (Gerzean)—of the Predynas-tic period remain moot.

Some scholars regard these three cultural phases as disjunctive and consider the Third Dy-nasty as the time at which canonical representa-tions in Egyptian art begin. This essay, however, suggests that these cultural phases form a contin-uum and that each develops from dynamics within Egyptian society, occasionally incorporat-ing as a catalyst influences from Mesopotamia. Recent scholarship has discredited the sugges-tion, popular in the early 1980s, of the primacy of Nubia in this development.

During the Badarian period (before 4000), two-dimensional representations take the form of in-cised decoration on red-polished black-top ware. These simple designs, perhaps intended to represent patterns found on basketry or harking back to the motifs from the Epipalaeolithic period, are replaced in the Naqada I period (about 4000–3500) by designs in white painted on red ware. Angular forms—zigzags, triangles, and the like—are popularly applied to these vessels, either randomly or accommodated to the shape of the area so decorated. Figural decoration includes Nilotic beasts, particularly the hippopotamus, and these are often found in association with human figures, on a smaller scale in relationship to their actual dimensions in real life relative to the depicted animals, in scenes apparently lacking principles of thematic organization. Each of the figures, reduced to an outline or silhouette, seems to be designed according to the fundamental Egyptian principle whereby the most characteristic view is the one selected for reproduction. Accordingly, mammals are depicted in side, or profile, views whereas reptiles and amphibians are represented in top views. These same vantages are employed for the designs of slate palettes, some of which were shaped to realize the silhouettes of animals depicted on them.

During the Naqada II period (3500–3300), the color scheme of Amratian pottery is reversed, with the result that the decoration now becomes red applied to the buff color of the vessels. The scenes become more complex, and their significance, to a modern scholar, more enigmatic. Equilateral triangles; designs resembling the letters N or Z, depending on how they are drawn on the pots; horned cervids; floral motifs resembling palm fronds; objects usually described as many-oared boats with "deck cabins"; and an assortment of humans in various poses are among the most frequent motifs. These are arranged in apparently random fashion across the surfaces of the vessels, but more often than not the human figures are confined to the top halves. Many of these same motifs appear as well on contemporary scraps of linen—the best collection of which is in Turin—and at Hierakonpolis (Kom al-Aḥmar, Nekhen) on the earliest mural painting. There is no consensus, despite any number of ingenious surmises, about the nature of their subject matter. The slate palettes now begin to be decorated with scenes in relief, some depicting hunts and other battles. The fig-

ures—human and animal alike—continue to be arranged in the same patterns.

From the seventh to the end of the fourth millennium, then, there appears to have been a progression in Egyptian art from simple abstract images to more ambitious efforts. These latter images incorporated figures and animals, each shown in its most characteristic view, in randomly structured compositions. During this period society became stratified as the means of production and the accumulation of wealth fell into the hands of a progressively smaller percentage of the population. Members of the emerging elite, responding perhaps to stimuli from Mesopotamia, forced these artistic tendencies into a codified visual system at the same time that its members developed the hieroglyphic system of writing. Written word and image, created at the same time by the same elite class, emerged as Siamese twins; thereafter, the one could not exist without the other.

TWO-DIMENSIONAL REPRESENTATION AND HIEROGLYPHS

An early example of this symbiosis of word and image is the Narmer Palette in the Cairo Museum (see illustration in the "History of Ancient Egypt: An Overview" chapter in Part 5). However, to make general observations about Egyptian two-dimensional representations, we turn to another illustration of this interdependency: several rows of hieroglyphs from the so-called Avant-Porte of the Temple of Mut at Karnak (fig. 1). The space is ordered as a series of bands, termed registers, and within those registers each sign is arranged by size and shape into a design in which natural scale is irrelevant. An owl, a blade of grass, and a human musician, all of which are of quite different size in the real world, have been grouped together into patterns without regard to their actual relative sizes. The signs exist in their own artistic world. That is, they are not placed in any perceptible environment but rather seem to exist in atemporal and nonspatial environments. For the sake of the design, signs have been placed in groups, often

Fig. 1. Detail of hieroglyph inscription on the outer portal of the temple of the goddess Mut, South Karnak, Ptolemaic period. THE BROOKLYN MUSEUM, NEW YORK

one group depicted above a second within the same register. There is no light source and there are no artistic devices—perspective, stacked planes, and the like—by which the spectator can gauge the relative distance between one object and the next. Furthermore, each and every sign is depicted as an archetype representing an object in a generic way without regard for specificity or individuality.

When these principles are applied to a two-dimensional representation, as in a scene from the Tomb of Nakht from the Eighteenth Dynasty (fig. 2), the images are arranged in registers; the space to be decorated is divided into a series of horizontal units, within which are placed smaller horizontal units. Compare, for example, the figures of Nakht and his wife, seated to the left, with the two groups of superimposed registers of their retainers, on a smaller scale, to their right. This disregard for the natural scale of things, inherent in the hieroglyphs, enables the craftsmen to render some figures larger than others, thereby emphasizing their importance. Each figure is shown in its most characteristic view, and certain images, such as those on the offering tables, can be placed one above the other, exactly as found in the hieroglyphs.

These conventions eschew concern for time and space, so that the environment in which these images exist is the neutral one of the hieroglyphic inscription. The sole exception is the use of overlapping for adjacent figures. Specificity is avoided because all individuals of any social stratum within a scene have identical generic features. In the design of two-dimensional compositions, the craftsman in charge, usually called the outline scribe, probably relied on pattern "books," the existence of which is, however, denied by some authorities. The composition would be elaborated on the basis of models in a pattern "book" in such a way as to fill the available space, which might be organized by the use of a grid, as seen in the reliefs decorating the exterior south wall of the fourth century BCE Granite Sanctuary of Philip Arrhidaeus in the Temple of Karnak.

Once designed, the contour of each image, hieroglyph, and representation would form a strong outline, comparable in some respects to those of coloring books. These contours would form color cells preventing a color in one section from spilling over into an adjacent space.

The Egyptians had but five color words: black; white; red; green; and variegated. As a result the distinctions that a modern critic would make, for example, between blue and green or yellow and orange might have little significance for an Egyptian. Despite the apparent lack of a complex terminology, color was important because it was imbued with symbolic value, a subject often overlooked in discussions of ancient Egyptian painting. Here, two caveats must be emphasized. The first is that the limited color terminology forced the Egyptians to adopt a pluralistic approach to their color symbolism. As a result, reds might equally connote either good (the sun) or evil (fire), depending on the context. The second is that most modern color reproductions of ancient Egyptian paintings are so unfaithful to the original that they should be used with extreme caution when making comments about their tones and hues.

The Early Dynastic (Archaic) Period

With the exception of designs on cylinder seals and scenes on stone stelae, there are very few examples of two-dimensional representations from the Early Dynastic period. Of these the

Fig. 2. A painting in the tomb of Nakht at Thebes (no. 52), west wall, north side, showing the deceased and his wife hunting and fishing, observing the vintage and the netting and preparation of birds, and receiving offerings. Painting on plaster. Eighteenth Dynasty, circa 1400 BCE. METROPOLITAN MUSEUM OF ART, NEW YORK

finest is the stela of King Djet in Paris. It represents the serpent, the hieroglyph for this king's name, with the serekh, or palace facade, on top of which is perched the falcon god Horus, symbolizing the divine protection enjoyed by the king. The design of this scene does not observe a strict vertical axis, the image of the falcon being slightly off center. However, consistent avoidance of strict bilateral symmetry is an intentional and enduring hallmark of Egyptian art. (See fig. 1 in "Palaces and Temples in Ancient Egypt" in Part 4, Vol. I for an illustration of the Djet stele.)

The Old Kingdom

Among the more aesthetically accomplished works from the Fourth Dynasty is the stela of Wepemnofret (fig. 3) from Giza, now in the Phoebe Hearst Museum of the University of California at Berkeley. The deceased is shown seated before an offering table to the left, which, as will be developed below, is the place of honor in Egyptian art. This lavishly painted monument well illustrates how the colors of any given object are shackled by color cells conforming to their contours. This is particularly evident in the rendering of the animals in the top register of signs, as well as in the depiction of the chair on which Wepemnofret sits. The painting of its legs, which resemble real bull's legs, attests to the ancient Egyptian penchant for puns.

The wafer-thin quality of this relief contrasts to the bold, raised relief found on other monuments from the Fourth Dynasty, of which the relief of Akhethotep in Brooklyn is perhaps most indicative (fig. 4). Here one sees even more clearly the inextricable relationship between hieroglyphs and figure. It was customary in hieroglyphic writing to place an ideogram, visually summarizing the word just written out, at the end of the string of signs composing that word. Such an ideogram is called a determinative. One might, therefore, expect to see a hieroglyph of a male figure to the left of the five signs in the field in front of Akhethotep's face that spell his name. Here, however, the figure of Akhethotep himself, in bold relief, becomes the expected determinative. This interplay between sign and image and the blurred boundaries between the two are characteristic of many two-dimensional representations from the Old Kingdom.

The principles just discussed apply in general to the decoration of the tombs at Saqqara dating to the Fifth and Sixth dynasties. Many of these contain vignettes termed "scenes of daily life" that allow one to catch fleeting glimpses of the elite ideals governing the society of the time. These should be viewed and studied as entire walls, rather than as excerpted passages, because of the compositional and thematic links not only between individual registers, but also between adjacent walls of rooms. For example, in the tomb of Neferirtenef, now reconstructed in Brussels, a scene on the east wall depicting craftsmen making beads is placed next to one of fishmongers removing roe from their catch. The implication seems to be that making beads is the more slippery task. In these and other scenes, the principles of two-dimensional representation are maintained as each member of the privileged elite adhered to a protocol in the choice of scenes and the conventions of their representations.

The First Intermediate Period

During the First Intermediate Period, political and economic dislocations altered the social pro-

Fig. 3. Stela of Wepemnofret from his tomb at Giza. The deceased is seated before a table of offerings. The inscriptions give his name and titles (large hieroglyphs), and lists of offerings in a table and in five columns. Painted limestone. Fourth Dynasty, circa 2500 BCE. PHOEBE HEARST MUSEUM OF ANTHROPOLOGY, THE UNIVERSITY OF CALIFORNIA AT BERKELEY

Fig. 4. Limestone relief of Akhethotep from his tomb at Saqqara, Third to Fourth dynasties, circa 2550 BCE. THE BROOKLYN MUSEUM, NEW YORK

file of the elite for which an art—termed by critics "folkloric" (at best) or "bad" (at worst)—was created. Some historians of Egyptian art avoid illustrating examples of this period's art altogether. The stela of Maaty in Brooklyn (fig. 5) is representative of the period's tendencies. One curator has suggested that the aberrations from the norm exhibited by such works are to be ascribed to the craftsmen's adherence to a canonical system different from that employed earlier, and that such departures were deliberate adherences to an as yet imprecisely defined alternative canon of proportions.

The Middle Kingdom

The stability of the state brought about during the course of the Eleventh Dynasty witnessed a flowering of the arts in the form of some remark-

able relief sculptures. The delicacy of the reliefs on the limestone sarcophagus of Kawit in the Cairo Museum is unsurpassed, not only in the beauty of the confidently sculpted contours but also in the discriminating way in which interior detail is added only to certain passages. One need only compare the figure of Kawit with that of a retainer who is offering her an ointment container to realize the finesse accorded the queen's figure (fig. 6). The detail of her coiffure, the sheerness of her shawl, and the gesture of her thumb and index finger set her figure apart from that of her less-embellished retainer, thereby underlining the difference in their social status. Equally appealing is the bold relief that characterizes some of the representations of Senwosret (Sesostris) I, as seen for example on his limestone pillar in Cairo. Here, again, one appreciates how the selective application of linear details to the kilt and headdress of this king call attention to his figure and emphasize his importance at the expense of the figure of the god Ptah, who nonetheless occupies primacy of place on the left-hand side of the composition.

The New Kingdom

The wealth and status enjoyed by a handful of courtiers of the New Kingdom is reflected by their tombs in Western Thebes and elsewhere. It would take volumes to address fully the artistic issues raised by these representations, but developments in the register system and in the elaboration of an already-existing painterly technique must be mentioned.

Although registers were usually horizontal from the Old Kingdom on, in the New Kingdom craftsmen introduced within the horizontal bands a series of undulating lines, doubtlessly intended to recall the hillocks of the Egyptian wilderness, the haunts of beasts and demons of all sorts. The desert hunt in the Old Kingdom tomb of Ptahhotep at Saqqara is representative of this tendency, which was further developed during the Eighteenth Dynasty. A secondary register in the tomb of Nakht is represented only as a continuous, sinuous line along which woodsmen fell trees. This concept appears to be pushed to its limits in a series of vignettes in the tomb of Qenamun, in which an ibex is brought to bay by a hound within a "pocket" of space. In a cattle scene in the tomb of Nebamun, the groundlines are totally removed for secondary

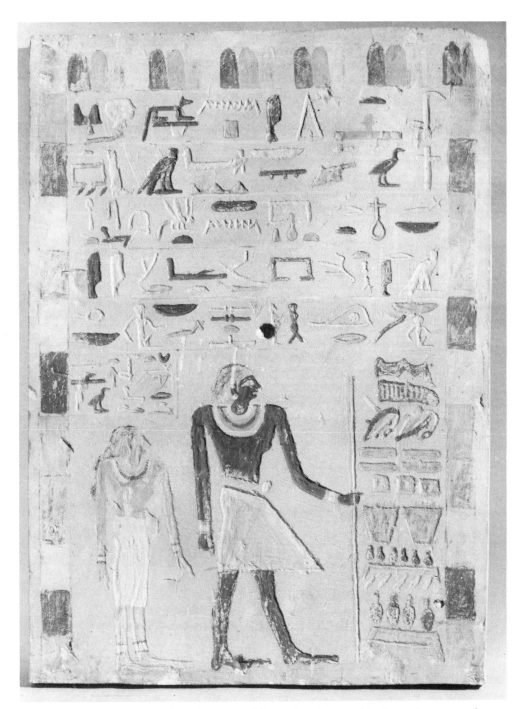

Fig. 5. Tomb stela of the official Maaty and his wife, who stand before a depiction of offerings that fills the register band. Above are five lines of inscription with an offering formula and the name and titles of the deceased. Painted limestone. Said to be from Nag‛ al-Dayr. First Intermediate Period, circa 2100 BCE. THE BROOKLYN MUSEUM, NEW YORK

registers, an artistic device encountered again in the Nineteenth Dynasty tomb of Ipuy; both of these seem to recall the scheme employed on the hunt palettes of the Naqada II period

mentioned above. The purpose of these experiments with the undulating or absent register lines was clearly to differentiate the fertile, productive landscape of the Nile Valley from the

Fig. 6. Detail or relief scene on the sarcophagus of the royal lady Kawit, who is shown seated holding a lotus flower to her nose and dipping her finger in a bowl of unguent proffered by a servant holding a fan. Limestone. From her tomb at Dayr al-Baḥri. Eleventh Dynasty, circa 1975 BCE. EGYPTIAN MUSEUM, CAIRO

wilds of the marginal land and deserts. One must, however, never lose sight of the fact that these experiments occurred within horizontal registers and never fully replaced them.

The dominance of the horizontal as an organizing principle in two-dimensional representations was successfully challenged by the artistic reforms of the Amarna period. One need only compare an entire scene from this period with

a scene from any other period, before or after, to appreciate the differences in approach. The lunette of Boundary Stela S at al-Amarna (fig. 7) is representative. Although the principal figures are arranged along a horizontal register line at the bottom, those depicted are arranged in ascending order, forming a triangular composition that rises obliquely up the picture surface, culminating in the centrally placed Aten (Aton). The

Fig. 7. Line drawing of the lunette relief of the rock-cut Boundary Stela S at al-Amarna, showing King Akhenaten with Queen Nefertiti and Meritaten and Meketaten, adoring the Aten depicted in the form of the solar disk. Eighteenth Dynasty, circa 1345 BCE. NORMAN DE GARIS DAVIES, *THE ROCK TOMBS OF EL AMARNA V* (1908)

movement up, as opposed to horizontally across, the picture plane and the concomitant replacing of the time-honored primacy of place at the left by an emphasis on the top center of the composition are revolutionary because they destroy the two invariable compositional concerns of all two-dimensional Egyptian representations both before and after. The experiment was short-lived and soon abandoned in favor of a return to orthodoxy. (See "Akhetaten: A Portrait in Art" in Part 5, Vol. II, and "The Hymn to Aten" in Part 8, Vol. III for more about Akhetaten and the Amarna period.)

At the same time that craftsmen were experimenting with the register system, the range of colors employed by the tomb painters appears to have increased significantly over what had previously been available. A modern critic recognizes a richness of hues and tones that far exceeds the preserved lexicographical nomenclature. One wonders, therefore, how the ancient Egyptians both perceived this apparently expanded palette and communicated with one another about the colors contained within. A great

deal more investigation is required before any answers can be found.

To experimentation with an expanded palette is to be added a second innovation, namely that of introducing—on a limited scale in some clearly defined passages within a tomb's decoration—a technique approximating a painterly approach in which color is allowed to bleed across color cells from one part of the image to the next. The genesis of this technique has been ascribed to a common practice of alternating lighter and darker values of the same hue in adjacent color cells for the skin tones of overlapping individual figures. This can be best observed in the coloring of the heads, fanned out like a deck of playing cards, in the tomb of Ramose (fig. 8). This juxtaposition of values of the same hue may have prompted some craftsmen to seek ways of representing the body emerging from beneath the gossamer costumes so popular in the New Kingdom. In one such scene, in the tomb of Nebamun, the artist painted the skin tones beneath the white garment a honey yellow, over which he then applied reddish lines indicating the folds of the

Fig. 8. Facsimile of a section of the funeral procession of the vizier Ramose, in his tomb at Thebes (no. 55), showing groups of men carrying grave goods and of mourning women. Painting on plaster. Eighteenth Dynasty, circa 1350 BCE. METROPOLITAN MUSEUM OF ART, NEW YORK

garments. The technique continued to be employed for this effect into the Twentieth Dynasty, at which time it was modified for the rendering of skin tones. The flesh of Nefertari in some, but not all, of the scenes in her tomb in the Valley of the Queens is rendered as a series of reddish values that blend into one in a way recalling the application of makeup. Although the motivation for and the significance of the appearance of this particular technique in this one tomb remain inexplicable, the rendering is a notable exception which represents virtually the only time in the history of ancient Egyptian painting when craftsmen attained chiaroscuro.

The artistic advances of the painters of the New Kingdom seem not to have survived the end of the Twentieth Dynasty. However, some of the vignettes in the tombs they decorated appear to have become classic, appreciated and perhaps even visited by later generations. Thus, the charming scene of a woman nursing her child beneath the shade of a tree, found in the Eighteenth Dynasty tomb of Menena (fig. 9), is repeated in the tomb of Montuemhat around 650, and the delightful scene of the three female musicians in the tomb of Nakht appears to have been varnished to protect it for the enjoyment of those who wended their way to the tomb in order to view it.

The Ptolemaic and Roman Periods

Few of the great temples of the pharaonic period are preserved well enough to permit a discussion of the designs and compositions of royal relief representations. Therefore, this section closes with a look at the pharaonic temples erected during the Ptolemaic and Roman periods whose form and function are fully tradi-

tional. It is becoming increasingly apparent that the designers of these temples used pattern books from which they derived cartoons and laid out grids on the walls in which to draw cartoons. Often scenes on the inner and outer faces of one and the same wall are linked both compositionally and thematically, despite the fact that an observer cannot see both images at the same time. This characteristic, termed a transparency because the mass of the intervening wall is disregarded, is indicative of the sophistication of the designers. Similarly, doorways seem to be

Fig. 9. Tomb of Menena at Thebes (no. 69), entrance hall, east wall, south section, detail showing a woman and child resting beneath a tree. Painting on plaster. Eighteenth Dynasty, circa 1400 BCE. RICHARD FAZZINI, *IMAGES FOR ETERNITY* (1975)

adorned with figures associated with ingress and egress, while supporting architectural elements are adorned with like-functioning deities. The decoration is, therefore, congruent with the function of the specific architectural feature.

SCULPTURE IN THE ROUND: GENERAL OBSERVATIONS

The three premises with which this essay was introduced also apply to sculpture in the round. The link between Egyptian hieroglyphs and two-dimensional representations, made above, includes sculpture as well.

Egyptian stone sculpture is the product of a process of attrition, whereby the surfaces of the statue are reduced by abrasion with a geologically harder material. As a result, this sculpture tends to be conceived as a series of broad planes that subtly merge into one another, all the more so since the hard stones employed by its craftsmen lacked tensile strength, which rendered it impossible to create images that broke out into the surrounding space in the manner of a Baroque statue by Bernini. For the most part, arms, legs, and attributes were shackled to the matrix of the block from which they were carved. Consequently, one encounters a greater amount of negative stone—that part of the block which remained behind after the statue was completed and which often served as a bridge, or link, that connected what would otherwise have been an element projecting into space with the composition proper. As a result, divisions between the planes of these different parts of the statue and their negative stone become blurred. It is not uncommon, therefore, for transitional areas, such as the intersection of an arm with a torso, to exhibit a lesser degree of finish than the rest of a piece.

Linear details, such as the incisions contributing to the emphasis of certain details and in the form of accompanying hieroglyphs, were usually added last, after which the image might be painted. In such a process effort was expended selectively on various parts of the statue so that each element did not receive the same amount of attention in design and execution. So, for example, heads may appear to have been more carefully crafted than the bodies to which they are attached, and on those heads individual features such as the ears may be emphasized at the expense of other features. The processes by which Egyptian sculpture was created did not demand that each passage of a statue be brought to the same level of completion and that each detail receive the same degree of attention in its design. Therefore, the criteria by which one judges the aesthetic achievement of Egyptian statuary are very, very different from the yardstick employed to measure the aesthetics of classical Greek art.

Statue Types

To these technical considerations must now be added those of form and function. Whenever one surveys the history of Egyptian sculpture, one is struck by its apparent invariability of types. So, for example, the male figure, confidently striding forward, arms held stiffly at its sides, has become, in its own way, an icon of ancient Egyptian statuary (fig. 10). When carved in stone, such images are usually provided with a back pillar, a rectangular section of the negative stone, running up the back of the statue in a line roughly corresponding to that of the spine, from the level of the feet to about that of the occipital bulge (it may terminate higher or lower), where it may end in a variety of shapes. The back pillar is normally inscribed with hieroglyphs containing a prayer and the name and titles of the owner. The meaning of the back pillar, which seems not to be specifically mentioned in surviving texts, is moot; but its appearance on striding as well as other types of statues is the clearest indication that such images were created for purposes other than mere visual commemoration.

The contents of the inscriptions on such statues generally conform to common cultural concerns of the elite of an historical period. None of these inscriptions, even the most blatantly biographical ones, celebrates the individual per se; all articulate pervasive societal concerns. The individual was subordinate to the social system so that no image was permissible which celebrated the role of one specific member at the expense of the community. There were no statues erected in "public squares" in commemoration of specific individuals for the performance

Fig. 10. Striding statue of the official Mitry, holding a staff and a scepter. Painted wood. From his tomb at Saqqara. Late Fifth or early Sixth Dynasty, circa 2350 BCE. METROPOLITAN MUSEUM OF ART, NEW YORK

of particular deeds. All of these sculptures were placed in exactly defined contexts, usually in temples or in tombs, in order to satisfy clearly articulated requirements, as formulated by the elite for whom they were commissioned.

Each succeeding historical epoch either adds a new element to the sculptural repertoire, eschews the use of an old one, or revives another long since dormant. It is, therefore, significant that the repertoire of types of monumental sculpture is, by any standard, relatively limited. And whereas one might suggest that images in smaller formats—those of servant figures and the like—seem to exhibit much more variety in their attitudes, it is well to remember that these smaller images are themselves but variations on established themes, comparable in their own way to the reworkings of themes in the concerti of Vivaldi.

Because of the nexus between Egyptian hieroglyphs and art, forms admissible in the former may appear as well in the latter. Since primacy of place is accorded the left in two-dimensional representations (fig. 4, Akhethotep, above), it should come as no surprise that the advanced "left" leg of such images is replicated by the advanced left leg of statues in the round. Moreover, hieroglyphs allow for truncated forms—a head, a foot, an eye. So, too, Egyptian art admits the existence of the bust as an independent artistic creation. During the Old Kingdom, the form of both the bust—as represented by that of Ankhhaef in Boston and that of the "reserve head" made from the neck upward (fig. 11)—were introduced. The significance of both remains moot, although the bust reappeared in the New Kingdom in contexts associated with ancestor worship. Its early appearance in the Fourth Dynasty antedates a parallel phenomenon in Roman art by more than two thousand years.

The block statue, first introduced in the Middle Kingdom, became an extremely popular type during the Third Intermediate Period and later. Some claim that the form is evocative of the original mound of creation that emerged from the waters of chaos when they were struck by the initial rays of the sun on the first day of the world. Others regard the image as an allusion to the resurrection of the god Osiris, who emerged from his burial box when he was revived. Whatever the interpretation, this type, once established, allowed for several variations. A secondary figure might be added in high relief to the front of the statue (fig. 12), or in the case of Senenmut, he might be shown holding a royal princess. Occasionally several figures, each in the block-

Fig. 11. Reserve head of Nefer. The head had been ritually mutilated before being interred within the tomb, as were almost all heads in this category. Limestone. From Giza. Fourth Dynasty, circa 2500 BCE. MUSEUM OF FINE ARTS, BOSTON

Egyptian hieroglyphs can be arranged in such as way as to form puns, notably by combining into one sign several different ones so that they "spell" out a message. Since the form of Egyptian sculpture is wed to that of the hieroglyphs, many statues could be designed as rebuses, or as visual puns in which elements might be combined in such a way as to create a plurality of meanings. Statues inscribed with the name of Senenmut are among the earliest of the type known, but that does not warrant ascribing their introduction to him, particularly since the exact meaning of his inscriptions, in which he alludes to having "invented" certain statue types, is vague. On a statue in the Brooklyn Museum, an inscription states that Senenmut is proffering an image of the cobra-goddess Renenutet to Montu. But when that offering is viewed from the front, its elements—human arms, the serpent, and cow's horns and sun-disk—as hieroglyphs spell one of the names of Hatshepsut, so that the whole thereby affirms Senenmut's fealty to that

Fig. 12. Block statue of Senwosretsenbefny, with a small female figure between its feet. Quartzite. Late Twelfth Dynasty, circa 1800 BCE. THE BROOKLYN MUSEUM, NEW YORK

statue pose, might be sculpted in a row from a single block of stone. Despite the popularity of the form, there are no known images of pharaohs as block statues, and women appear as such very rarely and only in association with block figures of men in the same statue group. During the Third Intermediate Period, block statues tend to be covered with innumerable inscriptions, which often also accompany elaborate scenes in relief.

2545

monarch (fig. 13). Similar rebus statues are common from the reign of Ramses (Ramesses) II and also in the Thirtieth Dynasty.

The standard-bearing statue represents a third type that was common in the New Kingdom. The standards are topped with heads either of deities or of the reigning monarch and serve several purposes (fig. 14). On one level they may commemorate the presentation of liturgical implements displayed during temple rituals; alternatively, they may be employed to assure the deceased of adequate provisions in the hereafter. As with block statues, woman are rarely represented as offering bearers, the sole known exception being an image perhaps to be identified as Nefertari, wife of Ramses II, in the Harer Collection.

Fig. 14. Striding statue of Saesi, bearing the standard of the god Wepwawet. Granite. Probably from Asyut. Nineteenth Dynasty, circa 1225 BCE. KUNSTHISTORISCHES MUSEUM, VIENNA

Fig. 13. Statue of Senenmut, kneeling and offering a rebus consisting of a uraeus with a crown of horns and disk and the *ka* hieroglyph underneath and forming the prenomen Maatkare of Queen Hatshepsut. Gray-black granite. From Armant. Eighteenth Dynasty, circa 1470 BCE. THE BROOKLYN MUSEUM, NEW YORK

These brief discussions of a few types illustrate how each was created to satisfy specific needs of an elite. One cannot, therefore, evaluate these statues from the contemporary artistic standards of the West, because few ancient Egyptians obtained permission to own a statue and fewer still were conversant with their fullest meaning. Linked to the hieroglyphs and expressing specific social concerns—at least to some ancient Egyptians if not to modern critics—Egyptian sculpture developed over time as a canonical enterprise relying on a limited range of types that, once introduced into the repertoire, remained invariable. This is the reason why "all Egyptian sculpture looks alike" is the common view of the general public. There were, however, perceptible changes over time, which the following diachronic survey will attempt to reveal.

A DIACHRONIC SURVEY OF EGYPTIAN STATUARY

The Predynastic Period

The history of Egyptian sculpture apparently begins with objects such as a remarkable terra-cotta head excavated in 1982 and dated to the late fifth millennium (fig. 15). This effigy of about ten centimeters (four inches) already exhibits two characteristics common to Egyptian sculpture of all periods: modeling in broad planes and a reduction of some features with a concomitant emphasis on others. Here the ears have been ignored, whereas the other orifices of the head—eyes, nostrils, and mouth—are boldly present.

The chronological sequence of figurines assigned to both of the Naqada periods is debated. For the moment, an ivory male figure has been assigned to Naqada I. Here again, certain fea-

Fig. 16. Female figurine with head resembling a bird and undifferentiated legs. Unfired clay. From Maʿmariya, near Hierakonpolis. Naqada II period, circa 3500 BCE. THE BROOKLYN MUSEUM, NEW YORK

Fig. 15. Painted terra-cotta head of the Merimda culture, one of the earliest pieces of sculpture from Egypt. From Merimda Benisalama. Late fifth millennium BCE. EGYPTIAN MUSEUM, CAIRO

tures are exaggerated at the expense of others and the introduction of secondary materials, in the form of inlays for the eyes, begins a tradition for such embellishment that will continue to the end of Egyptian sculpture in the first century CE.

Naqada II witnessed the continuation of these concerns, as seen, for example, in the figure of a bearded male figure that, to judge from the suspension loop in his hair or headdress, served as an amulet. The most evocative figures from this period are highly stylized female effigies with heads resembling those of birds. The figurines in Brooklyn (fig. 16) are exemplary. These, sculpted in clay which has not been fired, were painted and interred with the deceased; as many as sixteen have been found in a single grave. Although their significance is debated, these figures, like the head from the fifth millennium, exhibit an interest in sculptural values that are emphasized by modeling in broad planes and by the elimination of certain details in order to emphasize others.

These same concerns are evident in a remarkable group of colossal statues of the god Min, discovered by Sir William Matthews Flinders Petrie at Coptos, perhaps inscribed for several late predynastic kings, of whom the last was Narmer, a king traditionally associated with Egypt's unification. Pillar-like in their conception and conforming to the prevailing aesthetic dialectic of reduction and emphasis, these statues stand at the beginning of a long tradition.

Subsequent Development

As one surveys the surviving sculpture from the first three dynasties, one can observe how the craftsmen struggled to free the image from the block of stone from which it was wrought. The statue of a lion in Berlin from the Early Dynastic period or of the Third Dynasty kneeling priest in Cairo reveal this struggle of the craftsmen with their material. The processes of attrition enabled them to block out the major forms of the feline and the human figure, the toes and lower torso of which are allowed to coalesce into the garment belted about the waist. In a way, these images parallel the unfinished statues of Michelangelo in their effort to free themselves from their material.

With each new statue, the craftsmen sought new solutions to sculptural problems that arose. The solutions offered by these anonymous masters for the inclusion of attributes that in reality are often cantilevered into space are nothing short of ingenious. For example, on a statue in the British Museum, the adze, which symbolizes the trade of a shipbuilder, is placed so that the joint of the handle and its blade rests comfortably on his shoulder. The staff and baton carried by Sepa in his statues in the Louvre are pulled into the vertical plane of the statue in a novel way. The mace held by Mycerinus in one of his statues in Boston rests on the side of the throne on which the goddess Hathor sits, while the emblem of the goddess of the Hare Nome (prov-

ince) appears in high relief on the statue's back slab. In later times attributes were carefully selected so that they could be easily worked into sculptures.

Many of the types that were to become staples of the repertoire of Egyptian sculpture were introduced during this period. In addition to the striding male figure, one encounters seated figures, both for deities and royal personages and for male and female courtiers. As examples one may cite the Second Dynasty statues of Khasekhem in Cairo and Oxford; that of Mycerinus standing beside a seated Hathor in Boston; and the Cairo statues of Rahotep and Nofret. Images of seated figures in stone disappeared from the sculptural repertoire about 650 BCE and were briefly reintroduced around the time of the Roman emperor Augustus (30 BCE–14 CE) for statues of intercessors that are among the latest pharaonic statues sculpted in Egypt (fig. 17).

That a type, once introduced, might be long-lived and even translated into another medium is clear from a study of the statue of Chephren discovered in a pit in his Valley Temple (now in Cairo). In many ways this figure represents the culmination of all of the efforts of the preceding periods. The problems posed to the craftsmen of rendering into stone those attributes that project into space—and cannot be readily cantilevered by sculpting them in stone—was neatly solved by replacing all such objects in the fisted hand of the sovereign with a cylindrical object ending in two streamers that have been identified as a bolt of cloth. The body emerges from the matrix of stone, but the negative space remains visible between the feet and the throne and between the arms and the torso. Strict bilateral symmetry is subtly avoided by the dissimilar attitudes of the two hands. And the falcon peering up from behind as it protects the king becomes an icon repeated time and again both in sculpture in the round and in relief. From this period as well comes the image of the king kneeling as he proffers two *nw*-pots to a deity. The earliest example is that identified as Mycerinus, but the image is long-lived and frequently repeated in statues inscribed for Hatshepsut of the Eighteenth Dynasty.

The type of group statue depicting Mycerinus with a deity or nome personification was repeated by the craftsmen who did the group of

Fig. 17. Seated dignitary, one of the last statues in pharaonic style ever made in Egypt, circa 50–100 CE. The statue is made of black basalt and was found at Karanis, at the northern edge of the Faiyum. KELSEY MUSEUM OF ARCHAEOLOGY, UNIVERSITY OF MICHIGAN, ANN ARBOR

into the framework of existing types. Coeval with images of the physically handicapped and of the ideal type in the Old Kingdom are those that appear somewhat abstracted and stylized. An early example is one of the wooden statues of Methethy in Brooklyn (fig. 18). While often cited as an example of sensitively rendered introspection and vulnerability, these qualities would have originally been completely masked by the application of painted plaster that covered

Fig. 18. Statue of Methethy, one of a number presumably from his tomb, which was probably at Saqqara. Late Fifth or early Sixth Dynasty, circa 2350 BCE. Painted wood. THE BROOKLYN MUSEUM, NEW YORK

Pharaoh Sahure in New York and, on present evidence, provided the impetus for any number of the late Old Kingdom statues of family groups. Among the most accomplished is that of the dwarf Seneb ("he who is healthy") in which his physical disability is wonderfully disguised by placing his children in the position that a normal person's legs would occupy, which serves to affirm the appropriateness of his name. To this image may be added those of the obese, such as that of Ka-aper in Cairo, and of the hunchback. Such depictions are not clinically accurate records of the physical conditions shown; rather they are generic representations of certain states of existence that have been artfully manipulated

the surfaces, imparting an appearance totally different from what is now seen.

This brief survey of some sculptural types of the Old Kingdom reveals that several different artistic idioms were contemporary, and that they ran the gamut from the ideal to the more naturalistic to the stylized. One of the most vexing art historical issues is the explication of this dialectic; to date, no generally accepted theory has been formulated, as the following discussion of Middle Kingdom sculpture will show.

During the Middle Kingdom, new forms were introduced, the most novel of which is the appearance of signs of age on the faces of the monarchs, clearly revealed in certain images of Senwosret III (fig. 19). Termed "portraits" in the Western sense by some, interpreted in the Shakespearean sense of "heavy is the head that wears the crown" by others, these faces exhibit a facet of ancient Egyptian art which surfaces from time to time. Recent investigators have established that such visages first appear on statues of high officials, thereby effectively exploding the long-held axiom of art historians that royal workshops established types which the courtiers then imitated. In this case, the courtiers were in the van of artistic production. Since the creation of art is a canonical enterprise among members of the elite and since members of that elite did effectively challenge the political primacy of several of their members during the Middle Kingdom, one can cautiously suggest that the appearance of these images, marked by signs of age, represented an effort of this disaffected social group to visually distinguish itself by divorcing its chosen artistic style from that associated with the monarchs of the Old Kingdom—the latter style being the one used to depict the other members of the elite that the disaffected were challenging. In an art rooted in hieroglyphs, which are themselves based on manipulations of nature, visual manifestations of political statements could only be couched in modifications of tradition. Exaggerations in either direction from the norm, hyper-idealism or "super-realism," as in these images, are best regarded as political statements challenging the status quo rather than as expressions of artistic license or examples of ego images—that is, portraits in a Western sense.

One could defend such a position by survey-

Fig. 19. Small, seated statue of King Senwosret III. From Hierakonpolis. Late Twelfth Dynasty, circa 1820 BCE. Black Granite. THE BROOKLYN MUSEUM, NEW YORK

ing the art of the New Kingdom, particularly of the Eighteenth Dynasty. In an effort to establish their legitimacy as the new rulers of Egypt, the sovereigns and courtiers of the early Eighteenth Dynasty revived types current in the Middle Kingdom. Most of these were created in an idealizing style, as seen for example in an image of Thutmose (Tuthmosis) III in the Cairo Museum. With the passage of time, the image of the monarch was manipulated away from the norm toward what some have termed a more expressive style, as seen in certain faces of Thutmose IV, the slanted eyes of which anticipate those of Amenhotep (Amenophis) III. From this perspective the eyes of certain statues of Akhenaten (Amenhotep IV) are taken from a well-established tradition (the sandstone statues of Amenhotep IV from the peristyle court east of the Temple of Amun at Karnak compare with the Osiride statues of King Nebhepetre Montuhotep from Dayr al-Bahri, from the Eleventh Dynasty). This detail of the face is then incorporated into a visual system employing traditional typologies, the style of which has been fundamentally altered. The "ideal," characterizing much of the royal art of the early Eighteenth Dynasty, becomes "realistic" in the art of Akhenaten as the visual manifestation of his new policy. This emphasis on one of the polarities into which Egyptian sculpture can be divided coincides with the way the Amarna period witnessed the replacement of the horizontal register system with one emphasizing centrality in two-dimensional representations. In both instances the change from the traditional to the novel is a societal one, because art in ancient Egyptian civilization is subordinate to the concerns of the elite. Akhenaten and his coterie, however small, might, as the elite, manipulate the existing canonical image, which as transformed, was pressed into service as the new canonical image for a new societal agenda. The fall of Akhenaten and the excision of his name from official records coincided with the return to the canonical images of the pre-Amarna period. Thus art, religion, and society returned to the status quo ante.

The same conclusion appears to be valid for the "portraits" of private officials that characterize the art of the Late Period. Certain images from the Twenty-fifth and Twenty-sixth dynasties, such as those of Montuemhat (fig. 20, strid-

Fig. 20. Striding statue of Montuemhat, mayor of Thebes at the end of the Twenty-fifth Dynasty and the beginning of the Twenty-sixth, circa 650 BCE. Granite. Excavated at Karnak. EGYPTIAN MUSEUM, CAIRO

ing statue), and from the Ptolemaic period, with the head in the Bastis Collection being representative, depict members of the Egyptian elite in a time-honored style first introduced by their counterparts during the Middle Kingdom as an alternative to the style of the monarchs whose positions of authority and prestige the members of this elite have assumed. From a historical perspective, Montuemhat and the anonymous official represented in the Bastis head were the de facto rulers totally responsible for the administration of aspects of the nation's bureaucracy; in those areas the office of pharaoh existed only in the abstract. Far from being portraits in the

Western sense, these images, like those of the obese, the dwarf, and the hunchback of the Old Kingdom, define the elite in terms of an idiom that distances them from the traditional depictions of monarchs whose duties they are now discharging.

The art of the Third Intermediate Period, once considered to be provincial and backward, is now regarded as highly accomplished. Metal sculpture is known from the Old Kingdom in the form of the hammered sheet metal statue of Pepy I (Meryre) in Cairo and from the Middle Kingdom in the hoard of copper or bronze figures of kings and courtiers from the Faiyum now divided among museums of Paris and Munich, and the Ortiz Collection in Geneva. However, the metal statues of the Third Intermediate Period represent a high-water mark. Cast in bronze by the lost-wax method, these figures are often a meter high and embellished with inlays of either gold or silver. Several represent the human torso in tripartition, articulating the pectoral regions, rib cage, and lower abdomen, in contrast with the earlier tradition of bipartition, in which rib cage and lower abdomen coalesce into one form. Images of courtiers offering statuettes of deities (fig. 21) become popular and provide the model for the profusion of such statues in stone during the Late Period. It would appear, moreover, that this Egyptian technology was imported by Greeks visiting Egypt to the island of Samos and there used to give birth to the hollow-casting metal industry of an emerging Greece in the seventh century BCE.

Egyptian influence on the arts of other cultures quickened in the period after 650. Egyptian artists contributed substantially to the art of the Persian Empire. The statue of Darius, king of kings, discovered at Susa (biblical Shushan, modern Shush), was created for the monarch in Egypt by Egyptian craftsmen. (For a picture and further discussion of this statue, see the chapter "Art and Archaeology of the Achaemenid Empire," later in this section.)

The Persians, expelled in the fourth century, were soon followed by the aggressive rulers of the Thirtieth Dynasty, under whose patronage the arts flourished. To this period belong such wonderful creations as Brooklyn's "Dattari Statue" (fig. 22), representing a reinterpretation of the type first introduced during the Old King-

Fig. 21. Statue of the official Khonsumeh proffering an image of the god Osiris. Third Intermediate Period, late Twenty-first or early Twenty-second Dynasty, circa 925 BCE. Bronze, inlaid with electrum and silver. ÄGYPTISCHES MUSEUM, BERLIN

dom, and the Brooklyn Green head, indicative of the status of the elite at Karnak.

The annexation of Egypt by Alexander III "the Great" and the establishment of the Macedonian Greek monarchy in 305 by Ptolemy I Soter did not effectively alter the entrenched, privileged socio-economic position of the Egyptian elite with regard to its art. Numerous images characterized by signs of age were created, and these have now begun to be grouped into specific typologies. At least one new type, that of the striding, draped male figure, now appears for the first time in monumental stone sculpture, having been depicted earlier in both relief and

Fig. 22. Striding male statue from the reign of Nectanebo I (380–362 BCE), called the "Dattari Statue" after its first modern owner, a nineteenth-century collector of antiquities resident in Egypt. Black diorite. THE BROOKLYN MUSEUM, NEW YORK

small scale. More than 150 examples of such statues are known. These and seated figures (fig. 17) continued to be sculpted in Egypt until about 50 CE, when as far as we can tell, pharaonic sculpture ceased to be created. Three centuries later, the last hieroglyphic inscription was composed, and then a curtain of silence fell.

First-hand knowledge of ancient Egypt's culture was lost from the fourth century until the decipherment of the hieroglyphs by Jean François Champollion in the early nineteenth century (see "The Decipherment of Ancient Near Eastern Scripts" in Part 1, Vol. I). For fifteen hundred years, during which time the West was constantly reminded of the achievements of an-

cient Greece and Rome because their languages were not forgotten and could be translated and understood, the culture of ancient Egypt was transmitted via Greek and Roman sources in an imperfect and garbled fashion. Only in the late nineteenth and early twentieth centuries did scholars first began a systematic study of ancient Egyptian art history, and that history was modeled on patterns and prejudices of Western aesthetics that are still being improperly applied to the study of Egyptian art. (See "Egypt in European Thought" in Part 1, Vol. I.) This essay, which deliberately deviates from traditional art histories, is intended to suggest avenues of more productive investigation through integrating Egyptian art into the culture that produced it and simultaneously divorcing it from cultures with which it has nothing in common.

BIBLIOGRAPHY

The Theoretical Basis for a History of Egyptian Art

JOHN BAINES, "Color Terminology and Color Classification: Ancient Egyptian Color Terminology and Polychromy," *American Anthropologist* 87, no. 2 (1985), "Communication and Display: The Integration of Early Egyptian Art and Writing," *Antiquity* 63, no. 240 (1989); and "Restricted Knowledge, Hierarchy, and Decorum: Modern Perceptions and Ancient Institutions," *Journal of the American Research Center in Egypt* 27 (1990), "On the Status and Purposes of Ancient Egyptian Art," *Cambridge Archaeological Journal* 4, no. 1 (1994); ROBERT STEVEN BIANCHI, "An Ideal Image," in *Festschrift for Cyril Aldred*, edited by JOHN RUFFLE ET AL. (forthcoming); WHITNEY DAVIS, *The Canonical Tradition in Ancient Egyptian Art* (1989); HENRY GEORGE FISHER, *L'écriture et l'art de l'Égypte ancienne: Quatre leçons sur la paléographie et l'epigraphie pharaoniques* (1986), and "The Origins of Egyptian Hieroglyphs," in *The Origins of Writing*, edited by WAYNE M. SENNER (1989); and HERMAN TE VELDE, "Egyptian Hieroglyphs as Signs, Symbols, and Gods," *Visible Religion* 4–5 (1985–1986), and "Scribes and Literacy in Ancient Egypt," in *Scripta Signa Vocis: Studies About Scripts, Scriptures, Scribes, and Languages in the Near East, Presented to G. H. Hospers*, edited by H. L. J. VANSTIPHOUT ET AL. (1986).

Predynastic

MICHAEL A. HOFFMAN, *Egypt Before the Pharaohs: The Prehistoric Foundations of Egyptian Civilization*

(2nd ed., 1991); WINIFRED NEEDLER, *Predynastic and Archaic Egypt in the Brooklyn Museum*, Wilbour Monographs 9 (1984); and DIETRICH WILDUNG, *Ägypten vor den Pyramiden*, exhibition catalog, Munich (1981).

Old Kingdom

WILLIAM STEVENSON SMITH, *A History of Egyptian Sculpture and Painting in the Old Kingdom* (1946; 2nd ed. 1949), and CYRIL ALDRED ET AL., eds., *Le temps des pyramides: De la préhistoire aux Hyksos, 1560 av. J.-C.* (1978).

Middle Kingdom

JANINE BOURRIAU, *Pharaohs and Mortals: Egyptian Art in the Middle Kingdom* (1988); ELISABETH DE-LANGE, *Catalogue des statues égyptiennes du Moyen Empire, 2060–1560 avant J.-C.*, catalog Musée du Louvre (1987); and EDWARD L. B. TERRACE, *Egyptian Paintings of the Middle Kingdom: The Tomb of Djehuty-Nekht* (1968).

New Kingdom and Third Intermediate Period

CYRIL ALDRED ET AL., *L'Empire des conquérants: L'É-gypte au Nouvel Empire (1560–1070)* (1979); ROBERT STEVEN BIANCHI, "Nofertari, Her Life and Her Art," in *Nofertari for Whom the Sun Shines*, J. Paul Getty Museum (forthcoming); RICHARD A. FAZZINI, *Egypt:*

Dynasty XXII–XXV, in *Iconography of Religions*, edited by TH. P. VAN BAAREN ET AL., Section 16: Egypt, fascicle 10 (1988); *Ägyptens Aufstieg zur Weltmacht*, exhibition catalog Roemer-Pelizaeus-Museum Hildesheim (1987); *Egypt's Golden Age: The Art of Living in the New Kingdom, 1558–1085 B.C.*, exhibition catalog, Museum of Fine Arts, Boston (1982); and HOURIG SOUROUZIAN, *Les monuments du roi Merenptah*, Sonderschrift Deutsches Archäologisches Institut, Abteilung Kairo 22 (1989).

Ptolemaic and Roman Periods

CYRIL ALDRED ET AL., *L'Égypte du crépuscule: De Tanis à Méroë: 1070 av. J.-C.–IVe siècle apr. J.-C.* (1980), and ROBERT STEVEN BIANCHI ET AL., *Cleopatra's Egypt: Age of the Ptolemies*, exhibition catalog, The Brooklyn Museum (1988).

Illustrations of the Monuments

ARNE EGGEBRECHT, *Das Alte Ägypten: 3000 Jahre Geschichte und Kultur des Pharaonenreiches* (1984); RICHARD A. FAZZINI ET AL., *Ancient Egyptian Art in the Brooklyn Museum* (1989); MOHAMED SALEH and HOURIG SOUROUZIAN, *The Egyptian Museum Cairo*, official catalogue (1987); DONALD SPANEL, *Through Ancient Eyes: Egyptian Portraiture* (1988); and EDWARD L. B. TERRACE and HENRY GEORGE FISCHER, *Treasures of Egyptian Art from the Cairo Museum 22* (1970).

SEE ALSO **Artisans and Artists in Pharaonic Egypt** (Part 4, Vol. I); **Palaces and Temples of Ancient Egypt** (Part 4, Vol. I); **The History of Ancient Egypt: An Overview** (Part 5, Vol. II); **Jewelry and Personal Arts in Ancient Egypt** (Part 7, Vol. III); and various chapters in PART 5: HISTORY AND CULTURE, VOL. II.

Music and Dance in Pharaonic Egypt

ROBERT D. ANDERSON

IN ANCIENT EGYPT there was much concern to document many aspects of daily life, so the absence of any preserved musical notation or written hints on choreography from antiquity suggests that such texts did not exist. Yet the importance of music to the Egyptians is demonstrated in many ways. Many of Egypt's gods were closely associated with music; there are references to music, both serious and cautionary, in Egyptian literature and in writings about Egypt by classical authors; museum collections preserve musical instruments once used by the Egyptians, many of them lavishly crafted; music played its part in religious scenes on temple walls; and chamber groups were commonly and attractively represented in tomb scenes. The fact that at least from the time of the Old Kingdom court officials held titles involving music and dance implies that both were already highly organized. It seems probable, therefore, that as with so many Egyptian crafts, music and dance were traditional skills and maybe hereditary, learned by oral precept and practical example.

MUSIC AND THE GODS

Hathor

Deities mainly connected with music were the goddess Hathor, represented by a cow, and her son Ihy. Hathor's temple at Dendara (Iunet, ancient Tentyra) has columns shaped like an Egyptian sistrum. To the left of the sanctuary is "the shrine of the sistrum," containing hymns to Hathor and showing the goddess herself holding alternately the sistrum and the tambourine. In the Dendara crypts are depicted richly ornamented sistra that once formed part of the temple treasure, and it is the sistrum that Ihy usually carries. A late hymn at Dendara in Hathor's honor mentions her cult objects—such as the *menat,* a bead necklace with golden counterpoises—and links her worship with music and dance:

> We play the drum for your spirit,
> We dance for your majesty,
> We uplift you to the skies.
> For you are the mistress of the arched sistrum,
> Of the *menat* and the *naos* sistrum,
> The mistress of jubilation,
> For whose spirit music is performed.

A further text in the Dendara crypts implies orgiastic worship when Hathor is described as "leader of the choral dance, the bestower of the drunkenness that knows no end." It was indeed by her own drunkenness that the goddess was distracted in the Egyptian myth of the *Destruction of Mankind.* On that occasion she was the instrument of Re; as goddess of love, she also inspired his affection. (See "Myth and Mythmaking in Ancient Egypt" in Part 8, Vol. III.) This was pithily expressed in the *Contendings of Horus and Seth*. When Re is exhausted by the long court proceedings, Hathor comes before him, uncovers her private parts, and makes him laugh with such pleasure that he resumes the hearing. Hathor was also a goddess of foreign lands. In an Old Kingdom spell from the Pyramid Texts, the deceased king, who desires to reach the courts of Re, claims to be a "pygmy of 'the dances of god' who diverts the god in front of his great throne," pretending to be a pygmy from Hathor's Africa. On southern journeys Hathor took the form of a lioness; when she returned in peace, she was welcomed in her Greco-Roman period shrine at Philae by much music making and dance.

Among those performing for Hathor at Philae is the god Bes, dancing on this occasion to the music of a harp he is himself playing. A domestic god who helped at childbirth, Bes shakes his tambourine in jubilation in many a statuette, and his figure was sometimes tattooed on the legs of slave girl musicians and dancers (fig. 1).

Isis and Osiris

Greek tradition had a lofty view of Egyptian music. Philo of Alexandria (first century CE) maintained that Moses had been taught from Egyptian textbooks the lore of meter, rhythm, and harmony. Plato claimed that Egypt was the one country where the young might not pick up tunes or lyrics as they wished, since the goddess Isis had long since established melodic shapes of a natural truth and aptness. This high conception of Egyptian music influenced modern Europe, too, with Mozart giving maximum dignity to his priests' music in *The Magic Flute* and their hymning of Isis and Osiris. Plutarch wrote that Osiris civilized the world not by arms but by persuasive discourse and the power of music. Paradoxically, in Egypt itself, where Osiris was Lord of Silence, his rites might not be started by any singer or instrumentalist. At the raising of the *djed*-column, however, a public ceremony symbolic of the god's resurrection, exuberance was such that music was appropriate.

Isis, whose religion developed in the Mediterranean world a considerable austerity and moral

Fig. 1. Painted wooden statuette of Bes dancing and holding a tambourine. New Kingdom. Provenance unknown. BRITISH MUSEUM, LONDON

strength, could strike a sinner blind with her sistrum or, as in Apuleius's novel (second century CE), restore Lucius by means of it from ass to man. The potency of music among the gods is further illustrated by Plutarch's comment that the trumpet might not be played at Busiris, a place specially sacred to Osiris, since its sound was like the braying of an ass, an animal identified with the god Seth, brother and murderer of Osiris. A strange scene on a late Roman coffin in Berlin shows Isis playing the trumpet at her husband Osiris, perhaps to avert with his own instrument the evil influence of Seth and recall scenes from further north where the goddess 'Anat is shown serenading Baal. (See "Myth and Mythmaking in Canaan and Ancient Israel" in Part 8, Vol. III.)

MUSIC IN EGYPTIAN LITERATURE

Egyptian literature was fully aware of music's power and influence. The young scribe had to copy cautionary tales about pupils who had gone astray and become "like a broken rudder, like a shrine without its god." The reason was love of drink, learning to sing to the flute, pipe, and lyre, and sitting by a girl with garland awry until he started drumming on his paunch, was unable to stand, and fell prostrate in the mud. The hero of the Nakht-Sobek cycle of love poems knows that with song and dance, and wine and ale to confuse his girl, he will "gain her this night."

The Egyptians also understood that at moments of crisis, music might be a source of calm and solace. In the last of the stories about King Khufu and the Magicians, the four goddesses, Isis, Nephthys, Meskhenet and Heket, who are to aid the priest's wife Reddedet in childbirth and thus bring the Fifth Dynasty into being, disguise themselves as itinerant musicians. (See "Tales of Magic and Wonder from Ancient Egypt" in Part 9, earlier in this volume.) When their task was done, they caused to be heard from a sealed room "the sound of singing, music, dancing, and exultation" as a sign that the newborn babies would become royal. The *Story of Sinuhe* has the exiled hero of the title so altered on his return to Egypt that consternation ensued among the royal family. That was the moment for the young princes and princesses to hand the king their *menats*, rattles, and sistra with the words: "May your arms reach out to what is beautiful, O enduring king, to the ornaments of the Lady of Heaven." As comfort to Wen Amun (Wenamun), the Egyptian envoy thwarted in his search for cedar to make the boat of Amun, the prince of Byblos (modern Jubayl) sends Tanetne, an Egyptian songstress, with the instruction: "Sing for him: don't let his mind be preoccupied with worry."

THE INSTRUMENTS

Surviving musical instruments fall into four main groups: idiophones (percussion); membra-nophones (drums); aerophones (wind); and chordophones (strings). The first is the group most fully represented in museums; but there is no sure knowledge of the rhythms they and the membranophones defined. The most serious attempts to reconstruct ancient Egyptian music have been based on the wind and string instruments. The closest approximation has perhaps come from the bronze and silver trumpets found in the tomb of Tutankhamun (fig. 2). These have been sounded in modern times, but how far the skill and ambition of a contemporary bandsman matches or exceeds that of an ancient Egyptian is uncertain. Other wind instruments, made of reed or wood, have dried out and shrunk with age, so that the spacing of the holes is no longer a sure guide to the original sounds. With string instruments the main problem is that the actual strings are usually missing, and where they have survived, there is no information about the tension to which they were held.

Clappers, with either one or two held in each hand, are among the earliest idiophones. Fine examples from the beginning of the Dynastic period have their ends carved to represent animal heads or, occasionally, a bearded man. But the most common type is shaped to represent the human hand itself with the forearm, which symbolizes the most basic form of rhythmic activity. Such clappers are usually made from bone or wood, and the central feature is the face of Hathor (fig. 3). Many clappers are worked to a very high standard of craftsmanship, with roundel ornaments and hieroglyphic inscriptions. Some examples recovered from tombs seem too delicate for actual use; they are more like models or clappers for eternity.

The instrument that characterized Egypt for the ancient world was the sistrum. Virgil put the "native sistrum" (*Aeneid* 8) into the hands of Cleopatra VII Philopator when rallying her navy at the Battle of Actium, and this was the instrument that spread around the Roman world with the worship of Isis.

In Egypt proper the sistrum had two main forms, both associated with Hathor. One had the rods and sounding plates contained within an arch, the other within a small rectangular *naos* or shrine. The two sistrum types had a Hathor head represented above the handle; in the

attention of a god or warding off evil; models and votive instruments usually take this shape. In the hypostyle hall at Karnak, Hathor herself holds an arched sistrum; but often both types are represented together. There is a scene from Kom al-Hisn (ancient Imu) in which a teacher with an arched sistrum instructs a group of ten girls, each holding a *naos* sistrum (fig. 4). This may imply either that the pupils are going through the correct motions on model instruments or that little distinction was made between the arched and *naos* sistrum.

The importance of the sistrum in temple ritual may be gauged from the duties of the New Kingdom and Late Period god's wives of Amun. These were usually royal princesses, and it was among their responsibilities to play the sistrum

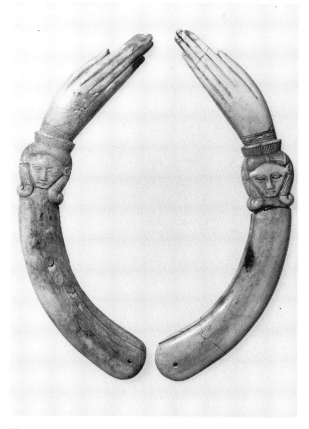

Fig. 2. Silver trumpet with its painted wooden core, found in the tomb of Tutankhamun, circa 1325 BCE; Cairo Museum. PHOTOGRAPH COURTESY OF HARRY BURTON

Amarna period, however, when Nefertiti is sometimes shown with the instrument, Hathor disappears and the handle assumes a plant form. The *naos* sistrum was confined to Egypt and had mainly religious significance in attracting the

Fig. 3. Pair of curved bone clappers in the form of hands with Hathor heads below. New Kingdom. Said to be from Thebes. BRITISH MUSEUM, LONDON

Fig. 4. Relief scene in the Middle Kingdom tomb of Khesuwer at Kom el-Hisn, showing a priest giving instruction in sistrum-playing and hand-clapping to ten girls. Drawing by Boris Eisenberg. ALBRECHT REITHMÜLLER AND FRIEDER ZAMINER, EDS., *DIE MUSIK DES ALTERTUMS* (1989)

before the state god. Its significance continued into Roman times, as is shown by its appearance in the hands of the emperors Augustus and Nero on the temple walls of Dendara.

Bells and cymbals were latecomers to Egyptian music, with most surviving instruments dating from the Roman period. Sometimes a bell had its body shaped to the features of the god Bes; in other cases a Bes head decorated the front of the bell and three animal heads adorned the rest of it. Bells and cymbals were usually of bronze, and some of the ancient shapes and sizes have survived in the Coptic church of Egypt.

Drums and tambourines of various shapes form the group of membranophones. A Twelfth Dynasty cylindrical drum from Beni Hasan is the earliest known to us. These instruments, most often barrel shaped, were suspended by a cord from the player's neck and struck at each end. Their use was mainly military, but they also appeared at the foundation ceremonies of temples.

A rectangular tambourine or frame-drum with concave sides was briefly popular during the Eighteenth Dynasty. It was played as part of the chamber ensembles at banquets and had an outdoor function at moments of celebration, especially at Akhenaten's capital, Akhetaten (modern Tell al-Amarna). The round tambourine is again a New Kingdom instrument but was common into Greco-Roman times. It was a favorite of the god Bes, who plays it exuberantly on the chair of Sitamun in the Cairo Museum; it was also used in outdoor rejoicings and for the expression of wild grief by professional mourners at funerals. A workshop in the Delta for the making of drums was found in the early 1980s. It dates from the Second Intermediate period, and the instruments made there were like the modern *darabukka*, an open-ended ceramic vase covered with a drum-skin.

The end-blown flute is the earliest attested among the aerophones. A fox or man in a fox mask plays it on a late Predynastic schist palette from Hierakonpolis (Kom al-Ahmar; Nekhen) in the Ashmolean Museum, Oxford. A nearby giraffe and ibex seem to be dancing to the music. These instruments usually had from four to six holes and in Old Kingdom chamber groups were played by men. Of considerable length, they

Fig. 5. A trumpeter (lower right) at the Battle of Qadesh (circa 1275 BCE); detail of relief in the Great Temple of Abu Simbel. CHRISTIANE DESROCHES NOBLECOURT ET AL., *GRAND TEMPLE D'ABOU SIMBEL, VOL. 2, LA BATAILLE DE QADESH* (1971)

were held across the body. Parallel pipes of the same period were fastened together by bitumen and twine. Their sound depended on the insertion of a single reed of the "clarinet" type. A New Kingdom innovation was a two-pipe instrument prominent in the female ensembles of the period. The pipes, often very slender, were held in the mouth at an acute angle to each other and played with double reeds of the "oboe" type. A Theban wall scene now in the British Museum shows the double reeds of the instrument picked out in white; it also shows the girl playing with crossed hands.

The trumpets or bugles of ancient Egypt were used in a military context. In the tomb of Ahmose (Amosis) at Amarna, a lone bugler summons a military detachment to join the royal procession on its way to the temple, while in the Great Temple at Abu Simbel, a similar bugler marshals Egyptian troops for the Battle of Qadesh (Tell Nebi Mend, Syria; see fig. 5). The military association is emphasized by the decoration on the two Tutan-khamun trumpets, which depicts the chief "regimental" gods of the country. There is a certain irony in the possession by Nebamun, chief of police on the Theban west bank in the time of Thutmose IV, of a trumpeter to lead his troops; among the tomb robbers caught in Ramesside times was a pair of such trumpeters. Terracotta rhytons, or "drinking horns," were used as musical instruments in the Greco-Roman period; and the Cairo Museum possesses a toylike ocarina, probably of the same date, in the shape of a monkey. (See "Pharaoh Ramesses II and His Times" in Part 5, Vol. II, for views of the battle of Qadesh and the Great Temple of Abu Simbel.)

The harp was the mainstay and only indigenous instrument among the chordophones, or strings. It took many shapes during its long history. In essence there were two main types, the arched and the angular. The former was the characteristic Egyptian harp, with neck and soundbox (at the lower end) forming part of a continuous curve. The angular harp, perhaps an import from Asia, had a vertical soundbox, with the horizontal neck at right angles to it (fig. 6). Later examples were sometimes shaped from three acute angles. The harp was both an ensemble and a solo instrument. In the tomb of Mereruka at Saqqara, it is shown in the hands of a royal princess, the daughter of King Teti of the Sixth Dynasty; alone and seated on a divan or bed, she plays to the high official, her husband. In Old Kingdom chamber groups the harpists are usually male; seven are shown playing together in a tomb at Dayr al-Gebrawi.

The Middle Kingdom tomb of Ukhhotep at Meir is the earliest to show a blind male harpist. Such musicians were to become common in the New Kingdom. Among the performers in the tomb of Nakht at Thebes, the male harpist is shown blind. At Amarna there was a choir of blind temple singers; for accompaniment they had either a blind harpist or blind lutenist (fig. 7). A curious commentary on this phenomenon is provided by the Nineteenth Dynasty tomb of Raia at Saqqara, where the owner is shown as sighted in most scenes but blind when he plays the harp. It is as if blindness here were a visual metaphor for inspiration. A characteristic banquet performance for such string players was "The Song of the Harper." The words urge a life of pleasure, since at the time of death "it is not given to man to take his goods with him. Behold, none who departs comes back again."

Fig. 6. Wooden statuette of a girl holding an angular harp, Ramesside period. BRITISH MUSEUM, LONDON

The other string instruments, the lyre and lute, probably came to Egypt from Asia. The lyre makes an initial appearance among members of a desert caravan shown in the Twelfth Dynasty tomb of Khnumhotep at Beni Hasan. The artist, fascinated by the new instrument, showed it in detail, clearly indicating the plectrum with which it was played. The lyre appears later in New Kingdom chamber groups and achieves considerable variety in shape and size at Amarna, where girls are shown practicing in a room given over to stringed instruments. At an Amarna royal banquet portrayed in the tomb of Huya, foreign men with flounced dresses and oriental caps play the lyre. One of the instruments, on an ornamental stand and with side struts shaped like spears, towers above its player. Sometimes two men performed on a giant instrument of this kind.

The Egyptian lute was of two types, both of which might appear together. One had a long wooden soundbox, the other a round soundbox made from a tortoise shell. The delicate instrument, with long neck and two or three strings, was played by both men and girls at banquets. It might also be played out of doors, as is clear from the depiction of celebrations of the festival of Opet in the Temple of Luxor.

OLD KINGDOM ENTERTAINMENT

By the Old Kingdom, royal music was highly organized. The Fifth Dynasty tomb of Nefer at Saqqara reveals a strong family connection with music. Like his father before him, Nefer was an overseer of singers. His brothers were both inspectors of singers, and his son Khenu became the director of singers in the Two Houses. A joint Fifth Dynasty tomb at Giza, belonging to Nimaetre and his wife Neferesris, concerns the music of the royal household. He was a priest of Re in the Sun Temple and overseer of singing in the Great House; she was overseer of the ladies of the Harem of the King and overseer of the Dancers of the King. A teacher of the Royal Singers is attested at Giza; also there was the tomb of an overseer of flautists. A statue in Munich represents a flautist of the Great House called Ipi. Singers were often among those involved in the cult of a dead king, as is made clear by such titles as "Inspector of singers of the Pyramid of Userkaf."

The chamber groups organized by such officials in the Old Kingdom consisted of the long end-blown flute that has survived into modern folk use as the *nayy*, the double parallel pipes, and the harp. Sometimes the instrumentalist faces another musician who seems to be directing the performance with hand gestures, perhaps indicating rhythm or mode. Such a chamber group is sometimes in close proximity to a dance scene. This is the case with the chapel of Werirniptah, now in the British Museum. In the upper register, a flautist and harpist each face a singer who seems also to conduct. Below are female

Fig. 7. Relief of a blind choir in the tomb of Meryre at Amarna. Reign of Akhenaten, circa 1340 BCE. NORMAN DE GARIS DAVIES, *THE ROCK TOMBS OF EL AMARNA*, VOL. 1 (1903)

dancers moving to the song of other women who clap their hands. Despite their apparent proximity, the two groups probably have no musical connection, and there is no reason to suppose the performances were simultaneous.

The dancers of ancient Egypt were more often women than men but their hair and dress were so cut that they might easily be taken for youths or boys. The hieroglyphic determinative of the word "to dance" is in fact that of a male dancer. It depicts a standing man with one leg crossed over the other at about the level of the knee. This is a dance step frequently shown in tomb scenes, and its persistence is demonstrated in the temple of Esna, where the Roman emperor Trajan (98–117 CE) is executing the same movement, dancing before Menhyt-Nebtu, a lioness-headed goddess who, like Hathor, journeyed to the south. Dance for the Egyptians also meant acrobatics. The same word was used for both, and the movements, though stereotyped, covered a wide range of expression.

The link with Hathor continues. The stately dances of the Old Kingdom often show the performers with their arms curved above the head in such a way that they might be taken to symbolize the horns of a cow. Considerable numbers may be involved. In the tomb of Sekhemkare (one of Chephren's sons) at Giza, fifteen women are engaged in the same solemn movement; and on a column of ʿAnkhtifi's tomb at al-Moʿalla (First Intermediate period), thirteen female dancers are shown hand in hand, as it were circling the pillar. Sometimes a dwarf is represented at the back of the dance groups, imitating their steps in his own clumsy way, and in the Sixth Dynasty tomb of Nunuter at Giza, a female dwarf carries a sistrum, with seven dancers apparently encircling her.

A mirror dance achieved some currency in the Sixth Dynasty. A fine example is in the tomb of Mereruka at Saqqara. The female dancers hold mirrors and clappers ending with a human hand. Both mirror and clapper had close associations with Hathor, and a characteristic movement in the dance seems to be the raising of the mirror to reflect the moment when the clappers touch. The same tomb has an energetic dance representing the "mystery of birth." Such acrobatic performances became popular in the later Old Kingdom. The female participants are often shown with a weighted ball or disk attached to the end of a long tress of gathered hair or, as in the tomb of Ibi at Dayr al-Gabrawi, fixed to the head by a band of white cloth.

In the tomb of Kagemni at Saqqara, the acrobatic dancers are shown in a position that could not be maintained without loss of balance. The artist has captured the moment of maximum daring, when the energy of the performers with the whirling disks has achieved its climax. Above the scene are fragments of a hymn to Hathor. Energy is shown differently in the tomb of Djau at Dayr al-Gabrawi, where in one register a group of naked female dancers is depicted. Two couples have joined hands and raised one leg so as to touch in the middle; behind each couple a solo dancer does a high kick to the level of the others' shoulders. Below this is a male dance, accompanied by rhythmic clapping, in which one man with legs apart seems to twist his companion round him, while another turns on the spot beneath the arm of his fellow.

MIDDLE KINGDOM DEVELOPMENTS

Middle Kingdom chamber groups were similar to those of the Old Kingdom. The double "clarinet" largely disappears, though it has survived into modern folk music as the *zummara*, and female musicians tend to play a larger part. The musical scene in the Twelfth Dynasty tomb of Amenemhet at Beni Hasan has three singers accompanied by two harps, a sistrum, and a rattle; only one of the harpists is male. From this period come enchanting wooden models of harpists entertaining their master. Two male harpists in a group from Saqqara squat wide-eyed on either side of the master and his wife; the clapping of three women accompanies their playing. A model from the Eleventh Dynasty tomb of Meketre at Thebes (in the Metropolitan Museum of New York) shows the chancellor of Nebhepetre Mentuhotep, on shipboard. He hears a report from the captain while at the same time listening to the music of a blind harpist and singer.

Dance in the Middle Kingdom was both more public and more private than before. It was performed outdoors, for instance, to celebrate in procession the dragging and installation of a tomb owner's statue; it also formed an integral part of funeral rites. An early occasion of jubilation over a statue is shown in a Louvre mastaba scene; but it is in the splendid provincial tombs at Beni Hasan in Middle Egypt that the details and implications of the dance are clearest. In the tomb of Amenemhet, men are depicted clapping as they dance; here, as in other Beni Hasan scenes, certain individual figures represent different stages in the movement of a single dancer. Women are shown executing the main types of movement inherited from the Old Kingdom. Some tread a classical measure with arms curved above the head; others are engaged in vigorous acrobatics, turning somersaults with one performer balanced on the back of another.

A statue celebration in the tomb of Khnumhotep at the same site includes a scene of subtle symbolism. Five female performers have their hair drawn high on top of the head so that they resemble the Muu ritual dancers who regularly attended Old and New Kingdom funerals. One of these women has grabbed another by the hair and has an arm raised behind her as if to mime the slaughter of an enemy by the king, an action often represented on the pylons of Egyptian temples. Two dancers bend like trees in the wind, and the last stands with arms raised gracefully before her. The hieroglyphic caption is "Wind beneath the two feet," a position usually reserved for subject foreigners. It has been suggested that the scene may also be connected with the "Song of the Four Winds," known from the Coffin Texts. The aim of the caption and the mimed performance was to gain control of the winds and ensure a favorable passage for the statue.

The inscriptions of Beni Hasan make no mention of Hathor; but at Cusae (al-Qusiya, Qis) near the tombs of Meir in Middle Egypt, she had an important cult center. The nomarchs, or provincial rulers, buried at Meir numbered among their titles "Overseer of prophets of Hathor, mistress of Cusae," and the tomb scenes show dances performed for the dead by musicians and priestesses of Hathor. Emblems of the goddess

Fig. 8. Dance of votaresses in honor of Hathor; painting in the tomb of Senet, mother of Antefoqer, at Thebes. Early Twelfth Dynasty, circa 1900 BCE. NORMAN DE GARIS DAVIES, *THE TOMB OF ANTEFOKER, VIZIER OF SESOSTRIS I* (1920)

are prominent in these tombs. Clappers, sistra, and the *menat,* for instance, can be seen in the tomb of Senbi. Three priestesses present to the dead man the "ornaments of the Lady of Heaven," just as in the *Story of Sinuhe.* The utterance of the third priestess emphasizes the vivifying power of the *menat,* in which Hathor herself was considered to be immanent: "For your *kas*! the *menats* of your mother Hathor, that she may prolong your life unto the years you desire!" A male harper praises the goddess and refers to the ritual attendants behind him: "Exalted is Hathor, (goddess) of love, O Ihuyu, O Ihuyu." These officials have pairs of clappers in each hand and have texts referring to Hathor as the Golden One. Three dancing men snap their fingers, one crouching low in the center and another in the traditional attitude that was eventually to be adopted by Trajan.

The early Twelfth Dynasty tomb of Antefoqer at Thebes has two main music and dance scenes. One depicts vigorous acrobatics that take place between registers dealing with the vintage and the counting of grain on its way to the granary. The central man among three leaps high into the air, and two women are apparently somersaulting. Elsewhere in the tomb, the funeral banquet is accompanied by music on flute and harp. Two men and a boy have the *menat* round their necks and emphasize the rhythm with clappers. While six women clap with raised hands, two pairs of young girls approach each other with a dance step. One pair has the characteristic long tress ending in a disk; the other pair has the close-cropped hair of young men. Dress is short, leaving the legs free. The dancers, as they near each other, at once eagerly and shyly, doubtless illustrate the texts above: "The doors of heaven open and the god comes forth" and "The Golden One has come." Perhaps there is an allusion in this dance to the mythical love of Re for Hathor. (See fig. 8 for a section of this scene.)

IMPERIAL MUSIC AND DANCE

The spread of the Egyptian empire in the New Kingdom not only brought new musical instruments to delight the Egyptians. In addition foreigners came to Egypt in large numbers, bringing exotic manners that included dance.

Newfound wealth enabled leading households either to have the service of their own permanent band of musicians or to hire a professional group for special occasions. A glance at the graceful chamber groups of the New Kingdom—in which rich jewelry is worn (though sometimes little else), in which the lithe movements suggest the practiced artist, in which the teamwork hints at a long-established ensemble—leads to the conclusion that music was now a discipline that required dedicated study.

Musical scenes are found in a quarter of the more than four hundred Theban tombs. Some depict more than one ensemble. The tomb of Thutmose III's vizier Rekhmire has three musical scenes. In a group of female musicians, two of the newer instruments are shown: the lute and a rectangular tambourine with concave sides. The male ensemble also has a lutenist. Elsewhere a female lutenist holds her instrument towards the ground, as if to support it for tuning purposes. In the slightly later tomb of Djeserkaresoneb, all three stringed instruments are being played by a female team. At the head of the group is a woman playing a large arched harp, with the point of the soundbox resting on the ground. A scantily clad lutenist sings and dances behind her. At the center is a near-naked girl dancer, and behind are players of the double "oboe"-pipes and the lyre (fig. 9). Three women sit cross-legged and clap the time.

These girl dancers of the New Kingdom banquets, whose only clothing is their jewelry, rely on grace and eloquence of movement for their effect. They operate within a confined space and at best could only weave in and out among the musicians. Occasionally there is a touch of wildness in the dance, when the performer bends low and whirls in a bravura movement; perhaps a Nubian or African may be the solo dancer, lending a flavor of the exotic to the occasion. Dancers were probably attempting to illustrate the theme of a banquet song. This is the case in the scene on a block from a Theban wall painting now in the British Museum, in which two intertwined dancers perform energetically beneath a text in praise of Ptah: "His beauty is in every body. . . . The earth overflows with love of him."

The influence of the dancers spreads to the players themselves, who make rhythmic move-

Fig. 9. Female musicians playing the harp, lute, double pipe, and lyre; scene in the tomb of Djeserkaresonb at Thebes. Mid Eighteenth Dynasty, circa 1400 BCE. DRAWING AFTER ROBERT HAY MSS IN THE BRITISH LIBRARY, LONDON; LISE MANNICHE, *MUSIC AND MUSICIANS IN ANCIENT EGYPT* (1991)

ments with beating foot and bending knee. The harpist is usually still because of the size of her instrument; but other members of a chamber group find it difficult to resist the lure of the music. Among notable dancing musicians are the supple, naked lutenist in the tomb of Nakht; the lyre player in the tomb of Nakhtamun, who holds the instrument vertically rather than horizontally and has her legs tattooed with the figure of Bes; and a player of the double "oboe"-pipe from Dayr al-Medina, a fragment of a slender figure performing within twining convolvulus. In the latter years of the New Kingdom, the dresses of the musicians become more flowing, loose-fitting gowns of transparent drapery. Convolvulus sometimes hangs from their arms, and the influence of Amarna art shows in the waving of branches and the expressive sweep of movement.

In many New Kingdom tombs, Hathor was represented as a cow emerging from the western mountain waiting to welcome the dead. Ritual Muu dancers gave the signal for the funeral procession to enter her precincts with the words,

"She has inclined her head"; a celebration in her honor was then held before the dead man. The Eighteenth Dynasty tomb of Amenemhet at Thebes (no. 82) preserves the dance association with Hathor. On this occasion the Muu dancers are captioned "Dancing for him by the people of Pe" and thus represent spirits from the primeval Delta capital of Buto (Tell al-Fara'in). Priestesses present sistra, *menat*s, and a sort of rattle; the two Ihuyu have human-headed clappers in each hand; and a male dancer leaps high into the air.

The dragging of a statue was still accompanied by dance. The tomb of Qenamun at Thebes has a number of such scenes. Men precede and follow a statue with arms crooked gracefully above the head in the manner familiar from the Old Kingdom. Priestesses with sistra and *menat*s are described as "ladies of the harem of Hathor."

New Kingdom dances of a religious nature were performed for other gods as well. In honor of Osiris, music and dance accompany the raising of the *djed*-column, as represented in the Theban tomb of Kheruef from the time of Amenhotep III. Royal princesses play sistra, and most of one register is taken up with symbolic fighting between groups of men, using fists and batons as supposed opponents and supporters of Osiris, while four women perform a classic Old Kingdom dance. Elsewhere in the tomb men wear animal masks, perhaps as Bes-figures, and women indulge in free expression dancing, each an individual with gesticulating arms and twisting torso. Blocks from the "Red Chapel" of Hatshepsut at Karnak show part of a procession with the bark of Amun. Acrobatic dancers are at hand, performing somersaults and cartwheels, while two girls stand ready for action, poised with hair fallen forward over the face.

Most vivid of all such religious scenes are the celebrations at the festival of Opet in the court of the Luxor Temple decorated under Tutankhamun. Tutankhamun's return to Thebes from Amarna was also cause for celebration, and the representations are propaganda for an Egypt in universal joy over the restoration of orthodoxy. Libyans are there, distinctive with feathers and boomerangs, black southerners leap to the accompaniment of a drummer, and Nubians perform a warrior dance at the behest of a trumpeter.

The appeal of exotic dance was well established in the New Kingdom. A Libyan-style dance is depicted in the temple of Hatshepsut. Two cylindrical drums are shown as accompaniment to a Nubian dance on a pylon of the Armant temple dating to Thutmose III. When Amenhotep (also called Huy), viceroy of Kush and governor of the south lands, visited his area of authority, he was welcomed by eight dancing musicians, two with rectangular tambourines. Their tall, slender figures suggest they were Nubians.

Music had become an essential adjunct to life in both its public and private spheres. A vizier in the time of Amenhotep II had with him when "hearing petitions" in the judgment hall not only his scribes to record the proceedings but also his harp player and lutenist.

SATIRE AND RIBALDRY

The prominence of music in Egypt made it fit material for the satirist. A fox on a British Mu-

seum papyrus of the Twentieth or Twenty-first Dynasty acts as goatherd with a basket over his shoulder; to beguile the time, he plays a double "oboe"-type pipe, like many a human counterpart in the tomb scenes. A Nineteenth Dynasty papyrus in Turin has an animal chamber group. A donkey manipulates a gigantic harp on the scale of the magisterial instruments depicted in the tomb of Ramesses (Ramses) III; a lion is in ecstasy at the lyre; a crocodile has the gentle lute; and a monkey plays the double pipes. Of similar mocking intent is the wooden statuette in the Fitzwilliam Museum (in Cambridge, England) of a monkey at an arched harp, apparently nonchalant in his mastery.

Similar high spirits might also be displayed using human figures. A steatite bowl of the Persian period (fifth century BCE) in the British Museum shows a procession to a Hathor shrine with tambourine, lyre, clappers, and double pipes. One member of the group has lifted her skirt and bangs her bottom in time to the music. Perhaps Hathor is also responsible for the erotic figurines that proliferated in the Greco-Roman period. Some are engaged in musical activities. The Fitzwilliam Museum has a group of male harpists from Antinoe playing angular instruments that rest on the performer's greatly enlarged phallus. Drummers discovered by Flinders Petrie at Memphis (modern Mit Rahina) and now in the Petrie Museum (University College London), all have their elongated phalluses wrapped round their necks.

PUBLIC AND PRIVATE MUSIC

Egypt was eventually to thrill to the six hundred singers and three hundred harpists organized for Ptolemy Philadelphus II in the third century BCE. Music and dance may well have played an important part in ritual dramas such as that shown on the walls of the temple of Edfu in honor of Horus. These Ptolemaic texts, certainly enshrining a much older tradition, suggest for the chorus moments of strong drama but also have lyrical passages that could only be enhanced by song.

But already in the New Kingdom, music could unite king and commoner. It was as integral to the great open-air ceremonies in honor of the state god as it was to the funerary banquets that took place beneath the western peak at Thebes. The guardian spirit there was the snake-goddess, Meretseger, "She Who Loves Silence," and she imposed her will on the many chamber concerts being performed at the foot of her slopes as well as on the temple ceremonies of the East Bank. The delicate wind instruments do now indeed "pipe to the spirit ditties of no tone," and we have reluctantly to accept that

> Heard melodies are sweet, but those unheard
> Are sweeter . . .

BIBLIOGRAPHY

Classical Literature

ATHENAEUS, *The Deipnosophists* (*The Learned Banquet*), edited and translated by CHARLES B. GULICK (1927; 2d ed. 1951); PLUTARCH, *De Iside and Osiride*, in *Plutarch's Moralia*, translated by FRANK COLE BABBITT (1962); and J. GWYN GRIFFITHS, *Plutarch's* De Iside et Osiride (1970).

Modern Studies

ROBERT D. ANDERSON, *Catalogue of Egyptian Antiquities in the British Museum*, vol. 3, *Musical Instruments* (1976); EMMA BRUNNER-TRAUT, *Der Tanz im Alten Ägypten* (1938; and 2nd ed. 1958); ELLEN HICKMANN, "Aspects of Continuity and Change in the Musical Culture of Ancient Egypt," in *Report of the Twelfth Congress, Berkeley, 1977, International Musicological Society* (1981); and forty-five articles on the music and musical instruments of Pharaonic Egypt in *Lexikon der Ägyptologie*, edited by WOLFGANG HELCK and WOLFHART WESTENDORF (1975–1986); HANS HICKMANN, *Catalogue général des antiquités égyptiennes du Musée du Caire: Instruments de musique* (1949), and 45 *siècles de musique dans L'Égypte ancienne*, Vies et travaux, 1 (1980); LISE MANNICHE, *Ancient Egyptian Musical Instruments*, Münchner ägyptologische Studien 34 (1975), *Musical Instruments from the Tomb of Tutᶜankhamūn* (1976), and "Symbolic Blindess," *Chronique d'Egypte* 53, no. 105 (1978); CURT SACHS, *Die Musikinstrumente des alten Ägyptens* (1921), *The History of Musical Instruments* (1940) and *The Rise of Music in the Ancient World: East and West* (1943); and CHRISTIANE ZIEGLER, *Les instruments de musique égyptiens au Musée du Louvre* (1979).

SEE ALSO **Private Life in Ancient Egypt** (Part 4, Vol. I) and **Costume in New Kingdom Egypt** (Part 4, Vol. I).

Aesthetics in Ancient Mesopotamian Art

IRENE J. WINTER

THERE ARE AT LEAST two good reasons why a comprehensive study of Mesopotamian aesthetics has not yet been undertaken. First is the apparent difference between Western definitions of "the aesthetic" and Mesopotamian cultural production; and second is the absence of cuneiform documents that present the "Mesopotamian view." To overcome these two hurdles, neither Western definitions of the aesthetic nor Western criteria for the aesthetic experience can be accepted uncritically. Rather, it is important to try to extract how such principles operated within a Mesopotamian vocabulary and worldview.

The literature on Western aesthetics makes a distinction between ordinary craft production (Greek *techne;* Latin *ars*) and what is commonly termed the "fine arts." A primary distinction is that to belong to the latter category, a work must be accessible through disinterested contemplation, divorced from any contextual function or utility, and its value as "art" must be intrinsic to its existence. This distinction, largely a product of eighteenth-century philosophical inquiry, was grounded in notions of property and value that were specific to the time. Aesthetic response was inherently tied to critical judgments of beauty and taste applied specifically to those objects designated as representatives of the "fine arts." While this view has undergone some

permutations through the nineteenth and twentieth centuries, the basic premises have not been challenged.

For the study of Mesopotamian art and aesthetics the above distinction of "fine" versus applied, or decorative, arts is problematic, as is the European classification system for what sorts of works are to be included in the "fine" category. Sculpture certainly has been recovered, but painting is rarely preserved. Large scale constructions identifiable as architecture have been excavated, but they exist only as largely incomplete ground plans, and so are not fully subject to analysis. Nor have we any exegetical texts that discuss the visual arts as abstract concepts. The same can be said about other products of the Mesopotamian imagination: examples of poetry have been recovered, but no treatise on poetic style or diction; elements of musical notation systems, but nothing like a score or even a classification of chords. Furthermore, the arts in Mesopotamia were never created "for their own sake," but existed within larger functional contexts. By European standards, then, they risk being dismissed as pendant, classified among "minor" or decorative arts by virtue of their utilitarian application. Finally, to accept Western concepts of beauty as the measure of art means becoming mired in hopeless comparisons between "our" manifestations of the aesthetic and theirs, a pursuit in which the ancient Near East, or indeed any culture removed from our own, cannot but emerge the loser.

To resolve this dilemma, it is essential to find appropriate criteria by which to assess Mesopotamian value and experience. This is at best a difficult undertaking, requiring study of both the artifactual and textual records of Mesopotamia—the most completely preserved assemblage of the ancient Near East. As a working definition, included among the visual arts is any work that is imaginatively conceptualized and that affords visual and emotional satisfaction, for which manufacturing skill is required and to which some established standards have been applied. The aesthetic quality of such a work can be judged not by how far it is removed from the functional, but by its affective properties according to Mesopotamian standards. For "beauty," the term we commonly use when responding today to a piece of art, we may then substitute concepts grounded in Mesopotamia's own lexicon.

It must be admitted that this task is daunting for, with no exegetical texts to aid us, we are left to wrestle with a vocabulary that is embedded in a broad range of documents and often is cast in highly formulaic and repetitive language. In many instances, particularly with respect to Sumerian texts, we must depend on lexical lists that rarely make perfect semantic matches between the Sumerian and Akkadian equivalents. The fully nuanced meanings of many important words not only elude us today, they also were occasionally beyond the grasp of the Akkadian scholars who collected and categorized them. This condition obviously has its consequences, for modern scholars are commonly forced to render loosely or poetically passages that escape complete comprehension; and this in turn limits our ability to understand the Mesopotamian aesthetic experience.

Nevertheless, it is possible to identify a number of attributes and responses related to aesthetic response, as preserved in texts that span the period from about 2500 to 500 BCE. Throughout this period, there is evidence for a surprising degree of continuity in both vocabulary and modes of perception and valuation, despite historical and political change. Three main categories of reference can be distinguished: con-

cerning the making and material treatment *of* a work; concerning the appearance and visual attributes inherent *in* a work; and concerning perception and responses *to* a work.

MAKING

Under this rubric fall terms related to the process of creation and manufacture. (Hereafter, words in *italics* are Akkadian, words in SMALL CAPS are Sumerian.) Sources are best for the Neo-Assyrian period, when we have both official inscriptions and letters that refer to works undertaken on behalf of royal patrons; however throughout our two-thousand-year period, texts consistently make reference to buildings, statuary, and objects serving the state or the cult. Verbs that deal with drawing (*eṣēru, esēqu;* ḪUR, ŠAB), carving (*naqāru, nuqquru;* GUL, BAL), mounting in (precious) metal (*uḫḫuzu;* GAR), building (*raṣāpu;* DU₃) are used in descriptions of works being produced. These include images in relief or freestanding sculpture or in paint; metal vessels, divine and royal insignia and appurtenances; and temples and palaces along with their appointments. In addition, verbs are attested that convey the more abstract notions "to create, fashion, form" (*banû, bašāmu, patāqu;* SA₇, AK) and "to execute according to a plan" (*šuteṣbû*), the latter often implying not only a blueprint for construction but the fact of careful thought and planning.

Care and planning are also revealed by the usage of terms that explicitly refer to preparation for tasks and to the skill or wisdom necessary to carry them out successfully: NAM.KU₃.ZU; *nēmequ* (knowledge[ably-], skillful[ly], expert[ly-made]). The god Enki (Ea) is seen as the source of inspiration and skill in craft design from the early texts and throughout our period. In the third millennium, inscriptions of Gudea of Lagash (circa 2100) attribute the plan or design of the Sumerian ruler's temple for the god Ningirsu to Enki; while Esarhaddon of Assyria (680–669) describes this god as "(he) who creates/shapes appearance, who fashions all things." Assigning mastery and inspiration to the god would presumably have been meant literally, not metaphorically, by the Mesopotamians and so is not equivalent to our tendency to regard creative genius or its results as a "gift from heaven." In general, Mesopotamians distinguished between moments in which the gods were directly involved in a creative effort and moments when human beings, especially rulers and other elite patrons, were vessels for this creative impulse. In some cases, as a document from Mari informs us, oracular quizzing of the gods preceded a decision on how to portray them visually, for example, "Regarding the god Lagamal, (this is an inquiry) whether to give him a human face and to set a tiara of 8 horns topped by a golden disk." A Sumerian couplet directly refers to an object as the product of its maker:

> My (awesome) object made by the skilled
>   carpenter;
> My (great) work fashioned by the skilled
>   metalworker!

Kings are especially likely to be credited with ingenuity, whether indirectly when marshaling the necessary craft to create a work and launch a project or directly when referring to work as the product of their own hands. No matter how the act of creation is presented, skill is always emphasized. Adjectives denoting skill, mastery, and ingenuity can be attached to the specific substantive or to a generic term meaning object or thing made (KIN, ME.DIM₂; *šipru, epištu*). In addition to the terms already noted, there are a number of alternative ways, in both Sumerian and Akkadian, of denoting the positive attributes of manufacture: GALAM; *nakliš, nikiltu* (masterful, artful, ingenious); *šipir nikilti* (expert, knowledgeable [work]); DIRIG (surpassing). In one instance, from the reign of Abisare of Larsa in the early second millennium, the whole array is called forth in a single text: As the king describes a silver and carnelian statue he has had made, he uses a circumlocution that brings the work close to the Western notion of "masterpice" (KIN.GAL.EŠ): "A great object, it is expertly fashioned; this work (is) a surpassing work, a thing beyond praise."

This emphasis on skill and expertise in craftsmanship and making is part of the value of the undertaking. Judgments of quality are inherent in the addition of terms of value to the work, as in ME.DIM₂.SA₆ and KIN.SA₆.GA, meaning markedly "good" or "auspicious" work. It is not uncommon in the Sumerian temple hymns, for example, to speak of temples built in an artful fashion. Similar references abound in later Assyrian texts. Esarhaddon tells us that he had silver and gold utensils expertly (artfully) fashioned with skillful techniques; in another instance, the same ruler claims credit for doing work on a crown for the god Assur, "which no one had (yet) formed into (such) a skillful piece of work." References of this sort are applied to the full range of objects commissioned by the elite, including palaces, temples, cult implements, temple and palace furnishings, and statuary. The assertion of skill in craftsmanship validates inspiration and expertise as part of the creative process and as part of the value inherent in the work.

In addition to skill and mastery as terms of value, there are a number of references to "decoration" as a positive attribute. We pursue below precisely what the qualities of decoration may be; but the *fact* of decoration is an inherent part of making. Verbs such as ŠU . . . TAG and ŠERKAN . . . du₁₁ or *zânu* (to decorate, adorn), *šarāḫu* (to make splendid), and *lapātu* (literally "to touch," but used for fashioning, decorating, even painting) are frequently included in descriptions, particularly in the case of elite buildings and cult

Silver vase of Entemena from Girsu. LOUVRE MUSEUM, PARIS

objects. The quality of being adorned or decorated (ŠERKAN.DI; *zu″u-nu*) is applied not only to buildings, but to precious objects and even persons. Kings refer constantly to the decoration lavished upon both temples and palaces. Other references include, in Sumerian, the attention paid to parts of buildings, stone and metal cult vessels, a ceremonial chariot for the god Ningirsu and a processional boat; in Akkadian, the investment in crowns for divine images, furniture and chariots. Comparable care was also devoted to the careful arrangement of works in their intended location, once the process of manufacture is completed. In one instance, an official in Mari presents a detailed report on placement to the king: "On a raised platform, to the left, stands the statue of the god Amurru, bearing a scimitar (*gamlum*); across from him stands my lord's statue in worship. Atop the statue (of the god?), there is a sun-disk and moon-crescent."

Despite the many historical and cultural changes occuring during the long span of Mesopotamian history, the value attached to decoration in precious metals and stones for thrones, beds, chariots, and sanctuary walls seems to have remained constant. Even the way Assyrian rulers described their deeds, in words or art, upon the walls of their palaces was part of this decorative tradition. The claim of rulers that they "made splendid" the buildings and works executed during their reigns is explicitly linked both to skilled and masterful work and to elaborate decoration, qualities that were perceptible visually as consequences of the creative process. Ibbi-Sin of Ur (circa 2020) speaks of the skillful and strange workmanship of a gold jar of ointment, the decoration of which was meant to provoke unending admiration. Shalmaneser III of Assyria (858–824) makes reference to an alabaster statue whose workmanship gave pleasure to behold. In both cases, mastery and decoration combine to give pleasure and confer "quality" on the finished product, and are therefore to be considered among the affective properties of the works in question.

APPEARANCE

A theory of aesthetics for the visual arts requires a developed concept of representation and an articulated relationship between representation and appearance. Essential is an understanding of the terms of ALAM in Sumerian and *ṣalmu* in Akkadian, terms whose primary meaning is "image." These terms are then applied to representations on freestanding sculpture, relief carving, or metal engraving as particular media. The terms can be used explicitly, as when kings record the fashioning of their own images (ALAM.LU-GAL; *ṣalam šarrūtiya*). Occasionally, imagery is understood, as when Ibbi-Sin speaks of his gold cult vessel decorated with wild bulls and serpents, or when Assurnasirpal II refers to "his great deeds" depicted on palace walls.

For analytical purposes, it is important to keep separate a notion of "representation" from one of appearance, or likeness. On Assurnasirpal II's great Banquet Stela, found in his Northwest Palace at Nimrud, he tells us specifically of his "royal image *like* (resembling) my (own) features." At first reading, this sounds very much like "portraiture" as we know it in the West—a topic that has been explored by Agnès Spycket and Betty Schlossmann for the ancient Near East. But study of the preserved sculptural images of Mesopotamian rulers makes clear that the representations adhere to an idealized standard of proportions and features, with only the occasional physiognomical trait serving as a "signature element" (for example, the chin of Gudea of Lagash) for a given individual.

Issues of "likeness" and "appearance" become relevant to aesthetics insofar as they are valued components of representation and affect response. In the Mesopotamian case, it would seem that likeness is not to be confused with Western notions of naturalism. Rather, resemblance, or "recognizable appearance," is likely to have also been conveyed by appropriate headgear, clothing, weaponry, and other attributes that we ordinarily regard as external to an individual, but that the Mesopotamians deemed inseparable from office, disposition, or identity. Furthermore, for royal and divine images at least, it is possible that their idealized features, as opposed to any idiosyncratic physical traits, actually were thought to constitute their "appearance" and signify identity. A remarkable text of Adad-nirari II of Assyria (911–891) tells us that the gods intervened to alter his appearance to one of lordly appearance, fixed and perfected his features, thereby making him fit to rule. Indeed, there is important continuity from the late third and early second millennium into the first in the way the gods were construed as actively engaged in shaping the royal "image." Thus, what the ruler wished to have perceived in his "likeness" was not necessarily his own personal physiognomy, but those ideal aspects of his appearance that had been molded by the gods, thereby attesting to his divinely sanctioned qualifications for rule, not just his individuality.

The same descriptive terminology associated with appearance is used for human and nonhuman subjects, and therefore suggests a shared domain of aesthetic value across subject matter. The terminology clusters around three primary groups of words: those denoting general physical attractiveness, those denoting light or luster, and those denoting intense radiance that carries with it aspects of power and awe.

Several terms in Sumerian and Akkadian clearly convey attractiveness. Modern scholars frequently translate them as "beauty" or "beautiful"; but each can be shown to represent a distinct underlying quality. Thus, sA$_7$/*banû* convey the sense of being at once "well-formed and well-bred"; sA$_6$.GA/*damqu* is used in the sense of being "good, auspicious"; TEŠ$_2$/*baltu* denotes "vigor, vitality"; and ḪI.LI/*kuzbu* is associated with being "luscious, alluring." Depending on context, beauty may sometimes be inferred, but only in some situations, and only as a "covert category," using circumlocution rather than direct reference to an attribute. Jack M. Sasson describes an analogy in some Arabic dialects in which beauty can be implied by words associated with "sweetness" and "savour," or by words with associations of "nicety" and "goodness." Especially in descriptions when more than one attribute are strung together, as in a person who is said to be *baltu kuzbu*, we may be more faithful to the original intent if we strive to ascertain what specific qualities were in mind than if we rely indiscriminately on a Western notion of and vocabulary for beauty.

Thus, we find qualities of vitality or vigor attributed to deities, humans, buildings, sculptural figures, and a crown in Mesopotamian texts; lusciousness and allure are attributed equally to the same range of beings and things. In all cases, what is conveyed is something attractive because it pulsates with vital energy and is filled with an elusive complex quality simultaneously signaling voluptuousness, luxuriance, lusciousness, and generative power. Similarly, the terms *banû* and *damqu* are frequently paired. Gods, humans, temples, and objects are all said to be "well-formed," while the gaze of a god or king, along with sculptural images and ornaments, are all termed "auspicious." This latter adjective would be visually manifest as physical grace. When a young woman is then said to be *ša kīʾam damqat kīʾam banât*, it is not unacceptable to translate it "so pretty, so fair"; yet when it is rendered more literally as "so auspicious/good, so well-formed/well-bred," we are better able to perceive the distinctly Mesopotamian characteristics that convey grace and physical presence.

To these positive physical attributes may be added the quality of radiant light. The same light that emanates from the principal astral bodies—Utu/Shamash (the sun), Sin/Nanna (the moon), and Inanna/Ishtar (the Venus star)—is frequently said to encircle persons, buildings, and diverse objects. This light or luminosity is viewed as particularly positive and auspicious. Objects that are holy or ritually pure and clean (KU$_3$/SIKIL; *ellu, ebbu*) are said to be imbued with light, their luminosity achieved through contact with the sacred or the divine. This imparted luminosity is the visible equivalent to the vital life force invested in and controlled by the gods. When applied to persons or noncultic objects, purity and cleanliness, as well as light, become the signs that someone or something has been touched by the sacred, or is prepared to come into contact with it. To the extent that the sacred is manifest as luminous, then that which is pure and holy will shine, and, conversely, that which shines manifests the sacred.

Simple terms for day, light, daylight (UD/U$_4$; *ūmu*); verbs governing actions like "to shine, become bright" (for example, *nabāṭu, namāru*; KAR$_2$, MUL); and their consequences, "shining, luminous, clear, radiant, bright" (ZALAG$_2$, DADAG, ŠERZI; *namru, napardû*) all carry a high aesthetic valance. Literally, of course, the sun-disk, the moon, and the stars all shine and so are inherently luminous, radiant, and bright. Used metaphorically, however, kings and princes, temples, sanctuaries, processional streets, palace gateway figures, and various objects and materials are also said to emit light, and often to "shine like the day."

When the same verbs and adjectives are used for astral bodies, to express positive emotions manifest as physical glow, and to describe positively charged works, all participate in a shared domain of value. Frequently, the characterization of cult objects and divine images as shining comes as the culmination of passages describing their manufacture, as if this quality represented the ultimate criterion of their physical value. In Esarhaddon's account of his renewal of the Babylonian gods in Assyria, we are told that the workmen fashioned the divine images more artfully than ever before, made them truly splendid, awesomely radiant with vitality, and made them shine like the sun. Sumerian temples are said to both go forth like moonlight and shine like the sun over the land. In later periods, Neo-Assyrian and Neo-Babylonian temples are said to shine like the sun, like the day, or like the sunrise. The brilliance that a temple shares with a heavenly body could be physically enhanced by covering the sanctuary walls with precious metals, white alabaster, or glazed brick. In this way, material undertaking and emotional investment join to achieve an aesthetic goal. Even when materials are not emphasized, a comparison with heavenly bodies is generally part of the description, and it is clear that to shine is good. It may also be *necessary*, as a sign of belonging to the class of earthly phenomena touched by the divine. In this way, luster or shine is ascribed not only to temples, divine statues, and cult implements but also to palaces, rulers, and royal accoutrements.

If bright was valued positively, then dark should correspondingly be negative. This is generally true; but the operative contrast is not so much light versus dark as luster versus dullness. In some cases, the term for the precious stone lapis lazuli (ZA.GIN$_2$; *uqnû*) is used to denote not the actual material, but the dark luster associated with the material as a positive attribute. Being multicolored (GUN$_3$) can also be stated as a quality of value, conveying properties of iridescence

A nineteenth-century lithograph of the restored palaces of Nimrud, from an 1853 publication of adapted on-site drawings made during an expedition to Assyria by Austen Henry Layard, M.P. A. H. LAYARD, *MONUMENTS OF NINEVEH* (1853)

and the sparkle of light. Whatever the source, light and luster were viewed as integral components of visual effect, and as such provoked a positive aesthetic response.

An additional group of qualities are also manifest as light, but with such an intensification of brilliance or radiance that the emanation has the power to provoke awe, dread, or terror. There are several terms associated with this emanating power, and all have at one time or another been translated as "radiance" or "awe." Each of the terms seems to correspond to a particular physical phenomenon: an encompassing aura (ME.LAM$_2$; *melammû*); general radiance (NI$_2$.GAL; *namrirrū*); rays (ŠERZI; *barīru*); sparks (*šarūru*, also rendered by NI$_2$.GAL and ŠERZI); shimmer, as light does on water (SU.ZI; *šalummatu*); or fiery glow (IIUŠ; *rašubbatu*). From their usage in both Sumerian and Akkadian texts, it would appear that these outward manifestations were inseparably linked to powers that generated emotional responses in those who viewed the outward physical sign. Those responses might be splendor, awe, fear, or dread. The translator is thus forced to reach for such awkward phrase-to-word equivalents as "awe-inspiring radiance," since modern vocabularies are ill-equipped to convey the subtle nuances of a culture that so richly distinguished variations in the appearance of the luminous and the awesome.

Gods are described as surrounded by all-encompassing auras, as are rulers. In the text of Adad-nirari II mentioned above, after the gods have altered his image to one worthy of rule, the king claims that they "raised me above crowned kings (and) covered my head with the aura of kingship." Temples are also amply possessed of auras, as are cultic paraphernalia. Most eloquent is the description of a crown made by Esarhaddon for the image of the god Assur: "This crown . . . clothed in (an) all-encompassing aura, adorned with vital energy (life-giving force), bearing shimmering awesomeness, bathed in radiance." The crown, artfully made of gold and precious stones (hence shining by virtue of the material), was thus deemed "fitting for the god." The attributes it manifests are nothing less than the sum total of awesome splendor attributed in other contexts to the gods themselves. The same could be said for temples and other works described as bearing these properties.

The more closely the works are associated with divinity, the more they are invested with intense radiance. However formulaic the phraseology, there does seem to be evidence that the ancient Mesopotamians distinguished a number of different sources of intense light, each of which presumably produced a distinctive sort of light phenomenon, which in turn produced a distinctive reaction in the viewer. Thus, while these phenomena were visually manifest, at the same time, they would have been understood as more than merely formal visual properties. Indeed, each term seems to have carried at least three levels of reference: first, the visible property by which it was manifest; second, the inherent internal characteristic or power to which the external sign corresponded; and third, the linked response of awe, fear, or terror provoked by each. Furthermore, the physical manifestation served as the sign of either divine presence or divinely endowed power. To the extent that awe and fear could be invested in objects, they simultaneously signaled intrinsic properties and also triggered a response in the viewer.

To summarize the preceding sections, then, a number of types of works, by virtue of their skillful manufacture, elaborate decoration, and visual effect fit our definition of art and also elicit aesthetic response. What is distinctive about Mesopotamian tradition, however, is the degree to which aesthetic and emotional responses are closely intertwined and the degree to which the sacred seems to be manifest through visually affective, hence aesthetic, qualities.

AFFECT

The Mesopotamian lexicon is rich in terms of value, but not all the terms are applied to works. Words such as GAL/*rabû*, "great," or *gitmālu* (AŠ), "unique, one of a kind," are frequently used to convey elevated status or large size when applied to gods, kings, or heroes; but they do not function similarly when applied to buildings or objects. More ambiguous are the terms such as MAḪ/*ṣīru*, which can be used to indicate rank or lofty status for deities and/or rulers, but can also at times suggest either scale or excellence and be applied to things.

Comparative judgments related to workmanship definitely imply standards of measure determined at least in part by aesthetic values. When, for example, DIRIG, "surpassing," is attached to work (as in the text of Abi-sare about his statue for the Temple of Nanna), and when this assessment follows rather complete descriptions of the materials and the skills employed in making the objects, then it is possible to suggest that these are judgments of value related to intrinsic (visual) properties of the work itself.

Reference to a work by a substantive that conveys special esteem is another way of indicating value. In some cases, the word for "star" (MUL, UL; *kakkabu*) takes on a sense of "treasure" or thing highly valued. In other cases, the statement that something is "praise-worthy" (literally, "suitable for praise," *simat tanādāti*) suggests that it has intrinsic value, as in a text of Nebuchadnezzar II of Babylon, who recorded that he gathered "silver, gold, precious stones, whatever was rare and splendid, treasures worthy of praise." In a long letter written to King Zimri-Lim of Mari, a trusted general lists jewelry he and other officers received from Hammurabi of Babylon. For each item, its actual weight (*šuqultum*) in gold or silver is given; in addition, its value (*nībum*), which is always fractionally higher than the weight, is noted, suggesting that the piece *qua* jewelry had value beyond the intrinsic value of the metal. Although we cannot know all of the criteria by which the "value" of a work is assessed, surely the quality of the workmanship and its aesthetic merit played a role. Similarly, the phrase "worthy of praise" is important in that it reveals that objects are valued not only for their material worth, but also as objects to which affirmative response is appropriate.

In Neo-Assyrian texts, rulers formulaically express pride and pleasure in completing a large-scale building project and, not incidently, convey their sense of the value of such undertakings, through a quadruple string of verbs: *arṣip*, "I built"; *ušeklil*, "I perfected"; *ušarriḫ*, "I made splendid"; and *usim*, "I made fitting." This attribution generally appears at the end of a long descriptive passage. The final assessment, "to be fitting/appropriate," reflects an aesthetic judgment incorporating all the aspects of fabrication, decoration, correctness, and affect mentioned in the description; it then also asserts the proper relationship between those properties and the ultimate purpose of the work in question.

It is important to remember that what we have preserved in Mesopotamia are not disinterested evaluations of works by external parties—in short, no reviews, no criticism, but rather quite interested assertions of value couched as reportage. Nevertheless, these official texts provide us with the criteria according to which positive evaluations of works were asserted: in part an assessment of visual attributes and affective qualities and in part a mental operation that required assessing the fit between a projected ideal or function and the realized phenomenon.

Needless to say, an aesthetic object can only be experienced and appreciated visually. Mesopotamian tradition, however, constantly reinforces the act of looking and seeing in the appreciation of the object. A plethora of verbs (IGI . . . DU$_8$, IGI . . . LA$_2$, IGI . . . BAR; *amāru, barû, dagālu, ḫâṭu, naṭālu, palāsu* [*naplusu*]) reflect as many nuances as obtain in modern languages: "to see, behold"; "to regard, look at, observe, inspect"; "to survey, explore, examine"; and "to stare." The occasions in Mesopotamian literature in which the act of looking is narrated or where visual inspection is invited range from heroic epics and love poetry, in which the gaze of the hero/lover or the display of the hero/beloved are explicitly foregrounded, to accounts of temple or palace building in which the finished product is presented to the viewer for admiration. (See "Love Lyrics from the Ancient Near East," in Part 9, Vol. IV.)

These invitations to inspect give prominence to the act of seeing, and thereby to the audience—divine, royal, or ordinary mortal—as the ultimate judge of an undertaking. Since the majority of such texts partake of royal rhetoric, the visual reaction to such inspection is stated in highly formulaic language, and is always recorded as overwhelmingly positive.

In inscriptions where the building of temples is the subject, the gods are specifically invited to inspect the achievements. They are not the only audience, however. On the colossal lion from the gateway of the Sharrat Nipkhi Temple in Nimrud, Assurnasirpal II records that he built the temple for the eternal gaze of rulers and princes. A text of Nebuchadnezzar (Nebucha-drezzar) goes even further, stating that "all the people" are welcome to admire the luxurious appointments of a newly built temple. This exhortation that gods and human beings should view and admire applies also to crafted objects. Nabonidus, for example, calls on Shamash to look joyously on the precious products of the king's hands. Assurnasirpal I assesses an ornate bed made for the inner chamber of the Temple of Ishtar as "suitable for viewing," that is, worth admiring. In this brief passage, the act of making, and particularly of ornamenting, is brought into focus. Once completed, the bed shines, a positive feature, and as such, it is worthy of regard in the same double sense of vision and esteem that one finds today. One should claim that such an expression of response to a royally commissioned object is merely formulaic, but the very status accorded to looking as the ultimate act of affirmation and appreciation underscores the power of visual cathexion (or investment of emotional energy in an object) in Mesopotamian tradition. In sum, through a combination of workmanship and visual attributes, value is achieved; and through seeing, value is perceived.

The positive viewing experience is explicitly said to produce a positive emotional reaction. Shalmaneser III declares a royal statue he has had made a "pleasure to behold," thus linking emotional gratification to beholding an artistically satisfying object. Surely, here, we come close to Western notions of aesthetics as engaging sensory—and not merely intellectual—delight.

Reactions to viewing are generally classified under two major rubrics: producing joy/delight or admiration/awe. These reactions are sustained differently depending on the audience involved. When the gods are the primary recipients of temple-building projects and of votive objects, they constitute the *intended audience* of the work. Their response is described in terms of direct gratification: joy, pleasure, delight. Joy ($\check{S}A_3.HUL_2(.LA)$; *hud libbi*, literally, "joy of the heart," and *hidâtu*, a derivative of *hadû*, "to rejoice") is clearly marked in Mesopotamian sources. It is most clearly an aesthetic response when the adverb *hadiš*, "joyously," is attached to verbs or states of looking upon works. The deities, it is hoped or asserted, are or will be happy with, and then *in*, their sanctuaries. How-

ever formulaic the phrases may be, the link between seeing and becoming joyful brings clearly into focus the delight associated with the experience of works.

Admiration or awe is the other positive response to an object, for which the terms $U_6.DI/$ *tabrītu* and $NI_3.ME.GAR/qâlu$ are used. When "the people" stand before a major work, they react to its qualities and overall effect as *spectators* rather than as primary recipients. The same temple or artifact that was greeted with joy by the gods evokes intense admiration when scrutinized by individuals, for they experience it not as a gift but in terms of its awesome impact on themselves and on their lives. Nowhere is this reaction clearer than when Gudea alludes to the Eninnu, the temple he built for the god Ningirsu in Girsu in his Cylinder A Inscription:

> The temple, its awesome radiance was cast over the land; its praise reached the mountains. The Eninnu, its dread covered all the lands like a garment.

It is then eulogized:

> Temple built in luxuriance for its king . . . Temple, like the sun(-god) shining forth over the land . . . like lush moonlight filling the assembly (place), like a well-formed mountain bearing luxuriance, established for admiration.

What is of particular interest in these passages is the temple's intrinsic ability to elicit admiration from the population of Lagash/Girsu, while to its patron deity, Ningirsu, it brings joy.

The rhetorical significance of the terms $U_6.DI$ and *tabrītu* as they occur in many royal texts is also evident. They call attention to a building or an object by claiming for it a powerful impact on its viewers. Such rhetorical devices serve to focus attention in much the same way as compositional considerations do in visual imagery, for example, as when the body of the Akkadian ruler, Naram-Sin, enhanced by scale and features, is placed centrally on the great Victory Stela bearing his name. Through the focus that statements about being admired or being joyously received achieve, the work's affect is at once asserted and established. At the same time, to report admiration and awe in the gaze of the people is a rhetorical strategy on the part of the particular Mesopotamian ruler that serves as the ultimate affirmation of his enterprise.

The Stela of Naram-Sin of Agade

The Victory Stela of Naram-Sin, discovered at Susa by Jacques de Morgan in 1898, remains one of the most powerful works of Mesopotamian art for Western audiences. It was created as a monument in celebration of a victory over eastern hill tribes by the Akkadian ruler (around 2240 BCE). In the twelfth century, the work was carried off as a battle trophy by the Elamite king Shutruk-Nakkhunte who reinscribed it as an offering to his own deity. (See also "Kings of Akkad" in Part 5, Vol. II.)

Modern viewers are engaged by the "beauty" of the lithe, supple body of the ruler, the attention to landscape elements, and the force of compositional vectors. All diagonals focus attention upon the king as he treads on the defeated enemy, dominates those who are about to flee, and victoriously faces his mountain. The dramatic power of the monument lies in the masterful manipulation not only of space but of time. The lines of Akkadian soldiers approach, the enemy flees, and the king emerges victorious all in a unified visual field—thereby adhering to classical Aristotelian precepts that underlie Western notions of coherence in a work of art (see, for example the masterful description of Henrietta Groenewegen-Frankfort). What is more, the overall compositional organization is familiar to us: One need only cite a work like Michelangelo's *Last Judgment*, in which the blessed rise at our left (as do Naram-Sin's soldiers) and point toward the central figure of Christ, while the damned fall at our right (just like Naram-Sin's enemy).

At the same time, our investigation of the Mesopotamian principles underlying works we call art illuminate what would have been seen as positive attributes in ancient times. Central to the work is, after all, an "image" (Akkadian *ṣalmu*) of the king. The well-formed (*banû*) body of the ruler conveys both breeding and the favor of the gods, which is manifested as grace. What would be less obvious to modern viewers is that there may be a cultural reason why the king is depicted in profile facing to our right. Mesopotamian incantations and omen texts all record that damage to the right side of the body bodes evil, not only for the individual but for the state and the ruler. That Naram-Sin's body is perfect, with the right side exposed to view, makes clear that the ruler is both well-formed and auspicious (*damqu*). More than any other monument preserved to date, his body is clearly apparent beneath his garments. The bold stance and powerful yet gracefully integrated musculature further denote the vigor (*baštu*) and allure (*kuzbu*) of the ruler. These are terms that are also used to describe the Mesopotamian hero-ruler, Gilgamesh, on whom many historical kings based their own image.

The multiple astral bodies (perhaps stars or suns) in the upper field have puzzled scholars; but it may be that they are intended to convey divine favor (since

Victory stela of Naram-Sin I, cast in red sandstone, found at Susa, circa 2240 BCE. LOUVRE MUSEUM, PARIS

the chief deity of Sippar, the city-state from which the Elamite ruler captured the monument, was the sun god, Shamash) as well as the positive attribute of radiant light or luminosity surrounding the ruler and his victory. Further evidence of divine favor may be seen in the neck-bead worn by Naram-Sin, known from textual references to be an auspicious amulet invoking divine protection.

Just as the ancient auditor of the Gilgamesh epic was explicitly invoked to "view" the body/person of Gilgamesh and see how auspicious and well-formed the hero was, so the ancient viewer of the monument can be imagined to have gazed on the figure and the victory monument of the king with admiration (*tabrītu*), finding it a "pleasure to behold" (*ana dagāli lullû*). This combination of awe, aesthetic delight, and appreciation—as response to the appearance and the impact of a work—helps us to touch not only what may appeal to us in individual monuments today but also what would have touched the ancient Mesopotamians.

CONCLUSION

The three categories of aesthetic investment and experience—making, appearance, and affect—reflect neither arbitrary nor idiosyncratic divisions; rather, they are interrelated aspects of the work, all of which were addressed in Mesopotamian texts. The first reflects an investment in aestheticized production, the second reflects the subclasses of positively coded aesthetic endowments, and the third reflects the range of aesthetic responses. Together they afford a glimpse into a coherent system of Mesopotamian aesthetics. Nevertheless, since this is a relatively new field of inquiry, it may be useful to conclude with considerations that need further exploration.

In reflecting on Mesopotamian aesthetics it has seemed important to take up the challenge of anthropologists and to discover, as Kris L. Hardin suggests, a "way of revealing, in indigenous terms, the culture-specific forms and foci of aesthetic evaluation." Our challenge has been to attempt to understand both the nature of and the role played by aesthetic experience in Mesopotamian culture. If anything, the links that the ancient Mesopotamians crafted between aesthetic affect and the sacred seem closest to what was obtained in Medieval Europe or in Hindu and Buddhist Asia, where a primary role of the aesthetic experience was to provide a conduit for encountering the divine. Some Mesopotamian artifacts presumed to be highly invested with aesthetic affect, such as finely carved cylinder seals made from precious material, are never mentioned in aesthetic terms in the texts. Perhaps this is because they functioned within the bureaucratic, not the religious, sphere of activities. This would not preclude their owners from taking pleasure in individual seals or their makers from investing the seals with affective qualities; but we cannot easily recover that information, for Mesopotamian texts give us no access to the personal realm of experience.

If, as Ian Hunter argues, aesthetics is one of the "contingencies" that not only represents and makes the culture but also socializes its members into directed channels of response, then "Mesopotamian" aesthetics is likely to be nowhere near as monolithic as is presented here: Changes in emphasis as well as innovation in elements of design and materials would have occurred both as natural developments in artistic tradition and as correlates of sociopolitical change. Nevertheless, the repetitive vocabulary and formulaic phraseology in which this aesthetic tends to be couched may in itself be information. Changes in form, style, and content may indeed have varied with cultural and historical change, but it is equally possible that because one of the principal rhetorical foundations of Mesopotamian tradition was continuity, the terms and qualities of "aesthetic value" and the general nature of aesthetic experience may well have remained relatively fixed through time.

BIBLIOGRAPHY

Theoretical Literature

The philosophical literature on aesthetics is vast. There are essentially two schools whose positions are relevant for us here. The first ties aesthetics to the contemplation of the "fine arts" and to judgments of quality (good, beautiful); the second, and more recent, links aesthetics to cultural expression and political systems of representation. Readers should consult any recent dictionary of art for a full bibliography.

In recent years, considerable scholarly attention has been placed on the importance of eliciting indigenous terms, concepts, and categories of aesthetic experience. An important early work is that by WARREN D'AZEVEDO, "A Structural Approach to Esthetics: Toward a Definition of Art in Anthropology," *American Anthropologist* 60, no. 4 (1958); and more recently, RICHARD L. ANDERSON, *Calliope's Sisters: A Comparative Study of Philosophies of Art* (1990) and IAN HUNTER, "Aesthetics and Cultural Studies," in *Cultural Studies*, edited by LAWRENCE GROSSBERG, CARY NELSON, and PAULA TREICHER (1992). The study of African art has been particularly concerned with these issues, for which see KRIS L. HARDIN, *The Aesthetics of Action: Change and Reproduction in a West African Town* (1993). In Western art, particular emphasis has been placed on inquiry into the learned debates on visual experience in the Medieval period, as, for example, in EDGAR DE BRUYNE, *The Esthetics of the Middle Ages*, translated by EILEEN B. HENNESSY (1969).

Sumerian and Akkadian Documents

As there are no philosophical or theoretical treatises on aesthetics in ancient Mesopotamia, the interested researcher must rely on literary, political, and even economic texts that contain references or allusions to visual works and experience. For the Sumerian terms discussed in this essay see the articles, as they appear, written for the *The Sumerian Dictionary of the University Museum of the University of Pennsylvania.* For the Akkadian materials, the more complete publications of *The Assyrian Dictionary of the Oriental Institute of the University of Chicago* are available, in which entries on individual terms can be consulted, with many cross-references as well as Sumerian equivalents provided. For the publications of inscriptions by periods, consult the bibliographies assembled in the "History" articles published in these volumes.

The cited Mari documents are extracted from articles by D. CHARPIN and J. DURAND, "Notes de lecture: *Texte aus dem Sinkāšid Palast,*" in *MARI: Annales de Recherches Interdisciplinaires* 7 (1993) and by P. VILLARD, "Parade militaire dans les jardins de Babylone," *Florilegium Marianum* 1 (1992).

On Mesopotamian Art and Aesthetics

General surveys of Mesopotamian art are found in HENRI FRANKFORT, *Art and Architecture of the Ancient Orient* (rev. ed. 1970) and ANTON MOORTGAT, *Art of Ancient Mesopotamia* (1969). Of the large picture books, EVA STROMMENGER, *5000 Years of the Art of Mesopotamia* (1964), is perhaps the most comprehensive.

Studies that pursue the particular nature of Mesopotamian representational systems include: PAULINE AL-BENDA, "Symmetry in the Art of the Assyrian Empire," in *La circulation des biens, des personnes et des idées dans le Proche-Orient ancien,* edited by D. CHARPIN and F. JOANNÈS, Rencontre Assyriologique Internationale, vol. 38 (1992); JULIA ASHER-GREVE, "Observations on the Historical Relevance of Visual Imagery in Mesopotamia," in *Histoire et conscience historique dans les civilisations du Proche-Orient ancien,* edited by ALBERT DE PURY (1989); GUITTY AZARPAY, "A Photogrammetric Study of Three Gudea Statues," *Journal of the American Oriental Society* 110, no. 4 (1990); ELENA CASSIN, *La splendeur divine: Introduction à l'étude de la mentalité mésopotamienne,* vol. 8, *Civilisations et Sociétés* (1968); PAUL GARELLI, "La concep-

tion de la beauté en Assyrie," in *Lingering Over Words: Studies in Ancient Near Eastern Literature in Honor of William L. Moran,* edited by TZVI ABUSCH, JOHN HUEHNERGARD, and PIOTR STEINKELLER (1990); HENRIETTA GROENEWEGEN-FRANKFORT, *Arrest and Movement: An Essay on Space and Time in the Representational Art of the Ancient Near East* (1951); THORKILD JACOBSEN, "Pictures and Pictorial Language," in *Figurative Language in the Ancient Near East,* edited by M. MINDLIN, M. J. GELLER, and J. E. WANSBROUGH (1987); BETTY SCHLOSSMANN, "Portraiture in Mesopotamia in the Late Third and Early Second Millennium B.C., Part I," *Archiv für Orientforschung* 26 (1978/1979) and "Part II," *Archiv für Orientforschung* 28 (1981/1982); AGNÈS SPYCKET, *La Statuaire du Proche-Orient ancien* (1981); IRENE J. WINTER, "The Body of the Able Ruler: Toward an Understanding of the Statues of Gudea," in *DUMU-E₂-DUB-BA-A: Studies in Honor of Åke W. Sjöberg,* edited by HERMANN BEHRENS, DARLENE LODING, and MARTHA T. ROTH, Occasional Publications of the Samuel Noah Kramer Fund, vol. 11 (1989). See also the important collection of studies in ANN C. GUNTER, ed., *Investigating Artistic Environments in the Ancient Near East* (1990), including JERROLD COOPER, "Mesopotamian Historical Consciousness and the Production of Monumental Art in the Third Millennium B.C.," ANNE D. KILMER, "Sumerian and Akkadian Names for Designs and Geometric Shapes," and JACK M. SASSON, "Artisans . . . Artists: Documentary Perspectives from Mari."

Special studies on architectural decoration and on the adornment of sculpture include DIETZ OTTO EDZARD, "Die Einrichtung eines Tempels in älteren Babylonien. Philologische Aspekte," in *Le temple et le culte* (1975) and SYLVIE LACKENBACKER, *Le palais sans rival: le récit de construction en Assyrie* (1990) for architecture; A. LEO OPPENHEIM, "The Golden Garments of the Gods," *Journal of Near Eastern Studies* 8 (1949) and W. F. LEEMANS, "Ishtar of Lagaba and Her Dress," in *Studia ad tabulas cuneiformes collectas a F. M. Th. de Liagre Böhl pertinentia* I/1 (1952). An early study on color in Mesopotamia was undertaken by BENNO LANDSBERGER, "Über Farben im Sumerisch-Akkadischen," *Journal of Cuneiform Studies* 21 (1967).

SEE ALSO **Artisans and Artists in Ancient Western Asia** (Part 4, Vol. I); **Reliefs, Statuary, and Monumental Painting in Ancient Mesopotamia** (Part 10, Vol. IV); and **Understanding Ancient Near Eastern Art: A Personal Account** (Part 11, Vol. IV).

Egyptian Art and Aesthetics

—JOHN BAINES

Whereas the monumental and visual record from ancient Egypt is incomparably rich, Egyptian texts are far less informative on aesthetic matters than are Mesopotamian ones. Aesthetic analysis therefore needs to start from works of art themselves. While such an approach risks imposing a Western perspective that will restrict discussion, not least by molding notions of what art is, points of comparison and divergence between the West and Egypt can be found and used to control interpretation.

The importance of art in Egypt is beyond question. The civilization had a central visual definition and high-cultural framework for public forms. In order to address aesthetic aspects of that definition and to relate them to particular works of art, it is necessary to compare the products of different hands, contexts, and periods and also to become familiar with the implicit norms and subtle variations through which meanings and values were expressed.

Audience and reception were not significant in the same way as in the West. Many works were not created primarily to be seen but to fulfill a religious function. They were objects of intense interest for patrons, especially during their lengthy manufacture, and more generally for artists; once created they were viewed by few, but those few included the gods and the dead.

Architecture was the premier artistic form. Building complexes absorbed huge expenditures and formed the setting for other works of art, no doubt including pieces made in luxurious perishable substances and performances such as dances. Both as a setting and in itself, architecture was a prime vehicle of meaning, and this emphasis on meaning grew with time. A brief text in the temple of Ramesses (Ramses) III at Medinet Habu runs: "As the sun disk continues to shine, the primeval waters to encircle the 'Ocean,' and the child moon to repeat manifestations, being rejuvenated perpetually, so the name of the King is in his temple for ever." While this statement is not directly aesthetic, it praises the temple by associating it with solar rhythms and with youth, an essential Egyptian value. The richly decorated Greco-Roman period temple of Dendara (Iunet, ancient Tentyra) is replete with symbolic solar groups that assimilate the structure to the image of the beautiful goddess of love, Hathor. The dazzling colors of a temple and the strong contrast between the dark interior and the constantly evoked sun outside circumscribe an aesthetic experience felt by both humans and deities. These aspects do not illuminate the decisions that went, for example,

into the choice of a temple's proportions, but they do set the world of the stone temple apart from the mud-brick of most other constructions. In creating an ideal microcosm, temples formed objects of beauty or perfection—ideas often conveyed by the same word in Egyptian.

The statuary that filled temples and tombs raises other aesthetic issues. Something of its ancient significance can be discerned through materials and quality of execution. The loss of the most precious substances—gold, electrum, silver, inlaid bronze, (semi)precious stones, and costly woods for inlay—makes it difficult to assess their aesthetic significance, but their importance is suggested by the extraordinary finds from the tomb of the minor king Tutankhamun (circa 1325 BCE).

Much large-scale statuary was made of hard stones. These were often valued for themselves more than for their visual qualities, since finished works were normally painted, rendering the material invisible. Use of these stones involved a comparable effort to precious metals. Richness of materials and virtuosity of planning and execution were valued both in aesthetic terms and—as with temples—for their eloquence in showing either the king's devotion to the gods, for whom many works were created, or his own or his elite's high status.

Works commissioned by different patrons exemplify the aesthetic significance of quality of execution. If modern critical judgments based on individual taste are left aside as irrelevant, this technical criterion is a valid indicator of ancient evaluation. There is a congruence between what kings and a few leading individuals commissioned and modern perceptions of what is of the highest quality—a congruence that would be lacking in untutored modern evaluations of some artistic traditions. Such a judgment is relatively straightforward for the gneiss statue of Khephren that appears as a masterpiece in surveys of Egyptian art. Its owner, who constructed the Second Pyramid at Giza (about 2500 BCE), was a powerful king who dedicated enormous resources to artistic production (comparable, for example, to the activities of Amenhotep III in the late Eighteenth Dynasty).

Most Egyptian statuary is idealizing, showing men very youthful, in still perfect early maturity, or, in a less widespread form, heavy with the success of age; women are almost always youthful. The slim, and for men often discreetly muscular, ideals of all but the Late Period are strikingly close to those of the modern

Continued on the next page.

Continued from the previous page.
West. Middle Kingdom royal works in particular illustrate that, although the Egyptians generally used a conventionally "beautiful" form, they had a more complex aesthetic. While the ideal and serene Old Kingdom Khephren embodies values of divinity indicated by the falcon enveloping the king's head cloth and asserts his calm dominion over the world, the haggard faces of statues of late Twelfth Dynasty kings, which are just as excellent technically, make a different statement. These works, which retain a perfect body, probably express iconographically the heavy responsibility of the king's role that is expounded in literary texts of the period, evoking a conception of society and of the world as threatened and in need of affirmation. The same facial types were used on sphinxes, in which the leonine element was more prominent than in other periods, creating images of great pensive ferocity. For an example of Twelfth Dynasty portraiture in sculpture, see fig. 19 of Senwosret III in "Ancient Egyptian Reliefs, Statuary, and Monumental Paintings," earlier in this section, this volume.

Many Late and Greco-Roman period nonroyal statues, superbly executed in prestigious hard stones, depict men with worn facial features. Both Twelfth Dynasty and Late Period works emphasize individual representation, if not portraiture, demonstrating an aesthetic interest in variety and in direct observation. In all periods, works exhibiting the highest technical skill tend also to be the most innovative, as well as showing the greatest range of human types and imperfections of the human form. The same principle is visible in the richly varied subordinate figures in reliefs of "daily life" found in the finest tombs.

Uses of the artistic past document aesthetic choices. Much Late Period statuary looks to models from the central Old Kingdom and the Twelfth and later Eighteenth dynasties—the periods of the works just cited. These later statues show both a deep knowledge of forebears and a complex response to them.

These few examples illustrate how, even though the living context of ancient aesthetic discussion and decision is lost, the comparison and study of ancient works and of their development over long periods can give access to some of the values and choices that informed Egyptian artistic tradition. These values are distinctive and different from those of other ancient near eastern civilizations.

Bibliography

MARIANNE EATON-KRAUSS and ERHART GRAEFE, eds., *Studien zur altägyptischen Kunstgeschichte* (1990) collects studies on the interpretation of Egyptian art; MAYA MÜLLER's "Die ägyptische Kunst aus kunsthistoricher Sicht," is particularly valuable. JOHN BAINES, "On the Status and Purposes of Ancient Egyptian Art," *Cambridge Archaeological Journal* 4, no. 1 (1994), discusses the position of art and artists in Egyptian society, partly in response to the essays in the volume just cited. ARIELLE P. KOZLOFF and BETSY M. BRYAN, *Egypt's Dazzling Sun: Amenhotep III and His World* (1992) is the catalogue of an exhibition of the art of Amenhotep III and gives a sense of the scale of the king's artistic undertakings. EDNA R. RUSSMANN, *Egyptian Sculpture, Cairo and Luxor* (1989) is an excellent study of statuary with a valuable introduction on artistic interpretation. JOHN BAINES, "Ancient Egyptian Concepts and Uses of the Past: 3rd to 2nd Millennium BC Evidence," in *Who Needs the Past? Indigenous Values on Archaeology*, edited by ROBERT LAYTON (1989) discusses artistic uses of the past. ROLAND TEFNIN, "Les Yeux et les oreilles du Roi," in *L'atelier de l'orfèvre: Mélanges offerts à Ph. Derchain*, edited by M. BROZE and P. TALON (1992), studies the sculpture of late Twelfth Dynasty kings. Other essays in this reference set—"Ancient Egyptian Reliefs, Statuary, and Monumental Paintings" (Part 10, Vol. IV); "Palaces and Temples of Ancient Egypt" and "Artisans and Artists in Pharaonic Egypt" (Part 4, Vol. IV); and "Akhetaten: A Portrait in Art of an Ancient Egyptian Capital"—present essential background, illustrations, and valuable discussion.

Reliefs, Statuary, and Monumental Paintings in Ancient Mesopotamia

AGNÈS SPYCKET

MESOPOTAMIAN CIVILIZATION developed in Sumer and then Akkad between the lower courses of the Euphrates and the Tigris rivers, and in Assyria along the upper course of the Tigris and its tributaries. The oldest sculptural and pictorial manifestations are not found in Mesopotamia. Actually, small clay figurines of humans and animals were created beginning in the seventh millennium BCE at Jarmo, in the mountains of Iraqi Kurdistan. Later, in the sixth millennium, and farther west, at Umm Dabaghiyeh, figures were created and animals were painted on the walls of dwellings. At about the same time, very small alabaster statuettes of nude women with conical heads and without mouths appeared at Tell al-Sawwan. It was not until the end of the fourth millennium that the Mesopotamians displayed their talent for hewing stone and decorating their walls with colored scenes.

RELIEFS

Fourth and Third Millennia

Statuary, which is sculpture in three dimensions, is different from the art of bas-relief, which requires translating reality into two dimensions. This explains certain conventions that the Meso-

potamians introduced and followed during their entire civilization. The head, the pelvis, the legs, and the feet are shown in profile, but the chest faces forward or, less commonly, is shown in three-quarter view. The face is in profile, but the eye remains in full view. The notion of perspective, as it is known to us, did not exist. From the very beginning artists used registers to separate the action, starting from the top. The hierarchy of values likewise imposes a certain number of conventions. Thus, the more important persons are depicted larger than the others. The gods are taller than the kings, who, in turn, tower over their subjects. When the king pits himself against an animal, the latter is shown smaller; however, if the point is to accent the valor of the king, then they do battle in equal size.

These design conventions are already employed in the oldest important relief known, which was found at Warka and is known as the Hunt Stela (height 80 centimeters [32 inches], in the Iraq Museum; fig. 1). Dating to the end of the fourth millennium, the relief is carved on a roughly oval block of basalt. The "priest-king" hunts the lion in two registers. In the upper register, he plants a long spear in the breast of a rearing lion; below, armed with a great bow, he has shot feathered arrows at two superposed lions. The bearded man, with his hair rolled into

Fig. 1. Basalt-block "Hunt Stela" showing a lion hunt, excavated from Uruk (modern Warka), circa 3000 BCE. IRAQ MUSEUM, BAGHDAD

a chignon and held by a rounded headband, is dressed in a wide skirt that falls to the knees and is gathered at the waist by a belt.

A type of relief peculiar to Early Dynastic Sumerian art is the perforated plaque, which is more or less square in shape. In a frame divided into two or three registers around a square or round hole, scenes centered on a religious theme unfold. The plaques must have been mounted on the walls by means of a peg of stone with a patterned head that passed through the central perforation. The plaques depict the commemoration of a ritual act of founding a temple; the celebration of a victory, in the form of a banquet in which the king and queen participate; or the king surrounded by his family. Not one of these plaques has been found in the location in which it was originally placed (not at Ur, Nippur, Girsu/Lagash, or the Diyala Valley). The great victory stela of Eannatum, a ruler of Lagash, found at Tello (ancient Girsu), is a good illustration of the care that monarchs took to perpetuate their exploits and to offer them to their gods, in

this case Ningirsu, the god of the city (height 1.88 meters [about 6 feet]). Sculpted on the top of this tall, arched stela, on each face and on the sides, are scenes in several registers. On one side, Eannatum is represented at the head of his army of foot soldiers and then in his chariot. The upper part is covered with vultures holding in their beaks the heads of conquered enemies. On the other side, the conqueror—or the god himself—has gathered the enemies in a large net and fells them with a mace under the watchful eye of a goddess. This fragmentary stela is interesting both iconographically and historically, because a long inscription tells the story of this victory over the neighboring city of Umma (modern Tell Jokha) toward the middle of the third millennium. (The stela appears in "The Deeds of Ancient Mesopotamian Kings" in Part 9, Vol. IV.)

Few changes are found in the sculpture of the Early Akkadian Dynasty. The victory stelas of King Sargon show the same use of registers as earlier works. It is not until the reign of his grandson, Naram-Sin, that noteworthy modifications are found. They are exemplified in the pink sandstone stela that was found at Susa, where it had been taken as booty by an Elamite king of the twelfth century (height 2 meters [about 6.5 feet]). The difference is obvious at first glance. The registers give way to a single scene. Under the protection of three stars representing the heavenly divinities—Sun, Moon, and Star (of Ishtar)—Naram-Sin, at the head of his army, ascends a mountain to conquer a tribe of pillaging nomads of whom four are already dead and three others beg for mercy. For the first time in Mesopotamian art, the king wears a helmet decorated with the two horns normally reserved for gods; this touch proves that he has been deified. Larger than his soldiers, Naram-Sin moves forward, climbing an undulating ground that brings him to the peak. The rising sweep in movement, from left to right, contrasts with the stagnant quality of the horizontal scenes as they had previously been depicted. Entirely new as well is the attempt to represent a landscape by mixing two large trees among the people. This artistic contribution of the Semitic conquerors shatters Sumerian rigidity, and while preserving the conventions of the predecessors, it brings realism and imagination to them. (The stela of

Naram-Sin is illustrated and discussed in "Aesthetics in Ancient Mesopotamian Art" above.)

The accession of the Third Dynasty of Ur opens the way for a Sumerian revival that lasts until the end of the third millennium. The rules of Gudea of Lagash and Ur-Nammu of Ur are marked by stelas designed in registers. The stela of Ur-Nammu, founder of the dynasty, is one example (height 3 meters [almost 10 feet]. Illustrated back and front, it shows King Ur-Nammu, who appears twice in a symmetrical scene of the second register, offering a libation before the moon-god Nanna and the goddess Ningal. (The stela of Ur-Nammu appears in "Furniture in Ancient Western Asia" in Part 7, Vol. III.)

Second Millennium

One of the most important monuments of Mesopotamian civilization is the basalt stela on which Hammurabi, the king of Babylon, had engraved the 282 laws of the code that bears his name (height 2.25 meters [about 7.4 feet]; illustrated in "King Hammurabi of Babylon" in Part 5, Vol. II). The perfect quality of the engraving of the long cuneiform inscription that takes up the greater part of the stone is more striking than the scene sculpted at the top. There, the sun-god Shamash, crowned with the tiara of four rows of horns, is seated on a stool, his feet on the mountain; he hands the ring and scepter, insignia of power, to the king. Hammurabi stands, his right hand at his mouth, and listens with reverence as the god dictates the laws to him. The king wears a long, open-fronted cloak with a double girdle and a headband, and the god wears a pleated robe; each has a very long beard.

The Kassite period during the second half of the second millennium produced few sculptural monuments, with the exception of the *kudurru*. The *kudurrus* are a special category of sculpted and inscribed stelae that were set up in the temples to invoke the protection of the gods on the transfer of royal property to a new owner. (See "The Kassites of Ancient Mesopotamia" in Part 5, Vol. II.) The stones were dedicated by kings of the dynasty. Several of the more than one hundred known *kudurrus* are inscribed with the name of Melishipak, who reigned in the twelfth century. On one, the king leads his daughter by the hand before an enthroned goddess to whom he will consecrate her as a priestess. Symbols

and animals emblematic of the gods of the Babylonian pantheon (height 90 and 68 centimeters [36 and 27 inches]) are laid out in registers on another stone (fig. 2). In the upper register, the crescent of the moon-god Sin, the star of Ishtar, and the sun-disk of Shamash appear over the two horned tiaras of the gods Anu and Enlil that lie on an altar. The emblems of Ea, a ram's front part on the fish-bodied goat, and of Ninkhursag, an upturned omega, also lie on the altar. On

Fig. 2. Black limestone *kudurru*, or boundary stone, of Melishipak, made in Babylonia, found at Susa, Kassite period. LOUVRE MUSEUM, PARIS

the succeeding register, Ninurta, Marduk, Nabu, Nusku, and Ningirsu are among other deities that are represented by their emblems.

First Millennium

Assyrian art supplanted Babylonian art during the first half of the first millennium. This was a result of the Assyrian domination of the entire Near East, from the Mediterranean to the frontiers of Elam and from Lake Van to the Persian Gulf. To commemorate their incessant military campaigns, all the Assyrian kings had themselves represented on stone stelae with an arched top or on rock reliefs. They are posed similarly, so that they would be unidentifiable were it not for the inscriptions that accompany them. Standing in profile with the right arm thrust forward, they are moving. Vested in their royal finery, they wear shawls with long fringes and tall tiaras topped with a little point. The beards and the hair, which falls to the shoulders, are finely curled. They wear necklaces with pendants, bracelets on their wrists, and arm bands at the elbow. Above them are shown various divine emblems. Other monuments include obelisks, which have four sides, each of which is sculpted with scenes arrayed in registers. These depict expeditions of two kings of the ninth century, Assurnasirpal II and Shalmaneser III. (See "Art and Ideology" above for the Black Obelisk of Shalmaneser.)

These indefatigable conquerors recorded their exploits for posterity on sculptural reliefs on the walls of their palaces. Their taste for the colossal could be satisfied because northern Mesopotamia furnished them with all the stone they needed. In this manner, the bas-relief took over the royal residences and exalted Assyrian power in narrative scenes. Each reign inscribed in stone the narrative of military campaigns as well as the life at the royal court.

By choosing different capitals, the rulers multiplied the occasions to recount their exploits (see "The Deeds of Ancient Mesopotamian Kings" in Part 9 earlier in this volume). In the ninth century, Assurnasirpal II (883–859). founded his capital at Kalkhu (modern Nimrud); the city remained the capital of Assyria through his successor, Shalmaneser III (858–824), and until Tiglath-pileser III (744–727). In the eighth century, Sargon II (721–705) chose Khorsabad as site for his capital Dur-Sharrukin, but his successors, Sennacherib (704–681), Esarhaddon (680–669), and Assurbanipal (669–630) settled at Nineveh. Buried in sand for more than two thousand years, it was not until the nineteenth century CE that these cities reemerged under the shovels of excavators.

The gates to the palaces of Nimrud and Khorsabad are guarded by winged genies, sculpted in high relief, with the body of a bull or a lion and the head of a bearded human, which is crowned with a divine tiara with horns (fig. 3). At Nimrud, over more than a hundred years under British excavation, the reliefs are much less prominent. The silhouettes of the king and of the genies are very slightly raised from the background, so that the cuneiform inscriptions could be engraved over the reliefs in a way that would not have been possible had the figures projected more. A large panel from the throne room portrays Assurbanipal twice in order to retain the symmetry. He is depicted on both sides of a stylized sacred tree with palm leaves, which is under the protection of the god Assur, who is shown within a winged disk. Dressed in robes of state, Assurbanipal is followed by a winged genie. Each genie holds in his right hand a pinecone, which he steeps in the water of a small bucket held in his

Fig. 3. Relief of human-headed, winged bull from the palace of Sargon II, Khorsabad, 721–705 BCE. ORIENTAL INSTITUTE, UNIVERSITY OF CHICAGO

left hand in order to fertilize the tree (height 1.70 meters [about 3.5 feet]; fig. 4). Beside these ritualistic scenes were those that portray military achievements: cities taken by means of rolling siege towers, ancestors of modern tanks; encampments; enemies in flight before the chariots. In Fort Shalmaneser, at Nimrud, the throne of Shalmaneser III (now in the Iraq Museum) is decorated with a sculpted scene that narrates a military campaign. At its center is a peace treaty, embodied in a handshake between the Assyrian king and a contemporary Babylonian king, probably Marduk-zakir-shumi. This unusual historical event allowed the depiction of two rivals, representing the northern and southern cultures. (The throne base appears in "Art and Ideology" above.)

In their residence at Imgur-Enlil (modern Balawat), Assurnasirpal II and Shalmaneser III commissioned monumental gates covered with panels of bronze (now in the British Museum and the Louvre; pictured in "Art and Ideology in Ancient Western Asia" above). Their military campaigns are modeled in repoussé in a very vivid style on superposed registers.

The excavation of the palace of Sargon II at Khorsabad began in 1843 under the direction of the French consul at Mosul, Paul-Émile Botta, with the cooperation of the artist Eugène Flandin. Victor Place undertook further work from 1852 to 1854. The site was cleared nearly a century later, from 1929 to 1934, by Henri Frankfort, who headed an expedition of the Oriental Institute Museum in Chicago. The reliefs include depictions of the king, crowned with his tiara, giving orders to his minister; servants transporting the royal furniture; and winged genies with human or animal heads sprinkling the sacred tree. In a scene that has no parallel, cedar trunks from Lebanon, for the roof of the palace, are transported by water (fig. 5). The trees are carried on barges or pulled with ropes behind the boats. A rocky islet surmounted by a temple situated along the Phoenician coast provides geographic precision, but great imagination rules the illustration of winged bulls and a genie-fish in the water alongside serpents, turtles, and fish.

While conquest largely occupied the time of the Assyrian rulers, they did have some moments for leisure. One of their favorite pastimes, the hunt, is depicted on several reliefs. The kings pit themselves against lions on foot, at the gallop on horseback, or else on two-wheeled chariots drawn by two or three horses. The seventh-century hunting scenes of Assurbanipal from Nineveh (now in the British Museum) are famous for the vivid scenes in low relief and for the beauty of animals modeled with restraint. The lioness, wounded by arrows that have paralyzed her hindquarters, yet roaring in fury and pain before collapsing, stands as a masterpiece from any era (fig. 6).

Scenes of daily life are rare. In one example in the British Museum, Assurbanipal enjoys a

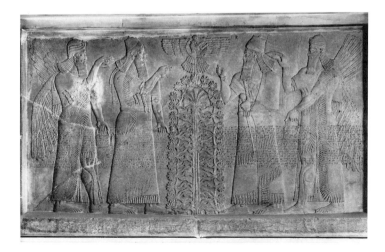

Fig. 4. Relief of Assurnasirpal II from the Northwest Palace at Nimrud, 883–859 BCE. BRITISH MUSEUM, LONDON

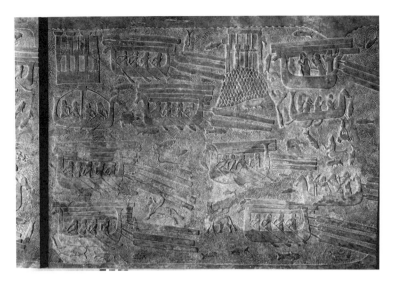

Fig. 5. A naval scene in which cedar trunks are being transported by water from Lebanon. Relief from the palace of Sargon II at Khorsabad, 721–705 BCE. LOUVRE MUSEUM, PARIS

well-earned rest under the arbor after the campaign against Elam. Lying on a bed, he takes his meal in the company of the queen, who is seated on a high-backed throne; he is surrounded by servants, some swatting flies while others play music. The head of the king of Elam dangles from the branches of a pine tree, symbolizing the omnipotence of Assyria.

Reaching ungovernable proportions, the Assyrian Empire collapsed under the blows of the Medes and the Babylonians, who seized Nineveh in 612. The Neo-Babylonian Empire, for

Fig. 6. Relief depicting a wounded lioness, from the North Palace of King Assurbanipal at Nineveh, circa 668–627 BCE. BRITISH MUSEUM, LONDON

all that it shone with great brilliance until the Persians' capture of Babylon in 539—and especially during the reign of Nebuchadnezzar II (604–562)—has left but few vestiges of its splendor. The monumental Gate of Ishtar and the Processional Way of Babylon were first built of baked brick and ornamented with rows of lions, bulls, and horned dragons in low relief. Then the walls were covered over with blue-enameled bricks; on this base, the animals stand out in yellow, beige, and white. Nothing remains of this grandiose concept but the reconstruction of the Gate of Ishtar at the Vorderasiatisches Museum in Berlin. (The Ishtar Gate is illustrated in "The Fortification of Cities in the Ancient Near East" in Part 7, Vol. III.)

STATUES

Third Millennium

In the period called Jemdet-Nasr (or the Protoliterate), stone statuary made its first appearance, at Warka (ancient Uruk) about 3000 BCE. Alongside statues of men that apparently depict priest-kings, with long hair wrapped into a chignon and topped by a broad headband, was a life-sized mask of a woman, magnificently modeled in white marble and intended to be attached to a vertical surface (fig. 7). Although the nose has

Fig. 7. Life-size mask of a woman, crafted in white marble, circa 3000 BCE, found at Uruk (modern Warka). The eyes and eyelids probably were once inlaid with stones, and the figure appears to have worn a headdress. IRAQ MUSEUM, BAGHDAD

been hammered and the eyes and eyebrows have lost their inlay of bitumen and shell, the work of the sculptor retains its seductive power. The sensitivity with which the cheeks and the eyebrows are rendered is particularly striking. (The statuary is also discussed in "Understanding Ancient Near Eastern Art" in Part 11, later in this volume.)

During the third millennium, in the Early Dynastic period, sculpture workshops were set up in the valley of the Diyala River, an eastern tributary of the Tigris, at Tell Asmar (ancient Eshnunna), Khafaje (ancient Tutub, Dur-Samsu-iluna, Tupliash), and Tell Agrab; in southern Mesopotamia at Nippur (modern Nuffar), Tello (ancient Girsu), al-Hiba (ancient Lagash), Uruk, and Ur (modern Tell al-Muqayyar); and in northern Mesopotamia at Asshur (modern Qalat Sharqat). Workshops also developed to the west, along the Euphrates and its tributaries at Mari (modern Tell Hariri) and Tell Khuera, and to the east, in Elam at Susa (modern Shush). The figures in the workshops were heavy and squat. Since stone was rare, especially in Sumer, the works, in limestone and alabaster, were small,

about 20 centimeters (8 inches) tall, but occasionally ranging up to double that height, as in some examples from Asmar. Copper and, later, bronze were also available to the sculptors.

The figures of men are most often portrayed standing barefooted on a pedestal; they are barechested and dressed in a *kaunakes* (a skirt with stylized woolly pleats that represent a goat- or sheepskin). They are either beardless with shaven head or bearded and wearing shoulderlength hair that is painted black with bitumen. More rarely, as came to be the fashion at Mari, the figure wears a beard and has his head shaved (Asshur, Khafaje). The eyes of both men and women can be carved, but more often they are inlaid with shell or marble, with the pupil in black stone or in lapis lazuli; the materials are secured in the eye socket with bitumen. The most common pose has clasped hands, for these statues were to perpetuate the prayers of the worshipers in the temples (fig. 8). Some male statues have an inscription in Sumerian cuneiform incised on the back that gives the name of the man, of the god, and of the temple in which the person dedicated his statue.

The women, on the other hand, are very rarely identified with an inscription. They stand or sit on a stool; their hands are clasped or they hold a branch, occasionally a bowl. A tunic, sometimes in one piece, sometimes a pleated *kaunakes*, leaves the right shoulder bare. The long hair is braided and crowns the head in a great variety of fashions; it can also be covered by a coiled turban (fig. 9). The absence of adornments at this period might be surprising: there are no necklaces, no bracelets, and only occasionally earrings. Given the presence of precious jewelry in certain tombs, it is reasonable to assume that the statues were sometimes decked out with real jewels that have subsequently disappeared.

The animals most frequently sculpted at this period are bulls and lions; sometimes the material is stone, sometimes copper or bronze. Other animals are represented as well, such as the two rampant bucks from a "royal" tomb at Ur (fig. 10). Leaning against a stylized tree, the wooden bodies are covered with gold and silver; the fleece is made of lapis lazuli locks of hair, as are the horns and the beard, and slivers of shells, which are analogous to the pleats of the *kaunakes* that clothe their contemporaries.

Fig. 8. Votive figurines, circa 2900–2600 BCE, from the Abu Temple at Tell Asmar that was excavated by Seton Lloyd in the 1930s. The sculptor purposefully made the eyes of two of them, which were inlaid with stones, quite large so that the statues appeared transfixed by the divine. Note the imprint of another statue on the figure in the front row, second from the left. ORIENTAL INSTITUTE, UNIVERSITY OF CHICAGO

The political change that ushered in the Akkadian Dynasty in the second half of the twenty-fourth century did not initiate any sudden modification of the character of the statuary; however, the rising power of the Semites is reflected in a greater variety in dress and a lesser rigidity in pose. A royal workshop produced pieces that illustrated this new tendency. One example is the life-sized bronze head of a man that was found at Nineveh (fig. 11). While it might portray any of the Akkadian Dynasty kings, the head very likely depicts Sargon (about 2334–2279), the founder of the dynasty. This identification was suggested by Sir Max Mallowan because the bronze head matches a representation of Sargon on a diorite stela now in the Louvre. Capped by a woven headband that keeps the hair tucked into a chignon, it has lost the inlay from the eyes; the beard, shaped into two parts, is entirely different from earlier works, and the modeling

of the cheeks attests to a new perception of the artist's task.

The changing style is obvious in a fine fragment of a large statue of King Manishtushu, who succeeded his brother Rimush. It is made of diorite, a hard, black stone highly valued by the kings henceforth from this period. The joined hands and the long skirt reveal a change in fashion: a supple fabric bordered with fringes replaces the woolly fleece of a *kaunakes* (fig. 12). Naram-Sin (about 2254–2218), Sargon's grandson, dedicated a well-modeled copper statue (now in the Iraq Museum) of which only the lower portion is preserved. Dressed only in a broad sash, the man is seated, legs folded, on a round base that is engraved with a long inscription recounting the foundation of several cities.

During the Third Dynasty of Ur, which lasted for more than a century at the end of the third millennium, the tendency toward large statuary

Fig. 9. Statuette of a female, from Khafaje, circa 2500 BCE. ORIENTAL INSTITUTE, UNIVERSITY OF CHICAGO

eyes are no longer inlaid, and the strongly emphasized eyebrows are given a herringbone pattern. The inscription carved on the robe indicates the name and the circumstances of the dedication to the god (another view of Gudea appears in "Proportions in Ancient Near Eastern Art" above).

A small female bust in black steatite, found at Tello and called, at the Louvre, "Woman with Scarf" (fig. 14), probably represents a princess whose name would have been written on the base of her skirt. The clothing, adorned with broad, decorative braiding, covers both shoulders. Her wavy hair is hidden by a fine, plain veil; the hair and the veil are gripped by a smooth headband that leaves the ears free. The neck is wholly encircled with a necklace of five

Fig. 10. Statuette from Ur of a ram and stylized foliage, circa 2500 BCE. THE UNIVERSITY MUSEUM OF ARCHAEOLOGY AND ANTHROPOLOGY, UNIVERSITY OF PENNSYLVANIA, PHILADELPHIA

continued. As before, stone was a luxury at Sumer and only the sovereigns used it. Diorite, known as "stone of Magan," was imported from a location that remains controversial. (For further discussion of Magan see "Distant Shores" in Part 6, Vol. III.)

Most of the statues of the *ensi* (governor) Gudea, sovereign of the kingdom of Lagash, and of his son Ur-Ningirsu come from Tello. In each of the score or so temples that he built or restored, Gudea installed a statue of himself that portrays him standing or seated on a low stool. He is dressed in a long one-piece shawl that is edged with a fringe and leaves bare the right shoulder and arm. His hands are joined in a pose of deference to a god (fig. 13). The head is shaved, and the full face, with a stubborn chin, is beardless. When he is not bareheaded, he wears a woolen hat with fine curls reminiscent of astrakhan. The

Fig. 11. Life-size bronze head of a man, presumed to be Sargon I, excavated at Nineveh, circa 2300 BCE. IRAQ MUSEUM, BAGHDAD

Fig. 12. Fragmentary diorite statue of King Manishtushu, third king of Akkad, brought as booty to Susa and excavated there, dating from circa 2260 BCE. LOUVRE MUSEUM, PARIS

Fig. 13. Fragmentary diorite statue of Gudea seated, found at Tello, circa 2130 BCE. LOUVRE MUSEUM, PARIS

rigid rings. From this period on, jewels are sculpted on both male and female statues. The hands assume the same pose as that of the men.

The surviving fragments of statues of kings of Ur have characteristics similar to those of Gudea. A limestone head from Warka is capped by the high, plain headband that was adopted by the rulers in the second millennium.

Statuettes of recumbent human-headed bison are also dated to this period. They are about 10

Fig. 14. Steatite bust from Tello of a "woman with scarf," circa twenty-second century BCE. LOUVRE MUSEUM, PARIS

2592

centimeters (4 inches) long and sometimes are inscribed. Crowned with the divine tiara of four rows of horns, their curly manes are stylized.

Second Millennium

Statues of divinities make their appearance at the beginning of the second millennium; they are recognizable by their tiaras decorated with several pairs of horns. One example now at the Louvre is a small, bearded head in terra-cotta from Tello (height 8.4 centimeters [about 3 inches]). The hair is tied in a chignon; on the head is a tiara with four rows of horns that join in an ascending movement. The remains of a necklace of large pearls are visible on the edge of the bust. This helps date the piece to the first centuries of the second millennium. While sculptures in this period were often painted, no paint is found on this example.

Two bronze statuettes from Tell Ishchali (ancient Neribtum) represent a four-faced god (height 17 centimeters [6.8 inches]) and goddess (height 16 centimeters [6.4 inches]). The god, clad in the old-fashioned *kaunakes*, is on the move; his left foot is placed on the back of a recumbent ram (fig. 15). Four bearded masks facing the four directions are set on the bust. They are topped with a flat cap edged with a single row of horns. The right arm falls along the body and holds a curved weapon. The goddess, seated on a four-legged stool, wears a long robe engraved with wavy lines. Her tall, cylindrical tiara is bordered by a pair of horns above each of her four faces. She holds to her knees a vase from which gush the fertilizing waters, a theme often represented in near eastern iconography (notably, in the "goddess with flowing vase" from Mari). Not a single known text clarifies the meaning of the four faces.

Several diorite statues of the kings of Eshnunna herald the art of the First Dynasty of Babylon, which was dominated by the strong personality of King Hammurabi in the eighteenth century. They were taken as booty to Susa in Iran, where they were recovered in damaged condition. There is no in-the-round equivalent to the representation of the king as on the stela of the Code of Hammurabi. However, at the Louvre, a small, diorite head (height 15 centimeters [6 inches]) of high quality, may represent the ruler at the end of his long reign of forty-three years. It depicts a bearded man, aged and gaunt, wearing the broad royal headband. This identification has been debated; the identification of a small bronze from Larsa at the Louvre has also been disputed. This man, kneeling on one knee, holds his right hand at his mouth. The right hand, the left fist, and the short-bearded face with inlaid eyes are covered with gold. A cap, which has been distorted by oxidation, must have been the royal headdress in the form of a broad band. A small, round basin is preserved on the front of the base. On the right side, in relief, a goddess seated on a high-backed throne receives a half-kneeling man, with his hand raised to his mouth, in the same pose as the statuette. On the left side of the base is carved a recumbent ram; behind it is an engraved thirteen-line inscription. The gold covering favors attributing the statue to a king, but it may also represent a person who has dedicated a statue of himself for the well-being of his king.

The most frequently represented animal in this period is the lion, who acts as guardian of the temples. Because of the scarcity of stone, large models were executed in clay, which were baked in sections. At Tell Harmal (ancient Shaduppum), fragments of six large lions have been

Fig. 15. Bronze statuette of a god with four faces from Tell Ishchali, Old Babylonian period, circa 1800 BCE. ORIENTAL INSTITUTE, UNIVERSITY OF CHICAGO

recovered; two have been reconstructed at the Baghdad Museum. The life-sized figures are sitting up with the front paws resting on the front of the slab that serves as a base; the wide-open mouths with four fangs are meant to be realistic and menacing, but the manes are stylized into striped tongues.

The Kassite Dynasty, which dominated the second half of the second millennium and ruled from Babylon, has left little in the way of an artistic legacy. A small, male head (height 4.3 centimeters [about 1.75 inches]) of great nobility was found in the royal palace of Dur-Kurigalzu (modern ʿAqar Quf) (fig. 16). It recalls the small terra-cotta head from Tello. Sculpted in clay, baked, and painted, it may date from the thirteenth century. The modeling of the face is fine, with a hooked nose, slanting eyes, and an edging of pointed beard. The hair, beard, eyebrows, eyelashes, and pupils of the eyes are painted black; the inside of the eyes is white, and the skin of the face is red.

In view of an execution that is more sensitive than what prevailed in the Assyrian north, a large limestone statue of a nude woman discovered at Nineveh must be Babylonian. The statue (height 94 centimeters [about 38 inches]), now at the British Museum, has no head or arms. Its

Fig. 16. Painted terra-cotta head, about 1.75 inches (4.3 cm.) high, of a man excavated at ʿAqar Quf, Kassite period. The head is currently in the Iraq Museum in Baghdad. HIRMER ARCHIVES, MUNICH

back is inscribed with the name of Assur-bel-kala, king of Assyria (1074–1057).

The lack of anatomical detail suggests that the statue depicts a goddess that would have been dressed in garments of state during ceremonies described in cuneiform texts. The custom of clothing statues of the Madonna and Child in sumptuous mantles at Christian pilgrimage sites would thus go back to a millennia-old tradition of the ancient Near East.

First Millennium

Assyrian power reached its height during the first centuries of the first millennium, and art was its beneficiary. The kings represented themselves in a worshiping attitude that gave sculpture in the round a conventional aspect. Because of the hazards of destruction and excavation, only statues of ninth-century rulers have so far been recovered. Thus, we have only one statue of Assurnasirpal II (883–859), from Nimrud (height 1.06 meters [about 3.5 feet], in the British Museum), and four statues of his successor, Shalmaneser III (858–823), two from Nimrud (height 1.03 meters [about 3.5 feet] and 1.40 meters [about 4.5 feet], in the Iraq Museum) and two from Asshur. The last group includes the only seated statue (height 1.35 meters [about 4.5 feet], in the British Museum). The seated statue is headless and made of basalt; the others are worked in limestone. The standing rulers are either bareheaded or crowned with a conical-bodied tiara, which is topped with a point. The curly hair falls to the shoulders and the long rectangular beard that broadly covers the cheeks descends in fine ringlets to the chest. One of the statues of Shalmaneser III from Nimrud retains the inlay in the wide-open eyes. He is clothed in a shawl bordered with a long, wavy fringe, which is wound diagonally around the body down to the sandal-shod feet, of which only the toes are visible. The monarch may wear bracelets and a necklace with pendants. Once again, the hands are clasped. Only Assurnasirpal II holds a scepter with a pommel and a curved weapon of state. Traces of black paint on the hair and beard are still perceptible in one case. All these royal statues are inscribed with the name of the ruler and rehearse the events of his reign. There is no question here of developing realistic portraits. Instead, the statues are symbols of Assyrian might—embodied in a compact, stiff appearance, as inexpressive as possible—which are meant to inspire fear and respect (fig. 17).

A bit more recent are six life-sized statues of guardian deities installed in the temple of the god Nabu at Nimrud. The deities are depicted standing with one hand in the other or holding a rectangular basin in front of them. They wear oval tiaras with one or two rows of horns, and a beard. These sculptures are massive, like those of gods holding a vase by the neck found at Khorsabad (height 1.60 meters [about 3 feet], in the Iraq Museum and the Oriental Institute Museum in Chicago).

The female statues of the Assyrian period are less numerous. A single complete example, in marble, comes from Asshur (height 70 centimeters [28 inches], in the Iraq Museum) and shows a full-figured woman with her hands joined who is dressed in a floor-length sheath dress with short sleeves. A plain headband binds the hair, which falls in curly masses to the shoulders. A sash, indicated by wavy lines, with a medallion hanging on the left side softens the compact and austere appearance, which is the same as that of the men (fig. 18).

Fig. 18. Marble statuette of a female, excavated at Asshur, Assyrian period. DRAWING BY CORNELIE WOLFF; IRAQ MUSEUM, BAGHDAD

While animals are handled with fine mastery in the Assyrian reliefs, only a few examples in the round survive. From Khorsabad, a recumbent bronze lion on a pedestal (length 41 centimeters [about 16.5 inches], in the Louvre) testifies to a gift for observation that has led to a realistic and powerful rendition of the musculature of the beast. Fixed in the earth, near a door of the palace, the strong ring it carries on its back probably was intended for attaching an awning above the entrance, which it guarded menacingly with open mouth.

WALL PAINTINGS

Throughout Mesopotamia, color has been applied to walls of houses, temples, and palaces for millennia. The distemper technique was used on mud-brick walls that were surfaced with mud, lime, or plaster. The fresco process (painting on a damp surface) was probably not used before the second half of the second millennium. The basic colors are red (iron oxide), white (gypsum), and black (bitumen), later supplemented by blue (lapis lazuli, copper oxide), green (mala-

Fig. 17. Limestone statue of Assurnasirpal II (883–859 BCE) from the Ninurta Temple at Nimrud. The statue's stiff appearance was meant to inspire fear and respect. BRITISH MUSEUM, LONDON

chite), and yellow and ochre (ferruginous earth). The color was mixed with water with a binder that could have been egg white or casein from milk.

The Neolithic village of Umm Dabaghiyeh, northwest of Asshur, has yielded dwellings from the beginning of the sixth millennium. Several small rooms preserve traces of wall paintings showing onager-hunting and wavy lines that are believed to represent birds' wings.

At Tell al-'Uqair, north of Babylon, a temple from the end of the fourth millennium includes a podium decorated with vertical yellow and white bands alternating with bands of geometric designs; it is flanked by animals, among them a reclining leopard and a seated leopard (fig. 19). Other rooms are decorated with a procession of people of whom only the lower portions are preserved. The colors brown, red, and orange predominate. (For the famous Mari wall paintings, dating to the eighteenth century BCE, see "Mari: A Portrait in Art" in Part 5, Vol. II.)

In the fifteenth century, the palace at Nuzi (Nuzu, modern Yorghun Tepe), where a Mitannian governor lived, was painted with friezes above the doors. On a white background, masks of women with a Hathoresque coiffure of Egyptian inspiration alternate with masks of bulls and palm leaves; above are rows of geometric motifs, including rectangles, triangles, dots, and twists. The colors used are red, pink, black, and gray. The inspiration is not much different in the palace constructed in the thirteenth century by Tukulti-Ninurta I, king of Assyria, near Asshur, at Kar-Tukulti-Ninurta. At ground level the walls are painted black; the next level is painted red; then, about 2 meters (6.5 feet) up, there are panels of palm leaves and rosettes surrounded by geometric motifs, as well as gazelles on either side of a stylized tree. Once again, the Assyrian penchant for symmetry is displayed (fig. 20). The motif of the rosette is the same as that on the enameled tiles used by the Middle Elamites at Choga Zanbil. The motifs, ringed in black, are painted red, blue, and white.

In contrast to the northern palaces, the palace at the capital of the Kassites, Dur-Kurigalzu, was decorated with paintings in the twelfth century by King Marduk-apla-iddina I. Lines of bearded men, half life-sized, are partly preserved in the halls leading to a court; they are surmounted by red bands on a light-blue base. The men are

Fig. 19. Wall painting from Tell al-'Uqair of a leopard on a temple podium, Uruk-Jemdet Nasr period. A. PARROT, *ASSUR* (1961)

Fig. 20. A wall painting from the palace of Tukulti-Ninurta I at Kar-Tukulti-Ninurta, 1244–1208 BCE. AFTER W. ANDRAE, *COLOURED CERAMIC FROM ASHUR* (1925)

painted in distemper on a cream base and are underlined in black; the skin and the details of the clothing are red; the hair, beard, and shoes are black. In another passageway appears a row of eight people in white clothing, with a sort of white fez on their heads; sometimes they are painted on a blue background. Some rooms of the palace are decorated with rosettes and red, yellow, and blue geometric designs on a cream base.

The most complete set of Assyrian paintings was found between 1929 and 1931 at Tell Aḥmar (ancient Til Barsip) by the François Thureau-Dangin expedition. They were found in a provincial palace of the eighth century and were attributed to Tiglath-pileser III. Copies were made on the spot by Lucien Cavro and are preserved at the Louvre. Thureau-Dangin identified two styles, the first quite similar to that of Sargon II at Khorsabad and the second showing resemblances with the reliefs of the palace of Assurbanipal at Nineveh.

To the first style belong the great panels of a large room measuring 24 by 8 meters (79 by 26.4 feet). The walls were decorated to a height of about 4.40 meters (14.5 feet) according to the following plan: a plinth of bitumen about half a meter (20 inches) high at ground level, bordered

with red bands framing rosettes at 0.10 meter (3.9 inches), surmounted by painted scenes at 1.50 meters (4.75 feet), then a decorative frieze of 2.30 meters (7.5 feet). In the longest scene, measuring 22 meters (73 feet) wide, the king in full costume is seated on a throne; he is followed by his soldiers, his chariot, and his saddle horses. Before the king, his minister is followed by functionaries, soldiers, and prisoners. These panels represent the end of a military campaign and the subsequent deportation of the enemy. In other passageways are found an eagle-headed, winged genie leading a bull. The high frieze was composed of quadrilaterals with concave edges between rows of palm leaves, rosettes, and pomegranates. A scene of an audience of tributaries before the enthroned king decorates another room of the palace.

The subjects change in the second style. The throne room is decorated with pairs of horses (white, red, or black) led by soldiers. One panel contains sketches of horsemen at the gallop that were never painted in. The sureness of the drawing and the deftness of the execution led Anton Moortgat (1959) to say they exhibit "an unmistakable touch of genius." Elsewhere, the king in his chariot, with blue horses at the gallop, hunts the lion; this painting is composed in a style that closely resembles the reliefs of Assurbanipal at Nineveh.

The conventions for drawing are the same as for the reliefs: the head and body are shown in profile, and the chest faces outward or in a three-quarter view. Friezes with geometric or floral decoration are used to frame scenes or decorate the bases of walls.

This classification scheme has been challenged by various archaeologists who suggest that what had seemed to be the first style could have been later. Nevertheless, the first style remains dated to the second half of the eighth century and the second style to the first two thirds of the seventh century. The drawing is drawn in black or, in the later panels, red. On the white background, now yellowed, red and blue predominate; they are sometimes blended to obtain a violet tint. There is no yellow or green.

From the ninth to the seventh centuries, all the palaces at Nimrud were decorated with figurative or geometric paintings. The vestiges that it has been possible to recover consist of motifs of palm leaves, rosettes, pomegranates, and full-face bulls. At Fort Shalmaneser, the decor of a throne room has been dated to Esarhaddon, but it seems to revive an older conception. The principal element is a column of the royal guard, long-haired, swords at their side, hands joined, and wearing long, fringed garments. The men, about 1.30 meters (4.3 feet) tall, march along a band of bitumen 0.45 meter (1.5 feet) high. Above them, five rows of decorative friezes reach 1.35 meters (4.5 feet). Reappearing there are the motifs of lotus blossoms, small circles, ornamented disks, and quadrilaterals with concave edges, which are painted blue, red, and black on a white background.

The palace of Sargon II at Khorsabad had been decorated with paintings, but the little that survived could not be saved. In 1852, Victor Place published a fragment of servants leading horses, beneath two friezes with geometric decoration. Despite the control of techniques vastly superior to those of earlier archaeologists, the excavators from the Oriental Institute of Chicago were unable to locate anything in the throne room but decorative elements consisting of rosettes, palm leaves, and geometric figures; the colors are red, blue, white, and black. On the other hand, an enormous panel, adorning a room 31 meters (102.3 feet) long in a residence, has been restored (fig. 21). In contrast to the decorations at Nimrud and Til Barsip, the decorative friezes run beneath the principal scene, which did not reach more than halfway up the panel. Separated and enclosed by numerous rows of rosettes, palm leaves, and lotus blossoms, three bands of symmetric representations are repeated indefinitely. In the middle is the motif of two bulls on either side of a quadrilateral with concave edges. Above and below are rows of half-kneeling winged genies. They are sprinkling an ornamented rosette with a pinecone that represents the sacred tree; the whole image symbolizes the fertilization of nature. This decorative part is 7.50 meters (24.75 feet) high, and the scene on top of it reaches about 6 meters (about 20 feet), including three people, each 3 meters (about 11 feet) tall. Below an arch decorated with friezes similar to those of the lower panel, a god standing on a podium receives a king followed by a minister.

Another form of colored decoration, in enameled brick, is found at Khorsabad on the facade of a temple. There, the king is represented standing; he is crowned with the pointed tiara. On another panel are depictions of an eagle, a bull, a fig tree, and a plow. The predominant colors here are different from those of the paintings. Here, yellow is the main color; it is used on a blue ground and augmented with touches of green.

Decoration with enameled bricks was first used at Asshur in the second half of the second millennium. It was particularly under the reign of Tukulti-Ninurta II, in the ninth century, that enameled but not sculpted decoration was used. Royal scenes in white, yellow, blue, and black are prevalent. These are the same colors that were used for a large panel at Nimrud that measures 4 by 3 meters (13.2 by 9.9 feet). The panel is dated to the reign of Shalmaneser III and has been reconstructed at the Baghdad Museum by Julian Reade. Rounded at the top, it comprises concentric friezes in an arch. Half-kneeling ibexes alternate with palm leaves; there are rows of lotus and pomegranate, flowers with twelve petals, braids, and rosettes. The motifs at the center are, from top to bottom, two rampant bulls (one on each side of a stylized tree), a four-line inscription, a row of flowers, and a winged bust

Fig. 21. Wall painting from Residence K, Khorsabad, of Sargon II and official standing before a statue of the god Assur, who holds a staff and circular emblem bearing his image, circa 721–705 BCE. G. LOUD AND C. B. ALTMAN, *KHORSABAD*, VOL. 2, *THE CITADEL AND THE TOWN* (1938)

of the god Assur above a double representation of the king face-to-face. As always, symmetry is important. This enameled panel uses no red, one of the essential colors in the paintings.

In the seventh century, Nebuchadnezzar II decorated the Gate of Ishtar and the Processional Way with animals in relief, covering with enameled brick those that previously had been worked in cast brick. Yellow lions, bulls, and horned dragons on a blue background are framed with rows of white and yellow rosettes. After conquering Babylon in the sixth century, the Achaemenid Persians imitated this decoration at Susa.

Mesopotamian art developed independent of that of its neighbors—be it Iran, Syria, or Anatolia. It exhibits a definite unity, despite a transition from a rigid Sumerian style to the more open and innovative Akkadian and Babylonian sensibility. The changes are not superficial, but reflect a new approach to nature and to overcoming restrictive conventions. When the Assyrian Empire was established, the royal studios followed new norms to respond to monarchic needs for power and hegemonic expansion. Rigidity regained its importance, at least in the royal portraits and in the sculpted decoration of the palaces. Only the depiction of animals escaped this style; at all times, their representation bears witness to the gifts of observation and the skills of the Assyrian artists.

Translated from the French by Peter T. Daniels

BIBLIOGRAPHY

General

PIERRE AMIET, *Art of the Ancient Near East*, translated by JOHN SHEPLEY and CLAUDE CHOQUET (1980); HENRI FRANKFORT, *The Art and Architecture of the Ancient Orient*, Pelican History of Art (repr. 1977); BARTHEL HROUDA, *Der Alte Orient* (1991); JEAN-LOUIS HUOT, *Les Sumériens* (1989); JEAN-CLAUDE MARGUERON, *Les Mésopotamiens*, 2 vols. (1991); ANTON MOORTGAT, *The Art of Ancient Mesopotamia* (1969); URSULA MOORTGAT-CORRENS, *La Mesopotamie* (1989); ANDRÉ PARROT, *Sumer* (1960) and *Assur* (1961).

Statuary

EVA ANDREA BRAUN-HOLZINGER, *Frühdynastische Beterstatuetten* (1977); GUDRUN COLBOW, *Zur Rundplastik des Gudea von Lagaš* (1987); HENRI FRANKFORT, *Sculpture of the Third Millennium B.C. from Tell Asmar and Khafājah* (1939) and *More Sculpture from the Diyala Region* (1943); BETTY L. SCHLOSSMAN, "Portraiture in Mesopotamia in the Late Third and Early Second Millennium B.C.," 2 pts., *Archiv für Orientforschung* 26 (1978/1979) and 28 (1981/1982); AGNÈS SPYCKET, *La Statuaire du Proche-Orient ancien* (1981); and EVA STROMMENGER, "Das Menschenbild in der altmesopotamischen Rundplastik von Mesilim bis Hammurapi," *Baghdader Mitteilungen* 1 (1960) and *Die neuassyrische Rundskulptur* (1970).

Reliefs

PAULINE ALBENDA, *The Palace of Sargon King of Assyria* (1986); RICHARD D. BARNETT, *Sculptures from the North Palace of Ashurbanipal at Nineveh (668–627 B.C.)* (1976); JUTTA BÖRKER-KLÄHN, *Altvorderasiatische Bildstelen und vergleichbare Felsreliefs*, 2 vols. (1982); BARTHEL HROUDA, *Die Kulturgeschichte des assyrischen Flachbildes* (1965); MAX E. L. MALLOWAN, *Nimrud and Its Remains*, 2 vols. (1966); and URSULA SEIDL, *Die babylonischen Kudurru-Reliefs* (1989).

On the Early Dynastic "perforated plaques," see DONALD P. HANSEN, "New Votive Plaques from Nippur," *Journal of Near Eastern Studies* 22 (1963); and JOHANNES BOESE, *Altmesopotamische Weihplatten* (1971). On the Eannatum's victory stela, see the articles by IRENE J. WINTER, "After the Battle Is Over: The 'Stele of the Vultures' and the Beginning of Historical Narrative in the Art of the Ancient Near East," in *Pictorial Narrative in Antiquity and the Middle Ages*, edited by HERBERT L. KESSLER and MARIANNA SHREVE SIMPSON, Studies in the History of Art 16 (1985), and "Eannatum and the 'King of Kiš'?: Another Look at the Stele of the Vultures and 'Cartouches' in Early Sumerian Art," *Zeitschrift für Assyriologie* 76 (1986). For a new presentation of the stela of Ur-Nammu at the University Museum in Philadelphia, see JEANNY VORYS CANBY, "A Monumental Puzzle: Reconstructing the Ur-Nammu Stela," *Expedition* 29 (1988).

Monumental Paintings

WALTER ANDRAE, *Coloured Ceramics from Ashur* (1925); ASTRID NUNN, *Die Wandmalerei und der glasierte Wandschmuck im alten Orient* (1988); ANTON MOORTGAT, *Alt-Vorderasiatische Malerei* (1959); AGNÈS SPYCKET, "Malerei," in *Reallexikon der Assyriologie*, vol. 7 (1988); and FRANÇOIS THUREAU-DANGIN and MAURICE DUNAND, *Til Barsib* (1936).

For Dur-Kurigalzu and Til Barsib, see YOKO TOMABECHI, "Wall Paintings from Dur Kurigalzu," *Journal of Near Eastern Studies* 42 (1983), and "Wall Paintings from Til Barsip," *Archiv für Orientforschung* 29–30 (1983/1984). On the Assyrian panel from Nimrud, see JULIAN READE, "A Glazed-Brick Panel from Nimrud," *Iraq* 25 (1963).

SEE ALSO **Artisans and Artists of Ancient Western Asia** (Part 4, Vol. I); **Mari: A Portrait in Art of a Mesopotamian City-State** (Part 5, Vol. II); **Art and Ideology in Ancient Western Asia** (Part 10, Vol. VI); **Aesthetics in Ancient Mesopotamian Art** (Part 10, Vol. IV); and **Understanding Ancient Near Eastern Art: A Personal Account** (Part 11, Vol. IV).

Music and Dance in Ancient Western Asia

ANNE DRAFFKORN KILMER

OUR SOURCES FOR ancient Mesopotamian music are surprisingly rich. We have hundreds of Sumerian and Akkadian cuneiform tablets inscribed with information relating to all aspects of music, in addition to iconographic representations and the remains of actual musical instruments recovered in archaeological excavations. Our information for dance, accompanied by music and song, is limited to iconographic representations and a body of terms that is much smaller than that for music.

MUSICAL INSTRUMENTS

Depictions of musical instruments occur on cylinder seals and stamp seals, painted pottery, terra-cotta and stone plaques, mosaics, wall paintings, ivory carvings, sculpture (in relief or in the round, of either clay or stone), and they are occasionally drawn on inscribed cuneiform tablets. These representations inform us that all the main categories of musical instruments existed: stringed instruments (chordophones), wind instruments (aerophones), drums (membranophones), and other, membraneless percussion instruments (idiophones). Of these categories, that of the stringed instruments appears to have been the most highly developed (harps, lyres, and fretted lutes are all well attested). Musicological texts that give us specific information

about the scales and tunings are closely associated with the stringed instruments.

Chordophones

The most impressive material remains of instruments are those found in the royal graves at Ur (approximately dating from the twenty-seventh century BCE). The eight lyres and two harps had been made of wood, but only the decorative overlaid and inlaid materials were preserved, the wood having decomposed.

Lyres varied in shape (symmetrical and asymmetrical) and ranged in size from small handheld examples (played while sitting, standing, or walking) to those large enough to be played by two standing musicians. Until the turn of the third millennium, the sound box was characteristically shaped like a bovine; after approximately 2000, a rectangular or trapezoidal shape of the sound box prevailed.

Harps were, in general, smaller than lyres, were played by the musician seated or standing, and could be held either in a horizontal or vertical position. The earliest harps are round (bow harps), while later ones are angular. Marching and playing harpists and lyrists are especially prominent in Neo-Assyrian palace reliefs; one Old Babylonian terra-cotta shows a dancing and playing harpist alongside another dancer.

The long-necked lute was introduced relatively late to the instrumentarium, or family of

Reconstructed Sumerian silver lyre from a twenty-fifth-century tomb at Ur. BRITISH MUSEUM, LONDON

instruments, being attested only shortly before 2000. King Shulgi of the Third Dynasty of Ur (twenty-first century) boasts that he was such a clever musician that he figured out how to play the lute immediately after it was put in his hands. Depictions of lutes vary with respect to the size of the sound box (generally quite small) and the presence of frets. Two-stringed lutes were the most common. Unlike harpists and lyrists, lutenists are often depicted nude and engaged in bending action with knees spread apart and other energetic bodily activity. Psalteries (ancient musical instruments resembling the zither) are represented on an ivory pot from the first-millennium Assyrian site of Nimrud (Kalkhu). They are played by dancing women in a garden entertainment scene.

Identification of the dozens of Sumerian and Akkadian words for the stringed instruments (and their parts) is attempted with difficulty, and scholars disagree about the translation of even the most common terms. The most usual translations are: (Sumerian terms are given in small capital letters; Akkadian terms are given in lowercase italics) BALAG/*balaggu*, "harp" (also "drummable resonator"); ZÀ.MÍ/*sammû*, "lyre"; GÙ.DI/*inu*, "lute." All the stringed instruments could be played with or without a plectrum.

Aerophones

The wind instruments were made of reed, wood, bone, and metal. Sizes varied from short to long, the shapes were straight or flared, and double pipes were common. We have no textual information about the pitches or graduated scales used in the pipes, but some music historians have tried to deduce the progressions from the distances between the finger holes. Our information is relatively scarce so that we are unable to say much about the use of reed mouthpieces or to distinguish with certainty between whistles or flutes, horns or trumpets. The vocabulary for wind instruments is smaller than that for the stringed instruments, and our identification of terms is imprecise. Common terms are: GI.GÍD (long reed)/*embūbu*, "reed pipe"; GI.DI.DA (sounding reed)/*malīlu*, "flute."

The fragmentary remains of a pair of silver flutes were found in the royal graves at Ur (modern Tell al-Muqayyar). Texts from the Third Dynasty of Ur mention GI.GÍD instruments made of bronze, silver, or gold. Bone-flute fragments with finger holes were found at the site of Tepe Gawra and date to prehistoric times. Pottery flutes/ocarina fragments with finger holes have also been excavated at several prehistoric sites.

The earliest representation of a rim-blown vertical flute is on a cylinder seal from the Old Akkadian Period (approximately 2200 BCE). Double pipes maintained their popularity from the second millennium to the last half of the first, while panpipes consisting of more than a pair were introduced from the West, late in the first millennium.

From the site of Tutub (Dur-Samsu-iluna, Tupliash, modern Khafaje) in the Early Dynastic period (3000–2500), we have a stone relief showing a trumpet being blown. The trumpet remained an instrument for loud blasts until the Neo-Assyrian Period when it was used for directing labor gangs.

One textual reference, a Sumerian temple hymn, refers to a bull's horn (SI.AM.MA.KE₄) as a musical instrument that made the sound "*gumga*". In another Sumerian hymn, the chief musician plays an ibex horn (Á.DA.RÀ) while others play lyres, drums, and clackers while singers sing. (Note that SI/*qarnu* is "horn." Although there are no musical references for Akkadian *qarnu*, we are told in the book of Daniel that Nebuchadnezzar's orchestra included a *qarnā*.) A musical animal horn seems to be depicted in an Old Babylonian wall painting from Mari (modern Tell Hariri), but the painting is too badly damaged to be certain. The horn (SI/*qarnu*) was also blown by heralds in the streets as the call to public announcements.

Membranophones

Drums of various shapes and sizes with skin drumheads are frequently depicted and are mentioned in many categories of texts.

Small, hand frame drums are among the earliest depictions of drums and are typically, but not exclusively, played by women (not infrequently nude). Frame drum players are often, especially on terra-cotta reliefs of the Old Babylonian period, depicted in dancing motion. The frame drum continued to be a part of musical ensembles until the last part of the first millennium. Neo-Assyrian stone reliefs frequently display larger frame drums being played by men in concert with strings and pipes amid military scenes. Rectangular frame drums are not attested with certainty until the Neo-Assyrian period. A late-fourth-millennium cylinder-seal impression from modern Khuzestan (southwestern Iran, ancient Elam, Susiana) shows a kettledrum placed on the ground being played by a seated man.

Two clear illustrations of footed kettledrums are available to us, one on an Old Babylonian terra-cotta relief that depicts boxing practice accompanied by the drum, and the other drawn on a Seleucid period (fourth to second century BCE) cuneiform tablet that provides ritual instructions for preparing an oxhide for the making of a kettledrum for cultic use. The tablet also names it for us: it is a LILIZ/*lilissu*. The *lilissu* was considered a sacred object in its own right and could be provided with the classification of "divinity."

A drummer playing a cylindrical drum is shown bringing up the rear in a line of marching Elamite musicians in an Assurbanipal relief of a military scene. The only example of a conical drum is found on another Assurbanipal relief, that of the king and queen feasting in a garden where the defeated Elamite king's head is hung in a tree. The drummer follows an attending harpist.

Giant drums (the diameter of the drumheads is as great as a man's height up to his shoulder) are attested, numbering seven representations (two very fragmentary), six from stone stelae and one from a cylinder seal. All samples belong to the early periods (approximately 2600 to 2000), and all show the drum lying on its side being beaten by hand or with drumsticks by two men, alternately, one at either side. Two scenes include a man playing cymbals. The scenes on the stelae depict temple-building operations and reflect ritual participation of royalty, priests, and gods.

A terra-cotta sculpture of a monkey (seventh

to sixth century) holds an object that may be our only example of a friction drum (an instrument of various shapes and materials, the membranes of which are caused to vibrate by friction, either by the fingers or a rosined pad, cord, or stick. In our example, the monkey appears to be vibrating the membrane with a stick).

Some common terms for drums are: MEZE/*manzû*, ŠEM/*ḥalḥallatu* for metal drums, Á.LÁ/*alû* for a wooden drum, and ÙB/*uppu* for a small frame drum.

Idiophones

Although less well attested than drums, the sistra, cymbals, clay rattles (round "piecrust" and various animal shapes), sickle-shaped clappers, and bells are known from the Early Dynastic period to the latest periods. Metal, wood, shell, and other materials capable of producing sound were used. We know the word for small, copper sickle-clackers: KIN.TUR/*niggallu*. PA.PA/*tāpalu* is a term used to denote a pair of wooden clackers of another type, probably mounted on sticks. Bells were common in the first millennium as jangles on the harnesses for royal horse trappings, as decoration on royal and cultic raiments, and in connection with cultic activities.

MUSICAL PERFORMANCE AND PERFORMERS

Music and song played a role in every aspect of life, ranging from unaccompanied lullabies and work songs to full temple orchestra and choral performances under the direction of professional cult musicians (GALA/*kalû*, NAR/*nâru*). The significance of the orchestra is illustrated by the fact that the event of fashioning musical instruments for the temple was honored by being used as an Old Babylonian date formula. (Babylonian years were designated by names that reflected a significant event during the preceding regnal year, e.g. "The year the chariot for Ninlil was made," and so on). Music was part of the school curriculum at least as early as the early Old Babylonian period (circa 1800).

Although we often know the names of the scribes who copied a text, most literary and musical compositions do not identify the author or composer. A notable exception is a Sumerian princess Enkheduanna, daughter of King Sargon (2334–2279), who, as a priestess of the moon-god Nanna and devotee of the goddess Inanna, composed several temple hymn cycles of recognized literary and stylistic merit.

Textual references mention lists of songs that include work songs, battle songs, love songs, hymns of praise, prayers accompanied by gestures, large sacred works, funerary songs, and magical incantations. One Middle Assyrian text (about 1100) lists more than 360 Sumerian and Akkadian song titles belonging to thirty-one different song types. From Sumerian and Akkadian literary texts, we derive descriptions of solo lead-singers, choirs, and orchestras, as well as technical terms referring to main and subsections, to antiphons, and to how the instruments in the orchestra were positioned. Royal correspondence concerning military matters informs us that singers and instrumentalists accompanied the army, that different categories of secular singers were in demand, and that captives (especially women) were trained to become vocal performers. Singers are sometimes depicted in art with one hand at the throat or cupped at the ear.

Men and women singers and instrumentalists performed in a variety of situations, both indoors and outdoors. The most commonly presented scene (from the earliest times to the late first millennium) is of a feast at which musical entertainment was provided by a small ensemble: a harp or lyre player, a piper, and a percussionist. Dancers are frequently present as well. Such scenes were sometimes cartooned to show performing animals in orchestras, in procession, in small ensembles, or as solo performers. (One Sumerian literary text is in the form of a letter from a music-hall monkey who complains to his mother that he is being mistreated.) Epics and myths were sung and accompanied by instruments. Music or song was performed at ominous or dangerous occasions as well: during a lunar eclipse, during childbirth, beside the sickbed, and during mourning rites.

Male or female lutenists and hand frame-drum players were not part of the large temple orchestras of harps, lyres, tympani, and wind instruments. They frequently performed in the nude, and occasionally they accompanied or themselves engaged in sexual activity while playing

Stone wall relief from Nineveh showing near life-sized Assyrian musicians, seventh century BCE. LOUVRE MUSEUM, PARIS

their instruments. Dancing and acrobatic performances of male lutenists and frame drummers are attested on Old Babylonian terra-cotta plaques, a valuable source for entertainment scenes. Also valued are the cylinder-seal representations which provide clear evidence for portable performance platforms for musicians, dancers, and other entertainers. Secular musicians performed in taverns and at social celebrations of all kinds. Palace musicians routinely received rations with other palace personnel, and some temples may have supported music schools. Secular musicians (and, presumably, instrument makers) lived in the artisan quarters of cities.

MUSICAL SCALES, TUNINGS, AND TECHNICAL VOCABULARY

The creator and water-god, Enki/Ea was the patron god of wisdom, magic, the musical arts, and water. It was he who created the GALA/*kalû*, the primary cult cantor and lamentation singer, in order to appease the wild mood of the goddess Inanna/Ishtar. Ea provided the GALA with two percussion instruments, the ÙB/*uppu* (hand frame drum) and the LILIZ/*lilissu* (kettledrum), which could appease the goddess by sounding *aḫulap!* "Mercy!/Condolences!/Oh woe!" Music, the lute, and several drums are listed among the MES, a Sumerian word (difficult to translate) used to describe the norms and customs of society as well as divine attributes and the arts.

General Terms

The Sumerian and Akkadian vocabulary referring to music does not necessarily include a single term that specifically means "music" as distinct from "song," "jubilation," or "revelry." The following words are commonly used:

NAM.NAR/*nârūtu*, "musicianship," "music"

GÙ.DÉ/*nagû*, "to exult," "sing joyously"

I.LU/*nigûtu*, "joyful music," "merry making"

Common verbs relating to music are:

TAG/*lapātu*, "to touch" (for playing stringed instruments and drums)

TUKU/*maḫāṣu*, "to strike, beat, tap" (used for playing percussion instruments and reed pipes)

ŠÌR/*zamāru*, "to sing," "to play" (said of strings and drums)

ḫalālu, "to wheeze," "pipe" (said of the throat and of reed pipes)

Technical Terms

It is highly probable that two different musical systems or traditions existed side-by-side. One is the less well-understood group of Sumerian technical terms used for Sumerian musical compositions, and the other is the better understood group of Akkadian terms (at least as old as the Old Babylonian period) that relate to a set of seven different heptatonic and diatonic musical scales.

The "Sumerian" System It is an educated guess that the Sumerian compositions practiced a "multi-modalism" in which different sections of a piece of music utilized different fixed modalities or tunings. The separate song-types themselves would have been associated with prescribed melodic and rhythmic patterns, all lost to us. The technical terms that are inserted in the written compositions (the "hymn rubrics" in scholarly parlance) identify the placement of the antiphons, label the different modes, locate the cadence, and provide us with the genre name of the composition. In short, song types deter-

mined modal patterns which the musicians had to learn by memorization.

The "Akkadian" System Eight cuneiform texts (ranging in time from the early second millennium to the middle of the first) provide us with a corpus of Akkadian technical terms relating to a set of seven musical scales and nine musical strings. SA/*pitnu* is the basic term for the musical string, but its meaning extends to "interval"/"chord" and "scale"/"tuning"/ "mode."

The names of the strings are:

1. fore string
2. next string
3. third (or third-thin) string
4. fourth (or Ea-creator) string
5. fifth string
6. fourth from the end string
7. third from the end string
8. second from the end string
9. the end string

Pairs of strings, in turn, define (generalized) intervals on the seven-note scale (see table).

The set of seven scales or tunings are the following (the corresponding Greek tunings are provided):

išartu, "normal" (Dorian)
  E F G A B C D

kitmu, "closed" (Hypodorian)
  E F# G A B C D

embūbu, "reed pipe" (Phrygian)
  E F# G A B C# D

pītu, "open" (Hypophrygian)
  E F# G# A B C# D

nīd qabli, "fall of the middle" (Lydian)
  E F# G# A B C# D#

nīš gabarî, "rise of the duplicate" (Hypolydian)
  E F# G# A# B# C# D#

qablītu, "middle" (Mixolydian)
  E# F# G# A# B# C# D#

We also know that the seven tunings were named after the interval that was used to begin the tuning process, which was done by a progressive series of fifths and fourths. In each tuning, the tritone (that is, the "discordant" interval like that between F and B on the white keys of the piano) was located in a different position in the

Intervals (Generalized) on the Seven-Note Scale

String Designations		Fifths and Fourths
	Fifths and Fourths	
1–5	*nīš gabarî*	"rise of the duplicate"
2–6	*išartu*	"normal"
3–7	*embūbu*	"reed pipe"
4–1	*nīd qabli*	"fall of the middle"
5–2	*qablītu*	"middle"
6–3	*kitmu*	"closed"
7–4	*pītu*	"open"
	Thirds and Sixths	
7–5	*šēru*	"song"
1–6	*šalšatu*	"third"
2–7	*rebūtu*	"fourth"
1–3	*isqu*	"throwstick/lot"
2–4	*titur qablītu*	"bridge of the middle"
3–5	*titur išartu*	"bridge of the normal"
4–6	*serdû*	"lamentation"

scale, thus changing the locations of the semitones (the distance between E and F on the white keys).

Notational Instructions

Three different types of verbal instructions that constitute musical notation (or perhaps instrumental tablature) have been observed, all using the same basic set of terms:

1. The first type is found in Old Babylonian performance instructions (fragmentary) for a Sumerian royal hymn that set forth the note on which to start the piece and the intervals and tunings to be used for each section of the hymn. It is probable that instructions for the end of the piece, the cadence, would also have been present had this tablet from Nippur (modern Nuffar) been completely preserved.

2. The second type is found in a complete hymn (about 1400) that was excavated (together with many fragments of similar hymns) at ancient Ugarit (modern Ras Shamra) and which provides instructions for performing the piece. The words of the hymns were all written in the Hurrian language (not related to Sumerian or Akkadian) in cuneiform script, but the musical instructions and the label ("colophon") of the hymn were written in the Akkadian language. The colophon tells us the type of hymn it is and gives us the scale used for the hymn, namely, the "fall of the middle" scale, which is the equivalent of the Greek Lydian tuning and our own modern major scale.

The notation section of the text follows the lyrics and consists of interval (string-pair) names followed by number signs. There are apparently no directions for rhythm or tempo. There have been several differing attempts to match the lyrics with the instructions and to render the words and notation in modern notational form. No general agreement has been reached as to which interpretation is "correct." However, because our knowledge of the intervals and scales is secure, all the renderings are euphonious in that they are operating within a familiar tonality: our major scale.

3. A different but related notational system appears on Akkadian hymns of the Neo-Babylonian period. In these texts, very abbreviated notation instructions (almost certainly related to the heptatonic scale terminology of type two) are found in the margins or in smaller

script within the body of the words of the hymns. This late system of musical instructions remains obscure.

Monody versus Harmony

Scholars differ in their opinions regarding the practice of homophony (only one note sounding at a time) as opposed to heterophony (two or more different notes sounding simultaneously), whether between voice and instrument or between the strings of one or more instruments. Double pipes imply a drone on one pipe and a melody on the other, while the existence of lyres with as many as twelve strings invites the possibility of melody (by voice or instrument) with harmonizing accompaniment. This evidence does not mean that homophonic performance was never practiced. One reason for arguing in favor of the knowledge of heterophonic performance is the very nature of the naming of the musical intervals as a pair of strings. Another reason is the observation that, in pictorial representations, musicians play the stringed instruments with both hands (one giant lyre is played by two men, four hands) where the fingers are shown plucking strings too far apart to represent stepwise movement, but at appropriate distances to represent two notes being sounded together. Finally, we observe that the discordant tritone interval is lacking in all the Hurrian hymn notations. At a more theoretical level, some musicologists explain that the very existence of consistent scales demands the concept of harmony because scales express the harmonious connection between notes.

Rhythm and Tempo

Unfortunately, none of the understood technical terms relates to rhythm or tempo. For the "Sumerian" system, as mentioned earlier, we assume that knowledge of song-type would have included melodic patterns, rhythm, and tempo. For the "Akkadian" system, no sure terms for "fast" or "slow," for example, have been identified as yet.

Metrical structures of poetic texts (hymns, myths, and other poetry) fall in the category of accented verse, and frequently exhibit four "beats" to each line of poetry, ending with a trochee. But inconsistencies and divergence from the four beats to the line prevent us from deducing musical rhythms for the compositions. It seems likely, however, that compositions named after drums were accompanied by drumbeats which may have set and guided the rhythms for the musicians.

Was There a "Philosophy" of Music?

Unlike the Greeks, the ancient Mesopotamians have left us no discussions of the ethnic, social, or psychological associations of the different modes and tunings, except to identify song-types as Sumerian or Akkadian, and to associate singing styles with foreigners.

That music was considered joyful, sad, or capable of soothing anger is apparent from many passages, but no detailed descriptions are available and no differentations are made as to the effect that any of the seven heptatonic scales were considered to have on the listeners. The frame drum and kettledrum were envisaged as being capable of calming the angry goddess Inanna or Ishtar. The "fall of the middle" tuning (the same as the Lydian, thought to be "effeminate" and "convivial" by the Greeks) was used exclusively for the Hurrian (non-Semitic, non-Sumerian) cult hymns of the middle of the second millennium, while the "open" tuning (Greek Hypodorian or "tender" mode) was used for part of a Sumerian royal hymn (about 1925 BCE). The evidence is thus too skimpy for us to believe that a "philosophy of music" existed.

DANCE

Just as "music" was not isolated from more general human social activities like "jubilation" or "revelry," "dance" was closely connected to casual "play," "frolic," or "gambol" on the one hand, and to organized cult activities and the arts of magic and healing on the other. The action of "dancing" is difficult to separate from "skipping," "hopping," "jumping," "running around," and "whirling." Although there are no textual descriptions that provide us with detailed information about dance motions or choreography, we may attempt to classify dance on the grounds of the meanings of the verbs of action and the nouns or adjectives used, and we can make use of the pictorial information which is less ample than the pictorial information for music.

The Vocabulary of Dance

(1) The Akkadian verb *raqādu* means "to skip," to "dance." Singers, actors, and dancers are mentioned together in many textual passages, both in literature and in lists of words. From the same Semitic root we have *raqqidu* or "(cult) dancer." If we assume an onomatopoeic origin for the verb "*riqqeda-riqqeda*," a tapping sound is implied. The Sumerian equivalent, however, of *raqqidu* is sùḫ.sùḫ; if it is onomatopoeic, we think of a soft sound instead (compare English "brush," "shuffle"). *Riqittu* (Sumerian sùḫ.saḫ₄.sar), is the noun "dance," as is *riqdu*.

(2) *Gâšu* means "to whirl"; *gūštu*, "whirling dance" (if onomatopoeic, relate these words to the sound of air moving and compare with English "gush" or "swish"). At the annual feast for the goddess Inanna/Ishtar/Gushea/Agushaya, whirling dances were done in her honor. We are led to believe that "whirling" was usually done by men, but that the male persona of Ishtar also engaged in whirling as did her male and female cult personnel, some of them as cross-dressed entertainers.

(3) DU₇.DU₇/*sâru* or "to form or dance in a circle." The Sumerian word means "to push each other back and forth." Unlike *raqādu* and *gâšu*, which are related to sound, *sâru* relates to form and arrangement. Most references to *sūrta sâru*, or "to form a circle," are to encircling ritual acts. It can be done *around* a sick person. Perhaps *circle* dances were used to expel sickness or were danced prophylactically on various, potentially ominous occasions. Normally, but not exclusively, circle dances were done by women.

(4) ḪÚB/*ḫuppû* "acrobat" or "acrobatic dancer." This word could be onomatopoeic, like the English word "hop." This energetic dancing was performed in the cult, together with wrestling and other action entertainment, by men.

Techniques of Dance and Dance "Steps"

Our pictorial sources for dance, like those for music, go back as far as preliterate periods, and are derived from painted pottery, stamp and cylinder seals, terra-cotta plaques, stone reliefs, and carved ivory. The richest periods for graphic representations of dance are the earlier ones (especially the early second millennium), for there is a relative paucity of such depictions by the first millennium.

Dancers are portrayed performing solo, in pairs, and in groups (in a row or circle). Dance steps or positions that have been identified are:

- spread apart, bent knees/bobbing
- squat dance (*à génuflexion inachevée*)
- foot-clutch dance (*à cloche pied*)
- jumps/leaps
- crossing one leg over the other

It is not always certain that a given static representation is one of dance as opposed to, for example, marching in procession, acrobatic performances, grappling, or hopping. In general,

Drawing of a cylinder-seal impression showing dancers with a seated instructor. The original seal is in the Louvre Museum. DRAWING BY M. MATOUŠOVÁ-RAJMOVÁ, "ILLUSTRATION DE LA DANCE SUR LES SCEAUX DE L'ÉPOQUE BABYLONIENNE ANCIENNE," *ARCHIV ORIENTALI* 46 (1978)

however, there are certain clues that observers use to identify dance motion:

- one or both feet leave the baseline
- pointed toes or tiptoes
- kneeling (or almost kneeling) on one knee with the other leg extended
- exaggerated posture in concert with music
- waist bends
- raised arms
- holding hands
- "conga line," holding person in front
- flying hair (depicting motion)
- performing on a table or platform
- balancing objects overhead (dance or balancing act?)
- "dance class," where a seated or standing figure with baton or time-stick directs a group of dancers and musicians.

Performance Places and Occasions for Dance

We may assume that any flat open space (such as a threshing floor) in or near a settlement could have been used as a place for dance and other performance for a variety of secular social occasions (tribal or family occasions, weddings, harvest feasts, and so forth). We know that dancers, musicians, and others sometimes performed atop a platform or table, and one scene shows dancing on a kettledrum laid on its side. Our

textual and pictorial evidence is richest for the highly organized cult festivals and action-filled worship services where costumed and masked performers danced, sang, acted, and performed special feats of skill (like juggling) in and around the temple. Mock battle dances were performed, and occasionally the dancers, armed with sharp weapons, would draw blood.

The priestly arts of magic and healing in and around homes and palaces could also be accompanied by dancers (sometimes in animal costumes) who participated in chasing away the disease or in protecting the living from any demonic influence at times of death and mourning.

Dancers and dancing musicians (sometimes with special headdress and coiffure) participated in scenes of explicit sexual activity by dancing around a copulating couple. These scenes may or may not be connected with cult activities, especially those of the goddess Inanna, or Ishtar, wherein circus acts, performing animals, all manner of carnival-like activities, gender cross-dressing, transvestite dancing, and singing occurred (as it does today, at weddings, for example, in Iraq and Iran).

No mixed-gender dancing is attested for any period, either in pairs or in groups. On the contrary, text passages tell us that different groups of dancers took turns dancing. When the women (and girls) danced, the men looked on and sang, and vice versa, and the old men took their turn

Cylinder-seal impression of dancers doing the "foot-clutch" step, Old Babylonian period. AFTER M. MATOUŠOVÁ-RAJMOVÁ, "ILLUSTRATION DE LA DANCE SUR LES SCEAUX DE L'ÉPOQUE BABYLONIENNE ANCIENNE," *ARCHÍV ORIENTÁLNÍ* 46 (1978)

separately from the young men (and boys). Likewise, certain types of dancing were normally gender-restricted: men did the "whirl" (compare the Sufi "whirling dervishes" of today); women were associated with the circle dance; and only men performed the "squat dance" (compare the cossacks' dance of today).

The foot-clutch dance was done by men. It is probably correct that the scenes depicting this action all represent dance; however, it is also possible that this same action refers to a balance contest or game in which one man (or boy) tries to knock the other down. Such a game (called "hopping on one leg") is still played among the marsh dwellers of southern Iraq.

The Dances

Ordinary folk danced on a variety of social occasions, as described above. For dance in the framework of cult worship and festivals, male and female dancers were chosen from among the cult personnel devoted to temple service. If the king participated in a festival activity, he was known to sing, but no dancing kings (as is the case of David) are mentioned in the texts. Deities and supernatural or monstrous creatures are seen in dance-like poses, and one text (eighteenth century BCE) refers to "dancing protective-*daimons*" (*Lamassu's*), perhaps a description of statues in dance positions.

For the entertainment in the palace and for the military troops in camp, musicians and dancers were often selected from captives. Some, especially females, were trained for the performing arts after their capture.

Instruments Held and Sounds Produced by Dancers

Women (and, less often, men) danced holding frame drums which they struck while dancing. There are depictions of a nude male dancer holding a lute, a nude female dancer playing a small lyre, and of two women in very short skirts playing psalteries while dancing. In addition to hand clapping and finger snapping, sickle clackers and other metal clappers (as well as those of other materials) were also used. Masquerade dancers sported whips and battle dancers

Terra-cotta plaque depicting a frame drummer and a nude lyre player, Old Babylonian period. STATE MUSEUM, BERLIN

wielded knives. Some dancers sang, and those dancers associated with the transvestite-cult performers uttered "twitters" and "chirps" while they danced. Yet, while metal ankle bracelets are known for women and girls, there is no direct evidence that ancient Mesopotamian dancers wore them.

An "Eyewitness" Account of "Assyrian" Dancing

In the third century CE, the Greek writer of romances, Heliodorus, repeated an account by one Calasiris of how "Phoenician" sailors from Tyre danced in Assyrian style:

> I left them there at their flute music and their dancing, in which they frisked to a tripping time given out by pipes in an Assyrian measure; now lightly springing aloft, and now crouching close to the ground and spinning the entire body round and round like possessed persons. (*The Aethiopica*, Book IV, translated by Sir Walter Lamb, 1961)

Even though this eyewitness account was made nearly eight hundred years after the fall of Babylon, it is a fitting description of three of the characteristic ancient Mesopotamian dance categories that have been reconstructed: acrobatic dancing, the squat dance, and the whirl.

Fragment from a steatite vase showing dancers and musicians in performance recovered from ancient Adab (modern Bismaya), Early Dynastic period. ORIENTAL INSTITUTE, UNIVERSITY OF CHICAGO

CONCLUSION

The world of dance in ancient Mesopotamia was and is still reflected in adjacent societies. Any study of dance in ancient, medieval, and modern Middle Eastern countries, in India, or in Africa (and in classical sources) reveals a range of dance that is at once familiar. All cultic, magic, folkloric, and social occasions and rites of passage are and were accompanied by music and dance, masks and costumes, as well as cross-dressing by male and female dancers with many variations on restrictions, depending on the context and the cultural traditions. The association of dancers with the broader "entertainment world," ranging from protected liturgical performance to secular prostitution, is attested from early cuneiform lists of professions and can be compared to similar associations in modern times.

The legacy of ancient Mesopotamian music, its scales and tuning procedures, its theory and practice, was transmitted (back and forth, with influences coming in as well as going out) to its near eastern neighbors (including Egypt), to Greece, and eventually to the modern world. The traditions have managed to endure for at least four thousand years.

BIBLIOGRAPHY

Sources

A comprehensive bibliography is provided in SUBHI ANWAN RASHID, *Musikgeschichte in Bildern*. Band II:

Musik des Altertums, Lieferung 2: Mesopotamien (1984), and in entries in the *Reallexikon der Assyriologie*. Sources for Akkadian vocabulary used in this article may be found in *The Chicago Assyrian Dictionary* and in *Akkadisches Handwörterbuch*. For the Sumerian vocabulary, see HENRIKE HARTMANN, "Die Musik der sumerischen Kultur" (Ph.D. diss., Johann Wolfgang Goethe-Universität, 1960).

Critical Studies

RICHARD L. CROCKER, "The Fragmentary Music Text from Nippur," *Iraq* 46 (1978); MANFRIED DIETRICH and OSWALD LORETZ, "Kollationen zum Musiktext aus Ugarit," *Ugarit-Forschungen* 7 (1975); MARCELLA DUCHESNE-GUILLEMIN, "Découverte d'une gamme babylonienne," *Revue de Musicologie* 49 (1963) and "A Hurrian Musical Score from Ugarit: The Discovery of Mesopotamian Music," *Sources from the Ancient Near East* 2 (1984); OLIVER ROBERT GURNEY, "An Old Babylonian Treatise on the Tuning of the Harp," *Iraq* 30 (1968); HANS GUSTAV GÜTERBOCK, "Musical Notation in Ugarit," *Revue d'Assyriologie* 64 (1970); ANNE D. KILMER, "A Music Tablet from Sippar (?): BM 65217 + 66616," *Iraq* 46 (1984) and "Musical Practice in Nippur," *Nippur at the Centennial*, Proceedings of the Thirty-fifth Rencontre Assyriologique Internationale (1992); ANNE D. KILMER and MIGUEL CIVIL, "Old Babylonian Musical Instructions Relating to Hymnody," *Journal of Cuneiform Studies* 31 (1986); ANNE D. KILMER, R. L. CROCKER, and ROBERT R. BROWN, *Sounds from Silence: Recent Discoveries in Ancient Near Eastern Music* (1976); THEO J. H. KRISPIJN, "Beiträge zur altorientalischen Musikforschung. 1. Shulgi und Musik," *Akkadica* 70 (1990); HANS MARTIN KÜMMEL, "Zur Stimmung der babylonischen Harfe," *Orientalia* 39 (1970); and MARIE MATOUŠOVÁ-RAJMOVÁ, "Quelques remarques sur la danse en Mésopotamie," *Archív Orientální* 38 (1970); "Illustration de la danse sur les sceaux de l'époque babylonienne ancienne," *Archív Orientální* 46 (1978); "La Position à génuflexion inachevée—Activité et Danse," *Archív Orientální* 47 (1979); "Der Tanz bei magisch-medizinscher Behandlung eines Kranken," *Archív Orientální* 55 (1987); "Die Darstellung einer Krankenbeschwörung auf dem 'Grossen Amulett'" and "Der Tanz auf kappadokischen Siegelbildern," *Archív Orientální* 57 (1989); "Tanzschulen im alten vorderen Orient?," and "Die tanzende Gottheit," *Archív Orientální* 60 (1992); see also SUBHI ANWAR RASHID, "Zur Datierung der mesopotamischen Trommeln und Becken," *Zeitschrift für Assyriologie* 61 (1971) and "Umdatierung einiger Terrakottareliefs mit Lautendarstellung," *Baghdader Mitteilungen* 6 (1973); AGNÈS SPYCKET, "La musique instrumentale mésopotamienne," *Journal des Savants* (1972); WILHELM STAUDER, "Ein Musiktraktat aus dem zweiten vorchristlichen Jahrtausend," *Festschrift Walter Wiora* (1967) and "Die Musik der Sumerer, Babylonier und Assyrier," *Orientalische Musik* (1970); RADUL VITALE, "La Musique suméro–akkadienne. Gamme et notation musicale," *Ugarit-Forschungen* 14 (1982); and DAVID WULSTAN, "The Tuning of the Babylonian Harp," *Iraq* 30 (1968), and "The Earliest Musical Notation," *Music and Letters* 52 (1971).

SEE ALSO **Private Life in Ancient Mesopotamia** (Part 4, Vol. I); **Clothing and Grooming in Ancient Western Asia** (Part 4, Vol. I); **Music and Dance in Pharaonic Egypt** (Part 10, Vol. IV); and **Music, Dance, and Processions in Hittite Anatolia** (Part 10, Vol. IV).

Art and Archaeology of the Achaemenid Empire

MARGARET COOL ROOT

THE ACHAEMENID PERSIAN DYNASTY (circa 559–330 BCE) controlled a vast, multicultural realm. Its imperial art brilliantly embraced diverse traditions in order to create a message that could successfully channel and support social and political mechanisms of authority among the conquered populations. In providing material for continuing archaeological and art historical interpretation of the empire along these lines, the great heartland cities in southwestern Iran—Pasargadae, Persepolis, and Susa (biblical Shushan, modern Shush)—remain critical. Simultaneously, there is now refined assessment of the Achaemenid presence in peripheral zones, ranging from diverse sites in Mesopotamia, Anatolia, the Levant, the Gulf area, Cyprus, and the remote eastern regions, to a host of isolated monuments particularly from Egypt.

Achaemenid art was not a static phenomenon, although it has often been characterized as such. During its two-hundred-year span, internal and external developments affected it. The Achaemenid achievement revalidated many earlier near eastern artistic manifestations and kept them alive for further adaptation in the centuries following the conquests of Alexander the Great. The empire also fostered fluid cultural cross-fertilizations within the Achaemenid period, which reflected sociopolitical attitudes over time.

Artistic patronage in the Achaemenid Empire can be tracked not only to the royal circle that commissioned state building programs and royal relief sculptures but also to people closely tied to the official workings of the empire and its reigning king. These patrons exhibit diverse tastes not necessarily dictated by canonical court modes.

Intended audience response on various levels is an important feature of the artistic product. Obviously official Achaemenid art projected an image and ethos of power that was meant to gratify the king. This art also addressed a wider audience of courtiers, among whom it reinforced bonds of allegiance and instilled a sense of prestigious participation in the imperial enterprise and ideology. Simultaneously, Achaemenid art aimed at impressing audiences, friendly or otherwise, composed of ambassadors from the subject lands or from hostile states. The mechanisms by which multiple voices in the official program were achieved are a critical area for study.

A paucity of surviving Achaemenid Persian texts on social customs, religion, mythology, court life, and historical narrative seriously challenges our ability to interpret the subtleties of Achaemenid art. Yet this lack of textual material magnifies the importance of the visual record as a primary source on Persian culture, serving as a check on and supplement to the classical texts, which have filled the void but present biases and interpretive problems of their own. (See "Social and Legal Institutions in Achaemenid Iran" in Part 4, Vol. I and "Darius I and the Persian Empire" in Part 5, Vol. II.)

Retrieval of the archaeological record of the Achaemenid Empire has been problematic in excavations at long-inhabited sites with complex stratigraphy. One reason for this difficulty is the fact that Greco-Roman construction often obliterated Achaemenid period levels. Other reasons for the difficulty involve the traditional directives of fieldwork: near eastern archaeology has focused on earlier phases, and classical archaeology in regions of the Achaemenid Empire has gravitated toward the Hellenistic and Roman periods. Furthermore, the interpretation of Achaemenid material once retrieved has frequently been obscured by biases in artifact classification, which have led to the identification of Achaemenid products from the western regions as "Greek."

Archaeology generally has focused until recently on the recovery of monumental and high-culture remains. The laudable current trend to investigate other aspects of the material record has posed a problem for field archaeologists of the Achaemenid period. Because the mundane debris of civilization across this vast empire is not easily distinguishable from what was used in the periods immediately before or after, the tendency has been to classify a stratum by terminology that is most suited to the cultures before or after the empire. Field and interpretive strategies have begun to address this unintentional muting of the Achaemenid phase.

PASARGADAE

Founded by Cyrus the Great, Pasargadae was the first dynastic capital of the empire. The name comes from the ancient Greek transliteration of an Old Persian form of still-disputed meaning. The site is referred to as Batrakataš on the Persepolis fortification tablets dating to Darius I.

The visible ruins were first identified as the Pasargadae of Greek sources by European travelers in the early nineteenth century. Scientific investigation began with Ernst Herzfeld, whose excavations in 1928 revealed important elements of the palatial compound. Subsequent archaeo-

logical work was undertaken first by Ali Sami of the Iranian Archaeological Service beginning in 1949 and then by David Stronach under the auspices of the British Institute of Persian Studies from 1961 to 1963.

Grandiose plans originally envisioned for the buildings on the citadel gave way upon the death of Cyrus to utilitarian functions. Under Darius I, the focus of imperial ceremonial construction shifted to Persepolis. Yet the Persepolis fortification tablets offer evidence of continuing activity at Pasargadae in treasury maintenance, religious ceremonies, and royal construction. A reused inscribed foundation document of Xerxes, plus numerous Achaemenid-period small finds certainly of post-Cyrus date, corroborates this. Similarly, Quintus Curtius records that Alexander III "the Great" extracted

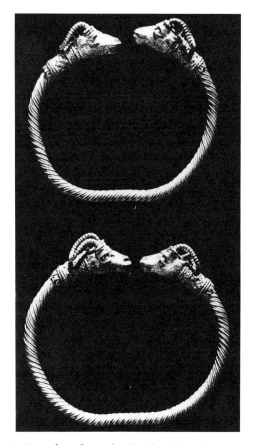

Fig. 1. Bracelets from the horde of jewelry excavated at Pasargadae, Achaemenid period. DAVID STRONACH, *PASARGADAE* (1978)

six thousand talents of treasure from Pasargadae in 330. An important jewelry hoard was found that included items of the mature Achaemenid period, plausibly buried hastily in their associated coarse earthen jar as Alexander pressed toward Pasargadae after sacking Persepolis (fig. 1).

Cyrus's capital is elegantly sited on the Dasht-i Morghab ("Plain of the Waterbird"). Structures in the plain include the tomb of Cyrus, an enigmatic stone tower (the Zendan) that may have been a repository for ritual paraphernalia, and a fire altar with adjacent worshiping platform. In addition, two hypostyle audience halls, two garden pavilions, and a gatehouse create an open-spaced compound surrounding landscaped waterworks. Pasargadae is the earliest preserved example of the Persian *parádeisos*, meaning beautiful garden (hence our term "paradise"). Xenophon described such a *parádeisos* belonging to Cyrus the Younger at Sardis. Although none has yet been systematically excavated, it is likely that satrapal palaces across the empire emulated royal gardens such as that preserved at Pasargadae. The continuity of this architectural tradition of porticoed palaces framing formal gardens is demonstrated by the well-preserved seventeenth-century-CE Chehel Sotun at Isfahan in Iran. (See "Palaces and Temples in Ancient Mesopotamia" in Part 4, Vol. I.)

The Tomb of Cyrus

The gable-roofed stone chamber of stark majesty that served as Cyrus's tomb rises from a stepped podium (fig. 2). The modest burial room measures roughly 10.2 by 7.2 feet (3.1 by 2.2 meters). Its lavish furnishings were described by classical authors; but as with the tombs of subsequent Achaemenid kings, this one was robbed long ago. Architecturally, Cyrus's tomb blends formal and symbolic allusions to traditions of several regions recently incorporated into the empire. The stepped base is evocative of the great ziggurats of Mesopotamia and Elam, with their highly charged value as symbolic mountains reaching for heaven. The form of the gable-roofed building recalls representations of Urartian temples and some features of Anatolian funerary structures. Masonry techniques, proportions, and molding forms (such as the *cyma reversa* that creates the transition from walls to roof) reflect

Ionic tradition. Their applications display total aesthetic sympathy with Ionic prototypes, but the resulting structure is unique.

Although Darius I and his successors used an altogether different tomb form, the freestanding monument of Cyrus became the model for a series of noble tombs, culminating during the fourth century in the famous tomb of the Carian satrap Mausolus (the Mausoleum at Halicarnassus). This use of Cyrus's tomb as a model reflects the increasingly heroic status accorded Cyrus as an ideal ruler even in the Greek world. (See "Soldiers to Pharaoh: The Carians of Southwest Anatolia" in Part V, Vol. II.)

The Takht

The Takht (Persian, "throne"), or citadel platform, formed around a core of roughly encased stone chips, has an outer wall made of massive drafted limestone blocks of equal height but variegated length. It forms a parallelogram measuring about 216 by 259 feet (65.8 by 78.8 meters) on north and west, rising some 48 feet (14.5 meters). A crowning stone parapet along a deeply recessed section on the south seems intended to complement a palace portico with a panorama of the plain.

As with the tomb, technical and stylistic features of the Takht masonry advertise the western reaches of imperial domain. In the 1960s Carl Nylander meticulously documented the application of Lydian and Ionian stone-working methods and forms here. As persuasively interpreted by Nylander, the result was a facade laden with allusion to the architectural splendor of archaic Asia Minor.

The Gatehouse

The rectangular Gatehouse (roughly 28.5 by 25.5 meters [94 by 84 feet]) had large doorways and four interior columns of stone. The connecting superstructure was mud-brick. Herzfeld reported remains of massive sculptures of Mesopotamian-type guardian bulls and man-bulls that would have projected from the doors of the main axis. The jamb of one of the two opposing side doors is extant. It is decorated with a relief of a winged human figure oriented as if walking into the Gatehouse (fig. 3). This creature sports a close-cropped beard and a

Fig. 2. Limestone-block tomb of Cyrus erected at Pasargadae, circa 529 BCE. Six steps lead to a simple building that can be entered by double doors. The inner chamber is windowless, and the structure has a gabled roof. ORIENTAL INSTITUTE, UNIVERSITY OF CHICAGO, CHICAGO

bobbed Elamite coiffure; he wears an elaborate robe of Elamite royalty, previously documented on the Assyrian reliefs of Assurbanipal's campaigns in Elam. He also wears an Egyptian triple "atef" crown. His feet are bare. Although lost in modern times, a cuneiform inscription above his head written in Old Persian, Elamite, and Babylonian once declared, "I am Cyrus, an Achaemenid." The use of these three languages for parallel texts on official Achaemenid monuments remained a standard practice.

Numerous theories have been suggested for the identity and meaning of the Gatehouse figure. His eclectic costume bespeaks carefully planned allusions to key cultural regions. Although Egypt was not conquered by the Persians until after the death of Cyrus, the Egyptian crown may well symbolize Cyrus's expansionist intentions. The Elamite coiffure and royal robe assertively reference this Iranian kingdom from which the Achaemenids assimilated much cultural and administrative expertise. The two pairs of wings recall Assyrian palace sculptures of cult genii. Yet it is tempting to read something more here. Herodotus tells of Cyrus's prophetic dream envisioning Darius I with two sets of wings—one shadowing Asia, the other Europe. This tale may transmit the kernel of a popular Persian legend of metaphorical imperial embrace.

Palace S

A rectangular hypostyle hall, Palace S has columned porticoes all around. The one completely surviving column is a tall, unfluted, white lime-stone shaft extending upward, with a slight taper from a slim astragal molding. The column bases are all of black stone and consist of two square plinths crowned by a torus molding. Herzfeld discovered evidence of four separate types of capitals of black stone that apparently belonged to the columns in the main hall. The capitals take the form of addorsed animal protomes (the heads and necks of two animals back to back). The hybrid leonine monster, lion, and bull are all capital forms found at Susa and Persepolis. (See plan of Achaemenid Palace at Susa erected by Darius I, fig. 7 in "The History of Elam and Achaemenid Persia: An Overview" in Part 5,

Vol. II.) The horse capital was apparently never repeated. Whereas the column bases and shafts owe much to Greco-Lydian traditions, these animal capitals seem to have been inspired by eastern imagery. No precise prototypes are known, but depictions of addorsed animals in the portable arts of Mesopotamia and Iran and Neo-Elamite animal protomes used as protruding architectural elements indicate possible sources of inspiration. The many-columned hall now has a firm pedigree in earlier first millennium Iranian architecture as a result of excavations at Godin Tepe, Baba Jan, Hasanlu, and Tepe Nush-i Jan.

Doorjamb reliefs once adorned all four entrances of Palace S, but only three doors are preserved at all. In every case, processional figures face the exterior of the building. The three extant variations (none preserved above the legs) are: a human figure with bare legs and feet preceding an eagle-footed monster, a fish-garbed priest figure preceding a rampant bull holding a staff, and two long-robed barefoot humans with a bovine quadruped alongside. Thus, Palace S evokes strong reminiscence of the cultic iconography of Neo-Assyrian times. Stylistically the sculptures show total artistic command of the Assyrian legacy of formal syntax, even as subtle adaptations are also apparent.

Palace P

A variation on the porticoed hypostyle hall, Palace P has column bases composed of a double plinth in white and black stone, crowned by a horizontally fluted torus molding. Column shafts are smooth, as in Palace S. No capitals are preserved. Evidence of curved painted plaster suggests the possibility that the uppermost elements were rendered in decorated wood.

The doorjambs of the two entrances are carved in relief with a staff-bearing royal figure followed by a smaller attendant. Only the bottom portions of these reliefs are preserved. The figures are clothed in the pleated Persian court robe familiar at Susa and Persepolis. Holes for metal attachment on the garment and shoes of the royal figures are a distinctive feature, reflecting actual elite sartorial accoutrements in decorative gold appliqué from tombs of Scythian chieftains in the Black Sea region, as well as Pasargadae itself, Sardis, and elsewhere. Inscrip-

Fig. 3. Nine-foot stone figure carved in the sixth century BCE on a doorjamb of the gatehouse at Pasargadae. COURTESY OF MARGARET COOL ROOT

tions added to the reliefs on the pleats of the royal robe identify the figure as Cyrus.

An inscription that once appeared above the reliefs seems to read that Cyrus built and decorated the palace, while Darius I added an inscription. This has been used to support a theory based on stylistic analysis (see below) to the effect that the Palace P reliefs were not carved until the reign of Darius. Darius may well have performed the pious (and self-aggrandizing) task of adding inscriptions, but the combined weight of evidence asserts the validity of Cyrus as artistic patron. Later at Persepolis, Xerxes similarly added inscriptions to monuments begun by Darius. The dating of the inscriptions at Pasargadae is a linguistic controversy centering on when Old Persian was first used in written form.

DARIUS I'S MONUMENT AT BEHISTUN

The rock relief and trilingual cuneiform inscription of Darius I at Mount Behistun (Bisitun, Bisutun) in northwestern Iran look down from a height of roughly 75 meters (250 feet) on the strategic ancient highway from Ecbatana to Babylon through a pass of the Zagros Mountains (see aerial view of Mount Behistun, Fig. 1 in "Darius I and the Persian Empire" in Part 5, Vol. II). Steps carved into the cliff for construction purposes were later cut away, leaving the monument visible only from a great distance (fig. 4).

Henry Rawlinson, working there from 1835 to 1847, was the first antiquarian to obtain good copies of the inscription and renderings of the sculpture from close range. Subsequent detailed documentation was obtained by George G. Cameron's missions in 1948 and 1957 and the work of a German team in the 1960s. (See "Darius I and the Persian Empire" in Part 5, Vol. II.)

The Behistun monument commemorates Darius's role as moral and military regenerator of the empire between 522 and 520. The last prisoner in the relief, a Scythian with pointed cap, was added after the original text and sculpture had been completed, necessitating the erasure of a section of inscription. Since the Scythian encounter symbolized by the added figure occurred in 519, this date provides a fixed point by which time the main part of the monument must have been completed. Behistun offers the only historical narrative surviving from the Achaemenids. Similarly the relief is the only surviving work of official Achaemenid art depicting a specific historical episode as distinct from a recurring ceremony or symbolic image.

Although the relief tells a story, it does so by presenting one emblematic, composite tableau

Fig. 4. Relief and much of text of Darius I from Mount Behistun. KELSEY MUSEUM OF ARCHAEOLOGY, UNIVERSITY OF MICHIGAN, ANN ARBOR

rather than a series of events. It illustrates the summary section of the long narrative text:

> Saith Darius the King: These are the provinces which became rebellious. The Lie made them rebellious, so that these (men) deceived the people. Afterwards Ahuramazda put them into my hand; as was my desire, so I did unto them.
>
> (Kent, *Old Persian*, p. 131)

In this summary text, as in the accompanying relief, historical detail has been distilled to focus on Darius's role as victor in collaboration with the Achaemenid patron god Ahura Mazda. Displayed within a smoothed panel approximately 3 by 5.5 meters (10 by 18 feet), the life-sized figure of Darius dominates the tableau. He stands with one foot pinning down the squirming, prostrate figure of Gaumata, a magus (Median priest) and pretender to the throne. While the king holds his great bow in one hand, the other is lifted up in acknowledgment of Ahura Mazda, who hovers above the earthly realm as a half-length figure within a winged disk. Behind the king, two noble weapon-bearers stand at attention, their slightly smaller size conveying their inferior status. Smaller still are the figures of nine captive rebels lined up in single file, attached together at their necks and with hands bound behind their backs.

Analysis of the rhetorical strategies of the relief reveals how important subtleties of the sources were exploited. The imagery of a victorious ruler pressing his foot on a prostrate foe—while other bound captives are brought forward by a deity—clearly quotes the late-third-millennium rock relief of a local king, Annubanini. This monument is still visible at Sar-i Pol-i Zohab, west of Mount Behistun along the same Zagros pass. The relief of Annubanini is a provincial monument reflecting the impact of contemporaneous Akkadian art such as the stele of Naram-Sin, with its forceful emblematic images of divinely sanctioned victory. Achaemenid adoption of visual symbolism favored by earlier rulers is not limited to the example of Behistun. It may indicate an informed revival of elements of Akkadian imagery to invoke the memory of imperial precedent. It surely indicates a range of shared goals in the depiction of military victory.

The sculptural style of Darius's relief invokes portrayals of Neo-Assyrian kings of the more re-

Fig. 5. Head of Darius I from the relief at Mount Behistun. See "Darius I and the Persian Empire" in Part 5, Vol. II, for a view of the site. KELSEY MUSEUM OF ARCHAEOLOGY, UNIVERSITY OF MICHIGAN, ANN ARBOR

cent past (fig. 5). The hair and beard of Darius are styled in a manner remarkably like those of Assurbanipal; significantly, they differ from the way these elements are rendered on the Persepolis sculptures. At Behistun the sculptural renditions of Persian robes are faithful to the belted garments with voluminous sleeves and many-pleated skirts that occur at Palace P, Susa, and Persepolis. Yet the Behistun version alters the feel of the costume by muting the heavy, multi-faceted lushness of the court robe and exaggerating a diagonal hemline.

It has traditionally been assumed that Achaemenid drapery style must have developed on an uninterrupted path from precanonic to canonic modes. For this reason, some have insisted that the Palace P reliefs at Pasargadae, although carrying the name of Cyrus, must postdate Behistun. It seems preferable to recognize the demonstrated tendency in Achaemenid art to make iconographic and stylistic choices depend on relevance to the intended message. Fragments of a full-scale copy of the Behistun relief found at Babylon repeat the Behistun style even though presumably carved later.

SUSA

With its great Elamite legacy, Susa was made a capital of the Achaemenid Empire under Darius I. This site presents myriad difficulties because of its long pre- and post-Achaemenid occupational history and because of problematic field methods of early excavations, when the French began to work at the site more than one hundred years ago. The talents and modern methods of the post–World War II French and international teams have made it possible to reinterpret the early records and to discover important new material from carefully controlled and documented contexts. Among the issues that modern investigation is attempting to clarify are the nature of continuity or discontinuity between Elamite and Achaemenid Susa (with evidence now suggesting the continued viability of Elamite occupation beyond the destructive Assyrian campaigns of 647 and bridging the gap into Achaemenid times) and the nature of urban environment and satellite settlement—as opposed to royal installation—in Achaemenid period Susa and its territory.

If we were to rely on classical Greek and biblical sources alone, Susa would loom as the focal point of all Achaemenid administrative, diplomatic, and courtly activity. Thus it is ironic that only a handful of Achaemenid administrative tablets has been retrieved from Susa. Very little in the way of portable goods of any sort has been found, in fact, although the recovery of ivory and Attic pottery fragments suggests that Susa was indeed a capital that satisfied diverse cosmopolitan tastes.

Palatial Remains

Despite the paucity of certain kinds of material evidence from Susa, the architectural remains of its Achaemenid palaces testify to life at court on a truly grand scale (the audience hall of Darius I measured about 250 meters [800 feet] square). Their most distinctive feature relates to the fact that Susa, like neighboring Mesopotamia, is an area poor in stone. Thus, only the elaborately carved soaring columns of the vast hypostyle halls were made of stone (on the order of those to be described for Persepolis). The stone had to be imported from the Zagros Mountains. What has been preserved of the surface architectural decoration of the Susa palaces was, on the other hand, primarily in the medium of bright glazed brick and molded glazed-brick relief, with a palette that emphasized blue, green, cream, yellow, and black. This technique has a secure pedigree in earlier Mesopotamian and Elamite architecture, its closest precedent being the extraordinary Processional Way at Babylon, built by Nebuchadnezzar (Nebuchadrezzar) II in the early sixth century.

In Achaemenid Susa, the repertoire of architectural decoration in glazed tile and brick includes files of food bearers, archers wearing richly ornamented robes that suggest the glories of near eastern textiles now lost, and lions and composite beasts, heraldically posed sphinxes, and contest groups showing a lion attacking a bull. A fragmentary inscription panel adjacent to the archer frieze preserves the name Otanes, a loyal supporter of Darius who is also mentioned in the Behistun text and given a prominent loyalist role in Herodotus's account of the rebellions faced by Darius. This suggests that the frieze of elegantly robed, spear-bearing men represented (in a generic mode) specific members of the Persian elite. While such files of court figures may seem like perfunctory space-fillers to the modern viewer, they must have been a source of pride and prestige to the powerful Persian families whose sons were, in effect, displayed in full regalia on the palace walls.

The Statue of Darius

In 1972 the French uncovered a monumental gatehouse and remains of a colossal statue of Darius I preserved almost up to the shoulders (fig. 6). It was probably one of an original pair of images positioned on either side of the entrance. The royal figure wears the Persian court robe and strapless royal Persian boots, and his bracelets and the dagger tucked in his belt are also typical Persian accoutrements. But in fact this statue is a remarkable hybrid. Its structure betrays Egyptian tradition: the figure is attached to a back pillar, with left leg placed forward in an Egyptian striding pose. Within the clenched right fist held down at the side, Darius holds a short sticklike implement of uncertain symbolism, typical of Egyptian statuary. His left arm is raised up and then bent at the elbow to lie flat and rigid against the chest in a line parallel with the ground, a position which evokes the aura of hieratic posturings of pharaonic "Osirid" sculptures.

Additional features point directly to manufacture on Egyptian soil (not merely to an embrace of egyptianizing motifs). The stone is Egyptian, possibly quarried in the Wadi Hammamat, from

Fig. 6. Headless, granite statue of Darius I from Susa, which was excavated in 1972. GERMAN ARCHAEOLOGICAL INSTITUTE, BERLIN

which Darius is known to have mobilized masons. Inscriptions on the garment are informative. In addition to a trilingual cuneiform text invoking Ahura Mazda, an Egyptian hieroglyphic text links Darius to the god Atum of Heliopolis and declares the prowess of the king in traditional Egyptian metaphor. The ends of the king's belt bear Darius's name in hieroglyphs within the royal cartouche. The rectangular base of the statue again includes a hieroglyphic inscription invoking Atum.

On either long side of the base appear twelve fortress rings upon which kneel personifications of the places named within the rings. The kneeling figures face toward the front of the base, their hands raised and turned palms up. Aspects of hairstyle, costume, and (to some extent) physiognomy differentiate them. Another hieroglyphic text, on the short sides of the base, is repeated four times, framing the traditional Egyptian representations of the paired fecundity figures binding the plants of the Two Lands. The text speaks for each fecundity figure:

> I have given you all life and power, all stability, all health, all joy. I have given you all flat lands and all mountain lands gathered under your sandals. I have given you Upper and Lower Egypt in adoration before your perfect face, as [before the god] Re, for ever. (Translated by J. Baines.)

This remarkable statue must have been commissioned for the temple of Atum at Heliopolis by Darius, probably while he was actually in Egypt. At some later point it was brought to Susa. Precedents exist in the ancient Near East for the transport and reinstallation of colossal royal images (for instance, the reinstallation by Esarhaddon or Assurbanipal of colossal statues of the Egyptian king Taharqa in a gateway at the Assyrian capital of Nineveh [Tell Kuyunjik, Nebi Yunus]).

The kneeling personifications on the statue base draw inspiration from an age-old Egyptian conceptualization of the traditional enemies of pharaoh as bound captives emerging from name rings ranged underfoot. Beneath Darius, however, the figures appear not as bound enemies but rather as figures willingly raising their hands up in adoration. This same message of harmonious support and praise of the king by the united lands of the empire is a leitmotif in the sculptural program of Persepolis. Designed for a specific

Egyptian audience, this statue conveys mainstream Achaemenid ideology through a visual code that adapts indigenous artistic traditions.

The Foundation Charter of Darius

In 1929 copies of a trilingual cuneiform text were unearthed from the debris of the palace of Darius I. It describes the construction of the palace and includes a listing of the nationalities of the artisans involved in specific tasks. The reference to Ionian and Sardian stonecutters has encouraged a notion that Achaemenid stone sculpture should be considered, in essence, a Greek achievement somewhat colored by Persian tastes. Recent scholarship has revised this approach, emphasizing the ideological creativity of Achaemenid art, its calculated embrace of a wide range of near eastern representational traditions, and the importance of placing in proper perspective the roles of multiethnic artisans in the implementation of the wishes of their imperial patron.

The Susa foundation charter must be interpreted as an imperial statement describing dominion in terms of human and material resources funneled to the imperial center, not as a strictly literal account of construction activities. Such statements have a long history in ancient Mesopotamia. The absence of Persians in the tally accords well with this interpretation, since the imperial statement involves a deliberate distinction between Persia and all the peoples and resources it controlled. Although the text does not express contractually literal specifications for the palace construction at Susa, it does convey a legitimate sense of the internationalism of the imperial work force. Furthermore, it remains valid as an index of the range of luxury materials such as gold, ivory, and ebony that embellished Achaemenid palaces.

PERSEPOLIS AND NAQSH-I RUSTAM

The sites of Persepolis and Naqsh-i Rustam were excavated and studied between 1931 and 1939 by the Oriental Institute of the University of Chicago: first under Ernst Herzfeld and subsequently under Erich Schmidt. Work continued under Iranian auspices, led by Ali Sami and his successors, and included the discovery and excavation of palatial complexes in the Persepolis plain just below the citadel. From 1964 through 1978 an Italian restoration team, led by Ann Britt and Giuseppe Tilia, made critical discoveries about the building history and techniques of construction and embellishment.

Persepolis was founded by Darius I, probably directly upon his return from the reconquest of Egypt in 518 (fig. 7). The site lies on the fertile Marv Dasht ("Plain of the Grassy Meadow") in Parsa (Persia). The name Persepolis is Greek, meaning "city of the Persians." The Achaemenids themselves referred to it simply (but definitively) as Parsa: symbolically equivalent to the greater homeland. It was the heart of the whole empire and the locus of coronations, royal burials, New Year's celebrations, and other imperial displays.

Persepolis was also the hub of a large administrative and agricultural region formed of many settlements and farming estates. This contextually diversified understanding of Persepolis is a recent development made possible through integration of information from the Persepolis fortification tablets with excavation and field survey data.

Like Pasargadae, Persepolis had palatial structures in the plain, dominated by a fortified Takht with imposing official buildings and rock-cut tombs of the last Achaemenid kings set in the cliffs above the citadel. But unlike Pasargadae, the citadel's intended role as a focal point of ceremonial display was actually achieved—to glorious effect.

Although Persepolis was sacked and burned by the army of Alexander the Great in 330, its ruins remained partially visible (and visited) throughout later history. Representational graffiti of the Sasanian period (224–651 CE) on the walls of the palace of Darius and the so-called harem of Xerxes bear witness to post-Achaemenid activity here. Motifs derived from the visible ruins of pre-excavation date became prototypes for Seleucid, Parthian, and especially Sasanian art in Persia and even enjoyed revivals in nineteenth-century CE sculptures commissioned at nearby Shiraz. Worked stone from Persepolis has been pilfered continuously since Alexander's destruction, with column bases and drums as well as relief slabs finding new uses at neighboring locations.

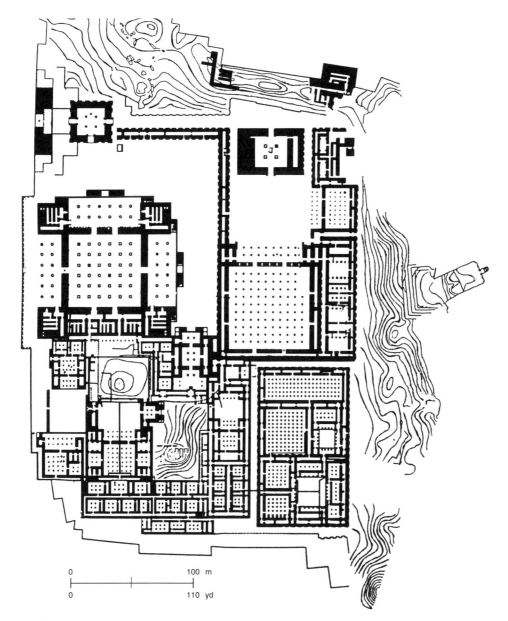

Fig. 7. Plan of Persepolis, which was founded by Darius I circa 518. The complex included the royal tombs set into the cliff at Naqsh-i Rustam, the Xerxes Gate, a treasury, a fortification wall, and many additional buildings. The University of Chicago's Oriental Institute excavated the site in the 1930s. COURTESY OF MARGARET COOL ROOT

Naqsh-i Rustam is a rocky enclave 6 kilometers (3.5 miles) north of Persepolis, where the tombs of Darius and three of his successors were carved into the cliffsides (fig. 8). A stone tower was built facing these tombs, replicating the Zendan at Pasargadae in form and presumably also in function. The majestic cliff formation marks an ancient spring that was sacred to the Elamite predecessors of the Achaemenids. Centuries

after the last Achaemenid tomb was carved there, it achieved renewed importance for the Sasanian Persian kings.

The Tomb of Darius

The choice of the symbolically charged site at Naqsh-i Rustam for the rock-carved tomb of Darius I enhanced the intrinsic significance of the

Fig. 8. Panorama of Achaemenid tombs from Naqsh-i Rustam with the tower at the extreme left. The site was excavated in the 1930s. ORIENTAL INSTITUTE, UNIVERSITY OF CHICAGO

monument and its message by linking it to indigenous traditions of cult and kingship. The tomb displays a cruciform facade 23 meters (75 feet) high, with the bottom edge about 15 meters (50 feet) above ground level. Rising above a smoothed lower section, the wide middle zone of the exterior depicts a palace facade similar to those at Persepolis. Its door is actually the entrance to the cavernous burial apartments hollowed out of the living rock. A vestibule 18.72 meters (61 feet) long runs parallel to the facade. Off this hallway three chambers, each containing three crypts, are carved deeper into the rock. The burial cists had massive stone lids and were clearly intended to accommodate interments. The coffins for the king and his close family members were probably made of metal or wood overlaid with metal.

Displayed in relief on the upper element of the cruciform tomb facade is a depiction of the king standing on a three-stepped platform worshiping before a blazing fire altar and an icon of Ahura Mazda in a winged disk. A lunar symbol is set in the field beyond the altar. This scene takes place on a massive and elaborately carved podium held above the level of the palace roof by labeled personifications of all the lands of the empire. Flanking Darius on the framing walls are members of his court: weapon-bearers behind him and robed figures with hands cupped toward their faces approaching him. In yet another instance of the royal practice of individualizing otherwise generic depictions of honored nobles, two of the weapon-bearers behind the king are named: Aspathines and Gobryas.

The main inscription on Darius's tomb (again in Old Persian, Elamite, and Babylonian) gives an account of the extent of empire bestowed upon Darius by Ahura Mazda, referring to the sculpted platform carriers as symbols of the vastness of his realm. The text also offers a series of rather personal royal statements about the all-embracing powers of Ahura Mazda, the nature of Achaemenid kingship, the ideal qualities of an Achaemenid ruler, and guidelines of good conduct for his people (including cooperative and truthful behavior).

The Citadel Platform

The Takht at Persepolis is nestled on the east against Mount Rahmat. Constructed from a bedrock and rubble core, it rises on its west side to about 14 meters (46 feet) above the plain. It forms an oblong quadrilateral with irregular sides, producing an expanse of about 428 meters (1400 feet) on the north–south axis and 300 meters (1000 feet) on the east–west axis. Mud-brick fortifications added another 10 to 15 meters (33 to 50 feet) to the height of certain segments of the citadel, and they extended along the mountainside at the back of the site.

The platform had massive stone-facing blocks articulating a masonry style radically different from that encountered at Pasargadae. Hewn from an adjacent gray limestone quarry, the blocks were brought to the construction site in rough, irregularly shaped and sized forms. The blocks were meticulously fitted together without mortar, their visible surface smoothed and polished. This construction was a labor-intensive feat compared with the neatly rationalized, modular construction of the platform at Pasargadae.

Beyond that, it is also possible that a symbolical message was intended by this masonry style. On the south side of the terrace wall, Darius I placed a Babylonian inscription that extols his god-given empire as a kingdom made whole out of diverse terrains, as a nation of many people speaking many languages. Several other texts he commissioned reiterate metaphorical allusions to an empire put together from disparate pieces; an empire likened to a restored architectural foundation.

A magnificent double-return staircase on the west gives slow ascent by steps with very short risers, forcing a lingering awareness of the mammoth polished blocks that dwarf the human visitor. At the top looms a colossal gatehouse with Assyrianizing guardian bulls and man-bulls. Begun by Darius and completed by his son Xerxes, this entranceway is named "Gate of All Lands": an explicit reiteration of the theme of imperial union out of many parts.

The Gate of All Lands had door frames and guardian sculptures, as well as four soaring columns, made of local limestone. The roofing was of wood; the walls linking the stone door frames were of brick with a decorative glazed surface. This is the basic formula for all the structures on the Takht, with the addition of stone stairways where relevant. The result is that the site, in its ruined state and denuded of walls and roofs, has the appearance of a vast forest of stone columns.

Occasional clearings are punctuated eerily by visions on the carved doorjambs and stairways of kings and courtiers.

The Sculptural Program

The columns of the great ceremonial buildings here (as at Susa) are elaborate composite creations (see fig. 9). Many of the bases are carved in the form of inverted bell-shaped flowers, with supporting lower margins set down into the floors so that they appear to rest on the very tips of the petals. Crisply fluted column drums are topped by an intricately ornamented complex capital consisting of a floral segment of drooping sepals crowned by a corona of palm leaves, a vertical member of four double volutes, and addorsed animal protomes forming saddles for the roof beams. (In architectural units where shorter columns were required, the animal protomes rested directly atop the shafts.) The most common animal protome is the bull. But man-bulls, lions, lion monsters, and griffins also stared down from their height (in the Apadana) of more than 17 meters (57 feet). Their own dimensions added another 2 meters (6 feet) to the total height.

These exotic sculpted columns represent a synthesis of elements from Egypt, Syria/Assyria, Ionia, and Iran. The Egyptianizing floral shapes on the complex capitals are striking. The individual parts of the columns come together to form a totally original creation. Given the emphasis on hypostyle halls at Persepolis and Susa, these columns take on great significance in their visual setting. The inverted-petal bases give the fantastic effect of massive, self-levitating pillars that seem merely to skim the surface of the floor in which they are actually rooted. The animal protomes suggest the harnessing of mighty creatures and monsters whose potentially destructive force can be constructively channeled to the support of the royal palaces.

The single most frequently used motif in Achaemenid architectural sculpture and portable arts is the image of the royal hero mastering or slaying powerful animals or monsters. At Persepolis, this emblem decorates doorjambs of several palaces—always in a manner that shows the hero protecting an interior chamber from the intrusive creature. Thus, the iconography of the column capitals reinforces the resolution of a conflict that is narrated in the passageways of many of the ceremonial buildings: threats are diverted, and instigators foiled (fig. 10).

Other sculptural motifs at Persepolis elaborate the theme of conflict resolution. The simplest one (echoing Palace P at Pasargadae) has the king in full regalia moving through doorways toward the exterior, followed by attendants bearing flywhisks and parasols. Combative labors carried out as scenes on doorjambs of the innermost regions of the buildings have been completed so that the king can emerge splendid and intact. Much more nuanced are the motifs that involve

the king in the context of explicitly imperial resolution.

In the Central Building and the Throne Hall, doorjamb reliefs display variations on the motif of the king held aloft on a dais supported by personified subject lands. This symbolism was presented in Egyptian style on the statue of Darius found at Susa. On the Persepolis palaces and also on the royal tomb facades, such personifications stand in the "Atlas" pose, holding the royal podium above their heads by the tips of their fingers. In the ancient Near East, this posture connotes cosmic support. The clear message offered here is an empire harmoniously

Fig. 9. Drawings of four orders of Achaemenid columns, Persepolis, which synthesized Egyptian, Ionian, Syrian, and Iranian elements.
ERNST HERZFELD, *IRAN IN THE ANCIENT NEAR EAST* (1941)

Fig. 10. View of Throne Hall, Persepolis, containing a relief of a hero, and the Central Building with its doorjamb relief of the king raised aloft. Achaemenid sculptural motifs like these emphasized a powerful royal hero and the theme of conflict resolution. COURTESY OF MARGARET COOL ROOT

ordered, in which all the constituent peoples raise the king up in communal praise.

The sculptures of Persepolis were planned at the highest level, to follow a program that dictated style as well as iconography. Certainly the king was directly involved in the creative planning process, working with a group of designers attuned to his interests and knowledgeable about the traditions of the subject lands to which he wished to allude. Exemplifying the type of expertise the royal patron must have gathered together, an Egyptian admiral, Udjahorresne, claimed in his biographical inscription to have

been an advisor to Darius, traveling between Egypt and the Persian sphere in this capacity.

The actual carving of the sculpture was done by crews, after the designs were drawn on the architectural blocks in paint or charcoal. Once roughly revealed by the chisel, figures emerged in progressively finer form, with intricate details left for last. Slots for the insertion of metal ornaments remain on numerous royal crowns, though none of the representations here repeats the use at Pasargadae Palace P of attachments on royal garments and shoes. The architectural sculptures were painted, with designs incised on headgear and garments functioning as guides. Several patterns (lions in procession, star and rosette emblems) are precisely paralleled in Achaemenid period carpets found in frozen tombs of Scythian chieftains in Siberia, who operated on the fringes of imperial control. (See "Textile Arts in Ancient Western Asia" in Part 7, Vol. III.)

Artisans from all over the empire worked at Persepolis in a variety of employment relationships ranging from bondage to more or less free agency. The lure of employment on a grandiose project also attracted itinerant artisans from non-imperial territory such as mainland Greece. The distinctive skills, individual expertise, native traditions, and training of this work force were channeled through careful planning and supervision to yield a conceptually and technically unified result.

The Apadana

The largest and highest palace is the Apadana, erected on its own platform about 2.6 meters (9 feet) above the level of the Takht. Its main hall measuring 60.5 meters (217 feet) square and supported by thirty-six columns, this edifice could conceivably have accommodated a standing audience of ten thousand. Grand pillared porticoes on the north, east, and west, plus a dense complex including courtyard, guard chambers, and service quarters at the south, greatly increase these dimensions. Under the foundations at the northeast and southeast corners two identically inscribed plaques of gold and silver were interred—each pair within a stone box. Several archaic Greek and Lydian coins were found below these boxes, probably meant to reflect Persian power or ambitions for power in these areas. A trilingual cuneiform inscription presents Darius I as king and describes an imperial domain anchored by four geographical corners, chiastically situated in relation to Persepolis: from the plains of Scythia-beyond-Sogdiana to Ethiopia (northeast to southwest); and from Sind to Sardis (southeast to northwest). Had Darius already conquered Thrace, this region rather than Sardis would have been listed as the farthest northwestern point of the empire. A date of about 515 for the foundation deposits fits the historical indicators.

The integrated rhetoric of text and material elements of the deposit fixes king, dynasty, royal palace, and numinous wealth at the conceptual as well as physical center of his domain. The

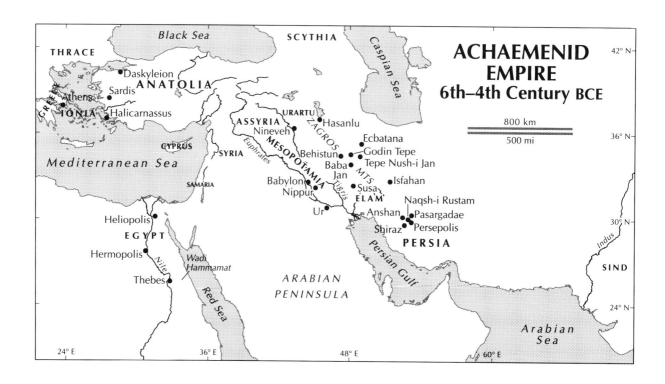

orientation of the corners of the palace point directly toward the four corners of the imperial frontier proclaimed in the foundation texts.

In their original state, the north and east stairways of the Apadana each displayed a relief of the enthroned king and court entourage receiving a bowing official. (At some later date these panels were removed to the interior of the Treasury.) Behind the king, a wing of sculptures depicts Persian nobles in alternating court robes and martial attire. Before him, files of delegates from twenty-three subject lands are poised to bring forward gifts of praise. The leader of each group is taken by the hand by a Persian courtier.

The pivotal motif on the Apadana reliefs is the hand-holding gesture. Like the "Atlas" posture for raising the Persian king aloft, this gesture has rich connotations in Egypt and the Near East. Specifically, it implies solemn, imminent presentation before a deity (or deified king) in the context of a reverential cult. The Persian use of the hand-holding imagery is grounded in Egyptian and Mesopotamian cult representations, brilliantly adapted so that the Achaemenid king assumes the position of the focal divinity, and the representatives from the subject lands assume the roles of pious petitioners.

The Apadana stairway facades present an elaborate metaphor of political ideology and cooperative social order cast as a gift-giving procession. Such a ceremony may well have occurred in actuality, for there is textual evidence from Sasanian Iran for processional gift-giving celebrations at the king's birthday. The sophisticated narrative on the Apadana may have served as a conceptual prototype for the Parthenon frieze carved about fifty years later in Athens, then at the height of Periclean imperial ambition following the repulsion of Persian forces from mainland Greece.

Finds

Thoroughly looted by Alexander and continuously picked over by visitors and antiquarians, Persepolis nevertheless yielded an important array of nonarchitectural material to controlled excavations. Finds from the sites of various buildings on the Takht include military paraphernalia and utilitarian pottery, occasional seals and coins, and beads of prized stones; fragments of gold jewelry, garment, and architectural orna-

ments; two silver vessels; and statuettes of bronze and lapis lazuli.

The Chicago expedition discovered two collections of clay administrative tablets and labels. The Persepolis fortification tablets (found in two rooms of the fortification system) include thousands of dated Elamite administrative tablets from 509 to 494. They record disbursements of food commodities from the imperial stores in the Persepolis region to personages of wide-ranging status, including members of the royal family, priests, and work groups involved with court-related activities. The Treasury tablets are a much smaller corpus of documents and labels from 492 to 458. These texts record payments by Treasury officials to workers. Both sets of tablets are important as documents on imperial administration and society. Furthermore, the seals applied both to the documents and to the many uninscribed labels are a major resource for the study of Achaemenid glyptic.

Stone statues of standing bulls and ibexes, seated mastiffs, and reclining felines were recovered. Textual sources supply additional information on the types of freestanding monuments that once graced Persepolis and other Achaemenid sites. Both Prince Arsam, satrap of Egypt, and Herodotus mention Achaemenid equestrian images. Herodotus also notes a gold statue of Artystone, the favorite wife of Darius I. Women do not figure in the representational imagery of the Persepolis reliefs. Yet the Persepolis fortification tablets shed light on the active court life of royal women, particularly Artystone. It is plausible that such women were indeed depicted in art, but that their images were placed in residential quarters not yet explored or were (like Artystone's statue) made of metal, long since melted down. The Middle Elamite tradition that has left us the marvelous life-sized bronze sculpture of Queen Napir-asu from Susa supports such possibilities. (See "The History of Elam and Achaemenid Persia: An Overview" in Part 5, Vol. II.)

At Persepolis, remnants of portable finds were concentrated in the Treasury. This building functioned not only as a storehouse for accumulated wealth in gold and silver, but also as a museum for other types of precious artifacts (diplomatic gifts, artworks, heirloom booty from many lands), as a repository for the tablets already mentioned, and as an arsenal.

Here, as elsewhere, Alexander's soldiers clearly intended to make a clean sweep. Plutarch's life of Alexander tells us that it took 10,000 mules and 5,000 camels to cart the loot from Persepolis. Diodorus and Quintus Curtius both report that 120,000 talents of gold and silver were seized there. This, combined with the smaller quantities located from other cities—40,000 to 50,000 from Susa, for instance—was the largest recorded amount of precious metal to change hands in all of antiquity. Indeed the Treasury was so completely emptied of its vast stores that no Achaemenian coins and only a small number of predestruction coins of other types were found. (See "Theology and Worship in Elam and Achaemenid Iran" in Part 8, Vol. III.)

A picture of the glorious Achaemenid metalwork which once enriched the Treasury must be drawn from other sources. Gift-bearing delegations portrayed on the Apadana reliefs carry vessels, jewelry, and ceremonial weaponry corresponding to actual items of precious metal known from finds (fig. 11). For instance, the bracelets with elaborately cast zoomorphic terminals brought by Medians, Lydians, and Scythians echo excavated examples from Pasargadae, Susa, Sardis, and Vouni (on Cyprus). Massive gold bracelets from the so-called Oxus Treasure exhibit intricate cloisonné decoration in multicolored inlay. (See "Archaeology and Artifacts in Iron Age Central Asia" in Part 5, Vol. II.)

Eight delegations on the Apadana bring metal vessels—the most elaborate being spouted jars with zoomorphic handles, closely paralleled, for instance, by a surviving silver example from a plundered Achaemenid-period burial at Duvanli, Bulgaria. One characteristic Achaemenid metalware shape is not depicted on the Persepolis reliefs: the horn-shaped drinking vessel (rhyton) terminating in a zoomorphic base. Although the rhyton shape was not new in the Near East, Achaemenid patronage encouraged unprecedented design elegance. The late-fourth-century tomb of Petosiris near Hermopolis (modern al-Ashmunein), Egypt, preserves paintings of local metalworkers making characteristic Achaemenid rhyta. The vessel form was also reproduced in local clay versions as a kind of "perserie" product both within the empire and even in fifth-century Athens.

Dissemination of precious-metal prototypes imitated in humbler media was widespread because of the Achaemenid royal practice of solidifying loyalty through gifts of gold and silver. Significant examples of metal tableware, often inscribed with the king's name, have been uncovered in controlled excavations throughout the empire, frequently in burials. This suggests that they were so highly valued for their personal meaning that families of the deceased recipients recognized the importance of allowing the costly metal to be removed from circulation.

Despite the paucity of surviving gold and silver in the Persepolis Treasury itself, the material that has been retrieved remains our most comprehensively informative excavated corpus of artifacts documenting the imperial Achaemenid contextual experience. One of several remarkable sculptural finds is a Greek marble statue of the seated "Penelope" type, dating to the mid fifth century, a rare example of an original Greek freestanding sculpture of the period. The image was treated roughly in the sack of Persepolis, for the right hand was found in a different room from the torso and the head never recovered at all.

A hoard of approximately six hundred vessels of prized stones, including alabaster and lapis lazuli, was found brutally shattered, perhaps because it had been decorated with gold. Several examples are inscribed with the names of pre-Achaemenid kings of Egypt and the Near East—including Assurbanipal of Assyria. Another fifty-three bear the trilingual cuneiform titulary of Xerxes as well as a version in Egyptian hieroglyphs. These vessels are related to stoneware inscribed with the names of Darius I, Xerxes, and Artaxerxes I discovered at various sites throughout the empire.

Fragments of molded and cut-glass vessels of clear fabric offer precious testimony of a luxury item attributed to the Persian court by Greek writers. Here again, shapes and decoration relate to examples in metal such as the lobed *phiale* for which several provenanced parallels in silver exist from Anatolia.

A corpus of green stone ritual vessels with ink notations in Aramaic includes mortars and pestles presumably for the grinding of the sacred *haoma* drug well attested in Zoroastrian ritual from the Sasanian period to the present. These artifacts raise important questions about the nature of religious practices at the Achaemenid

Fig. 11. Details of metal objects from a relief adorning the Apadana, or audience hall, at Persepolis. ERNST HERZFELD, *IRAN IN THE ANCIENT NEAR EAST* (1941)

Persian court and their relation to later orthodox Zoroastrianism.

SEALS AND IMPRESSIONS

During Achaemenid times the cylinder seal enjoyed renewed importance. Simultaneously, developments continued in the stamp seal and signet ring. Seals were made of coveted stones such as lapis lazuli, chalcedony, and agate, as well as more ordinary stones, clay, and glass. Rings of gold, silver, bronze, and iron bear a pointed or rounded elliptical surface for intaglio design. (See "Cylinder Seals and Scarabs in the Ancient Near East" in Part 7, Vol. III.)

Achaemenid-period seals based on near eastern artistic legacies display a great range of subject matter, including many types of ritual scenes and scenes of courtly life, erotic activity, hunting, and warfare, as well as human and animal figure studies and abstract devices. The single most frequent representational image in these seals is, however, some form of the age-old near eastern encounter scene between a heroic figure and one or more creatures (usually but not always animals or fantastic animal creatures). This image clearly enjoys a renaissance at all social levels and among women as well as men, undoubtedly inspired initially by fashions and ideas emerging from the royal circle. The pivotal renaissance occurred during the reign of Darius I. Evidence from a small corpus of dated early Achaemenid documents from Babylon shows the continuity of a typical Neo-Babylonian worship scene into this period—when, increasingly, the decorative repertoire of seals ratifying these documents adopts the hero motif. The official Achaemenid interest in this imagery may reflect a desire to evoke the memory of the Neo-Assyrian royal seal type that (in stamp form) portrayed the Assyrian king stabbing a rampant lion. Achaemenid patronage encouraged an amazing development of the hero theme—embroidering it with innumerable variations of style and iconography.

One important category of Achaemenid seals is the "court style" group, so designated because of a general similarity to the Persepolis sculptures (particularly in the use of the Achaemenid pleated and sleeved court robe and the dentate royal crown). A long-known cylinder seal in the British Museum, said to have come from Egyptian Thebes, is traditionally cited as the classic example of this style. (See cylinder seal of Darius I, Fig. 6 in "The History of Elam and Achaemenid Persia: An Overview" in Part 5, Vol. II.) It bears a trilingual cuneiform inscription of Darius (probably, though not explicitly stated, Darius I). Thus its date of manufacture can at least be confidently placed within the empire and its significance as a seal relating in some way to court authority can also be documented. Other surviving seals (mostly without secure provenance) have been loosely grouped with this seal.

Recent study of the many seal impressions preserved on the tablets excavated at Persepolis now makes accessible a corpus of closely dated court-style evidence from the imperial center. This material greatly enhances understanding of the origins of the court style and its relation to other styles in glyptic production fashionable in the heartland region from the late sixth century to the middle of the fifth century. Fortification Seal 7, bearing the trilingual cuneiform inscription of Darius, exemplifies the Persepolitan court style. Since it is first documented on a tablet of 503, its date of manufacture is fixed firmly within the last quarter of the sixth century. Although the ancient impressions preserve the seal imperfectly, a set of discernible characteristics offer a standard for the seals created in this idiom documented at Persepolis: a compact but balanced and elegant composition in which nega-

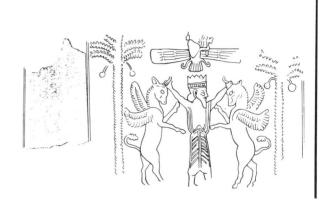

Fig. 12. Royal name seal of Darius I from Persepolis fortification tablets, Persepolis, which were found in the 1930s. COURTESY OF MARGARET COOL ROOT

tive spaces achieve a visual integrity that bonds the interactive forms of the design itself; powerful, graceful contours and smooth surfaces of the animals; a columnar human form exaggerated by the pleated robe and high crown; attention to minute details, for instance in the rendering of the hero's costume, the animals' wings, and the palm trees (fig. 12).

Twelve seals bearing royal name inscriptions of Darius I or Xerxes are now known from impressions on the Persepolis tablets. All of these seals are carved in the court style, as are numerous other seals used on the tablets by high-ranking officials there. There was no attempt to impose this style at the court universally, however. A seal owned by Parnaka, a member of the royal family and the chief administrator at Persepolis,

Fig. 13. Second seal of Parnaka from Persepolis fortification tablets. KELSEY MUSEUM OF ARCHAEOLOGY, UNIVERSITY OF MICHIGAN, ANN ARBOR

demonstrates that a variety of styles was current there. First applied on a tablet dated to 500, it is mentioned in this document as Parnaka's new seal. It is a brilliant Assyrianizing hero cylinder incorporating the official's name in Aramaic within a large frame (fig. 13).

Many heirloom seals were also used on the Persepolis tablets. Fortification Seal 93 displays an equestrian figure spearing one enemy while two slain foes lie beneath his charging steed. An Elamite inscription giving the name Cyrus of Anshan, son of Teispes, alludes to the grandfather of Cyrus the Great, a Persian vassal of the Assyrian Empire operating in formerly Elamite territory during the late seventh century (see fig. 14). The composition as well as the inscription link Seal 93 to a small number of late Neo-Elamite cylinders, but this seal is a masterpiece characterized by fine-tuned facial details, swelling volumes, and vigorously displayed dramatic action set in open space.

The majority of Persian period seals used on the fortification tablets are neither so restricted in forms and iconography as the court style nor so consciously archaizing as the Parnaka seal. On the corpus of slightly later tablets and labels from the Treasury, there is an increasing use of seals in hybrid Greek-Persian styles and in purely Greek style.

COINAGE

Achaemenid imperial coinage in gold and silver was developed in the reign of Darius I. Four types are known, all without inscription: one with the king, half-length, holding arrows, and three versions of the king full-length, in a kneeling or running pose, shooting a bow, holding a bow and spear, or holding a bow and arrows. Based on distribution patterns, the coinage seems to have circulated mainly in the western empire, despite the classical sources recording quantities of coinage found at Persepolis by Alexander. Although not a single Achaemenid coin was discovered in the excavations of Persepolis, a recently studied fortification tablet seal impression reveals it to have been made with an imperial coin of the bow-shooting type. This proves that the user (who was heading from the east toward Susa via Persepolis) had a royal archer coin at his disposal there in 500. (See "Methods of Exchange and Coinage in Ancient Western Asia" in Part 6, Vol. III.)

The iconography of the official coinage is purposefully restrictive. The emblematic presentation of the king-as-archer or spear-thrower on the coins departs radically from the ideal of ecumenical harmony which pervades the Achaemenid sculptural program and reinforces the widely held notion that Achaemenid imperial coinage was minted specifically for the purpose of paying soldiers.

Achaemenid coinage offers the earliest known use of a royal figure as coin emblem. Distinct from the imperial issue, coins minted in the western satrapies were decorated with a wider range of devices. One side of the coin often uses motifs invoking the Achaemenid dynasty through similarity to the imperial issue or to court-seal em-

Fig. 14. Royal name seal of Cyrus of Anshan from Persepolis fortification tablets, Persepolis. KELSEY MUSEUM OF ARCHAEOLOGY, UNIVERSITY OF MICHIGAN, ANN ARBOR

blems: royal archers, similar-looking royal figures in chariot processions, and hunt and hero scenes. The other side of several coin types from satrapies in Asia Minor, beginning in the fifth century, displays facial portraits of the satrap himself. The authority of the Achaemenid kings seems not to have been threatened by this. Rather, it appears that the satraps enjoyed great freedom to develop coinages focusing on their personal attributes.

These coin issues relate to the well-attested Achaemenid ethos of acknowledging close supporters with honorific representations. The network of reciprocal loyalties, the courtly affluence, and the relative regional autonomy characteristic of the Achaemenid Empire created a sociopolitical environment that fostered the emergence of expansive patron mandates. In the west (where we know them best) these regional patrons pushed Greek artists toward important new directions that were to have a profound effect on the history of Hellenistic and Roman imperial arts. Although the satrapal coin portraits are traditionally treated as Greek art because they display contemporaneous Greek style, they are conceptually, ideologically, and historically part of the story of the Achaemenid Empire. Their ambiguous status is paradigmatic of the difficulties and rewards awaiting the student of Achaemenid art.

BIBLIOGRAPHY

Achaemenid Art—General

PIERRE AMIET, "Glyptique élamite: À propos de documents nouveaux," and "La Glyptique de la fin de l'Élam," *Arts asiatiques* 26, 28 (1973), gives seminal discussions of the subtleties of interface in craft tradition between Elamite and Achaemenid times; JOHN BOARDMAN, *Greek Gems and Finger Rings: Early Bronze Age to Late Classical* (1970), see chapter 6, "Greeks and Persians," which remains a richly informative survey of "Graeco-Persian" (Greek-Persian hybrid) style in glyptic; RAYMOND DESCAT, ed., *L'or perse et l'histoire grecque, Revue des études anciennes* 91 (1989), has articles on coinage in the Achaemenid Empire (both imperial and satrapal issues) from multiple perspectives; MARK B. GARRISON, "Seals and the Elite at Persepolis: Some Observations on Early Achaeme-

nid Persian Art," *Ars Orientalis* 21 (1992), interprets numerous previously unpublished Persepolis seal impressions as artistic and administrative documents and provides extensive bibliography; and EDITH PORADA, *The Art of Ancient Iran: Pre-Islamic Cultures* (1965), is a valuable survey presenting Achaemenid art on an historical continuum with earlier and later Iranian traditions.

MICHAEL ROAF, "Sculptors and Designers at Persepolis," in *Investigating Artistic Environments in the Ancient Near East,* edited by ANN C. GUNTER (1990), summarizes the author's work on masons' marks and procedures of stone carving at Persepolis, with bibliography; MARGARET COOL ROOT, *The King and Kingship in Achaemenid Art: Essays on the Creation of an Iconography of Empire* (1979) offers detailed analysis of the royal ideology of Achaemenid art, with bibliography and documentation of official monuments empire-wide, and "Circles of Artistic Programming: Strategies for Studying Creative Process at Persepolis," in *Investigating Artistic Environments in the Ancient Near East,* revises theories on artist-patron relationships at the Achaemenid court based on new information from the Persepolis Fortification Tablets; and MARGARET COOL ROOT and MARK B. GARRISON, *Catalogue of the Seal Impressions on the Persepolis Fortification Tablets* (forthcoming in three fascicles).

HELEEN SANCISI-WEERDENBURG ET AL., eds., *Achaemenid History,* vols. 1–8 (1987–1994), is indispensable for the many articles on Achaemenid art and archaeology reflecting new perspectives in the field and brought together around specific themes such as "Centre and Periphery" (vol. 4); "Asia Minor and Egypt: Old Cultures in a New Empire" (vol. 6); "Through Travellers' Eyes" (vol. 7); "Continuity and Change" (vol. 8); and DENISE SCHMANDT-BESSERAT, ed., *Ancient Persia: The Art of an Empire* (1980), includes articles on the portable arts (problems of retrieval and documentation, Achaemenid glass, jewelry, and representations of women). Particularly important is OSCAR WHITE MUSCARELLA's "Excavated and Unexcavated Achaemenian Art."

Achaemenid Art—Impact in the Wider Sphere

MARGARET COOL ROOT, "The Parthenon Frieze and the Apadana Reliefs at Persepolis: Reassessing a Programmatic Relationship," *American Journal of Archaeology* 89 (1985), presents a case for the Greek emulation of the Achaemenid imperial program in monumental sculpture; and MARGARET C. MILLER, "The Parasol: An Oriental Status-Symbol in Late Archaic and Classical Athens," *Journal of Hellenic Studies* 112 (1992), is a case study in elite classical-period Athenian adoption of Persian court attributes. The author's Ph.D. dissertation on this theme (*Perserie: The Arts of the East in Fifth-Century Athens*, Harvard University, 1985) is forthcoming as an expanded monograph.

Selected Achaemenid Texts

GEORGE G. CAMERON, *Persepolis Treasury Tablets* (1948); G. R. DRIVER, *Aramaic Documents of the Fifth Century BC* (abridged and rev. ed., 1957), includes the letter of Prince Arsham to his sculptor; RICHARD T. HALLOCK, *Persepolis Fortification Tablets*(1969); and ROLAND G. KENT, *Old Persian: Grammar, Tests, Lexicon* (1950).

Heartland Capitals

PERSEPOLIS

ERICH SCHMIDT, *Persepolis*, vol. 1, *Structures, Reliefs, Inscriptions* (1953), vol. 2, *Contents of the Treasury and Other Discoveries* (1957), vol. 3, *The Royal Tombs and Other Monuments* (1970), publishes the Chicago expeditions of the 1930s; ALI SAMI, *Persepolis*, translated by R. N. SHARP (2nd ed. 1955), recounts finds from the Iranian excavations of the 1940s and early 1950s; ANN BRITT TILIA, *Studies and Restorations at Persepolis and Other Sites of Fārs*, Istituto Italiano per il Medio ed Estremo Oriente, *Reports and Memoirs* 16, 18 (1972, 1978), provides accounts of major archaeological discoveries plus detailed studies of technical aspects of architecture and reliefs; and W. M. SUMNER, "Achaemenid Settlement in the Persepolis Plain," *American Journal of Archaeology* 90 (1986), interprets settlement geography in the region through integration of archaeological and historical material (including the Persepolis tablets).

PASARGADAE

CARL NYLANDER, *Ionians in Pasargadae: Studies in Old Persian Architecture* (1970), offers aesthetic and technical analyses of Pasargadae structures, characterizing and assessing the historical significance of the various integrated traditions; and DAVID STRONACH, *Pasargadae* (1978), thoroughly documents and interprets the excavations of 1961–1963 and reviews the history of earlier explorations.

SUSA

RÉMY BOUCHARLAT, "Suse et la Susiane à l'époque achéménide: Données archéologiques," in *Achaemenid History*, vol. 4, *Centre and Periphery*, edited by HELEEN SANCISI-WEERDENBURG and AMÉLIE KUHRT (1990), gives a comprehensive overview of the archaeology of the Persian-period site, with an excellent bibliography. See also M. KERVRAN ET AL., "Une Statue de Darius découverte à Suse," *Journal Asiatique* 260 (1972); DAVID STRONACH ET AL., articles on the Susa statue of Darius I, in *Cahiers de la Délégation Archéologique Française en Iran* 4 (1974); and PRUDENCE O. HARPER, JOAN ARUZ, and FRANÇOISE TALLON, eds., *The Royal City of Susa: Ancient Near Eastern Treasures in the Louvre* (1992).

Peripheral Sites

P. R. S. MOOREY, *Cemeteries of the First Millennium BC at Deve Hüyük*, British Archaeological Reports International Series 87 (1980), provides an important case study in documentation and interpretive reassessment of Persian-period material from a site in Syria; and EPHRAIM STERN, "The Material Culture of the Land of the Bible in the Persian Period, 538–332 BC," *Bulletin of the American Schools of Oriental Research* 202 (1982), gives a survey of evidence of Achaemenid presence in this region.

SEE ALSO **Artisans and Artists of Ancient Western Asia** (Part 4, Vol. I); **Darius I and the Persian Empire** (Part 5, Vol. II); and **Archaeology and Artifacts in Iron Age Central Asia** (Part 5, Vol. II).

Anatolian Architectural Decorations, Statuary, and Stelae

KAY KOHLMEYER

FROM THE THIRD to the early first millennium BCE, sculptural production in Anatolia included primarily stelae, rock reliefs, carved architectural ornament in low relief, and a few large pieces of sculpture in the round, as well as numerous figurines in terra-cotta, stone, and metal. Such figurines are considered here only when large-scale sculpture is not attested for a particular period and when their realization distinguishes them from mundane crafts—that is, when they permit us to draw inferences concerning the development of artistic achievement.

ROOTS OF ANATOLIAN SCULPTURE

The beginnings of Anatolian sculpture may be summarized briefly: in 1944 the structuralist Guido Freiherr von Kaschnitz-Weinberg identified two main roots of ancient statuary form, first the menhir (megalith), which was a towering monument with a pronounced gravitational line (the "phallic" or "male" principle). Second, he contrasted it with an irregularly bounded, "hollow" conception of space exemplified by early corpulent female statuettes, which were subject to no system of order (the "female" principle).

This approach is still worth reflecting upon today, apart from the sex-specific designations.

The menhir, basically an unhewn block of stone, can, in principle—particularly when employed as a sculptural surface—assume one of two realizations of volume, that of a pillar or that of a column. The placing of an image on an upright block of stone is found in Anatolia already in the early stages of sedentarization and food production, as shown by recent finds from Nevali Çori (pronounced Nevali Chori), an Aceramic Neolithic settlement on a tributary of the Euphrates River. Within a cultic precinct of the late eighth and early seventh millennia, there originally stood limestone stelae, rectangular in section, one of which once had a height of 2.5 meters (8.25 feet). On its broad surfaces are depicted two arms in bas-relief, which meet in hands on the narrow side. On the fragment of the upper portion of a stela, which was subsequently reused, a life-sized head protrudes half in the round.

Small works, made completely in the round, were found at the same site. They exemplify the second conception of space. Similar works are attested for this period at Çayönü (pronounced Chayonu). These figurines of animals and humans, which cannot stand upright, have for the most part been reduced to a basic form. With bulging limbs, buttocks, breasts, and thighs, they stand in the Late Paleolithic tradition.

Similarly voluptuous but more naturalistically executed are numerous recumbent, seated, or squatting figurines of the Ceramic Neolithic period from Çatal Hüyük (pronounced Chatal Huyuk), some fifty kilometers (thirty miles) southeast of Konya (fig. 1). They have successors into the Chalcolithic Tell Halaf period. The broad spectrum includes sharply reduced figurines in which the menhir form may be at work. The gravitational lines of the body are emphasized, although the capacity to stand upright is not achieved. In contrast to Mesopotamia, it is not possible to determine precisely at what point the two principles genuinely merged so that the development of real statues was achieved.

It is worth noting that monumental sculpture conceived in three dimensions was already fashioned at Nevali Çori. A larger than life-sized limestone head was shaped as a slender oval, and a strand of hair in the form of a snake and ears like knobs were applied in relief (fig. 2).

Sculptural ornamentation of walls makes its first appearance in Neolithic Çatal Hüyük. The shrines of the settlement were adorned with gypsum reliefs representing at first animal heads—mostly of bulls—and later also complete animal forms and human figures, apparently exclusively female.

Fig. 2. Limestone head from Nevali Çori, Turkey, Aceramic Neolithic Age. COURTESY OF HARALD HAUPTMANN

EARLY BRONZE AGE

Sculptural production continued into the Early Bronze Age. From the early third millennium comes the upper portion of a limestone stela, 79 centimeters (31.6 inches) in height, in the form of a pillar with a stylized face. Only the heart-shaped outline, nose, and hair are represented. One eye is indicated by a double line; the other eye cannot be made out. A diagonal line on the

Fig. 1. Female statuette from Çatal Hüyük. MUSEUM OF ANATOLIAN CIVILIZATIONS, ANKARA

right cannot be interpreted with certainty. Perhaps it is a scepter. The piece was found in secondary reuse at Troy, Level I. A fragment of an offering table with basin-like hollows was reused nearby and may originally have been placed near the stela.

In its *pars pro toto* depiction of limbs, the stela stands in the tradition of the stelae from Nevalı Çori, although here the face is represented far more schematically. Faces are also stylized in the same manner on pottery, as on the "face pots" of Level II at Troy. This restriction to a few body parts in ceramic production persists until the beginning of the second millennium. On a double vase from Kanesh (modern Kültepe), gaping, thick-lipped mouths, ears, noses, eyes, and arms stand for the complete form.

The "twin shrines" of Beycesultan in western Anatolia show that aniconic stelae continued to be used in the Early Bronze Age. Corresponding to this is material from the Middle Bronze Age sanctuary of *kārum* Kanesh (Level Ib) and Middle Bronze Age Beycesultan. Here in Level V were found three large stone stelae, together with the base of an offering table. We will return to this cultic tradition in connection with Hittite rock reliefs.

We must look to neighboring northern Syria in order to interpret the bas-reliefs of southeastern Anatolia in the third and early second millennia. In general, the strong connections in architecture, ceramics, and probably also in the structures of social organization and religion that may be seen in the Early and Middle Bronze ages between southern—and to a certain extent central—Anatolia and northern Syria have, with the exception of the Assyrian trading colonies, not yet been sufficiently worked out. In contrast, instances of influence of the Mesopotamian Late Uruk culture on southeastern Anatolia during the final quarter of the fourth millennium are clearer because they may be defined as intrusive.

At the end of the last century two sculptured basalt stelae, today in the Louvre Museum, were discovered in Rumkale, north of Birecik (pronounced Birejik) on the west bank of the Euphrates. One depicts a naked man standing with bent knees, an ear of grain over his shoulder, holding an unidentified object. On the other is represented a man wearing a long, belted garment with a neckline and vertical central stripes, perhaps a border. The garment apparently ends in two points, although the frontal depiction is perhaps misleading and only the trailing portion of the textile may be intended, comparable to the wraparound garments of the Hittite Empire period. In the belt is a dagger, on the shoulder a palm frond. One hand grasps the short handle of a rectangular object with vertical segmentation, possibly a fly wisk. Both men have trimmed beards on chin and cheeks, effectively setting off the chin. A skullcap, or more likely a hairdo, rises above the forehead. The frontal representation of the body, including the thighs, is notable.

A stone shaft with relief from Onbir Lisan should be considered together with these two stelae. It shows a similar figure, this time seated. Dating of the stelae has fluctuated between the Protoliterate period, particularly in view of the similarity to bronze statuettes from Judaida (Amuq G to early H), and the end of the third millennium. Recently they have been characterized as later works emulating products of the ancient Near East.

The dating problem arises from the "primitiveness" of the representations, which far from the centers of ancient near eastern sculptural achievement allows us only to surmise the underlying models. Possible models should not be sought at too great a distance, and in any case in a related artistic genre, namely in representations in relief. Here, however, the greatest correspondences are with the carved basins of the early second millennium from Ebla (Tell Mardikh), particularly with the warriors on the narrow side of the basalt basin from sector B.

From the Edessa (Urfa) region come two very similar reliefs that have recently been connected by Ursula Seidl with the Mesopotamian Early Dynastic period. For these, too, a date in the post–ancient near eastern epoch, namely in the second or first century BCE, has been suggested.

In each case a broad rectangular border encloses the image, which depicts two seated men on either side of a cone, which they wrap around with bands. From the upper portion of the cone protrude two spade-shaped objects. The better-preserved relief reveals further details: the men wear only skirts with a narrow border and a thick roll at the waist, as well as a high *polos* (cylindrical headdress) made up of four rings. Their concave-seated stools are striated vertically and are provided with a central niche. Seidl cites parallels to Early Dynastic representations in the objects depicted and in the fashioning of the limbs; she also points to local peculiarities, such as the handle-shaped ears. The stool, upper body, and head are depicted frontally, but the lower body is in profile. The frontal view of the head is also a local peculiarity (fig. 3).

Seidl explains the cone as a stone monument such as was discovered not too far away in the Early Dynastic Ninni-zazza Temple at Mari and interpreted by the excavator, André Parrot, as belonging functionally to the *maṣṣebôt* (cultic pillars). Thus, there appears the second basic form to develop from the upright position of the menhir: not the basically rectangular structural mass of the stela or cult pillar but rather a cylindrical or conical form.

Spade-shaped objects are known from the temple cult of Early Dynastic Asshur (modern Qalat Sharqat). It is uncertain whether the wrapping of the cone, analogous to Early Dynastic seal representations, reflects a harvest ceremony.

Figurines of the Anatolian Early Bronze Age continue the development mentioned earlier. More naturalistically formed, anthropomorphic representations restrict their fullness, become more schematic, and accentuate their gravitational line. Particularly in western and central

Fig. 3. Relief from Vilayet Urfa depicting two seated men wrapping a cone with bands, Early Bronze Age. KUTLU EMRE ET AL., EDS., *ANATOLIA AND THE ANCIENT NEAR EAST: STUDIES IN HONOR OF TAHSIN ÖZGÜÇ* (1989)

Fig. 4. Alabaster idol from Kültepe, Early Bronze Age. ARNOLDO MONDADOR, ED., *ANATOLIA, IMMAGINI DI CIVILTÀ: TESSORI DALLA TURCHIA* (1987)

Anatolia there are also found flat figurines, round or violin-shaped, whose heads are modeled in the round, and which may be provided with genitalia. They are often referred to as "idols" because of their rather unrepresentational form.

One example of this style is a twenty-centimeter- (eight-inch-) high alabaster figurine from later Early Bronze Age Kültepe (ancient Kanesh) (fig. 4). On the round body with long neck and crudely modeled head is set another similar double grouping. The details have been added by carving and boring. Figurines of this type with two or three heads and necks are also known. A multiplicity of heads is also attested by terra-cottas from northern Syria; these are probably representations of divine families.

Artistically, the best figurines of the latter middle and late Early Bronze Age come from northeastern Anatolia, from the princely graves of Alaca Hüyük (pronounced Alaja Huyuk), Horoztepe, and Hasanoğlan. Although their origins have recently been questioned, these products of a highly developed metal craft should be attributed to the Hattic population. That is, they were created before the arrival of the Hittites. On a spiked base, which served for attachment to a support of some perishable material, stands a 52-centimeter (20.8-inch) high cast-bronze stag in the round (fig. 5). Geometric ornamentation in the form of circles and zigzag bands is inlaid in silver; the head, ears, and antlers are covered with silver foil. The abstract forms of the body contrast with naturalistic details, such as the ears and the base of the antlers. Other animals, such as the bronze stag of similar size with inlaid strips of electrum, anticipate in their abstraction sculptures of Picasso. The purpose of these figurines is unknown, but whether they crowned baldachins or chariots or served as crests for cultic standards, the featured animals (stag or bull) as well as the accessory animals (felines and red deer) were taken over into Hittite religion. They became theriomorphic (animal-like) manifestations of deities or were their associated beasts.

The breadth of variation of anthropomorphic statuettes is demonstrated by three examples from Alaca Hüyük, Hasanoğlan, and Horoztepe. The first two are made of silver with gold-foil appliqué, the third is made of bronze. Although the degree of abstraction of the bodies varies greatly, all three can stand upright. The most stable is the statuette of mother and child from Horoztepe, which is also the latest. The rendering of details varies from the use of simple geometric figures like circles for eyes and ears and

Fig. 5. Cast-bronze stag from Alaca Hüyük, Early Bronze Age. EKREM AKURGAL, DIE KUNST DER HETHITER (1961)

cones for breasts on the figure from Alaca Hüyük, to the articulated fingers of the other two female statuettes. The lack of proportion of the individual body parts, which show no real connection to one another, is striking, even in the case of the more naturalistic sculptures. An advance toward proportionality was apparently made in northern Anatolia only in the following period, as a result of the influence of Mesopotamian culture transmitted through northern Syria.

An interesting statuette of a woman may come from Horoztepe; it is now in Berlin. Seated on a four-legged stool with curved seat, she holds a bowl in her right hand. In texts describing Hittite divine images, it is almost always goddesses who assume this posture. Perhaps this figurine is an early forerunner of these later standardized depictions.

ASSYRIAN COLONIES: HITTITE OLD AND MIDDLE KINGDOMS

Through the irony of discovery, practically no large sculpture has been preserved from the period in which the basis of Hittite sculptural art was established. This was the time of intensive cultural contact with northern Syria and northern Mesopotamia brought about by the presence of Assyrian trading colonies in Anatolia. It is known as the *"kārum* period" (see "Kanesh" in Part 5, Vol. II). Influences that at first glance appear to be Egyptian, but which are in reality Syro-Palestinian, also contributed to Anatolian urban culture, or, to be more precise, to the artistic taste of court society. The number of genuine Egyptian imports was probably small and their influence on Anatolia was not considerable. Among these imports was a Twelfth Dynasty granite statuette from Kırıkkale, about sixty kilometers (thirty-six miles) east of Ankara.

Syro-Palestine and Mesopotamia exerted their influence mainly through minor arts: seals and carving. Of the latter, only a small part of the production in ivory has survived. Carving in other, more perishable, materials has been lost. Since both types of objects are discussed elsewhere (see the chapter "Jewelry and Personal Arts in Anatolia" in Part 7, Vol. III) it is not necessary to concern ourselves with them now, nor with small-scale anthropomorphic sculpture, inconceivable without forerunners in northern Syria and upper Mesopotamia.

Gaps in the finds prevent us from following the thread of Early Bronze Age animal figurines as exemplified by the pieces from the Alaca Hüyük burials. Zoomorphic terra-cottas, particularly those of oxen, bulls, and lions, show a development toward greater fidelity to the form of the bodies and away from abstraction. One of numerous examples from *karum* Kanesh is an approximately twenty-centimeters- (eight-inch-) high libation vessel in the shape of a standing lion with opened jaws and extended tongue. From the later *karum*-period Büyükkale of Khattusha (Boğazköy) come two cult ("citadel") vessels of about thirty centimeters (twelve inches) in height. They may represent altars in the shape of a pillar, topped by what appears to be an eagle. Four-footed animals crouch on top, and ram and bull heads protrude from the front; they are similar to the animal heads on the walls of the "shrines" of Neolithic Çatal Hüyük. They are also reminiscent of the aniconic pillar on a eighteenth-century stamp-seal impression from Acemhüyük, out of which project the foreparts of bulls. A worshiper stands in front and a goddess sits behind.

Hopefully our picture of the large-scale sculpture of this period will become clearer with the progress of excavation. At present the sole indication of the existence of this genre is the fragment of a basalt lion from a workshop in a house of *karum* Kanesh Ib, secondarily reused as the base of a pithos (large storage vessel) and therefore probably older than its context. This sculpture may have been placed in a gate, which puts it in the Mesopotamian tradition.

Finds from the Old Hittite period are decidedly scarce. The ability to model large terra-cottas in animal form reached a high level. Two figurines of about ninety centimeters (thirty-six inches) in height in the form of harnessed bulls from the Büyükkale of Khattusha are impressive examples of the mastery of a polished firing technique. Hollow and with a funnel-shaped spout on their backs, these figures are actually animal-shaped vessels. They were probably cultic utensils employed in connection with the storm-god.

Probably to be dated to the Old Hittite period (although most scholars regard it as Middle Hittite) is a poorly preserved, carved block of dark green gabbro, made up of four fragments. It is just over seventy centimeters (twenty-eight inches) high. The slanting contours of the representation are crudely executed. The surface is highly polished, and the shallow background has been left rough. The piece is obviously unfinished, but given the contemporaneous trend toward polychromy, the background may have been covered with a layer of colored plaster and the details of the raised figures may have been highlighted with color. A comparable relief fragment of gray limestone, which was found reused on Büyükkale as the cover for an early Empire-period sewer, shows traces of red and creamy-white paint. Judging from their form and size, the two blocks may have come from the same building.

The first block has two friezes. The one above features a chariot before which a fallen figure lies under the hooves of draught animals. This motif anticipates the scenes of triumph on the reliefs of Luwian minor kings of the first millennium. The lower frieze depicts a combat.

A decided liveliness characterizes these depictions, which do not shy away from a partial overlapping of the participants. The warrior of the lower scene bows slightly forward, so that his active posture is set diagonally to the field. Equally strong movement and a similar composition are found on the "Tyszkiewicz Seal," named after a former (modern) owner, and generally dated to the seventeenth century BCE. In fact, the relief gives the viewer a sense of a clumsy transposition of a seal image onto a scale that could not be mastered.

The evaluation of contemporary sculpture in the round is more complicated. Kurt Bittel, the greatest expert on Hittite art, hesitated between the Old Hittite period and the early Hittite Empire in the dating of a fragmentary half-sized female head of chlorite schist (fig. 6). The piece was reused as fill for the foundation of an Early Empire house in the northern Lower City of Boğazköy. It is dominated by a high, disk-shaped headdress characteristic of goddesses and the Great Queen under the empire. Several variants of this "cowl" are known, but it must be distinguished from the "Hathor kerchief" or "Hathor hairdo" with its pendant curls, which was of Egyptian inspiration.

Fig. 6. Female head made of chlorite schist, from Boğazköy. KURT BITTEL, *IIATTUSCIIA, IIAUPTSTADT DER HETHITER: GESCHICHTE UND KULTUR EINER ALTORIENTALISCHEN GROSSMACHT* (1983)

The voluminous cowl passes diagonally back across the eyebrows; therefore, the face has no forehead. Anatolian and northern Syrian Middle Bronze Age terra-cottas use a similar form. The triple-disk ornamentation of the ears also points to terra-cotta forerunners. An Old Hittite date for the head cannot be ruled out, but a final decision requires further evidence.

With the earlier dating of the carved block and the sculpture of the female head, we might ask what artistic creations may be assigned to the Middle Hittite period (mid fifteenth to early fourteenth centuries), but with our present state of knowledge, we cannot answer. All monuments discussed below can be dated with great probability to the Hittite Empire, the period beginning with Shuppiluliuma I.

HITTITE EMPIRE

The most extensive series of architectural sculpture comes from the Sphinx Gate of Alaca Hüyük, the monumental entrance to the inner city. Low reliefs decorate the socle (the base of the structure) of the outer and inner faces of the gate structure in front of the two portal sphinxes. These stand more than 2 meters (6.6 feet) high and have been formed simply as protomes (front parts of an animal body) on the gate piers. They are squarish and lack all internal proportionality (fig. 7). The very short legs contrast with the massively protruberant bodies. The headpiece, a cap that arches over the head with ribbons or locks ending in rosettes falling down at the sides, is an adaptation of the "Hathor kerchief" imported from Egypt via Syro-Palestine.

Traces of an impressive relief have been preserved on the interior face of the eastern gate pier. A double eagle—a symbol of power—grasps two hares in his talons. Above this figure one can just barely make out the lower rear portion of a long cloak, a foot, and traces of the curved staff that the Hittite Great King carried as a sign of office. It is reasonable to assume that the opposite pier face was once provided with a corresponding relief of the Great Queen. While the relevant area is now heavily damaged, Theodor Macridy-Bey, who in 1907 conducted the first extensive excavations at Alaca Hüyük, saw traces of a shoe and a garment, and John Garstang, who took part in these excavations, saw the head of an eagle below.

Only a portion of the excavated blocks of the gate structure remains in situ, and the full context of the scenes is therefore unknown. In addition, it is certain that some blocks have been lost. The underlying problem, however, is that the gate reveals at least two phases of construction involving an alteration in the conception of the relief program. This is most clearly demonstrated by the large unfinished sphinx on the side of the western gate pier facing the city wall, as well as by a number of other unfinished reliefs in the gate structure. It is possible that, as they were reused, blocks were placed differently than in the original conception.

The placement of scenes on the southern facade and the southwestern interior face is certain. They are all oriented toward the corner block, which depicts a bull on a pedestal; this is the theriomorphic form of the storm-god (fig. 8). To his left is an altar composed of a cylindrical slab on a conical base; an actual parallel to this altar is known from Emirgazi. King and queen stand in front in worship, followed by a scene break, after which a priest is depicted leading two files of sacrificial animals. Farther to the left are three more priests. King, queen, and priests wear different wraparound garments.

Fig. 7. Sphinx gate, Alaca Hüyük. COURTESY OF GREGORY MCMAHON

Also facing the right are the two smaller figures on the nearer half of the adjoining block. One depicts a man on a ladder, a second shows a man with raised arms. Beginning with the other half of the block, the orientation of the persons is to the left. They include a sword swallower and, on the next block, two men with an animal-shaped object and a lute. On this unfinished relief all persons wear a short, belted garment. Most also wear skullcaps featuring a hornlike curvature on the front, the purpose of which we do not understand. One participant in the religious ceremony has a long braid beginning at the forehead and pulled back over a shaved head. A similar coiffure is worn by Hittites in the Egyptian representations of the battle of Qadesh (Tell Nebi Mend, Syria), one scene of which is reproduced in "Pharaoh Ramesses II and His Times" in Part 5, Vol. II. At the end stands an unfinished bull with an attachment on his back.

The western interior face of the gate structure was decorated by a ritual scene that is difficult to interpret. Two pairs of men are depicted. On the right, one hands the other a staff with curved shaft; those on the left hold a simple staff. The opposite exterior face may be similarly reconstructed, although here priests and a seated goddess are depicted. Additional blocks with scenes of worship and cultic activity have been preserved; among these is a piece with six figures with heads shaved as described above; another shows two priests, the queen, and the king in the act of libation; and a third depicts the king before a seated god who is identified by the hieroglyph of the storm-god.

In contrast to these reliefs of extremely static composition are hunting scenes of almost dynamic tension. Hunters using bows and arrows pursue a boar and a stag, and others with spears and dogs stalk felines. There is also a depiction of a charging bull. Also preserved is a corner block with a lion springing upon a calf. The heads of both animals are rendered almost in the round. Beneath the lion's body is a winged sun-disk that must originally have crowned an inscription executed on a lower block, now lost. Another lion, probably once paired with the first, has a man beneath him.

It is difficult to date these reliefs. Kurt Bittel has pointed out that since Boğazköy is so near, we would expect a greater similarity with the sculptural works found here if they were contemporaneous; he concluded that the representations of Alaca Hüyük were created before the thirteenth century. This reasoning is valid, since variation in quality cannot be adduced to explain the difference between the reliefs of Boğazköy and those of Alaca Hüyük, and the latter indeed are in some ways reminiscent of Old Hittite work.

The resemblances are to be seen less in the correspondence of the tense movement of the hunting scenes to that of the battle relief from Boğazköy, which may be largely attributed to content. What corresponds most is the use of two friezes, which recalls the division into bands on Old Hittite relief vases as well as the battle relief. Beyond this, the depiction of the upper bodies of the priests and the offering bearers in frontal view corresponds to the artistic principles of the Old Hittite Kingdom. The stylization of animals and plants—for example, that of the grazing stag and the fallen calf—also points to an early date, since the influence of the minor arts of northern Syria, primarily of carved-furniture inlay, may still be felt. On the other hand, if the winged sun-disk crowned an inscription including the royal cartouche, this would indicate a date in the time of Arnuwanda I (late fifteenth century) or later, since it is not attested earlier in such a context. On the basis of the available evidence, Bittel's dating of the Alaca Hüyük

Fig. 8. Orthostat from Alaca Hüyük showing king and queen offering a gift to bull on a pedestal. EKREM AKURGAL, ED., *THE ART AND ARCHITECTURE OF TURKEY* (1980)

sculptures to the fourteenth century seems to be the most likely.

Through recent discoveries, a new starting point is given for the dating of the most famous architectural sculpture of the Hittite capital: the "Warrior God" of the King's Gate in the eastern circumvallation of the Upper City. The relief depicts a larger-than-life-sized male figure, naked but for a short kilt, a dagger in his wide belt, a pointed helmet with a bull's horn, and neck and cheek pieces. One hand is raised in greeting and the other holds an elaborately fashioned ceremonial ax.

The soft modeling, the precise shaping of the musculature (particularly that of the knees), and the detailed decoration of the kilt have given rise to speculation that the sculpture was not done by a Hittite, but by a foreign sculptor. It has also been remarked that in a letter to the Kassite king Kadashman-Enlil of Babylon, Khattushili III requests the dispatch of an artist. However, nothing in regard to the Warrior God is reminiscent of contemporary Kassite art. On the contrary, the layout of the figure displays all the principles of Hittite depiction of the human form. This is exemplified in the overlong legs and the slight elevation of the shoulder turned toward the viewer. This sculpture stands at the peak of the work of the Hittite Empire.

The new evidence for its dating is provided by a more than ninety-centimeter (thirty-six-inch) high block of limestone conglomerate found near a subsidiary structure—possibly a chapel—of Temple V in the Upper City. Its relief shows a spear-carrier walking toward the left; he wears a short skirt and a pointed hat with five pairs of horns. Above a hand raised in greeting is poised the cartouche of Great King Tudkhaliya; missing are the further titles, winged sun-disk, and hieroglyph for "hero" typical of the empire. One might presume that this is not Tudkhaliya IV but a Middle Hittite predecessor. However, titles are on occasion omitted in the empire, as on the rock relief of Khattushili III at Fıraktın (illustrated in "Khattushili III, King of the Hittites" in Part 5, Vol. II).

In any case, all misgivings have been dispelled by the discovery of an artificial "entrance to the underworld" on the Südburg ("Southern Fortress"). This chamberlike building was estab-

lished by Shuppiluliuma II as is proven by a long hieroglyphic inscription. This king is also depicted here as a warrior in a skirt and a pointed cap with three horns. In the writing of his name, both the winged sun-disk and the hero title are lacking. The relief of the king and that of the Warrior God in the gate agree in important details. In both instances the horned caps show that we are dealing with dead and divinized kings. On the front side of the artificial "entrance to the underworld" was placed another block, on which was carved a figure in the long wraparound garment of the king and the sun-god. He carries a curved staff in one hand and extends the other in greeting; the hieroglyph for "life" is carved above. As usual in the depictions of the sun-god, a broad-winged sun-disk hovers over his head.

When was the Tudkhaliya sculpture of Temple V executed? Tudkhaliya's own reign, as well as those of his successors, must be considered. The relief of Shuppiluliuma II must have been created during his own lifetime, since he was the final Hittite Great King before the fall of Khattusha. The question cannot be answered with certainty. If one compares the quality of the two works as royal depictions of equal rank, then one is not inclined to posit contemporary production.

Two name labels accompany the royal images in the rock sanctuary of Yazılıkaya: the "patron relief" of Chamber A and the representation of a ruler in the embrace of his protective deity Sharruma in Chamber B. In each case the elaborate "cartouche" indicates Tudkhaliya IV, Great King of the Hittite Empire.

The two Tudkhaliya reliefs of Yazılıkaya may be connected to the Warrior God of the King's Gate via the image from Temple V. The problem with the two Yazılıkaya reliefs is that the king wears a long garment that precludes a comparison of the modeling of the musculature of the legs. The protective deity wears a kilt, but he is badly damaged. However, the soft and vivid lines of the face of the "patron figure" indicate that the Warrior God of the King's Gate must be approximately contemporary. This is supported by the Tudkhaliya relief from Temple V, which displays the same characteristics in an excellent state of preservation. It is likely that under Tudkhaliya IV there was an active workshop of sculptors whose skills reached a level never before or afterward attained.

The other sculptures found in the defenses of the Upper City may also be attributed to this workshop. These include the Lion and Sphinx gates. The Sphinx Gate (Yerkapı) is a structure of central importance on the cultic way proceeding from the south in the direction of Nişantepe (Nishantepe) and the Südburg. Both sides of its outer passage were decorated with sphinx protomes. The inner passage had two examples executed almost completely in the round, of which the better preserved is now in Berlin, the other in Istanbul. The Berlin sphinx, 2.58 meters (8.5 feet) in height, came from the eastern side of the gate. (Above a horned cap it wears a head ornament consisting of three pairs of rosettes. The eyes were once inlaid. The body is incomparably better proportioned than those of the Alaca Hüyük sphinxes, although it still makes a heavy and massive impression.

Lions and sphinxes belong to the usual repertoire of Hittite architectural sculpture; they were also found in Temple III in the Upper City. Lion and bull protomes decorated water basins, the most important examples of which were among the finds from Temple I. To the furnishings of cultic buildings we must also assign two socle bases provided with slots on their upper surfaces. They are decorated with worshipers standing before altars with obviously aniconic double stelae.

The most impressive ensemble of Hittite sculpture is found in Yazılıkaya, about 2 kilometers (1.2 miles) northeast of Boğazköy. The limestone rock outcropping has two large Chambers (A and B), which were formed by geologic faults, as well as two subsidiary chambers. The main chambers are bounded by vertical rock faces. In the northwest a *temenos* (sacred precinct) wall was constructed around the rocks, and in the south there are adjacent architectural installations. Yazılıkaya thus constitutes a natural shrine, open to the sky.

In Chamber A, reliefs stretch along the western, northern, and eastern walls. The starting point for the representational scheme is the northern, central, face of the chamber, where the chief deities are depicted on a larger scale than those on the side walls. In the center is an almost life-sized storm-god Teshub and his spouse Khepat; they are identified by hieroglyphic labels. Both are supported by other figures: two mountain-gods and a feline, respectively. The storm-god, probably wearing a short kilt with sword to the side, shoulders a club. He wears an elaborate horned cap. Khepat is clothed in a long, pleated garment; from her *polos* with crenelations falls a long braid (fig. 9).

To the left of Teshub proceed forty-two deities on the western side of the chamber. All of them are male, with the exception of Ninatta and Kulitta, who are present as attendants of the male manifestation of Shaushga. With Khepat begins the column of at least twenty-one female deities. The exception here is Khepat's son Sharruma, who immediately follows her. Into this series may be inserted a relief found in nearby Yekbaz. The gaps were bridged with blocks, so that a complete reconstruction of the sequence of gods is not possible. The male deities face toward the right, the females toward the left. Tudkhaliya IV is depicted vis-à-vis the central panel. He stands upon mountains as befits his power.

The conception of this imagery and the ordering of the gods can be attributed with certainty to a particular time. As Emmanuel Laroche has pointed out, the order largely corresponds to that of Hurrian god-lists, which also differentiate by gender. This Hurrian conception is apparently violated only in the case of a single god, the Hittite sun-god of Heaven, who is inserted into the male procession.

Hurrian influence on Khatti occurred in two waves: in the Middle Hittite period, and after a time of conscious resistance, again only under Khattushili III, father of Tudkhaliya IV. Because their relatively certain proportions prove that the two reliefs in Chambers A and B, with hieroglyphic labels for Tudkhaliya IV, cannot be far separated in time from the other sculptures, a dating of the gods to the Middle Hittite period is excluded.

Could they already have been begun, however, under Khattushili III, as has recently been argued on the basis of art-historical considerations? The difficulty is that art-historical criteria, applicable in any case only to a limited extent in the study of ancient near eastern art, all too easily fail in connection with poorly preserved and often unfinished sculptures of varying material. For example, it has repeatedly been

Fig. 9. Portion of a rock carving from the open-air sanctuary at Yazılıkaya, circa 1260 BCE, showing the central scene. In the carving two processions of deities headed by the weather-god, Teshub, and the goddess Khebat astride a lion converge in the center of the chamber. The carving records the pantheon of gods and goddesses. KURT BITTEL ET AL., *DAS HETHITISCHE FELSHEILIGTUM YAZILIKAYA* (1975)

maintained that Hittite rock reliefs display a development toward greater relief—the earlier being flat, the later more rounded. However, the material can influence the depth of the relief; volcanic stones such as trachyte and andesite (the latter the material of the reliefs in Alaca Hüyük) require a different technique than limestone. Beyond this, the reliefs of Shuppiluliuma in the artificial "entrance to the underworld" are in low relief, and they belong to the end of the Hittite Empire.

Doubtless there are clear differences in the execution of the sculptures of Yazılıkaya, but these can be explained primarily by qualitative factors, comparable to the observations made for Neo-Assyrian reliefs, where the most important representations were the responsibility of the "masters," while the rest fell to the "journeymen." Despite this qualification, the assumption of a unified representational scheme for Chamber A and its dating rest basically on two pieces of data, which in the final analysis are not fully conclusive: the cult reform of Tudkhaliya as attested in written sources and the fact that only the name of this king is sculpted in the sanctuary. The position of his relief vis-à-vis the

chief gods, which tempts one to interpret it as a "donor representation," supports this line of argument.

The representations of Chamber A are usually understood as a "procession of deities"—a train of male divinities and a train of females—approaching one another. It is questionable whether such movement is intended, however. Bas-relief knows no other way of expressing standing than with the legs in a striding position. Thus, for example, are depicted the chief deities of Yazılıkaya, who certainly stand upon their bearing figures and do not stride above them. Behind this style lies an old and probably magical principle of ancient near eastern art, by which the human body must be represented intact with all limbs. Images in frontal view, which permit the impression of standing with simultaneous representation of both legs, are confined in low relief to a few traditional types such as the "naked goddess."

The positioning of the male deities toward the right and of the females toward the left constitutes only an "aid to the reader," similar to the practice by which signs of the hieroglyphic script face the beginning of a line. One must "read" two files of deities, beginning each time in the center of the chamber, in the middle of the frontal panel.

The group of twelve gods at the end of the male side prevents an interpretation of the relief program as a sequence of figures. Their depiction on tiptoes gives the impression of forceful striding. The group is tightly compressed by means of overlap, and the closest connection is achieved through the layering of insignificant limbs. Since the distortion of symmetrical parts of the body was avoided, the placement of the legs can only be explained by this principle of composition, intended to express an inner solidarity and unity of the group. The origin of the motif must be sought in Syria, where files of men in similar overlap are found in glyptic.

These reliefs did not function as cult images. Cult images were the object of daily attention: bathing, libations, feeding, and clothing. They are described in the "image description" texts as metal or wooden figures in the round. The temple was the site of their daily cult. In contrast, the reliefs of Yazılıkaya constitute formally nothing more than the consignment of rock face to deities; their function paralleled that of hieroglyphic inscriptions. This simply reflects the ancient conception that stones like stelae or rock faces could be the loci of divine presence. This may explain the rock benches in front of the reliefs. We learn from the texts that trails of cloth could be laid on the ground before the rocks, and oil or honey sprinkled on them in order to attract the deities. It is also possible that during certain rituals, cult images were set up in front of the reliefs.

These are the general arguments for an understanding of the sanctuary as a site for magical practice. Among the purificatory rituals there is one—the tenth tablet of the *itkalzi* ritual—in which incantations are addressed alternately to male and female deities, beginning with Teshub and Khepat. Alternatively, some excavators assign to Chamber A only the special function of a temple for the New Year Festival.

Between Chamber A and the passage to Chamber B is the small Chamber D, which is approximately triangular and enclosed by a wall. At its western entrance is the representation of two seated deities. Under the floor of the chamber were found the bones of a pig embryo that was covered by a bowl and surrounded by bronze pins. Pigs play a large role as substitute offerings in purificatory rituals. Covering over and nailing down could prevent the return to the upper world of animals rendered impure through ritual.

The entrance to Chamber B is flanked on either side by winged-lion composite monsters. On its western wall, Chamber B has a unified group of twelve gods that face a "sword god" (depicted as the hilt and beginning of the blade crowned by a god's head); as well as Tudkhaliya IV in the embrace of his protective deity Sharruma. Three deep niches have been hewn into the rock, one next to Tudkhaliya and two opposite him.

In the far northeast is the "cartouche" of Tudkhaliya IV. It may just as reasonably be connected to the small Chamber C immediately to the right as with the large stone block at the northern central face of Chamber B. It is likely that the block in Chamber B served as the base for the giant statue whose feet were carved on a basalt slab of similar size discovered at Yekbaz, and that the inscription referred to this image, which was constructed of several pieces. To judge from the feet, the piece from Yazılıkaya was of approximately twice human size and therefore almost matched the total height of the sword god.

The assumption of a colossal statue depicting Tudkhaliya lends weight to the old hypothesis that Chamber B was an installation of the type called É ^{NA4}*ḫekur* in Hittite. This term probably designated a rock sanctuary that may have been provided with buildings, and which as an institution controlled dependent localities providing for its upkeep. Such institutions played an important role in the cult of the dead. Shuppiluliuma II reports that he erected and "placated" an image of Tudkhaliya in the É^{NA4}*ḫekur*. The twelve gods, who can be understood as underworld deities, and the sword god, who probably represents Nergal, also point in this direction.

The decorative programs of the other Hittite rock reliefs may be divided into two groups. In the first group, deities are depicted at Gâvur Kalesi, Eflatun Pınar, and Akpınar. Gâvur Kalesi is a rock sanctuary; the latter sites are closely connected to springs, places of religious and magical character. Like the reliefs of deities at Yazılıkaya, this group exemplifies the conception that rocks and corresponding constructed stone monuments might be the residences of gods. In principle, therefore, they stand in the tradition of the *maṣṣebôt* cult of Anatolia, Syria, and Palestine.

The second group consists of mortals, who for the most part are depicted alone (Karabel A and B, Sirkeli, Hamide, and Taşçı [pronounced Taschi]), or before deities (Fıraktın, İmamkulu, and Hanyeri). Sometimes these reliefs are placed at cultic sites, but, more often, at places of geographic and strategic importance. This group belongs to the tradition of ancient near eastern rock reliefs depicting a ruler in a conspicuous location with propagandistic intent, as seen most clearly in the later Neo-Assyrian period.

The plateau-like rock outcropping of Gâvur Kalesı, about sixty kilometers (thirty-six miles) southwest of Ankara, was enclosed on three sides by cyclopean walls, thus integrating a large covered chamber to the north. On the south side and on an axis with this chamber, the image of a seated goddess was hewn from the rock. Seen in profile, she wears the headgear known as a "cowl," which at Eflatun Pınar is shown in frontal view. To her right, on a surface which has been only partly smoothed, are two male figures in kilts with swords at their sides and wearing horned caps with multiple articulations. The figure on the right has a beard. Since no labels are provided, we cannot identify the images. In the context of this chamber, one may see the seated female as a goddess of death, such as Lelwani or the sun-goddess of the earth, who would then be depicted without a winged sun-disk. The standing males might be the storm-god and his son, but the figure without a beard might also be a dead and deified king, who is being introduced to the seated goddess.

Although built of large blocks of stone, the spring sanctuary of Eflatun Pınar near Lake Beyşehir (Beyshehir) belongs to the category of rock sanctuaries, since the 7-by-4.2-meter (23.1-by-13.9-foot) southern facade serves only as a carrier of reliefs where a natural rock face is not available. Attempts to interpret the construction as the base for the stela of Fasıllar or for the sculpture in the round found nearby and known as Aslantaş (Aslantash, "Lion Rock") are mis-

guided because the composition of the facade will not accommodate additional divine images. According to religious traditions, nothing might be set above the crowning winged sun-disks, and if the images are placed on the rear surface of the structure in order to avoid this direct conflict, the overwhelming emphasis of the stela would remain, and from a distance it would dominate the sun-disks.

In the center of the facade are enthroned a male and a female figure, which are separated and flanked by pairs of composite monsters standing on top of one another and holding up two winged sun-disks. This scene is flanked by two lion-headed composite monsters who carry the large sun-disk covering the entire facade. In all probability the enthroned figures represent the sun-goddess of Arinna and the sun-god of heaven, recapitulated in their solar aspect by the large sun-disk. In contrast to the composite monsters, the seated figures do not follow the principles of bas-relief, but of sculpture in the round. They are designed to allow them to be seen from both side and front.

The 7.35-meter (24.3-foot) high, lion-flanked, trachyte stela from Fasıllar has a figure that follows the principles of sculpture in the round. It depicts a striding god with his foot on a smaller god. The latter may be recognized as a mountain-god, which makes it likely that the primary figure is the storm-god. His parabolic headgear is similar to that of the god of Eflatun Pınar and is possibly the product of a local workshop. The stela is pictured on the same scale as the fragmentary Aslantaş figure found overturned at the edge of the precinct of Eflatun Pınar. The impossibility of combining these two sculptures is demonstrated by the very dissimilarity of their dimensions.

The rock image of Akpınar on the northern slope of the Manisa Dağ (ancient Sipylos, southeast of Izmir) is probably that mentioned by Pausanias, who calls it "the very oldest pillar-image of the Mother of the Gods" in the land of the Magnetes on Sipylos. The image must have already been badly damaged in his time, for it actually depicts a bearded figure enthroned above a stylized mountain. The label seems to name a certain Kuwatnamuwa as donor. A second nearby inscription with titulary from the Hittite Empire supports the dating of the enthroned deity, probably a storm-god, to that period.

The reliefs of Karabel A and B, Hamide, and Sirkeli all show a single figure. The first three instances depict warriors—probably local rulers or princes. In the final case, King Muwattalli (Muwatalli) II is shown in a long wraparound garment with curved staff and skullcap, which is comparable to Tudkhaliya IV in Chamber A of Yazılıkaya.

In Hanyeri the image of the prince is complemented by a bull upon a mountain-god and an altar (fig. 10). As indicated by the label, the bull embodies the god Sharruma, "mighty king of the mountains." An Old Hittite story describes the creation of a path for the king through the Taurus Mountains by a bull who bends his horn in the process. Significantly, the relief of Hanyeri is set in a main pass of these very mountains.

On the other side of this col is the rock of İmamkulu, on which is carved a warrior and a large tableau of deities. The storm-god stands in a chariot drawn by bulls; it is supported by three lion-headed composite monsters and three bowing mountain-gods (fig. 11). The scene is completed by a winged goddess revealing her nakedness above a tree-like form. It was proposed to connect the scene to the mythological seduction of the storm-god by Ashertu. Interpretation, however, is very uncertain, above all because the scene consists of a combination of individual elements long known in glyptic. The prince bears the name Kuwatnamuwa, which is the same as the donor of the relief at Hanyeri as well as the rock image at Akpınar. This has not yet been explained.

Not far from İmamkulu are the very poorly preserved rock carvings of Taşcı (Tashji), which seemingly represent three priests and a priestess interceding on behalf of Khattushili III. We may also attribute to this ruler and his wife the rock relief of Fıraktın, which is only about 1 meter (3.3 feet) in height (it is shown in "Khattushili III, King of the Hittites" in Part 5, Vol. II). Very flatly carved into the trachyte wall, it is unfinished. On the left, Khattushili is depicted as a warrior with shouldered bow pouring a libation before a god. The latter, designated simply as a "deity," carries the symbol of well-being above one outstretched hand and with the other holds

Fig. 10. Rock relief from Hanyeri depicting a prince facing a bull upon a mountain-god.
DRAWING BY KAY KOHLMEYER

Fig. 11. Rock relief from İmamkulu showing a warrior (on the left) among many deities.
DRAWING BY KAY KOHLMEYER

a curved staff over his shoulder. Both figures wear a kilt and pointed cap with horns. Between them stands an altar covered by a cloth and offerings.

On the right, Pudukhepa pours a libation before the seated Khepat. The goddess holds a dish and the symbol for well-being. Both wear long garments and cowls. Once again there is an altar between the figures, but this time a bird perches on it. Further to the right a label reads, "Daughter of the Land of Kizzuwatna, Beloved of the God(s)," a propagandistic reference to Pudukhepa's origins.

The canon of representation of the human form in bas-relief during the Hittite Empire was very restricted and became ever more narrow as the rank of the person depicted became higher. There was no identity between an actual and a depicted body, that is, the figures have no real right or left side but rather simply sides turned toward or away from the observer. A figure turned toward the right corresponds in mirror image to one facing the left. This is similar to the practice in regard to the hieroglyphic script, whereby the signs face right or left according to

the direction in which the particular line is to be read. Legs are depicted in stride and heads in profile. The position of the arms and the view of the upper body vary.

Standing males of the statuary type (gods and members of the royal family) hold the arm nearest the viewer folded over the breast; that hand makes a fist with the thumb on top. The fist may grasp a weapon (gods: ax, club, sickle sword), a bow (king, prince, or local ruler), or the curved staff (king, sun-god). The arm away from the viewer is stretched out horizontally from the body, and the forearm may be bent upward. The hand again makes a fist and may carry an animal attribute or symbol (gods: a bird, or the symbol of well-being or of life) or a spear or staff (prince or local ruler; also a god at Yazılıkaya). The chest is seen from above. The shoulder nearest the viewer is generally placed a bit higher than the other. If a person of this type is engaged in activity, the schema is only slightly altered. In libation, the further arm is slightly lowered; in swinging a club, the near arm is raised and bent behind the head.

Standing females of the statuary type (goddesses and members of the royal family) also have the further arm stretched out from the body with the hand clenched in a fist. The other arm is held out somewhat higher, but the forearm is bent back toward the head so that the open hand points toward the face with palm in side view and thumb spread below. The upper body is viewed from the side, with the shoulder toward the viewer slightly displaced backwards, so that the other shoulder as well as the upper arm might be seen.

In the low-relief art of the empire, male, and especially female, seated deities are also attested. They are shown in profile. The position of the arms is similar to that of the standing females: The arm nearest the viewer is stretched out and bent so that the hand is near the chin. The hand is seen in side view and holds a bowl. The further arm is stretched out from the body and may again hold a symbol or animal attribute.

The occasional clumsy departures from this canon to be seen at Alaca Hüyük may be indications of the relatively early date of the reliefs at this site. However, the variations seen in the mountain-gods, in Ninatta and Kulitta at Yazılıkaya, and in the "naked goddess" at İmamkulu can be explained by their contents.

The Hittite "image description" texts also reveal a stereotyped canon: the gods hold a weapon in their right hand and an attribute or the symbol of well-being in their left—presumably in the form of a hieroglyphic sign. Goddesses are almost always described as sitting, with a GAL vessel in their right hand and the symbol of well-being in the other. From this we may conclude that the gods as well as the goddesses correspond to reality when depicted facing the right. Recognizing the analogy of the bowl held to the mouth with the hand in similar position, we see that the entire line of female deities in Chamber A of Yazılıkaya presents a mirror image of reality.

The correct representation of the king and sun-god, both in wraparound garments, follows from the logic that the left arm should rest in the fold of the cloth in order to leave the right arm free for action. This corresponds with the single known rendering of this image in the round on the ceremonial ax of Şarkışla (Sharkishla), now in the Vorderasiatisches Museum, Berlin. Thus, king and sun-god are shown correctly in terms of side when facing left, the position most often attested. This frozen canon of depiction is connected to the magical bond between image and actual person, whose integrity it was imperative to maintain.

LUWIAN AND ARAMAIC MINOR STATES

The collapse of the Hittite Empire did not entail the complete loss of these sculptural principles. At least some of the Luwian minor kingdoms continued the old traditions with certain modifications. While the low relief of the empire was basically carved on two planes, this now gave way to a more differentiated structure, possibly as a consequence of the change from bronze to iron tools. In the course of the first millennium, the sculptural production of Anatolia was exposed to completely new cultural influences that arose through contact with the Aramaic and Neo-Assyrian cultures.

In eastern Anatolia there occurred the Urartian transmission of both Neo-Assyrian and Syrian influences, while in central Anatolia, Phrygian culture developed, strongly marked at first by the ancient near eastern southeast and, later, by the Greek west. A detailed discussion of this development would exceed the bounds of this survey, so we limit ourselves to a few datable examples.

In the realm of the Luwian- and Aramaic-influenced minor states, the emphasis in bas-reliefs was on orthostats. They decorated city gates and external walls of temples, and in the later period also the entrances to palaces; unlike Assyria, they did not adorn interior rooms. In contrast to Phrygia, rock reliefs are rather rare. There are corner orthostats and column and pillar bases which are decorated with lions and sphinxes. They allow a view of two, three, or sometimes even four sides.

Also known are real sculptures in the round; they are usually connected with the cult for the dead. Stelae most often depict deities or banquet scenes, the latter also in relation to the cult for the dead. Some were probably erected as monuments over graves; others decorated gates. The most closely oriented toward the older empire canon and repertoire are the group of earlier orthostat reliefs from Malatya found in the Lion Gate. In one example, the center of the relief (fig. 12) depicts a libation before the storm-god by a ruler identified by a hieroglyphic label as PUGNIS-mili. On the left the same deity approaches in his chariot, while a bull for offering is shown on the right.

The storm-god and the same king are represented several times on the orthostats, the latter sometimes with a beard. Some orthostats depict offering scenes for other deities. Another features the battle of a god with a giant serpent, perhaps the struggle of the storm-god with Illuyanka. The royal name in the reliefs, PUGNUS-mili, of which only the second part may be read, occurs twice in the line of rulers of Malatya.

On the basis of the recent find of a seal impression in Lidar Hüyük, this ruling house may now be recognized with certainty as the collateral line of the kings of Karkamish of the empire (see "Karkamish and Karatepe" in Part 5, Vol. II). The first king of this name reigned in the second generation after Talmi-Teshub, who was himself a contemporary of Shuppiluliuma II, last Great King of Khattusha. The second PUGNUS-mili was the grandson of the first. Naturally we cannot

rule out the possibility that there was an additional ruler with this name, but all indications are that the reliefs of the Lion Gate should be attributed to PUGNUS-mili II. Two further monuments, the stelae of İspekçür (pronounced Ispekchur) and Darende, which may be connected to the earlier reliefs from Malatya in their mode of representation, name as their patron Arnuwanti, son of PUGNUS-mili II.

This elaborate justification for dating, dependent on David Hawkins's argument, is necessary here because the reliefs in question have until now been regarded as not closely datable, and certainly no earlier than the tenth century. Now, however, an assignment to the first quarter of the eleventh century must be considered very likely.

Three carefully modeled, multiplaned basalt slabs of the first half of the eighth century from Karkamish, now placed in the Archaeological Museum in Ankara, picture King Yariri and his family. On the right the youngest child is carried, and on the left the father leads his son Kamani. The flat representation of the Aramaean Barrakib of Sam'al (Zincirli, Zinjirli), produced around 730, more strongly assumes a knowledge of Neo-Assyrian bas-reliefs. The beard and hair-

Fig. 12. Orthostat from Malatya depicting a ruler making a libation to the storm-god. MUSEUM OF ANATOLIAN CIVILIZATIONS, ANKARA

Fig. 13. Basalt base from Adilcevaz showing guardian spirits and lions in mirror image, seventh century BCE. EKREM AKURGAL, ED., *THE ART AND ARCHITECTURE OF TURKEY* (1980)

style of the seated figure, who calls himself a true vassal of his Assyrian overlord, imitate Assyrian styles.

Created at about the same time is the approximately 6-meter- (19.8-foot-) high rock relief of Warpalawa, King of Tuwana—called Urballa by Tiglath-pileser—before the storm-god. Additionally, the inscription and a large bunch of grapes in his hand identify the deity as having characteristics related to a deity of vegetation. Here, in the northern foothills of the Taurus Mountains, Neo-Assyrian influence, for example, in the details of the heads, is joined with central Anatolian, expressed not only in the Phrygian royal clothing and fibula but possibly also in the rendering of the musculature of the god's legs.

URARTU

The few known examples of Urartean court relief art are inconceivable without Neo-Assyrian forerunners. This influence was mediated through Syrian minor arts, most importantly ivory carving. (See "The Kingdom of Urartu in Eastern Anatolia" in Part 5, Vol. II.)

Two pairs of guardian spirits stand in mirror image on either side of the basalt base of Adilcevaz from the time of Rusas II (fig. 13). Their fructifying gesture with pinecones appears directed toward the completely ornamental tree of life that stands before the central tower of a fortress. The composition of the scene is stiff, and the details are ornamental; they are comparable to a fragmentary relief in the Van Museum. Also found at the Van Museum is a stela with a most interesting representation of an empty chariot above a fallen fighter. This is the conquering chariot of Khaldi mentioned in Urartian historical texts from the eighth century.

The only known rock relief in Urartean territory was discovered at Doğubayazit on the Turkish-Iranian frontier. It is part of a burial chamber whose entrance is placed between two male figures, a worshiper and a helmeted personage, probably a minor king. The scene, which also includes a goat, cannot be interpreted and displays a strong local character.

PHRYGIA

Phrygian sculpture experienced two flourishing periods. In the late eighth and early seventh centuries, work of often very high quality was created under the influence of neighboring ancient near eastern states, but it also showed traces of the old central Anatolian tradition. Greek influence began with the incorporation of large portions of Phrygia into the Lycian Empire. The Greek influence made a strong impression on Phrygian sculpture during the second period of flourishing in the early decades of Persian hegemony. One example is the statuary group of Cybele accompanied by two musicians found near the Phrygian citadel gate in the Büyükkale area at Boğazköy.

CONCLUSION

The impulse of artistic creativity in Anatolia and the most important categories of sculpture produced there hark back to the Neolithic period. Until Greek influence began to have its effect in the Phrygian age, the range of styles and artistic themes are typical for what is found in the ancient Near East as a whole. Thus, in the Early and Middle Bronze ages, Anatolia and northern Syria had a great deal in common. Despite unmistakable features that are unique to the Hittite Empire, the sculptural art of the Late Bronze Age is inconceivable without the pictorial language and grammar created in earlier periods.

As the Hittite kingdom fell victim to enemy forces, the southeastern and eastern cultures bordering it gained increasing influence. Yet numerous artistic characteristics of the Hittite period survived, and it is possible to track elements of the old Anatolian pictorial world, especially its religious symbolism, long into the Roman period.

Translated from the German by Gary Beckman

BIBLIOGRAPHY

General Studies

HELMUTH THEODOR BOSSERT, *Altanatolien; Kunst und Handwerk in Kleinasien von den Anfängen bis zum völligen Aufgehen in der griechischen Kultur* (1942), contains an extensive collection of pictures. Overviews with bibliographies are found in: EKREM AKURGAL, *Die Kunst der Hethiter* (1961); WINFRIED ORTHMANN, "Hethitische Rundplastik" and "Hethitische Reliefkunst," in *Der Alte Orient*, edited by WINFRIED ORTHMANN (1975); MAURITS N. VAN LOON, "Urartäische Kunst," in *Der Alte Orient*, edited by WINFRIED ORTHMANN (1975); and KURT BITTEL, *Die Hethiter, die Kunst Anatoliens vom Ende des 3. bis zum Anfang des 1. Jahrtausends vor Christus* (1976).

Roots of Anatolian Sculpture

GUIDO FREIHERR VON KASCHNITZ-WEINBERG, *Die Grundlagen der antiken Kunst* (1944–1961), provides a structural analysis of early Mediterranean and near eastern art. JAMES MELLAART, *Çatal Hüyük: A Neolithic Town in Anatolia* (1967), studies Neolithic sites.

Early Bronze Age

For Early Bronze Age sites, see: REMZI OĞUZ ARIK, *Les fouilles d'Alaca Höyük, entreprises par la Société d'Histoire Turque. Rapport préliminaire sur les travaux en 1935* (1937); HÂMIT ZÜBEYR KOŞAY, *Ausgrabungen von Alaca Höyük, ein Vorbericht über die im Auftrage der Türkischen Geschichtskommission im Sommer 1936 durchgeführten Forschungen und Entdeckungen* (1944) and *Les fouilles d'Alaca Höyük, entreprises par la Société d'Histoire Turque. Rapport préliminaire sur les travaux en 1937–1939* (1951); HÂMIT ZÜBEYR KOŞAY and MAHMUT AKOK, *Ausgrabungen von Alaca Höyük; Vorbericht über die Forschungen und Entdeckungen 1940–1948* (1966) and *Alaca Höyük Excavations: Preliminary Report on Research and Discoveries, 1963–1967* (1973); TAHSIN

ÖZGÜÇ and MAHMUT AKOK, *Horoztepe: An Early Bronze Age Settlement and Cemetery* (1958); BURHAN TEZCAN, "New Finds from Horoztepe," *Anatolia* 5 (1960); and TAHSIN ÖZGÜÇ, "New Finds from Horoztepe," *Anatolia* 8 (1964).

URSULA SEIDL, "Zwei Frühdynastische Reliefs aus dem Vilayet Urfa," in *Anatolia and the Ancient Near East: Studies in Honor of Tahsin Özgüç*, edited by KUTLU EMRE, BARTHEL HROUDA, and MACHTELD MELLINK (1989), looks at Early Dynastic sculptures from southern Anatolia. JAK YAKAR, *The Later Prehistory of Anatolia: The Late Chalcolithic and Early Bronze Age* (1985), is the best summary of Early Bronze Age sites, chronology, and artifacts.

Period of Assyrian Colonies: Old and Middle Hittite Kingdom

TAHSIN ÖZGÜÇ, "Fragment of a Lion Statue Found in the Late Phase (Ib) of the Colony Period," *Belleten* 18 (1954), studies the monument from the Assyrian colony of Kārum Kanish. URSULA SEIDL, "Eine Stele aus der Nähe von Urfa," *Archäologischer Anzeiger* 1969, discusses the stelae from southern Anatolia; the dating is controversial. The sculptures of the Old Hittite Kingdom (dating controversial) are reviewed in PETER NEVE, "Ein älter-hethitisches Relief von Büyükkale," in *Boğazköy VI; Funde aus den Grabungen bis 1979*, edited by KURT BITTEL ET AL. (1984); and KURT BITTEL, "Kopf eines hethitischen Bildwerks aus der frühen Zeit des sogenannten Grossreichs," in *Boğazköy VI*, edited by KURT BITTEL ET AL. (1984).

Hittite Empire Period

For discussion of architectural decorations, see: MACHTELD J. MELLINK, "Observations on the Sculptures of Alaca Hüyük," *Anadolu (Anatolia)* 14 (1970) and "Hittite Friezes and Gate Sculptures," in *Anatolian Studies Presented to Hans Gustav Güterbock on the Occasion of His 65th Birthday*, edited by KURT BITTEL, P. H. J. HOUWINK TEN CATE, and E. REINER (1974); and ROBERT L. ALEXANDER, "A Great Queen on the Sphinx Piers at Alaca Hüyük," *Anatolian Studies* 39 (1989).

PETER NEVE, "Ausgrabungen in Boğazköy-Hattuša 1986," *Archäologischer Anzeiger* 1987, studies fragments of lions and sphinxes in Temple 3. KURT BITTEL, "Bemerkungen zum Löwenbecken in Boğazköy und zum Felsrelief von Sirkeli," in *Anatolian Studies Presented to Hans Gustav Güterbock on the Occasion of His 65th Birthday*, edited by KURT BITTEL, P. H. J. HOUWINK TEN CATE, and E. REINER (1974); HANS GUSTAV GÜTERBOCK, "Das Stierbecken von Dokuz," *Istanbuler Mitteilungen* 19/20 (1969/1970); PETER NEVE, "Ein hethitisches Stierrelief aus Derbent bei Boğazköy," in *Documentum Asiae Minoris Antiquae*, edited

by ERICH NEU and CHRISTEL RÜSTER (1988), basins with decoration discussed by Bittel, Güterbock, and Neve. The relief of Tudkhaliya IV in Temple V is studied in PETER NEVE, "Ausgrabungen in Boğazköy-Hattuša 1985," *Archäologischer Anzeiger* 1986. See his "Ausgrabungen in Boğazköy-Hattuša 1988" and "Ausgrabungen in Boğazköy-Hattuša 1989," *Archäologischer Anzeiger* 1989 and 1990, for sculptures of the artificial "entrance to the underworld." HÂMIT ZÜBEYR KOŞAY and MAHMUT AKOK, *Alaca Höyük Excavations: Preliminary Report on Research and Discoveries, 1963–1967* (1973) and PETER NEVE, "Ausgrabungen in Boğazköy-Hattuša 1982," *Archäologischer Anzeiger* 1983, look at fragments of large statues.

For the reliefs at Yazılıkaya, see: EMMANUEL LAROCHE, "Les dieux de Yazılıkaya," *Revue Hittite et Asianique* 27 (1969); VOLKERT THAAS and MARKUS WÄFLER, "Yazılıkaya und der grosse Tempel," *Oriens Antiquus* 13 (1974); HANS GUSTAV GÜTERBOCK, "Yazılıkaya: Apropos a New Interpretation," *Journal of Near Eastern Studies* 34 (1975); and KURT BITTEL ET AL., *Das hethitische Felsheiligtum Yazılıkaya* (1975). ROBERT L. ALEXANDER, *The Sculpture and Sculptors of Yazılıkaya* (1986). For a succinct rejection of Alexander's hypothesis, see KURT BITTEL, "Bemerkungen zum hethitischen Yazılıkaya," in *Anatolia and the Ancient Near East*, edited by KUTLU EMRE, BARTHEL HROUDA, and MACHTELD MELLINK (1989). PETER NEVE, "Einige Bemerkungen zu der Kammer B in Yazılıkaya," in *Anatolia and the Ancient Near East*, edited by KUTLU EMRE, BARTEL HROUDA, and MACHTELD MELLINK (1989), looks at the architecture, sculptures, and function of Chamber B, Yazılıkaya. See JUTTA BÖRKER-KLÄHN, *Altvorderasiatische Bildstelen und vergleichbare Felsreliefs* (1982) § 245–331 and KAY KOHLMEYER, "Felsbilder der hethitischen Grossreichszeit," *Acta Praehistorica et Archaeologica* 15 (1983), for rock reliefs and stelae.

Luwian and Aramaic Small States

Overviews with extensive bibliographies are found in EKREM AKURGAL, *Späthethitische Bildkunst* (1949) and WINFRIED ORTHMANN, *Untersuchungen zur späthethitischen Kunst* (1971). J. DAVID HAWKINS, "Kuzi-Tešub and the 'Great Kings' of Karkamiš," *Anatolian Studies* 38 (1988), discusses PUGNUS-mili.

Urartu

General studies are: MAURITS N. VAN LOON, *Urartian Art: Its Distinctive Traits in the Light of New Excavations* (1966) and PETER CALMAYER, "Some Remarks on Iconography," in *Urartu: A Metalworking Center in the First Millennium BCE*, edited by RIVKAH MERHAV (1991).

URSULA SEIDL, "Torschützende Genien in Urartu,"

Archäologische Mitteilungen aus Iran 7 (1974), looks at the relief in the Van museum. EMIN BILGIÇ and BÂKI ÖĞÜN, "Adilcevaz Kef Kalesi Kazıları," *Anadolu (Anatolia)* 9 (1965), discuss the sculptures of Adilcevaz. DIETRICH HUFF, "Das Felsgrab von Eski Doğubayazit," *Istanbuler Mitteilungen* 18 (1968), studies the relief of Doğubayazit.

Phrygia

See EKREM AKURGAL, *Phrygische Kunst* (1955); EKREM AKURGAL, "Chronologie der phrygischen Kunst," *Anatolia* 4 (1959) and FRIEDHELM PRAYON, *Phrygische Plastik* (1987), for overviews with bibliographies.

SEE ALSO **The History of Anatolia and the Hittite Empire: An Overview** (Part 5, Vol. II); **The Kingdom of Urartu in Eastern Anatolia** (Part 5, Vol. II); **Midas of Gordion and the Anatolian Kingdom of Phrygia** (Part 5, Vol. II); **Jewelry and the Personal Arts in Anatolia** (Part 7, Vol. III); and **Music, Dance, and Processions in Hittite Anatolia** (Part 10, Vol. IV).

Music, Dance, and Processions in Hittite Anatolia

STEFANO DE MARTINO

MUSIC

Hittite documentation about music is extensive, even though, given the official character of the Hittite archives, it is limited to the ritual sphere. We know very little about the role of music in Hittite private life. However, because Hittite treatment of the gods basically reflects their own human relations, we can infer that music may have played an important part on many occasions of private life.

For a reconstruction of Hittite music, it is of fundamental importance to study the corpus of cuneiform tablets; figurative documentation, even if more scarce, is also of great interest, particularly the İnandık vase, housed at the Archaeological Museum in Ankara.

Instruments

It is difficult to identify precisely the musical instruments mentioned in the Hittite texts. In fact, a great deal of testimony on the subject consists of generalized statements that say little about the musical instruments and even less about the type of music played. We lack documents of a technical character, and we do not know anything about the system of musical notation. For this reason, the typological classifica-tion of the instruments proposed here should be regarded as somewhat hypothetical.

The instrument most often attested is the GIŠ ᵈINANNA, which may be understood as "lyre." This Sumerogram corresponds to the Hattic term *zina/ir*, while we do not know the equivalent Hittite word. The interpretation of GIŠ ᵈINANNA as a stringed instrument is rather certain, however, partly due to the context in which the term appears, partly because this instrument is always used in accompaniment to song. Other studies propose an alternative, translating GIŠ ᵈINANNA as "harp." However, one should notice that while the lyre is amply documented in Anatolian iconography during the second and the first millennia BCE (on seals, vases, and reliefs), the harp is practically absent. If we were to accept the translation "harp," we would be contradicted by the documentation, since there are thousands of instances of this instrument (GIŠ ᵈINANNA) in the texts, but no iconographic evidence of harps in the plastic arts.

The GIŠ ᵈINANNA is illustrated earliest on the seals of the Assyrian colony period (circa 2000–1800) from Cappadocia, continuing to the end of the first millennium, for instance on the Kara-tepe reliefs. Particularly important for the Hittite period are the friezes on the previously mentioned vase from İnandık with depictions of six asymmetrical lyres, trapezoidal in shape, one of which is large, positioned on the ground and played by two musicians. On a ceramic fragment from Boğazköy (ancient Khattusha, later Pteria), there is a depiction of a symmetrical lyre with eight or more strings, played by one musician using both hands.

Taking all the data, both written and iconographic, into consideration, it is possible to get some idea of the typological variants of this instrument. The lyres can be of different dimensions, from small and portable to very large and probably stationary. Some of them are symmetrical, while others are asymmetrical; the number of strings varies from one example to the next. The structural elements are sometimes inlaid or covered with precious materials, while the arms and the yoke are sometimes decorated with animal figures.

It is not clear from the depictions whether a plectrum is used, but two different verbs are employed in connection with the GIŠ ᵈINANNA; the first is semantically linked to the action of "plucking/picking" (*ḫazziya-/ḫazzik(k)-*), while the second has the meaning of "strike/ beat" (*walḫ-*, a verb generally used in connection with percussion instruments). This information suggests different techniques for producing sounds, sometimes by using the fingers of the hand and sometimes a plectrum.

The other stringed instrument attested in Hittite music is the ᴳᴵˢTIBULA, probably a "lute," an instrument which is depicted in the figurative documentation as a small, circular body with an elongated neck.

The percussion instruments are more numerous. Three of them are always mentioned together, as if they formed a small orchestra: ⁽ᴳᴵˢ⁾*arkam(m)i-*, *ḫuḫupal*, and ⁽ᵁᴿᵁᴰᵁ⁾*galgalturi-*. The first can be identified with certainty as a "drum." The drum is made entirely or partially of wood, as demonstrated by the presence (although inconsistent) of the determinative GIŠ, "wood," and it exists in different sizes. The *ḫuḫupal* is a "cymbal." An interpretation for this term is arrived at by elimination, since in one text the *ḫuḫupal* is used as a container for liquids. The cymbal is also well documented in iconography: we find it depicted on the İnandık vase and in the frieze of the Hittite stag rhyton

of the Schimmel Collection displayed at the Metropolitan Museum of Art in New York (it is reproduced in "Theology, Priests, and Worship in Hittite Anatolia" in Part 8, Vol. III). The cymbal depicted on the Schimmel rhyton has incised decoration.

The instrument *galgalturi-* may represent "castanets." In some texts we find the mention of "a pair of *galgalturi-*," which works well with the translation "castanets," or at least with an instrument composed of two elements. The *galgalturi-* were made of metal or sometimes wood.

Another percussion instrument may be designated by the Sumerogram ᴳᴵˢBALAG.DI, which we think may be a type of drum, possibly a smaller one, or a tambourine. We can also identify the word ᴳᴵˢ*mukar* as "sistrum." This term never appears in connection with the verb "to play," but is used in loud accompaniment to magical recitals in order to "get the attention" of the deity. One ritual's text suggests that the *mukar* was made with sticks of wood. Metal sistra, however, are well known in pre-Hittite Anatolian culture, as is demonstrated by examples on view at the Archaeological Museum in Ankara.

In the case of wind instruments, there is textual evidence for the horn ⁽ˢᴵ⁾*šawatar/šawitra-* and the flute GI.DÙ. The musical function of the horn is limited because of its particular character and the narrow variation in sound it produces. It was mostly used to announce different rituals or to accompany songs or chants.

The flute is rarely attested in Hittite documentation, and when it is, it usually accompanies a song. The double flute is documented in Neo-Hittite reliefs from Carchemish (Karkamish), Karatepe (ancient Azatiwataya), and Zincirli (pronounced Zinjirli, ancient Sam'al).

Song and Recital

Songs were always accompanied by the sound of musical instruments, usually the lyre, more rarely percussion or wind instruments. Singing was a fundamental component of religious ceremonies; sometimes complete songs are set forth in texts, while at other times we have only the opening line or the "title," often determined by the name of the deity to which it is addressed, or by the ritual action for which it is intended (for example, "the song of the washing of the feet of the divinity").

In instances where the complete text or part of it is preserved, as in the case of a Hurrian song to Ishtar, we note the recurrent style of composition which uses alliteration and repetition of similar words. In another text, "the men of the city of Anunuwa" sing in the Hattic language accompanied not by the sound of musical instruments, but by the hitting or beating of swords. A similar rite presents a singer who begins his song to the sound of the lyre; then "the men of Anunuwa" sing while clashing their swords and, finally, the performers dance. One should mention here that two sword carriers also appear in the ritual procession depicted on the frieze of the İnandık vase. Furthermore, our interpretation of the two texts cited above may explain the images on the very fragmentary vase from Bitik, at the Archaeological Museum in Ankara, where two personages confront each other while holding short swords in their hands. This scene was earlier interpreted variously as a ritual duel or a sword dance.

Songs are integrated into the action of celebratory performances as in the case of a battle scene which we find enacted during the *(ḫ)išuwa* festival (to which we will return later). It is noteworthy here that the songs are accompanied by percussion, that is to say, by instrumentation that simulates the sound of war and conflict.

Songs were not only part of religious ceremonies but were also performed on a number of other occasions. An Old Hittite text belonging to the genre of the literary story, "the Chronicle of Pukhanu" narrates that while the Hittites prepare to defend against an awaited Hurrian attack, they ask two warriors ($^{LÚ.MEŠ}$*ḫulḫuliyanteš*) their opinion and prognosis of the war. These warriors then interrupt their preparation for war and, with apotropaic intention, intone a song with the opening words, "The clothes of Nesha."

Another Old Hittite text tells the story of the siege by the Hittites of the city of Urshu, and in the middle of the description of the various stages of the war, a song is announced. The text is in Akkadian, but the lines detailing the song are in Hittite. It is entitled "Song to the War God Zababa," and it is inserted into a ritual that we do not fully understand, but which seems to be related to the ongoing war and to the training of the troops.

Music not only accompanied song but also the recital of passages either in the Hittite language or in the other languages documented in the Anatolian written tradition of the second millennium: Luwian, Palaic, Hattic, Hurrian, and Babylonian. The musical accompaniment is usually with the lyre; sometimes, however, the texts specify that the recital begins only when the music stops. The speakers of the recited passages are therefore the "performers" ($^{LÚ.MEŠ}$ALAN.ZU$_9$), together with the other musicians (^{LÚ}*kita-* and ^{LÚ}*paluwatalla-*) who rhythmically pronounce their recitations with their voice and by clapping their hands.

During the rituals which took place during the funerals of kings, the passages recited by lyre-accompanied "performers" began on a loudly articulated ritual cry, "*aḫa*," before turning into a whisper as befitted a proper funeral rite.

The Musicians

We clearly distinguish between two categories of musicians: those who were specialists and those who had other functions but who occasionally also performed musical pieces. Professional musicians and singers are described by various terms, both Sumerograms and Hittite words. It is, however, difficult to distinguish specific traits among them: ^{LÚ}NAR, ^{LÚ}*ḫalli(ya)ri-*, ^{LÚ}*išhamatalla-*, ^{LÚ}*šaḫtarili-*, ^{MUNUS}SÌR (less often in the masculine form ^{LÚ}SÌR), and so on. Many of these designations are attested both in the masculine and the feminine form but it is noteworthy that in the Hittite documentation concerning musical matters there is a definite masculine predominance. A specific terminology indicates the players of certain musical instruments, the specificity of which makes us believe that to play these instruments one would have to have a certain technical ability or talent (for example, $^{LÚ/MUNUS}$*arkam(m)iyala-*, "male/female player of the drum"; LÚ.GI.GÍD, "flutist").

The lyre is always mentioned in abbreviated expressions, of the type "there is singing (with the accompaniment of) the lyre," which does not indicate to us who the players of this instrument are. One text mentions LÚ^{MEŠ}GIŠ ^{d}INANNA$^{HI.A}$ *Kaniš*, "the players of the lyre from the city of Kanesh" (Nesha, modern Kültepe).

The singers are distinguished according to the language in which they specialize: "singer of Hattic/Luwian/Hurrian," and so on. Sometimes the performers of songs or musical passages are called ^{LÚ.MEŠ}ALAN.ZU₉, a type of performer skilled in music, dance, and mime.

Musicians and singers were part of the personnel in temples and palaces. Probably every palatial or temple institution, whether in the capital of Khattusha or elsewhere, had a group of musicians at its disposal. It is possible to recover a hierarchical system among such personnel on the basis of titles such as "the master of singers" or "the superintendent of performers."

We know little about the system of recruitment for these performers. From administrative texts, we gather that the city or even a private individual could provide such specialized personnel to the palace or the temple. It is also possible that the musicians and singers circulated around Khatti or even moved in and out of nearby kingdoms. Perhaps the singers who sang or recited in a foreign language actually specialized in songs from their native traditions. Furthermore, our documents tell us of folkloristic groups, specializing in music and song. These are said to come from cities such as Anunuwa, Lallupiya, and Ishtanuwa, and this information may account for the local character of the cults they celebrated.

Alongside such specialized personnel, occasionally priests and other palace or temple functionaries are said to have played instruments, such as horns or tambourines, that were within the technical competence, apparently, of nonmusicians. Occasionally we read about instruments that were used less for their musical quality than for their perceived magical properties; their players apparently did not belong to orchestral groups.

Occasions for Music

Music was a fundamental element of religious ceremony. In the midst of festive rituals, music and song accompanies and articulates the various ritual acts. Usually the king or a high official gives the musicians the order to play, an order which can be recognized, for instance, in the calling out of the Hattic term *zina/ir*, or lyre.

First and foremost, the music accompanies a ritual action which seems to occur with great frequency: the king and queen, separately or together, occasionally also with priests or dignitaries, drink in honor of a deity. The texts give directions that specify not only at which point during the ritual the instruments must begin to sound, but also when they must stop or when their performance is optional. Musical accompaniment also occurs in processions when the king and queen, together with the court and priesthood, celebrate sacred ceremonies.

Moreover, specific instruments are likely to be more prominent in rituals belonging to one particular geographic or linguistic sphere than another. For example, the horn is used predominantly in Luwian and Hurrian rituals. At certain times during the festival the instruments are not played, but the musicians are expected to hold them in their hands. At other times instruments play incongruous roles. For example, the horn and the cymbal, which are obviously hollow in form, are turned into receptacles for libation.

Musical accompaniment is also required in rituals that are very different from what has so far been described here. A "physician," ^{LÚ}A.ZU, pierces himself with two needles while performing a dance to the sound of cymbals. The presence of the physician, the "beating" character of the music, and the whirl of the dance all lead us to believe that we are dealing with a magical, shamanistic action. It is even possible that magical powers were ascribed to the musical instruments themselves. In one ritual, for example, a physician recites an incantation while holding a sistrum in his hand.

DANCE

Dance is closely connected to music. Again, the documentation available to us is limited to dance in the cultic sphere. We do not know anything about dance in people's daily lives.

Hittite dance is better documented in the written records than iconographically, depictions being limited to the friezes on the İnandık vase and to a few decorated pottery fragments from Khattusha. As a final comparison some Neo-

Hittite fragments from Zincirli, Carchemish, and Karatepe are also of a certain interest.

Movements in Dance

In the tablets describing festivals, mention of dance is analogous to that of music, that is to say specific executed movements and steps of the dance are not always explained; instead, the texts say simply that at such and such a moment in the ceremony the dancers dance.

Nevertheless, a unique document that is possibly just an extract from a larger cultic text presents what we might call a "libretto of dance." It describes, in order, a series of dance steps, but unfortunately it does not recount the context in which the dance takes place. Some of the terms used remain incomprehensible to us, while others are sufficiently informative to allow a literal translation but not to form a visual image of what went on. For example, we read that "they danced in the style of the city of Lakhshan," or "in the style of the city of Khupishna [later Cybistra]".

Notwithstanding such difficulties, some movements of dance can be identified. In particular, it is possible to reconstruct a typology of dance steps based on the change between two series of movements, the first steps completed on the spot (*pedi*), while the second set of steps presupposes a leap from the original position to a distant point (*tūwaz*), sometimes a distance forward (*tūwaz para*). Thus, we are able to describe a dance, executed by a group of dancers who position themselves in parallel rows or concentric circles, and who first dance in place, then catch up with the row in front. Still today we find similar movements in folk dancing in many places around the Mediterranean.

Several kinds of dances are documented in the texts, and multiple verbs are used, not only *tarku(wai)-*, "to dance," but also *nai-*, "to turn"; *waḫnu-*, "to turn around"; *weḫ-*, "to make a turn"; *iya-*, "to run"; and *ḫinganišk-*, "to dance and mime," which make us realize that dance movements and steps had many variations. Furthermore, there are dances prescribing the bending of the knees (*ganenant-*), and others which imitate animal movements (*paršanili*, "in the manner of a leopard"). There are folkloristic

dances, if we can interpret the meaning of dances named after cities and countries ("the style of the city of Lakhshan"). Still other tablets give indications of positions: standing on the head or on the hands.

Some Old Hittite texts about festivals form a rather compact group from the point of view of content as well as the mention of specific divinities. In these texts, a dance accompanies a particular ritual action. After some movements in place, turning to the left and to the right, a boy or a girl "lets the message of the goddess Inara pass." The significance of this expression may seem rather obscure at first, but it becomes comprehensible when combined with what we know about the mythological tradition surrounding Inara. Following her disappearance, a bee is asked to search for Inara and to transmit a message from the mother goddess. It is therefore possible that during this festival the disappearance of Inara is reenacted and that dance steps mimed the part in which an insect or a bird flies in search of the divinity.

Music for Dance Choreography

The accompaniment to dance consists mainly of percussion and rhythmic music, but stringed instruments, like the lyre and the lute, may also play similar roles. Normally the dances have several dancers, all of whom perform the same movements. In one document, however, a single dancer separates himself from the group and performs an acrobatic solo. Acrobatic dancing is also documented in the pictorial evidence. On the upper register of the İnandık vase is depicted an orchestra with six instrumentalists playing the portable lyre, the lute, and four tambourines or cymbals. The musicians are followed by two dancers in movement, one of whom performs a kind of somersault while a women is keeping rhythm by clapping her hands. The scene is an exact visual transposition of one of the many scenes described in the festival texts where, normally, a corps of dancers perform to entertain the gods or royalty. In one ceremony, six female dancers line up in front of the king, dance and perform steps, first to the left, then to the right; never—as is specified in the text—are they to turn their back to the king. Perhaps this dance told a story and included movements of the face, the arms, or the hands that must be seen frontally by an audience; perhaps it was simply the custom in Khatti, as it was with us until just recently, never to turn one's back on royalty.

We have no information about the use of scenery or other theatrical props. Once, however, a dance is described as taking place on a wooden stage.

In dances of a mimic character, disguises or costumes were worn to indicate the roles of the performers (hunters, leopards, bears). We know that on other occasions the dancers were dressed in colorful clothes, or wore especially elaborate costumes. In one instance, however, the dancer is nude; this is the condition of the acrobatic dancer in the piece described above. It could be that cloth impeded the freedom of movement necessary for the act.

The Dancers

As with musicians, dancers can be divided between professional performers and those who only dance occasionally during a ritual. The first group consists of ^{LÚ.MEŠ}ḪÚB.BI/ḪÚB.BÍ, "dancers," joined by the ^{LÚ.MEŠ}ALAN.ZU₉, who are gifted performers with a certain versatility and who may alternate between being musicians, dancers, mimics, or actors. Also, mentioned are the ^{LÚ.MEŠ}ḫapi (y) a-, who sing, and the ^{MUNUS.MEŠ}zintuḫi-, who often both sing and dance. Both these categories of performers presumably have their origin in the Hattic tradition. Also, when the texts specify that "some women or girls" are required for the dance, we assume that these would be professional female dancers, since their identity should otherwise have been more clearly defined.

It happens, also, that nonprofessionals belonging to the cultic personnel are given to dance: the cook, the cupbearer, and members of the priesthood (for example, NIN.DINGIR, "lady of the god"). In two cases, the queen herself dances. Once the queen dances, and after her the dignitaries dance; on another occasion, the queen dances in a ritual during which she offers a deity an ax and a cloak that she held over her shoulder as she danced. Although people of both genders are said to dance, we read most often of males; whether they are adult or young is not always possible to know.

CULTIC PROCESSIONS

Music and dance play a fundamental role in the processions that initiate the celebration of festivals. An important example is the procession that takes place on the sixteenth day of the spring AN.TAḪ.ŠUM^{SAR} festival. The king and queen leave the palace preceded by several officials and a bodyguard. Behind them come all the court dignitaries. This procession is surrounded by the ^{LÚ.MEŠ}ALAN.ZU₉, who announce the proceedings while playing drums, cymbals, and castanets. Next to the king, a group of performers dances to the accompaniment of a lute; other performers dressed in colorful clothes first dance near the king and then encircle him. Before the royal couple arrives at the temple, the performers and their assistants take their places in front of the temple, evidently to be ready to receive the royal couple. When the king and queen arrive at the entry, a solo dancer performs a pirouette to welcome them after which they enter the courtyard of the temple.

Another example is the procession during the festival called KI.LAM. The king and queen walk together with officials and bodyguards. To musical accompaniment, ^{LÚ.MEŠ}ALAN.ZU₉ perform dances imitating the movements of leopards. The king takes his place at the entrance of the palace from which he watches a parade of oxen-pulled wagons carrying precious cultic ornaments. There follows a troop of ten dancers, among which a nude soloist performs an acrobatic dance. Next comes the priesthood of the deity LAMMA, and ritual objects, such as the sword and the hunting bags (^{KUŠ}kurša-), are carried forward. The sacred animals are presented one after the other. They are images, made of precious materials, representing the leopard, the wolf, the lion, the wild boar, and the bear. More music and songs follow, and then the presentation of the gold and silver images of four stags, one of which is without antlers. These animals belong to the cultural and iconographic tradition of Anatolia as demonstrated by the metal standards with figures of stags from Alaca (pronounced Alaja) Hüyük, now in the Ankara Museum. The involvement of the god LAMMA, the presentation of the images of wild animals, and the very character of the KI.LAM festival, are connected to the hunt. Thus, although hunting had lost the primary function it had held in an earlier subsistence economy, it remained alive in the religious sphere of Hittite culture and in its literary lore as well (The Saga of Kesshi).

We can identify a visual parallel to the KI.LAM festival text among the bas-reliefs at the sphinx gate, on the south side of Alaca Hüyük, a building that dates to the Empire period (circa 1400–1200). (The sphinx gate is pictured in "Anatolian Architectural Decorations, Statuary, and Stelae" above.) The friezes are arranged in two registers. (The orthostats were not found in their original place, and the arrangement of the stones is conjectural.) The lower register presents a procession of musicians and acrobats facing the altar and the image of a bull set on a pedestal. At the extreme opposite side, there is another image of a bull that is set on a wheeled base. The upper register, meanwhile, displays a hunting scene, with two archers and animals, including a wild boar and stags. These elements clearly indicate a connection between the cultic scene and the hunt, between processions and the wild animals—whether or not they were actual animals, actors in disguise, or statues.

DANCE AND MIME

There are some dances that are distinctly mimic in character and that recreate scenes from the hunt. In particular, two ceremonies should be mentioned that have to do with the cult of the Hattic deity Teteshkhapi. In the first, we find a hunter (LÚ*meneya*–) armed with a bow and another "actor" disguised as a leopard; in the second case, after a musician (LÚLUL-*šiya*–) has performed a dance with bending of the knees, the hunter (LÚ*meneya*–) dances with a bow in his hand pretending to shoot an arrow. Then another actor among the cultic personnel, dressed as a bear (LÚ*hartak(k)a*-), first bathes the feet of the performers with a liquid (*šerha*-, "animal urine"[?], real or imagined) and then performs a dance. Elsewhere we find a description of a similar scene, but with a female archer (MUNUS GIŠPAN) who readies to strike (the actor representing) the bear with an arrow. Since Teteshkhapi was a deity protective of wild nature, the frieze with the hunt becomes comprehensi-

ble, connecting such cultic representations to Hattic tradition. We may note that mural paintings at Çatal (pronounced Chatal) Hüyük about four thousand years before the Hittite period, depicting groups of men in movement—mainly without weapons and surrounded by wild animals—could also be interpreted as dancers in a hunt-related function or ritual.

Other mime performances display scenes of wrestling and battle. In the tenth tablet of the (*h*)*išuwa* festival, some musicians (LÚMEŠ BALAG.DI) dance while mimicking (*hinganiš-kanzi*) a battle and intone battle songs to the accompaniment of percussion instruments. In a different ritual we are presented with a true historical battle. The "actors" are divided into two groups, one representing "the men of Khatti" and the other representing "the men of Masha." The former carry arms of bronze, while the latter have weapons of reeds. The two groups fight, and naturally the men of Khatti are the winners. They take one of their adversaries prisoner and consecrate him to the storm-god.

Yet another text describes a wrestling match between the men of the city of Khallapiya and a group of "performers." They fight until, at a sign from the king, they are interrupted by one of the bodyguards. The men from Khallapiya are prevented from leaving and while the "performers" climb toward the city, the others stay where they are. We find an even more complete fighting match described elsewhere. A wrestling match, or perhaps a duel, takes place between an "enemy" and a Hittite, designated simply as "one of ours." Of course the fight is resolved in a manner unfavorable to the enemy and the audience shows its enthusiasm with either applause or yelling. At a sign from the king, a priest intervenes between the two combatants, doing something that is not entirely comprehensible to us. Thereupon, animals enter the stage, or rather, as usually happens, actors dressed up and masked as animals: two leopards and two bears. A wrestling match takes place (KITPALU *tiyanzi*). Two athletes represent champions of the enemy and of the Hittites; of course, the latter wins. A boxing match (LÚMEŠ GÉŠPU *tiyanzi*) follows.

The mention of weapons, even if only "stage weapons" are intended, recurs in another cult representation. Here the king comes out of his tent and positions himself near a fire by a bathing or washing installation. Two nude performers are hidden in the tub. Other cultic functionaries—the priestess of the deity Titiutti and the superintendent of the sacred prostitutes—run three times around the tub. The superintendent of the prostitutes has a wooden knife, and in front of him a priest of the god Titiutti stands with a stick. With the stick and perhaps with the knife (unfortunately the text does not say), they hit or threaten the two performers. Then a liquid, maybe a kind of beer, is poured on the performers' backs; finally they stand up, play the horn three times and leave the scene. Needless to say, we cannot confidently interpret what goes on.

SPORTS AND ATHLETIC PERFORMANCES

A horse race seems to signal the program of the AN.TAḪ.ŠUM festival, while another text mentions a prize to be given to the winner of a horse race. We have already caught a glimpse of wrestling and boxing matches in mime performances. Boxing matches (LÚ^MEŠGÉŠPU *tiyanzi*, GÉŠPU *ḫulḫuliya tiya-*) and free wrestling (*ḫulḫuliya tiya-*, or else KITPALU) are mentioned in several festival texts. Furthermore, running games and weight throwing are documented. In one rite, cult members sing and dance, while women hold on to a rope and rhythmic music is tapped on a drum. This may possibly indicate a gymnastic contest or perhaps a version of "tug-of-war."

In some festivals the wrestling contests occur during a banquet and for the entertainment of the god, "they eat (and) drink; they fill the goblets; in front of the deity they wrestle; they entertain (the deity)." That all those in attendance, including the king, the queen, and the officials who take part in the ceremony, derived pleasure from the theatrical performances offered to the gods goes without saying.

Two athletic activities merit attention. In an Old Hittite text, the "Palace Chronicle," there is a description of a team contest with archers performing for the king. The king is to judge the skill of the participants and thus select the best

among them for his personal service. The archers who hit the target receive wine as a prize, while those who miss are humiliated by having to fetch water naked.

In a ritual for erecting a building, the master builder (^LÚNAGAR) is asked to perform an acrobatic test. When the building is finished, the master builder uses a rope to climb up on the roof twice, while singers run around the hearth below. The third time that the master builder climbs the roof, he uncovers a silver ax and a silver knife, hidden under some material and tied to the roof of the building. The master builder gets to keep the ax and the knife as a reward, since this test of his courage was the final condition of receiving compensation for the completed building.

Music, dance, mime, and athletic performances played an important role in Hittite religion and in the celebration of festivals. It is obviously not possible to apply our term "theater" to the spectacle described, but it is certain that an elaborate choreography governed the performance of music and dance so that the gods would receive a rite with gratitude and the participants would be happy and involved in the activity. The different types of musical instruments, the songs, and the situations recreated by the mimes have their roots in ancient traditions and are mixed with Hattic, Hurrian, and Luwian elements, in keeping with the composite, yet original, character of Hittite culture.

Translated from the Italian by Ulla Kasten

BIBLIOGRAPHY

Music

ENRICO BADALÌ, "La musica presso gli Ittiti: un aspetto particolare del culto in onore di divinità," *Bibbia e Oriente* 28 (1986), "Beziehung zwischen Musik und kultischen Rufen innerhalb der hethitischen Feste," in *Zeitschrift der Deutschen Morgenländischen Gesellschaft, Supplement 7*, edited by EINAR VON SCHULER (1989), and *Strumenti musicali, musici e musica nella celebrazione delle feste ittite*, Texte der Hethiter 14 (1991); STEFANO DE MARTINO, "La funzione del *tarša(n)zipa-* nelle cerimonie cultuali ittite," *Hethitica* 5 (1983), "Il lessico musicale ittita II: ᴳᴵˢ ᵈINANNA = cetra," *Oriens Antiquus* 26 (1987), "Il lessico musicale ittita: usi e valori di alcuni verbi," *Hethitica* 9 (1988), and "Musik bei den Hethitern," *Reallexikon der Assyriologie und Vorderasiatischen Archäologie* 8 (1993); OLIVER GURNEY, *Some Aspects of Hittite Religion* (1977); CORD KÜHNE, "Hethitisch *ḫupišk-*," *Orientalia* 59 (1990); HANS MARTIN KÜMMEL, "Gesang und Gesanglosigkeit in der hethitischen Kultmusik," in *Festschrift Heinrich Otten*, edited by ERICH NEU and CHRISTEL RÜSTER (1988); TAHSIN ÖZGÜÇ, *İnandıktepe* (1988); and ANNA MARIA POLVANI, "Appunti per una storia della musica cultuale ittita: lo strumento *ḫuḫupal*," *Hethitica* 9 (1988), "Osservazioni sul termine ittita ⁽ᴳᴵˢ⁾ARKAMMI," *Oriens Antiquus* 27 (1988), and "A proposito del termine ittita *šawatar* 'corno'," *Studi Epigrafici e Linguistici* 6 (1989).

Dance and Mime

STEFANO DE MARTINO, *La danza nella cultura ittita*, Eothen 2 (1989), and "Il ᴸᵁALAN.ZÚ come 'mimo' e come 'attore' nei testi ittiti," *Studi Micenei ed Egeo-Anatolici* 24 (1984).

Sports and Athletic Performances

ALFONSO ARCHI, "Fêtes de printemps et d'automne et réintégration rituelle d'images de culte dans l'Anatolie hittite," *Ugarit-Forschungen* 5 (1973), and "Note sulle feste ittite," *Rivista degli Studi Orientali* 52 (1978); CHARLES CARTER, "Athletic Contests in Hittite Religious Festivals," *Journal of Near Eastern Studies* 47 (1988); JAAN PUHVEL, "Hittite Athletics as Prefigurations of Ancient Greek Games," in *The Archaeology of the Olympics*, edited by WENDY J. RASCHKE (1988); and AHMET ÜNAL, "Hittite Architect and a Rope-Climbing Ritual," *Belleten* 52 (1988).

SEE ALSO **Theology, Priests, and Worship in Hittite Anatolia** (Part 8, Vol. III); **Music and Dance in Pharaonic Egypt** (Part 10, Vol. IV); and **Music and Dance in Ancient Western Asia** (Part 10, Vol. IV).

Art and Architecture in Canaan and Ancient Israel

ANNIE CAUBET

INTERNATIONAL ART

The study of the material and artistic culture of the Levant results in the definition of a cultural community, an identity, or, in fact, a group of original identities. In this vast region of various populations and environments that were never politically united, one unifying factor is art expressed by the elite. In the case of an urban civilization organized into kingdoms, art is created by and for a courtly society. Royal families, officials, and priests were a choice clientele for the luxury arts. Long distance exchanges, alliances, and diplomatic marriages are well documented by economic texts and international letters. The written sources reflect the direct and frequent relationships established between the Mediterranean and the Euphrates, the Nile and the Amanus. The international ruling classes rivaled each other with opulent displays. This rivalry, which promoted a large increase in the demand for products representing social status, contributed to the flourishing of a truly "international" art.

The area covered by this international art varies slightly throughout time. It only really came into existence at the beginning of the second millennium, over a geographical zone that stretched from the Taurus Mountains in the north to the Gaza Strip in the south. From the second half of the second millennium onward, it extended from the Mediterranean (including Cyprus) eastward toward the middle Euphrates. This area, which is much larger than the sphere vaguely defined today as "Canaan," was also larger than the countries of Israel, Aram, and Phoenicia during the first millennium; the cultural designations only approximately coincide with the political, ethnic, and religious designations.

ARCHITECTURE AND URBANISM

The domains of architecture and urbanism, profoundly anchored in traditional surroundings and customs, are those which present the most local variation. Even without attempting a complete analysis, it is possible to indicate some common traits. Architectural techniques present specifically Levantine characteristics, notably the widespread use of stone and wood, which is clearly distinguishable from the Mesopotamian tradition of mud-brick. The use of wood is systematic, not only for roofing but also for the vertical structure of walls. Its use is more accessible to all social classes than in Mesopotamia or in Egypt, a sociological difference no doubt owing to the presence of the nearby forests of Lebanon and the Amanus Mountains. Construction stone, abundant all along the littoral and in the Syrian steppes, is used for foundations and walls in the form of small stones and hewed stones, also known as ashlar. The walls of dry stone are secured by timber frames and vertical reinforcements to protect against damage from frequent earthquakes. Dried mud-brick, omnipresent in Mesopotamia, only occasionally occurs in the Levant.

Urbanism reflects the compromise between the authoritarian planning of royal power and a certain anarchy inherent in the life of individuals, which is expressed by the encroachment of the private sector into the collective public space. At Ugarit (modern Ras Shamra), a layout of streets following the curves of the terrain was established in early times. Thoroughfares and back alleys gave access to small courtyards that were surrounded by blocks of houses. Increasing population brought about subdivisions of the living quarters. At the same time, buildings began to occupy the free spaces, until the crowding of the city and the blocking of the roadways obliged the royal authorities to demolish buildings and open large squares in the center of the urban network. Emar (modern Meskene) was built by the Hittite authorities on the west bank of the Euphrates. The city plan involved leveling the terrain into terraces that were used as small plots for private houses; these were all identical and connected by streets that were laid out before construction began.

The differences in organization between royal power and private initiative are also reflected in the water supply and sewer systems. In the palaces of Ugarit, rainwater was carried through pipes to large basins and pools, and capacious sewers drained the palatial complex. In the rest of the city, rainwater was collected in the courtyards to augment the water furnished by wells. These wells were shared among several houses at a time. Used water from private houses was emptied onto the street through short drains that were located near the doors. Royal activity explains the huge hydraulic works that are one of the characteristic features of the cities of Israel. Vast well-cisterns were accessible by stairs (Ha-

zor; modern Tell al-Qedah) or linked by a tunnel to a spring (Megiddo and Jerusalem). The famous tunnel dug by King Hezekiah channeled spring water inside the walls of Jerusalem from the Gihon spring in the Kidron Valley. These works entailed huge investments in manual labor that could only be obtained by a central power.

Most cities were provided with a rampart, not only as a consequence of the unstable political situation, but also as a demonstration of prestige, an affirmation of power. This feature has strongly marked the Syrian and Palestinian countryside. Even on nonexcavated sites, it is often the remaining rampart on an embankment that determines the roughly circular contour of the tells and maintains their relief. This defense system appeared systematically at the beginning of the Early Bronze Age toward the end of the third millennium (Tell Yarmuth); it includes many different types. The improvement brought about by the invention of sloping banks in brick (Tel Dan) or in stone (Ugarit) to reinforce the base of walls, undoubtedly dates back to the Middle Bronze Age. The cities of the Israelite monarchy developed casemate walls (a double wall with inner partitions) (Hazor). Gates in the rampart have a monumental aspect that is not only functional but symbolic as well. Often constructed in stone, the gate is surmounted by a tower and frequently boasts a complex of rooms with a pincer-shaped plan. This system existed from Ebla to Megiddo, from Tell Halaf (Gozan, Bit-Bakhiani) to Lachish. The direct tie established between the defensive function of the gate and its symbolic function, as an external demonstration of power, is often accentuated by the proximity of the palace to a gate in the rampart. Additionally, the palace needed its own entrance. At Ugarit, the tower flanked by a postern, the only part of the rampart excavated, belongs to the palace complex; the main entrances to the city still remain to be discovered. The protective and symbolic function of the gate was maintained during the first millennium, and such Neo-Hittite strongholds as Carchemish (Karkamish), Tell Halaf, or Sam'al (modern Zincirli) can be compared to the Israelite royal cities. The Biblical descriptions of the sieges carried out by the Assyrians, illustrated by sculpted reliefs on the walls of the conquerors at Nimrud (Kalkhu;

the siege of Gezer), Khorsabad, or Nineveh (the siege of Lachish), correspond to the plans uncovered by excavations.

The fortified royal cities of the Levant are generally of modest dimensions, much smaller than those of the Mesopotamian "megalopoleis." Nevertheless, royal ambition is expressed by the emphasis on the decorative scheme on the walls of the gate, which exhibits royal or religious propaganda prefiguring that of the Assyrians. In fact, during their conquests, the latter probably borrowed certain expressions of royal ideology from the Levant. The most striking elements are the guardian animals of the gateway. Lions, bulls, and sphinxes, all mythological monsters associated with concepts of divine and human royalty, are placed at the gates of Bronze Age cities like Hazor and Gezer, and, after having been adopted by the Hittite Empire, become characteristic of the fortified Neo-Hittite and Aramaean cities. (See also "Karkamish and Karatepe" in Part 5, Vol. II.)

Royal power is blatantly demonstrated in the construction of public buildings, particularly palaces. Few sites have been extensively explored to give a full understanding of their organization. In the third millennium, Mesopotamia inspired the official building of Ebla, probably destroyed by Sargon of Akkad (Agade) or Naram-Sin. The partial remains of this complex permit only an understanding of the administrative and archival function of the palace, whose monumental stairway in stone nevertheless marks its originality in comparison to those in Mesopotamia. The Amorite palace of Mari (nineteenth–eighteenth centuries), more completely excavated, is remarkable for its monumental entryway with a paved floor. Its several units serve different functions. The reception area is centered around the throne room, which is on the axis of a courtyard whose huge dimensions allow a large assembly of assistants. A sacred complex is located nearby, in order to facilitate the religious functions of the king. Arsenals, kitchens, and storerooms are placed in the back. The private apartments were apparently built on an upper story where residents could enjoy the free space offered by terraces and hanging gardens. The organization of rooms opening into a walled-in complex, except for a single entryway, is a feature borrowed from Mesopotamia. (See the chapter on Mari in Part

5, Vol. II.) Certain arrangements recall, however, the Mediterranean world and Cretan palaces; they are well illustrated at Ugarit (fourteenth–twelfth centuries). Pillared porches on one side of the major courtyards, which protect the adjoining rooms from the sun; illumination of inner rooms by a shaft; and the presence of basins and pools are all features that bear witness to a gentility of living that is rarely observed elsewhere than in Cretan palaces. The complexity of the royal palace plan at Ugarit also recalls the legend of the Cretan "labyrinth." (A plan of the palace of Ugarit appears on the next page.)

During the Israelite monarchy, a type of rectangular building supported by a double row of stone pillars appears (Hazor, Megiddo); its function is difficult to understand. Its identification at Megiddo as "royal stables" is not satisfactory. A comparison with the "Building of the Four Pillars" at Ugarit suggests that it might have a religious function related to the palace, serving, for example, as a locale for ceremonial banquets.

In south Palestine, which was subject to Egyptian influences, the palace plans are inspired by those of the New Kingdom with rooms distributed around a courtyard (thirteenth-century residence at Sharuhen [Tell al-ʿAjjul]). In the rest of the Levant, an original type of official building was developed, which archaeologists conventionally designate by the Assyrian term *bīt ḫilāni*. It is a freestanding building that opens onto a porch that is protected by two towers and consists of two rectangular rooms in a row juxtaposed along their long side. This plan becomes generalized from the Late Bronze Age onward and can be found, for example, at Alalakh (fourteenth century), where the base of the walls is reinforced by orthostats, that is, vertical slabs of stone. This style of building is used as far as the middle Euphrates, where it can be found at Emar in the thirteenth century. In the first millennium, it becomes a characteristic of the palaces built by the Aramaeans and the Neo-Hittites in northern Syria. There, the *bīt ḫilāni* becomes a support for sculpted decoration where religious and royal ideology are displayed. This imagery also appears at Carchemish (eleventh-tenth centuries) in front of the palace porch, which is preceded by a processional way adorned with sculpted orthostats in

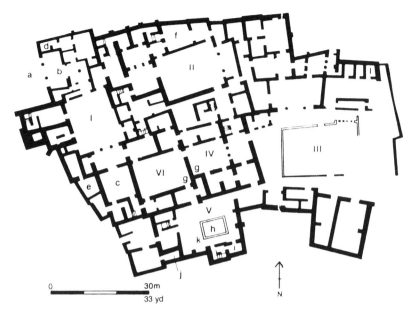

Plan of the royal palace at Ugarit. *a*, paved court; *b*, main entrance; *c*, throne room; *d*, western archive; *e*, annex office archives; *f*, tombs; *g*, central archives; *h*, shallow pool; *i*, southern archive; *j*, southwestern archive; *k*, oven(?) and tablets; *l*, eastern archive; **I, II**, courtyards; **III**, garden; **IV, V, VI**, courtyards. THE ANCHOR BIBLE DICTIONARY, VOL. 6

black basalt and white limestone. At Tell Halaf (Guzana; tenth–ninth centuries), the entrance porch of the palace of King Kapara is supported by statues of divinities in the form of caryatids. The conquest of the Levant by the Assyrians (ninth–eighth centuries), and then the Persian domination (sixth–fourth centuries), caused Levantine palatial architecture to lose its original and unitary character. There are occasional small versions of the Assyrian palace. At Til Barsip, in northern Syria, the frescoes are a painted imitation of sculpted historical and religious scenes that belong to Assyrian royal iconography (see "Reliefs, Statuary, and Monumental Paintings in Ancient Mesopotamia" above; the Til Barsip fresco is pictured in "Textile Arts in Ancient Western Asia" in Part 7, Vol. III). The Persian epoch introduces a regular architecture on a square plan around a large central courtyard. The residence of Lachish, for example, is very similar to the Persian palace of Vouni (Cyprus).

Temple architecture constitutes an authentic cultural tie throughout the Levant. Indeed, there are numerous local variants and different plans of sacred architecture, but it is in the Levant, in the Canaanite environment, that the freestanding temple, clearly visible in the urban landscape, was born. This concept, which prefigures that of the Greek temple, is quite different from that of the Mesopotamian complex, which shelters its sanctuary in the heart of a network of courtyards and annexes. The Syro-Palestinian temple is axial (rows of rooms arranged according to a straight axis), with a row of rooms, a porch or antechamber opening onto a small room, and, sometimes, a chapel or Holy of Holies in the back. The Temple of Jerusalem built by Solomon is described as a temple built in this style (a ground plan of this temple is reproduced in "Palaces and Temples in Canaan and Ancient Israel" in Part 4, Vol. I). Several examples of temples of this type have been excavated: the temple at Ebla dates from the second millennium; the Temple of Shechem goes back to the Hyksos period (seventeenth–sixteenth centuries); the two temples of Baal and Dagan at Ugarit located on the top of the acropolis probably date as early as the sixteenth or fifteenth

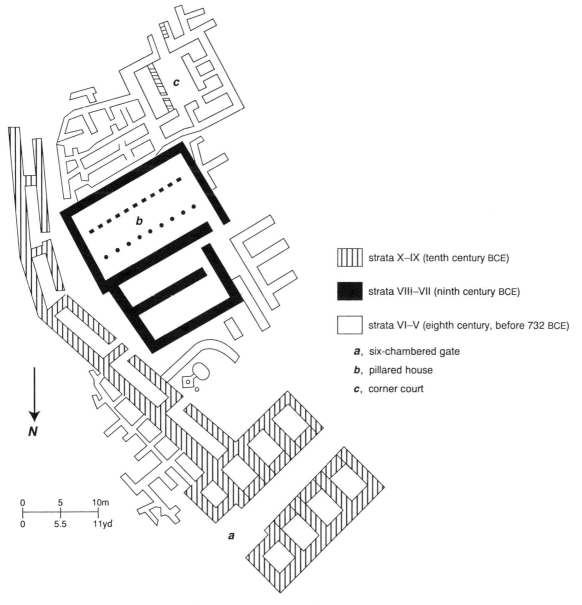

strata X–IX (tenth century BCE)

strata VIII–VII (ninth century BCE)

strata VI–V (eighth century, before 732 BCE)

a, six-chambered gate

b, pillared house

c, corner court

0 5 10m
0 5.5 11yd

N

Plan of the citadel at Hazor. Drawing after Y. YADIN, *ENCYCLOPEDIA OF THE ARCHAEOLOGICAL EXCAVATIONS IN THE HOLY LAND*, JERUSALEM.

centuries; the twin sanctuaries of Dagan and Ishtar at Emar date from the thirteenth century, as does the main sanctuary of the sacred complex at Kition (Cyprus). The width of the foundations and bases of the walls give them a powerful aspect that has often caused them to be called "fortress temples" (the Megiddo temple at Shechem), but this reinforcement of the base can also be interpreted as an architectural and functional necessity. In fact, certain ancient texts, such as the *Epic of Keret* from Ugarit, indicate that the temple is a raised edifice. When the legendary King Keret laments his lack of descendants, the god El appears in a dream ordering him to carry out a certain number of religious rites (to choose a sacrificial lamb and bird, to pour wine into a silver cup and honey into a golden cup), and tells him, "Climb to the top of the tower, mount the top of the wall, raise your hands toward the sky, sacrifice to your father El

2675

Reconstruction of the temple of Baal at Ugarit, sixteenth to fifteenth centuries BCE. LOUVRE MUSEUM, DRAWING BY OLIVIER CALLOT

the bull, honor Ba'al with your sacrifice" (*Epic of Keret;* see also "The Literatures of Canaan, Ancient Israel, and Phoenicia" in this volume and "Myth and Mythmaking in Canaan and Ancient Israel" in Part 8, Vol. III).

This interpretation agrees with architectural analysis of the archaeological remains and with that of the clay models of sanctuaries. These objects, which are a valuable source of information for the restitution of buildings for which

Reconstruction of the Ishtar and Dagan temples, Emar, thirteenth to twelfth centuries BCE. LOUVRE MUSEUM, DRAWING BY OLIVIER CALLOT

the only remains lie at ground level, probably belong to domestic cult furnishings and have been found on various sites: Megiddo, Selimiyé, Emar. They establish that many sanctuaries had at least one upper story. The base of the walls had to be capable of supporting the weight of stories and must have been especially thick. The sanctuary appeared like a sort of tower, visible from afar, and could serve as a landmark for the sending and receiving of smoke signals, a form of long-distance communication that is attested by the letters of Lachish. At Ugarit, the temple towers of the acropolis served as landmarks for sailors.

Occasionally the axial arrangement is interrupted by the presence of a chapel on the side of the main room, both units being lined with benches. This arrangement is found in the Fosse Temple at Lachish, various sanctuaries in the Plain of Sharon (Tell Qasile, Tel Mevorakh) during the twelfth and eleventh centuries, the Ingot God Temple at Enkomi (twelfth century), and the Temple of the Rhytons at Ugarit (thirteenth century).

The private house is a better reflection of the diversity of populations and ethnic groups than official architecture or the decorative arts, for which the clientele is mainly a cosmopolitan elite. This diversity means that it is difficult to treat private architecture otherwise than in detail. However, the constraints and the possibilities presented by the environment determine certain common factors. In these countries, which are usually warm, flat roofs of beaten earth laid on top of beams and mats were generally preferred because they promoted thermal insulation. The abundance of local stone and timber permitted the use, even in modest dwellings, of these materials, which were considered luxuries in Egypt and Mesopotamia. The overcrowding of the towns resulted in the development of the storied dwelling. The private apartments were typically located on the second floor in order to take advantage of the evening coolness on the terrace; outdoor activities such as washing and cooking also took place here. Shops, artisans' workshops, and storage rooms were located on the ground floor in the cool shade favorable to the preservation of perishable goods. Many styles were adopted over the course of time and from one region to another. Some reconstructions have been made possible by analyzing the architectural "models" in clay; thcir use may elude us, but they permit a better understanding of the organization of the dwelling.

The private house at Emar, a result of the authoritarian implantation of the Hittites on the middle Euphrates, follows a standard layout: a room in front opens onto two rooms in the back which support an upper floor. This floor opens onto a terrace on top of the front room. Part of the domestic activities undoubtedly took place on the terrace. These small living quarters, identical in their disposition, or plan, with one large room in front opening on two smaller rooms on the back, correspond exactly to the schema of the clay models. At Ugarit, the size and number of rooms vary according to the rank and wealth of the owners, but the total plan corresponds to certain criteria that are always the same: blind rooms on the ground floor house agricultural activities, pithoi storage, and sometimes shops or artisans' working quarters; and a small courtyard in the center of the house redistributes light to the living quarters on the upper floor (or floors). One particular aspect of Ugaritic houses is the almost universal presence of a family tomb, which was constructed in the basement at the same time as the house; it usually has an independent entryway. The wells, fewer than the dwelling units, are often located in rooms adjacent to neighboring dwellings in order to serve several

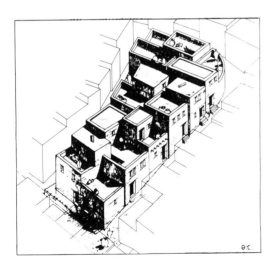

Reconstruction of a portion of a house at Emar, thirteenth to twelfth centuries BCE. LOUVRE MUSEUM, DRAWING BY OLIVIER CALLOT

households at the same time; it seems likely that the digging and maintenance costs were shared. Thus, alongside royal activity, which handles large collective works, individuals gather, when necessary, in small, communal efforts. From the Iron Age on, the private Palestinian dwelling is characterized by the appearance of the four-room Israelite house, which surrounds a central courtyard on three sides. This type is well represented at Tell al-Fara'in North (Tirzah) and at Tel Beersheba; the latter is a good example of urban planning with identical housing units, which were probably created by royalty for strategic and administrative reasons.

Like the private house, the tomb reflects the diversity of populations. There are no general rules for the arrangement of the cemeteries in relationship to the dwellings. One of the most widespread cultural features, perhaps with Canaanite origins, is the collective tomb under the floor of the house. This custom is observed at Lachish, Tell al-Fara'in North, Megiddo, Hazor, Ugarit, and Cyprus. The proximity of the living and the dead raises questions about cults of the dead (the Rephaïm of the Bible), which are mentioned in the Ugaritic texts. In the Gaza Strip, the Philistine populations seem to have adopted Egyptian funerary customs; their dead are buried in anthropoid clay sarcophagi. The tomb contents provide information concerning the society of the living. One of the traits common to the entire Levant is the almost universal presence of funerary gifts. Among these gifts, jewelry and personal objects are often exquisite examples of the decorative arts.

SCULPTURE

Monumental sculpture associated with architecture begins with the decoration of the city gate or public edifices. The guardian animals of the doorways—lions, sphinxes, bulls—appear on the city gates and official buildings as early as the middle of the second millennium. The body of the crouched lion found in the sanctuary at Hazor (fourteenth–thirteenth centuries) is sculpted in low relief on an upright block, while its head and the tips of its front paws are sculpted in the round. This combination of relief and

Orthostat of a life-size lion guarding the city-gate at Hazor, fourteenth to thirteenth centuries BCE. ISRAEL ANTIQUITIES AUTHORITY, JERUSALEM

sculpture in the round can also be found on miniature architectural monuments, such as the sarcophagus of Ahiram from Byblos. This sarcophagus is designed in the form of a rectangular building, which is protected on its sides by guardian lions. The lions flanking the buildings probably answered to profound beliefs that we do not understand now. This design was used in reduced scale for sarcophagi, chest, and boxes in the shape of miniature buildings. In another example, an ivory box from the Megiddo treasure is fashioned in the form of a square monument flanked by lions, sphinxes, and griffins. Here, too, the bodies appear in relief and the projecting heads are sculpted in the round. One of the characteristics of the decorative or minor arts of the Levant is its close iconographic and organic relationship to the monumental arts. At Ebla (eighteenth century), where the influence of Mesopotamian iconography is stronger than on the littoral, the basins in stone used for cult purposes in the temples depict mythological representations that are directly borrowed from the engravings of Mesopotamian cylinder seals. This adaptation of a miniaturist technique onto a major support is not universal, but reflects local temperaments and needs. In addition to the friezes representing gods in parade and cult scenes, the basins also exhibit the guardian lions with bodies in relief profile and heads sculpted in the round.

The use of protective guardian monsters at doorways has a long history in the Orient. Such figures are systematically used in the Hittite capital of Khattusha (modern Boğazköy; fourteenth–thirteenth centuries). Later, Neo-Hittites and Aramaeans of northern Syria and then the Achaemenid Persians use it as one of the outstanding features of their architecture.

On the Syro-Palestinian coast and on Cyprus, certain sculpted elements of public architecture, like proto-aeolic capitals, appear at the end of the Bronze Age (Megiddo, Ramat Rahel) and survive until the Assyrian epoch, notably on Cyprus. The capitals are not only found in public architecture but also in small works and furnishings. Ivory boxes and stools have these capitals, which are placed in an architectonic position. These works belong to the treasures of Megiddo (thirteenth century), Samaria (ninth–eighth centuries), and Arslan Taş (pronounced Arslan Tash; ninth–eighth centuries).

Architectural sculpture takes on a spectacular aspect in north Syria at the beginning of the first millennium. At Tell Halaf (ancient Guzana), the porch of the *bīt ḥilāni* is supported by caryatid statues representing divinities mounted on their animal attributes. The main passage is bordered with guardian sphinxes and orthostats that display mythological motifs. The basalt in which these sculptures are carved is one of the main reasons for their crude but powerful style. At Carchemish, a whole figurative program was set up by the kings who ruled from the eleventh century on. A panel represents the children of the king Yariri playing at knucklebones and with tops while servants bring them exotic animals. The king majestically presents the crown prince, his heir. This panel is incorporated into the monumental ensemble of the main processional way that mounts toward the palace; these works adorn walls that are also decorated with orthostats representing mythological subjects and triumphant warriors.

Sculpture in the round is rare anywhere in the Levant. This gap is perhaps due to the absence of stone suitable for direct stone carving: basalt is excessively rough and hard, whereas limestone is too soft. Ivory was used as early as the Chalcolithic period (fourth millennium), when residents of the Negev and the Dead Sea areas developed an art of ivory sculpting similar to that of predynastic Egypt. Mesopotamia exerted an influence on inland Syria, which followed iconographic traditions that were borrowed from the Sumerian culture of the mid third millennium. Instances of these traditions are the limestone statues of Mari or Tell Khuera that represent worshipers in prayer or carrying offerings; they are dressed in the Sumerian *kaunakes* (fleecy garment). Crudely anthropomorphic basalt megaliths are found throughout the hinterland, from northern Syria as far as Transjordan. These truly indigenous sculptures, difficult to date, seem to have persisted until the middle of the second millennium; they are perhaps precursors to the first monumental figurative art on stone of a truly Levantine character. Bronze Age effigies of dynasty founders or national gods are often carved in the basalt that abounds in northern Syria and on the frontier of Jordan. A god's head at the site of Jabbul, a depression near Aleppo, a statue of the governor Ishtup-ilum of

Mari (pictured in "Mari" in Part 5, Vol. II), and a statue of King Idrimi of Alalakh (pictured in "Autobiographies in Ancient Western Asia" above), all dating from the first half of the second millennium, are sculpted in large masses. The forms are heavy and the details omitted in favor of the general effect, which is accentuated by eyes with hollow orbits. The influence of Mesopotamian iconography is felt in the horned tiara that distinguishes the gods from mortals. Dynastic rulers wear a draped, fringed garment of Mesopotamian type, but the style and strength of the images are typically local.

Sculptures in the round are very rare during the second half of the second millennium; the very fine head thought to represent King Yarim-Lim of Alalakh, remains an exception. Cult images probably existed in the sanctuaries. The seated figure discovered surrounded by stelae in a sanctuary of Hazor offers an interesting parallel with the little stone statue of the god El found at Ugarit in 1988. The latter represents the god draped in a long garment with a banded border. The wrists are hollowed out, allowing the insertion of hands, which must have been made of another material. His back, leaning against the high back of the throne, is slightly bent; his shoulders are rather slouched. This figure has an aspect of weariness and age that is confirmed by the elongated face, the beard, and the high tiara. It is the image of El, the father of the gods, overwhelmed with the cares of the world, as he is described in the mythological texts of Ugarit. With his arms partially stretched out in a reconciling gesture, he belongs to the iconographic series of gods "of peace," which are represented also in bronze. The relationship between the minor arts and large sculpture is a determining factor in the domain of religious imagery as well.

In the middle of the second millennium, a particular type of stela appears: tall, narrow, often curved at the top, and sometimes with a forward-projecting base. The "obelisks" from Byblos betray an Egyptian influence but are, in fact, arched-top stelae with niches carved out at their base. Perhaps they are descendants of primitive cult stones (baetyls). Usually without pictorial representation, as at Hazor and Ugarit, these stelae are sometimes decorated with a simple figurative element (hands raised toward an astral crescent at Hazor, an astral symbol above

Stela of the weather-god Baal from Ugarit, circa fourteenth century BCE. LOUVRE MUSEUM, PARIS

a baetyl at Ugarit) or more complex ones. The weather-god Baal stela from Ugarit (about fourteenth century), is perhaps one of the most accomplished examples of Levantine Bronze Age art. The god, upright in a dynamic attitude, brandishes a club from which he releases lightning. In his other hand, he holds a spear pointed downwards, with a shaft transformed into a branch of vegetation, symbol of the beneficent effects of rain brought by storms. His feet rest on an altar, placed on top of wavy lines symbolizing the sea and his mountainous residence. The texts locate this at Mount Zaphon, a high mountain that rises directly above the sea. Under the protection of the arms of the god, there is a small upright figure in prayer, the king of Ugarit. The stela thus displays the divine protection accorded to the dynasty. The attitude and the costume of the king are identical to those found on a bronze

plaque in relief in a sanctuary at Hazor and are repeated on various clay cult stands of Ugarit. Throughout the Levant, the representation of the king involved in his religious functions and his relationship with the divine are amazingly homogeneous.

The appearance of Israelite monotheism contributed to the rarity of imagery in Palestine. Further to the north, the tradition of arched stelae persisted until the first millennium. In one example, the stela commonly known as the Amrit stela, found in the Phoenician kingdom of Arad (modern Arwad), is inscribed with the name of a healing god, Shadrapha. This document shows a juvenile god mounted on a lion and taming another smaller lion in his hands. The composition, which is also found on the stele of Qadmos, in the hinterland of Marathus, is directly derived from that of the weather-god Baal stela of Ugarit. During the Persian period, the votive stelae of divine images were gradually replaced on the Syro-Phoenician coast by other forms of cult monuments. The *naos*, a miniature model of a real building with an Egyptian-type facade, and the "Astarte thrones," stone thrones flanked by sphinxes, are good examples of the transfer of compositions from monumental architecture to the decorative arts.

Also on the Phoenician littoral, some freestanding sculptures carved in local sandstone show the adaptation of Egyptian compositions to local needs. The Sarepta statue and the colossi of the so-called Egyptian temple of Byblos are represented leaning on a dorsal pillar, wearing an Egyptian costume and headdress. Their position on the monument, as well as the style and the iconographic details indicate, however, that this Egyptianized shape was expressed by Phoenician artists working in the cities of Tyre, Sidon, Byblos, and Arad.

During the Persian period, the Syro-Palestinian littoral was exposed to the influence of the Ionian Greek world, an influence that is particularly obvious in the use of marble, a new building material imported from the Greek islands of Thasos and Paros. First worked by Greek artists for the needs of their Levantine clientele, marble was introduced into Phoenicia in a series of anthropoid sarcophagi destined for the Phoenician upper classes. The outward form is borrowed from Egypt, but the features of the faces and the coiffures are adaptations of Greek styles. During and after the fifth century, the influence of Athens was expressed by borrowing columns and pediments from western architecture for the production of stelae and sarcophagi in the form of miniature buildings. The famous sarcophagi of the royal necropolis of Sidon, now in the Istanbul Archaeological Museum, among them the so-called Lycian, Amazon, Satrap, and the sarcophagus said to belong to Alexander the Great, were carved for the royal Phoenician dynasty of Sidon, which had kept a certain measure of automony under the Persians. This autonomy was taken away by Alexander's conquest. Expressed from that point forth in a form borrowed from the Greek arts, the old tradition of the royal ideology reappeared in the hunting and battle scenes or images of the dynast reigning in majesty. The funerary sculptures of Sidon are good examples of how Syro-Palestinian artists assimilated and transformed their work when faced with the strong figurative arts coming from Egypt, Mesopotamia, and Greece. After Alexander's conquest, this adaptive capacity, combined with fidelity to the memory of a thousand-year-old, indigenous tradition, gave birth to a new culture, that of the hellenized Levant.

Given the rarity of stone sculpture in the round, the Levant found its own artistic form in small bronze statuary, which was exclusively religious in character. The application of gold leaf on the statuettes makes them even more precious. They correspond to well-documented rites that mention gold offerings made by the faithful to the image of the god. Despite the apparent diversity of costumes and coiffures, there is only a small number of divine iconographic types. The most popular is the juvenile god in a dynamic attitude, wearing a short kilt, walking in long strides, with one arm raised above his head, the other brandishing a weapon: the smiting god. Gold leaf sometimes covers his face or his headdress. It is easy to recognize in him one of the numerous incarnations of the weather-god, who appears in the texts as Reshep or Baal. The other most popular type shows a goddess, either dressed and carrying weapons, or naked (the naked goddess is more frequent in jewelry than in statuettes). These images were present throughout Canaanite territory, and correspond to the widespread cults of "Baals and

"Golden calf" from the weather-god temple at Byblos, seventeenth century BCE. LOUVRE MUSEUM, PARIS

Astartes" against which the prophets of Israel rose. It is also to the Baal cult that the images of the "golden calf" seem to refer. These statuettes of young bulls, made in bronze or silver, are covered with gold leaf. The biblical story of the adoration of the golden calf by the people led by Moses finds an echo in the mythological texts of Ugarit, which compare the triad of El, Baal, and Anat to an old bull, a young bull, and a heifer. Figurines of the young bull have been discovered at Ashqelon (thirteenth century), Byblos (seventeenth century), Ugarit (fourteenth–thirteenth centuries), and Emar as well. The El of the Ugaritic texts, represented as the father god, seated and giving his blessings, was also worshiped in the form of bronze and gold figurines. The statuettes representing a goddess on a throne are probably related to the cult of a companion to the father god. All these images, and there are many examples, testify to the remarkable unity of religious concepts stretching from Palestine to the Euphrates.

PAINTING

The conditions of preservation do not allow us to consider monumental painting, which the texts indicate was present on most of the edifices. The surviving examples at Mari (nineteenth–eighteenth centuries) show how black, brown, red, and sometimes green pigments were applied on the coating of white stucco that covered the mud-brick wall. The painted theme of the investiture of the king of Mari by the goddess Ishtar, of Mesopotamian inspiration, is treated with luxuriant additional motifs, including birds in stylized trees and mythological monsters. (See "Mari" in Part 5, Vol. II.) These figures, as well as the figure of the king in his characteristic tasseled dress and ovoid tiara, are found on contemporary Syrian cylinder seals. Small precious objects in faience also give a hint of what has been lost in the large-scale paintings. Some idea of the styles, the modes of composition, and the use of polychromy can be gleaned. The yellows, blues, and greens contrasting with large black zones are much evident in the faience works; on the other hand, the reds, undoubtedly present in the wall paintings, are practically unknown on Syrian faience.

Just as the "major arts," expression of a cosmopolitan cultural elite, reflect a certain Levantine artistic unity, so pottery is the expression of popular, local communities. Despite the diversity of styles and techniques, some common traits can be observed. Only a very small proportion of the enormous pottery production of the Levant has painted decoration. From the second to the first millennium, aside from the notable exception of the "bichrome" ware, which is an isolated phenomenon, the use of brown-red monochrome paint is general. The pigment is more or less dense so as to give a bichrome illusion (clear brown and dark brown) and the repertoire is extremely reduced, with a predilection for stylized floral and, occasionally, animal motifs. Rarely are there complex figurative scenes from daily life such as a *shaduf* for irrigation or subjects taken from mythology: exceptions include a vase from Kuntilat al-ʿAjrud that is painted with a scene associating Bes and Astarte, and a large goblet from Ugarit, which depicts a ruler wearing the Syrian ovoid tiara offering produce from the earth, water, and air to a god seated in front of a table laden with dishes of food. The painted "Philistine" pottery enriches this repertoire with birds inspired from the Aegean, some of which can be found on figural vases from Cyprus during and after the eleventh century. These were largely distributed on the Syro-Palestinian littoral. Pottery, the popular art par excellence, rarely reflects general tendencies of official art, and it is only on the imported ware, such as Mycenaean *kraters* of the fourteenth to thirteenth centuries, that an echo of courtly life can be found in the scenes of chariot hunting.

THE DECORATIVE ARTS

Decorative art objects that have appeared as a result of archaeological excavations confirm a taste for luxury among the Levantine elite that agrees with textual descriptions. In this domain, even more than that of monumental art, the unity reflected in luxurious furnishings is striking in these politically divided regions, where rivalries between kingdoms, cities, or tribes obliterate all consciousness of belonging to the same community. Nonetheless, at Byblos as at Ebla, at Ugarit as at Megiddo, the living and the dead surround themselves with the same artifacts, gold jewelry, alabaster tableware, and boxes of faience and ivory.

Given the homogeneous character of luxury goods, one wonders if they might be imports coming from such powerful neighbors as Egypt, where a strong artistic creativity accompanied the political supremacy exercised over the Levant. If, on the contrary, these works are the product of one or several local artistic centers, inspired when necessary by particularly appreciated foreign products, the strong resemblances between centers can perhaps be explained by the presence of itinerant artists, by the diffusion of the knowledge of masters via their apprentices, or, finally, by the circulation of drawn models.

As can be expected, the most beautiful creations of the goldsmiths were destined for royalty. It is in the princely tombs of Byblos and Ebla (nineteenth–seventeenth centuries) that one can judge the earliest examples, which often present Egyptianizing decorations. The pectoral made from embossed gold leaf from tomb III of Byblos is in the form of a falcon, the Egyptian royal emblem, spreading its wings in a frontal position. The falcon motif is also found on another pendant inscribed with the cartouche in Egyptian hieroglyphs of the king Ib-shemu-abi, from the local dynasty of Byblos (nineteenth–eighteenth centuries). The technique of this piece—gold cloisonné inlaid with colored enamels—is also of Egyptian inspiration. The tomb also contained a pair of gold sandals and a gold knife inlaid with silver; the design of waves and scales is rendered by the two metals of contrasting color. In addition to Egyptianizing works, the princely tombs of Byblos have yielded artifacts that indicate the relationship between the littoral and the Aegean world. The silver "teapot," a grooved vase with a long spout and a handle, and the silver cup decorated with spirals, from tomb I, are of Cretan inspiration. On the other hand, the narrative friezes that decorate the gold knife from the Reshep sanctuary at Byblos are specifically Levantine. The scabbard is decorated with a hunting scene inlaid in gold and silver on bronze. The main protagonist, perhaps the ruler of Byblos, is riding a donkey. The style, like the iconography, prefigures the narrative art of the ivory plaque from Megiddo, which is more recent (thirteenth century). The motif of the ruler on a donkey, a prestigious animal in the Near East before the appearance of the horse, is repeated on a bronze statuette from the Borowski collection. All the jewelry techniques are known and used at the beginning of the second millennium: cloisonné, inlay, granulation, embossing, and engraving. At Ebla, the

"Tomb of the Princess" contained bracelets, a pin made of twisted gold leaf, and earrings with a granulated decoration. In the same royal necropolis, the "Tomb of the Lord of the Goats," so named by the excavators of the Italian mission because of the crouching goats decorating the arms of a throne, was outstanding in its wealth of gold ornaments. A club handle is embellished with inlays of gold leaf in the form of monkeys adoring a solar disk. Hieroglyphs inlaid in gold leaf form the name of Hotepibreʿ, perhaps the Twelfth Dynasty pharaoh Hotepibreʿ Harnedjheriotef. It is an object imported from Egypt, perhaps a gift from the pharaoh to the ruler of Ebla. The garment of the corpse had buttons and gold leaves sewn onto it. A supple ribbon, perhaps a belt or a headband, from which hang circular medallions, is made of gold leaf decorated with filigree and granulations. The medallions, decorated in relief with granulations, depict a star with six pointed rays alternating with six globules. This motif, which can be interpreted as an astral symbol in relationship to the goddess Ishtar, is of Mesopotamian origin. It is comparable to a treasure of jewelry from the eighteenth century discovered at Larsa in Babylonia, and a necklace decorated with medallions now located in the Metropolitan Museum of Art in New York (see "Jewelry and Personal Arts in Ancient Western Asia" in Part 7, Vol. III, for an illustration of the Dilbat necklace). The Lord of the Goats tomb has also yielded a lapis lazuli

Jewelry from the royal tombs at Ebla, nineteenth to seventeenth centuries BCE. ITALIAN ARCHAEOLOGICAL MISSION, EBLA

pendant in the form of an eagle, a survival of Sumerian jewelry from the end of the third millennium. The adornment of the Ebla kings therefore combines Egyptian or Egyptianizing elements and pieces of Mesopotamian inspiration.

This diversity of technique did not last into the Late Bronze Age. Around the fifteenth century, the tombs of Tell al-ʿAjjul, in the Gaza Strip, still display the granulation technique, used on open-ring or falcon-shaped pendants. The two types of pendants that will be present in most of the wealthy tombs of the Levant until the end of the second millennium already begin to appear there. The first type of medallion has an astral motif of a star and globular planets deriving from the medallions of Larsa and Ebla. In the other type, the medallion is shaped like a rounded triangle, cut in such a way as to evoke female genitalia, and is decorated with a more-or-less stylized image of a woman. This engraved or embossed image shows a "naked goddess," sometimes holding flowers (Beth-She'an), sometimes holding serpents or goats

Gold jewelry from Ugarit depicting a naked goddess holding snakes and caprids, fourteenth to thirteenth centuries BCE. LOUVRE MUSEUM, PARIS

(Ugarit). She is sometimes reduced to just a few elements, a female mask and a pubic triangle, in some cases with the breasts and the navel represented by dots. These two types of pendants can easily be related to the planet Venus, the astral symbol of the goddesses of fecundity like Ishtar, Astarte, or Anat. They are often part of necklaces of carnelian beads that were formed in simple geometrical shapes or in the shape of poppy flowers. These high-quality creations are also astonishingly uniform in their style, technique, and iconography and are dispersed throughout a vast geographical area covering all the Syro-Palestinian littoral and Cyprus at the end of the second millennium.

In addition to this jewelry, some rare vessels in precious metals have come down to us; their small number contrasts with the large numbers mentioned in the texts. One tablet establishes the trousseau inventory of Queen Akhatmilku, the bride of a king of Ugarit:

A cup, a dish, a golden carafe, weighing 80 shekels . . . silver cups, weighing 1070 shekels . . . x bronze basins weighing 3 talents, x bronze plates, weighing 2 talents 1500 shekels, x bronze jars weighing 1 talent, five bronze pitchers, weighing 1 talent 600 shekels, . . . four bronze perfume pans weighing 1200 shekels, nine bronze crucibles with their bowls weighing 900 shekels, twenty bronze cups weighing 600 shekels, seven damper-lids (?) weighing 500 shekels.
(From Claude Schaeffer, *Le palais royal d'Ugarit*, vol. 3, 1955, pp. 182–186)

Their location and, in the case of figurative vessels, the iconography, relate such precious vessels to the royal court and family. The treasure of the level VII palace of Megiddo contained items of Egyptian inspiration: jewelry; a gold, shell-shaped bowl; and a cosmetic jar in obsidian encircled with gold and little Hathor-like masks in gold. The two gold cups discovered near the temple of Baal at Ugarit were probably offered to the god Baal by a royal person. These two cups seem complementary. One is hemispherical, embossed from the inside toward the outside, with a dense composition in concentric registers. The other, with a flat base and vertical sides, is decorated from the outside toward the inside with a clearly outlined hunting scene. The hero, perhaps a mythical king, shows his ability to drive his chariot, the reins passed through his belt, while his two arms are occupied with drawing his bow. The frantic chase after the game of wild bulls and goats, starting in front of the chariot, ends in a circle behind the hunter; there, a huge old bull charges the chariot with lowered horns.

This motif of the charging bull has an identical parallel on an ivory game box sculpted with a chariot hunting scene, which comes from Enkomi, Cyprus. Such details indicate the probable existence of drawn models for figurative compositions. A younger, slimmer male prevents the escape of a cow accompanied by her calf. This realistic image, which is one of a number of royal hunting scenes known from the Levant, probably hides a mythological allusion: the old god El and the young Baal are often described as "divine bulls" in the Ugaritic poems, and Anat is characterized as a "heifer." More than a simple hunt, the diversion of an elite, the cup illustrates the relationships between gods and humans. These relationships figure on the second gold cup from Ugarit with a frieze composition and iconography that evoke the art of the Syrian cylinder seals. The friezes, for example, are bordered with a row of pomegranates, in the Orient the symbolic fruit of fertility. A series of mythological combats between anthropomorphic heroes and monsters represents the confrontation between the forces of wild nature and those of a mythical humanity from the earliest ages. In the central register, bulls and lions passing under rows of pomegranates discreetly indicate the complicity between the gods and royal power.

The cup with bulls' heads executed in silver and inlaid with niello and gold discovered in a thirteenth-century tomb from Enkomi, Cyprus, carries over into precious metals one of the most popular local pottery types, the "milk bowl," with its characteristic wishbone handle. The frieze decorating the bowl displays bulls' heads seen from the front; the horns outline a large circle and small flowers are placed between the main motifs. The composition and the motif of a bull with large horns are of an Aegean inspiration (compare the frescoes of Knossos or Mycenaean vase painting, an example of which appears in "The 'Sea Peoples'" in Part 5, Vol. II), but the dots around the rim recall the stylization of Amarna painting from Egypt. Certain of these

stylistic elements can also be found in inland Syria, for example, on a fresco at Nuzi (Nuzu, modern Yorghun Tepe).

The mastering of vitreous materials is one of the triumphs of Levantine craftsmanship. The first technical developments obtained with sand and lime did not become the custom until the third millennium when these materials were used to make beads and small frit amulets. It is only during the first half of the second millennium that faience, and later glass, was commonly used to make larger objects such as vases or cosmetic boxes. In Palestine, Jericho, and Tell al-Far'a, this development was undoubtedly influenced by the Egyptian production of faience statuettes and containers during the Middle Kingdom. Initially imported, these works were then imitated locally. The same shapes and decorative techniques as in Egypt are found: little oval, narrow-necked bottles; conical goblets; lenticular flasks garnished with lotus petals drawn in black on a copper-blue background. At Byblos, statuettes of hippopotamuses and monkeys are also of Egyptian inspiration. In the north, as early as the seventeenth to sixteenth centuries at Ugarit, Alalakh, or Ebla, original figural shapes appear. The goblet in the shape of a woman's head from Ebla is the oldest known specimen of a series that becomes characteristic of the Late Bronze Age. The laboratory analyses carried out on the Ugaritic material show that the pieces were produced locally. Recipes for producing the color black (obtained with ferrous manganese) remain the same during the following periods.

At the height of the palatial civilization of the fourteenth to twelfth centuries, the number of faience vessels and statuettes increases and the social range of the owners of these luxury products broadens. From then on they can be found in private tombs and homes as well as in palaces and temples. The geographical distribution also broadens. Some types, like the goblets in the form of a feminine head or animal-head rhytons, can be found on Cyprus (Kition, Enkomi), on the Syrian (Ugarit) and Palestinian (Tell Abu Hawam) littorals, on the middle Euphrates (Emar), or as far as the Tigris (Asshur). The examples found on the shipwreck off the southern coast of Turkey, at Ulu Burun, show that these artifacts traveled on long-distance maritime

Faience vase in the form of a head of a woman from Minat al-Beyda, thirteenth century BCE. LOUVRE MUSEUM, PARIS

community of decorative shapes, and perhaps of thought, flourished during the second millennium. The Levant figures as a motor and a creative center rather than following in the wake of Egypt or Mesopotamia.

During the first millennium, after the disappearance of the palatial civilization around 1150, the faience makers' workshops, although they did not stop producing, waned in favor of glassmakers. The technique of making glass around a metal core lasted until the Greek conquest, and innovations like cut glass (from the eighth century onward) and then blown glass (from the Persian period?) secured the international reputation of the Levantine workshops.

Ivory carving was one of the major artistic expressions of the Levant. It appears as early as the Chalcolithic period in the Negev and the Dead Sea regions. The first artisans were expert in the use of hippopotamus ivory, skillfully employing parts of the canines and lower incisors. The presence of the hippopotamus is an indication of the southern Palestinian climate, fauna, and environment during these periods, as well as the relationship to the Nile Valley and protodynastic Egyptian art. During the Early Bronze Age (end of the third and beginning of the second millennium), this traditional craft continued in the southern Levant. Jericho, Ai, and Khirbet Kerak yielded furniture ornaments in the shape of bulls' or lions' heads. At the same time, craftsmen in inland and northern Syria preferred to use shell for making amulets and furniture appliqués; apparently, they were unacquainted with ivory. With the flourishing of international art at the end of the Late Bronze Age, there was a spectacular blooming of ivory work mainly based on hippopotamus tusks. The study of bone remains shows that the hippopotamus still lived in the swampy deltas of the little coastal rivers of Syria and Palestine. However, the pieces of exceptional size and quality are sculpted from elephant tusks. This rich ivory production in the Levant raises the problem of the Syrian elephant, whose presence is attested both in archaeological and faunal analyses as well as the royal hunting texts of the Egyptian and Assyrian kings. Its progressive disappearance at the end of the second millennium is probably due to extensive hunting and the deforestation brought about by the exploitation of the forests for timber. Appar-

trade routes, perhaps from (or toward) Cyprus, or toward Greece. Pendants in the shape of a feminine mask, made in faience inlaid with colored glaze, are another favorite type of object. Their symbolic significance is probably analogous to that of the gold medallions mentioned above. They are present from Cyprus (Hala Sultan Teke) to as far as Iran (Susa), passing along the Euphrates (Mari) and through Babylonia (Tell al-Rimah). The cups with a polychrome floral decoration, which juxtapose the yellow of lead antimony with the clear green of copper and the black of iron manganese, follow the same broad geographical distribution, with a heavy concentration on the Syrian littoral. It is probable that more than one local workshop operated in the centers and capitals of the numerous states strewn across this immense territory. But, concerning the minor arts, and particularly the faience technique, it is interesting to note that a

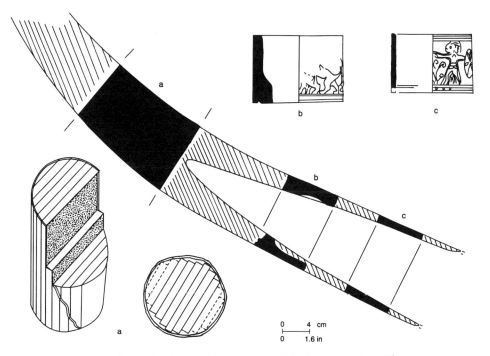

Diagram showing how elephant tusks were used in ivory carving. Plaques were cut from the solid part of the tusk (a), while the hollow portions (because of marrow cavity) were crafted to obtain thick-walled (b) or thin-walled (c) cylindrical pyxides (cosmetic boxes). DRAWING BY CAROLINE FLORIMONT, LOUVRE MUSEUM, PARIS

ently it was necessary to compensate for the lack of local resources by importing unworked tusks from Africa via Egypt and harbor cities like Ugarit.

The most characteristic examples of ivory works have been found in the private tombs of Ugarit, Megiddo, and Lachish. The spindle whorls, different small instruments, toilet articles, combs, and cosmetic or perfume boxes all point to a feminine clientele. The cylindrical or lenticular boxes have pivoting lids. The box shaped like a mother duck turning her neck to watch the baby ducks she carries on her back, undoubtedly of Egyptian inspiration, is a skillful use of the hippopotamus canine and its curve. The popularity of this shape is attested in the numerous examples found in the Levant at Alalakh, Ugarit, Kamid al-Loz, Acco, Megiddo, Enkomi, as well as among exports; it has been found in inland Syria (Tell Brak) as well as in Greece (Tiryns).

In the palaces, and sometimes in the sanctuaries, where they were undoubtedly royal offerings, the most valuable artifacts must have been the property of princesses. Ancient texts refer to these goods. For example, the trousseau of Queen Akhatmilku of Ugarit consisted of "three ivory-encrusted beds with their footstools . . . an ebony ivory-encrusted chair, with footstool . . . twenty ivory cosmetic boxes, four ivory salt cellars."

The ivory treasure of the level VIIB palace at Megiddo contained a pen box with a hieroglyphic inscription indicating that it belonged to "The Lady Kerker, the chief singer of Ptah of Ashqelon." In Egypt, this sacred title was reserved for women of royal blood; here it probably refers to a Canaanite princess. The furniture, like that of Queen Akhatmilku, was made of wood decorated with ivory; the wood has since disappeared, but sometimes the decorative plaques survive. The iconography of these furniture plaques is very homogeneous: sphinxes, the Egyptianized demon Bes, palmettes (see "Furniture in Ancient Western Asia" in Part 7, Vol. III). The headboard of a bed from Ugarit presents one of the rare narrative friezes. The only other examples are the Megiddo plaques and the En-

Ivory lid of a pyxis depicting possibly a goddess feeding caprids from Ugarit, thirteenth century BCE. LOUVRE MUSEUM, PARIS

komi game box. The headboard consists of a series of vertical panels and a large horizontal board, each of which corresponds to the width of the plaques sawed out of a single large elephant tusk. The horizontal frieze is decorated with a deer-hunting scene. On the panels, servants bow in front of a royal personage who wears an Egyptian crown and is represented in different aspects: as a hunter, as the lover of a beautiful young woman, as a warrior. In the center, a winged goddess, whose headdress recalls that of the Egyptian Hathor, nurses two young princes. The duplication of the prince is perhaps necessary for reasons of symmetry, unless it is an allusion to a mythological episode from the Ugaritic texts that mentions twin princes of divine origin. This superb piece, in an Egyptian style, is undoubtedly the work of a local artist drawing his inspiration from the royal ideology.

The most beautiful plaque from Megiddo, also discovered in the thirteenth-century palace, probably decorated a chest or a game box. It also depicts a scene exalting royal power. The ruler is represented twice. On the right, he is a conqueror who parades in his chariot, preceded by his vanquished enemies, naked and chained; on the left, he appears in majesty, seated on his throne while he is being offered a musical ban-

quet. The Enkomi game box, discovered in an exceptionally rich tomb, is not necessarily a royal furnishing, although the iconography of its decoration relates it to the two preceding pieces. A checkerboard is engraved on the upper side; it is a "game of twenty squares" well known in the Egyptian world of the New Kingdom. On the long sides are two chariot-hunting scenes. Bulls and deer are led by a figure drawing a bow, while a little stooped charioteer leads the armored horses. In front of them another hunter, on foot, stabs a lion with his lance. He wears a headdress, as does a second person on foot carrying a hatchet. The headdress is a sort of feathered crest on top of his head, resembling the headdress of the Sea Peoples represented on the temple of Ramesses (Ramses) III at Medinet Habu. This detail suggests that the protagonists sculpted on the Enkomi box are related to the elite warriors who took over the Levant during the twelfth century, soon to assimilate the cultural inheritance of the past. The image of the old wounded bull charging the chariot of his attacker, so similar to that on the gold cup from Ugarit, shows that these works were created by talented artists who were educated in the same traditions, who drew from the same sources of inspiration, and who worked for royal clients.

The social, political, and religious mutations that took place around 1200—the crisis of the Sea Peoples and the arrival of the Philistines—profoundly modified the geopolitical map. Consequently, the tastes and demands of the clients changed considerably. In the domain of ivory carving, which developed brilliantly during the ninth to seventh centuries, the technical traditions inherited from the Late Bronze Age were perpetuated, but not the sources providing the raw material. Henceforth, the ivory carvers used, almost exclusively, imported, unworked elephant tusks. Distribution of the goods seems from then on restricted to the royal sector. We know these treasures from the booty accumulated by the Assyrians when they conquered the Levant. The types of works indicate a masculine rather than a feminine clientele. They retain, however, a feminine connotation if one judges from the pejorative passage of the Bible that describes Ahab, the king of Samaria, as leading an effeminate life in his "ivory house" (1 Kings 22). The discoveries of the excavations at Sama-

Ivory plaque from Arslan Taş, depicting winged genies at the birth of the infant-god, nineteenth century BCE. LOUVRE MUSEUM, PARIS

ria illustrate this text. One official building yielded furniture appliqués and chests decorated with Egyptian motifs: winged genies, sphinxes. This same iconography appears everywhere in the Syro-Phoenician world. At Arslan Taş (ancient Khadatu) one of the ivory plaques is carved with an inscription of the name of Lord Hazael, no doubt the king of Damascus, which was allied to Samaria. It shows how these precious objects were likely to circulate from one court to another, either as gifts or as booty. The ivory furniture and utensils piled in the storerooms of the Assyrian palaces of Nimrud show that, during the epoch of Assurnasirpal II (883–859) and Shalmaneser III (858–824), the courts of the different indigenous kingdoms rivaled each other in luxuries before being gradually conquered by the Assyrian powers. The study of these ivories, in particular those of Nimrud, brings to light the existence of several distinct workshops, difficult to localize, working from the tenth century to the end of the seventh century. On Cyprus, during the brief period of Assyrian hegemony on the island, pieces of ivory furniture were deposited in the princely tombs at Salamis, Tamassos, and Paphos alongside weapons and bronze vessels of a splendor recalling the Homeric description of the funeral of Patroklos.

GLYPTICS

The birth and development of the art of cylinder seals in Syro-Palestine, from the end of the third millennium onward and during the whole Bronze Age, is yet another example of the cultural unity of these countries. The use of the cylinder seal supposes, in fact, identical administrative functions as well as the direction of the economy by central powers and their deputies; the introduction of this system to the Levant was the result of the economic and cultural expansion of Mesopotamia from the dynasty of Akkad and Ur III shortly before 2000. The engraved decoration on the Syro-Palestinian seals demonstrates the existence of a political and religious ideology inspired by Mesopotamia. Several main centers of engraving coexisted. From the end of the third millennium on, at Byblos and at Alalakh, the inspiration was drawn from a Mes-

2689

opotamian repertoire, to which were added Egyptianizing elements. At Ebla, the presence of cylinder seals in wood shows the probable existence of supports other than stone. During the first centuries of the second millennium, the influences created by the implantation of Assyrian colonies in Cappadocia favored the development of a style of glyptic characterized by the juxtaposition of miniaturist motifs; this style spread to Alalakh and crossed over to northern Syria. At Ugarit and Alalakh another style, derived from Babylonian models, reflects a brilliance of quality and imagination in the decor; one common figure is the ruler worshiping divinities, among whom the naked goddess and the weather-god are the most popular (an example is shown in "Cylinder Seals and Scarabs" in Part 7, Vol. III). At the apogee of the kingdom of Mitanni, which exercised its hegemony over the Levant toward the middle of the second millennium, an international style appears, with stereotyped motifs. Hard stone is replaced, from then on, by frit or faience, which could be mass-produced. These changes in style and the considerable increase in the number of seals in circulation can be related to the extension of administrative control over larger strata of social classes.

The cultural unity manifested in the Bronze Age glyptic lasted through the first millennium, but the technique of cylinder seals was progressively replaced by that of stamp seals with a lenticular shape, perhaps borrowed from the Egyptian scarab. The religious iconography remains varied in this reduced format: offering scenes, the sacred tree, astral symbols, and animal or mythological motifs persist. The image is often accompanied by an inscription, usually the name of the owner. This is often a member of a royal family or a high-ranking official. The names are those of dignitaries from Phoenicia, Aram, Israel, and Moab. Before the appearance of coinage, cylinder seals provide a precious source of information concerning the political history of the times. The Macedonian conquest, by opening the Levant to Greek administrative customs, brought this ancient tradition to an end.

The Levant, from its Bronze Age origins to the Greek conquest, is a remarkable bouquet of contradictions. It is surprising that a society divided in its political, ethnic, and religious spheres, could express such a cultural and artistic unity, a unity mainly observable in its official monuments and prestige items. Such a specifically original character is also surprising in a region so open, even subjected, to the influences of the great neighboring powers.

This unified character is expressed in shapes, techniques, and imagery. Certain identical types of public or private monumental architecture, sanctuaries, palaces, and built tombs can be found in places very distant from each other. Sophisticated techniques—faience, metallurgy, and particularly those concerning precious metals—are mastered from one end to the other of the Levant and are easily distinguishable from Egyptian or Mesopotamian styles. Carving using hippopotamus ivory is specifically Levantine. The sources of raw materials, the use of the materials, the types of objects created, and the choice of decorations give a characteristic physiognomy to the creations of Syro-Palestine. These technical and artistic traditions are of lasting quality and are often preserved until the Islamic epoch.

The unity of the imagery reflects a homogeneous type of courtly society trying to express its aspirations through the possession of prestigious works and rare or exotic products. This society, enmeshed in a network of international ties, ensured a wide distribution of the artistic creations that it gave rise to. In return, it was open to outside influences—factors of diversity and renewal. The artists of the Levant showed remarkable capacities for assimilation as well as for developing their own forms while borrowing from the dominant cultural powers of Egypt, Mesopotamia, and the Aegean world.

Translated from the French by Valery Cook

BIBLIOGRAPHY

International Art

CLAUDE BAURAIN, *Chypre et la Méditerranée orientale au Bronze Récent: synthèse historique*, Études Chypriotes, vol. 6 (1984); and E. PELTENBURG, "Ramesside Egypt and Cyprus," in *Acts of the International Archaeological Symposium "Cyprus Between the*

Orient and the Occident," Nicosia, 8–14, Sept. 1985, edited by V. KARAGEORGHIS (1986).

Architecture and Urbanism

OLIVIER CALLOT, Ras Shamra Ougarit, vol. 1, Une maison à Ougarit (1983); JEAN MARGUERON, "Emar: Un exemple d'implantation hittite en terre syrienne," Le Moyen Euphrate, zone de contacts et d'échanges: actes du Colloque de Strasbourg, 10–14 mars 1977 (1980), "Un exemple d'urbanism volontaire à l'époque du Bronze Récent en Syrie," Ktèma 2 (1977); and "Un 'hilāni' à Emar," Annual of the American Schools of Oriental Research 44 (1977); MARGUERITE YON, PIERRE LOMBARD, and MARGO RENISIO, "L'organisation de l'habitat," in Ras Shamra Ougarit, vol. 3, Le Centre de la ville (1987).

Sites

ALALAKH

LEONARD WOOLLEY, Alalakh: An Account of the Excavations at Tel Atchana in the Hatay, 1937–1949 (1955).

BYBLOS

NINA JIDEJIAN, Byblos Through the Ages (1968).

CARCHEMISH

J. D. HAWKINS, "Karkamiš," Reallexikon der Assyriologie, vol. 5 (1976–1980).

CYPRUS

JACQUES-CLAUDE COURTOIS, ELISABETH LAGARCE, and JACQUES LAGARCE, Enkomi et le Bronze Récent à Chypre (1986); VASSOS KARAGEORGHIS, ed., Excavations at Kition, vols. 1–5 (1974–1985); FRANZ GEORG MAIER and VASSOS KARAGEORGHIS, Paphos (1984).

EMAR

DOMINIQUE BEYER, ed., Meskéné Emar. Dix ans de travaux, 1972–1982 (1982).

EBLA

PAOLO MATTHIAE, Ebla: un impero ritrovato (1977).

KAMID EL LOZ–KUMIDI

ROLF HACHMANN, Frühe Phöniker im Libanon (1983).

LACHISH

OLGA TUFNELL ET AL., Lachish, vol. 2., The Fosse Temple (1940); Y. AHARONI, D. USSISHKIN, and OLGA TUFNELL, "Lachish," Encyclopedia of Archaeological Excavations in the Holy Land, vol. 3 (1977).

MEGIDDO

Y. YADIN, "Megiddo," Encyclopedia of Archaeological Excavations in the Holy Land, vol. 3 (1977).

UGARIT

MARGUERITE YON, ed., Ras Shamra Ougarit, vols. 1–9 (1983–1992).

Sculpture

MARGUERITE YON, "Les stèles de pierre," in Ras Shamra Ougarit, vol. 6, Arts et industries de la pierre (1991).

Decorative Arts

ANNIE CAUBET, "Ivoires de Cappadoce," in D. CHARPIN and F. JOANNÈS, eds., Marchands, diplomates, et Em- Shamra Ougarit, vol. 3, Le Centre de la ville (1985); ANNIE CAUBET, "Ivoires de Cappadoce," in D. CHARPIN and F. JOANNÈS, eds., Marchands, diplomates, et Empereurs (1991); GORDON LOUD, The Megiddo Ivories, University of Chicago Oriental Institute Publications, vol. 52 (1939); E. PELTENBURG, "The Glazed Vases," in Excavations at Kition, vol. 1, The Tombs (1974).

Cylinder Seals

P. AMIET, Ras Shamra Ougarit, vol. 9, Sceaux cylindres en hématite et pierres diverses (1992); DOMINIQUE COLLON, First Impressions: Cylinder Seals in the Ancient Near East (1987).

SEE ALSO **Palaces and Temples in Canaan and Ancient Israel** (Part 4, Vol. I) and **The History of Ancient Syria and Palestine: An Overview** (Part 5, Vol. II).

11

Retrospective Essays

Understanding Ancient Near Eastern Art: A Personal Account

EDITH PORADA

EDITH PORADA *Born in Vienna in 1912, Edith Porada received her Ph.D. from its University where, as a student of Viktor Christian, she began her lifelong study of ancient near eastern seal stones. After coming to the United States, Dr. Porada catalogued the near eastern seals in the collection of the Pierpont Morgan Library. The* Corpus of Near Eastern Seals in North American Collections, *published in 1948, remains a seminal work. Dr. Porada was named Honorary Curator of Seals and Tablets at the Morgan Library in 1956. Her teaching career began at Queens College, City University of New York; after 1958 she taught in the Department of Art History and Archaeology, Columbia University, where she was Arthur Lehman Professor of Art History and Archaeology. Her many honors, including the Award for Distinguished Archaeological Achievement from the Archaeological Institute of America, were tribute to Dr. Porada's vast knowledge, pioneering research, and abundant publications on near eastern art especially as expressed through cylinder seals. Until her death on March 24, 1994, Dr. Porada contributed imaginatively to a field of study she had founded in the United States.*

In writing a personal statement about my career in the field of ancient near eastern art, I will relate how my own studies progressed over half a century and explain my current views on some masterpieces from Mesopotamia. In discussing these artifacts I will cite the views and reactions of the early art historians who were the first to comment on great works of ancient near eastern art that were being revealed in the excavations. I do so because I want to draw attention to the work and insights of these previous generations of art historians and to show how each generation builds on the achievements of its predecessors.

For as long as I can remember, whether it was in the townhouse in Vienna or in my father's hunting lodge in the summers, I have liked things that could tell me something about their past, like petrified shells or stones.

In Vienna, archaeology is under one's feet. The camp of Emperor Marcus Aurelius was in what is now the center of town; and—much to the annoyance of the local taxi industry—excavations of Roman buildings are being carried out at present on the Michaeler Platz, a major thoroughfare in the inner city. My father encouraged my archaeological interests, and for my tenth birthday gave me a mammoth's tooth, one of several that had been found in the coal mines on whose administrative council he served.

While I was still in the Gymnasium (which in Europe corresponds to the American high school), the International Congress of Orientalists, which is held in a different European city every four years, met in Vienna. A distant cousin of my mother's, a professor of Arabic literature, came from Germany to attend this congress and suggested that I come along to some of the lectures. The one I remember was by Ernst Herzfeld, who reported on the excavation by Max, Baron Oppenheim at the site of Tell Halaf (Gozan, Bit-Bakhiani) in northern Syria. At that site was found pottery that we now know was from the fifth millennium BCE, as well as carved reliefs of the early first millennium, though the latter may have been made somewhat earlier. Herzfeld insisted that both reliefs and pottery were of the fourth millennium, as early as scholars were then willing to place objects that showed some technical skill. This claim aroused a violent debate, and I still see some of the bearded gentlemen walking out of the hall, shaking their heads and expressing doubts about Herzfeld's sanity.

I had lunch with my cousin, the Egyptologist Wilhelm von Bissing, and a third scholar whose name I cannot recall. At that luncheon my future was determined. The cousin, who had been informed by the family that I wanted to study archaeology, asked in which area I was planning to concentrate. "Crete and Mycenae," I radiantly answered. "Out of the question," thundered the cousin. "That field is overrun. You will study the ancient Near East. Your professor will be Viktor Christian."

I did exactly as I was told and went to see Professor Christian after I had finished the Gymnasium. Christian was even more precise than my cousin. He told me then and there that I would be working on seals of the Akkad period (circa 2340–2150), especially because the cousin's sister had a collection of ancient near eastern seals, dating from the third to the first millennium. As I think this over, it seems to me that there must have been some collusion, those sixty years ago, among the professors, who all knew one another as we, professors of near eastern studies in various countries, know one another

now. They had decided that a young, eager student was needed to work on the most abundant material of ancient near eastern art, the engraved seal stones, specifically on those which showed the most interesting representations, the cylinder seals of the dynasty of Akkad. Today my only regret is that I cannot start again on what is still the most interesting field, still waiting to be fully explored and understood.

Later, my background knowledge of seals enabled me to undertake the catalog of the collection of the Pierpont Morgan Library at the request of Belle da Costa Greene, the first director of the library. As I prepared the case for the 1991 exhibition of Masterpieces in the Pierpont Morgan Library, I gratefully thought of Miss Greene, who in 1946 entrusted to a young, unknown foreigner the work on what was then the greatest and finest private collection of cylinder seals, paralleled only by those of the British Museum and the Louvre. I was quite conscious then of the fact that such generous faith in an untried young scholar was possible only in the United States—and this I still believe.

At the University of Vienna, where I studied from 1930 to 1935, Viktor Christian taught Sumerian and Akkadian. It was a foregone conclusion that I would have to study the languages, though my memory is better for pictures than for words. Sumerian is an agglutinative language in which various elements of both meaning and grammatical relations are strung together. Writing may have been invented to serve Sumerian, though some scholars believe that an earlier language underlies the development of writing. If this was the case, writing was certainly modified at a subsequent stage to serve Sumerian. At first, single pictorial forms constituted the majority of the signs. The meaning of the pictorial form was expressed by words whose sounds were later used as syllables in writing abstract concepts. No change in the radicals of a Sumerian word expressed a concept of time. Specifications like time or person could be indicated only with prefixes or suffixes. (See the article by D. O. Edzard in Part 9 in this volume).

This basic structure of writing and language has always impressed me as a parallel to the structure of early Mesopotamian art. In figure 1 each characteristic element of the human head—its outline, its nose, eye, ear, lips, and

Fig. 1. Fragment of a limestone votive plaque of Eannatum I or II, Lagash, circa 2450 BCE. BRITISH MUSEUM, LONDON

chin—has its own distinctive form that is added to the others to create the timeless head of the ruler of Lagash, Eannatum (I or II), dated approximately 2450.

Akkadian, the second major language used in Mesopotamia, belongs to the family of Semitic languages, which seems to have a structure in which the basic elements are roots of three consonants that are manipulated by additions, doubling, and vowels to give rise to a vast number of derivative words in various tenses. The most dramatic representation of the ancient Near East, the victory stela of Naram-Sin of Akkad in the Louvre, appears to parallel the flexibility and the vitality of the Akkadian language. (The Stela

is pictured in "Aesthetics in Ancient Mesopotamian Art" in Part 10.)

Christian had a strong interest in archaeology and gave at least one course in that field in which he presented the available material, which he had carefully collected from the few publications of excavations available during my years of study in Vienna.

Excavations had started shortly before the middle of the nineteenth century at the Assyrian palaces of Kalkhu (modern Nimrud), Dur-Sharrukin (modern Khorsabad), and Nineveh (by Mosul) dated between about 880 and the destruction of Nineveh in 612. To the images of the Assyrians from the accounts of the Hebrew

Bible and the Greek historians, they brought the reality of the art created by the Assyrians who were responsible for the military installations, the battles, and the rituals and processions of the empire and its peoples.

With some gaps in the sequence of excavations as the result of financial and political constraints, there was a continuation of expeditions to Mesopotamia by the Americans (University of Pennsylvania, 1888–1898, to Nippur, modern Nuffar), by the French (1877–1933) to Tello (then thought to have been the town of Lagash, now known to have been the sanctuary site of Girsu), and by the Germans at Babylon (near modern Hilla, 1899–1917) and Asshur (modern Qalat Sharqat).

General interest in the excavated material of the texts, written in cuneiform on stone slabs and clay tablets, was far greater than in the statuary, reliefs, and seals that were being unearthed. The connection, actual or imagined, of the texts with those of the Hebrew Scripture—for example, an epic that contains elements of the deluge story—doubtless accounted for this widespread interest, which extended even to Gilbert and Sullivan, who had the major general in their *Pirates of Penzance* say, "I can write a washing bill in cuneiform."

The early history and evaluation of ancient Mesopotamian art were the work of scholars who had been trained in Greek art. Three individuals stand out. The first is Léon Alexandre Heuzey, whose earlier work had been in excavations in Macedonia and who had written on Greek statuary and terra-cottas. He devised an initial chronology of Mesopotamian art on the basis of the rather cursory French excavation reports of the site of Tello in southern Iraq in the book on which he collaborated with Ernest de Sarzec. In a book entitled *The Oriental Origins of Art* he reproduced, side by side, an Egyptian slate palette and a cylinder seal of about 3000, both showing monsters consisting of lions' bodies and serpents' necks, to illustrate the relation of these early cultures. This relation has been confirmed only since 1987, on the basis of remains of architectural painted cones of a type known from Susa in southwest Iran that were found at Buto in the Nile Delta. Heuzey's pioneering work was followed by two significant commentaries on the art of the ancient Near East, both appended to a far larger section on the art of Egypt: Walter

Andrae's "Die Kunst Vorderasiens," which followed Heinrich Schäfer's "Die Kunst Ägyptens" and Ludwig Curtius's "Vorderasien."

Andrae's was a very personal account, informed by his intimate knowledge of the countries that produced ancient near eastern art. His gradual approach to this art is interesting to observe. In speaking about one of his early excavations in Mesopotamia, he described his pleasure at finding Hellenistic-looking object among all the foreign-looking ones that were being turned up. The Hellenistic object was immediately intelligible to his Greek-trained eye, whereas at that stage in his career the ancient Mesopotamian works seemed dark and foreign.

Influenced by Heuzey's general chronological indications, Andrae divided the Mesopotamian material into an early period of the fourth millennium, followed by the works of the Akkad (Agade) and Gudea periods, which he called the golden age of Mesopotamia and dated in the middle of the third millennium. These dates are several hundred years earlier than the present datings; his dates for the late period in Babylonia and Assyria—the late second and early first millennia BCE—were like those now accepted.

Andrae recognized fine pottery as the artistic manifestation of the early period, not realizing the difference in time between the fifth-millennium pottery of Halaf and the fourth-millennium pottery of the Susa I period, which he considered the finest.

When he wrote his essay, Andrae thought that the earliest period known to him had no real architecture, that in the early third millennium BCE there were only reed huts. But he lived to learn of the magnificent temples built at Uruk (modern Warka) five hundred years earlier. One of Andrae's observations was the importance of the central courtyard around which rooms were built, an arrangement that lasted until the late Assyrian period. The main room lay on the south side. The oldest bricks known to Andrae were plano-convex, now known to have been introduced about 2900 BCE (though earlier ones of different types have since been identified).

Andrae saw the height of Mesopotamian art in the period of the Akkad Dynasty, represented by the victory stela of Naram-Sin, discovered at Susa, where it had been taken as booty from the sun-god's center of Sippar (modern Abu Habba)

in Babylonia. He also knew several of the magnificent cylinder seals of the period to which Joachim Ménant had drawn attention in one of the first books that used photographic reproductions for ancient near eastern cylinder-seal impressions.

Andrae linked the sculptures of Gudea (circa 2150; shown in "Proportions in Ancient Near Eastern Art" in Part 10, Vol. IV) with those of the period of the Akkad Dynasty (circa 2340–2150), in the golden age of Mesopotamia. The last work included by Andrae in his golden age was the stela with the law code of Hammurabi (pictured in "King Hammurabi of Babylon" in Part 5, Vol. II) which he lauded for its naturalism and precise rendering of the figures' profile views.

Andrae's suggestion of the existence of goldsmiths' work in the late period, for which he had very little factual proof but for which he assumed an international guild, reads almost like a presentiment of the gold treasures found in 1989 and 1990 by the Iraqi Antiquities Service in the tombs of Assyrian queens at Nimrud (fig. 2).

Fig. 2. Gold necklace ornamented with sixty-five bells from a tomb excavated at Nimrud. BARRY IVERSON/TIME MAGAZINE

In the discussion of the Assyrian reliefs Andrae showed his sensitive reaction to ancient near eastern art in his appreciation of the reliefs of Assurnasirpal II (883–859) (fig. 3). He spoke of the massive fullness of the figures, which never appear fat and mushy. He called it a style comparable only with the works of Michelangelo. Andrae devoted great care and understanding to the Late Hittite and Aramaean reliefs and sculptures in the round. By the time he wrote about these works, he had fully accepted the aesthetics of ancient near eastern art.

In contrast with Andrae, who was primarily an architect and may be said to have influenced the predominance of architecture in German archaeology, Ludwig Curtius was a historian of Greek and Roman art. His searching analysis of Egyptian and western Asiatic art was sparked by his desire to learn about the foreign influences on Greek art in the eighth and seventh centuries BCE. He therefore made a thorough study of the Assyrian reliefs, especially of the battle and hunting scenes, in which he made important statements about the pictorial structure of the representations.

Among the reliefs he chose for reproduction in *Antike Kunst* was one from the series in the palace throne-room of Assurnasirpal II at Nimrud (Kalkhu; known in the Bible as Calah), which shows fugitives swimming toward a city surrounded by water now is identified by Irene J. Winter as Carchemish (Karkamish) (fig. 4). Curtius described the relief as showing a unified perspective with a high viewpoint. He drew attention to the manner in which the single elements were reduced to their essential form to appear like symbols: the rocky embankment and the fortress, the trees, each single rippling wave, the archers and the garrison of the fortress. For such precise renderings of military undertakings Curtius used the descriptive term "annals written in pictures."

Even more obviously pictorial annals are seen in the bronze strips from the gates of Imgur-Enlil (modern Balawat), dating to the reign of Assurnasirpal's son Shalmaneser III (858–824), from which Curtius chose to reproduce the representation of the king at the source of the Tigris. He pointed out that this Assyrian creation of continuous historical narrative must have emerged from a specifically historical sense and

Fig. 3. Detail from an alabaster wall relief of Assurnasirpal II showing head and hands of Assurnasirpal and the hand of his cupbearer, from Nimrud, 885–860 BCE. METROPOLITAN MUSEUM OF ART, NEW YORK

Fig. 4. Relief of fugitives crossing a river at Carchemish from a wall of Assurnasirpal's throne room, Nimrud. BRITISH MUSEUM, LONDON

that it is not found again until the columns of Trajan and Marcus Aurelius. (See "Art and Ideology in Ancient Western Asia" in Part 10 for a scene from the Balawat Gates.)

Curtius found that the most grandiose attempts at constructing a new pictorial unit belonged to the art of kings Sennacherib (704–681) and Assurbanipal (668–627). Curtius assumed that there was only one palace at Nineveh, now called the Southwest Palace of Sennacherib, which Assurbanipal used before building his own North Palace.

The constraint of the single band of representation was abandoned in Sennacherib's reliefs in favor of a general mountainous background. Curtius was reminded of the Naram-Sin stela as well as of medieval paintings that show the sleeping apostles with Christ in the Garden of Gethsemane, all occupying the same landscape. Curtius called this the contracting manner of representation, which he also claimed to be an Assyrian discovery. The best example is the scene of the transport of a bull colossus (shown in "Material, Technology, and Techniques in Artistic Production" in Part 7, Vol. III). Above is a strip of the mountainous landscape with trees rendered with botanical accuracy. Below, another band shows the royal guardsmen. This, said Curtius, was still the old manner of representation, but now a completely new image appears: a great scene is viewed from a high vantage point. Far below is a river, and—the beginning of true perspective—the water scoopers are rendered at half the size of the other figures on the bank between the river and the canal. As Curtius pointed out, ancient art never again came as close to the solution of perspective. This image belongs to a large sequence, not entirely preserved, which shows the transport of a great, crudely blocked-out bull colossus, coming from the quarry on a path both on land and in the water.

According to Curtius, the battle and hunting scenes were themes taken over from the archaic style. In the representations of technical procedures, however, the interest of the period itself is evident. The Assyrian king enjoyed feelings of domination not only in military campaigns east and west but also in organizing vast building activities. This image, too, has its dramatic tension, which is expressed in the movements of

the engineers atop the colossus, and the effect is all the more visible because of the austere and factual rendering of the event.

In 1987, knowledge of Sennacherib's inscriptions and a renewed visual analysis of these reliefs enabled John Russell to write the article "Bulls for the Palace and Order in the Empire," interpreting these works as an outcome of the king's concepts of the meaning of his rule. Yet it is interesting to observe how much valid information Curtius was able to gain from merely examining the reliefs. He gave equally careful attention to the battle reliefs of Assurbanipal and concluded that art history ignores these works because they are difficult to access and demand an effort to understand them. Therefore, these great images have not received the place in the history of world art that is due to them. Though published in 1913, his view still has validity.

When I first came to the Metropolitan Museum of Art in 1944, I found the fragments of Sennacherib's and Assurbanipal's reliefs fascinating. They were only small pieces of the great panels that Curtius had discussed, but each one evoked an aspect of Assyrian life in which warfare played a major role. One of the reliefs shows cavalrymen leading their horses along a stream in mountainous country (fig. 5). Another shows a soldier with his horse fording a river by appearing to walk upright through the waves and among the fish. Still another fragment shows a boat carrying captive women guarded by an Assyrian soldier (fig. 6).

At that time, I mistakenly assigned this last fragment to Sennacherib. It was a few years later, when Margarethe Falkner of Graz took a few scholars through the gallery of the British Museum with the Sennacherib and Assurbanipal reliefs, that I learned from her how to differentiate between them. She had recognized differences in the military accoutrements, the most important of which for distinguishing the Metropolitan Museum of Art fragment is the length of the armor shirt, which ends at the waist in the reliefs of Assurbanipal. Of course, it was not only the small details but also the gestures, the composition, and, above all, the character of the scenes that made it possible to distinguish between the art of the two kings. For example, in the Assurbanipal relief, the woman sitting in the boat, raising her hands before her face and leaning

Fig. 5. Cavalrymen leading horses, from an alabaster relief in the palace of Sennacherib at Nineveh, circa 705–680 BCE. METROPOLITAN MUSEUM OF ART, NEW YORK

Fig. 6. Relief from the palace of Assurbanipal showing women, captives of the Assyrians, in a boat. The relief was found at Nineveh and dates from the eighth to seventh centuries BCE. METROPOLITAN MUSEUM OF ART, NEW YORK

forward in a pose of utter dejection, (fig. 6), is a more expressive figure than those seen in the marsh scene of Sennacherib. Margarethe Falkner had noted such difference in the approach of Assurbanipal's sculptors and those of Sennacherib. An early death terminated her promising career.

In order to understand Assyrian art, one should wonder about the motive behind the extraordinary effort of the kings, particularly Sennacherib and Assurbanipal, to have so much labor devoted to relief decoration. I believe that the answer may be forthcoming not directly from the representation of military victories but from those showing monstrous or demonic figures (fig. 7), for such reliefs are not as far removed in meaning from the military scenes as one might expect. In fact, our fragment with the captive women in a boat probably came from a room next to the one Richard Barnett called the "Susiana room" in his volume on the reliefs in the North Palace of Assurbanipal. This room, with a single entrance, contained reliefs on three walls depicting the assault and capture of the Elamite city of Hamanu (Khamanu) and the exodus of

Fig. 7. Relief of two Big-weather-beasts, *ugallû*, a human figure with a lion's head and eagle's feet, guarding the doorway to the North Palace, Nineveh. BRITISH MUSEUM, LONDON

prisoners from it, as well as apotropaic figures in the large recess in the northwest wall. The doorjambs had identical pairs of apotropaic figures.

In a Babylonian text about such figures, which F. A. M. Wiggermann called Big-weather-beasts, a person who may have been a conjuration priest is ordered to draw two figures of Big-weather-beasts (*ugallû*) on the gate and to invest them with the power to defend the gate against aggressors. The same procedure and the effect may be assumed for the gate in this room of Assurbanipal's palace. In addition, in the lower register under the Big-weather-beasts there was the relief showing a lion-man identified by Wiggermann as an *urmaḫlullû*, a creature thought to protect lavatories and bathrooms against Shulak,

a lion or lioness-demon who haunted such rooms (*Babylonian Prophylactic Figures*, p. 332).

In view of the magic powers that the monstrous figures in the reliefs were assumed to control, one may wonder whether the reliefs showing military victories and rows of prisoners fulfilled merely a commemorative purpose. More likely, by eternalizing the effect of the enemies' defeat and misery, they were also expected to influence future events.

Between the Gudea–Third Dynasty of Ur period and the Neo-Assyrian Empire (the twenty-first century and the early first millennium), Mesopotamian art is largely represented by small cylinder seals. These are the objects that Christian had asked me to study and that continue to fascinate me today.

The seals of the fourteenth to twelfth centuries BCE in northern Mesopotamia represent the art of the Middle Assyrian period. To appreciate the design engraved on a slender stone cylinder, it must be rolled over a flat surface of impressionable material such as Plasticene or some other product that can be hardened by baking. To illustrate how to appreciate a scene on a seal, I have chosen an example (fig. 8) that shows a lion menacing a fallen mountain sheep. The heavily muscled lion extends his body to touch the back of the sheep with one paw. He raises the other paw menacingly over his victim's head. A pine tree terminates the scene. A star fills what would otherwise be an empty space, but it may also be a meaningful symbol. Viewers of the small image should close their eyes and see if the memory of the image fills their entire inner vision. That is the way I see it. I assume other people working on seals have the same approach, and I venture to suggest that the ancient seal cutter, and probably the seal owner, saw not a small but an enlarged design that expressed both the drama and the beauty of the image. This is how seals should be viewed.

The meaning of scenes in which a lion or a hybrid monster attacks a horned game animal, which represent the majority of Middle Assyrian seal designs, is unknown. Perhaps they represent battles that were later pictured with human soldiers. The first person to draw attention to them and to the contemporary Kassite cylinders of Babylonia was Ernst Herzfeld, who had a very fine sense of style.

The seals of northern Mesopotamia and Syria in the fifteenth and early fourteenth centuries, the time of the Mitannian Empire, largely manifest a striking abstract style produced by mechanically rotated cutting wheels and drills (fig. 9).

For the Old Babylonian art of the twentieth to the seventeenth centuries there is the stela of Hammurabi (pictured in "King Hammurabi of Babylon" in Part 5, Vol. II), which has long been known and analyzed, and there are clay plaques with various religious and ritual representations. Nevertheless, it is through the cylinder seals of the period that many of the deities and their emblems became known not only to modern viewers but perhaps also to the ancients.

To interpret the meaning of the design on an Old Babylonian cylinder seal (fig. 10) I will cite a statement by F. A. M. Wiggermann in "The Staff of Ninšubura": "The representations on Old Babylonian seals reflect the religious interests of its bearer: defense against intruding evil, and good relations with the divine court, which insures divine protection and well-being. These themes are the constituting elements of Mesopotamian prayers and incantations of all times" (p. 24). The scene shows the sun-god as the chief justice of the world. He majestically places his foot on a hill, holding the saw with which he "cuts decisions" (a translation of the Akkadian phrase for judging). Placing his foot on a hill is

Fig. 8. Cylinder-seal impression of a lion attacking a mountain sheep, Middle Assyrian period. PIERPONT MORGAN LIBRARY, NEW YORK

Fig. 9. Cylinder-seal impression portraying a griffin and lion attacking horned animal, Syro-Mitannian, fifteenth to fourteenth centuries BCE. PIERPONT MORGAN LIBRARY, NEW YORK

an act symbolic of ascending in the morning from the lap of heaven. This subject is repeated from the most delicate engravings at Sippar (his principal cult center) to the crudest carvings from the provinces. Commonly the sun-god is approached by a king robed in a long mantle and offering a small goat. Cut on a smaller scale, a diminutive priest with pail and sprinkler may represent the seal owner in a priestly function. A goddess with hands raised in supplication stands behind the king as a protective figure whose prayer may be directed for the benefit of the seal owner. The role of the male deity to the left of the group cannot be determined. A goat placed beside a woman, to the right, helps us identify the latter as a goddess, inspirer of correct interpretations of omens appearing in sacrifices, who is mentioned in a Babylonian text on constellations, published by Christopher Walker and Her-

mann Hunger. The uncertainties reflected above exemplify the difficulties that we still face today in interpreting ancient near eastern imagery, even if we are at a stage far more advanced than at the beginning of the century.

Major sculptures that first attracted the attention of the world's art lovers to the ancient Near East derive from the time of Gudea of Lagash, now known to have been an elder contemporary of Ur-Nammu, the first king of the Third Dynasty of Ur (2112–2094). An incense burner, described in 1991 by Annie Caubet of the Louvre (fig. 11), bears a dedication rendered here in a free translation: "For the well-being of Gudea, ruler of Lagash, and for her own well-being as well, Nin-Alla, wife of Gudea, has dedicated this incense burner to Bawa, the gracious goddess, her mistress."

The small object, only 10.4 centimeters (about

Fig. 10. Cylinder-seal impression of a king positioned before the sun-god and other deities, Old Babylonian, circa 1800 BCE. PIERPONT MORGAN LIBRARY, NEW YORK

Fig. 11. Censer dedicated by the wife of Gudea, circa 2250 BCE. LOUVRE MUSEUM, PARIS

ents an effective contrast to the refinement of the female sculpture in figure 12. In a recent article Irene J. Winter harked back to verbal descriptions of Gudea's physical attributes, such as a strong arm, pointing out that the sculptures themselves emphasized the same features, thus both visually and verbally stressing the strength of Gudea as a ruler. The foundation figure of King Ur-Nammu (fig. 13) shows the same muscular power in the figure of the king, even when emulating the lowly act of carrying a basket of earth or bricks for the building of a temple. His action was first portrayed in a third-millennium relief from Tello, yet centuries later Assurbanipal, the last great Assyrian king, is still seen raising the basket "on his head like a holy crown," a phrase of Gudea's, in one of his building inscriptions.

To Henri Frankfort and Anton Moortgat, the two great art historians of the 1940s and 1950s, Gudea's sculptures seemed less interesting than the Akkadian works because they lacked the immediacy and vitality of the earlier style of the dynasty of Akkad. According to Frankfort, "the technical achievements of the Akkadian period are utilized, but of the aspirations of that time

4.2 inches) high, has a beautifully proportioned upper bowl. Its profile shows a smooth molding bordered above by a thin one and below by two more, one of which is slightly thicker and projects above the lower one. The bowl rests on a gently spreading support. The combination of these abstract forms expresses the refined taste of the period, as exemplified in the sculpted bust of a noble lady (fig. 12). Curtius called the style classic because it reflected natural forms, as in the soft folds of the garment over the arms, yet retained the calm effect of the large surfaces. He noted the hands with the long fingers folded in a gesture of worship but expressing complete self-control, thereby creating an expression of aristocratic refinement and inner nervous life. Curtius added that nothing like this had been seen before the articulation of limbs in archaic Greek art. His remarks about these objects, now long known, are worthy of repetition because they retain the same freshness and intensity of the impact on viewers as when they first appeared in photographs.

The powerfully muscular figure of Gudea pres-

Fig. 12. Fragmentary steatite statue of a woman, from the court of Gudea at Tello, circa 2250 BCE. LOUVRE MUSEUM, PARIS

Fig. 13. Detail of upper part of a copper figure carrying a basket, circa 2112–2075 BCE. PIERPONT MORGAN LIBRARY, NEW YORK

not a trace remains. Piety replaces vigour" (*Art and Architecture*, p. 47). As for Moortgat: "In no statue of Gudea, however, has diorite . . . been moved and animated by the same inner restlessness and burning desire for action sometimes shown in the period of Manishtushu" (Moortgat, *The Art of Ancient Mesopotamia*, p. 62). Articles in these volumes may show a slight shift in the level of admiration for the classic style of Gudea and Ur-Nammu, which we share with earlier art historians like Curtius.

The stela of Naram-Sin has amazed viewers since its discovery (see an illustration of the stela in "Aesthetics in Ancient Mesopotamian Art" in Part 10, Vol. IV). Curtius described it particularly vividly, and I use his description here in a very free rendering of the German text because I think that he grasped not only what the artist represented but also the message intended for the viewer four thousand years ago—which probably does not differ greatly from that for the viewer of today. In an open landscape, a steep mountain is scaled by a group of soldiers on

a narrow path. Gnarled trees characterize the rocky, wooded landscape. The king has sought to stage the decisive battle with the mountain peoples of the Lullubi on the summit, the pass where a tall rock rises. Now the decisive action has occurred. Two fallen enemies lie at the feet of Naram-Sin, almost in antithetical archaic postures. A third enemy has tumbled backward, straight down the steep incline. The man trying to pull the deadly spear out of his neck is surely the enemy king. With his death, resistance ceases. The enemy begs for mercy. One of them has broken his spear as a sign of submission; another, at the top, has thrown away his weapons and begs with raised hands, half in flight; a third, at a distance, waves, probably about to hide in the thicket and among the rocks.

Arsis (the rise) is created by soldiers ascending in identical stride, the lowest carrying the standards. *Akme* (the high point) is formed as the king stands alone, beside the mountain. Above are the constellations determining the event. The edge of the conical mountain defines the boundary between victor and vanquished. Here Naram-Sin places his foot on the corpses. The two main enemies are silhouetted against the conical plane of the mountain. In the descending composition, trees separate surrendering enemies from victorious soldiers. The king is the major figure. The ascending warriors look up to him; the defeated try to catch his eye. He is the first to have reached the top. Before him the power of the enemies has broken down.

As Curtius pointed out, all of this is actually shown by modest means. The soldiers are represented by one type, and another type characterizes the vanquished enemies. Naram-Sin is rendered like one of the soldiers but he surpasses his enemies in size. However, he is taller by just one head, as he may have been described at the time. The scene, therefore, retains the human scale that makes the rendering of the event believable. Some of the effect is due to the modeling of the royal figure in high relief so that it stands out from the low background, giving it dramatic motion.

The genetic predecessors of the stela are still unknown, as they were in the time of Curtius. Agade, the capital of the dynasty since Sargon founded it, remains to be discovered. Its palace may have contained wall paintings with composi-

Fig. 14. Cylinder-seal impression showing the flight of Etanna to heaven, Akkadian period, 2340–2150 BCE. PIERPONT MORGAN LIBRARY, NEW YORK

tions that extended beyond the horizontal bands that generally confined Mesopotamian compositions from monumental reliefs to small cylinder seals. Still, a few cylinders of the Akkad period (figs. 14–16) seem to transcend the horizontal rectangle that usually limited the design of a scene. For example, Etana, the shepherd king, is shown flying toward heaven with the help of an eagle (fig. 14). Dogs seated on the ground raise their heads to watch, and shepherds lift their hands in wonderment at the sight. The composition is thus unified in its upward extension.

In a cylinder seal of the same period, the upward extension of the picture plane in a hunting scene in the mountains is achieved by the outline of a mountain (fig. 15). Finally, in the seal of Adda in the British Museum (fig. 16), the moun-

tain pattern creates a common base for a group of gods. It also helps join Ishtar, whose abode is chiefly in heaven, with the sun-god Shamash, who rises from beneath the horizon, where he spends the night.

The preceding examples tend to show that the upward extension of a composition was used by seal engravers, prefiguring the same composition in the stela of Naram-Sin. While Curtius considered seal engraving to be an independent, minor art, Frankfort thought that in Mesopotamia "From Early Dynastic times decorative art in all its branches utilised the inventions of the seal cutters" (Cylinder Seals, p. 308). I agree with him to the extent that I do not believe there was a clear division within the craftsmanship of the Mesopotamian sculptors. That ivory workers could, on occasion, also work on major stone

Fig. 15. Cylinder-seal impression showing a hunt in the mountains, Akkadian, circa 2200 BCE. MUSEUM OF FINE ARTS, BOSTON

Fig. 16. Cylinder-seal impression of Adda with the rising
sun-god and other deities, Akkadian period, circa 2200
BCE. BRITISH MUSEUM, LONDON

sculpture is demonstrable from India. An inscription on the south gateway of the Sanchi Stupa states that the work was done by the ivory carvers of Vedisa, the nearby capital. The sculpture on the gateway was certainly larger than the usual scale of ivory working and there was, of course, considerable difference in the technique. Yet my colleague Vidya Dehejia informs me that in India the same craftsmen worked in both stone and bronze until about the ninth century CE.

Ludwig Curtius began his study of Mesopotamian art with an analysis of cylinder seals of the Early Dynastic period; his insights and thoroughness were unmatched until the work of Frankfort and Moortgat. Curtius's study was centered on seal impressions deriving from the court of the Sumerian ruler Lugalanda of Lagash (fig. 17). In

the course of his analysis he discovered some of the essential characteristics of the style that we now call Early Dynastic IIIB.

The seals Curtius studied show a frieze of struggling heroes, animals, and predators contained within the rectangular area of the mantle of a cylinder. The figures tightly fill the space, with vertical axes dividing the overlapping figures. All heads are kept at the same height, as if conforming to a law, the term for which is "isokephaly." There is a balanced relationship between the postures of the figures, which have a geometric character. The figures are not merely aligned in continuous friezes but also appear as compositional elements in heraldic motifs, best seen on the silver vase of Entemena, circa 2450, (see fig. 1 in "Aesthetics in Ancient Mesopotamian Art," Part 10, this volume.) These images

Fig. 17. Drawings of ancient impressions of the cylinder seals of Lugalanda of Lagash,
circa 2360 BCE. H. FRANKFORT, *A DOCUMENTARY ESSAY ON THE ART OF CYLINDER SEALS* (1939)

show a subjugation of the natural figure to formal concepts of rhythm and of a limiting space. They belong to a decorative style that Curtius recognized as the first of its kind in the history of art. He pointed out that the lion-headed eagle, which dominates the design in the Entemena vase, derives its timeless abstract character from its frontal stylization. The animals that the eagle grasps are as directionless as the principal figure because their movements balance each other. The single animals are deprived of their uniqueness by the repetition of the motif, and in the end they are transformed into a continuous frieze by the lions biting the horned animals. Curtius characterized this art as lacking every expression of the naïve, cheerful life that Egyptian art loved so dearly. In fact, he aptly described the art of western Asia as "humorless." Without having any factual evidence for a long development of art before the Entemena vase, he assumed that generations must have worked to develop the laws according to which the designs of the vase were composed. Indeed, almost a thousand years separate the beginning of Mesopotamian art in the Uruk period from the Entemena vase.

For the origin of Mesopotamian cylinder seals, of monumental architecture and sculpture, we have to go back to about 3300 BCE to the site of Uruk in southern Mesopotamia. There we also find the origins of a coherent narration in the Warka vase, later found again in the Naram-Sin stela.

The great alabaster vase was discovered at Uruk in the winter of 1933–1934 and published by Ernst Heinrich, whose text is used as a basis for the following description. The vase was part of a large collection of objects he called a "Sammelfund." There were animals sculpted in the round; cylinder seals, stamp seals, and seal impressions on lumps of clay; vessels of stone, plain and ornamented, and of pottery and metal; beads and pieces of jewelry; ornaments of structures, furniture, and tools; and various other items. The interpretation now favored of the circumstances leading to the "Sammelfund" is that an enemy plundered a storage place of movable temple inventory, which could have been a treasury. (The vase is illustrated in "Theologies, Priests, and Worship in Ancient Mesopotamia" in Part 8, Vol. III.)

The vase was produced from a large piece of alabaster by slow manual labor with stone instruments and abrasives. It is shaped like a chalice, having a conical foot with slightly everted rim. The height of the body with the reliefs measures about 92 centimeters (almost 37 inches). The representations are applied to three circular registers measuring 25, 17.5, and 20 centimeters (10, 7, and 8 inches) in width, the lowest bisected horizontally. The contents of the reliefs of the three registers obviously belong together; they apparently relate a gift to the Eanna sanctuary. The action begins in the top register.

The presence of the goddess Inanna is indicated by her symbol, the ring bundle, two examples of which occupy the entire height of the top register. Behind the symbols, offerings of all types are set up and laid down. These include two large vessels with the fruits of field and garden; two tall, footed chalices in shape similar to the great vase; two low, footed bowls, which surely contained some fine substance; two vessels in the form of small animal figurines, representing a gazelle and a lion; two square objects that cannot be interpreted; a bull's head; and an object that looks like a quiver with an attached lid. Most important is a curious group of figures: Two maned rams placed close together carry on their backs a two-stepped pedestal to which ring bundles are attached. These bundles associate the whole group with Inanna. On each step stands the figure of a man. One of them has his hands raised, grasping with one hand the wrist of the other. The other man holds in his outstretched hands an object, the form of which occurs in the older levels of Layer III and, according to Adam Falkenstein, is to be read EN, "lord."

In front of the large ring bundles stands a figure who appears to be characterized as female by her garment. It does not hang from the belt, as in the figures of men, but covers the upper body and the left arm. Only the right arm remains free. The garment seems to consist of a textile that is edged but not sewn in any other way. The woman's profile is differentiated only very slightly from that of the other figures: mouth and chin recede a little. Her hair falls in a wider bunch on the back than that of the men. She wears headgear that leaves a narrow strip of hair free on the forehead. On the back of her head there is a horn-shaped point, and there was surely a similar one in front that was lost in antiquity, along with a piece of the rim of the vessel. The woman has her right hand raised, much as do the deities in the presentation scenes on later cylinders. This gesture, as well as her position before the two Inanna symbols and her facing the people bringing the offerings, marks the woman as the person who accepts the donations, regardless of whether one interprets her as the goddess herself or as her representative, her priestess.

The first figure of the procession that moves toward the woman is a nude man who carries a vessel filled with fruit, very similar to those already set up behind the ring bundles. The following figure is obviously the principal one, the leader of the procession. Unfortunately, all that is preserved of that figure are one foot, a part of the garment, and the long plaited or woven belt with two large tassels at the end, which is carried by a servant behind him. The garment has a broad seam and is patterned by closely placed crossed lines.

The second register continues the row of offerers that begins above with the first figure of the procession. The third register shows the herds dedicated to the goddess, her gardens and fields. The wavy line below indicates the river. Above it is a row of the plants that grow from it. They were originally identified as ears of grain and date palms, but the latter have now been recognized as flax, which indicates a connection with an early textile industry.

This vase is the first extant monument that presents pictorially an orderly, continuous account of an event. In short, it is history's first narrative representation.

The relief of the vase is not the earliest at Uruk; fragments of artificial stone with considerable use of gypsum were found at Uruk by Heinrich Lenzen and discussed later by Eva Strommenger. These reliefs of artificial stone must have been cast. For them to be cast, there must have been a mold. Whatever technique was used for the mold, it was negative in relation to the figure that was to be produced. In other words, the artist went through the same creative process as did the seal cutter when carving a design. In his imagination he is inside the object that he models, working against its skin.

Now to a cylinder-seal design of the ruler figure (fig. 18) in what is referred to as the *Netzrock*, a mesh skirt, identified as a diaphanous garment because the legs are visible through it. I explain this representation in the following way: I believe that the ruler figure was designed as a whole. The Uruk artist saw the male body as an organic unit. He carved it as that and then dressed it in a skirt of patterned material, which he indicated by crisscrossing. The impressions of such seals seem to me to show that the dress was added secondarily. In my opinion, this has created the impression of a diaphanous material.

Turning to the representation of the ruler on the vase, I suggest that the fact the leg is outlined under the garment probably indicates that the technique in which it was carved derived both from the earlier, artificial stone, which was cast, and from carved cylinder seals. In both the body

Fig. 18. Cylinder-seal impression of ruler in a *Netzrock*, acting as a priest as he brings offerings to the gods, Uruk period, end of the fourth millennium BCE. ANTON MOORTGAT, *FRÜHE BILDKUNST IN SUMER* (1988)

Fig. 19. Upper part of a male statuette from Uruk, early Sumerian period, that is now in the Iraq Museum in Baghdad. HIRMER ARCHIVES, MUNICH

could have been modeled first, the garment carved over it later.

The concern with the attire of the figure indicates its importance. The image represents the dominant male personage of the period, a ruler. It is not surprising, therefore, that a three-dimensional sculpture of such a figure turned up in the excavations of Uruk several years after the vase (fig. 19).

Surely the latter part of the fourth millennium was the time of the self-realization of the Mesopotamian, symbolized by the figure of the ruler. There must have been a recognition of his potential and his responsibility for leadership, as a builder of lasting structures and as a being with the power to change and direct the life that nature had provided for him and his people.

In 1939, a life-sized female head was found at Uruk (pictured in "Reliefs, Statuary, and Monumental Paintings in Ancient Mesopotamia" in Part 10). The eyebrows and eyes, which were inlaid in a different material, have disappeared. Nevertheless, the effect of the head is extraordinarily vivid, which Lenzen, the excavator, ascribed to the natural carving of the eyelids. The

eyebrows repeat in beautifully curving lines the almond shape of the eyes. The cheekbones are broad and stressed but not exaggerated. The mouth is tightly closed, the chin is strong and softened by a slightly indicated double chin. Henri Frankfort noted that the artist's main interest seemed to have been the living flesh. In my opinion, the artist's aim was the rendering of the human being, as in the male torso. Even if the purpose was the rendering of a goddess, as is generally assumed, she was conceived in the image of a human woman by the artist who sculpted the work.

It is interesting to contrast my remarks with Frankfort's view of the style of the protoliterate period as represented in the sculptures and cylinders of Uruk in relation to the abstract style manifested in Early Dynastic sculptures from Eshnunna (modern Tell Asmar) in northern Mesopotamia. Having originally considered the style of Tell Asmar the first manifestation of Mesopotamian sculpture, Frankfort had to come to terms with the then newly found earlier and strikingly naturalistic works. He expressed the opinion that the Uruk style had been ousted

Edith Porada in the mountains of Austria near Hagengut in the 1950s. PHOTOGRAPH INSERTED BY THE EDITORS, COURTESY OF SYDNEY BABCOCK

(by the artists of Tell Asmar) when they came to believe that "the translation of the ever changing world of appearance into the stable form of sculpture could be achieved only by a bold grasp of essential shapes shorn of accidentals to such an extent that they approach geometrical forms." (These sculptures are pictured in "Reliefs, Statuary, and Monumental Paintings in Ancient Mesopotamia" in Part 10.) This view may be understood only as the result of the intellectual attitude that saw in the style of cubism an ultimate truth rather than a passing style of western European art. But, as has been shown in this essay (though it is expressly stated only in this instance), such "passing styles" influence the views of their times and the understanding of ancient art to which every generation makes its own contribution. Today we consider the Tell Asmar sculptures a provincial manifestation even though their creators produced some masterpieces. How they will be assessed by future art historians cannot be foretold.

BIBLIOGRAPHY

FRANÇOIS MAURICE ALOTTE DE LA FUYE, ed., *Documents présargoniques*, vol. 1 (1908), for seal impressions of Lugalanda and his court; WALTER ANDRAE, *Propyläen Kunstgeschichte*, vol. 2: *Die Kunst des alten Orients* (1925), and *Das wiedererstandene Assur*, 2nd ed. (1977); RICHARD D. BARNETT, *The Sculptures of the North Palace of Ashurbanipal at Nineveh (668–627 B.C.)* (1976); MANFRED ROBERT BEHM-BLANCKE, *Das Tierbild in altmesopotamischen Rundplastik*, Baghdader Forschungen 1 (1979), p. 53, for the present view concerning the origin of the "Sammelfund"; ANNIE CAUBET, "Un Autel dédié par Nin Alla, épouse de Goudéa, don du Baron E. de Rothschild," *Revue du Louvre et des musées de France* 41, no. 1 (1991); VIKTOR CHRISTIAN, *Altertumskunde des Zweistromlandes von der Vorzeit bis zum Ende der Achämenidenherrschaft* (1940); LUDWIG CURTIUS, *Die antike Kunst*, vol. 1: *Ägypten und Vorderasien* (1913); ADAM FALKENSTEIN, *Archaische Texte aus Uruk* (1936); HENRI FRANKFORT, *Cylinder Seals: A Documentary Essay on the Art and Religion of the Ancient Near East* (1939), *More Sculpture from the Diyala Region*, Oriental Institute Publications 60 (1943), and *The Art and Architecture of the Ancient Orient* (1954; 4th ed., rev. and enl., 1969), p. 47; WOLFGANG HEIMPEL, "The Sun at Night and the Doors of Heaven in Babylonian Texts," *Journal of Cuneiform Studies* 38, no. 2 (1986), in which the context of the phrase "lap of heaven" implies that the locality was found beneath the horizon.

ERNST HEINRICH, *Kleinfunde aus den archaischen Tempelschichten in Uruk*, Ausgrabungen der Deutschen Forschungsgemeinschaft in Uruk-Warka, 1 (1936); LÉON ALEXANDRE HEUZEY, *Les Origines orientales de l'art*, 4 vols. (1891–1915); ROBERT KOLDEWEY, *Das wiedererstehende Babylon*, 4th ed. (1925); HEINRICH LENZEN, "Ein Marmorkopf der Dschemdet Nasr-Zeit aus Uruk," *Zeitschrift für Assyriologie* 45 (1939): 85, *Vorläufiger Bericht über die . . . Ausgrabungen in Uruk-Warka* (1956), pl. 42a; DONALD M. MATTHEWS, *Principles of Composition in Near Eastern Glyptic of the Late Second Millennium B.C.*, Orbis Biblicus et Orientalis, Series Archaeologica 8 (1990), the best work on the cylinders of the Middle Assyrian period; JOACHIM MÉNANT, *Les Pierres gravées de la Haute Asie*, 2 vols. (1883); ANTON MOORTGAT, *The Art of Ancient Mesopotamia* (1969), p. 62; SVEND AAGE PALLIS, *The Antiquity of Iraq: A Handbook of Assyriology* (1956), see chap. 6 for a list of excavations from 1842 on; ANDRÉ PARROT, *Tello: Vingt campagnes de fouilles (1877–1933)* (1948); JOHN PUNNETT PETERS, *Nippur; or, Explorations and Adventures on the Euphrates*, 2 vols. (1897–1898); EDITH PORADA, "Reliefs from the Palace of Sennacherib," *Bulletin of the Metropolitan Museum of Art* 3, no. 6 (1945), "On the Problem of Kassite Glyptic Art," in *Archaeologica Orientalia in Memoriam Ernst Herzfeld*, 21, edited by BEULAH DIMMICK CHASE (1952), "Problems in Late Assyrian Reliefs," in *Essays in Ancient Civilization Presented to Helene J. Kantor*, edited by ALBERT LEONARD, JR. and BRUCE BEYER WILLIAMS, Studies in Ancient Oriental Civilizations 47 (1989).

JOHN MALCOLM RUSSELL, "Bulls for the Palace and Order in the Empire: The Sculptural Program of Sennacherib's Court VI and Nineveh," *Art Bulletin* 69, no. 4 (1987); ERNEST DE SARZEC, *Découvertes en Chaldée*, edited by LÉON ALEXANDRE HEUZEY, 2 vols. (1884–1912); BETTY L. SCHLOSSMAN, "Two Foundation Figurines," in *Ancient Mesopotamian Art and Selected Texts* (1976): 9–20; EVA STROMMENGER, "Kunststeinfragmente aus dem 'Riemchengebäude' in Warka," *Baghdader Mitteilungen* 6 (1973); THOMAS VON DER WAY and KLAUS SCHMIDT, "Tell el-Fara'in—Buto, 2. Bericht," *Mitteilungen des Deutschen archäologischen Instituts, Abt. Kairo* 43 (1987); CHRISTOPHER B. F. WALKER and HERMANN HUNGER, "Zwölfmaldrei," *Mitteilungen der Deutschen Orient-Gesellschaft* 109 (1977): 30–31, line 17; F. A. M. WIGGERMANN, *Babylonian Prophylactic Figures: The Ritual Texts* (1986), and "The Staff of Ninšubura: Studies in Babylonian Demonology, II," *Jaarbericht . . .*

ex oriente lux 29 (1987); IRENE J. WINTER, "The Throneroom of Ashurnasirpal II," in *Essays on Near Eastern Art in Honor of Charles Kyrle Wilkinson* (1983), fig. 6.

SEE ALSO Aesthetics in Ancient Mesopotamian Art (Part 10, Vol. IV) and various chapters in PART 10: VISUAL AND PERFORMING ARTS.

Assessing the Past Through Anthropological Archaeology

FRANK ARNOLD HOLE

FRANK ARNOLD HOLE *was born in Oak Park, Illinois, in 1931. He studied anthropology and archaeology with Robert Braidwood at the University of Chicago, taught at Rice University, and is now Professor of Anthropology and Curator of Archaeology, Peabody Museum of Natural History, Yale University. Dr. Hole has excavated in Iran and Syria and his many contributions to anthropological archaeology have earned him, among other honors, election to the National Academy of Sciences and the American Association for the Advancement of Science. Dr. Hole has pioneered the use in near eastern archaeology of flotation, a method for retrieving seeds from excavated soil, shedding new light on early agricultural village life. He has combined ethnographic study of nomads and archaeological fieldwork, yielding new insights on prehistoric nomadic pastoralism. His book* An Introduction to Prehistoric Archeology *(with Robert Heizer, 1965; 1973) has been published in several languages. As editor and contributor to* The Archaeology of Western Iran *(1987), Dr. Hole has reviewed decades of research in the area. In his many publications, he continues to contribute to the study of early agriculture and nomadic pastoralism.*

HISTORY, ARCHAEOLOGY, ANTHROPOLOGY

Anthropological archaeology in the Near East is relatively new. Nevertheless, its approaches promise to have a growing impact on the way fieldwork is carried out and on the problems scholars address. My experience in near eastern archaeology coincides with the first projects that were explicitly anthropological in their goals and methods. Nevertheless, while I have experienced much of this history and have contributed to the development of some of the approaches, I take a more general perspective here.

There are two diametrically different ways of studying the ancient cultures and civilizations of the Near East, textual and archaeological. In the former, archaeology is traditionally the agent by which texts are discovered, and is the source of some statuary, metalwork, and architectural monuments. Once we encounter written texts, archaeology is relegated to a supporting role, either to corroborate historically known places and events or to provide relics from the past.

For the prehistoric periods, artifacts alone must provide the materials for a narrative of the past, and they seldom convey the same information as texts. The inspiration for developing the narrative of prehistory has been anthropology, the scientific study of people and their cultures, with an emphasis on how people, common folk as well as the elite, lived. Anthropologists are concerned with factors that influenced the major changes in cultures and societies, the shift from small-scale, egalitarian societies to urban kingdoms, from simple hunting-and-gathering groups to agriculturalists. Anthropologists tend to look comparatively across regions and continents in search of common factors, and to regard as fundamental such mundane things as agriculture. They see the development of religion and social hierarchies—even literacy—as processes by which people adapt to changing conditions.

An archaeologist might seek to find a city named on a tablet, or wish to elucidate the temple architecture of a period and place; these are interesting but rather narrow concerns for an anthropologist, who would explore broader, more general kinds of issues. For example, what was the role of regional population increase in the development of more intensive agricultural systems or of urbanism? Are there ecological or environmental reasons, political factors, or economic interrelations that underlie the sudden intrusions of settlers from southern Mesopotamia into remote regions of the Near East as much as seven thousand five hundred years ago? In what ways did the impetus for the development of urban centers differ in northern as opposed to southern Mesopotamia? How did the office of kingship develop? Clearly, such questions cannot be answered merely by reference to one site or one period; they inherently require us to consider broad regions, review extensive periods of time, and deal with interrelations of people within and among sites. Moreover, they require an understanding of geographical as well as cultural factors.

Despite these differences in perspective, it is important to stress that the concerns of anthropologists and historians are complementary. Through anthropological inquiry and the application of modern methods of science, we have made enormous progress in our ability to learn about and understand the past. Today we can squeeze vastly more information out of less material, with greater accuracy. We expect that ad-

vances will continue to be made as we refine methodologies and subject our data to them.

Anthropology embraces every dimension of humankind, from contemporary to historical. While properly speaking there is no "anthropology of the ancient Near East," the study of contemporary peoples nevertheless has helped illumine the ancient world. But the potential that once was there scarcely exists today, for during the second half of the twentieth century, mechanization, transport, communication, and attempts to incorporate peoples of diverse cultures and religions into national political structures have all but obliterated traces of traditional ways of life.

It is significant that the first use of anthropology in the direct service of near eastern archaeology was to settle an important historical issue: the relation between irrigation agriculture and the centralization of political authority. Which came first, irrigation or the state? Some have argued that the organizational requirements of irrigation agriculture stimulated the development of centralized political authority, which became despotic when control of irrigation waters was ruthlessly applied. This theory, espoused by Karl Wittfogel in his influential *Oriental Despotism*, was tested by Robert Fernea, who settled into a village in southern Iraq to study how irrigation actually was organized. The result of his study—that irrigation need not depend on complex administration—was immediately used by Robert McCormick Adams in a broad-reaching consideration of irrigation civilizations in the Near East and elsewhere, and later in his detailed studies of settlement and political organization in southern Mesopotamia. He inferred that irrigation need have nothing to do with the genesis of a despotic state, however much it might potentially contribute to its success once established. In fact, as a result of Adams's archaeological surveys, it eventually became apparent that the administrative apparatus, so voluminously recorded in the cuneiform texts, came about long after irrigation had been well established in the ancient Near East. Thus the relevance of both ethnography and archaeology to an understanding of history was underscored.

The archaeological record, consisting of the

remains of temples and houses, the graves, the canals and roads, the implements used by people, and the refuse they discarded, is a natural counterpart to the texts. These things are tangible, are often immediately interpretable (though sometimes wrongly!), and exist in the absence of texts. Moreover, this evidence extends well beyond the normal subject matter of political history, dealing with the mundane as well as the exceptional and with the masses of people as well as with the ruling and literate elite.

TRADITIONAL ARCHAEOLOGY

During much of the nineteenth century, archaeology more closely resembled the scramble for mining claims during the gold rush than a scientific pursuit, as archaeologists in the Near East sought primarily to recover statuary and tablets. By the turn of the century, a shift toward more orderly operations had begun, though it was still too early to call most archaeology systematic, let alone "scientific." The change occurred when archaeologists became interested in architecture. Coupled with this new interest came an important advance in field technique: the systematic use of stratification. Archaeologists came to recognize that during the passage of time, sites build up in layers that successively record their history.

All of the great mounds of Mesopotamia have such layers (variously called Tell, Tel, Hüyük, or Tepe), which are composed of the ruins of buildings, yet archaeologists had failed to identify them unless they had been constructed of stone or baked brick. However, the favored material for construction in Mesopotamia was always unbaked mud-brick, a challenging material for an archaeologist, for the hardness, color, and texture of the bricks scarcely differ from the earth that encloses them. Before World War I, the Germans at Babylon under Robert Koldewey, trained a group of Arabs in the delicate art of revealing these bricks from seemingly featureless earth. Descendants of these individuals, whose skill has been handed down from father to son, still make up the skilled work force of excavation teams in Iraq.

Koldewey's techniques were adopted to varying degrees by other field archaeologists (often architects by formal training), who learned to excavate level by level and to draw detailed plans of structures. (See "Excavating the Land Between the Two Rivers" below.) Bit by bit, archaeologists discovered what they could learn through the process of digging, and more attention was placed on extracting information from remains in the ground. By the 1920s archaeologists had become aware that successive layers in diverse Mesopotamian sites consistently revealed a similar succession of pre-Sumerian artifacts, leading to the identification of distinct periods. The names by which we know these periods—Ubaid, Uruk, and Jamdat Nasr—came from the sites at which they were first found. The setting up of successive periods and the attempt to establish cross-correlations among regions began to dominate archaeology and provided the basis of present understandings of comparative developments. Until radiocarbon dating was invented in the 1950s, this cross-dating through comparison was the only way to establish the chronology of the prehistoric periods.

ANTHROPOLOGICAL ARCHAEOLOGY

Until World War II, there was an essentially unbroken continuity of activity, with techniques growing more refined but emphasizing the recovery of objects and architectural traces, and delineating the historical outlines of the regions that make up the Near East. The interruption of World War II provided a point of departure for the new approaches of the late 1940s and the 1950s.

The first of these, and the one that ultimately stimulated the others, was called by its originator, Robert Braidwood of the University of Chicago, "multi-disciplinary problem-oriented research." The problem in this case was to seek the origins of agriculture, a task to which Braidwood turned his attention in 1947. His project attempted to excavate sites dating from before, during, and after the advent of agriculture, so that he could witness the changes and circumstances that gave rise to this revolutionary development in human history. The sites in question were all small, few had pottery, and none had metal, tablets, statuary, or monumental architecture. The previous generation of near eastern archaeologists would not have recognized Braidwood's sites even if they had stood upon them.

There was much more to Braidwood's approach than just to dig at small sites. It required specialists with a knowledge of botany, zoology, and geology. In asking where and when agriculture began, Braidwood required answers from the natural sciences. He needed botanists to tell him where wild wheat and barley could have grown, and zoologists to establish the habitats of wild sheep, goats, cattle, and pigs. He had to learn from geologists whether there had been changes in the land and in climate that may have affected the locations of these natural habitats. All the information Braidwood gathered led to the conclusion that agriculture probably began somewhere in the foothills of northern Iraq or, as he put it, "in the hilly flanks of the fertile crescent."

Braidwood was the first near eastern archaeologist to take to the field a team of specialists in the natural sciences, and their interaction and collaboration have shaped the direction of a number of subsequent archaeological projects. The goal was to gain an understanding of how the fundamental change to agriculture came about, rather than primarily to recover cultural objects for display. The focus was natural science; and, for the first time, the principal funding was through the American National Science Foundation, not a museum or private donors. Since the time of Braidwood's Jarmo project, refinement of excavation methods has allowed more accurate interpretation of a site's history and the remains in it. But the most dramatic improvements have come through new analytical methods that extract previously unforeseen information from minute bits of pottery, obsidian, plant remains, and animal bones. As the potential yield of information has increased, the excavations themselves have become more focused and generally smaller in scale. This trend has been accentuated by a shift toward shorter digging seasons

resulting from academic schedules and declining budgets. Today, one is more likely to see reports with pages of stratigraphic sections and statistical tables than a lavish display of interesting objects.

Such was the case with my reports of the excavation of Ali Kosh, a small prehistoric site in western Iran. We had dug the site as part of the long-range program to investigate the origins of agriculture, a problem whose solution had been frustratingly impeded by our inability to find remains of ancient seeds. Most plant remains eventually decompose and are lost to archaeology; but when they are charred, they become impervious to decomposition. When we first excavated the site in 1961, we searched carefully for any traces of charred grains but were unable to find them. We reported, ruefully, that "plant remains were scarce." When we did find clusters of dark ash and earth that we thought might be dated by radiocarbon, we carefully wrapped them in aluminum foil and sealed them in plastic bags for transport to a laboratory in the United States.

Radiocarbon dating was just being tested in the early 1960s, and a number of laboratories were experimenting with methods. One such laboratory, in the research complex of Humble Oil Company (later Exxon) in Houston, agreed to date my carbon. Proudly I arrived at the laboratory and displayed my samples. The scientists there were quite unimpressed with the dark dust that I spilled out on the table; they told me that it seemed to be mostly ash and therefore not useful for dating. However, they said, if I could separate solid charcoal from the ash, they might be able to run some dates. I asked how to do so, and was told that if I poured the ash into water, the solid particles would separate from the ash which could be flushed down the drain.

Somewhat deflated, I went home to wash my samples in the kitchen sink. But as soon as I dumped the first sample into a pan of water, fat, black seeds miraculously popped to the surface. It was exciting and, for me, a moment of revelation. As I carefully scooped the seeds up and deposited them on a paper towel to dry, I knew that establishing radiocarbon dating would be strictly a secondary use of our seeds. I realized that we had a method for finding seeds and that we were, at the same time, on the threshold of achieving revolutionary results. If only we could get the seeds identified.

By a fortunate circumstance, when I worked in Iran as a member of Braidwood's team, it included the Danish paleobotanist Hans Helbaek. Hans, who was self-taught as a botanist, was paid as a low-level technician at the Danish National Museum despite his world-renowned work in paleoethnobotany, a field that he created to link botany, archaeology, and ethnography. As the pioneer in this field, Helbaek had made identifications of plants wherever he could find them: in caches and urns, as impressions on pottery and mud-bricks, and from the stomachs of "bog bodies" in Denmark. He became an authority on cereals, flax, and other plants, and he acquired an extensive knowledge of ecology as a result of his many collecting trips to the Near East.

So when I found the seeds, I wired Hans, who asked to see them. I sent them to him, and he immediately wired back that we had found emmer wheat. He said that these were the oldest and most exciting finds he had ever seen, and that we must return to Ali Kosh for further excavation. He would be part of the team.

As these events unfolded, there was another fortuitous happening. Stuart Struever, a fellow graduate student at the University of Chicago, had been experimenting in the American Midwest with flotation, a method of separating charred plant remains from the soil in which they lay, a technique similar to my washing ash in the sink but on a large scale. We decided to try his methods in Iran. These chance events set the course of my research and the course of many subsequent projects throughout the Near East. We secured funds to continue our excavation of Ali Kosh and oriented our digging to retrieve seeds rather than artifacts or architecture.

This was a fundamental shift in strategy, for our archaeological objectives and methods were determined by the search for seeds—what previously would have been considered almost a tangential result of excavation. We also wanted to follow a chronological sequence when excavating, in order to elucidate the development of agriculture from its earliest stages through the introduction of irrigation and the development of hybrid strains of grain. Building on

Braidwood's model, our approach was ecological. In large part this ecological orientation was shaped by Kent Flannery, whose previous training in zoology had led him to study the ecology of jumping spiders, but who now was concentrating on prehistoric archaeology. Our four-month survey of western Iran in 1961 heightened our appreciation for the ways different qualities of the mountain and valley landscape affected the development of cultures. This approach was then applied more narrowly in our intensive study of the Deh Luran plain, where we attempted to explore the interrelationships among technology, population, and changes in subsistence strategies, in connection with the changing physical and social environment over a long span of time. That we were able to accomplish this in Deh Luran, and that Braidwood met with similar success in Iraq, was a result both of careful selection of sites and of the generous permits granted by the local authorities, which allowed us to dig in several sites rather than just one. It would not be possible to duplicate this set of circumstances in most countries today.

A further fortunate circumstance of the Deh Luran project, which sharpened its impact on archaeology, was the speed with which we produced a report, *The Prehistory and Human Ecology of the Deh Luran Plain* (1969). Two factors were important. First, we were able to complete our excavations during one long season of fieldwork, and second, my two principal archaeological collaborators, Kent Flannery and James Neely, were able to join me for a summer in Houston, where we could give full attention to analysis and writing. The Iranians let us take the artifacts out of the country for analysis, a practice seldom permitted today.

The report contained a full description of our research at the sites of Ali Kosh, Tepe Sabz, and Tepe Musiyan, and introduced the notion of counting artifacts. This allowed us to detect and express numerically subtle changes in style and use in the artifacts. This approach had long been used in American archaeology, but in the Near East it had been traditional to publish only illustrative examples, disregarding quantities. Where potsherds might number in the hundreds of thousands, this disregarding of a vast quantity of artifacts made practical sense, but it missed information that could refine the chronology of the site and therefore lead to better understanding of its contexts.

The impact of our innovation was virtually immediate. Not long after our report was published, I visited the dig of a colleague and remarked that I was glad to see several students counting and recording potsherds. With a sigh of resignation, my colleague said, "It's because of you that we're forced to count all these damned things."

SURVEY

Fully implementing an ecological study requires both geographic and archaeological information on the region. The former is acquired through a local and regional survey; the latter, through studies of vegetation and local geology. A systematic survey attempts to record information about all sites in a given region.

The survey has always been an archaeological tool, and even the earliest explorers roamed the land looking for sites. But in those days only the most prominent mounds were noticed and recorded, and such surveys could hardly be described as either systematic or comprehensive. By the second quarter of the twentieth century a few archaeologists, among them Max E. L. Mallowan, carried out surveys, recorded the locations and ages of sites, and wrote some descriptive notes about them. They used this information chiefly as an aid in selecting promising sites for excavation; but they also recognized that the survey data could be developed into tangible history and that prominent sites might be evidence of trading centers, stops on caravan routes, or frontier fortifications.

Today, surveying has been considerably refined through searching for small as well as large sites, often with the aid of aerial photos. Most such surveys are now carried out on foot, so that even faint traces of former sites can be detected. Once on a site, the archaeologist walks systematically across it, carefully collecting and recording the pottery and other artifacts that indicate various periods in order to determine when the site was occupied. The survey is sometimes further refined by recording on a topographic map of

the site the areas occupied during each period, as determined by sherd scatter. In this way relative population sizes can be estimated. On some sites one can identify a citadel, an acropolis, and a town, as well as industrial facilities such as ceramic or brick kilns, canals, and quays. When hundreds of sites have been recorded in a region, the archaeologist can chart the changes in numbers and sizes of villages, towns, and cities; and can detect shifts in population from one region to another, or from village to city, and vice versa. Survey results therefore record the changing fortunes and patterns of settlements in one region over long periods of time.

To be maximally informative, the statistical data generated by these surveys must be related to their geological and modern ethnographic and historical contexts, as Robert McCormick Adams has done in his enormously influential surveys

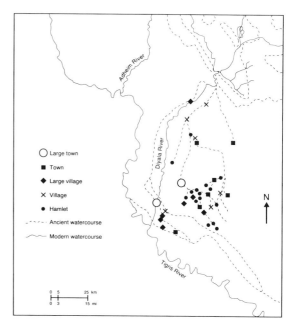

Fig. 1. Representation of the sites Robert McCormick Adams discovered in eastern Iraq with an indication of their size and possible function in a hierarchy of settlements. Data and maps such as these enable archaeologists to observe significant changes in overall population and degree of urbanization as well as to infer the development of irrigation systems and political integration. ADAPTED FROM ROBERT MCC. ADAMS, *LAND BEHIND BAGHDAD: A HISTORY OF SETTLEMENT ON THE DIYĀLĀ PLAINS* (1965)

of the southern alluvium of Mesopotamia (fig. 1). The landscape, the climate, and the water resources of each particular region determined to a large extent how cultural developments occurred. Mesopotamia is a harsh land of few natural resources that demanded enormous investments of human ingenuity and incessant labor in order to build and sustain civilized life. It is also a fragile environment that quickly shows signs of deterioration under heavy human use, and in which the major, life-giving rivers have repeatedly either catastrophically inundated vast stretches of land or, when they shifted courses, turned cities and whole agricultural regions into desert. Therefore, when survey information is related to the historical record, it may help locate a city mentioned in written texts, or it may more securely document historic changes, such as the abandonment of a city following agricultural disaster, the destruction of a canal, warfare, or a natural catastrophe. Survey information may suggest alternative explanations for political disruptions that have been revealed in the texts.

In short, survey provides a context in which the excavations of individual sites can be placed. None of the ancient cities, however large, was an entity unto itself. Each existed in a region of smaller, satellite settlements, and each was in contact with neighboring cities and polities whose growth and decline were intimately connected as part of larger systems (fig. 2). Some of the ramifications and interconnections are revealed through texts; but in the many cases in which written evidence is lacking or uninformative, it is the results of survey, coupled with excavation, that give us a fuller picture of their interdependence.

ETHNOARCHAEOLOGY

Despite all the advances in field methods and the use of scientific techniques by archaeologists, the remains of the past still give only a sketchy picture of life in the past. For this reason, some archaeologists look to contemporary peoples for insights into prehistoric life.

It has long been recognized that traditional peoples of the modern Near East bear some resemblance to those described in the Bible and in the documentation from Mesopotamia. Both the tribal organization and the preindustrial techniques of farming and herding practiced by these people are thought to represent ways of life that began in prehistoric times. Descendants of the "Tribes of Israel," or of the Akkadians, or of the Hurrians may well be dwelling in the same regions where their ancestors flourished, but this is difficult to prove because there were widespread and frequent migrations. For anthropologists, however, whether there is ethnic continuity in the Near East is an irrelevant issue. Rather than strict biological descent, they look for a close correspondence between the kind of environment people live in, the way they gain their livelihood, and their social and political organization. From this perspective, it is possible to observe diverse cultural aspects of antiquity among peoples who continue in traditional ways, whether in the Near East or elsewhere.

Early travelers to the Near East were well aware of this correspondence, yet systematic ethnographic studies that could be used to help interpret archaeological remains began only in

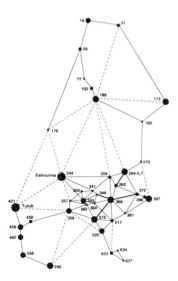

Fig. 2. This diagram attempts to show how sites are arranged around "central places," large sites with satellites, with the importance of connections between sites indicated by the width of the line. ADAPTED FROM GREGORY A. JOHNSON, "A TEST OF THE UTILITY OF CENTRAL PLACE THEORY IN ARCHAEOLOGY" IN *MAN, SETTLEMENT, AND URBANISM*, EDITED BY P. J. UCKO, R. TRINGHAM, AND G. W. DIMBLEBY (1972)

the 1950s. There is a difference between what a social anthropologist and an archaeologist see in a people under study. The former are more interested in social relations, whereas the latter are concerned with tangible things that might be recovered, such as tools and houses, as well as techniques of farming and herding. As a consequence, many studies written by social anthropologists have proved to be of little direct value to archaeologists. Recognizing this discrepancy, archaeologists took advantage of their own presence at villages near their digs, and of the availability of people who exemplified certain ways of life, to conduct their own ethnographic studies.

This was the context in which I carried out a study of nomadic pastoralists. The study was inspired by my excavations in Deh Luran, Iran, which provided much information on the development of agriculture but told little about the parallel development of stock raising. We had found bones of livestock in the sites, but we could not tell whether the animals had been raised in and around the village or had been bartered from nomadic pastoralists. Nor were we able to ascertain when transhumant pastoralism (seasonal movements with the animals from lowlands to mountain pastures and back again) began, or under what conditions nomadism became a fully specialized activity separate from village life. By studying modern nomads in the same terrain where I was digging, I hoped not only to gain insight into transhumant herding as a way of life but also to find ways of discovering the ancient sites of herders and to interpret their physical remains. (See also "Pastoral Nomadism in Ancient Western Asia" in Part 3, Vol. I.)

Although transhumant pastoralism was still much in evidence in the 1950s and 1960s, it was clearly a way of life under great stress, both politically and economically, and its days as a traditional mode of life were numbered. While I was excavating at a cave site near his village, I met a Luri man who was a member of one of these herder tribes. This young man, Sekandar Amanolahi Baharvand, was learning English and wanted very much to study in the United States. When he was able to do so, he enrolled in a graduate program in anthropology at Rice University, where I was teaching. For his dissertation he wished to study his tribe, which would

Fig. 3. Archaeological site of a tent camp in southwestern Iran that is about 8,800 years old. During the leveling of the field for agricultural irrigation, stones that formerly held bedding and other materials off the ground were exposed. The layout of the tents was almost exactly like that of today's nomads. Our excavation in 1973 revealed these sites. COURTESY OF FRANK HOLE

be the first and only scholarly study of these people. Since he was also interested in my research and was a native speaker of the necessary dialect, he agreed to help me organize and carry out my research. That was how, in 1974, Sekandar and I joined a camp of transhumant pastoralists, lived in their tents, participated in their activities, and migrated with them in the spring.

One of my goals was to learn how to find archaeological traces of ancient pastoralists, people who, by virtue of their mobility and presumed lack of pottery and other diagnostic artifacts, were thought to be irretrievably invisible archaeologically. I hoped to change this attitude and, through a fortunate set of circumstances, I did.

While I was traveling with the Luri pastoralists, there was a massive reconstruction of the fertile agricultural plain of Khuzestan, in southwestern Iran, undertaken to improve its irrigation potential. The project required the removal of most villages and the leveling of the land surface by huge scraping machines. One of my

Fig. 4. The Baharvand Luri nomads breaking their winter camp in 1973 in preparation for the spring migration. The winter tent sites are surrounded by low stone walls to help protect the interiors from the wind and cold. COURTESY OF FRANK HOLE

archaeological colleagues, Henry Wright, was surveying the plain in search of ancient irrigation canals when he discovered Neolithic pottery in a canal bank. Since he knew of my interests, he took me out to the site, where I immediately recognized pottery dating to about 8,800 years ago. I was intrigued and, because I knew that the land was about to be leveled, requested a permit to conduct a two-week sounding in the site. Then I resumed my wanderings with the Luri nomads.

By the time I had completed the ethnographic study, a permit was waiting for me; but when I returned to the site, I found it had been completely altered by the land-leveling—only a small fragment of the old canal bank with pottery could still be found. Nevertheless, on the newly leveled land surface, which had gone from a gently rolling, grassy plain to an absolutely flat surface covered with light tan, powdery dust, I could make out widely scattered patches of ash. On closer inspection I also found Neolithic sherds and large rocks protruding from the surface, many of them in straight lines. I realized then that the land leveling had inadvertently exposed the remains of nomads' tent sites (fig. 3).

Acting on this serendipitous occurrence, I was able to clear a number of these old tent sites and to establish beyond a doubt that they were about 8,800 years old. Sayid Ali, one of the older men who worked for me, asked why we were bothering to dig this place; it was, he said, "just a nomad camp." When I explained to him that it was

nearly nine thousand years old, he found that totally unremarkable because he assumed that his way of life went back to the beginning of time.

As we talked, I learned that he had camped near this very spot before his tribe was settled by the Shah's government. By looking at each of the uncovered tent sites and by observing its orientation to the prevailing wind, Sayid Ali could infer the season when it was occupied, and could tell by size and layout whether it belonged to a leader or to an average person. While we were cleaning out one of the tent sites, I asked him to show me where the fireplace was. He quickly oriented himself in relation to the back wall and, pointing to the ground, said, "Here." "Dig," I said. He did, and sure enough, there was the fireplace. So I said, "Then tell me where the ash was taken when the fireplace was cleaned out each day." He again oriented himself from the fireplace, took several steps to the front of the tent, veered a number of steps at an angle to the left, and announced, "Here." Again he dug, and of course he found the ash dump. The implications were clear. Even after the passage of 8,800 years, the spatial layout of a tent and of its surroundings had remained the same (fig. 4).

Our stay at this site was cut short before we were able to exploit it fully, but we had demonstrated that the nomad camps of antiquity could be found and, once found, could be recognized and interpreted for what they were.

Other ethnoarchaeological research has been conducted in agricultural villages. In fact, the first such study, by Patty Jo Watson, was closely related to Braidwood's archaeological project in 1959–1960 and involved a thorough study of the architecture, social organization, and artifacts found in a rural village. A similar study some years later by Carol Kramer led to a general review of how archaeologists can use ethnography to translate recovered evidence with a whole range of conclusions regarding architecture, population size, and settlement pattern.

It remained for Elizabeth Stone, a historical archaeologist, to put textual, architectual, and ethnographic evidence together to describe patterns of residence in Old Babylonian Nippur (modern Nuffar). Hers is an explicit attempt to combine the use of ethnographic analogy, architectural plans of houses recovered through excavation, and ancient texts to reconstruct the patterns of residence. Dr. Stone has related the testimony of cuneiform texts that told of ownership of houses and their division after inheritance and sales, to actual houses and rooms that had been recovered archaeologically. She found such a close correspondence between the texts, the ethnoarchaeological data, and the archaeology that she advanced the theory that virilocal extended family residence (married sons residing in their father's house) was normal in ancient Mesopotamia, but that there were also separate, nuclear households. In the houses of Old Babylonian Nippur about 1700 BCE, each individual had only about 17 square feet (about 1.5 square meters) of roofed space, small by our standards but apparently normal for many thousands of years in this region, as ethnographic studies have shown. (See the plan of Nippur in "The Development of Cities in Ancient Mesopotamia" in Part 3, Vol. I.)

Scattered studies of villages, abandoned as well as still occupied, assessments of a few remnant nomadic peoples, and a remarkable analysis of agriculture and plant processing round out the extent of ethnoarchaeology in the Near East. Today there is little left for us to study because traditional ways of life have nearly disappeared throughout the region. Neither tribal organization nor preindustrial technology can be said to flourish today except in the most vestigial ways.

ARCHAEOBIOLOGICAL STUDIES

A few generations ago, archaeologists drew on their own knowledge of natural history to identify bones and seeds found in excavations. Fortunately, early travelers and archaeologists had a rather broad and scientifically accurate knowledge of botany and zoology. Many archaeologists, however, were also content to depend on native workers to identify plant and animal remains. An amusing result was that the bones of animals pulling the wagons in the famous Ur death pit were incorrectly identified as those of oxen, a fact that was corrected only years later when a zoologist working in a museum identified them as belonging to onagers (a donkey-like equid). With the development of multidisciplinary projects it belatedly came to be appreciated that simple (even accurate) identification of

plant and animal remains was only a first step in trying to understand what these remains represented. The more difficult problem is with plants, for they can enter a site as fuel, as livestock forage and bedding, as construction material, and as food or medicine. Potentially, remains of plants carry information on the ecology of a site—what kinds of trees, grasses, and shrubs were growing nearby—on the way crops were grown, how the livestock were tended, how the food was processed, and what people ate.

None of these can be accurately ascertained until the relationship between charred and other material found in sites is established, and until the activities that brought the plants to where they were found are reconstructed. But to understand what the plant remains can tell us about ancient people requires study of modern people and how they handle plants under preindustrial conditions.

Gordon Hillman of the Institute of Archaeology in London is transforming the field of archaeobotany from one of identification to one of behavioral interpretation by asking a simple question: What does a particular sample of plant remains represent in terms of human activities? From 1970 to 1973, Hillman carried out a series of studies in central Anatolia. In the region surrounding a site, he surveyed the present-day vegetation, assessed the contemporary farming practices of the local villagers, and analyzed the way plants are processed once they have been brought into a village. The result of this painstaking study was a description of all that happens to plants between the time they are harvested and their discovery in an archaeological site. Hillman identified thirty distinct operations in the raising of one crop (glume wheat) to converting it to food, and he attempted to characterize each of them. Many of the steps, such as the initial separation of weeds from grain, dehusking, and cleaning before grinding into flour, leave characteristic traces that can be directly related to what is found in archaeological sites. For example, it is possible for an archaeobotanist to determine that the ash found in a fireplace consisted of weedy residue from grain being cleaned before consumption; or that the remains of plants in an ash heap came from dung, which was the primary fuel in the drier parts of Mesopotamia. And, from the composition of species in the harvested crop, it is possible to tell whether the fields were dry-farmed or irrigated.

Similarly, zoologists have developed techniques to discriminate between the bones of wild and domestic animals; they can now tell the ages and sexes of animals in herds, and establish whether they were used for meat, milk, or wool; and they can give information on the quality of the natural environment around the sites. (See "Animal Husbandry and Human Diet in the Ancient Near East" in Part 2, Vol. I.) By examining skeletons of the people, other analysts, known as biological anthropologists, can estimate their height, determine whether they had dietary problems, establish whether they were subjected to trauma, and estimate what their life expectancies were (see fig. 5). In short, through multidisciplinary collaboration, modern archaeologists have the potential to understand vastly more about the people of the past than could ever be revealed through the written texts alone (see fig. 6).

When I studied archaeology at the University of Chicago, I was interested in the prehistory of humankind, and I was attracted to Robert Braidwood's research into the origins of agriculture. Braidwood used to say that he had become

Fig. 6. Members of our interdisciplinary team at the archaeological site of Chagha Sefid, in Deh Luran, Iran, 1969. From left to right: Lynn Fredlund (archaeologist), Barbara Hole (camp manager), Frank Hole (director), Steven Hole, Jane Wheeler (zooarchaeologist), Colin Renfrew (archaeologist and obsidian specialist), Jane Renfrew (paleoethnobotanist), and Robert Hole. COURTESY OF FRANK HOLE

Fig. 5. Kent Flannery (archaeologist, archaeozoologist) butchering a wild pig whose bones were needed for our comparative faunal collections. Marianne Neely is adjusting the light and Mustafa Nargasi is handling the pig. Taken at our field camp near Ali Kosh in 1963. COURTESY OF FRANK HOLE

a prehistorian because he could not learn the ancient languages. In fact, he, like a number of others, had come into archaeology as an architect; and it is to his great credit that he had the initiative and insight to change the way prehistoric archaeology was carried out in the Near East. In any event, his personal interest waned at the threshold of literacy. As a result, anthropology students in those days generally did not take courses in the history of the Near East, and we ignored the later periods when we did fieldwork.

Fortunately, not all archaeologists wore the same blinders, and a series of projects in the Near East explored the first, second, and third millennia. With the exception of Robert McCormick Adams, however, none of the anthropologically trained archaeologists truly ventured into the realm of history, nor have historical archaeologists had much to do with prehistory, apart from an occasional deep sounding into the earliest levels of a site. There are good reasons for this lack of crossover. Prehistorians are usually not trained to read ancient languages, nor are they trained in the methods of historic inquiry; and historians and philologists are often not well trained in excavation and rarely in analysis of the archaeobiological finds.

Nevertheless, the characteristically anthropological concern with the ways people lived and with their social organization, as well as with a generalizing, comparative approach, have influenced deeper theoretical and interpretive works in all branches of archaeology. Those who studied early prehistory were preoccupied with hunter-gatherers whose ethnographic analogues were seen in remnant populations in the odd corners of the underdeveloped world. Among these archaeologists, the focus has shifted from assessing technology to discerning those changes in patterns of hunting which might reflect increasing knowledge, tighter social organization, and new ways of exploiting the environment. Those who were interested in the origins of agriculture shifted from finding Neolithic sites to finding causes: Why did people shift from the episodic but comfortable activity of the hunting and gathering existence to a life of unremitting toil as agriculturalists? A number of theories, most of them seeing agriculture as an attempt to overcome dietary stress, have been proposed. Similarly, anthropologists have promoted a series of ingenious theories to explain the rise to statehood from simple villages. In both cases, stress seems to be a precipitating factor, but anthropologists quarrel over why stresses arose and which stresses were the more crucial.

In essence, anthropological archaeology is concerned with the development and evolution of human cultures and societies. Its methods range from scientific to historical, and the results are tested through comparison. Both literary and ethnographic sources are needed for balance and insight, but there is also much to be learned from the scraps ancient peoples left in the ground. For the most part these supplement and are complementary to the information derived from texts. As the very rapid advances in understanding continue, we will find more and more that scholars on each side of the divide of literacy make greater use of the others' insights and knowledge.

BIBLIOGRAPHY

Historical Processes

ROBERT MCCORMICK ADAMS, *The Evolution of Urban Society* (1966), is a comparative study of the development of central Mexican and southern Mesopotamian civilizations. Adams's *Heartland of Cities* (1981) is the third in a series of interpretive monographs on his surveys of the Mesopotamian alluvial plain. This volume summarizes information from previous surveys and integrates a vast amount of geographical, agricultural, hydrological, archaeological, and historical data. KARL A. WITTFOGEL, *Oriental Despotism: A Comparative Study of Total Power* (1957), proposes a theory of the relations between management of irrigation and concentration of political power, whose implications for the Near East have been tested through ethnography and archaeology. ROBERT A. FERNEA, *Shaykh and Effendi: Changing Patterns of Authority Among the El Shabana of Southern Iraq* (1970), is a modern anthropological study of the organization of irrigation in southern Iraq that showed Wittfogel's hypothesis need not be true. ROBERT MCCORMICK ADAMS, "Early Civilizations, Subsistence, and Environment," in *City Invincible*, edited by CARL H. KRAELING and ROBERT MCCORMICK ADAMS (1960), evaluates the relationship between irrigation and the rise of dynastic authority.

Development of Archaeological Methods and Approaches

ROBERT J. BRAIDWOOD, BRUCE HOWE ET AL., *Prehistoric Investigations in Iraqi Kurdistan* (1960), and LINDA BRAIDWOOD ET AL., eds., *Prehistoric Archeology Along the Zagros Flanks* (1983) are reports on the research problem, fieldwork, and results of the first multidisciplinary investigation of agricultural origins. FRANK HOLE, KENT V. FLANNERY, and JAMES A. NEELY, in *Prehistory and Human Ecology of the Deh Luran Plain* (1969), develop an ecological approach to understanding the development of agriculture in the Near East. SETON LLOYD, *Foundations in the Dust: The Story of Mesopotamian Exploration* (1980), reviews the history of Mesopotamian archaeology up to World War II.

Ethnographic Analogy

PATTY JO WATSON, *Archaeological Ethnography in Western Iran* (1979), is a pioneering study of the houses, tools, and activities of a small Iranian village. CAROL KRAMER, *Village Ethnoarchaeology* (1982), is both a report on her field study and a general review of the archaeological implications of ethnographic studies. NORMAN N. LEWIS, *Nomads and Settlers in Syria and Jordan, 1800–1980* (1987), reviews historical and ethnographic evidence of the relations between nomads and settlers, and establishes models that can be used in archaeological interpretation. ELIZABETH T. STONE, "Texts, Architecture and Ethnographic Analogy: Patterns of Residence in Old Babylonian Nippur," *Iraq* 43 (1981) is a skillful use of data and inference to reconstruct the residence patterns in Nippur. ROGER CRIBB, *Nomads in Archaeology* (1991), reviews previous work and suggests ways it can aid archaeological interpretation. FRANK HOLE, "Pastoral Nomadism in Western Iran," in *Explorations in Ethnoarchaeology*, edited by RICHARD A. GOULD (1978), and "Rediscovering the Past in the Present: Ethnoarchaeology in Luristan, Iran," in *Implications of Ethnography for Archaeology*, edited by CAROL KRAMER (1979), give the principal results of an ethnoarchaeological study of Iranian nomads. FRANK HOLE, "Tepe Tūlā'ī: An Early Campsite in Khuzistan, Iran," *Paleorient* 2, no. 2 (1974), describes the excavation of a nomad camp eight thousand years old.

Paleobiological Studies

GORDON HILLMAN, "Traditional Husbandry and Processing of Archaic Cereals in Recent Times: Part I, The Glume Wheats," *Bulletin on Sumerian Agriculture* 1 (1984) and "Traditional Husbandry and Processing of Archaic Cereals in Recent Times: Part II, The Free-Threshing Cereals," *Bulletin on Sumerian Agriculture* 2 (1985), the classic ethnographic analysis of crop processing, which is widely used to interpret charred plant remains found at archaeological sites. NAOMI E. MILLER, "The Near East," in *Progress in Old World Palaeoethnobotany*, edited by WILLEM VAN ZEIST, KRYSTYNA WASYLIKOWA, and KARL-ERNST BEHRE (1990), is a comprehensive review, by country and period, focusing on the Near East. HENRY T. WRIGHT, NAOMI MILLER, and RICHARD REDDING, "Time and Process in an Uruk Rural Center," in *L'Archéologie de l'Iraq: Du Début de l'époque néolithique à 333 avant notre ère*, edited by MARIE-THÉRÈSE BARRELET (1980), is a multidisciplinary examination of the behavioral and seasonal implications of layers in a six-thousand-year-old trash pit. JOY MCCORRISTON and FRANK HOLE, "The Ecology of Seasonal Stress and the Origins of Agriculture in the Near East," *American Anthropologist* 93, no. 1 (1991), combines information from climatology, geomorphology, plant ecology, archaeology, and ethnography to place the origin of agriculture in the southern Levant.

SEE ALSO various chapters in PART 2: THE ENVIRONMENT.

Excavating the Land Between the Two Rivers

SETON LLOYD

SETON HOWARD FREDERICK LLOYD *is a fellow of the British Academy and Professor Emeritus at the University of London. He was born on 30 May 1902. Between 1926 and 1961 he participated in diverse excavations, including those of the Egypt Exploration Society and the University of Chicago Oriental Institute. In addition, he has served as Technical Adviser to the Directorate-General of Antiquities in Iraq (1939–1949) and as Director of the British Institute of Archaeology, Ankara, Turkey (1949–1961). Among his many honors is the Gertrude Bell Memorial Medal of the British School of Archaeology, awarded in 1971. Professor Lloyd has published extensively on Mesopotamian archaeology, architecture, and history. In 1986 appeared his touching and sensitive reminiscences,* The Interval: A Life in Near Eastern Archaeology.

AT ERIDU, NEAR THE southernmost limits of Iraq, a king of Ur built a ziggurat on the neglected site of a much more ancient shrine. Late in the winter of 1949, I found myself seated on a shoulder of mud-brick among its ruins. From that viewpoint I could see, in the remote distance, the similar staged tower of Ur itself. But beneath me also, I could look down into the immensely deep sounding, where, in three seasons of digging with my friend Fuad Safar, we had excavated the superimposed remains of sixteen previous temple buildings, starting with a miniature chapel, founded upon the clean sands of the Euphrates delta perhaps two thousand years before the time of King Shulgi. (See map in "Shulgi of Ur" in Part 5, Vol. II.) That occasion has special significance for me because, after twenty years of such work in Iraq, I was then about to transfer my professional activities to another country. In the present context also, the memory of that occasion leads to a reflection which may well simplify the handling of my present task. Its aim is to recall a particular phase in a long saga of Mesopotamian discovery.

At the time of my first arrival in Iraq there were eighteen foreign expeditions, European or American, already working in the country. Since World War II their numbers, as we know, have enormously increased, their sponsorship being extended to more remote seats of learning, for instance, Japan, Australia, and the Soviet Union. Libraries are filled with their painstaking reports and commentaries. Mesopotamian archaeology has become a degree subject in universities. For our present purposes, however, we must turn to a subject with which the world of scholarship has tended to be less concerned: we are to consider the lives and behavior of actual field archaeologists. And, since it is to this class of professional excavators that we owe the raw materials of historical research and learning, it would be natural to exploit the testimony of such eyewitness accounts as are still available, when evaluating the judgments of posterity. Due attention must of course be paid to cardinal discoveries; but a secondary aim should be to recapture the spirit of those who made them, to envisage the scenario against which they worked and the tensions generated by conflicting interpretations.

In all these respects I feel qualified to attempt the task. I have myself conducted or taken part in a score of excavations, all relevant and some vital to the understanding of Mesopotamian antiquity. When rearranged chronologically, they cover a wide spectrum of acquired knowledge and will surely serve as a vehicle for the story which has now to be told. In a word, a narrative approach may perhaps best serve our purpose.

My own introduction to near eastern archaeology had a prelude in Egypt. In 1929 I served as architect-surveyor in a team assembled by the Egypt Exploration Society at Tell al-Amarna. The leader of the expedition was Dr. Henri (Hans) Frankfort, a name with which I shall find myself greatly preoccupied. My arrival at his camp was in fact something of a surprise, since I had impulsively offered myself as substitute for a defecting colleague. Accepted a little ironically by Frankfort, I came very rapidly to understand the privilege of association with such a remarkable man. Admiration on my part and tolerance on his prolonged for many years the friendship which developed between us, and when, in 1954, he died prematurely, I could remind myself with gratitude of his direct responsibility for my change of profession. In view of the unique status that he had by then acquired in the realm of scholarship, something more may here be said about the scholar and the man— "Let us now praise famous men."

Contributing to Frankfort's stimulating personality were characteristics seldom apparent among denizens of the academic world. In the words of another devotee Thorkild Jacobsen— "The man no less than the scholar was concerned with cultural and human values. He had a deep love for, and need of, music, art and poetry, being thoroughly at home in all of them. His concern with values was never a detached one; rather it was a deep and vital involvement." At Amarna these qualities had a profound influence on my own thinking. Nor was it difficult for me, in return, to find ways of contributing to his cur-

rent research by bringing, I think, something new to the imperfectly understood problems of architectural reconstruction. All this being so, nothing could have pleased me more than the development which took place toward the end of the Amarna season.

Unexpectedly, our camp was visited by John D. Rockefeller, escorted by James Henry Breasted, the grand old man of American Egyptology. After they had left, Hans confided to me that Breasted, on behalf of the Chicago Oriental Institute, had offered him the directorship of a new Iraq expedition, inaugurating an ambitious program of excavations in that country. To my delight, Hans had accepted the offer on the condition that I should accompany him as assistant. Six months later, I joined him in Baghdad.

When I came as a stranger to Iraq in January 1930, my knowledge of the country was limited to gleanings from libraries, hurriedly visited before my departure from London. And now, since my story will clearly be in need of topographical background, I feel tempted to intrude the briefest possible review of what I had come to understand.

A century and a half ago, it was the discovery by Émile Botta of Assyrian sculptures at Khorsabad (modern Dur-Sharrukin) which initiated the quest for Mesopotamian antiquities. The country known to the Arabs as Iraq was then an impoverished state of the Ottoman Empire, and a further century was to elapse before it attained national status. In our own time, political emancipation and increasing mineral wealth have, in a few decades, combined to produce an almost miraculous transformation. Today the enrichment of its cities by industrial development and a thriving rural economy have changed the material aspect of the country almost beyond recognition. So, with us today is a phenomenon called modern Iraq. Yet, if we look further, behind the image which its rulers have created, something less ephemeral can be detected: the immemorial reality of Mesopotamian history and the immutable characteristics of the land and the climate. It is about these that something must first be said. (See the map in "The History of Ancient Mesopotamia: An Overview" in Part 5, Vol. II.)

In 1943 I published for wartime visitors an unpretentious history of Iraq, whose title used sometimes to reappear in the rhetoric of King Faisal II when referring to "my land of the twin rivers." In reality of course, the classical name applies only to the lower reaches of the Tigris and Euphrates. Both rivers have their sources high in the mountains of Anatolia, and the Euphrates, passing diagonally across Syria, has run over half its course before crossing the border into Iraq. Even then it is separated from the Tigris by a considerable tract of desert, and it is not until a point is reached a little to the north of Baghdad that the two draw together, to irrigate the land once called Babylonia. To the north is ancient Assyria, whose climatic characteristics differ considerably from those in the south.

Of Babylonia one Latin writer says, "The country is a plain, as flat as the sea and full of wormwood." He had forgotten the palm groves, but perhaps remembered an abstract meaning of wormwood—bitter mortification or its cause. More realistically, it is a country created by its own river. Like the delta of the Nile, it consists of fertile river-borne alluvium. Unlike the Nile, however, with its conveniently predictable flooding, the river water here requires artificial distribution. One sees then, particularly in aerial photographs, how the whole region is covered by a pattern of irrigation canals, ancient or modern, resembling the veins and arteries of the human body. These are central facts whose significance at once becomes apparent when studying the way of life adopted by dwellers in Mesopotamia from the earliest times. In a country of this sort, wood as well as stone must be imported from elsewhere. Date palms will grow, and certain shrubs, but other trees do not repay the water and labor necessary to irrigate them. Sun-dried brick or, for greater permanence, the kiln-baked variety, will invariably be the material used for building. Arches and vaults will be used to avoid the need for roofing timbers. And above all, earthenware will have taken its primary place in everyday life, so that pottery will be used for every conceivable purpose. Only the last of these characteristics applies equally to northern Iraq. North of Samarra, one finds oneself in an undulating hill country, with the mountains of Anatolia already remotely visible. The land is traversed by tributaries of the main rivers, and cereal crops can be cultivated almost without irrigation. Both wood and stone

are obtainable in the foothills; vines and fruit trees have replaced the date palm. Ethnologically, the predominant Arab population of the south is supplemented by Kurds and other minorities.

With these pictures in mind, we must now return to Baghdad, where Frankfort was energetically devising a strategy for the new expedition. Breasted's primary objective was to join in the many-sided inquiry into the civilization and antecedents of the Sumerians with which other scholars were at that time concerned. During the preceding decade, this investigation had been greatly stimulated by Woolley's striking discoveries at Ur. German excavators at Uruk (modern Warka) were throwing new light on events leading to the foundation of a Sumerian kingdom, and French soundings at Kish (Tell Ingharra/ Tell Uhaimir) confirmed its complicated heredity. Frankfort himself had contributed to the subject in his two-volume dissertation on near eastern pottery. He was also at that time preparing his more controversial work on *Archaeology and the Sumerian Problem,* more humorously referred to by some colleagues as "Sumerology and the Frankfort Problem."

In January 1930 Sidney Smith, of the British Museum, was acting as director of antiquities for the Mandatory Government, and it was he who first drew Hans's attention to a group of Sumerian mounds in the now barren country once irrigated by the Diyala River. The nearer of these, Khafajeh (Tutub), was then being heavily looted by illicit digging, and the premises of the Baghdad dealers were flooded with fragmentary Sumerian sculptures and cuneiform inscriptions. The digging was now stopped, after a paramilitary operation; but for Frankfort the task remained of repurchasing the accumulated loot.

In Baghdad, meanwhile, I had been joined by two further members of the expedition. One was Gordon Loud, whom I then described in a letter as "a sardonic Bostonian, rather short on conversation," and the other Thorkild Jacobsen: a tall, pale-haired Danish scholar, of whom I soon became rather fond. (Jacobsen's "Searching for Sumer and Akkad" follows this chapter.) While adapting ourselves to the eccentricities of local hotel accommodation, our arrival happened to coincide with a most appropriate public occasion, the unveiling of a memorial tablet to Gertrude Bell, in the museum to which her name had been given. Not unexpectedly, I wrote in a letter home,

> You wouldn't believe how real her "Letters" suddenly became. Many of her best friends were there, including even Sassoon Effendi and old Hajji Naji, whose garden she so loved. The High Commissioner made a speech, which was replied to by the King. Feisal is remarkable—very tall, elegant and nervous (Hans says "like a thoroughbred horse"). He spoke quietly and very sincerely, with an English interpreter: "The founding of this museum was not Miss Bell's only great work. She was, I consider, mainly—I will even say entirely responsible for establishing the Iraq nation." Then the tablet was unveiled, surmounted by a bronze bust of G.B.—a fine type of Englishwoman (even down to the high polish on her nose where the drapery had rubbed it!).

Of the three sites for which Frankfort had now obtained excavation permits the largest was a mound called Tell Asmar, which had already been identified as the capital city of an ancient state historically known as Eshnunna. This site, far out in the *chôl* ("once cultivated," in regional Arabic) desert, was now to be our headquarters, and an expedition house was to be built there. In the meanwhile, Frankfort had arranged for our little party of three to visit various excavations already in progress under foreign leadership, including Leonard Woolley's camp at "Ur of the Chaldees."

Our first journey, to Warka where the Germans were working, was a fairly rigorous introduction to the hazards of traveling in Iraq. Warka is twelve miles from the railway station at Khidr. It was dark and had been raining for three days, so the track was largely under water. Horses of a sort had been sent for us, and we should have been glad of the long sheepskin coats or *farwahs* which Hans had made us buy in the Baghdad *suq;* but no one had told us that, in rain, you turn the fleece outward, so they were permanently ruined. Our arrival under these conditions caused much amusement to the otherwise humorless Germans, who were living under a regime of incredible austerity. A thimbleful of ʿaraq hardly compensated for all the heel clicking and laughter. But when we left again, two days later, the entire staff turned out at four o'clock in the morning to see us off.

Next came the French camp at Kish, where we arrived in bright sunshine and were given a delicious lunch of francolin *panné* and a good deal of Mosul wine. Waterlin, the director, was helpful as well as hospitable; but my notes on method were on this occasion rather neglected, owing to the presence of Gerald Reitlinger, whom I now met for the first time. Gerald, who later became my close friend and collaborator, was an authority on, among other subjects, Islamic pottery. He was at Kish only by chance, as he was in fact supporting David and Tamara Talbot-Rice at the neighboring site of Hira. We had many friends in common, and our prolonged gossip rather obscured the purpose of my visit. By contrast, our reception at Ur seemed to us rather perfunctory. (Only later did we come to understand why visitors to an excavation in progress are usually regarded as a mixed blessing.) At lunch, we all stood behind our chairs until Lady Woolley was seated, and the conversation concerned itself with high persons in the Baghdad administration, none of whom we knew. After the meal, Woolley immediately disappeared, having assigned a staff member to show us around. Royal tombs were by that time a thing of the past, but at least we saw some splendid wall tracing in progress, of a sort which made digging at Amarna seem like child's play.

Another thing which I soon came to understand was Breasted's conception of an expedition headquarters. Tell Asmar was forty miles (sixty-four kilometers) east of Baghdad and twenty from the nearest cultivation. Provision had to be made for twelve or more people to live and work for up to six months of the year. Transport had to be arranged and the nearest source of water investigated. The actual building could not be completed until the following autumn, so we learned that our first winter season of work in Iraq was to take place at Khorsabad. There, in the hilly country to the north of Mosul, until recently other Americans had been re-excavating Sargon's palace among the ruins of his short-lived capital city. At Khorsabad one would encounter no problems of stratification, and the tracing of immensely thick mud-brick walls would provide us with useful experience. In Baghdad, Hans seemed to have completed his task and recovered the greater part of the Diyala antiquities. I paid a last visit with him to the *sûq* and can remember the old Jewish dealer, Samhiri, wringing his hands and complaining repeatedly, "Monsieur Frankfort m'a pris!" But all the sculptures and tablets from Khafajeh were safely delivered to Sidney Smith for the National Museum. We then set out by train for Mosul, transferring ourselves at Baiji, where the railway then ended, to a service of elderly Rolls-Royces.

My first letter from Khorsabad started with a long and excited description of Mosul, which has no place here, but indicates how little the town must have changed since Ottoman times. It continues, "Other than mandatory officials, the only visiting Europeans at that time were a party of British archaeologists, led by Dr. R. Campbell-Thompson from Oxford, who were making a deep sounding in the Kuyunjik mound at Nineveh on the other side of the river. Also among them were M. E. L. Mallowan and Robert Hamilton, . . ." both of whom later became my close friends, though, for reasons which I cannot recall, our party had no contact with them that year. I do however remember the model-T Ford which carried us precariously over the twelve-mile track to Khorsabad, ". . . a particularly attractive village in the last rays of the setting sun

and, silhouetted above it, the huge, table-shaped mound of Sargon's palace. On top was a group of buildings like a large farmhouse, whose contents of servants, donkeys, and saluki dogs came streaming down the side of the hill to meet us. Then, a wide courtyard with small, whitewashed rooms around it, a large dining-room with an open rafter ceiling—and a cloth laid for tea." Thus, our bachelor party's long sojourn at the Khorsabad site began.

We started work the next morning, having chosen a mound which clearly represented one of the minor gates in the great city wall. At first we could make no sense of it at all. A few days later, however, our party was joined by a fifth member, Pinhas (Pierre) Delougaz, who was able to throw more light on the situation. Pierre, whom I have elsewhere described as "an Israeli journalist and jack-of-all-trades," had previously been helping Edward Chiera (the excavator of Nuzi [Yorghun-Tepe]) to salvage damaged sculptures from the ruins of Sargon's palace. He had just completed the herculean task of transporting a winged-bull colossus by riverboat to Basra and so to America, and now became a permanent member of Frankfort's staff. Having taken a look at the spot where

Fuad Safar and Seton Lloyd, standing second and third from left, at Tell al-ʿUqair. COURTESY OF SETON LLOYD

our Kurdish laborers were wielding their picks, Pierre patiently pointed out that their present occupation amounted to no more than digging a deep hole in the mud-brick face of the city wall, which happened to be more than twenty meters (twenty-two yards) thick at that point. He now gave us our first serious lesson in wall tracing and, in time, the arched gateway could be completely exposed and recorded. We then moved to the main mound and re-excavated the huge throne room from which the winged bull had been extracted.

But at Khorsabad it was now indeed winter, and the rains had started. There were long periods when we could not dig at all and other occupations had to be sought, such as learning the Sumerian language from Thorkild Jacobsen. In fact, it was not until a year later that Gordon Loud, with the help of a large staff, was able to undertake the complete exposure of the newly discovered citadel and later to produce one of the Oriental Institute's most sumptuous publications.

It was Gordon, too, who during those rainy days at Khorsabad helped me to design a building for our projected expedition house at Tell Asmar. It was by no means a simple affair. Of its three courtyards, the largest had accommodations for the staff including tiled bathrooms and a library. Drawing office, conservation laboratory, and storeroom surrounded the second; servants' quarters and garages the third. Water would be brought from the nearest canal-head by truck and raised to storage tanks above the entrance tower, on which a beacon light would be fitted.

A contract for the actual construction of the building was signed by Frankfort before his departure for London, leaving me to choose the exact site and mark out the foundations. This I did, taking with me the contractor himself and, to be on the safe side, a local tribesman as guide. Nevertheless, on the return journey I was haunted by the appalling suspicion that I might have been taken to the wrong mound. This, I should add at once, was not so: for hardly a year later, Eshnunna had become a reality and the names of its rulers added to historical records.

In October of that year the actual building was almost complete, but I returned one month ahead of the main party to supervise the furnishing and installation of equipment. This was all

very well; but the weeks that followed were something that took a long time to forget. As I wrote home:

> I think I must have aged about ten years in the last fortnight; endless business in Baghdad, alternating with daily return-journeys to Asmar—eighty miles of dust and bumpy discomfort. One of many troubles has been that two German members of the expedition: Dr and Mrs Conrad Preusser arrived two weeks early and insisted on taking up residence at once in the unfinished house, where a nightmare of quarrels were still in progress between the hopelessly defaulting Arab contractor and an Israeli "supervisor" (knives and pistols much in evidence). I only managed to get the windows of their room glazed on the day they arrived—the kitchen without windows or doors and everything black with flies. Meanwhile seventy cases of household goods arrived by river in Baghdad, needing clearance through customs and transport to Asmar in a 3-ton lorry, with me driving and dealing with a broken spring on the way. . . . The problem of obtaining water from the nearest canal-head, ten miles away, also took some solving but . . . the day eventually came when, to everybody's amazement, water bubbled into the two main tanks and they were all able to rush around the house, turning on taps and flushing the smelly W.C.s. . . .

By that time Hans and Jettie Frankfort were due to arrive, and I planned one day's rest in Baghdad before handing it all over to them. But at eight the next morning there was a telephone message from Sidney Smith to say that the dealers were planning a digging raid on one of our sites; I was to warn Preusser at once and make sure that he had a gun. All this must have been sorted out after Hans's arrival, because the next letter is datelined Tell Asmar: "Now it is finished, there is time to take a more detached look at the house and to notice how near in reality it is to the original conception and design, yet having of its own accord acquired a romantic quality, which gives, to me at least, the most intense feeling of fascinated satisfaction."

Thorkild Jacobsen once said of Frankfort, "It was impossible to work for him: one always found one was working with him." The first task assigned to me on his behalf at Asmar was a group of Old Babylonian public buildings, roughly contemporary with Hammurabi, which

Excavation house at Tell Asmar, designed by Seton Lloyd in 1930 for the Oriental Institute's Iraq Expedition headquarters. ORIENTAL INSTITUTE, UNIVERSITY OF CHICAGO

came to be known as the Gimil-Sin Temple and the Palace of the Rulers. (Our German colleagues of course compared it to the "palace of the excavators"!) Those first two seasons at Asmar I now regard as my apprenticeship in near eastern excavation. In fact, at that time our instructors were a handful of Sharqati experts who had worked for Andrae at Asshur (modern Qalat Sharqat). As for our method of stratigraphy, it could at first only be described as empirical, based or acting on observation and experiment rather than theory. Disentangling the many rebuildings of the palace presented less difficulty because of the plentiful use of kiln-baked bricks stamped with the names of contemporary rulers and their fathers. But I have always suffered discomfort when faced by an unwisely published photograph, showing our discovery of the temple's vitally inscribed pivot-stone which, I think, the late Sir Mortimer Wheeler would have captioned "Chaos in the Middle East." In extenuation, I can only refer the reader to a book of mine, published thirty-one years later, which I myself (modestly) claim to be the definitive work on mound excavation, *Mounds of the Ancient Near East* (1963).

In 1931, a congress of orientalists at Leiden brought some order into the confused terminology then in use to denote successive phases in Sumerian history and prehistory. The latter were now to be called after sites at which they were first detected: Ubaid, Uruk, and Jamdat Nasr, while the monarchies of the Sumerian kinglist could be approximately associated with three archaeological phases: Early Dynastic (ED) I, II, and III. These terms were to take some time to be generally accepted, as shown by an experience of my own.

Among my fellow travelers in a boat sailing to Egypt that year, I met Flinders Petrie, then in his late seventies. Inadvisedly, I asked if he had been at the congress. In his reply, slightly obscured by wind and beard, I detected the words, ". . . too busy with my own excavation to chatter about other people's."

But the abbreviation ED had certainly caught on, and it was in an ED II temple at Asmar that I made my most sensational find. This was the well-known cache of twenty-one Sumerian statues, buried beneath the sanctuary pavement. (A group of these votive statues is shown in "Reliefs, Statuary, and Monumental Paintings in Ancient Mesopotamia" in Part 10, Vol. IV.) These could then be compared with an even larger assemblage of sculpture found at Khafajeh, where Delougaz was then excavating. Sumerian sculpture had till that time been most commonly judged by the so-called Gudea statues in the Louvre, which in fact represented the terminal phase of Sumerian culture. Frankfort now became interested in the stylistic implications of the Asmar group, suggesting that the geometrical simplification of its carving conformed with an earlier dating. His comments, partly concerned with aesthetic considerations, were not universally well received. One authority on contemporary art, R. W. Wilenski, objected that an archaeologist's duty was merely to record finds of this sort without aesthetic judgment: "When they stick to their business, as they occasionally do, they are useful to historians and critics. But they often indulge in art-criticism for which they are not equipped by their studies." He certainly underestimated Hans's "studies."

To return to Khafajeh on the banks of the Diyala River, Conrad Preusser had been in charge of the operations there during the first season. His initial sounding revealed building remains no more than eighteen inches deep, founded apparently on clean sand. When Delougaz took over during the following year, he was able to recognize a vast temple complex, of which the walls remained standing no more than two or three courses high. To trace them, he reverted to the German system, which involved the use of a pointed instrument to articulate every individual brick in turn. A gang of specially trained men was employed for this purpose and, working in rows, could cover wide areas of brickwork at surface level. In this way, the plan soon emerged of an oval-shaped temenos with double enclosure walls surrounding a rectangular brick platform upon which the central shrine had been raised, and the stairway approaching it. A section cut through the enclosure walls revealed a phenomenon without parallel in temple buildings elsewhere: before the foundations were laid, the entire area of the temenos had been excavated to a depth of more than four meters and then filled with clean sand. Delougaz estimated that 64,000 cubic meters (84,000 cubic yards) of sand had been moved in this way, perhaps in conformity with some ritual.

It was at that time beginning to be understood how, in a Sumerian city of this sort, the two primary requirements for the performance of religious ritual were, first, a small but important shrine raised on an artificial platform and, second, a larger, more congregational edifice at ground level, a convention which can indeed still be recognized, two thousand years later, in the ziggurat and Ninkhursag temples of Nebuchadnezzar's Babylon. As for the temenos enclosure, it occurred to Delougaz that this too must have parallels elsewhere. He remembered, in particular, the very similar temple platform at Tell al-Ubaid, near Ur, partially excavated by H. R. Hall in 1919. So, at the end of the Khafajeh season, I found myself whisked off by train to take another look at it. Within twenty-four hours, the two wall tracers whom we had brought with us had succeeded in locating a temenos wall and, after three days, tracing it in opposite directions, met again on the other side of the platform, having outlined a perfect oval and its entrance gate.

In the spring of 1933, our study of Sumerian temples was briefly interrupted by an independent operation which Thorkild and I were able to undertake alone, among the hills to the north of Mosul. Architecturally at least, this proved to be one of the most complete and satisfactory tasks that have ever come my way. (See also Jacobsen's own remarks on the undertaking in the chapter below.)

A succession of earlier travelers in those parts had reported the remains of some great stone structure, dating from Assyrian times, near the village of Jerwan, in the Ain Sifni district. We had visited the place while working at Khorsabad and had found a vast mass of masonry, straddling a valley with a stream called Gomel Su running through it. At the entrance to the village nearby, we found the old *mukhtar* (mayor) sitting outside his house on a large block of stone that bore an inscription in Assyrian cuneiform. Thorkild's first reading produced the words:

> Its . . . to it I added . . . I caused to be dug . . . over deep-cut ravines . . . white I spanned a bridge. . . . I caused to pass over upon it.

It was already known that, at some time in Sennacherib's reign, he became dissatisfied with the turgid waters of the Tigris and "brought clean water to Nineveh from the distant mountains." Even the source from which it was obtained had tentatively been identified at a place called Bavian, higher up the course of the Gomel Su, where the cliffs above the stream were adorned with rock sculptures and inscriptions. Our conclusion, then, which afterward proved right, was that the ruins we had found at Jerwan were less likely to be the remains of a bridge than those of an aqueduct. Now, therefore, with Hans's permission, having found accommodation in the village we enlisted about eighty Kurdish workmen and set about the total clearance of the Jerwan ruins. Our official sounding permit allowed us no more than one month's work; but in that time we completely exposed and recorded the surviving structure of our aqueduct, an astonishing example of Assyrian engineering, measuring 280 meters long by 22 meters wide (308 by 24 yards), with three pointed arches for the stream to pass under. The smallest blocks of "white" stone measured 50 cubic centimeters (3 cubic inches), and we calculated that more than two million of them had been quarried for the purpose.

It was already clear to us that the major supply of "clear" water for Nineveh must have its source at Bavian, where the whole story of the canal enterprise was recorded in rock inscriptions. But there were also indications that the quarry from which the "white" stone of the inscription had been obtained should also be sought at a canal head in the same locality. As for transport, the refinement of grading in the pavement over which the water flowed suggested a secondary use for wheeled vehicles.

All this was confirmed in the following spring, when a further short visit to Bavian became practicable. With time to examine the site more carefully, not only was the quarry immediately recognizable, but traces could also be found of a miniature barrage equipped with sluices by which the flow of water was regulated. My own job was to survey and record the whole setting, while Thorkild, suspended by rope from the top of the cliff, was recopying those inscriptions which dealt in part with the "opening ceremony" which the king attended.

By 1935 there were indications that the Iraq Expedition was running out of steam. This was sad for Delougaz, since at Khafajeh he had just located the main cemetery and was finding brick-vaulted graves, similar in date to the royal burials at Ur. But, from my own point of view, the Diyala region had a last prize in store, which bade fair to absorb my interest and energies for the whole of the following year. This was the site called Agrab.

During our first five years of residence at Asmar, we had been conscious of this neighboring mound, sixteen miles across the *chôl* to the east. Indeed, its outline could sometimes dimly be seen from the roof of our house, though often, owing to a whim of the local fata morgana, it would disconcertingly appear upside down. With our final departure from Asmar becoming imminent, a Sunday visit to Agrab on horseback was eventually arranged, with startling results. We found an oval-shaped mound, more than fifty feet high, measuring a quarter of a mile on its shortest axis: evidently a Sumerian walled city of considerable importance. Surface finds showed that its latest occupation must date from the last days of the Akkadian Empire, about 2200 BCE. But my own attention was attracted to a lower area, where the gray-white scattering of splin-

tered bones and votive pottery suggested a cemetery dating from the early Sumerian dynasties. Fragments of wall indicated that the graves had been dug into the remains of earlier buildings, which stood upon a horseshoe of raised ground, surrounding a low-lying amphitheater about a hundred yards across. Within this depression the color and texture of the soil suggested to a practiced eye the presence of a very large public building. If a temple, its site would conventionally have remained unoccupied after its destruction; later buildings and graves would then share the sanctity of its periphery. When I revisited the site a few days later, this assessment was rather dramatically confirmed.

I took with me Saleh Hussein, one of my best pickmen, and left him to scrape the surface at a point in the amphitheater where brickwork seemed visible, while I investigated other parts of the mound. Ten minutes later I heard him shout for me to return and knew, from this slight lapse of good manners, that he must have found something. I was right. He had not only located a clean, plastered wall-face, but his shovel had brought up a six-inch fragment of a relief carving in alabaster, a square plaque of the sort which is plugged to the wall of a temple. Among the figures carved on it, one could at once recognize the fleshy-nosed profile common to the Sumerians. During the following weeks, Frankfort was able to negotiate the inclusion of Tell Agrab in our excavation concession. It was then arranged that I should be put in charge of a two-month trial excavation, starting in January 1936.

Since the work was to be in the nature of a noncommital sounding, there was for the moment no question of my actually camping at the site itself. So I continued to use Tell Asmar as a base, driving to Agrab at sunrise and returning in the evening. Meanwhile the Sharqati workmen were housed in semi-underground dugouts covered with reed matting, while unskilled labor was transported six days a week from the nearest villages. The combined work of supervising, surveying, and controlling labor on a dig where up to a hundred workmen were employed would normally be considered overmuch responsibility for one person. But I had completed a rapid topographical survey of the mound before excavating began and, for the rest, I was supported by a team of experts at the Asmar base—draftsmen, conservators, photographers, and the like—who were available to assist me at any moment. In fact the whole excavation system had been so perfected during our past six years of work together that everything moved like clockwork. In the end it proved to be much more a question of whether the base staff could cope with the registration and treatment of the astonishing contributions which I brought home each evening than of my actually skimping the administration of the dig itself. The first few weeks of excavating the Shara Temple at Tell Agrab were some of the fullest and most exciting that I have ever spent.

During the first day's work it became clear that the wall face revealed by Saleh's pick belonged to a large and very important chamber. We soon traced the whole of its outline and, having located the doorway, decided to make a complete exposure, starting in the small antechamber through which it was approached. Since the walls were no more than a few inches high at this low point in the amphitheater, the pavement was very soon reached, and any doubts whether the building was a temple were

immediately dispelled, for the clay floor was littered with hundreds of beads and small amulets, mostly in the form of animals. The largest chamber itself, which indeed afterward proved to be the main sanctuary of the temple, was twenty meters long. As we approached the high, northern end we came upon two successive rows of small pedestals, upon which worshipers had apparently been accustomed to place their offerings. Around their bases was an even greater profusion of votive objects, including the first fragments of Sumerian sculpture. Beyond was the altar itself, with a vertical channel in one side leading to a sunken stone bowl, no doubt intended to catch the residue of libations.

Lying actually upon the altar was the severed head of a female statue, now a notable exhibit in the Iraq Museum in Baghdad. The lady of whom it was evidently a portrait wears a curiously shaped turban composed of fine cloth elaborately bound or pleated, around the edges of which her own hair appears, suggested by an inlay of bitumen. Her face has the strange, archaic smile of the period, her eyes and eyebrows are inlaid with lapis lazuli, and gold earrings

Seton Lloyd excavating the High Altar of the Shara Temple at Tell Agrab, 1936. COURTESY OF SETON LLOYD

would once have hung from the pierced lobes of her ears. One must, I suppose, imagine her as some great lady, whose likeness stood in an attitude of prayer before the cult statue (the small size of this effigy is characteristic of votive figures in the Early Dynastic period). When it was broken to pieces during a deliberate destruction of the building, the severed head must have remained on the altar and been covered by falling debris.

It was at this point also that we discovered a doorway leading to two small, intercommunicating chambers, literally full of damaged cult objects perhaps discarded by looters. There were scores of pear-shaped maceheads of the ritual kind that were carried in procession. They were carved out of every imaginable kind of stone or colored marble and sometimes quite elaborately decorated with animal or other motifs. There were many damaged statues and broken stone vessels, sculptured with scenes from Sumerian life. Often featured in the imagery was Gilgamesh, the herculean hero of the famous Sumerian epic and, as usual, the ritually naked figure of a priest. All these objects were buried with a litter of broken marble vessels and small amulets of every kind.

For nearly three weeks, the same pair of elderly Turkoman experts labored all day in these sacristy chambers, skillfully exposing and removing one object after another. Perhaps the most sensational find of all was made at the end of our second week. That morning I arrived after the men had started work and went straight to the rooms behind the altar, where I found the Turkomans already at their job. One of them was pointing excitedly to a lump of clay hardly bigger than an orange and using the Arabic word 'araba, meaning "carriage." Sure enough, when I looked more closely, projecting on one side was a tiny metal wheel. What emerged, after transport to the Asmar laboratory, was a two-wheeled chariot drawn by four onagers and driven by a bearded charioteer, perhaps a king. It was finely modeled in every detail and cast, as it now proves, by the cire perdue process. Needless to say, this object has been eagerly studied by many specialists in the subjects represented and even remodeled to a larger scale. A whole new chapter was thus added to the history of wheeled vehicles.

By the end of my fifth week's work, my funds were beginning to run short, so I had to start paying off my unskilled workmen. But by that time the antiquities storeroom at Tell Asmar was as full as it had ever been in the six years of our work there, and the crowded shelves gave great pleasure to the surviving members of the original staff. The stone maceheads, of which there were well over six hundred, had begun to be stacked in sackfuls, and beside them were tens of thousands of beads in cardboard boxes. Two perfect little statues of a man and a woman with inlaid eyes made a strange contrast to the broken foot of a life-sized statue, also of bronze. Meanwhile, the head and shoulders of a dog, easily recognizable as a saluki, finally established that breed as indigenous to Iraq. The broken alabaster vessels, now mostly mended, made a background for trays of cylinder seals. Some, which had perhaps been the property of priests, were nearly two inches in diameter and bore engravings of the sacred herd of cattle which was usually attached to temples like this one. Others showed hunting scenes, in which gazelles and ibex were depicted with a dexterity and sensibility rivaling that of Egyptian artists a thousand years later.

Clearly it was now imperative that a second and longer season of work at Tell Agrab should be arranged before the final liquidation of the Iraq Expedition. After negotiations, both in Chicago and in Baghdad, Frankfort contrived in the end to arrange that this should take place in November of the same year (1936), and for this purpose a small mud-brick building was constructed on the site.

On returning to the place after an interlude of some months in Europe, I was again struck by the extreme isolation of the mound as it survived at that time, and the impression that it gave of utter remoteness. No regular track passed within miles of it. The empty *chôl* stretched on all sides to the horizon, unblemished by a single tire mark. Far to the east the snow-covered mountains of Luristan hung like a hazy curtain, while in the nearer foreground a mirage undulated over a silver smear of water from the last rains. For the rest, there was rarely a bedouin or camel in sight, and the silence was broken only by such small sounds as the song of desert larks. By contrast, on our resumed digging we began

Four views of a copper quadriga found at the Shara Temple, Tell Agrab, circa 2800 BCE.
ORIENTAL INSTITUTE, UNIVERSITY OF CHICAGO

to find amulets in the form of fish, together with the actual copper hooks and net weights of fishermen. In the following months we completed the excavation of the Shara Temple, which proved to have been an enormous building of more than two hundred square feet (fifty-four square meters) with scores of rooms, including at least three subsidiary shrines and a suite of apartments for priests. The adjoining town wall also drew our attention, a structure of solid brick, more than fifteen feet (four and a half meters) thick with semicircular buttresses, of which we were able to trace the complete circuit. The impression which this created of a prosperous walled city, devoted to the worship of a single Sumerian god, was one that remained in our minds when the digging eventually came to an end and the site was pronounced abandoned.

For my own part, it had been a fairly exacting job and, after producing my own preliminary reports, I could allow the melodrama of Tell Agrab to fade from my memory.

Chronologically, the experiences related here cover a period of years in the 1930s, still identified in my memory as the Frankfort Era, but now to be regarded as a mere overture to my archaeological career. When it ended there was a interlude of similar work in Turkey and elsewhere which continued until 1939. In that year I returned to Iraq in a more official capacity, to share my newly acquired skills with the Iraqis themselves, and it must be admitted that, during the decades that followed, I again experienced highlights of discovery which seemed almost to excel those at Tell Agrab. Once more in the field of Sumerian studies, there was Tell al-ʿUqair, where much of the temple platform had survived, with its mural paintings still intact. In a later setting at ʿAqar Quf (Dur-Kurigalzu) there were the gigantic public buildings erected by Iraq's enigmatic Kassite rulers and, finally, our overwhelming successes in retrieving the marvels of prehistoric Eridu (Abu Shahrain).

At this point I am tempted to add some reference to my personal enjoyment of excavating, to record the unfailing pleasure that digging has afforded me over a period of more than forty years. I have known at times the sheer exhilaration of handling a team of experts and half a hundred unskilled men like a research instrument. What their work exposed could at first seem no more than an incoherent tangle of miscellaneous evidence; but an undisturbed hour of closer examination and intensive thought would occasionally lead to a welcome revelation, the rational interpretation that I had been seeking.

BIBLIOGRAPHY

P. DELOUGAZ and SETON LLOYD, *Pre-Sargonid Temples in the Diyala Region* (1942); HENRI FRANKFORT, *Sculpture of the Third Millennium B.C. in the Diyala Region* (1939), and *More Sculpture from the Diyala Region* (1943); THORKILD JACOBSEN and SETON LLOYD, *Sennacherib's Aqueduct at Jerwan* (1935); SETON LLOYD, *Twin Rivers* (1943), *Foundations in the Dust* (1947; rev. ed. 1980), *Mounds of the Ancient Near East* (1963), *The Archaeology of Mesopotamia* (1978), and *The Interval: A Life in Near Eastern Archaeology* (1987); GORDON LOUD and C. B. ALTMANN, *Khorsabad*, 2 vols. (1936–1938).

SEE ALSO **Searching for Sumer and Akkad** (Part 11, Vol. IV) and **Understanding Ancient Near Eastern Art: A Personal Account** (Part 11, Vol. IV).

Searching for Sumer and Akkad

THORKILD JACOBSEN

Born in Denmark in 1904, Professor Jacobsen studied Assyriology at the University of Copenhagen and completed his first doctorate at the University of Chicago's Oriental Institute in 1929. He later earned a second degree at Copenhagen in 1939. He served as professor and later as Director of the Oriental Institute at the University of Chicago. In 1962 he joined the Department of Near Eastern Languages and Literatures at Harvard University, where he served until retirement in 1974. Dr. Jacobsen continued to publish extensively as Professor of Assyriology Emeritus at Harvard University until his death in 1993.

MY FIRST SCHOLARLY ARTICLE was published in 1927. It was about the chronology of the Akkadian Dynasty and I was paid twenty shilling for it. Those were the days!

That same year, I passed my final exams for the degree of *magister artium* at the University of Copenhagen. The last of the requirements was a public lecture, and when I had finished it my wonderful teacher and mentor O. E. Ravn, who was always punctiliously correct in all his conduct, came up to me at the rostrum and said, "Jacobsen, now that you have your degree I can invite you to lunch." We went to a restaurant nearby, and when we were seated with the obligatory aquavit and beer before us, Ravn added:

"Jacobsen, now that you have your degree I can tell you that the first two years, after every session, I said to myself: 'The man is not stupid; he must see that this is not for him.'" But the man was.

That same year, 1927, a week after I got my degree, I married, and a week after that we left for Chicago on a fellowship of a thousand dollars from the American-Scandinavian Foundation. At that time it seemed to be a lot of money.

In Chicago I had intended to continue my studies under Daniel D. Luckenbill, but when I arrived I was told the sad news that he had died unexpectedly in London of a heart attack. Edward Chiera had been appointed but had not yet taken over. He was in Iraq finishing a season at Nuzi and opening a dig at Khorsabad from which the Institute obtained its huge winged bull. Work in Assyriology was thus at a standstill. Among the projects of the Institute then was one in Syriac, and since I had studied Arabic and Hebrew but not Syriac in Copenhagen, the latter seemed a useful language to add for etymological purposes. At that time etymology was still considered the prime key to the meaning of obscure Akkadian words. As a result, my American Ph.D. thesis came to be on a Syriac, rather than an Akkadian, subject: *The Commentary of Bar Salibi on the Book of Job,* both literal and spiritual.

The *Dictionary* (*The Assyrian Dictionary of the Oriental Institute of the University of Chicago*) was in the care of Frederik Geers, and soon after I arrived in Chicago, I spent much time with him among the filing cases. Geers was a most pleasant companion, kind, very learned, and slightly eccentric. He had an extraordinary aversion to publishing anything. I remember coming in one morning and finding him cleaning out his desk, throwing bits of paper in the wastebasket. When I asked what they were, he said they were notes about new sign values, joins of texts, and new meanings of words. He was not sure he could remember what they meant and they cluttered up the desk. I was horrified and made a quick dive into the wastebasket to rescue what I could. The result, together with some notes of my own, we published in a joint article in ZA, *Zeitschrift für Assyriologie,* penned, needless to say, by me. Years later when it was a matter of long-overdue promotion, he went through agonies when I. J. Gelb and I practically forced him to write his brief note on the important "Geer's Law."

The *Dictionary,* as I found it, had been planned along cost-economic lines. The scholars on the staff would transliterate and translate the texts and divide them into sections that would fill a file card. Clerical personnel would then mimeograph the sections on cards in as many copies as they had words. The scholars would then go over each card, underline a word, write it on the upper corner of the card, and parse it in an apparatus at the bottom of the cards. When all the cards had been thus treated, they would be filed by the clerical personnel, which at that time consisted of a single young woman. The texts on file in 1927 covered the Assyrian and Babylonian royal inscriptions, the Harper Letters in Leroy Waterman's translation (Robert F. Harper, *Assyrian and Babylonian Letters Belonging to the Kouyunjik Collection of The British Museum,* 14 vols., 1892–1910), the *Code of Hammurabi,* perhaps Arthur Ungnad's Old Babylonian Letters, and very little else. A drawback of the system was, apart from misfilings by persons not knowing Akkadian, that the purely mechanical way of filing tore apart shades of meaning that belonged together, so that the bulky files of fairly common words were more confusing than enlightening. Nor, indeed, was the level of translation very impressive.

When Chiera came back from the field and took over, all of this changed radically. It is not too much to say that he was the true founder of the *Dictionary,* setting the necessary standard of competence and finding the means to meet it. He made the *Dictionary* international. The body of materials was to be divided into genres and each genre was then assigned to a scholar who was already an expert on it so that the translation would reflect the best contemporary knowledge.

Chiera was a very inspiring person, always ready to share his ideas with others and for a young scholar it was exciting indeed to be present at the planning of a worldwide venture of such magnitude and of such crucial importance for the whole field of Assyriology. I was even allowed to be a part of it, for Chiera asked me to draw up the list of genres and scholars most competent to handle them. That list was, I think, generally followed; an improvement was Benno Landsberger's request for the lexical texts rather than the myths and epics assigned to him in the list. They went to Wolfram von Soden. The *Dictionary* thus gave Landsberger the incentive to undertake what is perhaps his most fundamental achievement, his work on the lexical texts.

The years working under Chiera in Chicago were a happy time for my wife, Rigmor, and me, but we knew we could not stay in the country long. Rigmor was here on a visitor's visa which had been renewed once and could not be extended again; I was here on a student visa but was soon to get my Ph.D. and so would not be a student any longer. There was no opening back in Denmark, so we could look forward only to living off our parents, which we did not like one bit. Then one day as I was working in the *Dictionary* room Chiera came in, and as he passed my desk he said: "Jacobsen, would you like to go on an excavation in Iraq?" to which I said, "Yes! Dr. Chiera." At that he swiveled around furious and said, "Damn it! I was not joking!" "Dr. Chiera, I was not joking either." "Then you shall go. I have just lost my fight to direct the Institute's project of excavation in Iraq so any little thing I ask for I shall get. I shall ask for you to go out as our representative." Thus miraculously, through Chiera's kindness and thoughtfulness, all our troubles were over and a wonderful new world of adventure and discovery lay before us.

We went back to Denmark awaiting the start of the expedition, which I was to join in January 1930. The leader of the expedition, I found out, was Henri Frankfort, whom I had long admired from afar as a consummate archaeologist. In getting to know him as a person I found that he was also a delightful companion, inspiring as leader of the expedition, and possessing a magic gift to make things come alive as he talked about them.

When I joined the expedition in Baghdad, Frankfort sent Seton Lloyd, Gordon Loud, and me on a tour south to visit the two great excavations then going on, Ur and Warka (Uruk). We gazed with awe at the empty holes in the ground that had held the fabulous royal tombs with all their golden treasures, and upon arriving at Warka on horseback—rain had made the desert impassable for cars—we admired the systematic work that had identified the Uruk period as the successor to the Ubaid period. The stunning marble head of Inanna had not yet been found. Greatly impressed with what could be discovered, we then went north to join Pinhas Delougaz and Frankfort in Khorsabad where we were to continue Chiera's earlier work. We cleared the throne room of Sargon of Assyria, a small room nearby with reliefs illustrating his campaigns, and excavated a city gate. We also learned the fine art of tracing a mud-brick wall embedded in debris of identical texture.

The following season we moved south to Tell Asmar (ancient Eshnunna). I was extremely happy that Rigmor had become a member of the expedition. She had studied archaeological photography in Copenhagen during the summer and was soon recognized as one of the best photographers on the expeditions then working in Iraq.

The years in Asmar were wonderful years and to try to recall them would demand far more space than is available here, so I shall limit myself to just three events of special concern to me. The first of these was the dig at Jerwan. A year or so after we had begun Asmar, Frankfort assigned the work at Khorsabad to Loud, so after each session Rigmor and I used to go up there for me to read the inscriptions found. It was on one such visit that it was borne in on me that I was holding in my hands a complete Assyrian Kinglist of the utmost importance for filling gaps in Assyrian chronology. I later copied it before it was sent on loan to Chicago where Arno

Poebel was to publish it. On the different occasion with which I am here concerned I was sitting watching the work when the foreman, whom I knew well, came up to me and told me of a village full of blocks of stone with cuneiform inscriptions; so with him as a guide I went to see it and found the inscriptions to be part of Sennacherib's name and titles. As we sat over tea hospitably provided for us, I was told that the inscribed blocks came from a long, ridgelike structure and that there was a place where there were many such blocks together. The villagers kindly uncovered it for me and there to my amazement and delight I read the words, "I spanned a bridge." The oldest bridge known then was one built by Nebuchadnezzar in Babylon and only one pier of it had survived. Here was one far older and, to judge from the looks of the ridge, in remarkable state of preservation.

Next year, at the end of the season, Lloyd and his wife, Joan, and Rigmor and I, went up into the Kurdish mountains to excavate it. It proved to be a very special bridge, one that was meant to

Thorkild Jacobsen at Tell Asmar during the 1934–1935 season. COURTESY OF KATRYNA JACOBSEN

carry a canal over a mountain arroyo, the earliest known aqueduct. Moreover, we were able to trace the network of canals to which it belonged and thus, utilizing other of Sennacherib's inscriptions, to reconstruct the magnificent canal system instituted by Sennacherib to provide his new capital, Nineveh, with abundant pure mountain water. The head of the system was on the Gomel River, marked by the monumental Bavian relief and inscription carved into the almost vertical mountainside there. The village in which the aqueduct was located, Jerwan, was inhabited by Yezidis, known as Devil worshipers. We found them friendly and pleasant and enjoyed visiting the picturesque villages of their coreligionists in the neighborhood. Actually they do not worship the Devil; they merely try to appease him.

The first seasons at Asmar I had been busy recording the tablets found with findspot and level. I think that was the first time this was done systematically on any excavation, and it allowed me by attention to the stratigraphy to establish the complete series of rulers of Eshnunna from the time of Ur III to that of Hammurabi. I also copied the tablets and had almost enough for a modest volume. It was thus a bit of a blow when I was suddenly informed that it had been decided that all tablets found there should remain unpublished to the end of the excavations, at which time Dr. Chiera and Professor Poebel would assign them. I might then, I was told, possibly be given some of the less important texts to publish. I do not think Chiera had anything to do with the decision; it was not like him. Frankfort, considerate as always, did what he could to cheer me by saying: "Thorkild, since you cannot publish tablets, would you like to take over a dig?" So I happily took charge of excavating Akkadian private houses in Tell Asmar with my good friend Harold Hill as architect.

Directly to the north of us Lloyd was digging up a small Early Dynastic temple where he came upon the most spectacular of our finds, the Asmar statues which at that time were the earliest ones known and so the finds were doubly exciting. (This find is detailed in "Excavating the Land Between the Two Rivers," above.) After the Akkad houses, which were so well preserved that walking around in them made one feel curiously

close to the ancients who had once lived in them, I was given charge of excavating Ishchali, another mound in the region. Here we uncovered a large temple complex of Isin-Larsa date dedicated to the goddess Inanna Kititum. It turned out to be crucial for understanding the development of the ancient Mesopotamian temple plan. Previous work by German archaeologists had distinguished a northern plan with "long-room" cella and bent-axis approach and a southern plan with "broad-room" cella entered by a gate in one of the long walls (see "Palaces and Temples in Ancient Mesopotamia" in Part 4, Vol. I for further discussion). Furthermore, while it was apparent that the living quarters of the deity were often situated on top of a high platform or a ziggurat, no plan of any historical period survived due to the extreme vulnerability to erosion of the top of the ziggurats and high terraces. Ishchali, remarkably, formed an exception, and we were able to recover the plan which showed that the "cella" was actually the deity's reception room, or *Iwan*, the public room of the house, while the private apartments, the living quarters, or *harēm*, lay behind it. The plan also suggested that the "broad-room" plan had developed out of the screened-in end of the "long-room" cella in the course of extreme enlargement of it. Finally it became clear that the remarkable Early Dynastic "Oval" temple plan discovered by Delougaz at Khafaje and Tell al-Ubaid developed through progressive squaring off into the standard plan of major temple complexes in later periods such as the Nanna Temple in Ur, the Enlil Temple in Nippur, and, of course, the Kititum Temple itself. All of that, as it gradually dawned on one as the temple and its plan emerged from the ground, was intensely fascinating.

The excavations of the Iraq Expedition came to an end in 1936, and as work drew to a close it seemed to me that while we had explored four major tells in depth, we really knew nothing about the Diyala region as a whole, and that before we left we ought to explore it to see where it had been occupied and where not. I spoke of this to Frankfort and with his usual openness to new ideas he agreed to let Rigmor and me stay over for such a survey.

Our procedure was to visit systematically every tell in the region, section by section, locate each one on the map, pace it off for size, and date it from pottery left on the surface. We then plotted the tells of each period on period maps and saw to our great delight that they made a pattern; they ranged themselves in lines which clearly stood for the rivers and canals on which the ancient towns and villages they covered had lain and on which they had depended for their existence.

The results of the survey were scheduled for the last volume of the expedition reports and so never got published. Instead they were made available to the Diyala Basin Archaeological Project in 1957.

An opportunity to try the survey method more widely came in 1953 when I was appointed Annual Professor of the Baghdad School and was asked to suggest a small project. I suggested an archaeological survey, the "Survey of Central Sumer." It was carried out with my old friend Fuad Safar and a new one, Vaughn Crawford, and it changed the ideas about ancient topography then current very substantially. We recovered the course of the important Iturungal canal and the "Canal going to Nina." We were able to rectify the universally held identification of Tello (Girsu) with Lagash (modern Tell al-Hiba) and to identify Bagara, Zabalam, and Bad-tibira.

The survey technique which Rigmor and I originated in 1936 had proved itself. It was a new thing in Mesopotamian archaeology in that it covered a region completely and systematically and in its use of dating by pottery, which Frankfort had introduced not long before.

(The last survey I undertook, years later, centered on the boundary canal separating Lagash and Ur. It was made together with my present wife Katryna and was very enjoyable and successful.)

Thinking back to the years in Asmar the exceptional character of that whole period is what stands out, with its full measure of nostalgia. As I wrote recently in a review of Seton Lloyd's autobiography *The Interval*, "the period . . . was unique in that it was one of basic initiations both archaeologically, politically, and socially, it had the feeling of laying foundations for great things whether of knowledge or of action. Lloyd mentions that it has been called the era of 'Great Excavations,' more correct would be the era of 'Basic Discovery.'" It is difficult now to realize

how little was known in 1930. Frankfort introduced dating by pottery and defined the Early Dynastic period. Later he organized and dated the cylinder seals, tablets were recorded with findspot and stratum for the first time at Tell Asmar, the Uruk period and the Ubaid period were identified in Warka and Ur, Lloyd established the Hassuna period. It was this sense of pioneering, of venturing into a great unknown past and finding out about it, of excitement and responsibility, that made the 1930s unique. Lloyd conveys it well in writing home about his discovery of the Asmar statues: "Personally it will take me a long time to forget the intense excitement of lying on my tummy for almost two days with the feeling of awful responsibility—knowing, especially in the case of the half-life-sized pair, which are apparently a god and goddess, that one is, in a sense, making history. . . . It is that sense, which can never be felt in quite the same way again, of the peak in Darien, that sets the thirties apart and will forever justify one as *laudator temporis acti*" (see Lloyd's account, "Excavating the Land Between the Two Rivers," above).

When the Iraq Expedition ended in 1936 I was transferred to Chicago to help in the preparation of the final reports, but not long after arriving there I learned to my dismay that my appointment would not be continued. As it happened however, owing to unforeseen events, I was taken on again as Research Associate on the *Assyrian Dictionary* together with the unforgettable Abe Sachs.

Work on the reports left me time for some independent research, and out of that grew my article "The Assumed Conflict Between the Sumerians and Semites in Early Mesopotamian History." Here a few words should perhaps be said to recall the intellectual climate of the times. There was virtual unanimity about what had shaped early Mesopotamian history, it was race, Sumerians fighting Semites. Races differed in physique and in character, so cranial measurements, shapes of noses, and even bearded or beardless were matters of moment. Eduard Meyer, Leonard King, and James Henry Breasted, to mention only a few names, thought so; even Frankfort devoted space to a discussion of crania in his *Archaeology and the Sumerian Problem* of 1932. I certainly shared the common opinion uncritically. In fact, already when I was still in my teens it had been a "project" of mine to determine precisely and in detail the differences between the two races on the basis of clear textual and other evidence; but it never got very far. It was not until 1937 or 1938 that in Chicago I returned to the problem thinking that it would make a good subject for a lecture I had been asked to give and found, rather to my surprise, that there *was* no such evidence and so, presumably, no such "racial conflict." Nor, I may add, has any such evidence turned up since. The conclusions I had thus reached were, for a time, widely shared and led to the abandonment of the racial frame for early Mesopotamian history. Fairly soon though, the old view was revived by the simple expedient of substituting the word "ethnic" for the word "racial." That does not, however, change the facts. All the conflicts we know of were political, conflicts between city-states and groupings of city-states, not ethnic, between ethnically differing units or groups. Rather, as we now know, the city Kish sided with Ur against Akkad throughout the early years of Naram-Suen's (Naram-Sin's) reign.

The article was published the next year, 1939, and so was a book I had been working on for some years, *The Sumerian Kinglist.* Walking around the Akkad houses in Asmar rekindled my interest in the chronology of the Akkadian Dynasty and from there in the kinglist as a whole. At that time, this list was thoroughly discredited since it assigned incredibly long reigns to some rulers and listed contemporaneous dynasties as successive. I tried to get an idea of what its sources would have been like and concluded that the dynasties of major centers like Kish, Uruk, and Ur came from a Kish, Uruk, and Ur source, respectively, so that the dynasties of each city were to be read as consecutive. The original lists, thus restored, could then be correlated through known synchronisms and would each show a clear point where mythical reigns changed to reigns of possible length.

Attending to synchronisms showed, among other things, that the Gutian Dynasty did not follow that of Akkad, as was then generally assumed, but began immediately after Naram-Suen. This lends some credence to the composition the *Curse of Agade,* which has the same timing. As for Naram-Suen, I found years later

to my utter surprise that Kish under Ipkhur-Kish and Ur under Anne must have been independent of Akkad during much of his early years, and a similar surprise was the realization that the breakup of the Ur III empire and the destruction of Ur itself did not constitute a single event but happened years apart. The more we know, the less simple things turn out to be. I submitted the kinglist book as a doctoral thesis to the University of Copenhagen and defended it in the tense atmosphere of Hitler's invasion of Poland and the beginning of the Second World War. As usual the Copenhagen newspapers reported the defense of a doctoral thesis on their front page. Ravn was official opponent and his magnificent tails and white tie were noted and duly commented on by the press.

In the war years, when fieldwork had necessarily come to a standstill, the Director of the Oriental Institute, John A. Wilson, gave a talk in which he suggested that we focus on institutions instead. I thought that was an excellent idea and told him so, only to find the next day a memo telling me that arrangements had been made for me to attend courses at the law school. That had not been what I intended, but there I was, caught. As it turned out, I found the courses engrossing, particularly one, Sociology of Law, given by Professor Max Rheinstein. So much of what I knew about ancient Mesopotamia came together in clear structures. It was what I learned in those courses that made me take up the problems of my articles "Primitive Democracy in Ancient Mesopotamia" (1943) and "Early Political Development in Mesopotamia" (1957). Their common theme is the effect of expansion of the human sociopolitical unit from village to city and city-state, kingdom, and empire, and I was pleased that this was the accepted theme for the "City Invincible" symposium called by Professor Carl Kraeling in 1958. At the symposium itself I tried to point up not only the effects of the expansion on the political forms but also the effects of these forms as patterns within culture generally: religion, art, and literature.

Much had happened, though, between my attending classes on law in 1942 and the symposium of 1958. In 1946 I was appointed Director of the Oriental Institute; in 1947 my beloved Rigmor died and life lost its meaning. All I could do was to bury myself in work.

At the time I was made director, the Institute was facing a number of problems. Excavations had come to a standstill, work on the *Dictionary* had, under Poebel's editorship, come to a complete halt, and there was a real need for senior appointments.

I began with trying to get excavations going again and the first expedition we sent out was that of Robert J. Braidwood to Jarmo in northeast Iraq. It established a new very early prehistoric period. Next was the problem of a site of historical importance in the heartland of Sumer or Akkad. I therefore went to Iraq to look for a possible site. It was summer and hot but Fuad did not mind driving all over the country, looking at tell after tell. In the end Nippur seemed the best choice, partly because of its unique importance as a political and religious center in antiquity, and partly for the promise it held out of yielding up tablets with Sumerian literary texts as it had done around the beginning of the century when Pennsylvania dug there.

Because of the moral claim to the site those excavations gave, it seemed only right to ask if the University of Pennsylvania was still interested in it and would consider a joint undertaking. I had therefore talked with Sam Kramer and he was able to persuade the director of the University Museum to accept. We were thus able to begin excavations there with Donald E. McCown and Carl Haines at the end of 1948. The excavation centered on the Ekur and the "scribal quarter," and in the third season our expectations of literary texts were richly rewarded. The tablets were baked in the field, a precaution first taken, I believe, in Asmar, and latex casts were made of them. This was a new additional safeguard. When the casts arrived in Chicago, Sam Kramer and I spent days going through them identifying both new compositions and duplicates that filled lacunae in old ones with the pure joy of discovery.

In addition to getting excavation going again, there was the problem of the *Dictionary* which had lain fallow so long, and here I was able to persuade Gelb to take over the editorship, which he conducted with great energy and devotion. Lastly there was the matter of appointments, and here the Institute had the extremely good fortune of being able to add to its staff scholars as eminent as Landsberger, Hans Güterbock, and

A. Leo Oppenheim. There were also losses, though; Frankfort was called to the directorship of the Warburg Institute in London.

In 1948 I was appointed dean of the Division of the Humanities and Kraeling took over as director of the Institute. I was able to return to scholarship in 1958. All I had been able to do of scholarly work till then was pondering Dumuzi texts. They accorded with my mood. I used to take a text volume down to a small restaurant where they did not mind that I stayed late after my dinner. The texts were often both moving and beautiful, but they were also very difficult and made it only too clear how partial was (and, for that matter, still is) our knowledge of Sumerian. Such basic understanding as we do have of the workings and structure of the language is due to Poebel and his great *Grundzüge des sumerischen Grammatik* of 1923, but, as Kramer has rightly written: "Now it might seem reasonable to expect that a fundamental and comprehensive grammar of this caliber would be received with deep appreciation by cuneiformists the world over. Not at all! It was not welcomed or even accepted by European scholars and was ignored in America." It was, in fact, only the younger generation of scholars who recognized it for what it was and became "Poebelians"; specifically, the triumvirate of Adam Falkenstein, Kramer, and me.

I had, of course, an undue advantage. Ravn, who was a very fine grammarian, had immediately recognized Poebel's excellence and had even gone to Rostock, Germany, to take one of his courses, so I was taught Poebel's grammar from the outset. Falkenstein was a student of Fritz Hommel but would, Landsberger told me, hear of nothing but Poebel; Kramer became an enthusiastic Poebelian when he was appointed to the *Assyrian Dictionary* and attended Poebel's courses, so much so, indeed, that for years he was known as "Poebel's Kramer." I had also had the privilege of attending a course by Poebel. It was shortly after Chiera had taken over the *Dictionary* and had invited Poebel over to prepare a report on the scholarly level of the translations in the *Dictionary* files. When I was told that we were to read *CT* 21 (*Cuneiform Texts from Babylonian Tablets in the British Museum*) I was disappointed. I had hoped for more advanced materials, but I prepared some twenty inscriptions for the first session; they seemed easy and straightforward. As it turned out, I think we got through only four or five in the whole course; every line raised fundamental questions to be explored. I still have my course notes and used to consult them for years until, by now, I know them by heart.

As it happened I came to disagree with Poebel on an essential point not long after. The first task I was given as epigrapher on the Tell Asmar expedition was to settle the question of the form of the ancient name of the site. I found that the final -k of the name Eshnunak was not rendered in texts following standard Sumerian orthography. It did occur, however, in texts outside that tradition; for example, Elamite and Kassite. This showed that it was *not* lost in the spoken language, so failure to render it must be a purely orthographical feature. This ran counter to Poebel's tenet that the writing rendered the underlying spoken forms exactly. I followed it up later, showing that such ellipticalness was a regular feature, particularly of the old inscriptions. Ur-Nanshe's, for instance, "omit" virtually all grammatical elements.

At present Poebel's view of the writing is generally accepted. Moreover, grammatical study of Sumerian considers the older texts basic and distrusts the more explicit renderings of the later ones. As the nature of the writing gets clarified this will, one hopes, radically change.

One of the most helpful group of later texts are the grammatical texts composed by the ancients themselves. They include organized lists of pronouns and paradigms of different kinds of verbal inflection. One such word, "to go," lists no fewer than 318 different forms the verb could take. Poebel appreciated their value fully and a great deal of his grammar was based on what was then available. A great addition were the so-called Crozer Texts bought by Chiera and entrusted by him to Poebel for publication. After Poebel's retirement they were taken over by Landsberger, who published them in *Materialien zum sumerischen Lexikon (MSL) IV* (1956), generously asking me to write the introduction to them. It was fascinating material, a true intellectual voyage of discovery into the unknown at the hands of the ancient teachers themselves. At a later date I tried to evaluate the intellectual contribution of these pioneering grammarians, the

first to deal with the structure of language, in an article I called "Very Ancient Linguistics."

Needless to say, the grammatical texts not only solved problems, they also raised new ones, and the Sumerian verb continued to fascinate me for years. It was the subject of my contribution to the volume honoring Landsberger in 1965, and I returned to its problems recently with a study of the verbal core.

When the introductions for *MSL IV* were finished I received an invitation from the Iraqi government to undertake a study of the history of salinization of the soil in Iraq. It was to concentrate on the Diyala region and to be a joint project of the Oriental Institute and the Department of Antiquities of Iraq. It was clear that such a program would have to draw on many and varied branches of knowledge, from hydraulic engineering and soil science to paleobotany, ethnography, archaeology, archaeological survey, and philology, and we were lucky in enlisting cooperation from experts in all of them. Of the many members of the project let me mention only a few from the field staff: Fuad Safar and Mohammed Ali Mustapha from the Department of Antiquities, Robert McC. Adams from the Oriental Institute, and Hans Helbaek.

We were able to show that the main cause of salinization was over-irrigation, which drew up salt from the salty water table through capillary action.

This simple explanation led to insights of many kinds; an unexpected one of interest to the historian was the likelihood that a canal cut by Entemena of Lagash to bring in Tigris water probably started over-irrigation and following salting up of the fields in the south and so led to the impoverishment and collapse of the heartland of the Ur III Empire, and with it, of Sumerian civilization itself.

Perhaps the most important, but also the most difficult, subject one has to deal with in the study of a civilization is its religion. Important because a civilization necessarily takes form from its understanding of man's relations with the ultimate powers governing existence, that is, from its religion, and difficult because the core of all religion, the numinous experience, can only be suggested in metaphors and cannot be described. For an outsider to a civilization its metaphors do not readily come to life and so one may easily lose their religious content altogether and be left with empty form.

It is thus understandable that I had to return to this challenging subject again and again, first in my chapters in *Before Philosophy* given in lecture form in 1946, then in a study of the dying god Tammuz, "Toward the Image of Tammuz" (1961). This was followed by attempts to recognize the major determinants in the development of the religion, its formative tendencies (1961), and central concerns (1963). Studies of the religious drama so focal in the cult, and of the significance of the cult statue were published in 1975 and 1987. A comprehensive statement I gave with my book *Treasures of Darkness: A History of Mesopotamian Religion* in 1976, and yet whether I have at all understood, not to say communicated, the sense of it, I can not rightly know.

One most enjoyable group of texts to work with is the one comprising myths and epics, and the one most deeply moving is the one with laments for the destruction of cities and temples. I remember the joy it was to leaf through Chiera's *Sumerian Religious Texts* which I bought in Paris in 1931 and shortly afterwards adding de Genouillac's *Textes religieux sumériens*. Later came Chiera's *Sumerian Epics and Myths* and *Sumerian Texts of Varied Content* with Kramer's introductions. These books have ever since been constant companions.

The need for publishing every fragment of literary texts, because only in this way could we hope to put the fragments together and restore the original composition, was realized first by Chiera, and he himself began the onerous task. These days when so much has been put together and new fragments are likely to have a niche to fit readily into, the sense of frustration in working only with unfitted fragments is difficult to convey. Nothing made sense or it broke off just before it would have done so. It was thus a dull routine job, but an essential one. The name that stands out here is that of Samuel Kramer. His patience, commitment, accuracy, and wonderful ability to recognize what went together is legendary. It was based, of course, on an unbelievably vast acquaintance with the farrago of bits and pieces we then had to work with. Personally I had the inestimable privilege of working closely with him for many years. He would send me

Thorkild Jacobsen at his home in New Hampshire reading *Daedalus*. COURTESY OF KATRYNA JACOBSEN

copies of new texts with his superb pioneering renderings. I would send my comments, and our discussion of moot points was always enjoyable and enlightening to me. At scholarly meetings, we would often sneak off to discuss Sumerian problems over drinks, both of us quoting long Sumerian passages by heart in support of our argument. I remember the puzzled faces of people at the neighboring tables who were trying to guess from our language where we came from.

Nobody ever came up to us and asked outright. Had anyone done so he might well have been even more puzzled to learn that we were committed, committed for life, to get to know even more about people so far away and so long dead—and we should have been hard put to answer why.

Actually, I suppose, on the deepest level it was not a rational choice at all, rather the listening to a compelling inner voice chanting lines like Rudyard Kipling's in "Explorer":

Something hidden, Go and find it,
   Go and look behind the Ranges—
Something lost behind the Ranges,
   Lost and waiting for you. Go!

Not that there were not perfectly good, rational reasons for commitment, but they would come after it had been made. First of all, of course, is the fact that the study of ancient Mesopotamia is pushing the beginning of history back for thousands of years, orients us in time as civilized beings, and gives us roots, evolves our background. In addition it rescues for us works of timeless beauty and value which, as we ponder them, enlarge our mind and tell us more about ourselves. Such works are the marble head of the goddess Inanna from Warka and the great "Lamentation over the Destruction of Ur," the Naram-Suen Victory Stela and the Gilgamesh epic.

So my search for Sumer and Akkad goes on. It has made me meet and work with great scholars who were also wonderful people; it has been not only searching but also finding. The joy in the deeply moving beauty of the great "Lament for Ur" is equaled by few great poems and would alone justify a lifetime's devotion.

BIBLIOGRAPHY

See SETON LLOYD, *The Interval* (1986) and SAMUEL N. KRAMER, *In the World of Sumer* (1986). Most of my earlier articles mentioned here are reprinted in WILLIAM L. MORAN, ed., *Toward the Image of Tammuz* (1970). Translations of Sumerian literary texts may be found in KRAMER, *History Begins at Sumer* (1981) and in my *The Harps That Once . . .* (1987).

SEE ALSO **Palaces and Temples in Ancient Mesopotamia** (Part 4, Vol. I); **Sumerian Literature: An Overview** (Part 9, Vol. IV); and **Excavating the Land Between the Two Rivers** (Part 11, Vol. IV).

Rediscovering Egypt of the Pharaohs

T. G. H. JAMES

T. G. H. JAMES *was born in Wales on May 8, 1923. He studied Classics and Egyptology at the University of Oxford and spent his professional career in the Department of Egyptian Antiquities in the British Museum in London, becoming Keeper in 1974 and retiring in 1988. He was elected a Fellow of the British Academy in 1976. Mr. James has held visiting professorships at the Collège de France in Paris and at Memphis State University, Tennessee. His publications include several epigraphic volumes on Egyptian monuments and on objects in museum collections; the* Ḥeḳanakhte Papers (1962), *a crucial group of papyri containing letters of an Eleventh Dynasty farmer to his family; and a number of works for general readers. He has also been very active as an editor of academic series.*

In writing this general review of the development of Egyptology and statement of how the discipline stands at the end of the twentieth century, I have chosen to emphasize particular advances and certain scholars without aiming to be comprehensive. It is a very personal review, and yet it does not incorporate all my own preferences—intellectual heroes, academic movements, significant publications. The inclusions are deliberate; the omissions are not intentional. I do not draw much attention to the weaknesses of the Egyptological discipline, of which there have been, and still are, many. I set out to underline the achievements of the past, to celebrate rigor in scholarship and the proper placing of Egyptology in the field of humane studies, as I observed them in the past and as I observe them in the present. I hope the review is positive without being bland and complacent.

Knowledge and understanding are of almost equal importance in the comprehension of a culture. Scholarship can provide the knowledge, but not necessarily the understanding, although there is little hope for the latter without the former. The ability to have insights about the ancient world that will survive the scrutiny of known facts is something which only some scholars possess, and few scholars exercise—for to have insight is often equivalent to sticking out your neck, with the possibility of having it chopped. Good scholars are masters of fact, and should rightly be cautious in formulating views that cannot easily be supported by convincing evidence; at the same time, because of their command of fact, good scholars are in the best position to have insights when the evidence may not be enough but, when combined with finely tuned intuition, points to persuasive conclusions. It is proper that scholars should, from time to time, stick out their necks, risk their reputations, hazard guesses, because in doing so they can advance understanding, stretch comprehension, and even redirect lines of inquiry.

One of the (apparently) dullest of Egyptologists was Francis Llewellyn Griffith (1862–1934), a man who, so it was said, lived a life absorbed by Egypt and Egyptian texts, whose formal contribution to the advancement of the study of ancient Egypt was formidable. His way of life was regular and austere; he had little interest in the arts; when in later life he discovered the cinema and began to keep longer hours, he did not last long. But he had such a feel for the language of ancient Egypt, for the modest products of its parochial literature, that he never wrote anything uninformed by understanding and sympathy, which even now, more than half a century after his death, does not inspire confidence. A careful scrutiny of Griffith's published work shows the range of his interests, and it is common knowledge that his contribution to paleography—to hieratic studies, the reading of demotic texts, to Meroitic, both cursive and hieroglyphic (scarcely better understood now than in his day), and Old Nubian—helped to establish its bases at quite crucial moments in the development of Egyptological studies.

Griffith was very much an autodidact—a self-taught scholar who was obliged to be so because of the inadequacy of the teaching possibilities in the Egyptological field in Britain. His own scholarly development occurred almost in a vacuum, in the years after the death of Samuel Birch (1813–1885), the learned Keeper of Oriental Antiquities in the British Museum, who had virtually single-handedly nurtured the tender Egyptological plant in Britain for almost fifty years. Griffith had a remarkable memory and, in his early years as a junior in the British Museum, indulgent superiors; he was able to set his own pace for development. In later life, with ample private means and an excellent library, he wasted little time. Everything he wrote was informed by understanding, and he never failed to stick out his neck if he had a good idea.

And in the world of ideas Griffith was profligate and generous. He had no false pretensions to scholarly priority; he scattered his intuitions with a lavish disregard for personal reputation. He was, as Georges Posener (1906–1988) once told me, someone whose footnotes alone might represent the achievement of less imaginative scholars. Posener, in fact, invoked Griffith *contra* Kurt Sethe (1869–1934)—footnotes to arti-

Painting of Samuel Birch, a Keeper of Oriental Antiquities in the British Museum during the nineteenth century. BRITISH MUSEUM, LONDON

cles. It was not, perhaps, a measured assessment, and not one that Posener might have wanted to defend to the death. But there was truth in it. Griffith leaped from knowledge to understanding; Sethe moved from knowledge by way of solid scholarship, analysis of evidence, and logical progression, to deeper knowledge.

THE EARLY DAYS

It is instructive to consider the state of Egyptology at the turn of the nineteenth–twentieth centuries. It was then, as it must have seemed at the time, that Egyptology came of age. During much of the nineteenth century, to which we shall return shortly, studies had developed in a somewhat disorganized manner. This was not altogether surprising, because at its inception Egyptology had been a kind of spin-off from classical studies combined with exercises in intellectual virtuosity that attracted clever men as much as scholars. At the end of the century there was, notably in France and Germany, a movement toward systematic studies which gave a superficial feeling that the discipline of Egyptology was just that, and not a disorganized intellectual grappling after elusive systems. The grammatical advances made by the German school, in particular, seemed to have tied down at last the uncertainties of Egyptian language, both grammatical and syntactic. The grammatical systematization of Adolf Erman (1854–1937) allowed students to examine the arcane mysteries of Egyptian hieroglyphs in a way that greatly surpassed the gropings of earlier Egyptologists. Sethe's studies of the Egyptian verb were, it seemed, conclusive and of permanent value. The fact that French scholars, headed by the magisterial Gaston Maspero (1846–1916), were more than a little skeptical about German certainties did not substantially alter the situation.

In the end, of course, what mattered was how you translated an Egyptian text; and that was still partly a question of magic and intuition.

It is a sobering matter to contemplate translation as an indication of success in the comprehension of Egyptian hieroglyphs. A brief retrospect of progress is both encouraging and somewhat disconcerting. One may still date the decipherment of hieroglyphs to 1822, to the *Lettre à M. Dacier,* in which Jean-François Champollion

Engraving of a painting by Sir Thomas Lawrence of Thomas Young, whose nineteenth-century work aided Jean-François Champollion's decipherment of hieroglyphs in 1822. NATIONAL PORTRAIT GALLERY, LONDON

(1790–1832) set out his understanding of the principles on which that fascinating script worked. It would not here be profitable to try to untangle how much Champollion owed his discovery to the work of others, particularly Thomas Young (1773–1829); but it can be stated without equivocation that what he announced in the *Lettre à M. Dacier* was entirely along the right lines. And it is to Champollion's credit—ingrate though he might have been to his coworkers—that he could see clearly what the principles of the script probably were, and that he pursued the matter until his principles matured from probability to certainty. So, by about 1830 students of Egyptian hieroglyphs had the possibility of exploiting Champollion's discovery, and set about finding out what all those strange texts in tomb and temple really meant. Almost inevitably they turned out to be quite different from the perverse conclusions of the late classical and Renaissance scholars who had applied esoteric theories to the selfsame texts.

From the perspective of today it seems extraordinary that the realization of the falsity of earlier views about decipherment should have been so complete. It came, it must be supposed, with the acceptance that in the Rosetta Stone a real basis for certainty had been discovered. Here was an inscribed slab with three texts, one of which, that in Greek, could be read with little difficulty. The two others, one in hieroglyphs and one in the cursive demotic script, known at the time as enchorial, were assumed to be versions of the Greek text in the two ancient Egyptian scripts. The first halting lines of inquiry appeared to support this view. Champollion's discoveries confirmed it; and in what now seems to have been no time at all, the identity of the three texts was fully confirmed, and the results were being applied to every text that scholars wished to read. The system worked!

It is hard now to appreciate what must have seemed almost a miracle in the 1830s and 1840s. You could, if you were a Sir John Gardner Wilkinson (1797–1875), or a Carl Richard Lepsius (1810–1884), go into an Egyptian tomb or a temple, look at a line of hieroglyphs at the heading to a scene, and actually read the name of a king and the description of what he was doing. You could make out, admittedly with some difficulty, the gist of a text; you could even provide a kind

The Rosetta Stone, which bore copies in hieroglyphic, demotic, and Greek of a decree promulgated in 196 BCE by the priests at Memphis. The basalt slab was recovered from Rosetta, Egypt, by Napoleon's troops and turned over to the British Army following Napoleon's defeat in 1801. This discovery provided the key to the decipherment of hieroglyphics. BRITISH MUSEUM, LONDON

of translation. If you were a Samuel Birch, with the already substantial riches of the British Museum at your elbow, you could be the first person in thousands of years to open a papyrus roll, penetrate the cursive difficulties of the hieratic or demotic text, achieve a very fair idea of the contents, and make a publication that remains, a century and a half later, not without usefulness.

There were, of course, doubters; there may even be a few today. Is there not more to hieroglyphs than the prosaic conclusions of the Egyptologists would allow? The idea that the Egyptians, particularly the priests, were the possessors of remarkable knowledge remains a strong belief within certain unsystematic sects and bodies devoted to the mystical interpretation of ancient texts. For such people Egyptologists are dull fellows who cannot see behind the first level of meaning. That view seems to be wholly misconceived. The "dull" Egyptologist who possesses any imagination—were not most Egyptologists trapped by the fascination of their study in their youths?—is constantly thrilled by

the knowledge he or she treasures, but is too sensible to allow the passion to control the understanding. How much more thrilling must it have been for the early workers in the field! They, few in number, unorganized, and often isolated—like Charles Wycliffe Goodwin (1817–1878), a virtual exile academically in his consular post in Shanghai but comforted by a small library, including the elephant folios of Lepsius's *Denkmaeler aus Aegypten und Aethiopien* (1849–1859)—relied greatly on the burgeoning international postal services. For Goodwin, to check a reference, to confirm a reading, to discuss a point of grammar or a possible etymology, he had to write along the trade routes to Europe. It is remarkable how much he was able to do in such circumstances. Herein lay true devotion to a study, remarkable persistence, and a genuine, even primitive, *philosophia*.

What difficulties the pioneers worked under! They had none of the tools of scholarship that are now available. To make any progress at all, the serious scholar had to compile his notes, write his cards, assemble his own word lists—in effect primitive dictionaries that were woefully inadequate for systematic study. It is true that in the nineteenth century the Egyptological library was small, capable of being housed on a very few shelves; it was within the capacity of a hardworking scholar to work his way through and to become familiar with all of the significant publications that would provide him with useful material in his work on, shall we say, new texts. The generation of Egyptologists who completed their studies before World War II had an enviable acquaintance with the monumental early publications like the *Geographische Inschriften altägyptischer Denkmäler* (1857–1860) and *Thesaurus inscriptionum aegyptiacarum* (1883–1891) of Heinrich Brugsch (1827–1894). To take down those weighty volumes requires a special kind of determination that many may now resist. Yet today, more than a century after publication, they remain worthy of quarrying, as does the apparently long-superseded *Dizionario di mitologia egizia* (1881–1886) of Ridolfo V. Lanzone (1834–1907). In a way, the many helpful reference works that lighten the task of modern scholars have made them far less adventurous and perhaps even less inquisitive than their predecessors.

T. G. H. James points out the name of Ptolemy V Epiphanes
in the demotic text of the Rosetta Stone in the galleries of the
British Museum. PHOTOGRAPH BY PETER HAYMAN, LONDON

THE CHANGING SCENE

In 1948 Alan Gardiner (1879–1963) wrote a brief
critique of the great *Wörterbuch der ägyptischen Sprache* (edited by Adolf Erman) in
which he concentrated on the first two pages of
that work. It was, as he readily admitted, something of a perverse hatchet job. He had in his
younger days been one of the Egyptologists who
had helped to collect the material for the dictionary, and he had participated in discussions with
the members of the small group of German scholars who ultimately compiled the work, for whom
he had the greatest admiration. But in the contemplation of years of using the *Wörterbuch*, he
was to see what mistakes of principle and of
execution had been made. Nevertheless, in spite
of Gardiner's strictures, what Egyptologist

would now be without this monumental work,
with its rich (though incomplete) reference to
texts published and unpublished? I am old
enough to remember the publication of the reference and supplementary volumes, and the expectation and disappointment with which they were
first used. Gardiner's plea for special studies of
particular categories of words has been only partially answered, and all scholars who are
concerned with lexicographical precision will
readily agree that imprecision in the determination of meaning remains one of the serious weaknesses of Egyptian linguistic studies.

Linguistic studies, however, have in the
fourth quarter of the twentieth century seriously
undermined the grammatical certainties of the
scholars who had apparently brought order to
the Egyptian language in the first half of the

century. There is, as I would see it, such divergence of opinion on structural matters, and on the proper bases of the analysis of Egyptian, that it will be a long time before a stable position is reached from which universally acceptable grammars may be written. What may not always be understood by the non-Egyptologist interested in using the ancient texts in translation is that modern developments have significantly modified what may be found in the older collections of versions. The longevity of works like the *Ancient Records of Egypt* (1906–1907) of James Henry Breasted (1865–1935) is as much a tribute to the care with which Breasted chose which texts to translate as to the abiding faithfulness of his versions. It is still the most commonly quoted book of its kind, a pity in many ways, not least because Breasted completed his compilation at a time when the first great grammatical studies were appearing. *Ancient Records* is now very out-of-date, lacking many important ancient inscriptions and texts on papyri that have substantially altered Egyptological conceptions of the country's ancient history. Yet, in the absence of any more modern compilation as large as Breasted's, it cannot be abandoned to the shelves holding important, but superannuated works.

In the fields of secular and religious texts the position is somewhat better. The interest and accessibility of Egyptian stories and so-called wisdom, or semiphilosophical, works have ensured frequent collections of translations since the late nineteenth century, and a regular reassessment of meaning and significance. It is good to be able to consult the versions by Maspero, Erman, Gustave Lefèbvre (1879–1957), Battiscombe Gunn (1883–1950), and those included in the useful updating of Aylward M. Blackman's English edition of Erman's *Die Literatur der Ägypter* (1927) by William K. Simpson. But especially valuable both for the sensitivity of the translation and for the very helpful notes and comments is Miriam Lichtheim's *Ancient Egyptian Literature* (1973–1980), a three-volume work that is well on the way to becoming a classic. The surviving body of secular compositions is surprisingly small, and possibly unrepresentative, one must conclude, of nearly three thousand years of lively and mostly settled culture. Not until the last centuries of

the pharaonic period, and the time of Ptolemaic and Roman rule, were imaginative writings produced that begin to match in quality what was being written in the contemporary cultures of the classical world. The reason probably lies to a great extent in the nature and character of Egyptian daily life, and the possible absence of a vigorous, intellectually oriented stratum of society.

There remains much work to be done on Egyptian society in general. In this respect there is, as far as the great periods of the pharaonic past are concerned, a serious paucity of evidence; and when evidence does exist in more than common quantity, it tends to be overinterpreted and used as the basis for conclusions too widely drawn. The classic case concerns the community of workmen who were employed on the making of the royal and other great tombs at Thebes—the inhabitants of Dayr al-Madina, the one recognizable urban site known to most visitors to Egypt. The villagers of Dayr al-Madina, far more skilled and accomplished numeratively and scribally than most of their contemporaries, cannot confidently be described as forming a cultured community, a kind of Hampstead, or Left Bank, or Greenwich Village enclave in a mostly rather uncultured land. Even Jaroslav Černý (1898–1970), who more successfully than most scholars got deep into the hearts and minds of the workmen of the Place of Truth, as the inhabitants of Dayr al-Madina were known in antiquity, never suggested that this somewhat isolated, and certainly protected, community would have been a good place to spend a few hours discussing the latest writings of the New Kingdom avant-garde.

Černý was such a master of the difficult hieratic handwriting practiced by the professional scribes of Dayr al-Madina that at least one colleague, Sir Alan Gardiner, a great friend and admirer of his skills, used to maintain that he could read a badly preserved text as well as someone today might read a faint or damaged piece of modern handwriting. Much of Egyptian writing was, of course, formulaic, and a deep acquaintance with the formulas and set expressions would understandably allow the interpretation of traces of ink with some certainty; but Černý could make the imaginative leap by filling in gaps in unformulaic contexts with otherwise irretrievable supplements. His deep interest in the mundane details of life in one suburb of ancient Thebes did not preclude an avid attraction to all things ancient Egyptian, evinced in a very wide and general knowledge, even of modest antiquities, which was not suspected by many Egyptologists who knew him only through his writings.

For the last twenty years of his life, unless trips to Egypt or elsewhere intervened, he came weekly to the British Museum. He rang the doorbell of the Egyptian Department with such a distinctive "ping" that his presence was known long before it was announced. The queries of the week could then be brought out, and the master would fall with eagerness on the problems. Out would come the ancient, and not very strong, lens, which Černý cherished beyond most of his possessions—a gift from his father in the days when he spent weekends away from the bank in Prague, copying hieratic texts in Turin. There was a dreadful moment sometime in the 1960s when he mislaid it during an examination of the Nash antiquities stored in Harrods Depository. He was as distracted and unwilling to be consoled by the promise of a replacement as the lady who led the rowers in Cheops's boat in the story in Papyrus Westcar, whose hair ornament of new turquoise was lost in the pleasure lake. Like her, Černý wanted no copy or replacement; happily it was found, not on a potsherd at the bottom of the Thames but on a packing case.

In the late 1940s Battiscombe Gunn used to hold a weekly class in his rooms in the Queen's College, Oxford, reading *Book of the Dead* with a small group including Gardiner, Černý, John Barns (1912–1974), and one or two awestruck students. It was like a corporate taking of medicine; nobody enjoyed the texts, but all felt that it was their duty to attend. Grammar, syntax, and vocabulary were the prime matters for attention. The neglect of the content of the texts reflected the general lack of interest in religious texts that prevailed in many academic circles at that time.

In Great Britain, I suppose, the devotion of Sir Ernest Wallis Budge (1857–1934) to such texts in some way diminished their importance; his casual attitude to grammar and lexicography—in spite of his compiling a not unuseful *Egyptian Hieroglyphic Dictionary* (1920)—seemed to have rubbed off on the texts themselves; they

had become casual, unreliable, compilations—put together by the ancient Egyptian equivalents of Budge. The study of religious texts, ritual, temple, and funerary, has required the devotion of a small number of single-minded and careful scholars, who are still in the process of establishing, organizing, analyzing, and translating what is the largest body of texts to have survived from Egyptian antiquity. A good case could now be made for claiming that some of these texts, especially in their earliest forms, like the *Pyramid Texts*, are among the most imaginative, even poetical, compositions to have survived.

There is no doubt that by change, development, poor textual transmission, misunderstanding, and the simple passage of time, many of their later forms (which exist in vast quantities) are confused, turgid, and difficult to comprehend. But it would be a mistake to evaluate these writings too lightly, or to dismiss them as meaningless collections of spells, hymns, invocations, and ritual procedures, drawn from disparate traditions and unworthy of study. Work begun some decades ago by Alexandre Piankoff (1897–1966) revealed that religious and mythical texts could be studied seriously, and without the panic that sometimes afflicted traditional scholars who could not come to terms with the allusive and elusive elements in such texts. The masterly work resulting from the comprehensive studies of scholars like Erik Hornung and Jan Assmann has further advanced the cause of this side of Egyptological studies, bringing sober assessments and sensible translation into the process of demystification.

DIRECTIONS IN FIELDWORK

The *Book of the Dead*, like pyramids and mummies, is one of the abiding points of reference between the general public and Egyptology. Another is excavation, typified in most people's minds by the discovery in 1922 of the tomb of Tutankhamun by Howard Carter (1874–1939). Nobody truly thinks that such a discovery will be made in Egypt again; yet nobody is brave enough to declare without equivocation that such will never happen. If you are an Egyptologist, and you are publicly identified as one, then it is at once assumed that you are an excavator. The romance of the subject seems to lie in the hunt in the field for a burial of untold magnificence and wealth. Indeed, until quite lately, most people who excavated in Egypt had at the back of their minds such a world-shaking discovery, and of those people, very few were competent to carry out an excavation even minimally up to the standards expected in Europe or in much of the Near East.

Even now it would not be impossible for a good Egyptologist whose competence lay in the field of linguistic studies to undertake the direction of an excavation; but such an apparently bizarre situation is far less common than it was formerly. In the history of excavation in Egypt there are a few examples of first-class scholars who have been able to bridge the gap between excavation and linguistic studies—one may think of Hermann Junker (1877–1962) and T. E. Peet (1882–1934)—but in general the presence of the desk scholar in charge of an excavation has been little short of disastrous. It has taken a long time for real professionalism to develop in Egyptian field archaeology. William M. Flinders Petrie (1853–1942), who in so many ways set the example and showed the way for others to follow, failed to sustain his own high standards, largely through impatience and an eagerness to move on to new sites and new challenges.

The strict methods developed by Herbert Winlock (1884–1950) and George Reisner (1867–1942), practiced by Howard Carter in the Tutankhamun excavation and by Guy Brunton (1878–1948) at al-Badari and elsewhere in Middle Egypt, and by Bernard Bruyère (1878–1971) at Dayr al-Madina, prepared the way for the postwar generation of stratigraphic, environmental excavations. Now a field expedition is no longer made up of a small number of semicompetents, but of many specialists headed by a director whose last purpose is to discover treasure. The search is now among the occupation sites of antiquity, not the tombs and temples of the past; it investigates how people lived, what they ate, where they deposited their rubbish, what animals they kept, what crops they grew, how they did things (see the chapter by Frank Hole above). High religion is out, art is out, inscriptions can be inconvenient and are almost out.

Painting of William M. Flinders Petrie (1853–1942) by Philip de Laszlo. Petrie strove to establish high standards in field archaeology in his surveys of Stonehenge, Egypt, and Palestine. It was he who first demonstrated the importance of such archaeological principles as stratigraphy, sequence-dating, and cross-dating. UNIVERSITY COLLEGE LONDON

The results of a season's work are measured in potsherds, linen fragments, seeds, excrement (ancient), foundations of walls, traces of fires, remains of industrial activities. The search remains exciting, but the excitement comes at a different level from that of the old days. The gleam of gold that once characterized the success of a season might now be distinctly unwelcome. The austerity provides great intellectual satisfaction and less aesthetic thrill. It might even be suggested that certain excavators would be inclined to rebury a treasure trove or a head of Nefertiti. It would be cruel to put them to the test.

The present-day emphasis on the excavation of occupation sites can only be welcomed. Many older Egyptologists would echo the call, so often made by Sir Alan Gardiner, to restrict the excavation of inscribed monuments until proper attention had been paid to the many visible standing monuments, much inscribed and sadly neglected, throughout Egypt. Gardiner would have applauded the excavation of Tell al-Dabʿa (Pi-Ramsese) in the Delta by Manfred Bietak, not least because it might throw light on the problem of the Delta Residence, which exercised him so greatly. He would perhaps have been less interested in the fruitful work of Barry Kemp at al-Amarna, though he would have recognized the importance of the discovery of the physical evidence in a site occupied by ancient Egyptians who were, for most practical purposes, untouched by the literate culture of the main Amarna city (Akhetaten). (For a discussion, see "Akhetaten: A Portrait in Art of an Ancient Egyptian Capital" in Part 5, Vol. II.) He would, however, have greatly approved of the increase in the work of recording standing monuments, many of which have been neglected because of the magnitude of the task and some because they seemed to offer insufficient scope for a serious campaign.

In the nineteenth century, when Egyptology was young and practiced by scholars and enthusiasts groping toward standards of recording and publication, herculean efforts were made by some to grapple with the vast areas of decorated and inscribed surfaces that were visible and available for copying. The outstanding product of the early years was the result of the great Prussian expedition led by Carl Richard Lepsius. The drawings in the massive *Denkmaeler aus Aegypten und Aethiopien,* made by good artists under scholarly supervision, were not to be equaled in quality for at least half a century, when the work of Howard Carter at Dayr al-Bahri on the West Bank at Thebes and of Norman de Garis Davies (1865–1941) in the tombs at al-Amarna and elsewhere, reintroduced artistry into epigraphy, combining it with close attention to the accurate reproduction of what was on the wall.

The spontaneity and liveliness that inform the best epigraphic work produced by single artists with good eyes for detail and sensitivity in the drawing of a line is to some extent lacking in the otherwise excellent volumes produced by the methods practiced and refined in the publications of the Oriental Institute of the University of Chicago. It would be more than unreasonable to complain about a certain lack of spontaneity in the splendid plates of the Chicago House series; for here are copies of style to which the scholar may go with almost complete certainty in the fidelity of the copying of what can be seen on the wall. The method is, nevertheless, very time-consuming and expensive.

More modest epigraphic campaigns in the Theban necropolis and at Saqqara, organized through the German Archaeological Institute, have made substantial advances in the recording of steadily deteriorating monuments. There are, further, scarcely adequate words to commend the epigraphic rescue of the apparently unrewarding tombs at al-Hawawish in Middle Egypt by Naguib Kanawati and his colleagues from Macquarie University in Sydney, Australia. Here systematic and comprehensive copying and study have preserved for scholarly exploitation a known but desperately neglected corpus of provincial material, which has turned out to be far more extensive, and distinctly more interesting, than was formerly comprehended. The work at al-Hawawish provides a very good example of how the modern approach to the *complete* recording of a site has yielded unexpectedly rich results. The somewhat superficial, selective examination and partial publication of Percy Edward Newberry (1869–1949) in the early years of the twentieth century had done little more than indicate what was there, and had scarcely demonstrated the potential importance of the site and the possibilities for more intensive examination.

The neglect of standing monuments cannot be blamed on the pioneers of Egyptology, and it is perhaps improper to blame the subsequent active practitioners of Egyptological fieldwork for not doing, fifty or one hundred years ago, what we might now appreciate to have had done. The size of the problem, combined with the modest size of the international community of Egyptologists, has in a sense defeated the best efforts of those whose dream has been to save the legacy of the past. When Francis Llewellyn Griffith first set out the aims and aspirations of the Archaeological Survey of Egypt in the 1890s, he fondly hoped that the whole of Egypt's standing monuments could be recorded for posterity in a matter of about five years. He could recall what he had been able to do with Flinders Petrie during a few weeks of feverish activity, traveling upstream from al-Minya to Aswan in 1886. What he had not allowed for was the difference between rapid recording in notebooks and careful copying for publication. One hundred years later finds the Archaeological Survey, one of the most enduringly important sides of the work of the Egypt Exploration Society, nowhere near finishing the task initiated by Griffith, in spite of many volumes and notwithstanding the massive contributions toward the same end published by many individual scholars and organizations from other countries.

Early Egyptologists who traveled in the country during the nineteenth century ranged the land, probed the sites, contemplated the monuments, copied inscriptions, even drew conclusions with a freedom from restraint and a seeming disregard of time unmatchable by modern scholars. In consequence, there was very little that missed their scrutiny, even if the results of this scrutiny were confined to brief notes and casual mentions in the modest outlets for the publication of "trivia" available at that time. Accounts of visits to ancient places in the Delta, in particular, indicate how catastrophic has been the subsequent failure of fieldworkers to tackle the problems of Delta excavation. Some standing monuments have totally disappeared in the intervening years, without having been more than sketchily recorded. It could be said that later generations of scholars have failed the pioneers by paying insufficient attention to what had already been noted and, to a considerable extent, suggested for future attention.

Unfortunately, lines of investigation and research cannot be dictated to scholars, especially young and ambitious scholars, by the requirements of urgent necessity or the moral imperatives of the dead. In the haphazard procedures of modern scholarly organizations there seems to be little possibility of achieving a system of organizing future work in Egypt and in the study that will secure both the proper attention to neglected monuments and the freedom for Egyptologists to pursue new lines of inquiry in fieldwork and in formal scholarship. Yet a good case could be made for a more structured attempt to fill the gaps, cover the neglected areas, and ensure that what may be identified as the priorities of work in the discipline of Egyptology are properly addressed.

NEW DIRECTIONS

One area of scholarship in which much has been achieved in the years since World War II, but which remains a much understudied field is art history. When Sir Joseph Banks (1743–1820) wrote dismissively to Henry Salt (1780–1827) about the views of the Trustees of the British Museum on the great head of Ramesses II, known erroneously as "the Younger Memnon," he voiced an opinion rooted in standards derived from the study of classical sculpture: "Though in truth we are here much satisfied with the Memnon, and consider it as a chef d'oeuvre of Egyptian sculpture; yet we have not placed that statue among the works of *Fine Art*." This attitude was so common throughout the nineteenth century, and persisted even into the mid twentieth century, that it affected Egyptologists with a kind of shamefaced, even withdrawn, acceptance of the moderate quality of Egyptian sculpture in particular. The problem lay far more in the absence of a well-developed connoisseurship in the Egyptian field than in any supposed inadequacy in the material itself.

The change has come about partly through the greater appreciation generally of what may be considered art, and partly through the systematic study of the products of Egyptian artists. The crucial examination of the principles underlying Egyptian artistic conventions was undertaken by Heinrich Schäfer (1868–1957), a scholar who also spanned more than two fields in Egyptian studies. His *Von ägyptischer Kunst* (1919, 4th ed. 1963; translated as *Principles of Egyptian Art* [1974]), in spite of dense argument whose opacity sometimes seems scarcely worth penetrating, presents an innovative way of examining the Egyptian approach to the visual world and to representing it in two dimensions especially, and has had a profound influence on the modern generation of art historians. The line from before the war is thin but clear, running from Schäfer and H. G. Evers (1900–1993) to Hans Wolfgang Müller (1907–1991), Bernard V. Bothmer (1912–), Jacques Vandier (1904–1973), and Cyril Aldred (1914–1991) and to a new but still inadequate scattering of the next generation. Studies in art history tend, perhaps properly, to be analytical rather than aesthetic in the old-fashioned sense, and it is difficult simply to stand back and admire a work of Egyptian art without seeking justification for one's judgment in the form of the uraeus or the shape of the back pillar. There remains, therefore, a gap in Egyptological literature waiting to be filled by a great work on Egyptian art, analytically based and aesthetically inspired.

My contemplation of Egyptological studies after forty years of continuous professional involvement inspires a rich mixture of memories, stiffened with thoughts of lost opportunities and misdirected efforts, but cheered by some successes, a few personal and far more those enjoyed by colleagues. The community of Egyptologists has changed very considerably in those forty years. It was already largely free from the amateur image that had survived from the days when Egypt was seen as the rich man's playground, and Egyptology his respectable pastime. That was almost always a false image, but one particularly aimed at British and American Egyptologists. Yet even for the so-called Anglo-Saxon countries the figures of Lord Carnarvon (1866–1923) and Theodore M. Davis (1837–1915) were not characteristic.

Still, the provision of university departments for Egyptological study in Britain and America has never matched what was available in continental Europe, especially in Germany. Consequently there has been a tenuous nature to the status of Egyptologists in Britain and America that needs further improvement for the future. It is a remarkable tribute to the devotion and tenacity of many young scholars, trained in Egyptological studies but unable to obtain a regular Egyptological appointment, that they still find niches in the academic world in which they can pursue their special interests, often in spite of their formal academic commitments.

It is easier to plow your individual furrow in an alien environment if you are a specialist rather than a generalist. One very noticeable development since the 1970s is the gradual disappearance of the Egyptologist who tries to remain in touch with many, if not all, branches of the subject. The flood of specialized literature alone makes it increasingly difficult to spread one's learning over more than a few areas. One may be a linguist, a historian, a student of religion and religious texts, a demotist, an hieraticist, a hieroglyphic paleographer, a specialist in Egyptian commerce or law or social life, an art historian, a ceramicist, an excavator—the list is almost without end. It is good for general comprehension of the idea of "ancient Egypt" to be able to encompass as many specialities as possible, and in attempting to do so, a scholar has a better chance to appreciate ancient Egyptian culture, and at the same time to enrich his or her understanding of a favored corner of interest.

A tendency that has developed with narrow specialization has been the proliferation of periodicals to accommodate the writings of Egyptologists who publish too quickly, too briefly, and too superficially. The trend stems partly from the pressure put by universities on scholars to demonstrate their "efficiency" by regular publication, measured by title and number but never by quality or necessity. It is also partly determined by an eagerness to publish a result before someone else does. Egyptologists are not chemists or physicists. Priority is for us far less important than proper presentation in a well-argued, well-documented piece. A large personal bibliography is no necessary mark of a scholar's true achievement. Consider the output of Battiscombe Gunn, who would never publish until he was completely satisfied that he had produced a truly finished work. The same was the case with Jacques Jean Clère (1906–1989). Such scholars, deeply learned and widely respected, have much to teach the young Egyptologist of today. Cyril John Gadd (1893–1969), the great Assyriologist and Keeper of the Department of Egyptian and Assyrian Antiquities in the British Museum when I joined that institution, once said to me, "Never write an article if you can write a book. A book is a thing of substance." It was a casual remark insofar as Gadd could ever have uttered anything casual; but it contained a real germ of sense.

A scholar should not, perhaps, coldly set out to write "a book," but it is proper that he or she should set out to pursue an idea or a topic in depth, to enter a field of inquiry, or to amass the material for a corpus—to engage, in short, in a scholarly activity that may lead to a substantial publication. In the course of studies one will from time to time come across something that may not be central to the main purpose but is worthy of publication as a short study or article; that event should be occasional and even unplanned. The goal, if one seeks to do work of lasting importance, should lie in the distance, to be approached slowly and richly. A good book is a real achievement, and will be added gladly to the list of distinguished publications that have made Egyptology such a rich and satisfying field of study.

BIBLIOGRAPHY

A conventional bibliography does not suit the foregoing essay. As it is wide-ranging and aims to give a personal view of the advances in the study of ancient Egypt over a period of some fifty years, it seems more suitable to list some of the books that have influenced my own thinking or represent my own scholarly viewpoint.

Starting with the Egyptian language it is impossible to omit ALAN H. GARDINER, *Egyptian Grammar* (1927; 3rd ed. 1957), even though it now represents the old tradition, and in its last revision is only slightly influenced by the seminal HANS JAKOB POLOTSKY, *Études de syntaxe copte* (1944).

For the understanding of Egyptian literature and its value for historical studies, no work has been more fruitful than GEORGES POSENER, *Littérature et politique dans l'Égypte de la XIIe Dynastie* (1956). The three volumes of MIRIAM LICHTHEIM, *Ancient Egyptian Literature* (1973–1980), provide a first-class collection of reliable versions.

Much of the best historical work is to be found in publications of texts and monuments; particularly valuable is JACQUES VANDIER, *Mo'alla: La tombe d'Ankhtifi et la tombe de Sébekhotep* (1950); also WILLIAM C. HAYES, ed. and trans., *A Papyrus of the Late Middle Kingdom in the Brooklyn Museum* (1955). A most useful, though awkwardly arranged, work on late chronology is KENNETH A. KITCHEN, *The Third Intermediate Period in Egypt* (1100–650 B.C.) (1973; 2nd ed. 1986).

In religion the one general account that I have found to be especially sympathetic and useful is that of SIEGFRIED MORENZ, *Ägyptische Religion* (1960), translated as *Egyptian Religion* by ANN E. KEEP (1973); and WARREN R. DAWSON, M. L. BIERBRIER, and ERIC UPHILL, *Who Was Who in Egyptology* (3rd ed. 1995).

HEINRICH SCHÄFER's important study, *Von ägyptischer Kunst* (1919; 4th ed. 1963), is now available in the translation by JOHN BAINES, *Principles of Egyptian Art*, edited with an epilogue by EMMA BRUNNER-TRAUT (1974; rev. ed. 1986). The best general account of Egyptian art remains WILLIAM STEVENSON SMITH, *The Art and Architecture of Ancient Egypt* (1958; 2nd ed., rev. by WILLIAM K. SIMPSON, 1982). The most useful specialized study has been *Egyptian Sculpture of the Late Period, 700 B.C. to A.D. 100* (1960), an exhibition catalog written principally by BERNARD V. BOTHMER.

In the publication of monuments there have been many splendid volumes. Two works dealing with basic problems are RICARDO A. CAMINOS and HENRY G. FISCHER, *Ancient Egyptian Epigraphy and Palaeography* (1976); and HENRY G. FISCHER, *The Orientation of Hieroglyphs*, vol. 1 (1977).

In cultural studies a work of profound learning and great influence is HERMANN KEES, *Das alte: Eine kleine Landeskunde Ägypten* (1955), translated as *Ancient Egypt: A Cultural Topography* by IAN F. D. MORROW, edited by T. G. H. JAMES (1961). More recently BARRY J. KEMP's *Ancient Egypt: Anatomy of a Civilization* (1989) has shown how the results of excavation can be used for new insights in cultural history.

Most used among the many reference works of recent years are the revised volumes of BERTHA PORTER and ROSALIND L. B. MOSS (with the help of ETHEL W. BURNEY and JAROMÍR MÁLEK), *Topographical Bibliography of Ancient Egyptian Hieroglyphic Texts, Reliefs and Paintings* (vol. 1, 1960, 1964; vol. 2, 1972; vol. 3, 1974, 1981). ALAN H. GARDINER, *Ancient Egyptian Onomastica* (1947) is a treasure house of information on geographical matters. ALFRED LUCAS, *Ancient Egyptian Materials and Industries* (1926; 4th ed., rev. by J. R. HARRIS, 1962) is a rich compendium of scientific information.

SEE ALSO **The Decipherment of Ancient Near Eastern Scripts** (Part 1, Vol. I).

Resurrecting the Hittites

HANS G. GÜTERBOCK

HANS GUSTAV GÜTERBOCK *was born on May 27, 1908, in Berlin and studied at the Universities of Berlin, Leipzig, and Marburg, receiving his doctorate in Leipzig in 1934. He served as epigrapher of the German expedition to Boğazköy from 1933 to 1935. Forced into exile by political developments in Germany, from 1936 until 1948 he was Professor of Hittitology in Ankara, Turkey. From 1949 he taught at the Oriental Institute of the University of Chicago, in 1976 retiring as the Tiffany and Margaret Blake Distinguished Service Professor. He is a member of the American Academy of Arts and Sciences, the American Philosophical Society, the Bavarian Academy of Sciences, and the British Academy. Professor Güterbock participated in the publication of ten volumes of copies of Hittite cuneiform inscriptions and is the author of many books and hundreds of articles on Anatolian and Assyriological topics. He is coeditor of the* Chicago Hittite Dictionary.

I GREW UP IN a household very much geared to the ancient Near East. My father was secretary of the German Orient Society and as such was in contact with many of the excavators and museum people. One of them, Professor Hans Ehelolf, curator of the tablet collection in the Berlin Museum and a pioneer in Hittite studies, intro-

duced me to Hittite, a language in which one had "to work from scratch." After one year I went to Leipzig to continue my studies under Professors Benno Landsberger in Assyriology and Johannes Friedrich in Hittitology.

I handed in my dissertation three days before Hitler seized power and passed my oral examination in the spring of 1933. At the Berlin Museum where I had hoped to work under Hans Ehelolf I was told that I could not be employed because I was half Jewish. My father came from a Jewish family; he himself had converted to Protestantism, but for the Nazis only the ancestry counted.

At this time it was felt that the ongoing new excavation at the Hittite capital of Khattusha (now Boğazköy) needed an epigrapher because tablets had been found and more were expected. I was an unemployed Hittitologist; but could I work on a German excavation? The director of the İstanbul branch of the German Archaeological Institute, Martin Schede, who was himself not a Nazi, said that he had no objection to my participation, as long as no government money was spent on it. So it was agreed that all other expenses of the excavation would be divided evenly between the Institute and the Orient Society, but that my transportation and my salary should be covered only by the private Orient Society.

Under these conditions, I went to Turkey for the first time in 1933. When I arrived at the German Archaeological Institute at İstanbul the director regretfully informed me that I could not be housed in the hostel of the Institute, but that a hotel room had been reserved for me. In those days one could only travel by train: three days from Berlin to İstanbul (the expedition did not pay for the Orient Express) and one overnight from İstanbul to Ankara. From Ankara the train left about 10:00 A.M.; it reached Yerköy after 5:00 P.M. From there one took a bus to Yozgat, the center of the province of the same name, where one had to spend the night.

The so-called hotel was extremely primitive, and one always had six-legged companions in bed. From Yozgat to Boğazköy there were two routes possible, one over a high mountain pass on an unfinished road, the other on a wide detour via Alaca (Alaja). Because in 1933 we had to transport much equipment, including tents and wheelbarrows, we had to use two minibuses to go the long road because they would not have been able to travel over the mountain. In subsequent years we traveled the forty kilometers (twenty-four miles) of the mountain road in the Turkish covered wagons of the time, called *yaylı*, which means "having springs."

The Hittites were really dead in the sense that they had been lost from the memory of later periods. For instance, Herodotus had heard of a rock relief in Asia Minor that we now know to be Hittite, but he ascribed it to an Egyptian king. The name of the Hittites does not occur in any Greek source except in the translation of the Old Testament. In Hebrew their name is *hittî* in the singular, *hittîm* in the plural, sometimes also "sons of Heth." They are among the tribes whom the Israelites found in the Promised Land. In the period of the monarchy, kings of the Hittites occur in 1 Kings, 2 Kings, and 2 Chronicles. Here they are obviously the rulers of foreign countries. We shall see later how these kings can be understood in the light of present knowledge.

In the nineteenth century, when the languages of Egypt and Assyria had been deciphered, the name of the Hittites was also found in documents of those countries. In Egyptian it is spelled with only the two consonants, *h* and *t*, a form that was arbitrarily vocalized *Kheta* by Egyptologists; in the cuneiform sources it is

Khatti. From these sources it was possible to learn that their land was somewhere in Asia, presumably in and around Syria, and that at times they must have been rather powerful. In 1870 five stones were found in the Syrian town of Hama (the biblical Hamath) that were inscribed in a script resembling hieroglyphs, but certainly different from the Egyptian hieroglyphs. Rock inscriptions in a similar script had already been reported from various places in the western part of Anatolia (present-day Turkey), and in 1876 Archibald Henry Sayce of Edinburgh proposed that this script and the language it represented should be attributed to the Hittites. One of the Anatolian monuments, depicting a whole row of deities with label inscriptions called by the locals Yazılıkaya ("the inscribed rock"), is situated near Boğazköy, a village about 130 miles (208 kilometers) east of Ankara.

The ruins of Boğazköy were discovered in 1834 by Charles Texier. They were visited several times thereafter throughout the nineteenth century. In 1893–1894 another Frenchman, Ernest Chantre, excavated some inscribed clay tablets at the site. They were written in cuneiform, the script known from Babylonia and Assyria, so they could be read, but as their language was unknown, they could not be understood. In 1887 cuneiform tablets had been discovered in Egypt at Tell el-Amarna, the capital of the heretic king Akhenaten (Amenhotep IV) of the fourteenth century BCE. With few exceptions, they were in Babylonian. Two of the tablets were written in an unknown language to and by, respectively, the king of Arzawa. Most diplomatic letters of those times began with a stereotyped set of greetings and blessings for the addressee, his wives, his sons, his troops, and so forth. They contained a number of word signs that were also present in one of the undeciphered letters. With the help of these word signs the Norwegian scholar J. A. Knudtzon was able to decipher the language in 1902 and to propose that it belonged to the Indo-European group. This claim was doubted by Indo-Europeanists, because in the syllabic spelling of the cuneiform script everything looked so strange. It was soon noticed that the unknown language of the Arzawa letters was the same as that of the tablets found by Chantre at Boğazköy. On these grounds the Assyriologist and historian

Hugo Winckler of the University of Berlin decided to go to Boğazköy in the hope of finding Arzawa.

In 1906 Winckler began excavations at Boğazköy together with Theodore Makridi, second director of the İstanbul Museum, and in the name of that museum. Funds came from private donors in Germany through the German Orient Society. During his first campaign Winckler found hundreds of tablets and fragments on the acropolis, locally known as Büyükkale ("great fortress"). Because some tablets were inscribed in Akkadian it was easy for the Assyriologist Winckler to see that these texts belonged to the kingdom of Khatti. As one of the sponsors of the expedition, who was a friend of my father, told me, one day he received a postcard postmarked in Yozgat, Turkey, which said, "Dear Dr. Hahn, Boğazköy is Khatti. Greetings, yours Winckler." This discovery was the beginning of the "resurrection" of the Hittites.

Winckler resumed his excavations in 1907, in which year he found tablets in the storerooms of the largest temple. In the same year an expedition of the German Archaeological Institute under the direction of Otto Puchstein mapped and partly excavated the monumental buildings of Boğazköy, especially the fortifications and the five temples. Winckler took up his excavations again in 1911, but in 1912 the work was interrupted by the outbreak of the Balkan War, soon to be followed by the First World War.

Early in 1914 two Assyriologists began copying Boğazköy tablets in the İstanbul Museum. Their work was interrupted by the outbreak of the war, but in 1915 Otto Weber, the director of the Near Eastern department of the Berlin Museum, arranged with the director of the İstanbul Museum, Halil Edhem, that the bulk of the tablets should be loaned to Berlin under the condition that they should be returned to Turkey once they were preserved, photographed, and published. This condition was faithfully kept by the Berlin Museum until almost the end of the Second World War. After the war no tablets were returned until 1989, when the East German government sent all tablets, published and unpublished, back to Turkey.

The cuneiform copies prepared by Assyriologists in İstanbul and Berlin were published in a series called *Keilschrifttexte aus Boghazköi* ("Cuneiform texts from Boğazköy") under the auspices of the German Orient Society. The first fascicle appeared in 1916. It contains state treaties in Akkadian and the so-called vocabularies, Sumero-Akkadian word lists provided with Hittite translations, which had already been edited in transliteration by Friedrich Delitzsch in 1914. The second fascicle soon followed with Hittite texts and fragments found in 1906 on Büyükkale. Unfortunately, after that the tablets from the various locations were mixed together without any record, so the findspots remained unknown until the unearthing of adjoining fragments in more recent controlled excavations revealed their places of discovery.

Winckler had already started the work of the decipherment of the Hittite language, but his last illness prevented him from completing the work. It was the Czech Assyriologist Bedřich (Frederick) Hrozný who achieved the decipherment of the Hittite language. At that time he was professor at the University of Vienna; after the war he went to the Czech University of Prague. He announced his results in an article of 1915 and published them in 1917 in a book called *Die Sprache der Hethiter*, whose title and subtitle may be freely rendered as "The language of the Hittites: its structure as part of the Indo-European family of languages." Hittite scribes separated words and paragraphs and used word signs for many common words, especially nouns. These patterns enabled Hrozný to determine verbal forms and nominal cases, connective particles, and the meanings of a number of words. As an instructive example, he quoted the following passage: *nu* NINDA-*an ezzatteni watar-ma ekkutteni*. NINDA is the Sumerian word sign for "bread," the added Hittite -*an* is the ending of the accusative. Hrozný had also found that -*teni* was the suffix of the second-person plural of the present-future. *nu* and -*ma* are connective particles like "and" or "but." The verb *ezzateni* reminded him of German *essen*, "to eat," especially with the object "bread." The second clause was obviously parallel, and the object *watar* could only be "water." The whole then reads: "Then you will eat bread and drink water."

Another scholar involved in the ongoing decipherment was Emil Forrer, a Swiss Assyriologist in Berlin. By 1919 both Hrozný and Forrer came to realize that the Boğazköy tablets contained a few more languages than just Akkadian and Hittite. In some places the texts would say, "He (that is, the priest or singer) says in such-and-such language," and there would follow a section in a non-Hittite idiom. The terms used for these languages are *luwili* (Luwian), a language spoken in the south of Anatolia, and *palaumnili* (Palaic), spoken in the north, both of which were also Indo-European; and *ḫurlili* (Hurrian), a non-Indo-European language of southeastern Anatolia and northern Syria. Ironically enough the word *ḫattili* ("in the language of Khatti") turned out to refer not to Hittite, but to an entirely unrelated language that must have been spoken by the original inhabitants of the country before the arrival of the Indo-Europeans. The latter began to worship Khattian gods and took some Khattic words into their language. The language we call Hittite was called *nešili* after Nesha, a city that was the capital of the Hittites in early times. The same city was also known as Kanesh, today Kültepe near Kayseri.

The claim that Hittite was an Indo-European language provoked a lengthy discussion, because many words had no immediate etymology, important terms were hidden behind word signs, and the writing system was so unfamiliar. One linguist decided to learn cuneiform and to familiarize himself with the texts in order to come to a clear conclusion. This was Ferdinand Sommer, who soon became one of the leading German Hittitologists. In the United States it was the Indo-Europeanist Edgar Sturtevant who, a little later, but for the same reason, learned Hittite.

While the publication of the *Keilschrifttexte* went on, Forrer persuaded the German Orient Society to publish texts directly in transliteration. This publication was meant to make Hittite texts more easily available to noncuneiformists and was called *Die Boghazköi Texte in Umschrift* ("The Boğazköy texts in transliteration"). The first volume appeared in 1922 under the title *Die Keilschrift von Boghazköi* and consisted of a complete sign list that long remained the only documented collection of all signs of cuneiform as written by the Hittites. The first fascicle of the second volume contained the historical texts of the Old Kingdom. The second volume was completed with sources of the New Kingdom in 1926. This series was not continued.

Keilschrifttexte was also discontinued after fascicle six because Ehelolf, the curator of the tablet collection of the Berlin Museum, persuaded Weber, director of the Near Eastern department, to have the museum itself start a new series. It was produced using an inexpensive method and in rapid sequence and, to distinguish it from the *Keilschrifttexte*, was named *Keilschrifturkunden aus Boghazköi* ("Cuneiform documents from Boğazköy"). Among the scholars who contributed hand copies to the latter series I mention only Arnold Walter, who had a preference for oracle texts and later taught Hittite at the University of Chicago, and Albrecht Goetze, who used to spend his vacations in Berlin in order to copy mainly historical texts. Goetze eventually migrated to the United States and taught at Yale University. The greatest number of volumes in this series were the work of Ehelolf; a few were produced by his students, J. Schiele, C. G. von Brandenstein, and myself. Ehelolf also wrote transliterations of all of the Boğazköy tablets not yet published, which were to serve as a basis for the selection of text groups for publication. Most of this tremendous work he did himself; only two groups of one thousand numbers each were done by von Brandenstein and by me. Ehelolf also started a comprehensive file collection of words in the hope that it would grow into a thesaurus and become the basis of a Hittite dictionary.

But at first there was no dictionary. Everyone had to make his own word file. When I began to study Hittite with Ehelolf in 1926, there were very few tools available. After Hrozný's first decipherment, Hittite grammar had been described in articles by Forrer and Friedrich. There were a few editions of texts in transliteration, with translation, philological commentary, and a glossary of all words occurring in the texts. So the student had to look for a certain word in all of these glossaries. There were also individual articles in learned journals, and somehow a student had to keep track of them too. Once, when I said to Ehelolf in class that I could not find a certain word, he replied, "Did you not know that Mr. X published something about it in such-and-such journal? You'd better sit down and put all these journal articles in your file." I did, but it took a long time. Soon after I had finished, Sturtevant's *Glossary* appeared.

Published in 1931, Sturtevant's work was modestly titled *A Hittite Glossary* with the subtitle *Words of Known or Conjectured Meaning*. For each word it gave a reference to the literature where the meaning had been established or suggested. Being a linguist, Sturtevant was, of course, most interested in the comparative aspect of his task, but he wisely refrained from giving any opinion in his brief glossary and only gave references to the literature pertaining to the linguistic aspects. The glossary was extremely useful, though it was not free of flaws caused by misunderstandings of the German literature. A few years later, when Hitler came into power, Goetze fled Germany, and Sturtevant later brought him to Yale as a professor of Assyriology, but also to teach Hittitology. The two scholars had many years of fruitful collaboration, one of the first results of which was a revised second edition of the *Glossary* (1936). Sturtevant published a supplement in 1939. In the meantime, he brought out a comparative grammar in 1933. This work was followed in 1935 by a chrestomathy coauthored with George Bechtel, which served as a useful tool for many generations of students.

Also in the 1930s Louis Delaporte brought out a manual in French for students comprising a sign list, a grammar, and a selection of texts in cuneiform with glossary. Beginning in 1930 he edited the *Revue hittite et asianique,* which became the leading periodical devoted to Hittitology. Delaporte died in a German concentration camp. After the war the *Revue hittite* continued publication under the editorship of Emmanuel Laroche until 1978. Editions of Hittite texts also appeared before the Second World War, in Germany as well as in other countries. In addition, the 1930s saw the resumption of field work in Boğazköy.

The end of the First World War had completely changed the political map of western Asia. It was some time before archaeological work could be taken up in what was now the Republic of Turkey, which was established in 1923 after the victorious War of Independence. In 1926 the German Archaeological Institute opened a branch in İstanbul, and already in 1926 Goetze visited Boğazköy, using the new railway

to Yerköy. Also in 1926 Forrer made a long exploratory trip through central Anatolia sponsored by the German Orient Society. James Henry Breasted, the director of Chicago's Oriental Institute, sent out the young German archaeologist Hans Henning von der Osten on an extended exploratory journey in 1926. From among the mounds visited, Alişar Hüyük was selected for the first controlled excavation in central Anatolia. It lasted from 1927 to 1932.

In the context of this interest in the early periods of central Anatolia, Schede, the director of the İstanbul branch of the Archaeological Institute, proposed that a controlled excavation should also be undertaken at Boğazköy, where the prewar excavations had only dealt with the remains of the Empire period. He proposed that, as in the old days, the Orient Society should be participating. Thus the new excavations started in 1931 as a joint enterprise of the German Archaeological Institute and the German Orient Society. The field director was Kurt Bittel, who had already participated in prehistoric excavations in Egypt. To start he selected the acropolis, Büyükkale, because he saw that it had a sufficient accumulation of earth to permit the observation of several levels. In his first campaign he hit a building that contained tablets, a fact that encouraged the Orient Society to continue. In 1931 Bittel found three hundred fragments; in 1932 he found eight hundred and saw that the building continued and must contain more tablets. He therefore insisted that a Hittitologist be added to his staff. As mentioned before, it was my good fortune to have been selected for this task, which is how, in 1933, I got to be in Boğazköy.

Boğazköy in those days was a very primitive village. It had one big landowner from a feudal family that in past centuries had been a ruling dynasty, named the Zülkadir Oghullari. Ziya Bey, who employed many of the local peasants as sharecroppers, owned a mansion known as a *konak,* which according to custom consisted of two buildings, one for the men where guests could be received, the other for women where the family was living at the time. Winckler had been a paying guest of the bey before building his excavation house at the foot of Büyükkale.

Bittel was also a paying guest of Ziya Bey in his first season, but the following year he preferred to camp near his excavation in a saddle south of Büyükkale, between the latter and the so-called *Südburg* (south fortress). When we arrived in 1933 there was already one small hut built of rough stones and mud plaster containing the kitchen, a darkroom, and one sitting room. The construction of a second hut was soon begun, but we slept in the tents. Over the years more such buildings were added, including bedrooms. Because timber was expensive and had to be brought in from a great distance, the budget did not at first allow for doors and shutters; so the rooms had simple openings that curtains could not really close.

There was no store in the village. From the peasants we could buy the flat unleavened bread called *yufka*, eggs, and the local vegetables—eggplant, green beans, tomatoes, and squash. The only meat we could buy was chicken; to have a lamb killed was useless for lack of refrigeration. There was, of course, no electricity at the time. There was milk and yogurt. Water was brought from a nearby spring in reused gasoline cans and cooled in earthenware pitchers. In season there were excellent grapes. The village had extensive vineyards, which were harvested in a festival for the preparation not of wine, but of a thick syrup called *pekmez*. This was the villagers' only sweetener, for the sugar made by the state-owned sugar factories was too expensive. Once a week a grocer from the nearby town of Sungurlu came by horse and brought in his packsaddle groceries that had been ordered the week before. I mention all of this because Boğazkale, as it is now called, is very different.

To be in Boğazköy was for me a great experience. Here I was at the heart of the Hittite Empire in a beautiful landscape. From Büyükkale one saw the whole area of the ancient city rising almost one thousand feet from the plain with buildings and gates built of cyclopean masonry. To the east one looked into the deep valley that protected the city on that side and onto the mountains beyond it. To the north one saw the fertile plain of the Budaközü, which was the economic base for the existence of Boğazköy.

The rock reliefs of Yazılıkaya left the deepest impression. I had, of course, seen photographs and the casts in the old near eastern department

Hans G. Güterbock leaving the Boğazköy excavation of 1936. In the background is a traveling wagon of the time. COURTESY OF ILSE BITTEL

of the Berlin Museum, but without any special feeling. Here, now, I found myself in a room, actually a natural rock formation that was shaped like a chamber, open in front and having three walls covered with rows of divine figures. One immediately got the feeling of being in a holy place. In subsequent seasons I had the opportunity to work there with Bittel.

Like everybody I had to do some fieldwork, which meant watching the workers and seeing to it that they collected potsherds and objects and did not remove stones that promised to be parts of a wall. This experience obviously did not make me an archaeologist, but it did provide occasions for long conversations with Bittel far from the ears of others. I found him as opposed to the Nazi regime as I was, and this shared worldview, together with the common goal of understanding the Hittites, became the basis for our lifelong friendship.

Bittel had asked for a philologist because he expected to find more tablets and because he hoped to learn something about their contents. The first expectation was fulfilled more amply than anybody could have hoped: a total of some two thousand six hundred tablets and fragments were found in the season of 1933 alone. Because of their sheer numbers it was impossible to read them all. In addition, parts of the surface were often covered by a thick lime incrustation that could only be removed chemically, not mechanically. All I could do was wash the baked tablets with water and a brush, give them numbers, and write file cards indicating their findspots. Nevertheless I got some impression of their contents. I remember Bittel's disappointment when I had to tell him that a large fragment or a complete tablet was "again a ritual." The few complete tablets were found in the central of the three rooms excavated that season. The same room had the highest accumulation of tablet fragments and yielded such texts as labels and shelf lists. We got the impression that this room probably was the original storage place, from which smaller quantities of fragments either had fallen into the neighboring rooms when the walls collapsed or had been moved there by later leveling.

As mentioned earlier, tablets had already been found in 1931 and 1932. They were sent to Berlin for preservation and study. Quite understandably, after the experience with Winckler's tablets, the unpublished bulk of which had stayed in Berlin for nearly two decades, the Turkish authorities tightly limited the lending periods. The tablets were now to be returned to the museum of Ankara, the new capital, and they all had to be photographed for identification.

The tablets of 1933 were sent to Berlin in three installments. In the Berlin Museum they were cleaned and photographed. Ehelolf copied in transliteration all of the tablets from the campaigns of 1931 through 1933, just as he had transliterated Winckler's tablets. Ehelolf soon began also to make cuneiform copies of some new tablets. They were published in four volumes of the *Keilschrifturkunden* series, some of them posthumously.

Bittel was fairly sure that the great find of 1933 had exhausted the tablets kept in the building he had selected at Boğazköy, and that such great numbers were not to be expected again. It was, therefore, decided that from now on the work on the tablets should be done at the excavation site. Thus we would avoid formalities and relieve Ehelolf of the heavy burden that the 3,700-odd new tablets already constituted for him. Therefore a worker from the museum laboratory was added to the staff, and I received detailed information from Mrs. Ehelolf, who had refined the technique of photographing cuneiform script, on how to instruct the photographer who joined us from İstanbul. In this way the tablets were cleaned and photographed on the spot, and in 1934 and 1935 I made the usual transliterations. In 1936 my own situation changed, as I shall now explain.

The seizure of power by the Nazis had an unexpected result for Turkey. Early in 1933 Hitler fired from the German universities all professors who were Jewish or of partly Jewish origin, or who had Jewish wives. They formed an emergency committee in Switzerland in order to look for employment in other countries. It so happened that the president of Turkey, Kemal Atatürk, planned at the time a radical university reform, in which the traditional institution in İstanbul was to be replaced by a modern research-oriented university. For the task of reorganization Professor Albert Malche of Geneva had been invited to Turkey in 1932. The refugee camp contacted him and as a result, one of its members, Professor Philipp Schwarz, was invited to Ankara by the minister of education, Dr. Reshit Galip. In one stroke thirty-two professors were hired. They formed the beginning of the İstanbul University; more German refugees were later added.

Apparently because this endeavor was a success, a similar policy was applied to the foundation of a new university in Ankara. Atatürk wanted to have a university in his new capital, and particularly one devoted to the study of those civilizations which in one way or another were relevant to the history of Turkish people or the country. The areas included Hittite, Sumerian, and Chinese, but also the classical languages, Old Indic, and Hungarian. I was encouraged by the Turkish students in Berlin to apply for a job, and at the end of the 1935 campaign at Boğazköy I signed a contract in Ankara. At that time I learned that my teacher, Professor Benno Landsberger, had been appointed to the chair of Assyriology or, as the Turks preferred to call it, Sumerology. After formalizing my emigration I started my job early in 1936.

Thus in the summer of 1936, as an emigrant,

I was no longer in the position of serving officially on the German excavation; nevertheless, Bittel invited me to participate for the whole campaign. The young Hittitologist Heinrich Otten joined the staff as epigrapher, and a little later Professor Ehelolf came for the greater part of the season. He had some unforeseen difficulties in reaching Boğazköy. He was not quite up to the primitive life in the camp, and the beginning of cold and rainy weather in the fall undermined his health. It was a traumatic experience for him. And what did Güterbock do in Boğazköy when two other Hittitologists had come to work on the tablets? There, good luck provided me very interesting and challenging work.

Already during the preceding seasons we had found so-called "bullae" bearing the impressions of royal seals. Bullae are lumps of clay used to secure a knot in a string and stamped with a seal. Hittite royal seals show the name of the king in hieroglyphs in the center and in cuneiform, sometimes with the genealogy, in one or more circles surrounding it. These seals made it possible to identify the hieroglyphic names of kings and thereby to date such reliefs as were provided with the same names. Going from reliefs thus dated by royal names and using stylistic comparison, it was possible to assign a number of uninscribed Hittite monuments to the period of the Empire. This breakthrough meant great progress. Only a few years earlier two books had appeared that had used different criteria and had come to results totally different from each other and from what we found.

Now in 1936 a hoard of about two hundred bullae was found in one storage room, some of them revealing new royal names but the majority bearing the seals of other individuals. It was my job to study and catalog the lot. After the excavation the question arose of who would publish the seals: neither the German Archaeological Institute nor the German Orient Society was allowed to print the work of a non-Aryan.

Bittel insisted that if at all possible I should do it, and no one else. But was it possible? It was also Bittel who approached the Assyriologist Ernst Weidner in Berlin, who at that time had no academic position and earned his living by working in the Ullstein Publishing Company. He published a scholarly journal, the *Archiv für Orientforschung*, using his own funds. He had

started a series of monographs entitled *Beihefte*, supplementary to the journal, and was willing to take my work into his series. He said that he had never been bothered by the Nazi authorities and did not care what they would do. My work therefore appeared during the war in two volumes, in 1940 and 1942, and I do not think that the publication caused him any difficulty.

In this particular publication of the seals I refrained from trying to read the hieroglyphs, for a very specific reason. The reading of some individual signs had by this time been determined. The very first royal seal we found in 1933 had a genealogy in cuneiform in three rings, but the king's own name was missing. It must have been contained in a fourth ring for which there had been no space on the small bulla. The genealogy made it absolutely clear that the owner of the seal was the king known from the texts as Urkhi-Teshub. (See "Khattushili III, King of the Hittites" in Part 5, Vol. II.) The hieroglyphs in the center, however, consisted of one sign known only as the logogram for "city," a vertical stroke, and a sign known as *li*. So I asked myself: How can it be possible that the name Urkhi-Teshub should be written by something ending in *li*? Therefore, I argued, some of the writings assumed to be names are something else: formulas of blessing, pious wishes, or symbols of some sort.

Among the seals of 1936 there were a number of impressions with a new royal name that according to the cuneiform inscription must have been Muwattalli. In fact there were hieroglyphs on the seal that could be read *mu-ta-li*. In the fall of the same year I received a letter from Professor John Garstang of the University of Liverpool, who was excavating a site near Mersin in southern Anatolia. He had been shown by Ali Rıza Yalgın, the director of the Adana Museum, a relief carved into a cliff overhanging the river Ceyhan (Jeyhan) near the village of Sirkeli. With the help of a scaffold erected in the water, Garstang got a close look at the relief and the accompanying inscription. He sent me photographs of the hieroglyphs and asked me whether I could provide a reading. I soon noticed that they included the same royal name that we had just read as *mu-ta-li*. I asked Professor Garstang whether I could visit him on our winter vacation, and he invited me to do so.

This time there was no scaffold. A ladder was held by a man who stood in the water, and I climbed up and got a close look. With my fingers I could also feel the signs worked in relief. There was no doubt that it was Muwattalli. But this name and its titles were followed by a second royal name. In such a case one expects a genealogy, but exactly where the word for "son" was expected the surface of the rock made a slight turn so that I could neither see it nor feel it with my hands. The strange circumstance was that the second name was the same as our Urkhi-Teshub, but Urkhi-Teshub was the son of Muwattalli, not his father. So it could not be a genealogy. But why would a king write the name of his son with the title "king" next to his own?

I was greatly puzzled. I actually played with the idea that the same hieroglyphs could also represent the name of Murshili who was Muwattalli's father. But at the time I did not dare draw this conclusion. It was only after the Second World War that an actual seal of Murshili II found at Ras Shamra (near Latakia, Syria) became known. It confirmed that they were indeed his hieroglyphs. Still later, at Boğazköy, another impression of the first "Urkhi-Teshub" seal was discovered that included the name Murshili in the outermost ring of cuneiform. The obvious conclusion was that Urkhi-Teshub had assumed the name Murshili when he became king without, however, giving up his Hurrian name. But all of these things were not known when I wrote the seal publication. It goes without saying that I have long since given up my skepticism and joined those who read the hieroglyphic seal legends as names. The first scholar who read a great many nonroyal seals by using my publication was Sedat Alp. He published his readings in German in a monograph for Ankara University in 1950.

In the seal publication I gave a list of the sign forms used in the Empire period and discussed the possible meanings of some signs that seemed to be logograms, such as the hieroglyphs for the god Sharrumma and the sun-god, or the stag as hieroglyph of the protective god. These identifications contributed to the understanding of the deities depicted at Yazılıkaya. I put all of this information in the seal book because I could not write for the 1941 official publication of Yazılıkaya.

Ankara, where I lived from 1936, was in those days an interesting place. For one thing it had a beautiful climate, completely free of the pollution that later plagued it. It was a small town in which it was easy to get around. There was a large community of Germans and Austrians, about fifty families, refugees like us who were employed at the university and the hospital, but also as consultants in many branches of government. There were also the musicians who taught at the conservatory and held the first chairs in the Philharmonic Orchestra. There was the feeling that Turkey was moving toward europeanization and that we were participating in that process. Personally I felt privileged to be in the country of the subject of my studies while remaining close to my teacher, Professor Landsberger. This reminiscence is not the place to describe our faculty, but I want to mention that von der Osten, having completed his work on the Alişar Hüyük excavations, was our colleague from 1936 to 1939.

The tablets that had been found at Boğazköy since 1931 were not accessible to me, because I was no longer a member of the German expedition. But this restriction did not apply to the tablets from Winckler's excavations kept in the İstanbul Museum. Some tablets had always remained there, and the Germans had recently returned a number of fragments, though they were not yet published. When after four years our first class of students graduated, two women who studied with me, Muazzezz Çığ and Hatice Kızılyay, were appointed to the İstanbul Museum. I made a point when spending my summer vacations in İstanbul of teaching them how to copy cuneiform. Together we started a series to publish the Boğazköy tablets in the İstanbul Museum. I was a coauthor for the first two volumes; after my departure they prepared a third volume, and many years later Mustafa Eren published the remaining fragments in a fourth one. In training these scholars, I think I did a service to cuneiform studies, for they later used their copying skills to help many Assyriologists and Sumerologists.

I was always interested in Hittite mythology. Ehelolf often hinted at a whole cycle of myths in which the Hurrian god Kumarbi was the central figure. In 1936 Emil Forrer published in transliteration and translation a tablet that told about divinities who one after the other held the kingship of the gods in heaven. The last three of these gods were Anu ("Sky"), Kumarbi, and the storm-god whose Hurrian name is Teshub.

During the war there appeared a new volume of the *Keilschrifturkunden* series, with mythological texts in handcopies by Heinrich Otten. The first part contains the texts of Anatolian myths to which Otten had already devoted a decisive study. The second part brought texts of Hurrian origin, among them many dealing with Kumarbi, and finally a handcopy of Forrer's text. When I read them I soon got the feeling that some isolated fragments dealing with Kumarbi seemed to belong to one coherent story. Otten had already seen that some fragments duplicated others. By arranging the fragments in such a way that those of one copy fell into the lacunae of another I was able to reconstruct a story. It was not complete, but the course of events was discernible. (See the chapter on the Kumarbi Cycle in Part 8, Vol. III.)

The story dealt with Kumarbi's attempt to regain the kingship from Teshub, who had wrested it from him. For this purpose he engendered a stone monster that threatened the world and the gods with destruction. Its name was Ullikummi, and the composition was called "The Song of Ullikummi." The gods are unable to defeat the stone until the wise Babylonian god Ea finds a way to break its supernatural power. I must confess that when I was able to reconstruct this myth in the midst of the Second World War, when another monster threatened the whole world with destruction, the story gave me some kind of hope.

Forrer had already seen the similarity between the "Kingship in Heaven" and the Theogony of Hesiod. I carried the parallel with Hesiod one step farther by comparing Ullikummi with the Greek monster Typhon. My work was published as one of a series of monographs founded by some refugee professors and printed in Turkey. Diverse academic fields were represented in this series, entitled *Istanbuler Schriften.* The production of my *Kumarbi* took a year and a half, so that it appeared only in 1946, after the Turkish edition.

Other work came to me during my Ankara years from another side. Ankara had no archaeological museum. There were projects, but no funds were available. In the bazaar quarter on the slope of the citadel were the ruins of two historic buildings. One was a bazaar building, called *Bedestan,* built by the grand vizier of Mehmed the Conqueror (middle of the fifteenth century). The other was a *khan* or caravansary of about the same period. Both ruins were inhabited by squatters. The governor of Ankara gave an ultimatum to the department of antiquities to restore these buildings or they would be razed. They obviously had to be saved, but that could only be done if they were put to use. Therefore the director-general of antiquities, Dr. Hamit Zübeyr Koşay, asked the dean of our faculty to delegate Professor von der Osten and me as consultants for planning an archaeological museum in the *Bedestan.* The building consisted of a central hall, forty-nine meters (54 yards) by nineteen meters (21 yards), and was originally covered with ten domes supported by four pillars along the middle. Only three domes remained. The central hall was surrounded by four bazaar streets with the typical small, vaulted shops.

Over the years the department had transported a great number of Hittite reliefs and inscriptions to Ankara and stored them temporarily in the cella of the temple of Augustus, while other pieces were still in situ. For example, in 1938 von der Osten had taken his students on a study trip on which he invited my students and me, which gave me the occasion to see Carchemish with many reliefs still in place. In trying to arrange the reliefs in the big hall I soon saw that it would be possible to imitate their original position. For the Lion Gate of Arslantepe near Malatya (ancient Melitene), Professor Delaporte kindly let me have copies of his plans and photographs before his book was published. The third volume of the Carchemish publication had not yet appeared, but I used a sketch map in an article by Herzfeld. In addition, Richard D. Barnett, who was stationed in Ankara during the war, provided valuable information and was influential in bringing to Ankara casts of those fragments in the British Museum which completed some of our pieces.

The work took a very long time. Not only were the funds limited but cement was rationed because of the war. Only slowly one small dome after the other could be erected in concrete, and then stone pedestals for the rows of reliefs could be built. One year it was only one dome and one row, but luckily that was not always so. The last set of reliefs, those of the Sphinx Gate at Alaca Hüyük, found its place only in 1948. The four adjoining tracts were restored without the shops and used for the exhibition of objects, but this work was done after my departure and without my participation. Its present shape is the work of Raci Temizer, who was director of the museum for many years. The *khan* houses the offices and storerooms. It is there that the tablets are kept.

In 1948 I left Turkey. I was invited to the University of Uppsala, Sweden, as guest lecturer for one year. I came to Chicago in November 1949. In 1952 Bittel was able to resume the excavations of Boğazköy. He invited me to join his staff again, now from Chicago, but it was clear that for the continuity of the Boğazköy enterprise a Hittitologist resident in Germany was needed. Bittel therefore also asked Otten to continue as epigrapher on the expedition. At first Otten was still in East Berlin, but after a few years he moved to the West and became professor at the University of Marburg. In some years he and I shared the work of transliterating the tablets. They were now cleaned locally by Turkish workers at the excavation site.

During the division of Germany it was obvious that the tablets from Bittel's excavations had to be published in the West. For this purpose the old series *Keilschrifttexte aus Boghazköi* was revived under the direction of Otten, who prepared most of the volumes. I also contributed a few volumes and parts of others. Otten also established a new center for Hittite studies, first in Marburg, then at the Academy of Mainz. One of this center's tasks is the preparation of a word file of all Hittite texts, published as well as unpublished.

During the first season after the war I had an interesting experience. That year the expedition was housed in the school. For the following years Bittel rented the *konak* unfurnished. The expedition stayed there until Peter Neve built the present modern expedition house near the museum. One day in 1952 I was sitting in the schoolhouse when a man brought me a tablet with a note from our architect, Rudolf Naumann, saying that this tablet was firmly dated to a level older than the Empire period. Could I say something about its contents? The piece, though only a fragment, was quite legible, and I soon found that its language had all the marks of the Old Hittite language, while the personal and geographic names mentioned in the text made me suspect that it might describe a war in the time of the Old Kingdom. This reading would fit the findspot very nicely, but that was not all. It struck my eyes that the cuneiform writing had a peculiar appearance. It looked denser, the individual wedges closer together than usual. The upper edges of the verticals were slanting to the right. I remembered at the time that I had seen this kind of writing elsewhere. So I asked myself whether this kind of handwriting might not be peculiar to the Old Kingdom. I mentioned my thoughts to Otten, and during the following years we both checked the evidence and found that, indeed, there were quite a number of tablets showing this kind of handwriting and that in all of them the language had the mark of Old Hittite. There simply was no example of an Empire period text written this way. This discovery considerably increased the size of the corpus of recognized Old Hittite texts, including cult texts and rituals that contained no reference to a historical period. Recent diachronic studies of Hittite draw on this corpus.

My observation was based on an overall impression. I did not at the time observe anything special about the shape of individual signs. This kind of detailed paleographic observation was added by Otten and his "school," in particular E. Neu and C. Rüster. For some cuneiform signs it is now indeed possible to follow a development of shapes from the oldest to the most recent period. These detailed observations became possible once the existence of the old script had been recognized.

So much for the recovery of the Hittite language. By now Hittitology has become truly international, as attested by the scholars from many lands who have contributed to these volumes on various aspects of Hittite civilization. But what about the Hittite hieroglyphs which, as mentioned earlier, were discovered first? For a long time they could not be deciphered. The breakthrough came only in the 1930s after the decipherment of Hittite, which provided a model for the kind of language to expect, and after the publication of more hieroglyphic inscriptions, especially those excavated by the

British Museum at Jerablus on the Euphrates. The greater part of those texts was published in the 1920s. The decipherment started from the recognition of place-names. From cuneiform sources it had been concluded that the ruins at Jerablus were the ancient Carchemish (Karkamish in Assyrian). When it was seen that the name mentioned near the beginning of many inscriptions began with two identical signs, the first of which was provided with an added stroke, it was tempting to read them as *ka+r-ka* and the following two as *mi-sa*. Similarly, inscriptions found at Maraş contained a name that also began with two identical signs of which the first had the added stroke. The area of Maraş was called Gurgum in the Assyrian records. Therefore scholars tentatively read the hieroglyphic name *gu+r-gu-ma*. These readings proved to be correct. They yielded some syllabic signs and the important recognition of the small added line as indicator of the consonant *r*. From here the decipherment progressed. The scholars who independently and at approximately the same time achieved the decipherment were H. T. Bossert (Berlin), E. Forrer (Berlin), P. Meriggi (then at Hamburg), B. Hrozný (Prague), and I. J. Gelb of the Oriental Institute of Chicago. In 1934 Meriggi had already published translations of many building inscriptions together with a glossary, followed in 1937 by a sign list.

A new discovery put the decipherment on a new basis. In 1946 H. T. Bossert, at that time professor at İstanbul, discovered and excavated a site called Karatepe, in the wooded hills of Cilicia. He found two gates decorated with sculptures and inscriptions in both hieroglyphs and Phoenician. On the basis of what had been deciphered by that time, Bossert and his assistant F. Steinherr soon saw that they were two versions of the same text, a real bilingual. (See "Autobiographies in Ancient Western Asia" in Part 9 above.) This find, of course, advanced the knowledge of the language considerably. It was clear by now that the language written in hieroglyphs was not the Hittite of the cuneiform texts, but a language related to it and most similar to Luwian.

The new evidence was utilized by Laroche in a new sign list in 1960 and by Meriggi in a revised edition of his glossary and sign list (*Hieroglyphisch-hethitisches Glossar*) in 1962. Meriggi also published a manual in Italian that contains a grammar and an edition of all texts with commentary (1966–1975). Unfortunately, this monumental work was overtaken by new developments even before it was completed.

Bossert, in an article published in *Orientalia* in 1961, toward the end of his life, already had the idea that some of the most common signs of the script should be read with values different from the accepted ones, and that the new readings would yield forms closer to Luwian. As his argumentation was rather involved, his thesis found no followers at first. It was only at a symposium held in 1970 in London that Günter Neumann and David Hawkins together with Anna Morpurgo-Davies independently propagated the same changes. To mention only one result, the endings of the nominative and the dative plural, which had been read *i* and *ī*, respectively, became *zi* and *za* as in Luwian. Now, finally, the hieroglyphic inscriptions can be read as representing a real language, the essentials of which are understood. We call it hieroglyphic Luwian. (See "Karkamish and Karatepe" in Part 5, Vol. II.)

The hieroglyphic script was already known in the second millennium, as is shown by the seal impressions discussed earlier in this essay. The excavations of 1990 and 1991 added more than 1,200 sealed bullae, which will increase our knowledge of the functioning of the administration. There exist a few coherent inscriptions of the thirteenth century BCE; their number increased through recent finds. But the majority of hieroglyphic monuments date to the period 1200–700 BCE, when rulers of small kingdoms in Anatolia and Syria carried on the Hittite tradition and wrote in Luwian. These Late Hittite kingdoms, as we call them, were conquered by the Assyrians shortly before 700 BCE, about the same time as the Northern Kingdom of Israel. Such Late Hittite rulers must be meant when the books of Kings speak of "kings of the Hittites."

BIBLIOGRAPHY

Grammar

The best grammar is still JOHANNES FRIEDRICH, *Hethitisches Elementarbuch*, part 1, *Kurzgefasste Grammatik*, 2nd ed. (1960).

Self-study

EDGAR H. STURTEVANT and GEORGE BECHTEL, *A Hittite Chrestomathy* (1935), contains text in both cuneiform script and transliteration with translation, preceded by a sign-list.

Dictionaries

JOHANNES FRIEDRICH, *Hethitisches Wörterbuch* (1952), with supplements (1957, 1961, 1966), though out of print, is still the only glossary of all words whose meaning was known at the time. Full dictionaries are being prepared but are far from completion. They are JOHANNES FRIEDRICH and ANNELIES KAMMENHUBER, *Hethitisches Wörterbuch* (2nd ed. 1975–), which at this writing covers the letters A, E, and part of H. JAAN PUHVEL, *Hittite Etymological Dictionary* (1984–); and so far covering the letters A, E, I, and H. HANS G. GÜTERBOCK and HARRY A. HOFFNER, *The Hittite Dictionary of The Oriental Institute of The University of Chicago* (1989–), starts in the middle of the alphabet in order not to duplicate the other dictionaries. One volume contains the letters L–N. While these dictionaries are incomplete, the following glossary may be used for quick orientation: JOHANN TISCHLER, *Hethitisch-deutsches Wörterverzeichnis*, Innsbrucker Beiträge zur Sprachwissenschaft, 39 (1982). It does not include the logograms (word signs), but a comprehensive list is given in the following sign list: ERICH NEU and CHRISTEL RÜSTER, *Hethitisches Zeichenlexikon* (1989).

For hieroglyphic Luwian see RUDOLF WERNER, *Kleine Einführung ins Hieroglyphen-luwische*, Orbis Biblicus et Orientalis, 106 (1991).

General

The best general work on Hittite history and civilization is still OLIVER R. GURNEY, *The Hittites* (1952; current revised reprint, 1990).

SEE ALSO **The Decipherment of Ancient Near Eastern Scripts** (Part 1, Vol. I) and **Indo-European Languages** (Part 9, Vol. IV).

Recovering Canaan
and Ancient Israel

CYRUS H. GORDON

CYRUS HERZL GORDON *was born on June 29, 1908, in Philadelphia, Pennsylvania, and received his doctorate at the University of Pennsylvania in 1930. He went to the Near East as a field archaeologist for the American School of Oriental Research (1931–1935) and participated in excavations at Tell Beit Mirsim, Tell Billa, Tepe Gawra, as well as in Moab and Edom with Nelson Glueck. He has taught at Johns Hopkins University, Smith College, Dropsie University, Brandeis University, and is presently Professor Emeritus at New York University. Professor Gordon has published extensively on a broad range of topics and issues dealing with the ancient and modern Near East.*

IN 1913, WHEN I WAS five years old, my father decided that I should embark on the study of the Bible, beginning with the book of Genesis in Hebrew. Since he had begun at three, he felt it was high time for me. He engaged a teacher, Mr. Abelson, who taught me the alphabet, and within a few days we plunged into the opening verses about the creation. Soon I was initiated into the narrative about Adam and Eve, and when I learned of the birth of Cain and Abel, I asked my teacher how babies come into the world. (I had obviously not been satisfied by the stork story my Victorian mother had told me.) Being an honest man, Mr. Abelson said, "They come out of ladies." I was fascinated, and at supper that evening I told my parents what I had learned. My mother was outraged and told my father to fire Mr. Abelson for teaching such immorality to a child of five. My father, who was the more worldly of my parents, was an intellectual physician and historian of medicine. He replied that Mr. Abelson had meant no harm and was a poor man who needed the salary for supporting his wife and two little daughters. My mother reluctantly agreed to retain his services on condition that he promise never again to expose me to corruption.

That was more than merely the start of my sex education. From then on, I was hooked on learning in general and on the great classic of Israel in particular. I did not yet realize how destiny was ineluctably leading me into the world of Canaan and indeed of the civilizations of the entire ancient Near East.

After graduating from high school in my native city of Philadelphia, I continued my studies at the University of Pennsylvania. My department at the university took an active interest in new discoveries and developments in archaeology. In the 1920s, Hittite was deciphered and became the subject of intensive investigation. One of the professors in the department, Dr. George A. Barton, though already a senior citizen, was young enough in spirit to embark on the study of Hittite, and, in collaboration with one of his students, published a Hittite grammar. It was not a good job, even for its time, but at least it kindled an interest among some of the students in an important new branch of near eastern studies. I got into Hittite in my university years and have taught it intermittently throughout my teaching career.

The Hittites entered the world of the Bible through Anatolia, where they established a powerful empire in the second millennium BCE. During much of the Amarna and Ramesside ages, Egypt and the Hittites were the two major powers on the international scene. One of the main features of the Israelite way of life is the Hebraic reaction against the practices and values of cultures with which they came into contact, including the Hittite. The significance of the text of the Hebrew Bible becomes clear only when we know the pagan institutions against which the Bible is reacting. The Hebrews abhorred bestiality of all kinds, regardless of the species of animal involved. Before creating Eve, God decided that "it is not good for man to be alone" (Genesis 2:18), whereupon He paraded all the animals before Adam and found that none was fit to be the proper mate for him (verse 20). Therefore Eve was fashioned as man's one and only proper mate. It is to be noted that the text disqualifies not merely some animals, but all of them. According to the Hittite Laws, by contrast, it was permissible to have sexual intercourse with some animals but not with others. For example, it was a capital crime to have intercourse with a sheep, pig, or dog (§§188, 199); but it was permissible with a horse or mule (§200A). The Hebrews were not interested in such subtle Hittite distinctions; they forbade every variety of bestiality. (See "Legal and Social Institutions of Hittite Anatolia" in Part 4, Vol. I.)

I assigned a dissertation on the Hittite Law code to one of my most gifted students, who is now the foremost American-born Hittitologist, Professor Harry A. Hoffner of the Oriental Institute at the University of Chicago, joint author of the Chicago *Hittite Dictionary,* which is now appearing in fascicles. When I retired at the age of sixty-five from Brandeis University, my students and friends honored me with a Festschrift, and Harry contributed an interesting and scholarly article entitled "Incest, Sodomy and Bestiality in the Ancient Near East." Two years later, in

1975, I was in Paris, where I called on Professor Emmanuel Laroche. Smiling broadly, he said, "How do you like the article that Hoffner dedicated to you in your Festschrift?" All I could say was, "I would have been quite satisfied with any one of the three topics."

My mentor at the University of Pennsylvania, Professor James A. Montgomery, had published a collection of Aramaic magic bowls that had been unearthed at Nippur in 1888 and 1889, when Iraq was part of the Ottoman Empire. Before I left Philadelphia for the Near East in May 1931, he showed me some additional fragments in the University Museum and got permission for me to publish them at some unspecified opportune time in the future. He added that the sultan had divided the antiquities between the University Museum and his Imperial Museum in Constantinople (now Istanbul). Montgomery advised me to spend enough time in Istanbul to study and copy the bowls that the sultan had kept in Turkey. He thought that the sultan had retained "the largest and fairest" specimens for his own museum. I arranged through Aziz Bey, the museum director, to work on the bowls during September 1931.

After spending the summer months of 1931 excavating at the Maccabean site of Beth-zur in Judea, I left Palestine for Turkey. On reaching Istanbul, I booked a room in one of the gracious old hotels called the Tokatlian, and the next morning I headed for the museum and asked to see Aziz Bey, a cultivated, europeanized Ottoman gentleman of the old school. He loved classical music and combined what was finest of the East and West. Aziz Bey had his staff assign a room to me for studying the bowls, all of which were brought to me the following day. The bowls were few in number, which surprised me because the collection the sultan had given to the American excavators was many times larger and better. I made an appointment to see Aziz and told him that I thought there must surely be more magic bowls stored somewhere in his museum. He asked why I thought so, to which I replied, "The sultan gave such a fine and large collection to the Americans, that he must have kept a still better one, or at least one as good, for himself." Aziz smiled and said, "I do not know what Americans mean by a gift, but for Turks a gift means the best." I learned a lesson.

Subsequent experience confirmed the noble generosity of the Turks, Arabs, and other near eastern peoples.

The Istanbul incantations were among the firstfruits of my published studies on bowl texts in European, Asiatic, and American collections. I feel that to understand any civilization, it is necessary to know it at various levels. It is not enough to read the belles lettres of a people to grasp that people's character. For every giant in literature or philosophy or fine art or science, there were hundreds of magicians catering to what we would call the superstitions of the populace. To arrive at a balanced estimate, I have found it of value to give my students at least some exposure to incantation texts, though we of course emphasized the loftier arts and sciences.

In coping with the problems of life, people prefer science to magic, if the science is available. Thus the Egyptians developed rational and effective techniques for setting broken bones. They accordingly entrusted the mending of fractures to competent specialists. By contrast, they could not deal rationally and effectively with nightmares and the machinations of enemies; for such afflictions they resorted to spells and exorcisms. Belief on the part of the patient in the efficacy of the sorcerer and his art is always necessary for obtaining satisfying results.

Under the corners of homes in Nippur (modern Nuffar), archaeologists often found incantation bowls exorcising the demons and demonesses that might otherwise harm the family and their possessions. Today we take out life, health, fire, theft, and other types of insurance and often gain thereby more peace of mind than actual security. Because in antiquity there were no insurance companies, the door was wide open for magicians. Just as we cannot describe modern life adequately without dealing with the roles played by insurance and psychiatry, we cannot understand ancient Canaan and Israel without delving into their magic.

At the end of September I headed south by railroad toward Mosul, the city nearest the village of Bahshiqa in Kurdistan. The religious majority in Bahshiqa and the neighboring village of Bahzani were not Muslims but Yezidis, who believe that God is capable only of good so there is no point in worshiping him; He wouldn't and couldn't hurt anyone. The source of trouble is the Prince of Evil, whom we call Satan and whom the Yezidis propitiate under the honorific title of the Peacock Angel. They avoid the very word "Satan" because it offends the Peacock Angel and can only incite him to mischief. This dualism is more widespread than is generally thought. Of course, Zoroastrianism is the best

Cyrus Gordon with two Yezidi workers at Tell Billa in Iraq Kurdistan during the 1931–1932 archaeological season. COURTESY OF CYRUS H. GORDON

2781

example of dualism, reckoning with two great deities: Ahura Mazda, the god of good and light, and Ahriman, the god of evil and darkness. The Bible and especially the Qumran scrolls often refer to the struggle between the forces of good (light) and the forces of evil (darkness). This major theme in Canaanite and Israelite thought deserves a more penetrating study than it has received. There were (and still are) two unequal ranks of legitimate priests in Israel: the higher rank, called *kôhănîm* (priests), serve God; the lower, called *lĕvîyîm* (Levites), have various roles, one of which we are about to probe.

The root of *lēvî* is *lwy*, from which is also derived *livyātān* (Leviathan), the dragon of evil. In both Hebrew and Ugaritic, Leviathan is called *nāḥāš bārĭaḥ* (the evil serpent). In Hebrew (Psalm 74:14) God, the deity of goodness, crushes the heads of Leviathan. In the Ugaritic myths Baal or his consort, Anath, representing the forces of good, crush Leviathan's seven heads. In Greek tradition the good Herakles slays the wicked Hydra, who has either seven or nine heads. The earliest version of this myth is recorded on a cylinder seal (from Eshnunna [modern Tell Asmar] in the valley of the Diyala River, a tributary of the Tigris), on which is carved a scene showing two heroes slaying the seven-headed dragon. What I am suggesting is a semantic and etymological connection between Leviathan and Levite, whereby originally the priests brought on the blessings of goodness while the Levites warded off the curses of evil.

Living among the Yezidis soon taught me that propitiators of Satan can be as noble as the best of the monotheists who worship God. Our foreman, Rashid, was the son of the mayor of Bahshiqa, Ṣaduq, who, more than a decade earlier, when Iraq was still part of the Ottoman Empire, did a good deed that was the measure of the man. The local Ottoman official, a Muslim Turk, cast a lustful eye on the wife of a Bahshiqa Christian and was bent on wresting her from her husband. Ṣaduq lost no time. He went to the pasha in Mosul with a substantial bribe from his own wealth, induced the Pasha to remove the corrupt official, and had him transferred immediately to a distant post. Virtue such as Ṣaduq's is long remembered.

In the evenings there was no place to go in Bahshiqa. The village had no lights, and the dogs were dangerous. Nothing resembling a coffee house or movie existed there. Most of the staff played cards, but a few of us preferred to read facsimiles of the Nuzi (or Nuzu) tablets together. Those documents of the fifteenth and fourteenth centuries BCE provide the most intimate and detailed record of private and public life in any ancient community. Wherever I have taught, I have included the study of the Nuzi tablets among my course offerings.

Although Nuzi is near Kirkuk, east of the Tigris in Iraq and quite far from Canaan, the tablets found there have had a profound effect on biblical studies, particularly on our understanding of the patriarchal narratives in Genesis. The tablets were written over four or five generations in the fifteenth and fourteenth centuries BCE. The Nuzi population was Hurrian ("Horite" in the English Bible) but the language of the tablets is Babylonian, the lingua franca of the period. Many of the laws and customs reflected in the tablets were, as is normally the case, of much older origin; and many continued to be in use for centuries to come with only gradual modifications, as is also quite normally the case. Part of the reason that the social institutions of Nuzi are so close to those of the Hebrew patriarchs is that the Hurrians were widespread, covering the area that included both Nuzi and the Harran region, whence the patriarchs migrated to Canaan.

A recurrent theme in the Nuzi wills is that only the chief heir, who is normally, but far from always, the firstborn son, is to inherit the household gods. This explains why Rachel stole her father Laban's teraphim (household gods); it was to secure the position of chief heir for her progeny. Not only did her older sister, Leah, have a better claim for her offspring, but there were sons of Laban (Genesis 31:1) who, as males, outranked their older sisters in succeeding Laban as chief heir. But one Nuzi will explains much more: it states that all of the chief heir's siblings will have to come to his house, where the household gods are kept, for all religious activities; and any of his siblings who makes gods of his own forfeits his inheritance. The purpose is clear; it is to hold the family together. This information adds a new dimension to the commandment not to make and worship graven images: it is a device to keep the people from fragmenting.

Cultic centrality for all Israel, with only one national shrine, is also built into the pentateuchal system (Deuteronomy 12:14). Such institutions are not merely abstract theological principles; they have down-to-earth practical functions.

The Nuzi tablets have also made clear the choice of alternative life-styles in Israelite society. Brothers could live together as a fratriarchal unit, or any one of them could leave and strike out on his own. The technical reference to a fratriarchal family is "when brothers are living together." Tradition has often misunderstood the phrase to refer to harmonious family relationships instead of designating a legal status. It is only when "brothers are living together" as a fratriarchal unit that the law of levirate marriage is operative (Deuteronomy 25:5). If, in such a unit, a brother dies childless, the widow is automatically mated with her brother-in-law and the first child of that union is considered the heir of the deceased, so that no man's name shall die out in Israel. The opening clause ("when brothers are living together") implies that the law of levirate marriage is not operative in the case of the widow of a brother outside the fratriarchal household. This distinction makes much sense if we compare the two scenarios. On the one hand, a widow in a fratriarchal unit is not dislocated but automatically retained in the family of which she is already a part. On the other, the widow of a brother who has detached himself from his siblings and moved away (perhaps far away) from his brothers is in a quite different situation. Moving her to a strange household, which she would enter as an outsider, would diminish her status and demand sudden adjustments on the part of the fratriarchal unit.

From 1931 to 1935 I was engaged in archaeological fieldwork. When I returned to the United States, the country was still in the Great Depression. I managed to secure a teaching fellowship at Johns Hopkins from 1935 to 1938. I then accepted a lectureship at Smith College for 1938–1939 and 1940–1941, where my main task was the publication of 110 cuneiform tablets in the Smith College collection. Working on the original clay documents was a valuable experience, for I wanted to know firsthand all the stages of my profession, among them digging, conserving, copying, translating, and interpreting.

The tablets belonged to the Smith College Library, whose director was Miss Mary Dunham. One day she called on me in my study and told me she was revising the first insurance policy for the library and wanted to know how much fire insurance she should take out for the tablets. She was surprised by my monosyllabic answer: "None." I then explained that burning improves unbaked tablets by making them hard as bricks, and in no way hurts the already baked tablets. As a librarian she realized for the first time why tablets endure for millennia while parchment and papyrus manuscripts, along with our books of paper, fall prey to the ravages of time. The poor quality of our newsprint and inks gives them a particularly short life span.

Late in the spring of 1938 I received an unexpected letter from the American-Scandinavian Foundation inquiring whether I "still" wanted to study in Sweden. Eleven years earlier, when I was completing a course in advanced Swedish and about to receive my A.B. at the University of Pennsylvania, I had applied for a fellowship to study Semitics in Sweden and had been turned down. My application was apparently kept on file until 1938–1939, when the clouds of World War II were gathering and Americans were not keen on going to Europe. I gladly accepted but only for the summer because I had already accepted a membership in the Institute for Advanced Study at Princeton for the academic year 1939–1940. I decided to spend the summer in Uppsala, preparing a grammar of the Ugaritic language. The university library, called Carolina Rediviva, is superb and had everything I needed for Ugaritic studies.

The state of Ugaritology was then chaotic. The decipherment of the Ugaritic alphabet was for all intents and purposes correct and complete. The language was obviously Semitic, but knowledge of the grammatical details was vague and, in retrospect, amateurish. Worst of all, the translators usually sought the meanings of problematic words in various dictionaries of sundry Semitic languages. The lexicon of biblical Hebrew happens to be the best, but even it can be misleading. For example, *yph* (pronounced *yāfēăh* or *yāfiăh*) was not known to be a noun meaning "a witness" in the Hebrew Bible though it does indeed have that meaning; it was thought to be a verb meaning "breathing, uttering." Whenever we deal with a text, every correct translation has to fit the context regardless of etymology. The Arabic lexica are particularly rich in words and various meanings for individual words, so much so that interpreting Ugaritic as though it were Arabic can yield an assortment of very different translations and interpretations for the same passage. Worse yet, one could quarry in August Dillmann's huge Ethiopic lexicon and come up with amazing mistranslations. Some scholars (including one of my own teachers) actually believed that the function of the researcher was to come up with a new and original rendering, rather than get at the original meaning of the ancient author. My *Ugaritic Grammar* in 1940 formulated the rules of the language that have stood the test of time. To be sure, my work has gone through four revised and enlarged editions since 1940 plus a later supplement, and as a result of new tablets being discovered and the contributions of many scholars, my opus should be periodically updated. Yet, when all is said and done, I did succeed in injecting law and order into an important but previously chaotic field.

Many important archaeological discoveries have been made in the Near East during the twentieth century, but none, in my estimation, equals that of the Ugaritic tablets. The latter include the sacred literature of Canaan against which the Bible was a conscious reaction. Ugaritic language and literature, including its poetic structures, were taken over by the Hebrews, who built upon a ready-made medium for expressing their original contributions. The Hebrew Bible turns out to be a new message in an old language and in old literary forms that the Hebrews found awaiting them when they entered Canaan as the Bronze Age was giving way to the Iron Age, circa 1200 BCE.

The Ugaritic epics have thrown considerable light on the patriarchal narratives. The common themes in the latter include the royal hero's recovery of his destined bride from another king's palace, the royal couple's overcoming difficulties in producing the right crown prince by enlisting divine help, and the eclipsing of the heir apparent by the more suitable younger child. But in addition to the literary aspects of the narratives, there is a historical dimension.

There is a dossier of tablets sent by the Hittite emperor Khattushili III (circa 1282–1250) to King Niqmepa of Ugarit to regulate the activities of the "merchants of Ur(a)" in Ugarit (modern Ras Shamra). There had been complaints from Ugarit against those merchants, and Khattushili had to address those complaints because the merchants were his subjects and Ugarit was a vassal state within his Hittite Empire. Three regulations were laid down. First, the merchants of Ur(a) were not to spend the entire year in Ugarit but only the harvest season. After the harvest they were to return to Ur(a) for the winter. Second, they were not to acquire real estate in Ugarit. Finally, they were to conduct their business in Ugarit and collect what the Ugaritians owed them. Thus the merchants of Ur(a), operating under the jurisdiction of the Hittite emperor, were not to have permanent residence or to own real property in Ugarit, but their right to conduct their business was guaranteed.

These three matters were what concerned the patriarchal community. For example, the Shechemites tried to induce Jacob to join them by offering them precisely those three rights: permanent residence, ownership of real estate, and conducting business throughout the land (Genesis 34:10). What is more, the biblical text specifies that Abraham's birthplace was "Ur of the Chaldees." Ur in Sumer is mentioned countless times in well-known cuneiform documents, in which it is never called "Ur of the Chaldees." Moreover, Ur of the Chaldees is described as beyond (that is, east of) the Euphrates, whereas Sumerian Ur is west of the river. Abraham's father, Terah, moved the family to Harran before Abraham's further move to Canaan. A look at the map shows that Harran cannot be on any reasonable route from Sumerian Ur to Canaan. Abraham's Ur must have been one of the many Urs far to the north of Sumer.

The evidence of these tablets reveals a development more important than the naming of the biblical Abraham in a cuneiform tablet would have been; it is the discovery of the wave of immigrants that brought the biblical Hebrews to Canaan. They came as merchant princes.

Muslim tradition regards Orrhai (modern Urfa, in the region of Haran) as Abraham's birthplace, even as it regards Hebron as the burial site of Abraham and his family. Until the middle of the nineteenth century CE, no one contested the northern location of Ur of the Chaldees. The decipherment of cuneiform led to the discovery of "Ur" in Sumer. The lure of novelty led some to identify that Ur with Abraham's birthplace in spite of all the evidence to the contrary. Finally, Leonard Woolley, who had an excellent sense of how to raise funds from biblical devotees, made the "definitive" identification. The error has taken hold so thoroughly that it will require a long time for the facts to prevail. Moreover, the royal tombs at Ur produced so much splendor in gold, carnelian, and lapis lazuli that it was "worthy of the Father of the three great monotheisms." You can lead a horse to water but you can't make him drink. My task is to get as close to the historic truth as the primary sources enable us.

The importance of Ugarit is many-sided. Thus a whole psalm (praising the lunar goddess Nikkal) complete with libretto and score has been unearthed at Ugarit. This means that already in the thirteenth century BCE musicography was cultivated at Ugarit, and that recordings (corresponding to our sheet music) were kept on file. Hitherto it was thought a "historic miracle" that David in the tenth century BCE became the greatest psalmist of all time. He was, according to the literary tradition, an all-around musical genius, who invented instruments and composed both the words and melodies of immortal songs. He was, in addition, a performing artist, and the innovator who gave the Judeo-Christian tradition the aesthetic component of its worship. Before him, the divine service consisted mainly of sacrificing animals. There is nothing aesthetic in the Tabernacle rituals. After David's reign his son, Solomon, built the Temple in which David's tradition of psalms was added to the sacrifices. The last of the Jerusalem Temples came to an end in 70 CE when Titus destroyed the one built by Herod. Since Judaism would only countenance sacrifices in the Temple, prayer in synagogues replaced Temple rituals. The psalms of David retained a prominent place in those prayers. Out of the early synagogues grew the churches, which continued the tradition of including psalms of David in the liturgy.

We can now understand the achievement of David as the culmination of a long and rich development. Music had been cultivated as an art in Canaan for centuries, not only as folk music but also as an academic discipline at centers such as Ugarit. (Scholars at the University of California at Berkeley have tried to reconstruct the sound by working backwards from the Gregorian chant. The result is uncertain, and in any case, the sound is monotonous.) Even as Bach was the culmination of Renaissance and medieval church music, David was the culmination of a great tradition that included what had been taught in the academies of Canaan since at least three centuries before his birth. We can explain David's achievement as we can Bach's. We still marvel at what they did, but we at last know what made it possible. To blossom, genius—like plants—requires the right soil.

The Ugaritic alphabet is particularly noteworthy. It appears at Ugarit, where it was used from about 1400 BCE, until the city was destroyed about 1185 BCE. It consists of thirty letters arranged in a fixed order, as we know from a number of school tablets on which the Ugaritic letters are always listed in the same sequence. The twenty-two letters that survived as the Hebrew-Phoenician alphabet appear in exactly the same sequence as in the Ugaritic alphabet. The first twenty-nine letters have distinctive phonetic values with no duplication; but the thirtieth letter has the same phonetic value as the nineteenth. In other words, the alphabet consists of either twenty-nine or thirty letters. The reason for this phenomenon is that the Ugaritic alphabet was used not only for consonantal spelling but also as a calendar with letters corresponding to the days of a lunar month. From one new moon to the next is a span of not quite twenty-nine and one-half days. Since the calendar does not reckon with fractions of days, a month consisted of either twenty-nine or thirty days.

Hugh A. Moran, a cultivated man acquainted with Sinology, noted that nations all over the Old World had variations of lunar zodiacs, in which the signs had alphabetic phonetic values. Moreover, he concluded that it was from the lunar zodiacs that the original alphabet had arisen. Impressed with Moran's book, David H. Kelley, an Americanist specializing in the Mayan inscriptions, noted that the indigenous peoples of Central America also had lunar zodiacs and that a Mayan zodiac included the direct sequence of a hand sign followed by a sign called *lamat* or *lambat*, after which came the water sign. "Hand" (specifically "palm of the hand") in northwest Semitic is *kappe*, which in Hebrew becomes *kaf*. *Kaf* is also the name of the Hebrew letter *k* and corresponds to the Greek *kappa*. Next comes the letter *l*, called *lamed* in Hebrew, *lambda* in Greek, and *lamat/lambat* in Mayan. Then comes "water," which is *mu* in Egyptian, Akkadian, and Greek and yields the letter *m*. Kelley calls attention to the striking direct sequence of *k-l-m* in the Phoenician-Hebrew, Greek, Latin, and Mayan alphabets, connecting the New World with the Old. Thus the evidence of the lunar zodiacs is of global application. I then added the Ugaritic evidence, showing that the alphabet of twenty-nine or thirty letters was the perfect example of the alphabet's correspondence to the days in a lunar month.

The centrality of the Ugaritic alphabet in the history of the alphabet that has eventually spread (with modifications) to the ends of the earth is the most striking index of the significance of Ugaritology. But how do we square the twenty-nine- or thirty-letter alphabet of Ugarit with the twenty-two-letter alphabet of the Northwest Semites? It happens that there is also a shorter alphabet at Ugarit in which pairs of phonemes (such as *ḥ/ḫ* and *ʿ/ġ*) have fallen together as in the Phoenician-Hebrew-Aramaic alphabet of twenty-two letters. Although we do not yet have school texts listing the letters of the shorter Ugaritic alphabet, there is no reason to doubt that it had twenty-two letters. Although the short alphabet was not extensively used at Ugarit, it was employed at distant sites such as Tel Taʿanak, Bet-Shemesh, and Mount Tabor in Palestine far to the south. The facts that the alphabet which spread throughout the ancient Near East was the short one, and that the order of the letters retained the Ugaritic order, indicate that our alphabet is derived from the short Ugaritic alphabet.

The spread of cuneiform during the second millennium BCE is phenomenal. In the Amarna period (late fifteenth and first half of the fourteenth centuries BCE) cuneiform Babylonian was the written lingua franca of the Near East, including pharaonic Egypt during the reigns of Amenophis (Amenhotep) III and IV. At Tell al-Amarna in Middle Egypt, the Babylonian tablets include about four hundred letters exchanged between those pharaohs and the rulers of Mesopotamia, Anatolia, Cyprus, and Canaan. In 1987 I received

a letter from Dr. Victor Mair, professor of Sinology at the University of Pennsylvania, informing me that according to all the evidence available, the beginnings of Chinese writing (as witnessed on the oracle bones) date to the late thirteenth century BCE. Moreover, twenty-two special graphs known as the "ten heavenly stems" and the "twelve earthly branches" already appear in the earliest Chinese writing. Moreover, those twenty-two graphs are still in use today. What Mair wanted to know was whether anything was happening about 1200 (or a bit earlier) in the Near East regarding the origin and spread of the twenty-two-letter alphabet. I told him about the short Ugaritic alphabet and its influence in the Near East outside Ugarit. He then sent me a chart of the twenty-two Chinese graphs with their variant forms. I noted that some of them are in Ugaritic cuneiform! For example, the letter *m* appears in the exact form that it appears in Ugaritic (►ᴛ). The Chinese letter that is transliterated *s* by Sinologists has the same shape as the cuneiform letter for *z* in Ugaritic (⧩). There are other cuneiform signs among the twenty-two Chinese graphs. Like the twenty-two letter Near East alphabet, the twenty-two Chinese graphs are used for calendrics—as a numerical system and for arranging (= "alphabetizing").

During my second year at the Institute for Advanced Study, the United States became involved in World War II, and I was approached by the Army Signal Corps based in Fort Monmouth, New Jersey. My background in linguistics and mathematics was the kind of experience they were looking for and I was assigned to cryptanalyze foreign intercepts. I began to work as a civilian employee of the Signal Corps around April 1942 and was commissioned as a Signal Corps officer on July 2 of that year. I spent nearly two years in Washington, D.C., where I organized America's first agency for cracking the codes and ciphers of the Arabic, Turkish, and Persian countries of the Near East. By the fall of 1943, all of the systems were solved. Since I had trained my assistants well, and I knew that my outfit could go on by its own momentum without me, I requested overseas service in the Middle East. I was transferred to the Persian Gulf Command, and as a professional orientalist I was assigned to the Office of Technical Information at Headquarters in Tehran. This gave me an opportunity to learn about the people, language, and culture of Iran and to travel widely in western Iran, from the Caspian Sea to the Persian Gulf.

Early in 1944, while I was still in Iran, I received a letter from Dropsie College (a graduate school of near eastern studies in Philadelphia) offering me a professorship in Assyriology and Egyptology. It was the first permanent job in my field that I had ever been offered. It came after fourteen years of working, hoping, and waiting since I had received my doctorate in 1930. From childhood I had felt a calling to be Semitist. That calling precluded my settling down and having a home and family of my own until 1946, when I was separated from active military service and embarked on my academic career as a professor and teacher at an advanced level, in my chosen field. Economically, those fourteen years were hard, but professionally they had been very productive.

In my new position, while working on a variety of different sources, I became more and more aware of the common background shared by the pre-classical Greeks and Hebrews. The first publication that resulted was my article "Homer and the Bible" in 1955, reprinted as a pamphlet in 1967. It was soon expanded into book form and eventually revised under the title *The Common Background of Greek and Hebrew Civilizations*. In 1953, while I was developing this theme, Michael Ventris deciphered Linear B, found in inscriptions on the island of Crete, as Greek. Since the earlier Linear A was in the same script, it became possible to pronounce words spelled syllabically in Linear A, thus opening the possibility of deciphering it, provided that the language was of a known linguistic family. In 1957 I demonstrated that Minoan Linear A was Semitic, which went a long way in explaining the common background of Greek and Hebrew civilizations. Both the Greeks and the Hebrews shared the same Northwest Semitic substratum. This conclusion was hailed enthusiastically by a few reviewers (including Arnold Toynbee) but was a priori unwelcome to many scholars who wanted Linear A to be at least Indo-European. If it couldn't be Greek, Hittite might do. But not something so alien or distasteful as Semitic or Egyptian. There was a hostile mind-set in much of academia.

While the controversy was raging, I discovered that the Eteocretan inscriptions from Dreros and Praisos, Crete, written in Greek characters especially during early Hellenistic times (circa 300 BCE), were in a Northwest Semitic language. I succeeded in reading many idiomatic phrases correctly, including one that was nine words long. The opposition (even from Semitists who should have known better) was derisive. What emboldened me to stand against the world, if necessary, was a Greek-Eteocretan bilingual from Dreros. The Greek version ended with a dedication "to his mother" (MATPI). MATPI can only be the Cretan dialectal form of the classical Greek dative μητρί. The Eteocretan version ends with ΛΜΟ. Because no Greek word can begin with *lm-*, no serious scholar thought that the Eteocretan could be Greek. But to me it was instantly clear that *lmo* corresponded to modern Hebrew *le'imo* (from the classical *le'immō*) "to his mother." This find ended all doubt for me, and the thrill of that moment is an experience that scholars who live within the shackles of consensus can never know. Decades of rebuff, denial, and outright scorn followed, but not doubt in my mind.

To be sure, some scholars not only accepted my decipherment of Minoan Linear A, but went on to make valuable contributions of their own. Foremost among them is Dr. Robert Stieglitz of Rutgers University. Another kind of support has been less enjoyable. One writer brazenly appropriated my decipherment as his own, even though many years earlier he himself had cited my writings on the subject and agreed with them in print. Few were taken in by his silly skulduggery.

In 1956 I left Dropsie and moved to Brandeis University, where I founded the Department of Mediterranean Studies, which flourished for about fifteen years. From the close of the McCarthy era to the student unrest in the late 1960s there were plenty of funds for higher education, and academicians were highly respected. Good students came to study under my tutelage from all over the United States and abroad. Their dissertations on a wide spectrum of topics were almost all published during those years. It was during my Brandeis years that my attention became more and more focused on the phenomenon of diffusion, and gradually I realized that global diffusion by land and sea had taken place so thoroughly by Neolithic times that no civilization (especially no high civilization) has ever arisen independently.

When I left Brandeis University in 1973 to take a five-year contract at New York University, little did I realize that my stay there would last sixteen years, for I did not retire from teaching at N.Y.U. until 1989. I was already a senior citizen in 1973, and I knew that to remain alive in mind as well as body, I would have to add a new area of academic inquiry to my vita. One can't keep reshuffling the same deck of cards without first boring his students and then himself. The new horizon was not long in coming. The Italians, under the leadership of Paolo Matthiae of the University of Rome, had undertaken the excavation of a large walled city (Tell Mardikh, which turned out to be ancient Ebla) a little more than thirty miles south of Aleppo, in Syria. Between 1974 and 1976 they discovered vast cuneiform archives from about 2300–2200 BCE. They uncovered about fifteen thousand tablets, which constitute the largest aggregation of written documents from anywhere in the world during the Early Bronze Age (3000–2000 BCE). The main language of the texts is called Eblaite. Actually it is a written lingua franca used also at many other sites, notably Mari, Abu Salabikh, and Kish. It contains both East Semitic (Akkadian) and Northwest Semitic (Ugaritic, Canaanite, and Aramaic) elements. I am now engaged in reconstructing "Eblaite." We must content ourselves here with a single indicator of how the Ebla archives are providing Early Bronze Age background for the origins of Canaanite and Israelite civilization.

A Ugaritic text describes a feared demon named Ḥaby as "possessing horns and a tail" and anticipating our iconography of the devil. Demonic names were frequently reduplicated, and an Eblaite incantation accordingly calls him Ḥabḥaby who also has horns and tail(s). Isaiah (26:20) still reckons with Ḥaby as a frightful demon; while Habakkuk (3:4) adds the suffix -ôn to his name so that he is called Ḥebyôn (whose horns are alluded to in the Hebrew text). Thus we discern some of our Judeo-Christian heritage can be traced to the Early Bronze Age through Canaan and Israel.

POSTSCRIPT

My studies began, in early childhood, with the Hebrew text of the Old Testament and proceeded without adherence to any school of thought. My first aim was to understand each passage as closely as possible to what it meant to the ancient author. Later, as my knowledge grew, I endeavored to grasp the significance of compositions as a whole. Theories did not attract me. I wanted the freedom to go wherever the facts might lead, regardless of consensus. I was, by nature, a loner in quest of the truth. My parents, particularly my father, came from a tradition of rationality that encouraged innovation. The mortal sin was not heresy but ignorance.

Next to my home environment, I owe most to the culture of my native city of Philadelphia as it was during the first third of the twentieth century. As a teenager I was trained in the Latin and Greek classics, which prepared me to see our West European culture as a product of the Mediterranean. The Bible imperceptibly made me aware first of Canaanite culture and then of the Ancient Near East, which embraces the Cuneiform World and Pharaonic Egypt. My ability to see relationships where others could not made me a comparativist; but unlike run-of-the-mill comparativists, I compared only what I knew from the primary sources.

The ecumene with which I dealt was constantly expanding. Seeing the Old Testament in the Canaanite sphere led to broader ecumenes. The Ugaritic tablets bridged the gap between early Greeks and early Hebrews; that is, between the Greeks reflected in Homer and the Hebrews reflected in the Patriarchal Narratives and in the Book of Judges. Then came the wider ecumene of the Ancient Near East. Gradually there emerged the global ecumene to which Israel and Canaan made seminal contributions including the most important single cultural invention: the alphabet.

The foregoing pages summarize what has been factually established and presented in already completed books and articles that have appeared or are in press. My current work incorporates additional factual data that should open new, hitherto unsuspected horizons. It all adds up to making possible a unified global history of mankind. The task will never be completed, but devotion to the quest for factual truth prevents us from abandoning the task.

BIBLIOGRAPHY

ALFONSO ARCHI, "Ebla and Eblaite," *Eblaitica* 1 (1987); MARTIN BERNAL, *Black Athena*, vol. 1, *The Fabrication of Ancient Greece 1785–1985* (1987); I. M. DIAKONOFF, "The Importance of Ebla for History and Linguistics," *Eblaitica* 1 (1987); CYRUS H. GORDON, *Adventures in the Nearest East* (1957), *The Ancient Near East* (1965), *The Common Background of Greek and Hebrew Civilizations* (1965), *Ugaritic Textbook: Grammar, Texts in Transliteration, Cuneiform Selections, Glossary, Indices and Supplement* (1967), *Homer and the Bible: The Origin and Character of East Mediterranean Literature* (1967), *Forgotten Scripts: Their Ongoing Discovery and Decipherment* (1968, rev. and enlarged 1987), *Before Columbus: Links Between the Old World and Ancient America* (1971), "Poetic Legends and Myths from Ugarit," *Berytus*, 25 (1977), "Semitic Inscriptions from Crete," *Hebrew Annual Review* 8 (1984), "Ebla, Ugarit and the Old Testament," *Orient* 25 (1989), and "New Directions in the Study of Ancient Middle Eastern Cultures," *Bulletin of the Middle Eastern Culture Center in Japan* (Anniversary issue honoring H.I.M. Prince Takahito Mikasa) (1991); also HARRY A. HOFFNER, ed. *Orient and Occident: Essays Presented to Cyrus H. Gordon on the Occasion of His Sixty-fifth Birthday* (1973); and HUGH MORAN and DAVID KELLEY, *The Alphabetic and the Ancient Calendar Signs*, 2nd ed. (1969).

SEE ALSO **Ugarit: A Second-Millennium Kingdom on the Mediterranean Coast** (Part 5, Vol. II); **Witchcraft, Magic, and Divination in Canaan and Ancient Israel** (Part 8, Vol. III); **The Story of the Semitic Alphabet** (Part 9, Vol. IV); and **Music and Dance in Ancient Western Asia** (Part 10, Vol. IV).

Contributors

William Y. Adams Professor Emeritus of Anthropology at University of Kentucky, Lexington. Author of *Shonto: A Study of the Role of the Trader in a Modern Navaho Community; Nubia: Corridor to Africa; Ceramic Industries of Medieval Nubia;* and (with E. W. Adams) *Archaeological Typology and Practical Reality.* Director of numerous archaeological excavations in Sudanese and Egyptian Nubia.
THE KINGDOM AND CIVILIZATION OF KUSH IN NORTHEAST AFRICA

Gösta W. Ahlström Until his death in January 1992, Gösta W. Ahlström was Emeritus Professor of Old Testament and Ancient Palestinian Studies at the Divinity School and in the Department of Near Eastern Studies at the University of Chicago. Author of numerous publications on the issues concerning the religion and history of ancient Israel, including *The History of Ancient Palestine from the Paleolithic Period to Alexander's Conquest,* which was published posthumously in 1993. He was also active in the American schools for Oriental research and participated in a number of archaeological excavations.
ADMINISTRATION OF THE STATE IN CANAAN AND ANCIENT ISRAEL

Bendt Alster Professor at the University of Copenhagen. Author of *Dumuzi's Dream, The Instructions of Šuruppak Instructions,* as well as other monographs, text editions, and articles on Sumerian literature.
EPIC TALES FROM ANCIENT SUMER: ENMERKAR, LUGALBANDA, AND OTHER CUNNING HEROES

Robert Anderson Extra-mural Lecturer in Egyptology at City University, London. Author of *Catalogue of Egyptian Antiquities in the British Museum, III: Musical Instruments.* Joint editor of *Egypt in 1800.* Former Honorary Secretary of the Egypt Exploration Society.
MUSIC AND DANCE IN PHARAONIC EGYPT

Alfonso Archi Professor of Hittitology in the Department of History, Archaeology, and Anthropology, The University of Rome. Author of numerous monographs and articles on Hittite and Hurrian culture as well as editor of texts from the royal archives at Ebla (Tell Mardikh). Editor of *Circulation of Goods in Non-Palatial Context in the Ancient Near East.*
HITTITE AND HURRIAN LITERATURES: AN OVERVIEW

Michael C. Astour Professor Emeritus of Historical Studies at Southern Illinois University, Edwardsville. Author of *Hittite History and Absolute Chronology of the Bronze Age* and *Hellenosemitica* and of numerous monographs and articles dealing with the history, geography, and literature of ancient Syria and northern Mesopotamia. Former president of the Middle Western Branch of the American Oriental Society.
OVERLAND TRADE ROUTES IN ANCIENT WESTERN ASIA

Hector Avalos Assistant Professor of Religious Studies at Iowa State University at Ames. Author of *Illness and Health Care in the Ancient Near East* and of several articles on the Bible and on the ancient Near East.

LEGAL AND SOCIAL INSTITUTIONS IN CANAAN AND ANCIENT ISRAEL

Guitty Azarpay Emerita Professor of Near Eastern Art at the University of California, Berkeley. Author of *Urartian Art and Artifacts: A Chronological Study; Sogdian Painting: The Pictorial Epic in Oriental Art;* and several articles on the art and architecture of Mesopotamia, Central Asia, and Iran.

PROPORTIONS IN ANCIENT NEAR EASTERN ART

Zainab Bahrani Lecturer in Ancient Art at the State University of New York at Stony Brook. Author of several articles on ancient near eastern art, Dr. Bahrani is collaborating with R. Maxwell-Hyslop on a new edition of *Western Asiatic Jewellery.*

JEWELRY AND PERSONAL ARTS IN ANCIENT WESTERN ASIA

John Baines Associate Editor of *Civilizations of the Ancient Near East.* Professor of Egyptology at the University of Oxford, England. Author of *Fecundity Figures: Egyptian Personification and the Iconology of a Genre;* translator and editor of Heinrich Schäfer's *Principles of Egyptian Art* and Erik Hornung's *Conceptions of God in Ancient Egypt;* coauthor of *Atlas of Ancient Egypt* and *Religion in Ancient Egypt.*

PALACES AND TEMPLES OF ANCIENT EGYPT; "Organization of Sacred and Secular Knowledge" in THEOLOGY, PRIESTS, AND WORSHIP IN ANCIENT EGYPT; "Elite Culture and Change" in MATHEMATICS, ASTRONOMY, AND CALENDARS IN PHARAONIC EGYPT; "Ancient Egyptian Conceptions of Language and Writing in Context" in ANCIENT EGYPTIAN AND OTHER AFROASIATIC LANGUAGES; and "Egyptian Art and Aesthetics" in AESTHETICS IN ANCIENT MESOPOTAMIAN ART

George F. Bass George T. and Gladys H. Abell Professor of Nautical Archaeology, Institute of Nautical Archaeology, at Texas A&M University. Author of *Archaeology Under Water; Cape Gelidonya: A Bronze Age Shipwreck;* and *Archaeology Beneath the Sea;* coauthor of *A History of Seafaring Based on Underwater Ar-*

chaeology and *Ships and Shipwrecks of the Americas.*

SEA AND RIVER CRAFT IN THE ANCIENT NEAR EAST

Richard H. Beal Research Associate on the Hittite Dictionary Project at the University of Chicago's Oriental Institute. Author of *The Organization of the Hittite Military* and of many articles on Hittite history, society, and language.

HITTITE MILITARY ORGANIZATION

Paul-Alain Beaulieu Research Scholar in Assyriology at Yale University, New Haven, Conn. Author of *The Reign of Nabonidus: King of Babylon, 556–539 B.C.* and of several articles on Babylonian culture, religion, and society of the first millennium BCE.

KING NABONIDUS AND THE NEO-BABYLONIAN EMPIRE

Gary Beckman Associate Editor of *Civilizations of the Ancient Near East.* Associate Curator of the Babylonian Collection at Yale University and has edited cuneiform and glyptic documents from Anatolia, Syria, and Mesopotamia. Author of numerous studies on second-millennium Anatolia and collaborator on the Hittite Dictionary Project of the Oriental Institute (University of Chicago).

ROYAL IDEOLOGY AND STATE ADMINISTRATION IN HITTITE ANATOLIA

Robert Steven Bianchi Art critic, archaeologist, and consultant, specializing in the arts of Egypt, Greece, and Rome. Author of numerous articles and books, including *Inside the Tomb of Nefertari; The Nubians;* and (with A. S. Mercatante) *Who's Who in Egyptian Mythology.*

ANCIENT EGYPTIAN RELIEFS, STATUARY, AND MONUMENTAL PAINTINGS

Carol Bier Curator, Eastern Hemisphere Collections, the Textile Museum, Washington, D. C. Author of *The Persian Velvets at Rosenberg* and a forthcoming work on pattern in Oriental carpets. Editor and contributing author to *Woven from the Soul, Spun from the Heart: Textile Arts of Safavid and Qajar Iran.*

TEXTILE ARTS IN ANCIENT WESTERN ASIA

Robert D. Biggs Professor of Assyriology at the University of Chicago. Author of many articles and monographs, including ŠÀ.ZI.GA: *Ancient Mesopotamian Potency Incantations* and *Inscriptions from Tell Abu Salabikh.* Editor of the *Journal of Near Eastern Studies;* associate editor of the *Chicago Assyrian Dictionary.*
MEDICINE, SURGERY, AND PUBLIC HEALTH IN ANCIENT MESOPOTAMIA

Jeremy A. Black Lecturer in Akkadian, University of Oxford, England. Author of *Sumerian Grammar in Babylonian Theory,* and (with Anthony Green) of *Gods, Demons, and Symbols of Ancient Mesopotamia: An Illustrated Dictionary.*
ARCHIVES AND LIBRARIES IN THE ANCIENT NEAR EAST

Edward Bleiberg Associate Professor and Director of Egyptian Art and Archaeology at the University of Memphis, Tennessee. Author of articles on the ancient Egyptian economy and a forthcoming book on gift-giving in ancient Egypt. Coeditor of *Fragments of a Shattered Visage.*
THE ECONOMY OF ANCIENT EGYPT

Joseph Blenkinsopp John A. O'Brien Professor of Biblical Studies at the University of Notre Dame, Notre Dame, Indiana. Author of many articles and of monographs that include *Gibeon and Israel; Prophecy and Canon; A History of Prophecy in Israel from the Settlement to the Hellenistic Period; The Pentateuch;* and a forthcoming monograph on leadership roles in ancient Israel.
AHAB OF ISRAEL AND JEHOSHAPHAT OF JUDAH: THE SYRO-PALESTINIAN CORRIDOR IN THE NINTH CENTURY

J. F. Borghouts Professor of Egyptology at the University of Leiden, The Netherlands. Author of many works, including *Ancient Egyptian Magical Texts.*
WITCHCRAFT, MAGIC, AND DIVINATION IN ANCIENT EGYPT

Jean Bottéro Professor Emeritus of Philology and Ancient History at the École Pratique des Hautes Études, Paris. Author of many articles and volumes, scholarly and popular, on diverse aspects of Mesopotamian culture including *Archives royales de Mari: Textes économiques et administratifs; Lorsque les dieux faisaient l'homme: Mythologie mésopotamienne* (with S. N. Kramer); *Mesopotamia: Writing, Reasoning, and the Gods; Naissance de Dieu: La Bible et l'historien; Mesopotamian Culinary Texts;* and *Il était une fois: La Mésopotamie* (with M. J. Steve).
AKKADIAN LITERATURE: AN OVERVIEW

Rémy Boucharlat Archaeologist and Director of the French Institute of Research in Iran. Author of a number of books and articles on the history and archaeology of Iran and the Arabian states of the Persian Gulf during the first millennium BCE and the beginning of the Christian era, including (with Jean-François Salles) *Arabie orientale, Mésopotamie et Iran méridionale: De l'Âge du fer au début de la période islamique.* Director of several archaeological programs in the United Arab Emirates from 1980 to 1992.
ARCHAEOLOGY AND ARTIFACTS OF THE ARABIAN PENINSULA

Burchard Brentjes Professor Emeritus at Martin Luther University, Halle, Germany. Author of numerous works on the ancient and medieval Near East and Inner Asia, including *Mittelasien; Vom Stamm zu Stadt, Der Knoten Asiens: Afghanistan und die Völker am Hindukusch; Völker an Euphrat und Tigris;* and *Drei Jahrtausende Armenien.*
THE HISTORY OF ELAM AND ACHAEMENID PERSIA: AN OVERVIEW

Pierre Briant Professor of History of Antiquities at the University of Toulouse II, Le Mirail, France. Author of numerous articles and monographs, including *Antigone le Borgne; Alexandre le Grand; Rois, tributs et paysans;* and *Une Histoire de l'Empire achéménide.*
SOCIAL AND LEGAL INSTITUTIONS IN ACHAEMENID IRAN

Trevor Bryce Deputy Vice-Chancellor at Lincoln University, New Zealand. Author of several books and of several articles on the ancient Near East, including *The Lycians: A Study of Lycian*

History and Civilisation to the Conquest of Alexander the Great and *The Lycians in Literary and Epigraphic Sources.*
THE LYCIAN KINGDOM IN SOUTHWEST ANATOLIA

Giorgio Buccellati Professor Emeritus of the Ancient Near East and History at the University of California, Los Angeles. Author of several books and articles on the history, languages, and archaeology of ancient Syria and Mesopotamia, including *The Amorites of the Ur III Period, Cities and Nations of Ancient Syria, Structural Grammar of Babylonian;* coauthor of *Terqa Preliminary Reports,* vol. 10, and *Mozan I.*
ETHICS AND PIETY IN THE ANCIENT NEAR EAST

Karl W. Butzer Dickson Centennial Professor of Liberal Arts at the University of Texas at Austin. Author of publications on the Islamic agronomists and on the environmental impact of the transfer of Mediterranean farming to the New World, including *Archaeology as Human Ecology* and *Early Hydraulic Civilizations in Egypt.* Recipient of many honors from professional societies, including the Royal Geographical Society, Society for American Archaeology, the Geologists Association of London, the American Geographical Society, and the Archaeological Institute of America.
ENVIRONMENTAL CHANGE IN THE NEAR EAST AND HUMAN IMPACT ON THE LAND

Jeanny Vorys Canby Research Associate in the Near Eastern section at the University of Pennsylvania Museum of Archaeology and Anthropology, Philadelphia, and former curator of Ancient Near Eastern and Egyptian Art at the Walters Art Gallery, Baltimore. Author of articles on Hittite, Syrian, Mesopotamian, and Egyptian art and archaeology and of *The Ancient Near East in the Walters Art Gallery.*
JEWELRY AND PERSONAL ARTS IN ANATOLIA

Annie Caubet Keeper, Department of Near Eastern Antiquities, Louvre Museum, Paris. Member of the French Excavation Teams at Ras Shamra, ancient Ugarit (Syria) and at Kition Bamboula (Cyprus). Papers in Report from the Department of Antiquities–Cyprus and coauthor in

the series *Ras Shamra—Ougarit,* Paris, ERC (vols. 3, 5, 7) as well as individual volumes such as *Les Antiquités de Chypre: Age du Bronze.*
ART AND ARCHITECTURE IN CANAAN AND ANCIENT ISRAEL

Dominique Charpin Professor of Ancient Near Eastern History at the University of Paris I (Sorbonne). Author of *Archives familiales et propriété privée en Babylonie ancienne* and *Le clergé d'Ur au siècle d'Hammurabi.* Participant in the publication of the *Archives Royales de Mari* series.
THE HISTORY OF ANCIENT MESOPOTAMIA: AN OVERVIEW

Miguel Civil Professor at the Oriental Institute, the University of Chicago. Author of numerous articles as well as of *The Sag-tablet, Lexical Texts in the Ashmolean Museum, Middle Babylonian Grammatical Texts, Miscellaneous Texts* and *The Farmer's Instructions. A Sumerian Agricultural Manual.*
ANCIENT MESOPOTAMIAN LEXICOGRAPHY

Dominique Collon Assistant Keeper of the Department of Western Asiatic Antiquities, the British Museum, London. Author of articles on the art and archaeology of the ancient Near East, including *The Alalakh Cylinder Seals: A New Catalogue of the Actual Seals Excavated by Sir Leonard Woolley at Tell Atchana, and from Neighbouring Sites on the Syrian-Turkish Border* and of *First Impressions: Cylinder Seals in the Ancient Near East.*
CLOTHING AND GROOMING IN ANCIENT WESTERN ASIA

James L. Crenshaw Robert L. Flowers Professor of Old Testament at Duke University, Durham, North Carolina. Author of numerous studies on the Hebrew Bible, including *Prophetic Conflict: Its Effect upon Israelite Tradition; Samson: A Secret Betrayed, a Vow Ignored; A Whirlpool of Torment: Israelite Traditions of God as an Oppressive Presence; Joel: A Commentary; Old Testament Wisdom: An Introduction;* and *Faith: Trembling at the Threshold of a Biblical Text.*

Former editor of Society of Biblical Literature monograph series.
THE CONTEMPLATIVE LIFE IN THE ANCIENT NEAR EAST

Frederick Cryer Professor at the University of Copenhagen. Author of a number of studies, including *Divination in Ancient Israel and Its Near Eastern Environment: A Socio-historical Investigation* and *The Productions of Time: Tradition History in Old Testament Scholarship.*
CHRONOLOGY: ISSUES AND PROBLEMS

Stephanie Dalley Shillito Fellow in Assyriology in the Oriental Faculty, University of Oxford, England. Author of numerous articles and studies, including *Old Babylonian Tablets from Tell Al-Rimah; Cuneiform Tablets in the Royal Scottish Museum; Mari and Karana: Two Old Babylonian Cities; The Tablets from Fort Shalmaneser;* and *Myths from Mesopotamia.*
ANCIENT MESOPOTAMIAN MILITARY ORGANIZATION

Peter T. Daniels Linguist and grammatologist; he has taught at the University of Wisconsin, Milwaukee, and at Chicago State University. Author of several articles on writing, general linguistics, and the history of decipherments. Translator and editor of *Introduction to the Semitic Languages: Text Specimens and Grammatical Sketches* by Gotthelf Bergsträsser; coeditor of *The World's Writing Systems.*
THE DECIPHERMENT OF ANCIENT NEAR EASTERN SCRIPTS

Johan de Roos Director of the Netherlands Institute for the Near East and a professor at the University of Leiden, The Netherlands. Author of a number of studies on Hittite culture, including the forthcoming *A Compendium of Treated Passages in Hittite Texts, 1917–1960.* Former Assistant Professor of Anatolian Languages at Amsterdam University and Visiting Professor at Northeast Normal University in Changchun, China.
HITTITE PRAYERS

Peter Der Manuelian Assistant Curator of the Department of Ancient Egyptian, Nubian, and Near Eastern Art at the Boston Museum of Fine Arts. Author of *Living in the Past: Studies in*

Archaism of the Egyptian Twenty-sixth Dynasty and *Studies in the Reign of Amenophis II.* Translator of the English edition of the *Egyptian Museum Cairo: Official Catalogue.*
FURNITURE IN ANCIENT EGYPT

William G. Dever Professor in the Department of Near Eastern Studies at the University of Arizona, Tucson. His publications include *Recent Archaeological Discoveries and Biblical Research* and *A Manual of Field Excavation: Handbook for Field Archaeologists,* as well as several reports on excavations in Israel and the surrounding region (Gezer, Sardis, Shiqmim).
PALACES AND TEMPLES IN CANAAN AND ANCIENT ISRAEL

Jacobus van Dijk Lecturer in Egyptology at the University of Groningen, The Netherlands. Author of *The New Kingdom Necropolis of Memphis: Historical and Iconographical Studies,* and of various articles on New Kingdom Egypt. Philologist on the joint Anglo-Dutch Expedition at Saqqara, Egypt.
MYTH AND MYTHMAKING IN ANCIENT EGYPT; "The Gods and Goddesses of Ancient Egypt" in THEOLOGY, PRIESTS, AND WORSHIP IN ANCIENT EGYPT (with Herman te Velde)

Paul Eugene Dion Professor of Near Eastern Studies at the University of Toronto. Author of *La Langue de Ya'udi* and *Dieu universel et peuple élu: L'Universalisme religieux en Israel depuis les origines jusqu'à la veille des luttes maccabéennes,* and of numerous articles on Israel and the Aramaeans during the Iron Age and Persian era.
ARAMAEAN TRIBES AND NATIONS OF FIRST-MILLENNIUM WESTERN ASIA

Trude Dothan Professor of Archaeology and Director of the Berman Center for Biblical Archaeology at the Institute of Archaeology of the Hebrew University, Jerusalem. Author of *The Philistines and Their Material Culture; Excavations at the Cemetery of Deir el-Balah;* and (with Moshe Dothan) *People of the Sea: The Search for the Philistines.*
THE "SEA PEOPLES" AND THE PHILISTINES OF ANCIENT PALESTINE

Rosemarie Drenkhahn Curator at the Kestner-Museum, Hannover, Lower Saxony, Germany, and Professor of Egyptology at the University of Hannover. Author of a number of studies, including *Darstellungen von Negern in Ägypten; Die Handwerker und ihre Tätigkeiten im alten Ägypten; Die Elephantine-Stele des Sethnacht und ihr historischer Hintergrund; Elfenbein im alten Ägypten;* and (with Renate Germer) *Mumie und Computer: Ein multidisziplinäres Forschungsprojekt in Hannover.*
ARTISANS AND ARTISTS IN PHARAONIC EGYPT

D. O. Edzard Professor at the Assyriology and Hittitology Institute of Munich University, Germany. Author of numerous articles, monographs, and text editions, including *Die <<Zweite Zwischenzeit>> Babyloniens; Altbabylonische Rechts- und Wirtschaftsurkunden aus Tell ed-Der in Iraq Museum, Baghdad;* and *Sumerische Rechtsurkunden des III: Jahrtausends aus der Zeit vor der III.* Editor of the *Reallexikon der Assyriologie.*
THE SUMERIAN LANGUAGE

Christopher J. Eyre Senior Lecturer in Egyptology at the University of Liverpool, England. Author of articles on social and economic history and linguistics, and of *A Late Egyptian Grammar* (with Sarah Israelit-Groll).
THE AGRICULTURAL CYCLE, FARMING, AND WATER MANAGEMENT IN THE ANCIENT NEAR EAST

Walter Farber Professor of Assyriology at the University of Chicago. Author of several articles and monographs on Mesopotamian magical, religious, medical, and literary texts, including first editions of previously unpublished cuneiform tablets: *Atti Ištar ša harmaša Dumuzi: Beschwörungsrituale an Ištar und Dumuzi* and *Schlaf, Kindchen, schlaf!: Mesopotamische Baby-Beschwörungen und -Rituale.*
WITCHCRAFT, MAGIC, AND DIVINATION IN ANCIENT MESOPOTAMIA

Benjamin R. Foster Professor of Assyriology at Yale University, New Haven, Connecticut. Author of *Umma in the Sargonic Period; Administration and Use of Institutional Land in Sargonic Sumer; Sargonic Texts from Telloh in the Istanbul Archaeological Museum* (with V. Don-

baz); *Before the Muses: An Anthology of Akkadian Literature* (condensed, paperback version, *From Distant Days: Myths, Tales, and Poetry* of Anthology of Akkadian Literature.
HUMOR AND WIT IN THE ANCIENT NEAR EAST

John L. Foster Professor of English at Roosevelt University, Chicago. Author of articles and monographs, including *Love Songs of the New Kingdom; Echoes of Egyptian Voices: An Anthology of Ancient Egyptian Poetry;* and *Thought Couplets in the Tale of Sinuhe.*
THE HYMN TO ATEN: AKHENATEN WORSHIPS THE SOLE GOD

Detlef Franke Fellow, Werner Heisenberg Stiftung, at the Ägyptologisches Institut, University of Heidelberg. Author of *Altägyptische Verwandtschaftsbezeichnungen im Mittleren Reich; Personendaten aus dem Mittleren Reich;* and *Das Heiligtum des Heqaib auf Elephantine.*
THE MIDDLE KINGDOM IN EGYPT

Sabina Franke Assistant of Ancient Oriental Studies at the University of Würzburg, Germany. Author of *Königsinschriften und Königsideologie: Die Könige von Akkade Zwischen Tradition und Neuerung.* Participated in excavations at Tell Chuera and Tell Halawa (Syria).
KINGS OF AKKAD: SARGON AND NARAM-SIN

Gabriella Frantz-Szabó Hittitologist, author of studies on Hittite culture and an editor of the *Reallexikon der Assyriologie und Vorderasiatischen Archäologie,* University of Munich and Bavarian Academy of Sciences. Author of several articles in *Reallexikon.*
HITTITE WITCHCRAFT, MAGIC, AND DIVINATION

Markham J. Geller Professor of Semitic Languages at the University of London. Author of *Forerunners to Udug-Hul: Sumerian Exorcistic Incantations;* editor (with J. Mindlin and J. E. Wansbrough) of *Figurative Language in the Ancient Near East,* and (with B. Alster) of *Sumerian Literary Texts (Cuneiform Texts from Babylonian Tablets in the British Museum, 58).*
THE INFLUENCE OF ANCIENT MESOPOTAMIA ON HELLENISTIC JUDAISM

Allan S. Gilbert Associate Professor of Anthropology at Fordham University, New York. Archaeologist and author of articles on the domestication and exploitation of animals in the Near East, the origins of pastoral nomadism, and the analysis of preserved organic substances from ancient buried bone.
THE FLORA AND FAUNA OF THE ANCIENT NEAR EAST

Jean-Jacques Glassner Research scholar at the National Center for Scientific Research, Paris. Author of many studies on Mesopotamian and Elamite culture, including *La Chute d'Akkadé: L'Événement et sa mémoire* and *Chroniques Mésopotamiennes*.
PROGRESS, SCIENCE, AND THE USE OF KNOWLEDGE IN ANCIENT MESOPOTAMIA

Cyrus H. Gordon Emeritus Professor at Brandeis University and New York University. Author of many books and of numerous articles including *Ugaritic Textbook; Before the Bible: The Common Background of Greek and Hebrew Civilizations; Adventures in the Nearest East; Evidence for the Minoan Language;* and *Forgotten Scripts.* Editor of the series *Eblaitica.* See also the introduction to his essay in Volume IV.
RECOVERING CANAAN AND ANCIENT ISRAEL

Gene B. Gragg Professor of Near Eastern Languages at the Oriental Institute, University of Chicago. Author of many works on Sumerian and East African linguistics, including (with Å. W. Sjöberg) *The Collection of the Sumerian Temple Hymns; Sumerian Dimensional Infixes;* and *Oromo Dictionary.* Director of the Cushitic-Demotic Etymological Database Project.
LESS-UNDERSTOOD LANGUAGES OF ANCIENT WESTERN ASIA

A. Kirk Grayson Professor of Near Eastern Studies at the University of Toronto. Author of numerous studies on Mesopotamian culture, including *Assyrian and Babylonian Chronicles; Babylonian Historical-Literary Texts;* and of chapters on Assyria for the *Cambridge Ancient History Series.* Director of the Royal Inscriptions of Mesopotamia Project in which he has also edited two volumes, *Assyrian Rulers of the Third and Second Millennia BC (to 1115 BC),* and *Assyrian Rulers of the Early First Millennium BC I (1114–859 BC).*
ASSYRIAN RULE OF CONQUERED TERRITORY IN ANCIENT WESTERN ASIA

Anthony Green G. A. Wainwright Research Fellow in Near Eastern Archaeology at the University of Oxford, England. He has excavated extensively in Iraq and writes on ancient Mesopotamian art and archaeology. Author (with Jeremy Black) of *Gods, Demons and Symbols of Ancient Mesopotamia: An Illustrated Dictionary.*
ANCIENT MESOPOTAMIAN RELIGIOUS ICONOGRAPHY

Crawford H. Greenewalt Professor in the Department of Classics, the University of California, Berkeley. Author of many studies, including *Ritual Dinners in Early Historic Sardis.*
CROESUS OF SARDIS AND THE LYDIAN KINGDOM OF ANATOLIA

Samuel Greengus Julian Morgenstern Professor of Bible and Near Eastern Literature at Hebrew Union College–Jewish Institute of Religion, Cincinnati, Ohio. Author of *Old Babylonian Tablets from Ishchali and Vicinity; Studies in Ishchali Document;* and various articles on legal institutions in Mesopotamia and ancient Israel.
LEGAL AND SOCIAL INSTITUTIONS OF ANCIENT MESOPOTAMIA

Edward L. Greenstein Professor of Bible at the Jewish Theological Seminary of America, New York. Author of *Essays on Biblical Method and Translation* and of several articles and reviews on the Bible and ancient near eastern language and literature. Coeditor of the *Journal of the Ancient Near Eastern Society* and former editor of the series *Society of Biblical Literature Semeia Studies.*
AUTOBIOGRAPHIES IN ANCIENT WESTERN ASIA

Mayer I. Gruber Senior Lecturer, Department of Bible and Ancient Near East, Ben-Gurion University of the Negev, Israel. Author of *Aspects of Nonverbal Communication in the Ancient Near East; The Motherhood of God and Other Studies; Rashi's Commentary on the Book of Psalms in English with Introduction and Supercommentary; Women in the Biblical World: A Study Guide;* and of several articles including a commentary on the Book of Amos.
PRIVATE LIFE IN ANCIENT ISRAEL

Ann C. Gunter Associate Curator of Ancient Near Eastern Art at the Freer Gallery of Art and the Arthur M. Sackler Gallery at the Smithsonian Institution, Washington, D.C. Author of *Gordion Excavations Final Reports: The Bronze Age;* coauthor of *Ancient Iranian Metalwork in the Arthur M. Sackler Gallery and the Freer Gallery of Art.* Editor of *Investigating Artistic Environments in the Ancient Near East.*
MATERIAL, TECHNOLOGY, AND TECHNIQUES IN ARTISTIC PRODUCTION

Hans G. Güterbock Professor Emeritus of Hittitology, the University of Chicago. Author of *Kumarbi: Mythen vom churritischen Kronos, Siegel aus Boğazköy; The Song of Ullikummi; Les hiéroglyphes de Yazilikaya* (with T. P. J. van den Hout); *Hittite Instruction for the Royal Bodyguard;* and of numerous articles on Hittite language, history, art, and civilization. With H. A. Hoffner, he is the editor of *The Chicago Hittite Dictionary.* See also the introduction to his essay in Volume IV.
RESURRECTING THE HITTITES

Volkert Haas Professor of Akkadian and the old Anatolian languages at the Free University of Berlin. Author of many books and articles on the Hittite religion and Hurrian texts, among which are *Geschichte der hethitischen Religion; Vorzeitmythen und Götterberge in altorientalischer und griechischer Überlieferung: Vergleiche und Lokalisation; Das reich Urartu; Magie und Mythen im Reich der Hethiter;* and *Aussenseiter und Randgruppen: Beiträge zu einer Sozialgeschichte des Alten Orients.*
DEATH AND THE AFTERLIFE IN HITTITE THOUGHT

William W. Hallo The William M. Laffan Professor of Assyriology and Babylonian Literature and Curator of the Babylonian Collection at Yale University, New Haven, Connecticut. His numerous works include *Early Mesopotamian Royal Titles; The Book of the People;* (editor) *Scripture in Context,* vols. I, II; *Heritage: Civilization and the Jews;* (coeditor) *The Tablets of Ebla: Concordance and Bibliography; Sumerian Archival Texts;* (with W. K. Simpson) *The Ancient Near East: A History;* and (with J. J. A. van Dijk) *The Exaltation of Inanna.* Translator of F. Rosenzweig's *The Star of Redemption.*
LAMENTATIONS AND PRAYERS IN SUMER AND AKKAD

Fekri A. Hassan Professor of Archaeology, University College, London. Author of many articles as well as *The Archaeology of the Dishna Plain, Egypt: A Study of a Late Paleolithic Settlement* and *Demographic Archeology.* Editor of *African Archaeological Review.*
EGYPT IN THE PREHISTORY OF NORTHEAST AFRICA

J. David Hawkins Professor of Ancient Anatolian Languages at the School of Oriental and African Studies, University of London, and Fellow of the British Academy. Author of numerous studies on hieroglyphic Hittite, including *Hittite Hieroglyphs and Luwian: New Evidence for the Connection,* and the three-volume *Corpus of Hittite Hieroglyphic Inscriptions.*
KARKAMISH AND KARATEPE: NEO-HITTITE CITY-STATES IN NORTH SYRIA

Brian Hesse Professor of Anthropology at the University of Alabama, Birmingham. Author of *Animal Bone Archaeology* (with P. Wapnish) and of various articles on the origins and development of domestic animals and pastoral husbandry in the Near East.
ANIMAL HUSBANDRY AND HUMAN DIET IN THE ANCIENT NEAR EAST

Harry A. Hoffner, Jr. Professor of Hittitology at the Oriental Institute at the University of Chicago. Author of *An English-Hittite Glossary; Alimenta Hethaeorum;* and *Hittite Myths.* Executive editor of *The Hittite Dictionary of the Oriental Institute of the University of Chicago;* editor of *Orient and Occident: Essays Presented to Cyrus H. Gordon* and *Kanissuwar: A Tribute to Hans G. Güterbock.* Translator of *Akkadian Grammar,* by Arthur Ungnad.
LEGAL AND SOCIAL INSTITUTIONS OF HITTITE ANATOLIA

Frank Hole Professor of Anthropology and Curator of Archaeology, Peabody Museum of Natural History, Yale University. Among his many published contributions to the study of agriculture and nomadic pastoralism is his *An Introduction to Prehistoric Archaeology* (with R. Heizer); other publications of his are *The Archaeology of Western Iran: Settlement and Society from Prehistory to the Islamic Conquest,* and *Studies in the Archaeological History of the*

Deh Luran Plain: The Excavation of Chagha Sefid. See also the introduction to his essay in Volume IV.
ASSESSING THE PAST THROUGH ANTHROPOLOGICAL ARCHAEOLOGY

Susan Tower Hollis Dean of the College, Sierra Nevada College, Nevada. Author of *The Ancient Egyptian "Tale of Two Brothers": The Oldest Fairy Tale in the World*, and articles on ancient Egyptian literature, religion, kingship and queenship, goddesses, and women; editor of *Feminist Theory and the Study of Folklore*.
TALES OF MAGIC AND WONDER FROM ANCIENT EGYPT

Erik Hornung Professor of Egyptology at the University of Basel, Switzerland. Author of numerous articles and monographs on pharaonic Egypt, including *Conceptions of God in Ancient Egypt; Idea into Image; The Tomb of Pharaoh Seti I; The Valley of the Kings;* and (with O.Keel) *Studien zu altägyptischen Lebenslehren*
ANCIENT EGYPTIAN RELIGIOUS ICONOGRAPHY

Theo P. J. van den Hout Professor of Hittitology and Anatolian History of the preclassic period, University of Amsterdam. Author of many studies on Hittite culture, including *Der Ulmitešub-Vertrag: Eine prosopographische Untersuchung* and (with H. H. Güterbock) *The Hittite Instruction for the Royal Bodyguard.*
KHATTUSHILI III, KING OF THE HITTITES

Philo H. J. Houwink ten Cate Emeritus Professor of Hittitology and History of the Ancient Near East, University of Amsterdam. Author of studies on Hittite civilizations such as *The Luwian Population Groups of Lycia and Cicilia Aspera during the Hellenistic Period* and *The Records of the Early Hittite Empire (c. 1450–1380 B.C.).*
ETHNIC DIVERSITY AND POPULATION MOVEMENT IN ANATOLIA

John Huehnergard Professor of Semitic Philology at Harvard University, Cambridge, Mass. Author of *Ugaritic Vocabulary in Syllabic Transcription; The Akkadian of Ugarit; A Grammar of Akkadian;* and of several articles on Semitic languages.
SEMITIC LANGUAGES

Fiorella Imparati Professor of Ancient Near Eastern History at the University of Florence, Italy. Author of *Le Leggi Ittite; I Hurriti; Una concessione di terre da parte di Tuthaliya IV;* and of numerous articles on Hittite civilization. Editor of *Letterature dell'Asia Minore, Testi del Vicino Oriente Antico* and coeditor of *EOTHEN, Collana di studi sulle civiltà dell'Oriente antico* and *Ricerche sulle lingue di frammentaria attestazione.*
PRIVATE LIFE AMONG THE HITTITES

Shlomo Izreʾel Senior Lecturer in Semitic Linguistics, Tel Aviv University, Israel. Author of *Amurru Akkadian: A Linguistic Study; The Amarna Scholarly Tablets;* (with Itamar Singer) *The General's Letter from Ugarit: A Linguistic and Historical Reevaluation of RS 20.33;* and articles on Akkadian linguistics and on the Amarna tablets.
THE AMARNA LETTERS FROM CANAAN

Thorkild Jacobsen Professor of Assyriology Emeritus at Harvard University until his death in 1993. Author of numerous contributions on Mesopotamian, and especially Sumerian, culture, including *The Harps that Once . . . Sumerian Poetry in Translation; The Sumerian King List; Toward the Image of Tammuz and Other Essays;* and *The Harab Myth.* See also the introduction to his essay in Volume IV.
SEARCHING FOR SUMER AND AKKAD

T. G. H. James Keeper Emeritus of the Department of Egyptian Antiquities in the British Museum and Fellow of the British Academy. He has taught at the Collège de France, Paris, and at the University of Memphis, Tennessee. Author of numerous books, including *The Hekanakhte Papers; Pharaoh's People: Scenes from Life in Imperial Egypt; Egypt: The Living Past; Howard Carter: The Path to Tutankhamun;* and *Excavating in Egypt: The Egypt Exploration Society, 1882–1982.* See also the introduction to his essay in Volume IV.
REDISCOVERING EGYPT OF THE PHARAOHS

Hans G. Jansen Physicist and archaeologist. Member of the Troia-Project (excavation at Troy/Turkey) in affiliation with the Universities of Tübingen and Cincinnati. Has conducted research into near eastern Bronze Age studies and geophysical prospection of archaeological sites.
TROY: LEGEND AND REALITY

Rosalind H. Janssen The Petrie Museum at University College London. Author of articles and monographs on Egyptian society, including *Growing Up in Ancient Egypt* and (as Rosalind Hall) *Egyptian Textiles*.
COSTUME IN NEW KINGDOM EGYPT

Francis Joannès Professor at the University of Paris VIII (Saint Denis) and Participant in the publication of documents from the Mari Archives. Among his published works are *Neo-Babylonian Tablets in the Ashmolean Museum* and *Archives de Borsippa: La Famille Ea-Ilûta-bāni, étude d'un lot d'archives familiales en Babylonie du VIIIe au Ve siècle av. J.-C.*
PRIVATE COMMERCE AND BANKING IN ACHAEMENID BABYLON

László Kákosy Head of the Department of Egyptology at Eötvös Lorand University, Budapest. Director of the Hungarian excavations in Egypt since 1983. Member of the Hungarian Archaeological Mission to Nubia in 1964. Author of many articles and of *La magia in Egitto ai tempi dei faraoni* and *Egyiptomi és antik csillaghit*.
EGYPT IN ANCIENT GREEK AND ROMAN THOUGHT

Barry J. Kemp Reader in Egyptology, University of Cambridge, and Fellow of the British Academy. Field Director of the Egypt Exploration Society excavations at Tell al-Amarna. Author of articles on Egyptian archaeology and of excavation reports on Tell al-Amarna; among his books are *Ancient Egypt: Anatomy of a Civilization;* (with R. Merrillees) *Minoan Pottery in Second Millennium Egypt;* and *Excavations at Malkata and the Birket Habu, 1971–1974*.
UNIFICATION AND URBANIZATION OF ANCIENT EGYPT

Anne D. Kilmer Professor in the Department of Near Eastern Studies, University of California, Berkeley. Author of numerous articles on Mesopotamian culture. Coauthor of *Sounds from Silence: Recent Discoveries in Ancient Near Eastern Music* (a lecture-demonstration on ancient near eastern music).
MUSIC AND DANCE IN ANCIENT WESTERN ASIA

Kenneth A. Kitchen Brunner Professor of Egyptology at the University of Liverpool. Author of *Šuppiluliuma and the Amarna Pharaohs; Ancient Orient and Old Testament; The Third Intermediate Period in Egypt, 1100–650 BC; The Bible in Its World; Pharaoh Triumphant: The Life and Times of Ramesses II King of Egypt; Catalogue of the Egyptian Collection in the National Museum, Rio de Janeiro;* and of numerous articles and reviews. Editor of *Ramesside Inscriptions, I–VIII* and *Ramesside Inscriptions Translated and Annotated*.
PHARAOH RAMESSES II AND HIS TIMES

Jacob Klein Professor of Assyriology and the Bible and Director of the Samuel Noah Kramer Institute of Assyriology at Bar-Ilan University, Israel. Author of many studies on Sumerian literature, including *Three Šulgi Hymns: Sumerian Royal Hymns Glorifying King Šulgi of Ur* and *The Royal Hymns of Shulgi King of Ur: Man's Quest for Immortal Fame*.
SHULGI OF UR: KING OF A NEO-SUMERIAN EMPIRE

A. Bernard Knapp Australian Research Fellow in Cypriot Archaeology at Macquarie University, Sydney, Australia. Author of *The History and Culture of Ancient Western Asia and Egypt; Copper Production and Divine Protection; Society and Polity at Bronze Age Pella;* and *Provenience and Politico-economic Change*. Editor of *Archaeology, Annales, and Ethnohistory* and *Prehistoric Production and Exchange: The Aegean and Eastern Mediterranean*.
ISLAND CULTURES: CRETE, THERA, CYPRUS, RHODES, AND SARDINIA

Heidemarie Koch Lecturer in Iranian studies at the University of Marburg, Germany. Author of *Die religiösen Verhältnisse der Dareioszeit; Verwaltung und Wirtschaft in persischen Kernland zur Zeit der Achämeniden; Vom Leben in persischen Grossreich; A Hoard of Coins from*

Eastern Parthia; Achämeniden-Studien; and (with W. Hinz) *Elamisches Wörterbuch.*
THEOLOGY AND WORSHIP IN ELAM AND ACHAEMENID IRAN

Philip L. Kohl Professor of Anthropology at Wellesley College, Wellesley, Massachusetts. Author of *Central Asia: Palaeolithic Beginnings to the Iron Age.* Editor of *The Bronze Age Civilization of Central Asia* and *Recent Discoveries in Transcaucasia.*
CENTRAL ASIA AND THE CAUCASUS IN THE BRONZE AGE

Kay Kohlmeyer Curator at the Museum für Vor- und Frühgeschichte, Berlin. Author of many articles on the art of the ancient Near East and of *Wiedererstehendes Babylon: eine antike Weltstadt in Blick der Forschung* as well as *Land des Baal: Syrien, Forum der Völker und Kulturen.*
ANATOLIAN ARCHITECTURAL DECORATIONS, STATUARY, AND STELAE

Rolf Krauss Associate Curator, Ägyptisches Museum, Staatliche Museen, Berlin. Author of studies on the art and history of the Amarna period, including *Das Ende der Amarnazeit,* and of *Sothis-und Monddaten.*
AKHETATEN: A PORTRAIT IN ART OF AN ANCIENT EGYPTIAN CAPITAL

Amélie Kuhrt Reader in Ancient History at University College London. Author (with S. Sherwin-White) of *From Samarkhand to Sardis: A New Approach to Seleucid History* and of *Hellenism in the East,* and an editor of several volumes of *Achaemenid History* and of *Images of Women in Antiquity.*
ANCIENT MESOPOTAMIA IN CLASSICAL GREEK AND HELLENISTIC THOUGHT

W. G. Lambert Emeritus Professor of Assyriology, the University of Birmingham, England. Author of *Babylonian Wisdom Literature; Atra-Hasis: The Babylonian Story of the Flood;* and other monographs, articles, and text editions on ancient Mesopotamian culture.
MYTH AND MYTHMAKING IN SUMER AND AKKAD

Mogens Trolle Larsen Associate Professor of Assyriology at University of Copenhagen. Author of *The Old Assyrian City-State and Its Colonies* and *Old Assyrian Caravan Procedures,* and contributing editor of numerous books on the social history of the ancient Near East, including *Centre and Periphery in the Ancient World; Power and Propaganda: A Symposium on Ancient Empires;* and *The State and Society: The Emergence of Social Hierarchy and Political Centralization.*
THE "BABEL/BIBLE" CONTROVERSY AND ITS AFTERMATH

Anthony Leahy Senior Lecturer in Egyptology, University of Birmingham, England. Honorary Secretary of the Egypt Exploration Society. Author of numerous articles on Egyptian history and art, and of *Excavations at Malkata: The Inscriptions;* editor of *Libya and Egypt: c. 1,300–750 BC.*
ETHNIC DIVERSITY IN ANCIENT EGYPT

René Lebrun Director of the École des Langues et Civilisations de l'Orient Ancien, Universitas Catholica Parisiensis, Paris. Director of the Collection Hethitica. Professor of ancient near eastern religions and of Anatolian philology. Author of *Samuha: Foyer religieux de l'empire Hittite; Hymnes et prières Hittites;* as well as of several articles on the Hittites and Asia Minor. Editor of *Le Langage dans l'antiquité.*
FROM HITTITE MYTHOLOGY: THE KUMARBI CYCLE

Erle Leichty Professor of Assyriology at the University of Pennsylvania and curator of Akkadian languages and literature at the University of Pennsylvania Museum of Archaeology and Anthropology, Philadelphia. Among his published works are *The Omen Series Šumma izbu, Teratological Omens in Ancient Mesopotamia* and (as a contributing editor) *A Scientific Humanist: Studies in Memory of Abraham Sachs.*
ESARHADDON, KING OF ASSYRIA

Niels Peter Lemche Professor of Old Testament Studies at the University of Copenhagen. Author of numerous articles and of *Early Israel: Anthropological and Historical Studies on the Israelite Society Before the Monarchy; Ancient Israel: A New History of Israelite Society;* and *The Canaanites and Their Land: The Tradition*

of the Canaanites. Editor of the *Scandinavian Journal of the Old Testament.*
THE HISTORY OF ANCIENT SYRIA AND PALESTINE: AN OVERVIEW

Ronald J. Leprohon Professor of Egyptology at the University of Toronto. Author of numerous articles on Egyptian history, administration, religion, and art, as well as a two-volume study of the stelae in the Museum of Fine Arts, Boston, in the *Corpus Antiquitatum Aegyptiacarum.*
ROYAL IDEOLOGY AND STATE ADMINISTRATION IN PHARAONIC EGYPT

Leonard H. Lesko Charles Edwin Wilbour Professor of Egyptology at Brown University, Providence, Rhode Island. Author of *The Ancient Egyptian Book of Two Ways; King Tut's Wine Cellar;* and *Index of the Spells on Egyptian Middle Kingdom Coffins and Related Documents.* Contributing editor of *Pharaoh's Workers: The Villagers of Deir el-Medina.* Editor (with B. Lesko) of *A Dictionary of Late Egyptian* (5 volumes) and *Egyptological Studies in Honor of Richard A. Parker.*
DEATH AND THE AFTERLIFE IN ANCIENT EGYPTIAN THOUGHT

Edward Lipiński Professor of Semitic Languages and Ancient Near Eastern Civilizations at the University of Louvain, Belgium. Author of *La Royauté de Yahwé dans la poésie et le culte de l'ancien Israël; Le Poème royal du Psaume 89; Studies in Aramaic Inscriptions and Onomastics; La Liturgie pénitentielle dans la Bible;* and of various articles on ancient Semitic languages and the history of Semitic religions. Editor of *State and Temple Economy in the Ancient Near East; Recherches archéologiques en Israël; Studia Phoenicia;* and *Dictionnaire de la civilisation phénicienne et punique.*
THE PHOENICIANS

Boris A. Litvinsky Chief of the Department of History and Culture of the Ancient East, Institute of Oriental Studies, Russian Academy of Sciences, Member of the Tajik Academy of Sciences, and Foreign Member of Accademia Nazionale dei Lincei, Rome. Author of many books and articles on archaeology, history, and culture of Central Asia and neighboring regions, dealing

with architecture, Buddhist and Manichaean religions, and cultural links of Central Asia with the Hellenistic world, India, and China. They include *Antike und frühmittelalterliche Grabhügel im westlichen Fergana-Becken, Tadzikistan; Eisenzeitliche Kurgane zwischen Pamir und Aral-See;* and (contributing editor) *Historiography of Tagikistan (1917–1969).* Head of excavations of Bronze Age monuments, ancient nomads, the Hellenistic-Bactrian temple of Takhti-Sangin, settlements of Kushan and medieval times, and ancient Buddhist monuments.
ARCHAEOLOGY AND ARTIFACTS IN IRON AGE CENTRAL ASIA

Mario Liverani Professor of the History of Antiquity at the University of Rome. Author of seminal studies on the ancient Near East, including *Storia di Ugarit; Prestige and Interest: International Relations in the Near East ca. 1600–1100 B.C.; Antico Oriente: storia, società, economia;* and *Three Amarna Essays*
THE DEEDS OF ANCIENT MESOPOTAMIAN KINGS

Seton Lloyd Professor Emeritus of Western Asiatic Archaeology at the University of London and Fellow of the British Academy. Served as Director of the British Institute of Archaeology, Ankara, Turkey. Among his extensive publications on Mesopotamian archaeology, architecture, and history are *The Art of the Ancient Near East; Foundations in the Dust: The Story of Mesopotamian Exploration;* and his reminiscences, *The Interval: A Life in Near Eastern Archaeology.* See also the introduction to his essay in Volume IV.
EXCAVATING THE LAND BETWEEN THE TWO RIVERS

Antonio Loprieno Professor of Egyptology and Chair of the Department of Near Eastern Languages and Cultures at the University of California, Los Angeles. Author of *Das Verbalsystem in Ägyptischen und im Semitischen; Topos und Mimesis;* and *Ancient Egyptian: A Linguistic Introduction.*
ANCIENT EGYPTIAN AND OTHER AFROASIATIC LANGUAGES

David Lorton Egyptologist, The Johns Hopkins University, Baltimore. Author of *The Juridical Terminology of International Relations in*

Egyptian Texts through Dynasty XVIII and of articles on Egyptian history, law, administration, literature, and religion. Coeditor of *Essays in Egyptology in Honor of Hans Goedicke.*
LEGAL AND SOCIAL INSTITUTIONS OF PHARAONIC EGYPT

John M. Lundquist The Susan and Douglas Dillon Chief Librarian of the Oriental Division at the New York Public Library. Author of *The Temple: Meeting Place of Heaven and Earth,* "Temple: Covenant and Law in the Ancient Near East and in the Hebrew Bible," "Tell Qarqur—The 1983 Season,"and of several articles on the Temple and on the archaeology of Syria. Member of the editorial board for the *Journal of Temple Studies.*
BABYLON IN EUROPEAN THOUGHT

M. C. A. Macdonald Member of the Oriental Faculty, University of Oxford, England. Epigraphist specializing in ancient North Arabian and Aramaic inscriptions. Author of *Nomads and the Hawran in the Hellenistic and Roman Periods* and of articles on epigraphy, Semitic philology, and history.
NORTH ARABIA IN THE FIRST MILLENNIUM BCE; "Wabar" in ARCHAEOLOGY AND ARTIFACTS OF THE ARABIAN PENINSULA

Gregory McMahon Associate Professor of History at the University of New Hampshire, Durham. Author of *The Hittite State Cult of the Tutelary Deities* and of various articles on Hittite history and culture. Associate Director of the Aliçar Höyük Excavation.
THEOLOGY, PRIESTS, AND WORSHIP IN HITTITE ANATOLIA

J. G. Macqueen Reader in Classical and Ancient Middle Eastern Studies at the University of Bristol, England. Author of many studies on Anatolian and classical antiquities, including *The Hittites and Their Contemporaries in Asia Minor.*
THE HISTORY OF ANATOLIA AND OF THE HITTITE EMPIRE: AN OVERVIEW

Maynard Paul Maidman Associate Professor of History at York University, Toronto, Canada, and editor of the *Journal of the American Oriental Society.* Author of many articles on Nuzi society and editor of Nuzi documents, such as *Two Hundred Nuzi Texts in the Oriental Institute of the University of Chicago* and (with E. R. Lacheman) *Joint Expedition with the Iraq Museum at Nuzi VII: Miscellaneous Texts.*
NUZI: PORTRAIT OF AN ANCIENT MESOPOTAMIAN PROVINCIAL TOWN

John R. Maier Professor of English at State University of New York College at Brockport. Author of many articles on the impact of the Ancient Near East on modern cultures, including *Desert Songs: Western Images of Morocco and Moroccan Images of the West; The Bible in Its Literary Milieu* (with John Gardner); *Gilgamesh* (translated from the Sin-leqi-unninni version; with S. N. Kramer); *Myths of Enki, the Crafty God* (with Samuel Noah Kramer); and (with V. L. Tollers) *Mappings of the Biblical Terrain.*
THE ANCIENT NEAR EAST IN MODERN THOUGHT

Michelle I. Marcus Research Associate at University of Pennsylvania Museum, Philadelphia. Author of various articles on the material culture of ancient Mesopotamia and Iran including *Emblems of Identity and Prestige: The Seals and Sealings from Hasanlu, Iran* and *The Personal Ornaments from Hasanlu, Iran.*
ART AND IDEOLOGY IN ANCIENT WESTERN ASIA

Jean-Claude Margueron Director of the French archaeological missions to excavate Mari and Emar, and Professor at the École Pratique des Hautes Études, IV Section, Paris. Author of numerous articles, archaeological reports, and monographs, such as *Recherches sur les palais mésopotamiens de l'âge du Bronze* and *Les Mésopotamiens* (2 vols.).
MARI: A PORTRAIT IN ART OF A MESOPOTAMIAN CITY-STATE

Stefano de Martino Professor in the Dipartimento di Scienze dell' Antichità, Università di Trieste, Italy. Author of *I Trattati nel mondo antico: Forma, ideologia, funzione; Die mantischen Texte: Corpus der hurritischen Sprachdenkmäler (ChS) I,* and *La danza nella cultura ittita.*
MUSIC, DANCE, AND PROCESSIONS IN HITTITE ANATOLIA

Frederick R. Matson Research Professor of Archaeology Emeritus at Pennsylvania State University at University Park. Author of more than one hundred papers. Editor of *Ceramics and Man*. President of the Archaeological Institute of America, 1975 and 1976. Recipient of the Pomerance Medal of the Archaeological Institute of America for Scientific Contributions to Archaeology, 1981.
POTTERS AND POTTERY IN THE ANCIENT NEAR EAST

Donald M. Matthews British Academy Postdoctoral Fellow in the Oriental Faculty, University of Oxford, England. Author of *Principles of Composition in Near Eastern Glyptic of the Later Second Millennium B.C.* and (with W. G. Lambert) *The Kassite Glyptic of Nippur*.
ARTISANS AND ARTISTS IN ANCIENT WESTERN ASIA

Amihai Mazar Professor of Biblical Archaeology at the Institute of Archaeology, Hebrew University, Jerusalem. Director of various excavations at Tell Qasile, Tel Batash, Tel Beth Shean, and other sites in Israel. Author of many articles, archaeological reports and monographs, including *Excavations at Tell Qasile; Archaeology of the Land of the Bible, 10,000–586 B.C.E.*; and (with A. Trone) *Voices from the Past*.
THE FORTIFICATION OF CITIES IN THE ANCIENT NEAR EAST

H. Craig Melchert Charles S. Smith Jr. Distinguished Professor of Linguistics at the University of North Carolina at Chapel Hill. Author of *Studies in Hittite Historical Phonology; Lycian Lexicon; Anatolian Historical Phonology;* and *Cuneiform Luwian Lexicon*.
INDO-EUROPEAN LANGUAGES OF ANATOLIA

Piotr Michalowski Professor of Near Eastern Studies at the University of Michigan, Ann Arbor, and editor of the *Journal of Cuneiform Studies*. Author of many papers on Sumerian literature and history, including *Letters from Early Mesopotamia* and *The Lamentation over the Destruction of Sumer and Ur*; contributor to the publication of M. T. Roth's *Law Collections from Mesopotamia and Asia Minor* and to *The Tablets of Ebla: Concordance and Bibliography*.
SUMERIAN LITERATURE: AN OVERVIEW

Lucio Milano Associate Professor of History of the Ancient Near East at the Università degli Studi di Venezia, Italy. Author of articles on society and food production in ancient Mesopotamia and of two volumes of texts in the series *Archivi Reali di Ebla—Testi*; editor of *Drinking in Ancient Societies: History and Culture of Drinks in the Ancient Near East*.
EBLA: A THIRD MILLENNIUM CITY-STATE IN ANCIENT SYRIA

James D. Muhly Emeritus Professor of Asian and Middle Eastern Studies at the University of Pennsylvania, Philadelphia. Author of studies on the trade and technology of the ancient world, including *Copper and Tin: The Distribution of Mineral Resources and the Nature of the Metals Trade in the Bronze Age; Cyprus at the Close of the Late Bronze Age;* and (with T. A. Wertime) *The Coming of the Age of Iron*.
MINING AND METALWORK IN ANCIENT WESTERN ASIA

William J. Murnane Associate Professor of History and Field Director of Karnak Hypostyle Hall Project at the Institute of Egyptian Art and Archaeology, the University of Memphis. Author of *The Penguin Guide to Ancient Egypt; Ancient Egyptian Coregencies; The Road to Kadesh; United with Eternity;* and *The Boundary Stelae of Akhenaten* (with C. C. Van Siclen III).
THE HISTORY OF ANCIENT EGYPT: AN OVERVIEW

Oscar White Muscarella Senior Research Fellow, Department of Ancient Near Eastern Art, the Metropolitan Museum of Art, New York City. Author of *Bronze and Iron: Ancient Near Eastern Artifacts in the Metropolitan Museum; Ancient Art: The Norbert Schimmel Collection; The Catalogue of Ivories from Hasanlu, Iran; Phrygian Fibulae from Gordion*, as well as of articles and reviews on near eastern, Anatolian, and Iranian art and archaeology, Greek and near eastern contacts and influences, and forgeries. Excavated at sites in the United States, Iran, and Turkey.
ART AND ARCHAEOLOGY OF WESTERN IRAN IN PREHISTORY

Hans J. Nissen Professor of Near Eastern Archaeology at Freie Universität, Berlin, and has

conducted fieldwork in Iraq, Iran, Pakistan, and Jordan. Author of *The Early History of the Ancient Near East, 9000–2000 BC; Mesopotamia before 5000 years;* (with Robert McC. Adams) *The Uruk Countryside;* and (with P. Damerow and R. K. Englund) *Archaic Bookkeeping: Early Writing and Techniques of Economic Administration in the Ancient Near East.* Contributing editor to the series "Die archaischen Texte aus Uruk."
ANCIENT WESTERN ASIA BEFORE THE AGE OF EMPIRES

David O'Connor Lila Acheson Wallace Professor of Egyptian Art at the Institute of Fine Arts, New York University. Author of many works, including *Ancient Nubia: Egypt's Rival in Africa;* (with D. P. Silverman) *Ancient Egyptian Kingship;* and (with B. G. Trigger, et al) *Ancient Egypt: A Social History.*
THE SOCIAL AND ECONOMIC ORGANIZATION OF ANCIENT EGYPTIAN TEMPLES

Gary H. Oller Associate Professor of Classics at the University of Akron, Ohio, and author of studies on Syria of the Middle and Late Bronze Age.
MESSENGERS AND AMBASSADORS IN ANCIENT WESTERN ASIA

Simon B. Parker Associate Professor of Hebrew Bible at Boston University. Author of *The Pre-Biblical Narrative Tradition: Essays on the Ugaritic Poems Keret and Aqhat* and of various articles on the literature and religion of ancient Syro-Palestine. General editor of *Writings from the Ancient World;* editor and one of the translators of a forthcoming volume of Ugaritic narratives.
THE LITERATURES OF CANAAN, ANCIENT ISRAEL, AND PHOENICIA: AN OVERVIEW

Laurie E. Pearce Research Affiliate in the Department of Near Eastern Languages and Civilizations at Yale University and in the Department of Near Eastern Studies at the University of California, Berkeley. Author on articles on scribes and scribal practices in Mesopotamia.
THE SCRIBES AND SCHOLARS OF ANCIENT MESOPOTAMIA

Olivier Perdu Ingénieur at the Collège de France, and Professor of Egyptologie, École du

Louvre, Paris. Author of studies on Egyptian biographies, especially of the Late Period.
ANCIENT EGYPTIAN AUTOBIOGRAPHIES

Geraldine Pinch Affiliated Lecturer in Egyptology in the Faculty of Oriental Studies at the University of Cambridge, England. Author of *Votive Offerings to Hathor* and *Magic in Ancient Egypt.*
PRIVATE LIFE IN ANCIENT EGYPT

Frances Pinnock Researcher in the Archaeology and Anthropology of Antiquity Department, the University of Rome. Author of studies on near eastern archaeology and the history of art, including *Le Perle del Palazzo Reale G (Materiali e Studi Archeologici di Ebla, 2),* and of articles on Syrian and Mesopotamian archaeology. Member of the Italian Expedition at Ebla since 1971.
EROTIC ART IN THE ANCIENT NEAR EAST

Holly Pittman Associate Professor in the Department of the History of Art, University of Pennsylvania, Philadelphia. Author of *Ancient Art in Miniature: Near Eastern Seals from the Collection of Martin and Sarah Cherkasky in the Metropolitan Museum of Art; Art of the Bronze Age: Southeastern Iran, Western Central Asia, and the Indus Valley;* and editor of *Essays on Near Eastern Art and Archaeology in Honor of Charles Kyrle Wilkinson.*
CYLINDER SEALS AND SCARABS IN THE ANCIENT NEAR EAST

Edith Porada Prior to her death in 1993, Dr. Porada was Arthur Lehmann Professor Emeritus of Art History and Archaeology and Senior Lecturer at Columbia University. Author of many monographs and of numerous articles, including *The Art of Ancient Iran* and *Man and Images in the Ancient Near East.* Recipient of the AIA's award for distinguished archaeological achievement. Former member of the American Philosophical Society, the British Academy, the German Archaeological Institute, and the Austrian Academy of Sciences. Curator of Seals and Tablets of the Ancient Near East at the Pierpont Morgan Library. See also the introduction to her essay in Volume IV.
UNDERSTANDING ANCIENT NEAR EASTERN ART: A PERSONAL ACCOUNT

J. Nicholas Postgate Professor of Assyriology in the Faculty of Oriental Studies, Cambridge University, and Fellow of the British Academy. Author of many works on the history and archaeology of ancient Mesopotamia, including *Early Mesopotamia: Society and Economy at the Dawn of History; Neo-Assyrian Royal Grants and Decrees; Taxation and Conscription in the Assyrian Empire;* and *Fifty Neo-Assyrian Legal Documents.* Editor (with M. A. Powell) of *Bulletin on Sumerian Agriculture.*
ROYAL IDEOLOGY AND STATE ADMINISTRATION IN SUMER AND AKKAD

Daniel T. Potts Edwin Cuthbert Hall Professor of Middle Eastern Archaeology at the University of Sydney. Author of *The Arabian Gulf in Antiquity; A Prehistoric Mound in the Emirate of Umm al-Qaiwain: Excavations at Tell Abraq in 1989; Further Excavations at Tell Abraq: The 1990 Season; Miscellanea Hasaitica; The Pre-Islamic Coinage of Eastern Arabia;* and *Supplement to the Pre-Islamic Coinage of Eastern Arabia.* Editor of *Dilmun: New Studies in the Archaeology and Early History of Bahrain* and *Araby the Blest.*
DISTANT SHORES: ANCIENT NEAR EASTERN TRADE WITH SOUTH ASIA AND NORTHEAST ASIA

Marvin A. Powell Presidential Research Professor of History at Northern Illinois University, De Kalb, Illinois. Author of numerous articles and monographs on the cultural history of ancient Mesopotamia, specifically metrology and early mathematics, and a forthcoming history of Sumerian agriculture. Editor of *Labor in the Ancient Near East* and (with J. N. Postgate) *Bulletin of Sumerian Agriculture.*
METROLOGY AND MATHEMATICS IN ANCIENT MESOPOTAMIA

John D. Ray Herbert Thompson Reader in Egyptology at the University of Cambridge. Author of *The Archive of Hor* and a study of the Achaemenid period in Egypt in *Cambridge Ancient History,* vol. 5. Since 1980 he has worked on the decipherment of the Carian script and language.
SOLDIERS TO PHARAOH: THE CARIANS OF SOUTHWEST ANATOLIA

Donald B. Redford Professor of Near Eastern Studies and the Director of the Akhenaten Temple Project, the University of Toronto. Author of many studies, including *Egypt, Canaan, and Israel in Ancient Times; A Study of the Biblical Story of Joseph (Genesis 37–50); Pharaonic King-Lists, Annals, and Day-Books: A Contribution to the Study of the Egyptian Sense of History;* and *Akhenaten, the Heretic King.*
ANCIENT EGYPTIAN LITERATURE: AN OVERVIEW

Jane Margaret Renfrew (Lady Renfrew of Kaimsthorn) Vice President of Lucy Cavendish College at the University of Cambridge, England. Prehistorian and paleoethnobotanist. Author of *Palaeoethnobotany: The Prehistoric Food Plants of the Near East and Europe* and (with M. Monk and P. Murphey) *First Aid for Seeds.* Editor of *New Light on Early Farming.* Trustee for the Royal Botanic Gardens at Kew and Wakehurst Place. President of the International Work Group for Palaeoethnobotany, 1983–1986.
VEGETABLES IN THE ANCIENT NEAR EASTERN DIET

Michael Roaf Professor of Near Eastern Archaeology, University of Munich. Author of the *Cultural Atlas of Mesopotamia and the Ancient Near East* and of studies on the art and archaeology of Mesopotamia, including *Sculptures and Sculptors at Persepolis.*
PALACES AND TEMPLES IN ANCIENT MESOPOTAMIA

John F. Robertson Professor of History at Central Michigan University, Mount Pleasant, Michigan. Author of articles on the organization of ancient Mesopotamian temples and economic structure in the ancient Near East.
THE SOCIAL AND ECONOMIC ORGANIZATION OF ANCIENT MESOPOTAMIAN TEMPLES

Gay Robins Associate Professor and Curator of Ancient Egyptian Art, Emory University, Atlanta. Author of *Women in Ancient Egypt; Proportion and Style in Ancient Egyptian Art; Egyptian Painting and Relief;* and (with C. Shute) *The Rhind Mathematical Papyrus.*
MATHEMATICS, ASTRONOMY, AND CALENDARS IN PHARAONIC EGYPT

Francesca Rochberg Professor of History at the University of California, Riverside. Author of

many studies on Mesopotamian astronomy, including *Aspects of Babylonian Celestial Divination: The Lunar Eclipse Tablets of Enūma Anu Enlil;* editor of *Language, Literature, and History: Philological and Historical Studies Presented to Erica Reiner;* and librettist for G. Rochberg's *Songs of Inanna and Dumuzi, for Contralto and Piano.*
ASTRONOMY AND CALENDARS IN ANCIENT MESOPOTAMIA

James F. Romano Curator in the Department of Egyptian, Classical, and Ancient Middle Eastern Art at the Brooklyn Museum. Author of *Death, Burial, and Afterlife in Ancient Egypt* and *Daily Life of the Ancient Egyptians;* coauthor of *The Luxor Museum of Ancient Egyptian Art.*
JEWELRY AND PERSONAL ARTS IN ANCIENT EGYPT

Margaret Cool Root Professor of Classical and Near Eastern Art and Archaeology at the University of Michigan, Ann Arbor. Author of *The King and Kingship in Achaemenid Art: Essays on the Creation of an Iconography of Empire* and the forthcoming *Persia and the Parthenon: Comparative Essays on the Art of Empire;* contributor to R. Hallock, *Persepolis Fortification Tablets.*
ART AND ARCHAEOLOGY OF THE ACHAEMENID EMPIRE

Karen Sydney Rubinson Associate Editor of *Civilizations of the Ancient Near East.* Research Associate at the University of Pennsylvania Museum, Philadelphia. Her scholarly work is focused on Central Asia and Transcaucasia, where she explores the role of art in the understanding of nonliterate cultures, issues in cross-cultural trade and transmission of ideas, and problems of chronology, especially in the Bronze and Iron ages. Also a field archaeologist, Dr. Rubinson has excavated in Turkey, Iran, and Armenia and is publishing materials from the Hasanlu Project excavations in Iran.

G. Kenneth Sams Professor of Classical Archaeology at the University of North Carolina at Chapel Hill. Author of several publications on Phrygia and Anatolia during the Iron Age. Director of the Gordion Archaeological Project. Editor of *Small Sculptures in Bronze from the Classical World: An Exhibit in Honor of Emeline Hill Richardson.*
MIDAS OF GORDION AND THE ANATOLIAN KINGDOM OF PHRYGIA

Heleen Sancisi-Weerdenburg Professor of Ancient History at Utrecht University, The Netherlands. Author of articles and monographs on the history of the Persian Empire, including *Geschiedenis van het perzische rijk* and *Persepolis en Pasargadae in wisselend perspectief: Iraanse oudheden beschreven en getekend door Europese reizigers.* Organizer of the Achaemenid History Workshops held in Groningen, London, and Ann Arbor, Michigan, and contributing editor to the periodical *Achaemenid History* (1–8).
DARIUS I AND THE PERSIAN EMPIRE

Jack M. Sasson Editor in Chief of *Civilizations of the Ancient Near East.* William Rand Kenan Jr. Professor of Religious Studies at the University of North Carolina at Chapel Hill. Author of *Ruth, Jonah,* and several articles on the ancient Near East, especially on the archives found at Mari. Member of a number of editorial boards of scholarly journals and reference works and former editor of *Journal of the American Oriental Society.*
KING HAMMURABI OF BABYLON; "Ishme-Dagan on His Own," in SHAMSHI-ADAD AND SONS: THE RISE AND FALL OF AN UPPER MESOPOTAMIAN EMPIRE; "Achaemenids, Persia, and Iran," in THE HISTORY OF ELAM AND ACHAEMENID PERSIA: AN OVERVIEW; and "Sartorial Pique," in TEXTILE ARTS IN ANCIENT WESTERN ASIA

Denise Schmandt-Besserat Professor of Middle Eastern Studies at the University of Texas, Austin. Author of articles on the archaeology and cultural and art history of the ancient Near East, including *Before Writing;* editor of *Ancient Persia: The Art of an Empire; The Legacy of Sumer;* and *Immortal Egypt.*
RECORD KEEPING BEFORE WRITING

Brian B. Schmidt Assistant Professor of Hebrew Bible and Ancient Levantine Cultures at the University of Michigan, Ann Arbor. Author of *Israel's Beneficent Dead: Ancestor Cult and Necromancy in Ancient Israelite Religion and*

Tradition and articles on ancient west Asiatic religions.
FLOOD NARRATIVES OF ANCIENT WESTERN ASIA

Alan R. Schulman Professor of History at Queens College, City University of New York. Author of *Ceremonial Execution and Public Rewards: Some Historical Scenes on New Kingdom Private Stelae* and *Military Rank, Title, and Organization in the Egyptian New Kingdom.*
MILITARY ORGANIZATION IN PHARAONIC EGYPT

Glenn M. Schwartz Associate Professor of Near Eastern Studies at Johns Hopkins University, Baltimore. Author of *A Ceramic Chronology from Tell Leilan: Operation I* and various articles on the development of urban civilization in Syria and Mesopotamia; editor of *Archaeological Views from the Countryside;* and codirector of the joint Johns Hopkins University/University of Amsterdam archaeological expedition to Syria.
PASTORAL NOMADISM IN ANCIENT WESTERN ASIA

JoAnn Scurlock Adjunct Assistant Professor of History at Elmhurst College, Elmhurst, Illinois. Author of a forthcoming work on magical means of dealing with ghosts in ancient Mesopotamia and of several articles on Mesopotamian magic, gynecology, and political and social history.
DEATH AND THE AFTERLIFE IN ANCIENT MESOPOTAMIAN THOUGHT

Elizabeth Simpson Associate Professor at the Bard Graduate Center for Studies in the Decorative Arts, New York City, a graduate program of Bard College. Director of the project to study, conserve, and publish examples of the wooden furniture from Gordion, Turkey, and in this capacity is a Research Associate at the University of Pennsylvania Museum, Philadelphia. Her publications include *Gordion Wooden Furniture, The Spoils of War* (as editor) and a number of articles on ancient furniture and the reconstruction of ancient works of art.
FURNITURE IN ANCIENT WESTERN ASIA

Mark S. Smith Associate Professor of Theology at Saint Joseph's University, Philadelphia. Author of many studies on West Semitic and Hebraic literature, including *The Early History of*

God: Yahweh and the Other Deities in Ancient Israel and *The Ugaritic Baal Cycle.*
MYTH AND MYTHMAKING IN CANAAN AND ANCIENT ISRAEL

Daniel C. Snell Professor of History at the University of Oklahoma, Norman, Oklahoma. Author of articles and monographs, including *Ledgers and Prices: Early Mesopotamian Merchant Accounts; The E. A. Hoffman Collection and Other American Collections; A Workbook of Cuneiform Signs; Twice-Told Proverbs and the Composition of the Book;* and (with C. H. Lager) *Economic Texts from Sumer.*
METHODS OF EXCHANGE AND COINAGE IN ANCIENT WESTERN ASIA

Wilfred H. van Soldt Assistant Professor of Assyriology at the University of Leiden, The Netherlands. Author of *Studies in the Akkadian of Ugarit* and *Letters in the British Museum* (an edition of Old Babylonian letters), as well as of several articles on Old and Middle Babylonia, Babylonian astronomy, and the western periphery, specifically Ugarit.
UGARIT: A SECOND-MILLENNIUM KINGDOM ON THE MEDITERRANEAN COAST

Walter Sommerfeld Professor of Assyriology at the University of Marburg, Germany. Author of *Der Aufstieg Marduks* and various articles on the Old and Middle Babylonian periods, including (with B. Kienast), *Glossar zu den altakkadischen Königsinschriften.*
THE KASSITES OF ANCIENT MESOPOTAMIA: ORIGINS, POLITICS, AND CULTURE

Agnès Spycket Archaeologist of Ancient Near East in the Départment des Antiquités Orientales, Musée du Louvre. Author of *La statuaire du Proche-Orient ancien; Les figurines de Suse;* and of numerous articles on Mesopotamian music, sculpture, and terra-cotta figurines.
RELIEFS, STATUARY, AND MONUMENTAL PAINTINGS IN ANCIENT MESOPOTAMIA

Rainer Stadelmann Professor of Egyptology at the University of Heidelberg, Germany. Director of the German Institute of Archaeology in Cairo. Author of *Die Ägyptischen Pyramiden; Die grossen Pyramiden von Giza; Syrisch-*

palästinensische Gottheiten in Ägypten; and many articles on history and archaeology of ancient Egypt.
BUILDERS OF THE PYRAMIDS

Marten Stol Professor of Akkadian and Ugaritic at the Vrije Universiteit, Amsterdam, The Netherlands. Author of many studies on Mesopotamian culture, including *Studies in Old Babylonian History; On Trees, Mountains, and Millstones in the Ancient Near East; Epilepsy in Babylonia; Letters from Yale* (edition of cuneiform letters at Yale); and (with F. A. M. Wiggermann) *Zwangerschap en geboorte bij de Babyloniërs en in de Bijbel.*
PRIVATE LIFE IN ANCIENT MESOPOTAMIA

Elizabeth C. Stone Professor of Archaeology at the State University of New York, Stony Brook, and author of many papers and monographs on the history and anthropology of Mesopotamia, including *Nippur Neighborhoods* and (with D. I. Owen) *Adoption in Old Babylonian Nippur.* Director of the Mashkan-shapir excavations project.
THE DEVELOPMENT OF CITIES IN ANCIENT MESOPOTAMIA

William John Tait Edwards Professor of Egyptology, University College London. He has published editions of Egyptian literary and documentary texts, and studies of Egyptian scribal practice. Author of *Papyri from Tebtunis in Egyptian and in Greek* and coauthor of *Saqqara Demotic Papyri.*
ARCHIVES AND LIBRARIES IN THE ANCIENT NEAR EAST, with Jeremy Black; "Demotic Literature" in ANCIENT EGYPTIAN LITERATURE

Jean-Michel de Tarragon Professor of Old Testament History, Ugaritic Literature, and Colloquial Arabic at the École Biblique Française de Jérusalem. Author of studies on Ugaritic and Hebrew religion, including *Le Culte à Ugarit;* editor of the *Revue Biblique.*
WITCHCRAFT, MAGIC, AND DIVINATION IN CANAAN AND ANCIENT ISRAEL

Karel van der Toorn Professor of Ancient Religions at the University of Leiden, The Netherlands. Author of many studies on the culture of

the ancient Near East and of the Hebrew Bible, including *Sin and Sanction in Israel and Mesopotamia: A Comparative Study; From Her Cradle to Her Grave: The Role of Religion in the Life of the Israelite and the Babylonian Woman;* (with J. Platvoet) *Pluralism and Identity;* and (contributing editor) *Dictionary of Deities and Demons in the Bible.*
THEOLOGY, PRIESTS, AND WORSHIP IN CANAAN AND ANCIENT ISRAEL

François Vallat Director of Research at the French National Center for Scientific Research, Paris, and author of several publications on the language and civilization of the Elamites; editor of *Contributions à l'histoire de l'Iran* and *Fragmenta Historiae Elamicae.*
SUSA AND SUSIANA IN SECOND-MILLENNIUM IRAN

James C. VanderKam Professor of Hebrew Scriptures at the University of Notre Dame, Notre Dame, Indiana. Author of articles on second-temple Jewish texts and of *Textual and Historical Studies in the Book of Jubilees; Enoch and the Growth of an Apocalyptic Tradition; The Book of Jubilees;* and *The Dead Sea Scrolls Today.* Member of the editorial boards of three journals and coeditor of the forthcoming *Oxford Encyclopedia of the Dead Sea Scrolls.*
PROPHECY AND APOCALYPTICS IN THE ANCIENT NEAR EAST

John Van Seters James A. Gray Professor of Biblical Literature at the University of North Carolina at Chapel Hill. Author of many studies, including *The Hyksos: A New Investigation; Abraham in History and Tradition; In Search of History; Historiography in the Ancient World and the Origins of Biblical History; Prologue to History: The Yahwist as Historian in Genesis;* and *The Life of Moses: The Yahwist as Historian in Exodus-Numbers.*
THE HISTORIOGRAPHY OF THE ANCIENT NEAR EAST

Herman L. J. Vanstiphout Associate Professor of Assyriology at Groningen University, The Netherlands. Author of articles on Mesopotamian literature and contributing editor to *Scripta signa vocis; Dispute Poems and Dialogues in the Ancient and Medieval Near East;* and *Mesopotamian Epic Literature: Oral or*

Aural?. Co-organizer of the"Groningen Group for the Study of Mesopotamian Literature."
MEMORY AND LITERACY IN ANCIENT WESTERN ASIA

Klaas R. Veenhof Professor of Assyriology at the University of Leiden, The Netherlands. Author of *Aspects of Old Assyrian Trade and Its Terminology;* coauthor of *Altassyrische Tontafeln aus Kültepe: Texte und Siegelabrollungen.* Editor of *Cuneiform Archives and Libraries.* Member of the editorial board of the *Journal of the Economic and Social History of the Orient.*
KANESH: AN ASSYRIAN COLONY IN ANATOLIA

Herman te Velde Professor of Egyptology at the University of Groningen, The Netherlands. Author of *Seth: God of Confusion* and of numerous articles on ancient Egyptian religion and culture.
THEOLOGY, PRIESTS, AND WORSHIP IN ANCIENT EGYPT

Pierre Villard "Maître de conference" at the University of Paris I (Sorbonne), author of studies on Neo-Assyria, and collaborator on the publication of documents from Mari.
SHAMSHI-ADAD AND SONS: THE RISE AND FALL OF AN UPPER MESOPOTAMIAN EMPIRE

Kent R. Weeks Professor of Egyptology, American University in Cairo. Weeks is the excavator of Tomb 5 in the Valley of the Kings at Luxor, believed to be the resting place of up to 50 sons of Ramesses II. Among his published works are *An Historical Bibliography of Egyptian Prehistory; Egyptology and the Social Sciences: Five Studies;* and (with J. E. Harris) *X-raying the Pharaohs.*
MEDICINE, SURGERY, AND PUBLIC HEALTH IN ANCIENT EGYPT

Edward F. Wente Professor of Egyptology at the University of Chicago. Author of *Late Ramesside Letters; Letters from Ancient Egypt;* and of articles on ancient Egyptian history and culture. Coeditor of *An X-ray Atlas of the Royal Mummies.*
THE SCRIBES OF ANCIENT EGYPT

Martin L. West Senior Research Fellow at All Souls College, Oxford. Author of *Early Greek Philosophy and the Orient; Textual Criticism*

and Editorial Technique; The Orphic Poems; Greek Meter; The Hesiodic Catalogue of Women; Ancient Greek Music; and various critical editions, commentaries, and translations of Greek poetic texts.
ANCIENT NEAR EASTERN MYTHS IN CLASSICAL GREEK RELIGIOUS THOUGHT

Joan Goodnick Westenholz Chief Curator at the Bible Lands Museum, Jerusalem. Author of *Legends of the Kings of Akkade,* "Oral Traditions and Written Texts in the Cycle of Akkade," "The Clergy of Nippur," and other articles on Mesopotamian literature and religion.
LOVE LYRICS FROM THE ANCIENT NEAR EAST

Helen Whitehouse Assistant Keeper in the Department of Antiquities, Ashmolean Museum, Oxford. Author of *The Dal Pozzo Copies of the Palestrina Mosaic* and articles on the interpretation of Egypt and its antiquities in Western culture from the Roman period onward. Editor in Chief of the *Journal of Egyptian Archaeology.*
EGYPT IN EUROPEAN THOUGHT

Robert M. Whiting Research Associate in the Department of Asian and African Studies at the University of Helsinki. Author of *Old Babylonian Letters from Tell Asmar,* "The Dual Personal Pronouns in Akkadian," and (with I. J. Gelb) *Earliest Land Tenure Systems in the Near East: Ancient Kudurrus.* Managing Editor of the State Archives of Assyria and associated series.
AMORITE TRIBES AND NATIONS OF SECOND-MILLENNIUM WESTERN ASIA

William D. Whitt Visiting Instructor of Religion at North Carolina State University at Raleigh. Author of articles on the Hebrew Bible and ancient Syro-Palestine.
THE STORY OF THE SEMITIC ALPHABET

F. A. M. Wiggermann Professor of Assyriology at the Vrije Universiteit, Amsterdam. Author of articles on Mesopotamian religious beliefs, including *Mesopotamian Protective Spirits: The Ritual Texts,* and a contributor to M. Stol, *Zwangerschap en geboorte bij de Babyloniërs en in de Bijbel.*
THEOLOGIES, PRIESTS, AND WORSHIP IN ANCIENT MESOPOTAMIA

Gernot Wilhelm Professor of Oriental Philology at the University of Würzburg, Germany. Author of numerous articles on Hurrian, Urartian, and Hurro-Akkadian grammar, on Akkadian texts from Boğhazköy, and on ancient near eastern history and chronology, including *Untersuchungen zum Hurro-Akkadischen von Nuzi; Hurritische und luwische Riten aus Kizzuwatna; Das Archiv des Šilwa-teššup* (vols. II–IV); *Sumerische und akkadische literarische Texte* (Keilschriftexte aus Boghazköi 36); *Medizinische Omina aus Hattusa;* and *The Hurrians.*
THE KINGDOM OF MITANNI IN SECOND-MILLENNIUM UPPER MESOPOTAMIA

Irene J. Winter Professor and Chairperson of Fine Arts, Harvard University, Cambridge, Massachusetts. Author of many studies that explore diverse aspects of ancient iconography and style, among them *Ingathering: Ceremony and Tradition in New York Public Collections* and *A Decorated Breastplate from Hasanlu, Iran: Type, Style, and Context of an Equestrian Ornament.*
AESTHETICS IN ANCIENT MESOPOTAMIAN ART

Paolo Xella Professor for Altorientalistik at the University of Tübingen and Chief Researcher at C. N. R. in Rome. Author of *Problemi del mito nel Vicino Oriente antico; I testi rituali di Ugarit; Baal Hammon; Gli antenati di Dio;* and of many articles and monographs on ancient near eastern religion, languages, and cultures.
DEATH AND THE AFTERLIFE IN CANAANITE AND HEBREW THOUGHT

K. Aslihan Yener Assistant Professor of Archaeology at the Oriental Institute, Chicago. Her forthcoming book is *Metal Technology and Social Organization: The Domestication of Metals.*
"Early Bronze Age Tin Processing at Göltepe and Kestel, Turkey" in MINING AND METALWORK IN ANCIENT WESTERN ASIA

Norman Yoffee Professor of Near Eastern Studies and Curator of Archaeology at the University of Michigan, Ann Arbor. Author of studies on the anthropology and economy of ancient Mesopotamia, including *The Economic Role of the Crown in the Old Babylonian Period* and *Old Babylonian Texts from Kish and Elsewhere in the Ashmolean Museum, Oxford.* Coeditor of *The Collapse of Ancient States and Civilizations; Early Stages in the Evolution of Mesopotamian Civilization;* and *Archaeological Theory: Who Sets the Agenda?*
THE ECONOMY OF ANCIENT WESTERN ASIA

Paul E. Zimansky Associate Professor of Archaeology at Boston University. Author of *Ecology and Empire: The Structure of the Urartian State.* Editor of *Mār Šipri,* the newsletter of the Committee on Mesopotamian Civilization at the American Schools of Oriental Research. He has excavated at Bastam (Iran) and directed excavations at sites in Iraq and Syria.
THE KINGDOM OF URARTU IN EASTERN ANATOLIA

Illustration
Acknowledgments

Charles Scribner's Sons Reference Books gratefully acknowledges the individuals and institutions who graciously allowed the use of drawings and photographs protected by copyright. Every effort has been made to contact the copyright owners of photographs and illustrations in these volumes; if the holder of the copyright of an illustration has not received a formal permission request he or she should contact Scribners. The credit printed in small capitals following each picture caption in these volumes acknowledges the source that provided Scribners with the image. The copyright holder from whom official permission was requested—sometimes identical to the source in the picture caption and sometimes not—will be found below. Illustrations not acknowledged below were prepared or significantly adapted especially for this project, or they are in the public domain.

VOLUME I

Part 1

P. 10, National Museum of Naples; p. 11, Museo Capitolino, Rome; p. 27, Harold Allen Archives, Chicago; p. 29, The Metropolitan Museum of Art, New York; p. 114, Louvre Museum, Paris; p. 115, Dante Gabriel Rossetti, *Astarte Syriaca,* © Manchester City Galleries, Manchester, England.

Part 2

Pp. 126, 133, and 146, courtesy of Karl W. Butzer; p. 156, courtesy of Willem Van Zeist, Biologisch-Archaeologisch Instituut, Groningen; p. 159, courtesy of Avi-noam Danin, Hebrew University, Jerusalem; p. 171, The Metropolitan Museum of Art, New York; p. 181, Griffith Institute, Ashmolean Museum, Oxford; p. 182, The University Museum of Archaeology and Anthropology, University of Pennsylvania; p. 194, The Metropolitan Museum of Art, New York; p. 197, Harriet E. W. Crawford, *Sumer and the Sumerians* (New York: Cambridge University Press, 1991).

Part 3

P. 238, Hillprecht Collection, Friedrich Schiller University, Jena; p. 240, courtesy of Elizabeth Stone; p. 246, courtesy of Elizabeth Stone, based on a drawing in *Iraq* 52 (British School of Archaeology in Iraq).

Part 4

P. 294, Oriental Institute, University of Chicago; p. 295, Griffith Institute, Ashmolean Museum, Oxford; p. 304, Louvre Museum, Paris; p. 307, courtesy of John Baines; p. 308, German Archaeological Institute, Cairo; p. 310, © Andromeda Oxford Ltd.; p. 314, The Metropolitan Museum of Art, New York.

Pp. 365 and 366 (top), Egypt Exploration Society, London; p. 366 (bottom), courtesy of Rosalind Janssen; p. 369, Nina Davies, *Scenes from Some Theban Tombs,* pl. 6 (Aris & Philips UK, 1963); p. 377, French Institute of Oriental Archaeology, Cairo; p. 386, Egyptian Museum, Turin; p. 388, Griffith Institute, Ashmolean Museum, Oxford; p. 390, Merseyside County Museums, Liverpool; p. 391, Egypt Exploration Society, London.

Pp. 424 and 425, Griffith Institute, Ashmolean Museum, Oxford; pp. 426 and 427, courtesy of Michael

Roaf; p. 428, Jeremy Black and Anthony Green, *Gods, Demons, and Symbols of Ancient Mesopotamia: An Illustrated Dictionary*, fig. 148, p. 176 (British Museum Press and University of Texas Press, 1992); p. 429, Oriental Institute Press, Chicago; p. 430 (bottom), P. Delougaz and Seton Lloyd, *Pre-Sargonid Temples in the Diyala Region* (Chicago: Oriental Institute Press, 1942); p. 434, Helen Leacroft and Richard Leacroft, *The Buildings of Ancient Mesopotamia* (Brockhampton Press, 1974); pp. 435 and 439, © British Museum, London; p. 438, Anton Moortgat, *The Art of Ancient Mesopotamia* (London: Phaidon Press Ltd., 1969).

P. 505, State Museum, Berlin; p. 506, Oriental Institute, University of Chicago; p. 509, Louvre Museum, Paris; pp. 511 and 513, © British Museum, London; p. 514, © British Museum; p. 536, Kurt Bittel et al., *Yazilikaya* (Berlin: Gebrüder Mann Verlag, 1975); p. 537, Claude F. A. Schaeffer, *Ugaritica III: Mission de Ras Shamra* (Paris: Librairie Orientaliste Paul Geuthner, 1956).

Pp. 558 and 559 (top), copyright unknown; pp. 559 (bottom) and 566, Museum of Anatolian Civilizations, Ankara; p. 564, Hirmer Photo Archives, Munich; p. 567, The Metropolitan Museum of Art, New York, Gift of Norbert Schimmel Trust, 1989 (1989.281.12); p. 594, Oriental Institute, University of Chicago; p. 634 adapted from Eretz Israel Museum, Tel Aviv; pp. 635 and 641, Israel Authority of Antiquities, Jerusalem; p. 637, Eretz Israel Museum, Tel Aviv; p. 640, Oriental Institute, University of Chicago; p. 642, Egypt Exploration Society, London.

VOLUME II

Part 5

Pp. 683 and 686, courtesy of John Ruffle; p. 694, Oriental Institute, University of Chicago; p. 695, Egyptian Museum, Cairo; p. 704, The Metropolitan Museum of Art, New York; p. 707, The Franco-Egyptian Center for the Study of the Temples of Karnak, Luxor; p. 708, Oriental Institute, University of Chicago; pp. 720, 723, and 733, © Rainer Stadelmann; p. 727, Rainer Stadelmann; pp. 729 and 731, John Ruffle; pp. 739, 740, 741, and 745, H. W. Müller Collection, Universitätsbibliothek, Heidelberg; p. 743, Louvre Museum, Paris.

Pp. 753, 755, and 760, Bildarchiv preussischer Kulturbesitz, Berlin; pp. 754 and 759, Egyptian Museum, Cairo; p. 756, Jürgen Liepe, Berlin; p. 757, NY Carlsburg Glyptothek, Copenhagen; p. 765, Egyptian Museum, Turin; p. 770, courtesy of John Ruffle; pp. 782, 784, 785, and 786 (left and right), courtesy of Professor Fritz Hintze; pp. 793, 799, and 800, © Hans J. Nissen; p. 796, S. A. Jasim, *Upon This Foundation*, Henricksen

and Thuesen, eds. (University of Copenhagen Museum, Tusculanum Press, 1989); p. 803 (top and bottom), courtesy of Dr. T. Cuyler Young, Royal Ontario Museum, Toronto.

P. 845, The University Museum of Archaeology and Anthropology, University of Pennsylvania; p. 852, The University Museum of Archaeology and Anthropology, University of Pennsylvania (obj. # CBS 10993); p. 860, Tahsin Özgüç, *Kültepe-Kaniš*, New Research at the Trading Center of the Ancient Near East (Ankara: Turk Tarib Kurum, 1959); p. 861, R. Naumann, *Architektur Kleinasiens von ihren Anfargen bis zum Ende der hethitischen Zeit* (Tübingen: E. Wasmuth, 1971); pp. 862 and 864, courtesy of Klaas R. Veenhof; pp. 889, 892 (top), and 896, Aleppo Museum; pp. 890 and 895, Louvre Museum, Paris; p. 891, André Parrot, *Mission archéologique de Mari* (Neuchâtel: Editions Ides et Calendes, 1953).

P. 906, Louvre Museum, Paris; p. 921, Louvre Museum, Paris; p. 927, © British Museum, London; pp. 932, 935, 936, 937, 939, and 943, Richard F. S. Starr, *Nuzi*, vol. 2 (Cambridge: Harvard University Press, 1937); p. 938, Corning Museum of Glass, Corning, New York; p. 953, State Museum, Berlin.

P. 985 (top), courtesy of Phil Smith; pp. 985 (bottom), 991, 996, and 997 (top), The Metropolitan Museum of Art, New York (#62.173.7, #60.20.15.16, #1986.121, and #43.102.7, respectively); pp. 986, 987, and 995, courtesy of Dr. T. Cuyler Young, Jr.; pp. 989, 990, 994 (bottom), and 997, courtesy of Oscar White Muscarella; pp. 992 and 993, Hasanlu Project, The University Museum of Archaeology and Anthropology, University of Pennsylvania.

P. 1002, Louvre Museum, Paris; p. 1007, courtesy of François Vallat; p. 1008, National Museum, Iran, photo courtesy of Ezat Negahban, Tehran; p. 1009, Louvre Museum, Paris, ©R.M.N.; p. 1016, David Stronach; p. 1017, courtesy of Dr. F. Krefter; p. 1018, © British Museum, London; pp. 1026, 1027, 1028, and 1032, courtesy of François Vallat; p. 1031, Louvre Museum, Paris; p. 1038, Oriental Institute, University of Chicago.

P. 1057, The State Hermitage Museum, St. Petersburg; pp. 1061 and 1063 (top and bottom), courtesy of Viktor Sarianidi, Archaeology Institute, Moscow; pp. 1071, 1075, 1076 (left and right), and 1077, courtesy of B. A. Litvinsky; p. 1111, courtesy of Dr. D. J. W. Meijer, Leiden; p. 1116, J. G. Macqueen, *The Hittites and Their Contemporaries in Asia Minor* (London: Thames and Hudson, 1986); pp. 1123 and 1124, Troy Project, Tübingen, Germany; p. 1126, courtesy of Hans G. Jansen.

Pp. 1150, 1151, 1153, and 1155, courtesy of the Gordion Archaeological Project, The University Museum of Archaeology and Anthropology, University of Pennsylvania; pp. 1165 and 1167, courtesy of Trevor R.

Bryce; p. 1177, courtesy of Crawford H. Greenewalt, Jr.; p. 1178, Philadelphia Museum of Art, Dr. Francis W. Lewis Collection, photo courtesy of The University Museum of Archaeology and Anthropology, University of Pennsylvania; p. 1188, Peter Clayton and Mary Price, *The Seven Wonders of the Ancient World* (London: Routledge, 1989); p. 1193, Egypt Exploration Society, London.

P. 1244, The Metropolitan Museum of Art, New York; p. 1248, drawing by Diana Stein-Wünscher; p. 1270, National Museum of Athens; pp. 1273, 1276, and 1277, Hebrew University, Jerusalem; pp. 1275 and 1278, Israel Authority of Antiquities, Jerusalem; pp. 1282 and 1289, National Museum of the Syrian Arab Republic, Aleppo; p. 1288, National Museum of the Syrian Arab Republic, Damascus; p. 1292, Louvre Museum, Paris.

P. 1301, © British Museum, London; p. 1316, Louvre Museum, Paris; p. 1317, *Biblical Archaeology Review* (1984); p. 1324, National Museum of Carthage, p. 1328, courtesy of F. Malha; p. 1330, private collection; pp. 1339, 1347, and 1348, French Archaeological Expedition in Abu Dhabi Emirate; p. 1344, French Archaeological Expedition in Kuwait; p. 1349 (top, left), Swiss Archaeological Expedition in Fujairah; p. 1349 (bottom, left; top, right), *Archaeology in the United Arab Emirates*, vol. 4 (1985); p. 1358, © British Museum, London.

VOLUME III

Part 6

P. 1424 (top), courtesy of The Carnegie Museum of Natural History, Pittsburgh (acc. 1842-1); p. 1424 (bottom), Diana Craig Patch and Cheryl Ward Haldane, *The Pharaoh's Boat at the Carnegie* (Pittsburgh: The Carnegie Museum of Natural History, 1990); p. 1427, © Frey/Institute of Nautical Archaeology, Texas A&M University, College Station; p. 1440 (left), Christos G. Doumas, *Thera: Pompeii of the Ancient Aegean—Excavations at Akrotiri, 1967–1979* (1983); p. 1440 (right), Christos G. Doumas, "The Wall-paintings of Thera" (The Thera Foundation, 1992); p. 1441, J.D. S. Pendlebury, *A Handbook to the Palace of Minos at Knossos* (Chicago: Aris Publishers, 1979); p. 1445, Giovanni Lilliu, *La Civiltà nuragica* (Sassari: Carlo Delfino Editions, 1982; p. 1454, Yale Babylonian Collection, Yale University, New Haven; p. 1489, Marvin A. Powell, DeKalb, Illinois; p. 1490, Institute of Nautical Archaeology, Texas A&M University, College Station.

Part 7

P. 1524, Cairo Museum, Cairo; p. 1530, Egypt Exploration Society, London; p. 1533, Oriental Institute, University of Chicago; p. 1534 (top), State Museum, Berlin; p. 1542 (top) and p. 1544, © British Museum, London; p. 1542 (bottom), The University Museum of Archaeology and Anthropology, University of Pennsylvania (neg. #54-141359); p. 1546, H. Hodges, *Technology of the Ancient World* (London: Penguin Press, 1970); p. 1548, Hirmer Archives, Munich; p. 1558, Oriental Institute, University of Chicago; pp. 1559 (top and bottom), 1560 (left and right), 1561, and 1563, courtesy of Frederick R. Matson.

P. 1569, Oriental Institute, University of Chicago; pp. 1576 and 1577, Sergei I. Rudenko, *The World's Most Ancient Artistic Carpets and Textiles* (Moscow: Iskusstvo, 1968); p. 1583 (top), The Metropolitan Museum of Art, New York; p. 1583 (bottom), © British Museum, London; p. 1584 (top and bottom), Louvre Museum, Paris; p. 1590, The Metropolitan Museum of Art, Gift of Martin and Sarah Cherkasky, 1983 (1983.314.16); pp. 1591 and 1599, British Museum, London; p. 1592 and 1598 (left), Louvre Museum, Paris; pp. 1593 and 1594, Holly Pittman, *Ancient Art in Miniature: Near Eastern Seals from the Collection of Martin and Sarah Cherkasky* (New York: The Metropolitan Museum of Art, 1987); p. 1597 (left), Iraq Museum, Baghdad; p. 1597 (right), courtesy of Holly Pittman; p. 1598 (right, top and bottom), D. J. Wiseman, "The Vassal-Treaties of Esarhaddon," *Iraq* 20 (British School of Archaeology in Iraq, 1958); p. 1602, Israel Museum, Jerusalem.

Pp. 1607, 1612, 1613, 1614, 1618, and 1619, The Brooklyn Museum, New York; pp. 1608 (left and right) and 1611 (left), Egyptian Museum, Cairo; pp. 1609, 1616, and 1617, The Metropolitan Museum of Art, New York; p. 1611 (right), State Museum, Berlin; p. 1627, Director's Contingent Fund, Museum of Fine Arts, Boston; p. 1628, Egypt Exploration Society, London; p. 1629, © British Museum, London; p. 1632, drawing by M. S. MacDonald-Taylor in Hollis Baker, *Furniture in the Ancient World* (New York: Macmillan, 1966); p. 1637, The University Museum of Archaeology and Anthropology, University of Pennsylvania; p. 1639, Iraq Museum, Baghdad; p. 1641, The Metropolitan Museum of Art, New York; p. 1648 (left), Museum of Anatolian Civilizations, Ankara.

P. 1648 (right), Pierpont Morgan Library, New York; pp. 1649 (left) and 1653, Louvre Museum, Paris; p. 1649 (right), The University Museum of Archaeology and Anthropology, University of Pennsylvania (neg. #S4-141197); pp. 1650 (top and bottom) and 1651, © British Museum, London; p. 1655 (left), K. Kenyon, *Jericho I, British School of Archaeology in Jerusalem*, 1960; p. 1655 (right), The Metropolitan Museum of Art, New York; p. 1660, reproduced by permission of the British School of Archaeology in Iraq from M. Mallowan and G. Hermann, *Ivories from Nimrud (1949–1963), Fascicule III: Furniture from SW.7 Fort*

Shalmaneser (1974); p. 1662, Department of Antiquities, Cyprus; pp. 1663, 1664, and 1665 (left; right, top and bottom), courtesy of Gordion Furniture Project, The University Museum of Archaeology and Anthropology, University of Pennsylvania; pp. 1667 and 1669 (bottom), St. Petersburg, The State Hermitage Museum, Oriental Department; p. 1669 (top), Archaeological Museum, Teheran; p. 1675, Istanbul Archaeological Museum; pp. 1677 and 1678, Museum of Anatolian Civilizations, Ankara; p. 1680, courtesy of Gordion Furniture Project, The University Museum of Archaeology and Anthropology, University of Pennsylvania (neg. #76500).

Part 8

P. 1703, E. Otto, *Osiris und Amun: Kult und heilige Statten* (Munich: Hirmer Verlag, 1966); p. 1705, Egyptian Museum, Cairo; p. 1706, A. Piankoff and N. Rambova, *The Tomb of Ramesses VI* (New York: Pantheon Books, 1954); p. 1712, Minneapolis Institute of Arts; p. 1713 (left), Collection Kofler-Truniger, Lucerne; p. 1713 (right), The Brooklyn Museum, New York; p. 1714 (left), © British Museum, London; pp. 1714 (right), 1715, 1717 (left and right), and 1721, Egyptian Museum, Cairo; pp. 1716 (left) and 1718, courtesy of Andreas Brodbeck; pp. 1716 (right) and 1723 (right), A. Piankoff and N. Rambova, *Mythological Papyri* (New York: Pantheon Books, 1957); pp. 1719 and 1722, A. Piankoff and N. Rambova, *The Tomb of Ramesses VI* (New York: Pantheon Books, 1954); pp. 1720 and 1726, Egypt Exploration Society, London; p. 1723 (left), courtesy of Barbara Lüscher; p. 1727, Collection Fraser-von Bissing, Antikenmuseum, Basel; p. 1728, courtesy of Hildi Keel-Leu; p. 1743, Harold H. Nelson and William J. Murnane, *The Great Hypostyle Hall at Karnak*, vol. 1, *The Wall Reliefs* (The Oriental Institute, University of Chicago, 1981).

P. 1754, Egypt Exploration Society, London; p. 1781, The Metropolitan Museum of Art, New York, Fletcher Fund, 1950 (50.85); p. 1791, Susan Weeks after P. E. Newberry, *Beni Hassan* (1891); p. 1792, Susan Weeks after Henri Wild, *Le Tombeau de Ti*, vol. 3 (1966).

P. 1801, © British Museum, London; pp. 1838 and 1848, J. Black and A. Green, *Gods, Demons, and Symbols of Ancient Mesopotamia* (London: British Museum Press, 1992); pp. 1844 and 1846, Louvre Museum, Paris; p. 1845, © British Museum, London; p. 1852 (left), Syrian National Museum, Damascus; p. 1852 (right), Iraq Museum, Baghdad; p. 1853, Bible Lands Museum, Jerusalem; p. 1868, courtesy of F. A. M. Wiggermann; p. 1897, Oriental Institute, University of Chicago.

P. 1905, © British Museum, London; pp. 1928, 1934, and 1936, courtesy of Francesca Rochberg; pp. 1948

(left and right), 1949 (left; right, top and bottom), 1950, 1951, 1952–1953, 1954, and 1956, courtesy of Marvin A. Powell; p. 1984, Kurt Bittel, *Die Hethiter* (Munich: Verlag CH Beck, 1976); pp. 1991 and 1992, Neriman Tezcan in S. Alp, *Beiträge zur Erforschung des hethitischen Tempels* (Ankara: Türk Tarih Kurumu Basimevi, 1983).

VOLUME IV

Part 9

Pp. 2098 (top) and 2101, German Archaeological Institute, Berlin; p. 2098 (bottom), pp. 2099 and 2102 (left), Louvre Museum, Paris; p. 2102 (right), Dr. T. Cuyler Young, Jr., Royal Ontario Museum, Toronto; p. 2126 (Aramaic), *Pshitta* vol. I, p. 19 (Leiden: Brill); p. 2127 (top), Mashaf Qeddus, *Bible in Amharic*, p. 8 (Addis Ababa: British Foreign Bible Service, rev. ed. 1967); p. 2127 (bottom), © 1953, Pontifico Instituto Biblico, Roma; pp. 2139, 2141, and 2142, Sir Alan Gardiner, *Egyptian Grammar: Being an Introduction to the Study of Hieroglyphs*, 3rd ed. (London: Oxford University Press, 1957); p. 2140, Serge Sauneron, *Le Temple d'Esna II* (Cairo, 1963); p. 2148, J. Osing, *Der spätägyptischen Papyrus BM 10808* (Wiesbaden, 1976).

P. 2152, H. Otten and C. Rüster, *Keilschrifttexte aus Boghazköy*, vol. 22 (Berlin: Gebrüder Mann Verlag, 1974); p. 2154, Piero Meriggi, *Manuale di eteo geroglifico*, part 2, 1st ser., #17 (Rome: © Edizioni dell'Ateneo, 1967); p. 2166, M.-J. Stève, *Tchoga Zanbil (Dur Untash)*, vol. 3, *Mémoires de la délégation archéologique en Iran*, text 41 (1967); p. 2173, F. W. Konig, *Handbuch der chaldischen Inschriften*, vol. 8, pl. 70, no. 90 (Osnabrück: Osnabrück Biblio-Verlag, 1967).

P. 2205, © French Institute of Oriental Archaeology, Cairo; p. 2213, courtesy of Egyptian Museum, Cairo; p. 2250, The Metropolitan Museum of Art, New York, Gift of Edward S. Harkness, 1912 (12.184); pp. 2267, 2269, and 2271, © British Museum, London; p. 2357, Louvre Museum, Paris; pp. 2380, 2382, and 2384 (left), Benjamin Sass, *The Genesis of the Alphabet and Its Development in the Second Millennium B.C.* (Wiesbaden: In Kommission bei O. Harrassowitz, 1988); p. 2383, Tel Aviv University; p. 2384 (right), *Ugarit-Forschungen* 23 (1991); p. 2391, Benjamin Sass, *Studia Alphabetica: On the Origin and the Early History of the Northwest Semitic, South Semitic, and Greek Alphabets* (1991).

P. 2424, © British Museum, London; p. 2462, © Fitzwilliam Museum, University of Cambridge; p. 2464, © British Museum, London; p. 2473, Oriental Institute, University of Chicago; p. 2475 (top), © British Museum, London; p. 2475 (bottom), E. Strommenger, *Festschrift hundert Jahre berliner Gesellschaft für Anthropologie, Ethnologie und Urgeschichte 1869–1969*, vol. 2 (Berlin, 1970).

Part 10

Pp. 2488, 2489 (top and bottom), 2490 (top), 2492, and 2502 (right), © British Museum, London; p. 2490 (bottom), Iraq Museum, Baghdad; p. 2491, British School of Archaeology in Iraq; pp. 2493, 2494, 2495, and 2498, courtesy of Hasanlu Project, The University Museum of Archaeology and Anthropology, University of Pennsylvania (neg. #s: S35-95153:11, S35-78114:18, S4-76304, and S4-93335A, respectively); pp. 2496 (top), 2499, 2500–2501, and 2504, courtesy of Hasanlu Project, The University Museum of Archaeology and Anthropology, University of Pennsylvania; p. 2496 (bottom), The Metropolitan Museum of Art, New York, Mrs. Constantine Sidamon-Eristoff Gift, 1961 (61.100.24); p. 2497, The University Museum of Archaeology and Anthropology, University of Pennsylvania (neg. #S4-139330); p. 2502 (left) Louvre Museum, Paris; p. 2503, Directorate General of Antiquities and Museums, Damascus.

Pp. 2511 and 2515 (top and bottom), Louvre Museum, Paris; p. 2512, courtesy of Guitty Azarpay; p. 2513, State Museum, Berlin; p. 2524 (bottom), Oriental Institute, University of Chicago; p. 2525 (right), © British Museum, London; p. 2526, State Museum, Berlin; pp. 2535, 2538, 2539, 2545 (right), 2546 (left), 2547 (right), 2549 (right), 2550, and 2553, The Brooklyn Museum, New York; pp. 2536, 2542 (top), and 2544, The Metropolitan Museum of Art, New York; p. 2537, Phoebe Hearst Museum of Anthropology, The University of California at Berkeley; pp. 2540, 2547 (left), 2551, and 2552, Egyptian Museum, Cairo; p. 2541, Egypt Exploration Society, London; p. 2542 (bottom), Richard Fazzinni, *Images for Eternity: Egyptian Art from Berkeley and Brooklyn* (San Francisco: Fine Arts Museum of San Francisco, 1975); p. 2545 (left), Harvard University-MFA Expedition/Courtesy of Museum of Fine Arts, Boston; p. 2546 (right), Kunsthistorisches Museum, Vienna; p. 2549 (left), Kelsey Museum of Archaeology, University of Michigan, Ann Arbor.

Pp. 2556, 2558 (right), and 2561, © British Museum, London; p. 2558 (left), Griffith Institute, Ashmolean Museum, Oxford; p. 2559, Boris Eisenberg in Albrecht Rietmuller and Frieder Zaminer, eds., *Die Musik des Altertums* (1989); p. 2560, Christiane Desroches Noblecourt et al., *Grand Temple d'Abou Simbel*, vol. 2, *La Bataille de Qadesh* (1971); p. 2562, Egypt Exploration Society, London; p. 2566, © Lise Manniche, *Music and Musicians in Ancient Egypt* (London: British Museum Press, 1991); p. 2571, Louvre Museum, Paris, ©

R.M.N.; p. 2578, Louvre Museum, Paris; pp. 2584, 2589, 2592 (top, left), 2595 (right), and 2596, Iraq Museum, Baghdad; pp. 2585, 2588 (top), and 2592 (left, bottom; right, top and bottom), Louvre Museum, Paris; pp. 2586, 2590, 2591 (left), 2593, and 2599, Oriental Institute, University of Chicago; pp. 2587, 2588 (bottom), and 2595 (left), © British Museum, London; p. 2591 (right), The University Museum of Archaeology and Anthropology, University of Pennsylvania (neg. #S5-23190); p. 2594, Hirmer Archives, Munich.

P. 2602, © British Museum, London; p. 2605, Louvre Museum, Paris; p. 2609, M. Matoušová, "Tanzschulen im alten vorderer Orient?" *Archív Orientální* 60 (Amsterdam: John Benjamins Publishing Co., 1992); p. 2610, M. Matoušová-Rajmová, "Illustration de la dance sur les sceaux de l'époque babylonienne ancienne," *Archív Orientální* 46 (Amsterdam: John Benjamins Publishing Co., 1978); p. 2611, State Museum, Berlin; p. 2612, Oriental Institute, University of Chicago; p. 2616, David Stronach, *Pasargadae*, pl. 147a (New York: Oxford University Press, 1978); pp. 2618 and 2626, Oriental Institute, University of Chicago; pp. 2619, 2625, and 2629, courtesy of Margaret Cool Root; pp. 2620 and 2621, Cameron Archive, Kelsey Museum of Archaeology, University of Michigan, Ann Arbor; p. 2623, German Archaeological Institute, Berlin; pp. 2628 and 2633, Ernst Herzfeld, *Iran in the Ancient Near East*, pls. 58 and 84 (New York: Oxford University Press, 1941 and 1958); pp. 2634 (top and bottom) and 2635, Kelsey Museum of Archaeology, University of Michigan, Ann Arbor, photo M. Root.

Pp. 2640 (bottom) and 2656, Museum of Anatolian Civilizations, Ankara; p. 2640 (top), courtesy of Harald Hauptmann; p. 2642 (left), Kutlu Emre et al., eds., *Anatolia and the Ancient Near East: Studies in Honor of Tashin Özgüç*, 1989; p. 2642 (right), Arnoldo Mondador, ed., *Anatolia, immaginidi civiltà: Tessrori dalla Turchia*, 1987; pp. 2643 and 2646, courtesy of Gregory McMahon; p. 2645, Kurt Bittel, *Hattuscha, Hauptstadt der Hethiter: Geschichte und Kultur einer altorientalischen Grossmacht* (Köln: DuMont Buchverlag, 1983); p. 2647, Ekrem Akurgal, ed., *The Art and Architecture of Turkey* (New York: Rizzoli, 1980) and Museum of Anatolian Civilizations, Ankara; p. 2657, Ekrem Akurgal, ed., *The Art and Architecture of Turkey* (New York: Rizzoli, 1980); p. 2650, copyright unknown; pp. 2653 and 2654, courtesy of Kay Kohlmeyer; p. 2674, *Anchor Bible Dictionary*, vol. 6 (New York: Doubleday, 1992); pp. 2676 (top and bottom), and 2677, Louvre Museum, Paris, drawing by Olivier Callot; p. 2678, Israel Antiquities Authority, Jerusalem; pp. 2680, 2681, 2684, 2686, 2688, and 2689, Louvre Museum, Paris; p. 2683, Italian Archaeological Mission, Elba; p. 2687, Louvre Museum, Paris, drawing by Caroline Florimont.

Part 11

Pp. 2697, 2700 (bottom), 2703, and 2709 (top), © British Museum, London; p. 2699, Barry Iverson/Time magazine; pp. 2700 (top) and 2702 (top and bottom), The Metropolitan Museum of Art, New York; pp. 2704, 2705 (top and bottom), 2707, and 2708 (top), Pierpont Morgan Library, New York; p. 2706 (left and right), Louvre Museum, Paris; p. 2708 (bottom), Harriet Otis Cruft Fund, courtesy of Museum of Fine Arts, Boston;

p. 2711, Anton Moortgat, *Frühe Bildkunst in Sumer* (Bonn: Rudolf Habelt Verlag, 1988); p. 2712 (left), Hirmer Archives, Munich; p. 2712 (right), courtesy of Sydney Babcock, Pierpont Morgan Library, New York; pp. 2722, 2723, and 2725 (left and right), courtesy of Frank Hole; pp. 2733 and 2738, courtesy of Seton Lloyd; pp. 2735 and 2740, Oriental Institute, University of Chicago; pp. 2745 and 2751, courtesy of Katryna Jacobsen; pp. 2754 and 2756, © British Museum, London; p. 2755, National Portrait Gallery, London; p. 2757, Peter Hayman, London; p. 2760, University College, London; p. 2770, courtesy of Ilse Bittel; p. 2781, courtesy of Cyrus H. Gordon.

Index

Titles and page ranges of articles in these volumes appear in boldface type. Italic page numbers refer to picture captions.

cuneiform alphabetic script for, 2384
decipherment of script, 85–87
Hazor documents in, 1205
Hittite ignorance of, 1091
international usage of, 812
Kassite loanwords, 926
as lingua franca, 2117, 2122, 2412,
    2414–2415, 2418
lurû, literary dialect of, 2313
Neo-Babylonian period, 970–971
phonemic writing system, 2185
scribal study of, 2270–2272
"silver" expressed in, 1491
Sumerian and, 2107, 2115
    aesthetic concepts in, 2570–2572
survival as literary language, 2294
in Susa, 1025
text example, *2127*
time span of, 43–44, 2117
titles, for scribes, 2272
in Ugaritic texts, 1263
vs. Amorite language, 1233
Akkadian literature, 2282. *See also* Hymns;
    Laments and lamentations
characteristics of, 835
disputations, 2295
for education and entertainment, 2298
fictional biographies of famous kings,
    2297–2298
forms of, 2300–2301
genres of, 2294–2300
    broad cultural perspective in, 2296
kings as subjects of, 2297
law codes, 2299
letters to the gods, 2295
lexicologic texts, 2299–2300
love as topic of, 2298
mathematical texts, 2299
medical treatises, 2299
myths, 2295
    literary qualities of, 2301
in Naram-Sin's reign, 835–836
narratives, literary qualities of, 2301
on the natural sciences, 2299
nature of, 2293
political and propagandistic works,
    2297–2298
propagandistic nature, 838
religious genres, 2296–2297
    divination manuals, 2299
    exorcism texts, 2298
Sumerian literature and, 2279
    adaptations of, 2295
    translations from, 2294–2295
technological treatises, 2300
time span of, 2293–2294
"wisdom" themes, 2297
Akkadian Literature: An Overview
    (Bottéro), **2293–2303**
Akkadian mythology. *See* Babylonian
    mythology
    Mesopotamian theology in, 1859

Akkadian Prophecies, 2091–2094
divinatory associations, 2093
Dynastic Prophecy, 2093
Jewish apocalypticism and
    differences, 2093–2094
    parallels, 2092–2093
revelation in, 2093
Shulgi Prophetic Speech, 2092
Text A, 2092
    cryptic language in, 2093
Uruk Prophecy, 2092
Akkadian religion. *See also* Prayer
Aramaean religion and, 1291
divinities, on cylinder seals, 1842
Hittite divination and, 1982
liturgical texts, 2477
mythological and ritual texts, 2295–2297
Sumerian religion compared, 2296
world order, 1820–1821
Akkhiyawa (Hittite place name), 1095,
    1097, 1117
Akhaiwa and, 1443
archaeological evidence, 1442–1443
    from Khattusha archive, 1129–1131
identification of, 1443
links to ancient Near East, 1446–1447
Akpınar, rock image of divinity from,
    2652–2653
Akroterion (roof type)
in Phrygian architecture, 1150–1151
as religious symbol, 1157
Akrotiri. *See also* Thera
destruction of, 1440
as trade center, 1440
urbanization, 1439
West House
    fresco, *1440*
    southwest-corner view, *1440*
Aksha Temple, cult statues of Ramesses
    II, 769–770
Aksumite Empire, language of, 2120–2121
al-. *See under next name component*
Alaca Hüyük
anthropomorphic statuettes, 2643
bronze objects from, 1676
    cast-bronze stag, *2643*, 2643
    female figurines, 1676
burials, 2642–2643
    animal figurines, 2644
ivory figure from, 1678
jewelry findings, 1673, 1675
metal artifacts from, 1508, 1514
orthostat of king and queen offering
    bull, *2647*
Phrygian inscriptions, 1157
Sphinx Gate, 2645–2647, *2646*
    dating of, 2647
    double eagle relief, 2645
    hunting scenes, 2647
    Khattusha reliefs and, 2647–2648
    phases of construction, 2645

placement and orientation of scenes,
    2645
reliefs, 2775
ritual scene on western interior face,
    2646
worship and cultic activities pictured,
    2646–2647
zoomorphic imagery at, 1990
Alakshandu, king of Wilushiya, Alexandros
    of (W)ilios and, 1117
Alala, Babylonian divinity, in Anu ancestry,
    1832
Alalakh (Tell Atchana)
craftsmen, houses of, 463
cylinder seals, 2689–2690
demographics, 1236
Eblaean sources from, 1225
furniture, 635
Khattushili I vs., 1089
lapis lazuli figure from, 1679
Mitanni archives in, 820
palace at, 606, 887
    rebuilding of, 606
social classes, status of craftsmen, 458
Sumerian language, 902
Syro-Palestinian sources from, 1196
temples at, 606, 610
Alarodians (Alarodioi), 2171
Urartians and, 1145
Alashiya. *See also* Cyprus
links to ancient Near East, 1446–1447
Alberti, Leon Battista, 2507
Alcaeus of Lesbos, 56
Alcoholic beverages. *See also* Beer; Wine
at Egyptian religious festivals, 368
Alder, 158
Aldred, Cyril, on Akhenaten, 1754
aleph, in Ugaritic script, 90
Aleppo. *See* Halab
Alexander III, king of Macedonia. *See*
    Alexander the Great
Alexander Polyhistor, compendium of
    histories by, 63
Alexander Romance, *Gilgamesh Epic* and,
    2335
Alexander the Great
Aramaic language and, 1293
in Babylon, 828
    restoration projects, 67
campaigns against Kassite tribes, 925
coinage of, 1496
conquests
    Egypt, 2552
    Lycia, 1170
    Tyre, 1322
in Egypt
    oracle received by, 1744
    takes over kingship, 286
at Granicus, 1104
orientalization of Greek thought
    and, 34

Alexander the Great (*continued*)
  in Persia
    battle with Darius, 1020
    destruction at Persepolis, 1049
    looting of Pasargadae by, 2616–2617,
      2632
    occupies central region, 1020
    Syro-Palestinian area under, 1215
Alexandria
  as capital of Egypt, 712
  Hellenistic, 7–8
Alexandros of (W)ilios, Alakshandu of
  Wilushiya and, 1117
Alikemektepesi, Late Chalcolithic painted
  ware, 1054
Ali Kosh, excavation of, 2718–2719
Alilat, Arabian divinity, 1360
Allakhad, kings of, government of district
  of Warad-Sin, 877
Allani, Hittite divinity
  Hattic counterpart, 2022
  in the netherworld, 2021
  in *Song of Remission*, 2373
Allatum, Akkadian divinity, in the
  netherworld, 2021
Allegory, in Egyptian literature, 2228
"All Gods." *See* Visai Baga gods
Alliances. *See* Matrimonial alliances;
  Treaties
Allocation of goods. *See* Redistribution of
  goods
Almanacs
  normal-star, 1938
  zodiac in, 1938
Alphabet. *See also* Alphabetic scripts;
  Phoenician alphabet; Semitic alphabet
  cuneiform writing of, 2384–2385
  language schemes using, 2181
  lunar calendars and, 2785–2786
  magical, 2079
  names of letters in, 2386
Alphabetic acrostics, 2391
Alphabetic numeration, 2386
Alphabetic scripts
  for Anatolian language subgroup,
    2156–2158
  earliest examples of, 2122
  indication of vowels in, 2390
  Near Eastern sites with inscriptions,
    2381 (map)
  for Old South Arabian languages, 2120
  origins of, 2379–2380
  versus ideographic or syllabic systems,
    2379
  writing materials and methods,
    2392–2394
Alster, Bendt, **2315–2326**
Altai Mountains, Pazyryk Valley, frozen
  tombs, furniture found in, 1668–
  1669

Altyn-depe
  archaeological record, 1060–1061
  craft quarters, 461
  social classes, 1061
Alû-demons, 1891
Alum, in mordants, 1550
Alwa, kingdom of, 789
Alyattes, king of Lydia
  Cimmerians vs., 1103–1104
  gifts to Greek sanctuaries, 1177
  Medes vs., 1176
  tomb of, 1181
  wives, 1178
ʾĀmâ (concubine), 625
AMA.GAL EN (Eblaean queen mother),
  power of, 1224
Amalkites, archaeological record and, 256
Amamet, the Devourer, in the *Book of the
  Dead*, 1769
Amanikhabale, king of Meroë, stela at
  Amun Temple, 784
Amanitore, ruler of Kush, temple building,
  785
Amarna. *See* Akhetaten (Amarna)
Amarna art. *See also* Relief art, Egyptian
  birds and animals in, 751–752
  canon of proportion, 758, 761
  contact figure, 756
  decorative, 751
  early and late styles, 756, 758
  in early excavations, 750–751
  eating depicted in, 368
  family stelae, 751, 760
  Flinders Petrie excavations, 751
  floor paintings, 752
  modern excavations, 752–755
  modern studies, 756–758
  naturalism, 752
  painted limestone bust, 752
  plaster heads, 753, 755
  polychrome effect, 751
  psychological unity, 756
  reforms of, 2540–2541, 2551
  role of Akhenaten in formulating, 758
  sfumato eyes, 752–753
  statuary, 761–762
    bust form, 761
    composite, 751
    private, 755–756
    sandstone colossus, 761
  Theban material, 756–758
  two-dimensional compositions,
    indication of movement, 750–751
Amarna gold hoard, 1383–1384
"Amarnaic" language (Canaano-Akkadian),
  2418. *See also* Canaanite languages
Amarna letters, 589, 1196, 1381, 2203
  Arzawa letters found in, 2766–2767
  Biblical Hebrew verses compared with,
    2416–2417

  from Canaan, 2122–2123, 2411–2419
    idiomatic language, 2413–2418
  cultural-linguistic background of,
    2412–2413
  cuneiform texts in, 2786
  delivery of, 1469
  epistolary conventions of, 2413–2416
  on exchange of artisans, 465
  furniture described in, 1656–1657
  historical setting of, 2411–2412
  international correspondence in, 819
  on *khabiru*, 1207–1208
  languages of, 2411–2419
  literary qualities of, 2238, 2413–2416
  messengers, detention and mistreatment
    of, 1467, 1470
  quotes from, 2413, 2415–2417
  Sea Peoples in, 1267–1268
  on Syro-Palestine, 1196, 1207
Amarna Letters from Canaan (Izreʾel),
  2411–2419
Amar-Sin, king of Ur, 856, 2282
Amasis, king of Egypt, 711, 1191–1192
Amaunet, Egyptian divinity, in
  Hermopolitan theogony, 1702
Ambassadors. *See also* Messengers
  negotiation, 1469
  selection of, 1466
Amedu (Bit-Zamani), Assyrian sources on,
  1286
Amel-Marduk, king of Babylon, 972
Amenemheb, Egyptian military hero, 295
Amenemhet, Egyptian official, tomb of
  autobiography in, 1246
  family history inscribed in, 2248–2249
Amenemhet (Ammenemes) I, king of
  Egypt, 698–699. *See also Teaching of
  Amenemhet*
  challenges to power of, 699
  predecessors of, 735–736
  reign of, 736, 738
  as the vizier Ameny, 1378
Amenemhet II, king of Egypt, 738, 742
  coregency, 281
Amenemhet III, king of Egypt, reign of,
  743–746
Amenemhet IV, king of Egypt, 746
Amenemhetankh, Egyptian official, 743
Amenemope, human plans and divine
  action in, 2453
Amenhotep, son of Hapu, Egyptian
  official, autobiography of, 2252
Amenhotep (Amenophis) I, king of Egypt
  problem of succession to, 703
  religious festivals, 369–370
Amenhotep II, king of Egypt
  accession ceremony, 277
  annals of, 2436
  on Nubians, 702
Amenhotep III, king of Egypt
  Aegean trade links under, 3

Arzawa king and, 1091
"book labels" of, 2200
cartouche of, 1512
foreign-born wives of, 229
international correspondence of, 819
jewelry given by king of Mitanni to,
1642
letter to Kadashman-Enlil I, 1628
al-Malqata palace of, 309, *314*, 314–315
marriage alliance of, 820, 2169
parents of. *See* Yuya and Tuya
reign of, 704
Shuttarna II and, 1250
slaves used for labor by, 229
stela of, materials used in, 341
Tushratta of Mitanni letter to, 1381
Amenhotep IV, king of Egypt. *See*
Akhenaten, king of Egypt
Ameni. *See* Amenemhet I, king of Egypt;
Ameny
Amenophis, kings of Egypt. *See*
Amenhotep
Amenuserhat. *See* Amun, Egyptian divinity
Ameny, Egyptian vizier, 1378. *See also*
Amenemhet I, king of Egypt
Amharic language, 2121
text example, *2127*
Amida (Diyarbakir), campaigns of Naram-
Sin against, 833
Ammenemes. *See* Amenemhet I, king of
Egypt
Ammianus Marcellinus, on Egyptian
obelisks, 15
Ammi-ditana, king of Babylon, 912
Ammi-saduqa, king of Babylon
dating of reign, 658
genealogy, 1239
mīšarum edicts, 912–913
Ammishtamru II, king of Ugarit
divorce, settlement of, 1259–1260
personal seal of, 2385
Ammiya, city of, joins 'Apīru, 589
Ammon, independence of, 1309
Ammonite language, 2123
Ammonite religion, divinities, 2034, 2047
Ammuladi, Qedarite sheikh, attack on
Assyrian vassal states, 1366
Ammuna, Hittite ruler, edict of, 2370
Ammunira of Beirut, letter by, 2413
Amorites (*Amurrû*, Martu, *Mar-tu*,
MAR.TU). *See also* Kings, Amorite
Aramaeans compared to, 821, 1281
Asshur vs., 1088
assimilation of Sumero-Babylonian
culture, 1235
in competition for political power, 1395
defined, 254
Early Bronze Age, 1200–1201
early second millennium, 1234–1236
Ebla under, 1216
in Egyptian and later sources, 1236

history, 812–817
sources for, 254–255
Hyksos and, 1205
language, classification, 1233
in Mesopotamia, 1232, 1234
military activities, 1235
Mukish under, 1203
names. *See under* Names, personal
Neo-Assyrian period, 1237–1238
as pastoral nomads, 254–255,
1239–1240
personal names in, 1222
pictorial representation, 1236
royal titles and tribal origins, 1239
sedentarization of, 255
settled populations and, 1239–1240
Sumer vs., 856
in tablet from Fara, 1234
terminology, 1201, 1231–1232
third millennium, 1234
tribes and tribal groupings, 1238–1239
Amorite Tribes and Nations of Second-
Millennium Western Asia
(Whiting), **1231–1242**
Amphictyony, Mesopotamian
BALA system, 402
for economic cooperation between
independent states, 399
Amu Darya River (Oxus River),
hydrological instability, 1058–1059
Amulets
Babylonian, magical uses, 1897, 1902
Egyptian, *1607*, *1607*, *1608*, *1610*
color of materials, 1725
for fertility and childbirth, 376–377
good luck, 1602
inscribed with oracular decrees, 1782
Old Kingdom, 1608
Predynastic, 1607
protective, 367
purpose of, 1725
quality of, 341
seal, 1714
symbolism, *1723*, 1724–1725
Hebrew, 2078–2079
of hand with fingers downward, 2079
protecting oneself by divine name,
2079
magical powers, 1600
magical uses, 1779
spells inscribed on, 2395
Mesopotamian, Pazuzu on, 1844
in mummification, 1766
scarabs as, 1601
seals as, 1600
Amun, Egyptian divinity
administration of affairs, 284–285
Akhenaten's campaign against, 749–750
cult of
in modern Luxor, 13
special relationship with king, 705

in Greek literature and mythology, 9
in Hermopolitan theogony, 1702
iconographic depiction, 1727
Phoenician dedication to, 1324
priesthood of, 284
in Kush, 779
as rulers of Upper Egypt, 708–709
selection of high priest, 1735
suppressed by Akhenaten, 1753
profile of, "the hidden one," 1736
rise of, 736
sacred barque of, 1379, 1698
sacrifices to, 227
as state deity of Kush, 785
temples of, 764
in Amun, 778
at Karnak, 292, *756*, *757*, 780
at Meroë, *783*, *784*
'Amuq. *See* Pattina
Amurrû. *See* Amorites
Amurru, kingdom of. *See also* Amorites
Egyptian-Hittite rivalry and, 1111–1112,
1207
Egyptian occupation of, 1094
formation of, 1236
form of government, 589
Hamath replaces, 1283
Hittite treaty with, 1096–1097
Neo-Assyrian period, 1237–1238
under Benteshina, 1117
Amurru, Mesopotamian divinity, 2046
on cylinder seals, Old Babylonian and
Kassite periods, 1847
symbols of, *1840*, *1841*
An, divinity. *See* Anum, Mesopotamian
divinity
Anahita, divinity, worship of, in
Achaemenid Iran, 1967
Analogous magic, 1991
Anam, ruler of Uruk, on relationship with
Babylon, 905
'Anat, Ugaritic divinity
in *Aqhat* myth, 2063, 2404
in *Baal Cycle*, 2032, 2405
divine consumption of enemies, 2032,
2037
"sister" of Baal, 2046
Yahweh and, 2037
Anatolia
agricultural practices, 2724–2725
Assyrians and
expansionism under Shamshi-Adad I,
813
rule by, 866–868, 1304
treaties with, 962
border regions, 259–260
bronze industry in, 1507
campaigns of Naram-Sin against, 833
Carians of, 1185–1194. *See also* Carians
ceremonial objects, Bronze Age, 1676
climate of, 260

spread of, 208
state-run enterprise system, 212
  wool production and, 212
Syro-Palestinian, 1197
technological innovation and, 204–205
three structures of, 210–212
Transcaucasia, 1053
village-based, innovations in agriculture
  and, 205
**Animal Husbandry and Human Diet in
  the Ancient Near East** (Hesse),
  203–222
Animals. *See also* Bestiality; Hunting;
  Sacrifice, animal; Sculpture, animal;
  Zoomorphic iconography; *specific
  kinds of animals*
  archaeozoological evidence of, 163
  in art
    Amarna period, 751–752
    Aramaic, 1289
    humorous depiction of, *2464*
    Mesopotamia, 2596, 2596–2597,
      2597–2600
    Mesopotamian sculptures of, 2589,
      2591, 2593–2594
  attitudes of herders and hunters toward,
    207
  bioarchaeological approach to study of,
    153
  domestication of, 1389. *See also*
    Animals, domesticated
  economic significance of, 203–206
  ethnoscience approach to study of, 154
  human bones scattered by, 1890
  humorous stories about, 2463–2465
  identifying remains in archaeological
    sites, 2724
  images of. *See also* Heraldry
    Babylonian, in European art, 74–75
    Babylonian and Aramaic demon
      composites, 50–51
  interspecies competition and
    adaptability of, 163
  laws concerning sexual intercourse with,
    2780
  mammals
    marine, exploitation of, 171
    species chart, *164–169*
  in Mesopotamian daily life, 498
  muricids, dye from, 172–173
  prehistoric, of eastern Sahara, 131–132
  sacred, Egyptian, 1735
  sacrificial, Syro-Palestinian, 2053
  size reduction of, 163
  surrogate burial of, 1883
  survey data on distribution of, 153
  unequal access to products, 205–206
  wild, 170–173, 203–204
Animals, domesticated. *See also* Animal
  husbandry; Herd animals; Pack
  animals; *specific animals, e.g.,* Cattle

choice of
  behavioral criteria in, 206
  and urbanization, 211, 221
economic significance of, 204–208
first appearance of, 206
as food source, 202
government managers and, 205
Israel, age of slaughter, 638
lack of biological diversity in, 208
Oman Peninsula, 1338
progenitors of, 163, 169–170
regional differences in stock, 209
ritual use of, 206–208
Secondary Products Revolution and, 205
selection in breeding of, 204–206, 209
state management of, 212
temple herds and flocks, 446–447
textual references to, 209
types of, 191
walled cities for protection of, 413
Anitta, Hittite king, 860
  achieves great prince status, 866
  expansionism of, 1088
  inscription of, 2369, 2436–2437
Ankara
  archaeological museum, 2774
  post-World War I, 2773
  under Midas's rule, 1157
Ankhmahor, king of Egypt, tomb of,
  circumcision festival, 378
Ankhsheshonq
  good deed in, 2453
  human plans and divine action in, 2453
  power of fate in, 2446
Ankh (Egyptian sign of life), 276,
  1725–1726
Ankhtyfy, Egyptian official, tomb
  biography of, 1383
Annals. *See* Chronicles
Annals of Murshili, 2372, 2374
Annals of Thutmose III, 384, 2436
Annuities, in Achaemenid Babylonia,
  1484–1485
Annulment of witchcraft. *See* Witchcraft
Annunitum, Babylonian divinity, temples
  to, 901
Anointing oils, in marriage ceremonies,
  1116
Anoukhva, ax from, *1057*
Anquetil-Duperron, Abraham Hyacinthe,
  Avesta, 72
Anshan (Tepe Malyan)
  Achaemenid settlement, 1040
  Elamite administrative texts, 2163
  Elamite settlement, 1004
  location, 1024
  nomadization of population of, 252
Anshan, Elamite settlement, 1004
Anshar, Babylonian divinity, in Sumerian
  mythology, 1830
AN.TAH.ŠUM^SAR festival, 1993, 2028
Antefoqer, Egyptian vizier, 741

Anthropological archaeology
  development of, 2717–2720
    natural sciences expertise and, 2718,
      2724–2725
  origins of, 2716
  survey methodology in, 2720–2721
Anthropologists, interests of, versus
  archaeologists, 2716
Anthropomorphism
  in Hittite iconography, 1990, 1994
  of Syro–Palestinian divinities,
    2044–2045, 2052
Antigonus, Macedonian general, control of
  Lycia, 1170
Antimenidas of Lesbos, 56
Antiochus I, Neo-Babylonian ruler,
  Berossus and, 62
Anti-Semitism, in modern Germany,
  103–105
Anti-Taurus Mountains, 260
Antiwitchcraft rituals. *See* Witchcraft
Antiyant- (son-in-law), 573, 576
Antiyanza ("bought" son-in-law), 559
Anu (Anum), Mesopotamian divinity,
  1860, 2332–2333, 2774
  ancestry, 1831–1832
  in *Atrakhasis Myth*, 1833
  in creation myth, 1819, 1830
  Hammurabi pronounced king by, 901
  in Kumarbi Cycle, 1974, 1982
  represented in art, 1846
  Shulgi and, 849–850
  symbols of, *1839*
Anu-belshunu, scribe of Uruk, 2276
Anubis, Egyptian divinity
  in funerary literature and tomb scenes,
    1772
  profile of, 1736
Anukis, Egyptian divinity, profile of, 1736
Anum. *See* Anu
Anumkhirpi, king of Mamma, in literature,
  2370
A.NUN.NA (netherworld deities), 2022
Anunnaki (Mesopotamian netherworld
  divinities), 1887–1888
Anzu, mythical bird, theft of Tablet of
  Destinies, 1843, 1851–1852
Aorn, Bactria city, 1071
Apadana palace, 2627
  architecture of, 2630–2631
  reliefs, 1044
    proportions, 2517
  textiles depicted in, 1585
Apedemak, divinity, 785
Aphlad, divinity, popularity of, 1291
Aphrodisiacs, 2078
Aphrodite, Babylonian. *See* Mylitta,
  Babylonian divinity
Apiculture, Hittite, 584
Apil-Ada, appeal to the "God of my
  father," 913

Assyrian siege of, 961
before Hammurabi, 903–905
biblical writings on, 73
bridge, 439
city layout of
  in European art, 76–77
  Herodotus on the, 58
  mythical descriptions of, 72
  predecipherment reconstructions of,
    76–77
destroyed by Sennacherib, 950–951
Elamite alliance with, 817
European writers on
  belles lettres, 72–74
  in early travel literature, 68–70
First Dynasty
  end of, 913
  foundation of, 903
  Hammurabi's reign, 905–907
  Kassites in, 917–918
  Mari and, 909 911
  political history, 901–903
first-millennium, 237–238
fortifications, 1533
German excavations at, 97
Isaiah's prophecy concerning, 98
modern remains, 902
Old Babylonian period, 902
Persian capture of, 826, 1039–1040
Processional Way, reliefs, 2588, 2599
rebuilt by Esarhaddon, 951–952
route to, via Euphrates, 1412
Southern Citadel, building plan, 435
Ziggurat of. *See* Tower of Babel
Babylonia. *See also* Chronicles,
    Babylonian; Mesopotamia *entries*;
    Neo-Babylonian Empire; Old
    Babylonian Empire
Achaemenid period
  agricultural land assignment to
    military families, 1482–1484
  Egibi family archives, 1475–1476
  Iddin-Nabu family archives, 1480
  private commercial and financial
    operations in, 1475–1485
alleged Sumerian-Akkadian conflict and,
    811
Arabs in, 1365–1366
Aramaeans in, 1282, 1286–1287
Assyrian territories under, 966
beer production in, 497
cultural influence of
  in Europe before the decipherment,
    67–79
  on Hellenistic Judaism, 43–53
  Selucid period, 44
daily life in, 485–499
  documentation on, 485–486
  Greek views of, 59
decline of Old Empire, 817
ecology of, 2731

ethics and morality, Delitzsch on, 103
feudalism, Kassite era, 923
Greek historians on, 58–64
historical sources. *See* Historical source
    material, Babylonian
Hittites and
  conquest of, 1089
  treaties with, 1095, 1108
  under Khattushili III, 1115
ideals regarding health and full life,
    1912
Indus Valley contacts, 1456–1458
inheritance. *See* Inheritance, Babylonian
Kassite era, 817, 819, 821, 917–918
  cultural influences, 925–926, 929
  political unification under dynasty,
    918–919
  relations between king and ruling
    elite, 922–923
  trade, 920
land rental in, 1495
Late Uruk period, 798–801
law. *See* Law, Babylonian
life expectancy, 487
magic in, influence on Hellenistic
    Judaism, 49–52
marriage customs, 488–490
mathematics in, influence on Hellenistic
    Judaism, 47
medical texts from, 1911–1912, 1915
medicine in, 1918, 1923
  influence on Hellenistic Judaism,
    48–49
monetary exchanges in, 1493
Nineveh captured by, 1103
palace regimes, 403–405
personal identification in, 487–488
populations deported from, 821, 1213
populations slain by Assurbanipal, 1890
record-keeping in, 656
scholarship in, influence on Hellenistic
    Judaism, 52–53
social institutions in, Greek writers on,
    58–60
social organization
  Kassite era, 928
  Old Babylonian period, 928
Sumerian domination of, 843
Syro-Palestinian vassals of, 1197
temples. *See* Temples, Babylonian
textile industry, 863
trade, with Egypt, 920
under Achaemenids, 826
under Assyrians, administration of, 965
under Esarhaddon, 824–825
under Nabu-apla-iddina, 823
under Shulgi, 844
under Sumu-la-el, 813
under Tiglath-Pileser III, 824
unit of road distance in, 1402
Urartians and, 1145

Uruk period, 801, 804–805
wagon use in, 1402
wine in, 199
witchcraft in, influence on Hellenistic
    Judaism, 50–51
Babyloniaca, 2342. *See also* Berossus,
    Chaldean priest
comparison to other flood narratives,
    2346–2347
as Greek history of Mesopotamia,
    2342
historiography in, 62–64
on swelling of earth's underground
    waters, 2345
"Babyloniamania," premodern European,
    factors discouraging, 67
Babylonian architecture
influence of, 71, 76–77
in Susa, 821
Babylonian art. *See also* Sculpture,
    Babylonian
reliefs, in Nineveh, 824
Uruk period, 800–801, 804
Babylonian Empire. *See* Neo-Babylonian
    Empire
*The Babylonian Job. See Poem of the
    Righteous Sufferer*
Babylonian language
chronological subdivisions of, 2119
cuneiform script for, 85
Eshnunna expansionism and, 813
literary dialect of, 2119
surviving texts, 2119
Babylonian literature
genres, 2194–2195
Hebrew Bible and, 98
Kassite period, 926–928
  collection and editing of, 926
  pessimism in, 927
  themes, 926–927
Old Babylonian mythology, 1825
Old Babylonian Version of *Gilgamesh
    Epic*, 2328–2330
"pseudo-autobiography" genre,
    2331–2332
Uruk period, 804–805
Babylonian mythology. *See also* Creation
    myths, Babylonian
on creation of humankind, 38
creation theme, 1827–1834
on destruction of humankind,
    38–39
development of meaning in, 1834
epic combats in, 1834
gods as portrayed in, 36
Greek myths and, 35–40
literary, 1825–1826
  on creation of human race, 1833
on man's loss of immortality, 38
matching numbers to gods, 912

Bittel, Kurt, as Boğazköy excavation
    director, 2769–2772, 2775
bītu (the Akkadian word), 1209
bītum (house), administration of, 878–879
Bitumen, in Mesopotamian construction,
    1545
Bit-Yakin tribe, Assyrian conflicts, 950
Bit-Zamani. *See* Amedu
Black, J. A., **2197–2209**
Black arts, the. *See also* Magic; Witchcraft
    Babylonian, 1896–1901
    Babylonian and Hellenistic Jewish
        practices, 50–51
Black magic. *See* Black arts, the
Black Obelisk of Shalamaneser III
    homage to the king, 2492
    Israelite apparel pictured on, 643
    textiles depicted in, 1585
Black Sea, in late Pleistocene, 125
Blacksmiths, 1514–1515, 1517
Blegen, Carl W., 1122
Bleiberg, Edward, **1373–1385**
Blenkinsopp, Joseph, **1309–1319**
The Blinding of Truth by Falsehood,
    1703–1704
Bloodguilt, 627–628
Blood offerings. *See* Offerings
Boatmen, of Lagash, 1421
Boats. *See* River craft; Sailboats; Ships,
    seagoing
Boatwrights
    construction techniques of, in Egypt,
        1423
    Phoenician, 1430
    wooden boat construction techniques of,
        1422
Bodrum. *See* Halicarnassus
Body, human. *See also* Human form in art
    Egyptian knowledge of, 1790
    Mesopotamian word lists for parts of,
        2311
Boğazköy. *See* Khattusha
Bolkar Maden, silver mining at, 260
Bone artifacts, production of, 1550
Bookkeeping techniques. *See* Accounting
    techniques
Book of Amduat
    depiction of time, 1722
    heavenly journey in, 1768–1769
    twelfth hour of the night, 1722
Book of Caverns
    heavenly journey in, 1768–1769
    punishment of the damned in, 1769
Book of Gates
    depiction of time, 1722
    heavenly journey in, 1768–1769
Book of Kells, "Chi Rho" monogram,
    Babylonian-Mesopotamian motifs
    in, 74
Book of Komit, 2215

The Book of the Cow of Heaven,
    1707–1708, 2230
    Hathor's drunkenness in, 2555
    source and content, 2228–2229
Book of the Dead, 1711, 2207, 2759
    Amamet the Devourer in, 1769
    burial of lesser personages, 1769
    creatures of, 1719
    depictions of beyond in, 1719–1720
    heart scarab in mummification, 1766
    judgment scene, vignettes, 1721
    Negative Confession, 376, 1768
    place of annihilation, 1719
    on *ushabtis*, 1773
Book of the Giants, Gilgamesh in, 2335
The Book of Traversing Eternity, 12
Books
    Egyptian, House of Life sacred,
        1747–1748
    wax writing board, 2269–2270
Books of the Netherworld, 1711,
    1718–1723
    central theme, 1718–1719
    Lake of Fire, 1719
Booty. *See* Pillage
Borchardt, Ludwig, 752, 755
Borghouts, J. F., **1775–1785**
Borsippa (Birs Nimrud)
    Ea-iluta-bani family archives, 1476,
        1478–1480
    misidentified as Tower of Babel, 69
    temple of Nabu, library of, 2206
Boscawen, W. St. Chad, on Deluge
    Tablet, 99
Bossert, H. T., work on hieroglyphic
    Luwian, 2775–2776
Botanists, role in archaeological research,
    2718–2719
Botta, Paul-Émile
    excavations of, 85, 96
    Monuments of Niniveh, 77
Bottéro, Jean, **2293–2303**
Boucharlat, Rémy, **1335–1353**
Boulaq papyri, 1374
Boustrophedon writing, 2120, 2381, 2390
Bow and arrow. *See* Archery, in warfare
Bow drill, for seal-making, 1593, 1594
Bracelets, Egyptian, 1607–1608,
    1610–1612
Brahmi script, decipherment of, 88
Braidwood, Robert, 2717–2718
Brak. *See* Taidu
Brass, accidental production of, 1502
Brazil, alleged Phoenician presence in,
    1331
Bread
    Babylonian, 496
    Egyptian, wages measured in,
        1379–1380
    Hittite, 583
    Israel, 639

    measurements, baking value units
        (Egyptian *psw*), 1379
    preparation techniques, 195–197
    temple needs for, 446
    types of, 196–197
Breasted, James Henry, 752, 1754
    Ancient Records of Egypt, 2758
    Iraq expeditions planned by, 2730–2731
Breast-feeding, in Egypt, 376–377
Brentjes, Burchard, **1001–1021**
Briant, Pierre, **517–528**
Brick grid
    Achaemenid, 2514–2516
        in Archer frieze at Susa, 2514–2516
        brickfist, 2515
        metrological equivalents of
            Persepolitan fist and forearms in,
            2516
        Old Persian mathematical ratios and,
            2514
        origins of, 2519
    Mesopotamian, 2513, 2513–2514
        as architectural and artistic standard,
            2514
Bricks. *See also* Mud-brick
    Achaemenid, frit, 2519
    Bactrian, 1072
        large unbaked, 1073
    Elamite, Achaemenid frit bricks and,
        2519
    enameled, first use of, 2598
    Mesopotamian
        making, 423–424
        standard proportions, 2513–2514
        as metrological standard in art and
            architecture, 2519
Bride-price. *See also* Dowries
    in Babylonia, 489
    Greek views of, 59
    Hittite. *See* kušata (bride-price)
Brides. *See* Marriage
Bridewealth, in Mesopotamia, 480
Bridges, in Mesopotamia, 439
Bristlecone pine, chronologies based on
    tree-ring studies of, 654
British Association for the Advancement of
    Science, 1511
British Isles, mining sites in, 1502
Bronze
    Anatolian production of, Assyrian
        imports in, 864–865
    casting and forging techniques, 1077
    early use at Troy, 1125
    in Hittite weaponry, 548
    Luristan culture, dating of, 1013
    Neo-Assyrian ingots, 1489
Bronze Age
    Aramaean expansionism in, 1281
    end of, 1100, 1516
    Hittite-Greek contacts in, 1117
    Mediterranean coast, 821

Bronze Age (*continued*)
  metals trade in, 1511–1514
    Anatolia, 1087
  Omani copper deposits and, 1506
  in Syro-Palestinian area, 1196,
      1199–1208, 1213–1214
  territorial states of, 1212–1213
  western Iran, 987–988
  in western Iran, 986–988
Bronze industry
  international trade crisis and, 1515
  in Mesopotamia, 1505
  tin in, 1506–1511
    from Anatolia, 1087
Bronzeware
  Bactrian
    dating of, 1007
    Elamite influence, 1007
    metal ax, *1007*
    Mitannian art and, 1008
  elemental analysis of, 1511–1512
  Neo-Assyrian casts, 1491
  Oman Peninsula, 1st millennium BCE,
      1346
  Phrygian, belts, 1154
  production of casts, 1517
Bronzeworkers, social status in
    Mesopotamia, 417, 459
Broom (plant), 156
Brothels. *See also* Prostitutes and
    prostitution
  Elamite holy (*aštam*), 1960, 1964
Brother gods, Egyptian, alphabetical list of
    names of, 1736–1740
Brothers, in Israelite family unit, 2783
Browne, Thomas, *The Garden of
    Cyrus,* 72
Brtakāmya, Median god, 1968
Brueghel, Pieter, the Elder, Babylon
    depicted by, 75
Brugsch, Heinrich, 2756
Brush, rush, for writing, 2211
Brutus, Roman general, siege of Xanthus,
    1171
Bryce, Trevor R., **1161–1172**
Buccellati, Giorgio, **1685–1696**
Buckelkeramik, 1127
Budge, Ernest Wallis, 2759
  on German interest in near eastern
    studies, 96
Buffalo, late prehistoric, 131–132
Builders of the Pyramids (Stadelmann),
    719–734
Building materials. *See also* Bricks; Stone-
    working
  earth, at Mari Palace of Zimri-Lim, 886
  marble, introduction into Phoenicia by
    Greeks, 2680–2681
  in Mesopotamia, 423–424
  mud-brick, in Mesopotamia, 2671

  stone, in Levant, 2671–2672, 2677
  wood, in Levant, 2671–2672, 2677
Bulgaria
  copper mining in, 1503
  gold from, 1508
Bull
  Egyptian worship of. *See* Apis Bull
  as motif in Levant, 2685
    Aegean inspiration for, 2685
  tail as Egyptian royal symbol, 275–276
Bullae
  as bookkeeping devices, 2183–2184
  defined, 2772
  with Hittite royal seals, Güterbock's
    work on, 2772–2773
  shapes of, 2269
Bull of Heaven (Sumerian mythological
    character), 2330, 2332–2333
Bundahishn, apocalypticism in, 2089
Bureaucracy. *See administration* entries
    under particular countries; Officials
BUR.GI (offering ceremony), 398
Burglary, Hittite law, 557
BUR.GUL (seals), 1601
Burial practices. *See* Funerary beliefs and
    practices; Tombs
Burial rites. *See* Funerary beliefs and
    practices
Burial sites. *See also* Cemeteries; Tombs
  in Basta, 794
  in Dinkha Tepe, 990
  in Hajji Firuz, 984–985
  Mesopotamian, 1885
    in southern cities, 242
  mounds
    Egyptian, 367–368
    in Transcaucasia, 1056
  Mycenaean, 1514
  pottery found in, 1553
  dating cities from, 1561
Burna-Buriash II, Kassite king
  Assur-uballit and, 820
  correspondence with Akhenaten, 1469
Burnishing, in pottery making, 1545
Burnouf, Eugène, decipherment of Old
    Persian cuneiform, 83
Business. *See* Merchants; Private
    enterprise; Trade
Butehamon, Egyptian scribe, egalitarian
    viewpoint of, 2220
Buto (Tell al-Fara'in)
  discovery of cones for wall mosaic at,
    304
  Predynastic sites at, 682–683, 686–687
  urbanization of, 687
Butzer, Karl W., **123–151**
Buying and selling
  in Achaemenid Babylonia, 1475–1485
    annuities and, 1484–1485
    archives of Ea-iluta-bani of Borsippa,
      1478–1480

  archives of Egibi of Babylon, 1480
  archives of Iddin-Nabu of Babylon,
      1480
  archives of Murashu of Nippur,
      1480–1485
  contracts, 1476–1478
    as disguised rentals, 1477
    silver used in, 1478
  commercial activities of Iddin-Nabu
    family, 1480
  concepts of, 1376–1377
  Egyptian, records of, 1373–1377,
      1379–1380, 1384
  seals used for, 1453–1454
Büyükkale, map of, *1096*
B'w (manifestation), 1777
Byblos (Gebal, Jubayl)
  alliance with '*Apīru,* 589
  cylinder seals, 2689–2690
  divinities, 2034
  Egyptian trade and, 1200, 1379
  Phoenician inscriptions from, 2123,
      2387
  pseudo-hieroglyphs of, 91–92
    decipherment attempts, 92
  royal tombs of
    artifacts with Aegean connections,
      2683
    Egyptianizing decorative arts in,
      2682–2683, 2685
  sarcophagus of Ahiram, 2678
  shipping to, 1511
  Syro-Palestinian deities of, 2047
Byron, George Gordon, Lord
  Babylonian themes in, 73
  Hebrew Melodies (poems), 73
  Sardanapalus (play), 73
Byzantine art, European art influenced by,
    Babylonian-Mesopotamian motifs in,
    74–75

C

Cabinetmakers. *See* Carpenters and
    cabinetmakers
Cactus, 157
Cafzeh Cave, Israel, *Homo sapiens*
    remains, 666
Cairo Geniza. *See* Geniza texts
Cairopol-Cyreskhata (Ura-Tyube),
    architectural structures, 1074
Calendar, Assyrian, lunisolar, 1932
  synchrony between lunar months and
    solar year, 1932
Calendar, Babylonian, 656–657,
    1931–1932
  automatic lunisolar, 46–47
  basic intervals structuring, 1931
  fixed-star, 1929–1930

proto-Tocharian migration, 1069
rise of states
  archaeological evidence, 1071–1072
  construction techniques, 1072–1073
  settlement types, 1071
  textual evidence, 1070–1071
settlement patterns
  comparison, Transcaucasia, 1064
  north-south migration, 1062
tin sources in, 1506
Central Asia and the Caucasus in the Bronze Age (Kohl), **1051–1065**
Centralization, political. *See also* Political organization, decentralized
  in Akkadian Empire, 810
  and decentralization, alternating cycles of, 253
  Ebla, 1221–1223
  in Egypt, 694–695, 1383
  irrigation agriculture and, 2716–2717
  in Mesopotamia, literary reflections of, 2296
  national/territorial states distinguished in, 1212–1213
  Sumerian, 844, 846
  in Syro-Palestinian area, 1198–1199, 1209, 1215–1217
  trade in relation to, 1398
  in Ur, 812–813
Central Taurus project, 1512–1513
Ceramics. *See* Pottery
Cereal grains. *See also* Beer; Bread
  Babylonian administration of, 801
  beer brewed from, 197–199
  contamination of, by toxic molds, 1922
  growing, 178, 180
  harvesting of, 195
  Hittite consumption of, 583–584
  Hittite imports of, 1097
  Hittite transactions with, 580
  monetary transactions with, 1488, 1491–1492
  origins and domestication of, 191
  preparation for use in diet, 195–199
  processing of, in ancient Palestine, 792
  progenitors of, 157–158
  in redistributive system, 353
  renting, in Elam, 1964
  as staple of diet, 195
  storage of, 439
  stores of
    as object of thievery, 413
    temple estates, 445
  wild, 158
  yields, 183–184
Černý, Jaroslav, Egyptian literary studies of, 2758–2759
Chadic languages, 2136–2137
Chaeremon, on Egyptian priests, 1735, 1745

Chagar Bazar
  copper mold from, *1546*
  textile production documentation from, 1581
Chagha Maran, Chalcolithic pottery of, *986*
Chairs. *See also* Stools
  Assyrian, with conical bases, 1658
  backed, 1652–1654, 1660
  Canaanite and Israelite households, 637
  carved sphinx legs, 1655
  with conical bases, 1658
  Egyptian royal, 1631
  ivory sheathing, 1661
  Syrian, with shell inlay, 1652–1653
Chalcolithic era
  counters. *See* Tokens
  metallurgy in ancient Palestine, 1504
  western Iran, 985–986
Chalcopyrite, *1514*
Chaldea. *See* Neo-Babylonian Empire
Chaldean dynasty of Babylon. *See* Neo-Babylonian Empire
Chambers, pyramid. *See also* Pyramids, Egyptian
  Egyptian
    building of, 721–733, *733*
    funerary temples and, 731–733
Champollion, Jean-François
  decipherment of Egyptian hieroglyphs, 17, 20, 84–85
  Lettre à M. Dacier, 2755
Chancellors, Sumerian. *See* SUKKAL (SUKAL).MAH
Chantre, Ernest, excavation of tablets at Boğazköy, 2766
Chants, religious, Ugaritic song to Baal, 2053–2054
Chaos, worship to forestall, 1731
Charcoal, in steelmaking, 1515
Charioteer class
  judiciary and, 941
  pauperization of, 941–942
Chariots and chariotry
  advantages of cavalry over, 297
  Assyrian, 418
  Egyptian, 290–291
    crew size, 297
    drawbacks of, 295–297
    economic aspects, 296–297
    horse strength, 296–297
    use as offensive weapons, 295
  Hittite
    clothing and weaponry, 548
    purpose of, 548
    terms of service, 547
  horsedrawn, 747
  Kassite, technological innovations, 925–926
  Mesopotamian, 414–417

Persian, 422
Philistine, 297, 1269
second millennium, 808
Sumerian, statue of chariot, 2739, *2740*
Charity
  Hittite edicts concerning, 2368
  Syro-Palestinian, temple centers of, 2051
Charms. *See also* Black arts, the
  beneficent, 2078
  in the Bible, 2078
  found in tombs, 2079
  harmful, 2078
Charon, mythical ferryman, Mesopotamian equivalent of, 1886
Charpin, Dominique, **807–829**
Chemistry, evidence for, 2060
Chemosh, Moabite divinity, 2034, 2047. *See also* Kamish (Kammush)
  cult of, 1315
  dedication of Ataroth and Nebo to, 1316
Cheops, king of Egypt. *See* Khufu, king of Egypt
Chephren (Khafre, Rekhaef), king of Egypt
  images of, 732, 2581
  pyramid of, building of, 732
  statue of, 275, *1727*, 2548
Chickens
  breeds of, 220
  domestication of, 220
  Israel, 639
Chiera, Edward, 2743
  Oriental Institute's *Assyrian Dictionary* and, 2744
Childbirth. *See* Pregnancy and childbirth
Childe, Vere Gordon, 1517
Childlessness
  in Babylonia, 491–492
  Egypt
    as grounds for divorce, 373–374
    social stigma, 376
Children. *See also* Funerary beliefs and practices, children; Stillborn children
  Egypt
    care of, 378
    play, 378
  Hittite, 579
    ancestral actions and, 1107
    of dissolved marriages, 574
    inheritance by, 576
    rituals associated with, 575
    social status of, 573
  Mesopotamian
    adoption of, 491–492
    diseases and illnesses of, 1917
    games of, 498
    nursing of, 491
    relationships with parents, 494

Crete (*continued*)
  Mycenaean Greek influence, 1441
  oxhide ingots and, 1513
  Philistines in, 1269
  Phoenician presence, 1324
  polities and economies
    agricultural, 1437
    archaeological evidence, 1436–1438
    settlement of, 1437–1438
    trade links with Egypt, 3
Crime. *See* Homicide; Robbery
Crocus, 584
Croesus, king of Lydia
  alliances, 1173
  defeat by Cyrus the Great, 976, 1039,
    1174
  family, 1174–1175
  gifts to Greek sanctuaries, 1176–1177,
    1181
  Greeks vs., 1104
  historical sources for, 1173
  legacy of, 1180–1181
  Lycian campaign, 1162
  military conquests, 1173
  palace at Sardis, 1180
  relations with Greece, 1173–1174
  Sardis gold and, 1508
Croesus of Sardis and the Lydian
  Kingdom of Anatolia (Greenewalt),
  1173–1183
Crowns, Egyptian dual, 680
Crozer Texts (Sumerian), 2750
Cryer, Frederick H., **651–664**
Cryptography, development of, 2191
Ctesias, Greek doctor
  history of Persia, 1039
  Persica
    influence of, 61, 63–64
    near eastern history in, 60, 64
Cubit rod, length of, 1810, 2509–2510
  standards compared, 2517
Cuisine, diet and, 213
Cult, meaning of in ancient Near East,
  1858
Cult images
  Egyptian, inner temple, 1732–1733
  Israelite, role in warfare, 1318
  Mesopotamian, rituals for, 1903
Cult of the dead
  Anatolian, sculpture in the round and,
    2655–2656
  Egyptian, 350, 1772
    as extension of family life, 348
Cults
  Central Asian
    burial, 1081
    of fire, 1081
  Egyptian
    activities determined by sacred
      calendars, 1775
    community participation in, 350

continuity in, 1776
list of gods and centers of, 1736–1740
  of Ramesses II, 769–770
relationship with divine in, 1775
solar, 1776
vs. magic, 1775–1776
Elamite, priests and, 1964–1965
Hittite, dance and, 2664–2668
Hurrian, influence on Anatolian religion,
  2004
Israelite
  replacement of Canaanite religion by,
    612
  shrines of, 611
Mesopotamian
  anthropomorphic, 1862
  chthonic, 1862
  common peoples' participation in,
    1866–1867
  cycles of nature and, 1862
  functionaries involved in, 1864
  in prehistoric society, 1867
  temple and, 1861–1862
Philistine, 1275–1277
  artifacts, 1276–1277
  sacrificial altars, 1276
Sumerian, state, 1869
Ugaritic, royal participation in, 1262
Cult stands, Philistine
  with bronze wheels, 1277
  Canaanite influence, 1276
  with human figures, 1276
Cultural contact, pottery as evidence of,
  1562–1564
Culture, individual consciousness and,
  1685–1686
Cultures, succession of, archaeological
  theories concerning, 683–684
Cult vase (Babylonian artifact), 801
Cuneiform. *See also* Archives,
  Mesopotamian; Behistun inscription;
  Old Persian cuneiform
  alphabetic writing from Ugarit,
    2384–2385
  Aramaic sources in, 821
  archives and libraries, 2206
    from Ebla, 2788
    nature and locations, 2197
    from Nuzi, 2782
    physical characteristics of, 2199–2200
  Boğazköy finds, 2766–2768
  changes over time, 2314
  content of texts in, 86
  creation of in Early Dynastic period,
    1406
  cylinder seals and, 1593
  decipherment of, 70, 85–87
    "translation competition" for, 87
  declining use of, 828
  for diplomacy and trade, 2412
  documentation for, 2181

evolution of, 2184–2187
  expansion of, 2186
  as written lingua franca, 2786
  Greco-Babyloniaca tablets, dating
    of, 44
  image not valued in, 2185–2186
  invention of, in Gilgamesh epics,
    2320–2321
  of Khattusha, 264
    inscription, 2152
  limitations of, 2313
  Mesopotamia, 2417–2418
  Mesopotamian tablets, and shaping of
    text, 2192–2193
  Nippur findings, 1481
  photographic techniques for recording,
    2771
  preservation of tablets, 2199
  private tablets, rarity of after reign of
    Xerxes I, 1476
  for record keeping, Sumerian,
    2101–2105, 2270
  scribal schools for, 2270–2272
  Second Type. *See* Elamite
  for Semitic languages, 902
  signs, student lists of, 2270–2271
  spread of, 2205
  for Sumerian language, 2310
  Third Type. *See* Akkadian
  types of, 85
  on Urartian ceramics, 1144
  use for Anatolian language subgroup,
    2151–2156
  widespread interest in findings, 2698
Cuneiform scholarship
  Mesopotamian cultural influence and,
    2417–2418
  of scribes, Mesopotamian, 2274–2276
Cupbearers
  Assyrian. *See rab šaqê*
  Hittite, 1991
Cupellation
  at Habuba al-Kabira, 1503
  lead by-products of, 1502
Currency. *See* Money and coinage
Curse of Agade (Akkad), 250, 839, 1871,
  2284, 2286
  Naram-Sin and, 811
  royal ideology in, 396
Curses
  against inscription effacement, 2425,
    2428–2430
  Assyrian, to assure succession, 956
  for breaching covenants, 618
  from breaking an oath, Babylonian
    influence on Jewish, 49
  Hittite, in Kumarbi Cycle, 1975
  sins and, Babylonian beliefs on,
    1898–1899
Curses upon Egypt of the Sixth Year of
  King Bocchoris, apocalypticism in,
  2087

Curtius, Ludwig
  Antike Kunst, 2699
  observations on Assyrian reliefs, 2699,
    2701
  on seal engravers' inventions,
    2708–2709
  on statue from court of Gudea, 2706
  on stela of Naram-Sin, 2706
  study of Mesopotamian art, 2709–2710
Cusae (al-Qusiya, Qis), tombs of Meir,
  cult center of Hathor at, 2564–2565
Cuscuta, 496
  as Babylonian flavoring agent, 497
Cushitic languages
  major groups, 2136
  morphology, 2136
Cyaxares. *See* Uakshater, king of the
  Medes
Cybele, Anatolian divinity, 1176, 1179
  Kubaba as, 1986
  rosette symbol, 1663
  statuary group, 2658
  Temple at Sardis, 1180
Cyclades, polities and economies
  agricultural, 1437
  archaeological evidence, 1436–1438
"Cycle of the disappearing god," human
  procreation and, 575
Cyclical patterns. *See* Diurnal cycles
Cylinder seals. *See also* Seals
  Akkadian, 2696
    Etana and the eagle story on, 1850
    Gilgamesh legend pictured on, 1851
    religious iconography, 1842–1843,
      1846
    scenes of bird-man brought before
      water-god on, 1851–1852
  Anatolian, 1678
  association with writing, 1593
  Babylonian, 800
  contact between Babylonia and Indus
    Valley, 1458
  death by, 1598
  depictions of temple activities on, 449
  description, 1591
  of Dilmun, 1453–1454
    economic transactions sealed with,
      1453–1454
  distribution of, 1592–1593
  Egyptian
    development of writing and, 1601
    as symbol of power and official status,
      1601
  imagery, representations of craftsmen
    in, 456
  impressions, 1591, *1592*, *1593*
  as information source on political
    history, 2690
  jar stoppers impressed with, *1601*
  Kassite
    iconography, 1847

  pictorial motifs, 1008
  prayer themes inscribed on, 928
  styles of, 457
  magical powers, 1600
  manufacture, on wall reliefs, *1593–1594*
  material used for, association with fate
    of owner, 1595
  Mesopotamian
    of copper, 1504–1505
    erotic art on, *2523–2524, 2524–2525,*
      2527
    of figure in "Netzrock," *2711,*
      2711–2712
    flight of Etana depicted on, *2708,*
      2708
    imagery, 1594–1595
    impression of Ishtar, 927
    Middle Assyrian scenes, *2704, 2704*
    Mitannian Empire abstract art on,
      2704, 2705
    viewing, 2704
    Old Babylonian, *2704–2705, 2705*
      iconography, 1847
      Ishtar on, 1843–1844
      monsters and demons on, 1847
    origin and early development of,
      1592–1593
    Persian, 2633–2634
    of Darius I, 1018
  rubbed down and redesigned, 459
  Sumerian, furniture depicted on, *1648,*
    1648, 1650
  suspended as necklace, *1597*
  Syrian, erotic art on, *2523–2524, 2527*
  Syro-Palestinian, 2689–2690
    Egyptianizing elements, 2690
    Mesopotamian ideology and,
      2689–2690
    replacement by stamp seals, 2690
  on toggle pins and armlets, 642
  uses for, 1590, 1600
**Cylinder Seals and Scarabs in the
  Ancient Near East** (Pittman),
  1589–1603
Cymbals
  Egyptian, 2559
  Hittite, 2662
  Mesopotamian, 2604
Cypria, mythical flood accounts in, 2344
Cypriot script, decipherment of, 88
Cyprus
  Assyrian presence, 1327
  conflict with Sea Peoples, 1436
  copper deposits in, 1502, 1505, 1510,
    1513
  Egyptian gold trade with, 1493
  environment and climate, 1433–1434
  Hittite conquest of, 550, 1097
  human colonization, 1434
  iron use on, 1515, 1517
  ironworking on, 1516

  links to ancient Near East, 1435,
    1446–1447
  merchants from. *See* Merchants, Cypriot
  multiethnic population, 1435
  Phoenician colonization, 1324
  polities and economies
    archaeological evidence, 1435–1436
    centralization of control, 1436
    documentary evidence, 1435
  vegetation of, 157
Cyrenaica, Egyptian attempt to conquer,
  1191
Cyropaedia, 1040
Cyrus II, king of Persia. *See* Cyrus the
  Great, king of Persia
Cyrus Cylinder, 1039–1040
Cyrus the Great, king of Persia. *See also*
  Pasargardae (residence of Cyrus)
  in Achaemenid kinglist, 1016
  adaptation of local customs and religion,
    1040
  building program, 1040
  conquests
    of Asia Minor, 1017
    Babylonia, 826, 976–977, 1003, 1017,
      1367, 1397
  Croesus and, 1104, 1174
  cultural and political background, 1040
  death of
    activities following, 1070
    end of Persian expansion, 1017
  declares himself Assyrian vassal, 1015
  defeats Astyages, 1016
  expansionist intentions of, 2618
  genealogy, 518
  location of rule, 1016–1017
  Median conflicts, 1039
  Palace P, *2619*, 2619–2620
  Palace S, 2618–2619
  portrayal of, 2617–2618
  prophetic dream of, 2618
  religion of, 1966
  tomb of, 1040, 2617, *2618*
Cyrus the Younger, king of Persia
  arming of chariots, 295
  brings Orontas before tribunal, 524
  Mesopotamia under, 827
  punishment, 525
Czechoslovakia, lead from, 1512

D

Dagan, Mesopotamian divinity
  bestows "banks of the Euphrates" on
    rulers, 400
  prestige of, 1291
  Sargon and, 810
  symbols of, 1846

Egyptian
  caloric value of, 1380
  of workers, 1379–1380
  fat in, fattening animals for, 211
  Hittite, 583–584
  origin of agriculture and dietary stress,
    2726
  social distinctions and, 213
  vegetables in, 199
Diffusion, cultural, importance of, 2788
Dignitaries, Hittite. *See Nakkeš*
Dijk, Jacobus van, **1697–1709**
Dilbat, Babylonian annexation of, 813
Dilmun
  civilization of, 1342–1343
  decline of, 1342
  divinities worshiped in, 1342
  emergence of, Indus Valley civilization
    and, 1342
  location of, 1455
  Mesopotamian copper trade and, 1506
  name changes, 1455
  seals from, 1453–1454
  settlements of, 1342–1343
  Sumerian myth *Enki and the World
    Order* on, 1452–1453
  temples of, 1342
  trade
    with Mari, 1454
    with Mesopotamia, 1425, 1452–1454
    Sumerian, in wood, 809
    with Ur, 813, 1454
Dimai (Soknopaiou), papyri from, 2207
Dimpikug, mythical scribe. *See*
  Geshtinanna, mythical scribe
dîn (judgment), 619
Dingil'dzhe, winemaking, 1077
DINGIR-sign (^d), Elamite, signifier of
  divinity, 1964, 1966, 1968
Dinkha Tepe
  Iron Age, 989, 990, 992
  Khabur ware of, 989
  Late Bronze Age, 988
Diodorus Siculus
  on Egypt, 15
  on Mesopotamia, 64
Dion, Paul E., **1281–1294**
Diorite
  import of, 1539–1540
  sculptures of, 2591, 2592
  source of, 2591
Diplomacy. *See also* Matrimonial alliances
  Assyrian, 960–961, 964–965
  gift giving and, 1380–1381
Diplomats. *See also* Messengers
  delivery of messages, 1468
  housing and gifts from recipient rulers,
    1469–1470
  returning home, 1470
  travel and transportation, 1466–1468
Diptychon, 1128

Disasters, natural. *See* Natural
  catastrophes
Disease
  diagnosis of, 1866
  during siege warfare, 552
  in Egyptian mythology, 1707
  etiology of, in Egyptian medicine,
    1788–1789
    putrefaction and, 1788
  infectious, in Mesopotamia, 1922
  knowledge of. *See* Medicine
  spiritual origin of, 1866
Displaced persons. *See* Deportations
*The Dispute Between a Man Tired of His
  Life and His Ba. See The Dialogue of
  a Man with His Ba*
**Distant Shores: Ancient Near Eastern
  Trade with South Asia and
  Northeast Africa** (Potts), 1451–1463
Distribution centers, Sumerian, 845
Diurnal cycles, in Egyptian mythology,
  1706
Divination. *See also* Black arts, the;
  Celestial divination; Extispicy;
  Witchcraft
  Akkadian texts, 2299
  animal sacrifice in, 1693
  appearance of sheep's liver, 1821
  Aramaean religion devoid of, 1292
  Canaanite and Israelite, 2071–2074
    Balaam, 2072–2073
    biblical references, 2072
    dreams, 2072
    extra-biblical evidence, 2073
    by lots, 2072
    means of, 2071–2072
    teraphim, 2073–2074
    terms for, 2072
  Egyptian
    calendars, 1782–1783
    by celestial phenomena, 1783
    dreams, 1783
    lecanomancy, 1783
    oracles, 1782
  Hittite, 1982, 1989, 2013, 2015–2017
    auguria oblativa and *auguria
      impetrativa*, 2013
    dreams, 2013, 2015
    omens and oracles, 2015–2017
  Lycian, interpreting fish behavior,
    1167–1168
  Mesopotamian, 1817
    Old Babylonian treatises, 1822
    religious beliefs and, 1895–1896
    in Sumerian royal hymnody, 853
  monotheism and rejection of, 2075
  rational universal order and, 1687–1688
  religion and, 2080
  Ugaritic, texts on, 2071
Divine judgment
  human execution of, 1861
  in Israelite wisdom literature, 2450

Divine oracles. *See* Oracles
Diviners
  Babylonian, 1904, 1906
  literacy of, 2188
Divine will, in didactic poetry, 2448
Divinities. *See also* Great goddess;
    Temples; *"divinities" subentry under
    religion; particular divinities; religion
    entry under particular countries;
    under particular divinities*
  attendants to, 444–445
  "care and feeding of." *See* Worship
  differentiation of kings from, 401
  divine kingship, 2044–2045
  freedom to act without external
    restraints, 2447
  gold associated with, 1605
  in the human world, 1731, 1896,
    2043–2044
  illness attributed to acts of, 1912–1913
  inheritance of, nations as, 2048
  intermediary, 804
  mythological monsters associated with,
    at city gates, 2673, 2677–2679
  national or patron, 2056–2057
  of the netherworld, 2021–2022
  piety directed towards, 1693–1694
  predictability controlled by, 1692
  restriction of wisdom to, 2447
  seal ownership, 1596
  symbols of, 1837, 1838–1840
    horns, 75
  theologies of exaltation of, 2056–2057
  worshiped with female consort, 1318
Division of labor. *See* Labor, division of
Divorce. *See also* Marriage
  Achaemenid Empire, 520
  Babylonian law, and Hellenistic
    Judaism, 45–46
  Egypt
    adultery not grounds for, 358
    demotic marriage settlements,
      373–374
    grounds for, 373–374
    property settlement, 372
    social status and, 374–375
  Hittite, 574
    between slaves and free persons, 565
    legal aspects, 560
  Israelite, requirements for, 622
  Jewish Hellenistic law, Babylonian
    influence on, 45–46
  Mesopotamian, 480–481, 490
  Ugaritic, between foreign powers,
    1259–1260
Diyala. *See also* Eshnunna
  systematic survey of, 2746–2747
Diyarbakir. *See* Amida
Djedkare Isesi, king of Egypt, as literate,
  2214

Djedkhonsefonkh, Mythological Papyrus of, *1712*
Djed (pillar of stability), 276
  as symbolic representation of Osiris, 1724
Djefaihapi, Egyptian governor, 741
Djeho, Egyptian dwarf, autobiography of, 2247
Djehutynefer, tomb of, Theban domestic chores depicted in, 384
Djer, king of Egypt
  iconographic depiction, 1712
  tomb of, jewelry from, 1607
Djeserkare, tomb of, painting of religious celebration on, 369
Djet, king of Egypt, stela of, *304*, 2536
Djoser, king of Egypt
  burial complex of, building of, 721–724, *723*
  importance of, 719, 733
  Step Pyramid of, 305, 696
Djzeserkaresoneb, Theban tomb of, musical scene in, 2565–2566
DNA analysis, in bioarchaeology, 153
Documents. *See* Archival documents
Dogs
  attitudes toward, 219
  breeds not established, 219
  progenitors of, 170, 218–219
Doğubayazit, rock relief, 2658
Dolerite
  in sarcophagi, 1884
  in stonemasonry, 1543
Domestic animals. *See* Animal husbandry; Animals
Domestic arts. *See* Cookery; Craft arts; Pottery; Weaving
Domitian, Roman emperor, Egyptian cults and, 10
Donkeys
  burials of, 747
  domesticated, 206–207
    complex record of, 216
    ritual offerings of, 207
    urbanization in relation to, 212
    uses of, 216
  in Israelite ceremonies, 1204
  of temple estates, 447
The Doomed Prince. See The Prince and His Fates
Doorways, of palaces and temples, 309, 315
Dor. *See* Tell Dor
Dorians, ironmaking by, 1516
Dothan, Trude, **1267–1279**
Dowries. *See also* Bride-price
  Babylonia, 45, 489
    Greek views of, 59
    under Achaemenids, 1477, 1479
  Canaanite and Israelite, 645

Egypt, 373
  linens, 367
  in Hellenistic Judaism, Babylonian influence on, 45
Hittite. *See Iwaru* (dowries)
Mesopotamia, 479–480, 489, 498
  jewelry included in, 1635, 1642
  women's ownership of, 45
Draft animals
  prices of, 581
  in stone transport, 1543
Drainage systems, in Mesopotamia, 1922–1923
Drauga (lie), 523
Dravidian language, Elamite and, 2177
Dreams
  divination by, 1783, 2072
    in Hittite society, 2037, 2039
  handbooks for interpreting, 1783
  interpretation of, 1687
  in Mesopotamian literature, 2342
  as omens, Babylonian and Hellenistic Jewish, 51–52
  in prayers, historical texts, and oracles, 2015
  revelation by, Syro-Palestine, 2055
  soul concept and, 1892
  unfulfilled vows in, 2015
Drenkhahn, Rosemarie, **331–343**
Dress. *See* Clothing
Dresses, Canaanite and Israelite, 641–643
Drought. *See also* Climate change
  in Syro-Palestinian area, 1197
  tribal-state relations and, 1199
Drugs. *See* Pharmacopeia
Drums
  Hittite, 2662
  Mesopotamian, 2603–2604
    common terms for, 2604
    depictions of, 2603–2604
Dualism
  in ancient near eastern religions, 2781–2782
  in Egyptian mythology, 680–681, 684
Dublamakh shrine at Ur, temple recyling workshop, 460
Duby, Georges, 810
Dugong, 171
DUGUD (magistrate), 562
Duma oasis (al-Jawf)
  deities of, 1360
  Minaic graffito found near, 1360–1361
  religious festivals, 1359
Dumuzi, deified king of Uruk. *See also* Tammuz, Akkadian divinity
  cults of, 1868
  Inanna and, poetry cycles, 2472–2474
  in *Ishtar's Descent to the Netherworld*, 1889
  lamentations for, 1874
  marriage to Inanna, 1844

mourning rites for, 1883–1884
represented in art, 1846
in Sumerian royal hymnody, 849
Sumerian sacred marriage rite and, 847–848
Dumuzi's Dream, 2285–2286
Dung beetle. *See also* Scarabs
  imagery on scarabs, 1601
Dungeon of Daniel (Babil), 69
Dunne, John S., on Mesopotamian and Egyptian myth, 109
Duperron, Abraham Hyacinthe Anquetil, decipherment of Avestan and, 84
Dur-Kurigalzu ('Aqar Quf)
  building of, 919
  Kassite buildings at, 2740
  Kassite palace at, 433–434, 819
    murals, proportional ratios in, 2514
    terra-cotta head found at, 2594, *2594*
    wall paintings, 2596–2597
  temple to Enlil, 928
  as the Tower of Babel, 69
Dur-Samsu-iluna. *See* Tutub
Dur-Sharrukin (Khorsabad)
  capital established at, 1397
  construction of, 824
  excavations at, 2697
    19th century, 2730
    in 1930s, 2732–2734, 2745
  fortifications, 1532, *1533*
  palace of Sargon II, 434, *434*, 436
    decorative elements, 2598, 2599
    reliefs from, *1534*, 2586
    temple in, 427
  plan of city, 244–245
  resources concentrated in, 822
  temple facade, enameled bricks on, 2502
  temple of Nabu, 2197
    library of, 2206
  walls of, sculpted reliefs on, 2673
Dur-Untash (Choga Zanbil)
  building history, 1009–1010
  building plan, *1027*
  construction of, 1026–1027
  Elamite seal impression, *1002*
  gods with temples in, 1960–1963
  temples to Elamite divinities, 1027
  temple tower (ziggurat), 1010, 1026
Dušk- (the Hittite word), 584
The Duties of the Vizier, 355
Duwayr. *See* Lachish
Dwellers, social class, 942
Dwellings. *See* Houses, private
Dyeing industry
  in Egypt, 384
  of Israel, 1580, 1639
  of Phoenicia, 1575
Dyes. *See also* Pigments
  evidence for use of, 504
  murex, 172–173, 1575

sources of colors, 1575, 1581
technology of, 1575
Dynastic Prophecy
Book of Daniel and, 2092
cryptic language in, 2093
Dynasties. *See under* Kings; *particular*
countries

E

É (Sumerogram), 571
Ea, Mesopotamian divinity. *See also* Enki,
Mesopotamian divinity
in *Atrakhasis Myth*, 1833
in Babylonian Flood Story, 2334
in *Creation Epic*, 1834
as creator, 1819
in *Erra and Ishum*, 2341
in *Gilgamesh Epic*, 2340
in *Kingship of the god* KAL/LAMMA,
1979
in Kumarbi Cycle, 1974, 1976–1978
origin of human race concept, 1832
symbols of, *1839–1840*, 1841, *1848*
Eagle and the serpent, Mesopotamian and
European images of, 74–75
Ea-iluta-bani family, archives, 1476,
1478–1480
Eanāsir, Ur merchant, 1506
Eanatum, ruler of Lagash, 2697
military victories, divine parentage and,
397
victory stela of, 2584
Eanna Precinct. *See* Uruk (Warka), Eanna
Temple Precinct of
Eannatum, ruler of Lagash. *See* Eanatum,
ruler of Lagash
Early Transcaucasian Bronze Age Culture.
See Yanik culture
Early Uruk period. *See* Cities,
Mesopotamian, Early Uruk period
Earrings. *See under* Jewelry
Earthquakes
Crete, 1441
Rhodes, rebuilding after, 1442
Eastern Desert. *See* Arabia Deserta
Eastern Mediterranean
decipherment of ancient scripts of,
88–91
multilingualism in, 2412–2413, 2415
Ebabbar, temple of Shamash, Nabonidus'
restoration of, 974
Ebarat, Elamite king
claimed divine status, 1005–1006
established crown at Susa, 1025
Ebartid dynasty, 1025–1026
imposes religion on Susiana, 1025
rule in Susiana, 1006
Eber nāri, 826–827

Ebla (Tell Mardikh)
accounting documents from, 2202
labeling system, 2199–2200
administration of, 1223–1224
Amorites in texts from, 1232
ancestor worship, 2060
archives at, 1406, 2788
Eblaite texts in, 2119–2120
lexical texts from, 2306
literary tablets, 2281
partial interrelatedness of, 2202
Semitic language texts, 2282
Syro-Palestinian documents from,
1196
Area D temple at, 605
carvings on stone basins found at, 2678
cylinder seals in wood, 2690
Dagan cult at, 1291
Delmun shekel and, 1506
in Early Bronze Age, 1220
economy of, 1224–1226
gate complex, *1527*, *1528*
Great Palace, furniture from, 1652
historical overview of, 1219–1230
historical significance of, 807
luxury items in, 1508
in myth, 2374
Naram-Sin vs., 1200, 1216
official building of, 2673
Palace G at, 605–606
urbanization evidenced in, 1220
Palace Q at, 606
ramparts, 1526, *1528*
royal tombs of
Egyptianizing decorations in,
2682–2683
jewelry from, 2683, 2683–2684
Lord of the Goats tomb, 2683–2684
"Tomb of the Princess," 2683
silver holdings of, 1491
Syro-Palestinian theology and gods of,
2043, 2045–2046
temple at, ground plan of, 2674
textile production documented from,
1581
tribute to Sargon, 832
Ebla: A Third-Millennium City-State in
Ancient Syria (Milano), **1219–1230**
Eblaean religion
chthonic gods, 2045–2046
divinities, 1225, 2045–2046
Eblaite language, 2119–2120
classification of, 1233
reconstruction of, 2788
Ecclesiastes (Hebrew Bible)
contrasts craftsmen with scribes and
rulers, 459
good deeds in, 2453
on old age, 2449
Eclipses
royal substitutes and, 1885

significance of
to Assyrian kings, 953
to Hittite kings, 2016
Ecological deterioration. *See*
Environmental change
Ecology
characteristics of regions, archaeological
data and, 2721
requirements for study of, 2720
Economic exchange. *See* Exchange
Economic prosperity. *See* Prosperity
Economics, invention of writing in relation
to, 2183–2184, 2186–2187
Economic sanctions. *See* Embargoes
Economic transactions. *See* Buying and
selling; Trade
Economy. *See also particular countries*
and regions; Prices; Trade; Wages
activities reconstructed through
archaeological research, 1387–1388
agricultural productivity and, 186–188
changes in
revolutionary nature of, 1390
social and political phenomena in
relation to, 1387–1388
development of, in Neolithic period,
1389
political, development of, 1387
textiles and, 1587
texts regarding
problems in study of, 1388
sources of, 1388
Economy of Ancient Egypt (Bleiberg),
1373–1385
Economy of Ancient Western Asia
(Yoffee), **1387–1399**
Edessa region, stone reliefs, 2641–2642
Edfu (Idfu), 747
urbanization of, 687
edh-Dibaʿi. *See* Tell edh-Dibaʿi
Edict of Khattushili, 2369–2370
Edict of Telipinu (Decree of Telipinu,
Proclamation of Telipinu),
2368–2370, 2440–2441
administration of lands, 539–540
on Hittite courtiers, 1286
prescription for royal succession,
534–535
rules and standards in, 2369
Edicts, Hittite
Akkadian versions, 2370
animal imagery in, 2368
principles of state organization
established in, 2368–2369
role of divinities in, 2369
works of charity, 2368
Edom
Dedan and, 1362
gods of, 2047
Israelite control, 1309
Edomite language, 2123

Engraving, as Eighteenth Dynasty
innovation, 1617
Enheduana, daughter of Sargon
as high priestess, 833, 2497
installation by father, 401
as scribe and author, 2266
works of, 835–836, 2279–2280
temple hymn cycles, 846, 2604
Ēni mahanahi (mother of the gods), 1166
Enkheduanna. *See* Enheduana
Enkhegal, prince of Lagash-Girsu, money
transactions of, 1491
Enki, Mesopotamian divinity, 1860. *See
also* Ea, Mesopotamian divinity
in *Atrakhasis Myth*, 2337
in Babylonian parody, 2463
creation of man by, 1859
in *Eridu Genesis*, 2339–2340
iconography, 1843
in netherworld, 1889
as patron god of music, 2605
relations with Inanna and Enlil, 1868
Enki and Ninhursag, 1453, 1459
Enki and Ninmakh, creation of human
race in, 1833
Enki and the World Order, 482,
1452–1453, 2286
Enkidu, mythological figure, 1888, 2327
in *Gilgamesh Epic*, 2317, 2329, 2333
Old Babylonian, 2328–2329
antiprimitivistic concept as basis of,
2327
humanization of, 2328
Enki's Journey to Nippur, 2286
Enkomi, Cyprus
craft areas, 461
God Temple at, plan of, 2676
Enlightenment, the. *See* European
Enlightenment
Enlil, Mesopotamian divinity
ancestry, 1830–1831
Dunnu version, 1831
in *Atrakhasis Epic*, 1833, 2339
as creator, 1819
cult of in Nippur, origin of human race
concept, 1832
curse of, 838
fates decreed by on Holy Mound, 1865
in *Gilgamesh Epic*, 2340
Hammurabi pronounced king by, 901
hymns to, 2281–2282
in Kassite religion, 928
in Kumarbi Cycle, 1977
"Lord Wind," 1961
Naram-Sin and, 834
political role and kingship
responsibilities, 399–400
relation to humans, 1860–1861
represented in art, 1846
separation of heaven and earth, 1828
Shulgi's devotion to, 849

succeeded by Enlil, 403
Sumerian kingship and, 848
Sumerian recognition of, 809
in Sumerian royal hymnody, 850–852,
854
support for Samsu-iluna, 912
temple at Nippur
embellishment, 464
transformation into national cult
center, 1868–1869
temples of, 834
Enlil and Ninlil, I and II, 2286
Enlil-bani, king of Isin, accession of, 1884
Enlil-nadin-akhi, Kassite ruler, rebels
against Elamites, 1010
Enlil-nadinshumi, puppet king of Babylon,
1010
Enmebaragesi, king of Mesopotamia,
transformed Enlil temple into
national cult center, 1868–1869
Enmerkar, heroic tales of, 2284
Enmerkar and Ensukhkeshdanna, 2316
chivalrous contests in, 2324–2325
invention of writing in, 2321
Enmerkar and the Lord of Aratta, 482,
846, 1391, 2184–2185, 2316
cuneiform writing invented in,
2320–2321
familiar themes and allusions in, 2320
historicity, 2323
intertextuality and, 2193
syntax, 2319
Enna-Dagan, on Ebla-Mari dispute, 1227
Ennead, Egyptian divinity. *See* Atum
Enneads. *See also* Egyptian religion
Egyptian divine extended families, 1732
Ennirzianna, princess of Sumer, Nanna
cult and, 844
Enoch, patriarch, *Proverbs of Ahiqar* and,
1290
ENSI (ruler), 396, 834
Akkadian replacements for, 810
during Akkadian Dynasty, 400
election of, 397
in Sumerian city-states, 809
in Sumerian provinces, 844
in Ur, 402, 811
Entemena, king of Lagash
canal of, 2750
Lugalkiginedudu and, 804
silver vase of, 2571, 2709–2710
victory stela, narration of war against
Umma, 2356, 2357
Entertainment
Egyptian. *See also* Dance, Egyptian;
Music, Egyptian
board games, 370
dancing and singing, 2225
inclusion of the dead, 369
music and dancing, 370
religious festivals, 368–370

at royal courts, 2236
segregation of women, 368–369
Hittite, 584–585, 1993
Mesopotamian, 498–499
Entrepreneurship
in Old Assyrian trading system,
1393–1394
in Old Babylonian period, 1395–1396
Enūma ana bīt marṣi āšipu illaku
(diagnostic omens compendium),
Mesopotamian, 1908
Enūma Anu Enlil (astrological forecasts
compendium), 1939
appearance and disappearance of planet
Venus, 913
on astrology, 1908
Babylonian priest scribes of, 46
eclipse omen repertoire, 1927
formulation of omens, 1927
lunar visibility, 1927–1929
organization of, 1926–1927
Tablet 14, 1927–1929
Venus Tablet, 658
Enuma Elish. See Creation Epic
EN UNŪTI, 578
Envelope, clay
for administrative documents, 2269
invention of, in *Sargon Legend*, 2321
the invention of writing on, 2101, 2105
prehistoric token system, 2101, 2105,
2269
Environmental change. *See also* Climate
change; Landscape modification
artificial irrigation and, 181, 185
climatic change and
after 3000 BCE, 134–136, 138–139
in late prehistoric period, 127–128,
130–134
climatic trends and, 123–124
deforestation and, 124, 147
in Holocene epoch, 124–147
human-induced, 162–163
land use activities and, 124
in late Pleistocene epoch, 124–126
research problems, 123
**Environmental Change in the Near
East and Human Impact on the
Land** (Butzer), **123–151**
Envoys of the City, 867
Eparti. *See* Ebarat
Epartid dynasty. *See* Ebartid dynasty
Ephemerides (astronomical data texts),
2274
Ephesian Ware, 1178
Ephesus, coinage of, *1494*
Epic literature
Hittite, legendary elements in,
2370–2371
Mesopotamian
concern for omens in, 2364
purpose of, 2434–2435
Ugaritic, themes of, 2784

Exorcism (*continued*)
  omens and, 53
    Babylonian, 1896–1902
    use of, 2781
"Exorcism" (Ugaritic conjuration text),
    2077
Expeditions, foreign
  mining, Egyptian, 739, 745
  trade
    Egyptian government promotion of,
      1381–1382
    Egyptian royal, 1377–1379
Expulsions of populations. *See*
    Deportations
Extispicy, 2016–2017
  of animal organs, in Babylonia, 1899,
    1904–1905, *1905*
  cost of, 2015
  to establish fitness of priests, 1865
  with rock partridge, 2017
Eye diseases, Babylonian and Hellenistic
    Jewish medical texts on, 48–49
Eye of Horus. *See also* Horus, Egyptian
    divinity
  Egyptian temple rituals named the,
    1744
Eyre, Christopher J., **175–189**
Ezekiel, Israelite prophet, quasi-mystical
    thinking, 2452
Ezekiel (Hebrew Bible), on temple gifts,
    1488
EZENS. *See* Religious festivals, Hittite
ʾēzôr (skirt), 641
Ezra (Hebrew Bible), 2443
  language of, 2124

F

Fables
  Egyptian, 2238
  Mesopotamian, entertainment function,
    2455
Faience
  beads, 1607
  Egyptian, 2685
  glazes on, 1548
  Levantine, 2685
    vessels, 2685–2686, *2686*
    workshops, 2686
  manufacture of by Egyptian jewelers,
    1606
  rings, 1612
  Syrian, colors used, 2682
Failaka Island
  Dilmun civilization settlements on,
    1343–1344
  Dilmun cylinder seals found on, 1453
  reoccupation in Achaemenid period,
    1349

stamp seals from, 1344
temple complex on, 1344
Fairy tales. *See* Folktales; Tales, Egyptian
Faith, in Israelite monotheism, 1691–1692
Faiyum Depression
  defined, 139
  fishing and cereal cultivation in, 139
  flood control in, 142
  land reclamation, 745
  land-use history of, 141–142
Fakhariya. *See* Sikan
Falaj irrigation system, in Arabian
    Peninsula, 1345–1346
Falcon motif, as Egyptian royal emblem,
    2682
Falkner, Margarethe, observations on
    Assyrian reliefs, 2701–2702
The Fall of Lagash, 1871
Fall of Man, Christian story of, Delitzsch's
    theory of Mesopotamian origin, 100
Family. *See also* Children; Divorce;
    Inheritance; Marriage; Pregnancy and
    childbirth; Widows
  in Achaemenid Babylonia, real estate
    and, 1478–1479
  in Achaemenid Empire, royal authority
    over, 521
  Assyrian, of traders, 869–870
  Canaanite, legal issues, 624–626
  Egyptian
    divine, temples for, 1732
    individuals as members of, 347–350
    number of children, 377–378
    obligations, 379–380
    priestly, 1734–1735
  Hittite, 572–577
    right to disinherit and reinstate, 567
  Israelite
    division of labor, 644
    inheritance, 646–647
    legal issues, 624–626
    size of, 646–647
  Mesopotamian, 1888–1889
    inheritance in, 478–480, 1395–1396
    religious interests, 1867
Family cults, in Mesopotamia, 479
Family gods. *See under religion entries*
Family law
  Hittite, 263
  in Mesopotamia, 478–481
Family structure
  Achaemenid, 521–522
    cohesiveness of, 521
    endogamy, 520–521
    marriage and divorce, 519–522
    polygamy, 520–521
    principle of familial responsibility, 521
  Egyptian, 370–371
    conjugal households, 370–371
    extended households, 370

mother-son relationship, 378
nuclear, as basic social unit, 347–348
Hittite, 566–567
Israelite, fratriarchal unit in, 2783
Khatti, 538
Lycian, matrilineality, 1169
Mesopotamian
  extended-family residence, 2724
  hierarchical organization, 1867
  nuclear, 488
  patriarchal authority, 478
Famine
  Anatolian, 584
  in Egypt
    local relief for, 1383
    water supply and, 185
  tribal-state relations and, 1199
Fara. *See* Shuruppak
Faraʿin (Tell al-). *See* Buto
Farber, Walter, **1895–1909**
Farmers
  documentation on, 186–188
  as rural sub-elite, 187
  working life of, 176
    in Egypt, 177
Farmer's Almanac (Sumerian document),
    182, 184, 193
Farming. *See* Agriculture
Fasıllar, trachyte stela, 2652
Fasting, in grief, 1886
Fate
  in *Oedipus the King*, 1694–1695
  polytheistic concept of, 1687–1688,
    1694
Fate, netherworld spirit, 1861
Fate-demons. *See Namtarus*
Father gods, Egyptian, alphabetical list of
    names of, 1736–1740
Fatherhood, godly and royal attribute of,
    2045
"Father of god" title, Egyptian, "servant of
    god" and, 1734
Fauna. *See* Animals
Feasts
  Elamite cult, *gušum*, 1965
  sacrificial, Syro-Palestinian, 2053
  Syro-Palestinian, worship and, 2053
Feather, as symbol of maʿat, 1723–1724
Feinan, copper mining at, 1501, 1504
Fergana Valley, Silk Road, 1060
Ferry service, Persian, 1419
Fertile Crescent, the. *See* Mesopotamia
Fertility, symbols of, 1846
Fertility cults
  erotic art and, 2527, 2530
  to secure prosperity, 398
Fertility myths. *See* Dumuzi, deified king
    of Uruk
Fertilizer, agricultural (*Sabbakh*), 687
Festivals. *See also* Parades; Sed-festival
  Egyptian, in community life, 350

Gordion (word), nomenclature, 1148–1149
Gordius, king of Phrygia, accession to
    throne, mythological basis for, 1149
Gordon, Cyrus H., **2779–2789**, *2781*
    The Common Background of Greek and
        Hebrew Civilizations, 2787
    Ugaritic Grammar, 2784
Goring Ox, legal paradigm of, 45
Government. *See administration entries*
    under particular countries
Governors. *See* Officials
Gozan. *See* Bit-Bakhiani
Graffiti, Egyptian, death-related, 1767
Gragg, Gene B., **2161–2179**
Grains. *See* Cereal grains
Granicus, battle of the, 1104
Granite massifs, 1508
Grapes. *See also* Wine
    cultivation of, 192, 199
    wild, 158
Grasslands, in late Pleistocene, 125
Graves. *See also* Tombs
    Bahrain, 1349
        construction types, 1342–1343
    Kushite
        burial goods, 788
        chamber, 781, 786
        nobility vs. common people, 781
        oval, 781
        pit, 781, 786
    Mesopotamian, goods placed in, 1884
    Oman Peninsula
        beehive type, 1338
        communal, 1340
        Hafit type, 1338
        Iron Age, 1346
        Wadi Suq period, 1344
    royal. *See also* Necropolises, royal
        early Egyptian, 720–721
Grayson, A. Kirk, **959–968**
Great Britain. *See* British Isles
Great Caucasus, geographical features,
    1051–1052
Great Goddess, images of
    in modern literature, 117–118
    women's studies and, 111
Great Overlord of the Nome, Egyptian
    official, 280
Great Pyramid (Giza)
    building of, 725, 728–731, *731*
    iron associated with, 1514
    measurements, 1810
Great Treasure. *See* Treasure of Priam
Great Tumulus of Ankara, 1157
Greco-Babyloniaca tablets, cuneiform,
    dating of, 44
Greco-Roman period, view of progress in,
    1802–1803
Greece, ancient. *See also* Greek *entries*;
    Greeks
    contact with Near East, pottery in study
        of, 1563

    Egyptian influence on, 3–14
        modern literature and, 118
    Egyptian trade objects in, 9
    Hesiodic and Homeric portrayal of
        gods. *See* Hesiod; Homer
    historical sources. *See* Historical source
        material, Greek
    medicine in, Babylonian influence on,
        47–48
    Mycenaean, 33–34
        maritime commerce, 1428–1429
    near eastern cultures and, 55–64
        Archaic period, 55–56
    orientalization of, sea routes to East
        and, 35
    Persian rule of, revolt against,
        1046–1047
    Persian War of 480–479 BCE, 57,
        1019–1020, 1048
    philosophy, Eastern links, 6
    Phoenician presence, 1327
Greek alphabet, 2379–2380
    adopted from Phoenicians, 2390
    Phrygian texts in, 1155, 2152
Greek art, archaic, orientalizing
    phase, 56
Greek inscriptions. *See* Inscriptions, Greek
Greek language. *See also* Mycenaean
    Greek
    in Egypt, 712
    in Palestine, ancient, 43
Greek literature. *See also* Poetry, Greek
    Egyptian literature influenced by, 2232
    historiography, Persian history in, 1046
    Mesopotamia in, 55–64
    near eastern cultures in, 55–56, 63–64
        Archaic period, 55–56
        Persia, 57–63
    romances, Mesopotamia in, 61
Greek mythology
    Carian deities and, 1187
    goddesses identified with Isis, 8
    Herodotus on Egyptian parallels, 6
    Kumarbi Cycle and, 1979–1980
Greek religion
    Babylonian myths and, 35–40
    divinities, of Lydian origin, 1179
    Egyptian influences, 8–9
    near eastern myths and, 33–42
        on death and the afterlife, 40–41
        flood myths, 39
        on moral decline of humanity, 37–38
        on relations between gods and
            humankind, 39–40
Greeks
    Anatolia colonized by, 1100
    coinage of, 1490, 1494–1495
    Croesus vs., 1104
    in Egypt
        during Saite period, 711

    Hellenistic period, 7–8
    military service, 228
    Gyges vs., 1102
    Hebrews (ancient Israel) and, cultural
        common background, 2787
    Hittite contacts with, 1117
    Ionian. *See* Ionians
    ironmaking by, 1516
    Persians vs., under Alexander, 1104
    in Syro-Palestine, 1215
Green, Anthony, **1837–1855**
Greenewalt, Crawford M., Jr., **1173–1183**
Greengus, Samuel, **469–484**
Greenstein, Edward L., **2421–2432**
Greetings, Achaemenid Empire, social
    differences, 518–519
Grey Minyan ware, from Troy, 1125
Griffith, Francis Llewellyn, 2754, 2761
Grinding stones, prehistoric Egypt, 670
    Final Palaeolithic sites, 668–669
Grooming. *See* Personal grooming
Grotefend, Georg Friedrich, decipherment
    of cuneiform and, 70, 83, 96
Groves, holy, Elamite, 1964–1965
Gruber, Mayer I., **633–648**
GU (mathematical term), 1951
Gubba. *See* Tell Gubba
Gudea, ruler of Lagash
    Architect with Building Plan, 2510
    Architect with Measuring Rule, 2510
    cultural achievements of, 811
    cylinder seal, 1844
        inscriptions, 2323
    defeated Anshan, 1004
    headdress of, 508
    hymn to goddess Gatumdug, 591
    incense burner dedicated to,
        2705–2706, *2706*
    Melukkha tin and, 1506, 1511
    Ningirsu temple built by, 2577
    poem about, 2282
    royal hymnody and, 855
    sculpture
        attributes of ruler and rendering of,
            2511
        proportional ratios in, 2510–2513,
            2511–2512
    stamped-brick inscription of, *2111*
    statue from court of, 2706, *2706*
    statues of, 2591, *2592*
Gudea Cylinders, 2282
Guilds
    craftsmen's, 463
    Ugaritic, 1262
Guilt offering (*'āšām*), Israelite, 2055
Gula, Mesopotamian divinity
    dogs and, 498
    hymn on activities of physician, 1918
    Isin as cult center of, 1918
    represented in art, 1845

on stages of woman's life, 486–487
symbols of, *1839*, 1841
Gungunum, king of Larsa, Ur conquered
by, 813
GÚN.MA.DA. *See* Taxation, of Sumerian
provinces
Gunn, Battiscombe, 2759
Gunter, Ann C., **1539–1551**
Günük. *See* Xanthus
GUR (unit of measure), king's, 834,
1955
Guran. *See* Tepe Guran
Gurgum
Assyrian annexation of, 1101
Neo-Hittite city-states, 1296
Gurparanzakh, epic of, Hurrian origin,
2373
Guruš (class), 458–459
Gush, House of. *See* Arpad (Bit-Agusi)
Gušum sacrifice and feast, Elamite, 1965,
1969
Güterbock, Hans G., **2765–2777**, *2770*
decipherment of Hittite inscriptions,
2770–2775
at excavation at Boğazköy, 2765,
2769–2773
Kumarbi, 2774
at university at Ankara, 2771–2775
work on Hittite royal bullae, 2772–2773
Gutians
invasion of Sumer and Akkad, literary
laments over, 1874
as pastoral nomads, 254
Shulgi vs., 844, 851
Ur-Nammu vs., 843
Utu-khegal vs., 811
Guti language, 2162
Gutium, dynasty of, 403
Guzana. *See* Bit-Bakhiani
Gyges, king of Lydia
expansionism of, 1102–1103
gifts to Greek sanctuaries, 1177
war on Greek states, 1175

H

ʾḤ (spirit), 1779
Haas, Volkert, **2021–2030**
Ḥabiru. See Khabiru
Habuba al-Kabira
cupellation at, 1503
as walled city, 1523–1524
Hacılar (Hajilar)
figurines from, 1674
fortifications, Neolithic, 1523
Hadad, Syro-Palestinian divinity. *See* Adad
(Hadad), Mesopotamian and Syro-
Palestinian divinity

Hadadezer (Adad-idri), king of Damascus
anti-Assyrian league under, 1285
deification of, 1286
Haditha Dam Salvage Project
(1978–1984), 437
Ḥadramitic language, 2120
Hadrian, Roman emperor, Egyptian visit
of, 10–11
Hafir (catchment basin), 783
Haftavan Tepe, polychrome ware of, 988
Hair, body, Egyptian removal customs,
1733
Hair styles
Canaanite and Israelite women, 643
Egyptian, wigs, 386
Mesopotamian, third millennium, 2589
of western Asia
Early Dynastic period, *506*, 506–507
Neo-Sumerian and Old Babylonian
periods, 508–509
prehistoric, 504
Uruk period, 505–506
al-Hajjar, graves at, 1351
Hajji Firuz
in Neolithic period, 984–985
textile finds, 1578
Halab (Aleppo, later Beroea)
conflict with Shamshi-Adad, 881–882
excavations unattempted in, 1196
god's head sculpture found near, 2679
Hittite conquest, 1249–1250
Khattushili I vs., 1089
Phoenician trading settlement, 1325
records of kingdom of Yamkhad, 1237
Tudkhaliya I vs., 1091
under Hittites, 1093, 1203
under House of Gush, 1283–1284
Zimri-Lim and, 816
Halab dynasty, fall of, 1247
Halaf. *See* Bit-Bakhiani
Halafian pottery, shards found in
Transcaucasia, 1054
Halaf region, cultural remains in, 795
Haldi, Urartian divinity
cult of, 1144
Urartian temple to, Sargon's destruction
of, 1140
Halévy, Joseph
on Babel/Bible controversy, 102
on Sumerian texts, 86
Halicarnassus (Bodrum)
Herodotus as native of, 1186
mausoleum at, *1188*, 1190
rulers of, 1188–1189
Hallo, William W., **1871–1881**
Hall of the Two Maʿats, judgment of dead
in, 1723
Halparuntiya II, ruler of Gurgum,
inscriptions on statue, 1300–1301
Ḥalṣum (district), 876
Halys River. *See* Kızıl Irmak

Hama. *See* Hamath
Hamadan, Iron Age, 995
Hamath (Hama)
Aramaeans vs., 1283
Assyrians vs., 1285
Hittite dynasty, Assyrian alliance, 1303
inscriptions from, 1298, 2766
Irkhuleni support for, 1284
Neo-Hittite dynasty, 1297
palace and temple remains, 1298
religion in, 1291
temples to, 1306
Hamide reliefs, 2653
Hamito-Semitic language. *See* Afroasiatic
languages
Hammada, uses of, 159
Hammamat. *See* Wadi Hammamat
Hammurabi (Hammurapi), king of
Babylon. *See also* Code of
Hammurabi
assumes kingship, 403, 907
Code. See Code of Hammurabi
consolidation of power, 905
depiction on stela, 2585
destruction of Mari Palace by, 898
devotion to justice theme, 901, 907
expansionism of, 813, 817
family relations, 909
historic treatment of, 913
internal rule, 907–909
legal decisions, 908–909
Mari-Qatna relations and, 1203
military campaigns, 906
attacks Mari, 1237
conquest of Larsa, 910–911
mīšarum, 905, 907
monumental inscriptions, 907
political coalitions, 906
political relations, 909–911
programmatic consolidation, 906
reading of name, 902
rebuilding projects, 907
reign of, 905–907
Shulgi Law Code and, 854
stela of, 2704
stool of Shamash pictured on, 1653
successors, 911–913
on waterways, 1403
Zimri-Lim and, 909–911
Hammurapi. *See* Hammurabi
(Hammurapi), king of Babylon
Ḥamuštum, 868
Hand axes, 666, 668
Acheulian, in western Iran, 984
Handel, George Frederick, *Belshazzar*
oratorio, 77–78
Hanging Gardens of Babylon. *See also*
Gardens, 194, 440, 971
doubts about existence of, 440
early descriptions of, 440
Hanigalbat (Mitanni), taxation of, 962

size of, 1213
water systems, 1314, 2672
Headbands
  Anatolian, gold foil, 1675
  Mesopotamian, sculptures capped by,
    2591–2592
Head ornaments
  Canaanite and Israelite, headband,
    642–643
  Egyptian, development of, 1610–1611
Headrests, Egyptian, *1627*, 1633
Healing arts. *See* Medicine
Health. *See also* Medicine
  Israelite legal issues, 624
  in Mesopotamia, 1922–1923
  Mesopotamian views on, 1911–1912
Heart, in Egyptian thought, 1764
  physiological view of, 1790
Heaven. *See* Death and the afterlife
Hebhepetre Mentuhotep. *See* Nebhepetre
  Mentuhotep, Egyptian ruler
Hebrew alphabet
  early inscriptions, 2388
  lapidary form, examples of, 2389
  Phoenician origins of, 2123
Hebrew Bible. *See* Bible (Hebrew Bible,
  Old Testament)
Hebrew language
  Aramaic language and, 1293
  consonants, 2128
  extinction and revival as spoken
    language, 2123
  Sumero-Akkadian influence on,
    2412–2414
  text example, *2126*
  Ugaritic language and, 2784
Hebrew literature. *See also*
    Apocalypticism, Jewish; Israelite
    literature
  forms of, 2400–2402
  incorporated into Hebrew Bible, 2400
Hebrew religion. *See* Israelite religion;
  Judaism
Hebrews. *See* Israel; Israelites; Jews;
  Judah
Hecataeus of Miletus, *Genealogiai*, 57
Hejaz
  settlement in, 1350
  under Achaemenids, 1350
Heka, Egyptian divinity
  Atum and, 1701
  personification of magic, 1776
  profile of, 1737
Hêkāl (big house), 595
Hekanakhte, Egyptian farmer, 1383
Helbaek, Hans, 2719
Helck, Wolfgang, 1384
Heliodorus, *Aithiopika*, 11
Heliopolis (On)
  cosmogony of, 1699–1701

pylon gateway, 764
temple at, 321
  construction of, 307
Hell, in Egyptian iconography, 1719
Hellespont (strait), 1121
Helmets
  crested, Carian, 1188
  electrum, *1548*
Hematite, 1503, 1514
  for seal-making, 1595
Hemerological texts. *See* Calendars, omen
Hemium, prince of Egypt, 730
Hem (royal Egyptian title), 275
Henotheism, definition of, 2056
Hepatoscopy. *See* Liver inspection
Heqaib, deified Egyptian official, *741*, *742*
Heqat (shepherd's crook), 276
Herakleid Dynasty, 1175
Herakleopolis (Ihnasya al-Madina), rivalry
  with Thebes for power, 698
Herakles, Greek mythical hero, temple at
  Gades, 1327
Heraldry. *See also* Animals, images of
  Babylonian images in, 74–75
Heralds, Assyrian. *See* Nāgir ekalli
Herbal medicines, in Mesopotamia, 1911,
  1914–1915, 1918–1919, 1923
Herbs, Hittite consumption of, 584
Herculaneum papyri, 2200
Herd animals. *See also* Nomadism,
    pastoral
  primary, in ancient Near East, 249
  secondary products of, and pastoral
    nomadism, 253
Herding. *See also* Nomadism, pastoral
  fallow, 210
  nomadic pastoralism and, 210
Herihor, ruler of Upper Egypt, 709
Hermes Trismegistus, Greek divinity
  persistence under Christianity, 13
  Renaissance view of, 16
  Rosicrucian tracts influenced by, 20
Hermopolis (al-Ashmunein)
  siege of, military tactics, 299
  temple of Ramesses II, relief blocks,
    758
  theogony at, 1702
Herodotus
  on African barter, 1488
  on Assyria, 58
  on Babylonia, 58–60
  on Carians, 1190
  Carians and, 1186
  on coinage, 1495
  on Croesus, 1173
  Cyrus's prophetic dream, 2618
  on Egypt, 15, 1384
    reliability of, 5–6
  Erythraean Sea named by, 1452
  on fortifications of Babylon, 1533
  historical sources, 1048

influence of, 64
legendary genealogies, 56
on Necho II's Phoenician
    circumnavigators, 1331
predecessors of, 57
Proteus myth in, 4
on road from Sardis to Susa, 1417–1419
on statue of Artystone, 2632
on Syro-Palestine, 1195
on Trojan war, 1131
Heroes
  captured, depicted in art, 1852–1853
  in Mesopotamian netherworld, 1888
  Sumerian. *See* Gilgamesh
Hesi. *See* Tell al-Hesi
Hesiod
  on creation of mankind, 38
  portrayal of Greek gods by, 36
  Theogony, 37, 1982
    Kumarbi Cycle and, 1972, 1979–1980
  Works and Days, 37
Hesse, Brian, **203–222**
Hesyre, tomb of, wall paintings showing
    furniture, 1624, *1625*, 1626
Hetepheres, queen of Egypt, tomb of
  furniture from, 1625–1626
  royal chairs from, 1631
Heuzey, Léon Alexandre, *The Oriental
    Origins of Art*, 2698
Hexes. *See* Black arts, the
Hezekiah, king of Judah, 961
  reorganization of cult, 598
Hiba. *See* Lagash
Hides. *See also* Leatherworking
  processing of, 1551
Hierakonpolis (Kom al-Ahmar, Nekhen)
  in Early Dynastic period, 329
  Egyptian Predynastic cemeteries at, 685,
    688
  funerary enclosure, 1525
  mortuary cult complex at, 305
  temple enclosure at, 306
  urbanization, 674
Hieratic writing, 2140, *2141*, 2205–2206,
    2208, 2213, 2215–2216
  arrangement of inscriptions in, 2207
Hieroglyphic writing, Egyptian,
    2138–2142, 2182, 2205–2206, 2216
  alphabetic elements in, 2380
  archives and libraries, 2198–2199,
    2203–2204, 2207–2208
  art and, 2533–2544
    pun formation, 2545–2546
  changes in Greco-Roman period, 2139,
    2141
  Classical or Middle period, 2140,
    2143–2144
  cryptography, 2140, 2140–2141
  cultural influences, 2140
  cursive varieties, 2139
  decipherment of. *See* Decipherment

Israelite
  Hebrew Bible and, 2441
  nation as main subject of, 2443
Mesopotamian
  historical omens in, 1874
  recent events, 2434–2435
  of remote past, 2438–2439
origin of
  external military encounters, narration of, 2356
  internal competition and, narration of, 2355–2356
Syro-Palestinian
  recent events, 2437–2438
  of remote past, 2441–2443
Historiography of the Ancient Near East (Van Seters), **2433–2444**
History
  European, Babylon in, 67–79
  uses of, in ancient Near East, 2433
History of Anatolia and of the Hittite Empire: An Overview (MacQueen), **1085–1105**
History of Ancient Egypt: An Overview (Murnane), **691–717**
History of Ancient Mesopotamia: An Overview (Charpin), **807–829**
History of Ancient Syria and Palestine: An Overview (Lemche), **1195–1218**
History of Elam and Achaemenid Persia: An Overview (Brentjes), **1001–1021**
Hit, Hammurabi and Zimri-Lin's dispute over, 910
Hittite and Hurrian Literatures (Archi), **2367–2377**
Hittite art. *See also* Sculpture, Hittite
  divinities in, stereotyped canon, 2655
  minor arts, 1679–1680
Hittite economy, 577–581
  state revenues, from military conquests, 538
Hittite Empire. *See also* Kings, Hittite; Military, Hittite; Neo-Hittite Empire; Neo-Hittite states; Qadesh, Battle of; Queens, Hittite
  administration, 539–541, 580
    feudal aspects, 541–542
    palace, 539
    provincial, 540
    religious, 540–541
    royal bureaucracy, 539
    of vassal states, 541
  Akkhiyawa (Achaia?) and, 1129–1131
  Amurru and, 1207
  Boğazköy as heart of, 2770
  collapse of, 708
  economy, state revenues, 538
  Egypt and, 706
  Egyptian provinces, 549

expansion of power, in legend, 2371–2372
14th–13th centuries BCE, 1110 (map)
historical overview of, 1085–1105
Hurrian culture, 1250
Kashkean assault, 1250
location of, 259
Mitanni vs., 820, 1249–1252
monetary exchanges in, 1493
Naram-Sin legends, 839–840
political development, 542
Syrian conquests, 1247
trade, state role in, 538
treaty with Ugarit, 1259
under Khattushili III, 1107–1120
Yamkhad and, 1203
Hittite Glossary (Sturtevant), 2768–2769
Hittite language, 261. *See also* Hieroglyphic writing, Hittite; Inscriptions, Hittite; Luwian hieroglyphics
  as chief administrative language, 2152
  chronological divisions, 2151–2152
  cuneiform script, 2367
    decipherment of, 87
  dictionary of, 2780
  etymology unclear, 2768
  grammar of, 2154–2155
    Barton and, 2779–2780
  Hattic and, 2174–2175
  Hurrian-Hittite bilingual tablets, 1253
  Hurrian influence, 2167–2168
  Luwian compared, 2155
  Old Hittite text sample, 2154
  sound inventory of, 2153
  trade relations and, 262–263
  vocabulary of, 2152
Hittite law. *See* Law, Hittite; Law, Old Hittite
Hittite literature
  annals and chronicles, 2369–2370
  edicts, 2368–2369
  Empire period, 2371–2373
  influence of foreign myths and poems on, 2367
  king's "manly deeds" genre, 2437
  Old Kingdom, formation of genres, 2368–2371
  plague prayers, 2000
  sagas and epics, 2370–2371
Hittite-Luwian languages, Carian as part of, 1193
Hittite Military Organization (Beal), **545–554**
Hittite music. *See* Music, Hittite
Hittite mythology, 2373–2377, 2773–2774
  of Anatolian origin, 2374
  Babylonian model, 1979
  behavioral standards in, 2373
  folkloric motifs in, 2376–2377
  of Hattic origin, 2375–2376

Hurrian influence, 2373–2374
  in magical rites, 2374
  in rituals, 2374–2375
  structure of, 2374
  Ullikummi, 1828
  vanishing god in, 2375
Hittite Old Kingdom, conquest of, 1246
Hittite Prayers (De Roos), **1997–2005**
Hittite religion
  dance in, 2665–2668
  divinities
    consulted for military advice, 546, 550
    daily care of statues, 2651
    dependence on human servants, 530
    family structure, 566, 566–567, 567
    of foreign origin, 1977
    gender equality, 567–568
    ordering of, 2649
    stereotyped canon of, 2655
    stone reliefs, 2651–2652, 2654
    tutelary, 1986, 1988–1989
  Hurrian influence, 1979, 1998–1999
  judgment in, 1999
  king's role in, 532–533
  music in, 2662–2664
  overview of, 1981–1995
  pantheon, 1977
  rites and ceremonies, 532–533
    musical accompaniment, 2664
  sin, passed from father to son, 1999, 2003
  singing in, 2662–2663
  texts
    Hurrian-Luwian influence in, 268
    languages of, 269
Hittites. *See also* Neo-Hittite *entries*
  ancestor cult, 2027–2029
  appearance of in Hebrew Bible, 2780
  clothing of, 510–511
    ceremonial robes, 510–511
  Egyptian spelling of, 2766
  Hattic language and, 261
  Hebrew name for, 2766
  historical sources. *See* Historical source material, Hittite
  households of, 571
  influence of foreign mythology on, 1979
  iron technology of, 1516
  Kassites and, 817
  location of land of, 2766
  matrilineality, 534
  personal names. *See* Names, personal, Hittite
  private life of, 571–586
  protohistoric phase, 262–264
  socioeconomic conditions, 538
  in Syria. *See* Syria, Hittites in
  Syro-Hurrian culture, 1245–1246
  in western Iran, 984
Hittite Witchcraft, Magic, and Divination (Frantz-Szabó), **2007–2019**

Irish art, Babylonian-Mesopotamian motifs
in, 74
Irkab-Damu, king of Ebla
property granted by, 1227
reign of, 1221
Irkalla, mythical being, 1887
Irkhuleni (Jarhuleni, Urhilenas), Hamath
independence and, 1284
Iron
cast, 1514
Central Asian deposits, 1067
early use of, 1514–1515
first millennium use of, 808
in Hittite weaponry, 548
products
gradual introduction of, 1546
storage of, 579
refining and use of, cultural and social
changes resulting from, 1067
smelting furnaces, 1077
technology of, on Cyprus, 1436
transition to, from bronze, 417
Iron Age
in Anatolia, 1100
Bronze Age transition to, 1516
in Mesopotamia, Aramaean
expansionism in, 1282–1284
in Syro-Palestine, 1209, 1211–1213
Aramaean expansionism in, 1284
religion in, 2043, 2046–2047
in western Iran, 989–994, 996
"Iron Letter"
on Hittite iron monopoly, 1516
on iron production, 1514
Iron oxide. *See* Hematite
Iron-sheep property (dowry), 45
Ironworkers, social position of, in
Mesopotamia, 417
Irra. *See* Erra
Irra-imitti, king of Isin, placed substitute
king on throne, 953
Irrigation. *See also* Water management
Arabian Peninsula, 1338
in Babylonia, in Uruk period, 798, 804
basin irrigation, 141
Central Asia, 1077
centralization of political authority and,
2716–2717
demarcation of rural occupations and,
186
in Egypt, 178–180, 193
farming techniques, 178–183
seed-crop ratio, 183–184
intensive, 182–183
large-scale, 180–182
in Egypt, 180–181
farming techniques, 181–182
in Mesopotamia, 180–183
in Nile Valley, 141
nomadic pastoralism linked to, 253

oasis-based systems, western central
Asia, 1059
Oman Peninsula, 1345–1346
Ptolemies and, 142
salinization and, 144–145
in Iraq, 2750
in southern Mesopotamia, 236–237
Sumerian conflicts over, 809
Transcaucasia, 1053
Irshirra divinities, 1975
Irtashduna, Persian princess, in Persepolis
tablets, 1045
Irtisen, overseer of Egyptian craftsmen
inscription extolling technical abilities,
339
stela of, 341
Irynefer, Egyptian woman, 1377
Isaac, biblical figure, courtship of, 1490
Isaiah, Israelite prophet, on Babylon, 98
Isaiah (Hebrew Bible)
monotheism in, 2057
necromancy in, 2074–2075
Psalm of Hezekiah, 1880
'Îš gibbôr ḥayil (clan member), 624
Ishan Bahriyat. *See* Isin
Ishar-Damu, king of Ebla, reign of, 1221
Ishar-Lim, king of Khana, 1236
Ishbi-Irra
foundation of Isin dynasty, 1234
Ibbi-Sin and, 856
Ishchali. *See* Nerebtum
Ished tree, royal titulary inscribed on, 277
Ishkhara (Išḫara), Mesopotamian divinity
priestess of, role in cremation ritual,
2027
symbols of, *1840*
Ishkhi-Adad, king of Qatna
Ishme-Dagan and, 1204
marriage of daughter to Yasmakh-Adad,
879–880
Shamshi-Adad I and, 1201
Ishkur, Sumerian divinity, 1860
hymn to, Akkadian and Hittite
translations, 2002
symbols of, *1838, 1840, 1841, 1843*
Ishme-Dagan, king of Assyria
after father's death, 882
Ekallatum under, 816, 874
Ishkhi-Adad and, 1204
refuge with Hammurabi of Babylon, 882
relations with brother, 876, 881
territories devolved to, 876
Ishme-karab, Elamite divinity, 1963
Ishtanu, Hittite divinity, hymn to, 2000
Ishtar, Mesopotamian divinity. *See also*
Astarte, Canaanite divinity; Inanna,
Mesopotamian divinity
Akkadian incantation dramas of, 2477
Ammi-ditana's hymn to, 912
of Arba'il, role of in battle, 421
chapel of, at Mari Palace, 886, 890–891

cult of, 499
association with sexual rituals, 398
cylinder-seal impression, 927
demonic aspects of, 1844
descent to netherworld, in art, 1851
in *Gilgamesh Epic*, 2332–2333
in Hittite religion, 1986, 1990
Inanna and Mount Ebikh, 835–836
jewels ornamenting, 1641
Khattushili III and, 1107, 1109,
1117–1119, 1989
in Kumarbi Cycle, 1976–1978
legends, 836
Naram-Sin and, 834
in Neo-Assyrian art, 1843–1844
in Neo-Babylonian Empire, 973
in the netherworld, 1844
"Ninmesharra" hymn, 835–836
on Old Babylonian seals and clay
plaques, 1843–1844
painting of, at Mari Palace, 886, 895
prayers to, Akkadian version of, 2002
Pudukhepa and, 1112
Samsu-iluna and, 912
Sargon and, 838
Shulgi and, 849
Sumerian kings and, 847
symbols of, *1839, 1841, 1843–1844*
sexual, 1843
temple at Asshur, erotic art in, 2525
temple at Nuzi, 936–937, 937
temple at Uruk, 799, 2331
facade, 920
royal donations, 922
Ur-Nammu mourned by, 843–844
Ishtaran, Mesopotamian divinity, 1860
symbols of, *1840*
Ishtar and Ishullanu, adapted from
Sumerian, 2295
Ishtar Gate, *1534*
reconstruction of, 2588
reliefs, 2588, 2599
Ishtar's Descent to the Netherworld, 1887,
1889
Ishtup-ilum, governor of Mari, statue of,
2679
Ishuwa
Khattushili III and, 1117
Shuppiluliuma I vs., 1092
Tudkhaliya I vs., 1090
Isin (Ishan Bahriyat)
Babylonia under, 821
control of southern Mesopotamia, 903
craft archives, 459
materials accounted for, 464
as cult center of Gula, 1918
foundation of Ur dynasty, 1234
Hammurabi's raids on, 906
Ishbi-Irra at, 856
Larsa vs., 813, 817
leatherworking in, 1540

location of temple, 238

political coalitions, 905

textile production from, 1581

Isin, dynasty of, literary lamentations over fate of, 1872

Isis, Egyptian divinity. *See also* Hathor, Egyptian divinity

attacks father Re with snake, 1781

birth of, 1700

in *The Contendings of Horus and Seth*, 1704

cult of

antiquities connected with, Roman sources of, 21

decline, 13–14

early Greek evidence of, 9–10

iconography of, 8

organization and rituals, 11–12

under Roman Empire, 10–12

Horus conceived by, *1703*

images

Roman relief of, *11*

Roman statue of, *10*

in Western art, 28

on Metternich stela, 1781

and music, 2556

myth of

Christian parallels, 13

Greek aretalogies, 9

Hellenized versus traditional Egyptian versions, 8–9

pictorial representation, *1718*, 1718

Osiris mourned by, 1702

Plutarch on, 1697

profile of, 1737

symbolic representations, 1724

worshiped in Kush, 785, 789

Iškaru (tax), 939

Islam, survival of Egyptian cults under, 13

Island Cultures: Crete, Thera, Cyprus, Rhodes, and Sardinia (Knapp), **1433–1449**

Isocrates, *Busiris*, on Egypt, 7

Isonomia, 1047

Israel, kingdom of. *See also* Canaan; Kings, Israelite; Palestine, ancient

administration, 598–602

Canaanite influence, 599

in districts, 602

districts of, 599

leaders of ten, 600

royal officials, 599–600

Assyrian deportations from, 961, 1213

Ben-Hadad defeat and, 1285

building program, 599

capital

palace administration, 595–596

temple administration, 596

consolidation under David, 1311

copper mining in, 1501, 1504

demographic data, 1312–1313

average settlement size, 646

economy, 1312

expeditions to Ophir for gold, 1460–1461

feudalism, 601

fortifications, in Iron Age, 1532

geography, 1312

historical source materials for

biblical, 1315

Gordon's studies of, 2779–2789

incorporation into Assyrian Empire, 1311

in international context, 1318

Iron Age, 1282

iron manufacture in, 1516

kingdom of Judah compared, 1312–1313

legal systems, 621

metal artifacts from, 1508, 1515, 1517

military campaigns, in southern Syria, 1310

national development of, 1211–1212

Philistines and, territorial conflicts, 1270–1271

prophetic intervention, 1311

queen mother, 597

recognition of independence, 1315

resident aliens and foreigners, laws affecting, 626–627

royal donkeys in, 1204

royal land grants, 601

rulers, 1311

schools, 644

social and political organization, 1313–1315

Syrian incursions, 1311

taxation in, 1488

corvée, 601

trade, 1312

tribal origins of, 1199

work and home economics

royal service, 644

work schedule, 644

work force

Amarna period, 601

organization of, 601–602

Zobah vs., 1284

Israelite literature. *See also* Hebrew literature; Poetry, Israelite

biblical, historical setting, 2402

dispute form, 2448

Egyptian influence, 1759

mythological tradition in, 2039–2040

narrative

of divine warrior-king, 2035

riddles in, 2447

sea monster motif, 2405

sexual behavior in, 2039

social contexts for, 2449–2450

theriomorphic deities, 2039

Israelite mythology

diminishing use of, 2039

early Israelite religion and, 2034–2035

paradise myth, 2038

parallelism between deity and king, 2038

political mythmaking, 2037–2038

seven-headed enemy, 2038

wisdom circles, 2038–2039

Israelite religion, 1315–1318. *See also* Judaism; Monotheism

Canaanite elements of, 1315–1316

covenantal relationship with God, 2086

cult of deceased ancestors, 2034–2035

divinities, 2034–2035. *See also* Yahweh

old Canaanite, 2034

theriomorphic, 2039

monotheism, 2056–2057

priests and worship, 2043–2057

resurrection in, 2037

rituals of, 2785

Israelites

Egyptian influence, 1311

Exodus from Egypt, 772

food and drink, 637–639

footwear, 643

furniture, 635–637

grooming, 643

houses. *See* Houses, Canaanite and Israelite

New Year Festival, 2050

private life, sources on, 633

recreation and leisure, 639–641

sports and hunting, 641

urban life, neighborhoods divided by craft, 635

Israel-Judah, united monarchy of, duration of, 1211

Issyk cemetery, 1080–1081

Istanbul, Archaeological Museum, Central Taurus project and, 1513

Istanbul Prism, Philistine history, 1271

Istanbul University, founding of (1932), 2771

Italy

Egyptian cults in, 10

Phoenician presence, 1327

unification of, 78

Itjtawy, 736, 739

as Middle Kingdom capital, 699

Twelfth Dynasty court and palace, 280

Itkalzi ritual, 2651

Itti-Marduk-balatu, scribe and businessman of Babylonia, 2273

Itur-Mer, Mari city-god, Shamshi-Adad's appeal to, 875

Iunet. *See* Tentyra

Iusaas, Egyptian divinity

Hathor and, 1701

profile of, 1737

Iversen, Erik, 2509–2510

Ivory
  Aramaean, *1289, 1291*
  artifacts
    materials for, 1539
    production of, 1550
  carvings, 2679
    Anatolian
      Hittite, 1679
      second millennium, 1677–1678
    decrease in from Levant, 2686–2687
    Levantine, 2686–2689, *2687*
  carvings of, 1644
  elephants as source of, 2687, 2688
  hippopotamus as source of, 2686–2687,
    2690
  plaque showing banquet and
    presentation scenes, *640*
  sculptures, Indian, 2708–2709
  sources of, 171, 218
  Syrian, at Hasanlu, 991, *2493*
  writing boards, cuneiform inscriptions
    on, 2269–2270
Iwaru (dowries), 573
'Izbet Sartah, alphabetic inscription from,
  2382–2383, *2383*
Izre'el, Shlomo, **2411–2419**

J

Jacobsen, Thorkild, **2743–2752**, *2745*,
  2751
  The Sumerian Kinglist, 2748
Jacoby, Felix, 63
Jaffa, conquest of, through deception,
  1531
James, T. G. H., **2753–2764**, *2757*
Jansen, Hans Günter, **1121–1134**
Janssen, Rosalind M. H., **383–394**
Jarhuleni. *See* Irkhuleni
Jarmo
  clay figurines, 2583
  lead bead from, *1503*
  textile finds, 1578
Jars
  Early Dynastic, jewelry portrayed on,
    1643
  Egyptian, gift, 1381
Jasbesh-gilead, oligarchic government, 590
Jawa, as fortified settlement, 1524
Jaynes, Julian, *The Origin of
  Consciousness and the Breakdown of
  the Bicameral Mind,* 110
Jazira (Syria region)
  Assyrian tax collection in, 966
  under Nabopolassar, 826
Jebel Barkal cemetery, 782
Jebel al-Silsila, Carian graffiti at, 1190
Jebel Sinjar, Zimri-Lim over, 816
Jehoshaphat, king of Judah
  alliance with Israel, 1314–1315

judicial hierarchy, 621
legal reforms, 599, 622
Jehovah. *See* Yahweh, Hebrew divinity
Jehu, king of Israel, purge of Omrids,
  1318
Jennens, Charles, *Belshazzar* oratorio text,
  77–78
Jerablus, ruins at, 2776
Jeremiah, Israelite prophet, quasi-mystical
  thinking, 2452
Jericho (Tell es-Sultan)
  animal use at, 207
  ceramic work in, 794
  city walls, 1523, 1527
  containers, *637*
  feasts, Middle Bronze Age, 639
  furniture, 1654–1655
    joinery, *1655*
    Middle Bronze Age, 636–637
  houses, Middle Bronze Age, 634
  Israelite booty from, 1490
  skull worship, 2060
Jeroboam I, king of Israel
  reorganization of cult, 598
  sanctuaries at Bethel and Dan,
    1315–1317
  secession from old Israelite confederacy,
    1311
  work force supervision, 601
Jeroboam II, king of Israel, expansionism
  of, 1285
Jerusalem
  administration, scribes, 600
  Assyrian siege of, 961, 1535–1536
  Babylonian capture of, 826, 1214
  Fish Gate, biblical references, 639
  in Iron Age, 1213
  neighborhood, 635
  population, 646
  temple of, 608–609, 611. *See also under*
    Solomon, king of Israel
    bronze snake as cult object in,
      2077–2078
    gods worshiped in, 2051
    materials for, 1488
    organization of, 2674
  as walled city, 1536
  water supply system, 2672
  well-cisterns, 2672
  Yahweh's marriage to, 2036–2037
Jervan. *See* Jerwan
Jerwan, Assyrian aqueduct at, 2736–2737,
  2745–2746
Jesus
  Beatitudes of, 1689–1691
  Jewishness denied by Delitzsch, 105
Jewelers
  Egyptian
    Predynastic, 1606–1607
    technology of, 1605–1606

Mesopotamian
  Mari texts on, 1641–1642
  productions of, 1637–1638, 1644
  profession of, 1638
  techniques of, 1637–1638, 1644
Jewelry
  gold, 1605
  Hebrew Bible on, 1490
  as literary image in poetry, 2474–2475,
    2478, 2482–2483
  women's, from Nimrud tombs, 512
Jewelry, Achaemenid
  bracelets from Pasargadae, *2616*
  signet rings, 2633
Jewelry, Anatolian
  Alaca Hüyük findings, 1673, 1675
  Bronze Age, 1675–1676
  gold, 1673, 1675
  Hittite, 1673
  Troy findings, 1673, 1675
Jewelry, Bactrian, 1077
Jewelry, Egyptian
  amulets, 1607, *1607*, 1610
  basic forms of, 1606–1608
  bracelets, 1607–1608, 1610–1612
  collars, *wesekh-,* 1611, *1612,* 1613
  conspicuous display of, 1607
  Early Dynastic period, 1607
  earrings, 1610–1611, *1611*
  Eighteenth Dynasty, 1612
  funerary items, 1607–1608, 1612
  materials used in manufacture,
    1605–1606
  Middle Kingdom period, 1608–1610
  New Kingdom period, 1611–1612
  Old Kingdom period, 1607–1608
  pectorals, *1609,* 1609–1610
  Predynastic, 1606–1607
  rings, 1610, 1612, *1613*
  scarab, 1610, 1612
  Seventeenth Dynasty, 1610–1611
  Third Intermediate and Late periods,
    1613
  Twenty-fifth Dynasty, 1613
Jewelry, Levantine
  cloisonné technique, 2683
  Egyptian influence on, 2683
  granulation technique, 2684
Jewelry, Mesopotamian, 1635–1645
  Akkadian, 1643
  amulets, 1640
  in archaeological record, 1635–1639
  from Assurnasirpal II's palace at
    Kalkhu, 1638–1639, *1639*
  Assyrian workmanship, 1638–1639
  booty of war, 1635, 1642
  breast ornaments (Akkadian *tudittu*),
    1641–1642
  in bridal dowries, 1635, 1642
  described, 1636–1638
  earliest known, 1635–1636

Early Dynastic, 1636–1637, 1643
earrings, 1636–1638
  on men, 1643
economic and historical textual records
  of, 1641–1642
excavated pieces, 1635–1639
exchange of, between rulers, 1642
functions of, 1635
gold, 1636–1638, 1641, *1641*, 1642
  necklace with bells, *2699*
Gudea Dynasty, 1643
inscriptions on, 1635–1636, 1639
from Larsa, 1637–1638
materials used in manufacture,
  1636–1638, 1642
metalworking techniques, 1637
necklaces, 1636, 1638, *1641*
Neo-Assyrian, 1643–1644
Neo-Babylonian, 1644
"Nimrud Jewel," 1638
Old Assyrian, 1638
Old Babylonian, 1637–1638, 1643
pendants, beneficent qualities attributed
  to, 1640
in representational arts, 1635,
  1642–1644
from Royal Cemetery of Ur,
  1636–1637, *1637*
Sumerian and Akkadian textual
  references to, 1639–1641
from Tepe Gawra burial sites, 1636
textual evidence regarding, 1635,
  1639–1642
Ur III period, 1637, 1643
Uruk period, 1636
vulvae-shaped ornaments (Akkadian
  uru), 1641
Jewelry and Personal Arts in Anatolia
  (Canby), 1673–1682
Jewelry and Personal Arts in Ancient
  Egypt (Romano), 1605–1621
Jewelry and Personal Arts in Ancient
  Western Asia (Bahrani), 1635–1645
Jewish literature. *See* Hebrew literature;
  Israelite literature
Jewish monotheism. *See* Israelite religion,
  monotheism
Jewish religion. *See* Judaism
Jews
  in Egypt
    military service, 228, 232
    as slaves of royalty, 229
    treatment of, 233
  funerary ideology, 2067
  in Germany before First World War,
    104
  Hellenistic
    Babylonian influence on, 43–53
    traditions on Nabonidus, 978
  in Persian garrison at Elephantine, 228,
    233

Philistines vs., 1516
Proverbs of Ahiqar and, 1290
Jezar. *See* Gezer
Jmj-rᶜ js (overseer of the workshop), 332
Jnw (Egyptian diplomatic gifts),
  1380–1381
Joannès, Francis, **1475–1485**
Job (Hebrew Bible)
  Mesopotamian "just-sufferer"
    compositions and, 1880
  social groups in, 2450
Joint rulership. *See* Co-regency, Egyptian;
  Kingship
Jokes. *See* Humor
Jokha. *See* Umma
Jordan
  copper mining in, 1501, 1504
  miniature ax from, 1515
Joseph, son of Jacob
  brothers of, 1494
  dreams of, 1687
  Proverbs of Ahiqar and, 1290
Josephus, Jewish historian, 2441
  Berossus quoted by, 62
  on Hazael, 1285
Josiah, king of Judah
  death of, 1214
  reorganization of cult, 598
Jsw (payment), 335
Jubayl. *See* Byblos
Judah, kingdom of
  access to trade, 1312
  Assyria and, 961, 1311
  Babylon vs., 1214
  Davidic Dynasty, 1311
    support for, 1315
  demographic data, 1312–1313
  desacralization of royal ideology,
    601
  division into administrative regions,
    1315
  economy, 1312
  Egyptian influence, 1311
  feudalism, 601
  geography, 1312
  history, biblical sources, 1315
  infant sacrifice, 1328
  in international context, 1318
  kingdom of Israel compared to,
    1312–1313
  national development of, 1211–1212
  Phoenician cities and, 1315
  political organization of, 1209
  puppet prince of, 1285–1286
  rulers, 1311
  Samaritans and, 1213
  schools, 644
  secession from old Israelite confederacy,
    1311
  social and political organization,
    1313–1315

theocracy under Yahweh, 602
work force, organization of, 601–602
Judaism, Hellenistic
  astronomy of, Babylonian influence on,
    46–47
  covenant with deity in, 2442
  divination by High Priest, 2072
  divorce law, Babylonian influence on,
    45–46
  exegetical tradition, 2452
  law and legal institutions, 44–46
  magic and, 49–52, 2075
  marriage law, 45–46
  mathematics in, 47
  medicine in, 47–49
  monotheism. *See* Israelite religion,
    monotheism
  scholarly methodology of, influence on,
    52–53
  witchcraft in, 50–51
Judean religion, 1315–1318
Judeidah. *See* Tell Judeidah
Judge, metaphor of the, Syro-Palestinian
  gods and, 2044, 2051
Judges
  in ancient Israel, authority for, 621
  in Israel
    elders and kinship groups as,
      622–623
    kings as, 621–622
    priests as, 622
  Mesopotamian, 473–474
  Persian royal, 524–525
Judgment. *See also* Last Judgment
  after death, in Egyptian thought, 1768
  in Hittite religion, 1999
  in Ugaritic thought, 2063
Juha stories, "clever fool" motif in, 2466
Julian, Roman emperor, Sarapis cult
  and, 13
Jum. *See* ʿEn-gedi
Jung, Carl G.
  ancient Near East cited by, 108–109
  concept of collective unconscious, 110
Jurisprudence, temples as centers of, Syro-
  Palestinian, 2051
Justice, administration of. *See* Legal
  system

K

Ka (soul), 1764
  in Egyptian iconography, 1720
Kaba-i-Zardusht, 1019
Kabul, cuneiform "coin" from, 1495
Kadashman-Enlil I, Kassite king, marriage
  alliance with Egypt, 704, 820
Kadashman-Enlil II, Kassite king,
  Egyptian relations with, 1115

Kadashman-Turgu, king of Babylonia,
    Khattushili III and, 1108, 1115
KÁ.DINGIR. RA *See* Babylon
Kahun. *See* Illahun
KÁ.KÁ (districts)
    rural/palace distinction in, 1224
    worker teams and, 1223
Kalaly-gyr, architectural structures, 1074
KALAM (the Land), 399
Kalkhu (Nimrud)
    arsenal, workshops in, 462
    art, plaque of woman looking out
        window, 2502
    Assyrian booty at, 1288
    Assyrian statues found at, 2594–2595
    Black Obelisk, decipherment of, 86–87
    capital established at, 1397
    citadel mound, 245
    construction of, 822
    excavations, 2697
    fortifications, 1532
    Fort Shalmaneser, 1660
    founding by Assurnasirpal II, 2586
    gold appliqués found in, 504
    ivory furniture, 1291
        fitters' marks, 457, 1659, 1661
        Fort Shalmaneser, *1660*
        gilded and inlaid plaques, 1659–1660
        Layard series, 1659
        Loftus group, 1659
        Phoenician and Syrian, 1658–1661
        sheathing, 1661
        stylistic groups, 1661
    jewelry findings at, 1638–1639, *1639*
    Late Assyrian palace at, 434
    layout, 245
    medical texts from, 1911
    military documents at, 824, 961
    Ninurta temple of. *See* Ninurta temple
        (Kalkhu)
    Northwest Palace
        relief of Assurnasirpal II, 2488, *2489*
        tombs in, 436
    palace of Assurnasirpal II, 199–200
        reliefs from, 2699, 2700, 2702
    palaces at
        ivories in, 2689
        reliefs from, 2586–2587, *2587*
        wall paintings, 2598–2599
    queens buried at, 1884
    Rassam Obelisk, 1657
    relief of Assurnasirpal II, *2586*
    Review Palace at, 419
        documentation on Assyrian army
            found at, 420
    storage of clay tablets at, 2199
    temple of Nabu
        library of, 2197, 2206
        records of, 2197
        throne room in, 427
    tombs, jewelry from, 512, 2699

walls of, 245
    sculpted reliefs on, 2672–2673
    writing boards from, 2393
Kalmuš (staff of office), 536
kalû (Sumerian singer), 1872
Kamani, king of Karkamish, 1303
Kamaru (mathematical term), *1948*
Kamid al-Loz. *See* Kumidi
Kamish (Kammush), Syro-Palestinian
    divinity, 2045–2047. *See also*
    Chemosh
Kamose, king of Egypt
    on Kushite and Hyksos invaders, 702
    military victory over Hyksos, 2436
Kämpfer, Engelbert, cuneiform named
    by, 70
Kamrushepa, Hittite divinity, 2375
Kanawati, Naguib, 2761
Kandalanu, king of Babylon, 825
Kandaulas, Lydian divinity, 1179
Kanesh (Kültepe, Nesha)
    administration
        bicameral structure, 867–868
        big men, 868–869
        solution of conflicts, 868
    Akkadian language in, 812
    alabaster idol, *2642*
    architecture, 862
    archives, 861–862, 1392–1393, 2203
        of Anatolian businessmen, 862
    building plan, *863*
    "Cappadocian tablets" and, 859
    city mound, earliest occupation,
        859–860
    destruction of, 865
    excavation of, 859–863
    figure from, *1678*
    Hattic population, 2175
    as Hittite capital, 2768
    identification of, 859
    kārum, 859–860
        authority of, 867
        contacts with Asshur, 867, 869–870
        decision-making procedures, 868
        economic issues, 867
        excavations, 860–861, *861*
        family hierarchies, 869
        government of, 867–868
        judicial duties, 867
        official letters, 867
        sanctuary remains, 2641
        sculpture and statuary, 2644
        statutes, 868
        traders' homes, 861, 862
    Kashkaean aggression against, 1109
    Kusshar aggression against, 1088
    protohistoric phase, 262–264
    queen of, in legend, 2370–2371
    textile production documentation from,
        1581

trade
    Assyrian, 813
    with Mari and Karkamish, 862
**Kanesh: An Assyrian Colony in
    Anatolia** (Veenhof), **859–871**
Kantuzzili, Hittite king, prayers of, 2002
    dreams in, 2013
    to personal god, 2001
Kapara, king of Gozan, orthostats collected
    by, 1288
Kaptaru. *See* Keftiu/Kaptaru
Karabel reliefs, 2653
Karadağ, royal inscriptions, 1302
Karaindash, Mesopotamian architect, 2513
Karashamb, burial mounds, 1056
Karatepe (Azatiwadiya, Azatiwataya)
    archaeological remains, 1299
    founding of, 2428–2429
    inscriptions at
        bilingual, 89–90, 1326, 2388
        hieroglyphic Luwian, 2776
        punctuation in, 2394
    sculptures, dating of, 1304
Karduniash. *See* Babylonia
Karkamish (Carchemish)
    Aramaeans vs., 1283
    archaeological remains, 1298
    architectural sculpture of kings at, 2679
    Assyrian rule of, 964, 1303
    cadet dynasty, 546
    campaign against Arzawa, 550
    deities, 1306
    Hittite era, 820, 1094, 1118, 1208
    King's Gate, hieroglyphic inscriptions,
        1300, *1301*
    kings of
        power over Syria, 1259
        under Hittite Great Kings, 541
    Kubaba cult in, 1986
    lapis lazuli figures from, 1679
    Nabopolassar's conquest of, 972
    Neo-Babylonian relief from, royal family
        depicted on, 513–514, *514*
    Neo-Hittite era, 1099–1101
        rulers, 1301–1302
        sculpture, 1302
    palace at, entrance porch, 2673–2674
    Processional Way, 1156
    rampart gate, 2672
    Shuppiluliuma I vs., 1092–1093
    stone reliefs, 2656
    Yamkhad empire and, 1201
**Karkamish and Karatepe: Neo-Hittite
    City-States in North Syria**
    (Hawkins), **1295–1307**
Karnak
    Great Temple of Amun
        colossi, 757
        Great Hypostyle Hall, *707*, 764
        processional ways, 780

L

Labarna (Hittite royal title), 532, 563
Labarna, mythical Hittite king, 1089
Labels, ivory, Egyptian gift, 1381
Labor, division of
  birth of city-states and, 1392
  Egyptian artisans and artists, 336–337
  Israelite work and home economics, 644
  pottery making, 797
  power struggles and, 1388
  Predynastic Egypt, 675
  in sedentary economies, 1390
Laborers. *See also* Wages; Workers
  agricultural, 181, 184–185
    scarcity of, 186
  deportees as, 961, 967
  Eblaean, 1223–1224
  Hittite, 574, 577–580
  on Mesopotamian temple estates,
    444–446
Labyrinths, Egyptian, pyramid, 742
Lachish (Tell al-Duwayr)
  alluvial fills, 137
  clothing and dress, 643
  conquest of, by Sennacherib, 1535
  dividing wall of, 1536
  early alphabetic inscription from, 2382
  Fosse Temples at, 610, 612, 2676
  Israelite "cult room" at, 611
  palace at, 607
  siege of, 824
  tombs of, ivory works from, 2687
"Lady of the City." *See* Ninali (Bēlē-ali),
    Elamite goddess
Lagamar, Elamite divinity, 1963
Lagash (Tell al-Hiba)
  administration, 397
  boatmen of, 1421
  depictions of warfare from, 414
  historical records from, 809
  legal texts from, 846
  local ideology, 396
  location of temple, 239
  monetary exchanges in, 1491–1493
  royal seals, 1596
  scribal school of, 855
  sculpture workshop at, 2589
  textile workshops of, 1570
  trade with Dilmun, 1453
  Umma and
    dispute with, 804
    lament about sack by Lugalzagesi,
      1871
    under Gudea, 811
    Ur-Nammu vs., 843
  Vulture Stela of Eannatum of, 1402
Lagash Epic, comparison to other flood
  narratives, 2346–2347
Lagash Kinglist, 2341–2343
  as response to *Sumerian Kinglist*, 2341

laḫmus (protective deities), represented in
  art, 1846, 1851
al-Lahun, housing, 364
Laish. *See* Dan
Lakes
  in late Pleistocene, 125–126
  late prehistoric ecology, eastern Sahara,
    131–132
Lakes, desert, in late prehistoric period,
  128, 130
  inferred flood trends, *133*
Lake Van, climatic fluctuations, 136, 138
Lake Zeribar, climatic fluctuations, 136,
  138
Lalḫuntalli-vessel, 2027
LAMAŘ, 1863
Lamashtu, Elamite divinity, 1897, 1960
  animal features, 1845
  iconography, *1844*, 1844
Lamassus (protective deities), *1848*
  represented in art, 1846–1847
Lambert, W. G., **1825–1835**
*The Lamentation over the Destruction of
  Sumer and Ur*, 1872, 2285–2286
  excerpt from, 1873
**Lamentations and Prayers in Sumer
  and Akkad** (Hallo), **1871–1881**
Lamentations (Hebrew Bible),
  Mesopotamian laments and, 1879
Lament of Khakheperresonb, 699
  on oratory, 2224
Laments and lamentations
  Akkadian, 1873–1875, 1877–1879
    city-laments, 1873–1874
    "just sufferer" prayers, 1878–1879
    bilingual Sumerian-Akkadian, "for
      appeasing the heart," 1877–1878
  Egyptian, 2225
    format of, 2233–2234
  Hebrew (Israelite), for kings,
    1879–1880
  Mesopotamian
    categories of, 1871
    congregational, 1871–1875
    individual, 1875–1879
    for kings, 1879–1880
  Mesopotamian royal ideology, 396
  Sumerian, 1871–1873, 1875–1877, 2296
    city-laments, 1872
    forerunners of, 1871–1872
    "hand-lifting," 1873
    tambourine-laments, 1873
  Syro-Palestinian, individual, 2055
Lamgi-Mari, king of Mari, hairstyle of, 507
LAMMA (protective divinity), 1986
  represented in art, 1846–1847
Lamps
  Egyptian
    oil, 367
    types of, 1633–1634
  funerary, 1884

Israel, pottery, 635
Syro-Palestine, 635
Land
  in Achaemenid Babylonia
    familial solidarity and, 1478–1479
    "feudal" system, 1481–1482
  Akkadian and Aramaic sale
    contracts, 45
  in Babylonia
    rental of, 1495
    use of, 804
  Canaanite and Israelite law regarding,
    629–630
  in Egypt
    reclamation of at Faiyum, 745
    rental rate and price, 353–354
    usufruct, 345, 354
  Hittite prices, 581
  private leases, 185
    Code of Hammurabi on, 187
  Egyptian, 184
  surveys of, revenue control maintained
    through, 183–184
  taxation of, Assyrian administration of,
    963
  transfers
    by barter, 1487
    Ebla/Emar, 1227
    Hebrew Bible on, 1494
    price calculation in, 1491
    ring money in, 1489
Land grants
  Kassite dynasty, 920–923
  curses on those interfering with,
    924–925
  economic importance, 925
  feudalistic features, 923
  holders of, 921–922, 924
  protection of privileges, 925
  reason for, 922
  size of properties, 922
  taxation, 922
  Ugaritic, to foreigners, 629
Land ownership
  Assyrian concentration of, 820
  in Ebla, 1225
  for economic purposes, 943
  Egypt
    in New Kingdom period, 319–320
    in Old Kingdom and Middle
      Kingdom periods, 325
  in Elam, by gods, 1964
  Hittites, royal deeds of gift, 538
  Israel, royal land grants, 601
  Judah, theological concept, 601
  private, 943, 945–946
    Nuzi, 945–946
  real estate transactions, 1480
  Sumerian conflicts over, 809
  women, 944
Landsberger, Benno, 2306, 2744, 2750

Lullubi, 2162
Lumber. *See* Wood
Lunar calendar. *See* Calendars, lunar
Lunar eclipse
    omens, 1926
    predicted in astronomical diaries, 1937
    recorded in *Enūma Anu Enlil*, 1927
Lunar theory, Babylonian
    definition of lunar cycle, 1931
    development of, 1928–1929
    dividing ecliptic into arcs, *1934*,
        1934–1935
    lunation, 1931
    in mathematical astronomical texts, 1927
    progress through sidereal ecliptic, 1937
    values for setting and rising of moon,
        1930
    visibility
        on any date, 1928
        over thirty-day equinoctial month,
            1927–1928, *1928*
    predicted intervals, 1937
    true lunar calendar, 1929
    zigzag function, 1928, 1934–1935
Lunar theory, Egyptian, agreement
        between lunar and Sothic year, 1811
Lunar zodiacs
    early alphabets and, 2785–2786
    Mayan, Semitic parallels, 2785–2786
Lundquist, John M., **67–80**
Lunisolar calendar. *See* Calendars
Luristan. *See also* Tepe Guran
    Bronze Age, 986
    bronzes of, 996–998
        dating of, 1013
Lur tribe
    breaking winter camp, 2723
    ethnographic study of, and ancient
        nomadism, 2722–2723
ᴸᵁSANGA, 1990
LÚ.Su, Ur vs., 812
Lutes
    Egyptian, 2559, 2563
    Mesopotamian, 2601–2602
Luwian art, sculptural principles,
    2655–2657
Luwian hieroglyphics, 2776
    characteristics of, 2155
    decipherment of, 88–89
    example of, *2154*
    grammar of, 2155–2156
    inscription of Azatiwada in, 2428–2431
    surviving texts, 2155
    text sample, 2156
    on Urartian storage jars, 1144
Luwian language, 2175, 2768
    cuneiform, 2154–2155
    descendants of, 1165
    earliest material, 267
    inscriptions. *See* Inscriptions, Luwian
    loanwords, 267

Lycian language and, 2156–2157
    Neo-Hittite period, 1297
    text material, 267–268
    writing systems used, 267
Luwian literature, "Istanuvian songs,"
    2155
Luwian religion, Hittite religion and, 1983,
    1986–1987
Luwians, arrival in Anatolia, 260
Luxor, Nile River near, *686*
Luxor Temple, dance scenes in, 2567
Luxury goods. *See also* Purple-dyed fabrics
    in Aramaean royal cities, 1288
    Assyrian plunder of, 962
    in Early Bronze Age trade, 1508
    glass simulation of, 1541–1542
    at Hasanlu IV, 991
    ivory for, 1550
    multiple components of, 1543
Lycia
    connections with Greece and Crete,
        1162
    in Delian League, 1163
    goods produced, 1169
    Greek and Roman observations on,
        1169–1170
    Greek influence, 1170
    Hellenistic period, 1170
    history, 1162–1164
    Late Bronze Age settlements, 1161
    legendary traditions, 1161–1162
    matrilineal family structures, 1169
    origins, 1161–1162
        of name, 1162
    political organization, 1164
    Roman rule, 1170–1171
    in satrap rebellion, 1163
    silver coinage, 1164–1165
    6th–4th centuries BCE, 1163 (map)
    subjection to Rhodes, 1170
    tombs and burial practices, 1168–1169
    in the Trojan war, 1161
    under Persian authority, 1163–1164
Lycian Kingdom in Southwest Anatolia
    (Bryce), 1161–1172
Lycian language
    Carian and, 1193
    dialects of, 2156
    interpreting, 1165–1166
    Luwian language and, 2156–2157
    sample inscription, 1165
    surviving texts, 2156
    texts, 267
Lycian League, 1171
Lycian religion, 1166–1167
    consulting of oracles, 1167
    divinities, function of, 1167
Lycians, arrival in Anatolia, 260
Lydia
    coinage of, *1494*
    hegemony over Phrygia, 1158

Hellenistic and Roman settlements,
    1175
military campaigns and alliances,
    1175–1176
Persian conquest of, 976
physical geography, 1175
precious metal resources, 1176
rise of, 1102–1104
royal gifts to Greek sanctuaries, 1177
wealth of, 1176, 1181
Lydian architecture
    masonry, 1178–1179
    monumental, 1176, 1178
    in Sardis, 1180
Lydian art
    Achaemenid motifs, 1178
    jewelry, 1178
    myth and legend depicted in,
        1179–1180
    pottery, 1178, 1180–1181
    vase shapes, *1177*
Lydian language, 261
    grammar of, 2157
    surviving texts, 2157
Lydian literature, funerary texts, 1179
Lydian mythology, depicted in art,
    1179–1180
Lydian religion, divinities, 1179–1180
    invoked to punish violators of tombs,
        1180
Lydians
    Anatolia colonized by, 260, 1100
    coinage, 1178, 1375
    culture of, 1175
        Anatolian influences, 1176
        impact of, 1180–1181
    defeat by Cyrus II, 1174
    funeral offerings, 1180
    Greek influence on, 1176–1178
    music and dance, 1179
    retail trade, 1178
    in Sardis, 1180
    status of women, Lydian vs. Greek,
        1177–1178
Lygdamis, as ruler of Halicarnassus, 1188
Lykopolis. *See* Asyut
Lyres
    Egyptian, 2557, 2563
    Hittite, 2661–2664
        shapes of, 2662
    Mesopotamian, 2601, 2602
    Sumerian, 2602

M

Maacah, queen mother, deposed by Asa,
    597
Maʿadi
    commercial zone, 674
    urbanization, 674

Ma'adi Culture, 687. *See also* Egyptian
culture
Naqada replacement of, 682–683,
685–686
Ma'at (Egyptian principle of harmony),
274, 277, 1721, 2448
in Amarna art, 752
Egyptian divinity, personification of
fate personified by, 1688
offering of, in iconography, *1728,*
1729
order and justice maintained by, 1741
presentation of, *1734, 1742*
profile of, *1737*
symbolic meaning of, 1700
as truth, *1734*
symbols of, 1723–1724
Maaty, stela of, 2538, *2538*
Macdonald, M. C. A., **1355–1369**
Macedonia
Anatolia under, 1104
conquest of Greece, 1020
Syro-Palestinian area under, 1215
war with Bactria, 1020
Mackenzie, Duncan, 1273
McMahon, Gregory, **1981–1995**
Macqueen, J. G., **1085–1105**
Madduwatta, Hittite ruler, 1090–1091
Madinat Madi, temple at, 307, 308
Madinet Ghurab. *See* Miwer
Madyas, Scythian king, Median submission
to, 1015
Maeonians, 1175
Magan
ancient literary texts on, 1452–1453
copper resources of, 1454–1455,
1505–1506
location of, 1345, 1456
Manishtushu's military campaign
against, 1455
Mesopotamian trade with, 1425
olivine-gabbro and diorite available in,
1455–1458
trade
with Mesopotamia, 1452–1453
with Ur, 1456
Maghzalia, fortification wall near, 437
Magic. *See also* Black arts, the; Exorcism;
Magical practice
analogic, 2011–2012
apotropaic, 2013
attraction, 2013
definition of, 1896
deflection, 2013
divination distinguished from, 1688
legal nature of, 49–50
in legends, 2076
medicine and, 2007–2008
miracles and, 2075–2076
principles of, 2011
religion and, 2007, 2075, 2080

role of women in, 2078
as a science, 2007
science and, in ancient Near East, 2781
therapeutic, 2076–2079
to cure snakebite, 2077
unacceptable, 1693
Magic, Babylonian, 1896–1902. *See also*
Magic, Mesopotamian
influence on Hellenistic Judaism,
49–52
medicine and, 1901–1902
prophylactic, 1896–1902
Magic, Canaanite and Israelite, 2075–2080
Aramaic magic bowls, Gordon and,
2780–2781
Ark of the Covenant, 2079–2080
charms, 2078–2079
Hellenistic Judaism, Babylonian
influence on, 49–52
magical alphabets, 2079
ordeal, 2078
therapeutic, 2076–2079
Magic, Egyptian, 1697
color symbolism, 1780
medicine and, 1777–1778
mythology and, 1781
netherworld, 1776
origins and characteristics, 1776–1777
physical vs. spiritual conception, 1776
procedures, 1777–1779
protective purpose, 1776–1777
reputation of, 11–13
spells
against dangerous animals, 1780
against headache, 1779
categories of enemies in, 1778
childbirth, 1780
to turn deceased into spirit, 1779
stories as charms against injury, 2231
for treatment of ailments, 1778–1779
invoking mythical precedents, 1779
use of symbolic elements, 1779
vs. cult worship, 1775
Magic, Hittite, 582–583, 1982, 1988, 1991,
2008–2009
harmful vs. defensive, 2008
origins, 2018
state control of, 2008
Magic, Israelite. *See* Magic, Canaanite and
Israelite
Magic, Mesopotamian
Akkadian love charms, 2477
apotropaic, 1889, 1896–1902
medicine and, 1911–1914
religious beliefs and, 1895–1896
Magic, Ugaritic, to prevent and heal
snakebites, 2077
Magical practice
Egyptian, 1775–1782
descriptions in literary texts, 1777

in funerary religion, 1779
spheres of operation, 1779–1782
Hattic, adopted by Hittites, 2008
Hittite, 2011–2013
against sexual impotence, 2014–2015
foreign sources of, 2008–2009
incubation, 2009, 2011, 2013
laws governing, 557
materials used, 2011
mythology in, 2374
occasions for, 2011
offerants, 2009
officiating priests and priestesses,
2009
rites of contact, 2012
rites of identification and substitution,
2012
in Yazılıkaya open-air sanctuary, 2651
Kizzuwatna, adopted by Hittites, 2008
manuscripts for, 2008, 2018
Magical wands, to protect young children,
1780
Magicians. *See also* Priests
in Achaemenid Iran, priests and, 1967
in Babylonia, *āšipu* professional,
1901–1904, 1908
Egyptian
professional, 1783–1784
as protagonists in tales, 2232
Median, 1967
Mesopotamian (*āšipu*), 1901–1904, 1908
as healer, 1911, 1919–1921
profession of, 1911, 1914, 1919–1921
physicians and, 1783
professional, 1783
Magico-religious thought, in Mesopotamia,
1895–1896
Magnetism. *See* Archaeomagnetological
studies
Magus, powers attributed to, 12–13
Maguš magicians, Median, 1967
Māhaī tusñti (Twelve Gods), 1167
Mahmatlar, silver ingots from, 1512
Mahu, Egyptian military hero. *See*
Amenemheb
Maidman, Maynard Paul, **931–947**
Maidum, Sneferu pyramid at, building of,
725–726
Maier, John, **107–120**
Maiunehes, population of, in New
Kingdom period, 320
Majordomos, Assyrian. *See* rab ša muhhi
ekalli, abu bītim
Maka. *See* Magan
Makouria, kingdom of, 789
Malachite
beads, Neolithic, 1674
mining for, 1503
Malatya. *See* Melid
Malgium, Hammurabi's raids on, 906

under Zimri-Lim, 816
wagon use in, 1402
wall paintings, earrings on men in, 1643
walls of, colors of pigment used on, 2682
wine trade, 199
Mari: A Portrait in Art of a Mesopotamian City-State (Margueron), **885–899**
Marib, inscribed stela from, *2391*
Mari Palace of Zimri-Lim, 885–888, 890–891, *891, 893–896, 895,* 1509
  architectural decor, 886–889
    materials used, 886
  architectural units, 885–886
  axial progression and asymmetrical progressions of, 887
  building plan of, *433*
  chapel of Ishtar, 886, 890–891
    mural from, *891*
  Court of the Palm, 887, *892,* 892–893
  destruction by Hammurabi, 898
  effect of natural lighting on, 888–889
  exteriors, 886–887
    doors and windows, 886–887
    porticos, 887
  Gate of the Palace, 891
  Great Sanctuary, 886, 889–890
    antiquity of, 890
    statue of god in, 889
    statue of Idi-ilum in, 889–890
    statue of warrior in, 889, *889*
  lighting effects, 880, 888–889
    clerestory and, 886
    emotional effects of, 887
  main entrance, 887
  material used for, 886
  monumental character of, 886
  paintings, 893–896, *895*
    scenes of sacrifice, 893
    technique, 893
  pictorial wall compositions, 887–888
    colors, 887
    in Court of the Palm, 893–896, *895*
    lime plaster walls and, 887
    porticos for protection of, 887
    in relation to architecture, 887–888
    survival during destruction of palace, 898
    in temple of Ishtar, 890–891, *891*
  plan of, *888*
  priests' role in, 889
  private apartments, 897
  as reflection of time, 898
  relief of goddess at, *890,* 891
  royal quarters, 891–892
  statue of Goddess of the Flowing Vase, 896, *896*
  throne room, 887, 897
  wall painting, 1584–1585

Marjoram, 156
Markasu (bond), 1842
Marketplaces, local
  in Egypt, 353
  pottery wares in, 1562
Markets
  demand of, and pastoral production, 211
  in domestic animals, 205
  multiple, of nomads, 210–211
  for pottery, 1562–1564
Markhashi (city-state), Shulgi and, 844
Marlik Tepe
  cemetery at, 994
  cylinder seals and metal vessels, *1008*
  Mitannian influence, 1008
Marqas (Marqasi, Maraş)
  hieroglyphic inscriptions found at, 2776
  Hittite population, 1296
  sculpture and inscriptions, Neo-Hittite period, 1302
Marriage. *See also* Adultery; Divorce; Matrimonial alliances; Sacred marriage; Weddings
  Achaemenid Empire
    dowries, 1477
    transmission of Persian nationality through, 520
    wedding customs and celebrations, 519–520
  Babylonian. *See also* Marriage, Mesopotamian
    Akkadian rituals for divinities, 2477
    Greek views of, 59
    incantations and, 1900–1901
    laws of, and Hellenistic Judaism, 45–46
  Egypt, 348–349
    absent husbands, 374
    adultery as private matter in, 358
    age of, 371
    ceremony, 372
    courtship, 371
    diplomatic, 769
    as economic activity, 353
    with family members, 372
    financial aspects, 372–374
    husband-wife relationship, 374
    partner selection, 371
    settlements, 367, 372–373
    to widowed and divorced women, 373
    wives' responsibilities, 374
    women's employment and, 374
  Hittite, 572–574
    betrothal contracts, 558–559, 566
    between different economic and social classes, 559–560
    between gods and goddesses, 566–567
    bought sons-in-law, 559
    counseling, 567

daughter's husband integrated into paternal family, 534
    dowry, 558–559
    legal aspects, 558–560
    of slaves to free persons, 565
  Israelite, 644–646
    arranged, 644–645
    betrothal stage, 645
    biblical laws affecting, 625
    biblical references, 646
    bride price, 625
    ceremony, 645
    consummation of, 646
    dowry and trousseau, 645
    Hellenistic period, Babylonian influence, 45–46
    infidelity, 645–646
    negotiations for, 625
    seven days of celebration, 645
    to slaves, 645
    wife's role, 624–625
  levirate. *See* Levirate marriage
  Mesopotamia, 488–492, 494
    dowries in, 479–480
    polygynous, 478–479
  Ugarit, negotiations, in myth, 2406–2407
Mar šipri (messenger), 1465–1466
Martensite, 1515
Martin, John, painter, 77
Martkobi, burial mounds, 1056
Martu (*Mar-tu,* MAR.TU). *See* Amorites
Martu-wall, in *Epic of Lugalbanda and Enmerkar,* 2323
Marx, Karl, *Das Kapital,* 108
Maşat Hüyük, Hittite texts from, 2151
Mashanauzzi, Hittite princess
  infertility of, 1116
  marriage of, 1108
Mashduri, king of Shekha River Land, Khattushili III and, 1109
Mashkan-shapir (Tell Abu Dhuwari)
  burial sites, 242
  Hammurabi's conquest of, 910–911
  layout of, *240–241*
  location of temple, 239
  manufacturing sites, 241–242
  organization of, 240
Mashtigga, Hittite woman, family counseling, 567
Masons
  marks, 456
  payment, 458
Maspero, Gaston, 2755
Maspians, Persian tribe, 517
Massa', tribe of, 1360
Maṣṣebôt (cultic pillars), 2642
Mass deportations. *See* Deportations
Mass spectrometry, in metals analysis, 1512

Mastabas. *See also* Pyramids, Egyptian
decoration, 1773
Egyptian, building of, 721–724, 723,
726
in nonroyal tombs, 1770
Master (Scholar), advisement of king on
religious matters, 1865
Mas'udu, king of Lihyan, 1362
Matanazi, Hittite princess. *See*
Mashanauzzi, Hittite princess
Matar, Phrygian divinity, 1156–1157
**Material, Technology, and Techniques
in Artistic Production** (Gunter),
1539–1551
Materials for the Sumerian Lexicon, 2306
Mathematics. *See also* Geometry
curriculums, scribal school, 2271, 2274
development of, record keeping and,
2103–2105
**Mathematics, Astronomy, and
Calendars in Pharaonic Egypt**
(Robins), **1799–1813**
Mathematics, Egyptian, 1800–1810
applications to daily life, 1812
approximations, 1808
in architecture, 1810–1811
contribution of, 1812–1813
division, 1803
fractions, 1812–1813
addition and subtraction of,
1803–1804
advantages and disadvantages of unit,
1807–1808
doubling of unit, 1804–1805
multiplication of, 1803, 1806–1807
geometry, 1808–1810
area of a circle, 1800, 1808–1809
formula for a frustum, 1809–1810
hieratic and demotic papyri, 1800
multiplication, 1801, 1803
of fractions by other whole numbers,
1806–1807
proportionality, 1811
Pythagoras's theorem, 1809
reciprocal relationships, 1804–1805,
1809
square roots, 1800
approximation of, 1808
surviving texts, 1800
uses of, 1800
value of pi, 1800, 1808
variant values, 1805–1806
volume of a cylindrical granary,
1800–1801
Mathematics, Jewish, Babylonian influence
on, 47
Mathematics, Mesopotamian. *See also*
Sexagesimal calculation
achievements and limitations of thought,
1944–1947
age and character of, 1943–1944

Akkadian texts on, 2299
algebraic logic, 1944–1945
sample problem, 1946
Babylonian, influence on Hellenistic
Judaism, 47
clay counters, 1949, *1951*
evidence for, 1941–1942
figures and fractions, 1819
geometry, 1945, *1951*
sample problem, 1946
metrological and geometric concepts in
reasoning, 1947
multiplication, *1949–1950*, *1951*
Old Babylonian period, 1943–1944
practical-life phrasebook, 1944
problem texts, 1944
protometric system, 1955–1956, *1956*
reciprocal calculation, *1954*, 1954–1955,
1955
sexagesimal vs. decimal notation, 1954
square root of 2, 1945
squaring, *1949*, *1951*
Sumerian counter system, *1948*
teaching of, 1944
tool texts, 1944
value of pi, 1945
zero concept, 1954
Mati'el, king of Arpad, treaties of, 1289
Mati''il, king of Dedan, 1361–1362
Matriarchy, Elamite, speculation on, 1960
Matrilineality
Elamite society, 1030
Lycia, 1169
Matrimonial alliances
of Assyrian kings, 965
of Ebla, 1224
of Khattushili III, 1117
of Shulgi, 844
of Zimri-Lim, 816
Matson, Frederick R., **1553–1565**
Mattān (marriage payment), 645
Matthews, Donald, **455–468**
Mausolus, satrap of Caria
conspired against by Arlissis, 527
control over Lycia, 1163
mausoleum designed by, *1188*,
1189–1190
Max Planck Institute for Chemistry, 1513
Max Planck Institute for Nuclear Physics,
1501, 1513
Maysar
copper mining and processing at, 1341
graves at, 1347
irrigation system (*falaj*) at, 1346
Mazar, Amihai, **1523–1537**
Mazdaism, 1042
Mazkîr (Israelite official), 600, 621–622
ME (Mesopotamian concept, *parṣu*)
Tablets of Destiny, 2447
traditional rules, 1865, 1868

Measurement
cubit rods in, 1810
in Egypt, baking value units (*psw*),
1379–1380
of land areas, 1810
in pyramid design, 1810–1811
Thera, 1440
unit of adulteration, 1812
unit of value, 1812
units of road distance
in Assyrian Empire, 1402, 1417
in Babylonia, 1402, 1417
in Persian, 1418
Meat
animals raised for. *See* Animal
husbandry; Animals, domesticated
in Babylonia, varieties of, 496
Canaanite and Israelite households
types of, 638
when eaten, 638
ME (lunar visibility interval), 1937
Mebamain, king of Kish, domain extended
to Khafaje, 398
Medes
Achaemenid conquest of, 976
in Anatolia, 1048
alliance with Persia, 1017
in annals of Shalmaneser III,
1011–1012
Assyrians and, 825, 1012
destruction of Assyrian Empire,
1015–1016
dynasty destroyed by Cyrus, 1016
Hasanlu architecture and, 990
Lydians vs., 1104
in western Iran, 989, 994–995, 998,
1012–1013
Media, history of, in Greek literature, 57
Median architecture, porticoes, 1016
Median religion
divinities, worship of in Achaemenid
Iran, 1967–1968
priests and magicians in, 1967
Medical terminology, Egyptian derivation,
1796
Medical texts
Akkadian, 2299
Mesopotamian, 1913–1914
as sources of information, 1911–1912
types of, 1913–1914
Medicine, Babylonian
Herodotus on, 59
influence on Hellenistic Judaism,
47–49
magic and, 1901–1902
omens compendium, 1908
under Kassites, 920
Medicine, Egyptian, 1116, 1708. *See also*
Anatomy, Egyptian knowledge of;
Pharmacopoeia, Egyptian; Physiology,
Egyptian knowledge of
demonic origin of ailments, 1779–1780

empirico-rational vs. magico-religious
approach, 1787–1788, 1796
etiology of disease, 1788–1789
legacy of, 1797–1798
magic and, 1777–1778
papyri, 1793–1797
pathology, 1790–1793
Greek and Latin sources, 1793
paleopathological studies, 1790
poor hygiene and spread of disease,
1791
representation of in art, *1791*,
1791–1792, *1792*
socioeconomic differences, 1792
wound treatment, 1794–1795
Medicine, Greek, near eastern and,
47–48
Medicine, Hittite, 581–583
Medicine, Jewish, Babylonian influence
on, 47–49
Medicine, magic and, 2007–2008
snakebite prevention and cure, 2077
Medicine, Mesopotamian, 1911–1924
changes in, over time, 1912
Greek medicine not derived from, 1923
herbal remedies, 1911, 1914–1915,
1918, 1923
identification of plants used in, 1915
home remedies, 1912
magical treatment methods, 1913–1914,
1919–1921
sources of evidence on, 1911–1912
surgical treatment, 1921–1922
treatment
for childbirth complications, 1917
dental problems, 1916
ear problems, 1915–1916
eye problems, 1915
gastrointestinal problems, 1916
for mental illness, 1917
skin problems, 1916–1917
urinary tract problems, 1916
veterinary, 1923
**Medicine, Surgery, and Public Health
in Ancient Egypt** (Weeks),
1787–1798
**Medicine, Surgery, and Public Health
in Ancient Mesopotamia** (Biggs),
1911–1924
Medinet Habu, temple of, relief of
Ramesses III naval victory, 299–300
Mediterranean islands
cultural sequence, dating of, 1434
environment and climate, 1433–1434
vegetation disturbance, 1433
human colonization, 1434
in Late Bronze Age, 1437 (map)
links to ancient Near East, 1446–1447
polities and economies, archaeological
evidence, 1434–1446

Mediterranean phytogeographical zone
Eu-Mediterranean vegetation, 154, 156
Oro-Mediterranean vegetation, 156–157
Mediterranean region. *See* Eastern
Mediterranean
history, periodization of. *See* Chronology
Megabyzus, Persian ruler
exile, 526
marital problems, 520
Megiddo (Tell al-Mutasallim)
blockade wall, 1530
building supported by pillars at, 2673
Canaanite palace, ivory furniture, 1656
city wall, 1526
defense systems, 1314
Egyptian siege of, 1248
textual accounts, 292–293
Thutmose III in, 299
gate houses, 1532
Gilgamesh Epic excerpts found at, 2343
Late Bronze Age II ivory showing king
on cherub-throne, 594
level VII palace, vessels found in,
2684–2685
silver hoard at, 1489
Temple 2048 at, 609
tombs of, ivory works from, 2687–2688
water systems, 1314
well-cisterns of, 2672
Mehri language, 2120
Me'il (fringed robe), 643
Meketaten, Egyptian princess, in art, 761
ME.LÁM (radiant light), 1842
Melchert, H. Craig, **2151–2159**
Melid (Arslantepe, Malatya, Melitene)
Assyrian tribute from, 1100
Kashka people at, 1099
Kummukh annexation of, 1101
Lion Gate, 1299
dating of, 1301
dynastic genealogies, 1300–1301
orthostat reliefs, *2656*, 2656
reliefs, 2774
Neo-Hittite period, 1296, 1299, 1301
Melishihu, Kassite king, *kudurrus* of,
2585, 2585–2586
Melitene. *See* Melid
Melôg (dowry), 645
Melqart, divinity
popularity of, 1291
Tyrian continuity with Ugaritic tradition,
2033
Melukkha
ancient literary texts on, 1452–1453
Indus Valley as possible location of,
1456–1458
language of, 1458
trade
with Babylonia, 1456, 1458
with Mesopotamia, 1452–1453, 1506,
1511

Memoirs. *See* Autobiographies
Memory, writing as replacement for, 2190
Memory and Literacy in Western Asia
(Vanstiphout), **2181–2196**
Memphis (Mit Rahina)
Assyrian capture of, 825
as First Dynasty capital, 694
Hyksos rule over, 747
Ionian and Carian mercenaries in, 1192
Middle Kingdom, 739, 742
palace of Apries at, 315
palace of Merneptah at, 314–315
Piye's siege of, 298, 300
temple sites at, 321
archaeological discoveries at,
1192–1193
theogony at, 1701–1702
Menats, 2557, 2565
defined, 2555
Menena, tomb of, woman nursing child
relief, *2542*, 2542
Menes (Aha?), king of Egypt. *See also*
Narmer, king of Egypt
as the first Dynastic king, 680, 686, 736
traditions about, 693–694
Menhir (megalith)
cylindrical or conical form, *2642*, 2642
male and female principles, 2639
pillar and column forms, 2639
Menkhyt-Nebtu, Egyptian divinity, 2563
Mensa Isiaca (Tabula Bembina), in study
of Egyptian iconography, 22
Menstruation
Babylonian beliefs and customs, 490
defilement concepts and, 2052–2053
Mentuhotep, Egyptian master builder, 741
Mercenary soldiers. *See* Soldiers
Merchants. *See also* Trade
Aramaean, in textile trade, 1287
Assyrian
in Anatolia, 864
Anatolian metals industry and, 1087,
1507–1508
cooperation policy of, 1088
Assyrian, in Kanesh
administrative role, 867–868
associations, 862
capital, 869
common values and competitive
behavior, 868–869
contacts with Asshur, 869–870
diversification, 869
with families in Asshur, 869–870
hierarchy of firms, 869
homes of, *861*, *862*
Old Assyrian period, 865
organization, 864
Cypriot, at al-Mina, 1284
Eblaean, Emar trade prohibited to,
1227
financing of, by royalty, 1451

Narunde, Elamite divinity, "Goddess of
Victory," 1960
Naruqqum (moneybag), 869
Naryasanga, Median divinity, 1968
Nasāḫu (mathematical term), 1949
Našû, 1949
Natakamani, king of Kush
Lion Temple relief, 786
temple building, 785
National states, defined, 1213
National theologies, concept of, patron
deities and, 2047–2048
Natnu, king of Nebayot, 1366
relations with Assyria, 1360
Natron (compound), uses of, 390
Natufian culture, 792
Natural catastrophes. *See also* Drought
retribalization and, 1199
worship to forestall, 1731, 1899
Natural resources
art materials from, 1539–1540
local availability of, 1451
of Mesopotamia, unequal distribution
of, 1397
obtaining through warfare, 413
Sumerian access to, 846
Syro-Palestinian, 1197–1198
Naukratis, Greek trade concentrated at,
711
Nauri Decree of Sety, 357–358
Naval warfare
Assyrian, 960
Egyptian
conduct of battles, 300
New Kingdom, 290
pictorial record, 299
ships, 1424
textual evidence, 299–300
titles and ranks, 300
Hittite, 549–550
merchant ships as naval vessels,
550
ships, 1421, 1424–1425, 1429–1430
Nazi-Maruttash, Kassite king, boundary
stone, 921
Nazlet Khater, Upper Paleolithic site, 668
Neanderthals, remains of, 792
Nebamun, tomb of
reliefs, secondary registers, 2538–2539
wall paintings, color usage, 2541–2542
Nebayot tribe, 1359–1360
Nebethetepet, Egyptian divinity
Hathor and, 1701
profile of, 1737
Nebhepetre Mentuhotep, king of Egypt,
735–736, 744
defeats northern dynasty, 280
reunification of Upper and Lower Egypt
under, 698
Nebi Mend. *See* Qadesh

Nebi Yunus (settlement mound). *See also*
Nineveh
site of, 246
Nebtawyre Mentuhotep, king of Egypt,
736
royal trade expedition for, 1378
Nebuchadnezzar (Nebuchadrezzar) I, king
of Babylon
destruction of Susa, 1013, 1028
Elam vs., 821, 1011
Nebuchadnezzar II, king of Babylon
Akkadian traditions, 831–832
Assyrian holdings of, 965
Babylon ziggurat restored by, 430–431
in Book of Daniel, Nabonidus as basis
for, 978
building program of, 826
enameled brick decoration by, 2599
extension of Babylonian authority,
971–972
fortification system, 1533
Wall of Media, 438
hanging gardens. *See* Hanging Gardens
of Babylon
invasion of Egypt, 1367
laws and judgments of, 470
military conquests, 972
Nabonidus and, 974
siege of Tyre, 1322
Nebuchadrezzar. *See* Nebuchadnezzar I,
king of Babylon
Necho II, king of Egypt, Phoenician
circumnavigators, 1331
Neck adornment, Egyptian, 1611, *1611*
Necklaces
cylinder seals as, *1597*
Mesopotamian, 1636, 1638, *1641*
from Nimrud tombs, 2699
Necromancy
in Canaan and Israel, 2069
biblical references to, 2074–2075
sentence for, 2075
Egyptian, 2075
Hittite, 2029
magic, Babylonian and rabbinic, 51
role of mediums and wizards in,
2074–2075
Necropolises, Egyptian
Middle Kingdom, 743
royal. *See also* Pyramids, Egyptian
early, 720
at Giza, 730
Nectanebo I, king of Egypt, 1376
Nedu, mythical gatekeeper. *See* Bidu,
mythical gatekeeper
Nefer
as overseer of singers, 2562
tomb of, 2562
Neferirkare Kakai, king of Egypt, funerary
temple of, documents from, 2204
Neferirtenef, tomb of, reliefs, 2537

Neferkare. *See* Pepy II, king of Egypt
Neferkare and the General Sisene, source
and content, 2227
Nefermaat, Egyptian prince, tomb of, 340
Nefertari, Egyptian queen, 769
tomb of, *1706*
in Valley of the Queens, 2542
Nefertem, Egyptian divinity, profile of,
1738
Nefertiti, Egyptian queen, 701, 749
in art
brown quartzite bust, 753, *754*, 761
Great Palace reliefs, 760
painted limestone bust, 753, *753*
"tired Nefertiti," 753, *755*
Nefrusobek (Sobeknefru), Egyptian queen,
746
Negev
forts, 1315
metalworking in, 1504
Nehemiah (Hebrew Bible), 2443
sources and style of, 2438
Neith, Egyptian divinity
glyphic on sanctuary of, *307*, 307
profile of, 1738
Nekhbet, Egyptian divinity
profile of
"She of Nekheb (Elkab)," 1738
in royal symbols, 275–276
Nekhebu, Egyptian architect,
autobiography of, 2247
Nekhen. *See* Hierakonpolis
Nēmequ (wisdom), 1816. *See also Ludlul
Bēl Nēmeqi*
Nemes (royal headcloth), 1725, 1727
Nemty, Egyptian divinity, in *The
Contendings of Horus and Seth*, 1704
Neo-Assyrian Empire
administration, 409–410
bronze casts of, 1491
bronze ingots of, 1489
conquest of Lower Egypt, 779–780
deportations by, 821
eunuchs employed by, 964
expansionist motives of, 962
historical overview of, 823–826
military exploits of, 960
military manpower of, 967
provincial governors, 409–410
obligations for Assur Temple
offerings, 410
provincial system, 409
Syro-Palestinian area under, 1213–1214
Tell Sheikh Hamad archives and, 820
treaties of, 965
tribute-payment ceremonies, 1470
Urartu and, 1139–1140
Neo-Babylonian (the term), 808
Neo-Babylonian Empire
Assyrians vs.
under Merodach-Baladan II, 824
under Shalmaneser III, 823

Nile River (*continued*)
  historical period
    documentation on, 136
    fluctuations in, 135–136
  in historical period, 135–136
    Early Dynastic, 135–136
    late prehistoric, *133*
    monsoonal rains and, 135–136
    reductions in, 136, 138
      disintegration of Old and New
        kingdoms and, 136
  in Heliopolitan cosmogony, 1700
  as major highway, 1421
  in Osiris myth, 1702
  river craft of, 1422–1425
  as subject of American literature, 30
  water sources, 142
  wetland plants of, 157
Nile River Delta
  about 300–200 BCE, 140 (map)
  Asiatic and Libyan nomads in, 226
  independence of, in Fourteenth
    Dynasty, 701
  natural landscape, 139
  penetration into ancient Palestine, 738
  role in economy, 225
  Sea Peoples in, 707–708
  Upper Egyptian expansion into, 694
  western Asian immigrants in, 1205
Nile Valley. *See also* Egypt; Faiyum
    Depression
  Acheulian artifacts, 666
  agriculture in, 139
  climatic changes, food production and,
    671
  as convex floodplain, 139
  introduction of agriculture
    environmental factors, 671–672
    political effects of, 671
  irrigation in, 141
  late prehistoric peoples, 133
  modification of by humans, 139–141
  Mousterian sites, 668
  natural landscape, 139–142
  populations localized in, 139
  Predynastic period
    community leaders, 675
    division of labor, 675
  prehistoric peoples, 668–669
  role in economy, 225
Nilo-Saharan language, distribution of
  prehistoric pottery and, 670
Nimaetreʿ, Egyptian priest, tomb at Giza,
  2562
Nimrud. *See* Kalkhu
Nimrud Black Obelisk, *2491*, 2535–2536
  state ideology expressed in, 2492–2493
Nimrud Throne Base, *2490–2491*
  state ideology expressed in, 2492–2493
Ninai-Negev area, nomadic herding, 671

Ninali (*Bēlēt-ali*), Elamite divinity, "Lady
  of the City," 1959–1960, 1965, 1969
Ninazu, Mesopotamian divinity, 1860
  association with Mushkhusshu dragon,
    1841
  in the netherworld, 2021
Nineveh (Tell Kuyunjik)
  Assurbanipal's palace at, relief from, *513*
  Assyrian musicians depicted at, 2605
  Babylonian-Mede-Scythian capture of,
    1103
  citadel mound, 244–245
  craft quarters, 461
  European art images of, 74–77
  European descriptions of, 72
  excavations, 2697
  the fall of, Greek writers on, 56, 60
  fortifications of, 245, 1532
  Gilgamesh Epic found at, 2330
  Hurrian rule, 1245
  Late Assyrian palace at, 434
  layout, 245, *246–365*
  Median capture of, 825–826
  messengers dispatched from, 966
  monuments of, influence on European
    artists, 77
  North Palace at, *435*
  palace of
    military scribes relief, 2267
    reliefs at, 2586
  relief art in, *1544*
    depiction of textiles, 1584
  resources concentrated in, 822
  Review Palace at, 419
  Sargon statue from, 1504
  settlement mounds, 246–247
  site of, 246–247
  size of, 1213
  Southwest Palace of Sennacherib,
    reliefs, 2701
  statue of nude woman found at, 2594
  temple of Nabu, library of, 2197, 2206
  textile production documentation from,
    1581
  under Sennacherib, 824
  walls of, sculpted reliefs on, 2673
  water supply of Sennacherib for,
    2736–2737, 2746
Ningal, Mesopotamian divinity
  depiction on stela of Ur-Nammu,
    2585
  temple at Ur, 427
Ningirsu, Mesopotamian divinity, 1860
  depiction on stela of Eannatum, 2584
  state ruler's connection to, 397
  symbols of, 1846
  temple of, 2577
Ningishzida, Mesopotamian divinity, 1860,
  1888
  association with Mushkhusshu dragon,
    1841
  symbols of, *1840*

Nin-Gubla, Akkadian divinity, offerings to,
  833
Ninisina, Mesopotamian divinity, 1860
Ninkasi, Hymn to, 198
Ninkhursag, Mesopotamian divinity, 1860
  symbols of, *1839*
Ninlil, Mesopotamian divinity
  Shulgi's devotion to, 849
  in Sumerian royal hymnody, 850, 854
  symbols of, *1839*
Ninmakh, Sumerian divinity, in *Enki and
  Ninmakh*, 1833
Nin-shata-pada, Sumerian princess, letter-
  prayer of, 1877, 2266
Ninshubur, Mesopotamian divinity,
  iconography, Neo-Assyrian and Neo-
  Babylonian periods, 1847
Ninsun, Sumerian divinity
  Lugalbanda and, 846
  as mother of Gilgamesh, 2327
  Shulgi and, 849, 853
Nintu, Mesopotamian divinity
  iconography, 1845
  symbols of, *1839*
Ninurta, Mesopotamian divinity, *1840*,
  1962–1963
  combat with Mushmakkhu dragon, in
    art, *1853*, 1853
  pursuit of Asakku monster, 1842–1843
    depicted in art, *1852*, 1852
  symbols, *1838*
  temple at Kalkhu
    monumental reliefs, 1842–1843
    royal annals at, 961
Ninus, king of Assyria, Ctesias on, 60
Ninus Romance (Hellenistic novel), 61
Nippur (Nuffar)
  academy at, 2189
  administration of, 919–920
  aristocratic life in, literary treatments of,
    1875
  as center of southern Mesopotamian
    alliance, 399
  clay model from, *1542*
  cuneiform tablets found at, 1481
  excavations at, 2698, 2749
  Farmer's Almanac found at, 193
  gardens of, 440
  great temple of, 811. *See also* Ekur
    Temple
    location, 238
  houses of, incantation bowls under,
    2781
  jewelry findings, 1637
  as literary center, 813, 1869
  literary texts from, 2281, 2283
  medical texts from, 1911
  Murashu family archives, 1476,
    1480–1485
  musical instructions found at, 2607
  Naram-Sin's treatment of, 834

patron divinity of, 809, 1962–1963
plan of, 238
priesthood of, perspective on Naram-
Sin, 838
private loans at, 1492
residence patterns in, 2723–2724
royal land grants, 923
scribal academy at, 2206
seal ownership, 1597
Sumerian kingship and, 848–849
Sumerian tablet from, 852
textile production documentation from,
1581
under Artaxerxes II, 827–828
Ur road to, 844
West Semitic population, 1481
ziggurat at, 429
Niqmaddu II, king of Ugarit
Hittite vassalage, 1259
personal seal of, 2385
treaty with Shuppiluliuma, Hittite Great
King, 2385
Niqmaddu III, king of Ugarit, Pudukhepa
and, 1112
Niqmepa of Ugarit
correspondence with Khattushili III,
2784
lawsuit of Iribkhazi against, 405
Nissen, Hans J., **791–806**
Nitokris, Egyptian queen, 746
Nitokris, queen of Babylonia, 58
in Handel's *Belshazzar*, 78
Njswt (royal Egyptian title), 275
Njswt-bjtj (royal Egyptian title), 275
Nofret, Egyptian queen, 742
statue of, 1608, *1608*
Nofru-Ptah, sister of Amenemhet IV, 746
Nomadism, pastoral. *See also* Nomads
archaeological records of, 2722–2723
meagerness of, 251–252
Caucasus, 1055, 1058
characterization of, 1359
continuity from ancient to modern
times, 2722–2723
development of, "secondary-products
revolution" linked to, 253
Egypt, 671
prehistoric times, 676
emergence of, 206
explanatory models for development of,
252–253
fallow herding and, 210
in historical period, 253–257
horizontal migratory patterns of, 249
migratory routes, 249
origins of, in western Iran, 252–253
pack animals and, 253
political decentralization and, 253–254
political organization of, 249–250
risks of, 210

sedentists' relationship with, 250–251,
254
as interdependent and antagonistic,
250–251, 254–257
mutually dependent nature of, 250
shift from sedentary lifestyle to, in
Arabian Peninsula, 1344
social stratification among, 252
tent camp site in Iran, 2722, 2723
textual sources on, 252–254
meagerness of, 252
tribal organization of, 249
vertical migratory patterns of, 1, 17
in western Asia, 249–258
in Zagros highlands of Iran, 252–253
Nomads. *See also* Nomadism, pastoral
Amorite, 1239–1240
animal husbandry in relation to, 207
Arabian, 256–257. *See also* Bedouins
Assyrian campaign against, 1366
early first millennium, 1364
first millennium, 1358–1359
Syrian attacks on, 1365, 1367
tribes, 1359–1360
warfare, 1363
camel nomads
Assyrians and, 256–257
trade and, 256
Central Asian
burial remains, 1078–1081
cultural contribution, 1083
geographical distribution, 1078
origin of culture, 1078
rituals and beliefs, 1081
weapons, 1081–1083
clan and kin relationships of, 469
interactions with Fertile Crescent
inhabitants, 1243–1244
military aggression by, against urban
states, 254–256
multiple markets of, 210–211
sedentarization of, among Amorites,
255
sedentists' relationship with, 257
trans-Arabian trade, 1359–1360
weaving looms used by, 1574
western Asian
Egyptian sources on, 1205
Mari tablets on, 1281
Nomarch (Egyptian official), 743, 1380,
1383
appointment and removal of, 281–282
independence of, under 11th and 12th
dynasties, 699
tomb inscriptions of, 2435
Nomes (Egyptian provinces), 739
administration of, 279–280
Late Period, 285
districts of the North, South, and Head
of the South, 282–283

division of, 280
political power in, 1383
religious freedom, 282
Nomos persikos (Persian law), 523
Nonferrous metals
in artistic production, 1546
casting of, 1547
Nonnus of Panopolis, myth of Typhon,
1978
Nora Stone, reference to Shardanu in,
1444
Norden, Frederick Ludvig, Nile
voyage, 18
Norris, Edwin, decipherment of Behistun
text, 87
Norşuntepe, copper workshop at, 1504
North Africa, history, seventh century,
1365–1367
North Arabia
history
early first millennium, 1364
eighth century BCE, 1364–1365
later first millennium, 1367–1368
sixth century BCE, 1367
Neo-Babylonian rulers, 974–975
North Arabia in the First Millennium
BCE (Macdonald), **1355–1369**
North Arabian languages, 2121
Northwest Semitic languages. *See*
Levantine languages
Notariqon system of word interpretations,
Babylonian and Hellenistic Jewish,
52–53
Nourishing Gods (Nap-ratep), Elamite
deities, 1960
Npš (vital element), 2063
Nubia
administration, 771
Egyptian influence and control
during Old Kingdom, 697
Middle Kingdom conquests of, 739,
743–744
military administration of, 283
reestablished under Eighteenth
Dynasty, 702–703
in Twelfth and Thirteenth dynasties,
700–701
in Egyptian mythology, 1708
forts found in, 1529, *1530*
gods of, 1736
horses of, 418
lower, 692 (map)
New Kingdom temples of, 308, 324
tribute by, 1489, 1493
Nubians
in Egypt, 231–232
change in pharaonic image and, 232
Egyptian depiction of, 226, 227
in Egyptian military, 228
rule of Egypt by, 232
male fashion, Egyptian adoption of, 385

O

inheritance of office, 346–347, 352, 695

inscriptions chronicling their achievements, 2435

merit in selection and promotion of, 695, 700

payment of by usufruct land, 345, 354

stability and continuity of, 701

Theban tombs of, 1380

Hittite, local cults and, 1994

as literate class, 2188

of Mesopotamian capitals, 239

Ogdoad, Egyptian collective divinity. *See* Nun, Egyptian divinity

in Heropolitan theogony, 1702

Oils. *See also* Olive oil

anointing. *See* Anointing oils

Egypt

for cooking, 368

for skin care, 368

vegetable. *See* Vegetable oils

Ointments. *See* Salves

Old age. *See* Elderly people

Old Akkadian language, royal records in, 810

Old Assyrian language, texts, 262

Old Babylonian period. *See* Babylon, First Dynasty; Babylonia

barter in, 1487–1488

bureaucracy, 817

monetary transactions in, 1492–1493

ring money in, 1488–1489

sacred marriage rite in, 848

Old Hittite Empire

Hattic loanwords, 262

historical overview of, 1088–1090

Kashka nomads in, 264

religion of, Palaic and, 265

sea borders mentioned in texts of, 260

Old Hittite Laws, family law, 263

Old Kingdom Pyramid Texts, 1711–1712, 2207

afterlife in, 1767

homosexual encounter in, 1704

joining of imperishable stars, 1770

mythological allusions in, 1698

offering lists in, 202

The Old Man and the Young Girl, 2449

Oldowan tool assemblage, 665

Old Persian cuneiform

decipherment of, 83–84

invention of, 1038

meager documentary sources, 85

Old Persian language

after reign of Xerxes, 1049

royal inscriptions, 1049

Old Testament. *See* Bible (Hebrew Bible, Old Testament)

Olduvai Gorge, Tanzania, Oldowan tool assemblage, 665

Oligarchy, Syro-Palestine, 590

Amurru, 589

Olive oil

keeping qualities of, 193

trading of, 192

Olive trees, 160, 162

in coastal regions, 201

domestication of, 192

growing of, 178

wild, 154, 160

Oller, Gary H., **1465–1473**

Olrik, Axel, epic laws, 2323–2324

Oman Peninsula, 1337 (map). *See also* Magan

agriculture in, 1338

in Assyrian and Achaemenid texts, 1345

copper mining and processing, 1341, 1455

Islamic era, 1505

ecology of, 1335–1336

graves, Iron Age, 1346–1347, *1349*

Harappan presence in, 1457–1459, *1461*

Iron Age culture of, 1344

irrigation systems, 1345–1346

mud-brick architecture, *1348*

settlements

1st millennium BCE, 1345–1346

3rd millennium BCE, 1338–1342

Wadi Suq culture, 1344

Omanum Emporium (ancient town), location of, 1348

Al-'Omari, burial sites, 674

Omens. *See also* Signs, divine

astronomical type, 2016

Babylonian, 1904–1908, 2015–2016

astrological, 1930–1931

influence on Hellenistic Judaism, 51–53

diagnostic, 1908

Egyptian

astrological, 1783

connected with months, 1782–1783

in Hellenistic Judaism, Babylonian influence on, 51–53

Hittite, structure and means of expression, 2016

liver models, 2016

Mesopotamian, 1692, 1904–1908

association of predicted events with celestial phenomena, 1926

astrological, 1925–1926

celestial, 1939

compendia of, 1907–1908

formulation of, 1927

lunar eclipse, 1926

nativity, 1932

birth omens and, 1933

public, 1907–1908

rituals and, Babylonian beliefs on, 1899–1900

solar signs, 2016

solicited, 1899, 1904–1906

unsolicited, 1899, 1906–1907

Omens, Babylonian. *See also* Omens, Mesopotamian

Omens, Mesopotamian. *See also* Omens, Babylonian

Omotic languages, 2137

Omri, House of, in Assyrian records, 1318

Omri, king of Israel

foundation of new capital, 1313

moves capital to Samaria, 1311

philophoenician policies, 1318

reign of, 1212

subjugation of Moab, 1316

On. *See* Heliopolis

Onagers

as chariot animals, from Tell Ajrab, *2739, 2740*

as wagon animals, in Ur death pit, 2724

Onbir Lisan, stone shaft with relief, dating of, 2641

On Isis and Osiris, 1782

apocalypticism in, 2089

Onomasticon of Amenemope

Philistines in, 1269

Shardanu in, 1444

Onomastics. *See* Names

Onuris, Egyptian divinity, profile of, 1738

Opening/Washing of the Mouth (*pīt/Mīs pî* ritual), 1732, 1781, 1903

Operas, European, Babylonian themes in, 77–78

Ophir

gold resources of, 1322, 1460–1461

location of, 1461

Opium poppy, origin and domestication of, 191

Oracle of Hystaspes, 2089

Oracles. *See also* Divination

augury, 2017

before treaties, 553

biblical references, against Egypt, 2075

consulted for military advice, 546, 550

Egyptian, 1782–1783

festival, 1744

temple, 1744

trials conducted by, 357

extispicy, 2016–2017

Hittite, 533

components, 2016

legal consultation, 622

linguistic difficulties, 2016

lot, 2016

for military advice, 2015

preconditions for, 2015

in private life, 2015

in the psalms, 2408

results of, 2016

rock partridge, 2017

snake, 2017

Papyrus Chester Beatty VI, 1794
Papyrus Ebers, 1793–1794
    Egyptian pharmacology and, 1795–1797
Papyrus Edwin Smith, 1793
    author of, 1795
    magical incantations in, 1787
    treatment of wounds in, 1794–1795
    withholding of treatment in, 1795, 1797
Papyrus 55001, eroticism in, 2522
Papyrus Great Harris, 2202
Papyrus Harris I, Philistines in, 1269
Papyrus Hearst, 1794
Papyrus Insinger, 371
    power of fate in, 2446–2447
    shame of begging in, 2453
Papyrus Kahun, 1793
Papyrus Kahun Vet, 1793
Papyrus Lansing
    on disciplining sons, 2454
    on life of Egyptian farmer, 177
Papyrus Med. London, 1794
Papyrus Ramesseum IV and V, 1793
Papyrus Reisner, arithmetical methods, 1806
Papyrus rolls
    access methods, 2200, 2202
    colophons at end of text, 2202
    environmental conditions and, 2200
    heights of, 2200
    lengths of, 2202
    manufacturing methods, 2201
    storage of, 2200, 2207
    surviving, 2199–2200, 2202, 2207
Papyrus scribes, 2270
Papyrus swamps, of Nile Delta and Valley, 139
Papyrus Turin 54003, 1793
Papyrus Westcar
    on Old Kingdom rulers, 697
    tales of the sons of Khufu, 2227, 2230
        plots of, 2260–2261
Papyrus Wilbour, 176, 2198
    on agricultural economy, 319
    temple count in, 321
    on temple lands, 323
Parables, 2448
Parades. *See* Processions
    Egyptian, diplomatic gift-giving, 1381
Paradise, in Hebrew Bible, Ugaritic and
    Mesopotamian motifs, 2038
Parasangs (Persian units of measurement),
    kinds of, 1418
Paríba (João Pessoa: Brazil), alleged
    Phoenician text, 1331
Paris of (W)ilios. *See* Alexandros of
    (W)ilios
Parīsu (unit of measure), 580
Parity treaties, defined, 1115
Parker, Simon B., **2399–2410**
Parks
    Assyrian, 440
    in Persian Empire, 1417–1418

Parrattarna I, king of Mitanni, 820
    authority over Nuzi, 934
    Egyptian conflicts, 1247
    Idrimi and, 2424–2425
Parry, Milman, theory of oral improvised
    composition, 2318
Parsa. *See* Persepolis
Parṣu (traditional religious rules), 1865
Parsua, in annals of Shalmaneser III,
    1011–1012
Parthia, Iron Age settlement with citadel,
    1069
Parthians, in Iron Age Central Asia, 1070
Pasargadae (Persian tribe), 518
Pasargadae (residence of Cyrus), 2617
    altar bases, 1041
    archaeological study of, 2616–2617
    architecture of, 1040
        columns, 435
        Gatehouse, 2617–2618
        Palace P, 2619–2620
        Palace S, 2618–2619
        Takht (citadel platform), 2617
    compound at, 2616–2620
    foundation of, 2616
    founding of, 2616
    gardens of, 440
    jewelry of, *2616*, 2617
    royal gardens of, 2617
Paser, Egyptian vizier
    responsibilities, 770
    Theban tomb of, statue of king Sety in,
        337
Pašiš rabû priests, Elamite, 1964
Paskuwatti, Arzawa woman, ritual against
    sexual impotence, 2014
Passports, issued to messengers by rulers,
    1467
Pastoralism. *See also* Agropastoralists;
    Animal husbandry; Herding;
    Nomadism, pastoral; Nomads
    competitive advantage of, 208
    economics of, 210–211
    expansion and elaboration of, 204
    expansion of nonpastoral societies into,
        207
    husbanding resources necessary to,
        207
    needs of, and agricultural needs,
        balancing, 209–210
    overgrazing, effects of, 157
    risks of, 210–211
    social networks and, 208
    state-run, 212
    wool and, 1587
Pastoral nomadism. *See* Nomadism,
    pastoral; Nomads
Pastoral Nomadism in Western Asia
    (Schwartz), **249–258**
Patili-priest, role in cremation ritual, 2027

Patriarchy
    Mesopotamia as, 488
    in Mesopotamian families, 478
Patrimony, mortgaged, in Achaemenid
    Babylon, 1478–1479
Patriotism
    Israelite religion and, 2048
    national theologies and, 2048
Patronage
    of art
        Egypt, 2581–2582
        Mesopotamia, 2571–2572, 2576–2577
    Assyrian, 963
Patron deities. *See under* religion entries
Patrōoi theoi (Lycian divinities),
    1166–1167
Pattern, representation of, 1585
Pattina ('Amuq, Unqi)
    Aramaeans and, 1284
    Assyrian annexation of, 1101
    Hittite state, 1297
Payment. *See also* Rewards and salaries;
    Wages
    to priests for sacrifices, Syro-Palestinian,
        2055
    vow, Syro-Palestinian, 2056
Pazarlı, Phrygian inscriptions, 1157
Pazuzu, Mesopotamian divinity, *1897*
    animal features, 1845
    iconography, 1844
    symbols of, *1849*
Pazyryk, Siberia, carpets found in, 1570,
    1576, 1576–1578
Pearce, Laurie E., **2265–2278**
Peasants
    herdsmen and, 186
    Hittite
        household structure, 538
        socioeconomic conditions, 538
    Syro-Palestinian, 1197, 1200, 1207
Pedagogy, scribal, Mesopotamian,
    2270–2272
Peet, T. Eric, 1376–1377
Pekah of Israel, Rakhianu and, 1285
Péladan, Joséphin, orientalism of, 73
Pella, miniature ax from, 1515
Pendlebury, J. D. S., 1383
Pens
    for alphabetic writing, 2392
    reed, Egyptian, 2200, 2211–2212
Penuel, oligarchic rule, 590
Pepy I, king of Egypt
    chapels dedicated to, 307
    decree listing Nubians in military, 228
    war against the Asiatic bedouin, 289
Pepy (Neferkare) II, king of Egypt,
    697–698, 1378–1379
    humorous story about, 2466
Per-aa (Egyptian palace), 276
Per ankh. See House of Life
Perdu, Olivier, **2243–2254**

raw materials needed, 1555–1556
as study area, 1555
mass production of, urbanization and,
  1560–1562
Meroitic, decoration, 787
Mesopotamian
  kilns for, 1545
  as sculpture models, 1541
  western Iranian ceramics and,
    985–986, 988
Mycenaean
  four successive styles, 1273
  in Near East, 1563
  on Rhodes, 1441–1442
  from Troy site, 1125
Neolithic, 794
  western Iranian, 984, 985
Oman Peninsula
  imported ware, 1340
  local production, 1340
  mass production of, 1348
Philistine
  decorated with birds, 1275
  jug with strainer spout, 1273
  from Tell al-Farah tomb, 1278
  workshops, 1275
Phoenician
  bichrome wear, 1324
  black-on-red (Cypro-Phoenician)
    ware, 1324
  chronology of Mediterranean
    expansion through, 1324–1325
  red-slip ware, 1324
  torpedo-shaped storage jar, 1324,
    1324
Phrygian
  gray ware, 1157
  Iron Age, 1154
  production of, 1154
polychrome. *See* Polychrome ware
production of, 1545
Samarra-Halaf region, 795
Sapalli, in Bactria, 1007
shapes of, similarities between, 1561,
  1563–1564, 1571–1572
shaping techniques, 1557–1558
similarities of, over wide area, migration
  and, 1556
surface decoration and design
  changes in, over time, 1554
  creation of, 1558–1559
  increasing demands for pottery and,
    1560–1561
  as study area, 1555
Syrian
  calciform, 1220
  Dinkha Tepe ceramics and, 988
thin-walled, 1557
from Troy site, 1125
Ubaid. *See* Ubaid ware
Urartian, inscriptions, 1144

Uruk
  early, 797
  in Syria, 1220
  uses of, 1553
  as study area, 1555
  wheel-made, 1557–1558, 1560–1562
    appearance of, 1555
    Leila-depe, 1054
Potts, D. T., **1451–1463**
Poverty, in Mesopotamia, 495–496
Powell, Marvin A., **1941–1957**
Power, political
  division of labor and, 1388
  royal, 2672–2673
    water supply systems and, 2672
  trade in relation to, 1451
"Praise," royal payments as, 1379
Pramesse, king of Egypt. *See* Ramesses I,
  king of Egypt
Prayer. *See also* Letter-prayers; Oaths;
  Religion; Worship
  Akkadian
    to goddess, to intercede with god,
      2476
    purpose of, 1878
  community, Syro-Palestinian, 2054–2055
  Hittite, 1981, 1992, 1994
    accompanying offerings to gods, 1998
    Akkadian influence, 2002
    Arkuwar, 1999–2000
    classification of, 1999–2002
    to escape the gods' penalties, 1997
    gestures accompanying, 1998
    Hurrian influence, 1998
    hymns inserted into, 2002
    individual goals and purposes served
      by, 2002–2003
    influence of Shamash Hymn on,
      2001–2002
    with introductory hymns, 2367
    Mesopotamian influence, 2001
    Mugawar, 2000–2001
    plague, 2000, 2002–2003
    relation to god expressed in, 2000
    Walliyatar, 2001–2002
    written by and for kings, 1997–1998
  individual and domestic, Syro-
    Palestinian, 2055–2056
  Mesopotamian, 1878
Prayer to the Gods of the Night,
  1693–1694
Prebends
  āšipu office, in Babylonia, 1904
  documentation on, 826
  Sumerian, 845–846
Precious metals
  ceramic imitation of, 1541
  in Ebla, 1226
  exchange of, 1490–1491, 1493, 1495
  hammering of, 1547

Lydia
  refining, 1176
  sources, 1176
  reuse of, 1546
  tin traded for, 1507
Precious stones. *See* Gems
Predictions. *See* Divination; Magic; Omens
Pregnancy and childbirth
  deities associated with, 1845–1846
  Egypt, 376–377
    birth ceremonies, 378
    miscarriage and infant mortality, 376
    on ostraca, 377
    tests for, 376, 1797
  Hittite, 574–575
    rituals, 575
  maternal death in, 1890
    Assyrian lament for, 1875
  Mesopotamia, 491, 1917, 1922
    customs, 490–491
    rituals, 1892
    spells, 1780
Prehistoric man, remains of, 791–792
Pre-market economies, 1375
Presentation gifts, to Assyrian kings, 962
Prices
  Hittite, 580–581
  Israelite (Hebrew), 1494
  in Mesopotamia, 481
  Ugaritic, 1493
Priestesses
  Babylonian, sorceresses, 1898
  dowries of, in Mesopotamia, 480
  Elamite, theology and cult, 1964
  as wife or concubine of a god, Syro-
    Palestinian, 2052–2053
Priest-kings, of western Asia, Uruk period,
  506
  depictions of, 34–3
Priestly Code, 616
  differing views on, 623
  health care laws in, 624
  judicial powers, 622
Priests. *See also* Magicians
  Achaemenid
    theology and worship by, 1965–1969
    titles of, 1967
  Aramaean. *See* Kumr
  Canaanite, legal and social role,
    623–624
  Egyptian, 1698
    autobiographies by, 1734, 1740–1741
    hierarchy of, 1734, 1747
    instruction for, 2216
    in New Kingdom period, 323
    nomination of, 1735
    preparation and schooling of,
      1745–1747
    state, 1731–1736, 1740–1741
    temple rituals by, 1741–1742
    theology of, 1745–1747

Priests (*continued*)
  titles of, 1734–1735, 1740,
    1744–1745, 1747
  worship by, 1741–1745
Elamite, theology and cult, 1964–1965
Hittite, 1990–1991, 1993
Israelite, 2052
  inherited positions, 623
  judicial power, 622
  legal and social role, 623–624
  Levites, 623, 2782
  two ranks of, 2782
jokes about, 2463
Mesopotamian, as reciters of
    lamentations, 1878
  as oracle-givers, 1744
  as philosophers, 1745
Syro-Palestinian, 2052–2053
  titles of, 2052
  women as, defilement concepts and,
    2052–2053
Primeval God (Egyptian cosmogony), 1701
Primeval Mound (Egyptian cosmogony),
    1699–1701
Primeval Waters (Egyptian cosmogony),
    1700, 1702, 1706–1707
The Prince and His Fates (*The Doomed
    Prince*), 2230
  Canaanite influences, 2231
  motifs in, 2257
  narrative structure of, 2257–2258
  source and content, 2228
Princes, Hittite, military responsibilities,
    546
Prinsep, James, decipherment of Brahmi,
    88
Prisoners of war
  of Assyria, treatment of, 419–420
  Egyptian, disposition of, 351
  female, as temple dependents, 445
  of Mesopotamia
    in second millennium BCE, 415–416
    in third millennium BCE, 414
Prisons, temples as, Syro-Palestinian, 2051
Privacy, lack of, in Egyptian homes,
    349–350
**Private Commerce and Banking in
  Achaemenid Babylon** (Joannès),
  1475–1485
Private enterprise. *See also* Buying and
    selling; Merchants; Money and
    coinage; Profit; Trade
  in Egypt, 1382–1384
  in Old Babylonian period, 1395–1396
Private life
  Egyptian, 363–381
  Hittite, 571–586
  Israelite, 633–648
  in Mesopotamia, 485–501
  Susa, 1032

Private Life Among the Hittites
  (Imparati), **571–586**
Private Life in Ancient Egypt (Pinch),
  363–381
Private Life in Ancient Israel (Gruber),
  633–648
Private Life in Ancient Mesopotamia
  (Stol), **485–501**
Processions
  Egyptian, sacred image, 1744
  Hittite, 2666–2667
    musical accompaniment, 2664
Proclus, hymns to Isis by, 13–14
Procreation. *See* Pregnancy and childbirth
Productivity, agricultural. *See* under
    Agriculture
Professions
  Hittite, 579
  Israel, 644
  Late Uruk period, 797
Profit, concept of in Egypt, 1375–1376,
    1379, 1383–1384
Prognostic omens. *See* Omens
**Progress, Science, and the Use of
  Knowledge in Ancient
  Mesopotamia** (Glassner), **1815–1823**
Promises to gods. *See* Vows
Promissory notes, in Achaemenid
    Babylonia
  in commerce and finance, 1476
  tablets, 1476
Property, damage to, Hittite law, 556
Property ownership
  dowries, in Babylonian and Hellenistic
    Jewish law, 45
  by foreign merchants, in Ugarit, 2784
  Khatti, patrilineal transmission of, 534
Property rights
  Egyptian
    disinheriting children, 379
    incest and, 372
    inheritance rule, 372–373
    marriage settlements, 372
  Israel and Canaan
    adoption by women with legal rights,
      625
    biblical laws, 629
    of daughters, 619
    royal distribution, 629–630
    state laws, 629
    transactions between successive
      generations, 625–626
Prophecy. *See also* Akkadian Prophecies
  apocalypticism and
    historical, 2090–2091
    literary and theoretical influences,
      2091–2094
  biblical, literary development, 2408
  definition and characteristics of, 2083
  Egyptian
    Admonitions of Ipuwer, 2084
    Prophecy of Neferti, 2084

Hebrew
  divination and, 2085, 2093
  international dimension, 2086
  political role, 2085–2086
Israelite, 2085–2086
Khatti, 2084
Mesopotamian, 2083–2084
  connection between earth and divine
    realm, 2084
  formulaic expressions, 2083
Syro-Phoenician, 2084–2085
  Report of Wen Amun on, 2085
  *Stela of Zakkur of Hamath and
    Luath*, 2085
**Prophecy and Apocalyptics in the
  Ancient Near East** (VanderKam),
  2083–2094
The Prophecy of Neferti, 699, 736–738,
    2084
  on oratory as entertainment, 2223–2224
  source and content, 2226–2227
Prophets
  Aramaean, 1292
  Egyptian high priest, 1743
    Greek name *prophetes* for, 1744
    inherited rank of, 1734–1735
  Israelite, 1691–1692
Prophylactic magic. *See* Magic
**Proportions in Ancient Near Eastern
  Art** (Azarpay), **2507–2520**
Proportions in art. *See also* Human form
    in art
  Achaemenid principles
    anatomical augmentation and
      standardization, 2518
    animal imagery, 2518
    brick grid, 2514–2516, 2519
    comparison of, 2516–2518
    Egyptian influence, 2516–2517
    metrological considerations,
      2515–2516
    modified for architectural needs, 2518
  Egyptian principles, 337
    grid system, 2507–2510
    metrology and, 2509
    stylistic differences between periods,
      2509
  Mesopotamian principles
    for divinities, 2513
    metrological considerations, 2510
    rule of sixteen fingers, 2510
    second and first millennia, 2513–2514
    standard brick, 2513
    temporal and regional variations, 2510
    third millennium, 2510–2513
  political continuity and standardization
    of, 2508
  sources for, 2507
Prosperity
  in Assyria, 822, 967
  in Babylon, 804, 813
  in Syro-Palestinian area, 1215

silver
  coinage anticipated by, 1488, *1489*
  from Tello, 1513
Rites of passage, Mesopotamian, music as
  accompaniment for, 2612
Ritual for Repelling the Aggressive One,
  2140
Ritual of Pashkuwatti, dreams in, 2015
Rituals. *See also* Incantations; Worship
  Assyrian
    connecting political and religious
      orders, 408
    coronation, 408
  Babylonian
    official, 1902–1903
    omens and undoing, 1899–1900
    potency, 1900–1901
  Central Asian
    burial cult, 1081
    sacrificial altars, 1081
  Egyptian
    for consecrating cult images and
      mummies, 1732, 1742
    power of language in, 2140
    temple, 1741–1742
    to ensure prosperity, 398
  Hattic, mythology in, 2374–2375
  Hittite, 575, 579
    birth, 2009, 2015
    to ingratiate oneself with divinities,
      2375
    itkalzi, 2651
    military, 2012
    mythology in, 2374–2375
    to placate offended divinities, 2375
    purificatory, pigs in, 2651
    substitution, 2016
  magic and, 2078
  Mesopotamian
    of ancestral cults, 479
    substitute king, 1927
    temple, 1862–1863
    treaties undertaken by means of, 482
    rulers' responsibilities for, 397–398
    sexual, 398
    substitute-king, 953–954, 2016
    temple attendants and, 444
    in temple household redistribution
      function, 448
    textiles in, 1568
  Ugaritic
    against snakebite, 2077
    death and afterlife issues, 2061
    in honor of deceased kings, 2062
    of undoing, 1899–1900
Ritual sacrifice. *See* Sacrifice
River craft
  canoes, 1422
  construction of
    in Egypt, 1422–1423
    in Mesopotamia, 1421–1422

in Egypt, 1422–1425
  funerary boats, Middle Kingdom, 1423,
    1424
  inflated animal skin, 1421–1422
  laws regarding, 1421, 1424
  in Mesopotamia, 1421–1422
  naval vessels, Egyptian, 1424
  quffas, 1422
  rafts, 1421–1422
  in Sumerian royal hymns, 849–850
  towing of
    on Nile, 1424–1425
    on Tigris and Euphrates, 1422
  wooden boats and barges, 1422–1425
    Egyptian, 1422–1425
    Mesopotamian, 1422
River ordeal. *See* Ordeal by water
Rivers. *See also* Euphrates River; Nile
  River; Tigris River
  determining courses of, through pottery
    analysis, 1554–1555
  Iranian, worship of, 1968
  traffic on
    in Egypt, 1422, 1424
    in Mesopotamia, 1421
RMP. *See* Rhind Mathematical Papyrus
Roads. *See also* Trade routes
  Assyrian, 966, 1416–1417
    royal, 966
  landmarks on, 1401–1402
  maintenance of, 1402
  paved, 1417
  repair of, 1401
  Sumerian, 844
  unpaved, 1401–1402
  Uruk period, 1404 (map)
  the Ways of Horus (Egypt-Levant trade
    route), 1382
Roaf, Michael, **423–441**
Robbery. *See* Theft
  tomb. *See* Tomb robbery
Robertson, John F., **443–454**
Robins, Gay, 758, **1799–1813**
Rochberg, Francesca, **1925–1940**
Rock carvings, prehistoric
  Arabian Peninsula, 1338
  Red Sea coast, 1350
Rock paintings, late prehistoric, savanna
  fauna representations in, 131
Rock tombs. *See* Tombs, rock
Rödiger, Emil, decipherment of
  Himyaritic, 87–88
Roeder, Günther, 755
Roman art, erotic, in Pompeian houses,
  2521–2522
Romance of Kesshi, Kumarbi in,
  1978–1979
Romances
  European, Babylonian themes in,
    72–74
  Greek literature, on Mesopotamia, 61

Roman Empire
  Cybele cult in, 1986
  in Egypt, relations with Kush, 787
  Egyptian cults in, 10–11
  Egypt in thought and literature of,
    3–14
  Palmyra captured by, 1293
Romanesque art, Babylonian influences
  on, 74
Romania, ironmaking in, 1516
Roman Kiosk Temple, 785
Romano, James F., **1605–1621**
Romanticism, 107
  orientalism in arts, 111–112
Rome, classical. *See also* Roman Empire
  historical sources. *See* Historical source
    material, Roman
Root, Margaret Cool, **2615–2637**
Rosetta Stone, 2756–2757
  decipherment of, 84–85, 2755
  discovery of, 20
Rosetti, Dante Gabriel, *Astarte Syriaca*,
  115
Rosh Hashana. *See* New Year Festival
Rosicrucianism
  Egyptian imagery in, 21
  hermetic doctrines and, 20
  orientalism in, 73
Rossini, Gioacchimo Antonio, 78
Routes, trade. *See* Trade routes
Royal Cemetery (Ur). *See* Ur, Royal
  Cemetery of
Royal estates. *See* Palace complex
Royal households
  Aramaean, 1287–1288
  Eblaean, 1224
Royal ideology
  Assyrian, 407–409
  Egyptian, 2435. *See also* Pharaoh
    changes in, 695–697
  Hittite Great Kings, 529–532
    divinization after death, 531–532
    relation to deities, 530–531
    standards of purity, 531
  Mesopotamian
    bias in sources on, 395–396
    divine order, 399
    hierarchical social order, 405
    internal order, 405
    palace regimes, 403–405
    written sources on, 396
  Syro-Palestine, 590–592
    administrative role, 592
    desacralization of, 601
    nationalistic function, 592
Royal Ideology and State
  Administration in Hittite Anatolia
  (Beckman), **529–543**
Royal Ideology and State
  Administration in Pharaonic Egypt
  (Leprohon), **273–287**

State. *See* Ideology, state
State chancellors, Sumerian. *See*
    SUKKAL(SUKAL) .MAḪ
State religion
  Achaemenid empire, 1966–1967
  Egyptian, 1732, 1745–1747
  Syro-Palestinian, 2051–2052
Status goods, trade in, 1390–1391
Steatite, 1548
Steel manufacture, 1515
Št' (Egyptian: mystery), 1698
  temple cult image as, 1732–1733
Stelae
  Anatolian
    aniconic, 2641
    Bronze Age, 2640–2643
    Neolithic, 2639–2640
    stylization of human form in, 2641
  Assyrian, 2586
  Caromemphite, 1192–1193, *1193*
  Egyptian
    inscriptions on, 346
    of King Djet, *304*, 2536
    Middle Kingdom, 737–738, 746
    of Ramesses II, 1382
    types of texts on, 2229
  from Hazor, 2679–2680
  Hittite, 1990, 1992
  inscriptions on as historical sources,
    2435
  Mesopotamian
    fourth and third millennia,
      2584–2585
    kudurrus, 2585, 2585–2586
    of Naram-Sin, 2578, 2697–2698,
      2706–2707
  at Nevala Cori, 792
  Phoenician, Amrit stela, 2680
  from Ugarit, 2680
Stela of the Vultures, 809
Step Pyramid (Saqqara), 696
  architecture of, 305
  gift jars for the king, 1381
Step pyramids. *See* Mastabas; Pyramids,
  Egyptian
Stereotypes of the Orient. *See also*
  Orientalism
  ancient Greek, 58–59, 61
  European, 77
Steward (Assyrian official). *See*
  Abarakku
Steward (Hittite official), 540
Steward (Israelite official), 595
Stillborn children, in Mesopotamian
  afterlife, 1888
Stock raising, research into development
  of, 2722–2723
Stol, Marten, **485–501**
Stone, Elizabeth C., **235–248**, 2723
Stonecarvers, Egyptian, 1615
Stone quarries. *See* Quarries

Stone reliefs. *See* Relief art
Stone vessels. *See* Vessels, stone
Stone-working
  Achaemenid, 2617–2632
  artistic aspects of, 1543–1544
  central Asia, 1064
    miniature columns, 1062–1063
Stoning, for adultery, 619
Stools, 1653
  Assyrian, 1658
  carved legs and sides, 1648
  Egyptian, 1630–1631
    carved, 1624
    depicted in statue of Ibikhil, *1648*
    folding, 1626–1627, 1631
    types of, 1630–1631
  joinery, 1655
  Persian, turned moldings, 1668
  Phrygian, *1666*
  rectangular, 637
  silver-plated, 1665–1666
  stretchers with bronze volutes,
    1665–1666
  Sumerian, depiction of, *1650*
  turned moldings, 1668
  Urartian
    silver-plated, 1665
    stretchers with bronze volutes,
      1665–1666
  wooden, 1654
Storage jars. *See also* Pithoi
  Phoenician, *1324*, 1324
Storehouses, in Uruk, 799, 801
Stories. *See* Folktales; Tales
Storm-gods
  conflict with cosmic sea, 2033
  multicultural manifestations of, 1983,
    1985
Story, William Wetmore, marble sculpture
  of Cleopatra, 29
The Story of Sinuhe, 225, 232, 275, 699,
    737–738, 1753, 2147, 2195
  accounts of western Asia in, 700
  fiction or reality of, 2422–2423
  language in, 2148
  music in, 2557
  on Palestine, ancient, 1205
  plot of, 2233
  source and content, 2227
Story of the Semitic Alphabet (Whitt),
  2379–2397
Strabo
  on Egypt, 15
  Geography, tale of Rhodopis, 2263
  on Mesopotamia, 64
  on Plato's visit to Egypt, 7
Stratigraphy, for establishing chronologies,
  654
Strauss, Richard, *Salome*, 112
Streets
  layout of, in Ugarit, 2672
  of southern Mesopotamian cities,
    239–240

Strouses, Persian satrap, resolution of
  Ionian disputes, 527
Studien zu den Anfängen der Metallurgie
  project. *See* SAM (*Studien zu den
  Anfängen der Metallurgie*) project
Sturtevant, Edgar H.
  Hittite Glossary, 2768
  work on Hittite language, 2768–2769
ŠÚ (lunar visibility interval), 1937
Subar (Subartu, Sibir) language, 2162
Subartu language. *See* Subar language
Sibir language. *See* Subar language
Subotnick, Morton, *The Wild Bull*
  (musical composition), 112, 114–115
Subsistence
  in Aceramic Neolithic era, 794
  in neolithic western Iran, 984
  in prehistoric Near East, 792
  in Samarra-Halaf region, 795
  Transcaucasia, 1053
  work and, 495–496
Succession of kings
  Egypt, 679–681, 685, 746–747. *See also*
    Kinglists, Egyptian
    coregencies, 699
    historical justifications offered for,
      2436
    matrilineal inheritance, 703
    pyramid ownership and, 725, 732
    queens and, 746
  Elamite, 1005–1006
  Hittite
    first-rank sons, 535
    matrilineal vs. patrilineal view, 534
    Old Kingdom, 533–534
    role of assembly in disputed, 534
    sons-in-law's claims, 535
  Hittite Great Kings, 533
    justifications for unorthodox choices,
      2437
    Proclamation of Telipinu, 2440–2441
  Mesopotamia, 397
  Sumerian. *See* Sumerian Kinglist
  Ugarit, 1260
Succoth, oligarchic rule, 590
Sudan
  climatic fluctuations, historical period,
    135
  Early Khartoum culture stage, 670
  in late prehistoric period, 130
  subsistence practices, Neolithic period,
    670
Suez Canal, opening of, Western interest
  in Egypt and, 17
Šufetīm (chief magistrate), 1329
Sugāgu, 1240
Suhi II, ruler of Carchemish, monumental
  inscriptions, 1302
Suicide
  in Egypt, 1766
  in Mesopotamia, 1890

Temple estates, Mesopotamian (*continued*)
in economic system, 1394–1395
growth in power in Old Babylonian period, 1395
land-tenure systems, 1394
livestock of, 446–447
management of, 445–448
Sumerian, 845
working land of, 445–446
Temple households, Mesopotamian. *See also* Temple estates
attendants to deity in, 444
as corporations, 447
as deity's household, 444–448
dependents of, 445–446
depictions of activities of, on seals, 449
early dynastic period, 450–451
function of, 448
funding economic needs of, 445
hierarchical organization of, 444–445
income of, 451–452
limitations of documentation of, 443–444
Old Babylonian period records, 451–453
origins and early development of, 448–450
redistributive economy of, 447–448
social and economic organization of, 443–454
social organization of, 444–445
Temple Hymns, 2285
on Ekhursag, 846
Temple of Hathor. *See under* Hathor, Egyptian divinity
Temple of Jerusalem. *See* Jerusalem, temple of
Temple of the Oxus
architecture, Achaemenid influence, 1073
cloisonné plaque of man leading camel, *1077, 1077*
decorated weapons, 1075–1076, *1076*
Greek and Achaemenid, 1076
ivory sword handle, *1076*
defensive armor found in, 1082
ivory rhyton, *1075, 1075*
jewelry found in, 1077
Temples. *See also* Priests; Temple estates; Temple households; Worship; Ziggurats
construction of, calculations for, 2217
economic functions of, 596, 2051
embellishment of
state workshops for, 462
supply and control of materials, 464
fortress, 596
furnaces for metal recycling, 460
juridical functions of, 2051

personnel
body ornaments, 2502
female, 2502–2504
political functions of, 2051
recognizability of, 607
record keeping in
scribes and, 2274
tokens for, 2105
relief sculptures, furniture shown in, 1623
ritual slaughters, 212–213
Temples, Assyrian. *See* Temples, Mesopotamian
Temples, Babylonian, 905. *See also* Temples, Mesopotamian
Aramaean destruction of, 821
cellas of, 426
government support for, 940
Kassite restoration of, 817, 819
Nabu-apla-iddina and, 823
Nebuchadnezzar II's restoration of, 826
preservation of scientific information, 1925
prostitution and, 493
Uruk period, 798–799
Temples, Eblaean, economic role of, 1224–1225
Temples, Egyptian
administrators of, in New Kingdom period, 323
agents of (*shuty*), 1383–1384
ancillary structures of, 323–324
archaeological sources on, 324–325
autobiographical inscriptions in, 2251–2252
purpose of, 2244, 2246
birth houses in, 1780
broken lintel, 751
Carian inscriptions at, studies of, 1192–1194
committees of priests, 771
completed by Ramesses II, 766–767
complexes of, 309
construction and decoration of, 304–316, *311–312*
craft workshops, 333–334, *334–335*
creation rituals in, 1706
cult buildings
in Old Kingdom and Middle Kingdom periods, 328
support of, in New Kingdom period, 320–321
cult statues in, 313
doorways of, 315
Early Dynastic and Old Kingdom, 306–307
enclosures, 306
niche paneling, 306
relief decorations, 307
symbolic markers at, 307
Early Dynastic periods, 328–329

funerary, 731–733
furniture of, 1623
god's temples, in Old Kingdom and Middle Kingdom periods, 327–328
granaries of, in New Kingdom period, 321, 323–324
Greco-Roman period, 309, 313–316
decoration of, 308–309
hierarchical organization of
in New Kingdom period, 323
in Old Kingdom period, 327
Houses of Life, 2216, 2219–2220
inscriptions on walls of, as information sources, 346
king and, in New Kingdom period, 321–322
lands of, 323
categorized, 323
libraries in, 2207, 2229
mortuary, 1770–1771
Early Dynastic, 328–329
location of, 1770
protection from robbery, 1770
New Kingdom period, 307–308, 321–324
decoration of, 308–309
settings of, 309–310, 312–314
as palaces of gods on earth, 1732
personnel in, 1734
pharaonic period, reliefs, 2542–2543
priestly worship in, 1731–1736, 1741–1745
priests of, in New Kingdom period, 323
production of goods for, 333
provincial
Early Dynastic, 329
in Old Kingdom and New Kingdom periods, 327–328
purpose of, 771
relief decorations, 307, 312–314
reliefs and paintings
hieroglyphic writing, 2141
production of, 336
religious iconography, 1711–1712
Greco-Roman period, 1712
royal mortuary temples, 1728–1729
revenues for support of
in New Kingdom period, 321–322
in Old Kingdom and Middle Kingdom periods, 327–328
ritual sacrifices depicted on walls, 227–228
royal chapels of, in Old Kingdom and Middle Kingdom periods, 328
royal funerary
in New Kingdom period, 324
in Old Kingdom and Middle Kingdom periods, 326–327
secret cult images in, 1698

Tigris River (*continued*)
Ishme-Dagan's control of region, 876
as major highway, 1421
navigation of, 966
river craft used on, 1421–1422
transport of goods on, 1403
Urukian settlements on, 1404
water sources, 142
Ti'innik. *See* Taanach
Til Barsip (Tell Ahmar, Kar-Shalmaneser)
Hittite population, 1296
palace at, frescoes of, 2674
sculpture and inscriptions, Neo-Hittite period, 1302
textiles in paintings at, 1584–1585
under Aramaeans, 821, 1283
under Assyrians, 822, 1303
wall paintings of Tiglath-pileser III, 2597–2598
Tillya-tepe, Kuchuk-tepe type artifacts, 1069
Timber
import of, by Egypt and Mesopotamia, 1451, 1453–1454
Lycian production of, 1169–1170
Melukkha as source of, 1456
Time
in Egyptian mythology, 1700
standardization of, with lunar calendar, 1398
Time, historical. *See* Chronology
Time cosmogony
Greek mythology and, 41
"Orphic" poems on, 36
various versions, 35–36
Timnah
copper from, 1504
trade with Egypt, 1362
Tin
in Anatolian bronze production, provenance of, 865
Anatolian industry, 1087
Assyrian trade in, 863–864
monopoly in, 865
bronze metallurgy and, 1506–1511
Caucasian sources, 1056
Early Bronze Age processing of, 1519–1520
imported into Oman Peninsula, 1341
Mari trade in, 1509–1511
processing of, in Early Bronze Age, 1519–1520
rarity of, 1515
silver traded for, 1393
in Taurus Mountains, 1502, 1513
trade in, transport from Cornwall to Mediterranean, 1444
in western Iran, Afghan sources of, 984
Tin bronzes, Mesopotamia, 1056
Tinstone. *See* Cassiterite
Tiribazus, Persian official, trial of, 524

Tisha-Lim, king of Emar, Eblaean property granted to, 1227
Tishpak, Mesopotamian divinity, 1860
Mushkhusshu dragon associated with, 1841
Titles
of priests, Egyptian, 1734–1735, 1740
of scribes, Mesopotamian, 2272
Tjeker (Sea Peoples), 1269
Tjkerbaal, prince of Byblos, trading by, 1379
To a Gallant Shepherd, 2298
Tobit, Book of, *Proverbs of Ahiqar* and, 1290
Toggle pins, Canaanite and Israelite, 642
Toilets
Egyptian night commode, 367
Nuzi, 935, 936
Tokens
location of, 2099 (map)
record keeping with, 2097–2101, 2268
clay tablets and, 2101–2105
shapes and markings on, 2097–2099
use of, in Egypt, 1379–1380
Token systems, development of writing systems and, 2184
Tomb-chapels, Egyptian
from epoch of Ramesses II, 771
wall scenes, provision for afterlife in, 771–772
Tomb robbery, 1384, 1771
protection from, 1770
Tomb-robbery papyri, Egyptian, 1771, 1773
on the *shuty*, 1384
translations of, 1376
Tombs. *See also* Graves
Achaemenid
of Cyrus the Great, 2617
of Darius I, 2625–2626
Canaanite and Israelite, objects found in with apotropaic uses, 2079
construction of, calculations for, 2217
of craftsmen, 456
Egyptian. *See also* Mastabas; Tutankhamun, king of Egypt
autobiographical inscriptions in, 346, 350, 2223. *See also* Autobiographies, Egyptian
decoration, 340
depiction of funeral on walls, 1771–1772
diminishing quality of, 2252
Eighteenth Dynasty, 1380
false doors, 1624
family, 367
First Dynasty kings, 673
furniture representations from, 1624–1626
guidebooks to the beyond in, 1769
imaginary divinity, 742, 744

location of, 688, 1770
Middle Kingdom, 736, 738, 741–743
of the nobles, 1771–1772
nonroyal, 1769–1770
of private citizens at Thebes, 1628, 1628
production of status and coffins for, 333
provincial, 2248
provision for afterlife, 771–772
reliefs and paintings, 336
reused for later burials, 1771
rock-cut, 1770
royal, 328
royal craftsmen, 341–342
at Saqqara, 1624–1625
shuty agents and the, 1384
star ceilings, 1723
stone in, 1769–1770
Levantine, under dwellings, 2677
Lycian
class differences, 1169
cliff sites, 1167–1168
house-tombs, *1167*, 1168
inscriptions, 1169
relief sculptures, 1168
sarcophagi, pillar, and monumental, 1168
Lydian, tumuli, 1178, 1180–1181
Mesopotamian
building styles and plans, 436
erotic figurines in, 2528
jewelry found in, 1636–1639
prehistoric, implications of funerary tokens in, 2105
rock, 741–743
royal. *See* Necropolises, royal; Pyramids, Egyptian
Syro-Palestinian, stools found in, 637
Ugaritic, family's living quarters next to, 2061
Tomyris, Massagetan queen, defeat of Cyrus, 1040
Tools
Bactrian, 1075
copper, 1550
Egyptian
for furniture making, *1628*, 1628–1630, *1629*
metal, 1617, 1619, *1619*
Hittite, 572
hominid, 665
iron, 1515, 1517
casting techniques, 1076–1077
metal, in artistic production, 1541
prehistoric, bifaces, 665
stone
Final Palaeolithic sites, 668–669
hand axes, 666, 668
microlithic, 668, 670

Verdi, Giuseppe
  Aïda, 29
  Nabucco or *Nabucodonosor* (opera), 78
Vessels
  Anatolian
    animal shapes, 1678
    gold, 1675
    pitcher from Kanesh, *1678*
    relief decoration on, 1678
    silver, 1675
    trick, *1675*
  chlorite
    Dilmun, 1342
    Oman Peninsula, 1340–1341, 1347,
      1349
  Egyptian, Early Dynastic slate toilet
    dish, *1616*
  Mesopotamian, made by jewelers and
    lapidaries, 1644
  metal, Egyptian, *1617*, 1618
  stone, Egyptian, 1615–1616
Veterinary medicine
  high status of, 216
  in Mesopotamia, 1923
Vice-chancellors, Assyrian. *See ummānu*
Vilayet Urfa, men wrapping cone, *2642*,
  2642
Villages
  agropastoral, and urbanization, 211–212
  early, localization of, 139
  Eblaean, 1225
  ethnoarchaeological research into,
    2723–2724
  Hittite, status of, 538
  mapping distribution of, *2720–2721*
  of Nile Delta, 139–141
Villard, Pierre, **873–883**
Vineyards, initial investment in, 183
Violence, theme of, in flood narratives,
  2348–2349
Virginity
  Egypt
    in brides, 371
    of priests, 1733
  Israelite laws, 619
  in Mesopotamia, 489–490
Virolleaud, Charles, decipherment of
  Ugaritic and, 90
Virtual bilinguals
  in decipherment of ancient scripts, 83
  example of false bilingual, 92
Visai Baga gods, worship of, in
  Achaemenid Iran, 1967–1968
Vishve Devah (Indian gods), 1967
Vision of the Netherworld, 2297–2298
Visual arts, aesthetics and, Mesopotamian,
  2569–2581
Vitruvius Pollio
  on Halicarnassus, 1186
  model of proportions, 2507

Vizier (Egyptian official)
  Late Period, 285
  Middle Kingdom, 280–281
  New Kingdom, 284, 320–321
  Old Kingdom, 279
  responsibility in Thebes, 770
Vocabularies, Mesopotamian. *See* Lexical
  lists, Mesopotamian
Volcanism
  Lydia, 1175
  on Thera, 1434, 1439
    economic consequences, 1440
Voltaire, François-Marie Arouet
  (pseudonym)
  Babylonized themes in, 72–73, 78
  La Princesse de Babylone, 72
  Sémiramis, 73, 78
  Zadig, 72
Vows. *See* Oaths

W

Wabālu (mathematical term), 1949
Wabar (ancient city)
  identity of, 1351
  medieval Arab legends, 1348
Wabartum (commercial settlement), 866
Wab "pure one" priests, Egyptian, 1734
Wad ban Naqa, archaeological ruins, 782
Wadi Araba, copper from, 1504–1505
Wadi Hammamat, stone quarries,
  inscriptions at, 2248, 2250
Wadi al-Hudi, amethyst mines,
  inscriptions at, 2250
Wadi Shatt al-Rigal, Carian graffiti at,
  1190
Wadjit, Egyptian divinity
  profile of, 1740
  in royal symbols, 275
  in royal titulary, 276
Wages
  in Egypt
    in baking value (*psw*), 1379–1380
    barter economy, 1377–1380
  gender differences, 560, 567
  for hiring animals, 560
  Hittite, 580–581
    laws governing, 560
  in Mesopotamia, 481
    calculation of, 495
  paid in kind, 1488
  paid in silver, 1491
  Persian, 1494
Wagons
  roads for, 1402–1403
  types of, 1402
  uses of, 1402
Wahb, campaign against Yauthaʿ, 1366
Waklum (overseer), 405

Walled cities. *See also* Fortifications, of
  cities; Fortresses; *and names of cities*
  casemate walls, 1536
  earliest, 1523
  Egyptian predynastic, 688
  for floodwater protection, 144
  habitation beyond, 349
  Iron Age, 1532–1536
  Israelite, 1532, 2672
  late fourth millennium, 1523–1524
  Levantine, 2672–2673
  Mesopotamian, 240, 243, 414, 436–437,
    471
    along Euphrates, 437–438
    plans of, 240
    reasons for, 413–414
  Neo-Assyrian, location of citadel
    mounds in, 245
  purposes of, 413–414
  second millennium, 1526–1532
  solid walls, 1536
  third millennium, 1524–1526
Walliyatar (hymn of praise), 2001–2002
Wall paintings, Mesopotamian. *See*
  Paintings, Mesopotamian
Walls
  cross-country, Mesopotamian, 438
  Egyptian Predynastic towns, 688
Walwaziti, Hittite scribe, Urkhi-Teshub
  and, 1113
War. *See* Warfare
Warad-Sin, district of, under Shamshi-
  Adad, 877
Warehouses. *See* Storehouses
Warfare. *See also* Fortresses; Military;
  Naval warfare; Psychological warfare;
  Siege warfare; Soldiers; Weapons
  Assyrian
    divinities' role in, 421–422
    strategies in, 960–961
    tactics used, 8, 28
  Egyptian. *See also* Megiddo; Qadesh,
    battle of
    conduct of, 291–293
    land, 293–294, 297
    Middle Kingdom, 739, 743–744
    naval, 299–300
    pictorial record, 292–293
    Predynastic, 684–687
    types of, 291
  Mesopotamian
    causes of, 413–414
    horses in, 415–418
    religious justification of, 416
    in second millennium BCE, 415–417
    in third millennium BCE, 413–414
Warka. *See* Uruk
Warka Vase. *See under* Uruk
Warnings, divine. *See* Omens; Signs,
  divine

Women (*continued*)
as property owners, marriage and, 45
religious role
Egyptian, 1734
as Hittite temple personnel, 567
Mesopotamian, 2503
Syro-Palestinian defilement concepts
and, 2052–2053
scribes, 2266, 2272
seal ownership, 1596–1597
in Susa, as legal witnesses, 1032
temple dependents, 445, 447
of Western Asia
clothing, 507
hairstyles and headdresses, 507
Women's studies, goddess images and, 111
Wood
in artistic production, 1549–1550
as building material, in Levant,
2671–2672
copper industry and, 1505
for furniture manufacture, in Egypt,
1628
import of, by Egypt, 1628
transport of, 1402
writing boards, cuneiform inscriptions
on, 2269–2270
Wood, Robert, and Dawkins, James, *The
Ruins of Palmyra, Otherwise Tedmor,
in the Desart*, 82
Wood, Robert, visit to Palmyra, 82
Woodlands, in late prehistoric period,
127–128
Wool
industry in Ebla, 1225
production of, 212
ecological constraints, 1570
use of, 1567
for clothing, 503–504
in Egypt, 383
Woolley, Leonard, on Eanāṣir, 1506
Wool Office at Ur, accounts of textile
industry, 462
Word lists. *See* Lexical lists
Workers. *See also* Laborers
Egyptian, wage measurements for,
1379–1380
Egyptian pyramid construction, 726
number of, 724, 731
paid, in Mesopotamia, 495–496
Workshops
archaeological remains, 459–460
ceramic, in Ashdod, 1275
craft areas, 460–462
specialist, 460
fixed installations, 459
home, 460
material hoards, 460
sculpture, Mesopotamian, 2589
seal cutters', 1593

state, 462, 466
tools, 459
World order, Mesopotamia
concentric vision of earth, 1821
conflicting forces in, 1821
levels of cosmos, 1820
Neo-Babylonian chronography and,
1822
regions dominated by chaos, 1821
two entities, 1821
World view, Egyptian, 226–228
in New Kingdom period, 320–321
of races of world, 226
races of world depicted on tomb of Sety
I, 226, 227
Wormwood, white, 157
Worship. *See also* Prayer
as care and feeding of the gods, 1731,
1741
Egyptian
by priests, 1731–1736, 1740–1741
temple ritual and, 1741–1745
purpose of, 1731
Syro-Palestinian, temple ritual and,
2053–2056
Wounds and injuries, Hittite compensation
for, 580
Wrestling contests, at Hittite festivals,
2668
Writing and writing systems. *See also*
Alphabetic scripts; Cuneiform;
Hieroglyphic writing; Literacy; Signs
advantages of using, 2190
Akkad
phonemic, 2185
political centralization and, 810
Babylonian oral literature and, 804–805
Chinese, 2182
classification of information and, 2190
complexity of, literacy level unrelated
to, 2188–2189
cultural contribution of, 2181
decorative uses of signs, 2191
defined, 2181
demotic, in Egypt, 2205–2206
development of, 1387–1388,
2182–2186, 2380
in Babylonia, 804
in Egypt, 685–686
location and time of origin, 2182
in Mesopotamia, 808, 2182–2186
monogenetic and polygenetic
hypotheses, 2182
in Sumer, 1815, 2101–2103, 2105,
2182
token theory of, 2184
economic uses of, 2183–2184
functional aspect of, 2181
grouping of documents and, 2190
image in, 2185–2186

importance of in ancient Near East,
2395–2396
nondocumentary function of, 2395
language and, 2181, 2187, 2190
material aspect of, 2181–2182
Maya, 2182
Mesopotamia
art production and, 1540
clay tablets, 2399–2400
preliterate Iranian culture and, 983
Uruk period, 797–798
operational aspect of, 2181
phonemic notation, 2181
phonetization and, 2181
Proto-Elamite, 2182
punctuation marks in, 2394
purpose of, 2187
record keeping before, 2097–2101
Semitic, in Ebla, 1221
Sumerian, 2182, 2696
grammatical forms in, 2185
interrelated sign systems in, 2183
teaching of, in schools, 2189–2190
in Susiana, 801
Thera, 1440
true, 2182
uses of
economic, 2186
noneconomic, 2186–2187
Writing boards
cuneiform inscriptions on, 2269–2270
Egyptian, 2200
Writing implements. *See also* Pens
Egyptian, 2211–2213
Mesopotamian, 2266–2270
Writing materials. *See also* Papyrus
for alphabetic systems, 2392–2394
Egyptian, 2200–2201
inks, 2211
ostraca, 2392
wooden boards, 2392–2393
Written records. *See* Archives; Clay
tablets; Inscriptions
Wrought iron, 1514–1515
Wᶜw (magician), 1783

X

Xanthian dynasty
coinage, 1164
disappearance, 1163
genealogy, 1164
promotion of Greek culture, 1170
tombs, 1168
Xanthus (Günük). *See also* Nereid
monument
conquered by Harpagus, 1163
dating of, 1162
Harpy tomb, 1168
Roman siege of, 1171

Index

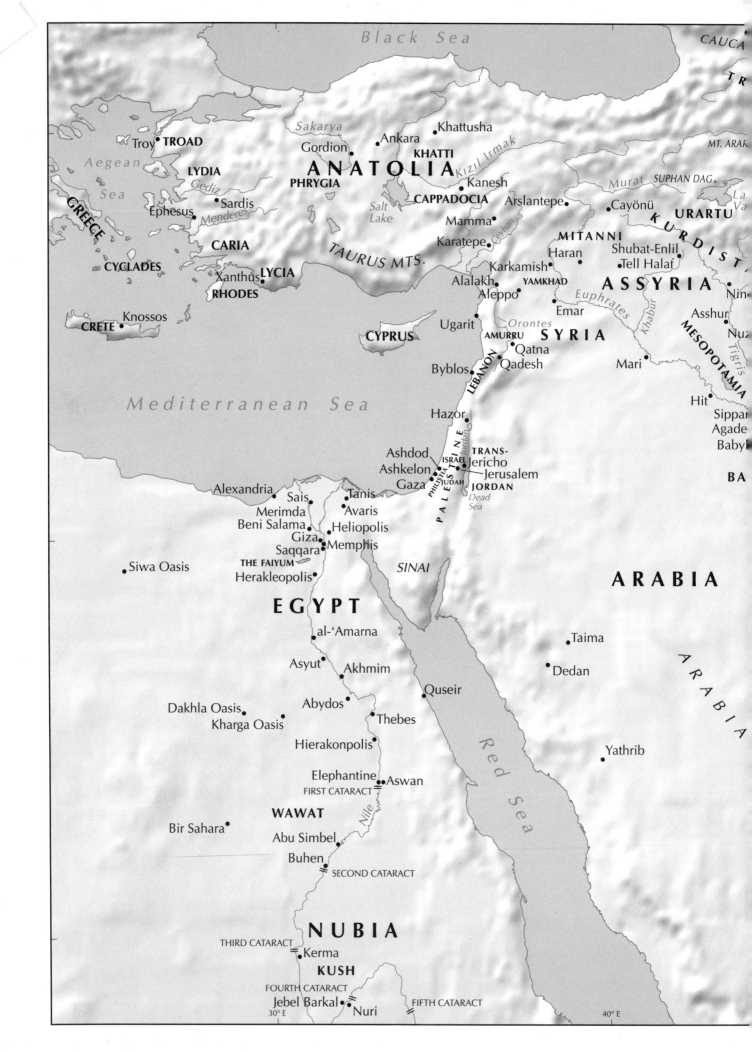